S0-BDA-545

TAX CONTROVERSIES: PRACTICE AND PROCEDURE
Third Edition

LEXISNEXIS LAW SCHOOL ADVISORY BOARD

TAX CONTROVERSIES:

PRACTICE AND PROCEDURE

THIRD EDITION

Leandra Lederman
William W. Oliver Professor of Tax Law
Indiana University at Bloomington
School of Law

Stephen W. Mazza
Professor of Law
University of Kansas
School of Law

Library of Congress Cataloging-in-Publication Data

Lederman, Leandra.
Tax controversies : practice and procedure / Leandra Lederman, Stephen W. Mazza. -- 3rd ed.
p. cm.
Includes index.
ISBN 978-1-4224-2263-2 (hardbound)
1. Tax administration and procedure--United States--Cases. 2. Tax Collection--United States--Cases. I. Mazza, Stephen W. II. Title.
KF6300.L43 2009
343.7304--dc22
2008045989

NOTE TO USERS

To ensure that you are using the latest materials available in this area, please be sure to periodically check the LexisNexis Law School web site for downloadable updates and supplements at www.lexisnexis.com/lawschool.

Editorial Offices
744 Broad Street, Newark, NJ 07102 (973) 820-2000
201 Mission St., San Francisco, CA 94105-1831 (415) 908-3200
www.lexisnexis.com

MATTHEW BENDER

(2009–Pub.1160)

Dedication

To my husband.
— LL

To my family.
— SWM

Preface

Unlike other areas of taxation you may have studied, tax procedure does not involve determining the tax consequences of particular transactions and events. Instead, a tax procedure course typically focuses on the process and procedure of both (1) our "voluntary compliance" system and its enforcement, and (2) federal tax disputes, including the chronology of a tax controversy from the filing of a return by the taxpayer through tax litigation. The course may also cover related issues, such as the taxpayer's and government's ability to access information about the other; relief from joint and several liability for taxes; ethical issues arising in tax cases; and tax research skills.

A thorough understanding of tax procedure is not only essential for a tax controversy expert, but is also extremely helpful for any tax practitioner. After all, tax planning includes an assessment of the risks of a transaction, including contemplation of possible disputes with the Internal Revenue Service regarding the transaction, and judgment about the likely outcome of those disputes.

The technical details of tax controversy procedure are illuminated by an understanding of the law's underlying conceptual framework. Throughout this book, we have tried both to explain the law and to put it in context, highlighting important theoretical considerations about tax controversies and current procedural rules. Strategic aspects of resolving a tax dispute are also very important. The book uses the "problem method" to promote application of the law to factual scenarios a tax practitioner might encounter, and to emphasize strategy considerations.

The Internal Revenue Service Restructuring and Reform Act of 1998 (the IRS Reform Act) made major changes to tax controversy law. More than a decade after the enactment of the IRS Reform Act, the effects of many of these changes continue to unfold, making this an exciting time to study tax procedure. We hope you enjoy the course.

Acknowledgments

This edition reflects a major overhaul of preceding editions. We appreciate the help provided by many people as we completed this edition. In particular, we would like to thank Leslie Book of Villanova Law School; Bryan Camp of Texas Tech University School of Law; William Henderson, Aviva Orenstein, and Carwina Weng of Indiana University School of Law–Bloomington; Philip N. Jones of Duffy Kekel LLP; J. Scott MacBeth and Eric S. Namee of Hinkle Elkouri Law Firm LLC; and Steve Ware of University of Kansas School of Law. For help with the graphics in Chapter 1, we are grateful to Frank Burleigh, Erin Cowles, Mark Newton, and Brian Smith. Erin Cowles and Michele Rutledge provided valuable assistance with the copyright permissions. We would also like to thank Tanner Coulter and Michala Irons of Indiana Law School, and Michael Dill and Pam Tull of Kansas Law School, for valuable research assistance on this edition. We also remain grateful to the many people who provided assistance with the previous two editions.

Table of Contents

Chapter 1

INTRODUCTION TO FEDERAL TAX CONTROVERSIES AND TAX ADMINISTRATION

§ 1.01 INTRODUCTION

Federal tax controversies generally involve disputes between private party "taxpayers,"[1] which may be individuals or entities such as corporations, and the Internal Revenue Service (IRS). The IRS is part of the Treasury Department, and is the administrative agency of the United States government responsible for administering the Internal Revenue Code (Code) and collecting federal taxes.

Other government entities in addition to the IRS are involved in the tax controversy process. Congress writes the tax law; the Joint Committee on Taxation must approve all refunds exceeding $2,000,000; the Treasury Department promulgates regulations to effectuate the laws; and the Department of Justice litigates all federal criminal tax cases and all federal civil tax cases in every court except the U.S. Tax Court. In general, however, the IRS is the primary government player in a tax controversy. It is the IRS that issues the forms on which taxpayers file returns, selects returns for audit, attempts to resolve tax controversies administratively, collects taxes, and handles the high percentage of litigated tax cases that are docketed in Tax Court. In addition, as discussed in Chapter 2, the IRS provides both public and private guidance to taxpayers to assist them in applying the Code.

Because of the importance of the IRS to tax procedure, this chapter first provides background information on the structure of the IRS. Next, the chapter introduces the rulemaking authority of the Treasury Department and the IRS, which is discussed further in Chapter 2. The chapter then outlines the tax controversy process, providing a framework for many of the issues addressed in subsequent chapters. Finally, the chapter considers the important issue of the gap between taxes due and those actually paid, along with the intriguing issues that tax evasion and other forms of noncompliance raise.

§ 1.02 STRUCTURE OF THE IRS

The IRS is an agency of the Treasury Department, one of the eleven bureaus of the federal government. The agency is headed by the Commissioner of Internal Revenue, who is appointed by the President and confirmed by the Senate. I.R.C. § 7802.[2] According to its mission statement, the IRS's purpose is to "[p]rovide America's taxpayers top quality service by helping them understand and meet their tax responsibilities and by applying the tax law with integrity and fairness to all."

Because some taxpayers find their obligation to report and pay taxes to be a burden, the IRS has often been viewed with some animosity. This animosity came to a head in the late 1990s when the IRS became the subject of intense Congressional scrutiny.[3] Taxpayers and IRS employees testified before congressional committees alleging misconduct and abusive practices by IRS auditors and collection agents. Although a subsequent government investigation raised serious doubts about the truthfulness of

---

[1] Anyone subject to federal tax is termed a "taxpayer" by the Internal Revenue Code. *See* I.R.C. § 7701(a)(14).

[2] Although the Code provides that it is to be administered and enforced by the Secretary of the Treasury, the Secretary has delegated much of this power to the Commissioner. I.R.C. § 7801(a). In addition, the Code specifies certain duties and powers for which the Commissioner takes responsibility. *See* I.R.C. § 7803.

[3] *See* National Commission on Restructuring the Internal Revenue Service, A Vision for a New IRS (1997).

charges of IRS abuse made at these hearings,[4] Congress responded to the allegations by enacting the Internal Revenue Service Restructuring and Reform Act of 1998 ("IRS Reform Act").[5] The IRS Reform Act contained many new and revised procedures that substantially changed the tax administration process. In fact, many of the procedures discussed throughout this book — including many that focus on taxpayer "rights" — were enacted or amended in that Act.

The IRS Reform Act also included a provision mandating that the IRS reorganize its operating structure. IRS Reform Act § 1001. Before the reorganization, the IRS employed a geographically-based structure. The National Office in Washington, D.C. oversaw four regional offices located throughout the country. The regional offices, in turn, oversaw district offices, each of which was responsible for applying the law to every taxpayer within the district office's geographic boundaries. The legislative history that accompanied the IRS Reform Act provides insight into the factors leading up to the call for a revised organizational framework.

> The Committee believes that a key reason for taxpayer frustration with the IRS is the lack of appropriate attention to taxpayer needs. At a minimum, taxpayers should be able to receive from the IRS the same level of service expected from the private sector. For example, taxpayer inquiries should be answered promptly and accurately; taxpayers should be able to obtain timely resolutions of problems and information regarding activity on their accounts; and taxpayers should be treated fairly and courteously at all times. The Commissioner of Internal Revenue has indicated his interest in improving customer service. The Committee should not only support the Commissioner's efforts, but also mandate that a key part of the IRS mission must be taxpayer service.
>
> The Commissioner has announced a broad outline of a plan to reorganize the structure of the IRS in order to help make the IRS more oriented toward assisting taxpayers and providing better taxpayer service. Under this plan, the present regional structure would be replaced with a structure based on units that serve particular groups with similar needs. The Commissioner has currently identified four different groups of taxpayers with similar needs: individual taxpayers, small businesses, large businesses, and the tax-exempt sector (including employee plans, exempt organizations and State and local governments). . . . The proposed plan would enable IRS personnel to understand the needs and problems affecting particular groups of taxpayers, and better address those issues. The present-law structure also impedes continuity and accountability. For example, if a taxpayer moves, the responsibility for the taxpayer's account moves to another geographical area. Further, every taxpayer is serviced by both a service center and at least one district. Thus, many taxpayers have to deal with different IRS offices on the same issues. The proposed structure would eliminate many of these problems.
>
> The Committee believes that the current IRS organizational structure is one of the factors contributing to the inability of the IRS to properly serve taxpayers and the proposed structure would help enable the IRS to better serve taxpayers and provide the necessary level of services and accountability to taxpayers. The Committee supports the Commissioner in his efforts to modernize and update the IRS and believes it appropriate to provide statutory direction for the reorganization of the IRS.

S. Rep. No. 105-174, 8–9 (1998). Is the comparison between the IRS and a private sector business a fair one to make? Should notions of customer service apply to the IRS?

---

[4] *See* Ryan J. Donmoyer, *Secret GOA Report Is Latest to Discredit Roth's IRS Hearings*, 87 TAX NOTES 463 (2000).

[5] Pub. L. No. 105-206.

The revised organizational structure referred to in the legislative history is now in place. Four operating divisions exist, each with end-to-end responsibility for all tasks affecting a group of taxpayers with similar needs, along with other service and enforcement functions. The operating divisions are supported by various information and financial officers, and interact with the Office of the Chief Counsel, appeals services, taxpayer advocate services, and others. The current organizational structure is illustrated in the chart below.

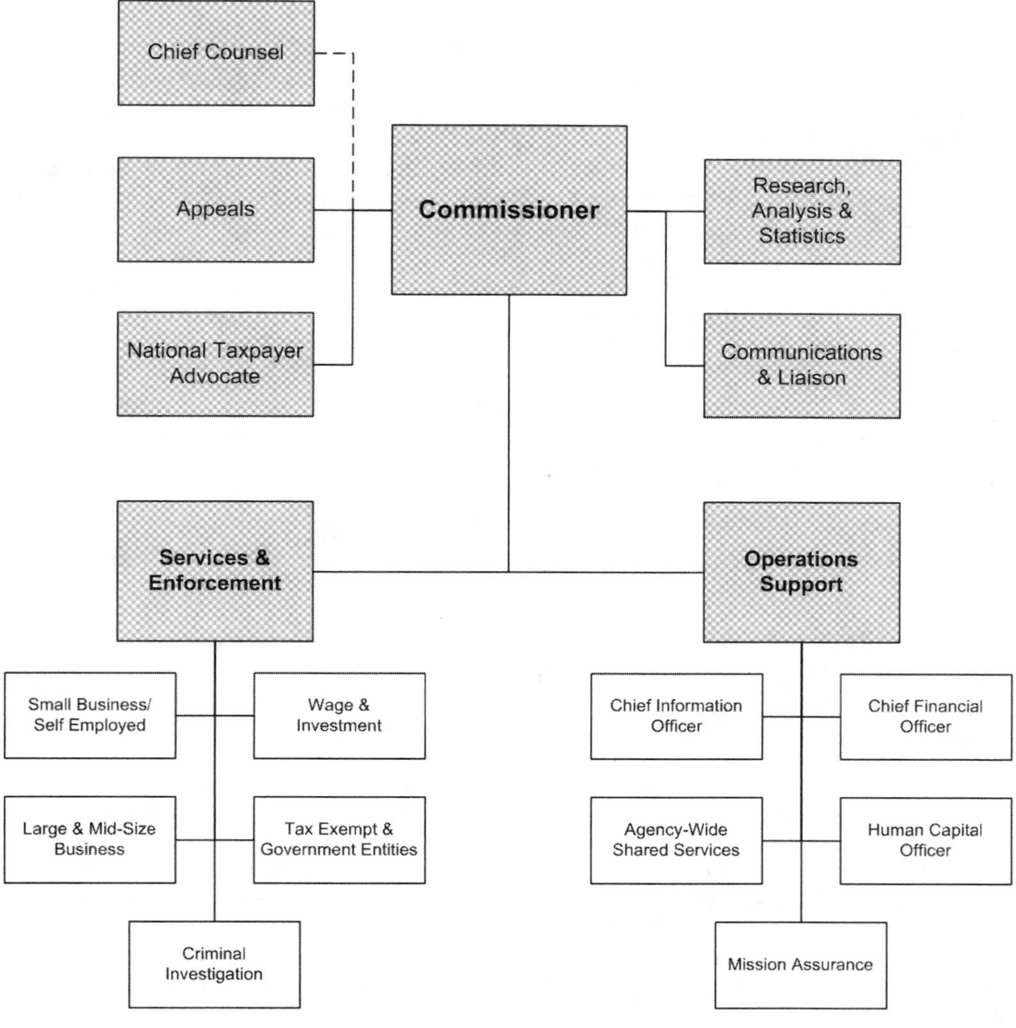

The IRS's National Headquarters in Washington, D.C. houses the office of the Commissioner of the IRS and is responsible for setting general policy, reviewing the plans and goals of the operating divisions, and developing major improvement initiatives. The Office of Chief Counsel consists of two components. Attorneys at the National Headquarters draft regulations, case-specific rulings and other guidance, and provide general legal advice to all components of the IRS. Attorneys in the field organization of the Chief Counsel's Office represent the Commissioner in Tax Court cases and in some bankruptcy cases.

The Office of Chief Counsel has established specialized groups of IRS field attorneys that are aligned with the four operating divisions. The structure consists of three tiers: a National Field Leadership Team, Area Teams, and Managing Counsel. The Field Leadership Team, which oversees allocation of field attorneys and supervises litigation projects with a national scope, includes attorneys from each of the major operating divisions. The Area Teams are assigned to geographic areas but include Area Counsel from each of the operating units. Managing Counsel has direct supervisory authority over groups of field attorneys. Overall, the new structure represents an organizational form designed to balance geographic and taxpayer classification concerns. *See* Donald L. Korb, *A New Approach to Managing Our Field Resources, at* 2006 TNT 43–54 (Mar. 3, 2006).

The four operating divisions responsible for serving specific groups of taxpayers are the Wage and Investment Division (W & I); the Small Business Self-Employed Division (SB/SE); the Large and Mid-Size Business Division (LMSB); and the Tax Exempt and Governmental Entities Division (TE/GE). W & I serves the approximately 88 million individual taxpayers who have only wage and investment income, almost all of which is reported to the IRS by third-party payors. W & I is organized into five segments: (1) Customer, Assistance, Relationships and Education (CARE), which focuses on providing pre-filing assistance, education, and filing support to taxpayers; (2) Customer Account Services (CAS), which is responsible for processing returns and payments; (3) Compliance, which conducts examinations; (4) Electronic Tax Administration (ETA), which delivers electronic tax administration products and services, including e-filing; and (5) a W & I Headquarters.

The SB/SE division is responsible for the 33 million taxpayers who are fully or partially self-employed, and the approximately 7 million small businesses (including C corporations, S corporations, and partnerships) with assets of $10 million or less. In addition to serving these taxpayer groups, SB/SE also handles estate and gift tax cases and, employment tax matters. SB/SE is organized into various segments, similar in function to those of the W & I operating division, although tailored to the needs and filing patterns of small businesses, which tend to have more frequent contact with the IRS than W & I taxpayers do.

The LMSB division includes the largest filers (C corporations, S corporations, and partnerships), each with assets over $10 million. Approximately 20 percent of LMSB filers are audited by the IRS each year, and the largest of these taxpayers interact with the IRS on a continual basis through the IRS's Coordinated Examination Program (CEP). LMSB filers tend to encounter the most complex issues relating to tax law interpretation, filing, and regulation. Many also have substantial international operations. Instead of being organized around function, LMSB traditionally has been divided into "industry segments": Retailers, Food, Pharmaceutical, and Healthcare; Natural Resources and Construction; Financial Services; Heavy Manufacturing and Transportation; and Communications, Technology, and Media. More recently, however, the LMSB division has moved its organizational structure from a strict industry focus to a more geographic alignment. Part of this move involves the creation of a revised industry issue focus (IIF) program. The IIF program identifies issues that involve a large number of taxpayers, significant dollar amounts at risk, and that have high visibility. IIF program coordinators then prioritize the surrounding issues and develop strategic guidance, such as audit guidelines and pre-filing assistance, in an effort to resolve issues common to LMSB taxpayers on a consistent basis. *See* Timothy J. Throndson & John Petrella, *LMSB Industry Issue Focus Program Raises New Considerations for Tax Executives*, DAILY TAX REP. (BNA), Apr. 18, 2007, at J-1.

The TE/GE division includes employee pension plans, exempt organizations, and governmental entities. These entities collectively remit to the government in excess of $220 billion in employment tax and income tax withholding. The TE/GE division includes a headquarters operation and a Customer Account Service division, responsible for customer service activities such as answering telephones and managing service center relations. The remaining three segments of the organization are aligned with three distinct "customer segments": Employee Plans (pension, profitsharing, and individual retirement plans); Exempt Organizations (public charities, private foundations, and section 527 political organizations); and Governmental Entities (federal, state, and local government agencies, including tax-exempt bond financing, and Indian tribes). The function of each of these segments is to educate their respective taxpayer groups, issue determination letters and rulings, and conduct examinations and other compliance checks.

The IRS also has several nationwide functional units that address specific issues. The Criminal Investigation Division, as the name suggests, works on potential criminal violations of the tax laws and related financial crimes. The Appeals unit, discussed in Chapter 5, is an independent administrative forum for dispute resolution with the authority to settle deficiency, refund, and collection cases. The Communication and Liaison office is responsible for disseminating information to Congress, professional organizations and the general public about IRS programs and policies. The Research, Analysis, and Statistics office gathers and disseminates statistical data on taxpayer compliance that the IRS uses to create enforcement programs.

The Taxpayer Advocate Service Division performs two functions. Its primary role is to ensure that, in those cases in which the IRS's standard procedures have broken down, taxpayer problems are resolved quickly and fairly. In such instances, taxpayers may request a Taxpayer Assistance Order (TAO) in order to resolve pending issues with the IRS. In addition to taxpayer-specific casework, Taxpayer Advocate Service coordinates with the operating divisions to identify potential administrative problems and implement solutions. Organizationally, the division consists of the National Taxpayer Advocate, headquartered in Washington, D.C.; a number of Area Advocate offices aligned with operating divisions; and a series of local Taxpayer Advocate offices that handle most of the casework.

Not shown in the chart is a nine-member IRS Oversight Board. *See* I.R.C. § 7802. The Board is composed of the Treasury Secretary, the Commissioner, a federal employee representative, and six members from the private sector. One motivating influence behind its creation in 1998 was to bring outside expertise in organizational development and management to the IRS and thereby provide a fresh perspective on the administration of the tax laws from a group of "outsiders." Among its responsibilities, the Oversight Board (1) approves annual and long-range strategic plans for the IRS; (2) reviews the operational functions of the IRS, including training and education, and outsourcing of work; and (3) reviews IRS operations to ensure proper treatment of taxpayers. The Board is prohibited from participating in the development of tax policy, and may not intervene in specific taxpayer cases.

§ 1.03 RULEMAKING AUTHORITY OF THE TREASURY DEPARTMENT AND THE IRS

The Treasury Department and the IRS have authority to promulgate various types of rules and pronouncements to assist taxpayers in interpreting and applying the Code. The precedential weight of these sources is discussed in more detail in Chapter 2, while Chapter 20 examines these sources within the context of the tax research process. A brief discussion of these items at this point should assist your understanding of the material in later chapters.

Section 7805(a) grants the Secretary (of the Treasury) the authority to "prescribe all needful rules and regulations" for the enforcement of the Code. Accordingly, it is the Treasury Department that officially promulgates interpretative and procedural regulations, although the job of initially drafting most regulations is performed by the Office of the Chief Counsel. Taxpayers may rely on regulations to support a reporting position, and courts will generally uphold the government's interpretation if it is reasonable.

Treasury regulations are numbered with a prefix, followed by the Code section number to which the regulation relates. The prefix indicates the regulation's basic subject matter. For example, income tax regulations carry the prefix "1"; estate tax regulations, the prefix "20"; and procedural and administrative regulations, the prefix "301." In addition, the IRS (without Treasury Department involvement) promulgates a separate set of procedural regulations applicable to its own internal processes. *See* Proc. Reg. § 601.101 *et seq.*

In addition to internal procedural regulations, the IRS releases published guidance in the form of Revenue Rulings, Revenue Procedures, and other announcements. Revenue Rulings provide guidance on substantive tax issues applicable to many taxpayers. The IRS uses a standard format. Each Revenue Ruling contains a set of facts, a statement of the issue, and the IRS's conclusion about the legal result. Taxpayers may rely on Revenue Rulings to determine the tax treatment of their own transactions as long as the facts and circumstances concerning their situations are substantially the same as those in the ruling. Proc. Reg. § 601-601(e). Revenue Procedures are similar, except that they provide guidance and instructions relating to procedural issues. For example, the first Revenue Procedure issued each year instructs taxpayers on how to apply for letter rulings. Revenue Rulings and Revenue Procedures are numbered by year and then by the order in which they were issued during the year. The first Revenue Procedure issued in 2008, for instance, was Revenue Procedure 2008-1. Revenue Rulings and Revenue Procedures are initially published in the Internal Revenue Bulletin, and are later collected in the Cumulative Bulletin, which is generally published twice each year.

The IRS also provides private guidance to taxpayers in the form of letter rulings and determination letters. Letter rulings and determination letters are responses written by the IRS to a particular taxpayer, and have no precedential value for other taxpayers. *See* I.R.C. § 6110(k)(3). Letter rulings (often referred to as "private letter rulings" or PLRs) are numbered according to the year of issue, week of issue, and order within that week. For example, PLR 200823003 would have been the third letter ruling issued during the twenty-third week of 2008. Taxpayers may obtain a letter ruling concerning the tax consequences of a pending transaction by following the procedures set forth in the first Revenue Procedure of the year and by paying the applicable fee. The third Revenue Procedure of the year sets forth matters on which the IRS will not rule.

Determination letters are similar to letter rulings, except that they advise taxpayers on a narrower set of issues. Most determination letters relate to the qualification of an organization for tax-exempt status under section 501 of the Code or to the qualification of retirement plans under Code section 401. In some instances, the IRS will issue a determination letter relating to a completed transaction, if it involves applying clearly established precedent to particular facts.

Several types of internal guidance exist, some of which only affect specific taxpayers, while other types affect broad categories of taxpayers. Technical Advice Memoranda (TAMs), for instance, are internal documents issued by the Office of Chief Counsel to the Appeals Division and other IRS offices for the purpose of clarifying technical and procedural issues arising during an audit, IRS appeal, or review of a refund claim. Issues commonly referred for technical advice are those for which there are inconsistent interpretations and those that are so unusual that they warrant the attention of the National Headquarters. A taxpayer involved in an IRS audit or appeal may also request that an issue be referred for technical advice. *See* Rev. Proc. 2008-2, 2008-1 I.R.B. 90. Like letter rulings, a TAM can be relied on only by the specific taxpayer to which it relates.

The Office of Chief Counsel also issues another category of internal guidance, known collectively as Chief Counsel advice. *See* I.R.C. § 6110(i). Chief Counsel advice is broadly defined as any legal or policy advice, substantive or procedural, prepared by attorneys in the Chief Counsel's office and disseminated to IRS field personnel. Examples of Chief Counsel advice include Field Service Advice, Generic Legal Advice memoranda, and

Case-Specific Legal Advice memoranda. Chapter 20 provides an explanation of these sources. Although Chief Counsel advice carries no precedential weight, the analysis contained within the document may reveal valuable insights into the IRS's litigating position with respect to a particular issue.

The IRS also publishes in the Internal Revenue Bulletin its position on adverse Tax Court opinions in the form of "acquiescence" (acq.) and "nonacquiescence" (nonacq). The IRS also prepares "action on decision" (AOD) recommendations when it loses on an issue in a Tax Court or district court case. The AOD contains a discussion of whether or not to appeal the decision, and the reasoning supporting that recommendation. The IRS issues AODs to enhance consistency in future litigation and dispute resolution.

Another important source of internal guidance is the IRS's own Internal Revenue Manual (IRM). The IRM may be thought of as an agency-wide employee handbook. It includes material relating to the organization and operations of the IRS, policy statements, and detailed instructions to IRS personnel concerning audits, appeals, and collection activity. It is, therefore, particularly helpful to practitioners in determining the IRS's approach to a particular issue or type of transaction. The IRM, like most of the other forms of internal IRS guidance, is released to the public under the Freedom of Information Act (FOIA). FOIA is discussed in Chapter 6.

§ 1.04 OVERVIEW OF THE FEDERAL TAX CONTROVERSY PROCESS

Reading Assignment: Skim or refer to when cited: I.R.C. §§ 6212(a), 6213(a), 6303, 6321, 6331(a)–(f), 6503(a), 6511(a)–(c), 6512, 6532(a), 7482(b).

Under the federal income tax system, a taxpayer whose gross income exceeds a specified amount must file an income tax return each year. I.R.C. § 6012. In order for the IRS to use administrative procedures to collect the tax owed, it must first "assess" it, which merely entails formally recording the tax liability.

The IRS can summarily (immediately) assess tax liability reported on a taxpayer's return. However, the IRS cannot assess a tax "deficiency" without first sending the taxpayer a written notice of deficiency. A deficiency can loosely be defined as an amount of tax the taxpayer allegedly owes the IRS in excess of any amounts reported on the taxpayer's return. *See* I.R.C. § 6211(a).

Because a notice of deficiency is a legal prerequisite for assessment of a deficiency, the notice must be sent within the statute of limitations on assessment. The IRS generally has three years from the date the return was filed within which to assess tax, though shorter or longer periods apply in some cases. *See* I.R.C. § 6501.[6]

Deficiencies generally arise out of IRS audits. As discussed below, each year the IRS audits a small percentage of all returns in order to enforce the tax laws and encourage voluntary compliance with those laws.[7] Because of the statute of limitations on assessment, the IRS typically needs to begin any audit within a few years after the tax return in question was filed.

If, on audit, an IRS revenue agent determines that a deficiency exists, and the taxpayer does not agree, the revenue agent prepares a detailed report known as a "Revenue Agent's Report" or "RAR." The IRS generally sends the taxpayer the RAR with a cover letter and a settlement agreement (Form 870) for the taxpayer to sign if he or she wishes to waive restrictions on assessment. The cover letter is known as a "30-day letter" because it informs the taxpayer of the right to request a conference with the IRS

---

[6] Statutes of limitations on assessment of tax are discussed in further detail in Chapter 7.

[7] Section 1.05[A][2] discusses the current overall audit rate for individuals, and the issues that low audit rates raise. Chapter 3 discusses the audit process in more detail.

Appeals Division within 30 days. Unlike the notice of deficiency, mailing of which is a legal prerequisite to assessment of a deficiency, the 30-day letter is not required by law.

A taxpayer who receives a 30-day letter faces a strategic decision whether to request a conference with Appeals, which, depending on the dollar amount in issue, may require a written "tax protest." The Appeals Division is highly successful at settling cases. Unlike revenue agents, Appeals Officers may consider the "hazards of litigation" in negotiating a settlement — that is, the likelihood that the IRS will lose the case if litigated. During the Appeals process, the statute of limitations on assessment continues to run against the IRS. If settlement discussions continue as the expiration of the limitations period approaches, the IRS typically will seek an extension of the limitations period from the taxpayer. Cases that are not settled in Appeals may be settled later in the process. Chapter 5 explores settlements, including settlements at the Appeals level, in more detail.

If a taxpayer requests an Appeals conference but the parties do not come to an agreement, or if the taxpayer simply ignores the 30-day letter, the IRS ordinarily sends the taxpayer a notice of deficiency. *See* I.R.C. § 6212. This "statutory notice" has numerous important effects that are explored in Chapter 9. First, it provides the taxpayer with several choices. One option is to pay the asserted deficiency and follow the refund procedures, which are discussed below and in Chapter 10. The notice also provides a taxpayer with the opportunity to petition the Tax Court to contest the claimed deficiency, generally within 90 days of the date the notice was mailed. Because of this time restriction, the notice of deficiency is commonly referred to as a "90-day letter."

Importantly, the mailing of the notice of deficiency also begins a period during which the IRS is prohibited from assessing tax. If the taxpayer petitions the Tax Court, the "prohibited period" continues until the Tax Court's decision is final. I.R.C. § 6213(a). This gives the taxpayer an opportunity to seek Tax Court resolution of the controversy prior to assessment and payment of the tax.

Because the IRS is prohibited from assessing tax during the prohibited period following the mailing of the notice of deficiency, the statute of limitations is suspended during that time. *See* I.R.C. § 6503(a). The provision suspending the limitations period also suspends that period for an additional 60 days, giving the IRS a grace period within which to assess tax. This and other issues relating to the statute of limitations on assessment are discussed in Chapter 7.

If the taxpayer petitions the Tax Court, the Tax Court can consider both the deficiency claimed by the IRS and any overpayment claimed by the taxpayer, though the amount the Tax Court can order to be refunded is capped at amounts that are designed to correspond with the amounts the taxpayer could have claimed as a refund within the statute of limitations on refund claims. *See* I.R.C. § 6512(b)(3). The statute of limitations on refund claims is discussed further below and in Chapter 10.

If the taxpayer petitions the Tax Court and the case has less than $50,000 in issue for each tax year involved, the taxpayer has the additional option of filing the case as a "small tax case." Small tax cases are considered under less formal procedures, in return for which the taxpayer waives the right of appeal. Tax Court cases and small tax case procedures are discussed further in Chapter 8.

Regardless of whether a taxpayer files a regular petition or small tax case petition with the Tax Court, if the taxpayer petitions the Tax Court without having previously had a conference with the Appeals Division, the Tax Court generally will send the case to Appeals, where it will be considered on a "docketed" basis. "Docketed" appeals should be contrasted with "nondocketed" appeals — those appeals made on a "protest" basis in response to a 30-day letter. The availability of docketed and nondocketed appeals presents another strategic choice, and is analyzed in Chapter 5.

This tax controversy process is reflected in the chart below.

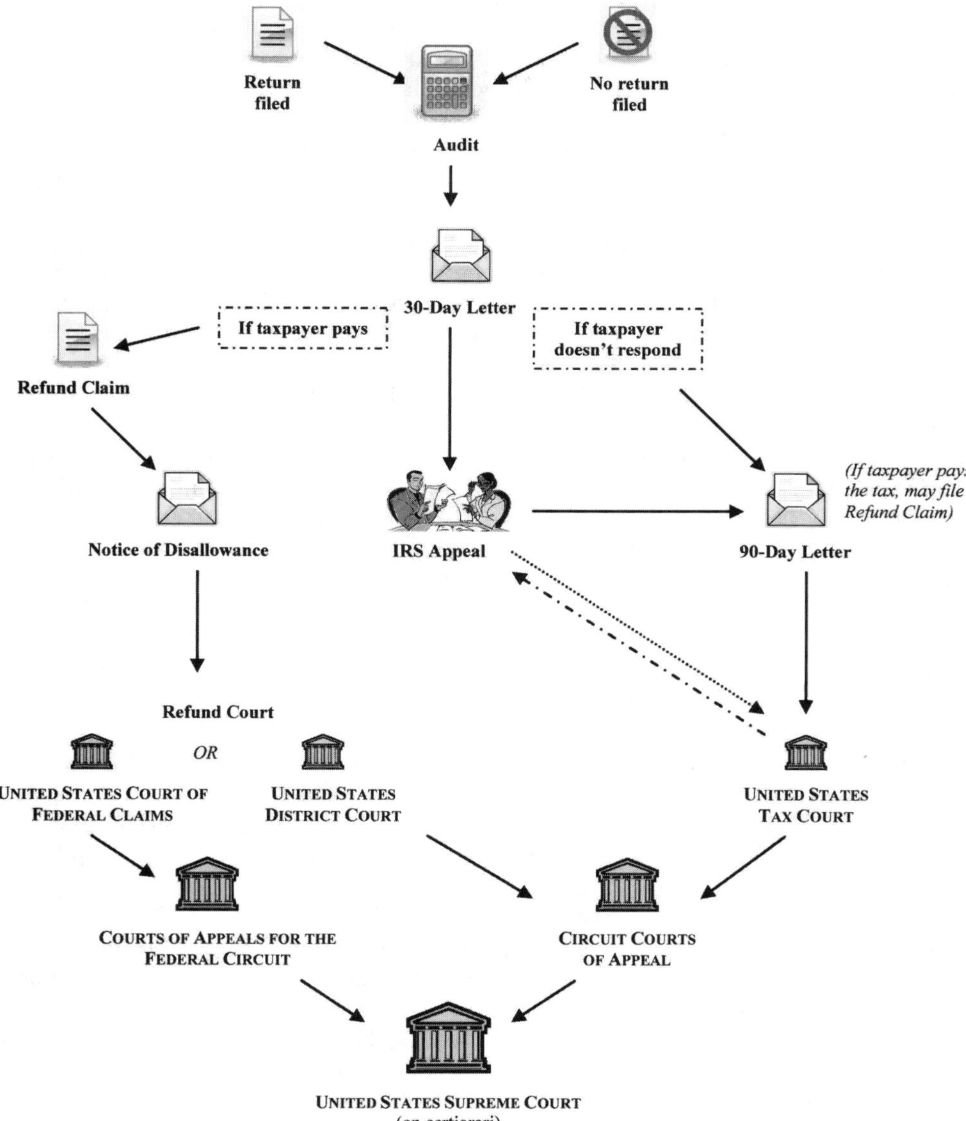

Note that at any point in the controversy process, the taxpayer has the option to pursue the refund procedures alluded to above. Refund procedures require (as a prerequisite to bringing suit) that the taxpayer first remit payment for the full amount at issue and claim a refund from the IRS. If this path is pursued in response to a notice of deficiency, for example, the taxpayer will have to pay the deficiency amount asserted in the notice, then file a refund claim. This pre-payment approach thus contrasts with the Tax Court route, for which payment in advance is not required.

Refund claims are subject to a statute of limitations that generally gives the taxpayer the longer of three years from the time the return was filed or two years from the date the tax was paid to file the claim. *See* I.R.C. § 6511. The three-year period generally corresponds to the general three-year statute of limitations on assessment, giving the taxpayer and the IRS similar periods within which to claim that the taxpayer's original return was erroneous. The period running two years from payment allows the taxpayer to claim a refund of amounts paid, even if more than three years has elapsed since the original return was filed. The use of the two-year period does not allow the taxpayer to claim a refund of amounts paid years earlier, however; a limitation on amount in Code section 6511 limits the amount that can be refunded to sums paid within applicable time periods.

After filing a refund claim, the taxpayer may not file a refund suit until either: (1) six months have elapsed from the time the claim was filed; or (2) the IRS has sent the taxpayer a notice of disallowance. I.R.C. § 6532. Furthermore, the taxpayer may not file suit later than two years from the date the IRS mails the notice of disallowance. *Id.* Tax refund suits may be filed in either the United States district courts or the Court of Federal Claims. The refund procedures are discussed further in Chapter 10, and the factors to consider in choosing a forum for tax litigation are discussed in Chapter 11.

If a taxpayer pursues the Tax Court option, the resulting decision may be appealed to the Court of Appeals for the Circuit within which the taxpayer resided at the time he or she filed the petition. *See* I.R.C. § 7482(b). District Court cases are similarly appealable to the Courts of Appeals. By contrast, Court of Federal Claims cases are appealable to the Court of Appeals for the Federal Circuit, resulting in the application of a different body of precedent in the Court of Federal Claims. Appeal from any of the Circuit Courts lies to the United States Supreme Court (on certiorari).

If a taxpayer does not respond to a notice of deficiency either by petitioning the Tax Court in the time provided by law or by paying the tax, the IRS can make an assessment. Once an amount is assessed, it becomes a debt of the taxpayer to the government. The IRS is required to give notice and demand for payment to the taxpayer as soon as practical and within 60 days of making an assessment. I.R.C. § 6303(a).

If a taxpayer refuses or neglects to pay the tax after notice and demand for payment, the amount of the tax liability becomes a lien on all of the taxpayer's real and personal property until it is paid. I.R.C. § 6321. If the taxpayer still refuses to pay the tax after receiving from the IRS the required pre-levy notices, the IRS can collect the tax by levying upon the taxpayer's property and selling it at auction. I.R.C. § 6331(a). Various procedures, including offers in compromise and installment agreements, are available to taxpayers who are unable to pay their entire tax liabilities immediately and in full. The procedures may allow the taxpayer, under specified circumstances, to spread tax payments over time or limit the amount the taxpayer pays for a given year. Collection procedures are explored further in Chapters 14–16.

§ 1.05 TAX COMPLIANCE, TAX EVASION, AND THE FEDERAL "TAX GAP"

[A] Introduction

The federal tax system in the United States is founded on the principle of "self assessment." The self-assessment (or "voluntary compliance") system does not mean that paying taxes is optional. Instead, it means that the IRS does not compute taxpayers' tax liabilities in the first instance. As discussed in further detail in Chapter 3, the Code requires taxpayers to determine their own tax liabilities, file returns reflecting those liabilities on proper forms, and pay the liabilities by specified dates. The

IRS enforces the tax laws through audits, civil tax penalties, and a number of tax collection tools, including seizure of property.[8]

[1] Voluntary Compliance Estimates

Currently, the overall voluntary compliance rate with respect to federal taxes is estimated to be around 83.7 percent, meaning that approximately 84 percent of taxes due are timely and voluntarily paid (not that 84 percent of taxpayers necessarily voluntarily comply).[9] "[M]ost [noncompliance] can be grouped into three general categories: (1) failure to file a required tax return (filing noncompliance); (2) failure to report on a filed return all taxes owed (reporting noncompliance); and (3) failure to pay over to the government taxes admittedly owed (payment noncompliance)." Leandra Lederman, *Tax Compliance and the Reformed IRS*, 51 Kan. L. Rev. 971, 971–72 (2003) (hereinafter, Lederman, *Reformed IRS*). Noncompliance can result from a host of different causes: perceptions about the fairness of the tax system; frustrations with the complexity of the substantive tax law; uncertainty surrounding the application of particular Code provisions; and tendencies towards self-interest and dishonesty, to name just a few. Does the estimated tax compliance rate surprise you? Does it seem low?

Of course, it would be unrealistic to expect a 100 percent rate of tax compliance. Yet, noncompliance is costly to taxpayers. The IRS's most recent estimates of the gross federal "tax gap" — the amount of federal tax liability for a particular year that is not voluntarily and timely paid — put it at around $345 billion for 2001. *See* IR-2006-28 (Feb. 14, 2006). It is this figure that gives rise to the estimated voluntary compliance rate of 83.7 percent. To put the tax gap figure in perspective, it "is approximately equal to the amount that the federal government pays each year for Medicare or the 2005 federal budget deficit. Examined another way, the tax gap increases the tax burden on every compliant individual taxpayer by $2,000."[10]

Which components of the federal tax system would you anticipate having the highest rates of noncompliance? Statistics from the most recent National Research Program study of noncompliance by the IRS show that, of the estimated $345 billion tax gap, $285 billion stems from underreporting, $33 billion from underpayment, and $27 billion from failure to file.[11] As the chart below shows, of the $285 billion of underreporting, $197 billion is attributable to the individual income tax, $54 billion to employment taxes, $30 billion to the corporate income tax, and $4 billion to estate and excise taxes.[12]

[8] Audits are discussed in more detail in Chapter 3; civil tax penalties are discussed in Chapter 12; and the IRS's tax collection tools are discussed in Chapter 14.

[9] U.S. Dept. Of the Treasury, Office of Tax Policy, *A Comprehensive Strategy for Reducing the Tax Gap* 5 (2006), http://www.ustreas.gov/press/releases/reports/otptaxgapstrategy%20final.pdf.

[10] Danshera Cords, *Tax Protestors and Penalties: Ensuring Perceived Fairness and Mitigating Systemic Costs*, 2005 B.Y.U. L. Rev. 1515, 1521–22 (footnotes omitted).

[11] These statistics and the ones that follow are from the Tax Year 2001 Federal Tax Gap, http://www.irs.gov/pub/irs-news tax_gap_figures.pdf.

[12]

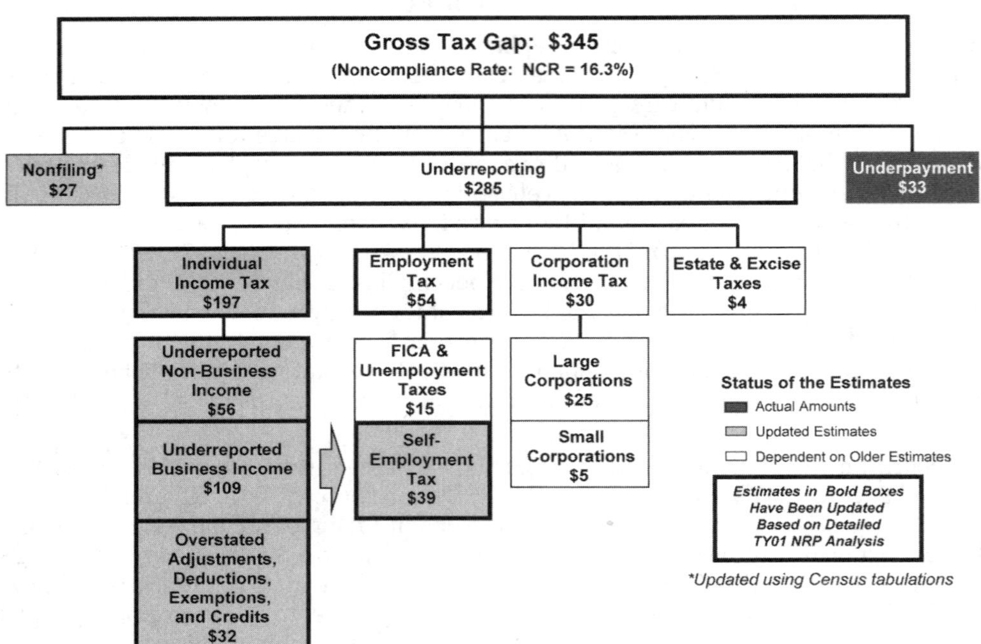

Thus, of the $345 billion estimated tax gap, an estimated $197 billion, or 57 percent, is attributable to underreported income on individual federal income tax returns. Why do you think unreported income makes such a large contribution to the tax gap in comparison to, say, inflated deductions?

Of course, despite its seeming precision, the federal tax gap is just an estimate, and noncompliance is not easy to measure. In 2005, the U.S. Government Accountability Office explained:

> The actual tax gap could be higher or lower due to various factors that affect IRS's certainty of the estimate. For example, due to a lack of reliable data, IRS's estimate does not include some types of noncompliance, such as corporate income tax nonfiling. Also, IRS is concerned with some of the outdated data and methodologies used to estimate the tax gap. Finally, it is difficult for IRS to identify and measure noncompliance, such as underreported income, when IRS has little or no information from third parties about payments made or taxes withheld.

United States Government Accountability Office, Report to the Committee on Finance, U.S. Senate, *Tax Compliance: Better Compliance Data and Long-Term Goals Would Support a More Strategic IRS Approach to Reducing the Tax Gap* 3 (July 2005).

A survey of taxpayer attitudes by the IRS Oversight Board in 2006 found that "[a]pproximately 86% of those taking part in the survey agreed that it is 'not at all' acceptable to cheat on your income taxes, down slightly by 2% from the previous year, but well within the 3% margin of error. And nearly three-out-of four respondents agreed that it is everyone's civic duty to pay their fair share of taxes (73%)." IRS Oversight Board, *2006 Taxpayer Attitude Survey Released; Compliance and Customer Service Valued Taxpayers Want Balance; Support Increased IRS Funding*, http://

www.treas.gov/irsob/press-posting_02202007.html. An earlier survey included a demographic breakdown, finding:

> While opinions about tax compliance are consistent across most demographic groups, there are a few notable differences. Women continue to feel stronger about compliance than men do (88% vs. 74% say no amount of cheating is acceptable). Although both have decreased since 2002, the drop among men has been greater (7 points vs. 3 points), resulting in an increase in the gender gap from a 10-point to a 14-point difference. Also, almost a third (30%) of young adults age 18–24 are among those most likely to feel that any amount of cheating is acceptable, an increase of 6 points since last year. The age groups that are the least likely to feel that any amount of cheating is acceptable are the 65+ group (10%), and interestingly the 35–49 age group (13%).
>
> The influence of income levels is not a reliable indicator of respondents' feelings regarding noncompliance. This is evidenced by the fact that those in the higher income levels are more in sync with the opinions of those at the lower income levels. Twenty percent of those with household incomes under $20,000, 21% of those in the $20,000 to $29,000 range, and 18% of those household incomes $50,000 and over feel that any amount of cheating is acceptable. Regionally, Midwesterners remain the least tolerant of cheating (only 13% feel any amount is acceptable) and those most tolerant have shifted from the West to the Northeast (21%). . . .

IRS Oversight Board, *2003 IRS Oversight Board Annual Survey of Taxpayer Attitudes* 4–5 (Sept. 2003).

What is the appropriate level of tax compliance, and how should the government go about achieving it? These questions exist within a difficult political context. On the one hand, a vigorous IRS striving to enforce the tax laws typically does not gain broad popular support. IRS enforcement activities can easily be perceived as cruel, especially if taxpayers identify with those who are the subject of enforcement activities. In fact, as noted above, in the late 1990s, Senator William Roth spearheaded an investigation of the IRS, collecting horror stories of abuses of power, and conducted televised hearings. An article in *Tax Notes Magazine* reported at the time:

> With the Grim Reaper looking on, House Republican leaders October 31 unveiled a new site on the World Wide Web to collect taxpayer horror stories.
>
> The site links from the House Republican Conference site. . . . It is intended to keep members informed about difficulties taxpayers encounter with the IRS, said Rep. John A. Boehner of Ohio, chair of the conference.
>
> "This Halloween, the Republican Congress is unmasking the IRS for what it really is: a bureaucratic monster stalking the American taxpayer," Boehner said.
>
> The lawmakers tried to associate the Web page to legislative efforts by the National Commission on Restructuring the IRS to overhaul the tax agency.

Ryan J. Donmoyer, *Hill Briefs: GOP Opens IRS Horror Story Web Site*, 77 Tax Notes 667 (1997).[13]

As indicated above, much of the testimony at the hearings was subsequently found to be unreliable, but not before the enactment of the IRS Reform Act. In the IRS Reform Act, Congress mandated a new organizational structure for the IRS and called for a revised compliance effort focusing on improved taxpayer service, pre-filing assistance, and early intervention programs designed to resolve potentially contentious issues before the taxpayer files the return. Congress also placed new limitations on the power of the IRS to utilize its collection enforcement techniques.

---

[2] Enforcement Statistics

Some policymakers believe that strong enforcement efforts on the part of the IRS encourage taxpayers to be compliant for fear of punishment. It is thus worth noting that enforcement efforts dropped dramatically after the IRS Reform Act was enacted in 1998. The decline in enforcement activity was primarily because the IRS was required to undertake a massive reorganization; train personnel in new procedures enacted as part of the Act; and, because of limited resources, redeploy personnel from enforcement to service. IRS figures show that its audit rates dropped beginning around 1998, as the following table shows:

IRS Audit Rates for Individuals and Corporations, Fiscal Years 1996–2007[14]

Fiscal Year*	Audit Rate for Individuals	Audit Rate for Corporations with Assets Under $10 Million	Audit Rate for Corporations with Assets Over $10 Million
1996	1.67 percent	1.88 percent	25.33 percent
1997	1.28 percent	2.22 percent	24.29 percent
1998	0.99 percent	1.67 percent	21.43 percent
1999	0.90 percent	1.16 percent	19.05 percent
2000	0.49 percent	0.77 percent	16.30 percent
2001	0.58 percent	0.60 percent	15.08 percent
2002	0.57 percent	0.59 percent	14.17 percent
2003	0.65 percent	0.49 percent	12.08 percent
2004	0.77 percent	0.32 percent	16.74 percent
2005	0.92 percent	0.79 percent	20.02 percent
2006	1.00 percent	0.80 percent	18.60 percent
2007	1.00 percent	0.90 percent	16.80 percent

* Fiscal year in this table refers to year of audit activity; generally returns examined in each year are those filed in the previous calendar year.

What patterns, if any, do you see in these audit rates?

---

[14] *See Internal Revenue Service Progress Report from the Commissioner of Internal Revenue* 43, http://www.irs.gov/pub/irs-utl/pub3970_2-2002.pdf (Dec. 2001) (1995–2001 statistics; percentages calculated by the authors); *Examination Coverage: Recommended and Average Recommended Additional Tax After Examination, by Type and Size of Return, Fiscal Year 2002*, Tbl. 10, http://www.irs.gov/pub/irs-soi/02db10ex.xls (corporate audit percentages calculated by the authors); *Examination Coverage: Recommended and Average Recommended Additional Tax After Examination, by Type and Size of Return, Fiscal Year 2003*, Tbl. 10, http://www.irs.gov/pub/irs-soi/03db10ex.xls (corporate audit percentages calculated by the authors); *Examination Coverage: Recommended and Average Recommended Additional Tax After Examination, by Type and Size of Return, Fiscal Year 2004*, Tbl. 10 http://www.irs.gov/pub/irs-soi/04db10ex.xls; *IRS Data Book: 2005*, Tbl. 10, http://www.irs.gov/pub/irs-soi/05databk.pdf; *IRS Data Book: 2006*, Tbl. 9, http://www.irs.gov/pub/irs-soi/06databk.pdf; *Examination Coverage: Recommended and Average Recommended Additional Tax After Examination, by Type and Size of Return, Fiscal Year 2007*, Tbl. 9, http://www.irs.gov/pub/irs-soi/07db09ex.xls. Portions of this table appeared in Leandra Lederman, *Tax Compliance and the Reformed IRS*, 51 Kan. L. Rev. 971, 984 & n.73 (2003).

The number of tax liens, levies on taxpayer assets held by third parties (such as bank accounts), and seizures of property held by taxpayers who were delinquent in paying their tax liabilities declined around the same time, as shown in the table below.[15]

Notices of Federal Tax Lien, Levies, and Seizures, Fiscal Years 1996–2006[16]

Fiscal Year	Notices of Federal Tax Lien	Levies	Seizures
1996	750,225	3,108,926	10,449
1997	543,613	3,659,417	10,090
1998	382,755	2,503,409	2,259
1999	167,867	504,403	161
2000	287,517	219,778	74
2001	426,165	674,080	234
2002	482,509	1,283,742	296
2003	544,316	1,680,844	399
2004	534,392	2,029,613	440
2005	522,887	2,743,577	512
2006	629,813	3,742,276	590

Does this table reveal similar patterns as the previous table?

A report by the Treasury Inspector General for Tax Administration (TIGTA) issued in 2007 found that the IRS's examination and collections efforts during 2006 were generally favorable:

> In FY [fiscal year] 2006, the level of compliance activities and the results obtained in many Collection function areas showed a continued increase. The use of liens and levies (collection enforcement tools) was greater, surpassing the FY 1997 levels. The use of seizures also increased, but it is unlikely that the use of seizures will return to the pre-1998 levels in the foreseeable future. Enforcement revenue collected continued to increase (to $48.7 billion), but the total dollar amount of uncollected liabilities also increased to $271 billion. However, the gap between new delinquent accounts and account closures narrowed slightly during FY 2006.
>
> * * *
>
> Some of the positive changes noted in this report might be attributed to management emphasis on the Collection and Examination programs. Over the last few years, the Small Business/Self-Employed Division has implemented reengineering and organizational changes that could have had a positive impact on enforcement efforts. In addition, both functions continue to work toward improved workload selection methods.

---

[15] Additional enforcement statistics are available in the Internal Revenue Service Data Books, which are published annually and are available on the IRS's website, www.irs.gov. Currently, the URL of the IRS Data Books is http://www.irs.gov/taxstats/article/0,id=102174,00.html.

[16] The statistics in this chart appear in *Trends in Compliance Activities Through Fiscal Year 2006* 4, *available at* http://www.treas.gov/tigta/auditreports/2007reports/200730056fr.pdf (1997–2006 statistics) and *Trends in Compliance Activities Through Fiscal Year 2003* 4, *available at* http://www.treas.gov/tigta/auditreports/2004reports/200430083fr.pdf (1996 statistics). Portions of this table appeared in Lederman, *supra* note 14, at 984.

> Despite actions the IRS has taken to improve its enforcement efforts, the Government Accountability Office regarded enforcement of tax laws (collection of unpaid taxes and Earned Income Tax Credit noncompliance) as 1 of the 26 high-risk areas in the Federal Government in its January 2007 update. However, as our report points out, the IRS has moved toward reversing many of the enforcement declines in both the Collection and Examination functions.

Treasury Inspector General for Tax Administration, *Trends in Compliance Activities Through Fiscal Year 2006* (2007-30-056) at 2–3 (March 2007) (footnotes omitted).

[B] Approaches to Tax Compliance

The question of how to narrow the tax gap is an important one that is of interest to many disciplines. Economists, political scientists, legal researchers, and others are all interested in this question. Relatively few empirical studies in this country involve actual federal tax data, but Australian researchers have conducted numerous field experiments with the cooperation of the Australian Taxation Office.[17] Researchers have studied such things as how demographic factors, taxpayer morale, trust in government, and the tone of communications from the taxing authority affect tax compliance.

Strict enforcement of the tax laws may be unpopular, as the Congressional hearings of the late 1990s on IRS reform show. Yet, the other side of the coin is that narrowing the tax gap can forestall tax increases and perhaps even allow a reduction in existing tax rates or narrowing of the tax base to which those rates apply. During the 1990s, the corporate tax shelter industry was blossoming. Formulaic, "cookie cutter" tax-minimization devices that produced tax benefits with little economic risk — many known by acronyms, such as CINS, LILO, and SILO — became prevalent. Some were even mass marketed by tax shelter promoters through cold calling.[18]

While the IRS Reform Act was being considered and ultimately enacted, one view was that enforcement need not be the principal mechanism used to prompt compliance; a softer, service-focused approach might be equally or more effective. More recently, the proverbial pendulum has swung back from the overriding emphasis in the late 1990s on service to a crackdown on at least certain types of noncompliance, such as tax shelters and tax evasion involving hiding funds offshore. Both the service and enforcement approaches to tax compliance are examined below.

[1] The Deterrence Model of Tax Compliance

Reading Assignment: Skim or refer to when cited: I.R.C. §§ 6662, 6663.

The basic economic model of tax compliance is a deterrence model under which a taxpayer decides whether to pay a tax known to be due or to evade it based on the expected penalty if the evasion is detected. Under that model, the taxpayer compares the cost of compliance with the expected cost of cheating. The expected cost of cheating discounts the amount that the taxpayer would owe if caught (typically the unpaid tax plus a penalty) by the probability of detection.[19]

If, for example, Jones owes $1,000 in taxes, the analysis is as follows: If Jones simply pays the tax due, the cost is $1,000. Assuming that, if caught cheating, Jones would owe the $1,000 plus a $200 fine, but Jones only has a 1 percent probability of being caught,

---

[17] *See* Centre for Tax System Integrity website, http://ctsi.anu.edu.au/.

[18] *See* Susan Cleary Morse, *The How and Why of the New Public Corporation Tax Shelter Compliance Norm*, 75 Fordham L. Rev. 961, 994–95 (2006).

[19] The basic form of the model assumes that the only punishment is financial and that the penalty is always imposed if the cheating is detected. *Cf.* Leandra Lederman, *The Interplay Between Norms and Enforcement in Tax Compliance*, 64 Ohio St. L.J. 1453, 1464 & n.49 (2003).

Jones's expected cost of cheating is only $12 ($1,200 × .01). In this scenario, the taxpayer faces a much lower cost from cheating than from compliance. Accordingly, the basic economic model predicts that Jones would cheat in this situation.

This model thus suggests that higher audit rates (which increase the probability that cheating will be detected) and higher penalties each should increase compliance, and studies support that notion.[20] Studies typically find that every dollar of tax collected through enforcement results indirectly in a positive multiple of that in increased compliance. For example, Professor Jeffrey Dubin found in a study of 1988–2001 IRS data that "doubling the [individual] audit rate would cost $323 million. However, doubling the audit rates is predicted to lead to an $18.71-billion increase in per annum reported collections . . . . Hence, an additional dollar allocated to audit would return $58 in general deterrence . . . ." Jeffrey A. Dubin, *Criminal Investigation Enforcement Activities and Taxpayer Noncompliance* 21 (2004), *available at* http://www.irs.gov/pub/irs-soi/04dubin.pdf. If increased enforcement pays for itself, why do you suppose there isn't more momentum to raise audit rates?

The economic approach to tax compliance provides a good starting point for examining the question of whether a voluntary compliance rate of 83.7 percent is lower or higher than we might expect. With civil tax penalty rates set at 20 percent of the unpaid tax (75 percent if the IRS establishes fraud), *see* I.R.C. §§ 6662, 6663, and an audit rate of around 1 percent — as the current average audit rate is for returns of both individuals and corporations with assets under $10 million — the economic model would predict that it would never be economically rational to comply with tax obligations.[21] Accordingly, from this perspective, a voluntary compliance rate of approximately 84 percent seems surprisingly high.

[a] The Role of Penalties in the Deterrence Model

Consider the Jones example, in which the audit rate was 1 percent. Even assuming that audits detect all noncompliance and the applicable penalty is always imposed when cheating is detected, the penalty would have to be greater than 99 times the tax owed for the expected cost of cheating to be more than the cost of compliance! Recall that if Jones owes $1,000 in taxes and simply pays it, the cost of compliance $1,000. If, instead, Jones cheats, is caught, and the penalty were 99 times the tax ($99,000), along with payment of the unpaid $1,000, the expected cost of cheating would be $1,000 ($100,000 × .01). The $99,000 penalty makes the expected cost of cheating equal the cost of compliance; thus, the penalty would have to exceed $99,000 in order for the expected cost of noncompliance to exceed the cost of simply paying the $1,000 due. Why do you think Congress has not increased penalties to 100 times the tax due (10,000 percent) instead of keeping most civil penalties at 20 percent?

Given the role of penalties in providing an incentive for compliance, can they be tailored to encourage increased compliance without necessarily increasing penalty rates? Professor Alex Raskolnikov has advanced a proposal for a compliance-fostering civil penalty:

> I argue that the government should counter taxpayers' incentives to conceal by creating nominal penalties that would vary inversely with the changes in probability of detection. If a nominal penalty prescribed in the statute is higher for the strategies that are harder to detect, it will offset a relatively low probability of detection, resulting in more uniform expected penalties, weaker incentives to conceal, and more effective deterrence.

---

[20] *See id.* at 1467 & n.74 (citing studies).

[21] Even an audit rate of 20 percent, which is approximately what corporations with assets of over $10 million have experienced in recent years, would only make the expected cost of cheating on $1,000 of tax, with a 20 percent penalty, $240 ($1,200 × .20), which is much less than the $1,000 cost of compliance.

The new type of penalty proposed here would accomplish this goal for a fairly wide (although limited) set of avoidance and evasion techniques that use various subtractions from gross income (such as losses, deductions, and credits) to reduce tax liability. The key insight is that subtraction items that are likely to raise questions on audit generally fall in one of two categories: They are either unusual for the taxpayer's business or personal situation, or they involve a drastic change in an otherwise typical item. The opposite is also true: Deductions, credits, and losses that are neither atypical nor significantly changed are less likely to invite additional scrutiny. Therefore, if a rational risk-minimizing taxpayer looks for an avoidance strategy that will be relatively difficult to detect, she is likely to choose one using those subtractions that are already present on her return, and that are present in a substantial amount.

For example, a suburban lawyer who has decided to overstate her deductions by $1,000 would probably choose to take an extra $1,000 charitable deduction in addition to a $10,000 charitable deduction she claims appropriately rather than taking a $1,000 farm loss that she has never claimed before. A 10% increase in a charitable deduction is less likely to attract an auditor's attention than an inexplicable farm loss, so the probability of detection, and, therefore, the expected future payment, is lower for the former strategy.

If this insight is correct (even if only in part), it is possible to raise nominal penalties for hard-to-detect strategies without knowing what they are in advance. We can do this by linking the statutory penalty for avoidance or evasion using a particular credit, deduction, or loss to the legitimate subtraction item of the same type. That is, the tax avoider (such as the lawyer) who decides to camouflage an illegitimate deduction by reporting it together with a similar legitimate one would be denied not only the tax item claimed inappropriately (the $1,000 charitable deduction), but also a fraction of the perfectly legitimate subtraction claimed on the same line of her tax return (e.g., 10% of the $10,000 charitable deduction).

The main strength of the proposed penalty — and its fundamental difference from any tax penalty existing today — is that it adjusts itself. If a taxpayer's avoidance strategy generates a deduction that has not appeared on her prior returns and is atypical for her business or personal circumstances, the strategy is more likely to be detected. The proposed nominal penalty in this case would be zero, however, because the total amount of the deduction and the amount of the improperly claimed deduction are the same. On the other hand, if a taxpayer inappropriately overstates a deduction that is and has been present on her return in a substantial amount, the overstatement would be much harder to find. However, the proposed self-adjusting penalty in this case would be significantly higher. As a result, the expected penalties for the two strategies become much closer than they are today, the payoff from hiding tax avoidance is reduced, and the overall deterrence is increased, all without any additional effort by the enforcement agency.

Many alternative nominal penalties may be devised based on the same fundamental insight. The self-adjusting penalty may be equal to the entire legitimate subtraction item of a type used in the avoidance arrangement, a fraction of that amount, or its multiple. It may or may not take taxpayer's fault into account. It may apply to all forms of avoidance and evasion, or only those using particular deductions, credits, or losses. It may be fine-tuned in many different ways, giving the government significant flexibility in influencing taxpayer decisions. In whatever form it is eventually adopted, the self-adjusting penalty is likely to improve tax compliance without consuming significant government resources while imposing relatively modest costs on most taxpayers.

Alex Raskolnikov, *Crime and Punishment in Taxation: Deceit, Deterrence, and the Self-Adjusting Penalty*, 106 Colum. L. Rev. 569, 571–73 (2006).[22] How would the proposed penalty differ from the civil tax penalty of Code section 6662, the amount of which is 20 percent of the tax underpayment?

[b] Accounting for Opportunity to Evade

Given the disconnect between low audit and penalty rates in the U.S. and relatively high compliance rates, it appears that the basic economic deterrence model must be leaving some important components of the tax compliance decision out of the calculus. This disconnect is pointed to as a "puzzle" in some of the economic and legal literature.[23] There are likely many reasons why compliance rates are higher than the economic model would predict, including overestimation of the likelihood of detection, fear of criminal prosecution, and moral factors that counsel compliance for many people. Yet, one critically important component of the high voluntary compliance rate with taxes such as the federal income tax is that much compliance does not depend solely on the taxpayer's honesty (or fear of being caught). The important mechanisms of withholding of taxes by payors, and, to a lesser extent, information reporting, pull much of the weight of "voluntary" compliance.[24]

The IRS has implemented an extensive withholding procedure through which a substantial portion of all collected tax is withheld by the payor and submitted directly to the government. In fact, when it comes to wages, the federal tax system is designed to overwithhold, which in turn requires taxpayers to file returns in order to obtain a refund. Under the IRS's information-reporting program, payors send both the payee and the IRS a form (such as Form W-2 for wages) stating how much the payor paid the payee. The IRS has the capacity to match the information-reporting form with the payee's tax return.[25]

Withholding taxes and information reporting are "structural" mechanisms that constrain compliance, meaning that they are systems that foster compliance without relying solely on taxpayers' honesty or moral compunction.[26] Payor withholding of taxes makes it very difficult for the taxpayer to evade taxes unilaterally. Information reporting facilitates detection through computerized return matching and suggests to the taxpayer the high likelihood of detection of any failure to report that income.

The estimated noncompliance rates with respect to various types of income subject to federal income tax are very revealing:

> Amounts subject to withholding (*e.g.*, wages and salaries) have a net misreporting percentage of only 1.2 percent. Amounts subject to third party information reporting, but not to withholding (*e.g.*, interest and dividend

---

[22] Copyright © 2006 Columbia Law Review Association, Inc. and Alex Raskolnikov. All rights reserved. Reprinted by permission.

[23] *See, e.g.*, James Alm, et al., *Economic and Noneconomic Factors in Tax Compliance*, 48 Kyklos 3, 3 (1995) ("[T]he puzzle of tax compliance is not so much 'Why is there so much cheating?' Instead, the real puzzle is 'Why is there so little cheating?' "); Eric Posner, *Law and Social Norms: The Case of Tax Compliance*, 86 Va. L. Rev. 1781, 1782 (2000) ("A widespread view among tax scholars holds that law enforcement does not explain why people pay taxes. The penalty for ordinary tax convictions is small; the probability of detection is trivial; so the expected sanction is small. Yet large numbers of Americans pay their taxes. This pattern contradicts the standard economic model of law enforcement, which holds that people violate a law if the benefit exceeds the expected sanction.") (footnote omitted).

[24] *See* Lederman, *supra* note 14, at 974–75; Lederman, *supra* note 19, at 1460; *see also* Edward K. Cheng, *Structural Laws and the Puzzle of Regulating Behavior*, 100 Nw. U.L. Rev. 655, 677 (2006).

[25] The information-reporting program is buttressed by penalties for failure to comply with information-reporting obligations. These penalties are discussed, in § 12.02[F] of Chapter 12.

[26] *See* Leandra Lederman, *Statutory Speed Bumps: The Roles Third Parties Play in Tax Compliance*, 60 Stanford L. Rev. 695, 697–98 (2007); Cheng, *supra* note 24, at 675–77.

> income) have a slightly higher net misreporting percentage of 4.5 percent. Amounts subject to partial third-party reporting (*e.g.*, capital gains) have a still higher net misreporting percentage of 8.6 percent. Amounts not subject to withholding or other information reporting (*e.g.*, Schedule C income or other income) are the least visible, with a much higher net misreporting percentage of 53.9 percent.[27]

These statistics provide more context for the 83.7 percent voluntary compliance rate. That figure is an overall rate that combines the extraordinarily high compliance with respect to income subject to withholding (around 99 percent) with the low compliance rate on such hard-to-tax income as small business income (around 46 percent).[28] These statistics also highlight the importance to tax administration of withholding and information reporting.

[2] Other Possible Influences on Tax Compliance

Withholding and information reporting do not explain all tax compliance, but they do need to be taken in account when evaluating the claim that compliance with the federal income tax is much higher than the basic economic model would predict. It is certainly true that taxpayers comply with their tax obligations for a variety of reasons, including some that have nothing to do with fear of detection. This section discusses additional factors that some have theorized may motivate tax compliance.

[a] Service to Taxpayers

In 1998, then-Commissioner of the IRS Charles Rossotti testified before Congress about IRS modernization. He emphasized the role that service to "customers" would play in the improved IRS. The idea was to "help people comply with the law" and "focus on the taxpayer's understanding and solving problems from the taxpayer's point of view." Concept for Modernizing the IRS — Excerpts from Commissioner Rossotti's Testimony Before the Senate Finance Committee — 1/28/1998, *available at* http://www.irs.gov/irs/article/0,,id=98144,00.html.

Does improved taxpayer service help increase tax compliance? For example, might taxpayers who face obstacles to compliance because of difficulties in understanding tax laws or forms increase their compliance if they are provided better service? More generally, can a focus on service help taxpayers feel better about the IRS and thus more inclined to pay their tax liabilities and cooperate with the IRS? One article distinguishes service to taxpayers from procedural fairness, a concept that "refers to issues such as due process and equality of treatment." Lederman, *Reformed IRS*, *supra*, at 991. It analyzes the results of studies of each of these attributes on tax compliance:

> *A. Service*
>
> * * *
>
> The results of experiments conducted by the Minnesota Department of Revenue and the IRS suggest that better service does not increase compliance. In the Minnesota study, taxpayers in a "service group" were mailed a letter offering them an increased level of service by the Minnesota Department of Revenue. They were sent a special phone number that they could use for assistance with federal as well as state tax returns. Normally, the Minnesota Department of Revenue did not provide assistance with federal taxes. The hours

---

[27] Charles P. Rettig, *Nonfilers Beware: Who's That Knocking at Your Door?*, 8 J. Tax Prac. & Proc. 15, 15–16 (2006).

[28] *See* Lederman, *supra* note 19, at 1460 & n.30.

of operation were the same as the hours of operation of the regular help line but represented an increase over prior years. This strategy, unlike certain other strategies tested in the study, had little effect on compliance.

The results of the IRS study are consistent with this — that study found that taxpayer phone calls to the help line had no measurable impact on voluntary compliance. In addition, the IRS study found that its speed of issuing refunds, the volume of the Taxpayer Service office's correspondence with taxpayers, and IRS educational outreach efforts all had no measurable effect on voluntary compliance.

Furthermore, in Minnesota, taxpayers in a "redesigned form" group received an expanded form (two pages instead of one) that facilitated additions and subtractions on the return without the necessity of referring to the instruction booklet or using worksheets. . . . The revised form also produced little overall difference in additions, subtractions, or taxes. Similarly, an Australian Centre for Tax System Integrity study that involved sending certain taxpayers with rental property a schedule to complete found that sending the schedule made no difference in the magnitude of deductions claimed where the taxpayers were not required to return the schedule. Thus, at least as measured thus far, increased service to taxpayers, in an effort to help them fulfill their compliance obligations, does not seem to affect compliance.

B. Procedural Fairness

An important focus of RRA '98 was procedural fairness to taxpayers.

* * *

With respect to areas of law other than tax compliance, Tom Tyler has shown that perceptions of procedural fairness impact compliance, although the impact may be attenuated. Given those findings and evident taxpayer willingness to oppose strongly perceived procedural unfairness on the part of the IRS, it seems likely that procedural fairness may impact tax compliance or at least normative commitments to compliance. Two studies suggest that the latter relationship exists. A study by Kent Smith found evidence that a higher level of perceived procedural fairness correlated with a lower normative acceptability of tax evasion. Similarly, Karyl Kinsey found that hearing from other people reports of unfair treatment by the IRS increased taxpayers' intentions of future noncompliance.

To what extent does increased acceptability of tax evasion or the intention not to comply correspond to actual noncompliance? Neither the study nor the Kinsey study reported a direct relationship between perceived procedural fairness and noncompliance. . . .

An Australian study compared the filing and payment compliance with respect to "Activity Statements" of recipients of a standard letter with recipients of letters designed to reflect two different types of procedural fairness. One set of letters focused on "informational justice" — the provision and transparency of explanations about procedures and decisions — and another set concerned "interpersonal justice," which refers to "politeness and respect, sensitivity to people's feelings and consideration of their circumstances." The study found that letters reflecting a format focused on procedural fairness had a modest effect on filing compliance with respect to individual taxpayers. However, for entities, "the reference to an interpersonal right tended to have a positive impact, but the combination of informational message and an informational right being made salient was counterproductive." With respect to payment compliance, the study found some evidence that, with respect to individual taxpayers, the informational fairness letter that also

> referenced principles of informational rights increased compliance, but the opposite was true for entities.
>
> * * *

Id. at 992–1003 (footnotes omitted).[29] What do the studies discussed in this excerpt suggest about the likely effects of IRS reform on tax compliance?

[b] Signaling by Taxpayers

Professor Eric Posner has argued that people may voluntarily pay taxes not so much because they fear detection and punishment if they fail to comply, but rather that by complying with tax obligations, they are signaling that the belong to a "good type," with whom others will want to form "cooperative relationships" such as friendships or business connections. *See* Eric Posner, *Law and Social Norms: The Case of Tax Compliance*, 86 Va. L. Rev. 1781, 1786 (2000). Professor Posner's argument is as follows:

> A good type wants partners [with whom to form cooperative relationships] because he values the long-term payoff from cooperation over many rounds. A bad type wants partners because he values the high first round payoff from cheating someone who attempts to cooperate. Everyone will therefore spend resources trying to persuade others that he belongs to the good type. This activity involves sending "signals."
>
> Signals are costly actions that are recognized as such by those who observe them, and they have the function of disclosing information about the person who sends the signal. An action is not a signal if the actor intrinsically enjoys the action (like eating ice cream) or obtains some benefit from it (like selling goods) independent of the information benefit. When a good type sends a signal to potential cooperative partners, he is, in effect, saying:
>
> > I can afford to send this signal only because I expect to receive a high discounted payoff from cooperating with you, but I can receive a high discounted payoff only if I have a low discount rate; therefore, you should match up with me and expect me to cooperate every round (unless you cheat me).
>
> If the signal is properly chosen, a bad type will not be able to mimic the good type, and in the resulting equilibrium (known as a "separating equilibrium"), only good types send the signal, and only good types match up with other good types. Bad types do not send the signal, and they do not match up with anyone, or at best match up with each other.
>
> * * *
>
> The particular signal that is relevant in the present context is that of compliance with the law. In a given community, it may be the case that compliance with the law, or with some laws but not others, serves as a signal of one's type. For this to be true, it is not necessary that everyone observe whether a particular person actually complies with the tax law at any given time. Such observation can come about indirectly. If a person does not comply with the tax laws, and he is subsequently detected and prosecuted, his failure to follow the tax laws becomes known. Tax compliance, then, is observable in a stochastic sense. The person who fails to comply is revealed (by the state) to be a bad type, and he is accordingly stigmatized.

---

[29]

> It is because detection of violation is so infrequent — it must involve a public prosecution following an audit, which, as we have already noted, is rare — that the response of potential cooperative partners is so severe. In mainstream society, the ex-convict is meticulously avoided. People know that many other people might be bad types and that they cannot avoid dealing with them sometimes even though they prefer not to, because the identities of the bad types are unknown. Once a person has been identified as a bad type, however, others have every reason to confine their dealings to those who remain in the (large) pool of the unstigmatized. . . . Stigma arises only when a behavior or its detection is rare. The fear of such stigma is the source of compliance.
>
> Because there is sometimes confusion about this, I should emphasize that stigmatizing or ostracizing does not necessarily come about through coordinated collective action. A person avoids a tax cheat because the tax cheat has shown that he has a high discount rate and is therefore a bad cooperative partner. It is not necessary that observers cooperate in order to stigmatize the tax cheat, because no observer has an incentive to deal with someone whom he cannot trust. . . .
>
> If this theory is true, it turns the basic model on its head. Suppose that at a given time a law is underenforced. Some people violate the law because the benefits of the illegal activity exceed the expected sanction. Other people, however, do not violate the law, and the reason is that by incurring the cost of not violating the law (which equals the benefit minus the expected sanction), they reveal that they belong to the good type — or, what is the same thing, they avoid the risk of being identified as a bad type. Now the government increases the expected sanction. Marginal members of the first group start obeying the law because the expected sanction rises above the benefit of the illegal activity. But marginal members of the second group start violating the law because the signal (compliance with the law) becomes weaker, so it becomes less effective at revealing type, and these people substitute to some other signal, such as wearing expensive clothes or making philanthropic gifts.
>
> * * *

Id. at 1787–91.[30]

Thus, Professor Posner argues that tax compliance may be a way to signal trustworthiness — or at least that noncompliance signals lack of trustworthiness and is thus stigmatized. Accordingly, he suggests that increasing sanctions for noncompliance might undermine compliance by those who were already complying to signal their trustworthiness, because their compliance will no longer send as strong a signal. In what contexts do we generally know how honest others are with respect to tax obligations? Do you think it would help compliance to limit the confidentiality that currently is afforded federal tax returns?[31] More generally, what do you think of the signaling theory of tax compliance?[32]

[c] Social Norms of Compliance or Noncompliance

One interesting area of academic study of compliance with tax and other legal obligations is the role of compliance "norms."

> Scholars generally define social norms as nonlegal rules or obligations that certain individuals feel compelled to follow despite the lack of formal legal

---

[30]

[31] Confidentiality of return information is discussed in Chapter 6.

[32] For a critique of the signaling theory of tax compliance, see Dan M. Kahan, *Signaling or Reciprocating? A Response to Eric Posner's Law and Social Norms*, 36 U. RICH. L. REV. 367 (2002).

> sanctions, whether because defiance would subject them to sanctions from others (typically in the form of disapproval, lowered esteem, or even ostracism) or because they would feel guilty for failing to conform to the norm (a so-called internalized norm). Put more positively, norms are nonlegal rules that certain individuals follow because they gain from doing so, either through increased inner satisfaction from doing the right thing or through approval they garner from others. In rational actor terms, violating a social norm imposes a cost on the violator that can tip the cost-benefit balance in favor of conformity with the norm.

Ann E. Carlson, *Recycling Norms*, 89 CAL. L. REV. 1231, 1238–39 (2001) (footnotes omitted).

Is it possible that if reporting all the taxpayer's income is the norm in a given community or industry, that norm, in and of itself, will foster tax compliance? If noncompliance is the norm, what effect might that have on someone deciding whether to comply with tax obligations? It could be that many people would feel like "chumps" if they diligently pay their taxes while nearly everyone else cheats. *Cf.* Janet Novack, *Are You a Chump?*, FORBES (Mar. 5, 2001). Professors Joseph Dodge and Jay Soled have argued that, in the United States, social norms regarding tax compliance may pull in opposite directions:

> The operation of norms has been advanced as an explanation of why tax compliance in the United States is higher than in most other countries. Honesty, law-abidingness, and cooperativeness are compliance-favorable norms that may well spill over into the tax area. There may even be some who adhere to a specific norm of complying with tax duties, believing that taxes are the price one pays for civilization or for being a citizen of the state.
>
> On the other hand, there may exist countervailing norms of an antigovernment, antitax, and/or tax-evasion character, which can be collectively referred to as libertarian norms. One kind of manifestation of libertarian norms is overtly political and can take such forms as (1) ideological commitment to libertarian principles,[n.187] (2) opposition to the U.S. government in all or most of its manifestations, and/or (3) adherence to the tax protestor movement. Another type of libertarian manifestation is the widespread attitude among the economic elite that the government is the adversary in a taxpayer's economic life. A related notion is that the system is too complex and burdensome for an honest person to follow. Another widely held belief is that most taxpayers in a position to cheat do cheat (and most get away with it), so that only fools strictly comply with tax obligations. If the IRS is so lax in enforcement that tax cheaters are willing to go public to boast about "getting away with it," why should ordinary citizens take their compliance duties seriously? In any event, a system in which there is significant noncompliance not only is unfair to those who do comply, but also does not deserve respect. Several of these attitudes and perceptions (or, if you will, rationalizations) can operate in a way such that even normally law-abiding citizens may feel justification in negligent or intentional noncompliance.
>
> Clearly, norms in the tax area pull both in the direction of compliance and against it, suggesting that norms do not operate very strongly, overall, to cause taxpayers to comply with tax duties when it is not in their perceived self-interest to do so. . . .

[n.187] Ideological libertarianism does not necessarily imply defiance of the law or tax evasion, but it implies a disrespect for much government activity financed by taxes and could thereby imply a jaundiced or minimalist view of tax compliance responsibilities.

Joseph M. Dodge & Jay A. Soled, *Debunking the Basis Myth Under the Income Tax*, 81 IND. L.J. 539, 575–77 (2006) (footnotes omitted).[33]

Can taxpayers' perceptions of compliance norms be manipulated so as to reduce the pull of norms against compliance? Both Australia and the state of Minnesota have studied the effects of letters sent to taxpayers explaining that tax compliance is higher than they might think. The purpose of the letters was to suggest that people are not chumps for complying with tax obligations. The studies found that these normative appeals have some success in increasing compliance, at least for some taxpayers.[34]

In line with the notion that taxpayers are more likely to comply with tax obligations when they believe that others are doing so as well, Professor Dan Kahan has advanced a "trust" model:

> A growing body of empirical research suggests that the willingness of individuals to contribute to public goods turns decisively on whether they trust each other. The disposition of individuals to reciprocate — to cooperate when they anticipate that others will cooperate and to withhold cooperation when they anticipate that others will withhold — is often stronger, this research suggests, than their drive to maximize their material wealth. Indeed, the introduction of material incentives can sometimes diminish trust, and hence dissipate voluntary reciprocal cooperation. When that happens, external incentives to contribute to public goods can produce self-defeating results that are extremely difficult to reverse.

Dan M. Kahan, *Trust, Collective Action, and Law*, 81 B.U. L. REV. 333, 335 (2001).

How does this model apply to tax compliance? Professor Kahan explains:

> Society collects taxes to finance a variety of goods — from education to highways to national defense — that benefit its members collectively but that self-interested individuals lack sufficient incentive to produce through voluntary transactions. Yet if we assume that individuals are motivated to behave in a materially self-interested fashion, then we should expect them to refrain from voluntarily paying their taxes as well. Accordingly, the conventional model of collective action prescribes the use of material incentives — in the form of penalties for tax evasion — to induce compliance.
>
> The alternative trust model, in contrast, suggests a very different analysis. As reciprocators, individual citizens, according to this model, will be motivated to pay their taxes or not based on their perception that other citizens are or are not inclined to pay. The behavior of others, the model predicts, will in fact loom much larger in individual decision-making than will the expected penalty for evasion. Indeed, the trust model implies that using penalties to induce compliance can easily backfire: through cueing, masking, and crowding out effects,[35]

---

[33]

[34] *See* Marsha Blumenthal, Charles Christian & Joel Slemrod, *Do Normative Appeals Affect Tax Compliance? Evidence from a Controlled Experiment in Minnesota*, 54 NAT'L TAX J. 125, 131 & tbl. 2 (2001); Stephen Coleman, *The Minnesota Income Tax Compliance Experiment: State Tax Results*, Minnesota Department of Revenue (Apr. 1996), http://www.taxes.state.mn.://us/legal_policy/research_reports/content/complnce.pdf; Michael Wenzel, *Misperceptions of Social Norms About Tax Compliance (2): A Field-Experiment* (Austl. Nat'l Univ., Austl. Taxation Office, Ctr. for Tax Sys. Integrity, Working Paper No. 8, 2001), http://ctsi.anu.edu.au/publications/WP/8.pdf.

[35] [These terms are explained in Dan M. Kahan, *The Logic of Reciprocity: Trust, Collective Action, and Law*, 102 MICH. L. REV. 71 (2003): "The simple existence of an incentive scheme can be seen as a cue that other individuals are not inclined to cooperate voluntarily: if they were, incentives would be unnecessary." *Id.* at 76. "[I]ncentive schemes tend to mask the extent to which individuals are inclined to contribute to public goods voluntarily, thereby weakening the tendency of observable cooperation to generate reciprocal cooperation by others." *Id.* at 72. Finally, "incentives can crowd out dispositions such as altruism by extinguishing the

conspicuous penalties for evasion can undermine the condition of trust on which reciprocal cooperation depends, generating a self-sustaining noncooperative equilibrium, in which even larger (and more costly to administer) penalties are likely to be of only modest effect.

The data on tax evasion turn out to be vast and much more consistent with the trust model than with the conventional one. In one study, for example, researchers attempted to determine how the 1986 Tax Reform Act had affected patterns of compliance. One hypothesis, suggested by conventional economic theory, was that individuals would become more or less willing to evade depending on whether the Act had increased or decreased their relative tax burden. The study found no such correlation. What did shift patterns of compliance, the researchers found, were the types of interactions that individuals had with other taxpayers in the months leading up to the reform: those who encountered others who expressed positive attitudes toward the Tax Reform Act displayed greater commitment to complying with it themselves, whereas those who encountered others who expressed negative attitudes displayed less commitment. This is exactly what one would expect to find if individuals' decisions to comply or evade were grounded in reciprocity dispositions.

Id. at 340–41 (footnotes omitted).[36] How does Professor Kahan's argument square with the empirical evidence discussed above on the effects that enforcement techniques, including audits and penalties, have on tax compliance?

[3] The Effect of Enforcement on Compliance Norms

Can efforts to foster compliance norms be used in conjunction with increased audit rates or penalties to produce higher compliance rates, or is increased enforcement of the law at odds with these other methods? Should one approach replace the other?

In support of their argument that tax compliance and noncompliance norms in the United States pull in opposite directions, Professors Dodge and Soled argue:

> Norms are evidently somewhat malleable, and there is good reason to think that a prevailing pro-tax-compliance norm could well "flip" to a prevailing noncompliance norm in an environment of antigovernment rhetoric and critically minimized enforcement.[n.190] Since the mid-1990s, Congress has bashed the IRS, starved it for funds, and redirected its mission towards "service" (rather than enforcement), resulting in an individual audit rate below one percent. Thus, compliance norms are likely to be in acute danger of being swamped by a combination of self-interest and anticompliance norms.

Dodge & Soled, *supra*, at 577–78.

By contrast, scholars such as Dan Kahan and Eric Posner, quoted above, have alleged that enforcement actually has a negative effect on tax compliance. To what extent do you think enforcement of the tax laws will undermine compliance? For example, might increased enforcement provoke taxpayers to behave more adversarially towards the IRS or feel more like "chumps" if they pay voluntarily and thus reduce compliance? Do the statistics above suggesting that "an additional dollar allocated to audit would return $58 in general deterrence," Dubin, *supra*, affect your answer?

One perspective on these questions takes into account the likelihood that there are some taxpayers who will not comply with the tax laws absent a near 100 percent likelihood of detection and imposition of a severe penalty. Conversely, there are some

---

opportunity of individuals to demonstrate (to themselves and to others) that they are willing to sacrifice material gain for the public good." *Id.* at 76–77. — Eds.]

[n.190] *See* [Lederman, *supra* note 19], at 1509–11.

taxpayers who will always comply as well as they can with their tax obligations because they believe it is the right thing to do. It is the large third group of "conditional cooperators" that can tip the balance to a norm of compliance or noncompliance. Enforcement sufficient to increase compliance to a critical mass through deterrence may prompt compliance by the conditional compliers, who are influenced by the actions of those around them. *See* Jon S. Davis, Gary Hecht & Jon D. Perkins, *Social Behaviors, Enforcement, and Tax Compliance Dynamics*, 78 Acct. Rev. 39, 56 (2003); Leandra Lederman, *The Interplay Between Norms and Enforcement in Tax Compliance*, 64 Ohio St. L.J. 1453, 1509–10 (2003) (hereinafter, Lederman, *Interplay Between Norms and Enforcement*).

The theory that some taxpayers are conditional compliers who are influenced by the behavior of others does not apply only to individual taxpayers. Professor Susan Morse has argued that enforcement helps sustain tax compliance norms for corporations:

> Commentators have previously observed a historical cycle of fraud, crackdown, compliance, a shift of focus from enforcement to service, and then more fraud. The observed recent increase in compliance with respect to tax shelters may simply represent a reaction to the "crackdown" portion of the cycle. . . .
>
> [T]his Article attributes the increased interest in compliance to top executives' and tax specialists' fear of enforcement action. . . .

Morse, *supra* note 18, at 1013–14 (footnotes omitted).

Moreover, for businesses, competitiveness is an issue. In industries in which noncompliance is pervasive, some businesses may find it hard to stay afloat without cheating.

> Cash businesses present not only great opportunities for tax evasion but also a strong financial incentive to do so. In fact, in their fascinating article on cash business owners, Professors Joseph Bankman and Stuart Karlinsky report that one of the justifications used by cash business owners for underreporting is the need to do so to remain competitive.[n.269] Because of rampant noncompliance in the cash business sector, "all else being equal, absent policy changes that lead to more accurate reporting (and a different before-tax return to labor and capital), an 'honest' taxpayer should do worse in the cash sector than other taxpayers in that sector, and worse than she would do in the non-cash sector."[n.270]

Lederman, *Interplay Between Norms and Enforcement*, *supra*, at 1504–05 (footnotes omitted). Accordingly, absent enforcement to bring a critical mass of noncompliant businesses into compliance, a noncompliance norm may be fostered by competitive pressures.

Competition may also affect the tax compliance of public corporations because they face pressure to lower effective tax rates.[37] "The marketplace rewards companies with lower effective tax rates than their peers, creating a powerful competitive pressure for executives to manage tax liabilities aggressively." *Developments in the Law-Corporations and Society*, 117 Harv. L. Rev. 2249, 2249 n.4 (2004). For both small businesses and publicly held companies, sufficient enforcement may "tip" the community norm from noncompliance to compliance.

[n.269] Joseph Bankman & Stuart Karlinsky, *Cash Business Owners and Their Tax Preparers* 15 (NYU Colloquium on Tax Policy and Public Finance, Working Paper, 2001); *see also* Christopher Bergin, *CID to Employment Tax Evaders: "We Will Catch You"*, 2001 TNT 94-9 (May 15, 2001) (with respect to employment taxes, "some employers turn to evading taxes to stay competitive in their industry. It is apparently a serious problem in the construction industry.").

[n.270] Bankman & Karlinsky, *supra* note 269, at 15.

[37] *See* Lederman, *supra* note 26, at 724 n.172.

Thus, a generally — though not uniformly — accepted view is that without visible and effective enforcement activities by the IRS, taxpayers may begin to take liberties with the law because they may perceive that others are doing so without adverse consequences. The government's recent focus on enforcement, which includes a well-publicized multi-faceted attack on the spread of corporate tax shelters and off-shore tax avoidance activity, accords with that view.[38]

[C] Where Do We Go From Here?

The materials in this section should have given you a feel for the multi-layered nature of issues relating to the tax gap and tax evasion and prompted you to think about how the government should address these issues. For example, given limited resources, should the most visible — or the most stubborn — forms of noncompliance be prioritized? Should specific types of claims with high error rates be prioritized for audit, even if the dollar amounts involved are low? The complex Earned Income Tax Credit (EITC) available to low-income taxpayers involves a notoriously high error rate but relatively small amounts of money.[39] EITC claims have experienced comparatively high audit rates compared to other claims. For example, "[i]n 2000, low-income taxpayers accounted for approximately forty-four percent of all IRS audits, with the odds of audit for low-income taxpayers approximately one in ninety while for everyone else the risk of an audit was approximately one in 370." Leslie M. Book, *The IRS's EITC Compliance Regime: Taxpayers Caught in the Net*, 81 Or. L. Rev. 351, 374 (2002).

Does this allocation of resources make sense? "[T]he increased audits of low-income taxpayers were set in motion by President Clinton as a political compromise with the Republican Congress in exchange for the continuation of the EITC." Dorothy A. Brown, *Race and Class Matters in Tax Policy*, 107 Colum. L. Rev. 790, 808 (2007). Note also that EITC claims, though administered through the tax system, raise issues that other types of tax claims may not:

> [T]ypical welfare programs are not funded based upon self-declared eligibility. The review process is much more rigorous. Generally applicants can't declare themselves eligible for transfer programs such as Temporary Assistance to Needy Families (TANF). A beneficiary must establish to the satisfaction of the government agency that he or she is eligible before receiving any benefits. In effect, there is a one hundred percent audit rate for traditional welfare programs.

Id. at 808–09.

Identifying the areas on which to focus government resources addresses only half of the question. Once the government has prioritized certain issues or types of returns, what techniques should the government use? Should it increase audits, penalties, service, structural mechanisms that constrain compliance, or some combination of these and other techniques?

The theme of how best to manage tax administration so as to achieve appropriate compliance with the tax laws with an efficient investment of resources runs throughout the book. Keep this framework in mind as you consider such issues as the content IRS guidance should contain, and to what extent courts should defer to that guidance; the appropriateness of audit rates and investigatory techniques; how much access citizens should have to government information and to what extent taxpayer information should

---

[38] Tax shelters are discussed further in Chapter 12. For additional reading on corporate tax shelters, including a discussion of the steps the government has taken to fight them, see Chapter 16 of Leandra Lederman, *Understanding Corporate Taxation* (2nd ed. 2006).

[39] *See* Leslie Book, *Preventing the Hybrid from Backfiring: Delivery of Benefits to the Working Poor Through the Tax System*, 2006 Wis. L. Rev. 1103, 1105–06 & n.13.

be kept confidential; the appropriateness of procedural hurdles in tax controversies and standards of review of government action; optimal levels of tax penalties; what constitute appropriate tax collection tools and limitations on tax collection power; and the ethical issues that can arise in tax representation.

PROBLEMS

1. What are the principal government entities involved in tax administration and the tax controversy process?
2. Alan, who is unmarried, has received a "30-day letter" from the IRS. Attached to the letter is a Revenue Agent's Report explaining adjustments to income that result in a $20,000 underpayment of tax. What are Alan's options in response to the 30-day letter?
3. Beatrice, a widow, has received a notice of deficiency in the amount of $40,000 from the IRS. What are Beatrice's possible responses to the notice?
4. The self-assessment system of taxation is sometimes referred to as a "voluntary compliance" system. Why is that?
5. What do you think the principal motivators for compliance with federal taxes are? What methods would you suggest for improving tax compliance, either generally, or for a specific subset of taxpayers?
6. Do you think that increasing the rate of audit of individual federal income tax returns from its current level would be appropriate and helpful? Why?
7. Suppose that Senator Smith has proposed raising penalties for tax understatements to 50% of the amount of the understatement. Do you think the proposal is likely to encourage or discourage tax compliance? Would it be more helpful to tailor penalties to aspects of the taxpayer's behavior, as Professor Raskolnikov's proposed self-adjusting penalty would do with respect to erroneous deductions and credits?

Chapter 2
IRS RULEMAKING

§ 2.01 INTRODUCTION

As you know from other tax courses, substantive tax law can be a highly technical and complicated subject. The fact that so many tax questions remain unanswered speaks to the complexity of the Internal Revenue Code and to the ingenuity of tax advisors seeking to minimize their clients' tax liabilities. To interpret the Code, tax practitioners turn not only to court cases, but also to Treasury regulations and to other guidance released by the IRS, including Revenue Rulings and Revenue Procedures. The next section of this chapter considers the taxpayer's ability to rely on these types of sources and the amount of deference a court will accord these pronouncements.

In some cases, tax practitioners may find it necessary to seek the views of the IRS in order to confirm how the Code should apply to a given set of facts. The chapter therefore discusses various types of taxpayer-specific guidance, with an emphasis on letter rulings (commonly referred to as private letter rulings or PLRs). The chapter also considers the letter ruling request process more generally, focusing on situations in which the IRS will and will not issue guidance, and on the type of information the requesting party must include in the letter ruling application. In addition, the discussion highlights some advantages and pitfalls associated with the taxpayer's decision to seek a letter ruling from the IRS.

§ 2.02 TAXPAYER RELIANCE ON PUBLISHED AUTHORITY

[A] Treasury Regulations

Reading Assignment: I.R.C. § 7805(a)–(b), (e); 5 U.S.C. § 553.

[1] Procedures for Enacting Treasury Regulations

The Code authorizes the Secretary of the Treasury to "prescribe all needful rules and regulations for the enforcement of [the Code]." I.R.C. § 7805(a). Although the Secretary has delegated much of this rulemaking authority to the IRS Chief Counsel's Office, which drafts most regulations, the Treasury Department actually issues those regulations. Treasury regulations represent official interpretations of the Code. In addition to explaining the statutory language to which they relate, regulations also may contain helpful examples of how and when a Code provision should apply.

There are two principal types of final regulations, interpretive regulations and legislative regulations. Regulations published pursuant to the general grant of Congressional authority in section 7805(a) are generally referred to as interpretive regulations. Those released under an express delegation of Congressional authority in the particular Code section they address are generally referred to as legislative. *See, e.g.*, I.R.C. §§ 263A(i), 385(a).[1]

Legislative regulations must be issued under the procedural requirements of the Administrative Procedure Act (APA), 5 U.S.C. § 553, which requires notice to the public

---

[1] Several scholars have argued that a distinction between interpretive and legislative regulations that rests on whether the Treasury issues the regulation pursuant to section 7805(a) is misguided. *See, e.g.*, Kristin E. Hickman, *Coloring Outside the Lines: Examining Treasury's (Lack of) Compliance with Administrative Procedure Act Rulemaking Requirements*, 82 NOTRE DAME L. REV. 1727, 1761–64 (2007); Noel B. Cunningham & James R. Repetti, *Textualism and Tax Shelters*, 24 VA. TAX REV. 1, 41, 45 (2004); Irving Salem et al., *ABA Section of Taxation Report of the Task Force on Judicial Deference*, 57 TAX LAW. 717, 738–39 (2004).

and an opportunity to comment on the regulations before they are finalized. Once comments are received, the regulations must be published in their final form in the Federal Register at least 30 days prior to their effective date. 5 U.S.C. § 553(b)(3), (d). Interpretive regulations, issued under the broad authority of section 7805, arguably are not subject to the 30-day notice and comment period, but the Treasury often follows that procedure anyway.[2]

In order to fulfill its obligations under the APA, the Treasury normally issues legislative and interpretive regulations initially in proposed form. The Treasury may also issue Temporary regulations when an immediate interpretation of a new statute is required. Temporary regulations are effective until superseded by final regulations, but in no event may they remain effective for more than three years after enactment. I.R.C. § 7805(e). Temporary regulations need not follow the usual APA notice and comment procedures. 5 U.S.C. § 553(b)(3)(B).

Until the 1990s, Code section 7805(b) allowed the Secretary of the Treasury to prescribe the extent to which, if any, a regulation would be applied *without* retroactive effect. However, the Taxpayer Bill of Rights 2, Pub. L. No. 104-168, § 1101, 110 Stat. 1452, 1468 (1996), removed this presumption of retroactivity. Under section 7805(b)(1)(B), final regulations generally do not take effect before the date on which related Proposed or Temporary regulations were published in the Federal Register.

[2] Courts' Deference to Treasury Regulations

While courts generally give deference to Treasury regulations, they do have the power to invalidate them. The leading case on courts' deference to the pronouncements of government agencies is *Chevron U.S.A., Inc. v. Natural Resources Defense Council, Inc.*, 467 U.S. 837 (1984), which is not a tax case. In that case, the Supreme Court stated:

> When a court reviews an agency's construction of the statute which it administers, it is confronted with two questions. First, always, is the question whether Congress has directly spoken to the precise question at issue. If the intent of Congress is clear, that is the end of the matter; for the court, as well as the agency, must give effect to the unambiguously expressed intent of Congress. If, however, the court determines Congress has not directly addressed the precise question at issue, the court does not simply impose its own construction on the statute, as would be necessary in the absence of an administrative interpretation. Rather, if the statute is silent or ambiguous with respect to the specific issue, the question for the court is whether the agency's answer is based on a permissible construction of the statute.

Id. at 843. The Court added in a footnote: "The court need not conclude that the agency construction was the only one it permissibly could have adopted to uphold the construction, or even the reading the court would have reached if the question initially had arisen in a judicial proceeding." *Id.* at 843 n.11 (citations omitted).

Considerable debate exists over the extent to which "*Chevron* deference" applies in tax cases. *Bankers Life and Casualty Co. v. United States*, 142 F.3d 973 (1998), discusses the issue of whether *Chevron* deference applies to Treasury regulations, as well as the issue of whether the level of deference varies between legislative and interpretive (which the court sometimes refers to as "general authority") regulations.

---

[2] Professor Hickman's study found that, although "Treasury purports to utilize notice-and-comment rulemaking in promulgating most Treasury regulations[,] . . . [a]lmost as often as not, Treasury does not follow the traditional APA-required pattern of issuing [a notice of proposed rulemaking], accepting and considering public comments, and only then publishing its final regulations." Hickman, *supra* note 1, at 1729–30. Specifically, she found that, in the three-year period she studied, the IRS issued temporary regulations simultaneously with the notice of proposed rulemaking in 84 of 232 rulemaking projects, and in 11 projects, it omitted the notice and comment process entirely. *Id.* at 1748–49.

On the latter question, the Supreme Court's subsequent decision in *United States v. Mead Corp.*, 533 U.S. 218 (2001), discussed below, largely confirms the Seventh Circuit's analysis.

BANKERS LIFE AND CASUALTY CO. v. UNITED STATES

United States Court of Appeals, Seventh Circuit
142 F.3d 973 (1998)[3]

TERENCE T. EVANS, CIRCUIT JUDGE.

* * *

Before explaining Bankers Life's substantive arguments or the government's responses, we need to cover the basic structure of a challenge to a tax regulation. Essentially, we must determine the degree of deference owed to a Treasury Regulation issued under I.R.C. § 7805(a) with notice and comment procedures. This seemingly simple inquiry leads us into a free-fire zone of judicial debate over the proper level of judicial deference to various IRS interpretations of the revenue laws. The basic question is whether *Chevron* deference (from *Chevron U.S.A., Inc. v. Natural Resources Defense Council , Inc.*, 467 U.S. 837, 81 L. Ed. 2d 694, 104 S. Ct. 2778 (1984), and its progeny) applies to tax regulations. *See, e.g.,* Central Pa. Sav. Ass'n v. Commissioner, 104 T.C. 384, 390–91 (1995) (discussing the "checkered career" of *Chevron* deference in the tax arena), *supplemented by*, 71 T.C.M. (CCH) 2724, 1996 WL 165489 (1996). In addition to the debate in the case law, the topic has generated heated scholarly commentary. *See* Ellen P. Aprill, Muffled Chevron: Judicial Review of Tax Regulations, 3 Fl. Tax Rev. 51 (1996) (describing and advocating a fusion of *Chevron* and *National Muffler*, 440 U.S. 472, 59 L. Ed. 2d 519, 99 S. Ct. 1304 (1979)); * * * John F. Coverdale, Court Review of Tax Regulations and Revenue Rulings in the Chevron Era, 34 Geo. Wash. L. Rev. 35 (1995) (arguing for distinct levels of non-*Chevron* deference for each type of tax interpretation); * * *.

The IRS interprets the tax code in four significantly different ways: (1) regulations issued pursuant to a specific directive from Congress, (2) regulations issued under the IRS's general authority to interpret the tax laws, (3) revenue rulings, and (4) private letter rulings. Each of these categories often receives different deference from the courts. While the first three categories constitute interpretations of general applicability, letter rulings apply only to the parties who specifically request them. Neither the courts nor the IRS may rely on letter rulings as precedent. *See* I.R.C. § 6110(j)(3) (1988) [currently I.R.C. § 6110(k)(3) — Eds.];* * *. At the other end of the spectrum from letter rulings are regulations issued under specific grants from Congress. The tax code contains a myriad of specific congressional instructions regarding rulemaking. *See* Coverdale, *supra*, at 52 (estimating the number of specific grants at over 1000 and providing examples). Pursuant to the Administrative Procedures Act ("APA"), the IRS issues these rules with full notice and comment. *See* 5 U.S.C. § 553 (1994). In the middle, between letter rulings and specific authority regulations, are general authority regulations and revenue rulings. The IRS issues general authority regulations under its power to "prescribe all needful rules and regulations." *See* I.R.C. § 7805(a) (1994). While the IRS takes the position that regulations issued solely under this general authority do not require notice and comment, the agency nevertheless usually follows full notice and comment procedures. *See* First Chicago NBD Corp. v. Commissioner, 135 F.3d 457, 1998 WL 28113, *2 (7th Cir. 1998). In contrast, the IRS does not follow notice and comment procedures for revenue rulings. Revenue rulings typically contain the IRS's interpretation of how the law applies to a set of hypothetical facts. Revenue rulings do not have broad application like regulations, but the IRS does consider them authoritative and binding. *See* Rev. Proc. 95-1, § 2.05 (codified at Treas. Reg. § 601.201 (West

[3] *Cert. denied*, 525 U.S. 961 (1998).

1998)); Rev. Proc. 89-14, § 7.01 (codified at Treas. Reg. § 601.601 (West 1998)).

Revenue rulings receive the lowest degree of deference — at least in this circuit. In *First Chicago,* we held that revenue rulings deserve "some weight," 135 F.3d at 459, and are "entitled to respectful consideration, but not to the deference that the *Chevron* doctrine requires in its domain," *id.* at 458 (citations omitted). In other circuits this question has generated inconsistent rulings ranging from *Chevron* deference to no deference. * * *

Determining the level of deference accorded to regulations is more difficult. Initially it may appear that we can resolve the problem by resorting to the APA's distinction between legislative and interpretive regulations. *See* 5 U.S.C. § 553(b)(3)(A) (1994). Administrative law scholars usually treat legislative regulations as rules of full legal effect — they create new legal duties binding on the parties and the courts and, therefore, require full notice and comment procedures. Interpretive rules, on the other hand, only clarify existing duties and do not bind; thus, they do not require notice and comment. In the tax world, however, these terms and classifications seem to provide more confusion than clarity. Tax experts refer to specific authority regulations as "legislative" and to general authority regulations as "interpretive." The confusion arises because the "interpretive" designation does not mesh with the characteristics of the IRS's general authority regulations. While the IRS calls its general authority regulations interpretive, the agency promulgates them according to the same formal procedures it employs for its specific regulations. Moreover, both the specific authority and general authority regulations, create duties and have binding effect. *See* Aprill, *supra,* at 55–56; Coverdale, *supra,* 48–50.

If this legislative versus interpretive distinction held up for tax regulations, we could apply the simple rule described in *Hanson v. Espy,* 8 F.3d 469 (7th Cir. 1993). In that case, we explained the distinction between nontax legislative and interpretive regulations and said that *Chevron* applied to legislative regulations only. *See id.* 472 n.3. General tax regulations seem to carry the force of law, they are developed according to notice and comment, and they have the imprimatur of a congressional delegation of authority. In substance, general tax regulations fall short of being full legislative regulations only because the congressional delegation is general rather than specific. This distinction, however, may not have any effect at all on the standard of deference because *Chevron* itself dealt with a regulation promulgated under an arguably general grant of authority to the EPA under the Clean Air Act. Furthermore, *Chevron* stated that its framework applied to implicit congressional delegations as well as to specific and explicit directives. *See Chevron,* 467 U.S. at 844.[n.4]

In any event, courts uniformly give tremendous deference to regulations issued under a specific directive from Congress. In fact, some courts give these regulations the same force as statutes, focusing only on whether the agency promulgated the regulation properly within its scope of authority. *See* Coverdale, *supra,* at 53 (citing cases). We basically follow the same approach. In *Gehl Co. v. Commissioner,* 795 F.2d 1324 (7th Cir. 1986), we explained that "a court's main focus in examining a legislative regulation issued under a specific statutory authority 'is whether the interpretation or method is within the delegation of authority.' " *Id.* at 1329 (*quoting* Rowan Co. v. United States, 452 U.S. 247, 253, 68 L. Ed. 2d 814, 101 S. Ct. 2288 (1981)). One commentator suggests that this level of deference accords even greater respect to the IRS's views than *Chevron. See* Coverdale, *supra,* at 55. We leave that hypothesis for another day.

[n.4] *Chevron* arguably, therefore, altered the understanding of a line of Supreme Court cases often applied to "interpretive" tax regulations. *See* National Muffler Dealers Ass'n v. United States, 440 U.S. 472, 59 L. Ed. 2d 519, 99 S. Ct. 1304 (1979); Rowan Co. v. United States, 452 U.S. 247, 68 L. Ed. 2d 814, 101 S. Ct. 2288 (1981); United States v. Vogel, 455 U.S. 16, 70 L. Ed. 2d 792, 102 S. Ct. 821 (1982). These cases all distinguished between regulations issued under specific grants of authority (full deference) and regulations issued under general grants of authority (less deference).

Where then does all of this leave tax regulations promulgated under general authority? The question would be easier if the IRS did not employ notice and comment rulemaking procedures — in other words, if general authority tax regulations more truly resembled interpretive regulations. In *Atchison, Topeka and Santa Fe Railway v. Pena*, 44 F.3d 437 (7th Cir. 1994) (*en banc*), *aff'd without discussion, Brotherhood of Locomotive Engineers v. Atchison, Topeka and Santa Fe Railway*, 516 U.S. 152, 133 L. Ed. 2d 535, 116 S. Ct. 595 (1996), we held that courts should accord only moderate deference to interpretive regulations issued without notice and comment by an agency without general rulemaking powers. *See id* at 442; *see also* Central Midwest Interstate LowLevel Radioactive Waste Comm'n v. Pena, 113 F.3d 1468, 1473 (7th Cir. 1997) ("we do not apply *Chevron's* 'rubber stamp' to interpretive rules"). As the *Atchison* court explained:

> Whatever degree of deference due these interpretive rules is dictated by the circumstances surrounding the agency's adoption of its statutory interpretation. "The weight given to an agency interpretation depends on many factors, including the validity of its reasoning, its consistency with earlier and later agency pronouncements and whether the administrative document was issued contemporaneously with the passage of the statute being interpreted." Doe v. Reivitz, [830 F.2d 1441, 1447 (7th Cir. 1987), *amended*, 842 F.2d 194 (7th Cir. 1988)]. In short, we look to "the thoroughness, validity, and consistency of the agency's reasoning." Orrego v. 833 West Buena Joint Venture, 943 F.2d 730, 736 (7th Cir. 1991) (*citing* United States v. Markgraf, 736 F.2d 1179, 1184 (7th Cir. 1984)).

Atchison, 44 F.3d at 442.

In accord with its emphasis on the "circumstances surrounding the agency's adoption" of the regulation, the *Atchison* court understood *Chevron* either to apply or not to apply based on the extent to which an agency follows full notice and comment rulemaking procedures. The court explained that the notice and comment process provides a critical component in our decision to grant *Chevron* deference:

> The principal rationale underlying [*Chevron*] deference is that in this context the agency acts as a congressional proxy; Congress develops the statutory framework and directs the agency to flesh out the operational details. But Congress typically does not permit the agency to run free in this endeavor; the Administrative Procedures Act establishes certain procedures that the agency must follow. Chief among them is the notice-and-comment provision of the APA. 5 U.S.C. § 553. This rulemaking process bears some resemblance to the legislative process and serves to temper the resultant rules such that they are likely to withstand vigorous scrutiny. It is this process that entitles the administrative rules to judicial deference.

Id. at 441–42.

In this regard *Atchison* is not unique. For instance, in *Pennington v. Didrickson*, 22 F.3d 1376 (7th Cir. 1994), we explained "[w]e are mindful of our obligation to defer to the interpretation of the agency whenever that interpretation can be said to embody a deliberate and considered interpretation of the legislative intent." *Id.* at 1383. When an agency undertakes notice and comment procedures it elevates the status of a regulation above mere interpretation. Similarly, in *Doe v. Reivitz*, 830 F.2d 1441, 1446–47 (7th Cir. 1987), *amended*, 842 F.2d 194 (7th Cir. 1988), we characterized regulations promulgated with the full panoply of procedures as "high powered" rules meriting *Chevron* deference. Thus, in this circuit it appears that rules developed pursuant to notice and comment procedures constitute full legislative regulations.

So, is there an answer to the question of whether we give *Chevron* deference to general authority tax regulations promulgated with notice and comment? At first it might appear that we shut the door on that question in *Bell Federal Savings & Loan*

Ass'n v. Commissioner, 40 F.3d 224, 226 (7th Cir. 1994). Unfortunately, that case does not provide definitive closure.

In *Bell Federal* we considered an IRS regulation promulgated under the general authorization statute, I.R.C. § 7805(a), just like the regulation in this case. We weighed whether to apply *Chevron* deference (as the Sixth Circuit did in *Peoples Federal Savings & Loan Ass'n v. Commissioner*, 948 F.2d 289, 304–05 (6th Cir. 1991)) or whether to apply a more narrow traditional rule of deference to tax regulations (as the Ninth Circuit did in *Pacific First Federal Savings Bank v. Commissioner*, 961 F.2d 800, 805–08 (9th Cir. 1992)). The *Bell Federal* court opted for the traditional rule apparently because it was more narrowly tailored to tax regulations:

> The proper test for the validation of a challenged regulation thus requires only that the regulation issued by the Commissioner constitute a reasonable implementation of Congress's mandate. The Commissioner's interpretation need not be the only, or even the most, reasonable interpretation possible as "the choice among reasonable interpretations is for the Commissioner, not the courts."

40 F.3d at 227 (*quoting* National Muffler Dealers Ass'n v. United States, 440 U.S. 472, 488, 59 L. Ed. 2d 519, 99 S. Ct. 1304 (1979)). *Bell Federal* continued by explaining that courts should inquire into whether the regulation " 'harmonizes with the plain language of the statute, its origin, and its purpose.' " *Id.* (*quoting National Muffler*, 440 U.S. at 477).

Bell Federal's choice of the traditional rule appeared eminently reasonable at the time. In *Cottage Savings Ass'n v. Commissioner*, 499 U.S. 554, 560–61, 113 L. Ed. 2d 589, 111 S. Ct. 1503 (1991), the Supreme Court conspicuously did not cite *Chevron* and appeared to apply the traditional rule of tax deference: "Because Congress had delegated to the Commissioner the power to promulgate 'all needful rules and regulations for the enforcement of [the Internal Revenue Code],' 26 U.S.C. § 7805(a), we must defer to his regulatory interpretations of the Code so long as they are reasonable." *Id.* at 560–61 (*citing National Muffler*).

The *Bell Federal* court equivocated, however, on whether there was any real difference between *Chevron* and the traditional rule. *Chevron* upholds a regulation if the agency based its interpretation on a permissible construction of a statute, *see* 467 U.S. at 843, while the traditional rule validates the regulation if the agency reasonably implemented Congress's mandate. Noting that "both approaches apply essentially the same test," the *Bell Federal* court stated that "the difference between these two approaches is negligible at best — any regulation which is 'based upon a permissible construction' of an ambiguous statute will almost always 'implement the congressional mandate in some reasonable manner' and vice versa . . . ." 40 F.3d at 227.

While *Bell Federal's* hedging about the difference between *Chevron* and the traditional rule gives us pause, we hesitate to apply the traditional rule for another reason. We think that the *en banc* decision in *Atchison* reopened the door that *Bell Federal* seemed to have shut. As Chief Judge Posner stated in *First Chicago*, "we consider [*Chevron's*] application to interpretive rules issued by the Treasury to be open in this circuit, since the Treasury has decided to use the notice and comment procedure for interpretive rules, though not required to do so by statute." 135 F.3d at 459 (citation omitted).

Atchison explained that the notice and comment procedure was the sine qua non for *Chevron* deference. Because the IRS promulgates general authority regulations through a notice and comment process, *Atchison* militates forcefully in favor of according *Chevron* deference to those regulations. Thus, after *Bell Federal*, *Atchison* altered the balance and tipped the scales in favor of *Chevron*.

Furthermore, we think *Bell Federal's* description of a "negligible" difference between the approaches might overstate the true extent of the divergence. *Chevron* held that "a court may not substitute its own construction of a statutory provision for a reasonable interpretation made by the administrator of an agency." 467 U.S. at 844. While the two approaches articulate the level of deference differently, they both come down to one operative concept — reasonableness. Thus, *Chevron* and the traditional rule constitute two different formulations of a reasonableness test. There may be some subtle difference in the phrasing of each framework, but we should be wary of attempts to discern too many gradations of reasonableness. As we explained in *Boyce v. Fernandes*, 77 F.3d 946 (7th Cir. 1996), "human ability to make fine distinctions is limited." *Id.* at 948 (describing the difficulty in distinguishing between the inquiries into a police officer's probable cause for an arrest and whether that officer receives qualified immunity). Viewed from this perspective at least, the supposed gap between *Chevron* and the traditional rule is a distinction without a difference.

* * *

This all leads us to the $64,000 question: If the deference test walks like *Chevron* and talks like *Chevron*, why shouldn't we just call it *Chevron*? Or, phrased differently, if the two standards are the same, does our denomination make any difference? Our answer lies with consistency. While we do not doubt that "foolish consistency is the hobgoblin of little minds, adored by little statesmen and philosophers and divines," Ralph Waldo Emerson, Self Reliance, Essays: First Series (1841), we hope that our emphasis on consistency does not qualify as foolishness. On the contrary, consistency in the law forms the backbone of effective jurisprudence. *See, e.g.*, Piper Aircraft Corp. v. WagAero, Inc., 741 F.2d 925, 937 (7th Cir. 1984) (Posner, J., concurring) ("The most important function of appellate review is to maintain the consistency of the law; if consistency is not a desideratum, the argument for appellate review is weakened."). Because the APA imposes uniform procedures on agencies that formulate rules, there is some incentive for courts to apply a uniform framework for challenges to regulations developed with notice and comment. A consistent approach might help alleviate the tensions evident in the now-resolved conflict between the Sixth Circuit and the Tax Court over *Chevron*. *See* Peoples Fed. Sav. & Loan Ass'n v. Commissioner, 948 F.2d 289, 304–05 (6th Cir. 1991) ("[W]e conclude that the Tax Court used the wrong standard to decide this case. Entirely ignoring *Chevron* . . . the Tax Court employed the standard in *National Muffler Dealers* which seemed to allow a plenary review of the legislative history without the deference requirements found in *Chevron* . . . ."). More practically, our decision signals an effort to move toward a resolution of the current circuit split on the issue. Currently the Sixth Circuit accords *Chevron* deference to all tax regulations. *See Peoples Federal.* Meanwhile, the Third and Fifth Circuits have rejected *Chevron* for general authority tax regulations. *See* E.I. du Pont de Nemours & Co. v. Commissioner, 41 F.3d 130, 135–36 & n.23 (3d Cir. 1994); Nalle v. Commissioner, 997 F.2d 1134, 1138–39 (5th Cir. 1993). Furthermore, we wish to avoid the situation in the Third Circuit — divergent treatment for notice and comment regulations depending on whether they are tax or nontax rules. *See* Elizabeth Blackwell Health Ctr. for Women v. Knoll, 61 F.3d 170, 182 (3d Cir. 1995) (applying *Chevron* to a nontax interpretive regulation), *cert. denied*, 516 U.S. 1093, 133 L. Ed. 2d 760, 116 S. Ct. 816 (1996). We see no reason that nontax regulations issued with notice and comment should receive *Chevron* deference while tax regulations promulgated with the same procedures receive something different.

More importantly, in contrast to our foregoing analysis of the similarities between the traditional rule and *Chevron*, there are some important differences. These considerations also argue in favor of *Chevron*. *Chevron* is the focus of ongoing development by the Supreme Court, especially regarding the scope of the initial inquiry into statutory meaning. *See, e.g.*, National R.R. Passenger Corp. v. Boston & Marine Corp., 503 U.S. 407, 417–18, 118 L. Ed. 2d 52, 112 S. Ct. 1394 (1992) (reformulating the first step of *Chevron* analysis by focusing on the plain language of the statute rather than the intent of Congress). We do not labor under the illusion that *Chevron* will provide monolithic certainty for all courts reviewing administrative rules — we recognize the Court's own inconsistency regarding *Chevron.* * * * We do hope, however, that by employing a uniform framework for challenges to administrative regulations we can better stay abreast of the Court's dictates.

We also favor *Chevron* because many courts contend that the traditional rule accords less than *Chevron* deference to tax regulations. The Sixth Circuit, for instance, characterizes *National Muffler* as allowing "plenary review" contrasted with *Chevron* deference. *See Peoples Federal,* 948 F.2d at 305. The Third and Fifth Circuits believe that the traditional rule entitles a regulation to "less deference" than under *Chevron. See E.I. du Pont,* 41 F.3d 130 at 135 n. 23; *Nalle,* 997 F.2d at 1139. As *Atchison* explains, we owe full *Chevron* deference to a regulation issued with the full deliberative procedures. Although we acknowledge the gulf between the idealized *Chevron* and the realized one, we do believe that the structure of *Chevron* encourages a court to defer rather than to interpret. We, therefore, prefer it.

Under *Chevron* deference we apply a two-step analysis: (1) We examine the text of the statute — in this case, the relevant section of the tax code. If the plain meaning of the text either supports or opposes the regulation, then we stop our analysis and either strike or validate the regulation. But if we conclude the statute is either ambiguous or silent on the issue, we continue to the second step: (2) We examine the reasonableness of the regulation. If the regulation is a reasonable reading of the statute, we give deference to the agency's interpretation. *See National R.R. Passenger Corp.,* 503 U.S. at 417–18; *Chevron,* 467 U.S. at 842–43, 81 L. Ed. 2d 694, 104 S. Ct. 2781–82.

While this circuit has examined legislative history during the first step of *Chevron, see* Illinois EPA v. United States EPA, 947 F.2d 283, 289 (7th Cir. 1991) ("To ascertain the intent of the law, we must examine the plain meaning of the statute at issue, the language and design of the statute as a whole, and, where necessary, less satisfactory indicia of congressional intent such as legislative history." (citations omitted)), we now seem to lean toward reserving consideration of legislative history and other appropriate factors until the second *Chevron* step, *cf.* Alex v. City of Chicago, 29 F.3d 1235, 1239 (7th Cir. 1994) ("when statutory meaning is clear with respect to the issue at bar judicial inquiry normally should end without heed to the embellishments of secondary materials like legislative history"). In the second step, the court determines whether the regulation harmonizes with the language, origins, and purpose of the statute. While not dispositive, a court may find various considerations informative — these considerations might include the consistency of the agency's interpretation, the contemporaneousness of the interpretation, and the robustness of the regulation following congressional re-enactment of the underlying statute. Although we sometimes describe *Chevron* as a "rubber stamp," *see Atchison,* 44 F.3d at 442, we know that agencies occasionally act unreasonably. Given the scope of the permissible inquiry under *Chevron's* second step, we believe that courts can rein in the excesses of unreasonable administrative rulemaking. With that said, however, we reiterate *Chevron's* fundamental dictate that a court must not "substitute its own construction of a statutory provision for a reasonable interpretation" by the agency in question. 467 U.S. at 84, 104 S.Ct. at 2782.

* * *

Bankers Life provides a valuable, albeit long-winded, exposition of both the "traditional" rule relating to tax regulations under *National Muffler* and the *Chevron* rule. Based on the court's analysis were you able to discern in the end which rule, at least according to the Seventh Circuit, gives more deference to regulations? Does it matter whether the regulation is interpretive or legislative?

[a] Which Deference Standard Applies, *Chevron* or *National Muffler*?

In *United States v. Mead Corp.*, 533 U.S. 218 (2001), discussed in more detail in Section 2.02[B], the Supreme Court set forth a test for when *Chevron* deference should apply to an agency interpretation. According to the Court, *Chevron* deference applies "when it appears that Congress delegated authority to the agency generally to make rules carrying the force of law, and that the agency interpretation claiming deference was promulgated in the exercise of that authority. Delegation of such authority may be shown in a variety of ways, as by an agency's power to engage in adjudication or notice-and-comment rulemaking, or by some other indication of a comparable congressional intent." *Id.* at 227. Under this test, would both legislative and interpretive tax regulations fall within those parameters?

Although the Supreme Court has had the opportunity to do so, the Court has not given a definitive indication of whether, in tax cases, the *Chevron* or the traditional (*National Muffler*) rule applies to Treasury regulations. *See* United States v. Cleveland Indians Baseball Co., 532 U.S. 200 (2001) (citing *National Muffler*, but not citing *Chevron*). In a case subsequent to *Mead*, the Court again failed to confront the issue head-on. In *Boeing Co. v. United States*, 537 U.S. 437 (2003), despite the lower court's reliance on *Chevron*, the Supreme Court apparently ignored both *Chevron* and *Mead*.

Boeing involved the validity of regulations under section 861, which provide rules for allocating research and development expenses between foreign and domestic sources. After a brief discussion of whether the regulations at issue were legislative or interpretive, the Court concluded that "[e]ven if we regard the challenged regulation as interpretive because it was promulgated under § 7805 (a)'s general rulemaking grant rather than pursuant to a specific grant of authority, we must still treat the regulation with deference." *Id.* at 448 (*citing* Cottage Sav. Ass'n v. Commissioner, 499 U.S. 554, 560–61 (1991)). The Court then compared the language of the regulation to that of the statute and concluded that the IRS's position was "surely not arbitrary." *Id.* at 449. The Court characterized the taxpayer's arguments relating to the statutory language as "plainly insufficient to overcome the deference to which the Secretary's interpretation is entitled." *Id.* at 451.

While the Supreme Court avoids the issue, debate among lower courts continues. The issue of whether *Chevron* applies to tax regulations was joined in *Swallows Holding v. Commissioner*, 126 T.C. 96 (2006) (reviewed by the court), *vacated and remanded*, 515 F.3d 162 (3d Cir. 2008). *Swallows Holding* involved the validity of regulations issued under the broad grant of authority in section 7805. Judge Laro, writing for the majority in the Tax Court, raised the interpretive/legislative distinction and concluded that the Tax Court has generally applied the traditional rule in *National Muffler* to interpretive regulations and the *Chevron* rule to legislative regulations. Responding to the issue of whether the Supreme Court intended *Chevron* deference to displace the traditional rule in tax cases, he asserted that:

> We have previously stated with respect to that question: "we are inclined to the view that the impact of the traditional, *i.e.*, *National Muffler* standard, has not been changed by *Chevron*, but has merely been restated in a practical two-part test with possibly subtle distinctions as to the role of legislative history and the degree of deference to be accorded to a regulation." . . . Here, we conclude likewise that we need not parse the semantics of the two tests to discern any substantive difference between them. While we apply a *Natl. Muffler* analysis, our result under a *Chevron* analysis would be the same.

126 T.C. at 131.[4]

---

[4] A vigorous dissent by Judge Holmes, joined by Judge Swift, raised the distinction between *Chevron* and the traditional rule.

On appeal, the Third Circuit rejected the Tax Court's conclusion about the validity of the regulations and its method of analysis. On the issue of whether *Chevron* applies, the Third Circuit stated:

> We note first that the deference owed to regulations issued under I.R.C. § 7805(a) has been described over the years in different ways. In *National Muffler*, of course, the Supreme Court listed factors such as whether the regulation was contemporaneous with the statute, the age of the regulation, and the consistency of its interpretation. 440 U.S. at 477. More recently, however, in *United States v. Cleveland Indians Baseball Co.*, 532 U.S. 200, 219, 121 S. Ct. 1433, 149 L. Ed. 2d 401 (2001), the Court remarked that "we defer to the Commissioner's regulations as long as they 'implement the congressional mandate in some reasonable manner.'" *Id.* at 219 (quoting *United States v. Correll*, 389 U.S. 299, 306–07, 88 S. Ct. 445, 19 L. Ed. 2d 537 (1967)).
>
> * * *
>
> Taxpayer argues . . . that the Secretary promulgated an interpretive regulation and that interpretive regulations, as a class, do not merit *Chevron* deference. We disagree. When determining whether Congress intends a particular agency action to carry the force of law, our inquiry does not hinge solely on the type of agency action involved. Rather, "[d]elegation of such authority may be shown in a variety of ways, as by an agency's power to engage in adjudication or notice-and-comment rule-making, or by some other indication of a comparable congressional intent." *Mead*, 533 U.S. at 227. . . . Here, the Secretary opened the rule to public comment, a move that is indicative of agency action that carries the force of law. *Id.* at 229–30; Cleary v. Waldman, 167 F.3d 801, 808 (3d Cir.1999). Accordingly, the resulting regulation is entitled to *Chevron* deference if it survives *Chevron*'s two prong inquiry.

515 F.3d at 168–70.

[b] If *Chevron* Applies, Then How?

Assuming that the *Chevron* standard controls, how should the two-part test be applied? In the final paragraph of *Bankers Life*, notice that the Seventh Circuit would reserve an inquiry into the legislative history of the statute underlying the regulation until the second step of the *Chevron* analysis. A Supreme Court decision involving the issue of whether the Food and Drug Administration has the authority to regulate tobacco as a "drug" (it does not), *FDA v. Brown & Williamson*, 529 U.S. 120, 132 (2000), indicates that a court should consider the legislative history of the underlying statute as part of its initial inquiry into whether Congress has already spoken to the specific question at issue. Does an examination of legislative history in step one of the *Chevron* analysis lead to greater or lesser deference to the agency's interpretation? *See* Irving Salem & Richard Bress, *Agency Deference Under the Judicial Microscope of the Supreme Court*, 88 Tax Notes 1257 (2000).

The Third Circuit's opinion in *Swallows Holding* provides further insight into how *Chevron* should apply and the distinction between *Chevron* analysis and the traditional rule. The interpretive regulations at issue in *Swallows Holding* were promulgated

---

> My disagreement with the majority is not just a disagreement about how to apply *National Muffler*. Instead, I think the problem lies in a very subtle distinction between *National Muffler* and *Chevron* — "reasonableness" using the *National Muffler* factors is taken to mean "is the Secretary construing the statute reasonably?," while under *Chevron* it means "is the Secretary behaving unreasonably by violating the statute in the course of exercising his delegated authority to set policy?" Both cases look to reasonableness, but in different ways. . . .

126 T.C. at 175 (Holmes, J., dissenting).

under Code section 882, which allows foreign corporations to deduct expenses related to real property investments held in the U.S. only in limited circumstances. The regulations in section 1.882-4 typically require a foreign corporation seeking to deduct expenses to file its return within 18 months of the filing deadline in section 6072(c), which is five and a half months after the end of the corporation's taxable year. A majority of the Tax Court judges had found that the regulations imposing the 18-month deadline exceeded the Treasury's rulemaking authority. The Tax Court, therefore, held the regulations invalid, thereby allowing the taxpayer to report its deductions even though it had filed its return after the deadline date. The IRS appealed.

The Third Circuit explained that the Tax Court's opinion had identified six factors set out in *National Muffler* that a court should consider when assessing the reasonableness of the agency's actions:

> (1) whether the regulation is a substantially contemporaneous construction of the statute by those presumed to have been aware of congressional intent; (2) the manner in which a regulation dating from a later period evolved; (3) the length of time that the regulation has been in effect; (4) the reliance placed upon the regulation; (5) the consistency of the Secretary's interpretations; and (6) the degree of scrutiny Congress has devoted to the regulation during subsequent reenactments of this statute.

Swallows Holding v. Commissioner, 515 F. 3d 162, 166 (3d Cir. 2008). The Tax Court had found that the regulations imposing the 18-month filing deadline failed to meet several of those factors, so the regulation was not a reasonable exercise of the Treasury's rulemaking authority. In particular, the Tax Court had found that the regulation was not a substantially contemporaneous construction of the statute; the regulation evolved after decisions by several courts had repeatedly held that the statute did not include a timely filing requirement; the regulations were issued after multiple reenactments of the statutory text; and the Treasury's statement accompanying the issuance of the regulations flew in the face of the prior court holdings and was a departure from a previous interpretation of earlier regulations. *Id.*

According to the Third Circuit:

> Our inquiry would be a simple one if, as the Tax Court suggested, the result of this case would be the same regardless of which standard we apply. This, however, is not the case. The Tax Court relied heavily on factors that, although relevant to the *National Muffler* standard, are not mandatory or dispositive inquiries under *Chevron*. As we set out above, the Tax Court reasoned that the challenged regulation was not a contemporaneous construction of the statute; the Tax Court found that the Fourth Circuit Court of Appeals and the Board of Tax Appeals had interpreted the statute as not including a timing element, and the Tax Court relied on the existence of several re-enactments of the statute without any change to the governing statutory language.
>
> Even if we were to assume that all of these observations are true, conclusive reliance on them is misplaced. When *Chevron* deference is owed, *Chevron*'s demands are clear. If the statutory text is ambiguous, an agency is given the discretion to promulgate rules that interpret the ambiguous provisions. Judicial deference to an agency's rule-making authority ends only when the agency's construction of its statute is unreasonable.

Id. at 167–68.

After concluding that the statutory language in section 882 was ambiguous — so the Treasury had the authority to issue regulations — the court shifted to the second part of the *Chevron* analysis:

> Our inquiry is not yet at its end, as we will only defer to the Secretary's action if it is a permissible construction of I.R.C. § 882(c)(2). *See Woodall*, 432 F.3d at 248 (citing *Chevron*, 467 U.S. at 842–43). We "need not conclude that the agency

> construction was the only one it permissibly could have adopted to uphold the construction, or even the reading the court would have reached if the question had arisen in a judicial proceeding." *Chevron*, 467 U.S. at 843 n.11. Often, a promulgated rule is the culmination of intense debate between the agency, Congress, other members of the Executive Branch and the public. Rules represent important policy decisions, and should not be disturbed if " 'this choice represents a reasonable accommodation of conflicting policies that were committed to the agency's care by the statute . . . .' " *Id.* at 845 (quoting *United States v. Shimer*, 367 U.S. 374, 382–83, 81 S. Ct. 1554, 6 L. Ed. 2d 908 (1961)). Further, Chevron deference is "even more appropriate in cases" that involve a " 'complex and highly technical regulatory program . . . .' " *Robert Wood*, 297 F.3d at 282 (quoting *Thomas Jefferson Univ. v. Shalala*, 512 U.S. 504, 512, 114 S. Ct. 2381, 129 L. Ed. 2d 405 (1994)). The Code is indisputably complex and technical, and we will adjust our inquiry accordingly.
>
> In this case, the Secretary has promulgated a rule that creates an eighteen-month window within which foreign companies must file a federal tax return in order to claim rental activity tax deductions. Taxpayer argues that previous cases upholding the disallowance of deductions under I.R.C. § 882(c)(2) involved filing deadlines that permitted at least a two year window within which foreign corporations could have filed timely tax returns. From this, Taxpayer draws the conclusion that it is unreasonable for the Secretary to promulgate a rule with a filing period of less than two years. We find Taxpayer's argument to be unpersuasive. The Secretary will, under the current regulation, allow a foreign company to file eighteen months after the filing was originally due. Moreover, because I.R.C. § 6072(c) already provides for a five and one-half month filing period, foreign companies have, in practice, twenty-three and one-half months to submit a "timely" return. It is not unreasonable for the Secretary to impose such a deadline.
>
> Additionally, we believe that drawing this temporal line is a task properly within the powers and expertise of the IRS. *Chevron* recognizes the notion that the IRS is in a superior position to make judgments concerning the administration of the ambiguities in its enabling statute. In this case, the IRS found that eighteen months served as a balance between its desire for compliance with the federal tax laws and a foreign corporation's desire to obtain valuable tax deductions. Therefore, we hold that the eighteen-month filing window created by Treas. Reg. 1.882-4(a)(3)(i) is a reasonable exercise of the Secretary's authority.

Id. at 171–72.

[c] What if the Regulation is Valid but Ambiguous?

What if the Treasury releases regulations, but those regulations do not specifically address the question raised? In other words, the issue is not so much the validity of the regulation, but how the regulation should be interpreted. The Supreme Court has held, outside the tax context, that a court, when determining the meaning of an ambiguous regulation, should give controlling deference to an interpretation presented by the agency as long as it is not plainly erroneous or inconsistent with the regulation. Auer v. Robbins, 519 U.S. 452, 457 (1997). The underlying rationale for this holding is that, as long as the agency's interpretation is consistent with the statute, any revised draft of the regulation containing the interpretation would necessarily be valid. *Id.* at 463. No cases involving tax regulations appear to have applied this approach, which is also known as *Seminole Rock* deference for the original case that addressed the issue, *Bowles v. Seminole Rock & Sand Co.*, 325 U.S. 410 (1945). Its applicability, therefore, remains unclear.

On a related note, if there are no regulations on point, should the IRS get the benefit of the doubt when it comes to interpreting the Code? Consider *United Dominion Indus., Inc. v. United States*, 532 U.S. 822 (2001), which involved the appropriate method for calculating net operating losses of an affiliated group of corporations electing to file a consolidated return. Responding to a specific grant of regulatory authority in Code section 1504(a)(5), the Treasury released voluminous regulations defining an affiliated group. These regulations, however, did not deal with the precise question of how the taxpayer should calculate net operating losses involving product liability claims. The majority ruled that the taxpayer's approach was correct, and rejected the Government's argument that its method of calculation, although not mandated by the regulations, was at least consistent with existing section 1504 regulations and therefore should be upheld. *Id.* at 834. Justice Stevens dissented:

> When a provision of the Internal Revenue Code presents a patent ambiguity, Congress, the courts, and the IRS share a preference for resolving the ambiguity via executive action. *See, e.g.,* National Muffler Dealers Assn., Inc. v. United States, 440 U.S. 472, 477, 59 L. Ed. 2d 519, 99 S. Ct. 1304 (1979). This is best achieved by the issuing of a Treasury Regulation resolving the ambiguity. *Ibid.* In this instance, however, the Secretary of the Treasury issued no such regulation. In the absence of such a regulation, the majority has scoured tangentially related regulations, looking for clues to what the Secretary might intend. For want of a more precise basis for resolving this case, that approach is sound.
>
> * * *
>
> In short, I find no answer to this case in the text of the statute or in any Treasury Regulation. However, the government does forward a valid policy concern that militates against petitioner's construction of the statute: the fear of tax abuse. *See* Brief for United States 40–42. Put simply, the Government fears that currently unprofitable but previously profitable corporations might receive a substantial windfall simply by acquiring a corporation with significant product liability expenses but no product liability losses. *See id.* at 40. On a subjective level, I find these concerns troubling. *Cf. Woolford Realty Co.*, 286 U.S. at 330 (rejecting "the notion that Congress in permitting a consolidated return was willing to foster an opportunity for juggling so facile and so obvious"). More importantly, however, I credit the Secretary of the Treasury's concerns about the potential scope of abuse. Perhaps the Court is correct in suggesting that these concerns can be alleviated through applications of other anti-abuse provisions of the Tax Code, . . . but I am not persuaded of my own ability to make that judgment. When we deal "with a subject that is highly specialized and so complex as to be the despair of judges," Dobson v. Commissioner, 320 U.S. 489, 498, 88 L. Ed. 248, 64 S. Ct. 239 (1943), an ounce of deference is appropriate.

Id. at 840-42 (Stevens, J., dissenting) (footnote omitted).

Justice Thomas filed a concurring opinion in which he took issue with Justice Stevens's approach:

> I agree with the Court that the Internal Revenue Code provision and the corresponding Treasury Regulations that control consolidated filings are best interpreted as requiring a single-entity approach in calculating product liability loss. I write separately, however, because I respectfully disagree with the dissent's suggestion that, when a provision of the Code and the corresponding regulations are ambiguous, this Court should defer to the Government's interpretation. *See post*, at 1–2. At a bare minimum, in cases such as this one, in which the complex statutory and regulatory scheme lends itself to any number of interpretations, we should be inclined to rely on the traditional canon that construes revenue-raising laws against their drafter. *See* Leavell v. Blades, 237

> Mo. 695, 700–701, 141 S.W. 893, 894 (1911) ("When the tax gatherer puts his finger on the citizen, he must also put his finger on the law permitting it"); United States v. Merriam, 263 U.S. 179, 188, 68 L. Ed. 240, 44 S. Ct. 69 (1923) ("If the words are doubtful, the doubt must be resolved against the Government and in favor of the taxpayer"); Bowers v. New York & Albany Literage Co., 273 U.S. 346, 350, 71 L. Ed. 676, 47 S. Ct. 389 (1927) ("The provision is part of a taxing statute; and such laws are to be interpreted liberally in favor of the taxpayers"). *Accord* American Net & Twine Co. v. Worthington, 141 U.S. 468, 474, 35 L. Ed. 821, 12 S. Ct. 55 (1891); Benziger v. United States, 192 U.S. 38, 55, 48 L. Ed. 331, 24 S. Ct. 189 (1904).

Id. at 838–39 (Thomas, J., concurring).

Justice Stevens responded:

> Justice Thomas accurately points to a tradition of cases construing "revenue-raising laws" against their drafter. However, when the ambiguous provision in question is not one that imposes tax liability but rather one that crafts an exception from a general revenue duty for the benefit of some taxpayers, a countervailing tradition suggests that the ambiguity should be resolved in the government's favor. *See, e.g.,* INDOPCO, Inc. v. Commissioner, 503 U.S. 79, 84, 117 L. Ed. 2d 226, 112 S. Ct. 1039 (1992); Interstate Transit Lines v. Commissioner, 319 U.S. 590, 593, 87 L. Ed. 1607, 63 S. Ct. 1279 (1943); Deputy v. Du Pont, 308 U.S. 488, 493, 84 L. Ed. 416, 60 S. Ct. 363 (1940); New Colonial Ice Co. v. Helvering, 292 U.S. 435, 440, 78 L. Ed. 1348, 54 S. Ct. 788 (1934); Woolford Realty Co. v. Rose, 286 U.S. 319, 326, 76 L. Ed. 1128, 52 S. Ct. 568 (1932).

Id. at 839 n.1 (Stevens, J., dissenting).

In response to the decision in *United Dominion*, would the Treasury be permitted to amend its section 1504 regulations to provide that its calculation approach, which was rejected by the majority, was the only permissible method of calculating net operating losses? In this regard, consider *Bankers Trust N.Y. Corp. v. United States*, 225 F.3d 1368 (Fed. Cir. 2000). In that case, the Federal Circuit held that an executive agency regulation cannot effectively construe a statute in a manner different from a prior definitive ruling of a court. The regulation at issue, Treasury Regulation section 4.901-2(f), adopted an interpretation that was in direct conflict with an earlier decision of the Court of Federal Claims. The Court of Appeals for the Federal Circuit held that the Court of Federal Claims erred in finding that the subsequently enacted regulation was a valid exercise of authority delegated to the IRS. *See Bankers Trust*, 225 F.3d at 1376. The Federal Circuit concluded that permitting the IRS, or any executive agency branch, to overrule an established statutory construction of the court by issuing regulations that are contrary to the court's prior decision would violate the "separation of powers" doctrine. *Id.* ("The *Chevron* doctrine, which requires us to defer to reasonable agency 'gap filling' interpretations of a statute as expressed in agency regulations, is not in conflict with stare decisis as it applies to this case, which requires adherence to precedential decisions of this court and of our predecessor courts.").

A 2005 Supreme Court decision, *National Cable & Telecommunications Ass'n v. Brand X Internet Services*, 545 U.S. 967 (2005), addressed the same issue. The following excerpt describing that case is from the Tax Court's opinion in *Swallows Holding*:

> In [*Brand X*], the Supreme Court decided the validity of a regulation that construed a statute inconsistently with a prior judicial interpretation. The Court held that "A court's prior judicial construction of a statute trumps an agency construction otherwise entitled to *Chevron* deference only if the prior court decision holds that its construction follows from the unambiguous terms of the statute and thus leaves no room for agency discretion." *Id.* at 2700. The Court stated: "Only a judicial precedent holding that the statute unambiguously forecloses the agency's interpretation, and therefore contains no gap for the

> agency to fill, displaces a conflicting agency construction." *Id.* at 2700. The Court noted that its decisions in *Neal v. United States*, 516 U.S. 284 (1996), *Lechmere, Inc. v. NLRB*, 502 U.S. 527 (1992), and *Maislin Indus., U.S., Inc. v. Primary Steel, Inc.*, 497 U.S. 116 (1990), "allow a court's prior interpretation of a statute to override an agency's interpretation only if the relevant court decision held the statute unambiguous." Natl. Cable & Telecomm. Association v. Brand X Internet Servs., 125 S. Ct. at 2700.

Swallows Holding, 126 T.C. 96, 143 (2006). In *Swallows Holding*, the Tax Court found that the Court's holding in *Brand X* did not apply. *Id.* at 144. The appellate court did so as well, but for different reasons. The Third Circuit concluded that, because no judicial opinion existed that unambiguously foreclosed the Treasury's authority to interpret the statute, it was not bound by previous judicial interpretations. *Swallows Holding*, 515 F.3d at 170.

[d] What About Temporary and Proposed Regulations?

As explained above, the Treasury releases most regulations first in proposed form. Proposed regulations are issued as Notices of Proposed Rulemaking, along with a statement soliciting comments on the regulations from the public. In cases in which the Treasury decides that the public needs immediate guidance on a particular issue — shortly after Congress enacts a new Code provision, for example — it may issue temporary regulations. Temporary regulations have the same force and effect as final regulations from the date of their issuance until the regulations are finalized, withdrawn, or expire (generally after three years). I.R.C. § 7805(e)(2). In 2003, the IRS issued Chief Counsel Notice CC-2003-014 (May 8, 2003), *available at* 2003 TNT 93-7 (May 14, 2003), that provides further insight into the IRS's view of the authority of temporary and proposed regulations:

> (a) Final or temporary regulations in force.
>
> If there are final or temporary regulations in force regarding an issue, Chief Counsel attorneys generally should follow the final or temporary regulations, even if the Service has subsequently issued proposed regulations addressing the issue, which might yield a different result if the proposed regulations were actually adopted and in effect. For example, if the application of the proposed regulations would have an adverse effect on the taxpayer by reaching a result that is not achievable under the final or temporary regulations, then the proposed regulations should not be applied in that situation. Proposed regulations do not operate to alter temporary or final regulations until they are finalized and adopted. Hence, where there are final or temporary regulations on an issue, as well as proposed regulations, Chief Counsel attorneys should follow the final or temporary regulations, not the proposed regulations.
>
> (2) Effect of proposed regulations.
>
> Proposed regulations have no legal effect unless and until they are adopted. This is so, even if there are no final or temporary regulations currently in force pertaining to the matter in question. Prior to adoption, proposed regulations can be withdrawn or modified at any time. Taxpayers generally should not rely on proposed regulations for planning purposes, except where there are no applicable final or temporary regulations in force and there is an express statement in the proposed regulations that taxpayers may rely on them currently. If there are applicable final or temporary regulations in force, taxpayers may only rely on proposed regulations for planning purposes in the limited circumstance where the proposed regulations contain an express statement permitting taxpayers to rely on them currently, notwithstanding the existence of the final or temporary regulations. In contrast, as set forth in rule (3), Chief Counsel attorneys should look to the proposed regulations to determine the office's position on the issue.

* * *

> (3) If there are no final or temporary regulations currently in force addressing a particular matter, Chief Counsel attorneys may not take a position that is inconsistent with proposed regulations.

CC-2003-014.

The statement in Chief Counsel Notice 2003-014 that IRS attorneys should follow proposed regulations if there are no final or temporary regulations in force is particularly interesting. Taxpayers may rely on proposed regulations to avoid the substantial understatement penalty in section 6662, Treas. Reg. § 1.6662-4(d)(3)(iii), but otherwise the precedential effect of proposed regulations is not completely clear. The Tax Court has ruled that proposed regulations carry "no more weight than a litigation position." *See, e.g.*, KTA-Tator, Inc. v. Commissioner, 108 T.C. 100, 102–03 (1997). If the IRS's Office of Chief Counsel has instructed its attorneys to follow proposed regulations, does this mean that taxpayers can rely on those regulations when planning transactions without the threat of the IRS litigating the validity of those regulations? The answer is no. The proposed regulations could be retracted or changed by the time the issue is litigated. Subsequent final regulations with a retroactive effective date would seem to take precedence over proposed regulations that are amended or withdrawn. *See generally* Sheldon I. Banoff & Richard M. Lipton, *IRS Chief Counsel Will Follow Prop. Regs. — But Don't Plan on Them!*, 98 J. TAX'N 187 (March 2003).

[B] IRS Authorities

Reading Assignment: I.R.C. § 7805(a)–(b), (e); Proc. Reg. § 601.601(d)–(e).

The IRS, independent of the Treasury Department, issues several forms of guidance to the public. For use by all taxpayers, the IRS publishes procedural regulations, Revenue Rulings, and Revenue Procedures. Those forms of guidance are discussed in this section. The IRS also provides private guidance to taxpayers in the form of letter rulings and determination letters. Furthermore, it issues internal guidance, ostensibly for use only within the agency, which is nonetheless made available to the public. Private and internal forms of IRS guidance are discussed in Sections 2.03 and 2.04.

[1] Procedural Regulations

The regulations in the IRS Statement of Procedural Rules, 26 CFR Part 601, are promulgated by the IRS, not the Treasury, and are not subject to the APA. These regulations generally address internal IRS "housekeeping" matters, yet may provide a valuable source of information on matters relating to IRS organization and procedure. *See, e.g.*, Proc. Reg. § 601.702, instructing a taxpayer how to make a Freedom of Information Act request to the IRS.

[2] Courts' Deference to Revenue Rulings

Revenue Rulings, also issued by the National Headquarters of the IRS, represent the IRS's official interpretation of the Code as it applies to a particular set of facts. *See* Rev. Proc. 2008-1, 2008-1 I.R.B. 1. The IRS describes the objectives of the Revenue Ruling program as promoting uniform application of the tax laws and assisting taxpayers in attaining maximum voluntary compliance. Proc. Reg. § 601.601(d)(2)(iii). Revenue Rulings serve as important sources of guidance that a taxpayer might use when planning a transaction and determining the tax results that flow from that transaction. As a general rule, taxpayers may rely on a Revenue Ruling to support a return position, assuming that the ruling has not been affected by subsequent legislation, regulations, cases, or other Revenue Rulings. A taxpayer's ability to rely on a Revenue Ruling is also contingent upon a substantial similarity between the taxpayer's facts and those reflected in the ruling. Proc. Reg. § 601.601(d)(2)(v)(e).

Given the purposes of the rulings program, the rulings that are chosen to be published as Revenue Rulings represent those that, in the opinion of the IRS, contain information and guidance that are likely to be important to a wide class of taxpayers. Topics for Revenue Rulings are often drawn from the IRS's annual business plan and, in some cases, the Treasury Department will suggest a topic for a Revenue Ruling to the IRS. Revenue Rulings are drafted and reviewed by attorneys in the Office of the Chief Counsel. After approval by the Chief Counsel, the Commissioner and the Treasury's Assistant Secretary (Tax Policy) review the proposed rulings. Because Revenue Rulings are not subject to APA procedures, the IRS does not generally afford the public an opportunity to comment on proposed rulings.[5] They are initially published in the Internal Revenue Bulletin, and then compiled as part of the semiannual Cumulative Bulletin.

As a general rule, Revenue Rulings may be applied on a retroactive basis. Section 7805(b) also permits the IRS the discretionary authority to *revoke* a Revenue Ruling retroactively. I.R.C. § 7805(b)(8); *see also* Dixon v. United States, 381 U.S. 68 (1965). The IRS has stated, however, that if a newly issued Revenue Ruling modifies or revokes a previously published ruling, the new ruling will not be applied retroactively to the extent that the revocation would have adverse tax consequences to the taxpayer. *See* Rev. Proc. 89-14 § 7, 1989-1 C.B. 814; *see also* Estate of McLendon v. Commissioner, 135 F.3d 1017 (1998) (reproduced below).

In many cases, Revenue Rulings are revoked or modified because subsequent legislation, court decisions, or Treasury regulations affect the underlying basis of the ruling's conclusion. When this happens, the IRS publishes this fact in the "Finding List of Current Action," which appears at the beginning of each Cumulative Bulletin volume. Even when a Revenue Ruling is not officially modified or made obsolete by the IRS as a result of a change in the law underlying the ruling, taxpayers must be careful to take into account the impact of the change on the ruling's continued validity.

If instead of seeking to rely on a Revenue Ruling, the taxpayer seeks to challenge the IRS's analysis contained in the ruling, how much weight will a court afford the IRS's view? The debate over the appropriate amount of deference to afford Revenue Rulings is nearly as heated as the question of whether *Chevron* deference applies to tax regulations. The Tax Court maintains that "[a]bsent exceptional circumstances, revenue rulings are viewed as 'merely an opinion of a lawyer in the agency', they are not considered to have the effect of law, and they are not binding on the Commissioner or the courts." Estate of McLendon v. Commissioner, T.C. Memo. 1996-307 (*citing* I.R.C. § 6110 and Foil v. Commissioner, 920 F.2d 1196, 1201 (5th Cir. 1990), *aff'g* 92 T.C. 376 (1989)). The Seventh Circuit in *Bankers Life*, *supra*, stated that Revenue Rulings deserve "respectful consideration, but not the deference that the *Chevron* doctrine requires in its domain." 142 F.3d at 978 (*citing* First Chicago NBD Corp. v. Commissioner, 135 F.3d 457, 458–59 (7th Cir. 1998)).

The Supreme Court's decision in *United States v. Mead Corp.*, 533 U.S. 218 (2001) — involving the appropriate level of deference to be afforded a tariff ruling letter issued by the U.S. Customs Service — suggests that Revenue Rulings should be afforded *Skidmore* deference, a standard that affords the pronouncement respect but less deference than *Chevron* would. Under *Skidmore*, the government agency's interpretation is accorded respect befitting "the thoroughness evident in its consideration, the validity of its reasoning, its consistency with earlier and later

[5] Occasionally the IRS does request comments on proposed Revenue Rulings. *See* John F. Coverdale, *Court Review of Tax Regulations and Revenue Rulings in the* Chevron *Era*, 64 Geo. Wash. L. Rev. 35, 79 & n.300 (1995) (pointing out that Announcement 95-25, 1995-14 I.R.B. 11, requested comments on a proposed Revenue Ruling).

pronouncements, and all those facts which give it the power to persuade, if lacking power to control." *Skidmore v. Swift & Co.*, 323 U.S. 134, 140 (1944).

In *Omohundro v. United States*, 300 F.3d 1065 (9th Cir. 2002) (*per curiam*), discussed further in Chapter 10, the Ninth Circuit applied *Skidmore* to uphold a Revenue Ruling that conflicted with one of the court's own earlier decisions. At the urging of both the taxpayer and the government, the Ninth Circuit rejected its earlier holding in *Miller v. United States*, 38 F.3d 473 (9th Cir. 1994) — that a two-year statute of limitations applies to a refund claim made on a delinquent return — and instead followed the IRS's conclusion in Revenue Ruling 76-511, 1976-2 C.B. 428, that a three-year limitations period applies to a delinquent return claiming a refund. The court found that Revenue Rulings were sufficiently analogous to the tariff rulings at issue in *United States v. Mead Corp.* to justify the same level of respect under *Skidmore*. The Ninth Circuit ruled that its failure to consider Revenue Ruling 76-511 in *Miller* and thereby afford it the level of respect *Skidmore* requires justified its decision to overturn *Miller*. The court then applied *Skidmore* to the Revenue Ruling:

> In light of the Supreme Court's intervening holding in *Mead*, we must decide whether Revenue Ruling 76-511 commands deference. We believe it does. First, the IRS's reasoning is valid. Although the IRS's interpretation of I.R.C. § 6511(a) may render the statute's time limitations somewhat "illusory," the look-back provisions of I.R.C. § 6511(b) effectively eliminate any danger of taxpayers recovering on stale claims. Every appellate court that has addressed this issue has reached the same decision as the IRS or has indicated it would do so. . . .
>
> Revenue Ruling 76-511 is consistent with later IRS pronouncements. In February of 2001, the Department of the Treasury and the IRS issued a final regulation regarding the application of the "mailbox" rule to late-filed returns including refund claims. The example in the regulation assumes a claim for a refund of overpaid 2001 taxes is timely under I.R.C. § 6511(a) when the claim was included in a return filed on April 15, 2005. *See* Timely Mailing Treated as Timely Filing/Electronic Postmark, 66 Fed. Reg. 2257 (Jan. 11, 2001) (to be codified at 26 C.F.R. pt. 301).
>
> The IRS's interpretation of I.R.C. § 6511(a) is supported by the legislative history of the statute. Under the 1954 version of the statute, the three-year period was intended to run from the date the taxpayer's return was due, not the date it was actually filed. . . . In 1958, Congress amended the statute, expressing concern that taxpayers had to file a timely return in order to benefit from the three year limitation period while the IRS had three years to complete assessments regardless of whether the return was timely. . . . By amending I.R.C. § 6511(a), Congress intended that "a claim for a refund or credit of any tax may be filed within three years from the time the return was actually filed (or, as under present law, within 2 years from the time of payment, whichever is later)."
>
> Subsequent legislation has also significantly undermined *Miller*'s reasoning. The *Miller* court found its holding was necessary to prevent taxpayers who received a deficiency notice from "forum shopping" between district court and tax court. The Taxpayer Relief Act of 1997 eliminated any disparity in deadlines between tax court and district court by amending I.R.C. § 6512(b)(3) to allow a three-year look-back period for a refund claim filed in tax court where no return has been filed and the mailing date of the deficiency notice is during the third year after the return due date. *See* I.R.C. § 6512(b)(3)(B), (C) (2002). Under the current statute, *Miller* actually creates a disparity since a taxpayer must file a return within two years of payment of the tax in district court, but need not do so in tax court.

> In light of the intervening Supreme Court decision in *Mead*, which requires that we accord *Skidmore* deference to revenue rulings, as well as the recent legislation that has obviated the *Miller* court's concern with potential forum shopping, we conclude we are no longer bound by *Miller*. Accordingly, we hold that under I.R.C. § 6511(a), a taxpayer's claim for credit or a refund is timely if it is filed within three years from the date his income tax return is filed, regardless of when the return is filed.

Omohundro, 300 F.3d at 1068–69 (footnotes omitted).

The Sixth Circuit has also ruled that, in light of *Mead*, Revenue Rulings warrant *Skidmore* respect. Aeroquip-Vickers, Inc. v. Commissioner, 347 F.3d 173, 181 (6th Cir. 2003). As part of its ruling, the Sixth Circuit asserted that the Tax Court erred by failing to acknowledge that Revenue Rulings deserve some deference. *Aeroquip-Vickers*, 347 F.3d at 181. Judge Clay, in his dissent in *Aeroquip-Vickers*, agreed with the majority that *Skidmore* should be applied to Revenue Rulings, but he disagreed over what level of deference *Skidmore* requires, if any:

> When the majority claims the Tax Court erred by failing to acknowledge that "*some* deference to revenue rulings is proper" (emphasis added), the majority overstates *Skidmore* "deference." *Skidmore* "deference" does not always involve "deferring" because the level of respect afforded the agency pronouncement depends on its "power to persuade." . . . An agency pronouncement with no persuasive power receives no deference. Therefore, because the Tax Court majority found the Treasury Department's justification for its revenue ruling unpersuasive, the Tax Court did not err by failing to acknowledge that "some deference to revenue rulings is proper." Likewise, to the extent this Court finds the Treasury Department's rationale unpersuasive, we have no obligation to defer. Exactly as the majority explains, "the amount of deference to be accorded to Revenue Ruling 82-20 ultimately turns upon the validity of its reasoning."

Id. at 186. Do you agree with Judge Clay's analysis?

[3] The IRS's Duty to Apply Revenue Rulings

The discussion in Section 2.02[B][2] considered the question of how much weight a court would afford a Revenue Ruling in the face of a taxpayer challenge. The *McLendon* decision, reproduced below, considers a slightly different issue: Under what circumstances may the IRS disavow one of its own Revenue Rulings?

ESTATE OF McLENDON v. COMMISSIONER

United States Court of Appeals, Fifth Circuit

135 F.3d 1017 (1998)

E. Grady Jolly, Circuit Judge:

The only question remaining in this appeal is whether Gordon B. McLendon was sufficiently close to death on March 5, 1986, to require him to depart from the actuarial tables published by the Commissioner of Internal Revenue (the "Commissioner") in valuing a remainder interest and related annuity. The Tax Court determined that he was, from which final decision McLendon's Estate appeals. We reverse.

I.

Although this case raises several contentious legal questions, the underlying facts are not in serious dispute. Through various partnership interests, McLendon was the principal owner and director of a vast broadcasting and entertainment empire. His interests ranged from the 458-station Liberty Broadcasting System to numerous individual radio stations, television stations, and movie theaters. Over his life time, McLendon became a very wealthy man.

Mortality hovers over the castle as well as the cottage, however, and in May 1985 McLendon was diagnosed with esophageal cancer. Although his condition initially improved following radiation therapy, the cancer recurred in September. At this point, McLendon's cancer was categorized as "systemic" — the most severe of three types of cancer growth. There is no dispute that the cancer was very likely terminal from this point forward, with a 2–3% overall survival rate. In particular, any remissions achieved after this point were generally expected by McLendon's doctors to be temporary.

Nonetheless, from October 1985 through March 1986, McLendon received six courses of chemotherapy at M.D. Anderson's world-renowned cancer treatment facility in Houston, Texas. On December 3, 1985, after three courses of chemotherapy, McLendon's doctor wrote on his discharge summary:

> The patient had an esophagogastroduodenoscopy on November 26, 1985, and it showed complete endoscopic remission confirmed by multiple biopsies of the affected area.

Despite this upbeat news, on December 5, 1985, McLendon attempted suicide by shooting himself in the head with a handgun. A suicide note reflected his belief that he would eventually succumb to the cancer and his desire not to prolong the suffering of his family. After being hospitalized for over a month for treatment of injuries from the failed suicide, McLendon began a fourth course of chemotherapy. He returned home in late January 1986 and began to receive periodic in-home examinations and treatment from a Dr. Gruebel. Her impression at the time was that he was doing well.

* * *

At the end of February, McLendon returned home under twenty-four hour care from a staff of private duty nurses. Notes taken by these nurses show that during the period from March 2 through March 5, McLendon was able to take short walks and perform minor tasks, but was at times sick to his stomach, was in constant need of pain medication, and was receiving artificial sustenance to ensure proper caloric intake. McLendon was examined at home on March 5 by the optimistic Dr. Gruebel. It was her impression at that time that McLendon was "markedly improved" and in the best condition since he had come into her care in January. The Commissioner subsequently presented undisputed expert testimony, however, that McLendon's chances of surviving for more than one year from this date were approximately 10 percent. This estimate was based principally on the likelihood of recurrence in a case like McLendon's.

On March 5, McLendon entered into a private annuity transaction with his son and the newly minted McLendon Family Trust. This transaction involved the transfer of remainder interests in McLendon's partnership holdings to his son and the Trust in exchange for $250,000 and an annuity to be paid to McLendon for life. The amount of the annuity was set such that its aggregate present value would equal the present value of the remainder interests. In valuing the remainder interests and the annuity, the parties referred to the Commissioner's actuarial tables for life expectancy then contained in Treas. Reg. § 25.2512-5(f). McLendon was sixty-five years old on March 5, 1986, resulting in an actuarial life expectancy of fifteen years from that date. Based on this figure, the parties ultimately determined that the remainder interests had a value of $5,881,695, and that the annuity would need to be $865,332 in order to match.

In late March, McLendon completed his final course of chemotherapy. In May, tests revealed a major recurrence of the cancer. Treatments were discontinued within a few weeks, and McLendon died at home on September 14. From the time that he was first admitted to M.D. Anderson in October 1985 until his death, McLendon survived longer than 75% of patients diagnosed with esophageal cancer.

II.

McLendon's estate tax return relied on a presumption that he had received an adequate and full consideration for the assets transferred in the private annuity transaction. The Commissioner disagreed with this presumption, taking issue with both the use of the actuarial tables and certain substantive aspects of the valuation of the partnership interests.

With regard to the actuarial tables, the Commissioner took the position that McLendon's life expectancy was sufficiently predictable on March 5, 1986, to make their use unnecessary and erroneous. Based on the medical evidence, the Commissioner further found that McLendon's actual life expectancy on this date was less than one year. Because this was significantly less than the fifteen-year figure used by the parties, the Commissioner concluded that the remainder interests had been so undervalued, and the annuity so overvalued, that the March 5 transfer had not been for an adequate and full consideration. As such, the Commissioner declared several million dollars in gift and estate tax deficiencies based on McLendon's erroneous use of the actuarial tables. Additional deficiencies were declared based on the substantive valuation issues.

McLendon's Estate took this dispute to the Tax Court, where the issues were reduced by joint stipulation to six discrete questions. One of these questions was whether it was proper for McLendon to apply the actuarial tables to determine his life expectancy in valuing the remainder interests and annuity. The rest of the questions concerned the substantive aspects of the valuation of the partnership interests. On September 30, 1993, the Tax Court issued its first opinion in this case, generally agreeing with the Commissioner and imposing $12.5 million in additional gift and estate taxes. Of significance to the instant appeal, the Tax Court held that use of the actuarial tables was improper because McLendon's life expectancy was reasonably predictable at the time the private annuity transaction occurred, being approximately one year.

McLendon's Estate appealed the Tax Court's ruling to this court. Estate of McLendon v. Commissioner of Internal Revenue, 77 F.3d 477 (5th. Cir. 1995). In an unpublished opinion, the panel reversed the Tax Court on the substantive valuation questions, but remanded as to use of the actuarial tables. Writing for the court, Judge Jones stated that:

> [W]e are unable to discern whether the Tax Court followed Revenue Ruling 80-80 or found reason to depart from it [in resolving the actuarial table question]. The Tax Court's opinion is both ambiguous and ambivalent regarding the revenue ruling, as it holds that Gordon had a life expectancy of one year, a finding that would suggest to us under the express language of the revenue ruling that death was not clearly imminent. We must remand for the court to clarify its position with regard to the applicability of Revenue Ruling 80-80 so that we will have a sounder basis for appellate review.

On July 8, 1996, the Tax Court issued its second opinion. It held that, although neither party had argued a position inconsistent with Rev. Rul. 80-80, the court had not felt obliged to follow that ruling, and had instead applied a standard gleaned from prior case law. It noted, however, that the result would have been the same under the ruling anyway. In the light of this clarification, McLendon's Estate now continues its appeal of the Tax Court's determination that use of the actuarial tables was improper.

* * *

IV.

As the prior panel foresaw, the remainder of this case turns on the applicability of Rev. Rul. 80-80. Because we hold that the ruling provides the legal test applicable to McLendon's situation, we find that his use of the actuarial tables was proper.

A.

The controversy in this case ultimately stems from 26 U.S.C. §§ 2036(a) and 2512(b). Under § 2036(a), a decedent's gross estate for estate tax purposes is defined to include any property transferred by him in which he retained a life estate, "except in case of a bona fide sale for an adequate and full consideration in money or money's worth." Similarly, under § 2512(b), a taxable gift is defined as a transfer of property "for less than an adequate and full consideration." Here, the transfer in question was the March 5 exchange of the partnership remainder interests for the cash and annuity. As the parties concede, the question whether that transfer was for "an adequate and full consideration" turns on the proper valuation of the remainder interests and the annuity.

At the time of the events in this case, Treas. Reg. § 25.2512-5 provided that "the fair market value of annuities, life estates, terms for years, remainders, and reversions transferred after November 30, 1983, is their present value determined in this section." Because the economic present value of these assets is dependent upon the predicted length of a measuring life, the regulation goes on to provide actuarial tables for life expectancy and instructions for using them to arrive at valuations of the assets in question. There is no dispute in this case over the valuation formulas contained in the regulation. The parties concede that the only question is whether the circumstances of McLendon's case allowed him to use a life expectancy figure derived from the tables of § 25.2512-5, or instead required him to use some other method to determine his "actual" life expectancy. * * *

B.

This question is less straightforward than it might seem. Despite their apparently clear command, Treas. Reg. § 25.2512-5 and its predecessors have not always been vigorously enforced by the courts. In particular, in *Miami Beach First National Bank v. United States*, 443 F.2d 116, 119–20 (5th Cir. 1971), this court held that "where there is sufficient evidence regarding the actual life expectancy of a life tenant, the presumptive correctness of the Treasury tables will be overcome."

At the time of the events in this case, the effective ruling was Rev. Rul. 80-80. It provides, in relevant part:

> The actuarial tables in the regulations are provided as an administrative necessity, and their general use has been readily approved by the courts.
>
> The actuarial tables are not based on data that exclusively involve persons of "good" or "normal" health. They reflect the incidence of death by disease and illness as well as by accident. The actuarial tables are properly applicable to the vast majority of individual life interests, even though the health of a particular individual is obviously better or worse than that of the "average" person of the same age and sex. Occasionally, however, the actual facts of an individual's condition are so exceptional as to justify departure from the actuarial tables.
>
> In view of recent case law, the resulting principle is as follows: the current actuarial tables in the regulations shall be applied if valuation of an individual's life interest is required for purposes of the federal estate or gift taxes unless the individual is known to have been afflicted, at the time of the transfer, with an incurable physical condition that is in such an advanced stage that death is clearly imminent. Death is not clearly imminent if there is a reasonable possibility of survival for more than a very brief period. *For example, death is not clearly imminent if the individual may survive for a year or more and if such a possibility is not so remote as to be negligible.*

Rev. Rul. 80-80, 1980-1 C.B. 194 (emphasis added, citations omitted).

McLendon's Estate argues that Rev. Rul. 80-80 clearly allows his use of the tables. In this regard, the Estate notes that the undisputed testimony of the Commissioner's own expert was that McLendon had a 10 percent chance of surviving for a year or more on March 5, 1986. As such, the Estate concludes that McLendon's possibility of surviving for a year or more from that date was not so remote as to be negligible, and that he therefore was permitted and required to use the tables under the clear terms of the ruling.

Although the Commissioner maintains that this court is not bound to follow Rev. Rul. 80-80, he also purports to take the position that the ruling does not mandate the result indicated by the Estate. The Commissioner argues that, although the ruling is a correct statement of the law, it cannot be taken at face value, and must be interpreted in the light of *Miami Beach First National Bank*. The Commissioner contends that under this reading McLendon's use of the tables was inappropriate since there was "sufficient evidence" of his actual life expectancy on March 5, 1986.

If Rev. Rul. 80-80 does govern this case, we, like the earlier panel of this court, find it undeniable that it supports the Estate's position. The ruling states a clear standard, expressed in language and example unneedful of further interpretation, and we are convinced that the 10 percent figure is sufficient to satisfy it. Whatever "negligible" might mean in a closer case, we are certain that it does not refer to a one-in-ten chance. As such, McLendon's use of the tables was clearly proper under the ruling.

The question, then, is whether Rev. Rul. 80-80 states the legal test applicable to McLendon's situation. If it does, then it is clear that McLendon's use of the actuarial tables was proper. The Tax Court ultimately chose not to apply Rev. Rul. 80-80 to this case. This choice was a purely legal decision, and is thus reviewed *de novo*.

C.

We note at the outset that the Tax Court has long been fighting a losing battle with the various courts of appeals over the proper deference to which revenue rulings are due. Whereas virtually every circuit recognizes some form of deference,[n.10] the Tax Court stands firm in its own position that revenue rulings are nothing more than the legal contentions of a frequent litigant, undeserving of any more or less consideration than the conclusory statements in a party's brief. Although the Supreme Court has not spoken definitively on the subject, its recent jurisprudence tends to support the view that the courts owe revenue rulings a bit more deference than the Tax Court would have us believe. Still, revenue rulings are odd creatures unconducive to precise categorization in the hierarchy of legal authorities. They are clearly less binding on the courts than treasury regulations or Code provisions, but probably (and in this circuit certainly) more so than the mere legal conclusions of the parties. Apart from that, little can be said with any certainty, and in the absence of a definitive statement from on high, the Tax Court continues its crusade to ignore them in toto.

This bit of background explains a great deal with regard to the posture of this case. In support of its general position on deference, the Tax Court went to great lengths to avoid applying Rev. Rul. 80-80 to McLendon's situation. The earlier panel of this court noticed this slight, and asked the Tax Court if it really wanted an open confrontation on the issue. Sticking to its guns, the Tax Court replied that it did. The result was the instant appeal.

As it turns out, however, this case does not require us to step squarely into the fray. Most questions of deference to a revenue ruling involve an argument by the taxpayer that a particular ruling is contrary to law. Here, however, the argument to ignore or minimize the effect of Rev. Rul. 80-80 comes from the Commissioner, the very party who issued the ruling in the first place.[n.13] In such a situation, this circuit has a well

---

[n.10] * * * In this circuit, revenue rulings are generally "given weight as expressing the studied view of the agency whose duty it is to carry out the statute." Foil [v. Commissioner, 920 F.2d 1196, (5th Cir. 1990)].

[n.13] The Commissioner's position is not entirely clear in this case. He purports to maintain that Rev. Rul.

established rule that is sufficient to resolve this case without probing the penumbrae of the general deference question.

In *Silco, Inc. v. United States*, 779 F.2d 282, 286 (5th Cir. 1986), we held that a taxpayer was entitled to rely on the legal standard implied by two revenue rulings extant at the time of his transaction, even though they had been subsequently abrogated. In reaching this conclusion, we noted that:

> Treas. Reg. § 601.601(e) provides that taxpayers may generally rely on published revenue rulings in determining the tax treatment of their own transactions, if the facts and circumstances of their transactions are substantially the same as those that prompted the ruling.

Id. at 286.[n.14] Because the statute, regulations, and case law were less than clear at the time of the taxpayer's transaction, we found that the rulings "provided the only insight available to [the] taxpayer at the time of [his] transaction as to the conceptual approach the [Commissioner] would use," and that the Commissioner acted improperly in subsequently applying a different test to that taxpayer. *Id.* at 287.

Silco stands for the proposition that the Commissioner will be held to his published rulings in areas where the law is unclear, and may not depart from them in individual cases. Furthermore, under *Silco* the Commissioner may not retroactively abrogate a ruling in an unclear area with respect to any taxpayer who has relied on it.[n.15]

Applying *Silco* to this case, it quickly becomes clear that Rev. Rul. 80-80 must govern our decision. McLendon went to great lengths to structure his transaction to comply with applicable law, and the Commissioner does not dispute that in so doing McLendon expressly relied on Rev. Rul. 80-80's clarification of the admittedly murky area of future and dependent interest valuation. The Commissioner ignored the clear language of his own ruling in declaring deficiencies, and it is precisely this kind of tactic that *Silco* declares to be intolerable. Because McLendon was entitled to rely on Rev. Rul. 80-80, the Tax Court was not at liberty to disregard it. Its decision to do so was error, and we

---

80-80 is an accurate statement of the law, yet would prefer the court decide the case based on the rule of *Miami Beach First National Bank.* This rule, he implies, is the same as that of Rev. Rul. 80-80. The Commissioner cannot eat his cake and have it too. As we explained above, Rev. Rul. 80-80 is unambiguous in its support for the Estate's position. To the extent that he argues for a rule inconsistent with the ruling's clear language, we construe the Commissioner's position to be that the ruling should not apply.

[n.14] Treas. Reg. § 601.601(e) states: "Taxpayers generally may rely upon Revenue Rulings published in the Bulletin in determining the tax treatment of their own transactions . . . ." Although not cited therein, *Silco* also finds support in Treas. Reg. § 601.601(d), which provides that revenue rulings "are published to provide precedents to be used in the disposition of other cases."

[n.15] This latter portion of *Silco* might be read to be in conflict with the Supreme Court's well established rule that the Commissioner may retroactively revoke certain revenue rulings, even where taxpayers may have relied on them to their detriment. *See* Automobile Club of Michigan v. Commissioner of Internal Revenue, 353 U.S. 180, 183–84, 77 S. Ct. 707, 1 L. Ed. 2d 746 (1957) (Brennan, J.); Dixon v. United States, 381 U.S. 68, 72–73, 85 S. Ct. 1301, 14 L. Ed. 2d 223 (1965) (Brennan, J.). For a number of reasons, however, we perceive no conflict.

First, the *Automobile Club* rule applies only where the Commissioner revokes a prior ruling that is contrary to the Internal Revenue Code. This was not the case in *Silco,* nor is it the case here. The *Silco* rule is expressly limited to areas where the Code does not provide a clear answer. Second, *Silco* is grounded on the Commissioner's invitation to taxpayers to rely on his revenue rulings as set out in Treas. Reg. § 601.601(e), a factor not present in the *Automobile Club* or *Dixon* cases. The essence of the *Silco* rule is that traditional notions of equity and fair play prevent the Commissioner from changing his position after inviting reliance with his own regulations. Finally, even if there were some tension between *Silco* and *Automobile Club,* we would be bound in this case by our past circuit precedent. "One panel of this Court may not overrule another (absent an intervening decision to the contrary by the Supreme Court or the en banc court . . .)." Hogue v. Johnson, 131 F.3d 466, 491 (5th Cir. 1997) (Garwood, J.) (emphasis added). *See also* United States v. McPhail, 119 F.3d 326, 327 (5th Cir. 1997) (Smith, J., dissenting), and cases cited therein. Supposed conflicts with *prior* Supreme Court precedent are grist for the en banc mill, but not for ad hoc panel revision. *See* 5th Cir. IOP to Fed. R. App. P. 35. For all of these reasons, we are content that *Silco* continues to be good law.

reverse on that basis. Furthermore, because the application of Rev. Rul. 80-80 clearly sustains the Estate's position, we need not remand yet again for further proceedings. Consistent with our discussion of the application of the ruling above, we render for McLendon's Estate.

V.

Where the Commissioner has specifically approved a valuation methodology, like the actuarial tables, in his own revenue ruling, he will not be heard to fault a taxpayer for taking advantage of the tax minimization opportunities inherent therein. Here, the Commissioner had no right to ignore Rev. Rul. 80-80 and the Tax Court was bound to apply it consistent with McLendon's right of reliance. The Tax Court's manifest failure to apply the ruling was clearly wrong, and, accordingly, we reverse its judgment and render for the Estate.

The issue of whether Revenue Rulings should be binding on the IRS was raised again in *Rauenhorst v. Commissioner*, 119 T.C. 157 (2002). Rauenhorst involved a charitable gift of warrants to purchase stock. The Commissioner, relying on the assignment of income doctrine, asserted that the taxpayers were required to report gains realized from the sale of the warrants. The Tax Court found that the Commissioner's position was contrary to an earlier position taken in Revenue Ruling 78-197, 1978-1 C.B. 83. According to Judge Ruwe, while the Tax Court is not bound by Revenue Rulings, it is not acceptable to permit the IRS to argue a position contrary to a Revenue Ruling when taxpayers had relied on the ruling to support their position. Judge Ruwe's criticism of the IRS's litigating position in *Rauenhorst* was pointed:

> Recently, the IRS, in a joint statement issued by the Commissioner, the Chief Counsel, and the Acting Assistant Secretary (Tax Policy) of the Department of the Treasury, has indicated its "continuing commitment to serve the public through the published guidance process." . . . To that end, the IRS has committed itself "to increased and more timely published guidance," in the form of revenue rulings and revenue procedures, in the hopes of achieving increased taxpayer compliance and resolving "frequently disputed tax issues." These stated goals will not be achieved if the Commissioner refuses to follow his own published guidance and argues in court proceedings that revenue rulings do not bind him or that his rulings are incorrect. Certainly, the Commissioner's failure to follow his own rulings would be unfair to those taxpayers, such as petitioners herein, who have relied on revenue rulings to structure their transactions. Moreover, it is highly inequitable to impose penalties, which respondent has done in this case. Accordingly, in this case, we shall not permit respondent to argue against his revenue ruling, and we shall treat his revenue ruling as a concession.

Rauenhorst, 119 T.C. at 183.

As a direct response to the Tax Court's concerns, the Office of Chief Counsel announced that its attorneys will be required in litigation matters to file legal positions that are consistent with IRS published guidance. *See* Chief Counsel Notice CC-2003-014 (May 8, 2003), *available at* 2003 TNT 93-7 (May 14, 2003).

[4] Revenue Procedures

Revenue Procedures are like Revenue Rulings except that they cover procedural processes. The IRS describes a Revenue Procedure as "an official statement of a procedure . . . that either affects the rights or duties of taxpayers or other members of the public under the Internal Revenue Code . . . or, although not necessarily affecting the rights and duties of the public, should be a matter of public knowledge."

Rev. Proc. 89-14, 1989-1 C.B. 814. The first Revenue Procedure issued each year describes the procedures for requesting a letter ruling or determination letter. *See, e.g.*, Rev. Proc. 2008-1, 2008-1 I.R.B. 1, a portion of which is reproduced below. Revenue Procedures, like Revenue Rulings, are first published in the Internal Revenue Bulletin, and then compiled as part of the Cumulative Bulletin.

Revenue Procedures are rarely contested in court, although when the Revenue Procedure's subject matter addresses a question of substantive law, disputes do arise. In *Federal National Mortgage Association v. United States*, 56 Fed. Cl. 228 (2003), *rev'd*, 379 F.3d 1303 (Fed. Cir. 2004), for instance, the Court of Federal Claims refused to apply *Chevron* deference to the IRS's position set forth in a Revenue Procedure. Instead, the court applied *Skidmore*. In doing so, the court rejected the IRS's position set forth in Revenue Procedure 99-43, 1999-2 C.B. 579, that "global" interest netting, which is discussed in Chapter 13, does not apply to periods before the enactment of section 6621(d) unless both the period of limitations on tax underpayments and overpayments remained open as of the date of the Code provision's enactment. The court concluded that "[b]ecause Revenue Procedure 99-43 contains no reasoning, cannot claim validity as a longstanding interpretation, and arguably conflicts with other IRS statements of procedure, we afford it little weight." *Fed. Nat'l Mortgage Ass'n*, 56 Fed. Cl. at 237. The Court of Appeals for the Federal Circuit agreed with the Court of Federal Claims that Revenue Procedures are not entitled to *Chevron* deference and also agreed that, applying *Skidmore*, the Revenue Procedure at issue was not persuasive. Fed. Nat'l Mortgage Ass'n v. United States, 379 F.3d 1303, 1307–09 (Fed. Cir. 2004).[6]

§ 2.03 TAXPAYER-SPECIFIC GUIDANCE

Reading Assignment: I.R.C. § 6110(a), (i), (k)(3).

One of the roles of the IRS is to provide taxpayer-specific guidance. This guidance is issued in three basic forms: Letter rulings, determination letters, and technical advice memoranda.[7] The most common type is a letter ruling. A "letter ruling" is a written statement issued to a taxpayer by the National Headquarters of the IRS that interprets and applies the tax laws to a specific set of facts described in the letter ruling request. Rev. Proc. 2008-1, 2008-1 I.R.B. 1. Letter rulings are often referred to as "private letter rulings," and are abbreviated "PLR." As explained below, taxpayers generally use letter rulings to determine how the IRS will treat a transaction.

A "determination letter" applies the principles and precedents previously announced by the IRS's National Headquarters to a specific set of facts. While similar to a letter ruling, a determination letter is issued by a designated director in the Operating Divisions, rather than the National Headquarters, and normally covers a completed transaction, rather than a proposed transaction. Determination letters most often relate to the qualification of an employee benefit plan as an exempt entity under Code section 401 or the tax-exempt status of an organization under Code section 501. The IRS has announced that it will issue a determination letter only when a determination can be made on the basis of clearly established rules in the statute, the regulations, or a published court decision. *See* Rev. Proc. 2008-1, at § 2.03. As a result, if the requested determination involves a novel issue or doubt exists concerning the application of precedent, the IRS will not provide a letter.

---

[6] The court reversed and remanded the case for further factual determinations based on a sovereign immunity issue that the appeals court raised *sua sponte*. *Fed. Nat'l Mortgage Ass'n*, 379 F.3d at 1311.

[7] Chapter 20 includes a discussion of other types of internal IRS guidance, including Chief Counsel advice and action on decision memoranda. These sources were also introduced in Section 1.03 of Chapter 1.

The IRS Office of Chief Counsel will also furnish advice during the examination stage of a tax controversy in response to requests from IRS field personnel and at the prompting of taxpayers. Technical Advice Memoranda (TAMs) are the written statements encompassing this advice. Like letter rulings, TAMs contain the IRS's views on how the Code, regulations, and judicial precedent should be applied to a specific fact pattern. The procedures for requesting technical advice and the circumstances under which it will be issued are described in an annual revenue procedure. *See* Rev. Proc. 2008-2, 2008-1 I.R.B. 90.

According to the Code, none of the three sources of taxpayer-specific guidance carry any precedential value except with respect to the taxpayer to whom the guidance relates. I.R.C. § 6110(k)(3). Nonetheless, the IRS publishes these items pursuant to section 6110, after any identifying details have been redacted. I.R.C. § 6110(c). Although the sources may not be used or cited as precedent by a third party, they can prove helpful to other taxpayers seeking to obtain a general idea of the IRS's position with respect to a particular issue. Moreover, the drafter's legal analysis contained in the document may prove to be a valuable exposition of the surrounding law. Letter rulings and TAMs are also included in the list of authorities that may help the taxpayer establish that his position has substantial authority, thereby avoiding the imposition of an accuracy related penalty. *See* Treas. Reg. § 1.6662-4(d)(3)(iii); *see also* Section 12.02[C] of Chapter 12.

§ 2.04 PRIVATE LETTER RULINGS

A taxpayer usually requests a letter ruling when the tax consequences of a transaction are unclear and the taxpayer wants some measure of certainty about how the IRS will treat it. The following sections explain when the IRS will issue a ruling, what the taxpayer must submit to obtain the ruling, and under what circumstances the taxpayer should consider making a ruling request.

[A] Areas in Which the IRS Will Not Issue Letter Rulings

The IRS's authority to decline a letter ruling request is, for the most part, discretionary. The stated policy of the IRS is to issue letter rulings only with respect to completed transactions for a year in which the taxpayer has yet to file a return and for prospective transactions that have not been consummated. Probably the most important fields in which the IRS will issue prospective rulings relate to the tax effects of corporate reorganizations and liquidations. There are certain topics on which the IRS has made it clear that it will not issue letter rulings. Generally, the third Revenue Ruling of each year lists the "no rule" areas for domestic taxation. Revenue Procedure 2008-3, 2008-1 I.R.B. 110, provides, in part, that the IRS will not rule on the following *general* areas:

(1) The results of transactions that lack a *bona fide* business purpose or have as their principal purpose the reduction of federal taxes.

(2) A matter upon which a court decision adverse to the Government has been handed down and the question of following the decision or litigating further has not yet been resolved.

(3) A matter involving alternate plans of proposed transactions or involving hypothetical situations.

(4) Whether under Subtitle F (Procedure and Administration) reasonable cause, due diligence, good faith, clear and convincing evidence, or other similar terms that require a factual determination exist.

(5) Whether a proposed transaction would subject the taxpayer to a criminal penalty.

(6) A request that does not comply with the provisions of Rev. Proc. 2008-1. . . .

* * *

Rev. Proc. 2008-3, § 3.02, 2008-1 I.R.B. 110, 115.

The Revenue Procedure also lists *specific* areas in which the IRS will not rule, including:

(17) Section 119. — Meals or Lodging Furnished for the Convenience of the Employer. — Whether the value of meals or lodging is excludible from gross income by an employee who is a controlling shareholder of the employer.

(18) Section 121. — Exclusion of Gain from Sale of Principal Residence. — Whether property qualifies as the taxpayer's principal residence.

* * *

(20) Section 162. — Trade or Business Expenses. — Whether compensation is reasonable in amount.

* * *

(26) Section 213. — Medical, Dental, Etc., Expenses. — Whether a capital expenditure for an item that is ordinarily used for personal, living, or family purposes, such as a swimming pool, has as its primary purpose the medical care of the taxpayer or the taxpayer's spouse or dependent, or is related directly to such medical care.

* * *

(29) Section 269. — Acquisitions Made to Evade or Avoid Income Tax. — Whether an acquisition is within the meaning of § 269.

* * *

(36) Section 312. — Effect on Earnings and Profits. — The determination of the amount of earnings and profits of a corporation.

* * *

(38) Sections 332, 351 and 368(a)(1)(A), (B), (E) and (F) and 1036. Complete Liquidations of Subsidiaries; Transfer to Corporation Controlled by Transferor; Definitions Relating to Corporate Transfers and Reorganizations; and Stock for Stock of Same Corporation. — Whether a transaction qualifies under § 332, § 351, or § 1036 for nonrecognition treatment, or whether it constitutes a corporate reorganization within the meaning of § 368(a)(1)(A) (including a transaction that qualifies under § 368(a)(1)(A) by reason of § 368(a)(2)(D) or § 368(a)(2)(E)), § 368(a)(1)(B), § 368(a)(1)(C), § 368(a)(1)(E) or § 368(a)(1)(F), and whether various consequences (such as nonrecognition and basis) result from the application of that section, unless the Service determines that there is a significant issue that must be resolved in order to decide those matters. * * *

SIGNIFICANT ISSUE: A significant issue is an issue of law that meets the three following tests: (1) the issue is not clearly and adequately addressed by a statute, regulation, decision of a court, tax treaty, revenue ruling, revenue procedure, notice, or other authority published in the Internal Revenue Bulletin; (2) the resolution of the issue is not essentially free from doubt; and (3) the issue is legally significant and germane to determining the major tax consequences of the transaction.

Id. at § 3.01. The final category enumerated above prevents taxpayers from getting "comfort" rulings when the tax consequences of a reorganization transaction are relatively clear.

The IRS also lists areas in which it "ordinarily" will not issue a letter ruling. These include:

(1) Any matter in which the determination requested is primarily one of fact, *e.g.*, market value of property, or whether an interest in a corporation is to be treated as stock or indebtedness.

(2) Situations where the requested ruling deals with only part of an integrated transaction. Generally, a letter ruling will not be issued on only part of an integrated transaction. If, however, a part of a transaction falls under a no-rule area, a letter ruling on other parts of the transaction may be issued. Before preparing the letter ruling request, a taxpayer should call the Office of the Associate Chief Counsel with jurisdiction over the matters on which the taxpayer is seeking a letter ruling to discuss whether a letter ruling will be issued on part of the transaction.

* * *

(4) The tax effect of any transaction to be consummated at some indefinite future time.

(5) Any matter dealing with the question of whether property is held primarily for sale to customers in the ordinary course of a trade or business.

(6) The tax effect of a transaction if any part of the transaction is involved in litigation among the parties affected by the transaction, except for transactions involving bankruptcy reorganizations.

Id. § 4.02.

[B] How to Request a Letter Ruling

To request a letter ruling, the taxpayer or the taxpayer's authorized representative must submit to the IRS a request containing specific information.[8] The first Revenue Procedure of each year describes the letter ruling request process, including what information must be included in the request and further guidance on when the IRS will or will not issue a ruling. Because Revenue Procedure 2008-1 is long and detailed, only portions of it are reproduced below. Notice in particular that the requesting party must furnish a complete statement of facts, a statement of supporting authorities, and copies of all relevant documents related to the transaction.

REVENUE PROCEDURE 2008-1

2008-1 I.R.B. 1

SECTION 7. WHAT ARE THE GENERAL INSTRUCTIONS FOR REQUESTING LETTER RULINGS AND DETERMINATION LETTERS?

This section provides the general instructions for requesting letter rulings and determination letters. . . .

Requests for letter rulings, closing agreements, and determination letters require the payment of the applicable user fee listed in Appendix A of this revenue procedure. . . .

Specific and additional instructions also apply to requests for letter rulings and determination letters on certain matters. Those matters are listed in Appendix E of this revenue procedure with a reference (usually to another revenue procedure) where more information can be obtained.

---

[8] The general procedures discussed below also apply to requests for determination letters.

.01 Documents and information required in all requests

Facts

(1) Complete statement of facts and other information. Each request for a letter ruling or a determination letter must contain a complete statement of all facts relating to the transaction. These facts include —

(a) names, addresses, telephone numbers, and taxpayer identification numbers of all interested parties. (The term "all interested parties" does not mean all shareholders of a widely held corporation requesting a letter ruling relating to a reorganization or all employees where a large number may be involved.);

(b) the annual accounting period, and the overall method of accounting (cash or accrual) for maintaining the accounting books and filing the Federal income tax return, of all interested parties;

(c) a description of the taxpayer's business operations;

(d) a complete statement of the business reasons for the transaction; and

(e) a detailed description of the transaction.

Documents and foreign laws

(2) Copies of all contracts, wills, deeds, agreements, instruments, other documents, and foreign laws.

(a) Documents. True copies of all contracts, wills, deeds, agreements, instruments, trust documents, proposed disclaimers, and other documents pertinent to the transaction must be submitted with the request.

If the request concerns a corporate distribution, reorganization, or similar transaction, the corporate balance sheet and profit and loss statement should also be submitted. If the request relates to a prospective transaction, the most recent balance sheet and profit and loss statement should be submitted.

* * *

Each document, other than the request, should be labeled and attached to the request in alphabetical sequence. Original documents, such as contracts, wills, etc., should not be submitted because they become part of the Service's file and will not be returned.

* * *

Analysis of material facts

(3) Analysis of material facts. The request must be accompanied by an analysis of facts and their bearing on the issue or issues. If documents attached to a request contain material facts, they must be included in the taxpayer's analysis of facts in the request, rather than merely incorporated by reference.

Same issue in an earlier return.

(4) Statement regarding whether same issue is in an earlier return. The request must state whether, to the best of the knowledge of both the taxpayer and the taxpayer's representatives, any return of the taxpayer (or any return of a related taxpayer within the meaning of § 267 or of a member of an affiliated group of which the taxpayer is also a member within the meaning of § 1504) that would be affected by the requested letter ruling or determination letter is under examination, before Appeals, or before a Federal court.

* * *

Statement of authorities supporting taxpayer's views

(8) Statement of supporting authorities. If the taxpayer advocates a particular conclusion, the taxpayer must include an explanation of the grounds for that conclusion and the relevant authorities to support it. Even if the taxpayer is not advocating a particular tax treatment of a proposed transaction, it must furnish views on the tax results of the proposed transaction and a statement of relevant authorities to support those views.

In all events, the request must include a statement of whether the law in connection with the request is uncertain and whether the issue is adequately addressed by relevant authorities.

Statement of authorities contrary to taxpayer's views

(9) Statement of contrary authorities. In order to avoid inevitable delay in the ruling process, contrary authorities should be brought to the attention of the Service at the earliest possible opportunity. If there are significant contrary authorities, it is helpful to discuss them in a presubmission conference prior to submitting the ruling request. The taxpayer is strongly encouraged to inform the Service about, and discuss the implications of, any authority believed to be contrary to the position advanced, such as legislation, tax treaties, court decisions, regulations, notices, revenue rulings, revenue procedures, or announcements. If the taxpayer determines that there are no contrary authorities, a statement in the request to this effect would be helpful. If the taxpayer does not furnish either contrary authorities or a statement that none exists, the Service in complex cases or those presenting difficult or novel issues may request submission of contrary authorities or a statement that none exists. Failure to comply with this request may result in the Service's refusal to issue a letter ruling or determination letter.

The taxpayer's identification of and discussion of contrary authorities generally will enable Service personnel more quickly to understand the issue and relevant authorities. Having this information should make research more efficient and lead to earlier action by the Service. If the taxpayer does not disclose and distinguish significant contrary authorities, the Service may need to request additional information, which will delay action on the request.

Statement identifying pending legislation

(10) Statement identifying pending legislation. When filing the request, the taxpayer must identify any pending legislation that may affect the proposed transaction. In addition, the taxpayer must notify the Service if any such legislation is introduced after the request is filed but before a letter ruling or determination letter is issued.

Deletions statement required by § 6110

(11) Statement identifying information to be deleted from copy of letter ruling or determination letter for public inspection. The text of letter rulings and determination letters is open to public inspection under § 6110. The Service makes deletions from the text before it is made available for inspection. To help the Service make the deletions required by § 6110(c), a request for a letter ruling or determination letter must be accompanied by a statement indicating the deletions desired ("deletions statement"). If the deletions statement is not submitted with the request, a Service representative will tell the taxpayer that the request will be closed if the Service does not receive the deletions statement within 21 calendar days.

(a) Format of deletions statement. A taxpayer who wants only names, addresses, and identifying numbers to be deleted should state this in the deletions statement. If the taxpayer wants more information deleted, the deletions statement must be accompanied by a copy of the request and supporting documents on which the taxpayer should bracket the material to be deleted. The deletions statement must indicate the statutory basis under § 6110(c) for each proposed deletion.

If the taxpayer decides to ask for additional deletions before the letter ruling or determination letter is issued, additional deletions statements may be submitted.

(b) Location of deletions statement. The deletions statement must be made in a separate document from the request for a letter ruling or determination letter and must be placed on top of the request.

(c) Signature. The deletions statement must be signed and dated by the taxpayer or the taxpayer's authorized representative. A stamped signature or faxed signature is not permitted.

(d) Additional information. The taxpayer should follow the same procedures to propose deletions from any additional information submitted after the initial request. An additional deletions statement is not required with each submission of additional information if the taxpayer's initial deletions statement requests that only names, addresses, and identifying numbers are to be deleted and the taxpayer wants only the same information deleted from the additional information.

(e) Taxpayer may protest deletions not made. After receiving from the Service the notice under § 6110(f)(1) of intention to disclose the letter ruling or determination letter (including a copy of the version proposed to be open to public inspection and notation of third-party communications under § 6110(d)), the taxpayer may protest the disclosure of certain information in the letter ruling or determination letter. The taxpayer must send a written statement to the Service office indicated on the notice of intention to disclose, within 20 calendar days of the date the notice of intention to disclose is mailed to the taxpayer. The statement must identify those deletions that the Service has not made and that the taxpayer believes should have been made. The taxpayer must also submit a copy of the version of the letter ruling or determination letter and bracket the proposed deletions that have not been made by the Service. Generally, the Service will not consider deleting any material that the taxpayer did not propose to be deleted before the letter ruling or determination letter was issued.

Within 20 calendar days after the Service receives the response to the notice under § 6110(f)(1), the Service will mail to the taxpayer its final administrative conclusion regarding the deletions to be made. The taxpayer does not have the right to a conference to resolve any disagreements concerning material to be deleted from the text of the letter ruling or determination letter. These matters may, however, be taken up at any conference that is otherwise scheduled regarding the request.

* * *

Signature on request

(12) Signature by taxpayer or authorized representative. The request for a letter ruling or determination letter must be signed and dated by the taxpayer or the taxpayer's authorized representative. A stamped signature or faxed signature is not permitted.

Power of attorney and declaration of representative

(14) Power of attorney and declaration of representative. Form 2848, *Power of Attorney and Declaration of Representative*, should be used to provide the representative's authority (Part I of Form 2848, *Power of Attorney*) and the representative's qualification (Part II of Form 2848, *Declaration of Representative*). The name of the person signing Part I of Form 2848 should also be typed or printed on this form. A stamped signature is not permitted. An original, a copy, or a (fax) of the power of attorney is acceptable as long as its authenticity is not reasonably disputed.

Penalties of perjury statement

(15) Penalties of perjury statement.

(a) Format of penalties of perjury statement. A request for a letter ruling or determination letter and any change in the request submitted at a later time must be accompanied by the following declaration: **"Under penalties of perjury, I declare that I have examined [Insert, as appropriate: this request or this modification to the request], including accompanying documents, and, to the best of my knowledge and belief, [Insert, as appropriate: the request or the modification] contains all the relevant facts relating to the request, and such facts are true, correct, and complete."**

(b) Signature by taxpayer. The declaration must be signed and dated by the taxpayer, not the taxpayer's representative. A stamped signature or faxed signature is not permitted.

The person who signs for a corporate taxpayer must be an officer of the corporate taxpayer who has personal knowledge of the facts and whose duties are not limited to obtaining a letter ruling or determination letter from the Service. If the corporate taxpayer is a member of an affiliated group filing consolidated returns, a penalties of perjury statement must also be signed and submitted by an officer of the common parent of the group.

The person signing for a trust, a state law partnership, or a limited liability company must be, respectively, a trustee, general partner, or member-manager who has personal knowledge of the facts.

* * *

Appendix A of Revenue Procedure 2008-1 contains a schedule of user fees, Appendix B contains a sample format for a letter ruling request, and Appendix C contains a detailed checklist entitled "Is Your Letter Ruling Request Complete?". The purpose of the checklist is to ensure that the taxpayer furnished all the necessary information and documents with the request. Appendix C provides that if the request is submitted by a representative, it will be returned if the checklist is not included.

A sample letter ruling request might look something like this, which is based on an actual PLR.[9] The "facts" and "analysis" sections of the request, depending on the issues involved, might be more detailed:

---

[9] This letter ruling request is loosely based on PLR 199933021.

SAMPLE LETTER RULING REQUEST

November 1, 2008

Internal Revenue Service
Associate Chief Counsel Domestic
Attn: CC: PA: T
P.O. Box 7604
Ben Franklin Station
Washington, D.C. 20044

Dear Sir or Madam:

The taxpayer, United Cancer Research Institute (the Institute) requests a ruling on whether certain research stipends it awards constitute payment for services within the meaning of section 117(c) of the Internal Revenue Code (the Code), whether the Institute will be required to withhold any taxes from the stipends, and whether the Institute will have reporting obligations with respect to the stipends.

A. STATEMENT OF FACTS

1. Taxpayer Information

The Institute is a Pennsylvania corporation that is exempt from Federal income taxation under Code section 501(c)(3). The complete address and telephone number of the Institute are:

United Cancer Research Institute
555 Main Line Drive
Philadelphia, PA 19010
(215) 526–9898

The Institute's employer identification number is 333-44-2222. The Institute keeps its books on a calendar year basis, and uses the accrual method of accounting.

2. Description of Taxpayer's Business Operations

The Institute conducts clinical and theoretical research, training, and educational programs on the development, progress, and treatment of cancer.

3. Facts Relating to Transaction

As part of its core research mission, the Institute conducts a nationally known training program designed to train postdoctoral fellows to become research scientists. The focus of the training program is the development and improvement of research skills. The training programs generally last from two to four years. To help defray the fellows' living expenses during their training, the Institute pays modest stipends. Each year, the Institute pays stipends to approximately 75 fellows. Research fellows are not required to have performed services or to agree to perform services for the Institute (such as working as a laboratory technician) as a condition to receiving a stipend.

B. RULING REQUESTED

The Institute requests a ruling that the research stipends awarded do not represent compensation for services within the meaning of section 117(c) of the Code, and that they do not constitute "wages" for purposes of section 3401(a). The Institute also requests a ruling that the stipends are not subject to section 3402 (withholding for income taxes at source), section 3102 (withholding under the Federal Insurance Contribution Act (FICA)), or section 3301 (Federal Unemployment Tax Act (FUTA)), and that the Institute is not required to file Forms W-2, or any information returns under section 6041, with respect to the stipends.

C. STATEMENT OF LAW

Code section 117 governs the federal income tax treatment of qualified scholarships and fellowship grants. Section 117(a) provides that gross income does not include any amount received as a "qualified scholarship" by an individual who is a candidate for a degree at an educational organization described in section 170(b)(1)(A)(ii). A qualified scholarship is defined as an amount expended for "qualified tuition and related expenses."

Section 117(c) of the Code provides that the exclusion for qualified scholarships shall not apply to that portion of any amount received which represents payment for teaching, research, or other services by the student required as a condition for receiving the qualified scholarship or fellowship. A scholarship or fellowship grant represents payment for services when the grantor requires the recipient to perform services in return for the granting of the scholarship or fellowship. A requirement that the recipient pursue studies, research, or other activities primarily for the benefit of the grantor is treated as a requirement to perform services. A scholarship or fellowship grant conditioned upon either past, present, or future services by the recipient, or upon services that are subject to the direction or supervision of the grantor, represents payment for services. *See* Bingler v. Johnson, 394 U.S. 741 (1969).

Although payments for research services are not excludable under section 117, not all payments for research activities represent payment for services. Under Code section 117 and the regulations thereunder, a qualified scholarship includes any amount paid or allowed to aid an individual in the pursuit of study or research. Accordingly, research activities by a student may qualify for exclusion from gross income. It is only where the research required by the grantor falls within section 117(c) that a payment must be included in gross income.

A scholarship or fellowship grant that is includible in gross income under section 117(c) of the Code is considered "wages" for purposes of section 3401(a). The grantor of such an amount is subject to certain withholding and reporting requirements respecting wages, including withholding for income taxes and the filing of Forms W-2. The application of Federal Insurance Contributions Act (FICA) and Federal Unemployment Tax Act (FUTA) taxes depends on the nature of the employment and the status of the grantor. *See* 1987-1 C.B. 475, Notice 87-31.

D. ANALYSIS

The Institute does not compensate research fellows for services, but rather subsidizes fellows' expenses as they learn to become research scientists. The stipends are disinterested grants to fellows to enable them to pursue research training independent of any benefit to the Institute. Therefore, the stipends do not represent compensation for services within the meaning of section 117(c) of the Code. *Cf.* Rev. Rul. 83–93, 1983-1 C.B. 364.

Because the stipends do not constitute payments for services under Code section 117(c), they are not "wages" for purposes of section 3401(a). In addition, they are not subject to section 3402 (relating to withholding for income taxes at source), section 3102 (relating to withholding under the Federal Insurance Contribution Act (FICA)), or section 3301 (relating to the Federal Unemployment Tax Act (FUTA)). Therefore, the Institute is not required to file Forms W-2 or any information returns under section 6041 with respect to the stipends.

E. CONCLUSION

The Institute's research stipends awarded do not represent compensation for services within the meaning of section 117(c) of the Code. The stipends also do not constitute "wages" for purposes of section 3401(a), and they are not subject to section 3402 (relating to withholding for income taxes at source), section 3102 (relating to withholding under the Federal Insurance Contribution Act (FICA)), or section 3301 (relating to the Federal Unemployment Tax Act (FUTA)). In addition, the Institute is not required to file Forms W-2, or any information returns under section 6041, with respect to the stipends.

F. PROCEDURAL MATTERS

1. Revenue Procedure 2008-1 Statements

a. The issue that is the subject of this letter ruling request is not reflected in any earlier return of the taxpayer or a predecessor, or in a return for any year of a related taxpayer.

b. The IRS has not previously ruled on the same or similar issue for the taxpayer, a related taxpayer, or a predecessor taxpayer.

c. No one, including the taxpayer, a related taxpayer, a predecessor, or any representatives previously submitted a request involving the same or similar issue but withdrew the request before a letter ruling was issued.

d. No one, including the taxpayer, a related taxpayer, or any predecessor taxpayer, has submitted a letter ruling request involving the same or a similar issue that is currently pending with the IRS.

e. Neither the taxpayer nor any related taxpayer is submitting another request to the IRS involving the same or a similar issue.

f. The law on the issues raised in this letter ruling request is certain, and is adequately addressed by existing authorities.

g. The Institute has been unable to find any contrary authorities.

h. The Institute requests a conference on the issues involved in the letter ruling request.

2. Administrative

a. The deletions statement and checklist required by Revenue Procedure 2008-1 are enclosed.

b. The required user fee is enclosed.

c. A completed Power of Attorney form is enclosed.

Very truly yours,

Frances Farnwell
Attorney for United Cancer Research Institute

November 1, 2008

Under penalties of perjury, I declare that I have examined this request, including accompanying documents, and, to the best of my knowledge and belief, the request contains all the relevant facts relating to the request, and such facts are true, correct, and complete.

United Cancer Research Institute

By: Daniel D. Doe
November 1, 2008

Although Revenue Procedure 2008-1 governs most letter rulings requests, the IRS has issued additional Revenue Procedures that cover ruling requests that relate to a particular type of transaction. Revenue Procedure 96-30, 1996-1 C.B. 696, as modified, for example, contains a checklist of additional information and representations that a taxpayer must submit in order to receive a ruling confirming that a distribution of a subsidiary's stock qualifies under section 355. Before submitting a ruling request, the taxpayer should carefully determine whether an additional pronouncement applies to the taxpayer's request. Appendix E of Revenue Procedure 2008-1 lists these additional Revenue Procedures and the transactions to which they relate.

[C] Requesting a Conference with the IRS

When pursuing a letter ruling request, a taxpayer is normally entitled to a conference with a representative from the Office of Chief Counsel, as a matter of right. If the taxpayer requests a conference, the IRS will notify the taxpayer of the time and place of the conference, which must then be held within 21 calendar days. The conference of right affords both the IRS representative and the taxpayer an opportunity to clarify the issues involved, and to request and respond to additional factual information or representations. *See generally* Rev. Proc. 2008-1, at § 10.

A taxpayer may request that the conference of right be held by telephone. A taxpayer might make this request if, for example, the taxpayer believes that the issue involved does not warrant incurring the expense of traveling to Washington, D.C. If a taxpayer makes such a request, the IRS will decide if it is appropriate in the particular case to hold the conference by telephone. If the request is approved, the taxpayer will be advised when to call the IRS representatives. *Id.* at § 10.08.

In addition to the conference of right, the IRS may offer the taxpayer additional conferences if the IRS feels they will be helpful. In general, the IRS will offer the taxpayer an additional conference if an adverse holding is proposed. During the conference, the taxpayer should furnish any additional documentation that was proposed by the taxpayer and discussed at the initial conference but not previously or adequately presented in writing. *See id.* at § 10.06. These conferences with IRS representatives prior to issuance of a ruling can, when conducted appropriately, significantly increase the taxpayer's chances of receiving a favorable ruling. The taxpayer's representative should come to the conference well prepared, having thoroughly researched the legal issues involved and with a full understanding of the relevant facts.

Occasionally the IRS will hold a conference before the taxpayer submits the letter ruling request in order to discuss substantive or procedural issues relating to a proposed transaction. Such conferences are held only if the taxpayer actually intends to make a request, only if the request involves a matter on which a letter ruling is ordinarily issued, and only on a time-available basis. *See id.* at § 10.07. Generally, the taxpayer will be asked to provide before the pre-submission conference a draft of the letter ruling request or other detailed written statements of the proposed transaction and the issues involved. As discussed more fully below, the taxpayer can use the pre-submission conference to gauge the likelihood that an adverse ruling may be issued, at which point the taxpayer may wish to either forego the ruling process or restructure the transaction. Any discussion of substantive issues at a pre-submission conference is advisory only, is not binding on the IRS, and cannot be relied upon as a basis for obtaining retroactive relief under the provisions of Code section 7805(b). *Id.*

[D] Taxpayer Reporting Requirements

A taxpayer who obtains a letter ruling must attach the letter ruling to the tax return for the year in question. A return submitted with an attached letter ruling may cause the IRS to take a closer than normal look at the return in order to confirm whether (1) the return properly reflects the conclusions stated in the ruling; (2) the representations upon which the letter ruling was based reflected an accurate statement of the material facts; (3) the transaction was carried out substantially as proposed; and (4) there has been no change in the law that applies to the period during which the transaction or continuing series of transactions were consummated. Rev. Proc. 2008-1, at § 11.03. If, for example, the actual facts surrounding the completed transaction are at variance with those represented in the letter ruling request, or if the taxpayer carries out the transaction in a manner different from that represented in the request, the ruling is effectively nullified. *Id.*

Although the IRS is not legally bound by a letter ruling, its longstanding policy has been to honor a ruling issued directly to a taxpayer. Unless it is accompanied by a closing agreement, however, the IRS may revoke or modify a letter ruling following (1) the enactment of legislation or ratification of a tax treaty; (2) a decision of the United States Supreme Court; (3) the issuance of temporary or final regulations; or (4) the issuance of a revenue ruling, revenue procedure, notice, or other statement published in the Internal Revenue Bulletin. *Id.* at § 11.04. If, on examination of the taxpayer's return, the IRS finds that a letter ruling should be revoked or modified, the findings and recommendations of the agent in charge will be forwarded to the National Headquarters for consideration before further action is taken. In most circumstances, the revocation will operate only prospectively, not retroactively. *Id.* at § 11.06.[10]

[E] Whether to Request a Letter Ruling and Whether to Withdraw a Ruling Request

As noted above, the letter ruling process essentially allows a taxpayer to ask the IRS to confirm the appropriate tax treatment of an item or proposed transaction. Such confirmation may be desirable where uncertainties exist in the law, and in cases where severe adverse tax consequences might result. If a ruling is requested and it is favorable, the taxpayer can proceed with the transaction with reasonable certainty of its tax consequences. Although a letter ruling may sound like a convenient method of resolving a potential dispute, a taxpayer should carefully consider the anticipated benefits and the potential drawbacks associated with initiating the ruling process.

One of the most important factors bearing upon whether the taxpayer should request a letter ruling is the likelihood of obtaining a favorable result. Once the taxpayer submits the formal request, the National Headquarters is made aware of a transaction, the tax consequences of which are, more likely than not, uncertain and important enough to the taxpayer to require special consideration. Experts will then scrutinize the transaction carefully in an effort to confirm the underlying facts and determine the appropriate tax consequences. Any flaws in the taxpayer's position, whether factual or legal, are much more likely to be discovered as part of the ruling application process as compared to a routine examination of the taxpayer's return.

While the taxpayer will normally be offered the opportunity to withdraw the letter ruling request if the IRS intends on ruling adversely, the taxpayer's withdrawal will not prevent the IRS from retaining the related files and possibly transmitting that information to the office that will have audit jurisdiction over the taxpayer's return. *See* ILM 200327041. As a practical matter, therefore, if the taxpayer is informed of or issued an adverse ruling, the taxpayer must be prepared to restructure the transaction, forgo it, or litigate the matter. Particularly when the taxpayer wishes to proceed with a transaction regardless of whether or not the tax consequences are favorable, a letter ruling request can present a serious risk.

In addition to the risks associated with an adverse determination, the taxpayer should also be advised of the costs related to the ruling process. These costs include not only the user fees imposed by the IRS, which can be substantial, but also the representative's billable time necessary to prepare and negotiate the request. Particularly when the issues involved are complex, preparation costs can mount quickly. The amount the taxpayer should be willing to spend on a letter ruling will vary, of

---

[10] A taxpayer who desires absolute certainty regarding the tax effects of a transaction must request that the IRS enter into a closing agreement. Closing agreements conclusively determine the tax treatment that should be accorded a particular transaction and can be revoked by the IRS only in the case of fraud or misrepresentation of a material fact. *See* I.R.C. § 7121. Closing agreements are discussed in more detail in Chapter 5.

course, with the potential tax liability in issue. In making this cost/benefit analysis, the taxpayer must also take into account the expense associated with an IRS examination if the transaction is selected for audit.

A final consideration relates to the time involved in obtaining a letter ruling. In some cases, the transaction cannot wait for a favorable ruling and must be consummated even though a ruling might lend the parties important peace of mind. Although no general rule exists, the estimated waiting period for a letter ruling in the income tax area is eight to twelve weeks. As the complexity of the issue and the potential tax liability involved increase, so generally does the waiting period.

Taxpayers can minimize the wait for a letter ruling by ensuring that the ruling request is submitted properly, with all required documentation. Revenue Procedure 2008-1, which was excerpted above, also permits a taxpayer to file a ruling request on an expedited basis. Expedited consideration will only be given when the taxpayer will suffer undue hardship or be irreparably prejudiced from taking certain actions if a prompt response to the ruling request is not issued. Self-imposed deadlines and other time limitations created by the taxpayer are not sufficient justifications for requesting expedited consideration. To obtain priority, the taxpayer must submit with the ruling request a separate letter that explains why expedited consideration is appropriate under the circumstances. Rev. Proc. 2008-1, at § 7.02(4).

Although the IRS may issue a letter ruling with respect to a completed transaction that has not yet been reported on the taxpayer's return, these types of rulings should be requested sparingly, given the risk of an adverse determination. In these cases, as in others in which timing and expense considerations are great, the taxpayer may be better off seeking an opinion letter from counsel relating to the tax consequences of the transaction, rather than a letter ruling. Tax opinion letters, as well as the practitioner's duties when advising a client about a reporting position, are discussed in more detail in Chapter 18.

§ 2.05 THE "DUTY OF CONSISTENCY"

Reading Assignment: Review I.R.C. §§ 6110(a), (k)(3), 7805(a).

One of the goals of the IRS's letter ruling program is to issue guidance in a timely manner to those taxpayers who request it and to apply the tax law on a uniform and consistent basis. If that is the case, why does the Code prevent third-party taxpayers from relying on the IRS's conclusions reached in a PLR or in other forms of taxpayer-specific guidance? *See* I.R.C. § 6110(k)(3).

Considering the non-precedential nature of the many forms of IRS guidance, *should* the IRS have a duty to treat similarly situated taxpayers similarly? Consider this excerpt from an article by Professor Zelenak:

Lawrence Zelenak, *Should Courts Require the Internal Revenue Service To Be Consistent?*[11]

40 Tax L. Rev. 411 (1985)

An administrative agency must follow its precedents or offer a reasoned explanation for departing from them; a court, faced with a departure from agency precedents which the agency does not satisfactorily explain and justify, will usually require the agency to adhere to its own precedents. What applies to other agencies, however, does not necessarily apply to the Internal Revenue Service. The Service takes the position that it need not treat similarly situated taxpayers consistently, and the courts have generally accepted the Service's contention.

The Service's claim for exemption from the requirement of administrative consistency is not as outrageous as it may seem. Two considerations peculiar to the Service support its position. First, the cases which impose a duty of consistency on other agencies are overwhelmingly concerned with situations where an agency's statutory mandate gives it broad discretion, and the agency could take any of several different positions without violating its governing statute. By contrast, most of the positions taken by the Service are interpretations of detailed statutes which vest the Service with little discretion in implementation. The question of whether a court should impose a duty of consistency on the Service arises when the Service asserts a position against one taxpayer which is justified under the court's interpretation of the relevant provisions of the Internal Revenue Code, but which the Service has not asserted and does not intend to assert against other similarly situated taxpayers. To impose a duty of consistency in those situations is to give taxpayers lenient treatment that is not justified under the substantive law. This is not a problem with the cases involving agencies given broad discretion by statute, since in those cases courts can require agencies to adhere to their precedents without violating the governing law. This distinction could explain and justify the Service's refusal to recognize a duty of consistency to taxpayers.

Second, section 6110[(k)](3) of the Internal Revenue Code states that private letter rulings issued by the Service "may not be used or cited as precedent." This could mean that private letter rulings issued to other taxpayers may not be used to show inconsistency on the part of the Service. If so, the Code itself relieves the Service of the duty of consistency.

I do not believe these special circumstances justify exempting the Service from the duty of administrative consistency. . . . [A] court should be willing to impose a duty of consistency even when the result of imposing the duty runs counter to that court's interpretation of the substantive law.

* * *

Professor Davis [in the second edition of his Administrative Law Treatise[12]] remarks: "Of all the agencies of the government, the worst offender against sound principles of administrative consistency may be the Internal Revenue Service." He argues that the same duty of consistency that applies to other agencies should apply to the Service. He harshly characterizes, almost ridicules, the Service's position: "Its basic attitude is that because consistency is impossible, an effort to be consistent is unnecessary; therefore it need not consider precedents, and it may depart from precedents without explaining why."

There is a crucial difference, however, between the cases noted by Professor Davis as establishing the duty of administrative consistency and the Service's situation. Virtually all of the cited cases involve statutory grants of authority giving broad discretion to the agencies; in these situations, a court can require agency adherence to precedent (if the agency fails to distinguish and declines to disavow its precedent) without countermanding the statutory command of Congress. But the vast majority of the cases involving the Service is different. Congress, in the Internal Revenue Code, has defined what is and what is not includible in or deductible from income. The Service views its task as determining and applying the one true meaning of that statute, not as exercising discretion in deciding what federal income tax policy should be.

The first step taken by a court in applying a duty of administrative consistency may be to remand the case to the agency for an explanation of its departure from its own precedent. This can be done even if the applicable statute is of the one true meaning variety (rather than one granting the agency a wide range of discretion), if the court thinks an explanation from the agency will help the court in determining that one true meaning. What would happen after a case had come back from remand, if the Service

---

[12] [K. Davis, Administrative Law Treatise § 8:12, at 206. — Eds.]

had failed to distinguish and declined to disavow its contrary precedents? If the court were serious about requiring the Service to be consistent, it would hold that the taxpayer in the case at issue must be treated in the same way the Service had treated all other similarly situated taxpayers. But what about the court's own interpretation of the substantive law? If the court agreed with the taxpayer and the Service's precedents on the proper interpretation of the relevant Code provisions, it could decide in the taxpayer's favor without even mentioning a duty of consistency. But if the court believed the proper interpretation of the law was that advanced by the Service in the present litigation, and that the Service's precedents and the position of the taxpayer were wrong, then, the court could enforce a duty of consistency only at the cost of not following its interpretation of the Code. In the context of a Code provision with one true meaning which is adverse to a taxpayer, a court can require the Service to be consistent only by giving the taxpayer a tax break which Congress did not intend to give him. This dilemma does not exist in the cases establishing the duty of consistency in the exercise of administrative discretion; precisely because administrative discretion is involved, courts can require those agencies to adhere to their precedents without thereby violating any statutory mandate laid down by Congress. Thus, it does not automatically follow . . . that a duty of consistency should be imposed on the Service.

* * *

Since the cases neither establish nor reject a duty of consistency on the Service, the question remains whether that duty should be imposed. It is not dispositive that cases have imposed a duty of consistency on other agencies because those cases do not involve the problem of whether a court should require consistency at the cost of failing to apply the court's interpretation of the substantive law.

I believe that there are circumstances in which it is appropriate for courts to require the Service to afford one taxpayer the same favorable treatment it has given all other similarly situated taxpayers, even if the treatment is inconsistent with that mandated by Congress. The facts of *Vesco*[13] are an example of an appropriate situation for elevating consistency over the substantive law. If the Service has not taxed, and has no intention of taxing, any other taxpayers on the value of relatives' trips on business flights of company jets, then it seems fundamentally unfair to allow the Service to tax Mr. Vesco, regardless of whether the trips fall within the broad sweep of the section 61 definition of gross income. I find equally compelling Professor Davis' hypothetical in which a college faculty member has his child's tuition at another college paid by his employer. Even if a court interprets section 61 to include such a fringe benefit in gross income, it should hold for the taxpayer if the Service has issued and continues to issue private letter rulings to other taxpayers, stating that those tuition payments are not taxable. I admit that my response is a visceral reaction; other people's viscera may react differently. Still, I think there are good reasons to seek equal justice over strict adherence to the substantive law.

* * *

There is another reason why the distinction between the range of discretion cases involving other agencies, and the one true meaning cases involving the Service, is more apparent than real. There is virtually no judicial review of a Service decision to be lenient. If the Service takes a position that it will not treat a particular item as income, or that it will allow a particular deduction, for practical purposes, that decision becomes the substantive law. This is because such a position cannot be challenged in court. Taxpayers directly affected will not challenge the position because it is favorable to them. The Service will not, of course, challenge its own position. Third parties may sue to prevent Service leniency toward other taxpayers (either out of high public minded-

[13] [39 T.C.M. (CCH) 101 (1979). — Eds.]

ness or because the taxpayers favored by the lenient position are competitors), but such suits are almost always dismissed for lack of standing. While Congress may have the power to create standing for third party challenges to lenient Service positions, the power has not been exercised.

Although the Code does not expressly grant the Service the discretion to decline to interpret the Code in a way which would extract every last permissible ounce of taxpayer flesh, the effect of the lack of third-party standing to challenge lenient Service positions is to give the Service this discretion. If, as a practical matter, the Service has discretion to interpret the Code leniently, then the case of the Service is not so different, after all, from that of the many agencies which have been held to a duty of consistency. The Service — in reality, if not in theory — has discretion to be lenient in its interpretations of the Code. If the Service exercises this discretion, it seems only fair that the Service should exercise this discretion consistently. It should not be allowed to interpret the Code strictly against a few taxpayers, while being lenient to other similarly situated taxpayers.

It seems to me that a court can decide a case in a taxpayer's favor on the basis of a consistency requirement, even when the court's interpretation of the substantive law supports the Service's litigating position, without necessarily subverting the intent of Congress. This is because the structure for judicial review of Service positions — a structure Congress most likely has the power to change — gives the Service the discretion to be lenient. If Congress has acquiesced in a system which permits the Service to interpret the Code leniently, lenient interpretations do not necessarily contravene the will of Congress. It follows that a judicially enforced consistency requirement need not subvert congressional intent. A consistency requirement merely ensures that the Service does not discriminate when it exercises its discretion to be lenient; if the Service can choose to be lenient without violating the will of Congress, a judicially enforced consistency requirement would violate the will of Congress only if one ascribes to Congress the unlikely intent to allow the Service to discriminate among similarly situated taxpayers when it chooses to be lenient.

I should make clear what I am not saying. I am not saying that once the Service has interpreted a Code section in a particular manner, it must continue to interpret it that way forever. The Service is always free to renounce a lenient interpretation, replacing it with a strict interpretation, as long as it does so for all similarly situated taxpayers and the strict interpretation is justified by the statute. The duty of consistency should merely prevent the Service from strictly interpreting the Code to the disadvantage of one or a few taxpayers, while continuing the lenient interpretation as to everyone else.

What reasons does Professor Zelenak give for imposing a duty of consistency on the IRS? Taken to its logical extreme, would a duty of consistency require the IRS to audit all taxpayers (or all taxpayers of a particular type) if it audits one taxpayer?

Duty of consistency issues sometimes arise in the context of retroactive revocation of a letter ruling, as in the *IBM* case, which is discussed in the following excerpt.

STICHTING PENSIOENFONDS VOOR DE GEZONDHEID v. UNITED STATES[14]

United States Court of Appeals, District of Columbia Circuit
129 F.3d 195 (1997)

TATEL, CIRCUIT JUDGE:

A Dutch pension fund jointly controlled by employers and unions and claiming to be a "labor organization" as described in section 501(c)(5) of the Internal Revenue Code

---

[14] *Cert. denied*, 525 U.S. 811 (1998).

challenges the Internal Revenue Service's denial of its application for exemption from federal income taxation. Because tax exemptions require unambiguous proof and because we can find no authority directly entitling the pension fund to an exemption, we affirm the district court's grant of summary judgment for the United States.

I.

Appellant Stichting Pensioenfonds Voor de Gezondheid, Geestelijke en Maatschappelijke Belangen (the "Fund") is a Dutch pension plan formed in 1969 following negotiations between labor unions representing hospital workers and the Dutch national hospital employers' association. Soon after the Fund's formation, the Dutch government granted it "compulsory treatment," thus requiring all private hospitals and their employees to participate. The Fund has since expanded to include fourteen health and social welfare sectors in the Netherlands. The Fund has no principal place of business in the United States, nor does it engage in any trade or business here.

* * *

The Fund invests in U.S. stocks and mutual funds. In 1993, its U.S. security custodians withheld and paid to the U.S. Treasury over eight million dollars in income tax. Claiming tax-exempt status as a labor organization under section 501(c)(5) of the Internal Revenue Code, *see* 26 U.S.C. § 501(c)(5) (1994), the Fund filed a claim [for refund] for this amount. Receiving no response from the Service, the Fund filed suit in the U.S. District Court for the District of Columbia.

Noting that taxpayers must prove exemptions "unambiguously," and finding that the Fund lacked "a sufficient nexus with a more traditional labor organization to qualify as a tax-exempt labor organization itself," the district court granted summary judgment for the United States. Stichting Pensioenfonds Voor De Gezondheid, Geestelijke En Maatschappelijke Belangen v. United States, 950 F. Supp. 373, 374, 379 (D.D.C. 1996). In doing so, the district court rejected the Fund's alternative argument that, even if not entitled to tax-exempt status, it should have received a refund pursuant to section 7805(b) of the Code, 26 U.S.C. § 7805(b) (1994) (superceded by 28 U.S.C.A. § 7805(b)(8) (West Supp. 1997)). *Stichting Pensioenfonds,* 950 F. Supp. at 381. We review the district court's grant of summary judgment *de novo.* Tao v. Freeh, 27 F.3d 635, 638, 307 U.S. App. D.C. 185 (D.C. Cir. 1994).

II.

* * *

We begin, of course, with the Internal Revenue Code. Section 501(c)(5) exempts labor, agricultural, and horticultural organizations from taxation. 26 U.S.C. § 501(c)(5). The Code neither defines the term "labor organization" nor elaborates on its meaning. The legislative history, moreover, provides no unambiguous guidance. The early twentieth-century congressional debates on whether to include the term "labor organization" in section 501(c)'s precursor had nothing to do with whether jointly controlled entities providing pension benefits should be exempt from federal taxation. Instead, the debates focused on whether the Code's exemption for "fraternal beneficiary societies . . . providing for the payment of life, sick, accident, or other benefits to members" would be understood as covering all labor organizations, a question that Congress answered negatively when it explicitly exempted labor organizations. *See* 44 Cong. Rec. 4154–55 (1909). We agree with the district court that this legislative history provides "little help" in understanding the scope of the term "labor organization." *See Stichting Pensioenfonds,* 950 F. Supp. at 375.

* * *

III.

We turn finally to the Fund's argument that even if not entitled to an exemption under section 501(c)(5), it should have received a refund pursuant to section 7805(b) of the Code, which gives the Service discretion to apply its rulings retroactively. *See* 26 U.S.C. § 7805(b). The Fund cites *IBM v. United States*, 343 F.2d 914, 170 Ct. Cl. 357 (Ct. Cl. 1965). After the Service granted Remington Rand, a direct IBM competitor, an excise tax exemption for its Univac computers, IBM applied for a similar ruling for its competing computer. Several years later, the Service denied IBM's request, at the same time revoking Remington's exemption. Invoking section 7805(b), the court held that the Service had abused its discretion by taxing IBM but not Remington in the years prior to the revocation of Remington's exemption. *Id.* Relying on this decision, the Fund argues that because the Service has exempted two similarly situated British pension funds in private determination letters, it likewise abused its discretion by failing to give the Fund a refund for the period in question, *i.e.*, 1993. We disagree.

To begin with, *IBM* applies only to direct competitors. In its very first sentence, the court stressed the competitive relationship between IBM and Remington Rand: "International Business Machines Corporation . . . and Remington Rand were, in the years 1951-1958, the two competitors in the manufacture, sale, and leasing of larger electronic computing systems." *Id.* at 915–16. Treating direct competitors similarly for tax purposes, the court emphasized, "is peculiarly essential to free and fair competition," *id.* at 923; *see also id.* at 921 n.8 (noting that IBM and Remington "were the only two competitors as to the type of devices involved in the Service's rulings"); *id.* at 923 (indicating that the Service's treatment "favor[ed] the other competitor so sharply that fairness called upon the Commissioner . . . to establish a greater measure of equality"). In view of this language, courts interpreting *IBM* have limited it to cases involving direct competitors. *See, e.g.,* Wilson v. United States, 588 F.2d 1168, 1172 (6th Cir. 1978) (characterizing *IBM* as applying to Service regulations or rulings that "would lead to inequality of treatment between competitor taxpayers"); Anderson, Clayton & Co. v. United States, 562 F.2d 972, 981 (5th Cir. 1977) (same). Because the Fund does not allege — as of course it could not — that it competes with the two exempt British funds, *IBM* has no applicability to this case.

We also doubt that section 7805 even applies here. By its terms, section 7805 only applies to a decision by the Service to limit the retroactive effect of a ruling. Here, the Service has simply denied a refund, taking no action whatsoever with respect to retroactivity. Moreover, neither the plain language of section 7805 nor any of the cases that the Fund cites stands for the proposition that once the Service has treated one taxpayer a certain way, it must thereafter treat every similarly situated taxpayer exactly the same way. In fact, to the extent that Treasury's new regulation denying section 501(c)(5) tax-exempt status to pension funds, * * *, represents a repudiation of the Service's previous decision to exempt the British funds, nothing requires the Service to perpetuate its original error by granting the same mistaken exemption to other taxpayers. *See* Sirbo Holdings, Inc. v. Commissioner of Internal Revenue, 509 F.2d 1220, 1222 (2d Cir. 1975) ("While even-handed treatment should be the Commissioner's goal . . . the making of an error in one case, if error it was, gives other taxpayers no right to its perpetuation.").

We affirm the district court's grant of summary judgment for the United States.

So ordered.

IBM v. United States, 170 Ct. Cl. 357 (1965), which is discussed briefly in the case reprinted above, is an unusual case, both on its facts, and in the holding for the taxpayer. In *IBM,* the IRS had issued IBM's sole competitor, Remington Rand, a favorable ruling exempting it from excise tax. The IRS waited more than two years to rule on IBM's similar request, and then denied the request. IBM and Remington Rand each applied for refunds of the excise taxes paid, and only Remington Rand was issued a refund. When the IRS subsequently revoked Remington Rand's ruling prospectively, this still left unequal treatment for roughly six years, at a cost of approximately $13 million to IBM. *Id.* at 372. The Court of Claims held that the IRS had abused its discretion under section 7805(b) based on an equality of treatment rationale. Thus, the court ordered the IRS to refund to IBM the excise tax paid for the period during which Remington Rand was exempt from the tax under the ruling. *Id.* at 372–73. By forcing the IRS to issue IBM the refund, did the court not grant precedential weight to Remington Rand's ruling exempting it from tax?

As illustrated by the discussion in *Stichting Pensioenfonds Voor De Gezondheid*, taxpayers have found little solace in citing *IBM* because courts have limited that case to its narrow facts. For example, in *Florida Power & Light Co. v. United States*, 375 F.3d 1119 (Fed. Cir. 2004), the taxpayer, a utility company, sought an excise tax refund based on the application of regulations that the IRS had favorably interpreted in private letter rulings issued to other utility companies. The taxpayer relied upon *IBM* for the proposition that, because these other utility companies were direct competitors, it was entitled to the same exemption. The Federal Circuit rejected the taxpayer's argument, noting that the court in *IBM* "rested its decision 'on the . . . basis that IBM, *having taken the pains to ask promptly for its own ruling*, was entitled to have the [IRS's] ruling, in response to that request, controlled by the standard of equality and fairness. . . .' " *Id.* at 1125 (*quoting IBM*, 343 F.2d at 924). Because the taxpayer in *Florida Power* did not seek its own letter ruling relating to the excise tax exemption, its circumstances were distinguishable from those in *IBM* and thus it was not entitled to relief. *Id.*

Should there be a duty of consistency on the part of the taxpayer? Courts have, in fact, recognized one. For example, in *Estate of Ashman v. Commissioner*, 231 F.3d 541 (9th Cir. 2000), a taxpayer who, when completing her return, took the position that she had timely rolled over a pension plan distribution into an IRA, when in fact she had not, was prevented from determining the tax consequences of a later, related transaction by assuming that the distribution had not been timely rolled over. According to the court, "The law should not be such a[n] idiot that it cannot prevent a taxpayer from changing the historical facts from year to year in order to escape a fair share of the burdens of maintaining our government." *Id.* at 544 (citation omitted). If the taxpayer has a duty of consistency, does that mean that the IRS should necessarily have a duty to apply the law consistently with respect to every taxpayer?

PROBLEMS

1. If challenged by a taxpayer, how much deference would a court likely afford the IRS's position set forth in the following types of authorities?
   - A. Treasury regulations issued under the general grant of authority in Code section 7805.
   - B. Treasury regulations issued under a Code section in which Congress specifically authorized the Treasury to issue regulations.
   - C. Treasury regulations inconsistent with a prior District Court opinion in which the District Court spoke to the question generally but did not resolve the question with any certainty.
   - D. A recent Revenue Ruling that construes a newly enacted Code provision relating to a highly technical substantive tax issue.
2. Assume that, in recent audits, IRS personnel have observed that a number of taxpayers have engaged in what the IRS believes were tax-motivated sham transactions. These transactions relied on what the IRS considers a distorted interpretation of a Code section that was repealed in 2008. The IRS would like to put a stop to the revenue loss caused by these shelter transactions. Its concern

is not prospective revenue loss, but rather lost revenue from the 2003–2007 tax years.

A. Following notice and comment procedures, can a Treasury regulation enacted today, but with an effective date of January 1, 2003, close the loophole?

B. Can the IRS instead issue today a Revenue Ruling that closes the loophole, and apply it to all transactions with respect to the pre-2008 provision that are now or will subsequently be under examination or in litigation?

3. Marvin is the majority shareholder of a small corporation. He is interested in entering into a complicated merger transaction that will result in diversification of his business and the acquisition of several subsidiaries. One of his former competitors, Dale, who retired last year, engaged in a very similar transaction two years ago. Dale told Marvin that she obtained a favorable letter ruling from the IRS before consummating the transaction. She is willing to send Marvin a copy of the ruling. Marvin asks you the following questions:

A. If he engages in exactly the transaction described in Dale's ruling, can Marvin rely on Dale's ruling, and simply carry out his transaction assured of favorable tax treatment?

B. Would he be better off, after engaging in the transaction described in Dale's ruling, to attach a copy of the ruling to his return with a statement that he expects the IRS to accord him the same treatment? Marvin is curious about whether that will create an enforceable obligation on the part of the IRS to treat his transaction in accordance with Dale's ruling.

4. Katrina has been breeding pedigreed hairless Sphynx cats for several years. The food and veterinary bills for the cats are costly, and Katrina has not been able to sell enough kittens to recoup her expenses. She has been content to run the cattery at a small loss because she makes a good income from her full-time job as a professor, from which she has been deducting her losses. Recently, a colleague who teaches tax courses mentioned to her that the cattery sounded more like a "hobby" than a true business, and that perhaps Katrina should not be deducting the cattery's losses. Katrina has come to you to ask whether she can and should obtain a ruling from the IRS on her cattery so that she will know how to treat it for tax purposes next year. What do you advise?

5. At the request of a client of his firm, Kenny has incorporated an entity that the client intends to run as a charitable organization that promotes friendly soccer and softball games between co-ed teams composed of children of divorced parents. The client would like to be assured that the intended activities of the corporation will not preclude tax exemption under Code section 501(c)(3). How can Kenny request such assurance from the IRS?

6. Dr. Murray H. Johnson, M.D. is a cash-method, calendar-year taxpayer. He is an employee (not a partner) of the Shelter Island Treatment Center in Shelter Island, Missouri. The Shelter Island Center is owned and operated by the Medical Group, a privately-held, limited partnership formed under Missouri law. The Medical Group contracts with the state of Missouri to house and care for individuals who have been declared wards of the state. Most of the patients housed at the Shelter Island Center suffer from some type of mental illness.

Johnson has served as head physician at the Shelter Island Center for the past two years. He is primarily responsible for overseeing a staff of ten nurses and more than two dozen assistants who care for patients. Johnson is the only member of the staff who is authorized to prescribe drugs. During the past year, a patient at the Center had a violent outbreak of mental delusion, causing on-site medical personnel to restrain the patient and summon Johnson from his home to administer drug therapy to calm the patient. After a second, similar outbreak by the same patient, Johnson prescribed heavy doses of amphetamines for the patient, and violent outbreaks have not recurred. No other such violent incidents have occurred in the Center's five-year history.

Towards the end of last year, the Medical Group and Johnson began renegotiating his employment contract. The new contract, effective January 1 of the current year, calls for Johnson to live at the Shelter Island Center on a "permanent" basis in order to handle patient emergencies. The Center is located on a 12-acre campus in rural southern Missouri, surrounded by an upscale resort community on one side and a national forest on the other. The nearest town, Miller Shoals, where most of the staff live, is located 20 miles to the west. The nearest hospital is located 60 miles to the east in the town of Sheffield. Ambulance service to the Center originates from the hospital. Prior to moving on-campus, Johnson lived in Miller Shoals.

On the Center's campus are a cluster of four buildings: The dormitory, where patients sleep and receive medical attention; the cafeteria, where all meals are served; the gymnasium, which also contains a library; and, prior to its conversion into a residence, which is discussed below, the facilities operations building. Patients have access to the entire campus and most are free to use walking trails that traverse the Center's grounds.

Shortly after Johnson tentatively agreed to the new employment contract, the Medical Group converted the facilities operations building into a three-bedroom, two-bath personal residence for Johnson, who is single, to live in on the grounds. At Johnson's request, the residence also contains a home office with internet access and an indoor pool and exercise room. Although the Medical Group retains fee simple ownership of the house, the new employment contract grants Johnson exclusive access to the residence on a rent-free basis; Johnson is required to pay only utility bills directly attributable to the residence. The residence sits towards the edge of the campus, about one-quarter of a mile from the dormitory.

Under the new employment contract effective this year, Johnson is expected to be present at the dormitory from seven in the morning until five in the afternoon, seven days each week. The contract also calls for him to be "on call" during the remainder of each day, although not necessarily present at the dormitory, in order to respond to patient emergencies. (Other medical personnel staff the dormitory in eight-hour shifts, with at least one nurse and one staff member present at all times.) Johnson is granted three weeks of vacation per year, the dates and times of which must be approved in advance by his employer. During the three weeks that Johnson is on vacation, the Center plans to contract with the hospital in Sheffield to provide emergency coverage should a Shelter Island Center patient incident occur. Compared to his prior employment contract, which did not require him to be on call after business hours or provide him with rent-free on-campus housing, the new contract specifies a $10,000 decrease in his annual salary. His cash wages for the current year total $150,000. He estimates the rent-free lodging to be worth around $20,000 per year.

A. What factors should Dr. Johnson consider in deciding whether to request a letter ruling from the IRS confirming his ability to exclude the value of the employer-provided housing from his gross income?

B. Based on the facts set forth above, draft a request for a letter ruling confirming that the value of the lodging provided to Johnson by the Medical Group is excluded from Johnson's gross income during the current calendar year. The letter ruling request must comply with the first Revenue Procedure of the current year. You do not, however, need to submit a Checklist as otherwise required by the Revenue Procedure, nor must you complete the fee certification. With respect to the Procedural

Matters section of the ruling request, you may answer all the inquiries in the negative, except that Johnson does wish to request a conference on the issues involved. Include a completed Power of Attorney Form 2848 (generate fictitious information as may be required to complete the form). Dr. Johnson's address is P.O. Box 4059, Shelter Island, MO 50596. His Social Security Number is 595-03-9506 and his telephone number is (816) 940-8692.

Chapter 3
TAX RETURNS AND EXAMINATIONS

§ 3.01 INTRODUCTION

As noted in Chapter 1, the federal income tax is a "voluntary compliance" or "self-assessment" system. Instead of the IRS billing taxpayers, the law requires taxpayers to file tax returns reflecting their tax liabilities and to pay those amounts by specified due dates. *See* I.R.C. §§ 6001, 6011; Treas. Reg. § 1.6011-1. The IRS enforces the self-assessment system in part by collecting information from payors to verify the amounts shown on taxpayers' returns; collecting tax throughout the year through withholding and estimated tax payments; and auditing a percentage of returns each year to ensure that taxpayers are reporting their tax liabilities correctly.

After this Introduction, the chapter begins by reviewing the taxpayer's filing obligations, focusing on what constitutes a valid return, when returns and payments are due, and how taxpayers may qualify for an extension of time to file the return or pay the resulting tax. The chapter then discusses the IRS's examination function. Section 3.03 reviews how the IRS selects returns for audits and how IRS employees normally carry out a typical income tax audit. After discussing special examination techniques applicable to large businesses and partnerships, the chapter then raises strategic considerations the tax practitioner should consider when representing a client during the audit process. Finally, Section 3.04 discusses the special techniques the IRS uses to reconstruct the taxpayer's income in cases in which the taxpayer's books and records do not exist or are inadequate. That section examines the various means of direct and indirect proof the IRS uses and how the representative can challenge those methods.

§ 3.02 TAX RETURNS AND PAYMENTS OF TAX

[A] Formal Requirements of a Return

Reading Assignment: I.R.C. §§ 6011, 6012, 6014, 6020(a)–(b), 6501(a)–(c), 6651(a)(1), 6702; Treas. Reg. § 1.6011-1(b).

Section 6011 mandates that all persons subject to tax file a return "according to the forms and regulations prescribed by the Secretary." For individual income taxpayers, the filing requirement generally applies once the taxpayer's gross income exceeds the combined amounts of the standard deduction and personal exemption. I.R.C. § 6012(a)(1)(A). The IRS's expectation is that taxpayers will submit their returns using the official forms the IRS prepares (for example, Form 1040 in the case of individual income tax). Treas. Reg. § 1.6011-1(b); *see also* I.R.C. § 6611(g)(2) (return is processible only if filed on a permitted form). The regulations recognize, however, that "[in] the absence of a prescribed form, a statement made by a taxpayer disclosing his gross income and the deductions therefrom may be accepted as a tentative return, and, if filed within the prescribed time, the statement so made will relieve the taxpayer from liability for the addition to tax imposed for the delinquent filing of the return, provided that without unnecessary delay, such a tentative return is supplemented by a return made on the proper form." Treas. Reg. § 1.6011-1(b).

Determining whether the document the taxpayer files constitute a "return" is important for several reasons. First, the taxpayer's failure to file a valid return by the prescribed due date can lead to a penalty in an amount equal to, typically, 5% of the amount of tax due for each month the return is late, up to a maximum penalty rate of 25%. I.R.C. § 6651(a)(1). Just as importantly, only a sufficient return starts the running of the statute of limitations on assessment against the IRS. *See* I.R.C. § 6501(c)(3); Blount v. Commissioner, 86 T.C. 383 (1986).[1] In the absence of a valid return, the IRS may assess tax liability at any time.

In the following case, the taxpayer submitted information using the official IRS form, yet the majority concluded that the submission was not sufficient to avoid the failure to file penalty. According to the majority, what elements must be present for a submission to constitute a valid return?

BEARD v. COMMISSIONER

United States Tax Court
82 T.C. 766 (1984)

WHITAKER, JUDGE: This case is before us on respondent's motion for summary judgment.* * *

In the notice of deficiency issued to petitioner, respondent determined a deficiency in petitioner's 1981 Federal income tax in the amount of $6,535. In the answer, respondent alleged that additions to tax were due under section 6651(a)(1) for failure to file a return, and section 6653(a) [currently I.R.C. § 6662 — Eds.] for negligence or intentional disregard of the rules and regulations. Additionally, damages pursuant to section 6673 for instituting proceedings before the Tax Court merely for delay were requested.

* * * Petitioner denies he was required to file a 1981 income tax return on or before April 15, 1982, in that he owed no tax liability for that year. He admits that the document in question in this case is the only submission he made to the Internal Revenue Service for the 1981 year, claiming that it is a return under section 6012 because it contains figures and numbers from which to compute a tax. * * *

FINDINGS OF FACT

Petitioner resided in Carleton, Mich., when the petition was filed in this case. During the 1981 taxable year, petitioner was employed by, and received wages from, Guardian Industries totaling $24,401.89. Such amounts were actually received by petitioner during that year.

He submitted to the Internal Revenue Service the below-described form and an accompanying memorandum dated February 22, 1982, as his 1981 return, thus indicating his protest to the Federal income tax laws. No other document alleged to be a return for the 1981 year was submitted. This document (the tampered form) was prepared by, or for, petitioner by making changes to an official Treasury Form 1040 in such fashion (by printing or typing) that the changes may not be readily apparent to a casual reader.

In that part of the first page of the official form intended to reflect income, petitioner deleted the word "income" from the item captions in lines 8a, 11, 18, and 20, and inserted in those spaces the word "gain." On line 21 of the form, he obliterated the word "income" from the item caption. In addition, in the margin caption to this section, petitioner deleted the word "Income" and inserted the word "Receipts."

In that part of the first page of the form intended to reflect deductions from income, he deleted the words "Employee business expense (attach Form 2106)" from line 23 of the form and inserted "Non-taxable receipts." In addition, in the marginal caption to this section, petitioner deleted the word "Income" and inserted the word "Receipts," so that the caption reads "Adjustments to Receipts" instead of "Adjustments to Income."

Petitioner filled in his name, address, Social Security number, occupation, and filing status in addition to the name, occupation, and Social Security number of his spouse. He

---

[1] The statute of limitations on assessment is discussed in detail in Chapter 7.

claimed one exemption on the tampered form. The relevant information entries are as follows: On line 7 entitled "Wages, salaries, tips, etc.," taxpayer inserted the amount of $24,401.89. On line 23, under the category of "Non-taxable receipts," petitioner claimed an adjustment to "Receipts" of $24,401.89. He therefore showed a tax liability of zero. On line 55, entitled "Total Federal income tax withheld," he showed an amount of $1,770.75. The total $1,770.75 that had been withheld from his wages was claimed as a refund. This tampered form was signed by petitioner and dated February 22, 1982. Petitioner's Form W-2 issued by Guardian Industries was attached.

Petitioner's scheme in submitting this tampered form apparently was to conceal from the IRS Center operators the fact that his inclusion of his wages on the tampered form was negated by his fabrication of "Non-taxable receipts" on line 23, thus simultaneously excluding the wages theoretically reported. The net effect of the two steps was to create a zero tax liability. Since his employer had withheld against the amounts paid to him for the 1981 year, this scheme allowed him to claim a refund for that year.

* * *

The instant case is one of 23 cases that were on the March 5, 1984, trial calendar for Detroit, Mich., in which tampered forms are at issue. Many other similar cases are pending before this Court. All of these 23 cases contain a fabricated adjustment for "Non-taxable receipts." All were submitted to the Internal Revenue Service in the year 1980 or 1981. All but 2 of the 23 were submitted with two- or three-page memorandums advocating that wages are not taxable income. Twenty-two of the petitions in these cases contained identical language except for entries relevant to the petitioners' personal data. The remaining case contained a handwritten, individually composed petition. In cases in which replies or responses to respondent's motion for summary judgment were filed, all but one were the same format and language, with minor deviations to suit the petitioners in each case. It is abundantly clear that these docketed cases and documents represent a coordinated protest effort — an attempt to obtain refunds where employers had withheld against amounts paid, as well as to drain further the limited resources of this Court with these frivolous contentions.

The Internal Revenue Service has been forced to develop special procedures to handle tampered forms like those in the group referred to above. The tampered forms are also referred to as "*Eisner v. Macomber* returns" because *Eisner v. Macomber*, 252 U.S. 189 (1920), is usually cited either in the form or in the literature attached. From a cursory look, they appear to be official Forms 1040, but upon closer inspection, definitively are not. Internal Revenue Service employees must identify and then withdraw these from the normal processing channels, and gather and deliver them to a special team for review. After such review, the person who submitted such a tampered return is often, but not always, informed that it is not acceptable as a return because it does not comply with the Internal Revenue Code. Petitioner was so informed by a letter dated July 16, 1982, stating that the tampered form was "not acceptable as an income tax return because it does not contain information required by law, and it does not comply with Internal Revenue Code requirements."

ULTIMATE FINDINGS OF FACT

Petitioner actually received $24,401.89 from his employer as wages during the 1981 taxable year. The only documents he submitted for the 1981 taxable year were the tampered form and its accompanying memorandum. Petitioner has extensively studied the rules and regulations regarding the income tax laws in addition to income tax cases and, thus, his actions were the product of informed deliberation.

OPINION

Summary Judgment Issue

The threshold issue is whether a motion for summary judgment is appropriate in this case. We conclude that it is. * * *

Failure To File

Respondent alleges an addition to tax under section 6651(a)(1) for failure to file a Federal income tax return for taxable year 1981. * * * Respondent maintains that the tampered form submitted by petitioner was not a return within the meaning of sections 6012, 6072, and 6651(a)(1), that it will not be accepted as such (and was not accepted in this case), and thus petitioner is liable for an addition under section 6651(a)(1). We agree.

The general requirements of a Federal income tax return are set forth in section 6011(a), in relevant part as follows:

> When required by regulations prescribed by the Secretary any person made liable for any tax * * * shall make a return or statement *according to the forms* and *regulations* prescribed by the Secretary. [Emphasis added.]

Regulations implementing this legislative mandate provide:

> (a) *General rule*. Every person subject to any tax, or required to collect any tax, under subtitle A of the Code, shall make such returns or statements as are required by the regulations in this chapter. The return or statement shall include therein the information required by the applicable regulations or forms.
>
> (b) *Use of prescribed forms*. Copies of the prescribed return forms will so far as possible be furnished taxpayers by district directors. A taxpayer will not be excused from making a return, however, by the fact that no return form has been furnished to him. Taxpayers not supplied with the proper forms should make application therefor to the district director in ample time to have their returns prepared, verified, and filed on or before the due date with the internal revenue office where such returns are required to be filed. Each taxpayer should carefully prepare his return and set forth fully and clearly the information required to be included therein. Returns which have not been so prepared will not be accepted as meeting the requirements of the code. * * *

[Treas. Reg. § 1.6011-1. — Eds.].

The statutory grant of authority to the Treasury requires that taxpayers make a return or statement according to the forms and regulations prescribed by the Secretary of the Treasury. These regulations mandate the use of the proper official form, except as noted below. The U.S. Supreme Court in the case of *Commissioner v. Lane-Wells Co.*, 321 U.S. 219 (1944), has recognized this mandate in stating:

> Congress has given discretion to the Commissioner to prescribe by regulation forms of returns and has made it the duty of the taxpayer to comply. It thus implements the system of self assessment which is so largely the basis of our American scheme of income taxation. The purpose is not alone to get tax information in some form but also to get it with such *uniformity*, *completeness*, and *arrangement* that the physical task of handling and verifying returns may be readily accomplished. [321 U.S. at 223; emphasis added.]

This discretionary authority outlined in the regulations at section 1.6011-1, Income Tax Regs., has also been recognized in the case of *Parker v. Commissioner*, 365 F.2d 792 (8th Cir. 1966). Although the facts of that case are distinguishable from the instant case, the court did note that —

> Taxpayers are required to file timely returns on forms established by the Commissioner. * * * The Commissioner is certainly not required to accept any facsimile the taxpayer sees fit to submit. If the Commissioner were obligated to do so, the business of tax collecting would result in insurmountable confusion. * * * [365 F.2d at 800.]

For years, the only permissible exception to the use of the official form has been the permission, granted from time to time to tax return preparers by the Internal Revenue Service, to reproduce and vary very slightly the official form pursuant to the Commissioner's revenue procedures. These revenue procedures require advance approval of a specially designed form prior to use as well as following the guidelines for acceptable changes in the form. The philosophy of the revenue procedure is and has been required forms to conform in material respects to the official form for the obvious reasons of convenience and processing facilitation but also to be clearly distinguishable from the official form, thereby removing the opportunity for deceit. * * *

On the tampered form, various margin and item captions, in whole or in part, have been deleted and most replaced with language fabricated by the petitioner. These changes were not in conformity with the Revenue Procedure[n.20] rules at section 5.01(2)(a)(1) requiring each substitute or privately designed form to follow the design of the official form as to *format*, *arrangement*, *item caption*, line numbers, line references, and sequence. Also, Revenue Procedure section 3.04(1) and (2) prohibits any change of any Internal Revenue Service tax form, graphic or otherwise, or the use of a taxpayer's own (nonapproved) version without prior approval from the Internal Revenue Service. Petitioner made no attempt to obtain such approval. Additionally, petitioner was required by Revenue Procedure section 6.01 to remove the Government Printing Office symbol and jacket numbers, and in such space (using the same type size), print the employer identifying number of the printer or the Social Security number of the form designer. Petitioner did not remove the symbol and numbers and did not insert in their place his appropriate number. The tampered form deceptively bore the markings of an official form. Section 8.01, Revenue Procedure rules, prohibits the filing of reproductions of official forms and substitute forms that do not meet the requirements of the procedure. The only filing made by petitioner for the 1981 taxable year was the nonconforming tampered form.

Petitioner's prohibited tampering with the official form, the net effect of which is the creation of a zero tax liability, adversely affects the form's useability by respondent. The tampered form, because of these numerous irregularities, must be handled by special procedures and must be withdrawn from normal processing channels. There can be no doubt that due to its lack of conformity to the official form, it substantially impedes the Commissioner's physical task of handling and verifying tax returns. Under the facts of this case, taxpayer has not made a return *according to the forms and regulations* prescribed by the Secretary as required by section 6011(a). The rejection of the tampered form was authorized by the regulations for failure to conform to the revenue procedure. But whether or not rejected in this case, the question remains — Is the Internal Revenue Service nevertheless required to accept and treat as a tax return this tampered form? We conclude that it is not.

There have been factual circumstances in which the courts have treated as returns, for statute of limitations purposes, documents which did not conform to the regulations as prescribed by section 6011(a). Since the instant case is one of first impression, we will consider these cases that were decided on the statute of limitations issue because a return that is sufficient to trigger the running of the statute of limitation must also be sufficient for the purpose of section 6651(a)(1).

The Supreme Court test to determine whether a document is sufficient for statute of

---

[n.20] Rev. Proc. 80-47, 1980-2 C.B. 782. . . . [The most current version of this Revenue Procedure to date is Revenue Procedure 2007-15, 2007-1 C.B. 300. — Eds.]

limitations purposes has several elements: First, there must be sufficient data to calculate tax liability; second, the document must purport to be a return; third, there must be an honest and reasonable attempt to satisfy the requirements of the tax law; and fourth, the taxpayer must execute the return under penalties of perjury.

It is important to consider the factual circumstances under which this test has been applied. In *Florsheim Bros. Drygoods Co. v. United States*, 280 U.S. 453 (1930), at issue was whether the filing of a "tentative return" or the later filing of a "completed return" triggered the statute of limitations. * * *

The Court recognized that the filing of a return that is defective or incomplete may under some circumstances be sufficient to start the running of the period of limitation. However, such a return must purport to be a specific statement of the items of income, deductions, and credits in compliance with the statutory duty to report information and "*to have that effect it must honestly and reasonably be intended as such.*" (Emphasis added.) Thus, the filing of the tentative return was not a return to start the period of limitation running.

This issue of whether the document was a return for the statute of limitation purposes was again before the Court in *Zellerbach Paper Co. v. Helvering*, 293 U.S. 172 (1934). Justice Cardozo, speaking for the Court, said:

> Perfect accuracy or completeness is not necessary to rescue a return from nullity, if it purports to be a return, is sworn to as such * * * and evinces an honest and genuine endeavor to satisfy the law. This is so even though at the time of filing the omissions or inaccuracies are such as to make amendment necessary. [*Zellerbach Paper Co. v. Helvering*, *supra* at 180. Citations omitted.]

* * *

The tampered form before us may purport to be a return in that it may "convey, imply or profess outwardly" to be a return. Black's Law Dictionary 1112 (rev. 5th ed. 1979). It was also sworn to. But it does not reflect an endeavor to satisfy the law. It in fact makes a mockery of the requirements for a tax return, both as to form and content. Whether or not the form contains sufficient information to permit a tax to be calculated is not altogether clear. We have held that the attachment of a Form W-2 does not substitute for the disclosure on the return, itself, of information as to income, deductions, credits, and tax liability. Reiff v. Commissioner, 77 T.C. 1169 (1981). Ignoring the Form W-2, the tampered form does show an amount of "Wages, salaries, tips, etc.," but with the margin description altered from "Income" to "Receipts." Similarly, in place of a deduction, the form has an amount for "Non-taxable receipts." Thus, to compute a tax from this tampered form, one must effectively ignore the margin and line descriptions, imagining instead the correct ones from an official Form 1040, or one must simply select from the form, including the Form W-2, that information which appears to be applicable and correct, and from the information so selected, irrespective of its label, compute the tax. We do not believe such an exercise is what the U.S. Supreme Court had in mind in *Commissioner v. Lane-Wells Co.*, *supra* at 222–223, and *Germantown Trust Co. v. Commissioner*, 309 U.S. 304, 309 (1940).

The tampered form here is a conspicuous protest against the payment of tax, intended to deceive respondent's return-processing personnel into refunding the withheld tax. Since such intentional tampering could go undetected in computer processing, respondent was forced to develop and institute special procedures for handling such submissions. The critical requirement that there must be an honest and reasonable attempt to satisfy the requirements of the Federal income tax law clearly is not met. * * *

The tampered form is not in conformity with the requirements in section 6011(a) or section 1.6011-1(a) and (b), Income Tax Regs., and it is not a return under the judicial line of authority set forth above.

* * * Respondent has met his burden of proving that petitioner did not file a return

for sections 6011, 6012, 6072, and 6651(a)(1) purposes, and thus an addition to tax is due.

* * *

Accordingly, we grant the motion for summary judgment.

CHABOT, J., concurring in part and dissenting in part:

* * *

From the majority's determination to grant summary judgment that the Form 1040 filed by petitioner was not a tax return, I respectfully dissent.

In *Badaracco v. Commissioner*, 464 U.S. [386] (1984), the Supreme Court confronted the contention of the taxpayers therein that the first documents they had filed "were 'nullities' for the statute of limitations purposes." In the course of its analysis, the Supreme Court stated as follows:

> a document which on its face plausibly purports to be in compliance, and which is signed by the taxpayer, is a return despite its inaccuracies. * * *
>
> *Zellerbach Paper Co. v. Helvering*, 293 U.S. 172 (1934), which petitioners cite, affords no support for their argument. The Court in *Zellerbach* held that an original return, despite its inaccuracy, was a "return" for limitations purposes, so that the filing of an amended return did not start a new period of limitations running. In the instant cases, the original returns similarly purported to be returns, were sworn to as such, and appeared on their faces to constitute endeavors to satisfy the law. Although those returns, in fact, were not honest, the holding in *Zellerbach* does not render them nullities. [464 U.S. at 396–97.]

An examination of the Form 1040 in question * * * shows the following: (1) It is a document which on its face plausibly purports to be in compliance with the law; (2) it is signed by the taxpayer (under penalties of perjury); (3) it does not make believe that only gold and silver coins need be reported; (4) it is not chock-full of refusals to provide information (indeed, it provides all the information requested as to petitioner's "Wages, salaries, tips, etc.", and respondent does not contend that petitioner had any other reportable income); (5) the income is reported on the correct line of the return; (6) an unwarranted deduction is reported on a line reserved for deductions; and (7) apparently the Form 1040 includes everything respondent needed in order to determine petitioner's income tax liability. Compare the instant case with *Reiff v. Commissioner*, 77 T.C. 1169, 1177–1179 (1981), and the cases cited therein. Nothing in the majority's opinion or on the face of the Form 1040 shows that respondent is led into error *because of the change in the text of any line on the Form 1040.*

I would hold that the document filed by petitioner constitutes a tax return under the standards adopted by the Supreme Court, as most recently articulated in *Badaracco v. Commissioner, supra.*

* * *

The majority's opinion * * * states that petitioner's alteration of the Form 1040 had "the net effect of * * * the creation of a zero tax liability" and that "because of these numerous irregularities, [it had to] be handled by special procedures and must be withdrawn from normal processing channels." This misdescribes the situation. Both the zero tax liability, and the requirement of special procedures, result from the unwarranted deduction. These problems would exist — because of the deduction — even if there were no alterations to the Form 1040.

* * *

The Form 1040 in question shows the necessary income information, and does so on the correct line, and that line has not been altered. This information is in accord with the Form W-2 (and not in conflict with it, as was the case in *Reiff v. Commissioner, supra,* relied on by the majority). There is no need to imagine the correct margin and line descriptions from an official Form 1040 because respondent's problems are no different, with the altered Form 1040, than they would be with an official Form 1040.

* * *

I understand and share the majority's frustration at having to deal with frivolous arguments. * * * However, this Court should not confuse the law as to what is a tax return, just to punish a particular individual or even a class of individuals. The Congress has given the courts more effective tools. We have used these tools to impose damages of up to $5,000 for frivolous or groundless actions. (Sec. 6673.) The District Courts have used these tools to uphold penalties of $500 for frivolous filings. (Sec. 6702.) As the majority note * * *, the injunction has been used to prevent conduct which interferes with proper administration of the Internal Revenue laws. (Secs. 7402(a), 7407.) When civil fraud is found, the sanction therefor now includes an additional amount under section 6653(b)(2).[2] The criminal fraud fine has been increased from a maximum of $10,000 to a maximum of $100,000 ($500,000 in the case of a corporation). (Sec. 7201.)

I would hold that petitioner's Form 1040 is a tax return. Since there is no finding that it was filed late, I would not impose an addition to tax under section 6651(a)(1). From the majority's contrary holding, I respectfully dissent.

How would, the majority and dissent rule in the case of a taxpayer who files a Form 1040 entirely filled in with zeros? Assuming the return were signed under penalties of perjury,[3] would this be a valid return? In *Coulton v. Commissioner*, T.C. Memo. 2005-199, the Tax Court applied the four-part test set forth in *Beard* to determine whether such a submission, accompanied by a document that contained tax protestor rhetoric, constituted a tax return. Focusing on the *Beard* requirement that "a document must be an honest and genuine endeavor to satisfy the tax law in order to be a return," the Tax Court found that the taxpayer's Form 1040 did not satisfy this requirement. *Id.*; *see also* C.C.A. 200651015 (instituting IRS policy of treating zero returns as invalid and frivolous). The requirement that a return must contain sufficient data to calculate the taxpayer's liability does not imply complete accuracy on the part of the taxpayer, but a document that does not make reference to income and deductions typically will not be treated as a valid return. *See, e.g.*, Ferrando v. United States, 245 F.2d 582 (9th Cir. 1957).

The dissent in *Beard* proposes several alternative ways, short of declaring the submission an invalid return, to punish the taxpayer for tampering with the IRS form. One option would be to apply a "frivolous return penalty." Section 6702 authorizes the imposition of a $5,000 penalty if the taxpayer files what purports to be a return but that (1) omits information on which the substantive correctness of the self-assessment may be judged; or (2) contains information that on its face indicates that self-assessment is substantially incorrect, and the taxpayer's conduct is due to a frivolous position or a

---

[2] [This is now section 6663. — Eds.]

[3] Under most circumstances, a return is not valid until it has been signed under penalties of perjury. I.R.C. § 6065. Joint returns require both spouses' signatures. Treas. Reg. § 1.6013-1(a)(2); *see Olpin v. Commissioner*, 270 F.3d 1297 (10th Cir. 2001) (holding that an unsigned joint return is not valid). However, there are special procedures for one spouse to sign the other's name where the other spouse is incapacitated and that spouse gives oral permission. *Id.* Code sections 6062 and 6063 contain rules for authorized signatories for corporate and partnership returns.

Under Code section 6064, a signature is presumed authentic. An agent with an appropriate power of attorney form may sign a return for an individual if the taxpayer is unable to do so because of disease or injury; is continuously absent from the United States for at least 60 days before the return is due; or the taxpayer requests permission in writing from the IRS, which then determines that good cause exists. Treas. Reg. § 1.6012-1(a)(5).

desire to impede the administration of the tax laws. I.R.C. § 6702(a). Wouldn't this have been the more appropriate remedy for the taxpayer in *Beard*?[4]

A taxpayer who files a return must also compute the amount of tax due unless he or she qualifies for and makes a special election under section 6014 to have the IRS perform the computation. *See* Treas. Reg. § 1.6014-2. In those instances in which the taxpayer can make such an election (primarily wage earners with taxable income less than $100,000), the IRS will compute the amount of the taxpayer's liability. *See* IRS Publication 967, *The IRS Will Figure Your Tax* (2007).

The IRS also has the authority under Code section 6020 to prepare a "substitute" return on the taxpayer's behalf if the taxpayer does not do so. *See* I.R.C. § 6020(a) ("If any person shall fail to make a return required by this title or by regulations prescribed thereunder, but shall consent to disclose all information necessary for the preparation thereof, then, and in that case, the Secretary may prepare such return, which, being signed by such person, may be received by the Secretary as the return of such person."), (b)(1) ("If any person fails to make any return required by any internal revenue law or regulation made thereunder at the time prescribed therefor, or makes, willfully or otherwise, a false or fraudulent return, the Secretary shall make such return from his own knowledge and from such information as he can obtain through testimony or otherwise."). A return prepared under section 6020(a) is generally treated as a "return" for all purposes. By contrast, a return prepared by the IRS under section 6020(b) does not start the running of the statute of limitations on assessment, but may prevent the imposition of certain penalties against the taxpayer. *See* I.R.C. § 6501(b)(3), Treas. Reg. § 301.6020-1(b)(3).

[B] Filing of Tax Returns

Reading Assignment: I.R.C. §§ 6072, 7502, 7503.

Individual calendar-year federal income tax returns are due on April 15 of the subsequent year. I.R.C. § 6072(a). Individual fiscal-year income tax returns are due by the 15th day of the fourth month following the close of the fiscal tax year. *Id.* Corporate calendar-year income tax returns are due March 15, I.R.C. § 6072(b), and corporate fiscal-year returns are due the 15th day of the third month following the close of the fiscal year, *id.* If the last day for filing the return falls on a Saturday, Sunday, or legal holiday, the return is still considered timely if it is filed on the next day that is not a Saturday, Sunday or legal holiday.[5] I.R.C. § 7503. For example, in years when April 15 falls on a Saturday, the filing date for that year is Monday, April 17.

Returns are generally considered filed when received by the IRS. However, timely mailing is considered timely filing if the requirements of section 7502(a) are met: (1) the postmark falls within the date for filing (including extensions); (2) the taxpayer deposits the return or other document in the mail in an envelope or wrapper properly addressed to the appropriate IRS office with postage prepaid; and (3) the return or other document is delivered to the IRS after it is due. The "timely mailed is timely filed" rule (sometimes

---

[4] The IRS now issues guidance identifying positions that it will treat as frivolous and that could trigger a $5,000 penalty. See Notice 2007-30, 2007-1 C.B. 883 (rejecting arguments that a "taxpayer may 'untax' himself or herself at any time or revoke the consent to be taxed and thereafter not be subject to internal revenue taxes" and that a "taxpayer may lawfully decline to pay taxes if the taxpayer disagrees with the government's use of tax revenues").

[5] If the return is filed before the due date, the statute of limitations begins to run on the actual due date (even if it was a Saturday, Sunday, or legal holiday). *See* Rev. Rul. 81-269, 1981–2 C.B. 243. If the return is filed on the extended due date (such as April 16 in a year that April 15 falls on a Sunday), then the statute of limitations starts to run only on the date the return is filed. If the statute of limitations runs on a Saturday, Sunday, or legal holiday, assessment on the next business day is timely. I.R.C. § 7503. *See* Chapter 7 for further discussion of statutes of limitations on assessment of tax.

also called the "mailbox" rule) applies not just to tax returns but also to refund claims, payments, petitions, and other documents. Under section 7502(f), a taxpayer can use a designated private delivery service (such as Federal Express, UPS, or Airborne Express) instead of the United States mail and benefit from the presumption in section 7502. *See* Notice 2004-83, 2004-52 I.R.B. 1030 (providing a list of designated private delivery services).

Note that one of the conditions associated with the mailbox rule in section 7502(a) is that the return must be delivered to the IRS. If the return is timely mailed but lost in transit, the burden of proving the date of mailing remains with the taxpayer. Consider the following excerpt from *Cardinal Textile Sales Inc. v. United States*, 88 A.F.T.R. 2d 5850 (N.D. Ga. 2001):

> On September 15, 1995, Jerome Maurer, a staff accountant with the Russe Firm, mailed the envelope containing plaintiff's Form 1120X refund claims for the 1988, 1989, and 1990 tax years from the United States Post Office in downtown Chattanooga, Tennessee. * * * Although the post office itself closed at 5:30 p.m. on September 15, 1995, the last mail pickup from the mail receptacle outside the post office was scheduled to occur at 7:00 p.m. * * * Mr. Maurer deposited the envelope containing plaintiff's Form 1120X refund claims[6] for the 1988, 1989, and 1990 tax years into the mail receptacle outside the post office after 5:30 p.m., but prior to 7:00 p.m., on September 15, 1995. * * *
>
> The IRS has no record of receiving Plaintiff's Form 1120X refund claims for the 1988, 1989, and 1990 tax years. * * * The claims were never returned to the Russe Firm. * * *
>
> Plaintiff argues that a genuine dispute exists whether Plaintiff filed its 1120X claims for refund for the 1988, 1989, and 1990 tax years. For the following reasons, the Court rejects Plaintiff's argument.
>
> First, Plaintiff did not send its claims for refund by certified or registered mail. Plaintiff therefore cannot rely upon § 7502(c) to show that its claims for refund were filed with the IRS.
>
> Second, the majority of courts interpreting § 7502(a) have concluded that § 7502(a) applies only if IRS actually receives the claims for refund. * * * It is not sufficient merely to place the claims for refund in a mail receptacle. * * * Because the undisputed evidence in the case shows that the IRS never received Plaintiff's claims for refund, § 7502(a) does not apply. * * *

As *Cardinal Textile Sales* suggests, if the taxpayer timely submits the return by registered or certified mail, the mailing receipt is considered to be prima facie evidence that the return was delivered to the IRS. I.R.C. § 7502(c). A taxpayer who does not use registered or certified mail bears the risk that a document deposited in the mail will be postmarked after the due date, and when arriving after the due date, will be deemed untimely. Treas. Reg. § 301.7502-1(c)(iii). Accordingly, mail stamped by private meter, to be timely, must be postmarked within the filing period and arrive within the time it would normally take a letter to arrive. If the arrival time is not reasonable, the taxpayer bears the burden of proving that it was deposited in the mails and the delay was caused by transmission of the post. Treas. Reg. § 301.7502-1(c)(1)(iii)(B).

The Treasury has issued proposed regulations providing that, other than direct proof of actual delivery, a registered or certified mail receipt is the only prima facie evidence of delivery that the IRS will accept. Prop. Reg. § 301.7502-1(e). This position is inconsistent with several court decisions, which would allow the taxpayer to present other forms of proof, beyond a certified or registered mail receipt, to establish that the

---

[6] [A Form 1120X is an amended corporate income tax return. Here, the amended returns were used to claim refunds. Refund claims are discussed in Chapter 10. — Eds.]

return was timely mailed on or before the deadline date. *See, e.g.*, Sorrentino v. IRS, 383 F.3d 1187 (10th Cir. 2004); Estate of Wood v. Commissioner, 909 F.2d 1155 (8th Cir. 1990).

Over the past several decades, the IRS has embraced electronic filing for many types of tax returns. Electronic filing for income tax returns was introduced in 1986, and by 1996, the electronic filing program was expanded so that taxpayers could file using their own personal computers. *See* IR 96-4. Congress set a goal of having 80 percent of all taxpayers electronically file by 2007. While the percentage of taxpayers who have done so has increased dramatically over the past decade, the IRS Oversight Board estimates that only about 58% of taxpayers electronically filed their returns in 2007. IRS Oversight Board, *Electronic Filing 2007 Annual Report to Congress*.

Beginning in 2003, the IRS established a free electronic filing system, Free File, available through the IRS's website. The program is based on an agreement between the IRS and a consortium of private companies in the electronic tax preparation industry. The agreement guarantees free online return filing for taxpayers with adjusted gross income under $50,000. *See* IR-2005-126, *available at* 2005 TNT 206-11 (Oct. 26, 2005). Until recently, the IRS also allowed some taxpayers to file tax returns over the telephone. The IRS eliminated the TeleFile program in 2005. *See* IR-2005-75, *available at* 2005 TNT 139-6 (July 21, 2005).

[C] Filing Extensions

Reading Assignment: I.R.C. § 6081.

Section 6081 grants the IRS the authority to extend the time for filing any return or document. I.R.C. § 6081(a). Individual taxpayers qualify for an automatic six-month extension of time to file an income tax return if they submit a completed Form 4868, *Application for Automatic Extension of Time to File U.S. Individual Income Tax Return*, on or before the regular due date for the return. Taxpayers do not have to sign the request or explain why they need the extra time. *See* Form 4868; Treas. Reg. § 1.6081-4(b). Although Form 4868 requires the taxpayer to make a good faith estimate of the net tax amount due for the year, technically the taxpayer need not pay any tax at the time of the extension request. However, the extension of time to file does not extend the time to pay tax.[7] Treas. Reg. § 1.6081-4(c). Therefore, it is advisable for the taxpayer to submit the estimated tax due with the extension request in order to reduce, to the greatest extent possible, accrual of interest and penalties.

Corporate taxpayers may also obtain an automatic six-month extension of time to file the taxpayer's income tax return by submitting Form 7004, *Application for Automatic 6-Month Extension of Time to File Certain Business Income Tax, Information, and Other Returns*, by the return's original due date. Like individual taxpayers, the corporation need not state a reason for the request. Corporate taxpayers must compute the total amount of their tentative tax on the extension request and, unlike individuals, must remit any balance due. Treas. Reg. § 1.6081-3.

---

[7] As a result, interest accrues on any amounts owed by the taxpayer during the period of the extension. The taxpayer may also be subject to a failure to pay penalty in section 6651(a)(2) even though the taxpayer obtained an extension of time to file. However, an extension of time to file may allow the taxpayer to avoid the penalty, provided that at least 90 percent of the tax due with the return is paid on or before the extended due date. *See* Treas. Reg. § 301.6651-1(c)(3). These interest and penalty issues are discussed, respectively, in Chapters 13 and 12.

[D] Amended Returns

A taxpayer has the option of amending the return if he or she discovers a mistake on the original return. If the taxpayer files an amended return on or before the return due date, the amended return is considered the taxpayer's return for that year. *See* Haggar Co. v. Helvering, 308 U.S. 389 (1940). By contrast, the IRS has the discretion to accept or reject an amended return filed after the due date. Rev. Rul. 83-86, 1983-1 C.B. 358. Even if the IRS accepts the amended return, the original return is the one relevant for statute of limitations purposes. *See* Badaracco v. Commissioner, 464 U.S. 386 (1984). As explained in more detail in Chapter 10, a taxpayer must file an amended return in order to claim a refund or credit of most tax overpayments.

What if the taxpayer discovers an omission on the taxpayer's original return: Does the taxpayer have an obligation to file an amended return correcting the mistake? Regulations provide that a taxpayer should file an amended return and pay additional tax due if the taxpayer discovers that an item of income should have been included in a prior tax year and the statute of limitations is open. *See* Treas. Reg. §§ 1.451-1(a), 1.461-1(a)(3).

[E] Tax Payments

Reading Assignment: I.R.C. §§ 6151(a), 6161(a), 6311, 6654; Treas. Reg. § 1.6161-1.

As noted above, an extension of time to file a return does not extend the time to pay tax. The date fixed for payment is the last day the return is due, determined without regard to extensions for filing. I.R.C. § 6151(a). Payments generally must be made by check or money order payable to the U.S. Treasury and collectible in United States currency.[8] *See* I.R.C. § 6311. In addition, the IRS accepts payment via the taxpayer's debit or credit card. Procedures and restrictions on the use of credit and debit cards are found in Treasury Regulation section 301.6311-2.

In unusual circumstances, the IRS may grant the taxpayer an extension of time to pay tax, generally for up to a six-month period. I.R.C. § 6161(a)(1). Interest on the amount of unpaid tax will, nevertheless, run from the due date of the return. I.R.C. § 6601(b)(1). Payment extensions are not freely given, and no extension is permitted if nonpayment was due to negligence, intentional disregard of rules or regulations, or fraud. The regulations require a showing of "undue hardship" to get the extension. Treas. Reg. § 1.6161-1(b). The taxpayer must file an application for an extension of time for payment before the original payment due date and must include supporting financial data (a balance sheet and income statement for three months). A taxpayer who is unable to pay the tax liability in full when due also may be eligible to enter into an installment agreement with the IRS, which allows the taxpayer to pay the liability over time. Installment agreements are discussed in more detail in Chapter 15.

In some cases, tax liability may actually be due earlier than the due date of the return. The Code provides for tax withholding from employees' wages so that the government receives tax on behalf of employees regularly throughout the year. *See* I.R.C. § 3402. In addition, taxpayers whose withholding is inadequate to cover their tax liabilities may be required to file "estimated tax" returns on a quarterly basis. In general, the amount due with each estimated tax form is twenty-five percent of the amount of tax due for the year.[9] I.R.C. § 6654(d). This is enforced through an "estimated tax penalty" if the

---

[8] Section 6657 provides a penalty for tendering a bad check.

[9] Each installment must be 25 percent of the "required annual payment." The "required annual payment" is generally the lesser of 90 percent of the tax liability for the current year or 100 percent of the tax liability for the prior year.

taxpayer owes too much tax with the annual return. *See* I.R.C. § 6654(a), (b). The estimated tax penalty is discussed in more detail in Chapter 12.

§ 3.03 EXAMINATIONS

[A] IRS Investigatory Authority

Reading Assignment: I.R.C. §§ 6001, 6201(a), 7602(a); Treas. Reg. § 1.6001-1(b).

In an effort to enforce the tax laws, the IRS examines taxpayers' returns in order to verify whether the return filed reflects the taxpayer's correct tax liability. The IRS's investigatory authority derives primarily from Code section 7602, which grants the IRS the power to "examine any books, papers, records, or other data which may be relevant" to determining the correctness of any tax return. I.R.C. § 7602(a)(1); *see also* I.R.C. § 6201(a) ("The Secretary is authorized and required to make the inquiries, determinations, and assessments of all taxes. . . ."). The authority in section 7602 is backed up by section 6001, which gives the IRS the authority to "require any person, . . . to make such returns, render such statements, or keep such records, as the Secretary deems sufficient to show whether or not such person is liable for tax." The IRS's power to require taxpayers to turn over those records through its summons authority is discussed in more detail in Chapter 4.

All taxpayers have an obligation to maintain records that substantiate the accuracy of their returns. Treas. Reg. § 1.6001-1(b). Recordkeeping requirements for business taxpayers (including most sole proprietors) are more detailed, requiring them to maintain books and records sufficient to establish gross income, deductions, and other items shown on the return. Treas. Reg. § 1.6001-1(a); *see also* IRS Publication 583, *Starting a Business and Keeping Records*. The Code and regulations also impose specific recordkeeping requirements for certain deductible expenditures. For example, the regulations under section 274 specify the type of documentation necessary to substantiate travel and entertainment expenses otherwise deductible under Code section 162. *See* Temp. Treas. Reg. § 1.274-5T. A taxpayer's failure to maintain supporting documentation can lead to a negligence penalty, *see* Treas. Reg. § 1.6662–3(b), and can prevent the taxpayer from shifting the burden of proof to the IRS under Code section 7491 if the tax controversy ends up in court, I.R.C. § 7491(a)(2).

[B] Audits

[1] Selecting Returns for Audit

According to the IRS, its primary objective in auditing returns is to promote voluntary compliance. I.R.M. 4.1.1.1. This objective is consistent with the basic deterrence model of tax compliance discussed in Chapter 1, which holds that the risk of audit, combined with the prospect of penalties for noncompliance, provide an incentive for taxpayers to report their income and expense items correctly. *See* Section 1.05[B][1] of Chapter 1. Another reason the IRS audits returns is to generate additional revenue. Therefore, those returns selected for audit are generally ones that the IRS expects will reflect a tax understatement.

[a] DIF Scores and Other Methods

The IRS uses various methods of selecting returns for audit. *See* IRS Publication 1, *Your Rights as a Taxpayer*. The most common method relies upon the Discriminate Function (DIF). The DIF is a mathematical technique used by the IRS to classify income tax returns as to their error potential. The DIF formula divides returns into various audit classes. For example, individual income tax returns are classed based on their total positive income figure shown on the return. The computer formula then assigns weights to certain return characteristics. Those weights are then added together to obtain a DIF score. The computerized scoring takes place at IRS Campuses (formerly known as Service Centers) where tax returns are sent for initial processing. Generally, the higher the DIF score, the greater the potential that the IRS will select the return for audit. *See* I.R.M. 4.1.3.2. Those returns with very high DIF scores are first flagged by the IRS's computerized system, then reviewed by IRS employees to determine whether the return should be audited and the type of audit that is appropriate. *Id.*

The specific weight that the DIF formula assigns to return characteristics is cloaked in secrecy. *See* I.R.C. § 6103(b)(2); I.R.M. 4.1.3.2(3). The formula was developed from data that the IRS gathered through a series of random taxpayer audits designed to detect common areas of noncompliance. The original audit program, called the Taxpayer Compliance Measurement Program (TCMP), involved very detailed, line-by-line audits. The IRS suspended the TCMP program in 1995 and eventually replaced it with a new, less-invasive program called the National Research Program (NRP). The first NRP study, relating to 2001 returns, involved audits of 46,000 randomly selected taxpayers.[10] The IRS expanded the program in 2005 to assess compliance by Subchapter S corporations. The IRS also announced plans to begin conducting NRP audits on an annual, rolling basis, selecting approximately 13,000 individual returns for audit each year, beginning in 2007. *See* IR-2007-113, *available at* 2007 TNT 110-9 (June 7, 2007). The information the IRS compiles through the NRP program allows the IRS to update its DIF formula to improve audit selection. *See* Stephen Joyce, *NRP Project Will Target Individual Returns in Push to Enhance Audit Work, Mazur Says*, 109 Daily Tax Rep. (BNA), June 7, 2007, at G-1.

The IRS has other methods of targeting returns for audit in addition to its DIF classification system. *See generally* I.R.M. 4.1.4. If a taxpayer files a claim for refund, for example, the IRS normally will screen the original return to determine whether an examination should be made to substantiate the claim. I.R.M. 4.1.5.1.5. The IRS's information return matching program (discussed in Chapter 1) may also trigger an audit if the receipt reported on the taxpayer's return differs in amount from that reported on the information return. *See Portillo v. Commissioner*, 932 F.2d 1128 (5th Cir. 1991). Audits may also arise from the process of "infection." If a corporation's tax return is being audited and there are discrepancies or other suspicious circumstances, this might lead the IRS to audit the shareholders of the corporation as well. Newspaper reports can also lead to audits.

[b] Whistleblowers

Reading Assignment: I.R.C. § 7623.

In addition to the methods of selecting return for audit discussed above, the IRS also has a long-standing informant program that rewards individuals who provide information leading to the collection of tax. *See* I.R.C. § 7623(a). In 2006, Congress enhanced this program with a new "whistleblower" provision that generally allows an individual who provides information submitted under penalty of perjury that results in the collection of tax to receive "an award at least 15 percent but not more than 30 percent of the collected proceeds."[11] I.R.C. § 7623(b)(1), (6). An award in the amount of 10 percent of the

---

[10] The results of the 2001 NRP study allowed the IRS to estimate the size of the tax gap at $345 billion for 2001. IR-2006-28, *available at* 2006 TNT 31-6 (Feb. 15, 2006). The meaning of the tax gap and the types of noncompliance that give rise to it are discussed in more detail in Chapter 1.

[11] "Prior law made the payments discretionary, depending on what the District Director 'deem[ed] to be

collected tax is also permitted for assistance that primarily involves information from public sources. *See* I.R.C. § 7623(b)(2). However, if the informant actually "planned and initiated the actions that led to the underpayment of tax," the IRS "may appropriately reduce [the] award." I.R.C. § 7423(b)(3). Furthermore, if the informant "is convicted of criminal conduct arising from the role described in the preceding sentence, the Whistleblower Office shall deny any award." *Id.* The informant can appeal IRS award determinations to the Tax Court. *See* I.R.C. § 7623(b)(4). Note that the new provision applies with respect to individuals "only if such individual's gross income exceeds $200,000 for any taxable year subject to such action." I.R.C. § 7623(b)(5)(A). Moreover, it only applies if the "amounts in dispute exceed $2,000,000." I.R.C. § 7623(b)(5)(B).

The legislation that enacted section 7623(b) also created an IRS Whistleblower Office to administer the program. The first Director of that office, Stephen Whitlock, has commented on the large claims that have been raised under the new provision:

> The idea behind the statute is that there are certain kinds of tax noncompliance cases that the Service may have difficulty identifying without the help of a knowledgeable insider. Some of the things we've received over the past few months are consistent with the statutory purpose, and people who were in a position to know what was going on inside a corporation have come forward and told us about it. In some cases, they're talking about tens and hundreds of millions of dollars. That's not what the program was getting very often in the preamendment days. Many preamendment cases were much smaller issues.

Jeremiah Coder, *Tax Analysts Exclusive: Conversations: Stephen Whitlock*, 116 TAX NOTES 98, 99 (2007) (reporting statements of Stephen Whitlock).

In Chief Counsel advice, the IRS has addressed issues that arise when an informant is the taxpayer's employee or representative. *See* CC-2008-011 (Feb. 11, 2008), *available at* 2008 TNT 42-16 (July 23, 2008). For employees of the taxpayer, the Chief Counsel advice adheres to the "one bite rule," under which "the government [can] legally use information received from a private party even if the private party obtained the information in an illicit or illegal manner as long as the government is a passive recipient of the information and did not encourage or acquiesce in the private party's conduct." *Id.* Accordingly, the IRS typically will meet with that informant only once. *Id.*

With respect to taxpayer representatives, the IRS will not accept information when an informant currently represents the taxpayer in a matter pending before the IRS or in litigation involving the IRS. *Id.* Furthermore, "[i]f a taxpayer's representative makes a direct or indirect overture to the Service or Counsel about becoming an informant, *e.g.*, either orally or by filing a Form 3949A, *Information Referral*, or Form 211, *Application for Reward for Original Information*, there will be no further dealings with that person as the taxpayer's representative and the informant must be informed of this outcome immediately." *Id.*

[2] Conducting the Audit

Once the IRS selects a return for audit, there are various ways in which the audit may be carried out. There are three main types of audits, known among practitioners as correspondence audits, office audits, and field audits. Correspondence audits (also called Campus audits) are normally conducted by mail; as a result, they are limited to issues that lend themselves to verification from records that can be forwarded to the IRS. I.R.M. 4.71.11.1. In most cases, employees at one of the IRS Campuses initiate and carry out correspondence audits. The Campus employee sends the taxpayer an initial contact letter requesting information, or explaining why the return had to be

---

adequate compensation in the particular case,' which generally did not exceed 15 percent of the amounts collected." Dennis J. Ventry, Jr., *Whistleblowers and Qui Tam for Tax*, 61 TAX LAW. 355 (2008) (*quoting* Treas. Reg. § 301.7623-1(c)).

corrected. If the taxpayer agrees with the correction, then the taxpayer generally pays the additional tax liability and the case is closed. Alternatively, if the taxpayer can explain the item in question and provide the information the IRS needs to verify the item, then the issue is resolved. Another possible response to a correspondence audit would be to request an interview. However, if the taxpayer requests an interview, the audit is transferred to an examining agent, which may lead to a more in-depth review of the return. *See generally* I.R.M. 4.71.11.5.

With respect to the other two types of audits, whether the IRS conducts a field audit or an office audit of a particular taxpayer will depend primarily on the complexity of the issues involved. Office audits are usually conducted at the IRS by a tax auditor. The initial contact letter usually contains a request that the taxpayer or the taxpayer's representative meet with the auditor at the IRS office. Normally the contact letter will also ask the taxpayer to bring specified pieces of information or documentation to support the treatment of a particular item. Returns selected for office audits generally involve issues that are too complex to be resolved by mail but not complex enough to warrant a field audit. I.R.M. 4.1.5.1.11.1(3). Office audits are used to handle such issues as unusual or large itemized deductions, dependency exemptions, travel and entertainment expenses, and the like. *Id.*

Field audits are reserved for more complex business and individual returns. They are conducted by revenue agents, usually at the taxpayer's place of business. A revenue agent is generally more experienced than a tax auditor and has more education. A taxpayer must be more sensitive when it comes to a field audit. Generally, the potential issues involved in a field audit are not as clear as in a correspondence audit or an office audit. Thus, the taxpayer should cooperate with the agent and provide the requested information, but the taxpayer should not be overly generous, given that the scope of the audit may expand later on.

The very largest corporate taxpayers in the U.S. are subjected to field audits essentially on a continual basis through the IRS's Coordinated Industry Case (CIC) program. I.R.M. 4.46.1.1. CIC exams are typically conducted at the taxpayer's place of business and require that the taxpayer provide the examining agent with office space and access to the taxpayer's files on a continual basis. Once the taxpayer is selected for a CIC exam, the team of examiners conduct a risk analysis to prioritize issues and create an examination plan. Specialized audit techniques, such as limited-scope audits, may be used to narrow the set of issues examined and focus resources on those issues that carry the highest potential for change. *See* I.R.M. 4.46.3.5.2.

[3] Specialized Audit Programs for Business Taxpayers

The IRS's Large and Mid-Sized Business Division (LMSB), which serves taxpayers with assets over $10 million, has developed a number of specialized audit techniques intended to speed up the examination process and encourage early dispute resolution. One program, the Compliance Assurance Program (CAP), assigns a team of examining agents who work with the taxpayer throughout the year to identify material transactions and issues that affect the tax return. As part of the program, the taxpayer agrees to provide ready access to records and individuals associated with the identified material transactions. The goal is to reach an agreement on those identified issues before the taxpayer files the return. After the return is filed, the IRS reviews the taxpayer's return to ensure that the taxpayer appropriately reflected the previously agreed upon issues on the return. If so, the examination is closed as to those issues without further inquiry. *See generally* Announcement 2005-87, 2005-5 C.B. 1144.

Another specialized audit process, the Limited Issue Focused Examination (LIFE), is designed to be quicker, less costly, and more cooperative than other audits. *See* IR-2002-133, *available at* 2002 TNT 234-7 (Dec. 5, 2002); I.R.M. 4.51.3. An eligible taxpayer who wishes to participate in the LIFE program must agree to comply with the terms of a memorandum of understanding between the IRS and the taxpayer regarding key aspects of the audit. Among other things, the taxpayer must agree to commit to certain response times for document requests to file claims by an agreed date and with supporting documentation; and to provide computations for recurring issues. The memorandum will also specify a monetary materiality threshold, established on a case-by-case basis, below which neither the IRS nor the taxpayer will raise issues or claims. Any LMSB taxpayer is eligible to use the LIFE procedure, but the IRS may terminate a LIFE agreement if the taxpayer consistently violates the memorandum of understanding. I.R.M. 4.51.3.1.1.

In addition to specialized audit techniques aimed at large business taxpayers, the IRS also maintains a variety of programs designed to resolve significant, recurring issues encountered by these taxpayers on a uniform basis. One such program, the Technical Advisory Program (TAP), involves the work of designated industry specialists at the IRS who coordinate audit programs and draft settlement guidelines that examining agents use when auditing a member of the industry. I.R.M. 4.40.1.1.1.7. Examples of information that the TAP initiative produces include: (a) identification of unique, industry-specific issues and the Service's position on those issues; (b) economic conditions of the industry; (c) descriptions of accounting and business practices in the industry; and (d) suggested audit procedures. *See* I.R.M. 4.40.1.1.1.5.

A related program, the Industry Issue Resolution (IIR) Program, is an IRS initiative designed to provide published guidance to business taxpayers relating to disputed issues that are common to a significant number of large and small businesses. *See generally* Notice 2000-65, 2000-2 C.B. 599. Its goal is to reduce the cost and burden of settling disputes by resolving them before an examination takes place. When selecting the types of issues to include in the IIR program, the IRS solicits input from taxpayers, industry associations, and other interested groups. Revenue Procedure 2003-36, 2003-1 C.B. 859, includes procedures taxpayers can use to submit a frequently disputed or burdensome business tax issue for consideration under the IIR program. Issues that are unique to one or a small number of taxpayers are not appropriate for consideration under the program. *See* IR-2007-141.

[4] Partnership Audit Procedures Under TEFRA

Reading Assignment: I.R.C. §§ 6221, 6223, 6226(a)–(b), 6227(a), 6228(a), 6231(a), 6240(a), 6241(a), (c), 6242(a)–(b), 6245, 6246(a), 6247, 6251, 6255(a)–(b).

Partnerships are not taxable entities, so, prior to 1982, the IRS was required to audit the return of each partner in order to adjust a partnership item. In 1982, Congress enacted the Tax Equity and Fiscal Responsibility Act (TEFRA),[12] to improve the audit procedures applicable to partnerships. In general, TEFRA applies to partnerships with more than ten partners. *See* I.R.C. § 6231(a)(1)(B). It provides special auditing and litigation procedures at the partnership level for partnership items, thereby enabling the IRS to audit a partnership without auditing each partner. The TEFRA rules, which also apply to limited liability companies taxed as partnerships, also provide a procedure for judicial review of adjustments to partnership items.

After making an adjustment determination, the IRS must send a notice of Final Partnership Administrative Adjustment (FPAA) to the "tax matters partner" (TMP). I.R.C. §§ 6223(a)(2), 6223(d)(2). In general, the TMP is either the general partner designated to the IRS as such, or the general partner having the largest profits interest in the partnership at the close of the taxable year involved. *See* I.R.C. § 6231(a)(7); *see also* Rev. Proc. 88-16, 1988-1 C.B. 691. The TMP is required to keep the other partners informed of the progress of administrative and judicial proceedings. I.R.C. § 6223(g).

---

[12] Pub. L. No. 97-248, 96 Stat. 324.

Within 60 days after the FPAA is sent to the TMP, the IRS must send copies to each notice partner. I.R.C. § 6223(d)(2). A notice partner is any partner whose name, address, and profit interest appears on the partnership return, and any partner that has furnished its name and address to the IRS at least 30 days prior to mailing of the FPAA to the TMP. I.R.C. §§ 6223(a), 6231(a)(8). The TMP has 90 days from the date the FPAA was mailed to petition the Tax Court, the Court of Federal Claims, or an appropriate federal district court. I.R.C. § 6226(a). Once the 90-day period expires, any notice partner can file a petition within the next 60 days. I.R.C. § 6226(b).

Any partner may file a request for administrative adjustment with the IRS within three years of the time the partnership return was filed, so long as the IRS has not already sent the TMP an FPAA. I.R.C. § 6227(a). The request for administrative adjustment is analogous to a refund claim. If the IRS does not grant the request in full, the partner can sue in Tax Court, district court, or the Court of Federal Claims. I.R.C. § 6228. The time limitations are similar to those discussed in Chapter 10 with respect to refund suits, *see* I.R.C. § 6228(a)(2)(A), except that no court petition may be filed after the IRS mails the partnership a notice of the beginning of an administrative proceeding, I.R.C. § 6228(a)(2)(B).

Many partnerships with over 100 partners may elect to be governed by simplified procedures. *See* I.R.C. §§ 775, 6240. The IRS is not required to notify the partners in an electing partnership that it has commenced an audit. I.R.C. § 6245(b). Unless the partnership designates a representative, the IRS can select any partner to represent the partnership. I.R.C. § 6255(b)(1). The representative can enter into a settlement agreement on behalf of the partnership that binds some or all of its partners, including past partners. I.R.C. § 6255(b)(2). Only the partnership can obtain judicial review of the IRS's adjustments. I.R.C. § 6247.

Adjustments to an electing large partnership will generally affect only the persons who are partners in the year the adjustment becomes final, rather than those who were partners in the year the item arose. I.R.C. § 6241(c)(1). Except for adjustments to partners distributive shares, *see* I.R.C. § 6241(c)(2), an electing partnership has the option of paying the deficiency, interest, and penalties directly, rather than passing it through to the partners. I.R.C. § 6242(b). The partnership must provide each partner with an information return by March 15 of the year after the close of the partnership's taxable year, regardless of when its own return is due. I.R.C. § 6031(b). A partner in an electing large partnership must report all partnership items in a manner consistent with the partnership's reporting, or it will be subject to penalties. I.R.C. § 6241(a).

[C] Audit Strategy

Reading Assignment: I.R.C. § 7521.

In theory, taxpayers should begin preparing for a possible audit on the first day of the taxable year by retaining documents and receipts, and documenting transactions. Of course, most taxpayers are generally neither that farsighted nor that diligent. Consideration of how to minimize the risk of audit should also occur at the return preparation stage. For example, assume that the taxpayer has an unusually large deduction for the year. Because of that large deduction, a likelihood exists that the return will be selected for examination. One strategy would be simply to file the return without any explanation of the deduction. An alternative strategy might be to attach a statement to the return explaining why the deduction is so large or attach a copy of the receipt confirming the amount expended. The theory behind the latter approach is that if the return receives a high DIF score, the examiner will look at the explanation and conclude that the matter is not worth pursuing. Practitioners disagree over whether taxpayers should take such measures aimed at reducing the possibility of an audit. Which approach do you think is better?

Once the taxpayer's return is selected for examination, many taxpayers allow their accountants to handle the audit; a taxpayer may call in an attorney only after receiving a notice of deficiency, or even after filing a Tax Court petition. Before an initial interview with the taxpayer, the IRS is required to provide the taxpayer with information about the audit process and the taxpayer's rights under that process. I.R.C. § 7521(b)(1). Unless the taxpayer is summoned, the taxpayer need not be present at the interview, and the taxpayer can be represented by a tax practitioner with a written power of attorney. I.R.C. § 7521(c). The power of attorney is usually reflected on Form 2848, Power of Attorney and Declaration of Representative.[13] Either the taxpayer or the IRS can record an audit conference, if that party notifies the other party in advance. *See* I.R.C. § 7521(a).

One of the best sources of information on how the IRS conducts an examination is the Internal Revenue Manual (IRM). The IRM is a resource intended primarily for internal use at the IRS, but it has been made available to the public under the Freedom of Information Act, discussed in Chapter 6. The IRM is divided into several different parts. Of special interest to taxpayers and their representatives is Part 4.10, which contains income tax audit guidelines for IRS examiners. These guidelines set forth audit procedures, along with exhibits and instructions to examining agents about commonly encountered taxpayer errors. The IRM can be very helpful to a tax practitioner in planning a taxpayer's response to an audit. If, for example, an office audit involves travel and entertainment expenses, the attorney can consult the section in the IRM that tells an auditor what questions to ask, what information to request, and the like. By knowing the likely approach of the auditor before the meeting, the attorney can prepare the client to answer the questions correctly and honestly, but without providing any additional information.

Audit strategy varies depending on the type of audit. For correspondence audits, the best course generally is to respond to the requests for information and documentation quickly and concisely in order to prevent the audit from being expanded to cover other issues. Resolving the matter with the employee at the IRS Campus means it is unlikely that a tax auditor or revenue agent will be assigned to the case. As a general rule, an office audit is limited to the issues that are listed in the initial contact letter. A tax auditor generally must get permission from a superior to expand the scope of the audit. I.R.M. 4.10.2.6.1(2). In contrast, a revenue agent conducting a field audit may use his or her own discretion to expand the audit. I.R.M. 4.10.2.6.1.1(8). In either case, it normally does not pay to antagonize the examiner.

With respect to strategy in dealing with an audit, one article suggests:

§ 32.04 AUDIT PLANNING TECHNIQUES

[1] — Pre-audit

For each actual or planned commercial transaction, the taxpayer should identify all potential litigation risks and, to the extent possible, structure the transaction such that it is supported by existing authority. For example, when transacting commercially with unrelated parties, taxpayers should allocate by contract each party's rights and obligations under a tax allocation provision. For significant transactions, taxpayers should consider obtaining a private letter ruling. * * *

---

[13] In order to facilitate return preparer resolution of certain basic return processing issues, an individual taxpayer can check a box on Form 1040 authorizing the preparer to resolve matters involving erroneous mathematical calculations reflected on the return, as well as matters relating to processing of payments and refunds.

The taxpayer should establish procedures for collecting and maintaining pertinent records. For corporate taxpayers, the taxpayer's tax or legal department should maintain files containing all relevant documents and identifying all knowledgeable witnesses.

[2] — During the Audit

[a] — Audits of Individuals and Smaller Companies

It is useful for the taxpayer or his representative to establish a good working relationship with the revenue agent conducting the examination. From the very first contact with the revenue agent, whether on the telephone or in person, a respectful (non-condescending) demeanor will set the right tone. It is preferable to have an initial telephone discussion with the agent to establish the ground rules for the audit. These include:

(1) submission of the representative's power of attorney if it has not previously been provided;

(2) determination of whether an extension of the statute of limitations is being solicited and, if so, the terms of the requested waiver;

(3) discussion of the issues that will be examined;

(4) determination of what material will be requested; and

(5) scheduling a meeting and learning the revenue agent's expected time frame for completing the examination.

Contact with the revenue agent also provides the opportunity to assess the agent's intelligence and level of experience. One also should be able to discern a number of other insights into the revenue agent, such as his or her attitude toward the job, any prejudices or preconceived notions that may cloud the agent's judgment about the particular case or issue, how aggressive or demanding he or she may be in requesting information or meeting deadlines, etc. The representative should be able to take cues from these perceptions that will help in steering the revenue agent through the audit and yielding a better resolution for the taxpayer in the end. Establishing rapport with the revenue agent can go a long way to making the audit less painful for the taxpayer and to achieving an agreed case.

Despite the taxpayer's or representative's best efforts to be cooperative and cordial, there are times when a revenue agent steps out of bounds or behaves irrationally. The taxpayer or representative cannot let these impulses go unchecked or let the revenue agent run amok. Thus, even at the risk of offending the revenue agent, it will be necessary to let the agent know that you wish to speak with his or her manager, and to do so. Managers will often support their agents but also know their agents' weaknesses and strengths. If the taxpayer's complaint is legitimate, the manager will usually intervene to fix the problem. Managers are also helpful in resolving issues over which the revenue agent may have little or no authority or experience.

When the audit has moved beyond the information-gathering stage, it is often helpful to meet with the manager to discuss the revenue agent's findings, particularly where the revenue agent appears not to understand the facts or the taxpayer's business, or the law. Contact with the manager or other personnel advising the agent can eliminate factual misimpressions that were conveyed by the revenue agent to his or her superiors and can provide an opportunity to address the substantive issues. The purpose for all of these efforts during the examination phase is to keep the audit as narrow as possible and to produce an agreed case at the end of the process.

[b] — The Large Case Audit

At the beginning of a large case audit, the Service's audit team, the Service's case manager, and the taxpayer typically meet. During the meeting, the taxpayer should attempt to establish an overall framework for the audit. Topics for discussion include:

(1) Identifying formal communication channels between the audit team and the taxpayer's tax or legal personnel.

(2) Reviewing with the Service's audit team, the team's proposed audit plan.

* * *

(5) Advising the Service of the taxpayer's position regarding the Service's requests for extending the I.R.C. § 6501(a) statute of limitations.

(6) Probing the degree to which the audit team intends to utilize specialists (e.g., economists). * * *

Taxpayers should provide the audit team with a comfortable working space (e.g., a private office), to avoid charges of hardship. The space should not be so comfortable, however, that the Service would prefer to spend time at the taxpayers' office over other offices. Taxpayers should control access to all documents and files, and should establish a system to funnel all information requests through the taxpayers' tax department. Each department should supervise the copying process and maintain a log of all information that the taxpayer turns over.

Barbara T. Kaplan, *Leveling the Playing Field in Federal Income Tax Controversies*, 56 N.Y.U. Ann. Inst. Fed. Tax'n 32-45 – 32-48 (1999).[14]

Another article adds the following:

One of the most important factors for success by the taxpayer at the audit level will be the quality of his or her documentation. Given that most audits occur a few years after completion of the transactions, the taxpayer should be instructed to be diligent in preserving potentially pertinent records and documents. If a taxpayer is notified of an audit and the records are not in the best condition, an attempt should be made to organize any supporting information which might exist.

If the requested documents do not exist, the representative should attempt to obtain corroborating evidence from outside parties. If there was absolutely no basis for the original tax position, the representative should simply concede the issue in the reply to the IRS. Although there is a risk that the IRS will then expand the scope of the audit in the belief that other areas of the taxpayer's return might also lack documentation, there is no viable alternative. Attempts to mislead the IRS may constitute professional misconduct for the representative, destroy his or her reputation with the IRS, and seriously damage the taxpayer's status with the IRS. * * *

The ability to present facts in a clear, concise, and convincing presentation is a factor that increases the chances for the taxpayer's success during an audit. This skill requires that the representative display a full understanding of all of the facts during the interview and be ready to rely upon an exhaustive research of the applicable law. In constructing the argument for each issue, the representative should outline legal authority. If the representative is able to direct the interview, usually the simple issues and those which present the strongest arguments in favor of the taxpayer should be discussed first. * * *

> There are two common negotiating techniques that often help the taxpayer. First, if the IRS has not taken a position on the issue in question and the examiner is not conceding the point, then the representative should consider requesting the examiner to seek technical advice from the National Office.[15] The examiner may be hesitant to delay the audit on the issue and might concede to the representative. Second, the representative should bring attention to any deductions which were not claimed. If a more beneficial method of tax computation is available to the taxpayer, the IRM directs the examiner to secure any information necessary to make the computation. This strategy might also help the taxpayer on other issues if the examiner believes this evidence shows the taxpayer is cautious in taking advantage of deductions and credits.

Thomas C. Pearson & Dennis R. Schmidt, *Successful Preparation and Negotiation May Reduce the Time and Breadth of an IRS Audit*, 40 Tax'n for Acct. 234, 235–236, 238 (1988).[16]

Controlling the flow of information to the IRS is an important part of the practitioner's job when it comes to representing the client during an examination. As explained in more detail in Chapter 4, the IRS has the authority to summon books and records from the taxpayer, forcing him or her to release the records involuntarily. In most cases, however, the IRS agent will first make an oral or written request for documents. Even if the taxpayer is inclined to comply with the request on a voluntary basis, it is wise to have the examiner issue an Information Document Request (IDR), Form 4564, setting forth the request in writing and listing the documents the examiner wishes to see. An IDR serves several purposes. It allows the representative to evaluate the request and negotiate its scope. It also may reveal a particular issue the examiner is considering, which helps in preparing an appropriate response. An IDR also provides the opportunity to respond with a cover letter that makes a favorable impression. *See generally* A. Steve Hidalgo & Percy P. Woodward, IRS Examinations and Appeals: Domestic and International Procedures (1993).

§ 3.04 RECONSTRUCTING A TAXPAYER'S INCOME

Reading Assignment: I.R.C. § 7602(e).

[A] Introduction to Direct and Indirect Methods of Reconstructing Income

How does the IRS go about determining a deficiency if a taxpayer has failed to keep adequate (or any) books and records, or the IRS believes the records are false? For example, what if the IRS believes that the taxpayer's business received more income than the taxpayer reported? Courts have ruled that the IRS may "reconstruct" the taxpayer's income using any of a variety of techniques. Common techniques include the specific items method, the net worth method, the bank deposits plus cash expenditures method (sometimes simply referred to as the bank deposits method), and the source and application of funds method.

The specific items method is the "direct" method of establishing unreported income. The Internal Revenue Manual explains, with respect to criminal investigations:

> (1) Among the various methods of proving unreported or underreported taxable income, the specific item method is the most preferred. Most subjects report their income and expenses by the specific item method using books and/or records in which their financial transactions are

[15] [Requests for technical advice are discussed in Chapter 2. — Eds.]

[16] Copyright © 1988 Warren Gorham & Lamont. All rights reserved. Reprinted by permission.

contemporaneously recorded. Their transactions are usually summarized and shown on the tax return.

(2) There are three broad categories of schemes which are suited to the specific item method of proof:

a. understatement of income;

b. overstatement of expenses;

c. fraudulent claims for credits or exemptions.

I.R.M. 9.5.9.2.1. Examples of unreported income that the IRS has included in the taxpayer's income using the specific items method are gambling winnings reported on Form 1099 in *Cooper v. Commissioner*, T.C. Memo. 1987-431, and proceeds from the sale of a partnership interest in *Maciel v. Commissioner*, T.C. Memo. 2004-28.

The other methods of reconstructing income are "indirect" methods. Each method seeks to establish the amount of taxable income earned by the taxpayer and to compare it to the return to determine the amount of unreported income. The source and application of funds method "is an analysis of a taxpayer's cash flows and comparison of all known expenditures with all known receipts for the period. Net increases and decreases in assets and liabilities are taken into account along with nondeductible expenditures and nontaxable receipts. The excess of expenditures over the sum of reported and nontaxable income is unreported taxable income." I.R.M. 4.10.4.6.4(1). The net worth method and the bank deposits plus cash expenditures method, which are commonly used by the IRS in income reconstruction cases, are discussed in further detail below. Note that the methods are not mutually exclusive. For example, the source and application of funds method can be used to help derive the taxpayer's opening net worth for purposes of the net worth method. It is discussed in that regard below.

[B] Limits on "Financial Status Audits"

Prior to 1998, the IRS had broad discretion to use indirect methods of reconstructing income. A government report explained:

> In the early 1990s, IRS became concerned that its auditors were not fully probing for income that should have been, but was not, reported on tax returns. This concern as well as others led IRS to reemphasize the need for its auditors to consider a taxpayer's financial status and to probe for unreported income. This reemphasis came to be known as the financial status audit program.
>
> IRS initiated the financial status audit program in late 1994 with a training course for auditors. In the training course, IRS stressed the importance of identifying unreported income by determining whether the taxpayer's reported income roughly conforms to his or her spending. Such an evaluation requires consideration of the taxpayer's spending patterns in addition to verifying items reported on tax returns. If reported income and spending patterns differ, the auditor is supposed to decide whether the difference is significant enough to warrant asking the taxpayer for an explanation.
>
> The training course stressed the importance of meeting with taxpayers, checking nontraditional data sources (such as state and local governments), and using four indirect audit techniques.

U.S. General Accounting Office, *Tax Administration: More Criteria Needed on IRS' Use of Financial Status Audit Techniques*, GAO/GGD-98-33, at 2–3 (Dec. 29, 1997), *available at* http://unclefed.com/GAOReports/ggd98-38.pdf (footnotes omitted).

The use of these "economic reality" techniques proved unpopular.

> By early 1995, IRS was receiving considerable criticism about audits using these financial status techniques. The American Institute of Certified Public Accountants (AICPA), Members of Congress, and various taxpayer groups were concerned that these audits were more time consuming and intrusive than

> other auditing techniques. AICPA officials had several concerns about the taxpayer burden and intrusiveness that they associated with IRS' use of financial status techniques. Specifically, they were concerned about IRS' practice of asking financial status questions at the initial interview before having any evidence of underreported income. Similarly, AICPA officials were concerned about IRS sending a request for personal living expense (PLE) information with the letter notifying the taxpayer of the audit, before finding any evidence of unreported income.

Id. at 3–4 (footnote omitted).

In response, Congress enacted Code section 7602(e) as part of the IRS Reform Act. Section 7602(e) provides, "[t]he Secretary shall not use financial status or economic reality examination techniques to determine the existence of unreported income of any taxpayer unless the Secretary has a reasonable indication that there is a likelihood of such unreported income."

What limitations does Section 7602(e) place on the IRS? How might those limitations apply? The IRS has issued the following internal Field Service Advice interpreting section 7602(e). Note its distinction between direct and indirect methods of reconstructing income.

INTERNAL REVENUE SERVICE NATIONAL OFFICE FIELD SERVICE ADVICE 200101030

(Oct. 25, 2000)

* * *

This Chief Counsel Advice responds to your request for advice. Chief Counsel Advice is not binding on Examination or Appeals and is not a final case determination. This document is not to be cited as precedent.

ISSUES:

1. Whether a revenue agent may drive by a taxpayer's house prior to having a reasonable indication that there is a likelihood of unreported income.

2. Whether a revenue agent may conduct a Lexis search to ascertain if the taxpayer purchased real estate during the year(s) at issue prior to having a reasonable indication that there is a likelihood of unreported income.

CONCLUSION:

1. A revenue agent may drive by a taxpayer's house prior to having a reasonable indication that there is a likelihood of unreported income.

2. A revenue agent may conduct a Lexis search to ascertain if the taxpayer purchased real estate during the year(s) at issue prior to having a reasonable indication that there is a likelihood of unreported income.

FACTS

Revenue agents have inquired whether they are still permitted to drive by a taxpayer's house or conduct a Lexis search to ascertain if the taxpayer purchased real estate during the year(s) at issue prior to having a reasonable indication that there is a likelihood of unreported income in light of the enactment of section 7602(e), which restricts the use of financial status audit techniques.

LAW AND ANALYSIS

The Internal Revenue Service Restructuring and Reform Act of 1998 (RRA '98), Pub. L. No. 105-206, section 3412, 112 Stat. 685 (July 22, 1998), added new I.R.C. section 7602(e), titled "Limitation on Financial Status Audit Techniques." Section 7602(e) provides that "[t]he Secretary shall not use financial status or economic reality examination techniques to determine the existence of unreported income of any taxpayer unless the Secretary has a reasonable indication that there is a likelihood of such unreported income."

* * *

The legislative history states that RRA '98 section 3412 merely prohibits the use of such audit techniques to determine the existence of unreported income until the Service has a reasonable indication that there is a likelihood of such unreported income. H.R. Conf. Rep. No. 105-599, at 270 (1998).

Prior to enacting section 7602(e), the Chairman of the House Committee on Ways and Means requested the General Accounting Office to report on the frequency and results of the use of financial status audit techniques to identify unreported income due to concerns over the treatment of and the burdens placed upon taxpayers. General Accounting Office Report GAO/T-GGD-97-186 (September 26, 1997), Tax Administration, Taxpayer Rights and Burdens During Audits of Their Tax Returns, at 3 and 9 (GAO Report). The term "Financial Status Audit Techniques" is not defined in the Code. As used in the GAO Report, financial status or economic reality audit techniques consist of indirect methods of examination such as the bank deposits method, the cash transaction method, the net worth method, the percentage of mark-up method, and the unit and volume method. GAO Report at 9; Examination of Returns Handbook, IRM 4.2.4.6. The General Accounting Office concluded that these techniques were never used alone and that they were used with other techniques that were used to explore issues other than unreported income, such as overstated deductions. GAO Report at 9.

There are two distinct types of methods of proof in tax cases, direct or specific item methods and indirect methods (financial status or economic reality examination techniques). In the direct or specific item methods, specific items are demonstrated as the source of unreported income. United States v. Hart, 70 F.3d 854, 860 n.8 (6th Cir. 1995); United States v. Black, 843 F.2d 1456 (D.C. Cir. 1988). With the specific item method of proof, the government uses "evidence of the receipt of specific items of reportable income . . . that do not appear on his income tax return." United States v. Marabelles, 724 F.2d 1374, 1377 n.1 (9th Cir. 1984). For example, the Service tracks funds from known sources to deposits made to a taxpayer's bank accounts rather than analyzing bank deposits to identify unreported income from unknown sources. *See* United States v. Hart, 70 F.3d 854, 860 (6th Cir. 1995) (tracing of unreported income from covert police fund is a direct method); United States v. Black, 843 F.2d 1456 (D.C. Cir. 1988) (monies traceable from dummy corporations to the taxpayer was evidence of specific items of income and not the use of the bank deposits or cash expenditures indirect method of proof). *See also* Pollak v. United States, 1998 U.S. Dist. LEXIS 16224 (N.D. Ill. 1998) (recognizing, in dicta, that directly tracing money transfers from an entity would not be a financial status or economic reality technique).

The Service does not use specific items to support an inference of unreported income from unidentified sources. The use of direct methods simply does not implicate the provisions of section 7602(e). Thus, there is no prohibition requiring the Service to have a reasonable indication that there is a likelihood of unreported income before resorting to such methods.

When using an indirect method, a taxpayer's finances are reconstructed through circumstantial evidence. United States v. Hart, 70 F.3d 854, 860 n.8 (6th Cir. 1995). For example, the government shows either through increases in net worth, increases in bank deposits, or the presence of cash expenditures, that the taxpayer's wealth grew during a tax year beyond what could be attributed to the taxpayer's reported income, thereby raising the inference of unreported income. United States v. Black, 843 F.2d 1456, 1458 (D.C. Cir. 1988). Indirect methods are used to support an inference of unreported income from unidentified sources.

The bank deposits indirect method is an analysis of bank deposits to prove unreported income from unidentified sources. This method, which computes income by showing what happened to the taxpayer's funds, may be considered to be a financial status technique when it is used without specific knowledge of a possible traceable source. As such, it is used to supply leads to possible unreported income from sources of such deposits. Examination of Returns Handbook, IRM 4.2.4.6.3.

With the cash transaction indirect method, the Service calculates the unreported income as the amount that the taxpayer's cash expenditures exceeded the taxpayer's sources of cash, including cash on hand at the beginning of the tax period in question, for the particular year. United States v. Hogan, 886 F.2d 1497, 1509 (7th Cir. 1989). The Service uses the taxpayer's tax return and other sources to ensure that adequate income has been reported to cover expenses. GAO Report at 9.

The net worth method requires establishing the taxpayer's net worth at the start of the taxable year by listing all assets, including cash on hand, and all liabilities, with the balance being the taxpayer's net worth. A similar analysis is made for the first day of the next taxable year. To any change in the net worth, the Service adds non-deductible expenditures for living expenses then deducts receipts from sources that are not taxable income and the amounts represented by applicable tax deductions and exemptions. If the increase in net worth, as adjusted, exceeds the reported taxable income, the inference is drawn that there is unreported income. United States v. Conway, 11 F.3d 40, 43 (5th Cir. 1993); United States v. Boulet, 577 F.2d 1165, 1167 n.3 (5th Cir. 1978).

With the percentage of mark-up method, the Service reconstructs income derived from the use of percentages or ratios considered typical for the business or item under examination. This method consists of an analysis of either sales or cost of sales and the appropriate application of a percentage of markup to arrive at the taxpayer's gross profit. By reference to similar businesses or situations, percentage computations are secured to determine sales, cost of sales, gross profit or even net profit. Likewise, by the use of some known base and the typical percentage applicable, individual items of income or expenses may be determined. These percentages can be obtained from analysis of Bureau of Labor Statistics data, commercial publications, or the taxpayer's records for other periods. IRM 4.2.4.6.6.

* * *

We have not been provided with any specific factual circumstances under which a revenue agent would drive by a taxpayer's house. Nonetheless, this activity would not be prohibited if used in determining whether there is a reasonable indication that there is a likelihood of unreported income so that the Service could resort to setting up unreported income under an indirect method. It should be noted that driving by a taxpayer's house would not be an intrusion on that taxpayer. It should also be noted that the Internal Revenue Manual cautions that due to privacy issues and the intrusiveness of inspecting a taxpayer's residence, such inspections should be limited. The purpose of inspecting the taxpayer's residence includes, but is not limited to, determining the validity of deductions for an office or business located in the residence and determining the taxpayer's financial status. IRM 4.2.3.3.5.

Conducting a Lexis search to ascertain if the taxpayer purchased real estate would be useful when using the net worth method. Such a search would not be prohibited if used in determining whether there is a reasonable indication that there is a likelihood of unreported income so that the Service could resort to setting up unreported income under the net worth method or any other indirect method. It should be noted that a search of property records that are available to the public is not an intrusion on a taxpayer.

Do you agree with the IRS's conclusion that driving by a taxpayer's house or performing a Lexis search for real property does not intrude on the taxpayer? Do you think it is appropriate to use these techniques as a means of finding a reasonable indication that the taxpayer failed to report income?

[C] Specific Indirect Methods

[1] The Net Worth Method

[a] In General

Holland v. United States, 348 U.S. 121 (1954), is the leading case on the net worth method. *Holland* involved criminal prosecution for tax evasion. Although the net worth method generally functions the same way in both civil and criminal cases, there are procedural differences between the two types of cases, including different burdens of proof. In criminal cases, the government bears the burden of proving the taxpayer's guilt beyond a reasonable doubt. In civil cases, the "preponderance of the evidence" standard applies in cases other than fraud cases, and, as discussed in Chapter 11, the taxpayer generally bears the burden of persuasion on issues other than fraud.

In *Holland*, before discussing the facts of the specific case, the Supreme Court provided the following information about the use of the net worth method of reconstructing income:

> In recent years, . . . tax-evasion convictions obtained under the net worth theory have come here with increasing frequency and left impressions beyond those of the previously unrelated petitions. We concluded that the method involved something more than the ordinary use of circumstantial evidence in the usual criminal case. Its bearing, therefore, on the safeguards traditionally provided in the administration of criminal justice called for a consideration of the entire theory. . . .
>
> In a typical net worth prosecution, the Government, having concluded that the taxpayer's records are inadequate as a basis for determining income tax liability, attempts to establish an "opening net worth" or total net value of the taxpayer's assets at the beginning of a given year. It then proves increases in the taxpayer's net worth for each succeeding year during the period under examination and calculates the difference between the adjusted net values of the taxpayer's assets at the beginning and end of each of the years involved. The taxpayer's nondeductible expenditures, including living expenses, are added to these increases, and if the resulting figure for any year is substantially greater than the taxable income reported by the taxpayer for that year, the Government claims the excess represents unreported taxable income. In addition, it asks the jury to infer willfulness from this understatement, when taken in connection with direct evidence of "conduct, the likely effect of which would be to mislead or to conceal." *Spies v. United States*, 317 U.S. 492, 499.
>
> . . . [W]e believe it important to outline the general problems implicit in this type of litigation. In this consideration we assume, as we must in view of its widespread use, that the Government deems the net worth method useful in the enforcement of the criminal sanctions of our income tax laws. Nevertheless, careful study indicates that it is so fraught with danger for the innocent that the courts must closely scrutinize its use.

One basic assumption in establishing guilt by this method is that most assets derive from a taxable source, and that when this is not true the taxpayer is in a position to explain the discrepancy. The application of such an assumption raises serious legal problems in the administration of the criminal law. Unlike civil actions for the recovery of deficiencies, where the determinations of the Commissioner have *prima facie* validity, the prosecution must always prove the criminal charge beyond a reasonable doubt. This has led many of our courts to be disturbed by the use of the net worth method, particularly in its scope and the latitude which it allows prosecutors. *E.g., Demetree v. United States*, 207 F.2d 892, 894 (1953); *United States v. Caserta*, 199 F.2d 905, 907 (1952); *United States v. Fenwick*, 177 F.2d 488.

But the net worth method has not grown up overnight. It was first utilized in such cases as *Capone v. United States*, 51 F.2d 609 (1931) and *Guzik v. United States*, 54 F.2d 618 (1931), to corroborate direct proof of specific unreported income. In *United States v. Johnson, supra*, this Court approved of its use to support the inference that the taxpayer, owner of a vast and elaborately concealed network of gambling houses upon which he declared no income, had indeed received unreported income in a "substantial amount." It was a potent weapon in establishing taxable income from undisclosed sources when all other efforts failed. Since the *Johnson* case, however, its horizons have been widened until now it is used in run-of-the-mine cases, regardless of the amount of tax deficiency involved. In each of the four cases decided today the allegedly unreported income comes from the same disclosed sources as produced the taxpayer's reported income and in none is the tax deficiency anything like the deficiencies in *Johnson*, *Capone* or *Guzik*. The net worth method, it seems, has evolved from the final volley to the first shot in the Government's battle for revenue, and its use in the ordinary income-bracket cases greatly increases the chances for error. This leads us to point out the dangers that must be consciously kept in mind in order to assure adequate appraisal of the specific facts in individual cases.

1. Among the defenses often asserted is the taxpayer's claim that the net worth increase shown by the Government's statement is in reality not an increase at all because of the existence of substantial cash on hand at the starting point. This favorite defense asserts that the cache is made up of many years' savings which for various reasons were hidden and not expended until the prosecution period. Obviously, the Government has great difficulty in refuting such a contention. However, taxpayers too encounter many obstacles in convincing the jury of the existence of such hoards. This is particularly so when the emergence of the hidden savings also uncovers a fraud on the taxpayer's creditors.

In this connection, the taxpayer frequently gives "leads" to the Government agents indicating the specific sources from which his cash on hand has come, such as prior earnings, stock transactions, real estate profits, inheritances, gifts, etc. Sometimes these "leads" point back to old transactions far removed from the prosecution period. Were the Government required to run down all such leads it would face grave investigative difficulties; still its failure to do so might jeopardize the position of the taxpayer.

2. As we have said, the method requires assumptions, among which is the equation of unexplained increases in net worth with unreported taxable income. Obviously such an assumption has many weaknesses. It may be that gifts, inheritances, loans and the like account for the newly acquired wealth. There is great danger that the jury may assume that once the Government has established the figures in its net worth computations, the crime of tax evasion automatically follows. The possibility of this increases where the jury, without

guarding instructions, is allowed to take into the jury room the various charts summarizing the computations; bare figures have a way of acquiring an existence of their own, independent of the evidence which gave rise to them.

3. Although it may sound fair to say that the taxpayer can explain the "bulge" in his net worth, he may be entirely honest and yet unable to recount his financial history. In addition, such a rule would tend to shift the burden of proof. Were the taxpayer compelled to come forward with evidence, he might risk lending support to the Government's case by showing loose business methods or losing the jury through his apparent evasiveness. Of course, in other criminal prosecutions juries may disbelieve and convict the innocent. But the courts must minimize this danger.

4. When there are no books and records, willfulness may be inferred by the jury from that fact coupled with proof of an understatement of income. But when the Government uses the net worth method, and the books and records of the taxpayer appear correct on their face, an inference of willfulness from net worth increases alone might be unjustified, especially where the circumstances surrounding the deficiency are as consistent with innocent mistake as with willful violation. On the other hand, the very failure of the books to disclose a proved deficiency might indicate deliberate falsification.

5. In many cases of this type, the prosecution relies on the taxpayer's statements, made to revenue agents in the course of their investigation, to establish vital links in the Government's proof. But when a revenue agent confronts the taxpayer with an apparent deficiency, the latter may be more concerned with a quick settlement than an honest search for the truth. Moreover, the prosecution may pick and choose from the taxpayer's statement, relying on the favorable portion and throwing aside that which does not bolster its position. The problem of corroboration, dealt with in the companion cases of *Smith v. United States*, *post*, p. 147, and *United States v. Calderon*, *post*, p. 160, therefore becomes crucial.

* * *

While we cannot say that these pitfalls inherent in the net worth method foreclose its use, they do require the exercise of great care and restraint. The complexity of the problem is such that it cannot be met merely by the application of general rules. *Cf. Universal Camera Corp. v. Labor Board*, 340 U.S. 474, 489. Trial courts should approach these cases in the full realization that the taxpayer may be ensnared in a system which, though difficult for the prosecution to utilize, is equally hard for the defendant to refute. Charges should be especially clear, including, in addition to the formal instructions, a summary of the nature of the net worth method, the assumptions on which it rests, and the inferences available both for and against the accused. Appellate courts should review the cases, bearing constantly in mind the difficulties that arise when circumstantial evidence as to guilt is the chief weapon of a method that is itself only an approximation.

Holland v. United States, 348 U.S. 121, 124–29 (1954).

[b] Establishing an Opening Net Worth

Critical to the application of the net worth method is establishment of an opening net worth. *Holland* discusses this issue as well as the taxpayers' claim that the government failed to account for a hoard of cash and stock:

We agree with petitioners that an essential condition in cases of this type is the establishment, with reasonable certainty, of an opening net worth, to serve as a starting point from which to calculate future increases in the taxpayer's assets.

The importance of accuracy in this figure is immediately apparent, as the correctness of the result depends entirely upon the inclusion in this sum of all assets on hand at the outset. The Government's net worth statement included as assets at the starting point stock costing $29,650 and $2,153.09 in cash. The Hollands claim that the Government failed to include in its opening net worth figure an accumulation of $113,000 in currency and "hundreds and possibly thousands of shares of stock" which they owned at the beginning of the prosecution period. They asserted that the cash had been accumulated prior to the opening date, $104,000 of it before 1933, and the balance between 1933 and 1945. They had kept the money, they claimed, mostly in $100 bills and at various times in a canvas bag, a suitcase, and a metal box. They had never dipped into it until 1946, when it became the source of the apparent increase in wealth which the Government later found in the form of a home, a ranch, a hotel, and other properties. This was the main issue presented to the jury. The Government did not introduce any direct evidence to dispute this claim. Rather it relied on the inference that anyone who had had $104,000 in cash would not have undergone the hardship and privation endured by the Hollands all during the late 20's and throughout the 30's. During this period they lost their café business; accumulated $35,000 in debts which were never paid; lost their household furniture because of an unpaid balance of $92.20; suffered a default judgment for $506.66; and were forced to separate for some eight years because it was to their "economical advantage." During the latter part of this period, Mrs. Holland was obliged to support herself and their son by working at a motion picture house in Denver while her husband was in Wyoming. The evidence further indicated that improvements to the hotel, and other assets acquired during the prosecution years, were bought in installments and with bills of small denominations, as if out of earnings rather than from an accumulation of $100 bills. The Government also negatived the possibility of petitioners' accumulating such a sum by checking Mr. Holland's income tax returns as far back as 1913, showing that the income declared in previous years was insufficient to enable defendants to save any appreciable amount of money. The jury resolved this question of the existence of a cache of cash against the Hollands, and we believe the verdict was fully supported.

As to the stock, Mr. Holland began dabbling in the stock market in a small way in 1937 and 1938. His purchases appear to have been negligible and on borrowed money. His only reported income from stocks was in his tax returns for 1944 and 1945 when he disclosed dividends of $1,600 and $1,850 respectively. While the record is unclear on this point, it appears that during the period from 1942 to 1945 he pledged considerable stock as collateral for loans. There is no evidence, however, showing what portions of this stock Mr. Holland actually owned at any one time, since he was trading in shares from day to day. And, even if we assume that he owned all the stock, some 4,550 shares, there is evidence that Mr. Holland's stock transactions were usually in "stock selling for only a few dollars per share." In this light, the Government's figure of approximately $30,000 is not out of line. In 1946 Holland reported the sale of about $50,000 in stock, but no receipt of dividends; nor were dividends reported in subsequent years. It is reasonable to assume that he sold all of his stock in 1946. In fact, Holland stated to the revenue agents that he had not "fooled with the stock market" since the beginning of 1946; that he had not owned any stocks for two or three years prior to 1949; that he had saved about $50,000 from 1933 to 1946, and that in 1946 he had $9,000 in cash with the balance of his savings in stocks. The Government's evidence, bolstered by the admissions of petitioners, provided convincing proof that they had no stock other than the amount included in the opening net worth statement. By the same token, the petitioners' argument that the Government failed to account for the proceeds of stock sold

> by them before the starting date must also fail. The Government's evidence fully justified the jury's conclusion that there were no proceeds over and above the amount credited to petitioners.

Id. at 132–35.

What do you think of the "cash hoard" defense raised in *Holland*? It is a common defense in net worth cases, as the *Holland* opinion mentioned in the excerpt above. The Internal Revenue Manual instructs IRS Special Agents with respect to criminal cases to gather detailed information about the taxpayer's net worth at the beginning of the period in question, including "cash on hand":

> (4) The establishment of cash on hand is critical. The inability to establish a firm and accurate amount of cash on hand can be fatal to the investigation. Uncertainty about the amount of cash on hand is a common defense in net worth investigations. It will be easier to refute this defense if the special agent has established a firm beginning and an ending cash on hand amount . . . . Cash on hand is almost always proved by circumstantial evidence.
>
> (5) The best source of information in establishing an accurate cash on hand figure may be obtained from the subject during an interview. The special agent may not always have the opportunity to interview the subject in every investigation. However, when the opportunity does exists, the special agent should attempt to establish the beginning and ending cash on hand. . . .
>
> (6) During the subject interview, the subject should be questioned in detail about cash on hand. The questioning should be preceded with an explanation of what constitutes cash on hand and elicit the subject's answer as to cash on hand. Cash on hand is coin and currency (bills, Federal Reserve notes, etc.) in the subject's possession, i.e., on the subject's person, in the subject's residence, or other place, in nominee hands, or in a safe-deposit box. It does not include any money the subject has on deposit in any account with any type of financial institution.
>
> * * *
>
> (9) The special agent may determine the amount of cash on hand by asking questions about the maximum amount of cash that the subject could possibly have had at any particular time. For example, such questions as, "Did you ever have more than $100 in cash on hand? More than $5,000? More than $10,000?," may result in admissions that can establish the total amount of cash on hand at a particular date.
>
> (10) Discussing the accumulation and purpose of the cash on hand may establish the minimum and maximum amount on a particular date. Determining the ultimate disposition of this cash on hand can provide a lead to a specific amount of cash on hand on a particular date. For example, a statement like "I used all my cash on hand to pay for my house in 1994" indicates how much cash the subject had on the date of payment. It also provides a cut-off date for cash on hand, since the subject evidently had no more cash after using all the cash on hand to pay for the house. The special agent should question the subject further to elicit an admission that the subject did not have any additional cash on hand as of the specified date.
>
> (11) The special agent's questioning should be directed toward developing:
>
> a. the maximum amount of cash on hand (undeposited currency and coin) claimed at the starting point and at the end of each year under investigation;
>
> b. the amount of cash on hand at the date of the interview. (This data is sometimes useful in computing cash on hand for earlier years.);
>
> c. how was the cash on hand accumulated and from what sources;

d. where the cash was kept

e. who knew about the cash;

f. whether anyone ever counted the cash;

g. when, where and for what was any cash spent;

h. whether any record is available with respect to the alleged cash on hand;

i. the denominations of the cash on hand;

j. was the cash shown on any net worth or personal financial statements;

k. ask to see the cash on hand . . . .

I.R.M. 9.5.9.5.5.

The source and application of funds method — aside from being used on its own as a means of reconstructing income — can be used as an indirect means of establishing the amount of cash on hand at the starting point of a year in question. The Internal Revenue Manual explains:

> (1) Another method of establishing a starting point for cash on hand is to analyze the subject's available finances for the years leading up to the starting point. Such a "source and application of funds" approach can also be used to bridge the years to the starting point from some point in time when cash on hand has been firmly established. The following is an example of how a source and application of funds computation can be used to establish a firm starting point in a net worth investigation.
>
> a. The subject filed bankruptcy in 1993. Immediately following the bankruptcy, the subject did not have any assets or liabilities. The starting point for the investigation is December 31, 1996, the prosecution years are 1997 and 1998. For the purposes of using the source and application of funds computation in determining a firm starting point (cash on hand figure on December 31, 1996), the years 1993 through 1996 would be treated as one unit.
>
> (2) First, the special agent must determine the total amount of funds available (taxable and nontaxable) during 1993 through 1996. From this amount, he/she will subtract the subject's personal expenditures for the period. This will yield the maximum amount of funds available for the subject's net worth at the beginning of 1997.
>
> (3) Second, the special agent subtracts the subject's beginning net worth figure (the amount the investigation revealed as of December 31, 1996, without the cash on hand figure) from the total funds available for net worth. This will account for non-personal living expenditure payments by reflecting the payments made to increase assets and decrease liabilities.
>
> (4) Funds used to purchase assets disposed of prior to the starting point can be included as funds applied, if their disposition is traced and the funds from the disposition are accounted for as funds available. The advantage of using this method is that the beginning net worth can be used as funds applied. If the subject has a large beginning net worth, it may be possible to overcome the subject's reported income for prior years and show that he/she could not have had cash on hand at the starting point. This can also be used to establish maximum possible cash on hand figure. It is important that the subject be given credit for all sources of funds available (both taxable and nontaxable) in the period for which the source and application method is used.
>
> (5) When using the one unit source and application of funds method to establish a firm starting point, the beginning net worth must be adjusted for any asset purchased and completely paid for prior to the source and application years. This is necessary because no funds were applied during the source and

application period to purchase the asset. This point is illustrated in the following example:

a. The subject purchased and paid off a residence 10 years prior to the starting point. The cost of the residence, $20,000, is included in the beginning net worth. The source and application of funds only covers a period of six years prior to the starting point. The beginning net worth must be adjusted by subtracting the cost of the residence because the residence was purchased with funds acquired by the subject prior to the years included in the computation. . . .

(6) This method can be used to establish cash on hand at the starting point if the subject does not cooperate during the investigation, or to corroborate the subject's admission of cash on hand. A source and application of funds cannot be used in every investigation but, in certain instances, can be a valuable tool in determining possible cash on hand.

I.R.M. 9.5.9.5.5.1.

[2] The Bank Deposits Plus Cash Expenditures Method

As indicated above, another method for reconstructing a taxpayer's income is the bank deposits plus cash expenditures method (sometimes termed the bank deposits method). One article describes this method as follows:

[The bank deposits] method is generally used when a business is examined or the IRS suspects the taxpayer operates a business without reporting income. To rely on the bank deposits method, the IRS must —

* establish the taxpayer engaged in an income-producing activity,
* establish the taxpayer made regular periodic deposits into an account, and
* make an adequate investigation to distinguish between taxable and nontaxable deposits.

Even if the IRS makes some classification errors, the court can still accept the overall use of the bank deposits method. The IRS assumes the taxpayer's gross income is the total of the deposits less obvious loan proceeds, transfers, and other nontaxable income. All business expenses, other allowable deductions, and exemptions are subtracted from gross income and the result is taxable income. Checks cleared through the account are the best source of business expenses. When there are cash deposits rather than check deposits, the IRS must establish the taxpayer's beginning cash position to meet its obligation of adequate investigation of nontaxable deposits.

Charles E. Price & Leonard G. Weld, *Income Reconstruction*, CPA JOURNAL (Aug. 1998), *available at* http://www.nysscpa.org/cpajournal/1998/0898/Features/f26898.html.[17]

The following case illustrates the application of the bank deposits plus cash expenditures method.

CHOI v. COMMISSIONER

United States Court of Appeals, Ninth Circuit

379 F.3d 638 (2004)

SCHROEDER, CHIEF JUDGE:

Taxpayers, Charles Y. Choi and his wife Jin Yi Choi, appeal the Tax Court's determination that they underreported the income from their Arizona grocery store on

---

[17]

their 1991 and 1992 federal tax returns and the imposition of a civil fraud penalty under 26 U.S.C. § 6663. It is undisputed that the Chois did not maintain adequate records for the store and that the Commissioner therefore was entitled to use an indirect method of reconstructing income to determine the amount of any deficiency. 26 U.S.C. § 446(b). The Commissioner used the "bank deposits plus cash expenditures" method of reconstructing income and assessed a deficiency of $59,106 for 1991 and $49,624 for 1992. The Commissioner found fraudulent intent and imposed a penalty. Indeed Mr. Choi, in 1996, pled guilty to criminal tax evasion for the 1992 tax year.

In challenging the deficiency and civil penalty determinations in the Tax Court, the Chois argued that the Commissioner was not allowed to use the "bank deposits plus cash expenditures" method to reconstruct their income. The Chois then provided expert testimony to establish that using a different method of reconstructing income, the Commissioner would not have found a deficiency for either tax year. They also challenged the fraud finding.

The Tax Court upheld the Commissioner's use of the "bank deposits plus cash expenditures" method of income reconstruction, rejected the Chois alternative method, and imposed a civil fraud penalty for 1991. The Tax Court ruled that Mr. Choi was barred by collateral estoppel from challenging the merits of the 1992 fraud penalty.

On appeal to this court, the principal challenge is to the use of the "bank deposits plus cash expenditures" method of income reconstruction. Under this method, gross income is derived by adding together all bank deposits made by the tax-payer during the tax year in question, subtracting nontaxable amounts, and adding expenditures made from cash that was never deposited into the bank. *United States v. Brickey*, 289 F.3d 1144, 1152 (9th Cir. 2002).

The Chois challenge the use of this method, arguing that the Commissioner did not properly subtract all nontaxable amounts. They contend that many of the bank deposits consisted of nontaxable amounts because the grocery store cashed payroll checks for its customers without charging a fee when the customer also purchased groceries. These checks were deposited into the grocery store's bank account. The portion of a check that was returned to a customer in cash is clearly not taxable income. Thus, the Commissioner could not permissibly include the full amount that was deposited into the store's bank account in the calculation of income. *See Kirsch v. United States*, 174 F.2d 595, 601 (8th Cir. 1949).

The Commissioner, however, did not include all of the store's deposits in the calculation of the Chois' income. Rather, the Commissioner correctly subtracted "identifiable non-income" and properly presumed the remainder of the deposits were taxable income. *See Burke v. Comm'r*, 929 F.2d 110, 112 (2d Cir. 1991).

As the Tax Court found, there were only two sources of cash that supplied the registers at the Chois' store: (1) cash from customers who bought groceries, and (2) cash returned from the store's bank account after checks were deposited. Any money received from the sale of groceries was clearly taxable. The only nontaxable activity that Taxpayers engaged in was the cashing of payroll checks for customers.

In 1991, the Chois deposited $2,066,381 into their bank account, none of it in cash. They then returned approximately $1,420,200 in cash to the register after processing the checks through their bank. Without additional cash entering the register from the sale of groceries, this $1,420,200 was the maximum amount available in the register to give to customers cashing payroll checks. Because they could only have cashed more than $1,420,200 in payroll checks if they received additional cash from customers who bought groceries, $1,420,200 is also the maximum amount of nontaxable money the Chois could have deposited into their bank account in 1991. The Commissioner properly subtracted the entire $1,420,200 from the calculation of the Chois' income.

We therefore affirm the Tax Court's holding that the use of the "bank deposits plus cash expenditures" method was proper because the Commissioner correctly subtracted "identifiable non-income." *Burke*, 929 F.2d at 112. We also affirm the Tax Court's ruling with respect to tax year 1992, which involved different dollar values but was computed in the same manner as tax year 1991 in all other respects.

We have reviewed similar challenges to the "bank deposits plus cash expenditures" method in appeals from criminal convictions and upheld the use of that method. *See Brickey*, 289 F.3d 1144; *Percifield v. United States*, 241 F.2d 225 (9th Cir. 1957). *A fortiori*, these authorities support our conclusion here. "Where the taxpayer fails to maintain adequate records for the government to determine the amount of actual income, the government may use indirect methods to establish income including the "bank deposits plus cash expenditures" method.

The Tax Court also properly rejected the Chois' alternative method of reconstructing income, the percentage markup method. Under this method, income is derived by multiplying the cost of goods sold by a business by the calculated average percent markup. *See Bernstein v. CIR*, 267 F.2d 879, 880–81 (5th Cir. 1959). The Tax Court gave no weight to the Chois' expert's testimony, which contained a reconstruction of the Chois' income using this method, because the calculation of the cost of goods sold was not supported by adequate records of the Chois' inventory and because the calculation of percentage markup was based entirely on interviews with the Chois. The Tax Court's determination of the credibility of this expert witness and the weight to be given to his testimony must be affirmed because it is not clearly erroneous. *See DHL Corp. v. CIR*, 285 F.3d 1210, 1216 (9th Cir. 2002); *Nor-Cal Adjusters v. CIR*, 503 F.2d 359, 362 (9th Cir. 1974).

The Chois only challenge to the imposition of a civil fraud penalty under 26 U.S.C. § 6663 is that there was no underpayment for 1991 or 1992. Because we have upheld the Tax Court's determination that there was an underpayment in both years, we also uphold the imposition of the civil fraud penalty.

The judgment of the Tax Court is AFFIRMED.

Does the IRS's approach seem fair? Did it adequately account for the cashing of customers' paychecks? Why was the Chois' argument for use of the percentage markup method unsuccessful?

[D] Defenses to Indirect Methods of Proving Income

How should the taxpayer respond when the IRS has used an indirect method to reconstruct income and the taxpayer feels it is inaccurate? One article explains:

> To prove an error exists in the income reconstruction and contest the deficiency or the amount of a refund, taxpayers have used several tactics. It is important for the taxpayer to focus on errors made by the IRS in applying the income reconstruction method, not the theory behind the method. All of the court-accepted methods are based on sound accounting principles.
>
> While lost or stolen records do not lessen the burden of showing the reconstruction was arbitrary or erroneous, the taxpayer can still be successful. When there are no records because of an innocent loss, the court will accept credible testimony. Testimony as to how the records were lost is important. If testimony can demonstrate the records would have shown the IRS's reconstruction to be arbitrary, capricious, or erroneous, the presumption of correctness may be overcome. The court may reject the income reconstruction, adjust the deficiency, or allow estimates under the *Cohan* rule.
>
> *Net Worth Method.* A common defense against the net worth method is that the opening net worth is too low. Taxpayers often claim the existence of a cash hoard that was not taken into account by the IRS. To be successful, the taxpayer must demonstrate a credible source for the cash hoard. Circumstantial evidence

such as regularly conducting business in cash, need for cash on a regular basis, documented distrust of banks, and large cash expenditure before the examination period, can all lend credence to a cash hoard defense. In addition, the taxpayer may be able to show there are other assets not included in the beginning net worth, e.g., inventory on consignment, receivables, or assets owned by the taxpayer but held by a third party.

The difference between beginning and ending net worth represents income. This income is reduced by the amount of any reported taxable and nontaxable income received by the taxpayer. The alleged unreported income can be reduced by the amount of any gifts, inheritances, tax exempt interest, capital loss carryovers, and loans not taken into account by the IRS. The taxpayer may also assert the IRS has overestimated personal living expenses or other nondeductible expenses, thereby reducing the amount of income to be explained.

Sources and Applications of Funds. The IRS must establish what funds were available to the taxpayer at the beginning of the year, funds acquired during the year, and then show the expenditures exceed the sum of those funds. As in the net worth method, the IRS must investigate all reasonable leads provided by the taxpayer as to nontaxable sources of funds and establish a likely source for the unreported income.

Again, the taxpayer may attempt to prove the beginning funds balance was understated because of a cash hoard or the existence of assets later sold for cash but not included in the analysis by the IRS.

Percentage Markup. This method has several weaknesses because the basis for comparison is an industry average. The taxpayer may claim IRS calculations do not take into account actual breakage, shoplifting, or employee theft. Also, asset size often explains differences in financial ratios. Location, the age of assets, new competition entering the market, experience of the operator, liberal discount policy, and product mix, can all account for a taxpayer failing to achieve industry profit margins.

Bank Deposits. As with the net worth method, the IRS must determine the taxpayer's beginning position and investigate leads offered by the taxpayer to explain nontaxable sources of cash. The best defense against this method is an alternative nontaxable source of the deposits. Sources such as loans, gifts, inheritances, transfers from other accounts, life insurance proceeds, sale of assets at a loss, tax exempt bond interest, or reimbursement for past expenditures can all explain deposits. However, testimony without corroborating evidence will not usually overcome the presumption of correctness attached to the reconstruction. Another defense is that the deposits are misclassified and actually belong to another tax year. Alternatively, the taxpayer may attempt to show that income related to the deposits was included on the return.

* * *

Charles E. Price & Leonard G. Weld, *Income Reconstruction*, CPA JOURNAL (Aug. 1998), *available at* http://www.nysscpa.org/cpajournal/1998/0898/Features/f26898.html.

Another commentator adds the following, in his analysis of *Kikalos v. United States*, 408 F.3d 900 (7th Cir. 2005), an opinion written by Judge Posner:

> Judge Posner notes that the estimation methods involved are typically used by the government to support the conclusion that the taxpayer had more income than reported. However, the estimation method proffered by the government can be turned into evidence supporting the taxpayer. Cross-examination can establish that the government's proffered estimation method was so sloppily performed that it is wholly irrational and unbelievable. In a Tax Court case, that would likely be sufficient to knock the government out altogether or at least

> shift the burden of persuasion to the government to permit the court to find the presence of a deficiency. *See* Helvering v. Taylor, 293 U.S. 507, 514 (1935). In a refund suit, at least conceptually, merely destroying the government's evidence does not establish that the taxpayer is entitled to a refund. Still, in the trial court's management of the litigation process and narrowing of the issues, if that is the only issue presented, the taxpayer may be able to prevail. But, more importantly for the present discussion, the cross-examination may not seek to destroy the method altogether but simply adjust it for taxpayer-favorable factors not properly considered by the government's expert. The net effect, if successful, is that the method, although initially proffered by the government, meets the taxpayer's burden of persuasion as to entitlement to a refund.
>
> . . . Judge Posner's discussion is a helpful reminder to the bar that, in appropriate cases, these methods (and other estimation methods that have the ability to persuade) may be used as affirmative evidence to rebut or test the IRS's estimation method in a civil or criminal tax case. For example, in a criminal investigation in which the CI [Criminal Investigation] special agent is hellbent on tagging your client with a crime for unreported income, those types of indirect methods if credible may be able to avoid a prosecution or conviction. One of the first things I do in a case in which the IRS special agent is trying to chase down additional income that my client denies (to me) having received is to have the Kovel accountant[n.13] perform some type of indirect method check (such as net worth or bank deposits) to test for unreported income.

John A. Townsend, *Judge Posner's Opinion in* Kikalos, 108 Tax Notes 593, 595–96 (2005).

In the *Choi* case, reproduced above, the taxpayer chose to respond to the IRS's reconstruction of income with a proposal to use a different method of reconstructing income. *Choi* is not unique in that regard. For example, in *Kikalos*, the case the excerpt above analyzes, the IRS used the percentage markup method of reconstructing the income of the taxpayers' retail stores. The taxpayers wanted to present expert testimony that the bank deposits method or net worth method would more accurately reflect the taxpayers' income from their stores. Judge Posner questioned the reliability of reconstruction of income based solely on the records the taxpayers chose to show their expert, but found that that would not make the expert's testimony inadmissible. *Kikalos*, 408 F.3d at 902–04.

PROBLEMS

1. Having put off for months filing her Year 1 income tax return, Jenny finally decides on the evening of April 15, Year 2 (a Friday), to make an effort to file. With no IRS forms at her disposal, she writes on a sheet of paper her name, address, social security number, and an estimate of her gross income and deductions for Year 1. She signs and dates the letter, includes a personal check for the estimated tax due, and rushes to the post office to mail the letter before midnight. Jenny mails the letter by regular mail, properly addressed, with a postmark of April 15. The letter arrived at the IRS Campus on Tuesday, April 19.
   A. On what day is Jenny treated as having filed the letter purporting to be her return?

[n.13] The use of a nonlawyer expert to assist an attorney deliver effective legal services and still preserve the attorney-client privilege was approved in the leading case of *United States v. Kovel*, 296 F.2d 918 (2d Cir. 1961). . . . [F]or those desiring an overview discussion [of Kovel experts], I have previously provided one in John A. Townsend, "The Accountant's Role and Risks in Koveling," CCH Tax Practice & Procedure (August/September 2000). [An excerpt from that article is included in § 4.03 of Chapter 4, which discusses the *Kovel* case in the context of privileges used to defend against IRS summonses. — Eds.]

B. By submitting the letter, has Jenny satisfied her filing requirements for Year 1?

C. Assume instead that Jenny decides to submit a request for an extension of time to file her Year 1 return. She properly completes Form 4868, Application for Automatic Extension, and mails the form to the IRS on Friday, April 15, Year 2. The extension request estimates her Year 1 tax liability but Jenny does not include any tax payment with the request. The IRS receives the extension request on April 18. When will Jenny's Year 1 income tax return be due?

D. Assume instead that Jenny mails the properly completed Form 4868 referenced in Part C on April 16, Year 2. The IRS receives the extension request on April 18. On what date is Jenny's Year 1 income tax return due?

2. Marc is the sole proprietor of a local bicycle repair shop in Los Angeles that has been in business for three years. During the previous year, Marc incurred a loss from the operation of the shop resulting primarily from a currently deductible repair expense he was forced to make on the building in which the shop is located. Marc also deducted other business-related expenses for the previous year, some for which he retained receipts and some for which he did not.

   A. Marc is concerned that the large repair expense will "red flag" his return and cause the IRS to select the return for audit. He asks you whether he might reduce his audit chances by attaching copies of receipts documenting the repair expense directly to his return. How would you advise Marc?

   B. Assume that Marc has received a letter from an employee at the IRS Campus questioning the deductibility of the repair expense and asking for documentation supporting the expense. What are Marc's options for responding to the letter? Would you advise him to request an interview with the IRS employee's supervisor to discuss the deduction in person?

3. Bubba Ellis operates the Texas Flight Training Academy (the "Academy"), a flight instruction school in Boline, Texas. Since its opening 10 years ago, the Academy's faculty has consisted solely of retired airline pilots. At all times, Bubba has treated the faculty members as independent contractors rather than employees, with the result that Bubba has not withheld on behalf of the faculty members federal income taxes, FICA (federal social security taxes), or FUTA (federal unemployment taxes). Instead, he has relied on the faculty members to comply with their tax obligations. Bubba recently received a letter from the IRS contesting the classification of the faculty as independent contractors and requesting a meeting at the IRS's offices to discuss the issue. As Bubba's representative, how might you prepare for the meeting with the examining agent? Specifically, what questions should you be prepared to answer on Bubba's behalf concerning the appropriate classification of the Academy's faculty? *See* Internal Revenue Manual 4.23.5; Form SS-8.

4. Field Service Advice 200101030, excerpted in Section 3.04, states that "[w]e have not been provided with any specific factual circumstances under which a revenue agent would drive by a taxpayer's house." Can you think of any context in which it might be helpful to a revenue agent to drive by a taxpayer's house as part of a determination of whether there is a reasonable indication of unreported income?

5. Rayanne owns a restaurant named *Chez Ray* in Coral Gables, Florida. The tax return she filed two years ago was recently audited, and the examining agent seemed concerned about the Schedule C she filed for the restaurant business.

   A. Rayanne has not kept very good books and records for the business. Given that fact, how might the IRS set about establishing that Rayanne has unreported income from the restaurant?

B. Would the IRS's ability to use any of the techniques available to establish the existence and amount of unreported income from *Chez Ray* depend on whether it had reasonable indication that Rayanne likely had failed to report all of the income from the restaurant?

Chapter 4
SUMMONSES AND PRIVILEGES

§ 4.01 INTRODUCTION

As explained in Chapter 3, the IRS has the authority to examine a taxpayer's return in order to verify whether that return accurately reflects the taxpayer's tax liability. To carry out this examination function, Congress has granted the IRS broad authority to "examine any books, papers, records, or other data which may be relevant" to determining the correctness of any tax return. I.R.C. § 7602(a). While the IRS normally seeks access to the taxpayer's books and records by making informal requests, the IRS does have summons power that enables the IRS to compel a taxpayer or third party to produce records or to testify under oath. I.R.C. § 7602(a)(2).[1]

This chapter first explores the scope of the IRS's summons authority, the procedures the IRS must follow to issue an enforceable summons, and the available remedies the taxpayer has to resist enforcement. Next, the chapter discusses the special procedures the IRS must follow when it seeks testimony and documents from third parties and the uses of John Doe summonses. Finally, the chapter examines the common law and statutory privilege claims available in a summons enforcement proceeding, including the attorney-client privilege, the work-product doctrine, and the federally authorized tax practitioner privilege of Code section 7525.

§ 4.02 IRS SUMMONS AUTHORITY

[A] Scope of Authority

Reading Assignment: I.R.C. §§ 6201(a), 7602, 7603, 7612(a)–(b).

When the IRS seeks access to the taxpayer's books and records, it will typically ask the taxpayer to provide them on a voluntary basis. If those efforts fail, the IRS may issue an administrative summons compelling the taxpayer to turn over the records. Nearly all IRS examination personnel are authorized to issue a summons. T.D. 6421; Delegation Order No. 4 (as revised).[2] The summons must be left at the taxpayer's "last and usual" place of residence. I.R.C. § 7603.

To be enforceable, a summons must contain the following information:

(1) The name and address of the person whose taxes are being inquired into along with the periods under consideration. . . .

(2) The identity of the person summoned. A summons directed at a corporation must be served on a corporate official, director, management agent or other person authorized to accept service of process. . . .

(3) A description of the items summoned, which must be described with reasonable certainty. I.R.C. § 7603. The summoned party must know what is required of him with "sufficient specificity to permit him to respond adequately to the summons." *United States v. Medlin*, 986 F.2d 463 (11th Cir. 1993); *United States v. Wyatt*, 637 F.2d 293, 302 n.16 (5th Cir. 1981).

---

[1] The IRS also has the authority outside of section 7602 to require taxpayers to maintain records and disclose those records upon request. For example, section 6112 requires organizers and sellers of potentially abusive tax shelter transactions to maintain lists of investors.

[2] As indicated in Chapter 14, the authority under Code section 7602 may also be used with respect to tax collection.

(4) The date, place and time for compliance. . . . The summons must provide at least 10 days for the party to respond. I.R.C. § 7605(a).

Barbara T. Kaplan, *Leveling the Playing Field in Federal Income Tax Controversies*, 56 N.Y.U. ANN. INST. FED. TAX'N § 32.01, at 32-11 (1999).

The IRS's summons authority is expansive. The following case considers the limits of the IRS's access to taxpayer information under its summons power:

UNITED STATES v. NORWEST CORPORATION

United States Court of Appeals, Eighth Circuit
116 F.3d 1227 (1997)

BEAM, CIRCUIT JUDGE.

In the course of an audit of Norwest Corporation, the Internal Revenue Service sought to enforce a designated summons directing Norwest to produce tax preparation software licensed to it by Arthur Andersen & Co., as well as related documents and data. Norwest and Andersen objected to the summons, claiming that the material was not within the scope of the IRS's authority, and that in any event it was not relevant to the audit. After a hearing, the magistrate judge issued an order enforcing the summons. The district court, adopting most of the findings and conclusions of the magistrate judge, affirmed the order. Norwest and Andersen appeal, and we affirm.

I. BACKGROUND

Norwest is a large bank holding corporation that has more than 300 subsidiaries in the financial services industry. Norwest files consolidated corporate federal income tax returns for all of its subsidiaries. Since at least 1983, Norwest has used tax preparation software in preparing its tax returns. In 1990, Norwest entered into a three-year licensing agreement with Andersen for use of Andersen's copyrighted "Tax Director" tax preparation software. Norwest first used Tax Director in preparing its 1990 returns, and used the program again for its 1991 returns.

A. The Tax Director Program

Tax Director is a group of related programs developed by Andersen that a corporation can use to calculate federal and state tax liability and prepare and print tax returns. Andersen has licensed Tax Director to approximately 700 corporate customers, including Norwest. The agreement between Norwest and Andersen states that Tax Director contains trade secrets and prohibits Norwest from transferring Tax Director to others or allowing others to use it. According to Norwest and Andersen, Tax Director operates in the following way. First, the company inputs year-end account balances from its books to be used in calculating the tax, either by manually entering the applicable figures or exporting this data from a previously compiled database. Next, the entered figures are assigned certain codes that instruct the program how they are to be classified for tax purposes. "Tax destination codes" (TDC codes) assign figures to particular lines on the return; for example, figures to be identified as gross rents are assigned the number "052.0." Similarly, "ALT codes" are used to identify figures with their proper destination on schedules to be attached to the return. All TDC and ALT codes to be assigned to particular entries are determined before the year-end balances are entered into Tax Director. In other words, how certain figures are classified for tax purposes is determined by the program's operator; Tax Director itself does not perform such classifications.

* * *

After the company's financial data is entered and the applicable codes and adjustments assigned, Tax Director generates the return and appropriate schedules. This process apparently involves simple arithmetical processes: Tax Director identifies all the information with a particular code, adds it up, and enters it on the appropriate line of the return. The program does, however, perform certain automatic adjustments to the information it receives. For example, Tax Director caps the figure calculated for reporting on the return as charitable deductions * * * as the Tax Code requires. The program also automatically reports taxable income as zero on the return if the data it receives would indicate a negative taxable income. Tax Director stores all of the entered data, including the account balances, codes, and adjustments, into data files which are segregated from the actual program. Tax Director thus does not itself retain any direct information about the company's finances or tax liability.

Tax Director can also generate and print certain "audit trail reports" based on the financial data it is given. These include the "Detail Spreadsheet Report" (R2 report) and the "Adjusting Entry Edit Report" (E3 report). The R2 report organizes and tabulates the year-end summary information for book balances and indicates for each account the TDC and ALT codes assigned, the Schedule M adjustments made, and the resulting adjusted tax balance. The E3 report likewise indicates the classifications and Schedule M adjustments assigned to each account. According to Norwest and Andersen, when Tax Director creates audit trail reports, it is not designed to save the data so that it may be viewed or manipulated by other commercially available software such as a spreadsheet program, nor is Tax Director itself designed to further view or edit this data. The program does, however, save this information as "print files." According to Norwest and Andersen, skilled computer technicians can convert these print files to spreadsheet-accessible files, and Norwest did in fact create such files for use in preparing its state income tax returns.

B. The Audit of Norwest

In April of 1992, the IRS began an audit of Norwest for the 1990 tax year. This audit later was expanded to included Norwest's 1991 tax liability. In the course of the audit, the IRS issued to Norwest numerous "Information Document Requests" (IDRs) requesting production of certain documents and records deemed relevant to the audit. On September 11, 1992, the agency issued IDR 26, requesting "a copy of the 'mapping' that takes place to translate the account totals on the [general ledger] report into line items on the tax return [including] Schedule M adjustments." Appellants' App. at 410. IDR 26 also indicated that "we anticipate that this process includes the use of Personal Computer based software of either an 'in-house' nature or a commercial package. Please provide a copy of these files in computer readable form." *Id.* In response to IDR 26, Norwest provided the IRS with a copy of an R2 report from the 1991 return.

In October of 1993, John Kuchera, the IRS computer audit specialist assigned to the Norwest project, orally requested that Norwest provide a copy of Tax Director. Norwest refused to produce Tax Director, but did provide the agency with two sets of computer diskettes. One set contained the unadjusted book balances entered into the program in completing the returns. The agency was able to easily access these files. The second set of diskettes were the adjusted tax balance files created by a Norwest employee from Tax Director's audit trail print files. These files presented the agency with some difficulty. Kuchera was eventually able to access the files, but testified that he was unable to verify whether they were accurate or complete.

The agency made no further requests for Tax Director until May 19, 1994, when it issued the designated summons at issue in this appeal. The summons directed Norwest to produce, among other things, the complete Tax Director program and all manuals and similar documents relating to the program. Norwest again refused to produce the software and its documentation. Instead, Norwest and Andersen met with agency auditors for several hours to demonstrate the program and its operation. This demonstration used generic data, and did not involve any Norwest-specific information.

Paragraph 2 of the summons requested "all data files, in machine sensible form, used by Tax Director to prepare the tax returns, or supporting computations, or upon which the Tax Director programs performed their functions." Appellants' App. at 16. In response to Paragraph 2, Norwest produced the original data files created by the program in creating the 1990 and 1991 returns. When the agency was initially unable to view these files, an Andersen employee explained that Tax Director itself had no capacity to manage the files, but instructed the agency computer specialists on how to convert these files into a readable format. When the agency was still unsatisfied with its access to the Paragraph 2 files, Andersen offered to construct a "bridge program" that would allow the agency to download and view the files. Andersen created such a program, but the agency refused to accept the program when Andersen and Norwest offered the bridge program on the condition that the agency accept it in lieu of Tax Director and that the agency agree not to pursue the summons.

With the statute of limitations for the 1990 audit on the verge of expiration, the agency initiated this enforcement action, which suspended the statute. Andersen intervened in the proceedings. Following a hearing, the magistrate judge concluded that the summons should be enforced, with certain limitations intended to protect Andersen's proprietary interest in Tax Director. The district court modified certain aspects of the magistrate judge's order, but affirmed enforcement. On appeal, Norwest and Andersen reiterate their position that this kind of software is not within the IRS's summons authority, that it is not material to the audit, and that the agency has acted in bad faith. Norwest and Andersen also argue that production of Tax Director will require that Norwest violate Andersen's copyright, and that this vitiates the agency's summons authority.

II. DISCUSSION

Under section 7602 of the Internal Revenue Code, the IRS has the authority to issue summonses requiring taxpayers to produce records, documents, or other material relevant to an audit or to give testimony. As it has done in this case, the agency may also issue a "designated summons" under IRC § 6503(j). During the enforcement period of a designated summons, the statute of limitations for issuing a notice of deficiency is suspended. IRC § 6503(j)(1). The IRS is entitled to summon material if it satisfies a deferential standard for relevancy. *United States v. Powell*, 379 U.S. 48, 57–58, 85 S. Ct. 248, 13 L. Ed. 2d 112 (1964).

No court has addressed whether the agency's summons authority encompasses tax preparation software that itself contains no direct information about a particular taxpayer. Therefore, we face two important questions of first impression: whether the section 7602 summons power applies to this situation, and, if so, whether the agency has shown that its summons for this material is enforceable under *Powell*.

A. The Applicability of Section 7602

Section 7602 authorizes the IRS to summon "any books, papers, records, or other data which may be relevant or material" to an IRS investigation. Given the agency's "broad mandate to investigate and audit 'persons who may be liable' for taxes," courts should be wary of "restricting that authority so as to undermine the efficacy of the federal tax system." *United States v. Bisceglia*, 420 U.S. 141, 145–46, 95 S. Ct. 915, 43 L. Ed. 2d 88 (1975). The Supreme Court has stated that " 'the administration of the statute may well be taken to embrace all appropriate measures for its enforcement, [unless] there is . . . substantial reason for assigning to the phrases . . . a narrower interpretation.' " *United States v. Euge*, 444 U.S. 707, 715, 100 S. Ct. 874, 63 L. Ed. 2d 141 (1980) (*quoting United States v. Chamberlin*, 219 U.S. 250, 269, 31 S. Ct. 155, 55 L. Ed. 204 (1911)). With these principles in mind, we must determine whether "books, papers, records, or other data" includes Tax Director.[n.6]

Norwest and Andersen argue that Tax Director is not a "record" or "other data" because the program itself does not contain or save any financial information particular to Norwest. Like any other computer program, it is a series of coded instructions that enable a computer to perform certain operations on data entered into it. The financial information that Tax Director used to generate Norwest's tax returns is not stored within the program, but is saved into completely segregated data files which have been provided to the agency. The copy of Tax Director the agency would receive from Norwest is no different from the software that Anderson licenses to hundreds of other corporate clients. Norwest and Andersen liken Tax Director to a calculator an individual taxpayer might use to complete a return, and argue that this kind of tool or asset is not within the agency's summons power.

Perhaps because it will usually be apparent whether a particular item is a "record" or "other data" under section 7602, there is a dearth of relevant case law.[n.7] *Euge*, however, suggests that "books, records, papers, or other data" under section 7602 cannot be defined as narrowly as Norwest and Andersen urge. In *Euge*, the Court considered "whether [the] power to compel a witness to 'appear,' to produce 'other data,' and to 'give testimony,' [pursuant to a section 7602 summons] includes the power to compel the execution of handwriting exemplars." 444 U.S. at 711. The Court held that this exercise of the summons power was "necessary for the effective exercise of the Service's enforcement responsibilities [and] entirely consistent with the statutory language." *Id.*

Norwest's and Andersen's arguments are reasonable, but they basically urge us to adopt a narrow interpretation of the types of information section 7602 encompasses. This is inconsistent with the approach in *Euge* and with our obligation "to liberally construe the powers given" the agency under the statute. *United States v. Giordano*, 419 F.2d 564, 569–70 (8th Cir. 1969). As Norwest itself states in its brief, "Tax Director consists of a set of instructions to the computer (i.e., algorithms) on how to sort and arrange financial data entered by a licensee, how to do simple arithmetic, and how to cause the data entered by the licensee to be printed on the lines of a federal income tax return." Appellant's Br. at 22. In light of the broad effect we are to give section 7602, a coded set of algorithms that sorts and arranges a taxpayer's financial information and then uses that information to generate the audited return can certainly be considered a "record" or "other data."

Norwest's and Andersen's argument that Tax Director is merely a "tool" such as a calculator is unpersuasive. First, simply labeling Tax Director a "tool" and pointing out that, in the end, numbers on the return are generated by arithmetical processes does not mean that the program is not also a "record" or "other data." Second, as the magistrate judge found, Tax Director is clearly much more sophisticated than a mere adding machine. It recognizes significant codes assigned to certain information based upon its intended tax treatment, organizes information based on those assignments, contains built-in limitations on the assignments a taxpayer can make, generates a return, creates files containing taxpayer financial data, and can generate detailed reports. We hold that the magistrate judge and district court correctly concluded that Tax Director was a "record" or "other data" under section 7602.

[n.6] The manuals, documents, and other written information related to Tax Director demanded in Paragraph 1 of the summons are obviously "books" or "papers." Thus, the only issue with regard to that material is whether it is relevant to the IRS's audit.

[n.7] We agree with Norwest and Andersen that two cases the IRS relies on are not entirely apposite. *See* United States v. Arthur Young & Co., 465 U.S. 805, 813–17, 104 S. Ct. 1495, 79 L. Ed. 2d 826 (1984) (upholding a summons for tax accrual workpapers retained by the taxpayer's accountant); United States v. Davey, 543 F.2d 996, 999–1000 (2d Cir. 1976) (enforcing a summons for magnetic tapes containing taxpayer-specific data). *Arthur Young* and *Davey* do, however, indicate the broad summons authority section 7602 gives the agency.

B. *Powell* Test

Under *United States v. Powell*, 379 U.S. 48, 57–58, 85 S. Ct. 248, 13 L. Ed. 2d 112 (1964), a court must enforce a section 7602 summons if the IRS shows: (1) that the investigation is for a legitimate purpose; (2) that the requested material is relevant to the investigation; (3) that the material is not already in the agency's possession; and (4) that the proper administrative steps have been followed.[n.8] Norwest and Andersen argue on appeal that the agency has not shown that the summoned material may be relevant, and that the summons was issued for an improper purpose.

1. Relevance

The agency points to a number of ways Tax Director may be relevant to the audit. For the returns at issue, Tax Director was the final step in translating the company's summary book income into the information reported on the returns. The agency thus contends that Tax Director is a critical link in the "audit trail," that is, the steps and processes that Norwest took in preparing its tax returns based on particular financial information. According to the agency, access to Tax Director may assist the audit team in gaining a "big picture" view of Norwest's returns and in identifying areas for more detailed investigation.

The agency also points out that Norwest's consolidated returns represent financial information from more than 300 subsidiaries and affiliates, and that the company's use of Tax Director was the most important step in organizing this vast amount of information. Tax Director itself contains algorithms that generate return information based upon interpretations of the Tax Code and that affect how the return is generated. While some of these functions, such as the automatic cap on charitable deductions, are clearly reflected on the return, others may not be; an Andersen employee testified that Tax Director contains other such automatic functions, but could not recall what they were. Finally, while Norwest did produce data files and audit trail reports created by Tax Director, the agency maintains that without Tax Director it is unable to verify whether this information is complete or accurate.

Norwest and Andersen offer a number of arguments for why they believe the agency's access to Tax Director will be unfruitful. "Relevance" under the *Powell* test does not depend, however, on whether the information sought would be relevant in an evidentiary sense, but merely whether that information might shed some light on the tax return. *Arthur Young*, 465 U.S. at 813–14 & n.11. The IRS need not state with certainty how useful, if at all, the summoned material will in fact turn out to be. *Id.* at 814. Furthermore, it is for the agency, and not the taxpayer, to determine the course and conduct of an audit, and "the judiciary should not go beyond the requirements of the statute and force IRS to litigate the reasonableness of its investigative procedures." *United States v. Clement*, 668 F.2d 1010, 1013 (8th Cir. 1982).

Norwest and Andersen also contend that the agency has never before felt a need to examine Norwest's tax preparation software in prior audits, and that the IRS can adequately "tie up" Norwest's returns to the book financial data by way of the data files and audit trail reports already provided. The issue, however, is not whether the IRS needs the software and supporting material in order to tie the final entries on the return to the detailed or summary financial data. There is, indeed, little question that it would be possible for the agency to tie the return information back to the input (that is, reconcile Norwest's tax income with its book income) without the software. But the agency's summons authority does not depend on whether the lack of certain information

---

[n.8] Norwest and Andersen argue that because Tax Director contains trade secrets of Andersen, we should apply a stricter test, and require the agency to show a "clear nexus" between the summoned material and Norwest's tax liability or that the material is necessary to complete the audit. Neither the statute nor the case law provides any basis for a higher standard of relevancy in this case, and we therefore reject this argument.

would make such reconciliation impossible, but whether the summoned material might "illuminate any aspect of the return." *Arthur Young*, 465 U.S. at 815. Under this broad standard, the agency has sufficiently shown that the material it seeks may assist the audit team in understanding the return and in focusing the investigation.

2. Legitimate Purpose

Norwest and Andersen contend that the agency's actual purpose in issuing the designated summons was to suspend the statute of limitations, which otherwise would likely have expired before the audit was completed. This, they maintain, was not a legitimate tax collection or determination purpose under the *Powell* test.

The appellants' arguments, however, basically boil down to repeating their position that the agency's stated purposes for seeking Tax Director are inadequate, and concluding from this that the IRS's real purpose could only be to extend the statute of limitations. Because we conclude that the agency's explanations for how Tax Director may be relevant to the audit are legitimate, we cannot accept appellants' premise. Because the audit was conducted in order to verify Norwest's tax liability for 1990 and 1991 and the IRS has demonstrated how Tax Director may be relevant to the audit, we hold that the summons was issued for a legitimate purpose. The IRS has therefore met its minimal burden under *Powell*, and is entitled to enforcement of the designated summons.

C. Summons of Copyrighted Material

Norwest and Andersen argue that because the summons forces Norwest to copy and produce to the IRS Andersen's copyrighted products, the summons will require Norwest to violate Andersen's copyright. Appellants maintain that this puts section 7602 in conflict with the Copyright Act, and that the district court thus should not have enforced the summons. The district court noted that appellants' argument is "essentially . . . that, when in conflict, the Copyright Act trumps the IRS's statutory authority to issue summonses." *United States v. Norwest Corp.*, 1995 U.S. Dist. LEXIS 21360, No. 4-94-MC-36, slip op. at 2–3 (D. Minn. Dec. 12, 1995). We agree with the district court that there is no authority for this proposition. Section 7602 does not indicate that a properly issued summons for relevant material is limited to uncopyrighted material. Nor does the Copyright Act indicate that copyright protection insulates either the copyright owner or the possessor of the particular item from producing that item in response to an IRS summons. To the extent that Andersen's proprietary interest in Tax Director may be threatened by enforcement of the summons, the restrictions imposed by the district court on the IRS's use of Tax Director adequately protect that interest.

* * *

III. CONCLUSION

For the reasons discussed above, we affirm the order of the district court in all respects.

Shortly after the *Norwest* case, Congress enacted section 7612, which places restrictions on the IRS's ability to obtain access to proprietary software, and helps ensure that trade secrets and other confidential information are protected. I.R.C. § 7612(b), (c). Note, however, that this section does not prohibit the IRS from issuing a summons for such software. C.C.A. 200550002.

Norwest suggests something about the broad scope of the IRS's summons authority. As another example, consider *United States v. Euge*, 444 U.S. 707 (1980), which was discussed in *Norwest*. In *Euge*, an IRS agent who was investigating Euge's income tax liability for years in which Euge had not filed any tax returns used the "bank deposits method" of reconstructing Euge's income.[3] The agent found only two bank accounts in Euge's name. However, he also found twenty additional bank accounts that appeared to be maintained by Euge under aliases. Accordingly, the agent issued a summons requiring Euge to appear and execute handwriting exemplars of the signatures appearing on the bank signature cards. In *Euge,* the Supreme Court enforced the summons, thus requiring Euge's production of the handwriting samples.

[B] Summons Enforcement

Reading Assignment: I.R.C. §§ 7210, 7402(b), 7604.

The IRS's summons is not self-enforcing. The IRS has several options if the taxpayer fails to comply voluntarily with the summons. In many instances, the IRS will decline to pursue the matter and will instead issue a notice of deficiency to the taxpayer proposing liability based on the information the IRS already has in its possession. Once the IRS sends the notice, the burden falls on the taxpayer to come forward with evidence to contest the asserted deficiency. *See* Philip N. Jones, *Has the Second Circuit Weakened Summons Enforcement Powers?*, 103 J. Tax'n 101 (2005). The IRS also has the option of seeking judicial enforcement of the summons. I.R.C. §§ 7604(a), 7402(b). To do so, the IRS must seek an order from a U.S. district court.

During the summons enforcement hearing, the prima facie case the IRS must present — essentially that it satisfied the four *Powell* factors, discussed above in *Norwest* — is easily satisfied in most cases. In fact, the IRS typically satisfies its burden under *Powell* by presenting a sworn affidavit of the IRS agent who issued the summons attesting to the satisfaction of each of the elements. The following case, involving efforts on the part of the IRS to obtain access to records of the taxpayer's offshore credit card activities, reflects this:

> "To obtain enforcement of an administrative summons issued pursuant to 26 U.S.C. § 7602(a), the IRS need only demonstrate 'good faith' in issuing the summons." *Lidas, Inc. v. United States,* 238 F.3d 1076, 1081–82 (9th Cir. 2001). The IRS can establish a prima facie showing of good faith by setting forth "(1) the investigation will be conducted for a legitimate purpose; (2) the inquiry will be relevant to such purpose; (3) the information sought is not already within the Commissioner's possession; and (4) the administrative steps required by the Internal Revenue Code have been followed." *Id.* (*citing United States v. Powell,* 379 U.S. 48, 57–58, 85 S. Ct. 248, 255, 13 L. Ed. 2d 112 (1964)). It is well established that the declaration or affidavit of an IRS director or agent satisfies the *Powell* requirements. *Lidas,* 283 F.3d at 1082 (citing *United States v. Stuart,* 489 U.S. 353, 360–61, 109 S. Ct. 1183, 103 L. Ed. 2d 388 (1989)); *United States v. Dynavac, Inc.,* 6 F.3d 1407, 1414 (9th Cir. 1993).
>
> To establish the prima facie case, the Government submitted [the IRS agent's] affidavit, in which she stated: (1) the investigation is being conducted for the legitimate purpose of assessing [taxpayer's] tax liabilities for the years 2002 and 2003, (2) that the inquiries may be relevant to that purpose, (3) that the information sought is not already within the Internal Revenue Service's possession, and (4) that the administrative steps required by the Internal Revenue Code have been followed. *See* Tsuha Decl. of 6/8/07 at PP 8, 19, 21. The Court concludes that the Petitioner has established a prima facie showing of good faith through [the] Revenue Agent['s] declaration.

---

[3] The bank deposits method of reconstructing income involves analyzing bank deposits to determine if they reflect unreported income. It is discussed in *Choi v. Commissioner,* 379 F.3d 638 (9th Cir. 2004), which is reproduced in Chapter 3.

> Once the IRS establishes its prima facie case, the burden shifts to the taxpayer to challenge the summons on any appropriate ground. *Lidas,* 238 F.3d at 1082 (*citing Powell,* 379 U.S. at 58). "The taxpayer bears a 'heavy burden' to rebut the presumption of good faith." *Lidas,* 238 F.3d at 1082 (quoting *United States v. Jose,* 131 F.3d 1325, 1328 (9th Cir. 1997) (en banc)). When challenging a summons, "[t]he taxpayer must allege specific facts and evidence to support his allegations of bad faith or improper purpose." *U.S. v. Jose,* 131 F.3d 1325, 1328 (9th Cir. 1997)(quoting *Liberty Financial Services v. United States,* 778 F.2d 1390, 1392 (9th Cir. 1985)).

United States v. Bright, 2007 U.S. Dist. LEXIS 67306.

The taxpayer is given the opportunity as part of the summons enforcement hearing to challenge the IRS's right to receive the records it seeks. Note that, in the case of a summons issued directly to the taxpayer, the taxpayer's ability to challenge the summons in court arises only after the IRS institutes the summons enforcement proceeding. In other words, the IRS must be the moving party: The taxpayer does not have standing to act preemptively to quash or enjoin the summons. *See* Schultz v. IRS, 395 F.3d 463 (2d Cir.) (*per curium*), *clarified on rehearing*, 413 F.3d 297 (2d Cir. 2005) (holding that District Court lacked jurisdiction over taxpayer's motion to quash summons when IRS had not yet attempted to enforce the summonses in court).

During the summons enforcement hearing, which is usually conducted by a magistrate judge, the taxpayer can challenge the summons by establishing that the IRS failed to meet the *Powell* factors. In addition, and as explained in more detail below, the taxpayer can resist enforcement based on a claim that the requested information is protected by one of the common law privileges, including the attorney-client and work-product doctrines. The latter set of issues tends to be the focus of many summons enforcement cases because the *Powell* factors are so easily established by the IRS in the typical case.

If the district court issues an order enforcing the summons, the taxpayer may appeal. If the taxpayer does not appeal or the appellate court upholds enforcement, and the taxpayer still refuses to comply, then the court may issue an order to show cause why the taxpayer should not be held in contempt for failing to comply with the summons. A taxpayer's failure to show cause at that stage will justify the entry of a civil contempt order. I.R.C. § 7604(b). The IRS can also seek to criminally prosecute the taxpayer for failing to comply. *See* I.R.C. § 7210 (nonappearing witness subject to fine of up to $1,000 and one year in prison). A taxpayer will typically be exposed to these latter two sanctions only in cases in which the taxpayer refuses to appear at the summons enforcement hearing or otherwise resists the summons in bad faith. *See* Jones, *supra*, at 103–105.

Can summonses be conditionally enforced? That is, can a court require compliance with a condition as a prerequisite to enforcement? In *United States v. Jose*, 131 F.3d 1325 (9th Cir. 1997) (*en banc*), the District Court had enforced certain summonses subject to the condition that the IRS notify the party summoned five days before circulating, transferring, or copying the summoned documents outside the Examination Division. The Ninth Circuit reversed, holding that the lower court was limited to enforcing or denying summonses. *See also United States v. Barrett*, 837 F.2d 1341, 1350–51 (5th Cir. 1988) (*en banc*), *cert. denied*, 492 U.S. 926 (1989) (regarding summons enforcement conditioned on compliance with Code section 6103).[4] In *Barrett*, the Fifth Circuit stated:

> In a summons enforcement proceeding, the district court's only task is to determine whether the summons should or should not be enforced. This inquiry

[4] An earlier decision in *Barrett*, 795 F.2d 446 (5th Cir. 1986), a suit under Code section 7431 alleging that the IRS sent to Dr. Barrett's patients letters disclosing confidential tax return information (the fact that he was under criminal investigation), is cited in *DiAndre v. United States*, 968 F.2d 1049 (1992), reproduced in Chapter 6.

> is limited to ensuring that the government has complied with the four *Powell* criteria, and that its process is not being abused. * * * There is no statutory authority, nor Congressional indication that existing statutes supply the authority, nor Supreme Court authority, to allow the district court to make any consideration except whether to enforce or not enforce the summons. * * * There is no middle ground because to create that remedy would unduly hamper the investigative efforts of the IRS.

Id. at 1350 (citation omitted).

[C] Third-Party Summonses

Reading Assignment: I.R.C. §§ 7602, 7609; Treas. Reg. § 301.7602-2(c).

The IRS's summons authority also extends to third parties — including the taxpayer's employer, bank, customers, and business associates — requiring them to give testimony or produce books and records. I.R.C. §§ 7602, 7609. Once the IRS issues a summons to the third party, notice of the summons typically must be given to the taxpayer within three days of the date on which the summons was served, and no later than the 23rd day before the date fixed in the summons as the day on which the records are to be examined.[5] The taxpayer then has the right, within 20 days after the notice is given, to bring a proceeding in district court to quash the summons and thereby prevent the third party from divulging the information. I.R.C. § 7609(a), (b)(2); *see also* Faber v. United States, 921 F.2d 1118 (10th Cir. 1990) (holding that 20-day period starts on the date the notice is mailed to the taxpayer). The taxpayer must also serve a copy of the petition to the person summoned and to the IRS. I.R.C. § 7609(b)(2)(B). The third party summoned can intervene in this proceeding, and is bound by the proceeding whether or not he intervenes. I.R.C. § 7609(b)(2)(C).

In addition to the right to bring a proceeding to quash the summons, the taxpayer identified in the third-party summons has the option of intervening in any proceeding brought by the IRS to enforce the summons. I.R.C. § 7609(b)(1). If the taxpayer intervenes or takes action to quash the summons, the statute of limitations on assessment is suspended during the enforcement proceedings and until all appeals are resolved. I.R.C. § 7609(e)(1); Treas. Reg. § 301.7609-5(b), (c).

The grounds for contesting a third-party summons, whether asserted by the taxpayer or the summoned party, are essentially the same as those that apply to information held directly by the taxpayer. Some courts, however, apply the *Powell* factors slightly differently in the case of third-party summonses. For example, in *United States v. Monumental Life Insurance Co.*, 440 F.3d 729 (6th Cir. 2006), a third-party summons proceeding, the IRS was investigating whether Johnson Systems had improperly deducted contributions made to its employee welfare benefit plan that were used to purchase Monumental life insurance products for Johnson Systems employees. *Id.* at 731. An IRS agent testified that the arrangements in question "are often used to disguise tax-avoidance schemes." *Id.* "[T]he administrative summons requested 172 categories of documents . . . ." *Id.* Monumental made a motion to quash the summons, which the district court dismissed. *Id.*

> Monumental delivered approximately 350 pages of documents to the IRS. Monumental also expressed a willingness to produce more documents if the IRS would place them under a protective order to keep the proprietary information confidential. This the IRS was unwilling to do. Moreover, the IRS was

[5] Section 7603 details the service of process requirements associated with the third-party summons and the notification to the taxpayer. Certain third-party summonses are not subject to the notification requirements. This category includes summonses issued only to determine whether or not records exist and those issued in aid of collection are not subject to the notification requirements in section 7609. I.R.C. § 7609(c)(2).

> displeased with Monumental's production of an insignificant portion of the requested documents, so it filed a petition to enforce the summons in April of 2001. . . .
>
> Monumental raised several objections to the enforcement of the summons, prompting the district court to refer the case to a magistrate judge. . . . The magistrate judge concluded that (1) the summons did not suffer from technical difficulties, (2) the IRS did not issue the summons in bad faith, (3) the government already had a portion of the requested documents in its possession because of [an investigation of another taxpayer], and (4) some of the documents that the government requested were irrelevant to the investigation. Because the magistrate judge did not believe that partial enforcement of the summons was legally permissible, he recommended that the district court deny enforcement in full. . . .
>
> The government then filed an objection to the magistrate judge's recommendation. In October of 2004, the district court declined to follow the recommendation of the magistrate judge and entered an order enforcing the summons in full.

Id. at 731–32.

On appeal from the decision of the District Court, the Court of Appeals for the Sixth Circuit reversed, denying enforcement of the summons because it agreed with Monumental that the IRS already had certain documents in its possession and "some of the documents requested by the IRS appear to be far removed from the investigation of Johnson's tax liability," *id.* at 737, and thus not relevant, *id.* at 736. On the relevance issue, the court explained that the "threshold is 'very low,' . . . , but judicial protection against sweeping or irrelevant orders is 'particularly appropriate in matters where the demand for records is directed not to the taxpayer but to a third-party.' " *Id.* (citations omitted). The court added:

> [I]n close cases, the "mere assertion of relevance" by an IRS agent will not necessarily satisfy the government's burden. *United States v. Goldman*, 637 F.2d 664, 667 (9th Cir. 1980). The present case exemplifies an exceptional circumstance where automatic reliance upon an agent's affidavit is not adequate because (1) the subpoena is directed to a third party, not to the taxpayer being investigated, (2) the IRS seeks a voluminous amount of highly sensitive proprietary information about Monumental's general administration of its products, (3) the IRS has opposed the imposition of a protective order, and (4) the magistrate judge, who spent years considering the scope of the summons, found that the IRS was seeking "some irrelevant information."

Id. at 736–37.

Not only is the taxpayer entitled to notice once the IRS serves a third-party summons, but the Code also requires the IRS to provide advance notice to the taxpayer before contacting third parties. I.R.C. § 7602(c)(1). The IRS must also provide the taxpayer, upon request, reports setting forth the names of third parties contacted with respect to the taxpayer's liability determination. I.R.C. § 7602(c)(2). Treasury regulations clarify the IRS's duties under section 7602(c). For example, the regulations clarify that third parties do not include the taxpayer's employees, officers, or fiduciaries as long as they are acting in their capacity as such. Treas. Reg. § 301.7602-2(c)(2). Further, an IRS agent may access databases and websites maintained by public and private entities without triggering the advance notification requirement. These would include records in county courthouses, county tax records, and library materials, whether maintained electronically or on a website. *Id.*

A taxpayer cannot avoid the intent of a summons for production of records held by a third party simply by having the third party transfer to his attorney records that were the subject of the summons. *See* Couch v. United States, 409 U.S. 322, 329 n.9 (1973). In addition, the third party who transfers the records in that context may be subject to criminal prosecution under 18 U.S.C. section 1503 for obstructing justice. *See* United States v. Curcio, 279 F.2d 681 (2d Cir.), *cert. denied*, 364 U.S. 824 (1960). If, however, the third party complies with the summons after being ordered by a court to do so or after being notified by the IRS that the taxpayer has not moved to quash the summons, then the summoned party cannot be held liable to the taxpayer for making the disclosure. I.R.C. § 7609(i)(3).

[D] John Doe Summonses

Reading Assignment: I.R.C. § 7609(f).

Code section 7609(f) contemplates summonses that do not identify the taxpayer whose liability is in issue — so-called "John Doe summonses." Under that section, issuance of a John Doe summons requires a prior court hearing in which the IRS establishes that:

(1) the summons relates to the investigation of a particular person or ascertainable group or class of persons,

(2) there is a reasonable basis for believing that such person or group or class of persons may fail or may have failed to comply with any provision of any internal revenue law, and

(3) the information sought to be obtained from the examination of the records or testimony (and the identity of the person or persons with respect to whose liability the summons is issued) is not readily available from other sources.

I.R.C. § 7609(f).

The IRS has used John Doe summonses to obtain documents relating to offshore, as well as domestic, transactions. For example, in 2000, a District Court judge authorized the IRS to serve summonses on MasterCard International and American Express Services in order to obtain customer records of unnamed United States taxpayers with accounts in the Bahamas, the Cayman Islands, Antigua and Barbuda that they may have been using to evade federal taxes. *See Judge Enforces IRS Summons to Obtain Credit Card Records*, Daily Tax Rep. (BNA), Nov. 1, 2000, at G-4. The IRS has also issued John Doe summonses in order to obtain the identity of those who invested in allegedly abusive tax shelter transactions. *See* Alison Bennet, *Jenkens & Gilchrist Refusing to Hand Over Shelter Investor Names Despite IRS Summons*, Daily Tax Rep. (BNA), June 23, 2003, at G-8.

Does the IRS need to comply with the requirements of section 7609(f) if a summons serves the dual purposes of investigating both a named taxpayer and unnamed persons? In *Tiffany Fine Arts, Inc. v. United States*, 469 U.S. 310 (1985), the Supreme Court ruled in a unanimous opinion that dual purpose summonses issued under section 7602 are not subject to section 7609(f) so long as the information sought is relevant to a legitimate investigation of the summoned taxpayer. The Court stated:

> The [Congressional] Reports [with respect to the enactment of section 7609(f)] discuss only one specific congressional worry: that the party receiving a summons would not have a sufficient interest in protecting the privacy of the records if that party was not itself a target of the summons. S. Rep. No. 94-938, at 368-369; H. R. Rep. No. 94-658, at 307. Such a taxpayer might have little incentive to oppose enforcement vigorously. Then, with no real adversary, the IRS could use its summons power to engage in "fishing expeditions" that might unnecessarily trample upon taxpayer privacy.

* * *

> When, as in this case, the summoned party is itself under investigation, the interests at stake are very different. First, by definition, the IRS is not engaged in a "fishing expedition" when it seeks information relevant to a legitimate investigation of a particular taxpayer. In such cases, any incidental effect on the privacy rights of unnamed taxpayers is justified by the IRS's interest in enforcing the tax laws. More importantly, the summoned party will have a direct incentive to oppose enforcement. In such circumstances, the vigilance and self-interest of the summoned party — complemented by its right to resist enforcement — will provide some assurance that the IRS will not strike out arbitrarily or seek irrelevant materials.

Id. at 320–21. Why do you think Congress was concerned that John Doe summonses might be used for "fishing expeditions"?

§ 4.03 DEFENSES TO SUMMONS ENFORCEMENT

As noted above, once the IRS demonstrates its compliance with the *Powell* factors during the summons enforcement proceedings, the burden shifts to the taxpayer to establish some defense to enforcement.

> Appropriate defenses include (1) the summons was issued after the IRS had recommended criminal prosecution to the Department of Justice . . . ; (2) the summons was issued in bad faith . . . ; (3) the materials sought are already in the possession of the IRS, . . . ; and (4) the materials sought by the IRS are protected either by the attorney-client privilege, . . . the work-product doctrine, . . . or other traditional privileges or limitations . . . . Although no blanket Fourth or Fifth Amendment privileges against testifying or producing documents are recognized . . . the taxpayer may assert those rights in response to specific questions asked or specific documents sought by the IRS.

United States v. Riewe, 676 F.2d 418, 420 n.1 (10th Cir. 1982) (citations omitted).

A commonly asserted defense is that particular materials sought by the IRS are protected by privilege. Why won't a claim that the information sought by the IRS is protected by the Fifth Amendment privilege against self-incrimination provide broad protection for the taxpayer? One court explained:

> As [the] Magistrate Judge . . . correctly pointed out, Respondents [Taxpayers] cannot invoke a blanket Fifth Amendment privilege, which must be asserted with specificity. "[T]he only way the Fifth Amendment can be asserted as to testimony is on a question-by-question basis. A taxpayer must present himself for questioning, and as to each question elect to raise or not to raise the defense. The District Court may then determine by considering each question whether, in each instance, the claim of self-incrimination is well-founded." *See United States v. Drollinger,* 80 F.3d 389, 392 (9th Cir. 1996) (internal quotations and citations omitted); *see also United States v. Bodwell,* 66 F.3d 1000, 1001 (9th Cir. 1995). Respondents, who did not appear for the interview, could not properly assert the Fifth Amendment in response to particular questions. *See Drollinger,* 80 F.3d at 392–93. Respondents' assertion of various defenses, including their rights under the Fifth Amendment, did not excuse their failure to appear on the scheduled date of their summonses or render the summonses unenforceable.
>
> Moreover, Respondents may not refuse to produce the documents regarding their offshore credit cards on Fifth Amendment grounds. Although in certain circumstances the act of producing evidence in response to a subpoena or summons is communicative, whether the communicative act falls under the protection of the Fifth Amendment depends upon whether the act of producing the documents is testimonial. *See Fisher v. United States,* 425 U.S. 395, 411, 96 S. Ct. 1569 (1976). The *Fisher* court concluded that when the existence of the

> documents is a "foregone conclusion," the taxpayer adds "little or nothing to the sum total of the Government's information by conceding that he in fact has the papers." *Id.* Thus, when the existence of the requested records is a foregone conclusion, the act of producing the documents is not testimonial and does not invoke the protection of the Fifth Amendment privilege against self-incrimination. *See United States v. Norwood,* 420 F.3d 888, 895 (8th Cir. 2005).

Bright, 2007 U.S. Dist. LEXIS 67306.

[A] Commonly Asserted Privileges

Because controversies with the IRS involve federal law, privilege issues in these cases are resolved under federal law, and specifically under federal common law. *See* Martin J. McMahon, Jr. & Ira B. Shepard, *Privilege and the Work Product Doctrine in Tax Cases*, 58 TAX LAW. 405, 406 (2005). In *United States v. Euge*, 444 U.S. 707 (1980), the Supreme Court stated, "[b]y imposing an obligation to produce documents as well as to appear and give testimony, we believe the language of § 7602 suggests an intention to codify a broad testimonial obligation, including an obligation to provide some physical evidence relevant and material to a tax investigation, *subject to the traditional privileges and limitations*." *Id.* at 714 (emphasis added). The two traditional privileges referred to are the attorney-client privilege and the work-product doctrine. This section provides an overview of these and other privilege claims. Note that it is not uncommon for a taxpayer to make multiple privilege claims with respect to the same item of information.

[1] The Attorney-Client Privilege

The attorney-client privilege has multiple requirements. The privilege applies:

> (1) Where legal advice of any kind is sought; (2) from a professional legal advisor in his capacity as such; (3) the communications relating to that purpose; (4) made in confidence; (5) by the client; (6) are at his instance permanently protected; (7) from disclosure by himself or by the legal advisor; (8) except the protection be waived.

8 J. WIGMORE, EVIDENCE § 2292 at 554 (*quoted in* United States v. Rockwell Int'l, 897 F.2d 1255, 1264 (3d Cir. 1990)).

Confidentiality is a critical aspect of the privilege. Because the purpose of the privilege is to protect confidential attorney/client communications, the privilege generally will not apply if the communication was not intended to be kept confidential or was actually disclosed to other parties. *See Rockwell Int'l*, 897 F.2d at 1265. Moreover, the disclosure of a portion of the communication generally will waive the applicability of the privilege to the entire communication. *Id.*

[a] Who is the Corporate "Client"?

If the client is a corporation, whose communications with the attorney are protected by privilege? *Upjohn Co. v. United States*, 449 U.S. 383 (1981), a leading case, addressed that question. The following is summary of the facts:

> Petitioner Upjohn Co. manufactures and sells pharmaceuticals here and abroad. In January 1976 independent accountants conducting an audit of one of Upjohn's foreign subsidiaries discovered that the subsidiary made payments to or for the benefit of foreign government officials in order to secure government business. The accountants so informed petitioner Mr. Gerard Thomas, Upjohn's Vice President, Secretary, and General Counsel. Thomas is a member of the Michigan and New York Bars, and has been Upjohn's General Counsel for 20 years. He consulted with outside counsel and R. T. Parfet, Jr., Upjohn's Chairman of the Board. It was decided that the company would conduct an

internal investigation of what were termed "questionable payments." As part of this investigation the attorneys prepared a letter containing a questionnaire which was sent to "All Foreign General and Area Managers" over the Chairman's signature. The letter began by noting recent disclosures that several American companies made "possibly illegal" payments to foreign government officials and emphasized that the management needed full information concerning any such payments made by Upjohn. The letter indicated that the Chairman had asked Thomas, identified as "the company's General Counsel," "to conduct an investigation for the purpose of determining the nature and magnitude of any payments made by the Upjohn Company or any of its subsidiaries to any employee or official of a foreign government." The questionnaire sought detailed information concerning such payments. Managers were instructed to treat the investigation as "highly confidential" and not to discuss it with anyone other than Upjohn employees who might be helpful in providing the requested information. Responses were to be sent directly to Thomas. Thomas and outside counsel also interviewed the recipients of the questionnaire and some 33 other Upjohn officers or employees as part of the investigation.

On March 26, 1976, the company voluntarily submitted a preliminary report to the Securities and Exchange Commission on Form 8-K disclosing certain questionable payments. A copy of the report was simultaneously submitted to the Internal Revenue Service, which immediately began an investigation to determine the tax consequences of the payments. Special agents conducting the investigation were given lists by Upjohn of all those interviewed and all who had responded to the questionnaire. On November 23, 1976, the Service issued a summons pursuant to 26 U. S. C. § 7602 demanding production of:

> All files relative to the investigation conducted under the supervision of Gerard Thomas to identify payments to employees of foreign governments and any political contributions made by the Upjohn Company or any of its affiliates since January 1, 1971 and to determine whether any funds of the Upjohn Company had been improperly accounted for on the corporate books during the same period.
>
> "The records should include but not be limited to written questionnaires sent to managers of the Upjohn Company's foreign affiliates, and memorandums or notes of the interviews conducted in the United States and abroad with officers and employees of the Upjohn Company and its subsidiaries." App. 17a–18a.

The company declined to produce the documents specified in the second paragraph on the grounds that they were protected from disclosure by the attorney-client privilege and constituted the work product of attorneys prepared in anticipation of litigation.

Id. at 386–88.

In considering the scope of the attorney-client privilege, the Court rejected the "control group" test, which applies the privilege only to the limited group of employees who have the responsibility for directing the firm's actions in response to legal advice. The Court explained:

> Such a view, we think, overlooks the fact that the privilege exists to protect not only the giving of professional advice to those who can act on it but also the giving of information to the lawyer to enable him to give sound and informed advice. See *Trammel* [v. *United States*, 445 U.S. 40 (1980)], *supra*, at 51; *Fisher* [v. *United States*, 425 U.S. 391 (1976)], *supra*, at 403. The first step in the resolution of any legal problem is ascertaining the factual background and sifting through the facts with an eye to the legally relevant. . . .

> In the case of the individual client the provider of information and the person who acts on the lawyer's advice are one and the same. In the corporate context, however, it will frequently be employees beyond the control group as defined by the court below — "officers and agents . . . responsible for directing [the company's] actions in response to legal advice" — who will possess the information needed by the corporation's lawyers. Middle-level — and indeed lower-level — employees can, by actions within the scope of their employment, embroil the corporation in serious legal difficulties, and it is only natural that these employees would have the relevant information needed by corporate counsel if he is adequately to advise the client with respect to such actual or potential difficulties. . . .
>
> The control group test adopted by the court below thus frustrates the very purpose of the privilege by discouraging the communication of relevant information by employees of the client to attorneys seeking to render legal advice to the client corporation. The attorney's advice will also frequently be more significant to noncontrol group members than to those who officially sanction the advice, and the control group test makes it more difficult to convey full and frank legal advice to the employees who will put into effect the client corporation's policy. *See, e.g., Duplan Corp. v. Deering Milliken, Inc.*, 397 F.Supp. 1146, 1164 (SC 1974) ("After the lawyer forms his or her opinion, it is of no immediate benefit to the Chairman of the Board or the President. It must be given to the corporate personnel who will apply it").
>
> The narrow scope given the attorney-client privilege by the court below not only makes it difficult for corporate attorneys to formulate sound advice when their client is faced with a specific legal problem but also threatens to limit the valuable efforts of corporate counsel to ensure their client's compliance with the law. . . .

Id. at 390–92.

The Court thus ruled in favor of Upjohn, stating:

> The communications at issue were made by Upjohn employees to counsel for Upjohn acting as such, at the direction of corporate superiors in order to secure legal advice from counsel. . . . The communications concerned matters within the scope of the employees' corporate duties, and the employees themselves were sufficiently aware that they were being questioned in order that the corporation could obtain legal advice. The questionnaire identified Thomas as "the company's General Counsel" and referred in its opening sentence to the possible illegality of payments such as the ones on which information was sought. App. 40a. A statement of policy accompanying the questionnaire clearly indicated the legal implications of the investigation. The policy statement was issued "in order that there be no uncertainty in the future as to the policy with respect to the practices which are the subject of this investigation." It began "Upjohn will comply with all laws and regulations," and stated that commissions or payments "will not be used as a subterfuge for bribes or illegal payments" and that all payments must be "proper and legal." Any future agreements with foreign distributors or agents were to be approved "by a company attorney" and any questions concerning the policy were to be referred "to the company's General Counsel." *Id.*, at 165a–166a. This statement was issued to Upjohn employees worldwide, so that even those interviewees not receiving a questionnaire were aware of the legal implications of the interviews. Pursuant to explicit instructions from the Chairman of the Board, the communications were considered "highly confidential" when made, *id.*, at 39a, 43a, and have been kept confidential by the company. Consistent with the underlying purposes of the attorney-client privilege, these communications must be protected against compelled disclosure.

> The Court of Appeals declined to extend the attorney-client privilege beyond the limits of the control group test for fear that doing so would entail severe burdens on discovery and create a broad "zone of silence" over corporate affairs. Application of the attorney-client privilege to communications such as those involved here, however, puts the adversary in no worse position than if the communications had never taken place. The privilege only protects disclosure of communications; it does not protect disclosure of the underlying facts by those who communicated with the attorney . . . .

Id. at 394–95. What is the "control group" test discussed in *Upjohn*, and why did the Court reject it?

[b] What is "Legal" Advice?

United States v. Rockwell Int'l, quoted above, goes on to explain that "[t]he *sine qua non* of any claim of privilege is that the information sought to be shielded is legal advice." *Rockwell Int'l*, 897 F.2d at 1264. What constitutes legal advice in the tax context? One article explains that it is critical to frame the question correctly:

> [A]sking whether something is tax advice is the wrong question. Rather, it is whether the advice is "tax law advice." If it is "tax law advice," then it is automatically legal in nature, despite the fact that it is also "tax advice." Interpreting the law is legal in nature, even if that law happens to relate to tax. Tax law is still law.
>
> Similarly, if "accounting advice" means advice rendered by accountants, then the analysis is certain to careen off track, because accountants perform functions that by any rational definition fall within the definition of legal advice. Tax Court litigation is one such example. Indeed, . . . [Code] section 7525 presumes that accountants perform some legal services. As such, concluding that something is "accounting advice" does not resolve the issue.
>
> To keep the analysis on track, the issue should be framed as follows: Whether the tax advice is "tax law advice" or "nonlegal tax advice."

Peter A. Lowy & Juan F. Vasquez, Jr., *Attorney-Client Privilege: When Does Tax Advice Qualify as "Legal Advice"?*, 97 Tax Notes 1335, 1344 (2002).

A recent summons enforcement case, reproduced below, indicates how fuzzy the line between legal advice and other advice can be in tax cases. Bear in mind that, with respect to tax accrual workpapers, the Supreme Court has stated:

> Nor do we find persuasive the argument that a work-product immunity for accountants' tax accrual workpapers is a fitting analogue to the attorney work-product doctrine established in *Hickman* v. *Taylor*, 329 U.S. 495 (1947). The *Hickman* work-product doctrine was founded upon the private attorney's role as the client's confidential adviser and advocate, a loyal representative whose duty it is to present the client's case in the most favorable possible light. An independent certified public accountant performs a different role. By certifying the public reports that collectively depict a corporation's financial status, the independent auditor assumes a *public* responsibility transcending any employment relationship with the client. The independent public accountant performing this special function owes ultimate allegiance to the corporation's creditors and stockholders, as well as to the investing public. This "public watchdog" function demands that the accountant maintain total independence from the client at all times and requires complete fidelity to the public trust.

United States v. Arthur Young & Co., 465 U.S. 805, 817–18 (1984).

UNITED STATES v. TEXTRON INC.

United States District Court, District of Rhode Island
507 F. Supp. 2d 138 (2007)

MEMORANDUM AND ORDER

Pursuant to 26 U.S.C. §§ 7402(b) and 7604, the United States has filed a petition to enforce an Internal Revenue Service (IRS) summons served on Textron Inc. and its subsidiaries ("Textron") in connection with the IRS's examination of Textron's tax liability for tax years 1998–2001. The summons seeks Textron's "tax accrual workpapers" for its 2001 tax year. Textron has refused to produce the requested documents on the grounds that (1) the summons was not issued for a legitimate purpose and (2) the tax accrual workpapers are privileged.

Because this Court finds that the requested documents are protected by the work product privilege, the petition for enforcement is denied.

Facts

Based on the pleadings, affidavits submitted by the parties, and the evidence presented at a hearing conducted on June 26, 2007, this Court finds the relevant facts to be as follows.

Textron, Inc. is a publicly traded conglomerate with approximately 190 subsidiaries. One of its subsidiaries is Textron Financial Corporation (TFC), a company that provides commercial lending and financial services. In 2001 and 2002, Textron had six tax attorneys and a number of CPAs in its tax department but TFC's tax department consisted only of CPAs. Consequently, TFC relied on attorneys in Textron's tax department, private law firms, and outside accounting firms for additional assistance and advice regarding tax matters.

Like other large corporations, Textron's federal tax returns are audited periodically at which time the IRS examines the returns for the tax years that are part of the audit cycle. In conducting its audits, the IRS, typically, gathers relevant information by issuing "information document requests" (IDRs) to the taxpayer. If the IRS disagrees with a position taken by the taxpayer on its return, the IRS issues a Notice of Proposed Adjustments to the taxpayer. A taxpayer that disputes the proposed adjustments has several options to resolve the dispute within the agency. Those options range from an informal conference with the IRS team manager to a formal appeal to the IRS Appeals Board. If the dispute is not resolved within the agency, the taxpayer may file suit in federal court. In seven of its past eight audit cycles covering the period between 1980 and the present, Textron appealed disputed matters to the IRS Appeals Board; and three of these disputes resulted in litigation.[n.1]

During the 1998–2001 audit cycle, the IRS learned, from examining Textron's 2001 return, that TFC had engaged in nine "sale-in, lease-out" (SILO) transactions involving telecommunications equipment and rail equipment. The IRS has classified such transactions as "listed transactions" because it considers them to be of a type engaged in for the purpose of tax avoidance. See 26 C.F.R. § 1.6011-4(b) (2). The IRS issued more than 500 IDRs in connection with the 1998–2001 audit cycle, and Textron complied with all of them, except for the ones seeking its "tax accrual workpapers."

[n.1] *See Textron, Inc. v. Comm'r*, 117 T.C. 67 (2001) (relating to federal income tax liability for tax years 1987 through 1992); *Textron, Inc. v. Comm'r*, 336 F.3d 26 (1st Cir. 2003) (appeal regarding a different issue raised in the tax court); *Textron, Inc. v. United States*, 418 F. Supp. 39 (D.R.I. 1976) (relating to tax years 1959 through 1962).

The Summons

On June 2, 2005, Revenue Agent Vasconcellos, the manager of the IRS team examining Textron's return, issued an administrative summons for "all of the Tax Accrual Workpapers" for Textron's tax year ending on December 29, 2001. The summons defined the "Tax Accrual Workpapers" to include:

> [A]ll accrual and other financial workpapers or documents created or assembled by the Taxpayer, an accountant for the Taxpayer, or the Taxpayer's independent auditor relating to any tax reserve for current, deferred, and potential or contingent tax liabilities, however classified or reported on audited financial statements, and to any footnotes disclosing reserves or contingent liabilities on audited financial statements. They include, but are not limited to, any and all analyses, computations, opinions, notes, summaries, discussions, and other documents relating to such reserves and any footnotes . . . .

Textron refused to produce its tax accrual workpapers, asserting that they are privileged and that the summons was issued for an improper purpose.

The Tax Accrual Workpapers

Because there is no immutable definition of the term "tax accrual workpapers," the documents that make up a corporation's "tax accrual workpapers" may vary from case to case.[n.2] In this case, the evidence shows that Textron's "tax accrual workpapers" for the years in question consist, entirely, of:

1. A spreadsheet that contains:

   (a) lists of items on Textron's tax returns, which, in the opinion of Textron's counsel, involve issues on which the tax laws are unclear, and, therefore, may be challenged by the IRS;

   (b) estimates by Textron's counsel expressing, in percentage terms, their judgments regarding Textron's chances of prevailing in any litigation over those issues (the "hazards of litigation percentages"); and

   (c) the dollar amounts reserved to reflect the possibility that Textron might not prevail in such litigation (the "tax reserve amounts").

2. Backup workpapers consisting of the previous year's spreadsheet and earlier drafts of the spreadsheet together with notes and memoranda written by Textron's in-house tax attorneys reflecting their opinions as to which items should be included on the spreadsheet and the hazard of litigation percentage that should apply to each item.

The evidence shows that while Textron may possess documents, such as leases, that contain factual information regarding the SILO transactions and other items that may be listed on the spreadsheet, its tax accrual workpaper files do not include any such documents.

As stated by Norman Richter, Vice President of Taxes at Textron and Roxanne Cassidy, Director, Tax Reporting at Textron, Textron's ultimate purpose in preparing the tax accrual workpapers was to ensure that Textron was "adequately reserved with respect to any potential disputes or litigation that would happen in the future." It seems reasonable to infer that Textron's desire to establish adequate reserves also was prompted, in part, by its wish to satisfy an independent auditor that Textron's reserve for contingent liabilities satisfied the requirements of generally accepted accounting

---

[n.2] Professor Douglas Carmichael, the government's expert, explained that the content of tax accrual workpaper files "does vary" because "Companies organize their records in different ways." Transcript of June 26, 2007 Evidentiary Hearing at 132. *See also United States v. El Paso Co.*, 682 F.2d 530, 533 (5th Cir. 1982) (noting the many names for tax accrual workpapers).

principles (GAAP) so that a "clean" opinion would be given with respect to the financial statements filed by Textron with the SEC.

Each year, Textron's tax accrual workpapers are prepared shortly after the corporation's tax return is filed. The first step in preparing the workpapers is that Textron's accountants circulate to Textron's attorneys a copy of the previous year's tax accrual workpapers together with recommendations regarding their proposed changes and/or additions for the current year. Textron's attorneys, then, review those materials, propose further changes to the spreadsheets and hazard litigation percentages which are returned to the accountants who compile the information and perform the mathematical calculations necessary to compute the tax reserve amounts. The attorneys and accountants, then, meet to give their approval so that the accountants may finalize the workpapers.

TFC goes through a similar process in preparing its tax accrual workpapers but, since TFC does not have any in-house attorneys, its accountants rely on tax advice obtained from outside accounting and law firms, before meeting with a Textron tax attorney to finalize the workpapers.

Once the tax reserve amounts for each item on the worksheets are established, those amounts are aggregated with other contingent liabilities and the total is reported as "other liabilities" on Textron's financial statements.

During the course of an audit conducted by Ernst & Young (E&Y), Textron's independent auditor, Textron permitted E&Y to examine the final tax accrual workpapers at issue in this case with the understanding that the information was to be treated as confidential.

Analysis

I. The Summons

A. Scope and Enforceability, in General

Section 7602 authorizes the IRS to issue administrative summonses for the production of "any books, papers, records, or other data which may be relevant or material" in "ascertaining the correctness of any return, . . . , determining the liability of any person for any internal revenue tax . . . , or collecting any such liability . . . ." 26 U.S.C. § 7602(a). The Supreme Court has described § 7502 as a "broad summons authority" reflecting a "congressional policy choice *in favor of disclosure* of all information relevant to a legitimate IRS inquiry." *United States v. Arthur Young & Co.*, 465 U.S. 805, 816, 104 S. Ct. 1495, 1502, 79 L. Ed. 2d 826 (1984).

When documents requested in a summons are not produced, the United States may petition a federal district court for an order compelling compliance. 26 U.S.C. § 7604. To obtain such an order, the IRS must show: (1) that there is a legitimate purpose for the investigation pursuant to which the summons is being sought, (2) that the inquiry or the materials sought may be relevant to that purpose, (3) that the information sought is not already within the Commissioner's possession, and (4) that the administrative steps required by the Code have been followed. *United States v. Powell*, 379 U.S. 48, 57–58, 85 S. Ct. 248, 255, 13 L. Ed. 2d 112 (1964).

The government may make a prima facie showing that those requirements have been satisfied "on the face of the summons and by supporting affidavits." *United States v. Freedom Church*, 613 F.2d 315, 321 (1st Cir. 1979). *See also United States v. Lawn Builders of New England, Inc.*, 855 F.2d 388, 392 (1st Cir. 1988) ("Assertions by affidavit of the investigating agent that the requirements are satisfied are sufficient to make the prima facie case.") (quoting *Liberty Financial Servs. v. United States*, 778 F.2d 1390, 1392 (9th Cir. 1985)). When the requisite showing has been made, the burden shifts to the party summoned to present evidence that the *Powell* requirements have not been satisfied or that there is some other reason why the summons should not be enforced. *Freedom Church*, 513 F.2d at 319 (citing, *inter alia*, *United States v. LaSalle Nat. Bank*, 437 U.S. 298, 316, 98 S. Ct. 2357, 57 L. Ed. 2d 221 (1978)).

In this case, Textron does not dispute that the documents sought may be relevant[n.3] or that the IRS has followed the necessary administrative steps in issuing the summons. Rather, Textron argues that the IRS seeks the documents for the purpose of using them as leverage in settlement negotiations and that the documents are privileged.

* * *

II. Applicability of Privilege

Satisfaction of the *Powell* requirements is not sufficient to warrant enforcement of an IRS summons if the documents sought are privileged. *Upjohn Co. v. United States*, 449 U.S. 383, 386, 101 S. Ct. 677, 681, 66 L. Ed. 2d 584 (1981) (refusing to enforce IRS summons because documents sought contained communications protected by the attorney-client privilege and also recognizing that "the work-product doctrine does apply in tax summons enforcement proceedings."). In general, when a claim of privilege is made, the party asserting the privilege "has the burden of establishing not only the existence of that privilege, but also that the privilege was not waived." *In re Raytheon Sec. Litig.*, 218 F.R.D. 354, 357 (D. Mass. 2003).

In this case, Textron argues that its tax accrual workpapers are protected by the attorney-client privilege, the tax practitioner-client privilege created by 26 U.S.C. § 7525, and the work product privilege.

A. Attorney-Client Privilege

The attorney-client privilege protects confidential communications between an attorney and client relating to legal advice sought from the attorney. *See United States v. Bisanti*, 414 F.3d 168, 171 (1st Cir. 2005); *Cavallaro v. United States*, 284 F.3d 236, 245 (1st Cir. 2002). Since the privilege may hamper the search for truth by preventing the disclosure of relevant evidence, it is narrowly construed. *In re Keeper of Records (XYZ Corp.)*, 348 F.3d 16, 22 (1st Cir. 2003) ("the attorney-client privilege must be narrowly construed because it comes with substantial costs and stands as an obstacle of sorts to the search for truth."). Narrow construction of the privilege is especially called for in the case of tax investigations because of "the 'congressional policy choice *in favor of disclosure* of all information relevant to a legitimate IRS inquiry.' " *Cavallaro*, 284 F.3d at 245 (quoting *Arthur Young*, 465 U.S. at 816).

Textron's affidavits state that its tax accrual workpapers are privileged because they were prepared by counsel and reflect counsel's legal conclusions in identifying items on Textron's return that may be challenged and assessing Textron's prospects of prevailing in any ensuing litigation. (Richter Aft. ¶¶ 13, 22.) The IRS argues that the workpapers are not privileged because, in preparing them, Textron's attorneys were not providing legal advice but, rather, were performing an accounting function by reconciling the company's tax records and financial statements.

It is true that, generally, the mere preparation of a tax return is viewed as accounting work and a taxpayer may not cloak the documents generated in that process with a privilege simply "by hiring a lawyer to do the work that an accountant, or other tax

---

[n.3] In *United States v. Arthur Young & Co.*, 465 U.S. 805, 104 S. Ct. 1495, 79 L. Ed. 2d 826 (1984), the Supreme Court held that an IRS summons satisfies the *relevance* prong of the *Powell* test if the documents sought " 'might have thrown light upon' the correctness of [the taxpayer's] return," *Arthur Young*, 465 U.S at 813–14, and that the "tax accrual workpapers" involved in that case, which were prepared by the taxpayer's outside auditor, satisfied that relevance standard. 465 U.S. at 815.

preparer, or the taxpayer himself . . . normally would do." *United States v. Frederick*, 182 F.3d 496, 500 (7th Cir. 1999). *See* E.G. Epstein, *The Attorney-Client Privilege and the Work-Product Doctrine* 246 (4th ed. 2001). On the other hand, it is equally true that communications containing legal advice provided by an attorney may be privileged even though they are made in connection with the preparation of a return.

> Determining the tax consequences of a particular transaction is rooted entirely in the law . . . . [Therefore] [c]ommunications offering tax advice or discussing tax planning . . . are 'legal' communications.

U.S. v. Chevron Texaco Corp., 241 F. Supp. 2d 1065, 1076 (N.D. Cal. 2002). *See* Epstein, at 249; Louis F. Lobenhoffer, *The New Tax Practitioner Privilege: Limited Privilege and Significant Disruption*, 26 Ohio N.U. L. Rev. 243, 252 (2000) (the attorney-client privilege should not be lost when true legal advice or lawyer's work is performed, albeit in support of an accounting or financial reporting function).

The Seventh Circuit explained the distinction, in the context of an IRS audit, by stating that where representation during an audit consists of "merely verifying the accuracy of a return," it is "accountants' work"; but, if the attorney participates in the audit "to deal with issues of statutory interpretation or case law" that may have been raised in connection with examination of the taxpayer's return, "the lawyer is doing lawyer's work and the attorney-client privilege may attach." *Frederick*, 182 F.3d at 502. Furthermore, in *United States v. El Paso Co.*, the Fifth Circuit addressed the distinction as it applies specifically to tax accrual workpapers by observing that, while preparation of tax accrual workpapers might be considered an accounting function, "we would be reluctant to hold that a lawyer's analysis of the soft spots in a tax return and his judgment on the outcome of the litigation on it are not legal advice."*United States v. El Paso Co.*, 682 F.2d 530, 539 (5th Cir. 1982).

Here, since the tax accrual workpapers of Textron and TFC essentially consist of nothing more than counsel's opinions regarding items that might be challenged because they involve areas in which the law is uncertain and counsel's assessment regarding Textron's chances of prevailing in any ensuing litigation, they are protected by the attorney-client privilege.

The IRS's reliance on *Arthur Young* is misplaced because, although *Arthur Young* deemed tax accrual workpapers pinpointing the "soft spots" on a corporation's tax return *relevant* to examination of the corporation's return, it did not hold the attorney-client privilege inapplicable to legal conclusions of counsel contained in the workpapers. On the contrary, *Arthur Young* expressly recognized that "§ 7602 is 'subject to the traditional privileges and limitations.' " *Arthur Young*, 465 U.S. at 816 (citation omitted). *Arthur Young* also is distinguishable on the ground that, there, the workpapers had been prepared by the corporation's independent auditor whose "obligation to serve the public interest assures that the integrity of the securities markets will be preserved." *Arthur Young*, 465 U.S. at 819. By contrast, Textron's workpapers were prepared by its counsel whose function was to provide legal advice to Textron.

* * *

Conclusion

For all of the foregoing reasons, the government's petition to enforce the summons is denied.

The *Textron* court distinguished *Arthur Young* on the ground that Textron's workpapers were prepared by its legal counsel while the workpapers in *Arthur Young* were prepared by its outside auditor. How does that square with the *Textron* court's recognition that "generally, the mere preparation of a tax return is viewed as accounting work and a taxpayer may not cloak the documents generated in that process with a privilege simply 'by hiring a lawyer to do the work that an accountant, or other tax preparer, or the taxpayer himself . . . normally would do' "? *Textron, supra* (*quoting* United States v. Frederick, 182 F.3d 496, 500 (7th Cir. 1999)).

[c] The Crime-Fraud Exception

The attorney-client privilege is subject to exceptions. In addition to the waiver doctrine, which was mentioned above, the "crime-fraud exception" applies "where the desired advice refers *not to prior wrongdoing*, but to *future wrongdoing*.' " United States v. Zolin, 491 U.S. 554, 562–63 (1989) (quoting 8 Wigmore, § 2298, p. 573 (emphasis in original)). The Supreme Court has further stated, "[i]t is the purpose of the crime-fraud exception to the attorney-client privilege to assure that the 'seal of secrecy,' . . . between lawyer and client does not extend to communications 'made for the purpose of getting advice for the commission of a fraud' or crime." *Id.* at 563 (*quoting* 8 Wigmore, § 2298, p. 573).

In summons enforcement litigation involving the accounting firm BDO Seidman:

> The IRS argues that the Intervenors cannot assert attorney-client privilege, tax practitioner privilege or the work product doctrine because the Intervenors were involved in fraudulent transactions by purchasing illegal tax shelters from BDO and BDO and the Intervenors attempt to inappropriately conceal these transactions from the IRS. The IRS supports its argument by pointing to the decision in *Denny v. Jenkens & Gilchrist*, where Judge Scheindlin determined that BDO had entered into a mutually fraudulent consulting agreement. 340 F. Supp. 2d 338, 346–47 (S.D.N.Y. 2004). The IRS also provides the declaration of IRS Revenue Agent Sandra Alvelo and a number of documents obtained through the IRS summonses from BDO.
>
> The IRS presents a picture of BDO, along with firms of Jenkens & Gilchrist, ("J&G"), Diversified Group, Inc., Helios, ICA-Bricolage and Gramercy, and Brown and Wood, ("B&W") as producers, marketers and implementers of allegedly illegal tax shelters. The IRS' argument is that BDO produces financial transactions or "tax products" that it markets to clients who are looking to evade their tax liabilities. By its continual reference to these transactions as "abusive," "pre-packaged," and "cookie cutter," the IRS is attempting to brand BDO as the proprietor of "off-shelf" prepackaged retail tax shelters sold to the Intervenors for the singular unlawful purpose of evading tax liability.
>
> In essence, the IRS alleges that everything done by BDO, the third party law firms and the Intervenors in these transactions, under the guise of a legitimate business purpose, is nothing more than an attempt to cover-up the unlawful purpose of the tax shelters. The IRS asserts this type of cover-up is necessary because the allegedly illegal tax shelters produced and marketed by BDO are the same or substantially the same as ones that have been previously determined to have been abusive in published IRS notices. The IRS concludes that since BDO and the Intervenors must be aware of the illegal nature of BDO's tax products, BDO and the Intervenors must be engaged in a practice of concealing its illegal activities and this deprives them of the benefits of attorney-client, tax practitioner and work-product privileges under the crime-fraud exception.

United States v. BDO Seidman, LLP, 2005 U.S. Dist. LEXIS 5555 (E.D. Ill. 2005) at *25–27. The District Court ruled that it would consider the applicability of the exception when it reviewed the documents *in camera*. *Id.* at *33. Ultimately, it found that a *prima facie* case for application of the crime-fraud exception existed with respect to only one document, Document A-40. *Id.* at *43. The court explained that "The privilege log states that Document A-40 is an e-mail sent from BDO employee Michael Kerekes to BDO employees Robert Greisman and Lawrence Cohen and a copy was provided to Paul Shanbrom. . . . " *Id.* at *43 n.8. The content of that e-mail is not made clear.

In a later decision, the court held that the crime-fraud exception applied to that document. *United States v. BDO Seidman, LLP*, 2005-2 U.S.T.C. ¶ 50,447 (N.D. Ill. 2005). On appeal, the Court of Appeals for the Seventh Circuit affirmed, stating:

> The crime-fraud exception places communications made in furtherance of a crime or fraud outside the attorney-client privilege. *United States v. Zolin,* 491 U.S. 554, 563, 109 S. Ct. 2619, 105 L. Ed. 2d 469 (1989). The exception is based on the recognition that the privilege necessarily will "protect the confidences of wrongdoers." *Id.* at 562. This cost is accepted as necessary to achieve the privilege's purpose of promoting the "broader public interests in the observance of law and the administration of justice." *Id.* (quoting *Upjohn Co. v. United States,* 449 U.S. 383, 389, 101 S. Ct. 677, 66 L. Ed. 2d 584 (1981)) (internal quotation marks omitted). However, when the advice sought relates "*not to prior wrongdoing,* but to *future wrongdoing,*" the privilege goes beyond what is necessary to achieve its beneficial purposes. *Id.* at 562–63 (quoting 8 John Henry Wigmore, Evidence In Trials At Common Law § 2298 (John T. McNaughton rev. 1961)) (internal quotation marks omitted) (emphasis in original).
>
> To invoke the crime-fraud exception, the party seeking to abrogate the attorney-client privilege must present prima facie evidence that "gives colour to the charge" by showing "some foundation in fact." *Al-Shahin,* 474 F.3d at 946 (quoting *Clark v. United States,* 289 U.S. 1, 15, 53 S. Ct. 465, 77 L. Ed. 993 (1933)) (internal quotation marks omitted). The party seeking to abrogate the privilege meets its burden by bringing forth sufficient evidence to justify the district court in requiring the proponent of the privilege to come forward with an explanation for the evidence offered against it. *See United States v. Davis,* 1 F.3d 606, 609 (7th Cir. 1993). The privilege will remain "if the district court finds [the] explanation satisfactory." *Id.*
>
> BDO and the Intervenors would require the party seeking to abrogate the attorney-client privilege to make out a prima facie case of each element of a particular crime or common law fraud to invoke the crime-fraud exception. Such a burden is inconsistent with our requirement that the party seeking to abrogate the privilege need only "give colour to the charge" by showing "some foundation in fact." *Al-Shahin,* 474 F.3d at 946 (quoting *Clark,* 289 U.S. at 15) (internal quotation marks omitted). The approach advocated by BDO and the Intervenors reflects the view of some circuits, which require enough evidence of crime or fraud to support a verdict in order to invoke the crime-fraud exception. *See In re Feldberg,* 862 F.2d 622, 625 (7th Cir. 1988). We expressly have rejected that approach. *See id.*
>
> We therefore must determine whether the district court abused its discretion in determining that the IRS had come forward with sufficient evidence to give color to its charge that Document A-40 was a communication in furtherance of a crime or fraud. The district court engaged in a document-by-document, *in camera* inspection of all 267 documents for which the Intervenors claimed a privilege to determine whether they fell within the crime-fraud exception. R.178 at 18. In determining whether there was prima facie evidence of criminal or fraudulent activity, the court looked at the totality of the circumstances, including the eight "potential indicators of fraud" discussed above.[n.10] *See id.* at

---

[n.10] As noted above, the eight potential indicators of fraud identified by the district court were:

> (1) the marketing of pre-packaged transactions by BDO; (2) the communication by the Intervenors to BDO with the purpose of engaging in a pre-arranged transaction developed by BDO or [a] third party with the sole purpose of reducing taxable income; (3) BDO and/or the Intervenors attempting to conceal the true nature of the transaction; (4) knowledge by BDO, or a situation where BDO

23. Based on the totality of circumstances, the district court found no prima facie evidence of crime or fraud with respect to 266 of the documents, a ruling that the IRS does not challenge.

Applying the same totality of the circumstance approach, the district court found prima facie evidence of crime or fraud with respect to Document A-40 and instructed the Intervenors to come forward with an explanation that would rebut the evidence. *Id.* at 24. The Intervenors responded and the IRS provided further evidence to rebut the Intervenors' response. After considering all of the evidence, the district court concluded that the Intervenors had failed to rebut the prima facie showing of crime or fraud. R.190 at 10.

The Intervenors now challenge the district court's ruling. First, the Intervenors point to the decision of the United States Court of Appeals for the Second Circuit in *Denney v. BDO Seidman, L.L.P.*, 412 F.3d 58 (2005), which reversed *Denney v. Jenkens & Gilchrist,* one of the cases from which the district court derived its potential indicators of fraud. *See Denney v. BDO Seidman,* 412 F.3d at 66. The Second Circuit's decision in *Denney v. BDO Seidman* does not draw into question the district court's totality of the circumstances analysis in this case.

In *Denney v. BDO Seidman,* the Second Circuit held that the District Court for the Southern District of New York had erred when it concluded, without factual support in the record, that the parties had agreed that their agreements were mutually fraudulent. *Denney v. BDO Seidman,* 412 F.3d at 66. The Second Circuit's decision did not address whether facts such as mention of the COBRA transaction, vaguely worded consulting agreements or failure to provide services under the consulting agreements, i.e., the factors that the district court in the present case derived from *Denney v. Jenkens & Gilchrist,* would be indicative of fraud. Moreover, the district court in the present case did not place dispositive weight on any one of the "potential indicators of fraud," nor did the court limit its analysis to the eight potential indicators. R.190 at 5.

The remainder of the Intervenors' challenge asserts that the IRS could not defeat the Intervenors' claim of privilege under the crime-fraud exception because the IRS had failed to allege a particular offense or the elements of common law fraud, and, in any event, the Intervenors had come forward with rebuttal evidence showing a legitimate purpose underlying the transactions in question. As we already have noted, our case law does not require a party seeking to invoke the crime-fraud exception to allege a particular offense or to make a prima facie showing with respect to each element of common law fraud. The IRS only was required to present sufficient evidence to "give colour to the charge" that the communication was made in furtherance of a crime or fraud by showing "some foundation in fact." *Al-Shahin,* 474 F.3d at 946 (quoting *Clark,* 289 U.S. at 15) (internal quotation marks omitted).

After concluding that there had been a prima facie showing that Document A-40 was a communication made in furtherance of a crime or fraud, the district court gave the Intervenors the opportunity to explain the communication. The Intervenors offered an explanation, but the district court did not find it satisfactory. Nor was the district court required to find the explanation satisfactory. Thus, the district court did not abuse its discretion when it concluded that the IRS had made a prima facie showing of crime or fraud which

---

should have known, that the Intervenors lacked a legitimate business purpose for entering into the transaction; (5) vaguely worded consulting agreements; (6) failure by BDO to provide services under the consulting agreement yet receipt of payment; (7) mention of the COBRA transaction; and (8) use of boiler-plate documents.

R.178 at 23.

the Intervenors failed to explain satisfactorily.

United States of America v. BDO Seidman, LLP, 492 F.3d 806, 818–20 (7th Cir. 2007).

[2] The Work-Product Doctrine

"The work-product doctrine traces back to *Hickman v. Taylor*, 329 U.S. 495 (1947). It is now codified in Rule 26(b)(3) of the Federal Rules of Civil Procedure . . . ." Peter A. Lowy & Juan F. Vasquez, Jr., *When Is the Work of a Tax Professional Done in Anticipation of Litigation and Thus "Work Product"?*, 98 J. TAX'N 155 (2003). Federal Rule of Civil Procedure 26(b)(3) provides:

> (A) Ordinarily, a party may not discover documents and tangible things that are prepared in anticipation of litigation or for trial by or for another party or its representative (including the other party's attorney, consultant, surety, indemnitor, insurer, or agent). But, subject to Rule 26(b)(4), those materials may be discovered if:
>
> (i) they are otherwise discoverable under Rule 26(b)(1); and
>
> (ii) the party shows that it has substantial need for the materials to prepare its case and cannot, without undue hardship, obtain their substantial equivalent by other means.
>
> (B) *Protection Against Disclosure.* If the court orders discovery of those materials, it must protect against disclosure of the mental impressions, conclusions, opinions, or legal theories of a party's attorney or other representative concerning the litigation.

The following excerpt provides an excellent overview of the application of the work-product doctrine in federal tax cases:[6]

Martin J. McMahon, Jr. & Ira B. Shepard, *Privilege and the Work Product Doctrine in Tax Cases*

58 TAX LAW. 405 (2005)[7]

Information that is not protected by the attorney-client privilege sometimes is protected from discovery by the work product doctrine. . . . The work product doctrine, as presently embodied in Rule 26(b)(3), protects from discovery documents (and other tangible things) concerning litigation, prepared by an attorney or other representative of a party in anticipation of litigation or for trial, subject to exceptions for "substantial need" or "undue hardship."[n.168] It also protects documents that would reveal the attorney's mental impressions, conclusions, opinions, or legal theories, which are immune even from the substantial need exception.[n.169]

The breadth and strength of the work product doctrine compared to the attorney-client privilege is illustrated by *In re Grand Jury Subpoena Dated October 22, 2001*,[n.170] in which the government sought to subpoena the testimony of an attorney regarding statements made by the attorney's client to Service agents in an interview at which the attorney was present. Even though the attorney-client privilege did not apply, the work product doctrine was invoked to bar compulsion of testimony that might tend to prove

---

[6] The article was published before the Federal Rules of Civil Procedure were restyled in 2007. The restyling changed the wording somewhat.

[7]

[n.168] *See* FED. R. CIV. P. 26(b)(3) . . . . *See also generally* Peter A. Lowy and Juan F. Vasquez, Jr., *When is the Work of a Tax Professional Done in Anticipation of Litigation and Thus "Work Product"?*, 98 J. TAX'N 155 (2003).

[n.169] *See id.*

[n.170] 282 F.3d 156 (2d Cir. 2002).

the client's guilt with respect to a past crime.[n.171] The court went on, however, to address a potential argument of the government that in the course of the interview the attorney witnessed, the client committed the crime of making false statements to government officials. With respect to a possible subsequent subpoena issued by a different grand jury seeking the attorney's testimony regarding the false statements claim, the court stated, "If the use of Attorney's testimony were limited to proving that General Counsel committed the crime of false statements in Attorney's presence, the Government would have strong arguments that the work product privilege should not bar a prosecutor's access to eyewitness testimony of the commission of criminal acts."[n.173] Nevertheless, the court continued, by suggesting that even if that were the case, the government probably could not show substantial need to compel the attorney's testimony before the grand jury.

> [The government] can easily establish probable cause as to [the taxpayer's] General Counsel's alleged false statements through the testimony of [Special] Agent Nass, regardless whether Nass's testimony is corroborated. Thus, the Government's arguments as to its substantial need for Attorney's testimony to resolve a swearing contest at trial are not directly pertinent to its need to compel Attorney's testimony before the grand jury).[n.174]

The circuits have conflicting views regarding the scope of the work product doctrine. A line of cases from the Fifth Circuit, including *United States v. Davis*[n.175] and *United States v. El Paso Co.*,[n.176] exemplifies a "primarily to assist in litigation" formulation of the type of documents protected by the doctrine. Several other circuits, however, have adopted a broader zone of protection that extends to documents prepared "in anticipation of litigation."[n.177] The Second Circuit's decision in *United States v. Adlman*[n.178] is a leading example of the application of this view of the work product doctrine in a tax case. In *Adlman*, an accounting firm's memorandum regarding the tax consequences of a proposed merger was covered by the work product doctrine. The memorandum was provided to the person who served as both the corporation's vice-president for taxes and in-house counsel. The court reasoned that because the taxpayer expected the Service to challenge its treatment of the transaction, the memorandum had been prepared "in anticipation of litigation," even if not "primarily to assist in litigation."[n.179] The work product doctrine applied because due to the anticipated litigation, the document had been prepared in a different form than it would have been prepared if it had been prepared solely to assist in making a business decision. The court expressly declined to follow the narrower version of the work product doctrine applied in *El Paso Co.*[n.180]

[n.171] *Id.* at 158.

[n.173] 282 F.3d at 160.

[n.174] *Id.* at 161.

[n.175] 636 F.2d 1028, 1040 (5th Cir. 1981) (denying protection to documents made in the course of preparation of a tax return).

[n.176] 682 F.2d 530, 534 (5th Cir. 1982) (denying protection to documents that analyzed prospective liabilities that might result from examination of its tax returns because the documents were not prepared to assist in litigation but to justify reserves in El Paso's financial statements).

[n.177] Fed. R. Civ. P. 26(b)(3) . . . ; *see also, e.g., In re* Sealed Case, 146 F.3d 881, 884–85 (D.C. Cir. 1998) (explaining that there is no requirement that a specific claim have arisen at the time the document was prepared); Martin v. Bally's Park Place Hotel & Casino, 983 F.2d 1252, 1260–61 (3d Cir. 1993) (explaining that documents prepared because of party's " 'unilateral belief' that litigation will result" are protected as "prepared 'in anticipation of litigation,' " as long as the preparer's anticipation of litigation was objectively reasonable); Logan v. Commercial Union Ins. Co., 96 F.3d 971, 976–77 (7th Cir. 1996) ("the document can fairly be said to have been prepared or obtained because of the prospect of litigation").

[n.178] 134 F.3d 1194 (2d Cir. 1998).

[n.179] *Id.* at 1199.

[n.180] *Id.* at 1198. *See also In re* Grand Jury Subpoena (Mark Torf/Torf Environmental Management), 357

Even the "in anticipation of litigation" standard has its limits. In *United States v. Davis*[n.181] a Fifth Circuit decision pre-dating *El Paso Co.*, the court applied the "in anticipation of litigation" standard and nevertheless denied work product protection to tax work papers prepared by an attorney in connection with return preparation. There was "no evidence that [the client] had reason to expect future trouble with the [Service].[n.182] Similarly, *United States v. Randall*[n.183] held that the work product doctrine did not attach to documents prepared by a taxpayer's attorney in connection with return preparation and which were turned over to the taxpayer's accountant to help him represent the taxpayer in an audit. "[T]he taxpayers were under civil audit by the [Service], the case had not yet been referred for criminal investigation[, and] nothing in the record suggest[ed] that any of the documents . . . were prepared in anticipation of litigation."[n.184] More recently, the District Court for the District of Columbia has observed that, "[m]ere mention of fear of being sued for an action or inaction is not the sort of 'anticipation of litigation' which is covered by the attorney work-product doctrine."[n.185]

On the other hand, *Adlman* also illustrates the very important principle that the work product doctrine can protect documents and information that are not protected by the attorney-client privilege. The accounting firm's memorandum that was shielded by the work product doctrine in *Adlman* was found by the court in the same opinion not to be subject to attorney-client privilege because the taxpayer did not communicate any confidential information to a lawyer for the purpose of obtaining the lawyer's legal advice.[n.186] However, because it was covered by the work product doctrine, the Service could not obtain the memorandum. Likewise, in *Long-Term Capital Holdings v. United States*, a tax opinion from King & Spalding, with respect to which the attorney-client privilege had been waived, was found (after in camera inspection) to constitute work product under the Second Circuit's application of the doctrine in *Adlman* to documents prepared in anticipation of litigation.[n.187]

The work product doctrine has limits, however. Documents used by an attorney-tax preparer solely in preparation of tax returns for clients are not protected by the work product doctrine.[n.188] In addition, the work product doctrine does not protect from discovery documents prepared in the ordinary course of business or those which would have been created irrespective of litigation.[n.189] In *Bernardo v. Commissioner*, the Tax Court articulated the principle as follows: "A litigant must demonstrate that the documents were created 'with a specific claim supported by concrete facts which would likely lead to [the] litigation in mind,' not merely assembled in the ordinary course of

---

F.3d 900 (9th Cir. 2004) (holding that a document that served both business purposes or which was required in order to comply with a law, but which was also prepared in anticipation of litigation, was protected under the work product doctrine because "litigation purpose so permeates any non-litigation purpose that the two purposes cannot be discretely separated from the factual nexus as a whole").

n.181 636 F.2d 1028, 1040 (5th Cir. 1981).

n.182 *Id.*

n.183 99-1 U.S.T.C. ¶ 50,596, 83 A.F.T.R.2d 2795 (D. Mass. 1999).

n.184 *Id.* at 88,619, 83 A.F.T.R.2d at 2798.

n.185 United States v. KPMG LLP, 316 F. Supp. 2d 30, 41 (D.D.C. 2004).

n.186 134 F.3d 1194, 1196 (2d Cir. 1998).

n.187 2003-1 U.S.T.C. ¶ 50,304, at 89,792, 91 A.F.T.R.2d 1139, 1147 (D. Conn. 2003).

n.188 United States v. Abrahams, 905 F.2d 1276 (9th Cit. 1990).

n.189 Fed. R. Civ. P. 26(b)(3) advisory committee's note; *see, e.g.*, United States v. Davis, 636 F.2d 1028, 1040 (5th Cit 1981) (noting that tax workpapers prepared by attorney in connection with return preparation where there was "no evidence that [the client] had reason to expect future trouble with the [Service]"); Nat'l Union Fire Ins. Co. v. Murray Sheet Metal Co., 967 F.2d 980 (4th Cir. 1992).

business or for other nonlitigation purposes."[n.190]

In *SABA Partnership v. Commissioner*[n.191] the Tax Court held that the work product doctrine did not apply to a memorandum to a corporation's officers from its in-house counsel describing a tax shelter investment that Merrill Lynch proposed to the corporation, but which did not contain any communications from the corporation's officers to its attorney or any legal advice or analysis. The memorandum was not work product material because it did not reflect the attorney's opinions, judgments, or thought processes, but merely addressed factual matters.

Furthermore, not all results of an attorney's work in the course of litigation are protected work product. *Hambarian v. Commissioner*[n.192] provides an example. In the course of a state criminal proceeding arising from the same transactions that gave rise to the Tax Court deficiency proceeding, the taxpayer's criminal defense lawyer selected 100,000 pages of documents from a much larger amount in the possession of the prosecuting attorney and converted the documents into computer searchable media. In the Tax Court proceeding, the Service sought production of the documents and computer searchable media, but the taxpayer resisted on the grounds that the criminal defense lawyer's selection of the particular documents reflected his mental impressions and was therefore protected work product. The Tax Court held that in light of the extraordinary number of pages of otherwise discoverable documents that was involved, it was highly unlikely that the attorney's mental impressions would be discernable, and the mere selection of particular documents by the taxpayer's lawyer did not automatically transmute the documents into work product.[n.193] Because the taxpayer failed to otherwise demonstrate how disclosure of the selected documents would reveal the defense attorney's mental impressions of the case, the requested documents and computerized electronic media were not protected by the work product doctrine.[n.194]

* * *

A factual work product voluntarily disclosed to all the involved parties will result in a waiver of protection under the work product doctrine.[n.199] Similarly, if a party claims that reliance on advice of counsel is an important component of his or her claim or defense, the attorney's work product may be discoverable.[n.200]

Although not technically within the scope of attorney work product, experts' work product in anticipation of or in preparation for trial is generally protected, unless (1) an expert's opinion may be presented at trial, in which case it must be disclosed,[n.201] or (2) due to "exceptional circumstances" it is impractical for the other party to obtain information on the same subject by other means,[n.202] in which case it is discoverable.

In *Black & Decker Corp. v. United States*,[n.203] the government sought discovery of numerous documents prepared by the accounting firm Deloitte & Touche, which the

---

[n.190] Bernardo v. Commissioner, 104 T.C. 677, 687 (1995) (quoting Linde Thomson Langworthy Kohn & Van Dyke v. Resolution Trust Corp., 5 F.3d 1508, 1515 (D.C. Cir. 1993)).

[n.191] 78 T.C.M. (CCH) 684, 1999 T.C.M. (RIA) ¶ 99,359.

[n.192] 118 TC. 565 (2002).

[n.193] *Id.* at 571.

[n.194] *Id.* at 572.

[n.199] In re Steinhardt Partners, L.P., 9 F.3d 230, 235 (2d Cir. 1993) (trader's voluntary submission of legal memorandum to the Securities and Exchange Commission, with whom the trader stood in adversarial position as subject of SEC investigation in connection with which memorandum was sought, waived protection of work product doctrine).

[n.200] *E.g.*, Donovan v. Fitzsimmons, 90 F.R.D. 583, 588 (ND. III. 1981).

[n.201] Fed. R. Civ. P. 26(a)(2).

[n.202] Fed. R. Civ. P. 26(b)(4).

[n.203] 2003-2 U.S.T.C. ¶ 50,659, 92 A.F.T.R.2d 6426 (D. Md. 2003).

taxpayer had retained to give advice regarding the transactions that gave rise to the refund claim. Although certain communications to the taxpayer's in-house counsel were not subject to attorney-client privilege under the *Kovel* doctrine,[8] the documents nevertheless were protected under the work product doctrine.[n.204] The government conceded that the documents had been prepared in anticipation of litigation, but argued that the "privilege" for work product had been waived.[n.205] Although the court held that as a matter of law the work product doctrine can be waived when the party puts the work "in issue," it found on the facts that the work product in question had not been put "in issue."[n.206] That the documents may have related to an opinion letter on which the taxpayer was going to rely in an effort to avoid penalties — and with respect to which the taxpayer thus waived the privilege — did not result in waiver of the work product doctrine, which is "broader and more robust than the attorney-client privilege."[n.207] However, the court did not explain how an accounting firm's work became "attorney" work product, which is significant because the section 7525 privilege (which was not expressly raised in the case) does not have a "work product" variant.

* * *

Note that the work-product doctrine generally provides less than complete protection for documents and tangible things prepared in anticipation of litigation (or for trial), as they are subject to a "substantial need" exception. *See* McMahon & Shepard, *supra*, at 429; Fed. R. Civ. P. 26(b)(3)(A)(ii). However, "[i]t also protects documents that would reveal the attorney's mental impressions, conclusions, opinions, or legal theories, which are immune from even the substantial need exception." McMahon & Shepard, *supra*, at 429; *see also* Fed. R. Civ. P. 26(b)(3)(B).

The McMahon & Shepard excerpt discusses the meaning of "in anticipation of litigation." More recently, in *United States v. Roxworthy*, 457 F.3d 590 (6th Cir. 2006), involving Yum Brands, Inc. ("Yum"), the Court of Appeals for the Sixth Circuit defined that phrase broadly. It adopted the "because of" test used by a majority of circuits — which protects documents prepared because of anticipated litigation — rather than the stricter "primary purpose" test that asks whether the documents in question were prepared "primarily or exclusively to assist in litigation," United States v. Adlman, 134 F.3d 1194, 1198 (2d Cir. 1998) (discussed above in the McMahon & Shepard excerpt). *See* Sheryl Stratton, *Work Product Alive and Well in the Sixth Circuit*, 112 Tax Notes 729, 731 (2006). The Court of Federal Claims has since adopted the "because of" test, as well. *See* Evergreen Trading, LLC v. United States, 80 Fed. Cl. 122, 133 (2007).

In *Roxworthy*, the Court of Appeals for the Sixth Circuit stated:

> We have yet to define "in anticipation of litigation." Other circuits have adopted the standard first articulated in Wright and Miller's Federal Practice and Procedures, asking whether a document was "prepared or obtained *because of* the prospect of litigation." *United States v. Adlman (Adlman II)*, 134 F.3d 1194, 1202 (2d Cir. 1998); *accord Nat'l Union Fire Ins. Co. of Pittsburgh v. Murray Sheet Metal Co.*, 967 F.2d 980, 984 (4th Cir. 1992); *Binks Mfg. Co. v. Nat'l Presto Indus., Inc.*, 709 F.2d 1109, 1119 (7th Cir. 1983); *In re Grand Jury Proceedings*, 604 F.2d 798, 803 (3d Cir. 1979). We have articulated and applied the "because of" standard in our unpublished cases . . . , and district courts from our circuit have also applied this test . . . . Today, we join our sister

---

[8] [The *Kovel* doctrine is discussed below. — Eds.]

[n.204] *Id.* at 89,496–97, 92 A.F.T.R.2d at 6430–31.

[n.205] *Id.* at 89,495, 92 A.F.T.R.2d at 6429.

[n.206] *Id.* at 89,496–97, 92 A.F.T.R.2d at 6430.

[n.207] *Id.* at 89,496, 92 A.F.T.R.2d at 6430.

> circuits and adopt the "because of" test as the standard for determining whether documents were prepared "in anticipation of litigation."
>
> Adopting this standard prompts the further question of when documents can be said to have been created because of the prospect of litigation. It is clear that documents prepared in the ordinary course of business, or pursuant to public requirements unrelated to litigation, or for other nonlitigation purposes, are not covered by the work product privilege. Fed. R. Civ. P. 26(b)(3) advisory committee's notes (1970); *Nat'l Union*, 967 F.2d at 984; *In re Sealed Case*, 146 F.3d 881, 888, 330 U.S. App. D.C. 368 (D.C. Cir. 1998). Thus, a document will not be protected if it would have been prepared in substantially the same manner irrespective of the anticipated litigation. *Adlman II*, 134 F.3d at 1205.
>
> Furthermore, courts applying the "because of" test have typically recognized both a subjective and objective element to the inquiry; that is, a party must "have had a subjective belief that litigation was a real possibility, and that belief must have been objectively reasonable." *In re Sealed Case*, 146 F.3d 881, 884, 330 U.S. App. D.C. 368; *see also Martin v. Bally's Park Place Hotel & Casino*, 983 F.2d 1252, 1260 (3d Cir. 1993) (requiring anticipation to be objectively reasonable); *Nat'l Union*, 967 F.2d at 984 (same); *Guardsmark*, 206 F.R.D. at 20-10 (following *In re Sealed Case*). We therefore embrace the test used by a number of the district courts in our circuit, including the district court in this case, which asks (1) whether a document was created because of a party's subjective anticipation of litigation, as contrasted with an ordinary business purpose, and (2) whether that subjective anticipation of litigation was objectively reasonable. *See, e.g., In re OM Group Sec. Litig.*, 226 F.R.D. at 584–85; *Guardsmark*, 206 F.R.D. at 209–10.

United States v. Roxworthy, 457 F.3d 590, 593–94 (6th Cir. 2006).

Most noteworthy is that the *Roxworthy* court found the subjective and objective anticipation of litigation aspects met with respect to the document in question, which was a tax opinion prepared by accounting firm KPMG. A tax opinion, normally used as protection against the imposition of penalties by the IRS, might not necessarily be considered a document prepared in anticipation of litigation. With respect to the objective test, the court stated:

> Although not every audit is potentially the subject of litigation, . . . a document prepared "in anticipation of 'dealing with the IRS' . . . may well have been prepared in anticipation of an administrative dispute and this may constitute 'litigation' within the meaning of Rule 26," *Hodges, Grant & Kaufmann v. IRS*, 768 F.2d 719, 719–22 (5th Cir. 1985).
>
> Here, Yum argues that it anticipated litigation because a yearly IRS audit of Yum was a certainty due to the company's size, the transaction at issue involved a $112 million discrepancy between tax loss and book loss, and the company had been advised by KPMG that the area of law was unsettled and that the IRS had recently targeted this type of transaction. Yum points to a case with analogous facts in which a district court upheld the work-product privilege. In *Chevron-Texaco*, 241 F. Supp. 2d at 1082, as here, the company's tax returns were routinely examined by the IRS, the company was engaged in a transaction involving "a very substantial amount of tax dollars," and the IRS "had previously questioned similar transactions." The court concluded that the withholding party "reasonably believed that it was a virtual certainty that the IRS would challenge the . . . transaction." *Id.*
>
> Likewise, in *United States v. Adlman*, 68 F.3d 1495, 1496 (2d Cir. 1995) (*Adlman I*), an accounting firm prepared documents evaluating the tax consequences and likely IRS challenges to a company's proposed reorganization in which the company would claim a capital loss of $290 million. The Second Circuit

> held that the district court erred in concluding that the prospect of litigation was too remote for work-product privilege to apply, observing that "[i]n many instances, the expected litigation is quite concrete, notwithstanding that the events giving rise to it have not yet occurred." *Id.* at 1501. The court remanded the matter for the district court to apply the proper standard.
>
> We find these factually analogous cases persuasive. As contemplated by *Adlman I*, Yum has demonstrated that the "expected litigation" here is "quite concrete" despite the absence of any overt indication from the IRS that it intends to pursue litigation against Yum. Yum has identified a specific transaction that could precipitate litigation, the specific legal controversy that would be at issue in the litigation, the opposing party's opportunity to discover the facts that would give rise to the litigation, and the opposing party's general inclination to pursue this sort of litigation. We believe that Yum has established that the memoranda at issue sought to protect Yum "from future litigation about a particular transaction," *see In re Sealed Case*, 146 F.3d at 885, that Yum has also established that KPMG and Yum had in mind a "specific claim supported by concrete facts which would likely lead to litigation," *see Coastal States*, 617 F.2d at 865, and that Yum has established that it "face[d] an actual or a potential claim following an actual event or series of events that reasonably could result in litigation," *Nat'l Union*, 967 F.2d at 984. Because we believe that Yum's circumstances clearly constitute objectively reasonable anticipation of litigation under any of the tests we have seen employed by our sister circuits, we need not decide which of these articulations is most useful.
>
> We therefore conclude that the district court committed an error of law in determining that Yum's anticipation of litigation was too remote to constitute a reasonable anticipation of litigation.

Roxworthy, 457 F.3d at 600–01. Does the court's analysis convince you that the KPMG tax opinion was prepared in anticipation of litigation?

United States v. Textron Inc., excerpted above, also discusses the work-product doctrine, including the meaning of "in anticipation of litigation." In *Textron*, the District Court applied the "because of" test because that is the test that was adopted by the Court of Appeals for the First Circuit. *See* Maine v. Dept. of the Interior, 298 F.3d 60, 68 (1st Cir. 2002). It found that Textron's tax accrual workpapers were prepared in legitimate anticipation of possible litigation with the IRS over several items on its tax return. *Id.* at 150. The court distinguished *El Paso*, which had found tax accrual workpapers to be business documents, because *El Paso* had applied the primary purpose test. *Id.* In the excerpt below from the *Textron* opinion, note the discussion of waiver of the work-product privilege and the "substantial need" exception to the privilege.

UNITED STATES v. TEXTRON INC.[9]

United States District Court, District of Rhode Island
507 F. Supp. 2d 138 (2007)

* * *

III. Waiver or Loss of Privilege

* * *

B. The Work Product Privilege

1. Waiver

Since the work product privilege serves a purpose different from the attorney-client or tax practitioner privileges, the kind of conduct that waives the privilege also differs.

The purpose of the attorney-client and tax practitioner privileges is to encourage the full and frank discussion necessary for providing the client with sound advice. That purpose is achieved by guaranteeing that confidential communications between the client and the advisor will remain confidential. Since disclosure to a third party is inconsistent with a claim of confidentiality, such disclosure waives the privilege.

By contrast, the purpose of the work product privilege is to prevent a potential adversary from gaining an unfair advantage over a party by obtaining documents prepared by the party or its counsel in anticipation of litigation which may reveal the party's strategy or the party's own assessment of the strengths and weaknesses of its case. Accordingly, only disclosures that are inconsistent with keeping the information from an adversary constitute a waiver of the work product privilege. *Gutter*, 1988 WL 2017926 *3 (S.D. Fl. 1998) ("While disclosure to outside auditors may waive the attorney-client privilege, it does not waive the work product privilege"). As the First Circuit stated in *United States v. Massachusetts Institute of Technology*, (*"MIT"*), 129 F.3d 681 (1st Cir. 1997):

> The [attorney-client] privilege is designed to protect confidentiality, so that any disclosure outside the magic circle is inconsistent with the privilege; by contrast, work product protection is provided against "adversaries," so only disclosing material in a way inconsistent with keeping it from an adversary waives work product protection.

129 F.3d at 687 (collecting cases). *See Jaffe Pension Plan*, 237 F.R.D. at 183 ("[T]he work product privilege may be waived by disclosures to third parties 'in a manner which substantially increases the opportunity for potential adversaries to obtain the information.' ") (citation omitted); *In re Raytheon Sec. Litig.*, 218 F.R.D. at 360 (D. Mass. 2003) ("[D]isclosure of a document to third persons does not waive the protection unless it has substantially increased the opportunity for potential adversaries to obtain the information.").

Most courts considering the question have held that disclosure of information to an independent auditor does not waive the work product privilege because it does not substantially increase the opportunity for potential adversaries to obtain the information. *In re JDS Uniphase Corp. Sec. Litig.*, 2006 WL 2850049 (N.D. Cal. 2006) (work product protection not waived when protected board minutes were disclosed to the independent auditor); *Jaffe Pension Plan*, 237 F.R.D. at 183 (Because an independent auditor does not have an adversarial relationship with the client, "[d]isclosing documents

[9] This case was decided before the Federal Rules of Civil Procedure were restyled in 2007.

to an auditor does not substantially increase the opportunity for potential adversaries to obtain the information."); *Frank Betz Assocs., Inc. v. Jim Walter Homes Inc.*, 226 F.R.D. 533, 535 (D.S.C. 2005) (disclosure to independent auditor of documents supporting reserve for copyright infringement litigation did not waive work product protection); *Merrill Lynch & Co., Inc. v. Allegheny Energy, Inc.*, 229 F.R.D. 441 (S.D.N.Y. 2004) (even though an auditor "must maintain an independent role," disclosure to auditor not a waiver of work product privilege because no likelihood that the independent auditors were a conduit to an adversary . . . or that accounting rules would "mandate public disclosure" of the documents); *Gutter*, 1998 WL 2017926 *5, *3 (S.D. Fl. 1998) (work product privilege not waived by disclosure to auditor of letters estimating cost of litigation "since the accountants are not considered a conduit to a potential adversary" and "there is an expectation that confidentiality of such information will be maintained by the recipient."); *In re Pfizer Inc. Sec. Litig.*, 1993 WL 561125 *6 (S.D.N.Y. 2003) (no waiver of work product privilege because auditor "not reasonably viewed as a conduit to a potential adversary.").

In this case, too, the disclosure of Textron's tax accrual workpapers to E&Y did not substantially increase the IRS's opportunity to obtain the information contained in them. Under AICPA Code of Professional Conduct Section 301 *Confidential Client Information*, E&Y had a professional obligation "not [to] disclos[e] any confidential client information without the specific consent of the client." Furthermore, *E&Y* expressly agreed not to provide the information to any other party, and confirms that it has adhered to its promise. (Weston Af. ¶ 3; Raymond Aft. ¶ 20.). Even if the AICPA Code coupled with E&Y's promise did not establish an absolute guarantee of confidentiality, they made it very unlikely that E&Y would provide Textron's "tax accrual workpapers" to the IRS and they negate any inference that Textron waived the work product privilege.[n.4]

The IRS cites *MIT* for the proposition that disclosure to an independent auditor waives work product protection but that reliance is misplaced because *MIT* is factually distinguishable from this case. The documents at issue in *MIT* were minutes of meetings of the MIT Corporation and some of its committees relating to bills submitted by MIT for services rendered pursuant to a contract with the Department of Defense (DOD). The documents were requested by the Defense Contract Audit Agency (DCAA) in order to confirm that the bills were justified and MIT provided the minutes due, in part, to the fact that DCAA "regulations and practices offered MIT some reason to think that indiscriminate disclosure was unlikely." *MIT*, 129 F.3d at 683. The First Circuit assumed, without deciding, that the documents were protected work product, but held that the documents had to be produced in response to an IRS summons because disclosure had been made to the DCAA, "a potential adversary." *Id.* at 687.

The difference between this case and *MIT* is that, in *MIT*, DOD was MIT's potential litigation adversary and DCAA, as DOD's audit agency, had both an obligation to DOD to determine whether the amounts charged by MIT to DOD were correct, and the authority to sue MIT in order to recover any overcharges. By contrast, in this case, E&Y was a truly independent auditor that had no obligation to the IRS to determine whether Textron's tax return was correct and no authority to challenge the return. In this instance, E&Y was seeking, only, to determine whether the reserve established by Textron to cover the corporation's contingent tax liabilities satisfied the requirements of GAAP. Since E&Y was not a potential Textron adversary or acting on behalf of a potential adversary, and, since E&Y agreed to treat the workpapers as confidential, disclosure to E&Y did not substantially increase the likelihood that the workpapers

---

[n.4] The IRS points out that Rule 301 provides that it shall not be construed to relieve an auditor of its obligation to adhere to applicable accounting standards set forth by GAAP or auditing standards set forth by GAAS, but there is no indication that compliance with those standards would have required disclosure in this case.

would be disclosed to the IRS or other potential Textron adversaries. *See Merrill Lynch*, 229 F.R.D. at 447 (finding no waiver where company shared internal investigative report of executive's theft with independent auditor, and distinguishing *MIT*: "The First Circuit, for example, found that the DOD's audit agency was an adversary because it could potentially dispute a billing charge and file suit against MIT, not because of its duty to review MIT's accounts."); *see also In re Pfizer Inc. Sec. Litig.*, 1993 WL 561125 *6 (finding Pfizer's disclosure to an independent auditor not a waiver of work product protection because "[Pfizer's independent auditor] is not reasonably viewed as a conduit to a potential adversary.").

2. Overcoming the Privilege

As already noted, the work product doctrine creates only a qualified privilege that may be overcome by a showing of (1) "substantial need" for the protected documents, and (2) an inability to otherwise obtain the information contained therein or its substantial equivalent without "undue hardship." Fed. R. Civ. P. 26(b)(3).

While establishing that protected documents relate to a legitimate IRS investigation may satisfy the "relevancy" requirement of § 7602, it is insufficient to establish the "substantial need" showing necessary to overcome the work product privilege. *See Davis v. Emery Air Freight Corp.*, 212 F.R.D. 432, 436 (D. Me. 2003) ("the fact that the documents sought might be relevant to [plaintiff's] claims is not enough under Rule 26(b)(3)."). That is especially true in the case of opinion work product, which consists of the "mental impressions, conclusions, opinions or legal theories" of attorneys, where the party seeking the materials must meet a heightened burden. *See Upjohn*, 449 U.S. at 401–2 ("a far stronger showing of necessity and unavailability by other means . . . would be necessary to compel disclosure" of attorneys' notes and memoranda regarding oral statements of witnesses which "reveal the attorneys' mental processes in evaluating the communications"); *see also* Fed. R. Civ. P. 26(b)(3) ("In ordering discovery . . . the court shall protect against disclosure of the mental impressions, conclusions, opinions, or legal theories of an attorney or other representative of a party concerning the litigation.").

Here, the IRS has failed to carry the burden of demonstrating a "substantial need" for ordinary work product, let alone the heightened burden applicable to Textron's tax accrual workpapers, which constitute opinion work product. While the opinions and conclusions of Textron's counsel and tax advisers might provide the IRS with insight into Textron's negotiating position and/or litigation strategy, they have little bearing on the determination of Textron's tax liability.[n.5] The determination of any tax owed by Textron must be based on *factual* information, none of which is contained in the workpapers and all of which is readily available to the IRS through the issuance of IDRs and by other means. The opinions of Textron's counsel, either favorable or unfavorable, would have little to do with that determination, and forced disclosure of those opinions would put Textron at an unfair disadvantage in any dispute that might arise with the IRS, just as requiring the IRS to disclose the opinions of its counsel regarding areas of uncertainty in the law or the likely outcome of any litigation with Textron would place the IRS at an unfair disadvantage. *See e.g. Delaney, Migdail & Young, Chartered v. IRS*, 826 F.2d 124, 127 (D.C. Cir. 1987) (upholding IRS assertion of work product privilege over "IRS memos advis[ing] the agency of the types of legal challenges likely to be mounted against a proposed program, potential defenses available to the agency, and the likely outcome.").

* * *

[n.5] At the evidentiary hearing, the IRS argued that it is entitled to the tax accrual workpapers because the hazards of litigation percentages would assist in determining whether Textron owes a penalty for underpayment of taxes. Since the IRS has not even asserted that Textron owes any further tax, this argument is premature, at best.

According to the District Court, why didn't Textron's disclosure of its tax accrual workpapers to its independent auditor, Ernst & Young, waive the work product privilege? Given the time period involved, *Textron* did not involve Financial Accounting Standards Board Interpretation No. 48 (FIN 48). "Under FIN 48, a reporting company has to identify all of its open tax positions and determine whether it is more likely than not that each tax position can be sustained on its technical merits and whether it is more likely than not that the full amount of the tax benefit will be sustained." David L. Click, *Taxing Standards: Recent Changes in the Practice of Tax Law*, 118 Tax Notes 293, 297 (2008).

FIN 48 is effective for fiscal years beginning after December 15, 2006. If it had existed at the relevant time period in the *Textron* case, might it have affected the outcome? One commentator argues that taxpayers have reason to be concerned:

> Under FIN 48, a company's determination of its income tax reserve may not take audit risk into account. FIN 48 mandates: "It shall be presumed that the tax position will be examined by the relevant taxing authority that has full knowledge of all relevant information" (FIN 48, para. 7.a). It follows that a company must determine its tax exposure and document its determination to the extent required by its auditors, regardless of whether it expects that the IRS or any other taxing authority will challenge, or even examine, its tax positions. For this reason, courts may conclude that FIN 48 generally undermines *Textron*'s determination that tax accrual workpapers would not be prepared but for the possibility of disputes.

Neil D. Kimmelfield & William C. Hsu, Textron, *the Work Product Doctrine, and the Impact of FIN 48*, 117 Tax Notes 871, 872 (2007). The article goes on to argue that specific documents might nonetheless be entitled to work produce protection. *Id.* It advises that "[a] company wishing to obtain work product protection for a document should therefore ensure that all persons to whom the document is disclosed, including outside auditors, agree to maintain the confidentiality of the document, and the company should consider ways of differentiating the document from documents it normally prepares as part of its FIN 48 compliance procedures." *Id.*

Will FIN 48 material itself be protected under the work product doctrine? Although neither *Roxworthy*, quoted above, nor *Textron* directly involved that issue, the Click article mentioned above argues that they are helpful for such a claim:

> *Textron* and *Roxworthy* suggest that FIN 48 analysis may be privileged under the work product doctrine even though traditionally tax workpapers have not been protected by other types of privileges. To realize a financial statement benefit for a tax position, FIN 48 requires that the position meet the more likely than not standard. Detailed analysis of each tax position will likely result in the sort of technical memorandum that was at issue in *Roxworthy*.

Click, *supra*, at 300.

[3] Privilege Protection for Accountants and other Tax Practitioners

[a] Kovel Agreements

The attorney-client privilege and work-product doctrine, discussed above, apply to attorneys. Over time, accountants have gained protections, as well. First, an important exception to the rule that disclosure to third parties waives the attorney-client privilege is the exception, recognized in *United States v. Kovel*, 296 F.2d 918, 919 (2d Cir. 1961), for an accountant hired by the attorney to facilitate communication with the client. In that case, the court explained:

> Kovel is a former Internal Revenue agent having accounting skills. Since 1943 he has been employed by Kamerman & Kamerman, a law firm specializing in tax law. A grand jury in the Southern District of New York was investigating alleged Federal income tax violations by Hopps, a client of the law firm; Kovel was subpoenaed to appear on September 6, 1961, a few days before the date, September 8, when the Government feared the statute of limitations might run. The law firm advised the Assistant United States Attorney that since Kovel was an employee under the direct supervision of the partners, Kovel could not disclose any communications by the client of the result of any work done for the client, unless the latter consented; the Assistant answered that the attorney-client privilege did not apply to one who was not an attorney.

Id. at 919. The court found that the attorney-client privilege applied:

> [T]he Government does not here dispute that the privilege covers communications to non-lawyer employees with 'a menial or ministerial responsibility that involves relating communications to an attorney.' We cannot regard the privilege as confined to 'menial or ministerial' employees. Thus, we can see no significant difference between a case where the attorney sends a client speaking a foreign language to an interpreter to make a literal translation of the client's story; a second where the attorney, himself having some little knowledge of the foreign tongue, has a more knowledgeable non-lawyer employee in the room to help out; a third where someone to perform that same function has been brought along by the client; and a fourth where the attorney, ignorant of the foreign language, sends the client to a non-lawyer proficient in it, with instructions to interview the client on the attorney's behalf and then render his own summary of the situation, perhaps drawing on his own knowledge in the process, so that the attorney can give the client proper legal advice. All four cases meet every element of Wigmore's famous formulation . . . .
>
> This analogy of the client speaking a foreign language is by no means irrelevant to the appeal at hand. Accounting concepts are a foreign language to some lawyers in almost all cases, and to almost all lawyers in some cases. Hence the presence of an accountant, whether hired by the lawyer or by the client, while the client is relating a complicated tax story to the lawyer, ought not destroy the privilege, any more than would that of the linguist in the second or third variations of the foreign language theme discussed above; the presence of the accountant is necessary, or at least highly useful, for the effective consultation between the client and the lawyer which the privilege is designed to permit. By the same token, if the lawyer has directed the client, either in the specific case or generally, to tell his story in the first instance to an accountant engaged by the lawyer, who is then to interpret it so that the lawyer may better give legal advice, communications by the client reasonably related to that purpose ought fall within the privilege; there can be no more virtue in requiring the lawyer to sit by while the client pursues these possibly tedious preliminary conversations with the accountant than in insisting on the lawyer's physical presence while the client dictates a statement to the lawyer's secretary or is interviewed by a clerk not yet admitted to practice. What is vital to the privilege is that the communication be made in confidence for the purpose of obtaining legal advice from the lawyer. If what is sought is not legal advice but only accounting service, as in *Olender v. United States*, 210 F.2d 795, 805–806 (9 Cir. 1954), *see* Reisman v. Caplin, 61–2 U.S.T.C. P9673 (1961), or if the advice sought is the accountant's rather than the lawyer's, no privilege exists. We recognize this draws what may seem to some a rather arbitrary line between a case where the client communicates first to his own accountant (no privilege as to such

> communications, even though he later consults his lawyer on the same matter, Gariepy v. United States, 189 F.2d 459, 463 (6 Cir. 1951)),[n.4] and others, where the client in the first instance consults a lawyer who retains an accountant as a listening post, or consults the lawyer with his own accountant present. But that is the inevitable consequence of having to reconcile the absence of a privilege for accountants and the effective operation of the privilege of client and lawyer under conditions where the lawyer needs outside help. . . .

United States v. Kovel, 296 F.2d 918, 921–23 (2d Cir. 1961).

It has become standard for the lawyer to enter into a formal arrangement with the accountant, called a Kovel agreement, when the accountant will be assisting an attorney with a tax matter.[10] The following excerpt explains why. While the excerpt focuses on a client with criminal tax exposure, Kovel agreements are also routinely used in the civil context.[11]

John A. Townsend, *The Accountant's Role — and Risks — in Koveling*

2 J. Tax Prac. & Proc. 20 (2000)[12]

Clients with potential criminal tax exposure often need both legal and accounting expertise to assist in managing the risk. Criminal tax exposure arises when a taxpayer has filed a fraudulent return (either false as to the amount of tax reported or false as to some material item required to be disclosed on the return) or has failed to file his or her return timely. Once a fraudulent return has been filed or a return is delinquent, the traditional way to avoid criminal tax exposure is to make a "voluntary disclosure" by filing an amended return or delinquent return, as appropriate. Voluntary disclosure is a separate topic. Suffice it to say here that voluntary disclosure requires that the taxpayer properly report his or her liability on an amended return(s) or delinquent return(s). That requires tax preparer expertise and, usually, accounting expertise to develop the information for reporting on the return(s).

[n.4] We do not deal in this opinion with the question under what circumstances, if any, such communications could be deemed privileged on the basis that they were being made to the accountant as the client's agent for the purpose of subsequent communication by the accountant to the lawyer; communications by the client's agent to the attorney are privileged, 8 Wigmore, Evidence, § 2317-1. See Lalance & Grosjean Mfg. Co. v. Haberman Mfg. Co., 87 F. 563 (C.C.S.D.N.Y., 1898).

[10] The use of a *Kovel* accountant is also mentioned briefly in Chapter 3 in connection with reconstruction of income. *See* § 3.04[D].

> [T]he Kovel rule has been extended beyond accountants to other third-party experts. Although few court decisions address Kovel's application to consultants other than accountants, it has been applied to communications with a psychiatrist, an operator of a polygraph, a patent agent assisting an attorney, and a public relations consultant who assisted an attorney. In Federal Trade Commission v. TRW, Inc., the D.C. Circuit Court of Appeals suggested that the Kovel privilege could apply to a situation in which a research institute was hired by an attorney for TRW, Inc., a credit reporting agency, to prepare a study of the company's computerized credit reporting system. The court, however, ultimately did not uphold the privilege: "Where, as here, we have not been provided with sufficient facts to state with reasonable certainty that the privilege applies, this burden is not met. As noted earlier, TRW's claim lies at an outer and indistinct boundary of the law of attorney-client privilege."

Carl Pacini, *Accountants, Attorney-Client Privilege, and the Kovel Rule: Waiver Through Inadvertent Disclosure Via Electronic Communication*, 28 Del. J. Corp. L. 893, 904–05 (2003) (footnotes omitted) (*quoting Federal Trade Commission v. TRW, Inc.*, 628 F.2d 207 (D.C. Cir. 1980)).

[11] The Townsend article also includes a checklist of items that should be incorporated in the Kovel agreement. *See* John A. Townsend, *The Accountant's Role — and Risks — in Koveling*, 2 J. Tax Prac. & Proc. 20, 24–25 (2000). For a sample Kovel engagement letter, see Martin A. Schainbaum & David B. Porter, *The Assistance of a Forensic Accountant in a Criminal Tax Case*, American Bar Association Center for Continuing Legal Education National Institute (2001).

[12]

Attorneys advising clients on how to mitigate or eliminate their criminal exposure usually engage independent accountants to perform the accounting and tax return preparation. The construct of the engagement is that the accountants assist the attorneys in rendering legal services to the attorneys' client. The reason this construct is used is to infuse the accountants' activity with the attorney-client privilege to the extent possible. The leading case that originally recognized the attorney-client privilege when accountants are engaged to assist in rendering legal services to a client was named *Kovel*, hence the accountants so engaged are referred to as Kovel accountants. The courts reason that in the complex and sometimes arcane tax area, accounting expertise is often required in order for the attorneys to provide adequate legal representation. The same theory could apply to other disciplines necessary for legal representation (*e.g.*, environmental engineers in legal representation related to environmental matters). But, here we focus on the Kovel accountants because that is the expertise most frequently encountered in tax representation.

The nuances of Kovel accountants are many and multifaceted. Here we can deal only with the highlights in a way that simplifies (at the risk of oversimplification) a complex subject. We will present the discussion in a question and answer format with a hypothetical accountant asking the questions.

* * *

Q: **Who am I working for if I enter a Kovel agreement?**

A: In the Kovel relationship, you work directly for the attorneys as an independent contractor. You do not work for the client except indirectly as part of the legal team rendering legal services to the attorneys' client. You are not practicing law but simply rendering accountant and tax preparation expertise to the attorneys so that they can deploy that expertise in delivering legal representation to the client. You will frequently deal directly with the client in developing the underlying information required for you to render your accounting and tax preparation services, but you will do so as an agent of the attorneys.

Q: **How can the privilege apply if I prepare the tax return (either amended or delinquent) that is then filed with the IRS?**

A: You have raised an excellent question and one that has some gray area because of the dearth of cases. Generally, there is no attorney-client privilege for tax return preparation services. For example, if a taxpayer engages an attorney to prepare a simple return and the attorney does nothing more than do what an ordinary tax return preparer would do, the attorney-client privilege does not apply. The privilege applies only to the rendition of legal services. Mere return preparation is not, ordinarily, the rendition of legal services. If, however, traditional legal services are provided in addition to mere return preparation, the privilege will apply to the legal services rendered. For example, if the presentation on the return is based upon legal advice as to whether a reorganization qualifies as a tax-free merger under Code Sec. 368(a)(1)(A), then that portion of the underlying services and communications between the client and the attorney or Kovel accountants should qualify for the privilege.

In a Kovel agreement, where major criminal tax concerns drive the preparation and filing of the return, significant areas of the work will relate to the rendition of legal services (as opposed, for example, to the mere compilation of data for presentation on the return). These are our conclusions as to the division between services to which the privilege applies and services to which it does not apply. In any given case, the dividing line may be hard to discern, but the foregoing is a very rough guide for discerning the line. The concept is that, as tax return preparer in the Kovel engagement, the Kovel accountants' services may ultimately be privileged as to some portions and not privileged as to others. Suffice it to say that because the cases are few and the IRS has not attempted to press matters in close cases, we do not have specific authority as to where the lines will be drawn. We think, however, that for purposes of addressing your concern, the foregoing is a good working summary.

We should note that there is one way to add some strength to the attorney-client privilege in this context, but it adds additional costs that the client may or may not be willing to incur. The Kovel accountants may work with and for the attorneys in developing the underlying return information and reporting strategies. After that information is developed, the Kovel accountants will not prepare the return. Rather, the attorneys will present the information to a separate, independent accountant, who has not been "Kovelized," for the actual return preparation. There are no cases addressing whether splitting the responsibilities and work efforts in this fashion will prevent the government from blowing out the privilege for communications with the Kovel accountants, but we think this offers an additional argument that, in an appropriate case, may be worth the cost. In the final analysis, the attorneys advise the client on the additional costs involved, the potential benefits that might be achieved, the projection of the likelihood of prevailing in court if the IRS were to press the matter, the projection of the likelihood that the IRS would press the matter (an issue separate from how a court may resolve the issues) and the risks if the taxpayer does not incur the additional costs. In short, the attorney helps the client consider costs, benefits and risks in making the decision whether to take this additional step and incur the additional costs. We have found that usually clients make the call not to take this additional step, but it is important that the client receive good advice and judgment based on considerable experience in making his or her decision. After all, it is the client's liberty and property that are at stake.

Q: **Is it necessary to have a written contract?**

A: The legal answer to the question is no. A Kovel agreement is simply a contract, and the law permits oral contracts. The practical answer to the question is *yes*. Proving the nature and parameters of an oral contract invites controversy and risks that can be easily and cheaply avoided. *Have a written Kovel agreement.* Moreover, having a written agreement provides a handy and objective reference for the attorneys and the Kovel accountants to periodically review their respective responsibilities.

Q: **When can I start work?**

A: Anytime after we enter a Kovel agreement. Of course, there may be preliminary discussions between you (the potential Kovel accountants) and the attorneys in determining whether to enter a Kovel engagement and some information may be shared at that stage. Generally, by analogy to attorney engagements, those preliminary discussions should be covered by the privilege, but it is the better part of wisdom to have some preliminary understanding that there is a limited engagement at the beginning of the discussion for which no charge will be made in the event a formal Kovel engagement is not entered. In all events, before the accountants set out on substantive work on the engagement, the Kovel agreement should be entered.

Q: What administrative actions are required by me as a Kovel accountant that I might not otherwise do in the normal course of my practice?

A: Broadly speaking, the attorney-client privilege applies only if the attorney-client communications are not divulged outside the scope of the persons having a need to know in the legal representation. This means that the information must be available only to the client, the attorneys and any person assisting the attorneys in the representation. The accountants must take action to insure the integrity of the files that the accountants maintain in the matter. Those files should not be available for access by accounting firm personnel not working on the engagement. We suggest that the Kovel accountants keep the files in red-ropes or other containers clearly marked that they are for limited access only and, if at all possible, be stored in a secure area of the accounting firm. Furthermore, it is important that the accountants be sensitive in discussing the engagement either with colleagues in the accounting firm or with outsiders. Keep in mind that colleagues within the firm should only be told such information as they have a need to know in furtherance of the legal representation of the client. This means that, on a routine basis, no information can be shared with colleagues.

There is one exception. The client's name can be shared within the accounting firm in order to permit it to run a conflicts check. There is a nuance here. You will recall that I said that the accountants are working for the attorneys, not for the attorneys' client. Technically, attorneys are the Kovel accountants' client. However, well-designed conflict checks usually include other parties in interest and, of course, the ultimate client (the taxpayer) is a party in interest. In an attorney-client relationship, the name of the client is usually not considered a confidential attorney-client communication, so disclosing the name of the ultimate client of attorneys poses no risk at least in terms of the Kovel accountants doing an internal conflict check (including consulting with colleagues as to any potential conflict).

We have encountered a second area of potential concern. Some, perhaps all, accounting firms do internal and external peer reviews of work performed. These reviews are performed by persons having no direct relationship to the delivery of services to the attorneys and the attorneys' delivery of legal services to the attorneys' client. There is some conceptual risk that such reviews could blow the privilege. We think, however, that a good argument can be made that such reviews do not blow the privilege. Basically, in the accounting environment, such reviews are a usual and needed (if not technically necessary) part of the rendering of services, and those persons performing the review should be within the scope of the privilege. We think that there are policy reasons that mitigate strongly against the government asserting that the mere disclosure to such review personnel would blow the privilege.

* * *

Q: Can I be a Kovel accountant if I am the taxpayer's regular accountant and/or tax return preparer?

A: The legal answer is yes. The practical answer is *no*.

The reason for this practical answer is that the attorney-client privilege does not apply to communications before the agreement is entered. Should the government summons or subpoena the accountants, the accountants will be allowed to assert the privilege (on behalf of the attorneys' client) only as to matters that the accountants learned while engaged as Kovel accountants. Our experience is that it is often very difficult, sometimes impossible, to establish what the accountants learned after being Kovelized and distinguish it from what they learned before being Kovelized. Moreover, the taxpayer's regular accountants may, in fact, have already learned information that could be damaging and that could not be protected if the IRS pressed the matter. (You are astute, and will have noted that this risk will be present even if new Kovel accountants are engaged, because the government can summons or subpoena the old accountants who were not Kovelized. Nevertheless, the subtle danger of using the old accountants is that, in the process of the Kovel engagement, the old accountants will inevitably learn additional information and nuances that cannot be divorced from their prior knowledge and will thus be difficult to avoid disclosing if the government presses the issue. In short, answering questions about their prior knowledge will disclose information or nuances learned later.) This injects considerable risk into engaging an accountant that was previously involved in the taxpayer's affairs. The general rule, therefore, is that a fresh accountant is Kovelized so that everything he or she knows is Kovelized.

Having said that, some taxpayers may strongly desire their regular accountants to do this work. The taxpayers' desires in this regard are almost always based upon financial reasons. The taxpayers reason that the accountants who already know the taxpayers' accounting and tax affairs can more expeditiously (and inexpensively) do the job. Our response is to strongly discourage that for the reasons noted. Moreover, if the old accountants are used, extra efforts (and costs) will be required (unless of course the taxpayer directs otherwise) to debrief the old accountants at the beginning of the engagement to establish what they knew (or even might have suspected) prior to the engagement. That debriefing could be inefficient and wide of the mark before the attorneys are aware of the full parameters of the underlying problems. Finally, it is conceivable that in order to mitigate the taxpayer's exposure, the taxpayer may have to argue that the old accountants did a sloppy job and thus are responsible (perhaps not criminally responsible, but nevertheless responsible as between them and the taxpayer). That will, in many cases, be a last resort and perhaps even a repugnant argument to the taxpayer, even if there is a factual basis for it. Nevertheless, at the early stages of the engagement before the underlying facts and nuances are known, it is highly risky to take action that might foreclose a wholly objective consideration of this potential defense.

For these reasons, we, as the attorneys, strongly urge that our client not engage his regular accountants. If the taxpayer chooses otherwise, we put our advice in writing (with a litany of all the risks that might be involved) and have the taxpayer (our client) expressly acknowledge our contrary advice and the taxpayer's knowing decision to proceed against our advice.

* * *

Note that Kovel agreements are not a panacea. A Court of Federal Claims case explains the limited scope of the *Kovel* doctrine:

> [S]ubsequent decisions in the Second Circuit and elsewhere make clear that "an attorney, merely by placing an accountant on her payroll, does not, by this action alone, render communications between the attorney's client and the accountant privileged." *Cavallaro*, 284 F.3d at 247; . . . . Rather, *Kovel* applies only "when the accountant's role is to clarify communications between attorney and client" — when he, in other words, acts "as a translator or interpreter of client communications." *United States v. Ackert*, 169 F.3d 136, 139 (2d Cir. 1999); *see also United States v. Adlman*, 68 F.3d 1495, 1499–1500 (2d Cir. 1995) (hereinafter "*Adlman I*"). In particular, a communication between an attorney and an accountant does not become shielded by the attorney-client privilege simply because "the communication proves important to the attorney's ability to represent the client." *Ackert*, 169 F.3d at 139; *see also Hickman*, 329 U.S. at 508. Further, in *Kovel*, the Second Circuit made clear that for the privilege to attach, the communication must be made "for the purpose of obtaining legal advice," adding that "[i]f what is sought is not legal advice but only accounting service . . . , or if the advice sought is the accountant's rather than the lawyer's, no privilege exists." *Kovel*, 296 F.2d at 922; *see also Cavallaro*, 284 F.3d at 247; *Adlman I*, 68 F.3d at 1500; *United States v. Brown*, 478 F.2d 1038, 1040 (7th Cir. 1973); . . . *United States v. ChevronTexaco Corp.*, 241 F. Supp. 2d 1065, 1072 (N.D. Cal. 2002) ("*Kovel* explicitly excludes the broader scenario in which the accountant is enlisted merely to give her own *advice* about the client's situation." (Emphasis in original)).
>
> It bears further noting that *Kovel* and most of its progeny deal only with the situation where an accountant was acting as an attorney's agent and not where an accountant is acting as the client's agent. *See Kovel*, 296 F.2d at 922 n.4; *In re Grand Jury Proceedings Under Seal*, 947 F.2d 1188, 1191 (4th Cir. 1991). In the latter situation, communications by the accountant to the attorney are viewed as equivalent to communications being made by the client to the attorney and hence are potentially covered by the attorney-client privilege. *See, e.g., id.* However, that conclusion does not necessarily shield such documents from discovery. If the documents are unprotected by privilege in the hands of the accountant or if the privilege is somehow waived other than by the communication from the accountant to the client's attorney, the documents may, nonetheless be discoverable. *See Heartland Surgical Specialty Hosp., LLC v. Midwest Div., Inc.*, 2007 U.S. Dist. LEXIS 53217, 2007 WL 2122440, at *4 (D. Kan. Jul. 20, 2007) (*Kovel* did not protect accountant's compilation of records that were subsequently provided to attorney); *In re Hyde*, 222 B.R. 214, 220 (Bankr. S.D.N.Y. 1998), *rev'd on other grounds*, 235 B.R. 539 (S.D.N.Y. 1999), *aff'd*, 205 F.3d 1323 (2d Cir. 2000) ("Neither *Kovel* nor any other case permits a party to hide unprivileged documents by given [sic] them to his attorney or forensic accountant."); . . . . The latter rule, of course, mirrors the rule that applies to attorneys — a party simply cannot prevent the disclosure of papers that would otherwise be discoverable by the simple expedience of transferring them to either an attorney or an accountant.

Evergreen Trading, LLC v. United States, 80 Fed. Cl. 122, 141–42 (2007).

Why is a *Kovel* arrangement particularly important for criminal tax cases and cases in which the client has possible criminal exposure? The discussion below on the statutory privilege of Code section 7525 helps answer that question.

[b] *Arthur Young* and the Section 7525 Privilege

Reading Assignment: I.R.C. § 7525.

The well-known *Arthur Young* case, decided by the Supreme Court in 1984, involved the question of whether tax accrual workpapers prepared by accountants were subject to a privilege similar to the work-product privilege that applies to attorneys. In holding that accrual workpapers had to be turned over to the IRS, the Court refused to recognize a work-product privilege for accountants. The Court also commented on its view of the proper role of attorneys and accountants in the self-assessment system:

> While § 7602 is "subject to the traditional privileges and limitations," . . . any other restrictions upon the IRS summons power should be avoided "absent unambiguous directions from Congress." *United States v. Bisceglia, supra*, at 150. We are unable to discern the sort of "unambiguous directions from Congress" that would justify a judicially created work-product immunity for tax accrual workpapers summoned under § 7602. Indeed, the very language of § 7602 reflects precisely the opposite: a congressional policy choice *in favor of disclosure* of all information relevant to a legitimate IRS inquiry. In light of this explicit statement by the Legislative Branch, courts should be chary in recognizing exceptions to the broad summons authority of the IRS or in fashioning new privileges that would curtail disclosure under § 7602. . . . If the broad latitude granted to the IRS by § 7602 is to be circumscribed, that is a choice for Congress, and not this Court, to make. See *United States v. Euge*, 444 U.S., at 712.
>
> The Court of Appeals nevertheless concluded that "substantial countervailing policies," *id.*, at 711, required the fashioning of a work-product immunity for an independent auditor's tax accrual workpapers. To the extent that the Court of Appeals, in its concern for the "chilling effect" of the disclosure of tax accrual workpapers, sought to facilitate communication between independent auditors and their clients, its remedy more closely resembles a testimonial accountant-client privilege than a work-product immunity for accountants' workpapers. But as this Court stated in *Couch v. United States*, 409 U.S. 322, 335 (1973), "no confidential accountant-client privilege exists under federal law, and no state-created privilege has been recognized in federal cases." In light of *Couch*, the Court of Appeals' effort to foster candid communication between accountant and client by creating a self-styled work-product privilege was misplaced, and conflicts with what we see as the clear intent of Congress.
>
> Nor do we find persuasive the argument that a work-product immunity for accountants' tax accrual workpapers is a fitting analogue to the attorney work-product doctrine established in *Hickman v. Taylor*, 329 U.S. 495 (1947). The *Hickman* work-product doctrine was founded upon the private attorney's role as the client's confidential adviser and advocate, a loyal representative whose duty it is to present the client's case in the most favorable possible light. An independent certified public accountant performs a different role. By certifying the public reports that collectively depict a corporation's financial status, the independent auditor assumes a *public* responsibility transcending any employment relationship with the client. The independent public accountant performing this special function owes ultimate allegiance to the corporation's creditors and stockholders, as well as to the investing public. This "public watchdog" function demands that the accountant maintain total independence from the client at all times and requires complete fidelity to the public trust. To insulate from disclosure a certified public accountant's interpretations of the client's financial statements would be to ignore the significance of the accountant's role as a disinterested analyst charged with public obligations.

United States v. Arthur Young & Co., 465 U.S. 805, 816–18 (1984).

In the excerpt from *Arthur Young* above, the Supreme Court quoted an earlier case as stating that "no confidential accountant-client privilege exists under federal law, and no state-created privilege has been recognized in federal cases . . . ." *Arthur Young & Co.*, 465 U.S. at 817 (*quoting* Couch v. United States, 409 U.S. 322, 335 (1973)). Over a decade later, as part of IRS reform, Congress did recognize such a privilege in the form of a tax practitioner-client privilege applicable to individuals authorized to practice before the IRS. Code section 7525 provides that "[w]ith respect to tax advice, the same common law protections of confidentiality which apply to a communication between a taxpayer and an attorney shall also apply to a communication between a taxpayer and any federally authorized tax practitioner to the extent the communication would be considered a privileged communication if it were between a taxpayer and an attorney," but only in "noncriminal tax matter[s] before the Internal Revenue Service; and . . . any noncriminal tax proceeding in Federal court brought by or against the United States." I.R.C. § 7525(a). Because section 7525 uses the term "federally authorized tax practitioner," the privilege often is referred to as the FATP privilege.

Once Congress enacted section 7525, there was some speculation that the new privilege afforded to nonlawyers would substantially change the way tax advice was provided, and by whom. Courts read the provision narrowly, however. For example, case law holds that "the § 7525 privilege is no broader than that of the attorney-client privilege, and 'nothing in § 7525 suggests that . . . nonlawyer practitioners are entitled to privilege when they are doing other than lawyers' work.' " United States v. BDO Seidman, 337 F.3d 802, 810 (7th Cir. 2003), *cert. denied sub nom.* Roes v. United States, 540 U.S. 1178 (2004) (*quoting* United States v. Frederick, 182 F.3d 496, 502 (7th Cir. 1999), *reh'g en banc denied*, 84 A.F.T.R.2d (RIA) 5760 (7th Cir. 1999), *cert. denied*, 528 U.S. 1154 (2000)). Moreover, section 7525 " 'does not protect work product'. . . . " United States v. KPMG LLP, 237 F. Supp. 2d 35, 39 (D.C. Cir. 2003) (*quoting Frederick*, 182 F.3d at 502).

United States v. BDO Seidman, LLP, 2005-1 U.S. Tax Cas. (CCH) ¶ 50,264, 2005 U.S. Dist. LEXIS 5555 (N.D. Ill. 2005), further explains:

> The tax practitioner privilege is interpreted based on the common law rules of the attorney-client privilege. United States v. BDO Seidman, LLP, 337 F.3d 802, 810–12 (7th Cir. 2003). The communications are made, however, for the purpose of tax advice instead of legal advice, *Id.* at 811, and the client's communication is with a federal authorized tax practitioner instead of an attorney. The statute defines a "federally authorized tax practitioner" as "any individual who is authorized to practice before the IRS" and "tax advice" means "advice given by an individual with respect to a matter which is within the scope of the individual's authority to practice" as described under the tax practitioners privilege. I.R.C. § 7525(a)(3)(A), (B).
>
> The tax practitioner privilege, like the attorney-client privilege, is not an absolute bar to disclosures, but instead contains limitations on the scope of the privilege. The tax practitioner privilege only applies to communications made on or after statute's enactment date of July 22, 1998. *Frederick*, 182 F.3d at 502. The language of the statute expressly limits the privilege to "noncriminal tax matters before the IRS," I.R.C. § 7525(a)(2)(A), and "noncriminal tax proceedings in Federal court brought by or against the United States." I.R.C. § 7525(a)(2)(B). The statute also prohibits the application of the tax practitioner privilege to "any written communication between a federally authorized tax practitioner" and client "in connection with the promotion of the direct or indirect participation of the person in any tax shelter (as defined in [I.R.C.] § 6662(d)(2)(C)(ii)).[13] I.R.C. § 7525(b). A tax shelter is defined as "a partnership

[13] [Until 2004, the tax shelter exception was limited to corporate taxpayers. What is the scope of the phrase

or other entity, any investment plan or arrangement, or any other plan or arrangement, if a significant purpose of such partnership, entity, plan or arrangement is the avoidance or evasion of Federal income tax." I.R.C. § 6662(d)(2)(C)(ii).

The limitations on the attorney-client privilege, such as the crime-fraud exception, are incorporated into the tax practitioner privilege through the application of the common law interpretations of the attorney-client privilege when interpreting the tax practitioner privilege. United States v. BDO Seidman, LLP, 337 F.3d 802, 810 (7th Cir. 2003). Furthermore, the phrase "tax advice," the communication covered under the tax practitioner privilege, "does not include communication regarding tax return preparation; it simply encompasses communication such as tax planning advice." United States v. BDO Seidman, LLP, 2003 U.S. Dist. LEXIS 1634, No. 02 C 4822, 2003 WL 932365, at *2 (N.D. Ill. Feb. 5, 2003) (citing In re Grand Jury Proceedings, 220 F.3d 568, 571 (7th Cir. 2000); United States v. Frederick, 182 F.3d 496 (7th Cir. 1999); United States v. KPMG LLP, 237 F. Supp. 2d 35, 2002 WL 31894130, at *4 (D.D.C. 2002)).

Id. at *20–22.

One commentator discusses concerns about courts' interpretation of the content of the section 7525 privilege, including the following:

Because the attorney-client privilege is designed to protect only those communications made in reliance on the privilege, the courts have insisted that the client maintain the confidentiality of her communications with her attorney. If a client reveals those communications to a third party, the natural inference is that her original statements were not made in confidence and that she would have made the statements regardless of the privilege. The courts have observed that the selective waiver doctrine is fundamentally inconsistent with the confidentiality requirement and does nothing to encourage full and frank communications between clients and their attorneys.

The FATP [federally authorized tax practitioner] privilege is quite different from the attorney-client privilege, however, and serves different purposes. To further those purposes, one must consider the unique scope of the privilege. It does not make sense to adopt attorney-client privilege principles in toto when determining the scope of the FATP privilege. In fact, strictly applying those principles may lead to odd contradictions.

Consider, for example, the application of the attorney-client privilege's "legal advice" requirement to the FATP privilege. Under attorney-client privilege principles, communications between taxpayers and their advisers are privileged only when the client seeks legal advice. However, the practitioners covered only by section 7525 are not licensed to practice law, and therefore cannot dispense legal advice. Thus, if the section 7525 privilege carries a "legal advice" requirement, taxpayers can never assert the privilege because they will be unable to show that they have sought legal advice from their nonattorney adviser. Congress could not possibly have intended that absurd result, and the statute's language — that the privilege applies only "to the extent the communication would be considered a privileged communication if it were between a taxpayer and an attorney" — must not be read literally. Under a

---

"promotion of the direct or indirect participation of the person in any tax shelter"? In an exchange in *Tax Notes* between Robert Aland, an adjunct professor in the Graduate Tax Program at Northwestern Law, and tax attorney (and former IRS Chief Counsel) B. John Williams, they agreed that advice rendered *after* the client had engaged in the tax shelter transaction would not fall within section 7525(b) because it would not involve "promotion" of participation in the shelter. *See Parsing the Practitioner Privilege*, 2005 TNT 79-47 (Apr. 26, 2005). — Eds.]

textual approach, literal interpretations are disfavored, particularly when they produce such silly results.

Indeed, courts have not imposed a "legal advice" requirement on the FATP privilege,[n.106] but they have insisted that the attorney-client privilege's confidentiality requirement does apply. But that insistence is misguided. Although the attorney-client privilege is a broad privilege, available during legal proceedings of any kind and against virtually all adversaries, the FATP privilege is available only in noncriminal tax proceedings and only against the IRS. Given that the privilege is usually unavailable to the client, protecting the confidentiality of her communications is nearly impossible and Congress could not possibly have required her to do so.

The close relationship between a taxpayer's state income tax liability and his federal tax liability illustrates the fragility of the FATP privilege. Whenever a taxpayer's federal income tax liability is at issue, his state income tax liability is also likely at issue — most states determine a taxpayer's income tax liability by referring to his federal income tax liability. Consequently, a state tax agency may seek disclosure of a taxpayer's communications with his adviser as part of its determination of the taxpayer's tax liability. Because state law generally does not provide a privilege comparable to section 7525,[n.111] the disclosure of those communications is easily compelled.

The communications produced by the client will almost certainly constitute "tax advice" within the meaning of section 7525 — that is, by complying with the request from the state revenue authority, the client will have revealed information pertinent to the determination of his federal tax liability.[n.112] The IRS could then argue that the client has waived the FATP privilege by disclosing the tax-related communications to the state revenue authority, and ask that a court compel disclosure.

It is hard to believe that Congress intended an "eggshell" waiver of the privilege. Congress could not have enacted section 7525 with the intention that it would be dead on arrival. A court's rejection of the selective waiver doctrine, however, could very well vitiate the privilege entirely.

The courts should recognize that the arguments for requiring a client to maintain the confidentiality of his communications with his attorney are inapposite to the client-tax practitioner relationship. Section 7525's text indicates that the substance of the taxpayer's communications will be freely discoverable by various federal and state agencies. A taxpayer will never make communications to her nonattorney tax adviser believing that those communications will be held confidential, and it is not sensible to impose a confidentiality

---

[n.106] *But see* United States v. Frederick, 182 F.3d 496, 502 (7th Cir. 1999) (stating in dicta, "Nothing in the new statute suggests that these nonlawyer practitioners are entitled to privilege when they are doing other than lawyers' work."). One court has cited *Frederick* for the "lawyers' work" proposition, but held only that tax return preparation did not qualify as lawyers' work, without further suggesting that a FATP must actually be engaged in the practice of law. United States v. KPMG, 237 F. Supp. 2d 35, 39 (D.D.C. 2002). It seems unlikely that a court will explicitly hold that a FATP must perform lawyers' work.

[n.111] While a few states do provide accountant-client privileges, the FATP privilege reaches communications made not only to accountants, but also to enrolled agents and enrolled actuaries. Communications made to agents and actuaries do not enjoy any state law privilege protections.

[n.112] See Jonathan Z. Ackerman, "With Privilege Comes Responsibility: The New Accountant-Client Privilege," Federal Bar Association Section of Taxation Report, Summer 1999, 1999-SUM Fed. B.A. Sec. Tax'n Rep. 1 ("Disclosures during the course of a state tax audit in a state without accountant-client privilege could leave a confidential client information prone to discovery in a subsequent IRS investigation."). A client could perhaps avoid that result by hiring one accountant to prepare his state tax return and another to prepare his federal tax return.

> requirement.[n.116] Section 7525 does not serve the broad purpose of encouraging full and frank communication between a taxpayer and her tax adviser, but simply provides limited privilege protections for tax-related communications during noncriminal tax proceedings.

Amandeep S. Grewal, *Selective Waiver and the Tax Practitioner Privilege*, 112 Tax Notes 1139, 1149–51 (2006) (selected footnotes omitted).[14]

Does Code section 7525 obviate the need for a Kovel agreement? The Townsend article, excerpted above, addresses that issue as follows:

> **Q: Why is "Koveling" important after Congress passed the practitioner privilege in Code Sec. 7525?**
>
> A: The Code Sec. 7525 practitioner privilege may only be asserted in noncriminal matters. The Kovel agreement is important only because there is risk of criminal exposure. If the IRS seeks to investigate or prosecute for tax crimes, Code Sec. 7525's practitioner privilege is not available. Accordingly, it is important to take extra steps to preserve the privilege for the type of information (particularly communications to and from the client) to which the accountants will have access while assisting the attorney in rendering legal services.
>
> We focus here on the attorney-client privilege, because, where applicable, it is absolute. It preserves the confidentiality of the information in all contexts, criminal or civil. There is one other privilege potentially applicable in this type of tax engagement. This is the work product privilege which is a qualified privilege, meaning that it generally applies but if the opposing party (here the government) could show a compelling need for the information, a court could order it disclosed. The work product privilege applies if the work is performed in anticipation of litigation (the possibility of litigation, not the certainty of litigation). The Kovel accountants' work in the context discussed here will qualify for the work product privilege. However, we do not focus on it here because it, like the Code Sec. 7525 privilege, is not an absolute privilege. Having said that, it should not be ignored in a Kovel engagement, and you and the attorneys should take the steps necessary to insure that it is available if needed (belt and suspenders approach).

John A. Townsend, *The Accountant's Role — and Risks — in Koveling*, 2 J. Tax Prac. & Proc. 20, 21 (2000).

[B] Court Review of Privilege Claims

Typically, "claims of attorney-client privilege must be asserted document by document, rather than as a single, blanket assertion." United States v. Rockwell Int'l, 897 F.2d 1255, 1265 (3d Cir. 1990) (*citing* United States v. First State Bank, 691 F.2d

---

[n.116] Indeed, as two practitioners observe, "Many accounting firms are no longer advising their clients that the privilege will protect their confidential communications." [Danielle M. Smith and David L. Kleinman, "The Federally Authorized Tax Practitioner Privilege: What Remains Under Section 7525?" BNA Tax Management Weekly Report (May 22, 2006).] It's hard to imagine that anyone would reveal his deepest-held confidences to his tax adviser, given that those confidences are protected only vis-à-vis the IRS. The privilege cannot possibly serve the purpose of encouraging full and frank communications between taxpayers and their tax preparers, and taxpayers should not be expected to guard communications as if it did. See also Smith, "After the Alamo: Taxpayer Claims of Privilege and the IRS War on Tax Shelters," Tax Notes, Jan. 13, 2003, p. 233, Doc 2003-1200, 2003 TNT 9-47 ("The privilege afforded to tax practitioners is so narrow and uncertain in its application that clients should exercise extreme caution before disclosing information to a nonattorney tax practitioner that is intended to remain privileged.").

[14]

332, 335 (7th Cir. 1982); United States v. El Paso Co., 682 F.2d 530, 541 (5th Cir. 1982), *cert. denied*, 466 U.S. 944 (1984)). Accordingly, a party who claims that a summons seeks documents that are protected from disclosure (typically because of a claimed privilege) will compile for the court and the government an index identifying each document and the protection claimed.[15] The index is called a "privilege log."

Information identifying a document typically includes the document's author, date, subject matter, nature (such as letter or memorandum), and recipient(s). *See, e.g.*, *United States v. United Technologies Corp.*, 979 F. Supp. 108, 113 (D. Conn. 1997) ("Document 16: A June 1982 memo from the head of UTC's tax department to the company's in-house counsel requesting legal advice on the significance and application of a tax ruling."); *United States v. Derr*, No. C-91-2782-EFL, 1991 U.S. Dist. LEXIS 17987, at *3 (N.D. Cal. 1991), *aff'd*, 968 F.2d 943 (9th Cir. 1992) ("The privilege log for each box shall describe for each document the privilege claimed and shall list the date, title, description, subject and purpose of each document and the name, position and last known addresses of the author(s) and recipient(s) of each document."). Generally, the party seeking to shield the documents from view will provide as little information as possible, and the amount of information required may be disputed.

It is possible that a court will conduct an *in camera* review of documents alleged to be protected. *See United States v. Zolin*, 491 U.S. 554, 565 (1989); *see also United States v. Frederick*, 182 F.3d 496 (7th Cir. 1999) (documents the subject of summonses issued to attorney/accountant were not protected by attorney-client privilege or work-product privilege; there is no protection for documents prepared for use in preparing tax returns), *reh'g en banc denied*, 84 A.F.T.R.2d 5760 (7th Cir. 1999), *cert. denied*, 528 U.S. 1154 (2000); *BDO Seidman*, 2005 U.S. Dist. LEXIS 5555 at *5 (finding that, of 267 withheld documents, all were privileged except document A-40, to which the crime-fraud exception applied). In *Derr*, cited above, the court ordered Chevron Corporation to submit each privilege log to the court and to submit for *in camera* review copies of the documents listed in the first privilege log so that the court could "inform the parties after reviewing the documents listed on the first privilege log whether Chevron shall lodge with the Court the documents from subsequently produced privilege logs." *Derr*, 1991 U.S. Dist. LEXIS 17987, at *3.

PROBLEMS

1. The IRS is in the process of auditing Jerry's Year 1 tax return. With respect to the issue of whether Jerry properly excluded payments he received under an annuity contract, the IRS revenue agent issues a summons to Jerry seeking that he provide "all documents relating to the annuity contract, including, but not limited to, the application for the contract; documents specifying the contract holder and any beneficiaries; and any documents describing, calculating, or analyzing the method for determining payments under the annuity contract."
   A. If Jerry does not want to comply with the summons, may he contest the IRS's authority to issue the summons as part of a court proceeding?
   B. If the IRS seeks to enforce the summons in court, what evidence must the IRS introduce in order to obtain an order enforcing the summons?

---

[15] Occasionally, a court will accept a privilege log that identifies documents in categories, rather than individually. *See, e.g.*, SEC v. Nacchio, 2007 U.S. Dist. LEXIS 5435, *31-*341 (D. Colo. Jan. 24, 2007) ("[T]he court concludes that a document-by-document privilege log is not required as to the documents specifically at issue in Defendant's Motion to Compel. Without a more particularized showing of need by Defendant Kozlowski, I will not require the SEC to list each and every document withheld on the basis of the work product doctrine . . . ."); United States v. Gericare Med. Supply, Inc., 2000 U.S. Dist. LEXIS 19662 *11–*12 (S.D. Ala. Dec. 11, 2000) ("The plaintiff provided a privilege log by category rather than by individual document. . . . A document-by-document privilege log would have revealed the identity of each person interviewed, information that itself would reveal the plaintiff's strategy and mental processes.").

C. Assume that the IRS obtains a court order enforcing the summons. What risks does Jerry run if he withholds the documents and ignores the court order?

2. Ruth Connely runs a real estate sales office through a sole proprietorship. She is currently under audit for allegedly having failed to report as income real estate commissions she received from several large sales. The IRS agent in charge of the audit would like to obtain information from Ruth's clients about commission payments they may have made to Ruth.

   A. If the IRS decides to issue a summons to the clients for information relating to commissions, what administrative steps must the IRS follow?

   B. May Ruth file a proceeding in court preemptively challenging the summons?

   C. If Ruth initiates a proceeding in court challenging the summons, may the clients intervene in that proceeding?

3. Assume that the IRS issues a summons to the Davis & Davis law firm seeking the names of all of the firm's clients who are suspected of having participated in a particular tax shelter transaction. Is the summons enforceable?

4. Brad, an attorney, was retained by Cabot, Inc. after Cabot received a 30-day letter. The IRS has identified issues involving $2 million, one of which is a recurring issue for Cabot's business. Brad has drafted a tax protest and requested a conference with the IRS Appeals Division. Brad also provided Cabot with a memo explaining certain arguments he opted not to include in the protest but rather to save for possible subsequent litigation. In the course of discussing this memo with Cabot's Chief Executive Officer (CEO), the Cabot CEO gave Brad some potentially damaging documents "for safekeeping." Assume that shortly after Brad files the protest, the IRS issues a summons to Cabot requesting both the memo and the other documents.

   A. Will the memorandum that Brad wrote to Cabot explaining the arguments he omitted from the protest to save for possible subsequent litigation likely be protected by privilege? If so, which privilege?

   B. Will the documents that Cabot's CEO gave Brad for safekeeping likely be protected by privilege? If so, which privilege?

   C. Is Brad's discussion with Cabot's CEO about the memo protected by privilege? If so, which privilege?

5. Carmen is a certified public accountant (CPA) who was retained by Bill Billionaire. Would the federally authorized tax practitioner privilege of Code section 7525 apply to protect from disclosure to the IRS the following documents created by Carmen for Bill?

   A. A worksheet used to prepare Bill's complicated federal income tax return.

   B. A memorandum providing tax advice on state income tax law to Bill to assist him in deciding where to locate the headquarters of his next business venture.

   C. An investment plan for Bill's billions.

   D. A letter to Bill encouraging him to invest in a tax shelter that Carmen has developed.

   E. A memorandum advising Bill of a possible strategy in a pending tax controversy with the IRS with respect to which Bill has received a notice of deficiency.

   F. Oral advice to Bill in the presence of his girlfriend of a possible litigation strategy if Bill should decide to take the pending tax controversy to Tax Court.

G. Oral advice to Bill on how to handle various aspects of a criminal tax investigation of Bill by special agents of the IRS.

6. Assume that Carmen, the CPA, is hired by Dana, an attorney, to assist Dana with the accounting issues of a complex civil federal tax controversy for Dana's client, Ernest. Carmen talks with Ernest about the relevant accounting issues and reports back to Dana. Under what circumstances, if any, would the conversation between Carmen and Ernest be covered by the attorney-client privilege?

Chapter 5
IRS APPEALS

§ 5.01 INTRODUCTION

Most disputes between a taxpayer and the IRS are settled or compromised in some way. In fact, tax controversies are no exception to the general policy favoring settlement of disputes. The IRS provides a taxpayer numerous opportunities after an examination has been completed to come to some agreement on the extent of the taxpayer's liability. In addition, formal processes exist that encourage and facilitate negotiation and settlement prior to trial, including the IRS Appeals process. In order to obtain the most favorable settlement possible, the taxpayer and his or her representative must understand these processes.

Probably the most important avenue for settlement with the IRS is the administrative dispute resolution process through the IRS Appeals Division. While personnel in the Appeals Division handle many different types of cases — including refund claims, collection due process hearings, offers in compromise, and interest abatement claims — the focus on this chapter is appeals arising from audits conducted by the IRS examination (now sometimes called the compliance) function. This chapter analyzes these appeals procedures from a strategic and planning standpoint. In doing so, the chapter explores alternative routes available within the IRS Appeals Division for contesting a proposed increase in the taxpayer's liability, and identifies factors that might make one route more favorable than another. In this regard, the chapter provides an introduction to Tax Court litigation, which is taken up in detail in later chapters. The chapter also considers how the Appeals Division views its role in the dispute resolution process and why an understanding of that view is helpful for obtaining a favorable settlement.

§ 5.02 SETTLEMENT OPPORTUNITIES DURING AND AFTER THE EXAMINATION PHASE

[A] Timing Issues

According to many tax practitioners, the earlier a case is settled, the better. Whether this is true depends, of course, on the terms of the settlement that can be obtained at the earlier juncture. Certain variables, however, are time-sensitive. Representation fees normally increase the longer a controversy remains unresolved, and eventually the taxpayer will encounter filing fees and other litigation costs. The taxpayer must also factor into this mix of variables interest charges that are imposed should the IRS's determination of a tax deficiency ultimately prevail. Unless the taxpayer takes steps to limit interest accrual by submitting payment or deposit, or the interest accrual is otherwise suspended, interest continues to build, compounded on a daily basis, until the additional tax liability is paid.[1] As explained below, extending the duration of the dispute resolution process also increases the risk that additional deficiencies may be asserted against the taxpayer.

In recent years, the IRS has created processes that allow taxpayers to resolve disputes at the earliest stages of the tax controversy process. In addition to the letter ruling request process discussed in Chapter 2, several procedures allow taxpayers to resolve potential issues before an examination begins or an affected tax return is even filed. For example, as part of its continuing efforts to combat tax shelter transactions, the IRS has begun making "global" settlement offers to taxpayers who invested in

[1] Interest on tax underpayments (deficiencies) is discussed in detail in Chapter 13.

transactions the IRS considers abusive. To participate in the settlement process, the taxpayer typically has to concede 100 percent of the tax liability owed as a result of the subject transaction, all accrued interest, and penalties of up to 20 percent of the resulting underpayment. *See, e.g.*, Announcement 2004-46, 2004-21 I.R.B. 964 (settlement initiative for Son-of-BOSS transaction); Announcement 2005-80, 2005-46 I.R.B. 967 (settlement initiative for a variety of transactions including inflated basis shelters). Taxpayers who invested in these transactions but do not participate in a global settlement face penalty rates as high as 75 percent.

The IRS's pre-filing agreement (PFA) program also allows taxpayers in the Large and Mid-Size Business Division to resolve potential issues before the taxpayer even files a return. Under this program, an eligible taxpayer can request the IRS to audit a specific issue related to the tax return before the return is timely filed. By requesting early consideration of an issue, the taxpayer and the IRS have ready access to records that will be relevant to the determination of the issue and the taxpayer has certainty about the tax treatment of the relevant item at an earlier time.[2] Details relating to the program are spelled out in Revenue Procedure 2007-17, 2007-1 C.B. 368.[3] Issues potentially suitable for pre-filing resolution include factual issues and the application of well-settled legal principles to known facts. Examples include asset valuation, capitalization issues, and inventory issues. Disagreements between a taxpayer and the IRS over legal interpretations of the Code, as well as most penalty issues, are not subject to the program.[4] A related, but more narrowly tailored initiative, the Advance Pricing Agreement (APA) program, gives taxpayers the opportunity to resolve potential inter-company "transfer pricing" disputes under Code section 482 outside the traditional audit process.[5] The taxpayer and the IRS enter into a binding contract whereby the IRS agrees not to seek a transfer pricing adjustment for transactions covered by the APA. *See* Rev. Proc. 2006-9, 2006-9 I.R.B. 278.

[B] Options at the Conclusion of the Examination

The procedures employed by the IRS following an examination of the taxpayer's return depend in part upon how the IRS conducted the examination. At the conclusion of most office and field audits, the revenue agent who conducted the examination will discuss his findings with the taxpayer or his representative before submitting a formal report. If the revenue agent concludes that no changes should be made to the taxpayer's liability, the agent will prepare a "no change" report and the case is usually closed. I.R.M. 4.10.8.2.4. If the revenue agent intends to propose an adjustment to the taxpayer's liability, the agent will normally prepare Form 5701, Notice of Proposed Adjustment, or a related form. I.R.M. 4.10.7.5.4. The agent may also prepare Form 886-A, which explains the items for which adjustments will be proposed, and attach it to Form 5701. I.R.M. 4.46.6.9. Although the revenue agent generally does not have formal settlement authority, the taxpayer normally is given an opportunity at the conclusion of the examination to reach a compromise with the agent or the agent's manager. Proc. Reg. § 601.105(b)(4). This compromise must be based on the IRS's published positions

---

[2] Another program for large business taxpayers, the Compliance Assurance Program (CAP), involves taxpayers who agree to be audited before filing a return. The goal is to resolve uncertainty in advance, thereby reducing or eliminating the need for a post-filing examination. *See* Announcement 2005-87, 2005-50 I.R.B. 1144.

[3] The parties memorialize their resolution of an issue in a pre-filing agreement (PFA). Revenue Procedure 2007-17 treats most PFAs as closing agreements under Code section 7121. *See* Rev. Proc. 2007-17 at § 7.02. As a result, the PFA is considered confidential return information under Code section 6103, and accordingly exempt from disclosure under the Freedom of Information Act. *Id.* at § 11.

[4] Questions regarding the interpretation of legal issues are more properly resolved by requests for letter rulings (discussed in Chapter 2).

[5] Section 482 authorizes the IRS to reallocate income and deductions among related corporations and other businesses if the taxpayers' treatment does not clearly reflect income.

with respect to legal issues (such as regulations or Revenue Rulings) and the examiner's determination of the facts involved.[6] According to one experienced tax practitioner:

> This is a very important stage in the processing of a tax case; many settlements are reached that might not be possible if discussions were deferred until after formal reports have been written or issued. Speculative and debatable questions of fact, which have no precise answer, may frequently be compromised on a fair basis, and quite often one doubtful legal question may be traded off against another.

HUGH C. BICKFORD, SUCCESSFUL TAX PRACTICE 206 (4th ed. 1967). Even where the likelihood of a compromise with the revenue agent seems remote, the taxpayer can use these informal proceedings as an opportunity to reiterate his or her arguments and to ensure that the agent correctly understands the relevant facts.

If negotiations at the examination level have stalled, the IRS has several specialized programs available to help the parties strike a settlement before the case is assigned to the Appeals Division. If, for instance, the parties have reached agreement on all but a single issue, the taxpayer might consider using the IRS's Early Referral Program. The Early Referral Program allows the taxpayer to request during the examination phase that a specific issue be transferred directly to the Appeals Division for resolution, while any remaining issues continue to be developed by the revenue agent. *See* I.R.C. § 7123(a). This procedure is designed to encourage quick resolution of key issues in the hope that such resolution might facilitate agreement on other outstanding issues. The procedures for initiating an early referral request are in Revenue Procedure 99-28, 1999-2 C.B. 109.

A related program, fast-track mediation, allows taxpayers in the Small Business/Self-Employed Operating Division (or the examining agent) to request the involvement of Appeals Division personnel to mediate the case while it is still undergoing examination. Under this procedure, if a taxpayer disagrees with the examining agent's findings, he or she may request that a mediator from within the Appeals Division be assigned to meet with the taxpayer and the examining agent's manager. The goal is to create an impartial forum for the taxpayer and the IRS in which to resolve the dispute. The role of the mediator is to encourage communication between the parties and to elicit information necessary to understand the nature of the issues. The mediator has no authority to require either party to accept a result. If unagreed issues remain, the taxpayer retains all appeals rights (discussed below). Procedures relating to the fast track mediation program are in Revenue Procedure 2003-41. 2003-1 C.B. 1047. The IRS has also established a similar program, fast-track settlement, primarily for taxpayers within the jurisdiction of the Large and Mid-Size Business Division. *See* Rev. Proc. 2003-40, 2003-1 C.B. 1044.

[1] Agreed Cases

If the taxpayer and the revenue agent can reach a mutually acceptable agreement at the conclusion of the examination, the taxpayer normally will be asked to evidence this agreement by signing Form 870, Waiver of Restrictions on Assessment and Collection of Deficiency in Tax.[7] *See* I.R.M. 4.10.8.4.[8] Review the Form 870 waiver agreement, reproduced below.

---

[6] *See generally* I.R.M. 4.10.7.5.3.1 ("Examination personnel have the authority and responsibility to reach a definite conclusion based on a balanced and impartial evaluation of all the evidence. . . . This authority does not extend to consideration of the hazards of litigation."). Examination personnel in the Small Business/Self-Employed and Large and Mid-Sized Business divisions do have limited settlement authority with respect to certain issues identified by delegation order if the settlement is consistent with prior settlements made at the Appeals level. *See, e.g.*, Delegation Order 4-25 (Mar. 11, 2005).

[7] Signing Form 870 also stops the accrual of interest on the underlying liability, such that no interest is

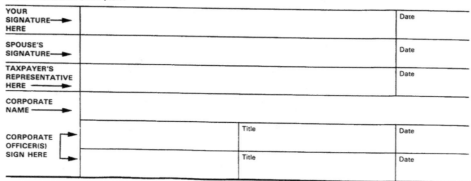

Form **870** (Rev. March 1992)	Department of the Treasury — Internal Revenue Service **Waiver of Restrictions on Assessment and Collection of Deficiency in Tax and Acceptance of Overassessment**	Date received by Internal Revenue Service

Names and address of taxpayers *(Number, street, city or town, State, ZIP code)*	Social security or employer identification number

	Increase (Decrease) in Tax and Penalties				
Tax year ended	**Tax**	**Penalties**			
	$	$	$	$	$
	$	$	$	$	$
	$	$	$	$	$
	$	$	$	$	$
	$	$	$	$	$
	$	$	$	$	$
	$	$	$	$	$

(For instructions, see back of form)

Consent to Assessment and Collection

I consent to the immediate assessment and collection of any deficiencies *(increase in tax and penalties)* and accept any overassessment *(decrease in tax and penalties)* shown above, plus any interest provided by law. I understand that by signing this waiver, I will not be able to contest these years in the United States Tax Court, unless additional deficiencies are determined for these years.

YOUR SIGNATURE HERE →			Date
SPOUSE'S SIGNATURE →			Date
TAXPAYER'S REPRESENTATIVE HERE →			Date
CORPORATE NAME →			
CORPORATE OFFICER(S) SIGN HERE →		Title	Date
→		Title	Date

Catalog Number 16894U — Form **870** (Rev. 3-92)

charged from a date 30 days after the taxpayer files the form. I.R.C. § 6601(c).

[8] In a fully agreed income tax case, the IRS may use Form 4549 to document the taxpayer's assent.

Instructions

General Information

If you consent to the assessment of the deficiencies shown in this waiver, please sign and return the form in order to limit any interest charge and expedite the adjustment to your account. Your consent will not prevent you from filing a claim for refund *(after you have paid the tax)* if you later believe you are so entitled. It will not prevent us from later determining, if necessary, that you owe additional tax; nor extend the time provided by law for either action.

We have agreements with State tax agencies under which information about Federal tax, including increases or decreases, is exchanged with the States. If this change affects the amount of your State income tax, you should file the required State form.

If you later file a claim and the Service disallows it, you may file suit for refund in a district court or in the United States Claims Court, but you may not file a petition with the United States Tax Court.

We will consider this waiver a valid claim for refund or credit of any overpayment due you resulting from any decrease in tax and penalties shown above, provided you sign and file it within the period established by law for making such a claim.

Who Must Sign

If you filed jointly, both you and your spouse must sign. If this waiver is for a corporation, it should be signed with the corporation name, followed by the signatures and titles of the corporate officers authorized to sign. An attorney or agent may sign this waiver provided such action is specifically authorized by a power of attorney which, if not previously filed, must accompany this form.

If this waiver is signed by a person acting in a fiduciary capacity *(for example, an executor, administrator, or a trustee)* Form 56, Notice Concerning Fiduciary Relationship, should, unless previously filed, accompany this form.

If the taxpayer is willing to agree to some of the revenue agent's proposed adjustments but not others, the taxpayer may file a waiver agreement covering only those agreed-upon issues. *Id.* As the language on the back of Form 870 makes clear, the taxpayer's execution of the Form 870 may not prevent the IRS from subsequently asserting an additional deficiency with respect to the same taxable year.[9]

An executed Form 870 allows the IRS to summarily assess the agreed-upon liability without complying with statutory restrictions that otherwise apply to tax deficiencies. *See* I.R.C. § 6213(d). In particular, the taxpayer waives his or her right to receive a statutory notice of deficiency, which, as explained in more detail below, will prevent the taxpayer from later contesting the liability in the Tax Court. By signing the Form 870 at this stage, the taxpayer also gives up the right to negotiate a settlement with the IRS Appeals Division. As a result, once the taxpayer signs the form, the IRS will assess the tax and begin the collection process. This is not to say, however, that the taxpayer has no recourse should he or she decide to challenge the adjustment later on. In order to do so, the taxpayer will have to pay the liability, make a timely claim for refund, and assert such claim in either the Court of Federal Claims or a United States district court.[10]

[2] Unagreed Cases

If the taxpayer and the revenue agent cannot come to an agreement, the agent normally will prepare and submit to the taxpayer a preliminary notice of deficiency, commonly called a "30-day letter." A sample is reproduced below. The 30-day letter is a form letter that sets forth the amount of the proposed adjustment to the taxpayer's liability. Included with the letter will be a copy of the revenue agent's report (RAR), which explains in detail the agent's findings and the basis for the proposed liability. Proc. Reg. § 601.105(d)(1). In the RAR, the agent describes his or her findings of fact and analyzes those facts in light of the agent's interpretation of surrounding law. The RAR may also include separate reports from IRS economists and appraisers addressing valuation and other technical calculations. The IRS will also include with the

---

[9] As a general matter, examination personnel are instructed not to reopen an agreed case to assert adjustments unfavorable to the taxpayer unless evidence of fraud or misrepresentation exists, or circumstances exist indicating that a failure to reopen the case would be a "serious administrative omission." Rev. Proc. 2005-32, 2005-1 C.B. 1206, at § 5.01. The term "serious administrative omission" could include transactions that present a significant potential for abuse as well as reportable transaction issues within the meaning of Treasury regulation section 1.6011-4(b). *Id.* at § 5.02.

[10] Refund procedures are discussed in detail in Chapter 10.

30-day letter an explanation of the taxpayer's appeal rights within the IRS (Publication 5) and an explanation of the collection process (Publication 594).[11]

After receiving the 30-day letter, the taxpayer has several options. The taxpayer may decide, having analyzed the revenue agent's report, to reconsider his or her potential exposure and agree to the agent's proposed adjustments. If so, the 30-day letter instructs the taxpayer to sign a Form 870 waiver. As noted above, agreeing to the agent's proposed adjustments and paying the resulting liability is also a viable option for a taxpayer who intends to pursue the matter as a refund action.

A second possible response to the 30-day letter is to contest the revenue agent's findings with the IRS Appeals Division. The taxpayer is granted 30 days (hence the preliminary notice's commonly used name) in which to request a conference with the Appeals staff. The procedures of the administrative appeals process are discussed below.

If the taxpayer elects not to pursue an appeal or otherwise fails to respond to the 30-day letter, he or she will eventually receive from the IRS a notice of deficiency (also referred to as a 90-day letter). Like the 30-day letter, the 90-day letter sets forth the additional amount that the IRS believes the taxpayer owes. The notice of deficiency also authorizes the taxpayer, within 90 days after the notice of deficiency is sent, to file a petition with the Tax Court to redetermine the amount of the proposed liability. In fact, if, at the conclusion of the examination, litigation in the Tax Court is the taxpayer's best option, he or she may consider forgoing the preliminary notice of deficiency, and request that the IRS issue a 90-day letter without additional delay. The advantages and disadvantages of pursuing Tax Court litigation without a prior administrative appeal are discussed below.

A 30-day letter typically looks something like this:

SAMPLE 30-DAY LETTER

Internal Revenue Service **Department of the Treasury**

Date:

Taxpayer Identifying Number:
Form:
Tax Period(s) Ended and Deficiency Amounts:
December 31, 20xx
$xx,xxx
Person to Contact:
Telephone Number:
Employee Identification Number:
Last Date to Respond to This Letter:

Dear Taxpayer:

We have enclosed an examination report showing proposed changes to your tax for the period(s) shown above. Please read the report, and tell us whether you agree or disagree with the changes by the date shown above. (This report may not reflect the results of later examinations of partnerships, "S" Corporations, trusts, etc., in which you may have an interest. Changes to those accounts could also affect your tax.)

If you agree with the proposed changes . . .

---

[11] The 30-day letter, unlike the notice of deficiency, is not required by statute and does not toll the running of the statute of limitations on assessment. As explained in Chapter 7, the IRS usually must send a valid notice of deficiency before making an assessment, and the notice of deficiency tolls the period of limitations for a specified time after it is issued.

1. Sign and date the enclosed agreement form. If you filed a joint return, both taxpayers must sign the form.
2. Return the signed agreement form to us.
3. Enclose payment of the tax, interest and any penalties due. Make your check or money order payable to the **United States Treasury**. You can call the person identified above to determine the total amount due as of the date you intend to make payment.
4. After we receive your signed agreement form, we will close your case.

If you pay the full amount due now, you will limit the amount of interest and penalties charged to your account. If you agree with our findings, but can only pay part of the bill, please call the person identified above to discuss different payment options. We may ask you to complete a collection information statement to determine your payment options, such as paying in installments. You can also write to us or visit your nearest IRS office to explain your circumstances. If you don't enclose payment for the additional tax, interest, and any penalties, we will bill you for the unpaid amounts.

If you are a "C" Corporation, Section 6621(c) of the Internal Revenue Code provides that an interest rate 2% higher than the standard rate of interest will be charged on deficiencies of $100,000 or more.

If you don't agree with the proposed changes . . .

1. You may request a meeting or telephone conference with the supervisor of the person identified in the heading of this letter. If you still don't agree after the meeting or telephone conference, you can:
2. Request a conference with our Appeals Office. If the total proposed change to your tax is:
   - $25,000 or less for *each* referenced tax period, send us a letter requesting consideration by Appeals. Indicate the issues you don't agree with and the reasons why you don't agree. If you don't want to write a separate letter, you can complete the Statement of Disputed Issues at the end of this letter and return it to us.
   - More than $25,000 for *any* referenced tax period, you must submit a formal protest.

The requirements for filing a formal protest are explained in the enclosed Publication 5, *Your Appeal Rights and How to Prepare a Protest If You Don't Agree.* We've also enclosed Publication 1, *Your Rights as a Taxpayer*, and Publication 594, *The IRS Collection Process.*

If you request a conference with our Appeals Office, an Appeals Officer will call you (if necessary) for an appointment to take a fresh look at your case. The Appeals Office is an independent office and most disputes considered by the Appeals Office are resolved informally and promptly. By requesting a conference with our Appeals Office you may avoid court costs (such as the Tax Court $60 filing fee), resolve the matter sooner, and/or prevent interest and any penalties from increasing your account.

If you decide to bypass the Appeals Office and petition the Tax Court directly, your case will usually be sent to an Appeals Office first to try to resolve the issue. Certain procedures and rights in court (for example, the burden of proof and potential recovery of litigation costs) depend on you fully participating in the administrative consideration of your case, including consideration by the IRS Appeals Office.

If you don't reach an agreement with our Appeals Office or if you don't respond to this letter, we will send you another letter that will tell you how to obtain Tax Court review of your case.

You must mail your signed agreement form, completed Statement of Disputed Issues, or a formal protest to us by the response date shown in the heading of this letter. If you decide to request a conference with the examiner's supervisor, your request should also be made by the response date indicated.

MAIL RESPONSES TO: **Internal Revenue Service**
Attn: J. Smith
200 Granby Hall Rm 539
Norfolk Federal Building
Norfolk, VA 23510

If you have any questions, please contact the person identified in the heading of this letter. We will be glad to discuss your options with you.

Sincerely yours,

Jane Doe
Director, Compliance Area 4-SBSE

Enclosures:

Copy of this letter
Examination Report
Agreement Form
Publications 5, 1, 594
Envelope
Letter 950 (DO) (Rev. 9-2000)

[C] Settlement at the IRS Appeals Division

[1] Background on the IRS Appeals Division

The appeals process involves an administrative review by an officer from the IRS Appeals Division, who negotiates with the taxpayer or the taxpayer's representative over the appropriate tax treatment of items on the return. The stated mission of the Appeals Division is to resolve tax controversies on a basis that is fair and impartial to both the government and the taxpayer, without litigation. I.R.M. 8.1.1.1. Statistics confirm the Appeals Division's apparent success in carrying out its mission. Statistics from the General Accounting Office reveal that over 85 percent of large cases handled by the Appeals Division are settled (representing 88 percent of the tax dollars in dispute). General Accounting Office, *Report on IRS Initiatives to Resolve Disputes Over Tax Liabilities*, GAO/GGD- 97-71 (May 9, 1997). If the taxpayer is unable to come to a compromise with the Appeals Division, the taxpayer's recourse is to pursue the matter either through Tax Court litigation or as a refund action.[12]

Under the IRS's organizational structure, the Appeals Division is integrated into the four operating divisions, but continues to function as an independent organization reporting directly to the IRS Commissioner. Appeals personnel are instructed to handle cases without favoritism or discrimination toward either the taxpayer or the government. Proc. Reg. § 601.106(f)(1). To ensure its independence from the examination function and other IRS units, procedures exist that prohibit an Appeals Officer and another IRS employee from conferring on a taxpayer's case outside the presence of the taxpayer or the taxpayer's representative. IRS Reform Act § 1001(a)(4). This prohibition primarily affects discussions between the Appeals Officer and the revenue agent who conducted the audit. It is not uncommon, in fact, for the Appeals Officer to remain in contact with the revenue agent during the appeals process. The prohibition against *ex parte* communications applies only to the extent such

---

[12] As noted above, the Appeals Division has jurisdiction to hear a variety of issues, not all of which stem from an assessment made after examination. For example, a taxpayer may also appeal a case to the Appeals Division after the taxpayer's refund claim is rejected or as part of the Collection Due Process (CDP) hearing procedures. Appeals procedures relating to these matters are discussed in Chapters 10 and 16, respectively.

communications appear to compromise the independence of the Appeals Division. As you become more familiar with the settlement techniques and procedures utilized at the Appeals Division, consider why Congress emphasized the need for independence and the appearance of independence of Appeals Officers.

Revenue Procedure 2000-43, 2000-43 I.R.B. 404, sets forth the IRS's current view on what constitutes a permissible or prohibited *ex parte* communication. As a general rule, the taxpayer or the taxpayer's representative must be given the opportunity to participate in communications, oral or written, between Appeals Officers and other IRS employees *unless* those communications relate to matters that are entirely "ministerial, administrative, or procedural" in nature. *Id.* Q&A 5. Communications addressing the "substance of the issues in the case" are prohibited unless the taxpayer is given an opportunity to participate (for example, attend a hearing or participate in a conference call). *Id.*

Specific examples of prohibited communications include: (1) "Discussions about the accuracy of the facts presented by the taxpayer and the relative importance of the facts to the determination"; (2) "Discussions of the relative merits or alternative legal interpretations of authorities cited in a protest or in a report prepared by the originating function"; and (3) "Discussions of the originating function's perception of the demeanor or credibility of the taxpayer or taxpayer's representative." *Id.* In the Revenue Procedure, the IRS takes the position that certain practices consistent with the function of the Appeals office are not affected by the prohibition. For instance, the revenue agent's act of transferring the taxpayer's administrative file to the Appeals Officer is not a prohibited *ex parte* communication. Similarly, the Appeals Officer's act of returning the case back to the examination function for further review or transferring to the revenue agent new information and evidence presented by the taxpayer is not a prohibited communication. If, however, as part of that process, the Appeals Officer wishes to discuss the strengths and weaknesses of the taxpayer's case, the taxpayer must be notified and be given an opportunity to participate in those discussion.

Revenue Procedure 2000-43 also limits *ex parte* communications between Appeals Officers and the Office of Chief Counsel in cases that have not been docketed in Tax Court (nondocketed cases).[13] Appeals Officers commonly rely on attorneys in the Chief Counsel's Office to supply legal advice concerning specific issues and settlement guidelines.

> Appeals employees should not communicate ex parte regarding an issue in a case pending before them with Counsel field attorneys who have previously provided advice on that issue [during the examination process]. * * * Counsel will assign a different attorney to provide assistance to Appeals. If an Appeals employee believes it is necessary to seek advice from any Counsel field attorney who previously provided advice to the originating function regarding that issue in the case, the taxpayer/representative will be provided an opportunity to participate in any such communications.
>
> Appeals' requests for legal advice that raise questions that cannot be answered with a high degree of certainty by application of established principles of law to particular facts will be referred to the Chief Counsel National Office and will be handled as requests for field service advice or technical advice, as appropriate, in accordance with applicable procedures. The response of the National Office to Appeals will be disclosed to the taxpayer in accordance with section 6110.
>
> Appeals employees are cautioned that, while they may obtain legal advice from the Office of Chief Counsel, they remain responsible for independently

---

[13] According to Revenue Procedure 2000-43, the prohibitions against *ex parte* communications do not apply in docketed cases.

> evaluating the strengths and weaknesses of the specific issues presented by the cases assigned to them, and for making independent judgments concerning the overall strengths and weaknesses of the cases and the hazards of litigation. Consistent with this assignment of responsibility, Counsel attorneys will not provide advice that includes recommendations of settlement ranges for an issue in a case pending before Appeals or for the case as a whole.

Id.

Revenue Procedure 2000-43 also confirms that taxpayers or their representatives may waive the prohibitions on *ex parte* communications by following specified procedures. But if the prohibitions are not waived and the Appeals office violates the *ex parte* rule, what is the appropriate remedy for the taxpayer? When it enacted the prohibition, Congress failed to specify a penalty should the Appeals office violate the prohibition. According to Revenue Procedure 2000-43, "[v]iolations will be addressed in accordance with existing administrative and personnel processes." The IRS has not issued further guidance on this issue and, possibly because violations are difficult to detect, few cases have addressed what an appropriate remedy would be.

In one instance involving an estate tax audit in which the valuation of closely held stock was at issue, the Appeals Officer contacted the examining agent in violation of the *ex parte* rules to instruct the agent to revise his stock appraisal. The taxpayer's attorney, having learned of the prohibited communication, requested that a different Appeals Officer be assigned to the case. Instead, the IRS assigned a new examining agent and restarted the audit. During the course of the new audit, the examining agent issued a series of third-party summonses. As part of the judicial proceedings in the case, both the district court and the Eighth Circuit refused to quash the summonses that were issued based on information that the IRS had obtained through *ex parte* communications. Robert v. United States, 364 F.3d 988 (8th Cir. 2004). The Eighth Circuit affirmed the district court's order enforcing the summonses, noting that Congress failed to include in the IRS Reform Act a remedy for the taxpayer should the IRS violate the *ex parte* rules. The court went on to explain that "[t]he Supreme Court has stated that courts should be slow to erect barriers to enforcement of [IRS] summonses where the summonses are being used to further [the IRS's] mission of effectively investigating taxpayer liabilities." *Id.* at 996 (*quoting* United States v. Euge, 444 U.S. 707, 711 (1980)).

The Tax Court has been more proactive on behalf of aggrieved taxpayers, rejecting on several occasions the IRS's argument that, as long as independent grounds exist for the Appeals Officer's determination, the prohibited communication should be ignored. Industrial Investors v. Commissioner, T.C. Memo. 2007-93; Moore v. Commissioner, T.C. Memo. 2006-171. In *Industrial Investors*, a case involving a prohibited communication that took place as part of a Collection Due Process hearing, Tax Court Judge Holmes remanded the taxpayer's case for a new hearing at the Appeals level. Judge Holmes specified further that the new appeals hearing should be conducted by an impartial Appeals Officer, in a face-to-face manner, and at the Appeals office nearest to the taxpayer. What other options might be available in a case in which the IRS violates the prohibition on *ex parte* communications?

[2] The Protest Letter

As a prerequisite to Appeals jurisdiction over proposed assessment cases, the taxpayer generally must request Appeals consideration. As the sample 30-day letter makes clear, the manner in which this is done primarily depends upon the amount of tax liability in controversy. If the amount of the proposed adjustment exceeds $25,000 for any taxable period, the taxpayer must file a formal written protest, as described below. If the amount at issue is $25,000 or less, the taxpayer can use the small case request procedures, which require the taxpayer merely to send a letter requesting

Appeals consideration and explain in the letter what the taxpayer disagrees with and why. *See* Publication 5, *Your Appeal Rights and How to Prepare a Protest if You Don't Agree.*

Where a formal written protest is required, it must be filed within 30 days from the date appearing on the 30-day letter. Although there is no official form for filing a written protest, the protest must include the following information:

- The taxpayer's name, address, and telephone number;
- A statement that the taxpayer wants to appeal the examination findings to the Appeals Division;
- A copy of the 30-day letter (or the date and symbols appearing on the 30-day letter);
- The taxable years involved;
- An itemized schedule of the adjustments with which the taxpayer disagrees;
- A statement of facts supporting the taxpayer's position on any contested factual issue;
- A statement setting forth the law and other authorities on which the taxpayer relies; and
- A specifically provided declaration under penalties of perjury that the factual representations are true and correct.

See id.

If the taxpayer's attorney or agent prepares the written protest, it must include a declaration indicating that the protest was prepared by a representative and a statement of whether the representative personally knows that the factual assertions included in the protest are true and correct. *See id.* If the protest is prepared by a representative who has not previously filed a power of attorney with the IRS on behalf of the taxpayer, the protest should also be accompanied by a power of attorney, Form 2848, executed by the taxpayer. A sample form for a protest letter is printed below.

SAMPLE PROTEST FORM

Internal Revenue Service
[Address]

[Date]

Re: Taxpayer's Name
Address
T.I.N. or E.I.N.

Dear Sir or Madam:

In response to your correspondence dated ____________________, asserting an income tax deficiency for the taxable year(s) ____________________, this letter protests certain findings in your letter and its attached examination report (copies of which are attached).

The following information is submitted in support of this protest:

1. Appeals Conference Request

   The taxpayer requests an appeals conference with an officer of the IRS Appeals Division for a time convenient to both parties.

2. Taxpayer's Name, Address and Telephone Number

   Name

   Address

   Telephone Number

3. Date and Symbols of the Transmittal Letter

Date

Symbols

4. Taxable Years Involved

Calendar (or Fiscal) Year(s) ________________

5. Schedule of Contested Adjustments

[Set forth in separately itemized paragraphs the adjustments included by the examining agent in the 30-day letter (including penalty assertions) with which the Taxpayer disagrees.]

6. Statement of Facts

[Set forth an organized description of the relevant facts surrounding each of the protested adjustments. Where appropriate, reference and attach affidavits and other supporting documents.]

7. Statement of Law

[Set forth the law applicable to each of the protested adjustments and apply the law to the facts of the case.]

The undersigned prepared this protest on behalf of the taxpayer but does not know personally whether the statement of facts contained in this protest is true and correct.

A Form 2848, Power of Attorney, authorizing the undersigned to represent the taxpayer in this matter, is also enclosed.

Respectfully yours,

[Representative]

Enclosures

Ideally, the protest letter should convey to the Appeals Officer the merits of the taxpayer's position and highlight the weaknesses in the revenue agent's analysis. From a more practical standpoint, the content of the letter will depend, to a large degree, on the amount in controversy and the drafter's familiarity with the taxpayer's case. (Frequently, a taxpayer does not consult a representative, particularly an attorney, until after the 30-day letter has been issued.) The amount of detail to be included in the protest letter also represents a strategic decision. One treatise explains:

> (2) The taxpayer has three options for filing a protest, which are:
>
> (a) a "skeletal" protest;
>
> (b) an agent's report responsive protest; and
>
> (c) a comprehensive protest.
>
> (3) The taxpayer should consider filing a skeletal protest that meets the minimum requirements for filing a protest when there is a concern for continued involvement of the agent at the examination level.

Steve Hidalgo & Percy P. Woodward, IRS Examinations and Appeals: Domestic and International Procedures ¶ 514 (1993).

In fact, a skeletal protest may be the only option when the representative has not had the opportunity to analyze all of the facts and issues by the time the protest is due. *Id.* Filing a skeletal protest, however, puts more pressure on the representative to make the taxpayer's case during the Appeals conference. An uninformative protest letter may also have the adverse effect of putting the Appeals Officer in the position of feeling less able to prepare for that conference. Michael I. Saltzman & Alan W. Saltzman, IRS Procedural Forms and Analysis ¶ 7.06[4][b] (2008).

> [T]he appeals officer who is made to feel ignorant may become defensive and "dig in his heels" when discussing a disposition of the case. This is more than a matter of psychology. As a practical matter, the appeals officer believes that the taxpayer has the burden of proving that the [IRS] made an improper determination. The taxpayer cannot begin to carry this burden by filing a skeleton protest and bringing up matters for the first time at a conference.

Id.

A report-responsive protest is one that is more developed than a skeletal protest but does not go beyond responding to the issues raised by the IRS in the RAR. *See* Hidalgo & Woodward, *supra*, at 514. This approach allows the taxpayer to respond to the RAR, and thus avoid leaving all of the arguments for the Appeals conference, but not inadvertently raise issues that have not been considered by the IRS. Submitting a report-responsive protest can also help the representative maintain the flexibility to develop arguments that will be the most persuasive to the particular Appeals Officer. Charles E. Hodges II, *Handling an IRS Estate or Gift Tax Audit and Beyond*, ABA Income and Transfer Tax Planning Group Roundtable (2006).

The third option, a comprehensive protest, also offers advantages to the taxpayer. One commentator argues:

> In nondocketed cases, taxpayers should put their best foot forward initially with a strong Protest. The facts and legal arguments in support of the taxpayer's position on each issue should be fully developed in the Protest. A strong, comprehensive and well-written Protest is the cornerstone of effective settlement negotiations. A strong brief can reveal fundamental weaknesses in Examination's case. Because Examination now has an opportunity to rebut the protest and Appeals can return a case to Examination when the RAR is fundamentally flawed, the taxpayer may be caught in the dilemma that a strong brief will result in further Examination activity. The only way to avoid this is to bypass the 30-day letter and take a statutory Notice of Deficiency.

Barbara T. Kaplan, *Corporate Income Tax Controversies: Procedures and Strategies for Audits, Appeals and Trials*, 796 PLI/Tax 633, 773 (2007). The option of initially bypassing Appeals is discussed below.

Although a comprehensive protest offers certain advantages, there also are associated risks. Note that the facts in a protest are sworn to under penalties of perjury, so they have the potential to be used against the taxpayer. *See* Hodges, *supra*. In addition, detailed factual assertions not previously considered during the audit might cause the Appeals Officer to return the case to the revenue agent for further investigation, I.R.M. 8.2.1.4, while detailed legal arguments run the risk of tipping off the Appeals Officer to legal theories he or she might not otherwise have considered. These latter risks are reduced somewhat by the IRS's own procedural rules that discourage an Appeals Officer from reopening issues previously resolved at the examination level, and from raising new issues or theories unless there are substantial grounds underlying the new issues and the potential effect on the taxpayer's liability is material. *See* IRS Policy Statement P-8-2 (Jan. 5, 2007).[14]

Although practitioners may disagree over how a protest letter should be drafted, and the particular circumstances of the case must always be considered, the general consensus seems to be that the taxpayer will start from a better negotiating position by preparing a protest that details the taxpayer's factual and legal arguments. At the very least, a strong protest letter lets the Appeals Officer know that the taxpayer has considered the issues seriously and is intent on pursuing the case aggressively.

---

[14] "The existence of unreported income, deductions, credits, gains, losses, etc. stemming from a tax shelter which is a listed transaction constitutes such a substantial ground with a material effect upon the tax liability." IRS Policy Statement P-8-2 (Jan. 5, 2007), *available at* http://www.irs.gov/pub/foia/ig/spder/p-8-2.pdf.

[3] Docketed Versus Nondocketed Appeals

If the taxpayer chooses to file a protest letter, it is forwarded by the examining agent, along with the administrative file prepared by the agent, to the Appeals Officer who will participate in the negotiations. If the taxpayer chooses not to protest the 30-day letter, the IRS will ultimately issue a notice of deficiency, which permits the taxpayer to file a petition in the Tax Court. If the taxpayer follows this course of action, initially bypassing the Appeals process and filing directly in the Tax Court, the taxpayer will still be provided an opportunity to settle the case administratively. Under IRS procedures designed to encourage case resolution before trial, the IRS attorney handling the Tax Court case must refer it back to the Appeals Division for possible settlement before the case is scheduled for trial. *See* Rev. Proc. 87-24, 1987-1 C.B. 720. As indicated above, cases that are protested directly to Appeals in response to the 30-day letter are referred to as "nondocketed" cases. Cases that reach Appeals after a Tax Court petition has been filed and the case has been entered on the Tax Court's calendar (the docket) are referred to as "docketed" cases.[15]

The settlement guidelines and policies that the Appeals Officer is instructed to follow generally do not vary based on whether the case is presented as a docketed or nondocketed case. I.R.M. 8.2.1.1. The Internal Revenue Manual instructs the Appeals Officer to maintain impartiality with respect to the taxpayer and the government regardless of the context. Unlike a revenue agent negotiating at the examination level,[16] an Appeals Officer may compromise issues based on the "hazards of litigation," that is, the possibility that the IRS's stated position may not be sustained if litigated. Proc. Reg. § 601.106(f).[17] As a result, even if the taxpayer's position is contrary to a published ruling or regulation, it is not uncommon for an Appeals Officer to concede the issue if the applicable case law supports the taxpayer's position. Determining the hazards of litigation, of course, requires a careful analysis of IRS rulings and pronouncements, court decisions, as well as pending court cases addressing similar fact situations.

Another policy of the Appeals Division is that it will not consider a settlement based on the nuisance value of a case. I.R.M. 8.6.4.1.3. Likewise, the Appeals Officer is instructed not to concede penalty assertions in exchange for concessions by the taxpayer on unrelated matters. Chief Counsel Notice CC-2004-036 (Sept. 22, 2004) ("Penalties can and should still be settled, but the settlement should be based on the merits and the hazards surrounding each penalty issue standing alone.")[18]

With respect to nondocketed cases, the Appeals Officer retains exclusive settlement authority. For docketed cases, settlement authority is divided between the Appeals Division and the IRS attorney handling the case. Once a docketed case has been referred to the Appeals Division for settlement, Appeals has sole settlement authority until such time as the case is returned to IRS counsel. The Appeals Division generally must return a case to the IRS attorney when it becomes clear that no progress is being made toward settlement or when the case is placed on the Tax Court trial calendar. When returned, IRS counsel takes up authority to dispose of the case by trial or settlement. *See* Rev. Proc. 87-24, *supra*.

---

[15] The IRS requires that the limitations period during which the IRS can assess additional liability (generally three years) remain open during the Appeals process. If, at the time the Appeals Division considers the case, the statute of limitations will expire in 150 or fewer days, the taxpayer will be asked to extend the limitations period to permit a full consideration of the case. If the taxpayer refuses to extend the limitations period, he or she will be sent a 90-day letter and may lose the ability to negotiate the issues in a nondocketed posture. I.R.M. 8.21.3.1.3.1. The statute of limitations on assessment is discussed in Chapter 7.

[16] *See* Section 5.02[B], *supra*.

[17] While most Appeals Officers are not attorneys, they are generally capable of understanding the relative risks of taking a case to trial.

[18] Penalties are discussed in Chapter 12.

Given that a taxpayer's case will be routed through the Appeals Division eventually, why might the taxpayer decide to defer Appeals consideration until after a petition has been filed in the Tax Court? This approach, like many of those in this chapter, represents an important strategic decision based upon a broad range of factors; there are no clear answers. One author explains these considerations as follows:

> There are a number of potential advantages of docketing a case in Tax Court rather than filing a Protest as the route to the Appeals Office. In a Docketed Case, a taxpayer often can selectively brief issues. Further, selective disclosure of facts in response to requests by an Appeals Officer is possible. The taxpayer also can get an initial reading of the Appeals Officer's position based upon his review of the Petition. In contrast, where the taxpayer goes directly to Appeals, the Protest describes fully its factual and legal positions about each issue before meeting the Appeals Officer. Prior docketing of a case in the Tax Court should help convince the Appeals Office of the taxpayer's determination to litigate one or more issues if necessary to achieve the appropriate result.
>
> For cases that ultimately go to litigation, docketing in the Tax Court before Appeals Office consideration should result in an earlier trial date. In this regard, the periodic receipt of trial status notices tends to put additional pressure on an Appeals Officer to grapple with the issues. For issues that go to litigation, prior docketing in the Tax Court forces the IRS to begin to lock in its position before the Tax Court (via the Notice of Deficiency) without the benefit of further development of its position through Appeals Office consideration. While the Tax Court will allow the IRS to amend its Answer to raise new issues or allege new facts, the IRS will bear the burden of proof with respect to any "new matter." Tax Ct. R. 142(a).[19] * * * The involvement of an IRS trial lawyer may inject more realism about the hazards of litigation for the IRS. Docketing of the case before the Appeals Office's consideration also may avoid delays and other consequences of the IRS's practice of having the Examination Division prepare a rebuttal of the protest. * * *
>
> There also are potential disadvantages of prior docketing in the Tax Court. The taxpayer must await issuance of a Notice of Deficiency and filing of the Petition and Answer before the case comes before the Appeals Office. The Petition will lock in the taxpayer's position as to any facts or legal conclusions set forth therein to a greater extent than a Protest or informal discussions with an Appeals Officer. While the taxpayer can amend its pleadings before the Tax Court as freely as the government, it may lose credibility with the court. Docketing a case in the Tax Court before Appeals Office consideration will lock in the Tax Court as the forum for any litigation. Obviously, the taxpayer should docket a case in the Tax Court before Appeals Office consideration only if it has already decided that the Tax Court is the preferred forum for litigation. Prior docketing in the Tax Court will preclude a possible "second chance" for Appeals Office consideration. Despite the IRS's practice of referring a docketed case to the Appeals Office if the case has not already been before Appeals, this practice is discretionary and the Chief Counsel may determine not to forward the case. The taxpayer has no recourse if this decision is made. The case will move to the trial preparation phase.

Kaplan, *supra*, at 765–67.

Once an IRS attorney becomes involved in a docketed case, he or she may emphasize litigation-related issues such as discovery procedures, admissibility of evidence, and burden of proof more heavily than the Appeals Officer. Whether this slightly different perspective will facilitate or impede a settlement depends on the particular facts of the case. As noted in Chapter 11, the burden of persuasion in a litigated tax case generally

---

19 [Now Tax Court Rule 142(a)(1). — Eds.]

falls on the taxpayer unless the taxpayer can meet the statutory requirements necessary to shift that burden to the IRS.[20] I.R.C. § 7491(a). However, even if the taxpayer does not succeed in shifting the burden to the IRS under Code section 7491, in a Tax Court case, the IRS bears the burden of persuasion with respect to issues that are not included in the notice of deficiency (commonly called "new matter"), as explained above. TAX CT. R. 142(a)(1). Procedurally, new matters generally are presented by the IRS in its answer to the taxpayer's Tax Court petition or in an amended answer.[21] How might this procedural rule affect the decision to approach Appeals through docketed versus nondocketed status?

As noted at the beginning of this chapter, time delays and expense are also important factors to consider in determining whether to pursue a nondocketed appeal. While litigation is expensive, if the taxpayer can predict that the case will ultimately be brought to trial, he or she may not wish to waste time and resources protesting a potential adjustment, but instead should focus on drafting the Tax Court petition and preparing for trial. Docketing the case in Tax Court will also result in an earlier trial date. Conversely, if the taxpayer foresees settlement possibilities, prior docketing in Tax Court can delay Appeals consideration until after the IRS files an answer to the taxpayer's Tax Court petition. Once at Appeals, however, docketed cases generally take priority over nondocketed cases in order to ensure sufficient time to explore settlement possibilities before the scheduled trial date arrives. This priority may also result in additional pressure on both the taxpayer and the IRS to achieve a prompt settlement.

Keep in mind that if a case is not settled, the taxpayer is not precluded from litigating the case after the conclusion of the Appeals process. By docketing the case in Tax Court without requesting prior Appeals consideration, the taxpayer locks in the forum choice. By comparison, filing a protest in response to the 30-day letter allows the taxpayer additional time to consider whether the Tax Court or one of the refund fora is more advantageous should settlement negotiations break down. Choice of forum issues are discussed in more detail in Section 11.03 of Chapter 11.

Privacy and confidentiality concerns may also dictate whether the taxpayer pursues the appeal on a docketed versus nondocketed basis. As explained in Chapter 6, tax return information is confidential and may not be disclosed by IRS personnel except in limited circumstances. I.R.C. § 6103. The protest letter the taxpayer files remains confidential return information, while a Tax Court petition becomes a matter of public record. As a result, the taxpayer's desire to avoid publicity or protect sensitive information may provide an incentive to reach a settlement before litigation commences.

[4] Statutory Provisions Affecting Appeals Consideration and Settlements

Reading Assignment: I.R.C. §§ 6673, 7430(a)–(c), (g); Treas. Reg. §§ 301.7430-1(b), 301.7430-7(a)–(c).

The IRS Appeals process presents an opportunity to resolve disputes more quickly and with less cost than through litigation. Concerned particularly about the size of the Tax Court's "inventory" of cases, Congress has taken legislative steps to encourage

---

[20] One of the statutory conditions necessary to cause the burden of proof to shift to the IRS is that the taxpayer fully cooperate with reasonable requests by the IRS for documents and information within the taxpayer's control. The legislative history to section 7491 specifies that a necessary element of full cooperation with the IRS is that the taxpayer must exhaust available administrative remedies, including any appeal rights provided by the IRS. S. Rep. No. 105-174 (1998). The legislative history does not specify whether the taxpayer must pursue the appeal as a nondocketed case, or whether engaging in negotiations with the Appeals Division after the case is docketed with the Tax Court fulfills this condition. *See id.*

[21] These issues are discussed in more detail in Chapter 9.

taxpayers to negotiate with the Appeals Division before filing a Tax Court petition. Section 7430, for example, which is discussed in more detail in Chapter 11, allows a taxpayer to recover from the IRS reasonable administrative and litigation costs, including attorney's fees, if the taxpayer was the "prevailing party" and the position maintained by the IRS during administrative and court proceedings was not "substantially justified." *See* I.R.C. § 7430(a), (b). The award is conditioned upon a number of requirements, including the taxpayer's exhaustion of administrative remedies with the IRS. For example, if the IRS issues a 30-day letter and invites Appeals consideration, the taxpayer must participate in an Appeals conference prior to filing a petition in the Tax Court in order to establish that this condition was met. Treas. Reg. § 301.7430-1(b)(1). Therefore, in most cases, the possibility of recovering costs under section 7430 hinges upon pursuit of Appeals consideration on a nondocketed basis.[22]

Section 7430 also contains a provision designed to encourage settlement that is similar to Federal Rule of Civil Procedure 68's "Offer of Judgment."[23] Under section 7430(c)(4)(E), a taxpayer may be entitled to recover reasonable administrative and litigation costs if the taxpayer makes a "qualified" settlement offer to the government, the government rejects the settlement offer, and the taxpayer's liability subsequently determined by a court is less than or equal to the amount that was offered.[24] I.R.C. § 7430(c)(4)(E); Treas. Reg. § 301.7430-7(b). To recover fees under the qualified offer rule, the taxpayer must still exhaust administrative remedies, which, as otherwise required under section 7430, means that the taxpayer must pursue the case with Appeals on a nondocketed basis. *See* Haas & Assoc. Accountancy Corp. v. Commissioner, 117 T.C. 48 (2001), *aff'd*, 2003-1 U.S.T.C. ¶ 50,253 (9th Cir. 2003) (unpublished op.).

A "qualified offer" must be in writing; must specify the offered amount of the liability; must be designated as a qualified offer; and must remain open for acceptance by the government during the period beginning on the date the offer is made and ending on the earliest of (1) the date the offer is rejected, (2) the date the trial begins, or (3) the 90th day after the date the offer is made. I.R.C. § 7430(g)(1). The taxpayer must specify the amount of the liability in such a manner that, if accepted by the government, it would resolve the taxpayer's liability for the type of tax specifically at issue in the proceeding. The taxpayer may do so based on a specific dollar amount or a percentage of the adjustments at issue. Treas. Reg. § 301.7430-7(c)(3). In addition, the offer must be made during the "qualified offer period," which is the period that begins on the date on which the taxpayer is first notified of the opportunity for Appeals consideration and that ends on the date that is 30 days before the date that the case is first set for trial. I.R.C. § 7430(g)(2); Treas. Reg. § 301.7430-7(c)(7). The taxpayer may make multiple qualified offers while the qualified offer period remains open. A new offer supersedes any offers

---

[22] The regulations set forth limited instances in which the requesting party need not establish that the party exhausted all administrative remedies in order to recover costs. For example, the requirement does not apply when the taxpayer failed to receive a 30-day letter before the IRS issued a notice of deficiency; and the failure was not due to any action on the part of the taxpayer; and the taxpayer did not refuse to participate in an Appeal conference while the case was docketed before the Tax Court. Treas. Reg. § 301.7430-1(f)(2). The IRS can also waive the requirement of exhaustion of administrative remedies. Treas. Reg. § 301.7430-1(f)(1).

[23] Under Federal Rule of Civil Procedure 68:

> More than 10 days before the trial begins, a party defending against a claim may serve on an opposing party an offer to allow judgment on specified terms, with the costs then accrued. . . . If the judgment that the offeree finally obtains is not more favorable than the unaccepted offer, the offeree must pay the costs incurred after the offer was made.

Fed R. Civ. P. 68(a), (d).

[24] If these conditions exist, the taxpayer is treated as a "prevailing party." The qualified offer rule also renders irrelevant an IRS claim that it was "substantially justified" in its position. *See McGowan v. Commissioner*, T.C. Memo. 2005-80.

previously made. Only the last qualified offer is compared to the amount of the judgment to determine whether the determined liability was equal to or less than the amount of the qualified offer and only fees and costs incurred on or after the date of the last qualified offer are recoverable. I.R.C. § 7430(c)(4)(E)(iii); Treas. Reg. § 301.7430-7(c)(6).[25]

Note that, although the qualified offer rule applies only when there is a judicial determination of the taxpayer's liability, the taxpayer can make a qualified offer before litigation is instituted. As early as the date the 30-day letter was mailed, a taxpayer may make a written settlement offer to the IRS that could result in an eventual award to the taxpayer of administrative and litigation fees if the IRS rejects the offer and subsequently fails to obtain a higher amount in court. If, however, the taxpayer settles the liability with the government before the entry of a judgment, he or she will not be able to recover fees under the qualified offer rule. Some practitioners view the qualified offer rule not so much as way of setting the stage for a recovery of fees but as an effective means of settling a case:

> We normally recommend that a qualified offer be considered after the first meeting with the IRS appeals officer. It cannot be made any later than 30 days before trial, but that is somewhat late in the game for the typical tax case in which substantial costs are incurred in attempting to get at the facts and to negotiate a settlement. However, making an offer before getting enough information to evaluate the strength (and weakness) of the case is hazardous. An appeals officer who has done his homework may well accept an offer that is too high and the taxpayer will pay more tax than was justified. An offer that is too low will not accomplish much, either. It is apt to be rejected and will accomplish nothing if the final outcome of the case is a tax liability that is greater.
>
> After the first conference with the appeals officer, the practitioner should have a better understanding of the government's stance in the case than before the conference. With some additional digging into the facts and some additional research, it should be possible for the practitioner to come up with an educated estimate of what it might take to reach a meeting of the minds and settle the case, and what the range and likelihood of possible outcomes of litigation might be if a settlement cannot be reached. The practitioner should also be conscious that the qualified offer can be worded to expire in 90 days unless sooner accepted (unless, of course, the offer is sooner rejected or trial begins). As with expiring statutes of limitations, the advantage of an imminent expiration date to an offer is to encourage the appeals officer to pay attention to the case. Note that an unlimited number of qualified offers can be submitted, allowing fine-tuning as the practitioner gets a better feel for the likely outcome if the case were to go to litigation. How can there be multiple offers? Even though a taxpayer's offer to settle for $100,000, for example, may not have expired and has been neither accepted nor rejected, further information and discussions with the appeals officer have led the practitioner to estimate an offer of $120,000 would better represent the litigating value of the case. Another qualified offer for that amount can be submitted. While there are now two qualified offers open, the second offer has effectively replaced the first. . . . If the case goes to litigation, and the tax liability found by the court is $115,000, the $120,000 offer can be used in support of a claim for fees and expenses incurred from the date of that offer.

---

[25] The net worth limitations and the types and amounts of costs recoverable under section 7430 are discussed further in Chapter 11. For now, note that costs incurred while negotiating with the revenue agent during the examination process, as well as costs incurred in connection with a private letter ruling request, are not recoverable, even under the qualified offer rules. *See* I.R.C. § 7430(c)(2); Treas. Reg. § 301.7430-3(a).

Burgess J.W. Raby & William L. Raby, *Qualified Offers and Settlement of Tax Controversies*, 113 Tax Notes 455 (2006).

Another statutory provision, Code section 6673, grants the Tax Court authority to award up to $25,000 in damages against a taxpayer where it appears to the Tax Court that the taxpayer unreasonably failed to pursue administrative remedies. I.R.C. § 6673(a)(1)(C). The underlying purpose of the statute, according to the Tax Court, is "to penalize taxpayers who needlessly involve the Tax Court in a dispute that should have been resolved in the Appeals Division of the IRS." Birth v. Commissioner, 92 T.C. 769 (1989). The Tax Court normally imposes the section 6673 penalty in tax protestor-type cases. The IRS has not sought to impose this penalty merely because a taxpayer pursues an appeal as a docketed rather than a nondocketed case.

[5] Negotiating a Settlement with Appeals

An Appeals Officer is afforded a great deal of flexibility in determining whether to accept a final settlement offer from the taxpayer. The Officer may resolve each issue individually based on an assessment of the hazards of litigation, or may reach a overall settlement on the basis of concessions by both parties. A general discussion of offer and concession techniques is included in Section 19.04 of Chapter 19.

The Internal Revenue Manual recognizes two broad categories of settlements at the Appeals level: mutual concession and split issue. I.R.M. 8.6.4.1.1, 8.6.4.1.2. A mutual concession settlement, as the name implies, results when neither party is willing to concede an issue in full but the parties are willing to negotiate a compromise. The amount compromised on each side will depend upon the relative level of uncertainty regarding how a court would interpret and apply the law to the facts of the case. Valuation issues, for instance, lend themselves to mutual concession settlements because the parties may agree to a final valuation somewhere between their initial valuation numbers. A split-issue settlement, on the other hand, is normally used when an issue involved, if litigated, would result in a complete victory for one of the parties, such as whether the taxpayer's incorporation transaction qualifies under the nonrecognition rule of section 351. A split-issue settlement may be reached based on a percentage or stipulated amount of the asserted deficiency.

These two broad categories of settlements allow for creativity and old-fashioned horse-trading. As the following excerpt makes clear, the negotiating techniques and procedures used during the Appeals conference will vary. Tips on preparing for an Appeals conference are also included in the excerpt.

Robert C. Carlson, How to Handle and Win a Federal Tax Appeal: A Complete Guide for a Tax Professional[26]
¶¶ 2.05, 2.06 (1989)

¶ 2.05 BETWEEN THE PROTEST AND THE CONFERENCE

* * *

[b] Taxpayer Strategies

Several times in this chapter the importance of carefully drafting the protest and preparing for the appeals conference have been emphasized. This section describes in more detail the preparation that is recommended for the conference.

---

[26] Robert C. Carlson, How to Handle and Win Federal Tax Appeals: Complete Guide for Tax Professionals, 1st Edition © 1988, pp. 15–18. Adapted by permission of Pearson Education, Inc., Upper Saddle River, NJ.

Many taxpayer representatives appear at conferences unprepared because several features of the conference mislead representatives. The conference is a fairly informal meeting between the appeals officer, the representative, and perhaps the taxpayer. Rules of evidence do not apply, and there is no formal structure to the conference. In addition, while the appeals officer serves in effect as judge during the conference, representatives frequently forget that the officer also will be serving as an adversary during the proceeding. The officer's judge-like role occurs mainly after the conference when the hazards of litigation are balanced to determine an acceptable settlement. During the conference the appeals officer will be a staunch advocate of the IRS's position.

The representative can best protect the taxpayer's interests by preparing for the conference as though it were a trial. The steps described in this section should be familiar to representatives experienced in litigation.

The taxpayer should be interviewed thoroughly. This means asking questions that will elicit all unfavorable information from the client and ensure that the facts are not being hidden or distorted. After the interview, all records and documents should be reviewed to check the accuracy of the taxpayer's statements. Frequently even taxpayers with strong cases will color their statements to strengthen their cases. Such actions can damage the credibility of both the representative and the taxpayer and must be avoided. Any witness other than the taxpayer also should be interviewed, and their statements should be checked against any other evidence available. An intensive investigation of the facts can give the taxpayer's representative a substantial edge over the appeals officer, because the officer will not conduct a separate investigation of the facts. The facts known to the officer will be those uncovered and reported by the audit agent. These agents are frequently the least experienced and knowledgeable of the IRS employees who deal with substantive tax matters, so a skilled practitioner can expect to prepare a superior case.

Investigation of the facts should be followed by legal research. Then, once the facts and the law have been collected, an outline of the points to be made at the conference can be prepared. This outline should be a checklist of the points that must be proved according to the law and the evidence that supports each point. The points that will be made by the appeals officer also must be anticipated and counter-arguments should be prepared. Unlike the protest, the conference should focus on the taxpayer's strongest arguments. A weak argument that is made in writing is less damaging to credibility than one that is made in person.

Whenever possible, third-party evidence such as affidavits and reports should be used. This will add to the credibility of taxpayer-generated evidence. Exhibits and documents should be used at the conference whenever possible so that the appeals officer will have more to rely on than the oral statements of the taxpayer and counsel. Any independent support for the taxpayer's positions will enhance the credibility of all the taxpayer's statements and should be used.

After preparing the case, settlement proposals should be prepared. The proposals should be structured issue-by-issue because the appeals officer is not permitted to trade concessions on one issue for concessions on another. On each issue there should be an initial proposal that reflects the doubt created by the taxpayer's presentation and that shows a good faith intention to settle the case based on the hazards of litigation. Several proposals should be prepared on each issue, because the best proposal should not be offered first. The taxpayer should determine in advance the maximum amount on each issue that will be conceded in order to avoid the time and expense of litigation. Each settlement proposal should compute the exact amount of additional tax that would be due under the proposal. It is critically important that all settlement offers be stated in terms of the likelihood of the taxpayer's winning the issue in litigation or the uncertainty of the outcome.

* * *

¶ 2.06 THE APPEALS CONFERENCE

Procedure at a conference varies between appeals officers but is always informal. Generally the parties begin discussing the issues, gradually find their areas of agreement and disagreement, and work their way towards discussing specific settlement possibilities. In most cases all this is done in one conference, though sometimes the officer will refer the case back to the district for additional fact finding. Cases involving complicated legal issues or fact situations can be expected to take more than one conference. Whether the taxpayer or the appeals officer makes the first presentation and the exact format of the presentations depend entirely on the individuals involved. The taxpayer or representative might want to discuss such procedural matters with the officer when scheduling the conference.

The IRS issued updated guidelines on appeals conference procedures in 1986. The guidelines say that the conferences are to be informal "to promote frank discussion and mutual understanding." Appeals officers "must handle cases objectively" with the goal of reaching a decision based on the "merits of the issues in dispute and not with the attitude that settlements must be made." The new procedures also state that "ideological kinds of arguments" have no place in a conference. The guidelines emphasize two additional points. First, the conference is to be an informal procedure. Second, the appeals officer is not to be an advocate or a rubber stamp for the auditor's positions. While the appeals officer's objective posture might not be clear during the conference, the officer will try to settle a case that the government is not likely to win at trial.

All physical evidence that supports the taxpayer's position should be brought to the conference. Evidence should be brought even when the taxpayer believes that it would not be admissible in court, because the rules of evidence do not prevail at an appeals conference. It is important that copies of the evidence be presented to the officer because any settlement proposal must be sent to a reviewing officer, who must be convinced that the settlement conforms to the IRS's standards. Further, a graphic presentation of the taxpayer's evidence should make the appeals officer more amenable to a favorable settlement. A carefully prepared conference presentation also can convince the officer that the taxpayer is willing to litigate the issues if a favorable settlement is not reached. An inadequate presentation at the conference, however, will give the officer little reason to believe that there are hazards in litigating the case.

After the issues and evidence have been discussed, the appeals officer will either state that the parties are too far apart for a settlement to be possible or will ask the taxpayer for a settlement offer. Usually the taxpayer makes the first offer. If that offer is rejected, the officer should state a proposal that would be acceptable. If not, the taxpayer should ask what the officer would consider acceptable. Through this exchange of offers the parties can gradually move toward a mutually acceptable settlement or conclude that a settlement is not possible.

Even if the taxpayer and the Appeals Officer are unable to resolve all issues, efforts should be made to resolve as many as possible. Before agreeing to a full or partial settlement, however, the taxpayer should carefully consider how the settled issue might affect the taxpayer's exposure for past and future taxable years. If the settlement involves issues that have a continuing effect, such as the taxpayer's basis in property, the impact of these issues on other years should be included in the settlement agreement.

Traditionally, most appeals conferences involved face-to-face meetings between the Appeals Officer and the taxpayer's representative. While still available, many appeals conferences are now conducted over the telephone or through correspondence.

[6] Alternative Dispute Resolution

Reading Assignment: I.R.C. § 7123.

In recent years, the IRS has established a series of programs designed to encourage settlement at the Appeals level through the use of alternative dispute resolution techniques, including arbitration and mediation. For example, if the Appeals Officer and the taxpayer have been unable to negotiate a settlement between themselves during the normal appeals process, the parties may request binding arbitration to resolve unsettled factual disputes. *See* I.R.C. § 7123(b)(2). The arbitrator may be a member of the Appeals Office or an agreed-upon third party. Because arbitration is optional, both parties must agree to be bound by the process. The type of factual issue appropriate for arbitration is one that is susceptible to resolution based upon a combination of (1) a finding of fact and (2) an agreement between the parties as to any applicable interpretation of law, regulation, ruling, or other legal authority. Examples of the type of issue appropriate for arbitration include valuation questions and reasonable compensation disputes. Because binding arbitration is final, neither side can appeal or contest the arbitrator's factual findings in court. *See* Rev. Proc. 2006-44, 2006-44 I.R.B. 800 (containing a model arbitration agreement). Originally targeted at taxpayers in the Large and Mid-Size Business (LMSB) Division, the arbitration program is now available to any type of taxpayer who cannot resolve factual issues with the Appeals Division.

The IRS Appeals Division also offers a post-Appeals mediation program for most nondocketed cases. *See* I.R.C. § 7123(b)(1); Rev. Proc. 2002-44, 2002-2 C.B. 10 (containing a model mediation agreement). Unlike arbitration, mediation is nonbinding: The mediator has no authority to impose a decision on the parties. Instead, the mediator functions as a neutral party to promote settlement by helping the parties define the issues. Also unlike arbitration, some legal issues, as well as factual issues, are eligible for mediation.[27] Revenue Procedure 2002-44 specifies that the mediator must be chosen from within the IRS, although the taxpayer can bring in an independent co-mediator at the taxpayer's own expense. If a final settlement agreement between the parties still cannot be reached, the IRS will issue a notice of deficiency and the case will proceed as any other unresolved nondocketed case would.

In addition to arbitration and mediation, the IRS has established a series of more specialized programs, aimed primarily at large corporate taxpayers, that are designed to expedite case resolution. A pilot initiative called the Comprehensive Case Resolution program, established under the auspices of the LMSB Division, involves revenue agents, Appeals Officers, and IRS Counsel working in teams to resolve disagreements with large business taxpayers. 2001-6 I.R.B. 514, Notice 2001-13, provides the criteria for participation and other details. According to the Notice:

> The goal of the Comprehensive Case Resolution program is to help taxpayers that have tax years under examination by LMSB and in Appeals (including docketed cases under Appeals jurisdiction) resolve all open issues in all such years through an IRS Comprehensive Case Resolution process (CCR process). In some situations, it may also be appropriate to include tax years which are docketed before the Tax Court and not under Appeals' jurisdiction. The effect of this program will be to expedite the taxpayer's LMSB years, where the audit is substantially complete, into a resolution process. This CCR process will constitute the taxpayer's formal administrative appeal for the LMSB years . . . . The CCR process will plan aggressive timelines for completion, with a target of closing all years within six to twelve months. If agreement

---

[27] The fast-track mediation procedure mentioned in Section 5.02[B], above, is for cases that are still in the examination phase. The mediation procedures in Revenue Procedure 2002-44 are for cases already in Appeals but that have not been docketed with the Tax Court.

> cannot be reached using this process, Appeals will not again consider the unagreed issues from the years under examination by LMSB.

Notice 2001-13.

The Appeals Division also plans to implement a new case resolution process called the "Mutually Accelerated Appeals Program" (MAAP). The program will require taxpayers to agree on an audit schedule and to a commitment of specified resources that will be devoted to reaching a settlement. If an agreement can be reached, the IRS will create special appeals teams to handle the case on an accelerated basis. *See* IR-2000-42. The MAAP procedure is available only in cases involving $10 million or more in disputed tax liability.

[7] Disposing of a Case at Appeals

Reading Assignment: I.R.C. § 7121; skim I.R.C. §§ 6501(a), (c), (e), 6511(a).

If the taxpayer and the Appeals Division can reach a mutually acceptable settlement, the parties normally memorialize that settlement by signing Form 870-AD, Offer to Waive Restrictions on Assessment and Collection of Tax Deficiency (a copy of which is reproduced below). Form 870-AD contains substantially the same terms as Form 870, discussed above, with the addition of "offer" and "acceptance" language. As a result, while the Form 870 is effective when received by the IRS, the Form 870-AD is effective only when it is accepted by the IRS.[28] Moreover, Form 870-AD contains a statement to the effect that, once the agreement is accepted by the IRS, the IRS agrees not to reopen the case for the taxable years involved except in certain specified circumstances.[29] In return, the taxpayer agrees to the assessment of any settled liability and commits not to file a claim for refund for the taxable year in issue.[30]

---

[28] Signing Form 870-AD suspends the accrual of interest on the underlying liability from a date 30 days after the waiver is accepted by the IRS and becomes effective. *See* I.R.C. § 6601(c).

[29] The IRS has also issued a series of policy statements explaining when an agreed-upon case may be reopened by the IRS. If the case was closed on the basis of concessions made by both the IRS and the taxpayer (a mutual concession case), the IRS will not reopen the case unless the case involved fraud, malfeasance, concealment, misrepresentation of facts, an important mistake in mathematical calculations, or discovery of certain tax shelter items. In nonmutual concession cases, the permitted bases for reopening the case are similar. However, the IRS also has the authority to reopen a case settled on a basis other than mutual concession in the event that circumstances indicate that failure to reopen would be a serious administrative omission. Penalty Policy Statement P-8-3 (Jan. 5, 2007), *available at* http://www.irs.gov/pub/foia/ig/spder/p-8-3.pdf.

[30] Form 870 may be used to conclude a case with Appeals where the settlement does not involve mutual concessions or where the amount of tax liability in issue is not large. Form 870-AD, however, may be used only in Appeals. *See* I.R.M. 8.6.4.3.

Form **870-AD** (Rev. April 1992)

Department of the Treasury—Internal Revenue Service

Offer to Waive Restrictions on Assessment and Collection of Tax Deficiency and to Accept Overassessment

Symbols	Name of Taxpayer	SSN or EIN

Under the provisions of section 6213(d) of the Internal Revenue Code of 1986 (the Code), or corresponding provisions of prior internal revenue laws, the undersigned offers to waive the restrictions provided in section 6213(a) of the Code or corresponding provisions of prior internal revenue laws, and to consent to the assessment and collection of the following deficiencies and additions to tax, if any, with interest as provided by law. The undersigned offers also to accept the following overassessments, if any, as correct. Any waiver or acceptance of an overassessment is subject to any terms and conditions stated below and on the reverse side of this form.

Deficiencies (Overassessments) and Additions to Tax

Year Ended	Kind of Tax	Tax				
		$	$	$		
		$	$	$		
		$	$	$		
		$	$	$		
		$	$	$		
		$	$	$		

Signature of Taxpayer		Date
Signature of Taxpayer		Date
Signature of Taxpayer's Representative		Date
Corporate Name		Date
By Corporate Officer	Title	Date

For Internal Revenue Use Only	Date Accepted for Commissioner	Signature
	Office	Title

Cat. No. 16896Q **(See Reverse Side)** Form **870-AD** (Rev. 4-92)

This offer must be accepted for the Commissioner of Internal Revenue and will take effect on the date it is accepted. Unless and until it is accepted, it will have no force or effect.

If this offer is accepted, the case will not be reopened by the Commissioner unless there was:

- fraud, malfeasance, concealment or misrepresentation of a material fact
- an important mistake in mathematical calculation
- a deficiency or overassessment resulting from adjustments made under Subchapters C and D of Chapter 63 concerning the tax treatment of partnership and subchapter S items determined at the partnership and corporate level
- an excessive tentative allowance of a carryback provided by law

No claim for refund or credit will be filed or prosecuted by the taxpayer for the years stated on this form, other than for amounts attributed to carrybacks provided by law.

The proper filing of this offer, when accepted, will expedite assessment and billing (or overassessment, credit or refund) by adjusting the tax liability. This offer, when executed and timely submitted, will be considered a claim for refund for the above overassessment(s), if any.

This offer may be executed by the taxpayer's attorney, certified public accountant, or agent provided this is specifically authorized by a power of attorney which, if not previously filed, must accompany this form. If this offer is signed by a person acting in a fiduciary capacity (for example: an executor, administrator, or a trustee) Form 56, Notice Concerning Fiduciary Relationship, must accompany this form, unless previously filed.

If this offer is executed for a year for which a joint return was filed, it must be signed by both spouses unless one spouse, acting under a power of attorney, signs as agent for the other.

If this offer is executed by a corporation, it must be signed with the corporate name followed by the signature and title of the officer(s) authorized to sign. If the offer is accepted, as a condition of acceptance, any signature by or for a corporate officer will be considered a representation by that person and the corporation, to induce reliance, that such signature is binding under law for the corporation to be assessed the deficiencies or receive credit or refund under this agreement. If the corporation later contests the signature as being unauthorized on its behalf, the person who signed may be subject to criminal penalties for representating that he or she had authority to sign this agreement on behalf of the corporation.

Notwithstanding the language to the contrary in Form 870-AD, taxpayers have, on occasion, sought to reopen a case by filing a refund claim arising from issues covered by the agreement. As discussed in *Kretchmar*, reproduced below, courts have reached differing conclusions over whether and under what circumstances the taxpayer's commitment not to seek a refund is binding.

KRETCHMAR v. UNITED STATES

United States Claims Court
9 Cl. Ct. 191 (1985)

REGINALD W. GIBSON, JUDGE:

In this tax refund action, plaintiffs, Frank R. and Bertha M. Kretchmar, jointly seek a refund of federal income taxes, interest, and penalties in the amounts of $19,006.05, $27,404.64, and $24,250.02 for the taxable years 1976, 1977, and 1978, respectively. * * *

Without addressing the merits of these claims as to any of the foregoing years, defendant, in moving for summary judgment, avers that (1) plaintiffs' previous execution of IRS Form 870-AD, Offer of Waiver of Restrictions on Assessment and Collection of Deficiency in Tax and of Acceptance of Overassessment, now estops plaintiffs from seeking a refund for each of said taxable years. As for the taxable years 1976 and 1977, we find that the plaintiffs are barred from litigating the merits of their refund suit on the grounds that the doctrine of equitable estoppel, stemming from their previous execution of IRS Form 870-AD, is a complete impediment.

FACTS

Plaintiffs, husband and wife residing in West Brookfield, Massachusetts, filed timely federal income tax returns for the taxable years in question, 1976, 1977, and 1978. Schedule C of each of said returns described plaintiffs' business, euphemistically, as "novelty sales," and reported gross receipts and net income in the identical amounts of $11,700, $19,140, and $30,000, for the taxable years 1976, 1977, and 1978, respectively.[n.4]

[n.4] "Euphemistically" is the appropriate adjective given subsequent revelations as to the real source of the understated income. From the documentation reflected in defendant's exhibits, it appears that on January 18, 1978, the Massachusetts State Police conducted a raid on plaintiffs' residence at which time $50,000 in cash was

No deductible expenses were claimed as having been incurred in connection with earning these amounts of income.

During the calendar year 1980, Internal Revenue Agent (IRA) Robert B. Puzzo conducted an audit of the plaintiffs' 1976, 1977, and 1978 returns. That audit report (December 12, 1980) resulted in plaintiffs being assessed income tax deficiencies of $12,156.76, $13,867.49, and $24,180.99, for the taxable years 1976, 1977, and 1978, respectively. In addition, plaintiffs were also assessed civil fraud penalties * * *.

Plaintiffs rejected, *i.e.*, refused to execute, the Form 870 settlement offer and appealed the foregoing proposed deficiencies to the Appeals Office of the Internal Revenue Service (IRS). Upon further settlement negotiation, the IRS agreed in 1982 to *decrease* plaintiffs' assessed gross income by the amount of $6,000 for 1976, and $20,000 for 1978. No adjustment, however, was made for 1977 given the agreed diminution in 1976 and 1978. As a result of said readjustments by the Appeals Office, plaintiffs' reassessed taxes and penalties were reduced to $14,063.52, $20,801.24, and $20,104.15, for the three taxable years in question or an aggregate amount of $54,968.91. As evidence of the results of the compromise/settlement negotiations, and in order to preclude future assessments against such taxable years, plaintiffs executed Form 870-AD on January 29, 1982, which was accepted for the Commissioner of Internal Revenue on February 9, 1982. * * *

In spite of plaintiffs' promise in the Form 870-AD that "no [future] claim for refund or credit shall be filed . . . . other than for amounts attributed to carrybacks" for the years in issue after the execution of the Form 870-AD, they nevertheless filed a timely claim for refund (Form 1040X), for each of the years in question, "other than for amounts attributed to carrybacks" with the Boston Appeals Office of the IRS on or about May 23, 1983. At that date, despite plaintiffs' previous execution of several forms extending the general three-year limitations period for deficiency assessment for 1976 and 1977 to December 31, 1982, defendant's right to assess any further deficiency as to all years under *the general three-year period* of limitations (§§ 6501(a) and (c)(4)) had then expired. On each such Forms 1040X, plaintiffs claimed, *inter alia*, that the originally reported income amounts on their returns for each year were correct; that the Form 870-AD was executed by a representative of plaintiffs who was acting outside the scope of his authority; that the Form 870-AD was itself illegal as it was executed beyond the three year statute of limitations contained in 26 U.S.C. § 6501; and that no grounds existed to assess civil fraud penalties pursuant to 26 U.S.C. § 6653(b). The IRS rejected plaintiffs' contentions and disallowed all of plaintiffs' refund claims on December 12, 1983.

Plaintiffs, thereafter, commenced a refund action in this court on February 3, 1984. The petition here did not seek refunds "for amounts attributed to carrybacks," but rather requested refunds of the same amounts for each year which were sought in plaintiffs' earlier appeal to the Appeals Office dated May 23, 1983. In opposition, on January 22, 1985, defendant moved for summary judgment in which it invoked the doctrine of equitable estoppel for all years as a result of plaintiffs' execution of Form 870-AD, and also averred that this court lacks jurisdiction with regard to the claim respecting the taxable year 1978.

For reasons hereinafter delineated, we find that judgment should be granted in favor of defendant on its motion for summary judgment as to all taxable years in issue.

---

confiscated. A five-count indictment relating to illegal gambling activity followed therefrom, and plaintiff, Frank Kretchmar, pleaded guilty to each count. The Service, therefore, contends that given the fact that no income from the admitted gambling activities was listed on either of the 1976, 1977 or 1978 returns, the subsequently discovered unreported cash must have emanated from said illegal activity. * * *

DISCUSSION

* * *

B. Equitable Estoppel

1. Background

Defendant has * * * moved for summary judgment on plaintiffs' refund claims (the taxable years 1976-1977) on the ground that their previous execution of IRS Form 870-AD equitably estops plaintiffs from litigating these now compromised and settled claims. In short, defendant avers that it would be most inequitable and unjust, in the face of the bargained-for-concessions implicit in Form 870-AD signed by plaintiffs on January 29, 1982, and approved by defendant on February 9, 1982, to permit plaintiffs to file an efficacious claim for refund (May 23, 1983) long after the running of the general three-year statute of limitations (26 U.S.C. § 6501(a)) on additional assessments. Conversely, and in opposition, plaintiffs argue that (1) any estoppel of their claims would be "inequitable" given the fact that no compromise of their claims was made through the execution of Form 870-AD; (2) no prejudice would be visited on defendant should the agreement be revoked inasmuch as the statute had not run on additional assessments at the time plaintiffs filed their claims to the extent the defendant can prove either fraud or an omission in excess of 25 percent of the amount of gross income originally reported; (3) in fact the Form 870-AD was executed by an unauthorized person; and (4) the Form 870-AD is not valid because the statute of limitations (§ 6501(a)) expired prior to January 29, 1982.

Research discloses that the application of the doctrine of equitable estoppel, to bar the prosecution of tax refund claims settled and concluded by the execution of a Form 870-AD, has provoked not only controversy but outright inconsistency among various federal circuits. On the one hand, there are those courts which strictly hold, according to the Supreme Court in *Botany Worsted Mills v. United States*, 278 U.S. 282, 49 S. Ct. 129, 73 L. Ed. 379 (1929), that the only binding form of tax settlement is one which conforms to the finality prescribed through a settlement agreement pursuant to 26 U.S.C. § 7121 (1982). The justification for this conclusion is apparently premised on the fact that Form 870-AD specifically states that it is not such an agreement. Absent strict adherence to the formality envisioned in § 7121, these courts, therefore, reject the application of the doctrine of equitable estoppel relying instead on the Supreme Court's admonishment that "when a statute limits a thing to be done in a particular mode, it includes the negative of any other mode." *Botany*, 278 U.S. at 289. *Cf.* Uinta Livestock Corp. v. United States, 355 F.2d 761 (10th Cir. 1966); Associated Mutuals, Inc. v. Delaney, 176 F.2d 179, 181 n. 1 (1st Cir. 1949); and Bank of New York v. United States, 170 F.2d 20 (3d Cir. 1948).

On the other hand, there are also those courts which have a tradition of affirmatively applying the doctrine of equitable estoppel to bar the litigation of claims previously concluded through the taxpayer's execution of a settlement Form 870-AD. These courts, *infra*, in essence, acknowledge the continued vitality of *Botany*, but they persuasively distinguish its holding by arguing that that case did not present the estoppel issue squarely to the Court. In support of this position, they refer to the following often cited *dicta* in *Botany*, to wit:

> It is plain that no compromise is authorized by this statute which is not assented to by the Secretary of the Treasury. For this reason, if for no other, the informal agreement made in this case did not constitute a settlement which in itself was binding upon the Government or the Mills. *And, without determining whether such an agreement, though not binding in itself, may when executed become, under some circumstances, binding on the parties by*

> *estoppel, it suffices to say that here the findings disclose no adequate ground for any claim of estoppel by the United States.*

Botany, 278 U.S. at 289 (emphasis added, citations omitted). Since the Supreme Court has expressly reserved the issue of what circumstances might ultimately raise the execution of a Form 870-AD to a binding settlement, certain courts have consequently held that *Botany* does not estop the courts from developing their own law on the subject. Thus, it is on the foregoing premises that a properly executed Form 870-AD has become a recognized impediment, in certain circuits, to estop taxpayers from litigating the merits of tax refund claims settled therein. *Cf.* Stair v. United States, 516 F.2d 560 (2d Cir. 1975); * * * Elbo Coals, Inc., v. United States, 763 F.2d 818 (6th Cir. 1985).

2. Equitable Estoppel in the Predecessor Court of Claims

Research further discloses that the predecessor Court of Claims saw fit on a number of occasions to apply the doctrine of equitable estoppel on facts arising out of a taxpayer's previous execution of a Form 870-AD. *See* Guggenheim v. United States, 77 F. Supp. 186, 111 Ct. Cl. 165 (1948); H.W. Nelson Co., Inc. v. United States, 308 F.2d 950, 158 Ct. Cl. 629 (1962); D.D.I., Inc. v. United States, 467 F.2d 497, 199 Ct. Cl. 380 (1972); McGraw-Hill, Inc. v. United States, 224 Ct. Cl. 324, 623 F.2d 700 (1980) (doctrine affirmed but not applied on the specific facts of the case). In so doing, said Court of Claims made particular mention of the language cited from *Botany, supra*. For example, in the seminal case adopting the doctrine in the predecessor Court of Claims, *Guggenheim v. United States*, all of the formalities required for executing an efficacious Form 870-AD were present. *Guggenheim*, 77 F. Supp. at 196. Both parties had signed, and the form was properly accepted by the Commissioner on the same day. *Id.* at 194. There, the court noted in contradistinction to *Botany* that:

> Many of the elements in the formal agreement involved in this case [*Guggenheim*] were lacking in that case [*Botany*]. Moreover, we do not understand that case to hold, as plaintiff contends, that under no circumstances will a closing agreement be held binding unless executed in accordance with Section [7121] . . . .

Guggenheim, 77 F. Supp. at 196. Having effectively distinguished *Botany*, the Court of Claims in *Guggenheim* went on to dismiss the tax refund action therein holding that cause of action to be equitably barred due solely to the plaintiff's previous execution of Form 870. *Id.* at 197.

* * *

3. Application of the Doctrine — Equitable Estoppel

As outlined above, we apply the doctrine of equitable estoppel to preclude the litigation of plaintiffs' claims as to the taxable years 1976 and 1977. * * * The discussion which follows demonstrates that in accordance with Court of Claims precedent, plaintiffs did, by executing the Form 870-AD, waive their right to further litigate the 1976 and 1977 claims, so that to reopen them at this juncture would significantly prejudice the defendant. On such facts, we find that equity favors the enforcement of plaintiffs' agreement.

In general terms, binding precedent teaches that the doctrine of equitable estoppel, arising out of the execution of a Form 870-AD, may be applied to hold a taxpayer to his bargain if the following three criteria are established: (1) the execution of the Form 870-AD was the result of mutual concession or compromise; (2) there was a meeting of the minds that the claims be extinguished; and (3) that to allow the plaintiff to reopen the case would be prejudicial given the defendant's reliance on the extinguishment thereof. *Guggenheim*, 77 F. Supp. at 196; *H.W. Nelson Co.*, 308 F.2d at 956–59; *D.D.I.*,

Inc., 467 F.2d at 500–01; *McGraw-Hill, Inc.*, 623 F.2d at 706. As the pleading of the doctrine raises an affirmative defense, the burden is on the defendant to establish these criteria by the requisite quantum of proof.

a. Mutual Concession and Compromise

With respect to the first criterion, mutual concession or compromise, the defendant's documentary evidence clearly establishes this fact for all taxable years with striking similarity to the facts in *Guggenheim*. In *Guggenheim*, the court stated in that connection that:

> Plaintiff protested the proposed disallowance and thereafter conferences were held with plaintiff's representatives. A further investigation was made by a revenue agent. As a result of these discussions, the representatives of the Commissioner agreed to recommend for allowance a deduction . . . . claimed by plaintiff. Plaintiff abandoned his contention that the other deductions claimed were allowable. The Commissioner's representative also agreed to make an adjustment in plaintiff's favor on account of certain dividends.

Guggenheim, 77 F. Supp. at 194. In the case at bar, plaintiffs similarly protested the audit report which initially assessed them some $75,307 in deficiencies (taxes and penalties) in December 1980 for all of the years in issue. Likewise, as in *Guggenheim*, a further investigation was held in which an IRS report was issued containing the following revelations:

> *Taxpayers, in an effort to close this case, propose that the Government accept in the year 1976 a reduction of $6,000* as representing a repayment of the loan to Ray Heck as outlined above. *Taxpayers concede all adjustments in 1977. In 1978, it is proposed that the Government concede the inclusion of $13,661* deemed to have been for the purchase of JTC stock. *In the year 1978, taxpayers also propose that an amount of $6,339 be considered as cash on hand. It is recommended that this proposal of settlement be accepted as a reasonable conclusion to this case.*

Appeals Transmittal Memorandum and Supporting Statement, Feb. 12, 1982 (emphasis added). This paraphrase of the ongoing dialogue between plaintiffs and defendant as contained in the referenced IRS report, evidencing the negotiations leading to the final adjustments which were then recorded on Form 870-AD, persuasively belies plaintiffs' assertion that "the numbers placed on the Form 870-AD were not a compromise at all." Indeed, as in *Guggenheim*, it is clear beyond cavil, and we so find, that plaintiffs' settlement, manifested by the execution of Form 870-AD in this case, was a bilateral process driven by mutual concession and compromise.

* * *

b. Meeting of the Minds

The second criterion cited above requires that, concomitantly, there must also be a meeting of the minds to the effect that the right to raise any prospective claims or to otherwise reopen the case, for such years, be extinguished (save exceptions not here relevant). In *Guggenheim*, the court added substance to the evaluation of this concept by examining two additional factors: (1) the parties' course of conduct; and (2) the express language adopted by the parties on the Form 870-AD. *Guggenheim*, 77 F. Supp. at 195. As to course of conduct, the court stated:

> The conclusion is inescapable from the evidence that there was a meeting of minds as to the final disposition of the case. When that occurred, the Commissioner recomputed plaintiff's tax liability and transmitted to plaintiff

> the settlement document wherein was set out a deficiency for each of the years. In transmitting that document to plaintiff at that time, the Commissioner stated that he was accepting plaintiff's "proposal for settlement," and also referred to the document as an "agreement" when executed by plaintiff and approved on his behalf. In returning the document after execution, plaintiff likewise referred to it as an "agreement."

Id. at 195. In *Guggenheim*, at no time did either party objectively manifest a belief that what was being negotiated was anything less than a complete settlement for the taxable years in issue. While no correspondence similar to that in *Guggenheim* has been presented to the court in the case at bar, neither has any demonstrative evidence been submitted supporting plaintiffs' contention that a definitive settlement was not intended for all taxable years. In fact, on this issue the documentary evidence is thoroughly supportive of defendant's position, particularly when we examine defendant's Form 5278, Statement-Income Tax Changes, prepared by the Appeals Office of the IRS which contains a box plainly checked "settlement computation." Similarly, in the Appeals Transmittal Memorandum and Supporting Statement, *supra*, the words "Proposal of Settlement" are used consistently throughout to characterize the nature of the procedural posture of plaintiffs' appeal. While plaintiffs may, as an afterthought, *now* contend otherwise, the evidence is wanting and it strains credulity to contend that the lengthy and detailed negotiations, which led to the preparation and execution of Form 870-AD, were conducted with any purpose other than that they were aimed at a definitive settlement.

Moreover, in reviewing the undeniable language contained in the Form 870-AD together with other referenced evidence, *supra*, the ultimate intentions of the parties leave no room for doubt. This conclusion is compelled when one carefully reviews the Form 870-AD, wherein the following unambiguous statement appears directly above the plaintiffs' signatures:

> *If this offer is accepted for the Commissioner, the case shall not be reopened* in the absence of fraud, malfeasance, concealment or misrepresentation of material fact, an important mistake in mathematical calculation, or excessive tentative allowances of carrybacks provided by law; *and no claim for refund or credit shall be filed or prosecuted for the year(s) stated above other than for amounts attributed to carrybacks provided by law.*

Appendix B to the Memorandum for the United States in Support of Its Motion for Summary Judgment, January 22, 1985, Exhibit C (emphasis added). Thus, by signing the Form 870-AD containing the referenced language, plaintiffs, in essence, waived all further rights to contest the assessment for the stated taxable years, save for the specific exception not present in this case. While the Form 870-AD was drafted by the defendant, no ambiguity exists as to the clear import of the intendment of the parties, *i.e.*, each side *expressly* waived its right (with exceptions not pertinent here) to subsequently litigate the settlement contained therein. For this court to find otherwise, at this posture, would contravene and directly ignore the clearly exhibited objective manifestations of the signatories.

* * *

c. Detrimental Reliance

The third, and final, criterion defendant must establish to effect the application of the doctrine of equitable estoppel is that of detrimental reliance. In the precise context of this case, to meet this burden, the proof must show that defendant detrimentally relied upon plaintiffs' execution of the Form 870-AD in question. The degree of detrimental reliance sufficient to support the application of the doctrine of equitable estoppel has been characterized by the courts in various ways. In *McGraw-Hill*, for example, the court stated that "equitable estoppel [is to be applied] whenever the IRS cannot be placed in the same position it was when the agreement was executed." *McGraw-Hill*, 623 F.2d at 706. More specifically, perhaps, is the definition given in *D.D.I.* wherein the court states that detrimental reliance is the result which obtains "where the statute of limitations has run on the collection of further deficiencies between the time an informal compromise agreement was executed and the time the refund claim was filed. . . ." *D.D.I.*, 467 F.2d at 500.

Quite logically, the predecessor Court of Claims has also, by implication, suggested the necessity for the defendant's reliance to have been reasonable under the circumstances. In this regard, the key variable is the timing of the defendant's knowledge regarding the plaintiff's decision to change its position, *i.e.*, whether the repudiation of the Form 870-AD occurs at a time when the statute of limitations on assessment has expired. Or, on the other hand, the question is whether such knowledge preceded the running of the statute of limitations to the extent that the Service could be restored to the "same position," *i.e.*, by expeditiously effecting an additional assessment within the general three-year period of limitations (§ 6501(a)). The case of *Erickson v. United States*, 309 F.2d 760, 159 Ct. Cl. 202 (1962), is particularly instructive on this issue. In *Erickson*, the Court of Claims estopped the plaintiff from seeking a refund of deficiency interest made payable under a compromise agreement proposed by the taxpayer as a settlement of a claim being litigated in the Tax Court. The settlement agreement contained an award of interest, yet the Tax Court in ratifying the agreement, omitted the award of interest. In accordance with the written settlement agreement itself, the Commissioner collected the interest. In estopping plaintiff from suing for a refund of the interest, the Court of Claims commented on the reasonableness of the defendant's reliance as follows:

> Taxpayer tells us that his counsel orally indicated to representatives of the defendant in October 1958, before the Tax Court orders had become final, that he intended to sue for most of the interest assessed and not refunded. This, he says, was sufficient warning to the Government that his position had changed. *But such informal oral statements, even if strongly asserted, would not change the reliance which the Government had already placed on the prior written agreement and could rightfully continue to place, at least until the agreement was formally repudiated in writing.*

Id. at 764–65 (emphasis added). Consistent with the foregoing statement by the court in *Erickson*, we construe the quoted language of *D.D.I.*, cited *supra*, to mean that the cut-off date for the defendant to claim detrimental reliance is certainly the date the Form 870-AD is "formally repudiated in writing." Thus, the prejudice to defendant emanating from detrimental reliance because of the running of the three-year limitations period, must have accrued at the date just prior to the time the claim for refund was filed with the IRS, or just prior to the date when any other written notice of repudiation was served on defendant, whichever occurs first. For defendant to proceed in allowing the three-year statute to run, after having received such written notice of repudiation, would clearly not be reasonable, nor indicative of the requisite prejudice required to be caused by the plaintiff. In other words, equity will only estop a plaintiff based on that prejudice which is traceable to its own action or inaction, not for that which is self-imposed by the defendant.

Plaintiffs insist that at the time they repudiated the Form 870-AD and filed their refund claims with the Service on May 23, 1983 (as well as at the date plaintiffs' petition was filed here (February 3, 1984)), the defendant was in no worse position to assess further deficiencies than it was in at the date the Form 870-AD became effective (February 9, 1982). That is to say plaintiffs argue that defendant was then "in the same position it was when the agreement was executed," as contemplated in *D.D.I.*, *supra*, and it is, therefore, not barred from effecting additional assessments for taxable years 1976 and 1977 upon the proof of fraud (26 U.S.C. § 6501(c)(1)); nor would it be so barred upon proof of an omission of income in excess of 25 percent of reported gross income (26 U.S.C. § 6501(e)). Defendant, on the other hand, has strenuously insisted that due to the running of the general three-year statute of limitations on assessment on December 31, 1982 (26 U.S.C. § 6501(a)), and a concomitant shift in the burden of proof relative to the necessity of proving fraud as a basis for assessing a *deficiency* for the taxable years 1976 and 1977, defendant was *not* in the *same* position on May 23, 1983, as it was in at the time the Form 870-AD was executed (*i.e.*, January 29, 1982 and February 9, 1982). As discussed below, we find that at the date on which defendant received notice of plaintiffs' repudiation of the Form 870-AD (May 23, 1983), defendant had previously sufficiently relied to its detriment on the Form 870-AD so as to support the application of equitable estoppel to plaintiffs' refund claims. Therefore, regarding the existence of this final element — detrimental reliance, we agree with defendant as to both taxable years 1976 and 1977.

The detriment which we find sufficient to support defendant's claim of estoppel is both traditional, as contemplated under the standards articulated by *Guggenheim* and *D.D.I.*, and unique to the peculiar facts of this case. Starting with an examination of the facts as of the critical date of notice, May 23, 1983, we note that at that date, the three-year statutory period (inclusive of plaintiffs' extensions) had clearly run for both taxable years 1976 and 1977. For each of these two years, plaintiffs' consent to an extension of the three-year statutory period on assessment was effective up to December 31, 1982. The three-year period of limitations on assessments as extended for each year, therefore, expired approximately five months *before* plaintiffs filed their May 23, 1983 claims with the IRS. Consequently, on these facts, we find the precise prejudice which is cited to by the court in both *D.D.I.* and *McGraw-Hill*. Defendant cannot be put back in the "same position" today (or at any time after December 31, 1982) as it held before the Form 870-AD was signed simply because the *general statute* of limitations on additional assessments (§ 6501(a)), extended by § 6501(c)(4), which had *not* then run on February 9, 1982, had in fact expired at the date plaintiffs' claims for refund were filed.

On the foregoing, we are convinced that the *Guggenheim* case is, therefore, dispositive of this issue because substantially the same facts present here gave rise to a finding of prejudice there by the Court of Claims. Citing *cf.* to the case of *R.H. Stearns Co. v. United States*, 291 U.S. 54, 54 S. Ct. 325, 78 L. Ed. 647 (1934), the predecessor court stated:

> At the time the agreement in this case was executed the statute had not run on the collection of further deficiencies, but when the claims for refund were filed the statute had run. It would obviously be inequitable to allow the plaintiff to renounce the agreement when the Commissioner cannot be placed in the same position he was when the agreement was executed. A clear case for the application of the doctrine of equitable estoppel exists and should be applied.

Guggenheim, 77 F. Supp. at 196. For the reasons discussed *infra*, and contrary to plaintiffs' assertions in the case at bar, it is to the running of the *general three-year statute of limitations* (where extended, of course, by § 6501(c)(4)), and *only* to that statute, that we must look to determine the existence of the necessary prejudice to the defendant.

* * *

CONCLUSION

The foregoing outlines the various forms of prejudice inuring to defendant which we have found based upon the detailed facts as presented in this case. Since we have also found the requisite concession or compromise, and a meeting of the minds with regard to extinguishing of the claim, we see no legal basis for denying defendant's motion for summary judgment. In short, the following language in *Guggenheim* thoroughly summarizes our position:

> A reasonable interpretation of the entire document is that what the parties sought to do was to close the case in such a manner that it could not be reopened either for a refund or for the assessment of deficiencies except in the case of fraud, malfeasance, etc. We see no reason for interpreting the document otherwise. * * *

Guggenheim, 111 Ct. Cl. at 181. * * *

It is so ordered.

What if the Kretchmars had offered, just prior to the Claims Court trial, to waive the statute of limitations on assessment so that the IRS could have timely asserted additional deficiencies against the Kretchmars to offset their claimed refund? Would the waiver have prevented the IRS from using the estoppel defense? *Cf. Ihnen v. United States*, 272 F.3d 577 (8th Cir. 2001) (taxpayer's offer to waive an expired statute of limitations on assessment made for the first time during oral arguments at the appellate level held untimely).

The *Kretchmar* case highlights the danger of relying on the possibility of litigating an issue once a Form 870-AD has been signed. If the taxpayer wants to reserve the right to file a refund claim on other issues — whether they are known or unknown at the time the 870-AD is filed — the taxpayer might wish to raise those issues and alter the Form 870-AD agreement accordingly, or use a Form 870 settlement agreement instead. Intervening court cases, legislation, or administrative determinations could generate a refund possibility after the fact.

From an ethical perspective, should an attorney counsel a client to enter into a settlement agreement with the intention of later repudiating that agreement?

§ 5.03 CLOSING AGREEMENTS

Reading Assignment: I.R.C. § 7121.

As noted in *Kretchmar*, it is the existence of the closing agreement procedures under Code section 7121 that has led some courts to conclude that any agreement that does not conform to the section 7121 requirements does not provide the taxpayer with absolute finality with respect to a particular issue or item. Once executed, a formal closing agreement prevents either party from reopening the case absent a showing of fraud, malfeasance, or the misrepresentation of a material fact.[31] "A closing agreement determining tax liability may be entered into at any time before such liability determination becomes a matter within the province of a court of competent jurisdiction and may thereafter be entered into in appropriate circumstances when authorized by the court (*e.g.*, in certain bankruptcy situations)." Rev. Proc. 68-16, 1968-1 C.B. 770. Closing agreements under section 7121 of the Code are ordinarily reflected on Form 906 (for final determination of specific matters) and, in rarer cases, on Form 866 (for final determination of tax liability).

"A closing agreement may be entered into in any case in which there appears to be an advantage in having the case permanently and conclusively closed. . . ." Treas. Reg.

---

[31] A closing agreement relating to a period after the date of the agreement is executed is subject to alteration based on a change in the law enacted after that date. Treas. Reg. § 301.7121-1(c).

§ 301.7121-1(a). The regulations provide the following example of when a closing agreement might be appropriate:

> A owns 500 shares of stock in the XYZ Corporation which he purchased prior to March 1, 1913. A is considering selling 200 shares of such stock but is uncertain as to the basis of the stock for the purpose of computing gain. Either prior or subsequent to the sale, a closing agreement may be entered into determining the market value of such stock as of March 1, 1913, which represents the basis for determining gain if it exceeds the adjusted basis otherwise determined as of such date. Not only may the closing agreement determine the basis for computing gain on the sale of the 200 shares of stock, but such an agreement may also determine the basis (unless or until the law is changed to require the use of some other factor to determine basis) of the remaining 300 shares of stock upon which gain will be computed in a subsequent sale.

Treas. Reg. § 301.7121-1(b)(4) Ex.

Revenue Procedure 68-16, 1968-1 C.B. 770, provides further discussion of appropriate uses of closing agreements:

> .01 A determination of tax liability by closing agreement may be entered into for good reasons shown by the taxpayer where there is no disadvantage to the Government or where desired by the Government. Representative of acceptable reasons for entering into such agreements are the following circumstances:
>
> 1. The taxpayer wishes to definitely establish its tax liability in order that a transaction may be facilitated, such as the sale of its stock.
> 2. The fiduciary of an estate desires a closing agreement in order that he may be discharged by the court.
> 3. The fiduciary of a trust or receivership desires a final determination before distribution is made.
> 4. A corporation in the process of liquidation or dissolution desires a closing agreement in order to wind up its affairs.
> 5. A taxpayer wishes to fulfill creditors' demands for authentic evidence of the status of its tax liability.
> 6. Where proposed assessments are contested on the theory that the years are barred and the parties wish to agree, with finality, to some portion or all of the assessments.
> 7. A taxpayer wishes to assure itself that a controversy between it and the Service is conclusively disposed of.
> 8. To determine personal holding company tax in order to permit deficiency dividends under section 547 of the Code.
>
> .02 A determination of one or more specific matters may be accomplished by closing agreement for good reasons shown by the taxpayer where there is no disadvantage to the Government or where desired by the Government. A few examples of circumstances that may merit entering into such closing agreements are as follows:
>
> 1. To determine cost, fair market value, or adjusted basis as at a given past date.
>
> * * *
>
> 5. To determine the amount of a net operating loss.
> 6. To provide determinations for disposition of cases involving sections 1311 to 1315 of the Code.
>
> * * *

8. To prevent inconsistencies in "whipsaw" situations such as those that could result where a related taxpayer concedes an issue (with the result that the other related party obtains a benefit) and then subsequently, after the statutory period of limitations has expired against the other related party, contests the issue by filing a claim.

* * *

10. To determine the amount of income from a transaction, the amounts of deductions or the year of includibility or deductibility.

* * *

As you can see from the Revenue Procedure excerpted above, closing agreements are limited to specific situations that are much narrower than the situations in which a Form 870 or 870-AD might be used to settle a case. Appeals officers are instructed to use closing agreements only when the case involves mutual concessions and the subsequent tax effect is material. I.R.M. 8.6.4.1.8. As a general matter, closing agreements are fully enforceable in accordance with their terms, and their interpretation is governed by ordinary principles of contract law. *See* Rink v. Commissioner, 100 T.C. 319 (1993), *aff'd*, 47 F.3d 168 (6th Cir. 1995).

Closing agreements may be used by IRS personnel during the examination and appeals process, and occasionally by IRS counsel. Special procedures exist for cases that settle only after being docketed in court. For further discussion of post-docketing settlements, see Section 11.05 of Chapter 11.

PROBLEMS

1. Sylvester, who is single, is a highly successful labor attorney with a large Washington, D.C. law firm. During Year 1, Sylvester received numerous "business gifts" from one of his clients, including a new BMW roadster and the use of the client's beach house during the month of July. Sylvester consulted with the firm's tax department about the tax consequences of the "gifts." He was told, incorrectly, that the rental value of the beach house did not constitute gross income. He was advised correctly that the fair market value of the BMW should be reported. Nevertheless, Sylvester decided not to report either "gift" on his Year 1 tax return. Excluding the gifts, Sylvester reported on his Year 1 return $220,000 of gross income, $5,000 of which represented interest and dividend income and the remainder of which was salary income.

   Sylvester also deducted on his Year 1 return various charitable contributions, including weekly contributions of $20 in cash to his church (for which Sylvester did not maintain a bank record or receive a receipt from the church acknowledging the gifts) and a one-time contribution of 100 shares of stock in a closely held corporation to his alma mater. The book value of the stock was $25 per share. Although Sylvester's ownership in the closely held corporation represented a minority interest, he deducted the value of the stock at its book value, without reducing the valuation for a minority discount. Sylvester's tax return preparer explained to him the risk of reporting the cash contributions without supporting documentation and the potential controversy over the appropriate valuation of the gifted stock.

   During Year 4, the IRS audited Sylvester's Year 1 tax return, which he had timely filed on April 15, Year 2. At the conclusion of the audit late in Year 4, Sylvester received a 30-day letter asserting that the value of the BMW was reportable as gross income and that the appropriate value for the contributed stock was $15 per share. The 30-day letter contained a recalculation of his Year

1 tax liability (with interest) resulting from the failure to report the BMW and the stock revaluation. No penalties were asserted. The examining agent did not ask Sylvester about the use of the beach house, nor did the agent mention the charitable contributions to Sylvester's church. Moreover, neither of these issues was mentioned in the Revenue Agent's Report attached to the 30-day letter. Sylvester believes he has a possibility of establishing that the BMW did not constitute gross income. He also believes that, under applicable law, the minority discount imposed by the IRS was excessive and should not have exceeded 10 percent. With respect to Sylvester's use of the beach house, Sylvester's accountant recently learned about it and suggested to Sylvester that he should have reported it.

A. Should Sylvester pay the asserted deficiency in the 30-day letter and settle on that basis? How would you advise him?

B. Regardless of your advice in part A, Sylvester would like to continue settlement negotiations with the IRS. If a settlement is not reached, he would prefer to contest the deficiency in Tax Court, rather than pay the asserted amount and sue for a refund. Having received the 30-day letter, would Sylvester be better off procedurally (a) requesting an Appeals hearing in response to the 30-day letter or (b) ignoring the 30-day letter and waiting for (or even requesting) a notice of deficiency and filing suit in Tax Court? What factors should he consider?

2. Following the conclusion of a recent audit of Elizabeth's Year 1 tax return, the IRS sent to her a 30-day letter proposing a $10,000 deficiency with respect to her Year 1 return. Elizabeth hired Monty to represent her during the controversy. Monty is not confident that Elizabeth will be able to obtain a settlement with the IRS Appeals Division, but instead believes that the matter is likely to end up in Tax Court. Based on the facts and applicable law, Monty believes that a 50 percent likelihood exists that the Tax Court will find that Elizabeth owes no deficiency. Monty is considering making a qualified settlement offer to the IRS on Elizabeth's behalf in the hope that, if the matter is resolved judicially, Elizabeth will be entitled to recover applicable fees and costs under section 7430.

A. At what point in the controversy process may Monty make a qualified settlement offer, and what terms and conditions must it contain?

B. If Elizabeth decides to forgo Appeals consideration on a nondocketed basis, will she be allowed to recover fees and costs based on the qualified settlement offer?

C. What dollar amount should Monty offer to settle the case, and why?

3. Altaf participated in an investment that was marketed to him as a tax shelter. He has been audited by the IRS. After Altaf received a 30-day letter and filed a tax protest, the IRS Appeals Division offered him a settlement. The settlement would allow Altaf to claim 10 percent of the losses he reported from the shelter investment. Altaf thinks a judge might be sympathetic to allowing a larger share of the deductions. He asks you the following questions.

A. If he decides to settle the case on the IRS's proposed terms, should he memorialize the settlement on Form 870 or Form 870-AD?

B. If he signs an 870-AD, does this preserve his right to petition the Tax Court should he decide to do so after the settlement?

C. If he signs an 870-AD, does this preserve his right to pursue a refund claim for the amounts he will pay over to the IRS with the 870-AD?

4. For many years, Laura Black worked in a high school cafeteria, earning approximately $20,000 per year. In Year 1, the school experienced budget problems and let her go. After looking for a similar job for months, Laura decided to devote herself full-time to the activity she had previously pursued only

in the summer months, deep sea fishing. During the previous ten years, Laura had fished for two months every summer, reporting approximately $5,000 per year as income from fishing.

Laura had never owned a boat but had always rented a small boat for the months she needed one. In Year 2, she decided to try to purchase a boat. Her savings were minimal, so she decided to try to buy a new boat with financing from the seller. However, she soon discovered that the payments would be more than she could comfortably manage. She began looking to buy a used boat and soon found an appropriate one for a reasonable price, $100,000. She looked into obtaining a bank loan but discovered that interest rates were more than she could afford.

After the summer of Year 2, during which Laura again rented a boat, Laura called her relatives and asked to borrow some money. Several of her relatives were surprisingly generous, particularly her extended family living overseas. In addition, one of her former co-workers, Dan, took up a collection at the high school and gave Laura a check totaling $2,000, representing the funds he had collected. Laura discovered that the used boat was still available and agreed to buy it. With the $2,000 check, a little of her own money, and the approximately $96,000 her relatives had furnished, some of which was in cash, Laura purchased in Year 2 a cashier's check from her bank, made payable to the owner of the boat.

In Year 5, Laura was audited and the IRS sent Laura a revenue agent's report and a 30-day letter asserting that the $100,000 used to purchase the cashier's check was unreported income from her fishing activity. Laura tells you that most of the $96,000 was loans, although she does not have documentation in all instances and has not paid any interest. She tells you that her extended family is very close and generally does not require documentation of loans to family members. She also tells you it is their custom not to pay interest but to repay the loan as soon as possible, and perhaps pay a "bonus" at the end to the lender, if that is financially feasible. Laura thinks some of her relatives may not expect repayment at all, but she intends to repay them when she can. Laura said she knows that Dan and her former co-workers at the high school intended to give her a gift, and she does not plan to pay them back. She tells you that although it is possible to make $100,000 in a summer of deep sea fishing, her operation is too small to earn that much. According to Laura, she has tried to be honest in reporting her earnings on her tax return, but she cannot be sure she was completely accurate because she was often paid in cash and did not always keep good records.

Draft a protest letter for Laura. Laura's address and telephone number are 1478 Hickory Drive, Macon, GA 38746; 912-752-5555. Her Social security number is 878-46-4827. Assume that the 30-day letter is dated August 3 of the current year, and the symbols of the letter of transmittal are "Letter 951(DO)." In the protest letter, ignore any below-market loan issues.

5. Refer to the facts appearing in Problem 6 of Chapter 2.

Assume that Dr. Johnson decides not to request a letter ruling relating to the employer-provided lodging. Assume also that he decides not to report as gross income the value of that lodging on his Year 1 income tax return, which he timely filed.

During the current year, the IRS audits Johnson's Year 1 return. The revenue agent conducting the examination submits a preliminary notice of deficiency that includes the following determinations:

Johnson may not exclude the value of the employer-provided housing from his gross income because:

a. The residence does not constitute a part of the employer's business premises because Johnson does not perform the majority of his business activities within the home office;

b. The employer-provided housing is not absolutely necessary for Johnson to perform properly his duties as head physician because adequate housing is available within a reasonable distance that would still allow him to respond to emergencies in a timely manner;

c. Dr. Johnson's allowance of three weeks of vacation per year, during which time no one at the school can adequately respond to potential emergencies, evidences the fact that the employer-provided housing is not a business necessity;

d. The occurrence of only two patient outbreaks prior to the time the parties renegotiated Johnson's employment contract does not evidence a business necessity for the employer-provided housing;

e. The indoor pool and exercise room outfitted for Dr. Johnson evidence an intent on the part of the employer that the residence was provided to him for a compensatory purpose.

The revenue agent proposes a $9,270 deficiency in Johnson's income tax (along with interest and penalties, which you may ignore).

Having received the revenue agent's report and the preliminary notice of deficiency reflecting the above determination (dated November 2 of the current year; symbols 435 (DO) 2-45), Johnson decides to protest the 30-day letter to the Appeals Office. Draft a formal protest letter for Johnson contesting the revenue agent's conclusions. You do not need to attach the 30-day letter to the protest letter, nor do you need to submit a power of attorney. Also, address a cover letter to Johnson explaining the type of protest submitted (skeletal, report-responsive, or comprehensive) and the strategic reasons for doing so. The Appeals Office address is 1465 Southwest Blvd., Kansas City, MO 50694.

Chapter 6
TENSION BETWEEN CONFIDENTIALITY AND DISCLOSURE

§ 6.01 INTRODUCTION

As part of its effort to achieve the highest level of taxpayer compliance possible, the IRS collects and assembles millions of pages of information each year pertaining to virtually every citizen of the United States. While the IRS obtains the vast majority of this information from voluntarily submitted tax and information returns, it also obtains a considerable amount of information involuntarily through its examination, collection, and summons authority. Moreover, the IRS prepares internal memoranda and other materials intended primarily for use by the IRS's own personnel.

Efforts by taxpayers to obtain or control the release of information collected and generated by the IRS have taken place on many fronts, and involve a tangle of statutory provisions. As you will see, some of these provisions favor taxpayers' privacy interests, while other provisions support full disclosure by the IRS to the public. In part, this chapter raises the issue of how the current statutory scheme affecting confidentiality and disclosure of information operates to reconcile these competing interests.[1] The chapter also considers remedies for violations of the various non-disclosure statutes.

As you read the remainder of the chapter, consider these fundamental questions: Under what circumstances should information be disclosed, to whom, and for what purposes? More specifically, should the nature of the information sought or the identity of the requesting party play a role in determining whether the IRS should release the information? In addition, how might a policy of full disclosure by the IRS affect a taxpayer's willingness to provide complete and accurate financial information to the IRS?

§ 6.02 ACCESS TO IRS INFORMATION

Reading Assignment: 5 U.S.C. § 552.

Taxpayers may obtain information from the IRS through a combination of Internal Revenue Code provisions and other statutes. This section describes these statutory provisions and highlights the connections among them.

[A] Disclosure Under the Freedom of Information Act

[1] Categories of Information Subject to Disclosure

Congress enacted the Freedom of Information Act ("FOIA"), 5 U.S.C. § 552, to provide the general public with ready access to information held by government agencies, including the IRS, relating to the organization, procedures, and policies of the agencies. FOIA describes the broad categories of information and records subject to disclosure and the methods by which the information must be made available by the government agency. *Id.* § 552(a). The statute also expresses Congress' intent not to allow agencies to withhold information or limit the public's access to government records, except as specifically stated in the statute. *Id.* § 552(d). This "spirit of disclosure" has been reinforced through judicial interpretations of FOIA, resulting in

---

[1] The related question of what information the IRS can compel the taxpayer, the taxpayer's representative, or a third party to disclose to the IRS for purposes of examining the taxpayer's return or collecting tax liability is discussed in Chapter 4, which addresses summonses and privileges.

more and more information being released by the IRS.[2] As a result, FOIA remains a taxpayer's primary means of compelling the IRS to disclose information.[3]

Three categories of agency information must be made available. The first category includes descriptions of the agency's organizational structure and operations, procedural rules, available forms, and statements of general policy and interpretations. *Id.* § 552(a)(1). Because of its broad appeal, this type of information must be published on a current basis in the Federal Register. Pursuant to this mandate, for example, the IRS publishes proposed, temporary, and final Treasury regulations in the Federal Register the day after they are issued. The second category of information, described in section 552(a)(2), need only be made available by an agency for public inspection and copying, or for sale.[4] This category includes final opinions and orders made during the processing of a case, administrative staff manuals, and instructions to employees that might affect a member of the public.[5]

The final category of information consists of "agency records." Unlike the documents that fall into the first two categories, the types of agency records contemplated in section 552(a)(3) need not be disclosed automatically. In order to obtain access to these types of records from the IRS, a taxpayer must request the information in accordance with the published rules described below. Agency records encompass a wide array of information, from statistical studies derived from data submitted by thousands of taxpayers to a revenue agent's report prepared in connection with the audit of a single individual. As the following case confirms, agency records are not limited to items or information prepared by officials or employees of the agency from which the information is being requested.

UNITED STATES DEPARTMENT OF JUSTICE v. TAX ANALYSTS

United States Supreme Court
492 U.S. 136 (1989)

JUSTICE MARSHALL delivered the opinion of the Court.

The question presented is whether the Freedom of Information Act (FOIA or Act), 5 U.S.C. § 552 (1982 ed. and Supp. V), requires the United States Department of Justice (Department) to make available copies of district court decisions that it receives in the course of litigating tax cases on behalf of the Federal Government. We hold that it does.

I.

The Department's Tax Division represents the Federal Government in nearly all civil tax cases in the district courts, the courts of appeals, and the Claims Court. Because it represents a party in litigation, the Tax Division receives copies of all opinions and orders issued by these courts in such cases. Copies of these decisions are made for the Tax Division's staff attorneys. The original documents are sent to the official files kept by the Department.

---

[2] In the tax area, Tax Analysts, a publisher of several tax magazines, has been at the forefront of FOIA litigation. *DOJ v. Tax Analysts*, which is reproduced in this chapter, describes one of Tax Analysts' interest in bringing these lawsuits. On a more general level, the litigation represents the Tax Analysts organization's long-held position that the public has a right of access to the IRS's internal documents.

[3] FOIA has generated considerable litigation involving government agencies other than the IRS. Cases involving these other administrative agencies establish principles that necessarily influence the IRS's obligations under the statute. However, this chapter is confined, for the most part, to those cases specifically bearing upon the IRS's duties under the statute.

[4] For records created on or after November 1, 1996, the IRS must make these records available by computer telecommunications; that is, on the IRS's website.

[5] Much of the information within the second FOIA category is published commercially by private firms such as Commerce Clearing House and Tax Analysts. Chapter 20 identifies these sources.

* * *

Respondent Tax Analysts publishes a weekly magazine, Tax Notes, which reports on legislative, judicial, and regulatory developments in the field of federal taxation to a readership largely composed of tax attorneys, accountants, and economists. As one of its regular features, Tax Notes provides summaries of recent federal-court decisions on tax issues. To supplement the magazine, Tax Analysts provides full texts of these decisions in microfiche form. Tax Analysts also publishes Tax Notes Today, a daily electronic data base that includes summaries and full texts of recent federal-court tax decisions.

In late July 1979, Tax Analysts filed a FOIA request in which it asked the Department to make available all district court tax opinions and final orders received by the Tax Division earlier that month. The Department denied the request on the ground that these decisions were not Tax Division records. Tax Analysts then appealed this denial administratively. While the appeal was pending, Tax Analysts agreed to withdraw its request in return for access to the Tax Division's weekly log of tax cases decided by the federal courts. These logs list the name and date of a case, the docket number, the names of counsel, the nature of the case, and its disposition.

Since gaining access to the weekly logs, Tax Analysts' practice has been to examine the logs and to request copies of the decisions noted therein from the clerks of the 90 or so district courts around the country and from participating attorneys. In most instances, Tax Analysts procures copies reasonably promptly, but this method of acquisition has proven unsatisfactory approximately 25% of the time. Some court clerks ignore Tax Analysts' requests for copies of decisions, and others respond slowly, sometimes only after Tax Analysts has forwarded postage and copying fees. Because the Federal Government is required to appeal tax cases within 60 days, Tax Analysts frequently fails to obtain copies of district court decisions before appeals are taken.

Frustrated with this process, Tax Analysts initiated a series of new FOIA requests in 1984. Beginning in November 1984, and continuing approximately once a week until May 1985, Tax Analysts asked the Department to make available copies of all district court tax opinions and final orders identified in the Tax Division's weekly logs. The Department denied these requests and Tax Analysts appealed administratively. When the Department sustained the denial, Tax Analysts filed the instant suit in the United States District Court for the District of Columbia, seeking to compel the Department to provide it with access to district court decisions received by the Tax Division.

The District Court granted the Department's motion to dismiss the complaint, holding that 5 U.S.C. § 552(a)(4)(B), which confers jurisdiction in the district courts when "agency records" have been "improperly withheld,"[n.2] had not been satisfied. 643 F. Supp. 740, 742 (1986). The court reasoned that the district court decisions at issue had not been "improperly withheld" because they "already are available from their primary sources, the District Courts," *id.*, at 743, and thus were "on the public record." *Id.*, at 744. The court did not address whether the district court decisions are "agency records." *Id.*, at 742.

The Court of Appeals for the District of Columbia Circuit reversed. 845 F.2d 1060, 269 U.S. App. D.C. 315 (1988). It first held that the district court decisions were

---

[n.2] Section 552(a)(4)(B) provides:

> "On complaint, the district court of the United States in the district in which the complainant resides, or has his principal place of business, or in which the agency records are situated, or in the District of Columbia, has jurisdiction to enjoin the agency from withholding agency records and to order the production of any agency records improperly withheld from the complainant. In such a case the court shall determine the matter de novo, and may examine the contents of such agency records in camera to determine whether such records or any part thereof shall be withheld under any of the exemptions set forth in subsection (b) of this section, and the burden is on the agency to sustain its action."

"improperly withheld." An agency ordinarily may refuse to make available documents in its control only if it proves that the documents fall within one of the nine disclosure exemptions set forth in § 552(b), the court noted, and in this instance, "[n]o exemption applies to the district court opinions." *Id.*, at 319, 845 F.2d, at 1064. As for the Department's contention that the district court decisions are publicly available at their source, the court observed that "no court . . . has denied access to . . . documents on the ground that they are available elsewhere, and several have assumed that such documents must still be produced by the agency unless expressly exempted by the Act." *Id.*, at 321, 845 F.2d, at 1066.

The Court of Appeals next held that the district court decisions sought by Tax Analysts are "agency records" for purposes of the FOIA. The court acknowledged that the district court decisions had originated in a part of the Government not covered by the FOIA, but concluded that the documents nonetheless constituted "agency records" because the Department has the discretion to use the decisions as it sees fit, because the Department routinely uses the decisions in performing its official duties, and because the decisions are integrated into the Department's official case files. *Id.*, at 323–324, 845 F.2d, at 1068–1069. The court therefore remanded the case to the District Court with instructions to enter an order directing the Department "to provide some reasonable form of access" to the decisions sought by Tax Analysts. *Id.*, at 317, 845 F.2d, at 1062.

We granted certiorari, 488 U.S. 1003 (1989), and now affirm.

II.

In enacting the FOIA 23 years ago, Congress sought " 'to open agency action to the light of public scrutiny.' " Department of Justice v. Reporters Committee for Freedom of Press, 489 U.S. 749, 772 (1989), quoting Department of Air Force v. Rose, 425 U.S. 352, 372 (1976). Congress did so by requiring agencies to adhere to " 'a general philosophy of full agency disclosure.' " *Id.*, at 360, quoting S. Rep. No. 813, 89th Cong., 1st Sess., 3 (1965). Congress believed that this philosophy, put into practice, would help "ensure an informed citizenry, vital to the functioning of a democratic society." NLRB v. Robbins Tire & Rubber Co., 437 U.S. 214, 242 (1978).

The FOIA confers jurisdiction on the district courts "to enjoin the agency from withholding agency records and to order the production of any agency records improperly withheld." § 552(a)(4)(B). Under this provision, "federal jurisdiction is dependent on a showing that an agency has (1) 'improperly' (2) 'withheld' (3) 'agency records.' " Kissinger v. Reporters Committee for Freedom of Press, 445 U.S. 136, 150 (1980). Unless each of these criteria is met, a district court lacks jurisdiction to devise remedies to force an agency to comply with the FOIA's disclosure requirements.[n.3]

In this case, all three jurisdictional terms are at issue. Although these terms are defined neither in the Act nor in its legislative history, we do not write on a clean slate. Nine Terms ago we decided three cases that explicated the meanings of these partially overlapping terms. Kissinger v. Reporters Committee for Freedom of Press, *supra;* Forsham v. Harris, 445 U.S. 169 (1980); GTE Sylvania, Inc. v. Consumers Union of United States, Inc., 445 U.S. 375 (1980). These decisions form the basis of our analysis of Tax Analysts' requests.

[n.3] The burden is on the agency to demonstrate, not the requester to disprove, that the materials sought are not "agency records" or have not been "improperly" "withheld." *See* S. Rep. No. 813, 89th Cong., 1st Sess., 8 (1965) ("Placing the burden of proof upon the agency puts the task of justifying the withholding on the only party able to explain it"); H.R. Rep. No. 1497, 89th Cong., 2d Sess., 9 (1966) (same); *cf.* Federal Open Market Committee v. Merrill, 443 U.S. 340, 352 (1979).

A

We consider first whether the district court decisions at issue are "agency records," a term elaborated upon both in *Kissinger* and in *Forsham. Kissinger* involved three separate FOIA requests for written summaries of telephone conversations in which Henry Kissinger had participated when he served as Assistant to the President for National Security Affairs from 1969 to 1975, and as Secretary of State from 1973 to 1977. Only one of these requests — for summaries of specific conversations that Kissinger had had during his tenure as National Security Adviser — raised the "agency records" issue. At the time of this request, these summaries were stored in Kissinger's office at the State Department in his personal files. We first concluded that the summaries were not "agency records" at the time they were made because the FOIA does not include the Office of the President in its definition of "agency." 445 U.S., at 156. We further held that these documents did not acquire the status of "agency records" when they were removed from the White House and transported to Kissinger's office at the State Department, a FOIA-covered agency:

> "We simply decline to hold that the physical location of the notes of telephone conversations renders them 'agency records.' The papers were not in the control of the State Department at any time. They were not generated in the State Department. They never entered the State Department's files, and they were not used by the Department for any purpose. If mere physical location of papers and materials could confer status as an 'agency record' Kissinger's personal books, speeches, and all other memorabilia stored in his office would have been agency records subject to disclosure under the FOIA." *Id.*, at 157.

Forsham, in turn, involved a request for raw data that formed the basis of a study conducted by a private medical research organization. Although the study had been funded through federal agency grants, the data never passed into the hands of the agencies that provided the funding, but instead was produced and possessed at all times by the private organization. We recognized that "[r]ecords of a nonagency certainly could become records of an agency as well," 445 U.S., at 181, but the fact that the study was financially supported by a FOIA-covered agency did not transform the source material into "agency records." Nor did the agencies' right of access to the materials under federal regulations change this result. As we explained, "the FOIA applies to records which have been in fact obtained, and not to records which merely *could have been* obtained." *Id.*, at 186 (emphasis in original; footnote omitted).

Two requirements emerge from *Kissinger* and *Forsham*, each of which must be satisfied for requested materials to qualify as "agency records." First, an agency must "either create or obtain" the requested materials "as a prerequisite to its becoming an 'agency record' within the meaning of the FOIA." *Id.*, at 182. In performing their official duties, agencies routinely avail themselves of studies, trade journal reports, and other materials produced outside the agencies both by private and governmental organizations. *See* Chrysler Corp. v. Brown, 441 U.S. 281, 292 (1979). To restrict the term "agency records" to materials generated internally would frustrate Congress' desire to put within public reach the information available to an agency in its decision-making processes. *See id.*, at 290, n.10. As we noted in *Forsham*, "The legislative history of the FOIA abounds with . . . references to records *acquired* by an agency." 445 U.S., at 184 (emphasis added).

Second, the agency must be in control of the requested materials at the time the FOIA request is made. By control we mean that the materials have come into the agency's possession in the legitimate conduct of its official duties. This requirement accords with *Kissinger's* teaching that the term "agency records" is not so broad as to include personal materials in an employee's possession, even though the materials may be physically located at the agency. *See* 445 U.S., at 157. This requirement is suggested by *Forsham* as well, 445 U.S., at 183, where we looked to the definition of agency records in the Records Disposal Act, 44 U.S.C. § 3301. Under that definition, agency records include "all books, papers, maps, photographs, machine readable materials, or other documentary materials, regardless of physical form or characteristics, made or received by an agency of the United States Government *under Federal law or in connection with the transaction of public business. . . .*" *Ibid.* (emphasis added).[n.5] Furthermore, the requirement that the materials be in the agency's control at the time the request is made accords with our statement in *Forsham* that the FOIA does not cover "information in the abstract." 445 U.S., at 185.

Applying these requirements here, we conclude that the requested district court decisions constitute "agency records." First, it is undisputed that the Department has obtained these documents from the district courts. This is not a case like *Forsham*, where the materials never in fact had been received by the agency. The Department contends that a district court is not an "agency" under the FOIA, but this truism is beside the point. The relevant issue is whether an agency covered by the FOIA has "create[d] or obtaine[d]" the materials sought, *Forsham*, 445 U.S., at 182, not whether the organization from which the documents originated is itself covered by the FOIA.

Second, the Department clearly controls the district court decisions that Tax Analysts seeks. Each of Tax Analysts' FOIA requests referred to district court decisions in the agency's possession at the time the requests were made. This is evident from the fact that Tax Analysts based its weekly requests on the Tax Division's logs, which compile information on decisions the Tax Division recently had received and placed in official case files. Furthermore, the court decisions at issue are obviously not personal papers of agency employees. The Department counters that it does not control these decisions because the district courts retain authority to modify the decisions even after they are released, but this argument, too, is beside the point. The control inquiry focuses on an agency's possession of the requested materials, not on its power to alter the content of the materials it receives. Agencies generally are not at liberty to alter the content of the materials that they receive from outside parties. An authorship-control requirement thus would sharply limit "agency records" essentially to documents generated by the agencies themselves. This result is incompatible with the FOIA's goal of giving the public access to all nonexempted information received by an agency as it carries out its mandate.

The Department also urges us to limit "agency records," at least where materials originating outside the agency are concerned, "to those documents 'prepared substantially to be relied upon in agency decision-making.'" Brief for Petitioner 21, quoting Berry v. Department of Justice, 733 F.2d 1343, 1349 (CA9 1984). This limitation disposes of Tax Analysts' requests, the Department argues, because district court judges do not write their decisions primarily with an eye toward agency decision-making. This argument, however, makes the determination of "agency records" turn on the intent of the creator of a document relied upon by an agency. Such a *mens rea* requirement is nowhere to be found in the Act. Moreover, discerning the intent of the drafters of a document may often prove an elusive endeavor, particularly if the document was created years earlier or by a large number of people for whom it is difficult to divine a common intent.

[n.5] In *GTE Sylvania, Inc. v. Consumers Union of United States, Inc.*, 445 U.S. 375, 385 (1980), we noted that Congress intended the FOIA to prevent agencies from refusing to disclose, among other things, agency telephone directories and the names of agency employees. We are confident, however, that requests for documents of this type will be relatively infrequent. Common sense suggests that a person seeking such documents or materials housed in an agency library typically will find it easier to repair to the Library of Congress, or to the nearest public library, rather than to invoke the FOIA's disclosure mechanisms. *Cf.* Department of Justice v. Reporters Committee for Freedom of Press, 489 U.S. 749, 764 (1989) ("[I]f the [requested materials] were 'freely available,' there would be no reason to invoke the FOIA to obtain access"). To the extent such requests are made, the fact that the FOIA allows agencies to recoup the costs of processing requests from the requester may discourage recourse to the FOIA where materials are readily available elsewhere. *See* 5 U.S.C. § 552(a)(4)(A).

B

We turn next to the term "withheld," which we discussed in *Kissinger*. Two of the requests in that case — for summaries of all the telephone conversations in which Kissinger had engaged while serving as National Security Adviser and as Secretary of State — implicated that term. These summaries were initially stored in Kissinger's personal files at the State Department. Near the end of his tenure as Secretary of State, Kissinger transferred the summaries first to a private residence and then to the Library of Congress. Significantly, the two requests for these summaries were made only after the summaries had been physically delivered to the Library. We found this fact dispositive, concluding that Congress did not believe that an agency "withholds a document which has been removed from the possession of the agency prior to the filing of the FOIA request. In such a case, the agency has neither the custody nor control necessary to enable it to withhold." 445 U.S., at 150–151.[n.9] We accordingly refused to order the State Department to institute a retrieval action against the Library. As we explained, such a course "would have us read the 'hold' out of 'withhold. . . . A refusal to resort to legal remedies to obtain possession is simply not conduct subsumed by the verb withhold.' " *Id.*, at 151.[n.10]

The construction of "withholding" adopted in *Kissinger* readily encompasses Tax Analysts' requests. There is no claim here that Tax Analysts filed its requests for copies of recent district court tax decisions received by the Tax Division after these decisions had been transferred out of the Department. On the contrary, the decisions were on the Department's premises and otherwise in the Department's control, *supra*, at 146–147, when the requests were made. * * * Thus, when the Department refused to comply with Tax Analysts' requests, it "withheld" the district court decisions for purposes of § 552(a)(4)(B).

The Department's counterargument is that, because the district court decisions sought by Tax Analysts are publicly available as soon as they are issued and thus may be inspected and copied by the public at any time, the Department cannot be said to have "withheld" them. The Department notes that the weekly logs it provides to Tax Analysts contain sufficient information to direct Tax Analysts to the "original source of the requested documents." Brief for Petitioner 23. It is not clear from the Department's brief whether this argument is based on the term "withheld" or the term "improperly."[n.11] But, to the extent the Department relies on the former term, its argument is without merit. Congress used the word "withheld" only "in its usual sense." *Kissinger*, 445 U.S., at 151. When the Department refused to grant Tax Analysts' requests for the district court decisions in its files, it undoubtedly "withheld" these decisions in any reasonable sense of that term. Nothing in the history or purposes of the FOIA counsels

---

[n.9] Although a control inquiry for "withheld" replicates part of the test for "agency records," the FOIA's structure and legislative history make clear that agency control over requested materials is a "prerequisite to triggering any duties under the FOIA." *Kissinger*, 445 U.S., at 151 (emphasis added); *see also id.*, at 152–153; Forsham v. Harris, 445 U.S. 169, 185 (1980).

[n.10] *Kissinger's* focus on the agency's present control of a requested document was based in part on the Act's purposes and structure. With respect to the former, we noted that because Congress had not intended to "obligate agencies to create or retain documents," an agency should not be "required to retrieve documents which have escaped its possession, but which it has not endeavored to recover." 445 U.S., at 152 (citations omitted). As for the Act's structure, we noted that, among other provisions, § 552(a)(6)(B) gives agencies a 10-day extension of the normal 10-day period for responding to FOIA requests if there is a need to search and collect the requested materials from facilities separate from the office processing the request. The brevity of this extension period indicates that Congress did not expect agencies to resort to lawsuits to retrieve documents within that period. *See id.*, at 153.

[n.11] The Court of Appeals believed that the Department was arguing "that it need not affirmatively make [the district court decisions] available to Tax Analysts because the documents have not been *withheld* to begin with." 845 F.2d 1060, 1064-1065, 269 U.S. App. D. C. 315, 319–320 (1988) (emphasis in original).

contorting this word beyond its usual meaning. We therefore reject the Department's argument that an agency has not "withheld" a document under its control when, in denying an otherwise valid request, it directs the requester to a place outside of the agency where the document may be publicly available.

C

The Department is left to argue, finally, that the district court decisions were not "improperly" withheld because of their public availability. The term "improperly," like "agency records" and "withheld," is not defined by the Act. We explained in *GTE Sylvania*, however, that Congress' use of the word "improperly" reflected its dissatisfaction with § 3 of the Administrative Procedure Act, 5 U.S.C. § 1002 (1964 ed.), which "had failed to provide the desired access to information relied upon in Government decision-making, and in fact had become 'the major statutory excuse for withholding Government records from public view.' " 445 U.S., at 384, quoting H.R. Rep. No. 1497, 89th Cong., 2d Sess., 3 (1966). Under § 3, we explained, agencies had "broad discretion . . . in deciding what information to disclose, and that discretion was often abused." 445 U.S., at 385.

In enacting the FOIA, Congress intended "to curb this apparently unbridled discretion" by "clos[ing] the 'loopholes which allow agencies to deny legitimate information to the public.' " *Ibid.* (citation omitted); *see also* EPA v. Mink, 410 U.S. 73, 79 (1973). Toward this end, Congress formulated a system of clearly defined exemptions to the FOIA's otherwise mandatory disclosure requirements. An agency must disclose agency records to any person under § 552(a), "unless they may be withheld pursuant to one of the nine enumerated exemptions listed in § 552(b)." Department of Justice v. Julian, 486 U.S. 1, 8 (1988). Consistent with the Act's goal of broad disclosure, these exemptions have been consistently given a narrow compass. *See, e.g., Ibid.;* FBI v. Abramson, 456 U.S. 615, 630 (1982). More important for present purposes, the exemptions are "explicitly exclusive." FAA Administrator v. Robertson, 422 U.S. 255, 262 (1975); *see also Rose*, 425 U.S., at 361; *Robbins Tire & Rubber Co.*, 437 U.S., at 221; *Mink, supra*, at 79. As Justice O'Connor has explained, Congress sought "to insulate its product from judicial tampering and to preserve the emphasis on disclosure by admonishing that the 'availability of records to the public' is not limited, 'except as *specifically* stated.' " *Abramson, supra*, at 642 (dissenting opinion) (emphasis in original), quoting § 552(c) (now codified at § 552(d)); *see also* 456 U.S., at 637, n. 5; H.R. Rep. No. 1497, *supra*, at 1. It follows from the exclusive nature of the § 552(b) exemption scheme that agency records which do not fall within one of the exemptions are "improperly" withheld.[n.12]

The Department does not contend here that any exemption enumerated in § 552(b) protects the district court decisions sought by Tax Analysts. The Department claims nonetheless that there is nothing "improper" in directing a requester "to the principal, public source of records." Brief for Petitioner 26. The Department advances three somewhat related arguments in support of this proposition. * * *

First, the Department contends that the structure of the Act evinces Congress' desire to avoid redundant disclosures. An understanding of this argument requires a brief survey of the disclosure provisions of § 552(a). Under subsection (a)(1), an agency must "currently publish in the Federal Register" specific materials, such as descriptions of

[n.12] Even when an agency does not deny a FOIA request outright, the requesting party may still be able to claim "improper" withholding by alleging that the agency has responded in an inadequate manner. *Cf.* § 552(a)(6)(C); *Kissinger v. Reporters Committee for Freedom of Press*, 445 U.S., at 166 (Stevens, J., concurring in part and dissenting in part). No such claim is made in this case. Indeed, Tax Analysts does not dispute the Court of Appeals' conclusion that the Department could satisfy its duty of disclosure simply by making the relevant district court opinions available for copying in the public reference facility that it maintains. *See* 269 U.S. App. D.C., at 321–322, and n.15, 845 F.2d, at 1066–1067, and n.15.

the agency, statements of its general functions, and the agency's rules of procedure. Under subsection (a)(2), an agency must "make available for public inspection and copying" its final opinions, policy statements, and administrative staff manuals, "unless the materials are promptly published and copies offered for sale." Under subsection (a)(3), the general provision covering the disclosure of agency records, an agency need not make available those materials that have already been disclosed under subsections (a)(1) and (a)(2). Taken together, the Department argues, these provisions demonstrate the inapplicability of the FOIA's disclosure requirements to previously disclosed, publicly available materials. "A fortiori, a judicial record that is a public document should not be subject to a FOIA request." *Id.*, at 29.

The Department's argument proves too much. The disclosure requirements set out in subsections (a)(1) and (a)(2) are carefully limited to situations in which the requested materials have been previously published or made available by the agency itself. It is one thing to say that an agency need not disclose materials that it has previously released; it is quite another to say that an agency need not disclose materials that some other person or group may have previously released. Congress undoubtedly was aware of the redundancies that might exist when requested materials have been previously made available. It chose to deal with that problem by crafting only narrow categories of materials which need not be, in effect, disclosed twice by the agency. If Congress had wished to codify an exemption for all publicly available materials, it knew perfectly well how to do so. It is not for us to add or detract from Congress' comprehensive scheme, which already "balances, and protects all interests" implicated by Executive Branch disclosure. *Mink, supra*, at 80, quoting S. Rep. No. 813, 89th Congress, 1st Sess., 3 (1965).

It is not surprising, moreover, that Congress declined to exempt all publicly available materials from the FOIA's disclosure requirements. In the first place, such an exemption would engender intractable fights over precisely what constitutes public availability, unless the term were defined with precision. In some sense, nearly all of the information that comes within an agency's control can be characterized as publicly available. Although the form in which this material comes to an agency — *i.e.*, a report or testimony — may not be generally available, the information included in that report or testimony may very well be. Even if there were some agreement over what constitutes publicly available materials, Congress surely did not envision agencies satisfying their disclosure obligations under the FOIA simply by handing requesters a map and sending them on scavenger expeditions throughout the Nation. Without some express indication in the Act's text or legislative history that Congress intended such a result, we decline to adopt this reading of the statute. * * *

III.

For the reasons stated, the Department improperly withheld agency records when it refused Tax Analysts' request for copies of the district court tax decisions in its files. Accordingly, the judgment of the Court of Appeals is

Affirmed.

JUSTICE BLACKMUN, dissenting.

The Court in this case has examined once again the Freedom of Information Act (FOIA), 5 U.S.C. § 552. It now determines that under the Act the Department of Justice on request must make available copies of federal district court orders and opinions it receives in the course of its litigation of tax cases on behalf of the Federal Government. The majority holds that these qualify as agency records, within the meaning of § 552(a)(4)(B), and that they were improperly withheld by the Department when respondent asked for their production. The Court's analysis, I suppose, could be regarded as a fairly routine one.

I do not join the Court's opinion, however, because it seems to me that the language of the statute is not that clear or conclusive on the issue and, more important, because the result the Court reaches cannot be one that was within the intent of Congress when the FOIA was enacted.

Respondent Tax Analysts, although apparently a nonprofit organization for federal income tax purposes, is in business and in that sense is a commercial enterprise. It sells summaries of these opinions and supplies full texts to major electronic data bases. The result of its now-successful effort in this litigation is to impose the cost of obtaining the court orders and opinions upon the Government and thus upon taxpayers generally. There is no question that this material is available elsewhere. But it is quicker and more convenient, and less "frustrat[ing]," * * * for respondent to have the Department do the work and search its files and produce the items than it is to apply to the respective court clerks.

This, I feel, is almost a gross misuse of the FOIA. What respondent demands, and what the Court permits, adds nothing whatsoever to public knowledge of Government operations. That, I had thought, and the majority acknowledges, * * * was the real purpose of the FOIA and the spirit in which the statute has been interpreted thus far. *See, e.g.*, Forsham v. Harris, 445 U.S. 169, 178 (1980); NLRB v. Robbins Tire & Rubber Co., 437 U.S. 214, 242–243 (1978). I also sense, I believe not unwarrantedly, a distinct lack of enthusiasm on the part of the majority for the result it reaches in this case.

If, as I surmise, the Court's decision today is outside the intent of Congress in enacting the statute, Congress perhaps will rectify the decision forthwith and will give everyone concerned needed guidelines for the administration and interpretation of this somewhat opaque statute.

Notice that the majority's analysis of whether the district court decisions were improperly withheld by the Justice Department did not take into account Tax Analysts' motivation for requesting the information (a point that seemed to concern Justice Blackmun). As a general matter, a taxpayer who requests information under FOIA need not specify a reason for doing so or otherwise explain how the materials requested may be relevant to the taxpayer. *See* EPA v. Mink, 410 U.S. 73, 79, 92 (1973); NLRB v. Sears Roebuck & Co., 421 U.S. 132 (1975). Instead, as explained in footnote 3 of the majority's opinion, the burden of proof falls on the government agency to specify the reason for withholding all or a portion of the requested documents. What other procedural safeguards has Congress included in FOIA to help ensure full disclosure of government information?

[2] FOIA Exemptions Most Relevant to Tax Practice

Reading Assignment: Review 5 U.S.C. § 552(b); read I.R.C. § 6103(a)–(b).

The IRS's burden of justifying its failure to make requested agency records available for inspection normally plays out in the context of the nine exemptions from disclosure listed in section 552(b).[6] These exemptions specify circumstances under which the IRS may deny access to records. Many of these exemptions are either relatively uncontroversial or are not particularly relevant to the field of tax practice.[7] Those exemptions of principal importance to tax administration are Exemption 3 (relating to information

[6] FOIA also contains a series of exclusions permitting the IRS to respond to a request by claiming that the requested records do not exist. *See* 5 U.S.C. § 552(c). These limited exclusions may be used by the IRS where disclosure would reveal the identity of an informant participating in a criminal investigation or identify the subject of the investigation.

[7] These include the exemption for documents relating to national defense and foreign policy, trade secrets, and information that would result in an unwarranted violation of personal privacy. 5 U.S.C. § 552(b)(1), (4), (6).

specifically exempted from disclosure by other statutes), Exemption 5 (relating to agency memoranda), and Exemption 7 (relating to documents gathered for law enforcement purposes).

Courts have consistently ruled that each of the FOIA exemptions must be narrowly construed in favor of disclosure. *See, e.g.,* Vaughn v. Rosen, 523 F.2d 1136 (D.C. Cir. 1975). Moreover, if a requested document contains information that is exempt from disclosure under the statute, the IRS must attempt to segregate the portion that is exempt and disclose the remaining material. 5 U.S.C. § 552(b); *see also* King v. United States Department of Justice, 830 F.2d 210, 224 (D.C. Cir. 1987) ("[T]he withholding agency must supply 'a relatively detailed' justification, specifically identifying the reasons why a particular exemption is relevant and correlating those claims with the particular part of a withheld document to which they apply."). Only when the nonexempt material is "inextricably intertwined" with the exempt material may the IRS properly withhold the entire document. Schiller v. NLRB, 964 F.2d 1205, 1209 (D.C. Cir. 1992).

[a] FOIA Exemption 3

Under Exemption 3, the IRS may withhold information if that information is specifically exempted from disclosure by another statute. With respect to FOIA requests made to the IRS, the principal statute implicated by Exemption 3 is Code section 6103. *See* Chamberlain v. Kurtz, 589 F.2d 827 (5th Cir.), *cert. denied*, 444 U.S. 842 (1979). Section 6103 seeks to ensure that a taxpayer's return and tax return information remain confidential and not subject to disclosure except where disclosure is specifically permitted by the statute. Accordingly, FOIA does not require disclosure of information that may not be lawfully disclosed by the IRS under section 6103. The operation of section 6103 as a confidentiality statute and the scope of its many exceptions are discussed in more detail in Section 6.03 below.

[b] FOIA Exemption 5

Pursuant to Exemption 5, the IRS may refuse to disclose interagency or intra-agency memoranda that would not be available by law to a private party in litigation with the IRS. 5 U.S.C. § 552(b)(5). The Supreme Court interprets FOIA Exemption 5 to exempt from disclosure those documents that would otherwise be privileged and not discoverable by a party requesting the information as part of a hypothetical civil case. NLRB v. Sears Roebuck & Co., 421 U.S. 132 (1975). The privileges incorporated into Exemption 5 include the (1) attorney-client privilege, (2) the attorney work product privilege, and (3) to a limited extent, the deliberative process privilege.

As explained in Chapter 4, the attorney-client privilege encourages communication between client and attorney by assuring that a client's confidences to his or her attorney will not be disclosed without the client's consent. Coastal States Gas Corp. v. Dept. of Energy, 617 F.2d 854, 862 (D.C. Cir. 1980). The privilege extends to situations in which a client seeks an attorney's counsel on a legal matter. *Id.* The federal courts also extend the privilege to an attorney's written communications to a client, to ensure against disclosure of information that the client has previously confided to the attorney. Mead Data Central, Inc. v. United States Dept. of Air Force, 566 F.2d 242, 254 n.25 (1977). However, the privilege is narrowly construed and is limited to those situations in which its purposes will be served; it "protects only those disclosures necessary to obtain informed legal advice which might not have been made absent the privilege." Fisher v. United States, 425 U.S. 391, 403 (1976).

The attorney work product privilege was established by the Supreme Court in *Hickman v. Taylor*, 329 U.S. 495 (1947). The privilege protects documents prepared in contemplation of litigation, providing an attorney with privacy within which to prepare the case and plan litigation strategies. *Coastal States Gas Corp.*, 617 F.2d at 865. "Whatever the outer boundaries of the attorney's work-product rule are, the rule clearly applies to memoranda prepared by an attorney in contemplation of litigation which set forth the attorney's theory of the case and his litigation strategy." *Sears Roebuck & Co.*, 421 U.S. at 154. These types of documents are therefore protected from disclosure under Exemption 5.

The deliberative process privilege covers " 'all papers which reflect the agency's group thinking in the process of working out its policy and determining what its law shall be.' " Arthur Andersen & Co. v. Internal Revenue Service, 679 F.2d 254, 257 (D.C. Cir. 1982) (*quoting Sears Roebuck & Co., supra*). Courts have limited the privilege to materials that are both "predecisional" and "deliberative." *See* Tax Analysts v. Internal Revenue Service, 117 F.3d 607, 616 (D.C. Cir. 1997). Documents protected from disclosure by Exemption 5 typically include some type of legal or policy analysis. Factual information gathered by the IRS, on the other hand, is generally considered to be outside the scope of Exemption 5 because it is non-deliberative.

The issues of whether requested information is pre- or post-decisional, and deliberative or non-deliberative, are illustrated in *Tax Analysts v. Internal Revenue Service*, 97 F. Supp. 2d 13 (2000), excerpted below.[8] In that case, the District Court for the D.C. District granted the IRS's motion for summary judgment on the issue of whether FOIA compelled the IRS to disclose "legal memoranda" (LMs). LMs are documents prepared by attorneys in the Office of Chief Counsel (referred to by the court as "docket attorneys") to assist in the preparation of a proposed Revenue Ruling. The memorandum contains the drafter's legal research as well as the drafter's evaluation of the strengths and weaknesses of the proposed ruling. The memorandum ultimately serves as briefing material for IRS reviewers before the Revenue Ruling is finalized. The court explained:

> The IRS contends that LMs are shielded from disclosure by the executive or governmental deliberative process privilege, which is one of three privileges incorporated by FOIA's Exemption 5. * * * The deliberative process privilege protects only those "government 'materials which are both predecisional and deliberative.' " Tax Analysts v. Internal Revenue Svc., 117 F.3d 607, 616 (D.C. Cir. 1997) (*quoting* Wolfe v. Department of Health & Human Svcs., 839 F.2d 768, 774 (D.C. Cir. 1988)). As a general rule, a document is predecisional if it was "generated before the adoption of agency policy" and deliberative if it "reflects the give-and-take of the consultative process." *Coastal States*, 617 F.2d at 866; *Tax Analysts*, 117 F.3d at 616 (same). Thus, the IRS must establish that the withheld LMs "contain 'the ideas and theories which go into the making of the law' and not 'the law itself.' " Arthur Andersen & Co. v. Internal Revenue Svc., 679 F.2d 254, 258 (D.C. Cir. 1982) (*quoting* Sterling Drug, Inc. v. FTC, 450 F.2d 698, 708 (D.C. Cir. 1971)). "An agency will not be permitted to develop a body of 'secret law' used by it in the discharge of its regulatory duties and in its dealings with the public, but hidden behind a veil of privilege . . . ." *Coastal States*, 617 F.2d at 867. Accordingly, this "exemption is to be applied 'as narrowly as consistent with efficient Government operation.' " *Id.*, 617 F.2d at 868 (*quoting* S. Rep. 89-813 at 9 (1965).
>
> * * *
>
> Applying this Circuit's law to these undisputed facts, the Court finds that the deliberative process privilege protects from disclosure those portions of LMs that do not reflect the official position of the Office of Chief Counsel. In this regard, the Court finds that LMs function like the Background Information

[8] After several motions from both parties relating to the disposition of this case, the D.C. Circuit Court of Appeals eventually affirmed the district court's ruling that the LMs at issue were protected from disclosure by the deliberative process privilege. Tax Analysts v. Internal Revenue Service, 294 F.3d 71, 76 (2002).

Notes ("BINs") at issue in *Arthur Andersen*, 679 F.2d 254, 258 (D.C. Cir. 1982).[9] Like LMs, BINs are part of a proposed revenue ruling's publication package. After conducting an *in camera* review of the contested draft Revenue Rulings and their accompanying BINs, the D.C. Circuit noted that "the flow of the documents was from subordinate to superior. Because approval was required at each higher level, all the participants up to the Commissioner were without authority to make a final determination." *Arthur Andersen*, 679 F.2d at 259; *see also* Pies v. Internal Revenue Svc., 668 F.2d 1350, 1353 (D.C. Cir. 1981) (protecting draft proposed regulations and a draft transmittal memorandum that were "never subjected to final review, never approved by the officials having authority to do so, and never approved within the Legislation and Regulations Division"). Because the drafters lack ultimate authority, their views are necessarily pre-decisional. Similarly, LMs are directed upward from docket attorneys to reviewers and, ultimately, to the Office of the Assistant Secretary (Tax Policy) at the Department of Treasury. Although LMs are sometimes returned to their drafters for revisions, they are not officially approved, nor do they emanate from the Office of Chief Counsel with any appearance of authority. Instead, the Court finds that LMs "reflect the agency 'give-and-take' leading up to a decision that is characteristic of the deliberative process." 679 F.2d at 257; *see also Coastal States*, 617 F.2d at 868 (emphasizing that documents are predecisional if they are produced in the process of formulating policy).

Contrary to Plaintiff's characterization, the Court finds that LMs are distinguishable from the General Counsel Memoranda ("GCMs") at issue in *Taxation with Representation Fund v. Internal Revenue Service*, 646 F.2d 666 (D.C. Cir. 1981) ("TWRF") and the Field Service Advices ("FSAs") at issue in *Tax Analysts v Internal Revenue Service*, 117 F.3d 607 (D.C. Cir. 1997). Whereas GCMs and FSAs are used to promote uniformity in IRS policy, *see, e.g., Tax Analysts*, 117 F.3d at 617, LMs are tools for formulating policy. Unlike GCMs, which are "revised to reflect the final position of the Assistant Commissioner (Technical)"; "widely distributed throughout the agency," and "constantly updated to reflect the current status of an issue within the Office of Chief Counsel," *TWRF*, 646 F.2d at 681–82, LMs are not updated, officially reconciled, or widely distributed. Furthermore, LMs do not necessarily reflect the official position of the Office Chief Counsel on a given issue. This treatment stands in sharp contrast to the procedures utilized with GCMs, which "are retained by the Office of Chief Counsel, and extensively cross-indexed and digested, as well as 'updated,' much like the service provided by Shepard's." *Id.* at 682. Whereas LMs flow "upward" from staffers to reviewers, FSAs flow "outward" from the Office of Chief Counsel to personnel in the field. *See Tax Analysts*, 117 F.3d at 617. The FSA case is also distinguishable because LMs are not used to guide personnel in the field or elsewhere. Admittedly, IRS attorneys sometimes retain LMs for future reference, but such use does not automatically convert LMs to "agency law." *See Pies*, 668 F.2d at 1353–54 (noting that use as a research tool, without more, does not convert unfinalized or unapproved materials into agency working law).

In keeping with these general principles, the IRS has redacted portions of LMs that reflect the opinions and analysis of the author and did not ultimately form the basis of the final revenue ruling. Because the Court finds that this approach to segregability is consistent with the D.C. Circuit's mandate that the

---

[9] [The Background Information Notes at issue in *Arthur Andersen* were described by the court as follows: "On their face there appear the number, identities and titles of the various persons in successively higher positions to whom the drafts were submitted for 'approval' and the alterations these persons made in the text of the background note and revenue ruling." *Arthur Andersen*, 679 F.2d at 259. — Eds.]

deliberative process privilege be applied as narrowly as possible, the Court shall grant IRS's motion for summary judgment as to LMs.

Tax Analysts, 97 F. Supp. 2d at 15–18.[10] Do you find the court's "upward" versus "outward" distinction helpful?

[c] FOIA Exemption 7

The remaining exemption from FOIA's disclosure requirements that is of significance to tax practice is the exemption in section 552(b)(7). Exemption 7 applies to "records or information compiled for law enforcement purposes." The phrase "law enforcement purposes" encompasses both civil and criminal proceedings, including civil audits and criminal tax investigations. Prior to 1974, the IRS successfully used the exemption for investigatory files as an excuse for refusing to disclose broad categories of information, including most of the records compiled by the IRS in connection with an audit of a taxpayer's return. *See, e.g.,* Williams v. Internal Revenue Service, 479 F.2d 317 (3d Cir.), *cert. denied sub nom.* Donlon v. Internal Revenue Service, 414 U.S. 1024 (1973). Fearing that FOIA was being used more often as a withholding statute rather than a disclosure statute, Congress enacted amendments in 1974 designed to narrow the exemption. *See* Pub. L. No. 93-502, § 2(b), 88 Stat. 1561, 1563–64 (1974) (codified at 5 U.S.C. § 552(b)(7) (1976)).

Under current law, the IRS may withhold investigatory records under Exemption 7 when it can establish that disclosure of such records could result in, among other effects, interference with law enforcement proceedings. 5 U.S.C. § 552(b)(7)(A). This exemption most commonly applies where a party subject to an ongoing criminal investigation seeks documents compiled by the IRS in order to defend against a future enforcement proceeding.[11] Based on the argument that disclosure during a pending investigation could hamper the agency's inquiry, the IRS has successfully asserted this exemption to deny access to documentary evidence collected during the inquiry. Witness statements, as well as internal memoranda that would reveal investigative techniques and procedures pertaining to the case, have also been protected from disclosure. *See generally* Kanter v. Internal Revenue Service, 478 F. Supp. 552 (N.D. Ill. 1979); Barney v. Internal Revenue Service, 618 F.2d 1268 (8th Cir. 1980).

[3] Using FOIA During the Tax Controversy Process

Reading Assignment: I.R.C. §§ 6103, 6110.

Over the years, FOIA has been used by taxpayers to compel the IRS to disclose letters, memoranda, and other materials that provide important insights into the agency's internal operations and procedures. During the 1970s, for example, FOIA lawsuits resulted in the release of extensive portions of the Internal Revenue Manual, which provides instructions to IRS agents and employees for handling such matters as audits, appeals, and collection actions. As discussed below, FOIA suits also led to the

---

[10] As part of the same suit, Tax Analysts sought disclosure of litigation guidance memoranda (LGMs), technical assistance bulletins, and tax litigation bulletins. Because those documents fell within the definition of Chief Counsel advice under Code section 6110, which trumps FOIA for documents covered by that section, the court held that it did not have subject matter jurisdiction over those FOIA requests. Tax Analysts v. Internal Revenue Service, 2000-1 U.S.T.C. ¶ 50,370 (D.D.C. 2000). The interaction between the disclosure mandate in section 6110 — particularly with respect to Chief Counsel advice — and FOIA Exemption 5 is discussed below in Section 6.02[C].

[11] The exemption in 5 U.S.C. section 552(b)(7)(A) generally applies only to pending enforcement proceedings, rather than closed investigations. Once the investigation of the taxpayer is closed or abandoned, the exemption no longer applies. Moreover, should the IRS institute legal proceedings against the taxpayer, much of the information otherwise protected by (b)(7)(A) may be obtained through pretrial discovery.

enactment of Code Section 6110, which requires the IRS to release documents such as letter rulings and technical advice memoranda. As explained in more detail in Chapter 2, these types of sources (sometimes referred to as the IRS's "secret" or "agency" law) contain a wealth of useful information for the taxpayer and the taxpayer's representative. Audit guidelines contained in the Internal Revenue Manual, for instance, tip the taxpayer off to issues the IRS is likely to raise during examination and thus allow the taxpayer to prepare for the examination in advance.

[a] Access to Administrative Files Prepared by the IRS

The IRS voluntarily discloses copies of the Internal Revenue Manual, letter rulings, technical advice memoranda, and other related sources on a continuing basis and they are widely available from commercial publishers without the need for a formal request to the IRS. However, if a taxpayer wishes to obtain materials that were prepared by the IRS during an investigation of the taxpayer's own return, the taxpayer may have to make an individual FOIA request.[12] Restrictions in section 6103 and FOIA Exemption 7 limit a taxpayer's access to information about his or her own case while the examination is still in progress. *See* I.R.C. § 6103(e)(7) (disclosure authorized if it will not seriously impair tax administration); 5 U.S.C. § 552(b)(7)(A). Once the examination has concluded and the IRS issues a 30-day letter, it is common practice for the IRS to make the materials contained in the taxpayer's administrative file prepared by the examining agent available to the taxpayer. Before the IRS turns over the administrative file, however, the revenue agent will delete otherwise confidential third-party information and any material relating to a potential criminal investigation of the taxpayer. If the IRS does not voluntarily turn over the file, the taxpayer may submit a FOIA request seeking access to the materials. *See* I.R.M. 4.2.5.

A taxpayer's administrative file becomes an important source of information during the settlement process. The administrative file will normally contain a copy of the agent's working file, which may include workpapers, notes, intra-agency memoranda, affidavits, and interview transcripts. The file also contains all records compiled by the agent during the audit, including records obtained from third parties. Although much of this information will be reflected in the revenue agent's report issued to the taxpayer at the conclusion of the audit, significant facts and alternate legal theories may be buried in the administrative file. A taxpayer who hopes to settle the case with the IRS Appeals Division, rather than litigate the matter, can use this information to decide what to include (or not include) in the protest letter submitted to the Appeals Division. As explained in Chapter 5, the taxpayer's negotiating position during the settlement process is also greatly improved if the taxpayer is aware of all of the facts known by the IRS.

[b] Requesting Information Under FOIA

Reading Assignment: Proc. Reg. § 601.702(a), (c).

The IRS has issued detailed regulations specifying the procedures a taxpayer should follow when requesting information under FOIA. These regulations also describe the required contents of a FOIA request. Proc. Reg. § 601.702(c). Among other requirements, a FOIA request must be submitted in writing, signed by the requesting taxpayer, and addressed to the appropriate IRS disclosure officer. Proc. Reg. § 601.702(c)(4)(i).

---

[12] A taxpayer is entitled to receive a copy of the taxpayer's record of assessment, which includes the date of assessment, the character of the liability, the taxable period, and the amounts assessed. I.R.C. § 6203; Treas. Reg. § 301.6203-1. The taxpayer can request a copy of previously filed tax returns using Form 4506 ($39 fee in 2008), or obtain a transcript of previously filed tax returns (which contains most of the line entries on the return) for free by filing Form 4056-T.

The requesting party must also "reasonably describe" the records sought. A reasonable description is one that would "enable the Internal Revenue Service employees who are familiar with the subject matter of the request to locate the records without placing an unreasonable burden upon the IRS." Proc. Reg. § 601.702(c)(5)(i). The IRS has indicated that a request for "all records concerning me" would be rejected as overly broad. I.R.M. 11.3.13.5.4.

Where the potential exists that the IRS may deny access to the requested records because the records fall within one of the FOIA exemptions, the requesting party should include with the initial request sufficient identification or authorization to confirm the requesting party's right of disclosure. As an example, a partner seeking to obtain access to information returns filed by the partnership under the exception in section 6103(e)(1)(c) should submit documentation identifying him or herself, such as a notarized statement or a statement signed under penalties of perjury confirming that he or she is, in fact, a member of the partnership. Proc. Reg. § 601.702(c)(5)(iii). Similarly, a request made by a representative on behalf of a taxpayer should include a copy of the representative's power of attorney (Form 2848). *Id.* If a FOIA request does not conform to the requirements set forth in the regulations, it will be returned to the requesting party with a statement notifying the party of any defects. Proc. Reg. § 601.702(c)(4).

A sample FOIA request is reproduced below:[13]

SAMPLE FOIA REQUEST

IRS FOIA Request

[Address][14]

[Date]

Re: [Taxpayer's name,
Social Security number,
Tax years]

Dear ____________________:

I, ____________________, am the attorney for the taxpayer named above; I have attached a power of attorney and declaration of representative. Under the authority of the Freedom of Information Act, 5 U.S.C. § 552, I request a copy of each of the following records:

(1) All workpapers, correspondence, and other documents relating to the examination and investigation of the federal income tax liability of the taxpayer named above, for the taxable years ____________________, including but not limited to [detailed description of records].

(2) All statements given by the taxpayer named above to the Internal Revenue Service (IRS) during the course of its examination, including all written statements; all oral statements reduced to writing by any employee of the IRS, whether or not verbatim, and whether or not signed by the taxpayer; and all oral statements of the taxpayer that were recorded by any mechanical device.

My return address is:

____

____

____

---

[13] The regulations in section 601.702 also include a schedule of fees imposed by the IRS for search and duplication of the requesting materials. Proc. Reg. § 601.702(f). As part of the FOIA request, the requesting party must state his or her willingness to pay the resulting fees. *Id.* at § 601.702(c)(4)(H).

[14] Disclosure office addresses are listed in procedural regulation section 601.702(h). *See also* Proc. Reg. § 601.702(c)(4)(c) (instructions for determining appropriate address).

I agree to pay the hourly search fee and the current fee per copy obtained pursuant to this request. I attest under penalty of perjury that I am not in any of the following categories: (A) commercial use requester, (B) news media requester, (C) educational institution requester, or (D) noncommercial scientific institution requester, but instead that I am a category (E) other requester.

Very truly yours,

____

[Name of representative]

Once the FOIA request is received by the IRS, the agency normally has 20 days within which to notify the requesting party of its initial determination to grant or deny the request. 5 U.S.C. § 552(a)(6). The IRS may request additional time. Proc. Reg. § 601.702(c)(11). If the IRS denies the request, in whole or in part, a notification letter is sent to the requesting party informing him or her of the denial. The notification letter includes a brief statement of the grounds for denial (normally based on a FOIA exemption) and informs the requester of the right to appeal the matter administratively. Proc. Reg. § 601.702(c)(9)(iv).

In order to trigger the administrative appeals process, the taxpayer must submit a letter to the IRS within 35 days after receipt of the denial letter. In the appeals letter, the taxpayer should describe the records requested, identify the office to which the initial request was submitted, and include copies of both the initial FOIA request and the letter denying the request. Proc. Reg. § 601.702(c)(10). The appeals letter should also include any arguments the requesting party may have in support of the right of access. *Id.* These arguments normally take the form of a statement rebutting the disclosure officer's use of a FOIA exemption to deny the request.

The IRS typically has 20 days in which to grant or deny the appeal. Proc. Reg. § 601.702(c)(10)(iii). If the IRS denies the appeal or fails to respond within the specified time periods, the requesting party may file an action in a United States district court seeking an order requiring the IRS to release any document improperly withheld. 5 U.S.C. § 552(a)(4)(B); Proc. Reg. § 601.702(c)(13). In the disclosure proceedings, the district court reviews the matter *de novo* and may examine the contents of the requested records *in camera* in order to determine whether the IRS has sustained its burden of proving that the records are exempt from disclosure. *Id.*

Where the volume of records at issue is great, rather than requiring the IRS to produce copies of each disputed record at trial, the court normally allows the IRS to submit an itemized index of the documents withheld, along with a corresponding explanation of the IRS's justification for withholding the documents. This "*Vaughn* Index," named for the *Vaughn v. Rosen* case in which the technique was first applied, 484 F.2d 820 (D.C. Cir. 1973), can also prove very useful for the party seeking disclosure. The index not only specifies the IRS's claimed exemptions with respect to each item or category of items requested, but also describes the specific nature of the documents being withheld. With this information, the requesting party should be able to rebut the IRS's arguments more effectively. A requesting party who prevails in the FOIA suit may be entitled to recover attorney's fees and other costs. 5 U.S.C. § 552(a)(4)(E).

[c] Relationship of FOIA to Discovery Rules

As discussed above, under FOIA, a taxpayer is entitled to obtain agency records that do not fall within one of FOIA's nine exemptions. In litigation, a taxpayer may also obtain access through the discovery process to relevant government documents as long as the documents are not privileged. Because FOIA and discovery provide the taxpayer with separate methods for obtaining government documents the question of whether a taxpayer should be able to use FOIA as a discovery tool in litigation often arises.

Although FOIA was not intended to serve as a mechanism for litigation discovery, *see, e.g.*, Renegotiation Board v. Bannercraft Clothing Co., 415 U.S. 1, 24 (1974), courts have pointed out that a FOIA requester's right of access to agency records is independent of any discovery rights in litigation, Morgan v. Dep't of Justice, 923 F.2d 195, 198 (D.C. Cir. 1991). As a result, IRS attorneys are instructed not to issue blanket denials of FOIA requests made during litigation. I.R.M. 11.3.13.7.2.7; *see also* Chief Counsel Notice CC-2006-016, *available at* www.irs.gov/pub/irs-ccdm/cc-2006-016.pdf (outlining procedures for IRS coordination of parallel FOIA and discovery requests). If the litigant's FOIA request remains unresolved while the court case proceeds, the litigant can request, but is not automatically entitled to receive, a continuance or stay of the proceedings until the FOIA request is resolved. Any request from a petitioner to the Tax Court to compel the IRS to release records under FOIA will be rejected, as the Tax Court has no jurisdiction over FOIA disputes. *See* 5 U.S.C. § 552(a)(4)(B).

Some courts have ruled that an exemption available to the government under FOIA does not necessarily preclude discovery. *See, e.g.*, United States v. Murdock, 548 F.2d 599, 602 (5th Cir. 1977); Millennium Marketing Group LLC v. United States, 238 F.R.D. 460 (S.D. Tex. 2006) (rejecting government's contention that discovery cannot be permitted because it would short-circuit the FOIA process). By contrast, seeking access to documents through FOIA generally will not result in greater access than would the discovery process. This is because FOIA Exemption 5 (discussed above), which incorporates the privileges of civil discovery, likely will preclude a taxpayer-litigant access under FOIA to material the taxpayer cannot obtain through discovery procedures.

[B] Access to Information Under the Privacy Act of 1974

Reading Assignment: 5 U.S.C. § 552a.

In addition to FOIA, there is a second, although less commonly employed, avenue that an individual taxpayer may use to obtain disclosure of information from the IRS. This is the Privacy Act of 1974. 5 U.S.C. § 552a. The Privacy Act leads, in effect, a double life. To protect against unwarranted invasions of personal privacy, the legislation imposes restrictions on federal government agencies, including the IRS, relating to the use and dissemination of personal information. *Id.* § 552a(b). The Privacy Act also grants an individual the right, upon request, to gain access to records or information compiled with respect to that individual. This right of access applies only to individuals and only with respect to the individual's own records. The Privacy Act does not permit a taxpayer to gain access to third party records or to internal agency documents. *Id.* § 552a(d).

Exemptions in section 552a severely limit the usefulness of the Privacy Act as a means of obtaining tax-related information from the IRS. Section 552a(d)(5), for example, denies access to "any information compiled in reasonable anticipation of a civil action or proceeding." Furthermore, the Act permits the IRS to promulgate rules exempting from disclosure a wide variety of information, including investigatory materials compiled for law enforcement purposes. *Id.* § 552a(k)(2). The IRS has used this grant of authority to exempt from disclosure under the Privacy Act most tax records compiled by the agency during the audit and appeals stage of a tax controversy. I.R.M. 2.11.3.15.5.[15] And while the Privacy Act also permits an individual to request that the agency correct any records that the individual believes are not accurate or complete, section 7852(e) of the Code specifically prohibits the individual from using this correction provision to seek a redetermination of the taxpayer's liability for taxes or penalties. As a practical matter, therefore, the Privacy Act rarely provides an individual access to tax-related information from the IRS greater than that otherwise available under FOIA.

---

[15] As discussed above, this type of information is routinely available under FOIA.

See Gardner v. United States, 213 F.3d 735 (D.C. Cir. 2000), *cert. denied*, 531 U.S. 1114 (2001) (section 6103 preempts Privacy Act regarding claims that the IRS made unauthorized disclosures of taxpayer's return information to a third party); Lake v. Rubin, 162 F.3d 113 (D.C. Cir. 1998) (taxpayers cannot rely on Privacy Act to gain access to tax return information but must instead rely on the more specific provisions in Code section 6103).

[C] Access to Written Determinations Under Section 6110

Reading Assignment: I.R.C. § 6110(a)–(e), (i).

In addition to the statements and pronouncements voluntarily disclosed by the IRS under the first two prongs of FOIA, another important source of "agency law" is the material subject to inspection under section 6110 of the Code. As a general matter, section 6110 requires the IRS to make available for inspection copies of letter rulings, technical advice memoranda, determination letters, and Chief Counsel advice (referred to collectively in the statute as "written determinations"). Closing agreements entered into under section 7121, however, are excluded from the category of information that must be disclosed under section 6110. I.R.C. § 6110(b)(1)(B) (referencing section 6103(b)(2)).

Enacted as part of the Tax Reform Act of 1976, section 6110 was largely the result of a series of FOIA lawsuits brought by taxpayers seeking access to letter rulings. *See, e.g.*, Fruehauf Corp. v. Internal Revenue Service, 566 F.2d 574 (6th Cir. 1977). The original goal of section 6110 was to dispel the notion that the IRS, through its letter ruling program, was developing a body of "secret" internal agency law to which only some practitioners, particularly those in large law and accounting firms, had access. Another concern was that some parties might try unfairly to influence the IRS to issue a favorable ruling, and, because the entire process remained secret, such influence would never come to light. *See* Joint Committee on Taxation, General Explanation of the Tax Reform Act of 1976, at 301–03.

The IRS voluntarily releases most items that fall within the definition of a written determination under section 6110 and these items are subsequently published in complete form by commercial services. These sources are most easily accessed via the IRS's website, www.irs.gov, or an online research service. The statute also makes available "background file documents," which include written information submitted in support of the requested letter ruling or determination letter, as well as other material compiled by IRS personnel to support the IRS's ultimate conclusion. I.R.C. § 6110(b)(2); Treas. Reg. § 301.6110-2(g). Background file documents are available only upon written request by the taxpayer.

In 1998, Congress amended section 6110 to include "Chief Counsel advice" within its disclosure requirements. IRS Reform Act § 3905(a) (enacting I.R.C. § 6110(i)). The amendment was in response to a FOIA lawsuit, this one seeking access to "Field Service Advice memoranda" (FSAs) — case-specific legal advice from the IRS's Chief Counsel's office to IRS personnel. Tax Analysts v. Internal Revenue Service, 117 F.3d 607, 620 (D.C. Cir. 1997). Chief Counsel advice ("CCA") encompasses not only FSAs but also any other written advice issued by the Office of Chief Counsel to IRS personnel if the advice contains a legal interpretation or Counsel position or policy with respect to a revenue provision. I.R.C. § 6110(i).[16] The broad scope of the term has led the IRS Chief Counsel's office to issue a series of notices specifying what does and does not fall within the

[16] Chief Counsel advice also includes litigation guideline memoranda, service center advice, tax litigation bulletins, and general litigation bulletins, among other sources. Chapter 2 contains a discussion of the precedential value of written determinations and their usefulness when planning transactions.

category of CCA. *See, e.g.*, Chief Counsel Notice CC-2003-22 (entitled "Procedures for Processing Taxpayer-Specific Chief Counsel Advice That Will Be Withheld in Full From Public Disclosure").

In one notice, CC-2004-012, the IRS sought to shield from the disclosure requirements in section 6110(i) legal advice prepared within less than two hours. In *Tax Analysts v. Internal Revenue Service*, 495 F.3d 676 (D.C. Cir. 2007), the D.C. Circuit Court of Appeals, affirming a lower court decision, rejected the "two-hour rule" and determined that emails containing legal advice that lawyers in the Office of Chief Counsel sent to IRS field personnel were CCA, regardless of the time it took to prepare the emails. In reaching this conclusion, the court rejected the IRS's attempt to distinguish between formal advice and "the informal, unreviewed advice of an individual lawyer." *Id.* at 680.

> [CCA] requires no particular form or formality. Nor does it distinguish between advice a lawyer renders in less than two hours and advice that takes longer than two hours to prepare. Thus, given the broad definition of "Chief Counsel advice" in section 6110(i)(1)(A), we believe that the temporal distinction the IRS draws in its two-hour disclosure rule is contrary to the unequivocal statutory directive that a "written determination," defined to include "Chief Counsel advice" without exception, "shall be open to public inspection," 26 U.S.C. § 6110(a). The IRS cannot, therefore, consistent with the plain language of 26 U.S.C. § 6110, rely on the two-hour rule to avoid disclosing legal advice rendered in under two hours.

Id. at 681; *see also* Chief Counsel Notice CC-2008-002 (instructing IRS attorneys, in light of D.C. Circuit's decision, to use email only for answering routine and simple questions and not for issuing formal legal advice), *available at* www.irs.gov/pub/irs-ccdm/cc-2008-002.pdf.

The intersection between the FOIA and section 6110 has also generated controversy. If both FOIA and section 6110 potentially apply to a request, the rules in section 6110 generally control. *See* I.R.C. § 6110(m). Section 6110(i), however, incorporates several FOIA Exemptions, including Exemption 5, that permit the IRS to withhold information that might otherwise fall within the scope of CCA. In *Tax Analysts v. Internal Revenue Service*, 391 F. Supp. 2d 122 (D.D.C. 2005), for example, the D.C. District Court held that the IRS could withhold CCA memoranda because each item was prepared by the IRS in its entirety in the context of litigation and thus protected by the attorney work product privilege. According to the court, the work product doctrine, as developed under FOIA Exemption 5, was incorporated into section 6110. *Id.* at 127; *see* I.R.C. 6110(i)(3).

For those forms of advice that must be made available to the public, section 6110 sets forth detailed procedures the IRS must follow. In order to protect taxpayer confidentiality, the statute contains a series of exemptions from disclosure. Most notably, section 6110(c)(1) requires that, before any material is made available for public inspection, the IRS must delete "the names, addresses and other identifying details of the person to whom the written determination pertains and of any other person, . . . identified in the written determination or any background file document." As further protection against disclosure of otherwise confidential information, the IRS must notify the person to whom the written determination pertains and allow that person an opportunity to discuss with the IRS, prior to disclosure, what information should be deleted. I.R.C. § 6110(f); Treas. Reg. § 301.6110-5. These confidentiality protections are backed up by section 6110(j), which permits a taxpayer to file an action against the United States in the Court of Federal Claims if the IRS publicizes a written determination without first making the required deletions.[17]

---

[17] These protections apply more restrictively in the case of Chief Counsel advice. *See* I.R.C. § 6110(i)(4).

As noted above, the purpose behind the disclosure requirement in section 6110 is to provide greater transparency when it comes to the IRS's operations. This, in turn, fosters confidence in the agency's activities by helping to ensure the public that the agency operates fairly and even-handedly. But does forcing the IRS to release all written determinations, including every email sent by an IRS attorney to another IRS employee about a particular case impair the IRS's ability to effectively administer the federal tax law? Does the fact that these documents generally may not be used or cited as precedent affect your view?

§ 6.03 PRESERVING TAXPAYER CONFIDENTIALITY: CODE SECTION 6103

[A] Disclosure Prohibitions Under Section 6103

Reading Assignment: I.R.C. § 6103(a)–(b).

As discussed above, the primary function of section 6103 is to implement Exemption 3 of FOIA. In this role, the statute limits a taxpayer's access to information held by the IRS. Section 6103 also operates independently of FOIA as a confidentiality provision, limiting the circumstances under which, and to whom the IRS may disclose information about the taxpayer. Policymakers maintain that preserving the confidentiality of taxpayer information promotes tax compliance. The inverse, that violating a taxpayer's privacy expectations reduces a taxpayer's willingness to comply, they maintain, also holds true. A Privacy Commission study explains:

> [T]he Commission believes that the effectiveness of this country's tax system depends on the confidentiality of tax returns and related information. . . . [T]he Commission believes that widespread use of the information a taxpayer provides to the IRS for purposes wholly unrelated to tax administration cannot help but diminish the taxpayer's disposition to cooperate with the IRS voluntarily. This is not to say that the taxpayer will decline to cooperate, but that his incentive to do so may be weakened. Such a tendency in itself creates a potentially serious threat to the effectiveness of the Federal tax system.

Privacy Protection Study Commission, Personal Privacy in an Information Society 540 (July 1977).

[1] The Scope of Return Information

Reading Assignment: I.R.C. § 6103(b)(2).

The confidentiality protections contained in section 6103 are expansive. The statute mandates that tax "returns and return information" remain confidential and, except as authorized by the statute, cannot be disclosed. For these purposes, a taxpayer's return is broadly defined to include any tax or information return, amended return, declaration of estimated tax, or claim for refund, as well as any supporting schedules or attachments. I.R.C. § 6103(b)(1). As a fine example of inclusive statutory drafting, section 6103(b)(2) defines the term "return information" to mean:

> [A] taxpayer's identity, the nature, source, or amount of his income, payments, receipts, deductions, exemptions, credits, assets, liabilities, net worth, tax liability, tax withheld, deficiencies, overassessments, or tax payments, whether the taxpayer's return was, is being, or will be examined or subject to other investigation or processing, or any other data, received by, recorded by, prepared by, furnished to, or collected by the Secretary with respect to a return or with respect to the determination of the existence, or possible existence of liabilities (or the amount thereof) of any person under this title for any tax,

penalty, interest, fine, forfeiture, or other imposition, or offense.

This formulation would encompass virtually all information collected by the IRS as part of an audit of the taxpayer's return.

The one limitation on the definition of return information appears in section 6103(b)(2). This exception, commonly known as the Haskell Amendment, excludes from the category of return information any data in a form that cannot be associated with, or otherwise identify, a particular taxpayer. The following case considers the scope of this limitation. Notice, in particular, the interaction of the section 6103(b)(2) limitation and FOIA.

CHURCH OF SCIENTOLOGY OF CALIFORNIA v. INTERNAL REVENUE SERVICE

United States Supreme Court
484 U.S. 9 (1987)

CHIEF JUSTICE REHNQUIST delivered the opinion of the Court.

Section 6103 of the Internal Revenue Code, 26 U.S.C. § 6103, lays down a general rule that "returns" and "return information" as defined therein shall be confidential. "Return information" is elaborately defined in § 6103(b)(2); immediately after that definition appears the following proviso, known as the Haskell amendment:

> "[B]ut such term does not include data in a form which cannot be associated with, or otherwise identify, directly or indirectly, a particular taxpayer."

Petitioner Church of Scientology of California, seeking disclosure under the Freedom of Information Act, contends that the Haskell amendment excepts from the definition of "return information" all material in the files of the Internal Revenue Service (IRS) which can be redacted to delete those parts which would identify a particular taxpayer. Respondent IRS in opposition argues that the mere redaction of identifying data will not, by virtue of the Haskell amendment, take the material out of the definition of "return information." We agree with the IRS.

Petitioner filed a request with respondent under the Freedom of Information Act (FOIA), 5 U.S.C. § 552, for the production of numerous documents. Among the materials sought by petitioner were "[c]opies of all information relating to or containing the names of, Scientology, Church of Scientology, any specific Scientology church or entity identified by containing the words Scientology, Hubbard and/or Dianetics in their names, L. Ron Hubbard or Mary Sue Hubbard in the form of written record, correspondence, document, memorandum, form, computor [sic] tape, computor [sic] program or microfilm, which is contained in" an extensive list of respondent's case files and data systems. FOIA Request Dated May 16, 1980, App. 20a27a. Petitioner also requested similar information from the offices and personal areas of a number of respondent's officials.

Dissatisfied by the slow response to its request, petitioner filed suit in the United States District Court for the District of Columbia to compel release of the materials. In the District Court the parties agreed — as they continue to agree here — that § 6103 of the Internal Revenue Code is the sort of statute referred to by the FOIA in 5 U.S.C. § 552(b)(3) relating to matters that are "specifically exempted from disclosure by statute . . . "; thus, if § 6103 forbids the disclosure of material, it may not be produced in response to a request under the FOIA. Respondent argued that many of the records were protected as "returns" or "return information" under § 6103.

* * *

The District Court, after an *in camera* review of representative documents, held that respondent had correctly limited its search for and disclosure of materials requested by petitioner. *See* 569 F. Supp. 1165 (DC 1983). Petitioner appealed that decision to the

United States Court of Appeals for the District of Columbia Circuit. Following briefing and argument before a three-judge panel, the Court of Appeals *sua sponte* undertook en banc review of the meaning of the Haskell amendment and the modification it works upon § 6103(b)(2). The Court of Appeals concluded that, by using the words "in a form," Congress contemplated "not merely the deletion of an identifying name or symbol on a document that contains return information, but agency *reformulation* of the return information into a statistical study or some other composite product. . . ." 792 F.2d 153, 160, 253 U.S. App. D.C. 85, 92 (196) (emphasis in original). Thus, the court held, before respondent may produce documents otherwise protected, the Haskell amendment requires that some modification have occurred in the form of the data contained in the documents. "[M]ere deletion of the taxpayer's name or other identifying data is not enough, since that would render the reformulation requirement entirely duplicative of the nonidentification requirement."[n.1] *Id.*, at 95, 792 F.2d, at 163.

We granted certiorari, 479 U.S. 1063 (1987), to consider the scope of the Haskell amendment and its relation to the confidentiality provisions of §§ 6103(a) and (b). Petitioner believes that the Haskell amendment makes significantly greater inroads on the definition of "return information" than did the Court of Appeals. It makes two interrelated contentions: first, that the Haskell amendment removes from the classification of "return information" all data which do not identify a particular taxpayer, and, second, that 5 U.S.C. § 552(b) — requiring that "[a]ny reasonably segregable portion" of a record be provided to a requestor after deletion of the portions which are exempt — compels respondent to redact "return information" in its files where possible so as to bring that material within the terms of the Haskell amendment. We reject both of these arguments.

We are told by the IRS that, as a practical matter, "return information" might include the report of an audit examination, internal IRS correspondence concerning a taxpayer's claim, or a notice of deficiency issued by the IRS proposing an increase in the taxpayer's assessment. Tr. of Oral Arg. 24–25. Petitioner asserts that the segregation requirement of the FOIA, § 552(b), directs respondent to remove the identifiers from such documents as these and that, once the materials are purged of such identifiers, they must be disclosed because they no longer constitute return information described in § 6103(b)(2).

We find no support for petitioner's arguments in either the language of § 6103 or in its legislative history. In addition to the returns themselves, which are protected from disclosure by § 6103(b)(1), § 6103(b)(2) contains an elaborate description of the sorts of information related to returns that respondent is compelled to keep confidential. If the mere removal of identifying details from return information sufficed to put the information "in a form" envisioned by the Haskell amendment, the remainder of the categories included in § 6103(b)(2) would often be irrelevant. The entire section could have been prefaced by the simple instruction to respondent that the elimination of identifiers would shift related tax data outside the realm of protected return information. Respondent would then first determine whether the information could be redacted so as not to identify a taxpayer; only if it could not would the extensive list of materials

---

[n.1] The decision of the District of Columbia Circuit was thus in substantial agreement with the Seventh Circuit's opinion in *King v. IRS*, 688 F.2d 488 (1982), and the Eleventh Circuit's determination in *Currie v. IRS*, 704 F.2d 523 (1983). The Seventh Circuit concluded in *King* that § 6103 "protects from disclosure all nonamalgamated items listed in subsection (b)(2)(A), and that the Haskell Amendment provides only for the disclosure of statistical tabulations which are not associated with or do not identify particular taxpayers." 688 F.2d, at 493. Similarly, in *Currie* the Eleventh Circuit held that the Haskell amendment does not obligate the IRS, in a suit under the FOIA, to delete identifying material from documents and release what would otherwise be return information. 704 F.2d, at 531–532.

The Ninth Circuit, however, reached a different result in *Long v. IRS*, 596 F.2d 362 (1979), *cert. denied*, 446 U.S. 917 (1980). In *Long*, the court found that the Haskell amendment removes from the category of protected return information any documents that do not identify a particular taxpayer once names, addresses, and similar details are deleted. *See* 596 F.2d, at 367–369.

that constitute "return information" become pertinent. And if petitioner correctly interprets the intent of the Haskell amendment, Congress' drafting was awkward in the extreme. The amendment exempts "data in a form" that cannot be associated with or otherwise identify a particular taxpayer. A much more natural phrasing would omit the confusing and unnecessary words "in a form" and refer simply to data.

* * *

The legislative history of the Tax Reform Act of 1976, Pub. L. 94-455, 90 Stat. 1520, of which the amendments to § 6103 are a part, also indicates that Congress did not intend the statute to allow the disclosure of otherwise confidential return information merely by the redaction of identifying details. One of the major purposes in revising § 6103 was to tighten the restrictions on the use of return information by entities other than respondent. *See* S. Rep. No. 94-938, p. 318 (1976) ("[R]eturns and return information should generally be treated as confidential and not subject to disclosure except in those limited situations delineated in the newly amended section 6103"). Petitioner's suggestion that the Haskell amendment was intended to modify the restrictions of § 6103 by making all nonidentifying return information eligible for disclosure would mean that the amendment was designed to undercut the legislation's primary purpose of limiting access to tax filings.

The circumstances under which the Haskell amendment was adopted make us reluctant to credit it with this expansive purpose. During debate on the Senate floor, Senator Haskell proposed that § 6103(b)(2) be amended to make clear that return information "does not include data in a form which cannot be associated with, or otherwise identify, directly or indirectly, a particular taxpayer." He then added this explanation of his proposal:

> "[T]he purpose of this amendment is to insure that statistical studies and other compilations of data now prepared by the Internal Revenue Service and disclosed by it to outside parties will continue to be subject to disclosure to the extent allowed under present law. Thus the Internal Revenue Service can continue to release for research purposes statistical studies and compilations of data, such as the tax model, which do not identify individual taxpayers.
>
> "The definition of 'return information' was intended to neither enhance nor diminish access now obtainable under the Freedom of Information Act to statistical studies and compilations of data by the Internal Revenue Service. Thus, the addition by the Internal Revenue Service of easily deletable identifying information to the type of statistical study or compilation of data which, under its current practice, has [sic] been subject to disclosure, will not prevent disclosure of such study or compilation under the newly amended § 6103. In such an instance, the identifying information would be deleted and disclosure of the statistical study or compilation of data be made." 122 Cong. Rec. 24012 (1976).

After these remarks, the floor manager of the legislation, Senator Long, added that he would "be happy to take this amendment to conference. It might not be entirely necessary, but it might serve a good purpose." The Haskell amendment was then passed by voice vote in the Senate and became part of the conference bill.

We find it difficult to believe that Congress in this manner adopted an amendment which would work such an alteration to the basic thrust of the draft bill amending § 6103. The Senate's purpose in revising § 6103 was, as we have noted, to impose greater restrictions on the disclosure of tax data; a change in the proposed draft permitting disclosure of all return information after deletion of material identifying a particular taxpayer would have, it seems to us, at a minimum engendered some debate in the Senate and resulted in a rollcall vote. More importantly, Senator Haskell's remarks clearly indicate that he did not mean to revise § 6103(b)(2) in this fashion. He refers only to statistical studies and compilations, and gives no intimation that his amendment would require respondent to remove identifying details from material as it exists in its files in order to comply with its requirement. All in all, we think this is a case where common sense suggests, by analogy to Sir Arthur Conan Doyle's "dog that didn't bark," that an amendment having the effect petitioner ascribes to it would have been differently described by its sponsor, and not nearly as readily accepted by the floor manager of the bill.

We thus hold that, as with a return itself, removal of identification from return information would not deprive it of protection under § 6103(b). Since such deletion would not make otherwise protected return information discloseable, respondent has no duty under the FOIA to undertake such redaction. The judgment of the Court of Appeals is accordingly affirmed.

[2] Does the Source of Information Matter?

Reading Assignment: Skim I.R.C. § 7431.

Should the source of the information released by the IRS play a role in the decision of whether the information remains confidential under section 6103? Consider the following excerpt.

RICE v. UNITED STATES

United States Court of Appeals, Tenth Circuit
166 F.3d 1088 (1999)[18]

Baldock, Circuit Judge:

In March 1994, a jury convicted Plaintiff Jerry V. Rice on two counts of filing a false tax refund claim and three counts of making and subscribing a false tax return in respective violation of 18 U.S.C. § 287 and 26 U.S.C. § 7206(1). The district court imposed a thirty-month term of imprisonment on Rice, ordered him to pay restitution, and fined him $20,000. Consistent with its policy of publicizing successful tax prosecutions, the Internal Revenue Service (IRS) issued two press releases regarding the criminal proceedings against Rice. The first release, issued March 2, 1994, reported Rice's conviction. * * * The second release, issued June 13, 1994, reported Rice's sentence. * * *

Rice, a certified public accountant and lawyer, subsequently filed a *pro se* civil action against the United States, the IRS, and those officials responsible for issuing the press releases, alleging that Defendants wrongfully disclosed confidential tax information about him. The district court dismissed all but three of Rice's claims pursuant to Fed. R. Civ. P. 12. Remaining were (1) a claim against the United States arising under the Internal Revenue Code, 26 U.S.C. §§ 6103 & 7431; (2) a claim against the United States arising under the Federal Tort Claims Act, 28 U.S.C. §§ 2671–80; and (3) a claim against the IRS arising under the Federal Privacy Act, 5 U.S.C. § 552a.

Following discovery, the United States and IRS moved for summary judgment pursuant to Fed. R. Civ. P. 56 on the remainder of Rice's claims. In a thorough memorandum opinion, the district court concluded that no genuine issue of material fact existed as to whether the two press releases disclosed confidential tax information about Rice. The court found that all the information contained in the press releases came from public documents and proceedings. Specifically, the court found that to prepare the releases, an IRS public affairs officer had reviewed the indictment against Rice, attended his trial and sentencing, and researched the possible criminal penalties for his crimes. These the court found were the only sources for the information contained in the press releases. Accordingly, the district court held that Rice had no

---

[18] *Cert. denied*, 528 U.S. 933 (1999).

claim against the United States or the IRS for violating the confidentiality provisions of the Internal Revenue Code. The court further determined that because the IRS had not released confidential taxpayer information about Rice from its records, but obtained the information for the releases from public sources, he similarly had no claim against Defendants under the Federal Torts Claim Act or the Federal Privacy Act.

On appeal, Rice raises two issues worthy of review. First, Rice contends that because the information contained in the press releases was, as a matter of law, confidential tax return information, Defendants necessarily violated the confidentiality provisions of the code by issuing the releases. In the alternative, Rice contends that genuine issues of material fact precluding summary judgment exist as to the source of the information contained in the press releases. Our jurisdiction arises under 28 U.S.C. § 1291. We review a grant of summary judgment de novo employing the same legal principles as the district court. Kane v. Capital Guardian Trust Co., 145 F.3d 1218, 1221 (10th Cir. 1998). Applying these principles, we affirm.

I.

Section 6103(a) of the Internal Revenue Code prohibits disclosure of tax return information unless expressly authorized by an exception. *See generally* Baskin v. United States, 135 F.3d 338, 340–42 (5th Cir. 1998) (discussing history of disclosure prohibition). * * * One of the numerous exceptions to § 6103's general prohibition allows disclosure of "return information" in federal court where "the taxpayer is a party to the proceedings." *Id.* § 6103(h)(4)(A).

Section 7431(a) of the code in turn provides a cause of action to an aggrieved taxpayer for a violation of § 6103: "If any officer or employee of the United States knowingly, or by reason of negligence, . . . discloses any return or return information with respect to a taxpayer in violation of any provision of section 6103, such taxpayer may bring a civil action for damages against the United States . . . ." 26 U.S.C. § 7431(a)(1). Subsection (b) of § 7431 provides an exception to liability where the officer's or employee's disclosure "results from a good faith, but erroneous interpretation of section 6103." *Id.* § 7431(b)(1).

II.

Rice complains that the press releases contain "return information" as defined in § 6103(b) because they identify him, his accounting firm, and the fact that he unlawfully claimed tax refunds for the years 1988 and 1989, based on false withholdings. Regardless of the source of the information contained in the releases, Rice claims that the government's dissemination of such information without his authorization violated § 6103(a). In other words, Rice asks us to hold that an IRS press release which contains information about a taxpayer's criminal tax liability necessarily constitutes an unauthorized disclosure of tax return information, exposing the government to liability under § 7431. We decline to do so.

The Seventh Circuit rejected an identical argument in *Thomas v. United States*, 890 F.2d 18 (7th Cir. 1989). In that case, the taxpayer claimed a violation of § 6103, although he admitted that the immediate source of the information contained in an IRS press release about him was a tax court opinion. The court acknowledged that the disclosed information may have come *indirectly* from the taxpayer's tax return. Notwithstanding, the court stated:

> Nothing in the background of the statute suggests so broad a scope as Thomas is urging and so direct a collision with the policies that animate the free-speech clause of the First Amendment . . . . [W]e believe that the definition of return information comes into play only when the immediate source of the information is a return, or some internal document based on a return, as these terms are defined in § 6103(b)(2), and not when the immediate source is a public document

> lawfully prepared by an agency that is separate from the Internal Revenue Service and has lawful access to tax returns.

Thomas, 890 F.2d at 21. We adopt this reasoning. If, as the government claims, the two press releases about which Rice complains were based solely on public documents and proceedings, *i.e.* the IRS public affairs officer's review of the indictment, her attendance at trial and sentencing, and her research into the possible criminal penalties, then Rice's assertion that the government violated § 6103 by issuing the press releases must fail.

Despite Rice's assertion, our decision in *Rodgers v. Hyatt*, 697 F.2d 899 (10th Cir. 1983), is not to the contrary. In *Rodgers*, we rejected the government's argument that the disclosure of return information in a public record bars a taxpayer from complaining about any subsequent disclosure of such information. *Accord* Chandler v. United States, 887 F.2d 1397, 1398 (10th Cir. 1989); * * *. Instead, we held that an IRS agent's prior "in court" testimony at a hearing to enforce an IRS summons did not alone justify the agent's subsequent out of court statement to a third party regarding an ongoing investigation of the taxpayer. *Rodgers*, 697 F.2d at 904–06. We upheld the jury's verdict in favor of the taxpayer and its implicit finding that the agent had not obtained his information from the court hearing — a public proceeding, but rather had obtained it from internal documents based on the taxpayer's tax return. Thus, under both *Thomas* and *Rodgers*, whether information about a taxpayer may be classified as "return information" invoking application of § 6103 turns on the immediate source of the information.

* * *

The judgment of the district court as to both Rice and JVR Accounting, Inc., is affirmed.

The analysis applied in *Rice* to determine whether the disclosure violated section 6103 has been termed the "immediate source" test. *See also* Johnson v. Sawyer, 120 F.3d 1307 (5th Cir. 1997) (adopting a similar test). Read section 6103(b) carefully. Do you see any reference to source in section 6103(b)? If the information the IRS discloses is already in the public domain, why should it matter whether the information comes directly from the IRS's own internal files as opposed to from some outside source?

Not every court agrees with the analysis in *Rice*. In fact, the test applied in *Rice* represents the middle ground position in the debate over whether information already in the public domain retains its confidentiality under section 6103. At one extreme in this debate is the Ninth Circuit's position in *Lampert v. United States*, 854 F.2d 335 (9th Cir. 1988), *cert. denied*, 490 U.S. 1034 (1989). In *Lampert*, the Ninth Circuit considered the consolidated appeal of several district court cases, each denying the taxpayer's request for damages under section 7431 for wrongful disclosure based on press releases prepared by the IRS. Despite the absence of an exception in section 6103 specifically permitting disclosure, the Ninth Circuit concluded that the government did not violate section 6103 when it issued the press releases concerning the taxpayers' criminal conduct. According to the Ninth Circuit, "once return information is lawfully disclosed in a judicial forum, its subsequent disclosure by press release does not violate [section 6103]." In reaching this conclusion, the court considered the taxpayer's privacy interests in the return information: "We believe that Congress sought to prohibit only the disclosure of confidential tax return information. Once tax return information is made a part of the public domain, the taxpayer may no longer claim a right of privacy in that information." *Id.* at 338. The "public records" exception in *Lampert* differs from the immediate source test in that it looks only to whether the information has already been disclosed, not the source of the disclosure.

At the other extreme in the debate is the Fourth Circuit's position in *Mallas v. United States*, 993 F.2d 1111 (4th Cir. 1993). In *Mallas*, the Fourth Circuit affirmed the government's liability for damages in a wrongful disclosure suit involving efforts by the IRS to publicize the criminal conviction of a tax shelter promoter. The Fourth Circuit rejected the government's arguments that "the Ninth Circuit's public records exception strikes a better balance between the Government's legitimate interests in disclosing return information to administer the tax laws and a taxpayer's reasonable expectation of privacy." *Id.* at 1120. According to the Fourth Circuit, it is Congress's job to balance these interests, not the courts':

> Section 6103(a) prohibits the disclosure of taxpayers' "return information" "except as authorized by this title" . . . . In so providing, Congress strictly circumscribed the contexts in which Government officers or employees may disclose such information. Unless the disclosure is authorized by a specific statutory exception, section 6103(a) prohibits it. The Government points to no such exception — and we are aware of none — permitting the disclosure of return information simply because it is otherwise made available to the public.

Id. at 1119. Does a taxpayer have a legitimate privacy interest worth protecting if the information has already been disclosed in the public domain? *See* Stephen W. Mazza, *Taxpayer Privacy and Tax Compliance*, 51 Kan. L. Rev. 1065 (2003) (arguing, in part, that the manner in which the information became public matters).

To what extent can disclosure improve voluntary compliance by taxpayers? Several state revenue agencies, including the Louisiana Department of Revenue (LDOR), have initiated efforts to publicly identify delinquent taxpayers. According to the LDOR, its "Cybershame" program, an Internet site that lists the names of taxpayers with past due accounts, generated $700,000 in overdue tax payments within the first six months. *See* Mazza, *supra* at 1132–33. The General Accounting Office studied the question of whether such a disclosure program might work at the federal level and did not support it. *See* GAO, *Tax Administration: Few State and Local Governments Publicly Disclose Delinquent Taxpayers* (GAO/GGD-99-165), *reprinted at* 1999 TNT 164-14 (Aug. 25, 1999). Is the fear of being publicly shamed for not complying with one's tax obligations an effective incentive for compliant behavior? Even if the person who is being identified for noncompliance is unaffected, would the disclosure efforts help support compliance norms among those who do comply?

[B] Exceptions Under Section 6103 Permitting Disclosure

Having established the general rule that taxpayer information should remain confidential, section 6103 then proceeds to list circumstances under which information may be made available without subjecting the IRS to liability for wrongful disclosure. For example, returns and return information may be disclosed by the IRS (1) to a third party designated by the taxpayer to receive the information and (2) to a person having a material interest in the return or return information. I.R.C. § 6103(c), (e). This latter authorization permits the taxpayer to obtain a copy of his or her own return, each spouse to obtain a copy of a jointly filed return, and a partner to obtain a copy of the partnership's return. Section 6103 also authorizes the IRS to exchange taxpayer information (including names, social security numbers, addresses, and wage information) with various federal, state, and local agencies. These agencies are entitled to use this information for several specified purposes, such as administering state tax programs, enforcing child support payments, and conducting criminal investigations. *See, e.g.*, I.R.C. § 6103(i), (j), (k), (l).

On a broader level, these exemptions under section 6103 highlight the tension between the need for other government agencies and third parties to use tax return information for legitimate purposes and the taxpayer's need for some assurance that the information he or she submits to the IRS will remain private. As you read the statutory language, notice the limitations on the release of return information and the elaborate procedures employed by the IRS to ensure that the information, once in the hands of the recipient, remains confidential. The regulations under section 6103 and the Internal Revenue Manual provide additional specific examples of when and for what purpose information may be disclosed. *See, e.g.*, Treas. Reg. § 301.6103(c)-1; I.R.M. 11.3.21.

[1] Disclosures Permitted During an Investigation

Reading Assignment: I.R.C. § 6103(k)(6); Treas. Reg. § 301.6103(k)(6)-1(c).

As discussed in Chapter 4, the IRS has broad authority to summon records and testimony from third parties during the course of an investigation of a taxpayer. To what extent may the IRS reveal return information during the investigation? Consider the following case:

DIANDRE v. UNITED STATES

United States Court of Appeals, Tenth Circuit

968 F.2d 1049 (1992)[19]

EBEL, CIRCUIT JUDGE:

In this appeal, we consider whether, and to what extent, section 6103 of the Internal Revenue Code ("I.R.C.") (26 U.S.C. § 6103) limits the scope of an Internal Revenue Service ("IRS") investigation. We hold that IRS circular letters sent to the taxpayer's customers requesting information on all payments made to the taxpayer did not violate section 6103. Accordingly, we reverse the district court's judgment awarding damages to the taxpayer under I.R.C. § 7431 (26 U.S.C. § 7431) based upon an alleged violation of I.R.C. § 6103.

I.

This suit arises out of an IRS criminal investigation of a corporation, plaintiff-appellee Metro Denver Maintenance Cleaning, Inc. ("MDMCI"), and its owner, plaintiff Anthony F. DiAndrea, concerning possible tax fraud. MDMCI provided janitorial services primarily to corporate customers.

In July 1985, the IRS began auditing DiAndrea and MDMCI. The investigation apparently remained dormant for some time, but resumed in early 1986. The agent assigned to the audit was unable to reconcile the corporation's records with its tax returns. In addition, he observed evidence of potential fraud: DiAndrea appeared to be intentionally uncooperative with the audit; there appeared to be two sets of profit and loss statements containing different figures for the same time period; DiAndrea allegedly admitted that he habitually inflated his travel and entertainment expense deductions; and DiAndrea appeared to be living beyond his means based on the income he declared on his tax returns. However, the agent did not suspect that MDMCI or DiAndrea was receiving unreported cash payments from customers. Appellant's App. at 178. On the basis of the other badges of fraud, the agent referred the case to the IRS's Criminal Investigation Division ("CID").

In September 1986, Shirley Kish Thomas, a CID Special Agent, undertook the criminal investigation of MDMCI and of DiAndrea. Agent Thomas issued a summons to DiAndrea and MDMCI for all of MDMCI's books and records, bank statements, deposit slips and cancelled checks, information on all bank accounts, and all financial statements for the period under investigation.

As part of her investigation, Agent Thomas prepared a "circular letter," a type of form letter, to obtain information from MDMCI customers. This letter, which appeared

[19] *Cert. denied sub nom.* Metro Denver Maintenance Cleaning v. United States, 507 U.S. 1029 (1993).

on CID letterhead, provided in relevant part:

> The Internal Revenue Service is conducting an investigation of Metro Denver Maintenance, Inc., Lakewood, Colorado, for the years 1983 through 1985. Mr. DiAndrea is an officer of Metro Denver Maintenance whose address is 6800 West 6th Avenue, Lakewood, Colorado, 80215.
>
> During the course of our investigation, we noted transactions between you and Metro Denver Maintenance, Inc. and/or Mr. DiAndrea for [the] previously mentioned period. As part of our investigation, we need to verify the purpose of these transactions. Your assistance is needed in determining all payments made to or on behalf of Metro Denver Maintenance and/or Mr. DiAndrea for the previously mentioned period. We would appreciate you furnishing the information indicated on Attachment 1, for use in a Federal tax matter.

Appellant's App. at 91. Attachment 1 requested the following information: "the date, check number, amount and form of all payment(s). By form of payment, it is meant if the payment(s) was made in cash, check, money order, etc." *Id.* at 94. Attachment 2, which was a form upon which the required information was to be entered, specified that the response should include "any payments made in the form of cash." *Id.* at 95.

Agent Thomas mailed this letter to all MDMCI customers. She subsequently issued a summons to all of DiAndrea's and MDMCI's banks for all records pertaining to either of them.

Using the bank records together with the MDMCI records, Agent Thomas and an accountant were substantially able to reconcile the records with MDMCI's and DiAndrea's tax returns. In addition, the bank records revealed that DiAndrea had several money market accounts, which explained his apparent ability to live beyond his means. The responses to the circular letters failed to reveal any further pertinent information. Agent Thomas ultimately concluded that the amount of potential underreporting of income did not meet the IRS's guidelines for criminal prosecution. The criminal investigation was then terminated.

DiAndrea and MDMCI filed suit against the United States pursuant to I.R.C. § 7431. The plaintiffs alleged that by mailing the circular letters, Agent Thomas had wrongfully disclosed confidential tax return information in violation of I.R.C. § 6103. The district court conducted a bench trial, at the end of which it orally entered its findings of fact and conclusions of law.

In its ruling, the district court found that the circular letters did not disclose any of DiAndrea's personal return information. The court found, however, that the circular letters did disclose a number of items of MDMCI's return information: the name of the taxpayer (MDMCI), the taxpayer's address, that DiAndrea was an officer of the taxpayer, that the IRS was investigating the taxpayer, that it was a criminal investigation, and that IRS records revealed transactions between the taxpayer and the recipient of the circular letter. The court further found that certain information sought via the circular letters — the payments cleared through DiAndrea's and MDMCI's banks — was reasonably available using bank and corporate records. The court rejected the government's argument that the circular letters were necessary to obtain information on unrecorded cash payments that may have been received by DiAndrea or MDMCI for undocumented "side jobs." The court specifically noted the absence of any evidence indicating that customers were making undocumented cash payments, except for statements by a former employee that DiAndrea had large amounts of cash available to him. Moreover, the court found that normal IRS procedure required that its agents first attempt to account for discrepancies in a tax return using bank records prior to sending out circular letters. Because Agent Thomas was not focusing specifically on cash payments at the time she sent out the circular letters, the court concluded that the government's argument that cash payments could not be discovered through examination of the bank records was "a belated attempt to justify what the special agent was doing at the time." Appellant's App. at 225.

The district court concluded that, in revealing MDMCI's return information, the disclosures violated section 6103 and that at least some of the information disclosed did not result from a good faith, but erroneous, interpretation of the section. The court accordingly awarded damages and entered judgment in favor of MDMCI. Because the circular letters had revealed none of DiAndrea's personal return information, the court dismissed DiAndrea's complaint.

The United States filed a timely notice of appeal. We have jurisdiction pursuant to 28 U.S.C. § 1291.

II.

The statute under which DiAndrea and MDMCI brought suit, section 7431 of the Internal Revenue Code, permits a taxpayer to bring a civil action against the United States if a federal employee or official violates that taxpayer's rights under section 6103. I.R.C. § 7431(a)(1). However, section 7431 provides that the United States is not liable if the violation occurred because of "a good faith, but erroneous, interpretation of section 6103." I.R.C. § 7431(b). The government argues that no violation of section 6103 occurred. Alternatively, it argues that if a violation did occur, it resulted from a good faith, but erroneous, interpretation of the statute, and that therefore the government has no liability.

Congress enacted section 6103 of the Internal Revenue Code to protect taxpayers' privacy and to prevent the misuse of the confidential information obtained in the course of collecting taxes. *See* S. Rep. No. 938, 94th Cong., 2d Sess. 19, 317–18 (1976), *reprinted in* 1976 U.S.C.C.A.N. 3439, 3455, 3746–47. * * *

Section 6103 provides a safe harbor for IRS agents that is relevant here:

> An internal revenue officer or employee may, in connection with his official duties relating to any audit, collection activity, or civil or criminal tax investigation or any other offense under the internal revenue laws, disclose return information to the extent that such disclosure is necessary in obtaining information, which is not otherwise reasonably available, with respect to the correct determination of tax, liability for tax, or the amount to be collected or with respect to the enforcement of any other provision of [the Internal Revenue Code].

I.R.C. § 6103(k)(6). Thus, an IRS agent may disclose return information during an investigation in order to obtain information, provided three requirements are met: (1) The information sought is "with respect to the correct determination of tax, liability for tax, or the amount to be collected or with respect to the enforcement of any other provision of [the Internal Revenue Code]." (2) The information sought is "not otherwise reasonably available." (3) It is necessary to make disclosures of return information in order to obtain the additional information sought.

The parties do not dispute that Agent Thomas disclosed return information by sending out the circular letters. Whether, in doing so, she violated section 6103 depends on whether her actions fell within the safe harbor of section 6103(k)(6). Accordingly, we must determine whether the three requirements of section 6103(k)(6) were met.

It should be self-evident that the first requirement — that the information sought related to determining tax liability — was met in this case. Information regarding all payments made to a taxpayer clearly relates to a determination of tax liability.

The parties dispute whether the second of these requirements was met: that the information sought must not be otherwise reasonably available. The circular letter requests information on "all payments," including those "made in cash." *See* Appellant's App. at 91, 94, 95. Cash payments do not appear to be the primary focus of the circular letter, but the letter clearly does request information on this subject. Information on receipt of undocumented cash payments was not available from any source other than from the payor, thereby meeting the second requirement. Although the circular letter also requested information that was potentially available from other sources, section 6103 does not prohibit requesting additional information beyond that not otherwise reasonably available if the additional request requires no further disclosure.

The final requirement — that the disclosures were necessary to obtain the information sought — was also met. There is no dispute that obtaining the information sought from MDMCI's customers required disclosure of all the return information contained in the circular letter, with the possible exceptions of the taxpayer's address and the fact that the tax investigation underway was criminal in nature. With regard to the former disclosure, given the necessity of revealing the taxpayer's identity, we hold that, under the circumstances of this case, disclosure of nonsensitive public information such as a business address to aid in identification was appropriate and necessary and therefore not a violation of section 6103. *Cf.* I.R.C. § 6103(b)(6) (taxpayer identity includes name, mailing address, and taxpayer's identifying number). With regard to the latter disclosure, the district court concluded that the government was protected by the good faith exception of section 7431(b). *Accord* Diamond v. United States, 944 F.2d 431, 435–37 (8th Cir. 1991). MDMCI does not appeal that ruling, so we do not review it here.

The district court strayed beyond the parameters of section 6103 when it sought to determine Agent Thomas' subjective intent and when it concluded that insufficient justification was shown to warrant delving into whether cash payments were made. That inquiry misperceives the function of section 6103(k)(6), which is to limit disclosures to those necessary to obtain the information sought. The section does not require the IRS to justify the appropriateness or need for the information sought so long as such information relates to the determination of tax liability and is not otherwise reasonably available. In other words, section 6103 does not provide a vehicle to test the probable cause or any other level of justification to investigate. *See* Barrett v. United States, 795 F.2d 446, 451 (5th Cir. 1986) ("in a section 7431 action, the court does not inquire whether the information sought is necessary"); *cf.* United States v. Powell, 379 U.S. 48, 57, 85 S. Ct. 248, 13 L. Ed. 2d 112 (1964) (IRS does not require probable cause to issue summons); United States v. MacKay, 608 F.2d 830, 832 (10th Cir. 1979) (same). The plain language of section 6103 does not limit in any way what information the IRS may seek in the course of an investigation. Section 6103 merely imposes certain restrictions on the IRS's ability to make disclosures in seeking that information. *See Barrett*, 795 F.2d at 451 ("We do not question the right, wisdom, or necessity of a particular IRS investigation. We do question, however, the means of investigation, but only to the limited extent consistent with section 7431."). The three requirements that section 6103(k)(6) imposes to permit an IRS agent to disclose return information were all met here. Thus, we hold that section 6103 did not prevent Agent Thomas from seeking information regarding cash payments even if she did not suspect cash payments and even if the badges of fraud could be legitimately explained.

We do not hold — indeed, we do not mean even to imply — that the IRS may investigate any subject and seek any information it wishes based on mere whim, caprice, or malice. Section 6103(k)(6) permits disclosures of return information only to obtain information relating to tax liability. Whatever other limits there may be on the scope of an IRS investigation, *cf., e.g.,* United States v. LaSalle Nat'l Bank, 437 U.S. 298, 313, 98 S.Ct. 2357, 57 L.Ed.2d 221 (1978) ("the IRS must use its summons authority in good faith"); *Powell*, 379 U.S. at 58 (court may refuse to enforce summons if issued for an improper purpose such as to harass or to apply pressure in a collateral matter); United States v. Malnik, 489 F.2d 682, 686 n.4 (5th Cir.) ("enforcement of an unclear and overly broad summons would violate the Fourth Amendment's proscription of unreasonable searches and seizures"), *cert. denied*, 419 U.S. 826, 42 L. Ed. 2d 50, 95 S. Ct. 44 (1974), it is not section 6103 that imposes those limits.

Because we conclude that no violation of section 6103 occurred, we need not and do not address the government's arguments regarding a good faith, but erroneous, interpretation of section 6103.

Accordingly, we reverse the judgment of the district court and remand with instructions to enter judgment for the United States.

Treasury regulations under section 6103(k)(6), issued after *DiAndrea* was decided, clarify the standards used to determine whether an IRS agent's disclosures during an investigation are necessary to obtain information not otherwise reasonably available. *See* T.D. 974 (July 11, 2006). The standards set forth in the regulations are largely consistent with the Tenth Circuit's analysis. For example, disclosure is "necessary" when, at the time of disclosure, the IRS agent "reasonably believes" disclosure is necessary to obtain information that permits the agent to carry out the investigation. *See* Treas. Reg. § 301.6103(k)(6)-1(c)(1). Furthermore, the term "necessary," as used in section 6103(k)(6), does not refer to the "necessity of conducting an investigation or the appropriateness of the means or methods chosen to conduct the investigation." Disclosure by the agent is necessary when it is "appropriate and helpful" in obtaining the information sought. *Id.*

Notice the Tenth Circuit's conclusion in *DiAndrea* that disclosure of the taxpayer's identity was necessary to carry out the investigation and that, "given the necessity of revealing the taxpayer's identity," the act of disclosing the taxpayer's address, which it characterized as "nonsensitive public information," did not result in a violation of section 6103. Recognizing that a taxpayer's identity is return information within the meaning of section 6103, could an IRS agent obtain information about the taxpayer from a third party *without* revealing the taxpayer's identity?

In *Snider v. United States*, 468 F.3d 500 (8th Cir. 2006), during the course of an investigation of the taxpayers for failing to pay income and employment taxes, the IRS Special Agent contacted the taxpayers' employees and business associates and revealed to them the taxpayers' names and that the taxpayers were being investigated for tax and nontax crimes. *Id.* at 505–06. A majority of the Eighth Circuit panel affirmed the district court's finding that the government did not show that revealing the taxpayer's identity was necessary to the investigation. *Id.* at 507–08. The IRS has issued an Action on Decision setting forth its nonacquiesence in the Eighth Circuit's holding. A.O.D. 2007-03, 2007-30 I.R.B. 4 ("In order to conduct an effective interview with a third-party witness in a tax investigation, it is certainly appropriate and, therefore, necessary to disclose the identity of the taxpayer under investigation to the third-party witness to obtain information from the witness. *See* Treas. Reg. §§ 301.6103(k)(6)-1(c)(1) Ex. 1; 301.6103(k)(6)-1(c)(3). The disclosure of the identity of a taxpayer under investigation will avoid confusing a third-party witness about the nature and scope of the investigation and help to ensure the accuracy and reliability of the information provided by the third-party witness.").

When is taxpayer information "otherwise reasonably available" within the meaning of section 6103(k)(6)? Must the IRS investigator seek information from the taxpayer or the taxpayer's representative first, before contacting third parties who might have the information? *Payne v. United States*, 289 F.3d 377 (5th Cir. 2002), *cert. denied*, 545 U.S. 1105 (2005), involved a lawyer who, in compensation for legal services, received stock in a corporation that operated a topless dance club under the name "Caligula XXI." During the course of an investigation of the corporation, the IRS agent contacted the lawyer's employees, relatives, clients, and former clients. The lawyer filed suit seeking damages for wrongful disclosure in violation of section 6103 and the district court awarded damages to the lawyer. On appeal, the Fifth Circuit rejected the government's argument that "IRS special agents need never consider the taxpayer under investigation as a source from whom information is 'reasonably available.' " The Fifth Circuit indicated that the taxpayer, if asked, could voluntarily provide sources of corroborating evidence, thereby negating the need to contact third parties. "We do not hold that the taxpayer is always such a fruitful and reliable source of information that IRS agents may never approach third-parties for necessary information. We hold only that such a determination must be made in light of the 'facts and circumstances of the case,' and that the taxpayer's cooperation legitimately forms part of the inquiry." *Id.* at 383–84. *Cf.* A.O.D. 2007-03, *supra* ("[A]n agent is not required to seek information from a taxpayer or his attorney before contacting a third-party witness.").

[2] Disclosure to Persons with a Material Interest

Reading Assignment: I.R.C. § 6103(e).

Code section 6103(e) allows the taxpayer to receive or inspect the return of another party in specified circumstances where the taxpayer has a legally relevant interest in that return. In the context of a passthrough entity such as a partnership or S corporation, does return information pertaining to the entity's operations belong the entity itself or to the equity holder? Resolving this issue is important for purposes of applying the exception in section 6103(e). The following case illustrates the dilemma.

MARTIN v. INTERNAL REVENUE SERVICE
United States Court of Appeals, Tenth Circuit
857 F.2d 722 (1988)

SEYMOUR, CIRCUIT JUDGE:

Robert J. Martin filed suit under the Freedom of Information Act (FOIA), 5 U.S.C. § 552 (1982), to compel the Internal Revenue Service (IRS) to disclose to him tax protests filed by three other individuals. The protests concerned proposed adjustments to those individuals' tax returns based on proposed adjustments to the returns of certain passthrough corporate and partnership entities in which Martin and the other individuals had interests. The district court ordered the IRS to disclose the protests to Martin. Because we conclude that the protests are not "return information" of the corporate entities within the meaning of 26 U.S.C. § 6103 (1982 & Supp. IV 1986), we reverse.[n.1]

I.

From 1980 to 1983, Robert J. Martin, Robert L. Mehl, Patrick D. Maher, and Jordan R. Smith were shareholders in Western Oil Marketing (WOM), a subchapter S corporation. They were also partners in a limited partnership, Industrial Energy Partners (IEP). WOM and IEP were the sole partners in a general partnership, Western Operating Joint Venture (WOJV). All of these entities are passthrough entities. They file information returns with the IRS but pay little or no tax. Their partners/shareholders are primarily responsible for the tax consequences of the entities' income and expenses. 26 U.S.C. §§ 701, 1372 (1982). Any adjustments to the entities' returns thus affect the liabilities of their partners/shareholders. Martin severed his relationship with the entities in 1983.

The IRS audited the returns of the three entities and proposed adjustments to the income and expenses reported by each from 1980 through 1983. A copy of the revenue agent's report proposing the adjustments was sent to each of the partners/shareholders. The IRS then audited and sought adjustments to the returns of these

[n.1] It is undisputed in this case that if section 6103 prohibits disclosure of this information, it is exempt from disclosure under FOIA. *See* 5 U.S.C. § 552(b)(3) (FOIA does not apply to matters that are "specifically exempted from disclosure by statute").

individuals.[n.2] Martin alleges, and the IRS has not denied, that Mehl, Maher, and Smith filed protests with the IRS contesting these proposed adjustments.[n.4] The IRS agent auditing Martin's returns has stated that she will adopt the same position as that taken by the IRS in response to Mehl, Maher and Smith's protests in her audit of Martin's returns. Rec., doc. 5, at 10, para. 7. Martin therefore seeks disclosure of the protests, to the extent they relate to the entities' returns, in order to prepare his own response to the IRS.

After exhausting his administrative remedies, Martin filed this FOIA suit seeking disclosure of such parts of the protests as relate to the entities. A magistrate recommended that his request be granted with respect to WOM and IEP and denied as to WOJV, because Martin is not a partner or shareholder of WOJV. The district court granted the request as to all three entities and ordered the IRS to redact information identifying the taxpayers who filed the protests. After the court denied the IRS's motion to suspend the injunction pending appeal, the IRS made an emergency motion to this court for stay pending appeal. We granted the stay, conditioned on an IRS extension of time for Martin to respond to his 30-day letter, and expedited the appeal.

II.

Section 6103 of the Internal Revenue Code, 26 U.S.C. § 6103, governs the confidentiality and disclosure of tax returns and return information. It provides that returns and return information may not be disclosed except as authorized by title 26. *Id.* § 6103(a). * * * Partners and shareholders may obtain access to returns and return information of their partnerships and corporations pursuant to section 6103(e), which governs disclosure to persons having a material interest. That section authorizes a partner to examine the return of his partnership, *id.* § 6103(e)(1), and a shareholder of a subchapter S corporation to examine the return of that corporation, *id.* § 6103(e)(1)(D)(v), upon written request. They may examine the return information of such partnerships or corporations if the Secretary determines that such disclosure would not seriously impair Federal tax administration. *Id.* § 6103(e)(7).

The parties agree that the same item of information may be the return information of more than one taxpayer. They also agree that the source of that information is not controlling. Therefore, data supplied to the IRS by A that may affect B's tax return may in theory be return information of A alone, of A and B, of B alone, or of no one. The parties disagree on how to determine whose return information such data would be in any given case. Martin argues that the key factor is whose tax liability may be affected by the data. The IRS argues that the key factor is whose tax liability is under investigation by the IRS. Specifically, the IRS defines "any person," as the term is used in the definition of return information, as "the person or persons whose liabilities are under investigation and as to whom information collected by the IRS is germane to a

---

[n.2] After an audit, a revenue agent's report is sent to those under audit along with a letter explaining the taxpayers' alternatives. IRS regulations provide that if audited taxpayers disagree with the revenue agent's proposed adjustments to their tax returns, they may file a response to the IRS letter. This response must be sent within 30 days; thus, the letter is known as a 30-day letter. One form of response is to file a protest and appeal to an IRS appeals officer. 26 C.F.R. § 601.105 (1988). Mehl, Maher and Smith have responded by filing protests.

[n.4] The parties' statements of facts are not entirely clear as to whether the protests were filed in response to the proposed adjustments to the entities' information returns in themselves, or whether they contest the resulting proposed adjustments to Mehl, Maher and Smith's own returns. While the distinction between these is technical, it is significant. Protests that were filed in direct response to proposed adjustments to the entities' information returns would be return information of the entities. * * * Finally and most significantly, although Martin asserts in his brief that the protests were furnished to the IRS with respect to the entities' returns, he does not contest the IRS's argument that the protests are return information of Mehl, Maher and Smith. We thus assume that the protests were submitted by Mehl, Maher and Smith to contest adjustments to their own tax liability.

determination of their tax liabilities." Brief for the Appellant at 11–12.

The facts of this case make Martin's argument very appealing. Passthrough entities are to a large extent legal fictions in the tax context and that is particularly evident here. One could say with some justification that Martin is in fact contesting his tax liability with his former copartners/shareholders. The IRS agent auditing his returns has stated that she will adopt the same approach to his returns as the IRS adopts with respect to Mehl, Maher and Smith's returns. While Martin may appeal this approach if it does not favor him, both with the IRS and in court, the IRS may already have considered and rejected the arguments he is likely to make before he gets that opportunity. It may seem both unjust and contrary to common sense to read the statute to allow Mehl, Maher and Smith to attempt to affect Martin's tax liabilities without permitting him to know their arguments and to reply to them.

To counter this argument, the IRS stresses the privacy rights that section 6103 is designed to protect. The Government points out that information supplied by one taxpayer with respect to his own tax liability often affects the liability of another taxpayer, and that such information does not thereby become disclosable to the second taxpayer merely because of its possible effect. At oral argument, counsel for the IRS drew a mental picture that illustrates the IRS' position. Suppose the IRS has a basket for each taxpayer and corporate entity. When the IRS makes a determination about an entity's return, the report is placed in the entity's basket. Under the authority of section 6103(e), it is also placed in the baskets of the entity's partners/shareholders. Individual reactions to the report are placed only in the basket of that taxpayer. If the IRS then reacts to the protests and changes the entity's return, that information is again placed both in the entity's basket and in those of its partners/shareholders.

We have found only two circuit cases, one of them ours, that have considered whether a specific item of information is the return information of a corporate entity. *See* MidSouth Music Corp. v. United States, 818 F.2d 536 (6th Cir. 1987); First Western Gov't Securities v. United States, 796 F.2d 356 (10th Cir. 1986). *MidSouth* and *First Western* do not provide us with much guidance, however, because of significant differences between their facts and the facts of this case. Those cases concern information released by the IRS; the communications did not reveal that the information supplier was under investigation or the substance of the legal basis for the IRS determination; and the information was arguably corporate information released to investors. Here, on the other hand, a third party is seeking information the IRS has determined to be nondisclosable; the information would necessarily reveal that Mehl, Maher and Smith are under investigation, and the substance of their legal arguments;[n.5] and the information is that of individual taxpayers and would be released to a corporate entity.[n.6] Furthermore, *MidSouth* and *First Western* concluded that the information in question was not the return information of the supplier. Here there can be no doubt that the protests are the return information of Mehl, Maher and Smith.

[n.5] The IRS describes tax protests as follows:

> "A taxpayer's written protest may . . . be argumentative and adversarial in nature. The taxpayer . . . may cite and argue from precedent, may argue that the agent has misconstrued or misunderstood facts and transactions, and may attempt to cast the facts relied upon by the agent in a light more favorable to his own position. Even if a taxpayer used the return information of an entity in formulating his protest, that information may have been recast, reformulated or reorganized by an advocate . . . Thus, a protest, although based upon the [revenue agent's report] issued by the agent, consists primarily of the analyses, interpretations and conclusion of the taxpayer or his attorney."

Brief for the Appellant at 27–28.

[n.6] Martin argues that the protests are return information of the entities. Martin's right to the protests, if any, derives from his status as a partner/shareholder; if the entities are entitled to the information, he is as well, to the extent permitted by section 6103(e)(7).

Two cases with facts more similar to those of this case are *Church of Scientology v. Internal Revenue Service*, 484 U.S. 9, 108 S. Ct. 271, 98 L. Ed. 2d 228 (1987) (rejecting attempt by Church to require IRS to disclose information relating to Church in IRS case files and data systems) and *Ryan v. Bureau of Alcohol, Tobacco and Firearms*, 715 F.2d 644, 230 U.S. App. D.C. 170 (D.C. Cir. 1983) (rejecting attempt to require IRS to disclose information supplied by liquor bottle manufacturers in aid of determination of tax liabilities of liquor manufacturers). In those cases, however, the issue was whether the information was return information at all. It is not disputed here that the protests are the return information of Mehr, Maher and Smith. The question we address is whether they are also the return information of the entities; that is, our question is whose return information it is, not whether it is return information. We note that *Ryan* explicitly rejected the argument made by the IRS in this case, although with respect to an arguably different term, and held that information supplied to the IRS is the return information of "any person with respect to whom information is received." *Ryan*, 715 F.2d at 647.

Ultimately, we are convinced by two arguments. First, we agree with the IRS that the mere fact that information supplied by one person may affect the tax liability of another is insufficient to give the second a right to see that information. If one considers tax returns rather than return information, that principle is not difficult to accept. It is frequently the case that one transaction is reflected in many tax returns. If two taxpayers' returns were based on different allocations of resulting tax liability from a transaction, that difference in itself would not give one taxpayer a right to see the other's return. The right to see return information is no greater than the right to see tax returns. *See* 26 U.S.C. § 6103(e)(7).

Second, given the structure of section 6103, acceptance of the argument made by Martin would render section 6103(e) superfluous. Pass-through entities are to a large extent legal fictions for tax purposes. They pay little or no tax themselves. The information they submit is useful to the IRS primarily insofar as it affects the tax liabilities of their partners/shareholders. They present perhaps the quintessential case for Martin's argument that the key factor in determining access to return information should be whose liability is at stake. Were that argument the basis on which section 6103 is constructed, however, the returns submitted by pass-through entities to the IRS would automatically be the return information of their investors, the taxpayers. No statutory provision other than section 6103(c), which provides for the disclosure of a taxpayer's return and return information to that taxpayer or his designee, would be needed.

In fact, however, entity returns and return information are disclosable to partners/shareholders only because of section 6103(e), which provides for the access of *third parties* to the return information of *others*. Congress recognized that persons with a material interest, as defined by statute, in another's tax return or return information, have a legitimate basis for disclosure. Partners and shareholders in subchapter S corporations are included in the class of such persons. Since we must give meaning to this statutory provision, and since Martin's argument would make section 6103(e) unnecessary in this context, we must reject it. If Congress thinks it necessary to specify that partners are persons with a material interest in a partnership, it cannot be the case that partners can automatically obtain access to partnership returns or return information on the ground that it is their own return information. The reverse must also be true. In short, the returns and return information of pass-through entities are disclosable to the taxpayers whose liability is actually at stake only because Congress so provided in explicit terms. We do not think that we can read the statute to permit such information to flow in the other direction — from partners shareholders to entities — without a corresponding explicit statutory provision.[n.8]

[n.8] This statutory construction cannot be evaded by asserting that Martin has a material interest in Mehl,

III.

The parties raise additional arguments which we do not address given our disposition of this case. In particular, Martin argues that disclosure is warranted under section 6103(h)(4)(C).[n.9] *See First Western*, 796 F.2d at 360–61. After reviewing the record, we conclude that this argument was not raised below, and we do not address it.

As directed in our order staying the judgment below, Martin has two weeks from the date of this judgment to respond to his 30-day letter.

Reversed.

Is *Martin* a section 6103(e) case? Why did the court disagree with Martin's argument?

[C] Remedies for Unlawful Disclosure Under Section 6103

Reading Assignment: I.R.C. §§ 7213, 7431.

In order to give teeth to the prohibition in section 6103, Congress established both civil and criminal liability for wrongful disclosure of return and return information. Section 7431 affords an aggrieved taxpayer a cause of action against the United States for damages resulting from any disclosure of return or return information knowingly or negligently made by an employee or officer of the United States. I.R.C. § 7431(a)(1).[20] Concerned about reports that IRS employees were browsing through files containing taxpayer information, Congress expanded Code section 7431 to impose liability not only for unauthorized disclosure, but also for unauthorized inspection of return information. Liability on the part of the government does not arise, however, where the IRS can prove that the unauthorized disclosure or inspection resulted from a good faith, but erroneous, interpretation of section 6103. I.R.C. § 7431(b).

The cause of action under section 7431, arising in a U.S. district court, must be brought within two years after the taxpayer discovers that an unauthorized disclosure has been made. I.R.C. § 7431(d). The measure of damages available includes actual damages sustained by the taxpayer, court costs, and possibly reasonable attorney's fees. At a minimum, the statute specifies a damage award of not less than $1,000 for each act of unauthorized disclosure. Punitive damages are also available in situations where the unlawful disclosure is willful or where disclosure results from gross negligence. *Ward v. United States*, a portion of which is reproduced below, provides an example of how a district court determines the government's liability under section 7431.

Maher and Smith's tax protests insofar as they contain information relating to the entities. The meaning of the term "material interest" is defined by statute. A partner has a material interest in his partnerships' return and return information under 26 U.S.C. § 6103(e)(1)(c) & (e)(7); he does not have a material interest in the return information of a copartner because no provision so provides.

[n.9] Section 6103(h)(4)(C) provides:

> "(4) Disclosure in judicial and administrative tax proceedings. — A return or return information may be disclosed in a Federal or State judicial or administrative proceeding pertaining to tax administration, but only — . . .
>
> (C) if such return or return information directly relates to a transactional relationship between a person who is a party to the proceeding and the taxpayer which directly affects the resolution of an issue in the proceeding . . . "

26 U.S.C. § 6103(h)(4)(C).

[20] Liability also extends to a narrowly defined group of private individuals (specified in section 6103(a)) if such individuals violate section 6103. I.R.C. § 7431(a)(2).

WARD v. UNITED STATES

United States District Court, District of Colorado
973 F. Supp. 996 (1997)

DOWNES, DISTRICT JUDGE:

[The plaintiff apparently owned a chain of stores known as Kid's Avenue. She alleged that IRS agents told various employees and customers that she had not paid her taxes, was using several different Social Security Numbers and aliases, that she had been on a number of trips to South America, and that she was suspected of money laundering and/or involvement with drugs. *See Ward*, 973 F. Supp. at 998–999. She also alleged that the IRS posted similar information in the windows of some Kid's Avenue stores. The court did not give credence to this testimony, but focused on the IRS' admitted disclosures of return information on a live radio talk show, to Inside Edition, and in a letter to the editor of a newspaper. The court rejected the Government's argument that a consent executed by the plaintiff to a reporter for the radio station served to authorize disclosure under section 6103(c). — Eds.]

* * *

The Court will briefly outline the issues. Plaintiff, Carol Ward, has filed suit against the United States Internal Revenue Department, asserting that the IRS and its employees and agents made unauthorized disclosures of her "return information" in violation of 26 U.S.C. § 6103(a) and seeks damages pursuant to 26 U.S.C. § 7431. Plaintiff alleges five instances of unauthorized disclosure of "return information" by Defendant: (1) verbal disclosures by IRS employees to Plaintiff's customers and to Citadel Mall management; (2) the alleged posting of "return information" in the windows of three "Kid's Avenue" stores operated by Plaintiff's son; (3) disclosure of "return information" on August 3, 1993, during a live radio talk show on KVOR radio in Colorado Springs by the IRS District Director, Gerald Swanson and IRS employee Patricia Callahan; (4) disclosure of Plaintiff's "return information" in an IRS "fact sheet" provided to Inside Edition/American Journal (*See* Pltf.'s Exhibit No. 19); and (5) disclosure of "return information" in a published letter to the editor of the Colorado Springs Gazette Telegraph by James Scholan, a revenue officer in the Colorado Springs office of the IRS (*See* Pltf.'s Exhibit No. 21.).

* * *

FINDINGS OF FACT

* * *

Radio Talk Show

4. Defendant has conceded and this Court finds that Defendant, through IRS employees Gerald Swanson and Patricia Callahan, disclosed Plaintiff's "return information" during their August 3, 1993, appearance on a live talk show broadcast on KVOR radio. The Court further finds that Mr. Swanson and Ms. Callahan's disclosures were negligently made. As this Court previously found, Defendant's reliance upon the written consent by Plaintiff was mistaken and, in light of the IRS's own regulations, 26 C.F.R. § 301.6103(c)-1, it cannot be found to be a "good faith, but erroneous, interpretation of section 6103" exempt from liability under 26 U.S.C. § 7431(b). *See* Barrett v. United States of America, 51 F.3d 475 (5th Cir. 1995) *citing with approval* Huckaby v. United States Department of the Treasury, 794 F.2d 1041, 1048–49 (5th Cir. 1986). Furthermore, pursuant to *Rodgers v. Hyatt*, 697 F.2d 899, 906 (10th Cir. 1983), the Court finds that Plaintiff's prior disclosure of return information, including debating the merits of the jeopardy assessment with Swanson and Callahan while on the radio talk show, did not waive the confidentiality of Plaintiff's return information. Nonetheless, the Court

finds that Mr. Swanson and Ms. Callahan's disclosures were not willful or the result of gross negligence supporting an award of punitive damages. *See* Barrett v. United States, 100 F.3d 35, 40 (5th Cir. 1996) (defining willful conduct as that which is done without ground for believing that it was lawful or conduct marked by careless disregard of whether one has a right to act in such manner and grossly negligent as conduct which is willful or marked by wanton and reckless disregard of the rights of another). The Court finds that, prior to the radio broadcast, Defendant sought and received advice (although incorrect), as to whether disclosure of Plaintiff's return information was authorized in light of the prior consent executed by Plaintiff. (*See* Pltf.'s Exhibit No. 71, Declaration of Michael S. Perkins.)

5. Over the objection of Defendant the Court accepted the testimony of Mr. Greg Sher. Mr. Sher is the director of sales for the Citadel Group which owns and operates KVOR and other radio stations. Mr. Sher testified that, based upon his review of Arbitron Company ratings, there were approximately 3,200 to 3,300 listeners tuned into the KVOR radio talk show on which Mr. Swanson and Ms. Callahan appeared and discussed Plaintiff's return information. (*See* Pltf.'s Exhibits No. 25 and 74.) The Court finds that Mr. Sher's estimate is too speculative to support a finding by this Court that 3,200 to 3,300 listeners were tuned into the radio talk show. Nonetheless, based upon the evidence and a review of the taped radio show, the Court finds that Mr. Swanson and Ms. Callahan each committed an act of disclosure in violation of 26 U.S.C. § 6103. (*See* Pltf.'s Exhibit 16).

Fact Sheet

6. Based on Defendant's concessions, this Court finds that a disclosure of Plaintiff's return information was made when Defendant provided Inside Edition with a "fact sheet" concerning Plaintiff's dispute with the IRS. (*See* Pltf.'s Exhibit No. 19.) As with the disclosure made on KVOR radio, the Court finds that Defendant's disclosure was negligent, but not willful or grossly negligent, supporting an award of punitive damages. Ms. Callahan, who had provided the "fact sheet" to Inside Edition, testified that prior to release she had checked with the IRS disclosure officer, Mike Perkins, who incorrectly advised her that Plaintiff's prior consent authorized the disclosure of Plaintiff's return information. The Court rejects Plaintiff's suggestion that the material contained in the fact sheet made intentional misstatements of the "facts" surrounding Plaintiff's case. Accordingly, the Court finds that one act of unauthorized disclosure was made as a result of the "fact sheet" being provided to Inside Edition.

Letter to the Editor

7. This Court finds that the letter written to the editor of the Colorado Springs Gazette Telegraph by the Colorado Springs IRS Revenue Officer, James Scholan, which was published in the October 12, 1993 edition of that paper contained "return information." (*See* Pltf.'s Exhibit No. 21.) Based upon the testimony of Tom Miller and James Scholan, this Court also finds that this return information was obtained by Mr. Scholan in his capacity as a revenue officer for the IRS.

Mr. Miller testified that Mr. Scholan would have had to have been "in a coma" not to have known that there was a collection action going on involving Plaintiff. In addition, contrary to his declaration, which was filed with this Court, Mr. Scholan was forced to acknowledge that he did serve a levy for Mr. Miller, making ¶ 2 of his declaration inaccurate. (*See* Pltf.'s Exhibit No. 68.) Mr. Scholan also acknowledged that ¶ 3 was inaccurate in that he did become aware of Plaintiff's tax information, partly based upon his official duties. In fact, Mr. Scholan testified that he knew from his job as a revenue officer that there had been a seizure against Plaintiff because of her outstanding tax liability. Finally, Mr. Scholan testified that ¶ 6 of his declaration was inaccurate, in that he did have access to Plaintiff's return information gathered by the IRS. Mr. Scholan testified that, despite his prior IRS training concerning the disclosure of return information, he thought that he was not disclosing return information because of Plaintiff's prior letter to the editor and her appearance on the radio. Mr. Scholan testified that he learned only recently that a taxpayer's disclosure does not allow a subsequent disclosure by an IRS official. However, Defendant offered no evidence to show that Mr. Scholan, unlike Mr. Swanson and Ms. Callahan, sought a determination as to whether his writing of the letter would be a violation of pertinent tax laws or IRS regulations. Moreover, it is not suggested that Mr. Scholan knew or even relied upon Plaintiff's prior execution of a release.

The Court finds that Mr. Scholan's conduct constituted a blatant violation of 26 U.S.C. § 6103. In addition, the Court finds Mr. Scholan's conduct was grossly negligent, meriting an award of punitive damages. Mr. Scholan's conduct, in light of his prior training and IRS regulations, was in reckless disregard of the law and the rights of Plaintiff. *See* Barrett v. United States, 100 F.3d at 40.

Damages

8. Plaintiff seeks to recover the greater of her statutory or actual damages. Based upon the findings set forth above, the Court finds that Plaintiff is entitled to recover $4,000.00 in statutory damages for four acts of wrongful disclosure made by Swanson, Callahan and Scholan. Plaintiff is also entitled to punitive damages.

Plaintiff claims actual damages as a result of Defendant's wrongful disclosures in the form of mental distress and emotional damages, humiliation, loss of the Citidel Mall lease and loss of peripheral vision in Plaintiff's right eye as a result of a grand mal seizure.

The Court finds that Plaintiff has failed to prove that the injury to her eye was caused by Defendant's conduct. Plaintiff testified that she had previously suffered grand mal seizures (five in the last eighteen years) and has suffered from epilepsy since she was twenty-eight. The evidence offered is insufficient to show that Plaintiff's seizure and resulting vision loss were caused by Defendant's wrongful conduct. * * *

The Court finds that Plaintiff's claims for mental distress, emotional damages and humiliation have merit. *See* Hrubec v. National Railroad Passenger Corporation, 829 F. Supp. 1502, 1504–06 (N.D. Ill. 1993) (analyzing the issue of whether emotional distress damages are available under 26 U.S.C. § 7431(c)(B)). The evidence offered by Plaintiff establishes that Defendant's wrongful conduct caused Plaintiff's personality to change. She became bitter and consumed by a battle with the IRS in an effort to establish that what Defendant's agents and employees had said and done was incorrect. As stated by Plaintiff's mother, Ms. Altavilla, Plaintiff was so enraged and obsessed by Defendant's conduct that "we all began to hate her." Similar testimony was offered by Plaintiff's son, Tristan Ward and her daughter, Kelly Gilmour. Plaintiff's daughter testified that as a result of Defendant's actions, her mother became irritable and she frequently cried. Plaintiff also testified that the information released by Defendant caused a number of her friends and family members to question whether Plaintiff really was a drug dealer and/or tax protestor. The Court finds that, as a result of Defendant's wrongful disclosures, Plaintiff suffered actual damages in the form of emotional distress. The Court further finds that $75,000 will fairly compensate Plaintiff for the damages she suffered as a result of Defendant's wrongful conduct over a three month period.

9. Based upon this Court's finding, that Mr. Scholan's conduct was grossly negligent, Plaintiff is also entitled to recover punitive damages pursuant to 26 U.S.C. § 7431(c)(1)(B). Considering the conduct of Mr. Scholan, the harm inflicted upon Plaintiff; the deterrent aspect of a punitive damage award and the public medium through which Plaintiff's return information was disclosed, this Court finds that Plaintiff is entitled to recover $250,000 in punitive damages. *See* Continental Trend Resources, Inc. v. OXY USA, Inc., 101 F.3d 634 (discussing factors to be considered in an award for punitive damages).

As a public employee and a revenue officer for the IRS Mr. Scholan holds a position of trust and power. Along with that trust and power comes a high degree of responsibility. Part of that responsibility requires that you accept criticism, however inaccurate and/or unjustified, in silence and that you act in accordance with the law. While admittedly equipped with 20/20 vision, every other revenue officer, when asked, acknowledged that Mr. Scholan's conduct was clearly inappropriate in light of the disclosure laws. In addition, the Court notes that the medium which Mr. Scholan used was expected to and did reach a public audience, resulting in a wide dissemination of Plaintiff's return information. *See* Miller v. United States, 66 F.3d 220, 224 (9th Cir, 1995).

The conduct of our Nation's affairs always demands that public servants discharge their duties under the Constitution and laws of this Republic with fairness and a proper spirit of subservience to the people whom they are sworn to serve. Public servants cannot be arbitrarily selective in their treatment of citizens, dispensing equity to those who please them and withholding it from those who do not. Respect for the law can only be fostered if citizens believe that those responsible for implementing and enforcing the law are themselves acting in conformity with the law. By this award, this Court gives notice to the IRS that reprehensible abuse of authority by one of its employees cannot and will not be tolerated.

CONCLUSIONS OF LAW

In addition to those findings of law which are included in the Court's findings of fact set forth above the Court makes these additional findings of law:

1. Plaintiff contends that she is entitled to recover the $1,000 statutory damage for each listener to the KVOR radio talk show on which Mr. Swanson and Ms. Callahan appeared. Plaintiff takes the position that there was an act of disclosure for each listener. The Court disagrees. Pursuant to 26 U.S.C. § 7431(c)(1)(A), Plaintiff is only entitled to recover $1,000 "for each act of unauthorized disclosure." (emphasis added). Under 26 U.S.C. § 6103(b)(8) "[t]he term 'disclosure' means the making known to any person in any manner whatever a return or return information."

In *Mallas* [*v. United States*, 993 F.2d 1111 (4th Cir. 1993)], the district court found and the Fourth Circuit Court of Appeals affirmed that an act of disclosure occurred for each named person to which the IRS mailed return information. *Mallas*, 993 F.2d at 1124–25. In making this finding the district court found that two acts of disclosure were committed where only one envelope was sent, but the envelope was addressed to two named persons. In its affirmance, the Court of Appeals, after reviewing § 7431(c)(1)(A) and § 6103(b)(8), concluded:

> that the "act" to be counted for computing damages is the "making known to any person in any manner whatever" the return information. Each time the Government "makes known" return information to a person in violation of 6103, it has committed an "act of unauthorized disclosure." If the IRS addresses and mails a single RAR to two people, it makes the information in the RAR known to each of them no differently than if it had decided to use two copies of the RAR, two envelopes, and two stamps . . . .

Id. at 1125. Liability is triggered under § 7431(c)(1)(A) by the "act" of "making known to any person in any manner whatever a return or return information." In *Mallas*, Defendant committed 73 different "acts" by addressing and placing in the mail envelopes that were addressed and directed to seventy-three different individuals. Thus, Defendant committed 73 separate "acts" of disclosure. In the case at bar Swanson and Callahan each committed an act of disclosure when they discussed Plaintiff's return information on the radio. Nevertheless, to the extent that *Mallas* could be interpreted as holding that an act of disclosure is committed for every person who learned about

Plaintiff's return information, as a consequence of Swanson and Callahan's act of appearing on the radio, this Court disagrees with such an analysis. It is the "act" of disclosure, not the receipt of information which triggers liability. Moreover, taken literally, the analysis applied in *Mallas* is inconsistent with the implicit finding made in *Rodgers v. Hyatt*, 697 F.2d 899 [10th Cir. 1983], where plaintiff was found to be entitled to only $1,000 for a single disclosure made by an IRS official in a meeting at which two Amax officials were present. *Id.* at 905–06. It is for these reasons that the Court further rejects Plaintiff's argument that she is entitled to $1,000 for every listener to the KVOR radio talk show.

* * *

Therefore, it is ordered that, based upon the foregoing findings of facts and conclusions of law, Plaintiff is entitled to a Judgment in her favor and against the Defendant in the amount of $325,000 and the Clerk of Court is hereby directed to enter the Judgment. * * *

Courts have disagreed about the appropriate method for calculating damages under section 7431. In *Snider v. United States*, 468 F.3d 500 (8th Cir. 2006), discussed above in Section 6.03[B], an Eighth Circuit panel also disagreed about whether a single act of wrongful disclosure by the IRS special agent to more than one person constituted multiple violations of section 6103(a), as well as whether a single disclosure that contained more than one item of return information (an interview between the IRS agent and a third party during which the agent disclosed six separate pieces of return information) counted as more than one act of disclosure for purposes of calculating damages under section 7431:

> The government urges that we hold that: (1) a disclosure to more than one person at a time amounts to one act of disclosure; and (2) a disclosure of more than one piece of return information in a single interview constitutes a single act of disclosure. We disagree. Increased culpability warrants increased punishment. Direct disclosures to multiple persons multiplies the harm to the taxpayer. Our sister circuit has held that one disclosure to two people counts as two separate disclosures. *Mallas v. United States*, 993 F.2d 1111, 1125 (4th Cir. 1993). As *Mallas* recognized, § 7431(c)(1)(A) imposes statutory damages for "each act of unauthorized disclosure of . . . return information," and § 6103(b)(8) defines "disclosure" as "making known to any person in any manner whatever a return or return information." *Id.* Accepting the government's position would nullify the language "in any manner whatever." *Id.* If a government official directly discloses a taxpayer's return information to two listeners at the same time, the official has informed both listeners and caused as much harm as telling them separately. *Id.* We see no reason why the government should benefit from a wider audience, especially where a wider audience means an increased injury to the taxpayer's privacy. The same reasoning applies to the quantity of information disclosed.
>
> At the same time, we recognize the concerns addressed in *Miller v. United States*, 66 F.3d 220 (9th Cir. 1995). In *Miller*, the Ninth Circuit held that the IRS's disclosure of return information to a Los Angeles Times reporter, who subsequently published 184,000 newspapers containing the information, represented a single act of disclosure rather than 184,000 acts of disclosure. . . . The court reasoned that § 7431 "punishes 'disclosure,' not subsequent disseminations" and declined to extend *Mallas* to such a situation. . . . We agree that the proper limitation of liability is the initial act of disclosure, not secondary disclosures made by others such as the media. . . .

> However, we do not agree with the Ninth Circuit's holding in *Siddiqui v. United States*, 359 F.3d 1200, 1202–03 (9th Cir. 2004), which extended *Miller* and declined to impose liability for an agent's unauthorized disclosure of return information in a speech to a party of 100 people. As discussed above, we believe that liability should track culpability and injury. A disclosure to 100 people is certainly more egregious than a disclosure to one person, and we believe that Congress drafted the statute to scale damages to injury and culpability with respect to the agent's own acts of disclosure. . . . The method of counting performed by the district court is affirmed.

Id. at 508–09. Thus, the majority found that the IRS agent committed six acts of unauthorized disclosure.

The dissenting judge in *Snider* believed that each statement the IRS agent made constituted a single act of disclosure, regardless of how many people heard the statement:

> I would find that § 7431(c)(1)(A) limits the statutory damages for disclosures to the number of specific acts of disclosure. When there are no actual damages, the number of violations for purposes of determining statutory damages is based on "each act of unauthorized inspection or disclosure of a return or return information with respect to which such defendant is found liable." 26 U.S.C. § 7431(c)(1)(A) (emphasis added). A statement by a special agent is a single "act," regardless of the number of people who hear the statement or the number of separate items of return information included in the statement. Even if one oral disclosure is heard by numerous people, it is still one "act" of disclosure. *Siddiqui v. United States*, 359 F.3d 1200, 1202–03 (9th Cir. 2004) (holding that an oral disclosure to 100 people did not equal 100 disclosures). . . .
>
> Under the Court's expansive reading of the statute, the statutory damages for a single act of disclosure could result in an unimaginable windfall to a taxpayer for a disclosure disseminated to a large number of recipients over the internet, television, or radio. For instance, a single disclosure of a taxpayer's return information to one million people on national television would result in $1,000,000,000 in statutory damages. This surely was not the result Congress intended when it provided for statutory damages of $1,000 per act of improper disclosure in the absence of actual damages. The Court's concern that counting only the agent's "act" would "nullify the language 'in any manner whatever' " and not adequately "track culpability and injury" is unfounded. . . . The statute provides for actual damages where dissemination to multiple listeners or of multiple items of return information results in more substantial injury. Because a taxpayer can use evidence of widespread dissemination to prove actual damages, there is no disproportionality to culpability or injury. The taxpayer is free to prove that the disclosure resulted in actual damages to the extent that actual damages exceed the statutory damage amount of $1,000 for the act of improper disclosure.

Id. at 516–17.

The IRS's nonacquiesence in *Snider* also took issue with how the court had calculated damages. A.O.D. 2007-03, 2007-30 I.R.B. 4 ("The Eighth Circuit's holding creates the anomalous result that mentioning two items of return information in a conversation constitutes two acts of disclosure, but disclosing an entire tax return only constitutes a single act of disclosure.") How would the majority in *Snider* calculate the damages the plaintiff in *Ward* suffered when the IRS agent disclosed her return information during a live radio talk show with approximately 3,200 to 3,300 listeners?

In addition to civil liability under section 7431, the statute makes unauthorized disclosure of a return or return information by an IRS employee a felony and imposes a fine of up to $5,000 a jail term of up to five years, or both. I.R.C. § 7213. It is also a felony, subject to the same penalties, for other persons who obtain return information under the auspices of section 6103 (for example, state employees, one percent shareholders of a corporation) to disclose that information to unauthorized parties. I.R.C. § 7213(a)(2)–(5). Somewhat reduced criminal penalties (a $1,000 fine/one year of imprisonment) may apply in the case of unauthorized inspection by IRS employees of return information. I.R.C. § 7213A.

§ 6.04 THE TENSION BETWEEN FOIA AND SECTION 6103

Section 6103, as it applies to FOIA requests made by taxpayers for tax return information, has been used by the IRS as a shield against disclosure. This interrelationship between the FOIA disclosure statute and the section 6103 confidentiality statute has led to disagreement over which statutory provision should take precedence over the other and, more broadly, whether privacy concerns or the public's right of access to information should control the analysis. From a policy standpoint, should section 6103 preempt FOIA when it comes to releasing a taxpayer's return or return information or should section 6103 merely implement FOIA Exemption 3?

The preemption question raises a number of issues, including the standard of review a court should apply when reviewing the IRS's refusal to release information that otherwise falls within the auspices of section 6103. As noted above, a district court reviewing a denial of a FOIA request does so on a *de novo* basis. Conversely, if section 6103 takes priority over FOIA with regard to disclosure of tax return information, the district court would be limited to a determination of whether the IRS's decision to withhold documents was arbitrary or an abuse of discretion. *Compare* Zale Corp. v. Internal Revenue Service, 481 F. Supp. 486 (D.D.C. 1979) (section 6103 is the sole standard governing the release of returns and return information), *with* Grasso v. Internal Revenue Service, 785 F.2d 70 (3d Cir. 1986) ("It is thus evident that section 6103 was not designed to displace FOIA."); *see also* White v. Internal Revenue Service, 707 F.2d 897 (6th Cir. 1983).

Because of the abuse of discretion standard of review, the IRS would generally prefer that section 6103 take precedence over FOIA. The Joint Committee on Taxation made such a recommendation to Congress as part of a study into the confidentiality and disclosure provisions relating to tax administration. *See* Volume I, Joint Committee on Taxation, Study of Present-Law Taxpayer Confidentiality and Disclosure Provisions as Required by Section 3802 of the Internal Revenue Service Restructuring and Reform Act of 1998 (2000). The recommendation suggested that section 6103 become the sole means by which returns and return information could be requested. The Joint Committee explained the recommendation as follows:

> While the courts have tried to harmonize section 6103 and the FOIA through FOIA exemption 3, it is an imperfect fit. The purpose of the FOIA is to provide information about agency operations. In contrast, the purpose of section 6103 is to maintain the confidentiality of returns and return information of a taxpayer. The FOIA provides information to the general public without a showing of need. The intended use of the information or the requester's identity generally has no bearing on who has access to agency records under the FOIA. On the other hand, section 6103 only permits disclosure of returns and return information if the person seeking the information meets certain criteria. Thus under section 6103, examining the identity of the person requesting returns or return information is a prerequisite to disclosure.
>
> The core purpose of the FOIA is to contribute significantly to public understanding of the operations or activities of the government. Taxpayer representatives often use the FOIA as an alternate means to obtain information the IRS has collected in building its case against their clients. Very little, if any, information about IRS operations, however, is gleaned from the release of a specific taxpayer's return or return information in response to a FOIA request.

The disclosure of returns and return information of specific taxpayers is not consistent with the main purpose of FOIA.

* * *

The staff of the Joint Committee recognizes that the FOIA has several important administrative provisions that are not contained in section 6103. These include response time limitations and administrative appeal of the IRS decision to withhold documents. The FOIA also affords a requester the opportunity for *de novo* judicial review by a U.S. District Court. The staff of the Joint Committee recommends that these provisions should be incorporated into section 6103. This will provide persons seeking disclosure of returns and return information with the same administrative protections and remedies currently available to them under FOIA.

Do you agree with the Joint Committee's statement that little information about the IRS's operations has been gleaned from the release of a specific taxpayer's return information in response to a FOIA request? What about the FOIA litigation in *Tax Analysts & Advocates v. Internal Revenue Service*, 362 F. Supp. 1298 (D.D.C. 1973), *modified*, 505 F.2d 350 (D.C. Cir. 1974), and *Fruehauf Corp. v. Internal Revenue Service*, 522 F.2d 284 (6th Cir. 1975), *vacated on other grounds*, 429 U.S. 1085 (1977), which led to the release of private letter rulings and technical advice memoranda? Would these actions have been heard by the courts if the preemption recommended by the Joint Committee had actually been in place?

A few months after the release of the Joint Committee study, the House of Representatives unanimously passed the Taxpayer Bill of Rights 2000, H.R. 4163, which incorporated the Joint Committee's recommendation concerning section 6103's preemption over FOIA. The bill was not introduced in the Senate. The House drafters described the bill as simply a clarification of existing law and not a substantive change.[21] Some Circuit Courts of Appeal (including the First, Third, Fifth, Ninth, Tenth, and Eleventh) might be surprised to hear of this "clarification," having held that section 6103 is an Exemption 3 statute under FOIA. *See, e.g.*, Aronson v. Internal Revenue Service, 973 F.2d 962 (1st Cir. 1992); *Grasso, supra*; Chamberlain v. Kurtz, 589 F.2d 827 (5th Cir. 1979); Williamette Indus. v. United States, 689 F.2d 865 (9th Cir. 1982); DeSalvo v. Internal Revenue Service, 861 F.2d 1217 (10th Cir. 1988); Currie v. Internal Revenue Service, 704 F.2d 523 (11th Cir. 1983).

PROBLEMS

1. Sally runs a housekeeping business called Hire-a-Maid. She has heard a rumor that her competitor, Maid-for-Hire Corporation, has been in litigation with the IRS over the question of the corporation's treatment of its maids as employees rather than independent contractors. Unaware that she can obtain copies of judicial decisions at the local law library, Sally files a FOIA request with the IRS to obtain copies of all regular Tax Court decisions in which Maid-for-Hire was the petitioner. She hopes to use the information she receives to spread negative rumors about her competitor. Can Sally use FOIA to obtain access to those Tax Court decisions from the IRS? If the IRS denies her request, what remedies might she have to compel the agency to release the records?
2. Jerry is having a dispute with his neighbor Newman. Believing that Newman is not reporting all his income, Jerry makes a FOIA request to the IRS seeking a copy of Newman's income tax returns filed during the previous five years. Must the IRS disclose copies of Newman's returns to Jerry?

---

[21] The bill did not incorporate the procedural protections and remedies that are now available to the requesting party only through a FOIA request.

3. Pauline and Roy, a married couple, filed a joint return last year. They have subsequently separated. Pauline asked Roy for a copy of the couple's return, but he has refused to give her one. If Pauline submits a request to the IRS under FOIA for a copy of the return, must the IRS disclose it to her?

4. Clara is requesting a letter ruling on behalf of a corporate client. Her client is concerned that the letter ruling will be made public under FOIA and that competitors will find out that the company is engaging in the transaction in question. How can Clara reassure her client?

5. Patrick represents a celebrity client who is concerned that IRS employees might look through her tax returns out of curiosity about her private life. Can Patrick provide his client any measure of assurance that this will not happen?

6. Janine was convicted of tax fraud, and the IRS issued a press release publicizing the conviction. All of the information in the press release was correct, including Janine's full name, the name of her employer, and the counts on which she was convicted. The IRS employee who drafted the press release obtained the information about Janine's conviction from notes the employee took while viewing the criminal trial. The local newspaper in the area in which Janine lives published the press release.

   A. Does Janine have a viable cause of action against the federal government for wrongful disclosure?

   B. If the local newspaper has a circulation of 50,000, what would be the measure of damages that Janine might be entitled to receive?

7. You represent Alan Wright, a client whose return was recently audited. The IRS has issued a 30-day letter proposing a $10,000 deficiency in Alan's income tax liability for Year 1. You did not represent Alan during the course of the examination and thus do not have copies of transcripts of interviews Alan gave to the revenue agent. In an effort to advise Alan properly about whether he should protest the proposed deficiency on a docketed or nondocketed basis, you would like to see copies of the interview transcripts. Draft a FOIA request to the IRS for these transcripts, as well as any other documents the IRS collected or generated in connection with the examination of Alan's return. Alan's Social Security number is 215-55-0955. He resides at 507 Oakwood Boulevard, Falls Church, Virginia 22043.

Chapter 7
RESTRICTIONS ON ASSESSMENT OF TAX

§ 7.01 INTRODUCTION

Reading Assignment: I.R.C. §§ 6203, 6303(a).

"Assessment" is merely the IRS's formal recording of a tax liability. *See* I.R.C. § 6203. In essence, it is nothing more than a bookkeeping entry. However, assessment is a key act; the IRS cannot legally collect tax through its administrative collection powers without first assessing it.[1] As discussed in Chapter 14, the IRS's lien and levy powers depend on a notice and demand for payment, *see* I.R.C. §§ 6321, 6331(a), the issuance of which, in turn, cannot be made prior to assessment, *see* I.R.C. § 6303(a). This chapter discusses the various types of assessments, the statutes of limitations on assessment of tax, and the statutory mitigation provisions, which, in certain circumstances, can allow reopening of a year closed by the statute of limitations.

§ 7.02 TYPES OF ASSESSMENTS

Reading Assignment: I.R.C. §§ 6201(a)(1), 6213(a).

Assessment takes place once an IRS officer signs a summary record of assessment (Form 23C) containing identifying information about the taxpayer and the character and amount of the tax liability. Treas. Reg. § 301.6203-1. There are four main types of assessments: summary assessments, deficiency assessments, jeopardy assessments, and termination assessments. The IRS can summarily assess an admitted tax liability, such as the amount a taxpayer reflects in the tax return for the year. Deficiency assessments require that the IRS first send the taxpayer a timely notice of deficiency, and give the taxpayer the period required by statute, generally 90 days, to petition the Tax Court. I.R.C. § 6213(a).

For reasons discussed more fully below, the procedures leading to assessment and collection of a deficiency may take months or even years to complete. Although these procedures are designed to give taxpayers a means of contesting the IRS's proposed assessment before collection proceedings begin, taxpayers may be tempted to utilize these delays to avoid paying tax that is properly owed. The interest provisions, discussed in Chapter 13, reduce this incentive but may not eliminate it. Therefore, Code sections 6851 and 6861 allow for immediate assessment where the IRS believes that assessment or collection of the tax will be jeopardized by delay. Section 6851 further allows the IRS to terminate the taxpayer's tax year mid-year. Procedures for summary, deficiency, jeopardy, and termination assessments are discussed in further detail below.

[A] Summary Assessments

Most tax receipts are assessed based on a taxpayer's "voluntarily" submitted tax return. Code section 6201(a)(1) authorizes the IRS to summarily (immediately) assess and collect any tax shown to be due on a taxpayer's original tax return, as well as any

---

[1] In a recent opinion, the Supreme Court stated, "Under a proper understanding of the function and nature of an assessment, it is clear that it is *the tax* that is assessed, not the taxpayer." United States v. Galletti, 541 U.S. 114, 123 (2004) (emphasis in original). That case involved an assessment of tax against a partnership, which the Court found sufficient to extend the collection statute of limitations; the tax did not need also to be assessed against the partners.

additional taxes shown to be due on a subsequently filed amended return.[2] The summary assessment procedure does not require the IRS to send the taxpayer a notice of deficiency. Professor Bryan Camp explains:

> The summary procedure is the general rule, authorized by section 6201. All other assessment procedures are either statutory or administrative exceptions to the summary assessment process. It is called the summary procedure because the IRS simply and summarily records the taxpayer's liability, payments, and credits, based on the information before it, and then notifies the taxpayer if there is a balance due. The most typical example is when the IRS makes an assessment based on the taxpayer's return, such as the Form 1040 for income taxes or the Form 941 for employment taxes. The form might also be generated by an IRS employee.

Bryan T. Camp, *The Mysteries of Erroneous Refunds*, 114 TAX NOTES 231, 234 (2007).

The IRS may also use its summary assessment authority in other instances. If the taxpayer waives the statutory restrictions on deficiency assessment — by filing Form 870, for example — or otherwise fails to take advantage of the deficiency procedures within the time period specified in the Code, the IRS may immediately assess the tax and proceed with collection activities. I.R.C. § 6213(c), (d).

In addition, the Code authorizes the IRS to summarily assess any additional tax due as a result of a mathematical or clerical error made by the taxpayer on the return. However, before so doing, the IRS must notify the taxpayer of the alleged error and include an explanation of the basis for recomputation. The taxpayer is given 60 days from the date the notice of assessment is sent to contest the error by filing a request for an abatement of the assessment. Whether or not the IRS agrees with the taxpayer's position, it must abate the proposed summary assessment upon receipt of the request. At that point, any attempt by the IRS to reassess the tax must be made pursuant to the deficiency procedures. I.R.C. § 6213(b). The statute defines a "mathematical or clerical error" to include arithmetic errors, inconsistent entries on the return, omissions of information necessary to properly substantiate a return item, and deductions or credits that exceed limits provided in the Code. I.R.C. § 6213(g)(2).

[B] General Restrictions on Deficiency Assessments

Reading Assignment: I.R.C. §§ 6212(a), 7421(a).

Before assessing a deficiency in income, estate, or gift taxes,[3] and before assessing most penalties, the IRS must first send the taxpayer a "notice of deficiency" or "statutory notice," provided for in Code section 6212.[4] The formal requirements of a notice of deficiency (also called a 90-day letter) are discussed in more detail in Chapter 9.

---

[2] Chapter 10 considers the question of whether the IRS is legally obligated to refund to the taxpayer a voluntary remittance of tax made while the statute of limitations was open but never formally assessed before the statute expired.

[3] At a very general level, a "deficiency" is the difference between tax reported and tax due. *See* I.R.C. § 6211(a).

[4] A fundamental element of the deficiency procedures is the right afforded the taxpayer to seek judicial review (in the Tax Court) prior to assessment. In other cases — most commonly employment taxes imposed under Subtitle C of the Code — the IRS can immediately assess tax without a notice of deficiency and without granting the taxpayer the opportunity for pre-assessment judicial review. Once employment taxes have been assessed, the taxpayer's sole remedy is to follow the refund procedures in order to recover the previously paid tax. Certain types of civil tax penalties, including the preparer and information reporting penalties, also may be assessed by the IRS without regard to the deficiency procedures.

Once the IRS sends the taxpayer a notice of deficiency, it cannot assess the tax during the 90-day period (or 150-day period, if applicable) following the mailing of the notice (commonly called the "prohibited period"). I.R.C. § 6213(a). This assessment delay gives the taxpayer an opportunity to contest the deficiency by petitioning the Tax Court, which is the only court that grants taxpayers pre-assessment review. If the taxpayer petitions the Tax Court, the "prohibited period" lasts until the Tax Court's decision becomes final.[5] *Id.* If the IRS violates this prohibition, the taxpayer can obtain an injunction and a refund of any tax collected, as this is a stated exception to the Anti-Injunction Act (Code section 7421). *See* I.R.C. §§ 6213(a); 7421.

> *Example:* The IRS mails Blake a notice of deficiency on Thursday, March 1. It is sent to his last known address in Chicago, Illinois. Blake receives the notice on Monday, March 5. Unless Blake signs a Form 870 permitting immediate assessment of the deficiency, the IRS is prohibited from assessing the deficiency until Thursday, May 31, because Blake has until May 30 to petition the Tax Court. If Blake petitions the Tax Court, the IRS cannot assess any deficiency determined by the Tax Court until after the Tax Court's decision becomes final.

[C] Jeopardy and Termination Assessments

Reading Assignment: I.R.C. §§ 6851(a)(1), (4), (b), 6861(a)–(b); skim I.R.C. § 7429(a)–(b).

Section 6861 allows for immediate assessment where the IRS believes that assessment or collection of the tax will be jeopardized by delay. The IRS will then send notice and demand for payment, I.R.C. § 6861(a), and if it has not already sent a notice of deficiency, the IRS must mail one to the taxpayer within 60 days of the assessment, I.R.C. § 6861(b). Treasury regulations set forth the most commonly encountered conditions under which a jeopardy assessment may be made: (1) the IRS believes the taxpayer is designing to depart quickly from the United States or to conceal himself or herself; (2) the IRS believes the taxpayer is planning to quickly place his or her property beyond the reach of the government by concealing the property, dissipating it, transferring it to other persons, or removing it from the country; or (3) the IRS believes the taxpayer's financial solvency is imperiled. *See* Treas. Reg. § 301.6861-1 (referring to the conditions described in Treas. Reg. § 1.6851-1).

For these same reasons, the IRS may make a termination assessment against the taxpayer pursuant to section 6851. For the most part, the procedures relating to jeopardy and termination assessments are the same. A jeopardy assessment is employed when a deficiency is determined by the IRS after the end of the taxable year to which the assessment relates. A termination assessment, in contrast, is utilized when collection is put in jeopardy before the taxpayer's taxable year has ended. As its name implies, a termination assessment terminates the taxable year for the purpose of computing the amount of tax to be assessed and collected. Section 6851(b) requires the IRS to mail the taxpayer a notice of deficiency for the full taxable year within 60 days of the later of the due date of the taxpayer's return or the date the return is filed.

Under the Code, the Chief Counsel of the IRS or his delegate must approve, in writing, any jeopardy or termination assessment. I.R.C. § 7429(a)(1)(A). Because of the drastic consequences resulting from these types of assessments, Congress enacted an expedited administrative and judicial review process. *See* I.R.C. § 7429. Code section 7429 requires the IRS, within five days of making such an assessment, to provide the taxpayer with a written statement of the information on which the IRS relied in making

---

[5] In general, a Tax Court decision becomes final when the time for all appeals has run. *See* I.R.C. § 7481. However, assessment and collection are not stayed during a taxpayer's appeal unless the taxpayer files a bond. *See* I.R.C. § 7485.

the assessment or levy. I.R.C. § 7429(a)(1)(B). The taxpayer then has 30 days to request administrative review. I.R.C. § 7429(a)(2). Section 7429(b) provides for expedited follow-up judicial review in the United States district courts. In these proceedings, the IRS bears the burden of establishing that it acted reasonably. I.R.C. § 7429(g). The taxpayer also has the option of filing a bond to stay collection. *See* I.R.C. § 6863.

§ 7.03 THE STATUTES OF LIMITATIONS ON ASSESSMENT OF TAX

[A] General Rules

Reading Assignment: I.R.C. § 6501(a).

Section 6501 contains the statutory periods for assessing tax. The general rule is that the IRS must assess tax within three years of when the return was filed.[6] I.R.C. § 6501(a). The date of assessment is the date that the assessment officer signs the summary record of assessment. Treas. Reg. § 301.6203-1. To confirm that date, the taxpayer may request a copy of the summary record, which section 6203 requires the IRS to furnish.

[B] Return Filing Date

Reading Assignment: I.R.C. §§ 6501(b)(1), 7502(a)–(d), 7503.

Because filing a return commences the running of the statute of limitations under section 6501, it is important to know what constitutes a return, and when that return is deemed filed. What constitutes a "return" for purposes of section 6501 is discussed in Chapter 3 in connection with the *Beard* case, and in this chapter in the *Badaracco* case, reproduced below.

For purposes of section 6501, an early return is deemed filed on its due date. I.R.C. § 6501(b)(1). For example, the statute of limitations on a Year 1 return, which was due April 15, Year 2, and was actually filed on April 2, Year 2, would expire on April 15, Year 5.[7] An amended return filed after the due date, although it modifies or adds to the original return, generally has no effect on the period of limitations.[8] Thus, when an original return is subsequently amended, the statute of limitations normally begins to run from the date the original return was filed, not from the date the amended return was filed. Zellerbach Paper Co. v. Helvering, 293 U.S. 172 (1934).

---

[6] If a partnership or S corporation is audited pursuant to the TEFRA procedures specified in section 6229, the statute of limitations for assessing tax against a partner or S corporation shareholder with respect to an item of income or deduction generated at the entity level is calculated based on the time the entity files its information return. I.R.C. § 6229(a)(1). If the unified audit procedures do not apply, the statute of limitations is based on the time the individual equity holder files his own return. *See* I.R.C. § 6501. For example, assume that a calendar-year partnership files its Year 1 information return on March 1, Year 2. An individual partner in the partnership does not file an individual return reporting his or her share of the partnership's income for Year 1 until April 15, Year 2. The limitations period with respect to that individual's share of partnership items begins to run on April 16, not March 2.

[7] If April 15, Year 5 is a Saturday, Sunday, or legal holiday, the statute will expire on the next business day. I.R.C. § 7503.

[8] However, when a taxpayer files an amended return reflecting additional income tax liability within 60 days before the last date for assessment, the IRS is granted an additional 60 days beyond the applicable limitations period in which to assess tax. I.R.C. § 6501(c)(7).

The filing date of a return is generally the date on which the return is delivered to the IRS.[9] However Code section 7502, which allows a taxpayer who properly mails his or her return to rely on the postmark date as the date of delivery, applies to determine the date of filing if the return arrives after the due date.[10] Hotel Equities Corp. v. Commissioner, 65 T.C. 528 (1975), *aff'd*, 546 F.2d 725 (1976). If the return is mailed late, section 7502 cannot operate, so the return is not considered filed until it is actually received by the IRS.

> *Example:* Tara mails her return to the IRS on Friday, April 15, and it arrives on Monday, April 18. Because Tara mailed her return on time but it arrived late, her return is deemed filed on April 15, assuming she complied with the mailing requirements of section 7502. If, instead, Tara had mailed her return on Monday, April 18, and it had arrived on Thursday, April 21, her return would have been deemed filed on April 21.

There is currently some question about what method of mailing a taxpayer must use in order to benefit from Code section 7502:

> [S]ection 7502(c) provides that for documents sent by U.S. registered mail, the registration is prima facie evidence that the document was delivered to the IRS and that the date of registration is deemed the postmark date. Also, section 7502(e)(2) permits the IRS to treat certified mail as prima facie evidence of timely filing. Therefore, if a document is sent by certified mail and is postmarked by the postal employee to whom the document is presented, the date of the U.S. postmark on the receipt is treated as the postmark date. Specifically, reg. section 301.7502-1(c)(2) provides:
>
> > If the document is sent by United States registered mail, the date of registration of the document shall be treated as the postmark date. If the document is sent by United States certified mail and the sender's receipt is postmarked by the postal employee to whom such document is presented, the date of the United States postmark on such receipt shall be treated as the postmark date of the document. Accordingly, the risk that the document will not be postmarked on the day that it is deposited in the mail may be overcome by the use of registered mail or certified mail.
>
> Reg. section 301.7502-1(1)(e)(1) then states that certified as well as registered mail is prima facie evidence of filing* * *.
>
> * * *
>
> Although the IRS has consistently taken the position that registered or certified mail is the exclusive means to prove the filing of a tax return or other document to the IRS, some courts have permitted other evidence to establish the time of the posting (and therefore delivery) of the document to the IRS. Thus, for example, in *Estate of Wood v. Commissioner*, the Eighth Circuit held that taxpayers may present evidence other than registered or certified mail to prove that a tax return was filed on a certain date. Other courts, however, have

[9] Note that the Document Locator Number (DLN) stamped on a document such as a return can provide information about when the IRS received it because the DLN contains a "Julian date" that uses a unique number from 1 to 365 (366 for a leap year) for each day of the year. *See* Hale E. Sheppard, *Little-Known IRS Notation May Establish Tax Return, Filing Date*, 78 Prac. Tax Strategies 4 (Jan. 2007).

[10] For example, in *Natalie Holdings, Ltd. v. United States*, 2003-1 U.S.T.C. ¶ 50,233 (W.D. Tex. 2003), the tax matters partner in a partnership proceeding argued that the statute of limitations had expired prior to the date on which the IRS had mailed the Final Partnership Administrative Adjustment (FPAA). The IRS had mailed the FPAA to the tax matters partner on September 7, 2001. The returns in question were due, under valid extensions, on October 15, 1998. They were mailed on September 3, 1998 and delivered on September 10, 1998. The District Court found that, because the returns were timely, section 7502, by its terms, did not apply. The returns had therefore been filed on September 10, 1998, and the September 7, 2001 FPAA was timely.

held that registered or certified mail is the only means to prove when a tax document was filed.* * *

Noting the conflict among the circuits as to whether section 7502 provides the exclusive means to establish prima facie evidence of delivery of a document to the IRS or Tax Court, the IRS, on September 21, 2004, released the following amendment to the end of reg. section 301.7502-1(e)(1):

> Other than direct proof of actual delivery, proof of proper use of registered or certified mail is the exclusive means to establish prima facie evidence of delivery of a document to the agency, officer, or office with which the document is required to be filed. No other evidence of a postmark or of mailing will be prima facie evidence of delivery or raise a presumption that the document was delivered.

Also, prop. reg. section 301.7502-1(g)(4) states that when finalized, the above amendment making registered or certified mail the exclusive means to prove delivery absent proof of actual delivery will apply retroactively to all documents mailed after September 21, 2004. In the preamble to the proposed regulation, the IRS explained that making the effective date of the proposed rule effective before the rule itself is finalized was appropriate because the IRS currently accepts only a registered or certified mail receipt to establish a presumption of delivery if the IRS has no record of ever having received the document in question. Accordingly, the IRS reasoned that because the proposed regulation merely "clarify and confirm" current IRS practice, the effective date of the regulation should be September 21, 2004, even though it might be many months before the rule itself is finalized.

Donald T. Williamson & A. Blair Staley, *Are the Proposed Timely Mailing/Timely Filing Regulations Timely?*, 108 TAX NOTES 597, 598–99 (2005) (footnotes omitted).[11]

In addition to section 7502, section 7503, relating to due dates falling on a Saturday, Sunday, or legal holiday, may also apply to determine the date on which the return was filed. Assume, for example, that April 15, the required filing date for individual calendar-year taxpayers, falls on a Saturday. Pursuant to section 7503, the taxpayer's return would still be considered timely if filed on Monday, April 17. Assume that the taxpayer mails a return from the Post Office on Saturday, April 15, and it arrives on April 18, so it is deemed filed on April 15 under section 7502. In the latter case, for purposes of calculating the statute of limitations under section 6501, does the three-year period begin to run on April 15 or April 17? The following Revenue Ruling addresses that question.

REVENUE RULING 81-269

1981-2 C.B. 243

ISSUE

When will the period of limitation for assessment of tax expire in the following situations?

FACTS

Situation 1. A, an individual taxpayer, files his or her federal income tax return on a calendar year basis. A filed the return for 1978 with the Internal Revenue Service on March 1, 1979.

---

[11] Copyright © 2005 Tax Analysts, Donald T. Williamson and A. Blair Staley. All rights reserved. Reprinted by permission.

Situation 2. B, an individual taxpayer, also files on a calendar year basis. B filed the return for 1978 on Monday, April 16, 1979.

LAW AND ANALYSIS

Section 6072(a) provides that individual income tax returns made on the basis of the calendar year must be filed on or before April 15 of the following year.

Section 6501(a) of the Code provides the general rule that tax must be assessed within 3 years after the return was filed.

Section 6501(b)(1) of the Code provides that, for purposes of section 6501, a return filed before the last day prescribed by the Code or regulations is considered as filed on the last day.

Section 7503 of the Code provides that when the last day for performing any act falls on a Saturday, Sunday, or legal holiday, performance of the act is considered timely if it is performed on the next day that is not a Saturday, Sunday, or legal holiday.

The purpose of section 7503 of the Code is to extend the time for filing a document when the last day for filing is a Saturday, Sunday, or legal holiday. Section 7503 does not change the date prescribed for performing an act, nor does it provide that an act performed on the day following a Saturday, Sunday, or legal holiday will be deemed to have been performed on the actual due date. Rev. Rul. 75-344, 1975-2 C.B. 487.

In *Situation 1,* section 7503 of the Code does not operate to change the "date prescribed for filing" to April 16. Accordingly, because an early return is deemed filed on the date prescribed for filing the return, which remains April 15, 1979, the period of limitations under section 6501(a) starts running from April 15.

In *Situation 2,* while the return filed on April 16 is considered timely filed under section 7503 of the Code, it is not deemed to have been filed on April 15. In this case, the period of limitations under section 6501(a) starts running from the actual date of filing, or April 16. *See* Brown v. United States, 391 F.2d 653 (Ct. Cl. 1968).

HOLDINGS

Situation 1. The period of limitation for assessment of tax (or mailing of the notice of deficiency) will expire April 15, 1982.

Situation 2. The period of limitation for assessment of tax (or mailing of the notice of deficiency) will expire April 16, 1982.

Note that section 7503 may apply to the *expiration* of the statute of limitations, as well. That is, if the last day of the statute of limitations on assessment were to fall on a Saturday, Sunday, or legal holiday, section 7503 of the Code would operate to extend that period to the next day that is not a Saturday, Sunday, or legal holiday.

In *Estate of Mitchell v. Commissioner,* 250 F.3d 696 (9th Cir. 2001),[12] a case involving the valuation of stock held by the estate of hair stylist Paul Mitchell, the Estate had received a six-month extension of time to file its estate tax return, postponing the filing deadline from January 21, 1990 to July 21, 1990. In 1990, July 21 fell on a Saturday. The Estate actually mailed the return on Friday, July 20, 1990, and it arrived at the IRS on Monday, July 23, 1990.

Both the Tax Court and the Court of Appeals for the Ninth Circuit held section 7502 inapplicable because the fact that the filing deadline would otherwise end on a Saturday rendered section 7503 applicable to extend the deadline to Monday, July 23, 1990. As

---

[12] Much of *Estate of Mitchell* is reproduced in Chapter 9 in connection with its discussion of arbitrary notices of deficiency.

discussed above, section 7502 only applies when a timely mailed document arrives *late*. Under the courts' analysis, the return arrived on time, and therefore was deemed filed on the date it was *received*, Monday, July 23, 1990. The IRS mailed its notice of deficiency to the Estate on July 21, 1993. Was it timely? What if the Estate's return, mailed on Friday, July 20, 1990, had arrived at the IRS on Tuesday, July 24, 1990 — would a notice of deficiency mailed to the Estate on July 21, 1993 have been timely?

[C] Exceptions to the Three-Year Statutory Period

Reading assignment: I.R.C. § 6501(c)(10).

Although the general limitations period on assessment of tax is three years, there are several exceptions to that general rule.[13] A number of the exceptions are discussed below.

[1] Request for Prompt Assessment

Reading assignment: I.R.C. § 6501(d).

Under section 6501(d), the executor of an estate or a liquidating corporation may make a "request for prompt assessment" that will shorten the limitations period to 18 months. In the case of an estate, the prompt assessment procedures apply to any tax (other than estate tax) for which a return is required and for which the decedent or the estate may be liable. An executor might request prompt assessment in order to close the estate before making distributions to the beneficiaries. A corporation that has dissolved or is being dissolved will request prompt assessment for the benefit of its shareholders or, if it has been the target of an acquisition, the acquiring corporation. The procedural prerequisites for a request for prompt assessment are in section 6501(d).

[2] Substantial Omission of Items

Reading assignment: I.R.C. § 6501(e)(1)–(2).

Statutory limitations periods longer than three years apply in certain cases. Under section 6501(e), if the return reflects a "substantial omission of items," a six-year period applies. A "substantial omission of items" includes an omission "from gross income [of] an amount properly includible therein which is in excess of 25 percent of the amount of gross income stated in the return," I.R.C. § 6501(e)(1)(A).[14]

According to the Supreme Court, the six-year period under section 6501(e) does not apply unless an *entire item* is omitted. *See* The Colony, Inc. v. Commissioner, 357 U.S. 28 (1958). The deficiencies in *The Colony, Inc.* arose out of a determination that the taxpayer had understated the amount of its realized gain resulting from the sale of certain lots. The understatement resulted from the taxpayer's overstatement of its adjusted basis in the lots by including unallowable development costs in the basis. The Tax Court held that the extended statute of limitations under section 6501(e) applied,

---

[13] Section 6501 also contains subsections relating to various specialized limitations periods that are not further discussed in this chapter, such as limitations periods applicable to holding companies and foreign tax credits.

[14] The IRS has stated in a legal memorandum that to compute the amount of gross income in a tax return for purposes of Code section 6501(e), capital gains are included, and they are not reduced by capital losses. ILM 200609024, *available at* 2006 TNT 43-26 (Mar. 6, 2006). An article criticizes the legal memorandum for not citing *The Colony, Inc.*, and argues that it "ignores that there must be an omission, which is not merely a computational matter." M. Todd Welty, et al., *Tax Shelters and the Six-Year Statute of Limitations: "Omission of Gross Income" and* The Colony *Revisited*, 8 J. TAX PRAC. & PROC. 33, 35 (2006).

taking "the view that the statutory language, 'omits from gross income an amount properly includible therein,' embraced not merely the omission from a return of an item of income received by or accruing to a taxpayer, but also an understatement of gross income resulting from a taxpayer's miscalculation of profits through the erroneous inclusion of an excessive item of cost." The Supreme Court took a different view:

> The Commissioner also suggests that in enacting § 275(c) [currently I.R.C. § 6501(e) — Eds.] Congress was primarily concerned with providing for a longer period of limitations where returns contained relatively large errors adversely affecting the Treasury, and that effect can be given this purpose only by adopting the Government's broad construction of the statute. But this theory does not persuade us. For if the mere size of the error had been the principal concern of Congress, one might have expected to find the statute cast in terms of errors in the total tax due or in total taxable net income. We have been unable to find any solid support for the Government's theory in the legislative history. Instead, * * * this history shows to our satisfaction that the Congress intended an exception to the usual three-year statute of limitations only in the restricted type of situation already described.
>
> We think that in enacting § 275(c) Congress manifested no broader purpose than to give the Commissioner an additional two [now three — Eds.] years to investigate tax returns in cases where, because of a taxpayer's omission to report some taxable item, the Commissioner is at a special disadvantage in detecting errors. In such instances the return on its face provides no clue to the existence of the omitted item. On the other hand, when, as here, the understatement of a tax arises from an error in reporting an item disclosed on the face of the return the Commissioner is at no such disadvantage. And this would seem to be so whether the error be one affecting "gross income" or one, such as overstated deductions, affecting other parts of the return. To accept the Commissioner's interpretation and to impose a five-year [now six-year — Eds.] limitation when such errors affect "gross income," but a three-year limitation when they do not, not only would be to read § 275(c) more broadly than is justified by the evident reason for its enactment, but also to create a patent incongruity in the tax law. * * *

The Colony, Inc., at 36–37.

Notice also section 6501(e)(1)(A)(ii), which provides that "[i]n determining the amount omitted from gross income, there shall not be taken into account any amount which is omitted from gross income stated in the return if such amount is disclosed in the return, or in a statement attached to the return, in a manner adequate to apprise the Secretary of the nature and amount of such item."

> The adequate disclosure test of § 6501(e) has been described differently by different courts. Some courts interpret the test as being whether the return provides a "clue" as to the omitted item. *See Benderoff v. U.S.*, 398 F.2d 132, 136 (8th Cir. 1968). Other courts interpret adequate disclosure to be more than "simply a clue which would be sufficient to intrigue a Sherlock Holmes," but less than "a detailed revelation of each and every underlying fact." *Quick Trust v. Comm'r*, 54 T.C. 1336, 1347 (U.S. Tax Ct. 1970) (internal quotation marks omitted). There are still other variations of the meaning of adequate disclosure.

Brandon Ridge Partners v. United States, 2007-2 U.S.T.C. ¶ 50,573 (M.D. Fla. 2007). In *Brandon Ridge Partners*, the court found that despite disclosure of several steps in a tax shelter transaction, the disclosure was inadequate where it did not reveal relevant basis adjustments and thus did not allow the IRS to determine the correct amount of capital gain on the sale of certain stock. *Id.*

Under *The Colony, Inc.*, what is the result if the taxpayer reports a receipt as gross income, but understates the amount of that receipt? Does or should the extended period apply under these circumstances? Why or why not? Would it change your answer if the omitted item were a portion of the taxpayer's gain on the sale of an asset because the taxpayer claimed an inflated basis in the item?

This last question is the source of some confusion. Code section 6501(e) hinges on an omission from gross income. That section further provides that, "in the case of a trade or business, the term 'gross income' means the total of the amounts received or accrued from the sale of goods or services (if such amounts are required to be shown on the return) *prior to diminution by the cost of such sales or services . . . ,*" I.R.C. § 6501(e)(1)(A)(i) (emphasis added). This language would seem to encompass basis in goods. *The Colony, Inc.* itself involved a sale of goods, and was decided in favor of the taxpayer, which might seem to resolve the issue, but it was decided under the 1939 Code, which did not contain the language quoted immediately above. However, in *The Colony, Inc.*, the Supreme Court addressed that language in dicta. It stated, "without doing more than noting the speculative debate between the parties as to whether Congress manifested an intention to clarify or to change the 1939 Code, we observe that the conclusion we reach is in harmony with the unambiguous language of § 6501(e)(1)(A) of the Internal Revenue Code of 1954," and quoted I.R.C. § 6501(e)(1)(A), including (A)(i). *The Colony, Inc.*, at 37.

Despite the Supreme Court's statement that its holding for the taxpayer was "in harmony with the unambiguous language of § 6501(e)(1)(A)," the IRS has taken the position that "gross income is determined after reducing sales proceeds by basis except in the case of a sale of a good or service; the sale of property used in a trade or business is not a sale of a good or service for such purposes." ILM 200537029, *available at* 2005 TNT 180-36 (Sept. 19, 2005); *see also* ILM 200628021, *available at* 2006 TNT 152-17 (Aug. 8, 2006). ILM 200628021 states in part, "I.R.C. section 6501 applies *Colony*'s gross receipts test only to trade or business income arising from the sale of a good or service. This partial definition implies that Congress did not intend the gross receipts test to apply to other types of income." *Id.* Does this make sense, given the Supreme Court's focus in *The Colony, Inc.* on whether the item appeared on the face of the return?

In *Bakersfield Energy Partners, LP v. Commissioner*, 128 T.C. 207 (2007), a case involving sales using overstated basis, the Tax Court disagreed with the IRS's position and held for the taxpayer on this issue, stating:

> We are unpersuaded by respondent's attempt to distinguish and diminish the Supreme Court's holding in *Colony, Inc. v. Commissioner*, 357 U.S. 28 . . . (1958). We do not believe that either the language or the rationale of *Colony, Inc.* can be limited to the sale of goods or services by a trade or business. As petitioners point out, the Supreme Court held that "omits" means something "left out" and not something put in and overstated.

Id. at 215; *see also* M. Todd Welty et al., *Tax Shelters and the Six-Year Statute of Limitations: "Omission of Gross Income" and* The Colony *Revisited*, 8 J. Tax Prac. & Proc. 33, 34 (2006) ("*The Colony* did not decide what constitutes 'gross income' — be that gain or gross receipts. Rather, *The Colony* stands for the proposition that, where gross receipts of a sale are fully disclosed, there is no 'omission' of income.").

If the six-year period does apply, does it apply only to the omitted item that triggered section 6501(e), or to the taxpayer's entire tax year? The Tax Court tackled that question in *Colestock*:

COLESTOCK v. COMMISSIONER

United States Tax Court
102 T.C. 380 (1994)

Panuthos, Chief Special Trial Judge:

This matter is before the Court on a motion for partial summary judgment filed by Stephen G. Colestock and Susan F. Colestock (petitioners). Petitioners seek partial summary judgment that an increased deficiency and related additions to tax asserted by respondent in an amendment to answer are time barred by virtue of the general 3-year period of limitations prescribed in section 6501(a).

The issue for decision concerns the scope of the 6-year period of limitations prescribed in section 6501(e)(1)(A). Specifically, we must decide whether section 6501(e)(1)(A) extends the assessment period with respect to a taxpayer's entire tax liability for a particular taxable year or whether the provision simply extends the period for assessment with respect to those items constituting a substantial omission of gross income.

* * *

BACKGROUND

On or about April 22, 1985, petitioners filed a joint Federal income tax return for the 1984 taxable year. Petitioners filed an amended return for 1984 on or about October 28, 1985.

By statutory notice of deficiency dated April 15, 1991, respondent determined deficiencies in and additions to petitioners' Federal income tax. * * * The deficiency in tax is attributable to respondent's determination that petitioners failed to report taxable income arising from transactions involving a corporation known as Hunter Industries, Inc.

Petitioners filed a timely petition for redetermination with this Court. The petition includes an affirmative allegation that respondent erred in issuing a deficiency notice to petitioners more than 3 years after the filing of petitioners' tax return for the 1984 taxable year. Respondent filed a timely answer to the petition, including therein an allegation that the 6-year period of limitations set forth in section 6501(e)(1)(A) is applicable in this case. Petitioners filed a reply to respondent's answer in which they allege that the 6-year period of limitations does not apply.

Respondent subsequently filed a motion for leave to file an amendment to answer out of time and lodged an amendment to answer with the Court. We granted respondent's motion for leave to file an amendment to answer out of time over petitioners' objection, and respondent's amendment to answer was filed. Respondent's amendment to answer includes allegations that petitioners are liable for an increased deficiency and additions to tax as the result of the disallowance of a portion of a depreciation deduction claimed on petitioners' 1984 return. Petitioners filed a reply to respondent's amendment to answer in which they deny the allegations set forth in the amendment to answer and allege that respondent is barred by the applicable period of limitations from claiming the increased deficiency.

In their motion for partial summary judgment, petitioners argue that the general 3-year period of limitations prescribed in section 6501(a) bars respondent from seeking the increased deficiency and additions to tax set forth in respondent's amendment to answer. In conjunction with this argument, petitioners maintain that respondent cannot rely on the 6-year period of limitations prescribed in section 6501(e)(1)(A) because that provision only applies to items of omitted gross income in excess of 25 percent of the amount of gross income reported in the particular return. Respondent objects to petitioners' motion for partial summary judgment asserting that the 6-year period of limitations does apply to the increased deficiency, notwithstanding that it is attributable to a disallowed depreciation deduction, so long as respondent can otherwise establish a substantial omission of gross income on petitioners' 1984 return.

DISCUSSION

* * *

In sum, respondent generally may claim an increased deficiency any time at or before trial in the Tax Court if such deficiency could have been included in the original notice of deficiency mailed to the taxpayer. Smith v. Commissioner, 925 F.2d 250, 254 (8th Cir. 1991), *affg.* T.C. Memo. 1989-432; Teitelbaum v. Commissioner, 346 F.2d 266, 267 (7th Cir. 1965), *affg.* T.C. Memo. 1964-141.

As indicated, petitioners assert that the increased deficiency and additions to tax set forth in respondent's amendment to answer could not have been included in the original deficiency notice that was mailed to petitioners almost 6 years after the filing of their 1984 return. In petitioners' view, a deficiency notice issued under the 6-year period of limitations prescribed in section 6501(e)(1)(A) may only include deficiencies in tax directly attributable to items constituting a substantial omission of gross income. Because the increased deficiency and related additions to tax that respondent asserts in her amendment to answer are attributable to the disallowance of a depreciation deduction (as opposed to an item of omitted gross income), petitioners contend that the 6-year period of limitations under section 6501(e)(1)(A) is not applicable and that respondent's determination with respect to the depreciation item is otherwise barred under section 6501(a). Respondent reads section 6501(e)(1)(A) more broadly.

* * *

Neither party cites a case involving the specific question presented.

As a preliminary matter, we observe that the parties' comparisons of the various provisions set forth in section 6501 result in conflicting, yet fairly plausible, interpretations of section 6501(e)(1)(A). Nonetheless, an analysis of the provision in conjunction with a review of its legislative history compels the conclusion that petitioners' interpretation must fail.

It has been said that limitations statutes barring the collection of taxes otherwise due and unpaid are strictly construed in favor of respondent. *See* Badaracco v. Commissioner, 464 U.S. 386, 391–392 (1984); *see also* Bufferd v. Commissioner, 506 U.S. [927], 113 S. Ct. 927, 930 n.6 (1993); Northern Ind. Pub. Serv. Co. v. Commissioner, 101 T.C. 294, 300 (1993); Estate of Smith v. Commissioner, 94 T.C. 872, 874 (1990). Further, it is a well-established rule of statutory construction that statutes are to be construed so as to give effect to their plain and ordinary meaning unless to do so would produce absurd or futile results. United States v. American Trucking Associations, 310 U.S. 534, 543–544 (1940).

* * *

Notably, the prefatory language of subsection (e)(1) provides that the provision covers "any tax imposed by subtitle A" — a reference to the Federal income tax. In this regard, we interpret the phrase "the tax may be assessed * * * at any time within 6 years after the return was filed" as referring to any tax imposed by subtitle A for the particular taxable year. Sec. 6501(e)(1)(A). In other words, if the taxpayer omits the requisite amount of gross income from his return, the taxpayer's entire tax liability for the particular taxable year is subject to the 6-year limitations period.

* * *

We reject petitioners' interpretation of section 6501(e)(1)(A) under which the phrase "the tax may be assessed" is read as referring solely to a deficiency in tax resulting from an omission of gross income from the return. In our view, Congress would have used more exacting language if petitioners' interpretation were intended. *Cf.* sec. 6501(h). In the absence of such exacting terms, we decline to otherwise limit the scope of section 6501(e)(1)(A).

Our interpretation of section 6501(e)(1)(A) finds support in the legislative history of the provision. Section 6501(e)(1)(A) was originally codified as section 275(c) under the Revenue Act of 1934, ch. 277, tit. I, 48 Stat. 680. As originally introduced in a preliminary report of a subcommittee of the House Committee on Ways and Means, however, a proposal was made to add the provision to then-existing section 276 of the Revenue Act of 1934. The preliminary report states in pertinent part:

> Section 276 provides for the assessment of the tax without regard to the statute of limitations in case of a failure to file a return or in case of a false or fraudulent return with intent to evade tax.
>
> Your subcommittee is of the opinion that the limitation period on assessments should also not apply to certain cases where the taxpayer has understated his gross income on his return by a large amount, even though fraud with intent to evade tax cannot be established. It is, therefore, recommended that the statute of limitations shall not apply where the taxpayer has failed to disclose in his return an amount of gross income in excess of 25 percent of the amount of the gross income stated in the return. The Government should not be penalized when a taxpayer is so negligent as to leave out items of such magnitude from his return. [Preliminary Report to the House Comm. on Ways and Means, 73d Cong., 2d Sess. 21 (Comm. Print 1933).]

* * *

The subcommittee's proposal was adopted by the House Committee on Ways and Means as reflected in H. Rept. 704, 73d Cong., 2d Sess. 35 (1934), which states:

> Section 276(a). No return or false return: The present law permits the Government to assess the tax without regard to the statute of limitations in case of failure to file a return or in case of a fraudulent return. The change in this section continues this policy, but enlarges the scope of this provision to include cases wherein the taxpayer understates gross income on his return by an amount which is in excess of 25 percent of the gross income stated in the return. It is not believed that taxpayers who are so negligent as to leave out of their returns items of such magnitude should be accorded the privilege of pleading the bar of the statute.

The Senate Committee on Finance took a slightly different approach to the issue as reflected in S. Rept. 558, 73d Cong., 2d Sess. 43–44 (1934), which states in pertinent part:

> Your committee is in general accord with the policy expressed in this section of the House bill. However, it is believed that in the case of a taxpayer who makes an honest mistake, it would be unfair to keep the statute open indefinitely. * * * Accordingly, your committee has provided for a 5-year statute[15] in such cases.

In sum, the Committee on Finance resolved that, in fairness to the taxpayer, the period of limitations should be held to 5 years as opposed to allowing the assessment period to stay open indefinitely. H. Conf. Rept. 1385, 73d Cong., 2d Sess. 25 (1939), 1939-2 C.B. (Part 2) 627, 634, reveals that the Committee on Ways and Means accepted the change proposed by the Senate.

Viewed in its entirety, the legislative history indicates that Congress intended for the extended period of limitations under former section 275(c) to apply broadly in the same general manner as in the case of a fraudulent return. * * * Neither [the statute's] text nor legislative history limits the scope of the statute as petitioners contend.

Based on the preceding discussion, we conclude that, if the 6-year period of limitations is otherwise applicable, respondent was not barred at the time of the issuance of the deficiency notice in this case from determining a deficiency attributable to the disallowed depreciation deduction. It follows that respondent is not precluded from claiming an increased deficiency with respect to that item in her amendment to answer. *See* Teitelbaum v. Commissioner, 346 F.2d 266, 267 (7th Cir. 1965), *affg.* T.C. Memo. 1964-141. Of course, should respondent fail to prove that there was an omission of more

---

15 [The five-year period no longer exists. — Eds.]

than 25 percent of the amount of gross income stated in petitioners' return, then respondent would be barred from assessing both the deficiency determined in the notice of deficiency and the additional deficiency asserted in the amendment to answer.

To reflect the foregoing, an order denying petitioners' motion for partial summary judgment will be issued.

[3] False or Fraudulent Return

Reading assignment: I.R.C. § 6501(c)(1)–(3).

If the taxpayer does not file a return, or files a "false or fraudulent return with the intent to evade tax," the statute of limitations is unlimited. I.R.C. § 6501(c)(1)–(3). Note that the period is unlimited if the taxpayer fails to file a return even if that failure was completely inadvertent. How can the taxpayer cure the filing of "no return" in order to start the statute of limitations running?

What if a taxpayer files a fraudulent return but later files an amended, nonfraudulent return — which limitations period applies? The United States Supreme Court resolved that issue in the following case:

BADARACCO v. COMMISSIONER
United States Supreme Court
464 U.S. 386 (1984)

JUSTICE BLACKMUN delivered the opinion of the Court.

These cases focus upon § 6501 of the Internal Revenue Code of 1954, 26 U.S.C. § 6501. Subsection (a) of that statute establishes a general 3-year period of limitations "after the return was filed" for the assessment of income and certain other federal taxes. Subsection (c)(1) of § 6501, however, provides an exception to the 3-year period when there is "a false or fraudulent return with the intent to evade tax." The tax then may be assessed "at any time."

The issue before us is the proper application of §§ 6501(a) and (c)(1) to the situation where a taxpayer files a false or fraudulent return but later files a nonfraudulent amended return. May a tax then be assessed more than three years after the filing of the amended return?

I.

No. 82-1453. Petitioners Ernest Badaracco, Sr., and Ernest Badaracco, Jr., were partners in an electrical contracting business. They filed federal partnership and individual income tax returns for the calendar years 1965–1969, inclusive. "[For] purposes of this case," these petitioners concede the "fraudulent nature of the original returns." App. 37a.

In 1970 and 1971, federal grand juries in New Jersey subpoenaed books and records of the partnership. On August 17, 1971, petitioners filed nonfraudulent amended returns for the tax years in question and paid the additional basic taxes shown thereon. Three months later, petitioners were indicted for filing false and fraudulent returns, in violation of § 7206(1) of the Code, 26 U.S.C. § 7206(1). Each pleaded guilty to the charge with respect to the 1967 returns, and judgments of conviction were entered. United States v. Badaracco, Crim. No. 766-71 (NJ). The remaining counts of the indictment were dismissed.

On November 21, 1977, the Commissioner of Internal Revenue mailed to petitioners notices of deficiency for each of the tax years in question. He asserted, however, only the liability under § 6653(b) of the Code, 26 U.S.C. § 6653(b) [currently I.R.C. § 6663 — Eds.], for the addition to tax on account of fraud (the so-called fraud "penalty") of 50%

of the underpayment in the basic tax. *See* App. 5a.

Petitioners sought redetermination in the United States Tax Court of the asserted deficiencies, contending that the Commissioner's action was barred by § 6501(a). They claimed that § 6501(c)(1) did not apply because the 1971 filing of nonfraudulent amended returns caused the general 3-year period of limitations specified in § 6501(a) to operate; the deficiency notices, having issued in November 1977, obviously were forthcoming only long after the expiration of three years from the date of filing of the nonfraudulent amended returns.

* * *

II.

Our task here is to determine the proper construction of the statute of limitations Congress has written for tax assessments. This Court long ago pronounced the standard: "Statutes of limitation sought to be applied to bar rights of the Government, must receive a strict construction in favor of the Government." E.I. du Pont de Nemours & Co. v. Davis, 264 U.S. 456, 462 (1924). *See also* Lucas v. Pilliod Lumber Co., 281 U.S. 245, 249 (1930). More recently, Judge Roney, in speaking for the former Fifth Circuit, has observed that "limitations statutes barring the collection of taxes otherwise due and unpaid are strictly construed in favor of the Government." Lucia v. United States, 474 F.2d 565, 570 (1973).

We naturally turn first to the language of the statute. Section 6501(a) sets forth the general rule: a 3-year period of limitations on the assessment of tax. Section 6501(e)(1)(A) (first introduced as § 275(c) of the Revenue Act of 1934, 48 Stat. 745) provides an extended limitations period for the situation where the taxpayer's return nonfraudulently omits more than 25% of his gross income; in a situation of that kind, assessment now is permitted "at any time within 6 years after the return was filed."

Both the 3-year rule and the 6-year rule, however, explicitly are made inapplicable in circumstances covered by § 6501(c). This subsection identifies three situations in which the Commissioner is allowed an unlimited period within which to assess tax. Subsection (c)(1) relates to "a false or fraudulent return with the intent to evade tax" and provides that the tax then may be assessed "at any time." Subsection (c)(3) covers the case of a failure to file a return at all (whether or not due to fraud) and provides that an assessment then also may be made "at any time." Subsection (c)(2) sets forth a similar rule for the case of a "willful attempt in any manner to defeat or evade tax" other than income, estate, and gift taxes.

All these provisions appear to be unambiguous on their face, and it therefore would seem to follow that the present cases are squarely controlled by the clear language of § 6501(c)(1). Petitioners Badaracco concede that they filed initial returns that were "false or fraudulent with the intent to evade tax." * * * Section 6501(c)(1), with its unqualified language, then allows the tax to be assessed "at any time." Nothing is present in the statute that can be construed to suspend its operation in the light of a fraudulent filer's subsequent repentant conduct. Neither is there anything in the wording of § 6501(a) that itself enables a taxpayer to reinstate the section's general 3-year limitations period by filing an amended return. Indeed, as this Court recently has noted, Hillsboro National Bank v. Commissioner, 460 U.S. 370, 378–380, n.10 (1983), the Internal Revenue Code does not explicitly provide either for a taxpayer's filing, or for the Commissioner's acceptance, of an amended return; instead, an amended return is a creature of administrative origin and grace. Thus, when Congress provided for assessment at any time in the case of a false or fraudulent "return," it plainly included by this language a false or fraudulent *original* return. In this connection, we note that until the decision of the Tenth Circuit in *Dowell v. Commissioner*, 614 F.2d 1263 (1980), *cert. pending*, No. 82-1873, courts consistently had held that the operation of § 6501 and its predecessors turned on the nature of the taxpayer's original, and not his amended, return.[n.8]

The substantive operation of the fraud provisions of the Code itself confirms the conclusion that § 6501(c)(1) permits assessment at any time in fraud cases regardless of a taxpayer's later repentance. It is established that a taxpayer who submits a fraudulent return does not purge the fraud by subsequent voluntary disclosure; the fraud was committed, and the offense completed, when the original return was prepared and filed. *See, e.g.,* United States v. Habig, 390 U.S. 222 (1968); Plunkett v. Commissioner, 465 F.2d 299, 302–303 (CA7 1972). "Any other result would make sport of the so-called fraud penalty. A taxpayer who had filed a fraudulent return would merely take his chances that the fraud would not be investigated or discovered, and then, if an investigation were made, would simply pay the tax which he owed anyhow and thereby nullify the fraud penalty." George M. Still, Inc. v. Commissioner, 19 T. C. 1072, 1077 (1953), *aff'd,* 218 F.2d 639 (CA2 1955). In short, once a fraudulent return has been filed, the case remains one "of a false or fraudulent return," regardless of the taxpayer's later revised conduct, for purposes of criminal prosecution and civil fraud liability under § 6653(b). It likewise should remain such a case for purposes of the unlimited assessment period specified by § 6501(c)(1).

We are not persuaded by [Petitioners' suggestion] that § 6501(c)(1) should be read merely to suspend the commencement of the limitations period while the fraud remains uncorrected. The Tenth Circuit in *Dowell v. Commissioner, supra,* made an observation to that effect, stating that the 3-year limitations period was "put in limbo" pending further taxpayer action. 614 F.2d, at 1266. The language of the statute, however, is contrary to this suggestion. Section 6501(c)(1) does not "suspend" the operation of § 6501(a) until a fraudulent filer makes a voluntary disclosure. Section 6501(c)(1) makes no reference at all to § 6501(a); it simply provides that the tax may be assessed "at any time." And § 6501(a) itself contains no mechanism for its operation when a fraudulent filer repents. By its very terms, it does not apply to a case, such as one of "a false or fraudulent return," that is "otherwise provided" for in § 6501. When Congress intends only a temporary suspension of the running of a limitations period, it knows how unambiguously to accomplish that result. *See, e.g.,* §§ 6503(a)(1), (a)(2), (b), and (d).

The weakness of petitioners' proposed statutory construction is demonstrated further by its impact on § 6501(e)(1)(A), which provides an extended limitations period whenever a taxpayer's return nonfraudulently omits more than 25% of his gross income.

Under petitioners' reasoning, a taxpayer who *fraudulently* omits 25% of his gross income gains the benefit of the 3-year limitations period by filing an amended return. Yet a taxpayer who *nonfraudulently* omits 25% of his gross income cannot gain that benefit by filing an amended return; instead, he must live with the 6-year period specified in § 6501(e)(1)(A). We agree with the conclusion of the Court of Appeals in the instant cases that Congress could not have intended to "create a situation in which persons who committed willful, deliberate fraud would be in a better position" than those who understated their income inadvertently and without fraud. 693 F.2d, at 302.

We therefore conclude that the plain and unambiguous language of § 6501(c)(1) would

---

[n.8] The significance of the original, and not the amended, return has been stressed in other, but related, contexts. It thus has been held consistently that the filing of an amended return in a nonfraudulent situation does not serve to extend the period within which the Commissioner may assess a deficiency. *See, e.g.,* Zellerbach Paper Co. v. Helvering, 293 U.S. 172 (1934); National Paper Products Co. v. Helvering, 293 U.S. 183 (1934); National Refining Co. v. Commissioner, 1 B.T.A. 236 (1924). It also has been held that the filing of an amended return does not serve to reduce the period within which the Commissioner may assess taxes where the original return omitted enough income to trigger the operation of the extended limitations period provided by § 6501(e) or its predecessors. *See, e.g.,* Houston v. Commissioner, 38 T.C. 486 (1962); Goldring v. Commissioner, 20 T.C. 79 (1953). And the period of limitations for filing a refund claim under the predecessor of § 6501(a) begins to run on the filing of the original, not the amended, return. Kaltreider Construction, Inc. v. United States, 303 F.2d 366, 368 (CA3), *cert. denied,* 371 U.S. 877 (1962).

permit the Commissioner to assess "at any time" the tax for a year in which the taxpayer has filed "a false or fraudulent return," despite any subsequent disclosure the taxpayer might make. Petitioners attempt to evade the consequences of this language by arguing that their original returns were "nullities." Alternatively, they urge a nonliteral construction of the statute based on considerations of policy and practicality. We now turn successively to those proposals.

III.

Petitioners argue that their original returns, to the extent they were fraudulent, were "nullities" for statute of limitations purposes. *See* Brief for Petitioners in No. 82-1453, pp. 22–27; Brief for Petitioner in No. 82-1509, pp. 32–34. Inasmuch as the original return is a nullity, it is said, the amended return is necessarily "the return" referred to in § 6501(a). And if that return is nonfraudulent, § 6501(c)(1) is inoperative and the normal 3-year limitations period applies. This nullity notion does not persuade us, for it is plain that "the return" referred to in § 6501(a) is the original, not the amended, return.

Petitioners do not contend that their fraudulent original returns were nullities for purposes of the Code generally. There are numerous provisions in the Code that relate to civil and criminal penalties for submitting or assisting in the preparation of false or fraudulent returns; their presence makes clear that a document which on its face plausibly purports to be in compliance, and which is signed by the taxpayer, is a return despite its inaccuracies. * * * Neither do petitioners contend that their original returns were nullities for all purposes of § 6501. They contend, instead, that a fraudulent return is a nullity only for the limited purpose of applying § 6501(a). *See* Brief for Petitioners in No. 82-1453, p. 24; Brief for Petitioner in No. 82-1509, pp. 33–34. The word "return," however, appears no less than 64 times in § 6501. Surely, Congress cannot rationally be thought to have given that word one meaning in § 6501(a), and a totally different meaning in §§ 6501(b) through (q).

Zellerbach Paper Co. v. Helvering, 293 U.S. 1972 (1934), which petitioners cite, affords no support for their argument. The Court in *Zellerbach* held that an original return, despite its inaccuracy, was a "return" for limitations purposes, so that the filing of an amended return did not start a new period of limitations running. In the instant cases, the original returns similarly purported to be returns, were sworn to as such, and appeared on their faces to constitute endeavors to satisfy the law. Although those returns, in fact, were not honest, the holding in *Zellerbach* does not render them nullities. To be sure, current Regulations, in several places, *e.g.*, Treas. Reg. §§ 301.6211-1(a), 301.6402-3(a), 1.451-1(a), and 1.461-1(a)(3)(i) (1983), do refer to an amended return, as does § 6213(g)(1) of the Code itself, 26 U. S. C. § 6213(g)(1) (1976 ed., Supp. V). None of these provisions, however, requires the filing of such a return. It does not follow from all this that an amended return becomes "the return" for purposes of § 6501(a).

We conclude, therefore, that nothing in the statutory language, the structure of the Code, or the decided cases supports the contention that a fraudulent return is a nullity for statute of limitations purposes.

IV.

Petitioners contend that a nonliteral reading should be accorded the statute on grounds of equity to the repentant taxpayer and tax policy. "Once a taxpayer has provided the information upon which the Government may make a knowledgeable assessment, the justification for suspending the limitations period is no longer viable and must yield to the favored policy of limiting the Government's time to proceed against the taxpayer." Brief for Petitioner in No. 82-509, p. 12. *See also* Brief for Petitioners in No. 82-1453, p. 17.

The cases before us, however, concern the construction of existing statutes. The relevant question is not whether, as an abstract matter, the rule advocated by petitioners accords with good policy. The question we must consider is whether the policy petitioners favor is that which Congress effectuated by its enactment of § 6501. Courts are not authorized to rewrite a statute because they might deem its effects susceptible of improvement. *See* TVA v. Hill, 437 U.S. 153, 194–195 (1978). This is especially so when courts construe a statute of limitations, which "must receive a strict construction in favor of the Government." *E.I. du Pont de Nemours & Co. v. Davis*, 264 U.S., at 462.

We conclude that, even were we free to do so, there is no need to twist § 6501(c)(1) beyond the contours of its plain and unambiguous language in order to comport with good policy, for substantial policy considerations support its literal language. First, fraud cases ordinarily are more difficult to investigate than cases marked for routine tax audits. Where fraud has been practiced, there is a distinct possibility that the taxpayer's underlying records will have been falsified or even destroyed. The filing of an amended return, then, may not diminish the amount of effort required to verify the correct tax liability. Even though the amended return proves to be an honest one, its filing does not necessarily "remov[e] the Commissioner from the disadvantageous position in which he was originally placed." Brief for Petitioners in No. 82-1453, p. 12.

Second, the filing of a document styled "amended return" does not fundamentally change the nature of a tax fraud investigation. An amended return, however accurate it ultimately may prove to be, comes with no greater guarantee of trustworthiness than any other submission. It comes carrying no special or significant imprimatur; instead, it comes from a taxpayer who already has made false statements under penalty of perjury. A responsible examiner cannot accept the information furnished on an amended return as a substitute for a thorough investigation into the existence of fraud. We see no "tax policy" justification for holding that an amended return has the singular effect of shortening the unlimited assessment period specified in §§ 6501(c)(1) to the usual three years. Fraud cases differ from other civil tax cases in that it is the Commissioner who has the burden of proof on the issue of fraud. *See* § 7454(a) of the Code, 26 U.S.C. § 7454(a). An amended return, of course, may constitute an admission of substantial underpayment, but it will not ordinarily constitute an admission of fraud. And the three years may not be enough time for the Commissioner to prove fraudulent intent.

Third, the difficulties that attend a civil fraud investigation are compounded where, as in No. 82-1453, the Commissioner's initial findings lead him to conclude that the case should be referred to the Department of Justice for criminal prosecution. The period of limitations for prosecuting criminal tax fraud is generally six years. *See* § 6531. Once a criminal referral has been made, the Commissioner is under well-known restraints on the civil side and often will find it difficult to complete his civil investigation within the normal 3-year period; the taxpayer's filing of an amended return will not make any difference in this respect. *See* United States v. LaSalle National Bank, 437 U.S. 298, 311–313 (1978); *see also* Tax Equity and Fiscal Responsibility Act of 1982, Pub. L. 97-248, § 333(a), 96 Stat. 622. As a practical matter, therefore, the Commissioner frequently is forced to place a civil audit in abeyance when a criminal prosecution is recommended.

We do not find petitioners' complaint of "unfair treatment" persuasive. Petitioners claim that it is unfair "to forever suspend a Sword of Damocles over a taxpayer who at one time may have filed a fraudulent return, but who has subsequently recanted and filed an amended return providing the Government with all the information necessary to properly assess the tax." Brief for Petitioner in No. 82-1509, p. 26. *See* Brief for Petitioners in No. 82-1453, p. 16. But it seems to us that a taxpayer who has filed a fraudulent return with intent to evade tax hardly is in a position to complain of the fairness of a rule that facilitates the Commissioner's collection of the tax due. A taxpayer who has been the subject of a tax fraud investigation is not likely to be surprised when a notice of deficiency arrives, even if it does not arrive promptly after he files an amended return.

Neither are we persuaded by [the taxpayer's] argument that a literal reading of the statute "punishes" the taxpayer who repentantly files an amended return. *See* Brief for Petitioner in No. 82-1509, p. 44. The amended return does not change the status of the taxpayer; he is left in precisely the same position he was in before. It might be argued that Congress should provide incentives to taxpayers to disclose their fraud voluntarily. Congress, however, has not done so in § 6501. That legislative judgment is controlling here.

V.

Petitioners contend, finally, that a literal reading of § 6501(c) produces a disparity in treatment between a taxpayer who in the first instance files a fraudulent return and one who fraudulently fails to file any return at all. This, it is said, would elevate one form of tax fraud over another.

The argument centers in § 6501(c)(3), which provides that in a case of failure to file a return, the tax may be assessed "at any time." It is settled that this section ceases to apply once a return has been filed for a particular year, regardless of whether that return is filed late and even though the failure to file a timely return in the first instance was due to fraud. *See* Bennett v. Commissioner, 30 T. C. 114 (1958), *acq.*, 1958-2 Cum. Bull. 3. *See also* Rev. Rul. 79-178, 1979-1 Cum. Bull. 435. This, however, does not mean that § 6501 should be read to produce the same result in each of the two situations. From the language employed in the respective subsections of § 6501, we conclude that Congress intended different limitations results. Section 6501(c)(3) applies to a "failure to file a return." It makes no reference to a failure to file a timely return (*cf.* §§ 6651(a)(1) and 7203), nor does it speak of a fraudulent failure to file. The section literally becomes inapplicable once a return has been filed. Section 6501(c)(1), in contrast, applies in the case of "a false or fraudulent return." The fact that a fraudulent filer subsequently submits an amended return does not make the case any less one of a false or fraudulent return. Thus, although there may be some initial superficial plausibility to this argument on the part of petitioners, we conclude that the argument cannot prevail. If the result contended for by petitioners is to be the rule, Congress must make it so in clear and unmistakable language.

* * *

Justice Stevens, dissenting.

The plain language of § 6501(c)(1) of the Internal Revenue Code conveys a different message to me than it does to the Court. That language is clear enough: "In the case of a false or fraudulent return with the intent to evade tax, the tax may be assessed, or a proceeding in court for collection of such tax may be begun without assessment, at any time." 26 U.S.C. § 6501(c)(1). What is not clear to me is why this is a case of "a false or fraudulent return."

In both cases before the Court, the Commissioner assessed deficiencies based on concededly nonfraudulent returns. The taxpayers' alleged prior fraud was not the basis for the Commissioner's action. Indeed, whether or not the Commissioner was obligated to accept petitioners' amended returns, he in fact elected to do so and to use them as the basis for his assessment. When the Commissioner initiates a deficiency proceeding on the basis of a nonfraudulent return, I do not believe that the resulting case is one "of a false or fraudulent return."

* * *

In light of the purposes and common-law background of the statute, as well as this Court's previous treatment of what a "return" sufficient to commence the running of the limitations period is, it seems apparent that an assessment based on a nonfraudulent amended return does not fall within § 6501(c)(1). Once the amended return is filed the rationale for disregarding the limitations period is absent. The period of concealment is over, and under general common-law principles the limitations period should begin to run. The filing of the return means that the Commissioner is no longer under any disadvantage; full disclosure has been made and there is no reason why he cannot assess a deficiency within the statutory period.

* * *

Whatever the correct standard for construing a statute of limitations when it operates against the Government, *see ante*, at 391–392, surely the presumption ought to be that some limitations period is applicable.

> "It probably would be all but intolerable, at least Congress has regarded it as ill-advised, to have an income tax system under which there never would come a day of final settlement and which required both the taxpayer and the Government to stand ready forever and a day to produce vouchers, prove events, establish values and recall details of all that goes into an income tax contest. Hence, a statute of limitation is an almost indispensable element of fairness as well as of practical administration of an income tax policy." Rothensies v. Electric Storage Battery Co., 329 U.S. 296, 301 (1946).

However, under the Commissioner's position, adopted by the Court today, no limitations period will ever apply to the Commissioner's actions, despite petitioners' attempts to provide him with all the information necessary to make a timely assessment.

* * *

If anything, considerations of tax policy argue against the result reached by the Court today. In a system based on voluntary compliance, it is crucial that some incentive be given to persons to reveal and correct past fraud. Yet the rule announced by the Court today creates no such incentive; a taxpayer gets no advantage at all by filing an honest return. Not only does the taxpayer fail to gain the benefit of a limitations period, but at the same time he gives the Commissioner additional information which can be used against him at any time. Since the amended return will not give the taxpayer a defense in a criminal or civil fraud action, *see ante*, at 394, there is no reason at all for a taxpayer to correct a fraudulent return. Apparently the Court believes that taxpayers should be advised to remain silent, hoping the fraud will go undetected, rather than to make full disclosure in a proper return. I cannot believe that Congress intended such a result.

I respectfully dissent.

Does the position of the majority with respect to a fraudulently filed return discourage a taxpayer from making an effort to meet the taxpayer's reporting obligations by filing an accurate amended return? On the other hand, what might a rule that allowed subsequent honesty after filing a fraudulent return to trigger the three-year statute of limitations encourage taxpayers to do?

In *The Colony, Inc. v. Commissioner*, 357 U.S. 28 (1958), discussed above, the Court held that the six-year statute under section 6501(e) does not apply unless an entire item is omitted, presumably because partial reporting of the item by the taxpayer discloses that item to the IRS, which then requires less investigatory time. Compare the majority's opinion in *Badaracco* with this principle of *The Colony, Inc.* If the policy behind the unlimited assessment period for false or fraudulent returns is similarly to grant the IRS additional time in which to discover the taxpayer's fraudulent behavior, should an amended return that provides the IRS enough information to make an accurate assessment trigger some sort of limitations period? How does the *Badaracco* majority respond to this potential inconsistency?

Also consider *Badaracco* in light of the holding of *Bennett v. Commissioner*, 30 T.C.

114 (1958), which is cited approvingly by the Court. In *Bennett*, the Tax Court ruled that where a taxpayer fraudulently fails to file a return at all, a subsequently filed nonfraudulent return is sufficient to trigger the three-year statute of limitations. Under *Bennett*, if the IRS discovers a taxpayer's failure to file and begins an investigation, the taxpayer need only file a nonfraudulent return in order to start the limitations period. Which of these two scenarios — a fraudulently filed return or a fraudulent failure to file — seems more threatening to the system of voluntary compliance? Do these cases mean that a taxpayer intent on perpetrating a fraud is better off filing no return at all rather than filing a fraudulent return?

The Tax Court has held that the "fraudulent return" provision applies even if the fraud is that of the return preparer, not the taxpayer.[16] *See* Allen v. Commissioner, 128 T.C. 37 (2007). In that case:

> Petitioner, a truck driver for UPS during 1999 and 2000, timely filed his returns for 1999 and 2000 (the years at issue). Petitioner gave his Form W-2, Wage and Tax Statement, section 401(k) statement, mortgage interest statement, and property statements to Gregory D. Goosby (Mr. Goosby), who prepared petitioner's returns for the years at issue and filed them with respondent.
>
> Mr. Goosby prepared petitioner's returns for the years at issue and claimed false and fraudulent Schedule A, Itemized Deductions, for both years. The false deductions included deductions for charitable contributions, meals and entertainment, and pager and computer expenses, as well as various other expenses. Petitioner received complete copies of petitioner's returns for the years at issue after they had been filed, but he did not file an amended tax return for either year.

Id. at 37–38. In Tax Court, "[t]he parties . . . agree[d] that petitioner himself did not have the intent to evade tax, but Mr. Goosby claimed the false deductions for the years at issue on petitioner's returns with the intent to evade tax." *Id.* at 38. The court found:

> Nothing in the plain meaning of the statute suggests the limitations period is extended only in the case of the taxpayer's fraud. The statute keys the extension to the fraudulent nature of the return, not to the identity of the perpetrator of the fraud. Nor do we read the words "of the taxpayer" into the statute to require the taxpayer to have the intent to evade his or her own tax.

Id. at 40. Do you agree with the court? For an argument that the Tax Court got the *Allen* case wrong, see Bryan T. Camp, *Tax Return Preparer Fraud and the Assessment Limitation Period*, 116 Tax Notes 687, 697 (2007). What would be the downside of a rule that return preparer fraud does not extend the statute of limitations on assessment?

[D] Tolling of the Statute of Limitations on Assessment

Reading Assignment: I.R.C. § 6503(a)(1); Treas. Reg. § 301.6503(a)-1(a)(2) Ex.

The IRS must assess tax before the statute of limitations on assessment expires, or any amount assessed must be refunded to the taxpayer. *See* I.R.C. § 6401. Because the notice of deficiency is a prerequisite to assessment of a deficiency, the notice must be sent before the expiration of the statute of limitations on assessment. As discussed above, the notice triggers a "prohibited period," and the statute of limitations is tolled during the period that the IRS is prohibited from assessing tax, plus 60 days. *See* I.R.C.

---

[16] The holding is contrary to FSA 200104006, *available at* 2001 TNT 19-46 (Jan. 29, 2001), in which the IRS determined that only the taxpayer's intent was relevant, so fraud committed by a tax return preparer was insufficient to hold open the statute of limitations on assessment.

§§ 6213(a), 6503(a). Determining the timeliness of an assessment therefore can require counting days fairly precisely. Note that the statute of limitations is suspended beginning on the date the notice of deficiency was mailed. Treas. Reg. § 301.6503(a)-1(a)(2) Ex.

> *Example:* Gary filed his Year 1 return on April 1, Year 2. On February 1, Year 4, the IRS mailed a notice of deficiency with respect to Gary's Year 1 tax year to Gary's last known address in New York City. Gary receives the notice on February 7, Year 4, but does not respond to it. On these facts, the notice of deficiency was mailed within the three-year period under section 6501. That period runs from the due date of the Year 1 return, which was April 15, Year 2. (In the absence of a notice of deficiency, the limitations period would have expired on April 15, Year 5.) The *first* day the IRS can assess tax is when the prohibited period expires, May 3, Year 4 (because the 90-day period within which Gary can file a Tax Court petition runs through May 2, assuming Year 4 is not a leap year). The *last* day the IRS can assess tax, assuming the three-year limitations period applies, is September 12, Year 5. That is, the statute of limitations was tolled for 150 days (the 90-day prohibited period plus the 60-day grace period). Therefore, instead of expiring on April 15, Year 5, the statute is extended 150 days — until September 12, Year 5.

If, in response to a notice of deficiency, the taxpayer signs Form 870, permitting immediate assessment of tax, that cuts short the prohibited period. That, in turn, will shorten the time period during which the statute of limitations is tolled. The 60-day tolling period still applies, and it starts to run on the date the Form 870 was filed. Rev. Rul. 66-17, 1966-1 C.B. 272.

> *Example:* On January 5, Year 1, the IRS mails a notice of deficiency to Joanne's last known address in Miami, Florida. Joanne receives the notice on January 8. On February 1, Year 1, she signs a Form 870, waiving restrictions on assessment of the deficiency. The statute of limitations on assessment is tolled for 86 days (the 26 days from January 5 through January 31, plus 60 days).

Section 6503 provides that "if a proceeding in respect of the deficiency is placed on the docket of the Tax Court," the statute of limitations on assessment is tolled "until the decision of the Tax Court becomes final[], and for 60 days thereafter." What if the taxpayer argues that the person who filed a responsive petition was not authorized to do so? In *Martin v. Commissioner*, T.C. Memo. 2003-288, the Tax Court, applying the reasoning of a prior case, held that the docketing of a proceeding responding to a notice of deficiency tolls the statute of limitations even if the proceeding is docketed by an unauthorized party. The Court of Appeals for the Tenth Circuit affirmed. Martin v. Commissioner, 436 F.3d 1216 (10th Cir. 2006).

What is the rationale for tolling the statute of limitations during the prohibited period plus an additional 60 days?

[E] Extensions of Time to Assess Tax

Reading Assignment: I.R.C. § 6501(c)(4).

It is often the case that the IRS is unable to complete an examination of the taxpayer's return during the prescribed assessment period. Even when the case has progressed to the Appeals stage, an expiring limitations period may give the Appeals Officer very little time in which to consider the taxpayer's protest letter and attempt to settle. If the statutory period is about to expire before an assessment has been made, the IRS commonly requests that the taxpayer sign a consent extending the general statute of limitations. It is not uncommon, in fact, for the IRS to request seriatim extensions of the statute of limitations as each extension nears expiration.[17] Section 6501(c)(4) provides that where, before the expiration of the limitations period, both the taxpayer and the IRS agree in writing to its extension, the tax may be assessed at any time prior to the expiration of the agreed-upon period. Note that an extension is only valid if executed prior to the expiration of the statute of limitations. *See* I.R.C. § 6501(c)(4). Why might the taxpayer agree to extend the statutory period?

Extensions can be made on Form 872, Consent to Extend the Time to Assess Tax, or Form 872-A, Special Consent to Extend the Time to Assess Tax. Form 872 (the "fixed-date" consent) provides for an extension for a finite period of time stated in the agreement, typically one year or less. Form 872-A (the "open-ended" consent) is an unlimited extension of time, which terminates 90 days after (1) the IRS receives a Form 872-T from the taxpayer, (2) the IRS mails the taxpayer a Form 872-T, or (3) the IRS mails the taxpayer a notice of deficiency. In the last case, the extension period will not expire until 60 days after the prohibited 90-day period specified in section 6213. Form 872-A is discussed further below.

The fundamental question of whether a taxpayer should agree to sign an extension does not lend itself to an easy answer. If the taxpayer refuses to extend an expiring limitations period, the IRS will very likely issue the taxpayer a notice of deficiency. As discussed in subsequent chapters, the notice of deficiency sets into motion the litigation phase of the tax controversy process and forces the taxpayer to consider within a relatively short period of time whether to pursue the case in Tax Court or one of the refund fora. A taxpayer's failure to consent to an extension may also place pressure on the IRS to prepare the notice of deficiency based on an investigation that may be ill-developed or incomplete. In such a case, the examining agent's response may be to include in his or her report all items that the agent believes are questionable, even if the items have a weak legal or factual basis.

Houlberg discusses one circumstance in which the IRS might seek an extension of the statute, and also illustrates the kinds of questions that taxpayers may raise after the fact about the validity of consents to extend the statutory period. What does the case indicate about whether a taxpayer has a "right" to a conference with the IRS Appeals Division?

HOULBERG v. COMMISSIONER

United States Tax Court
T.C. Memo. 1985-497

GERBER, JUDGE:

By statutory notice, respondent determined the following deficiencies in petitioners' Federal income tax:

Year	Deficiency
1976	$7,443
1977	5,553
1978	3,276
1979	9,895

The issues for decision are (1) whether the period of limitations on assessment for 1976 and 1977 was extended by valid consents or had expired prior to issuance of the notice of deficiency, and (2) whether the notice of deficiency was issued by a person

[17] Concerned that taxpayers were unaware of their right to refuse to extend the statute of limitations, the IRS Reform Act required the IRS, on each occasion when the taxpayer is asked to sign an extension consent, to notify the taxpayer of the taxpayer's right to refuse to extend the statutory period, and to notify the taxpayer of his or her right to limit the extension to a particular issue or period of time. *See* I.R.C. § 6501(c)(4)(B).

lacking proper authority and, therefore, was invalid.

FINDINGS OF FACT

Some of the facts have been stipulated. The stipulation of facts and accompanying exhibits are so found and incorporated by this reference.

Petitioners are husband and wife and resided in Los Angeles, California, when they filed their petition. They timely filed joint Federal income tax returns for 1976, 1977, 1978, and 1979.

In November 1979, petitioners received a Form 872 (Consent to Extend the Time to Assess Tax) to extend the period of limitations on assessment for 1976 until September 30, 1981. The form provided in part: "MAKING THIS CONSENT WILL NOT DEPRIVE THE TAXPAYER(S) OF ANY APPEAL RIGHTS TO WHICH THEY WOULD OTHERWISE BE ENTITLED." The form was accompanied by a cover letter from the Internal Revenue Service (IRS) notifying petitioners that the return of K. T. Associates, a partnership with which they were involved, was under examination. The letter in part stated:

> We do not expect to receive the results of the entity(s) audit before the expiration of the normal statute of limitations. Generally, a delay in time is the result of the taxpayers exercising their right to appeal the IRS decision. In order to allow time for adequate consideration of your case in conjunction with the audit of the entity(s), we request that you sign the enclosed consent * * *.

After consulting with their accountant, Michael J. Ravin, petitioners signed the form and returned it to the IRS which accepted the consent.

In May 1981, petitioners received a Form 872A (Special Consent to Extend the Time to Assess Tax), which in part provided that any tax due for 1976 could be assessed on or before the 90th day after the IRS mailed a notice of deficiency. The form and its accompanying cover letter contained the same language regarding appeal rights as cited above. After consulting with Ravin, petitioners signed the form and returned it to the IRS which accepted the consent.

In October 1980, a Form 872A was sent to petitioners for 1977. Ravin advised petitioners to sign the consent and prepared a letter to be used by them in forwarding the consent to the IRS. The letter, dated December 5, 1980, provided in part:

> Our signing this extension of time is expressly contingent upon the fact that we are not waiving any of our rights to the normal administrative procedures afforded to us by the Internal Revenue Service in connection with audit of our 1977 income tax return.

The following language was added to the bottom of the last page of the Form 872A: "SUBJECT TO THE ATTACHED LETTER DATED Dec. 5, 1980."

On receipt of the letter and conditional extension, an IRS representative called Ravin and advised him that the IRS would accept only an unmodified consent. Ravin then suggested to petitioners that they sign an unaltered consent, which they did. The signed Form 872A and the cover letter sent with respect to 1977 contained the language regarding appeal rights previously cited.

In October 1981, a Form 872A was sent to petitioners with respect to 1978. Petitioners refused to sign it.

On April 15, 1982, petitioners were sent a notice of deficiency covering 1976, 1977, 1978, and 1979. The notice bore the District Director's name, and was initialed by Jerold M. Ching, a Quality Review Section Chief, Grade GS-13.

Petitioners did not have a conference with the IRS prior to issuance of the notice of deficiency. Subsequent to issuance of the notice, an administrative hearing was held between counsel for petitioners and a representative of respondent's appeals division, at which time the parties agreed that the deficiencies for the taxable years at issue were as follows:

Year		Deficiency
1976	....	$474
1977	....	5,553
1978	....	3,276
1979	....	0
	TOTAL:	$9,303

The parties agree that, if this Court rules for respondent with respect to the validity of the consents and the notice of deficiency, the deficiencies are as above.

OPINION

Validity of Consents

Petitioners argue that the period of limitations on assessment for 1976 and 1977 expired prior to issuance of the notice of deficiency. They assert that they consented to extend the period of limitations in return for administrative review and the opportunity to present their views before issuance of a statutory notice, and that the consents are invalid because this condition was not met. Respondent maintains that the period of limitations was extended by valid consents. We agree with respondent.

Section 6501 states the general rule that a tax must be assessed within three years of the filing of a return. Section 6501(c)(4) permits the IRS and taxpayers to extend the period of limitations on assessment by written agreement. Since petitioners timely filed their tax returns for 1976 and 1977, the notice of deficiency, issued April 15, 1982, was barred unless the assessment period had been validly extended.

Petitioners maintain that they received both oral and written assurances that they would receive a hearing prior to issuance of a deficiency notice. At trial, petitioner Jens Houlberg (Houlberg) testified that towards the end of 1979, he was notified by mail that the IRS was conducting an audit of calendar years 1976 through 1979. Houlberg stated that he called Ravin, who told him that he would be afforded an opportunity to be heard before a notice of deficiency was issued. Houlberg further testified that other than his wife, Ravin, and counsel, he had not discussed the extensions with anyone. When asked the basis of his understanding, other than from his discussions with Ravin, that he would receive a pre-notice hearing, Houlberg described his experience with past audits. At no time did Houlberg testify that the IRS promised him a pre-notice hearing for the taxable years at issue.

Ravin, petitioner's accountant, also testified at the hearing. He stated that after receiving a copy of the first extension request, he called the IRS representative whose name appeared on the accompanying cover letter. Ravin related:

> I asked him at that point in time * * * [if] signing of the consent would preclude the Service from sending a notice of deficiency prior to Mr. Houlberg or myself * * * expressing our position before and during the normal administrative review procedure.
>
> And he told me that this would in no way preclude that.

Ravin further related that he had spoken with another IRS representative regarding the requested extension for 1978. Ravin stated:

> [I] reiterated the taxpayers' position with appeal rights being confirmed, that this is no way would jeopardize their ability to go through the normal administrative appeals prior to the notice of deficiency being issued.

Ravin continued that he had contacted still another IRS representative regarding the extension requested for 1977. He stated:

> [I] again reiterated the same position, with respect to the administrative appeal rights. She agreed with me.

Ravin further testified that he was contacted by an IRS representative regarding the modified Form 872A petitioners had sent to the IRS. According to Ravin, the IRS representative —

> said that they could not accept a conditional extension, and that they would be sending out a normal extension of time requesting Mr. Houlberg to sign it. And at that point in time, I asked, well, did they understand that they were not waiving their appeal rights. And they said they certainly did, and it was very evident in the letter that I had sent — or Mr. Houlberg had sent.

At no time did Ravin testify that an IRS representative promised petitioners a hearing prior to issuance of a notice of deficiency. He essentially related that he was told that by signing the consents petitioners would not harm their appeal rights.

The final witness at the hearing was Glenn Marker. During 1981, Marker was chief of a unit involved with solicitation of consents to extend the period of limitations on assessments. Marker testified that he did not recall having had any conversations with petitioners or Ravin. He stated that he had never indicated to a taxpayer or a taxpayer's representative that by extending the statute of limitations they would be guaranteed an appeals conference prior to issuance of a deficiency notice. Marker further testified as to what taxpayers were told would occur if a taxpayer chose to extend the statute:

> We would go on further to explain that if they chose to extend the statute, the case would then be retained in the Suspense Unit, awaiting the resolution of partnership adjustments, depend [sic] upon the outcome of the adjustments. If it was in the government's favor, we would try to solicit an agreement from the taxpayer, based upon the results of the partnership audit. And if the taxpayers then chose not to, the case would be moved forward for issuance of the 30-day letter.
>
> The 30-day letter would then be issued, and they would have 30 days to file a protest to the government's position. And then, if they had not filed that letter, then it would go default to the 90-day section for against [sic] the issuance of the statutory notice of deficiency.

Marker was subsequently asked if —

> the process is the consent is signed, you finish up your audit, you then contact the taxpayer, the taxpayer is given an opportunity to settle it at that level, if he can't, then he is allowed to protest?

He responded affirmatively. He stated that he knew of no cases in which a consent was signed and a notice issued before an appeals conference was allowed. Later, however, he stated that although it was normal procedure to issue a 30-day letter, there were instances where statutory notices went out without such letters being sent. He described these instances as —

> cases where we have determined them [the cases] to be litigating vehicles, that they cannot be resolved at the appellate level * * *. The manager looks at the case and makes a determination, and can actually recommend the issuance of a 90-day letter, because he doesn't feel that anything could be resolved at that level, the 30-day level.

Marker's testimony does not demonstrate that respondent promised petitioners pre-notice of deficiency appeal rights in return for petitioners' consent to extend the period of limitations, as petitioners assert. On the contrary, Marker stated that no such promises are made to taxpayers. Marker indicated that although pre-notice conferences are commonly held, taxpayers are not always afforded such meetings.

The waiver forms and accompanying cover letters similarly contain no explicit promise for a pre-notice conference. Like the oral communications with IRS representatives that petitioners note, these written communications merely did not rule out the possibility of such a meeting.

The same contention petitioners make regarding the conditional nature of their consents was made previously by their accountant, Ravin, in his own case which was decided by this Court. Ravin v. Commissioner, T.C. Memo 1981-107, *affd. without published opinion* 755 F.2d 936 (9th Cir. 1985). In *Ravin v. Commissioner, supra,* we held that consents signed by Ravin were valid, even though an IRS agent had made, and a letter from the IRS contained, inaccurate statements concerning his appeal rights. With respect to the effect to be given statements of IRS agents to taxpayers, we stated:

> [t]he often stated general rule is that a revenue agent does not have the authority to bind the Commissioner. *See* United States v. Stewart, 311 U.S. 60 (1940); Bornstein v. United States, 345 F.2d 558, 170 Ct. Cl. 576 (1965); Wilkinson v. United States, 304 F.2d 469, 157 Ct. Cl. 847 (1962). A claim of estoppel is usually rejected, although the taxpayer contends that he followed the erroneous advice of an agent and acted in reliance upon it. *Cf.* Montgomery v. Commissioner, 65 T.C. 511, 522 (1975); Boulez v. Commissioner, 76 T.C. 209 (1981). [41 T.C.M. at 1064, 1066, 50 P-H Memo T.C. par. 81, 107 at 81-381]

We further observed, with respect to the same language on the Forms 872 and 872A regarding appeal rights that we quote in this case, that —

> [this language] does not state that any conferences will be automatically provided, but it merely states that by signing the Form 872 the taxpayer retains the same rights to an appellate conference prior to the issuance of the notice of deficiency as all other taxpayers. Put differently, it is nowhere indicated on the Form 872 that by signing it a taxpayer will improve his appeal rights. [41 T.C.M. at 1066, 50 P-H Memo T.C. at 382–81.]

In *Ravin v. Commissioner, supra,* we additionally pointed out that procedural rules with respect to administrative appeals are merely directory, and compliance with them is not essential to the validity of a notice of deficiency. *See also* Luhring v. Glotzbach, 304 F.2d 560, 563 (4th Cir. 1962); Rosenberg v. Commissioner, 450 F.2d 529, 532 (10th Cir. 1971), *affg.* a Memorandum Opinion of this Court; Collins v. Commissioner, 61 T.C. 693, 701 (1974); Flynn v. Commissioner, 40 T.C. 770, 773 (1963). Accordingly, we find that the IRS did not violate its procedural rules by not conferring with petitioners prior to issuing a deficiency notice and, consequently, the requirements of section 6501(c)(4) have been met.

Petitioners further suggest that the consents are ineffective because petitioners signed them under the mistaken belief that a pre-notice hearing would be held.[n.3] As is implicit in our opinion in *Ravin v. Commissioner, supra,* a consent is valid where no hearing is held, even though a taxpayer expects such review. We know of no authority holding that a valid waiver of the period of limitations on assessment requires knowledge that a pre-notice administrative hearing may not be held. Petitioners note that they are not accountants. Petitioners were represented by an accountant (Ravin) and we are not persuaded that petitioners' backgrounds should dictate a different result than that reached in *Ravin v. Commissioner, supra,* with respect to the effectiveness of the waivers.

The Code imposes no general requirement on the IRS to confer with a taxpayer who

---

[n.3] Petitioners were under no duress to sign the waivers. *Compare* Robertson v. Commissioner, T.C. Memo. 1973-205 (taxpayers, who had never previously dealt with the IRS, signed consents under threat of seizure of their property and without the opportunity to consult with their attorney).

has signed a waiver prior to issuing a notice of deficiency. For the reasons we have stated, we do not find that pre-notice administrative review was required in the specific circumstances of this case. Accordingly, we hold that the period for assessment for 1976 and 1977 was extended by valid consents.

Authority to Issue Deficiency Notice

Petitioners argue that Jerold M. Ching, the Quality Review Section Chief (Grade GS-13), who issued the deficiency notice, lacked properly delegated authority to do so, and that the notice therefore is invalid. Respondent maintains that Jerold M. Ching had the delegated authority to issue the notice. We agree with respondent.

In *Ravin v. Commissioner, supra,* the taxpayers also argued that the IRS representative who issued the statutory notice did so without authority. The circumstances in which the statutory notice was issued are very similar in the two cases and, accordingly, *Ravin v. Commissioner, supra,* provides appropriate precedent for this case.

In *Ravin v. Commissioner, supra,* we pointed out the authority by which certain IRS representatives could issue deficiency notices:

> Section 6212(a) provides that if the Secretary determines that there is an income tax deficiency, he is authorized to send a notice of deficiency to the taxpayer by certified mail or registered mail. The term "Secretary" is defined in section 7701(a)(11)(B) as the "Secretary of the Treasury or his delegate." The phrase "or his delegate" is defined in section 7701(a)(12)(A)(i) as "any officer, employee, or agency of the Treasury Department duly authorized by the Secretary of the Treasury directly, or indirectly by one or more redelegations of authority, to perform the function mentioned or described in the context." Under the provisions of section 301.7701-9(b), Proced. & Admin. Regs., when a function is vested by statute in the Secretary of the Treasury or his delegate, and the Treasury regulations provide that such function may be performed by a district director, then the provision in the regulations constitutes a delegation by the Secretary to the district director of the authority to perform such function. Section 301.6212-1(a) [Proced. & Admin. Regs.] provides that if a district director determines that there is an income tax deficiency, he is authorized to notify the taxpayer of the deficiency. Thus, the authority to issue notices of deficiency has been delegated by the Secretary to district directors. Under section 301.7701-9(c) [Proced. & Admin. Regs.] an officer authorized by regulations to perform a function has the authority to redelegate the performance of such function except to the extent that "such power to do so redelegate is prohibited or restricted by proper order or directive."

* * * Since the authority of a District Director to delegate his authority to issue notices of deficiency is derived from sections 301.6212-1(a) and 301.7701-9, Proced. & Admin. Regs., the fact that Delegation Order LA-41 (Rev. 9) referred to Delegation Order 77 (Rev. 14), which had been superseded by Delegation Order 77 (Rev. 15) at the time the notice of deficiency was issued, is irrelevant to the validity of the notice. *See Estate of Brimm v. Commissioner,* 70 T.C. 15, 19–22 (1978), and *Ravin v. Commissioner, supra.* In both *Estate of Brimm v. Commissioner, supra,* and *Ravin v. Commissioner, supra,* although the District Director's delegation order in effect at the time the deficiency notice was issued cited as authority a superseded revision of Delegation Order No. 77, we found no jurisdictional defect. * * *

Accordingly, we hold that the delegation to Jerold M. Ching was proper, and that he had authority to issue the notice of deficiency.

To reflect the foregoing, decision will be entered for respondent.

Because Form 872-A extends the statute of limitations on assessment indefinitely, taxpayers should be cautious about signing a Form 872-A. The following short case suggests the difficulty that taxpayers have in arguing that a statute kept open under a Form 872-A has nonetheless expired:

MUIR v. COMMISSIONER

United States Court of Appeals, Eighth Circuit
11 F. App'x 701 (2001) (unpublished)

Per Curiam.

On his 1980 and 1981 federal tax returns, Ross M. Muir claimed losses arising from an investment in a limited partnership. In 1984 and 1985, he executed Form 872-A, consenting to an extension of the three-year statutory period in which the Commissioner of Internal Revenue ("Commissioner") could assess taxes against him for the 1980 and 1981 tax years, respectively. *See* 26 U.S.C. §§ 6501(a) (time limit for assessing tax); 6504(c)(4) (Commissioner and taxpayer may agree to extend normal limitations period). Form 872-A provided that the extension agreement would be terminated when either Muir or the Commissioner executed a notice of termination (Form 872-T), or when the Commissioner mailed Muir a notice of deficiency. In 1988, the Commissioner issued Muir a notice of deficiency, disallowing the claimed partnership losses. Muir then petitioned the tax court, challenging the assessment and the rate of interest payable on the alleged underpayment of tax in 1980, and contending that the notice of deficiency was time-barred. The tax court rejected his arguments and he appeals. We affirm.

On appeal, Muir renews his argument that the statutory period for assessment had expired. Having carefully reviewed the record and the parties' briefs, *see Campbell v. Commissioner*, 164 F.3d 1140, 1142 (8th Cir.) (standard of review), *cert. denied*, 526 U.S. 1117, 119 S. Ct. 1765, 143 L. Ed. 2d 796 (1999), we agree with the tax court that the notice of deficiency was not time-barred, because the Form 872-A extension was a valid agreement and the statutory period of limitations did not expire by operation of law. *See Stenclik v. Commissioner*, 907 F.2d 25, 27–29 (2d Cir.) (Form 872-A constitutes agreed-upon extension as contemplated by § 6501(c)(4), and fact that extension granted by Form 872-A does not expire on date certain does not undermine its validity. Form 872-A is hardly silent as to duration, which is expressly provided for and is as definite as taxpayer needs it to be since he is empowered to commence termination period at any time by filing Form 872-T), *cert. denied*, 498 U.S. 984, 112 L. Ed. 2d 528, 111 S. Ct. 516 (1990).

We also reject Muir's argument that the Commissioner unreasonably delayed enforcement of the deficiency: Muir had the power to terminate the extension and commence assessment at any time, to limit the accumulation of interest, and to settle his case with the Commissioner while the matter was pending before the tax court. *See Stenclik*, 907 F.2d at 28 (rejecting taxpayer's claim that Commissioner unreasonably and unjustifiably delayed issuing notice of deficiency, because Commissioner was entitled to rely on explicit terms of Form 872-A agreement for termination and assessment).

Accordingly, we affirm.

What did *Muir* hold? Other cases have held that the equitable doctrine of laches does not bar an assessment for a year open under a Form 872-A, even after a long period of time has elapsed. *See* Stenclik v. Commissioner, 907 F.2d 25, 28 (2d Cir.), *cert. denied*, 498 U.S. 984 (1990); Mecom v. Commissioner, 101 T.C. 374, 391 (1993), *aff'd without op.*, 40 F.3d 385 (5th Cir. 1994). However, in *Fredericks v. Commissioner*, 126 F.3d 433 (3d Cir. 1997), *acq.*, 1999-1 I.R.B. 5, on unusual facts, the Court of Appeals for the Third Circuit applied equitable estoppel to bar the IRS from assessing tax. In that case:

In October 1980, the IRS sent Fredericks a Form 872-A, Special Consent to Extend the Time to Assess Taxes, requesting him to extend for the 1977 tax year the three-year statute of limitations within which the government must assess deficiencies. J.A 22a. *See* 26 U.S.C. § 6501(a). On October 17, 1980, Fredericks signed and returned the Form 872-A. . . .

According to the government's "received" date stamp on the Form 872-A, it was received by the Audit Division of the Manhattan District Director's Office on November 3, 1980, and signed and dated by the IRS on November 4, 1980.

In January 1981, an IRS agent telephoned Fredericks and requested him to sign a Form 872, Consent to Extend the Time to Assess Tax, for the 1977 tax year. According to Fredericks' trial testimony:

> [The] IRS agent . . . indicated that he was reviewing my tax return involved in the audit of my 1977 tax return, and . . . the statute of limitations was about to run and that the Government needed an extension of that statute. . . . I told the . . . agent that I had already executed and returned . . . an extension. . . . He told me he was in charge; he had my file and there was no extension in the file. He asked me did I receive . . . a copy of the extension back from the IRS signed. I said I did not. He indicated . . . that therefore the Government did not have it, it was probably lost in the mail, and that he needed me to execute another extension, otherwise the Government was going to assess the tax. But they didn't want to do that. They wanted time to review, and would I send them an 87 — a new form. We did not mention numbers.

J.A. 81a–82a. The IRS did not contradict this testimony.

Consistent with Fredericks' testimony, the government sent a Form 872, which he signed and returned to the IRS. The Form 872 expressly extends the statute of limitations for only one year, whereas the Form 872-A authorizes an indefinite, although revocable, extension of the statute of limitations. This first Form 872 executed by the IRS and Fredericks extended the statute of limitations until December 31, 1982.

The agents telephoned Fredericks on two additional occasions and requested him to sign and return two additional Forms 872. On June 13, 1982, Fredericks signed and returned a consent to extend the statute of limitations to December 31, 1983; and on February 3, 1983, Fredericks signed and returned a Form 872 agreeing to extend the statute of limitations until June 30, 1984. Each of these Forms 872 was received and signed by an agent of the IRS Newark District Director's Office, and copies of these signed forms were subsequently forwarded to, and received by, Fredericks.

On July 9, 1992 — eight years and nine days after the June 30, 1984 expiration date — the IRS mailed a notice of deficiency to Fredericks and his former wife alleging they were liable for $28,361 in income tax, plus interest for the 1977 tax year. Fredericks filed a petition in the Tax Court challenging the deficiency assessment on grounds that it was barred by the June 30, 1984 statute of limitations agreed to in the third Form 872. Thus, Fredericks claimed the Commissioner was estopped from relying on the Form 872-A to avoid the statute-of-limitations defense, which completely bars the assessment of any deficiency.

The Tax Court held a trial at which Fredericks testified and the Commissioner presented no witnesses. Significantly, the IRS presented no evidence as to the date it discovered its possession of the Form 872-A which it invoked to assess Fredericks' 1977 return in 1992. This is the same form the IRS affirmatively represented to the taxpayer as non-existent. Moreover, the IRS does not dispute that it waited until 1992 to notify the taxpayer that it had the

> Form 872-A and intended to rely on that form instead of the third Form 872 signed by the parties. At oral argument, counsel for the IRS stated that she did not know when the IRS discovered the Form 872-A or when it decided to rely on that form.

Id. at 436–37.

Reversing the Tax Court, the Court of Appeals found that all of the elements of estoppel were met:

> We conclude that Fredericks has met his burden of establishing the traditional elements of estoppel. The IRS misrepresented its possession of a Form 872-A indefinite extension of the statute of limitations and confirmed that misrepresentation by obtaining three Forms 872. The IRS' conduct constituted affirmative misconduct when it remained silent upon realizing its mistake and upon deciding to change its course of action to rely on the previously lost Form 872-A without notifying the taxpayer. Its decision to effectively revoke the third Form 872 without notice to the taxpayer also adds to the affirmative misconduct here. Fredericks relied upon the IRS' oral and written representations as to the relevant statute of limitations and lost his right to terminate the Form 872-A. His detriment is compounded by the IRS' assessment of an increased penalty rate of interest covering the entire duration of its protracted investigation.
>
> We have addressed the special factors that must be considered in governmental-estoppel claims and we conclude that they favor estopping the IRS here. The impact on the public fisc is minimal and consistent with Congress' enactment of enforceable statutes of limitations. The acts and omissions of the IRS agents were authorized; the errors involved misrepresentations of fact, not law, and do not contravene any statutory or regulatory requirements. The government benefitted from its misrepresentations; and Fredericks relied on those misrepresentations to his detriment, irretrievably losing the benefit of the statute of limitations, the benefit of the contracts he entered with the IRS, and the right to terminate the Form 872-A that the government repeatedly and affirmatively represented as non-existent.

Id. at 450.

Note that whether a taxpayer agrees to a fixed-date or open-ended consent, the taxpayer can seek to limit the extension agreement to specific items or issues on the return. I.R.C. § 6501(c)(4)(B). Revenue Procedure 68-31, 1968-2 C.B. 917, lists the circumstances under which the IRS will allow the taxpayer to restrict an extension agreement. The practical effect of a restrictive consent is to allow the statute of limitations on assessment to expire except with respect to those issues specified in the agreement. A restrictive consent is best accomplished by typing on the form itself a contractual limitation. Because courts interpret these types of limitations based solely upon the language in the consent, the restriction should be drafted in a clear and unambiguous manner and should be signed by both the taxpayer and the appropriate IRS official.[18] The Internal Revenue Manual offers the following suggested language: "The amount of any deficiency assessment is to be limited to that resulting from any adjustment to (description of the area(s) of consideration), including any consequential changes to other items based on such adjustment."[19] I.R.M. 25.6.22.8.12. From a

[18] Although a consent to extend the period of limitations results in a unilateral waiver of a defense by the taxpayer, contract principles are significant because section 6501(c)(4) requires that the IRS and taxpayer reach a mutual agreement over the terms of the extension. Piarulle v. Commissioner, 80 T.C. 1035 (1931).

[19] This language is not necessarily unambiguous. Compare the differing interpretations of the term "adjustment" in *Mecom v. Commissioner*, 101 T.C. 374, 391 (1993), *aff'd without op.*, 40 F.3d 385 (5th Cir. 1994) and *Powell v. Commissioner*, T.C. Memo. 1990-329. The differing interpretations resulted in opposite holdings in those cases.

procedural standpoint, a restrictive consent not only limits the taxpayer's overall exposure to adjustments by the IRS, but affords the taxpayer an opportunity to negotiate further with the IRS over the scope of continued examination or appeal activity.[20]

[F] Abatement of Assessments

Reading Assignment: I.R.C. § 6404(a)–(d).

An assessment, once made, can be abated by the IRS in certain circumstances, including erroneous or illegal assessment. *See* I.R.C. § 6404. In *Mackey v. Commissioner*, T.C. Memo. 2004-70, the taxpayer received notices of deficiency for 1995 through 1999, years for which he had not filed returns. The taxpayer timely mailed a Tax Court petition in response to the notices.

Code section 6213 prohibits assessment of a deficiency during the period the taxpayer has to petition the Tax Court and, if a Tax Court case is docketed, until the Tax Court's decision is final. Timely mailing is timely filing if the requirements of section 7502 are met, and, in *Mackey*, the taxpayer's petition was timely. However, it took an unusually long time to arrive at the Tax Court, and, in the meantime, the IRS assessed the tax, believing that the taxpayer had not petitioned the Tax Court.

> Following receipt of a copy of the petition, however, respondent's counsel, by letter dated April 8, 2002, notified petitioner of the assessments and stated that he had requested abatement thereof. Respondent abated the assessments on May 13, 2002.
>
> Also on May 13, 2002, respondent's Austin Service Center notified petitioner by letter that it had credited petitioner's account for 1996 in the amount of $35,694.86 [the amount assessed] and that such amount would be refunded to him if he "[owed] no other taxes or other debts we are required to collect". Petitioner received a $39,229.76 refund [$35,694.86 plus interest] shortly thereafter.
>
> By letter dated June 7, 2002, respondent's Austin Service Center responded to an unspecified inquiry from petitioner regarding his 1999 taxable year. The letter states in part: "You don't need to do anything further now on this matter.* * * If you receive or have received additional notices about this account, please disregard them."

Mackey, supra (footnote omitted).

In Tax Court, the taxpayer argued that "respondent's continued assertion of the deficiencies and additions to tax remaining at issue is not 'fair,' based on respondent's allegedly misleading actions and statements in connection with the premature assessments of the amounts set forth in the notices." *Id.* The Tax Court explained that:

> [W]hile, in effect, acknowledging unreported income in excess of the deductions allowed by respondent for 1995, 1996, and 1997, petitioner does not want to pay the resulting deficiencies in tax (and section 6654(a) additions to tax), claiming that respondent's actions led him to believe that his case had been resolved, thereby prompting him to discard records that would have substantiated additional deductions. Although not phrased in so many words, petitioner's argument essentially amounts to a claim of estoppel.

Id. The Tax Court ruled against the taxpayer, finding the absence of reliance by the taxpayer. Thus, a premature assessment that was abated did not preclude the possibility of a later assessment of the tax.

---

[20] Unless otherwise suspended, interest continues to accrue during the period the extension was granted. Interest is discussed in further detail in Chapter 13.

In *Mackey*, the assessment was correctly abated because it had been improperly assessed after the taxpayer petitioned the Tax Court. What happens if an assessment is erroneously abated (as a result of IRS error) and is subsequently reinstated, but after the statute of limitations on assessment has expired? In *Becker v. IRS*, 407 F.3d 89 (2d Cir. 2005), a bankruptcy case, the Court of Appeals for the Second Circuit (in a 2-1 decision) affirmed the District Court's holding that reinstatement of the assessment was not barred either by the statute of limitations on assessment or by equitable estoppel.

§ 7.04 EXCEPTIONS TO THE STATUTES OF LIMITATIONS

[A] The Statutory Mitigation Provisions

Reading Assignment: I.R.C. §§ 1311, 1312(1)–(4), 1313(a)–(b), 1314(a)–(b); skim I.R.C. § 1314(c).

By their nature, statutes of limitations cut off otherwise valid claims. To prevent a double benefit to either the taxpayer or the government, Code sections 1311 through 1314, the statutory mitigation provisions allow reopening, in specified circumstances, of a year otherwise barred by the statute of limitations. In general, if the taxpayer has received the double benefit, the mitigation provisions may allow the government to reopen a year barred by the statute of limitations on assessment (a "closed" year), so as to make an assessment. On the other hand, if the government received the double benefit, the mitigation provisions may allow reopening of a year barred by the statute of limitations on refund claims. *See generally* Treas. Reg. § 1.1311(a)-1(b). The statute of limitations on refund claims is discussed in detail in Chapter 10.

The mitigation provisions are technical and complex. The Tax Court has explained:

> In the aggregate, sections 1311 through 1314 set forth a highly complicated and confusingly interrelated set of provisions authorizing the correction of error which is otherwise prevented by operation of law, *e.g.*, the expiration of the statutory period of limitations for assessment. Considerably oversimplified but nevertheless sufficiently accurate for present purposes, sections 1311–1314 were designed to prevent a windfall, in specified circumstances, either to the taxpayer or to the Government arising out of the treatment of the same item in a manner inconsistent with its erroneous treatment in a closed year. Thus, provision is made to correct an error in the closed year where, for example, the same item was erroneously included or excluded from income or where the same item was allowed or disallowed as a deduction in a barred year. The authorized mechanism for correction is an "adjustment," a term of art the meaning and scope of which emerges from the mitigation provisions of sections 1311–1314.

Bolten v. Commissioner, 95 T.C. 397, 402–403 (1990).

In general, an "adjustment" is the change made to correct the erroneous reporting in the year barred by the statute of limitations. *See* I.R.C. §§ 1311(a), 1314(a)–(b). The statutory regime also requires, as a prerequisite to an adjustment, a "determination" that is inconsistent with the previous tax treatment of an item. I.R.C. § 1311(a); *see also* I.R.C. §§ 1312, 1313(a). The determination can consist of a court decision that has become final; final disposition of a refund claim made by the taxpayer; a closing agreement that meets the requirements of Code section 7121;[21] or, under regulations, an agreement between the IRS and the taxpayer relating to the taxpayer's tax liability. Treasury regulation section 1.1313(a)-4 sets forth the requirements such an agreement must meet.

---

[21] Closing agreements are discussed in Chapter 5.

The regulations provide the following example of an adjustment that will result in a refund or credit to the taxpayer:

> *Example:* A taxpayer who keeps his books on the cash method erroneously included as income on his return for 1954 an item of accrued interest. After the period of limitations on refunds for 1954 had expired, the district director, on behalf of the Commissioner, proposed an adjustment for the year 1955 on the ground that the item of interest was received in 1955 and, therefore, was properly includible in gross income for that year. The taxpayer and the district director entered into an agreement which meets all of the requirements of § 1.1313(a)-4 and which determines that the interest item was includible in gross income for 1955. The Commissioner has maintained a position inconsistent with the inclusion of the interest item for 1954. As the determination (the agreement pursuant to § 1.1313(a)-4) adopted such inconsistent position, an adjustment is authorized for the year 1954.

Treas. Reg. § 1.1311(b)-1(b) Ex. In this example, the taxpayer would be entitled to a refund for 1954 because of the interest income that was erroneously included in that year.

The following example provides a more detailed illustration of the application of the statutory mitigation provisions:

> *Example:* Jeanne and Peter entered into a contract under which Peter paid Jeanne for architectural services. In Year 1, they had a dispute over whether Jeanne had earned $10,000 of her fee for the year. Peter paid Jeanne but sued her in state court for return of the $10,000. Although Jeanne filed her Year 1 return on time, she did not include the $10,000 in her Year 1 gross income because she was uncertain of the outcome of the lawsuit. In Year 3, Jeanne won the suit, which Peter did not appeal. Jeanne filed her Year 3 return on April 5, Year 4, but did not include the payment in her gross income for Year 3, having decided that it actually should have been included in her gross income for Year 1.
>
> On January 10, Year 5, the IRS sends Jeanne a notice of deficiency for the Year 3 tax year. Its deficiency is based on the $10,000 fee, which the IRS asserts should have been included in Jeanne's Year 3 gross income. In response to the notice of deficiency, Jeanne petitions the Tax Court. Assume that Jeanne wins the litigation, based on her argument that Year 1 was the proper year for her to include the amount in gross income. Assuming that the statute of limitations on assessment applicable to Jeanne's Year 1 return is three years, it will have expired by the time the Tax Court renders its decision.
>
> The Tax Court decision, once it is final, constitutes a "determination" for purposes of section 1311(a). I.R.C. § 1313(a)(1). The double exclusion of the amount from gross income is the situation described in section 1312(3)(B). At the time the IRS sent the notice of deficiency to Jeanne, assessment for her Year 1 tax year was not barred, as provided in section 1311(b)(2)(A). Therefore, section 1311 applies to permit an "adjustment" under section 1314. Under section 1314(a), the adjustment is to Jeanne's Year 1 tax, in the amount of the increase in tax determined by adding $10,000 to her Year 1 gross income. The resulting tax liability can be assessed and collected in the same manner as a deficiency. I.R.C. § 1314(b).

Finally, consider the following case, which involves both a District Court decision and a Tax Court decision.

GILL v. COMMISSIONER

United States Court of Appeals, Fifth Circuit
306 F.2d 902 (1962)

JONES, CIRCUIT JUDGE.

The two proceedings here before us for decision involve federal income tax liability of Robert S. Gill and his wife, Sara Louise Gill who is now deceased. All of the transactions from which the asserted tax liability arose were those of Robert S. Gill and he will herein be referred to as the taxpayer. Mrs. Gill was, and her executor is, a party because of the filing of joint husband and wife returns. The original controversy was before this Court in 1958. Gill v. United States, 5 Cir., 258 F.2d 553. The taxpayer had been a partner in Gill Printing and Stationery Company. It reported income on a fiscal-year basis, closing its books as of April 30 of each year. In July of 1945 the taxpayer became the sole proprietor of the business. He continued to file his income tax returns, as before, on a calendar-year basis but continued to report the earnings of the printing business on the basis of the accounting periods previously employed. Thus his return for a particular calendar year would include the net earnings of the business for the fiscal year beginning on May 1st of the prior year through April 30 of the current year. He filed claims for refund for the years 1949, 1950, 1952, and for a period of 1951 ending April 30 of that year. In support of his claim for refund of tax paid for 1949, and it is with the 1949 tax that we are concerned, the taxpayer made a recomputation of his income by excluding two-thirds of the income of the business for its accounting year ending April 30, 1949, and adding two-thirds of the business income for the fiscal year ending April 30, 1950. These adjustments put the Gills' tax computation for the 1949–1952 period on a calendar-year basis except for the two-thirds of the business income for annual period ending April 30, 1949.

The claim for refund was disallowed, suit was brought and judgment was for the Government in the district court. This Court reversed, and by its decision, *supra*, determined that the taxpayer's income should be computed on a calendar-year basis. As a result, a judgment of the district court was entered, following the remand of this Court, which eliminated from the taxpayer's 1949 computation the business income for the May 1 to December 31, 1948, period. No amended return for 1948 was filed, no waiver of limitations has been made for the year 1948, and no charge of fraud has been asserted. On September 28, 1958,[22] a notice of deficiency was sent to the taxpayer proposing an increase in the tax for 1948 by the inclusion in that year the business income which had been excluded from the 1949 determination. In so doing the Commissioner invoked the provisions of Sections 1311–1314 of the Internal Revenue Code of 1954 usually referred to as the mitigation provisions. We first consider whether the assessment was made within a year after the "determination" of the error in computing the 1949 tax. To be collectible the assessment must have been made, under the provisions of Section 1314(b), within a year.

The taxpayer contends that the "determination" was made by the opinion of this Court, issued on July 18, 1958, in which it was held that the tax on all of the income of the taxpayer should be computed on an annual basis. The taxpayer takes the position that a determination was made on July 18, 1958, the date of the opinion, and the deficiency notice mailed on September 28, 1959, was sent too late. The Tax Court was of the opinion that there was no "determination" until the expiration of the time for applying to the Supreme Court for certiorari. It held the notice was timely. An opinion of a Court of Appeals permits a losing litigant to seek a rehearing or to apply to the Supreme Court for a writ of certiorari, or both. In the absence of any action by the Supreme Court, a Court of Appeals retains jurisdiction, and none is relinquished to the district court, until a mandate or judgment is issued. 36 C.J.S. Federal Courts § 301(32),

---

22 [This date apparently should read September 28, 1959 instead of 1958. — Eds.]

p. 1370 et seq.; 5B C.J.S. Appeal & Error § 1959, p. 530 et seq. The mandate of this Court was issued on September 29, 1958, and this is the earliest date at which it could be said there was a "determination." Louis Pizitz Dry Goods Company v. United States, D.C.N.D. Ala. 1950, 185 F. Supp. 186, *aff. sub. nom.* Louis Pizitz Dry Goods Co., Inc. v. Deal, 5th Cir., 1953, 208 F.2d 724, *cert. den.* 347 U.S. 952, 74 S.Ct. 676, 98 L.Ed. 1097; Bishop v. Reichel, D.C.N.D. N.Y. 1954, 127 F. Supp. 750, 54 A.L.R.2d 532, *aff.* 2 Cir., 221 F.2d 806, *cert. den.* 350 U.S. 833, 76 S.Ct. 68, 100 L.Ed. 743, 2 Mertens Law of Federal Income Taxation, ch. 14, p. 48 *et seq.* § 14.12. The notice of deficiency was given on September 28, 1959, and so was within the year prescribed by the statute. It is not necessary to consider whether the time of the determination might have been postponed until the right to apply for certiorari had expired. Since our 1958 review was of a district court judgment, we do not express any view with respect to the statutes which relate to the time when decisions of the Tax Court become final. 26 U.S.C.A. (I.R.C. 1939) § 1140; 26 U.S.C.A. (I.R.C. 1954) § 7481. It was suggested that, in view of the provisions of the remand of this Court as set out in the opinion of July 18, 1958, the determination was made by the district court's judgment after the remand. The disposition we have made of the "determination" issue makes it unnecessary to pass upon this question.

The taxpayer makes a contention that the mitigation provisions of the statute are specific and limited, that they cannot be extended or enlarged, and that they do not cover the situation. He asserts, in connection with this contention, that the adjustment made by the exclusion from 1949 taxable income of the amount which should have been included in 1948 income was not an "item" within the meaning of the statute. It was, though, a stated sum specified by the taxpayer. "Item" as used in the statute, has been construed "to include any item or amount which affects gross income in more than one year, and produces, as a result, double taxation, double deduction or inequitable avoidance of the tax." Gooch Milling & Elevator Co. v. United States, 78 F. Supp. 94, 111 Ct. Cl. 576. *See* H.T. Hackney Co. v. United States, 78 F. Supp. 101, 111 Ct. Cl. 664; Dubuque Packing Co. v. United States, D.C.N.C. Iowa 1954, 126 F. Supp. 796, *aff.* 8 Cir., 233 F.2d 453. Under this principle the mitigation provisions of the Internal Revenue Code were properly invoked.

The taxpayer finally argues that, if unsuccessful on his other contentions and the Government is permitted, under the mitigation statute to adjust his 1948 tax by the inclusion for the year of the income excluded from 1949 income by this Court's determination, there should be a complete reopening of the 1948 tax computation so as to permit the exclusion of the May 1 to December 31, 1947, business income. The difficulty with the taxpayer's position is that the statute does not permit the doing of that which he would have done. The statute authorizes adjustments only with respect to the items involved in the determination. The statute of limitations precludes reopening as to any item which was not involved in the determination. First National Bank of Philadelphia v. Commissioner, 18 T.C. 899, *aff.* 3 Cir., 205 F.2d 82; Central Hanover Bank 3 Trust Co. v. United States, 2 Cir., 163 F.2d 60.

We find no basis for disturbing the decision of the Tax Court in the one case or the decision of the District Court in the other. Each is

Affirmed.

Why does *Gill* involve both a District Court decision and a Tax Court decision? Where in the mitigation provisions does it require the IRS to send a notice of deficiency within one year of the determination that triggered the applicability of the provisions? More specifically, what was the taxpayer's argument in *Gill* about that one-year limitation period and how does the Court of Appeals resolve it?

[B] Equitable Recoupment

Another doctrine that alleviates the harshness of an expired limitations period is called "equitable recoupment." In general, it allows a party, the IRS or the taxpayer, to defend against a claim of the other by offsetting a time-barred amount owed to the first party that arises out of the same transaction. For example, assume that the IRS has issued a notice of deficiency in estate tax based on an increased valuation of certain property included in the estate, the estate had sold some of that property using its valuation as its basis, and the statute of limitations has run on the potential income tax refund claim. The estate might be able to use the defense of equitable recoupment to offset any deficiency in estate tax with the time-barred overpayment of income tax. *See* Estate of Branson v. Commissioner, 113 T.C. 6 (1999), *aff'd*, 264 F.3d 904 (9th Cir. 2001), *cert. denied*, No. 01-928 (2002); Estate of Mueller v. Commissioner, 101 T.C. 551 (1993).[23] Equitable recoupment may arise in refund cases, as well. In that regard, it is discussed further in Chapter 10.

PROBLEMS

1. During Year 1, Amy received from her employer, in addition to her annual salary of $100,000, an antique work of art as additional compensation.
   A. Assume that Amy properly reported the artwork as gross income on her Year 1 return, which she filed on April 15, Year 2. Her return reflected her valuation of $10,000. The IRS audited Amy's return. On February 1, Year 5, which is not a leap year, the IRS mailed to her a notice of deficiency reflecting its determination that the correct value of the artwork, includible in her gross income, was $30,000. Amy has not responded to the notice of deficiency.
      i. When is the last day that the IRS can assess additional tax with respect to Amy's Year 1 return?
      ii. When is the last day for the IRS to assess additional tax with respect to Amy's Year 1 return if Amy had filed her return on March 1, Year 2 instead of April 15?
      iii. When is the last day for the IRS to assess additional tax with respect to Amy's Year 1 return if Amy had filed her return on June 2, Year 2 instead? Does it matter whether Amy had obtained an extension of time to file?
      iv. When is the last day for the IRS to assess additional tax with respect to Amy's Year 1 return if Amy's annual salary were $40,000 instead of $100,000?
   B. Assume instead that Amy did not report the receipt of the artwork on her Year 1 return, which she filed on April 15, Year 2. On February 1, Year 5, which is not a leap year, the IRS mailed to her a notice of deficiency reflecting its determination that Amy has $30,000 of additional gross income, attributable to the artwork.
      i. Assume Amy was unaware that the artwork constitutes gross income to her, and that is why she did not report it on her return.
         a. If Amy does not respond to the notice of deficiency, when is the last day the IRS may assess additional tax with respect to Amy's Year 1 return?
         b. If Amy responds to the notice of deficiency on March 10, Year

---

[23] By statute, the Tax Court now has equitable recoupment authority "to the same extent that it is available in civil tax cases before the district courts of the United States and the United States Court of Federal Claims." I.R.C. § 6214(b).

5 by signing a Form 870 waiving restrictions on assessment of tax, when is the last day the IRS may assess additional tax with respect to Amy's Year 1 return?

c. Assume that Amy responds to the notice of deficiency by filing a Tax Court petition on April 3, Year 5. The Tax Court hears the case on May 4, Year 6, and its decision, which is adverse to Amy, becomes final on February 1, Year 7. Assuming Years 5, 6, and 7 are not leap years, when is the last day the IRS may assess additional tax with respect to Amy's Year 1 return?

ii. If Amy had instead intentionally failed to report the value of the artwork as gross income, and she does not respond to the notice of deficiency, when is the last day the IRS may assess additional tax with respect to Amy's Year 1 return? How would your answer change if Amy had filed an amended return on June 16, Year 2, reporting $30,000 of gross income from the receipt of the artwork?

iii. Assume that Amy had her return prepared by an accountant who intentionally failed to report the value of the artwork as gross income and Amy was unaware that the artwork had to be reported. When is the last day the IRS may assess additional tax with respect to Amy's Year 1 return?

C. Assume that Amy fraudulently failed to file a return for Year 1. She subsequently filed the return on June 1, Year 5. When is the last day the IRS may assess tax with respect to Amy's Year 1 tax year?

2. Assume that the statute of limitations on José's return will expire in three months. José is currently negotiating a settlement with the IRS Appeals Division. The Appeals Officer has requested that José extend the statute of limitations on assessment for an additional six-month period.

   A. What factors should José consider in deciding whether to agree to extend the statute of limitations?

   B. If José does agree to extend the statute, should the extension be made on Form 872 or Form 872-A?

3. Although she left her job in November of Year 1, Patrice was entitled to a year-end bonus. On December 30, her former boss called her to let her know the check was available. Patrice did not pick up the check until January 3, Year 2. Her W-2 for Year 1 did not include the bonus, so Patrice did not include it in gross income for her Year 1 tax year when she filed the return on April 15, Year 2. In Year 2, she received a W-2 in the amount of the bonus, but Patrice decided that she should have included it in her Year 1 gross income because she "constructively received" it in Year 1. Therefore she did not include it in her Year 2 return, which she filed on April 15, Year 3.

   On May 1, Year 5, the IRS mailed Patrice a notice of deficiency for her Year 2 tax year based on the unreported bonus. Patrice petitioned the Tax Court, and on June 1, Year 6, the Tax Court's decision in Patrice's favor became final. The decision was made on the ground that the bonus should have been income for Patrice's Year 1 tax year. The statute of limitations on assessment for Year 1 expired in Year 5.

   A. What recourse does the IRS have?

   B. If the IRS has an option under Part A, what action would it have to take, and by what deadline?

4. Gail filed her Year 1 return on April 15, Year 2. On March 3, Year 5, the IRS asked Gail to agree to extend the statute of limitations on assessment. On March 5, Year 5, Gail signed a Form 872, specifying an extension of the statute until

April 15, Year 6. Subsequently, Gail signed additional Forms 872, on April 1, Year 6 and May 1, Year 7, each providing an additional 1-year extension. When is the last day that the IRS can send Gail a notice of deficiency as a prerequisite to assessing tax with respect to Gail's Year 1 tax year?

5. The IRS has asked Drake to extend the statute of limitations on a tax year that is under audit. In deciding whether to agree to extend the statute, Drake would be interested in ascertaining whether taxpayers who agree to extend the statute of limitations obtain better settlements or better results in court than those who do not. Would Drake likely be able to obtain this information under FOIA?

Chapter 8
THE UNITED STATES TAX COURT

§ 8.01 THE U.S. TAX COURT: AN INTRODUCTION

This chapter focuses on the court that hears the vast majority of litigated federal tax cases, the United States Tax Court (Tax Court). The chapter begins with a discussion of the court's basic structure and procedures. The next section examines the breadth of Tax Court jurisdiction and the volume of its inventory. The chapter then considers Tax Court pleading requirements; its discovery procedures, which are more restrictive than those applicable in district court; the question of which precedent should apply in Tax Court cases; and the "small tax case" procedure. The chapter also examines both (1) the charges of bias that have often been lodged against the Tax Court and (2) the controversy over secret factfinding in certain large tax cases. The chapter concludes with a discussion of the extent of the Tax Court's equitable powers.

[A] Structure

Reading Assignment: I.R.C. §§ 7441, 7443(a)–(c), (e), 7443A(a)–(b).

The Tax Court's history harkens back to an independent administrative agency in the executive branch. In 1924, Congress established that agency, the Board of Tax Appeals.[1] It was renamed twice over the years, becoming the United States Tax Court in 1969 — the point at which Congress also declared it to be a court.[2]

Numerous proposals existed over the years to make the Tax Court an Article III court, but they were met with strong opposition. *See* Harold A. Dubroff, The United States Tax Court: An Historical Analysis 184–204 (1979). Congress instead made the Tax Court an Article I court. Accordingly, unlike their Article III counterparts, Tax Court judges do not have life tenure and do not have the salary protections of Article III. Congress also opted not to make the Tax Court subject to the Administrative Office of U.S. Courts or the U.S. Judicial Conference. S. Rep. No. 91-552, at 304 n.3 (1969). The Tax Court is thus largely self-governing.

By statute, the Tax Court is allowed 19 judges. I.R.C. § 7443(a). These judges are appointed by the President with the advice and consent of the Senate, *id.*, each for a 15-year term, I.R.C. § 7443(e). The Code also allows the Chief Judge of the Tax Court to appoint "special trial judges." I.R.C. § 7443A(a). Special trial judges hear "small tax cases" — those under a specified dollar limit — as well as other cases, as authorized by statute. *See* I.R.C. § 7443A(b).

[B] Procedures

Reading Assignment: I.R.C. §§ 7441, 7443(a)–(c), (e), 7443A(a)–(b).

The Tax Court is based in Washington, D.C., but its judges travel to hear cases on regular calendars in various cities around the country, and also may travel additional times or to additional locations for "special sessions" of the court, if warranted. *See* I.R.C. § 7446. At trial, the taxpayer may be represented by anyone admitted to practice

---

[1] *See* Revenue Act of 1924, ch. 234, sec. 900, 43 Stat. 253, 336–338. In 1942, the Board of Tax Appeals was renamed the Tax Court of the United States. Revenue Act of 1942, ch. 619, sec. 504, 56 Stat. 957.

[2] Tax Reform Act of 1969, Pub. L. No. 91-172, 83 Stat. 487, 730–736.

before the Tax Court, which includes non-attorneys who have passed an examination. *See* I.R.C. § 7452. The IRS is represented in the Tax Court by attorneys from the IRS Chief Counsel's Office.

Under Code section 7453, the Tax Court applies "the rules of evidence applicable in trials without a jury in the United States District Court of the District of Columbia" and follows its own procedural rules, which generally are based on the Federal Rules of Civil Procedure. The Tax Court's Rules of Practice and Procedure are available on the Tax Court's website, www.ustaxcourt.gov. *See* TAX CT. R. 1.

Several months prior to trial, the Tax Court judge will provide to the parties a notice of the date and location of the trial, as well as a Standing Pretrial Order. *See* TAX CT. R. 131(b). The order contains instructions for preparation for trial. *See id.* Unexcused failure to comply with that order can subject the noncomplying party to sanctions. *Id.*

[C] Opinions and Decisions

The Tax Court issues three types of opinions: Division Opinions, which have precedential value and are officially published; Memorandum Opinions, which have no official precedential value, but are privately published; and Summary Opinions in small tax cases, which have no precedential value but have been privately published since 2001. It is up to the Chief Judge to determine whether to issue a decision as a Division Opinion or Memorandum Opinion. *See* I.R.C. § 7460. Division Opinions are generally the Tax Court's first pronouncement on a question of law, while Memorandum Opinions generally apply clear law to new facts.

The Chief Judge can also refer a Division Opinion for review by the entire court.[3] *Id.* A reviewed case is not retried *en banc*, but rather the Tax Court judges reconsider the case in conference from the written record. Such opinions are labeled "reviewed by the Court." Court-reviewed cases are generally ones that (1) decide legal issues not previously considered by the Tax Court; (2) invalidate a Treasury Regulation; (3) would conflict with existing Tax Court case law; (4) involve a legal issue not previously considered by the Tax Court, and, as written, would conflict with the decision of a Court of Appeals other than the one to which appeal would lie; or (5) involve an issue on which the Tax Court was previously reversed by a circuit other than the one to which appeal would lie.[4]

If the taxpayer and the IRS settle a case after it was docketed with the Tax Court, the settlement is entered by the court as a stipulated decision. "In fact, unlike in District Court, once a taxpayer properly commences a case in Tax Court, only the court can remove the case from its jurisdiction. Thus, the Tax Court refuses to allow voluntary dismissal or 'removal' to District Court." Leandra Lederman, *Equity and the Article I Court: Is the Tax Court's Exercise of Equitable Powers Constitutional?*, 5 FLA. TAX REV. 357, 396 (2001) (footnotes omitted) (citing cases).

[D] Appeals of Tax Court Decisions

Reading Assignment: I.R.C. § 7482(a)(1), (b)(1)(A)–(B).

Appeals from the Tax Court go to the United States Courts of Appeals, just as those from the district courts do. *See* I.R.C. § 7482(a)(1). Tax Court appeals are taken to the Court of Appeals for the circuit in which the taxpayer resided at the time he or she filed the Tax Court petition. I.R.C. § 7482(b)(1).

---

[3] In fiscal year 2006, for example, the Tax Court produced 288 memorandum opinions, 204 Summary Opinions, and 36 Division Opinions, five of which were reviewed by the court. *United States Tax Court Fiscal Years* 1996–2006 Annual Report, Tbl. 6.

[4] NINA CRIMM, TAX COURT LITIGATION: PRACTICE AND PROCEDURE, at ¶ 10.2[2][c][iv] (1999).

[1] Appeal of Fewer Than All Tax Years

An issue that sometimes arises with respect to appeals from Tax Court cases is whether a Court of Appeals has jurisdiction over a matter in which certain tax years have been disposed of by the Tax Court (and appealed) while others remain undecided. In district court, Federal Rule of Civil Procedure 54(b) allows the district court in such a case involving multiple claims to "direct entry of a final judgment as to one or more, but fewer than all, claims . . . if the court expressly determines that there is no just reason for delay. . . ." FED. R. CIV. P. 54(b). The Tax Court has its own Rules of Practice and Procedure, which have no analog to Rule 54(b). However, the Tax Court has the power, in the absence of an applicable Rule, to "prescribe the procedure, giving particular weight to the Federal Rules of Civil Procedure to the extent that they are suitably adaptable to govern the matter at hand." TAX CT. R. 1. Thus, the question of whether appeal can be pursued at a point in which one or more tax years remain before the Tax Court is more complicated than it would be in district court, although, as discussed below, Congress has made Tax Court decisions reviewable in the same manner as district court decisions.

In *N.Y. Football Giants, Inc. v. Commissioner*, 349 F.3d 102 (3d Cir. 2003), the Court of Appeals for the Third Circuit explained:

> The question raised in this appeal is whether a court of appeals has jurisdiction to review an order of the Tax Court dismissing some, but not all, of the disputed years in a petition. Although this is a question of first impression in this circuit, it has been addressed by several of our sister circuits, resulting in three distinct approaches. The D.C. Circuit permits appellate review of orders that finally dispose of any particular claims. *InverWorld, Ltd. v. Comm'r*, 979 F.2d 868, 875, 298 U.S. App. D.C. 319 (D.C. Cir. 1992). The Fifth, Seventh, and Ninth Circuits permit appellate review of orders dispensing of claims only where the Tax Court makes a Rule 54(b) determination that judgment as to those claims is final and immediately appealable. *Nixon v. Comm'r*, 167 F.3d 920 (5th Cir. 1999) (*per curiam*); *Brookes v. Comm'r*, 163 F.3d 1124 (9th Cir. 1998); *Shepherd v. Comm'r*, 147 F.3d 633 (7th Cir. 1998). Finally, the Second and Sixth Circuits do not permit appellate review of an order that does not dispose of the entire case. *Schrader v. Comm'r*, 916 F.2d 361, 363 (6th Cir. 1990) (*per curiam*); *Estate of Yaeger*, 801 F.2d 96, 97 (2d Cir. 1986).
>
> Both the Giants and the IRS urge us to adopt the position of the D.C. Circuit in *InverWorld* and to exercise jurisdiction over this appeal. The parties argue that the tax liability for each fiscal year establishes a separate cause of action, *Commissioner v. Sunnen*, 333 U.S. 591, 598, 92 L. Ed. 898, 68 S. Ct. 715 (1948), the disposition of which should be immediately final and appealable though the entire case is not concluded.
>
> Our consideration of the three approaches taken by the various circuits that have addressed this issue leads us to the conclusion that the Seventh Circuit's decision in *Shepherd* provides the correct approach. . . . We believe that, if we are to exercise jurisdiction under section 7482(a)(1) "in the same manner and to the same extent" as under [28 U.S.C.] section 1291 [relating to appeals from district court cases], a judgment disposing of less than all claims is not appealable unless it is accompanied by a determination that the order is final and that there is no just reason to delay. *Shepherd*, 147 F.3d at 635 (holding that, absent such a determination, "we do not have jurisdiction if our appellate jurisdiction over decisions by the Tax Court is to be modeled closely on our appellate jurisdiction over decisions by district courts"). We hold that, without such a determination, a judgment disposing of less than all claims is not final and appealable under section 7482(a)(1).

Id. at 106–07. Might efficiency concerns counsel allowing or prohibiting an appeal from a single tax year in a multi-year case?

[2] Deference to Tax Court Decisions

Reading Assignment: Review I.R.C. § 7482(a)(1); read I.R.C. § 7482(c)(1).

During the time that the Tax Court was an administrative agency, the Supreme Court held that the Courts of Appeals must accord deference to Tax Court decisions, both with respect to the Tax Court's findings of fact, and, "when the court cannot separate the elements of a decision so as to identify a clear-cut mistake of law, the decision of the Tax Court must stand." Dobson v. Commissioner, 320 U.S. 489, 502 (1943).

The holding of *Dobson* was unpopular, and Congress purported to reverse it by statute in 1948. What is now Code section 7482(a) provides, in part, "The United States Courts of Appeals (other than the United States Court of Appeals for the Federal Circuit) shall have exclusive jurisdiction to review the decisions of the Tax Court, except as provided in section 1254 of Title 28 of the United States Code, in the same manner and to the same extent as decisions of the district courts in civil actions tried without a jury. . . ." Thus, as indicated above, review of Tax Court decisions was expressly made comparable to review of district court decisions, to which no special deference is required. Yet, Congress did not repeal the predecessor of Code section 7482(c)(1), which provides, "Upon such review, such courts shall have power to affirm or, if the decision of the Tax Court is *not in accordance with law*, to modify or to reverse the decision of the Tax Court, with or without remanding the case for a rehearing, as justice may require." I.R.C. § 7482(c)(1) (emphasis added). Arguably, this subsection suggests that appellate courts do not have the power to modify or reverse the Tax Court's findings of fact.

One scholar has argued:

> The predominant view of the modern cases is that Tax Court decisions on questions of law (including mixed questions that are characterized as questions of law), like district court decisions on questions of law, are subject to de novo review. This view, of course, is consistent with the language of section 7482(a) adopted by the 1948 amendment, but leaves unexplained the existence of section 7482(c). Many decisions simply rely on section 7482(a), suggesting that the courts have either ignored or overlooked the other provision as *Dobson* has faded into history.

David F. Shores, *Deferential Review of Tax Court Decisions: Dobson Revisited*, 49 Tax Law. 629, 655 (1996). Another scholar explains:

> The legislative history does not rescue us from the conundrum. It appears that "the Senate intended to overrule *Dobson* with respect to questions of fact only, while the House intended to overrule *Dobson* with respect to questions of fact as well as law." Whose intent, then, should control? Since the language that eventually became the statute originated in the Senate, Shores maintains that the Senate's intent should predominate. If so, *Dobson* would survive at least to this extent: appellate courts should defer to the Tax Court on issues of law unless the Tax Court's view thereof is plainly unreasonable.

Steve R. Johnson, *The Phoenix and the Perils of the Second Best: Why Heightened Appellate Deference to Tax Court Decisions Is Undesirable*, 77 Or. L. Rev. 235, 252 (1998) (footnotes omitted). Given the Tax Court's current status as a trial court, rather than an administrative agency, do you think appellate courts ought to defer to the Tax Court's views on issues of law?

§ 8.02 THE TAX COURT'S JURISDICTION AND CASELOAD

Reading Assignment: I.R.C. §§ 6211(a), 6512(b)(1).

Much of the Tax Court's caseload consists of cases involving tax deficiencies, with respect to which the taxpayer received a notice of deficiency. A deficiency can generally be understood as an understatement (as opposed to an underpayment) of tax.[5] *See* I.R.C. § 6211(a). The Tax Court also has jurisdiction to hear overpayment claims in cases in which it has deficiency jurisdiction.[6] *See* I.R.C. § 6512(b). This allows for the efficiency gained from consolidating claims in one court.

The Tax Court also has jurisdiction over several other types of cases, including certain declaratory judgment actions, such as those relating to the tax-exempt status of an organization; disclosure actions under Code section 6110; and actions for relief of joint and several liability ("innocent spouse" determinations).[7] An increasingly important area of the Tax Court's jurisdiction is Collection Due Process cases (which the Tax Court Rules refer to as "Lien and Levy Actions").[8]

As the chart below reflects, over the last decade, the Tax Court's inventory of cases pending declined steadily through the 2000 fiscal year and then began to increase. The aggregate dollar amounts in dispute in Tax Court cases have varied more.[9]

Fiscal Year	1997	1998	1999	2000	2001	2002	2003	2004	2005	2006
Number of Cases Pending in Tax Court (dockets in thousands)	29.6	24.7	21.9	16.6	18.3	20.5	22.4	23.9	24.9	26.2
Dollars in Dispute in Cases Pending in Tax Court (in billions)	$33.2	$33.8	$32.8	$28.9	$29.8	$35.9	$22.7	$19.7	$29.3	$27.7

---

[5] The statutory definition is more technical because it takes into account assessments and rebates. *See* I.R.C. § 6211(a).

In *Bocock v. Commissioner*, 127 T.C. 178, 180–82 (2006), the Tax Court held that it had no jurisdiction over the issue of whether the IRS improperly applied payments intended for a couple's 2002 tax year to the husband's 1978 tax year. The court found, in part, that the payments were payments of "estimated taxes." It found that estimated tax payments are not considered in calculating the amount of a tax deficiency, under section 6211(b). *Id.* at 182. Accordingly, the Tax Court had no basis for jurisdiction.

[6] Overpayment claims are discussed in detail in Chapter 10, which covers the various methods of pursuing a refund of overpaid taxes.

[7] Innocent spouse litigation is discussed in Chapter 17.

[8] Tax Court rulemaking is discussed below. Collection Due Process litigation, which is now consolidated in the Tax Court, *see* I.R.C. § 6330(d), is discussed in Chapter 16.

[9] The figures in the chart are from the following sources: Report of Office of Chief Counsel, Internal Revenue Service, prepared for American Bar Association Tax Section Court Procedure Committee, Kissimmee, FL (Jan. 30, 2004) at 2, 3 (fiscal years 1997 through 2003); Chief Counsel Workload: Tax Litigation, by Type of Case, Fiscal Year 2005 (Table 29) (fiscal years 2004 and 2005), *available at* http://www.irs.gov/taxstats/compliancestats/article/0,,id=132165,00.html; Chief Counsel Workload: Tax Litigation, by Type of Case, Fiscal Year 2006 (Table 27) (fiscal year 2006), *available at* http://www.irs.gov/taxstats/article/0,,id=168593,00.html.

§ 8.03 TAX COURT PLEADING REQUIREMENTS

Tax Court jurisdiction over federal tax deficiencies is based on a notice of deficiency mailed by the IRS to the taxpayer and a timely responsive petition by the taxpayer. *See* IRC § 6213(a); *see also* Tax Ct. R. 20, 34. To initiate litigation, the taxpayer must file the petition with the Tax Court, generally within 90 days of the date the IRS mails the notice of deficiency.[10] The taxpayer need not pay the amount in dispute in order to obtain Tax Court jurisdiction — an important difference from refund litigation, which is discussed in Chapter 10.[11]

As indicated above, under Code section 6512(b), the taxpayer can also claim in the petition a refund of an overpayment. Tax Court rules provide for calculation of the amount of the deficiency or overpayment, which is necessary in any case in which the judgment (including any concession) is not entirely for one party — petitioner or respondent. (In Tax Court, the taxpayer is the "petitioner" and the IRS is the "respondent.") The calculation is referred to as a "Rule 155" calculation, and the resulting decision is entered under Tax Ct. R. 155.

The taxpayer's petition must include the taxpayer's legal name and state of residence (or, for a corporation, its principal place of business); the taxpayer's mailing address; the office of the IRS with which the return in question was filed; the date of the notice of deficiency; the amount of the alleged deficiency; the type of tax involved; the tax years or periods in issue; clear and concise assignments of the IRS's errors; clear and concise lettered statements of the facts on which the taxpayer bases the errors; a prayer for relief; the signature, mailing address, and telephone number of each taxpayer or each taxpayer's counsel, and counsel's Tax Court bar number; and a copy of the notice of deficiency, redacted to remove the taxpayer's Taxpayer Identification Number. Tax Ct. R. 27, 34(b).[12]

The IRS's responsive pleading is called an answer. The petition and answer are generally the only two pleadings in Tax Court; in most cases, the taxpayer does not have to file a reply. *See* Tax Ct. R. 30, 37, 38. At times, the IRS may file an amended answer.

A Tax Court petition generally looks something like this one, which was filed in an actual case.

SAMPLE TAX COURT PETITION

JANE PARKER,
Petitioner,
v.
COMMISSIONER OF INTERNAL REVENUE,
Respondent.

PETITION

The Petitioner hereby petitions for a redetermination of the deficiency set forth by the Commissioner of Internal Revenue in his Notice of Deficiency (bearing symbols "SS:ESP MD:STP") dated December 14, 1998, and as a basis for the petitioner's case alleges as follows:

---

[10] The fee for filing a Tax Court petition is $60. *See* I.R.C. § 7451.

[11] The taxpayer is not precluded from paying the deficiency, however. *See* I.R.C. § 6213(b)(4) ("In any case where . . . amount [paid as a tax] is paid after the mailing of a notice of deficiency under section 6212, such payment shall not deprive the Tax Court of jurisdiction over such deficiency determined under section 6211 without regard to such assessment.").

[12] Tax Court Rule 34(b) no longer calls for inclusion of the taxpayer's Taxpayer Identification Number. Instead, Rule 20(b) requires a Statement of Taxpayer Identification Number. The Statement will not be included in the public case file, in order to protect taxpayer privacy.

1. The Petitioner has a legal residence at 125 Oak Street, Jordan, Minnesota, 55352-9307. Petitioner Jane Parker's taxpayer identification number is [TIN OMITTED]. The return for the period ending December 31, 1996 was filed with the Office of Internal Revenue Service at Kansas City, Missouri.

2. The Notice of Deficiency for the tax year ending December 31, 1996 (a copy of which is attached hereto and marked as Exhibit "A") was mailed to the Petitioner on or after December 14, 1998, and was issued by the office of the Internal Revenue Service at St. Paul, Minnesota.

3. The deficiency as determined by the Commissioner is in income tax and additions to tax pursuant to the Internal Revenue Code Section 6662 as follows:

Tax Year Ended	Deficiency	Additions to Tax IRC Section 6662(a)
12/31/96	$30,825	$6,615

all of which is in dispute.

4. The determination of addition to tax set forth in the Notice of Deficiency is based upon the following errors:

A. The Commissioner erred in determining that Petitioner received funds from the Estate of Robert Bennett as compensation or income from services.

B. The Commissioner erred in determining that the addition to tax provided by Section 6662 is applicable.

5. The facts upon which the Petitioner relies as the basis for her case are as follows:

A. The Petitioner's first husband, John Parker, died from malignant brain cancer in 1964. Petitioner and her first husband operated a restaurant "Parker Cafe" in Plato, Minnesota for many years which Petitioner continued to operate after the death of her first husband.

B. Petitioner met Mr. Robert Bennett in 1966. In 1977, Mr. Bennett persuaded Petitioner to retire from active business, sell the restaurant, move to Jordan, Minnesota and establish a common household with him in a house that he was building in Jordan, Minnesota.

C. Petitioner helped Mr. Bennett complete the construction of the house by contributing funds, materials and her time and efforts to completing the construction of the house.

E. Petitioner provided most of the furnishings, appliances and utensils used in the house by this couple in an amount greater than $50,000.00.

F. During the years during which they maintained their common household, Petitioner met her own personal living expenses and also contributed significantly more to the couple's joint living expenses than Mr. Bennett did. For example, for the period from August 23, 1989 through early 1996, Petitioner contributed in excess of $50,000.00 to the couple's joint living expenses.

G. Mr. Bennett was aware of Petitioner's large and disproportionate contributions to their joint living expenses. Also, Mr. Bennett wished to express his love for Petitioner and gratitude for the life they shared. Therefore, he verbally promised Petitioner that upon his death, in his will, he would give her the house that they had built, furnished and lived in from its construction.

H. Mr. Bennett died on February 7, 1996. No will for Mr. Bennett was ever found.

I. Mr. Bennett's brother, a Mr. Richard Bennett, became the administrator of Mr. Bennett's estate.

J. Mr. Richard Bennett refused to honor Mr. Robert Bennett's promise to bequeath the house to Petitioner.

K. As a result, Petitioner filed a claim against the estate in the probate proceeding for Mr. Robert Bennett.

L. Petitioner and the estate of Robert Bennett settled this claim by transferring the house to Petitioner. The parties agreed the house had a fair market value of $138,000 as per an appraisal. Petitioner paid $35,000 in cash to the estate and the estate agreed to credit $103,000 against the value of the house.

M. Petitioner paid more towards the construction and furnishing of the house and their joint living expenses than the $103,000 credited towards the purchase price of the house.

N. Therefore, the $103,000 represented a reimbursement of expenses incurred and funds advanced by Petitioner and an expression by the decedent of love and gratitude toward Petitioner for the life they had shared.

O. Therefore, none of the $103,000 credited to the value of the house in the settlement agreement is attributable to compensation for service.

P. Petitioner informed her return preparer about the bequest that she had received from the estate of Robert Bennett in the form of a credit against the purchase price of the house at the time the 1996 Federal Income Tax Return was prepared. Therefore, in not reporting this amount as income, she relied upon the advice of her return preparer and accountant.

Q. The accountant's treatment of this transaction as a bequest rather than as compensation for services was correct as a matter of fact and law.

WHEREFORE, it is prayed that the Court hear this case and determine that there is no deficiency and no addition to tax due from Petitioner for the taxable year of 1996.

Dated: January 21st, 1999

By:
Attorney for Petitioner
Address
Telephone Number
Attorney No.

[Attachments omitted.]

Because a petition is required for Tax Court subject matter jurisdiction, a Tax Court case will be dismissed if the taxpayer was sent a valid notice of deficiency but filed his or her petition late.[13] In addition, although the Tax Court may allow the taxpayer to file an amended petition, if the petition is in the name of someone other than the taxpayer, it is better for the proper party to file the petition in the first instance so that obtaining permission to amend the petition is not necessary. *See* Tax Ct. R. 60(a)(1); *see also* Fletcher Plastics, Inc. v. Commissioner, 64 T.C. 35 (1975) (amendment to reflect proper petitioner allowed); Great Falls Bonding Agency, Inc. v. Commissioner, 63 T.C. 304 (1974) (case dismissed for lack of jurisdiction because petitioning corporation had legally ceased to exist two years prior to petitioning Tax Court); Starvest U.S., Inc. v. Commissioner, T.C. Memo. 1999-314 (appropriate parties ratified filing of petition).

One type of case that raises the issue of whether parties properly petitioned the Tax Court involves married taxpayers who filed a joint return and received a notice of deficiency in both names but filed a petition in one name only. *See, e.g.,* Holt v. Commissioner, 67 T.C. 829 (1977) (court found that husband was acting as his wife's agent as well as on his own behalf); Beaumont v. Commissioner, T.C. Memo. 1986-373 (court found that letter from husband was imperfect petition with respect to both

[13] Issues of Tax Court subject matter jurisdiction are discussed in more detail in Chapter 9.

spouses). In Martin v. Commissioner, T.C. Memo. 2000-187, the Tax Court upheld Alfred Martin's argument that because he had not authorized his name to be included on a Tax Court petition for tax year 1980, the Tax Court lacked jurisdiction over him. The court therefore dismissed him from the case. Mr. Martin's accountant had received a notice of deficiency, and sent a copy of it to a law firm that then included his name on the petition, along with the name of his ex-wife.

§ 8.04 DISCOVERY IN TAX COURT

As indicated above, while the Federal Rules of Evidence apply in Tax Court, the Tax Court has established its own Rules of Practice and Procedure. *See* I.R.C. § 7453. Discovery is somewhat more limited in Tax Court than in the district courts. A key difference between Tax Court discovery and discovery in other courts is that the Tax Court relies heavily on stipulations of facts. The parties to a Tax Court case are required to stipulate to the facts to the fullest extent possible. *See* Tax Ct. R. 91. This includes stipulations of the evidence, so that key documents such as tax returns typically are attached to the stipulation of facts as exhibits. It is therefore unnecessary for the Tax Court to take the time for the taxpayer to testify in order to lay a foundation for the taxpayer's return to be admitted as evidence. The Tax Court also encourages the use of informal discovery as much as possible. Consider the following case:

THE BRANERTON CORPORATION v. COMMISSIONER

United States Tax Court
61 T.C. 691 (1974)

Dawson, Judge:

This matter is before the Court on respondent's motion for a protective order, pursuant to Rule 103(a)(2), Tax Court Rules of Practice and Procedure, that respondent at this time need not answer written interrogatories served upon him by petitioners in these cases. Oral arguments on the motion were heard on February 20, 1974, and, in addition, a written statement in opposition to respondent's motion was filed by the petitioners.

The sequence of events in these cases may be highlighted as follows: The statutory notices of deficiencies were mailed to the respective petitioners on April 20, 1973. * * * Petitions in both cases were filed on July 2, 1973, and, after an extension of time for answering, respondent filed his answers on September 26, 1973. This Court's new Rules of Practice and Procedure became effective January 1, 1974. The next day petitioners' counsel served on respondent rather detailed and extensive written interrogatories pursuant to Rule 71. On January 11, 1974, respondent filed his motion for a protective order. The cases have not yet been scheduled for trial.

Petitioners' counsel has never requested an informal conference with respondent's counsel in these cases, although respondent's counsel states that he is willing to have such discussions at any mutually convenient time. Consequently, in seeking a protective order, respondent specifically cites the second sentence of Rule 70(a)(1) which provides: "However, the Court expects the parties to attempt to attain the objectives of discovery through informal consultation or communication before utilizing the discovery procedures provided in these Rules."

It is plain that this provision in Rule 70(a)(1) means exactly what it says. The discovery procedures should be used only after the parties have made reasonable informal efforts to obtain needed information voluntarily. For many years the bedrock of Tax Court practice has been the stipulation process, now embodied in Rule 91. Essential to that process is the voluntary exchange of necessary facts, documents, and other data between the parties as an aid to the more expeditious trial of cases as well as for settlement purposes.[n.1] The recently adopted discovery procedures were not intended in any way to weaken the stipulation process. *See* Rule 91(a)(2).

Contrary to petitioners' assertion that there is no "practical and substantial reason" for granting a protective order in these circumstances, we find good cause for doing so. Petitioners have failed to comply with the letter and spirit of the discovery rules. The attempted use of written interrogatories at this stage of the proceedings sharply conflicts with the intent and purpose of Rule 70(a)(1) and constitutes an abuse of the Court's procedures.

Accordingly, we conclude that respondent's motion for a protective order should be granted and he is relieved from taking any action with respect to these written interrogatories. The parties will be directed to have informal conferences during the next 90 days for the purpose of making good faith efforts to exchange facts, documents, and other information. Since the cases have not been scheduled for trial, there is sufficient time for the parties to confer and try informally to secure the evidence before resorting to formal discovery procedures. If such process does not meet the needs of the parties, they may then proceed with discovery to the extent permitted by the rules.

An appropriate order will be entered.

As *Branerton* points out, interrogatories and other discovery procedures, such as requests for admissions and depositions, are available in Tax Court. *See* Tax Ct. R. 70–76, 90. However, they are available only if necessary after the parties have conducted discovery through informal means. *Branerton* is a leading case on Tax Court discovery. Letters making an informal request for information or for a conference to communicate informally have become known as *Branerton* letters. *See, e.g.,* DeLucia v. Commissioner, 87 T.C. 804, 807 (1986); Williams v. Commissioner, T.C. Memo. 1997-541, *aff'd*, 176 F.3d 486 (9th Cir. 1999).

In *Schneider Interests, LP v. Commissioner*, 119 T.C. 151 (2002), the Tax Court criticized the IRS for failing to allow time for informal discovery before pressing Schneider Interests to respond to formal discovery requests. In that case, Schneider Interests filed a motion for a protective order, seeking a stay of formal discovery until the parties had an opportunity to engage in meaningful informal discovery. *Id.* at 153. The court granted the motion, stating, in part:

> *The actions of respondent's counsel in the instant case lead us to believe that he does not fully appreciate the importance of our* Branerton *opinion.* His insistence on compliance with his formal discovery requests in advance of any conference between the parties does not effectively present an opportunity for the "discussion, deliberation, and an interchange of ideas, thoughts, and opinions between the parties" that our rules contemplate.

Id. at 156 (emphasis added).

It is interesting to note that in *Branerton*, the taxpayer sought discovery, although the taxpayer generally should have superior access to the facts. *See* Philip N. Jones, *Tax Court Discovery and the Stipulation Process*: Branerton *30 Years Later*, 100 J. Tax'n 29, 30 (2004). By contrast, it was the IRS that sought discovery in *Schneider Interests*.

[n.1] Part of the explanatory note to Rule 91 (60 T.C. 1118) states that —

> "The stipulation process is more flexible, based on conference and negotiation between parties, adaptable to statements on matters in varying degrees of dispute, susceptible of defining and narrowing areas of dispute, and offering an active medium for settlement."

§ 8.05 PRECEDENT APPLICABLE TO TAX COURT CASES

Reading Assignment: I.R.C. § 7482(a)(1), (b)(1)(A)–(B), (2).

The Tax Court is a national court yet its appeals lie to the various Courts of Appeals. What precedent should apply in Tax Court cases — Tax Court precedent or Court of Appeals precedent? The Tax Court answered this question in the following case.

GOLSEN v. COMMISSIONER

United States Tax Court
54 T.C. 742 (1970)[14]

The Commissioner determined a deficiency of $2,918.15 in petitioners' income tax for 1962. The only issue is whether a $12,441.40 payment made by petitioner Jack E. Golsen to the Western Security Life Insurance Co. is deductible as an interest payment pursuant to section 163, I.R.C. 1954.

OPINION

RAUM, JUDGE:

This case involves an ingenious device which, if successful, would result in petitioner's purchase of a substantial amount of life insurance for the protection of his family at little or no aftertax cost to himself, or possibly even with a net profit in some years. The device is based on an unusual type of insurance policy that appears to have been specially designed for this purpose in which the rates were set at an artificially high level with correspondingly high cash surrender and loan values to begin immediately during the very first year of the life of the policy. The plan contemplated the purchase of a large amount of such insurance, the "payment" of the first year's premium, the simultaneous "prepayment" of the next 4 years' premiums discounted at the annual rate of 3 percent, the immediate "borrowing" of the first year's cash value at 4 percent "interest," and the immediate "borrowing" back of the full reserve value generated by the "prepayment," also at 4-percent "interest." Each year thereafter, the plan called for the "borrowing" of the annual increase in the loan or cash value of the policy at 4-percent "interest"; such increase, as a result of the artificially high premium, was more than sufficient to "prepay" the discounted amount of the premium which would become due 4 years thereafter. The net result of these complicated maneuvers would be that the insured's net out-of-pocket (pretax) expenditures each year would be equal to the true actuarial cost of the insurance benefits that he was purchasing (*i.e.*, net death benefits in substantial amounts even after the policies had been stripped of their cash surrender values) — although, in form, he appeared to be paying large amounts of "interest." At the heart of the device is the deduction allowed in section 163(a) of the 1954 Code with respect to "interest paid * * * on indebtedness." * * *

The precise question relating to the deductibility of "interest" like that involved herein has been adjudicated by two Courts of Appeals. In one case, *Campbell v. Cen-Tex., Inc.*, 377 F.2d 688 (C.A. 5), decision went for the taxpayer; in the other, *Goldman v. United States*, 403 F.2d 776 (C.A. 10), *affirming* 273 F. Supp. 137 (W.D. Okla.), the Government prevailed. *Goldman* involved the same insurance company, the same type of policies, and the same financial arrangements as are before us in the present case. *Cen-Tex* involved a different insurance company but dealt with comparable financing arrangements. Despite some rather feeble attempts on the part of each side herein to distinguish the case adverse to it, we think that both cases are in point. It is our view that the Government's position is correct.

---

[14] *Aff'd*, 445 F.2d 985 (10th Cir.), *cert. denied*, 404 U.S. 940 (1971).

Moreover, we think that we are in any event bound by *Goldman* since it was decided by the Court of Appeals for the same circuit within which the present case arises. In thus concluding that we must follow *Goldman*, we recognize the contrary thrust of the oft-criticized[n.13] case of *Arthur L. Lawrence*, 27 T.C. 713. Notwithstanding a number of the considerations which originally led us to that decision, it is our best judgment that better judicial administration[n.14] requires us to follow a Court of Appeals decision which is squarely in point where appeal from our decision lies to that Court of Appeals and to that court alone.

Section 7482(a), I.R.C. 1954,[n.16] charges the Courts of Appeals with the primary responsibility for review of our decisions, and we think that where the Court of Appeals to which appeal lies has already passed upon the issue before us, efficient and harmonious judicial administration calls for us to follow the decision of that court. Moreover, the practice we are adopting does not jeopardize the Federal interest in uniform application of the internal revenue laws which we emphasized in *Lawrence*. We shall remain able to foster uniformity by giving effect to our own views in cases appealable to courts whose views have not yet been expressed, and, even where the relevant Court of Appeals has already made its views known, by explaining why we agree or disagree with the precedent that we feel constrained to follow. * * *

To the extent that *Lawrence* is inconsistent with the views expressed herein it is hereby overruled. We note, however, that some of our decisions, because they involve two or more taxpayers, may be appealable to more than one circuit. This case presents no such problem, and accordingly we need not decide now what course to take in the event that we are faced with it.

Decision will be entered for the respondent.

WITHEY, J., dissenting: While I agree with the conclusion of the Court on the merits of this case, I dissent on the reversal of this Court's position on *Arthur L. Lawrence*, 27 T.C. 713, by the majority.

Note that if two similar cases are governed by conflicting Court of Appeals precedent, the *Golsen* decision allows the possibility of inconsistent Tax Court decisions, even if the two cases are decided by the same Tax Court judge. Therefore, when analyzing any Tax Court case, it is important to determine whether a Tax Court case reflects the Tax Court's application of its own rule or of binding circuit precedent. *See, e.g.*, Perryman v. Commissioner, T.C. Memo. 1988-378 ("Despite our holding in [a prior Tax Court case],

---

n.13 *Norvel Jeff McLellan*, 51 T.C. 462, 465–467 (concurring opinion); *Automobile Club of New York, Inc.*, 32 T.C. 906, 923–926 (dissenting opinion), *affirmed* 304 F. 2d 781 (C.A. 2); *Robert M. Dann*, 30 T.C. 499, 510 (dissenting opinion); Del Cotto, "The Need for a Court of Tax Appeals: An Argument and a Study," 12 Buffalo L. Rev. 5, 8–10 (1962); Vom Baur & Coburn, "Tax Court Wrong in Denying Taxpayer the Rule Laid Down in His Circuit," 8 J. Taxation 228 (1958); Orkin, "The Finality of the Court of Appeals Decisions in the Tax Court: A Dichotomy of Opinion," 43 A.B.A. J. 945 (1957); * * *.

n.14 The importance of the *Lawrence* doctrine in respect of the functioning of this Court has been grossly exaggerated by some of the critics of that decision. That case was decided Jan. 25, 1957, and this is the first time during the intervening period of somewhat in excess of 13 years that the Court has ever deemed it appropriate to face the question whether or not to apply the *Lawrence* doctrine.

n.16 SEC. 7482. COURTS OF REVIEW.

> (a) Jurisdiction. — The United States Courts of Appeals shall have exclusive jurisdiction to review the decisions of the Tax Court, except as provided in section 1254 of Title 28 of the United States Code, in the same manner and to the same extent as decisions of the district courts in civil actions tried without a jury; and the judgment of any such court shall be final, except that it shall be subject to review by the Supreme Court of the United States upon certiorari, in the manner provided in section 1254 of Title 28 of the United States Code.

we will follow the precedent established in the court to which appeal would lie.").

§ 8.06 THE TAX COURT'S SMALL TAX CASE PROCEDURE

Reading Assignment: I.R.C. §§ 7443A(b)(2), 7463(a), (b), (d), (f).

Section 7463 of the Code provides for an elective, informal procedure for cases involving relatively small amounts of money. For deficiency cases, this small tax, or "S case," procedure is available if neither the deficiency placed in dispute nor any claimed overpayment exceeds $50,000 for any one taxable year.[15] I.R.C. § 7463(a). Cases involving claims for relief from joint and several liability (innocent spouse claims) can be heard as S cases if "the amount of relief sought does not exceed $50,000." I.R.C. § 7463(f)(1). Collection due process appeals under Code section 6330(d)(1)(A) can be heard as small tax cases if "the unpaid tax does not exceed $50,000."[16] I.R.C. § 7463(f)(2). As of 2007, S cases comprised about 50 percent of the Tax Court's docket. *See* United States Tax Court Press Release (Jan. 12, 2007), *available at* http://www.ustaxcourt.gov/press/011207.pdf.

To obtain eligibility to elect the small tax case procedure in a deficiency case, the taxpayer can concede amounts that exceed the jurisdictional cap. Kallich v. Commissioner, 89 T.C. 676 (1987), *acq.* 1988-2 C.B. 1. For example, if a notice of deficiency reflects a deficiency of $55,000, the taxpayer can concede $5,000 of it and be eligible to have the case heard under the small tax case procedure. By contrast, the Tax Court has held that in a CDP case, the unpaid tax — not the amount of that tax in dispute — must be $50,000 or less for the case to be eligible for the S case procedure. *See* Leahy v. Commissioner, 129 T.C. 71, 76 (2007).

The taxpayer has the option to elect the small tax case procedure, so long as the Tax Court agrees. I.R.C. § 7463(a). In general, the Tax Court will agree to the designation as a small tax case unless the case involves a recurring issue for which precedent is needed — as indicated below, S case opinions have no precedential value.

In deciding whether to elect the small tax case procedure, taxpayers and their representatives should consider the several ways in which S cases differ from regular cases. First, S cases are conducted more informally than regular cases, *see* I.R.C. § 7463(a). The Federal Rules of Evidence do not apply in those cases. *See id.* In addition, the Tax Court travels on a regular basis to more cities to hear S cases than it does to hear regular cases. *See* Tax Court Rules Appendix III. Special Trial Judges, rather than regular Tax Court judges, hear most of the S cases, I.R.C. § 7443A(b)(2), and write Summary Opinions in those cases, *see* I.R.C. § 7463(a). Also very important is that (1) there is no appeal from an S case, and (2) the decision has no precedential value. I.R.C. § 7463(b).[17]

Taxpayers must file a petition to invoke the Tax Court's jurisdiction, but, until 2007, the IRS did not have to file an answer in S cases. The Tax Court changed that by rule.

---

[15] When the small tax case procedure was first enacted, it was limited to disputes involving no more than $1,000. Tax Reform Act of 1969, Pub. L. No. 91-172, § 957, 83 Stat. 487, 730–36. Congress has increased that over the years, most recently in 1998 from $10,000 to its present level of $50,000, as part of the IRS Reform Act.

[16] CDP appeals are discussed in Chapter 16.

[17] In January 2001, the Tax Court began posting Summary Opinions in S cases on its web site. The S case opinions are available at the same site as other Tax Court opinions, www.ustaxcourt.gov/ustcweb.htm. Division and Memorandum Opinions are available from January 1, 1999, and Summary Opinions are available from January 1, 2001. Opinions on the Tax Court website became searchable by key word in May 2003. *See ABA Tax Section Meeting: Court Clerks Present Procedural Wish List*, 2003 TNT 91-19 (May 9, 2003).

See TAX CT. R. 173(b). The IRS subsequently issued Chief Counsel Notice CC-2007-009, *available at* 2007 TNT 53-11 (Mar. 19, 2007), specifying updated procedures for filing answers in Tax Court cases.

§ 8.07 OUTCOMES IN TAX COURT CASES AND ALLEGATIONS OF BIAS

The Tax Court has often been accused of bias against taxpayers.[18] Typically, allegations of Tax Court bias focus on the outcomes in Tax Court cases.[19] More sophisticated analyses compare Tax Court case outcomes to those of federal tax cases heard by other courts. For example, Professor Deborah Geier compared the outcomes of the Tax Court and the federal district courts for various years spanning 1965 to 1986. Deborah A. Geier, *The Tax Court, Article III, and the Proposal Advanced by the Federal Courts Study Committee: A Study in Applied Constitutional Theory*, 76 CORNELL L. REV. 985, 998 (1991). She found that "the government won or partially won an average of 70.5% of district court cases in the years indicated, and no particular trend is discernible. . . . [T]he percentage of cases won or partially won by the government in the Tax Court averaged 90.4% for the same period — a full twenty-point difference — evidencing a decided pro-government trend in recent years." *Id.*

Particularly because the taxpayer often has a choice of forum, as discussed in Chapter 11, a comparison of case outcomes can be relevant to the strategic choice of where to docket a case. However, the jurisdictional prerequisites are not the same for the Tax Court and the refund fora. Comparing outcomes across fora will not result in an apples-to-apples comparison if, for example, weaker cases disproportionately go to Tax Court. Notably, the taxpayer need not pay the deficiency to docket the case in Tax Court, which could result in frivolous cases disproportionately being brought there.

A comparison of outcomes also does not control for other factors, such as whether or not the taxpayer is represented by counsel. Tax Court cases are procedurally complex, and unrepresented taxpayers may make mistakes that put them at a disadvantage. One study of a sample of Tax Court cases found that the presence of an attorney for the taxpayer decreased the government's recovery rate by 17.9 percentage points, on average. Leandra Lederman & Warren B. Hrung, *Do Attorneys Do Their Clients Justice? An Empirical Study of Lawyers' Effects on Tax Court Litigation Outcomes*, 41 WAKE FOREST L. REV. 1235, 1255 (2006). "This means, for example, that if the IRS would otherwise have recovered 78% of the amount of tax it claimed was due, representation would lower that amount, on average, to about 60%." *Id.* Moreover, the taxpayer's results improved with the years of experience of the attorney. *Id.* at 1260 ("each additional year of attorney experience decreases the IRS's recovery ratio by approximately 9/10 of a percentage point, and this is statistically significant."). The study found that, in cases that settled after being docketed in Tax Court, attorneys had no statistically significant impact on settlement amounts. *Id.* at 1262.

In 2008, the Tax Court stated that "approximately 75 percent of [its] petitioners are pro se individuals. . . ." Tax Court Press Release (Jan. 15, 2008), *available at* http://www.ustaxcourt.gov/press/011508.pdf, at 12. This figure includes small tax cases, but is suggestive of the frequency of pro se litigation in regular Tax Court cases. By contrast, one study found that in ten U.S. District Courts, 21 percent of the filings were

---

[18] Professor James Maule describes the history of those accusations in his article, James Edward Maule, *Instant Replay, Weak Teams, and Disputed Calls: An Empirical Study of Alleged Tax Court Judge Bias*, 66 TENN. L. REV. 351, 354–63 (1999).

[19] For example, in Glenn Kroll, *Are Tax Court Judges Partial to the Government?*, 45 OIL & GAS TAX Q. 135 (1996), the author, then a law student, started the article by arguing that "one cannot help but think that their chances of winning their case should be better than 14.3 percent." *Id.* at 135. That figure was obtained by averaging figures in the Annual Report of the Commissioner of Internal Revenue from 1986 to 1993. *Id.* at 135 n.2.

pro se. Of a sample of 52,885 pro se cases they reviewed, only 37 percent involved nonprisoner civil actions. *See* David Rauma & Charles P. Sutelan, *Analysis of Pro Se Case Filings in Ten U.S. District Courts Yields New Information*, 9 FJC Directions 5, 6 (1996). If substantially fewer tax cases in the federal district courts and Court of Federal Claims involve pro se taxpayers — which seems likely, in part because the IRS's notice of deficiency mentions only the Tax Court option, not the refund court option — then any greater success in refund courts may in part be due to the influence of taxpayer counsel.

Another complicating factor is the relevant basis of comparison. As the figures Professor Geier cites suggests, many cases are "won" by neither party, but rather reflect a split decision (the financial result of which is computed under Tax Court Rule 155). Should wins and losses in those cases be determined according to who won the greatest number of issues, the most important issues, or some other way? One seemingly straightforward way to compare cases is to look at the percentage of dollars in dispute that are recovered by the government (or, conversely, are retained by the taxpayer). Even that gets complicated, however, where the taxpayer claims an overpayment or time-sensitive penalties are involved; how much is actually in dispute in those cases? For example, if the IRS has asserted a deficiency of $100,000, the taxpayer claimed an overpayment of $10,000, and the court determines that the taxpayer owes nothing and had a $5,000 overpayment, what percent of the dollars in dispute were recovered by the government and by the taxpayer?

According to Tax Court statistics, the IRS recovery rates in opinion decisions for fiscal years 1996–2005 are as follows:

Fiscal Year	IRS Recovery Rate, All Cases	IRS Recovery Rate, Regular Cases[20]	IRS Recovery Rate, S Cases
1996	23.6%	23.6%	74.5%
1997	39.4%	39.4%	68.9%
1998	17.0%	16.9%	73.3%
1999	11.7%	11.6%	62.6%
2000	30.2%	30.0%	68.5%
2001	12.9%	12.8%	73.1%
2002	15.0%	14.9%	74.6%
2003	41.4%	41.2%	64.9%
2004	8.9%	8.7%	71.5%
2005	7.7%	7.6%	76.0%

Note that the blended figures in the left column closely track the results in regular opinion decisions, but the outcomes in S case opinion decisions are substantially different. What do these statistics show about how taxpayers' recoveries compare to those of the government in regular cases? Why might the government do so much better in small tax cases?

Professor Maule countered the allegations of Tax Court bias with his own study, which examined the possibility of bias both in the court as a whole, and by individual judges. Among other tests, he "select[ed] . . . several issues presenting opportunities for a judge's alleged bias to influence the result. Of the most ideal candidates, reasonable compensation, charitable contribution valuation, and estate tax valuation were selected as issues among those most vulnerable to bias and ones that would occur with sufficient frequency so as to permit the accumulation of a useful quantity of data. . . . " James E.

---

20 [Percentages calculated by the authors. — Eds.]

Maule, *Instant Replay, Weak Teams, and Disputed Calls: An Empirical Study of Alleged Tax Court Judge Bias*, 66 TENN. L. REV. 351, 367 (1999). He concluded, with respect to this analysis:

> Turning to the issues in which there is a bias opportunity, taxpayers prevailed in 29% of the sampled issues from memorandum opinions and split with respect to nine percent of the issues. Taxpayers prevailed with respect to 48% of the sampled issues from regular opinions and split with respect to 1% of the issues. The weighted average of 42%, which takes into account the different number of such issues in each of the two types of opinions, is not much lower than the 50% one would expect if the judges merely flipped an unbiased coin with respect to each issue. These findings suggest that Kroll's lament [in footnote 16, above — Eds.] in begging for a taxpayer's chance of success exceeding 14.3% is an unnecessary one. . . . [T]he only way that the overall taxpayer "issue success rate" could approximate 50% or more is for the Court to hold in favor of the taxpayers with respect to every issue other than those involving tax protesters; taxpayers who fail to appear, file documents, or otherwise proceed; and issues appealable to Circuit Courts previously deciding the same issue in another case. . . .

Id. at 391 (footnotes omitted).[21]

Professor Maule then considered outcomes on the issues he studied in terms of IRS recovery rate:

> Because the three examined issues do not have an "all or nothing" quality, there is more utility in measuring the average extent to which the taxpayer prevailed with respect to the issues. . . .
>
> [C]onsidering all 407 issues included in the examined data, taxpayers averaged 56.7% of the amount in dispute. In other words, if, in the average charitable contribution deduction valuation issue, the taxpayer claimed a value of $100,000 and the IRS determined that the value was $20,000, on average the court held that the value was $65,360. Lest the 56.7% amount make it appear that the Court is simply "splitting the difference," the distributional characteristics of the data need to be considered. Only 11.6% of the issues fell into the .50001 to .75 range and only 18.4% fell into the .25001 to .50000 range. . . .

Id. at 392 (footnotes omitted).

Ultimately, Professor Maule concludes:

> The Tax Court is not biased in favor of the IRS. If anything, it might be biased in favor of taxpayers, but that is an issue deserving its own empirical study. The Tax Court consists of judges who come from many different backgrounds that enrich the Court. The judges are much more experienced at representing taxpayers than in any other endeavor and have served with distinction, free of scandal, corruption, or prejudice.

Id. at 425–26. Are you convinced one way or the other on the issue of claimed Tax Court bias? If not, what evidence would you want to analyze in order to reach a conclusion?

---

§ 8.08 REVIEW OF LARGE CASES HEARD BY SPECIAL TRIAL JUDGES

Reading Assignment: I.R.C. § 7443A(c); Tax Ct. R. 183.

As discussed above, the Tax Court is composed not only of presidentially appointed judges, it also has on its staff special trial judges, judicial officers appointed by the Chief Judge, who serve as employees at will. *See* I.R.C. § 7443A(a). Although they typically hear S cases, special trial judges have the authority to hear any case assigned to them by the Chief Judge. I.R.C. § 7443A(b). They are not empowered to enter decisions in cases involving over $50,000 in dispute for any tax year, however. *See* I.R.C. § 7443A(c). In those large cases, a Tax Court Rule provides that the special trial judge must submit a "report" on the case for review by a regular judge of the Tax Court. *See* Tax Ct. R. 183(b) (currently providing "After all the briefs have been filed by all the parties or the time for doing so has expired, the Special Trial Judge shall file recommended findings of fact and conclusions of law and a copy of the recommended findings of fact and conclusions of law shall be served in accordance with Rule 21").

For about two decades until 2005, the Tax Court's rules did not provide an opportunity for the parties to the case to see the special trial judge's report. The Supreme Court ultimately reviewed and criticized that practice. The case that ultimately went to the Supreme Court, *Investment Research Associates Ltd. & Subs. v. Commissioner*, T.C. Memo. 1999-407, was decided under the version of Tax Court Rule 183 that did not provide for disclosure to the parties of the special trial judge's report. Special Trial Judge Couvillion presided over the trial and authored the report, and Judge Dawson, a senior judge, served as the reviewing judge.

The official Tax Court opinion in *Investment Research Associates* found three individuals liable for over $30 million dollars in taxes, penalties, and interest based on a finding of fraud. Declaration of Randall G. Dick in Investment Research Associates v. Commissioner (August 21, 2000), *available at* 2004 TNT 230-11 (Nov. 30, 2004). When the opinion was released, Randall Dick, one of the taxpayers' attorneys, "said he thought that [it] sounded as if it had been written by two people. He said a friend, Julian I. Jacobs, a judge on the tax court, and, later, a special trial judge, Peter J. Panuthos, told him that the final opinion had reversed Judge Couvillion's initial findings." Louise Story, *A Glimpse Inside U.S. Tax Court and How It Made a Decision*, N.Y. Times, July 23, 2005, at 4.

Mr. Dick therefore made a series of motions to obtain disclosure of Judge Couvillion's report. The Tax Court denied all of these motions, including a motion to include the report in the record on appeal. *See* Tax Court Order dated Apr. 26, 2000, *reprinted at* 2001 TNT 23-31 (Feb. 2, 2001); Tax Court Order dated Aug. 30, 2000, *reprinted at* 2001 TNT 23-30 (Feb. 2, 2001). The third motion included an affidavit from Mr. Dick stating that he had been informed that Special Trial Judge Couvillion's original report had found in favor of the taxpayers. The Tax Court stated in its Order, "[a]lthough Mr. Dick states in his declaration that some judges commented about the procedures involved in handling these cases, whatever may have been said to Mr. Dick is irrelevant and immaterial." Tax Court Order dated Aug. 30, 2000, *supra*.

Investment Research Associates was appealed to three Circuits. In *Ballard v. Commissioner*, 321 F.3d 1037 (11th Cir. 2003), *rev'd*, 544 U.S. 40 (2005), the Court of Appeals for the Eleventh Circuit affirmed the Tax Court. On the issue of disclosure of the Special Trial Judge report, the court stated, in part:

> Even assuming [taxpayer counsel Randall] Dick's affidavit to be true and affording Petitioners-Appellants all reasonable inferences, the process utilized in this case does not give rise to due process concern. While the procedures used in the Tax Court may be unique to that court, there is nothing unusual about

judges conferring with one another about cases assigned to them. These conferences are an essential part of the judicial process when, by statute, more than one judge is charged with the responsibility of deciding the case. And, as a result of such conferences, judges sometimes change their original position or thoughts. Whether Special Trial Judge Couvillion prepared drafts of his report or subsequently changed his opinion entirely is without import insofar as our analysis of the alleged due process violation pertaining to the application of Rule 183 is concerned. Despite the invitation, this court will simply not interfere with another court's deliberative process.

The record reveals, and we accept as true, that the underlying report adopted by the Tax Court is Special Trial Judge Couvillion's.

Id. at 1042–43. The taxpayers petitioned for certiorari on the Special Trial Judge report issues.

In *Estate of Kanter v. Commissioner*, 337 F.3d 833 (7th Cir. 2003), *rev'd sub. nom. Ballard v. Commissioner*, 544 U.S. 40 (2005), the Court of Appeals for the Seventh Circuit affirmed the Tax Court in part and reversed in part. On the issue of the Special Trial Judge's report, the Seventh Circuit affirmed the Tax Court's refusal to disclose it. Judge Cudahy filed a lengthy dissent on this issue, arguing that the omission of the Special Trial Judge's report from the record on appeal "creates legitimate due process concerns with respect to [the Court of Appeals'] review." *Id.* at 887 (Cudahy, J., concurring in part and dissenting in part). The taxpayers in *Estate of Kanter* also petitioned for certiorari.

The third of the three Circuits to which *Investment Research Associates* was appealed was the Fifth Circuit. In *Estate of Lisle v. Commissioner*, 341 F.3d 364 (5th Cir. 2003), the Court of Appeals for the Fifth Circuit reversed the Tax Court's finding that the taxpayers had committed fraud. That resulted in elimination of the underlying deficiency for one tax year because of expiration of the statute of limitations. *See id.* at 367. Neither party petitioned for certiorari in that case.[22]

The Supreme Court granted certiorari in *Ballard* and *Estate of Kanter*.[23] *See* Ballard v. Commissioner, 544 U.S. 40 (2005). The Court held that the Tax Court may not exclude the Special Trial Judge's report from the record on appeal, under the language of Tax Court Rule 183. In a 7-2 opinion written by Justice Ginsburg, the Court explained:

Petitioners are taxpayers who were unsuccessful in the Tax Court and on appeal. They object to the concealment of the special trial judge's initial report and, in particular, exclusion of the report from the record on appeal. They urge that, under the Tax Court's current practice, the parties and the Court of Appeals lack essential information: One cannot tell whether, as Rule 183(c) requires, the final decision reflects "due regard" for the special trial judge's "opportunity to evaluate the credibility of [the] witnesses," and presumes the correctness of that judge's initial fact findings.[24] We agree that no statute authorizes, and the current text of Rule 183 does not warrant, the concealment

---

[22] The Court of Appeals "remand[ed] the case to the Tax Court for the limited purpose of recalculating the deficiencies and additions to tax, consistent with [its] opinion." *Id.* at 385. On September 23, 2003, it issued a mandate in that regard. *See Counsel Asks Fifth Circuit to Recall Estate of Lisle Case from Tax Court*, 2005 TNT 150-21 (Aug. 5, 2005).

[23] Professor Lederman filed an amicus brief in the Supreme Court in support of the petitioners in the consolidated cases of *Ballard v. Commissioner* and *Estate of Kanter v. Commissioner*.

[24] [The rule provided:

The Judge to whom or the Division to which the case is assigned may adopt the Special Trial Judge's report or may modify it or may reject it in whole or in part, or may direct the filing of additional briefs or may receive further evidence or may direct oral argument, or may recommit the report with instructions. Due regard shall be given to the circumstance that the Special Trial Judge had the opportunity to evaluate the credibility of witnesses, and the findings of fact recommended

> at issue. We so hold, mindful that it is routine in federal judicial and administrative decision-making both to disclose the initial report of a hearing officer, and to make that report part of the record available to an appellate forum. A departure of the bold character practiced by the Tax Court — the creation and attribution solely to the special trial judge of a superseding report composed in unrevealed collaboration with a regular Tax Court judge — demands, at the very least, full and fair statement in the Tax Court's own Rules.

Id. at 46–47.

The Court also commented on the possibility that the Tax Court might subsequently change its rules expressly to allow for off-the-record collaboration: "The idiosyncratic procedure the Commissioner describes and defends, although not the system of adjudication that Rule 183 currently creates, is one the Tax Court might some day adopt. Were the Tax Court to amend its Rules to express the changed character of the Tax Court judge's review of special trial judge reports, that change would, of course, be subject to appellate review for consistency with the relevant federal statutes and due process." *Id.* at 65.

In a concurring opinion in which Justice Scalia joined, Justice Kennedy addressed various possibilities regarding what might happen following the Supreme Court's opinion:

> If the Tax Court deems it necessary to allow informal consultation and collaboration between the special trial judge and the Tax Court judge, it might design a rule for that process. If, on the other hand, it were to insist on more formality — with deference to the special trial judge's report and an obligation on the part of the Tax Court judge to describe the reasons for any substantial departures from the original findings — without requiring disclosure of the initial report, that would present a more problematic approach. It is not often that a rule requiring deference to the original factfinder exists, but the affected parties have no means of ensuring its enforcement.
>
> That brings us to the questions of how these cases should be resolved on remand and how the current version of the Rule should be interpreted in later cases. As to the former, this question is difficult because we do not know what happened in the Tax Court, a point that is important to underscore here. From a single affidavit, the majority extrapolates "a novel practice" whereby the Tax Court treats the initial special trial judge report as "an in-house draft to be worked over collaboratively by the regular judge and the special trial judge." *Ante*, at 14. I interpret the opinion as indicating that there might be such a practice, not that there is. The dissent, in contrast, appears to assume that any changes to the initial report were the result of reconsideration by the special trial judge or informal suggestions by the Tax Court judge. *Post*, at 4 (opinion of Rehnquist, C.J.). Given the sparse record before us, I would not be so quick to make either assumption, particularly given that the Commissioner, charged with defending the Tax Court's decision, is no more privy to the inner workings of the Tax Court than we are.
>
> Given the lingering uncertainty about whether the initial report was in fact altered or superseded, and the extent of any changes, there are factual questions that still must be resolved. If the initial report was not substantially altered, then there will have been no violation of the Rule. If, on the other hand, substantial revisions were made during a collaborative effort between the special trial judge and the Tax Court judge, the Tax Court might remedy that breach of the Rule in different ways. For instance, it could simply recommit the

---

by the Special Trial Judge shall be presumed to be correct.

Tax Ct. R. 183(c). — Eds.]

> special trial judge's initial report and start over from there. More likely in these circumstances, the remedy would be for the Tax Court to disclose the report that Judge Couvillion submitted on or before September 2, 1998.
>
> This leads to the question of how Rule 183 should be interpreted in future cases. Rule 183's requirement of deference to the special trial judge surely implies that the parties to the litigation will have the means of knowing whether deference has been given and of mounting a challenge if it has not. Thus, a reasonable reading of the Rule requires the litigants and the courts of appeals to be able to evaluate any changes made to the findings of fact in the special trial judge's initial report. Including the original findings of fact in the record on appeal would make that possible.

Id. at 66–68 (Kennedy, J., concurring).

Chief Justice Rehnquist, joined by Justice Thomas, dissented. He argued, in part:

> [C]onsistent with its practice during the more than 20 years since Rule 183 was adopted in its current form, the Tax Court interprets Rule 183 as not requiring disclosure of "any preliminary drafts of reports or opinions." . . .
>
> Because this interpretation of Rule 183 is reasonable, it should be accepted. An agency's interpretation of its own rule or regulation is entitled to "controlling weight unless it is plainly erroneous or inconsistent with the regulation." *Bowles v. Seminole Rock & Sand Co.*, 325 U.S. 410, 414, 65 S. Ct. 1215, 89 L. Ed. 1700 (1945). . . .

Id. at 70 (Rehnquist, C.J., dissenting) (citations omitted).

After the Supreme Court issued its opinion, the taxpayers in *Estate of Kanter* filed with the Court of Appeals for the Seventh Circuit a motion "requesting an order of production directed to the Tax Court regarding the Special Trial Judge Report; requesting the record on appeal to be supplemented with that report; and, requesting that this court set a schedule for briefing the merits of the appeal in light of the report. . . ." Estate of Kanter v. Commissioner, 406 F.3d 933, 934 (7th Cir. 2005). The IRS filed a motion "requesting that the case be remanded to the Tax Court for further proceedings consistent with the Supreme Court's decision. . . ." *Id.* The Seventh Circuit denied the taxpayers' motions and remanded the case to the Tax Court. *Id.*

In the Seventh Circuit, Judge Cudahy dissented again, stating, in part:

> The essential issue in this case was whether the Tax Court was within its rights in refusing to include in the record on appeal the report of the special tax court judge who presided over the trial. The Supreme Court has now decided that the rules of the Tax Court do not authorize the suppression of this document. This report must be included in the record, and I see no reason why it cannot be produced without further delay. It was improperly withheld, and that nondisclosure ought to cease — now.
>
> The Commissioner argues that the Court also disapproved the "collaborative" procedure followed by the Tax Court in dealing with the special trial judge's report. Therefore, apparently before the undisclosed report is produced, the Commissioner seeks a remand so the Tax Court can somehow deal with the Supreme Court's disapproval of its procedure. But this seems to me to put the cart before the horse. The "collaborative" procedure was only adopted in light of the decision to keep the report secret, in order to deal with the requirement that the findings of the report be granted due deference.

Id. (Cudahy, J., dissenting).

The parties made similar motions in *Ballard*. In contrast to the Seventh Circuit, the Eleventh Circuit granted the taxpayers' motion to supplement the record and ordered the Tax Court to produce Special Trial Judge Couvillion's original report within 14 days.

See Court Orders Addition of Special Trial Judge's Report to Record in Ballard *Case*, 2005 TNT 99-26 (May 24, 2005) (reproducing Eleventh Circuit's Memorandum to Counsel or Parties).

In response to the Eleventh Circuit's order, the Tax Court released the report. *See* Ballard *Special Trial Judge Opinion Released to Eleventh Circuit*, 2005 TNT 107-16 (June 6, 2005). In stark contrast with the official Tax Court opinion in the case, Special Trial Judge Couvillion's report found no evidence of fraud. The report states, in part:

> There is not [sic] showing that taxes were evaded or avoided on any of the payments made by "The Five". Quite the contrary, respondent's witnesses, including its own agents, testified that all of the payments by "The Five" had been reported on Federal income tax returns, and the taxes due thereon had been paid. The evidence does not establish that the parties reporting such income were not the proper earners of that income. . . . Moreover, in the Court's view, certain transactions that respondent cited . . . in asserting petitioners are liable for these additions to tax for fraud, at best, amount to only respondent's suspicious [sic] of fraud. The Court, however, does not consider these transactions as even rising to the level of suspicion of fraud.

Id.

In addition to serving a copy of the report on the parties, the Tax Court also took the unusual step of releasing explanations by Special Trial Judge Couvillion; Judge Dawson, the reviewing judge; and Judge Cohen, who was the Chief Judge at the time *Investment Research Associates* was decided. *See Tax Court Releases Judges' Clarifying Statements in* Kanter, Ballard, 2005 TNT 140-19 (July 22, 2005).

Following the release of Special Trial Judge Couvillion's report, the *Chicago Tribune* requested copies of the original reports in other cases tried since 1983 under Rule 183. Maurice Possley, *Tax Court Case Stirs Multiple Questions; Request for Judges' Trial Findings Rebuffed*, Chi. Trib., July 10, 2005, Zone C, at 1. The *Chicago Tribune* reported that out of more than 900 such cases, only 117 original reports could be located, and of those, five, including the one in *Ballard*, reflected differences between the original findings and the Tax Court's opinion. Maurice Possley, *Tax Court Findings Secretly Changed in at Least 5 Cases*, Chi. Trib., Sept. 1, 2005, Zone C, at 1; *see also* Sheryl Stratton, *In* Ballard*'s Wake, Tax Court Releases Initial Reports*, 2005 TNT 175-2 (Sept. 8, 2005). How should the Tax Court and the IRS handle these cases?

The Tax Court served the reports on the parties to the 117 cases, along with an order stating that the original decisions remained in effect (except in three cases that were still pending before the Tax Court or on appeal). *See Sample Tax Court Order for All Identified Draft Rule 183(b) Reports*, 2005 TNT 174-25 (Sept. 9, 2005); CC 2005-017, *available at* 2005 TNT 188-11 (Sept. 29, 2005). The IRS issued a Chief Counsel Notice describing its procedures for addressing any motions by taxpayers to vacate decisions or for a new trial. *See* CC 2005-017, *supra*.

Does it bother you that the Tax Court could not locate original reports in approximately 800 cases? In 2005, Judge Gerber, who was the Chief Judge at that time, reportedly explained:

> A thorough search was made, including inquiries of retired judicial officers, and all computers were searched for electronic copies, he said. The search yielded 117 STJs' initial draft opinions, as submitted to the chief judge, he said. Most of the 117 are relatively contemporaneous, in that many judges and STJs tended to discard their deliberative materials after the decisions in those cases become final, he explained. Judge Dawson, who was one of the principal reviewing and adopting judges, maintained all of those documents since May 2001, when the issue of the status of the STJs' reports became prominent, he said.

ABA Tax Section Meeting: Tax Court Chief Judge Speaks out on Ballard *Procedure*, 108 Tax Notes 1510, 1512 (2005).

After reviewing Special Trial Judge Couvillion's initial report, the Court of Appeals for the Eleventh Circuit remanded the case to the Tax Court with instructions that included the following: "The original report of the special trial judge is ordered reinstated; . . . [and] The Chief Judge of the Tax Court is instructed to assign this matter to a regular Tax Court Judge who had no involvement in the preparation of the aforementioned 'collaborative report'. . . ." Ballard v. Commissioner, 429 F.3d 1026, 1027 (11th Cir. 2005).

On remand, the cases were assigned to Tax Court Judge Haines, who had been appointed to the Tax Court in 2003. *See Tax Court Reinstates Trial Judge's Report in* Kanter, 2005 TNT 246-16 (Dec. 23, 2005). Judge Haines issued his opinion in 2007. *See* Estate of Kanter v. Commissioner, T.C. Memo. 2007-21, *rev'd sub nom.* Ballard v. Commissioner, 522 F.3d 1229 (11th Cir. 2008). Like the 1999 opinion, but unlike the Special Trial Judge's original report, the 2007 opinion found that the taxpayers committed fraud. Does that outcome surprise you?

Judge Haines's 2007 opinion documented "departures from the recommended findings of fact in the STJ report . . . [with] a comment either in the text or in the margin (including appropriate citations of the record)," as well as putting additional findings of fact in bold type. *Id.* at *32–*33. On appeal, the Court of Appeals for the Eleventh Circuit reversed. *See Ballard*, 522 F.3d 1229. The Eleventh Circuit ordered the Tax Court to enter Special Trial Judge Couvillion's report as the court's opinion. Do you agree with that outcome?

In 2005, in response to the Supreme Court's *Ballard* opinion, the Tax Court proposed several amendments to its Rules of Practice and Procedure, including adoption of a notice and comment process for its rulemaking and amendments to Rule 183. The post-*Ballard* version of Rule 183 includes a transparent procedure under which the Special Trial Judge's report is served on the parties and they have an opportunity to file objections to it.[25] *See* Tax Court Press Release (Sept. 21, 2005), *available at* http://www.ustaxcourt.gov/press/092105.pdf. Accordingly, the report is also included in the record on appeal. Do these changes seem helpful? Are they sufficient, in your opinion?

§ 8.09 EQUITY IN THE TAX COURT

Reading Assignment: I.R.C. § 6214(b).

As indicated above, the Tax Court is an Article I court. The boundaries of the Tax Court's jurisdiction are strictly determined by statute. The Code does not contain a provision authorizing the court to use equitable principles to mitigate otherwise harsh results in deficiency cases. In fact, in 1987, the Supreme Court stated, "the Tax Court is a court of limited jurisdiction and lacks general equitable powers." Commissioner v. McCoy, 484 U.S. 3, 7 (1987). Nonetheless, the Tax Court has applied a number of equitable doctrines since then, most notably equitable recoupment,[26] a doctrine that allows allow the taxpayer or the government to essentially recover an amount otherwise barred by the applicable statute of limitations offsetting it against an amount owed to the other. *See* Mann v. United States, 552 F. Supp. 1132, 1135 (N.D. Tex. 1982). Equitable recoupment is discussed in Chapter 10.

---

[25] This transparent procedure is comparable to the procedure the Tax Court followed under an old version of the rule, which was amended in 1983 to remove the provisions for service of the report on the parties and inclusion of the report in the record on appeal.

[26] For a discussion of other equitable doctrines applied by the Tax Court and an argument that the Tax Court's use of equity is improper, see Leandra Lederman, *Equity and the Article I Court: Is the Tax Court's Exercise of Equitable Powers Constitutional?*, 5 Fla. Tax Rev. 357 (2001). Portions of the discussion here about the Tax Court's equitable powers are adapted from that article and are used, as adapted, with permission.

The Supreme Court stated in 1943, with respect to the Tax Court's agency predecessor, the Board of Tax Appeals:

> The Internal Revenue Code, not general equitable principles, is the mainspring of the Board's jurisdiction. Until Congress deems it advisable to allow the Board to determine the overpayment or underpayment in any taxable year other than the one for which a deficiency has been assessed, the Board must remain impotent when the plea of equitable recoupment is based upon an overpayment or underpayment in such other year.

Commissioner v. Gooch Milling & Elevator Co., 320 U.S. 418, 422 (1943). For years after *Gooch Milling* was decided, the Board (and then the Tax Court) expressed the view that it lacked jurisdiction over equitable recoupment claims. *See, e.g.*, Estate of Schneider v. Commissioner, 93 T.C. 568, 570 (1989); Poinier v. Commissioner, 86 T.C. 478, 490–91 (1986), *aff'd in part and rev'd in part*, 898 F.2d 917 (3d Cir.), *cert. denied*, 490 U.S. 1019 (1988); Estate of Van Winkle v. Commissioner, 51 T.C. 994, 999–1000 (1969); Vandenberge v. Commissioner, 3 T.C. 321, 327–28 (1944), *aff'd*, 147 F.2d 167 (5th Cir.), *cert. denied*, 325 U.S. 875 (1945). The IRS shared that view. *See* Rev. Rul. 71-56, 1971-1 C.B. 404, 405 ("the Tax Court lacks jurisdiction to consider a plea of equitable recoupment").

In 1990, in *United States v. Dalm*, 494 U.S. 596, 611 n.8 (1990), a tax refund suit, the Supreme Court stated that because the taxpayer had not raised the issue in her prior deficiency litigation, the Court had "no occasion to pass upon the question whether Dalm could have raised a recoupment claim in the Tax Court." In dissent, Justice Stevens also raised the possibility that the Tax Court might have equitable recoupment jurisdiction. *See id.* at 615 n.3 (Stevens, J., dissenting).

Subsequent Tax Court decisions applying equitable recoupment resulted in a split in the circuits on this issue. *Compare* Estate of Mueller v. Commissioner, 153 F.3d 302 (6th Cir. 1998) (Tax Court lacked jurisdiction to apply equitable recoupment), *cert. denied*, 525 U.S. 1140 (1999), *with* Estate of Branson v. Commissioner, 113 T.C. 6 (1999), *aff'd*, 264 F.3d 904 (9th Cir. 2001) (Tax Court had power to apply equitable recoupment), *cert. denied*, 535 U.S. 927 (2002).

In 2006, Congress resolved this particular issue by statute, amending Code section 6214(b) to state, "[n]otwithstanding the preceding sentence the Tax Court may apply the doctrine of equitable recoupment to the same extent that it is available in civil tax cases before the district courts of the United States and the United States Court of Federal Claims." The amendment, though important, does not address the question of the Tax Court's equitable power more generally.

One reason some courts have given for allowing the Tax Court to apply equitable doctrines is that the federal district courts, which also have jurisdiction over tax cases, have that power. For example, Judge Posner used this approach to uphold the Tax Court's power to apply equitable estoppel, stating, "[w]e are given no reason to suppose that statutes of limitations are intended to be administered differently in the Tax Court than in the federal district courts, which share jurisdiction in federal tax cases with the Tax Court." Flight Attendants Against UAL Offset, 165 F.3d 572, 578 (7th Cir. 1999). Does this analysis persuade you? In *Lundy*, a statute of limitations case discussed in Chapter 10, the Supreme Court noted numerous procedural ways in which the Tax Court and refund fora differ. It stated, in part:

> We assume without deciding that . . . a different limitations period would apply in district court, but nonetheless find in this disparity no excuse to change the limitations scheme that Congress has crafted. The rules governing litigation in Tax Court differ in many ways from the rules governing litigation in the district court and the Court of Federal Claims. Some of these differences might make the Tax Court a more favorable forum, while others may not.

Commissioner v. Lundy, 516 U.S. 235, 252 (1996).

PROBLEMS

1. Darcy has received a notice of deficiency from the IRS in the amount of $20,000.
   A. What should Darcy do if she wishes to dispute the notice in Tax Court?
      i. Does she have to pay the deficiency at this point?
      ii. Is she precluded from paying the deficiency at this point?
   B. Assume that Darcy believes that the notice is incorrect, and that she is actually entitled to a refund of $10,000. May she litigate in Tax Court both the issues in the notice and the issues she believes entitle her to a refund?
2. Alice and Alan Andrews own and operate as a sole proprietorship a small soda distributing company called Mom and Pop's One Stop Pop Shoppe. They report the tax events in the life of the business on their Form 1040, Schedule C. Last month, the Andrews received a timely notice of deficiency reflecting a deficiency of $20,000 for their Year 1 tax year and $35,000 for their Year 2 tax year. The notice of deficiency contained an adjustment for a business deduction they took on the advice of their daughter, an accountant. Their daughter has advised the Andrews to file a petition in the United States Tax Court, contesting the deficiencies. The Andrews do not plan to hire an attorney, but instead represent themselves with the informal assistance of their daughter.
   A. Are the Andrews eligible to file a petition to have their case responding to the Year 1 and Year 2 notice of deficiency heard as a small tax case? Would your answer change if the Andrews planned to include an overpayment claim for Year 1, claiming a refund of $25,000?
   B. Assume that the Andrews are eligible to file a small tax case petition in the Tax Court, and they consult you informally on how to proceed. The only issue they plan to raise is the deduction questioned in the notice of deficiency. Would you advise the Andrews to file a small tax case petition or a regular petition with the Tax Court?
      i. Would your answer to Part B change if the amounts in issue were instead only $3,000 for each tax year?
      ii. Would your answer to Part B change if the Andrews were to tell you that they take the business deduction in question every year, and that they hope to take it again each year going forward?
      iii. Would your answer to Part B change if the Andrews told you that their daughter believes that the deduction in issue is taken by all similar businesses, including some very large ones, and that the IRS may be using the Andrews' case to establish a precedent?
      iv. Would your answer to Part B change, if, after speaking with you, the Andrews decide to hire an attorney to represent them in the Tax Court?
3. What effects would making the Tax Court an Article III court have, as a structural matter? Would you support or oppose such a proposal, and why?
4. Ellen and Robert Green were legally divorced on May 3, Year 1. Their property settlement, which was incorporated into their divorce decree, awarded to Mr. Green Mrs. Green's half-interest in the Greens' personal residence. Pursuant to the property settlement, Mr. Green was required to pay Mrs. Green $50,000 per year plus 10 percent interest for 10 years. He issued a promissory note to her, and also conveyed to her a mortgage deed on the residence as security for the debt. The deed was subordinate to a preexisting mortgage on the property from First State Bank. Mr. Green deducted the interest of $5,000 per year on the promissory note on his federal income tax return as an itemized deduction for

qualified residence interest under section 163.

On the first day of last month, the Atlanta, Georgia IRS office sent Robert Green a notice of deficiency for the years Year 4 through Year 8 in which it denied the $5,000 interest deduction for each year, arriving at a deficiency of $1,500 for each of the five years in question. (Assume that the statute of limitations was open for each of those years and that the notice is valid.) The notice of deficiency contained the symbols "SP:END MP:SLD."

The explanation attached to the notice of deficiency stated that the interest deduction was disallowed because the interest was not qualified residence interest under section 163(h) of the Code. Mr. Green still resides in the residence in question, located at 765 Peach Street in Atlanta, GA 30319, which is where he received the notice. His social security number is 999-88-7777. Draft a Tax Court petition for him.

5. Dr. Murray Johnson,[27] the client in the Private Letter Ruling problem in Chapter 2 and the Tax Protest problem in Chapter 5, has been unable to come to a settlement with the IRS concerning Dr. Johnson's position that he should not have to include the value of his employer-provided lodging in gross income. With the statute of limitations running out, the IRS Wage and Investment Division office in Kansas City, Missouri recently mailed to Dr. Johnson the attached 90-day letter. (Assume the IRS does not assert interest or penalties.)

   Draft a petition to be filed in the United States Tax Court on Johnson's behalf contesting the IRS's deficiency set forth in the 90-day letter. Although Johnson's case otherwise qualifies for the small tax case procedure, he decides to conduct the proceeding as a regular Tax Court case in order to preserve his right to appeal an adverse decision. The Tax Court petition must be typed and otherwise comply with United States Tax Court Rules 20–34 and Forms 1 and 5. Dr. Johnson wishes to select Kansas City as the place of trial.

[27] His address and Social Security number appear in the notice of deficiency below. His telephone number is (816) 555-8692.

Internal Revenue Service
Department of Treasury
Wage and Investment Division
Kansas City, Missouri

Symbols: IRS-73069
Date: February 1, Year 3

Taxpayer Identification Number:
595–03–9506
Person To Contact:
Andrew Cushman
Contact Telephone Number:
(816) 555–0000

Last Date to Petition Tax Court:
May 2, Year 3

Dr. Murray H. Johnson
P.O. Box 4059
Shelter Island, MO 50596

Tax Year Ended: December 31, Year 1
Deficiency: $9,270 Income Tax

Dear Taxpayer:

We have determined that there is a deficiency (increase) in your income tax as shown above. This letter is a NOTICE OF DEFICIENCY sent to you as required by law. The enclosed statement shows how we determined the deficiency.

If you want to contest this deficiency in court before making any payment, you have until the **Last Date to Petition Tax Court** (90 days from the above mailing date of this letter or 150 days if addressed to you outside of the United States) to file a petition with the United States Tax Court for a redetermination of the amount of your tax. You can get a petition form and the rules for filing a petition from the Tax Court. You should file the petition with the **United States Tax Court, 400 Second Street, NW, Washington, D.C. 20217**. Attach a copy of this letter to the petition.

The time in which you must file a petition with the Court (90 or 150 days as the case may be) is fixed by law and the Court cannot consider your case if your petition is filed late. As required by law, separate notices are sent to spouses. If this letter is addressed to both a husband and wife, and both want to petition the Tax Court, both must sign the petition or each must file a separate, signed petition.

The Tax Court has a simplified procedure for small tax cases when the amount in dispute is $50,000 or less for any one tax year. You can get information about this procedure, as well as a petition form you can use, by writing to the Clerk of the United States Tax Court at the Washington, D.C. address shown above. You should write promptly if you intend to file a petition with the Tax Court.

If you decide *not* to file a petition with the Tax Court, we would appreciate it if you would sign and return the enclosed waiver form. This will permit us to charge your account quickly and will limit the accumulation of interest. The enclosed addressed envelope is for your convenience. If you decide not to sign and return the waiver and you do not timely petition the Tax Court, the law requires us to bill you after 90 days from the above mailing date of this letter (150 days if this is addressed to you outside the United States).

If you have questions about this letter, you may call the Contact Person whose name and telephone number are shown in the heading of this letter. If the number is outside your local calling area, there will be a long distance charge to you. If you prefer, you can call the Internal Revenue Service (IRS) phone telephone number in your local directory. An IRS employee there may be able to help you, but the office at the address shown on this letter is most familiar with your case.

When you send information we requested or if you write to us about this letter, please provide a telephone number and the best time to call you if we need more information. Please attach this letter to your correspondence to help us identify your case. Keep the copy for your records.

The person whose name and telephone number are shown in the heading of this letter can access your tax information and help you get answers. You also have the right to contact the Taxpayer Advocate. You can call 1-877-777-4778 and ask for Taxpayer Advocate Assistance. Or you can contact the Taxpayer Advocate for the IRS Office that issued this Notice of Deficiency by calling (816) 555-5500 or writing to:

Kansas City Center
Taxpayer Advocate
P.O. Box 9553
Kansas City, Missouri 84957

Taxpayer Advocate assistance is not a substitute for such established IRS procedures as the formal appeals process. The Taxpayer Advocate is not able to reverse legally correct tax determinations, nor extend the time fixed by law that you have to file a petition in the United States Tax Court. The Taxpayer Advocate can, however, see that a tax matter that may not have been resolved through normal channels gets prompt and proper handling.

Thank you for your cooperation.

Sincerely,

Commissioner
By: Shiro Kawashima
Director of Individual Taxation

Enclosures:
Copy of this letter
Explanation of Deficiency
Waiver
Envelope

* * *

EXPLANATION OF DEFICIENCY
FOR TAXPAYER, MURRAY H. JOHNSON
SS# 595-03-9506

Taxable year Ended December 31, Year 1

Taxpayer has failed to satisfy the qualifications under Internal Revenue Code section 132. Accordingly, the value of your employer-provided lodging is included in your gross income.

Amount of Deficiency: $9,270 Income Tax

Chapter 9
THE NOTICE OF DEFICIENCY

§ 9.01 INTRODUCTION

Reading Assignment: I.R.C. § 6213(a).

Most tax litigation will not begin until after the IRS sends the taxpayer a letter known as a "notice of deficiency." Code section 6212 governs notices of deficiency. It provides, in part:

> If the Secretary determines that there is deficiency in respect of any tax imposed by subtitle A or B or chapter 41, 42, 43 or 44, he is authorized to send notice of such deficiency to the taxpayer by certified mail or registered mail. Such notice shall include a notice to the taxpayer of the taxpayer's right to contact a local office of the taxpayer advocate and the location and phone number of the appropriate office.

Although it may sound from this statutory language as if a notice of deficiency is optional, the IRS generally cannot assess a deficiency without first sending a valid notice to the taxpayer. *See* I.R.C. § 6213(a); *see also, e.g.*, Philadelphia & Reading Corp. v. United States, 944 F.2d 1063, 1072 (3d Cir. 1991). In fact, the "authorization" language refers only to the method of delivery.

A notice of deficiency (also commonly called a 90-day letter) generally resembles the one reproduced below. Schedules attached to the notice typically explain the calculation of the deficiency and penalties.[1]

SAMPLE NOTICE OF DEFICIENCY

Department of Treasury
Internal Revenue Service
Philadelphia, PA 19255

Letter Number: [redacted]
Letter Date: May 29, 2007

[Taxpayer name and address]

Taxpayer Identification Number:
[redacted]
Tax Form: 1040
Tax Year Ended and Deficiency:
December 31, 2005
[deficiency redacted]
Contact Person: [redacted]
Contact Telephone Number:
(866) 583–3251 Toll Free

Hours to Call: 7:00 A.M. — 11:00 P.M.
Last Date to Petition Tax Court:
August 27, 2007

Dear Taxpayer:

We have determined that there is a deficiency (increase) in your income tax as shown above. This letter is a NOTICE OF DEFICIENCY sent to you as required by law. The enclosed statement shows how we figured the deficiency.

---

[1] "An explanatory paragraph in a notice of deficiency should reflect a twofold purpose: (a) to inform the taxpayer in clear and concise language of the adjustment; and (b) to state the position or positions of the Service with respect to the adjustments being made." I.R.M. 8.7.4.11.1.

If you want to contest this deficiency in court before making any payment, you have until the **Last Date to Petition Tax Court** (90 days from the above mailing date of this letter or 150 days if addressed to you outside the United States) to file a petition with the United States Tax Court for redetermination of the amount of your tax. You can get a petition form and the rules for filing a petition from the Tax Court. You should file the petition with the **United States Tax Court, 400 Second Street, NW, Washington, D.C. 20217**. Attach a copy of this letter to the petition.

The time in which you must file a petition with the Court (90 or 150 days as the case may be) is fixed by law and the Court cannot consider your case if the petition is filed late. As required by law, separate notices are sent to spouses. If this letter is addressed to both a husband and wife, and both want to petition the Tax Court, both must sign the petition or each must file a separate, signed petition.

The Tax Court has a simplified procedure for small tax cases when the amount in dispute is $50,000 or less for any one tax year. You can get information about this procedure, as well as a petition form you can use, by writing to the Clerk of the United States Tax Court at 400 Second Street, NW, Washington, DC 20217. You should write promptly if you intend to file a petition with the Tax Court.

If you decide *not* to file a petition with the Tax Court, please sign and return the enclosed waiver form to us. This will permit us to assess the deficiency quickly and will limit the accumulation of interest. We've enclosed an envelope you can use. If you decide not to sign and return the statement and you do not timely petition the Tax Court, the law requires us to assess and bill you for the deficiency after 90 days from the above mailing date of this letter (150 days if this letter is addressed to you outside the United States).

If you have questions about this letter, you may call the Contact Person whose name and telephone number are shown in the heading of this letter. If the number is outside your local calling area, there will be a long distance charge to you. If you prefer, you can call the Internal Revenue Service (IRS) telephone number in your local directory. An IRS employee there may be able to help you, but the office at the address shown on this letter is most familiar with your case.

When you send information we requested or if you write to us about this letter, please provide a telephone number and the best time to call you if we need more information. Please attach this letter to your correspondence to help us identify your case. Keep the copy for your records.

The person whose name and telephone number are shown in the heading of this letter can access your tax information and help you get answers. You also have the right to contact the Taxpayer Advocate. You can call 1-877-777-4778 and ask for Taxpayer Advocate Assistance. Or you can contact the Taxpayer Advocate for the IRS Office that issued this Notice of Deficiency by calling (215) 516-2499, or writing to:

PHILADELPHIA IRS CENTER
TAXPAYER ADVOCATE
P.O. BOX 16053, DP #1300
PHILADELPHIA, PA 19114

Taxpayer Advocate assistance is not a substitute for established IRS procedures such as the formal appeals process. The Taxpayer Advocate is not able to reverse legally correct tax determinations, nor extend the time fixed by law that you have to file a petition in the United States Tax Court. The Taxpayer Advocate can, however, see that a tax matter that may not have been resolved through normal channels gets prompt and proper handling.

Thank you for your cooperation.

Sincerely yours,

Commissioner
By: /s/ Cheryl Cordero
Cheryl Cordero
Director, Philadelphia Compliance Center

Enclosures:
Copy of this letter
Explanation of Deficiency
Waiver
Envelope

§ 9.02 THE NOTICE OF DEFICIENCY: FUNCTIONS AND VALIDITY

The notice of deficiency is probably the single most important document in tax procedure. As explained in more detail below, the IRS's assessment authority typically hinges on its timely mailing a legally valid notice of deficiency. In addition, because assessment is generally a legal prerequisite for collection of tax, a notice of deficiency is also a prerequisite for collection of any tax deficiency under the IRS's administrative collection procedures.[2]

This section considers the multiple roles the notice of deficiency plays in tax controversies; the requirements the IRS must meet for the notice to be valid; and the nature and consequences of challenges to the validity of the notice. Even if the notice is valid, it may be arbitrary or otherwise defective, which can affect which party bears the burden of proof in a Tax Court case. This chapter discusses that issue, and Chapter 11 discusses the more general burden of proof rules that apply across the three tax litigation fora.

[A] The Multiple Functions of the Notice

The notice of deficiency serves multiple functions in the tax controversy process. First, it is an indispensable prerequisite to Tax Court subject matter jurisdiction. I.R.C. § 6213(a); *see also* Tax Ct. R. 20, 34. In fact, courts sometimes refer to the notice as the taxpayer's "ticket to the Tax Court."[3] *See, e.g.,* Commissioner v. Shapiro, 424 U.S. 614, 630 (1976); Corbett v. Frank, 293 F.2d 501, 503 (9th Cir. 1961); Bourekis v. Commissioner, 110 T.C. 20 (1998). Second, and equally important, the notice of deficiency informs the taxpayer of the IRS's claim, analogous to legal process. In an ordinary civil suit, legal process is the notice to the defendant of a pending action. *See* R. Griggs Group, Ltd. v. Filanto Spa, 920 F. Supp. 1100, 1103 (D. Nev. 1996).

If a case is docketed in Tax Court, the notice serves yet a third function — it becomes part of the Tax Court pleadings. "Issuing a notice is in many ways analogous to filing a civil complaint." Clapp v. Commissioner, 875 F.2d 1396, 1403 (9th Cir. 1989). "Like a complaint, the statutory notice generally identifies the amount in issue and helps frame the issues in dispute in any subsequent Tax Court proceeding." Leandra

---

[2] Notice and demand for payment cannot be made prior to assessment. *See* I.R.C. § 6303(a). The IRS's lien and levy powers follow the notice and demand for payment. *See* I.R.C. §§ 6321, 6331(a). These issues are discussed in Chapter 14.

[3] As discussed in Chapter 1, the taxpayer has a forum choice on receipt of the notice because the taxpayer can pay the deficiency in full and follow the refund procedures as a prerequisite to litigation in one of the refund fora. The refund procedures and refund fora are discussed in Chapter 10.

Lederman, *"Civil"izing Tax Procedure: Applying General Federal Learning to Statutory Notices of Deficiency*, 30 U.C. DAVIS L. REV. 183, 198–99 (1996) (footnotes omitted).

In addition to these three primary functions, the notice of deficiency has other effects on the tax controversy process. Once the IRS sends the notice, the IRS is prohibited from assessing tax during the time period the taxpayer has to file a Tax Court petition (generally 90 days), and if the taxpayer does file a petition, until the Tax Court decision becomes final. I.R.C. § 6213(a). Not surprisingly, the notice tolls the statute of limitations on assessment during the period the IRS is prohibited from assessing tax (plus an additional 60 days). I.R.C. § 6503. A notice of deficiency also terminates an indefinite waiver of the statute of limitations made on Form 872A. *See* Roszkos v. Commissioner, 850 F.2d 514 (9th Cir. 1988), *cert. denied*, 489 U.S. 1012 (1989). Furthermore, as discussed below, the notice of deficiency plays an important role in the allocation of the burden of proof.

[B] General Requirements of the Notice

Reading Assignment: I.R.C. §§ 6212(a), 7522.

Case law establishes that a valid notice of deficiency must identify the taxpayer and the taxable year involved, indicate that a deficiency has been determined, and specify the amount of the deficiency. *See, e.g.*, Estate of Yaeger, 889 F.2d 29 (2d Cir. 1989), *cert. denied*, 495 U.S. 946 (1990); Scar v. Commissioner, 814 F.2d 1363, 1367 (9th Cir. 1987); Abrams v. Commissioner, 787 F.2d 939, 941 (4th Cir.), *cert. denied*, 479 U.S. 882 (1986). The notice must also notify the taxpayer of the "right to contact a local office of the taxpayer advocate and the location and phone number of the appropriate office." I.R.C. § 6212(a). In addition, the notice must specify the deadline date for filing a Tax Court petition. IRS Reform Act § 3463(a).

Because a deficiency assessment is a nullity if the IRS failed previously to send a valid notice of deficiency, many taxpayers have challenged the validity of the notices they received by petitioning the Tax Court and making a motion to dismiss the case for lack of subject matter jurisdiction.[4] *See* TAX CT. R. 53. If the Tax Court finds the notice invalid, it must dismiss the case for lack of jurisdiction. *See, e.g.*, Pietanza v. Commissioner, 92 T.C. 729, 735 (1989), *aff'd*, 935 F.2d 1282 (3d Cir. 1991); Keeton v. Commissioner, 74 T.C. 377, 379 (1980). The IRS theoretically can send a new notice if one is invalidated, but by then, the statute of limitations on assessment often has expired. *See* I.R.C. § 6501.[5] If the Tax Court finds that it does not have subject matter

[4] This is the most common approach for challenging defective notices, but it is not the only one. Taxpayers have sometimes sought injunctive relief to restrain assessment or collection of the tax, particularly for violations of the last known address rule of section 6212. *See, e.g.*, Cool Fuel, Inc. v. Connett, 685 F.2d 309 (9th Cir. 1982); Williams v. United States, 264 F.2d 227 (6th Cir.), *cert. denied*, 361 U.S. 862 (1959); Ponchik v. Commissioner, 1986 U.S. Dist. LEXIS 16870 (D. Minn. 1987); Garmany v. Baptist, 1979 U.S. Dist. LEXIS 8072 (N.D. Ala. 1979). Code section 7421(a), which is known as the Anti-Injunction Act, provides that "no suit for the purpose of restraining the assessment or collection of any tax shall be maintained in any court by any person." However, it includes exceptions for the provisions of Code sections 6212(a) and 6213(a). Section 6213(a) expressly provides that collection or assessment during the "prohibited period" may be enjoined.

The United States Supreme Court has held that in order to obtain injunctive relief in a tax case, the taxpayer must show that (1) "under the most liberal view of the law and the facts . . . under no circumstances could the Government ultimately prevail," (2) the taxpayer "would suffer irreparable injury if collection were effected" and (3) "equity jurisdiction otherwise exists." Enochs v. Williams Packing & Navigation Co., 370 U.S. 1, 7 (1962). Taxpayers have therefore not generally been successful in injunction actions based on invalid notices of deficiency. *See, e.g., Cool Fuel, supra*, at 314 (Cool Fuel's admitted ability to pay the deficiency precluded equitable relief).

[5] The statute of limitations on assessment is discussed in Chapter 7.

jurisdiction in the first instance, how can it make a determination that the notice was not valid? For purposes of ruling on the validity of the notice, the Tax Court has "jurisdiction to determine jurisdiction."

Many taxpayer challenges to notices of deficiency have been unsuccessful. For example, courts have refused to invalidate a notice that was not signed by an IRS official, Urban v. Commissioner, 964 F.2d 888, 889 (9th Cir. 1992); Commissioner v. Oswego Falls Corp., 71 F.2d 673, 677 (2d Cir. 1934); or that related to a full tax year despite its reference to only part of the tax year, Estate of Scofield v. Commissioner, 266 F.2d 154 (6th Cir. 1959). Similarly, a notice was valid where it covered a period longer than the one asserted by the taxpayer to be the proper period, and the notice included the taxable event in question. Sanderling v. Commissioner, 571 F.2d 174 (3d Cir. 1978).

Judge Learned Hand stated that the purpose of the notice of deficiency "is only to advise the person who is to pay the deficiency that the Commissioner means to assess him; anything that does this unequivocally is good enough." Olsen v. Helvering, 88 F.2d 650, 651 (2d Cir. 1937). In fact, when Congress added what is now section 7522, which requires that notices of deficiency and other notices include a description of the basis for and the amounts of any tax due, interest, penalties and the like, it stated, "[a]n inadequate description under the preceding sentence shall not invalidate such notice." Why might Congress have been concerned about the possibility of invalidation of the notice for such an omission? Consider what the purpose of the description requirement is and the consequence of invalidation of the notice.

Several cases have involved notices of deficiency that did not contain the deadline date for filing a Tax Court petition as required by section 3463(a) of the IRS Reform Act (an off-Code provision). In *Rochelle v. Commissioner*, 116 T.C. 356 (2001), *aff'd*, 293 F.3d 740 (5th Cir. 2002), a court-reviewed opinion with a concurrence and three dissents, Rochelle, an attorney, received a notice of deficiency on July 23, 1999 that was dated July 20, 1999. The notice failed to specify the last day for filing a Tax Court petition but did contain the standard language setting forth the 90-day period for filing a petition. Rochelle mailed his petition to the Tax Court 143 days after the mailing of the deficiency notice, and it was received 3 days later. Judge Vasquez, joined by nine other judges, rejected the taxpayer's argument that the notice was invalid, noting that he had received it in time to meet the deadline. The majority also rejected the taxpayer's argument that failure to include the deadline date rendered his petition timely.

Compare *Rochelle* with *Elings v. Commissioner*, 324 F.3d 1110 (9th Cir. 2003), in which the taxpayer timely filed the Tax Court petition. The Court of Appeals affirmed the Tax Court's holding for the government, stating that it concluded "that the IRS's failure to include the calculated date does not invalidate a notice when the taxpayer suffers no prejudice, as a result." *Id.* at 1112. What is the "prejudice" to the taxpayer in this context? Do you think that the Ninth Circuit would find late filing of a petition (as in *Rochelle*) to constitute "prejudice" to the taxpayer, thus counseling invalidation of the notice of deficiency?

Note that the consequence of filing an untimely Tax Court petition in response to a valid notice of deficiency is likely dismissal of the case for lack of subject matter jurisdiction — eliminating the opportunity for the taxpayer to contest the deficiency in Tax Court. In order to contest it, the taxpayer will have to pay it in full and follow the procedures for litigation in a U.S. district court or the Court of Federal Claims. Those procedures are discussed in Chapter 10.

If the IRS alleges that the taxpayer's petition was untimely and the taxpayer alleges that the notice of deficiency is invalid, whose claim should be considered first? In such a case, the parties will each be arguing that the Tax Court should dismiss the case for lack of subject matter jurisdiction. The Tax Court considers the taxpayer's motion first, and does not consider dismissal based on a late-filed petition unless it finds that the IRS's notice of deficiency was valid. *See* Dubin v. Commissioner, 99 T.C. 325, 326 (1992); Heaberlin v. Commissioner, 34 T.C. 58, (1960), *acq.* 1960-2 C.B. 5. How do the consequences of dismissal differ if the Tax Court dismisses based on an invalid notice of deficiency rather than based on an untimely petition?

[C] The Notice of Deficiency and the Burden of Proof

As discussed in Chapter 11, the "burden of proof" has two components: The burden of going forward and the burden of persuasion. Both burdens apply only to factual questions. The burden of going forward requires the party who bears the burden to produce sufficient evidence to make a *prima facie* case. Once one party makes a *prima facie* case, the case proceeds. The party who bears the burden of persuasion must persuade the court that its version of the relevant facts is the correct version. In a Tax Court case, both burdens generally fall on the taxpayer, but the notice of deficiency plays a role in allocating each of these burdens.

[1] Can a Court "Look Behind" the Notice of Deficiency?

The notice of deficiency traditionally has benefitted from a "presumption of correctness," Welch v. Helvering, 290 U.S. 111, 115 (1933), which requires the taxpayer to come forward with evidence rebutting the IRS's determination. In line with the presumption of correctness afforded the notice, case law has established that courts generally will not "look behind" the notice of deficiency to examine the motives or methods of the IRS in determining the deficiency. The following case lays out the rationale:

GREENBERG'S EXPRESS, INC. v. COMMISSIONER
United States Tax Court
62 T.C. 324 (1974)

Tannenwald, Judge.

These cases are before us on petitioners' motion for a protective order under Rule 103(a)(10), Tax Court Rules of Practice and Procedure. We deny the motion for the reasons stated below and append some additional comments which we hope will facilitate the further proceedings in these cases.

The substantive gravamen of petitioners' complaint is that the deficiency notices involved herein stem from second examinations of the books and records of the corporate petitioners under section 7605; that such second examinations, although ultimately made in compliance with the formal requirements of section 7605(b), were not instituted or conducted in good faith and for a legitimate purpose; and that such second examinations and the deficiency notices which issued as a result thereof were based upon discriminatory selection of petitioners because two of their number are the sons of one Carlo Gambino, a purported target of a governmental investigation into organized crime. In support of this claim, petitioners allege that the revenue agent in charge of the second examinations, and a member of the Strike Force, stated, "Your trouble is that 'The Godfather' got so much publicity, everybody was breathing down everybody's neck and we were told that we had to do something to take the heat off, so we went out to get a Gambino." Petitioners further allege that the deficiency determinations in themselves were arbitrary, unreasonable, and capricious because of respondent's failure to follow his established audit procedures and, in the case of certain of the corporate petitioners, his blanket disallowance of claimed business expense deductions and/or increases of round dollar amounts of taxable income.

On the basis of the foregoing, petitioners seek an order directing respondent to produce and deliver into the custody of the Court, and thereby make available for inspection by the petitioners prior to trial, all documents (whether in the custody of the Commissioner of Internal Revenue, the Secretary of the Treasury, the Attorney General of the United States, or any of their agents or designees) relating to the audit of petitioners' Federal income tax returns for 1966 through 1968 and any investigation of petitioners Thomas Gambino and Joseph Gambino by the Department of Justice, the Internal Revenue Service, or the Federal Strike Force Against Organized Crime operating in New York City. Petitioners assert that such an order is necessary to prevent the possible destruction or concealment of the documents involved and to enable the petitioners to prove, by such documents, the allegations of their amended petitions that respondent's determination of deficiencies in each of their Federal income tax liabilities for 1968 arose from official actions violating their constitutional rights.

Petitioners also ask us, in the event that their allegations are established, to declare respondent's determinations null and void and therefore decide that there is no deficiency due from any of them for 1968; alternatively, petitioners ask that we shift to respondent the burden of proof or the burden of going forward with the evidence.

In terms of petitioners' primary request herein — to wit, an impounding order under Rule 103(a)(10) — we are satisfied that they are not entitled to such relief. * * *

We come now to what we consider the crux of the matter before us: if petitioners were able to establish their allegations of discrimination in their selection as objects of an otherwise legitimate tax audit, would they be entitled to the benefit of any of the requested forms of relief? If not, such allegations would be immaterial to the resolution of the instant cases and petitioners would, therefore, not be warranted in their attempts to compel the production of any documents sought to establish those allegations. *Cf.* William O'Dwyer, 28 T.C. 698, 702–704 (1957), *affd.* 266 F.2d 575, 581 (C.A. 4, 1959).

As a general rule, this Court will not look behind a deficiency notice to examine the evidence used or the propriety of respondent's motives or of the administrative policy or procedure involved in making his determinations. Human Engineering Institute, 61 T.C. 61, 66 (1973), on appeal (C.A. 6, Jan. 2, 1974); Efrain T. Suarez, 58 T.C. 792, 813 (1972). Thus, we will not look into respondent's alleged failure to issue a 30-day letter to the petitioners or to afford them a conference before the Appellate Division. Cleveland Trust Co. v. United States, 421 F.2d 475, 480–482 (C.A. 6, 1970); Luhring v. Glotzbach, 304 F.2d 560 (C.A. 4, 1962); Crowther v. Commissioner, 269 F.2d 292, 293 (C.A. 9, 1959), *affirming* 28 T.C. 1293 (1957). The underlying rationale for the foregoing is the fact that a trial before the Tax Court is a proceeding de novo; our determination as to a petitioner's tax liability must be based on the merits of the case and not any previous record developed at the administrative level. *William O'Dwyer, supra.*

This Court has on occasion recognized an exception to the rule of not looking behind the deficiency notice when there is substantial evidence of unconstitutional conduct on respondent's part and the integrity of our judicial process would be impugned if we were to let respondent benefit from such conduct. *Efrain T. Suarez, supra.* But even in such limited situations, we have refused to declare the deficiency notice null and void, as petitioners would have us do. *See Efrain T. Suarez*, 58 T.C. at 814. *See also* Marx v. Commissioner, 179 F.2d 938, 942 (C.A. 1, 1950), *affirming* a Memorandum Opinion of this Court dated Jan. 24, 1949.

In the area of the criminal law, "mere selectivity in prosecution creates no constitutional problem." *See* United States v. Steele, 461 F.2d 1148, 1151 (C.A.9, 1972). On the other hand, "While the Fifth Amendment contains no equal protection clause, it does forbid discrimination that is 'so unjustifiable as to be violative of due process.' " (Citations omitted.) *See* Shapiro v. Thompson, 394 U.S. 618, 642 (1969). Even the conscious exercise of some selectivity is not in and of itself a Federal constitutional violation. *See* Oyler v. Boles, 368 U.S. 448, 456 (1962). Within these boundaries, the Federal courts have developed the test that before the complainant is entitled to relief, it must appear that the law has been "applied and administered by public authority with an evil eye and an unequal hand" (*see* Yick Wo v. Hopkins, 118 U.S. 356, 373–374 (1886), or with "questionable emphasis" (*see* United States v. Steele, 461 F.2d at 1152), through the use of an unjustifiable criterion such as race, religion, or expression of unpopular views. *See also* Two Guys v. McGinley, 366 U.S. 582, 588 (1961); United States v. Falk, 479 F.2d 616 (C.A. 7, 1973).

Assuming without deciding that a similar standard should be applied to civil tax litigation (*cf.* Hugo Romanelli, 54 T.C. 1448 (1970), *reversed in part* 466 F.2d 872 (C.A. 7, 1972), and John Harper, 54 T.C. 1121 (1970)), it is conceivable that there may be situations where a taxpayer should be accorded some relief, if he were able to prove that he was selected for audit on a clearly unjustifiable criterion. But we think that such situations will be extremely rare and we are satisfied that petitioners' allegations, even if true, would not be sufficient. Petitioners do not deny — indeed, they assume for the purposes of their motions — that the audits involved herein stemmed from the Government's attempts to deal with organized crime. Nor do they at any point assert that the deficiency notices are without foundation, i.e., that they owe no tax. *Cf.* Enochs v. Williams Packing Co., 370 U.S. 1, 7 (1962); Miller v. Nut Margarine Co., 284 U.S. 498, 510 (1932). *Compare* Bob Jones University v. Simon, 416 U.S. 725 (1974).

* * *

We are also satisfied that the circumstances alleged herein do not constitute unconstitutional action on the part of the respondent which would justify, at least at this stage of the proceeding, shifting to respondent the burden of proof or of going forward with the evidence as we did in *Efrain T. Suarez, supra.* Nor do the allegations of blanket disallowances of deductions and/or increases of round dollar amounts of taxable income, in the case of the corporate petitioners, dictate any such action. To be sure, the evidence presented at the trial may be such that the Court will be required to determine the extent of petitioners' tax liabilities, if any, on the basis of the record before it and not merely on the basis that petitioners have failed to sustain their burden of proof. Helvering v. Taylor, 293 U.S. 507 (1935); *Marx v. Commissioner, supra*; Durkee v. Commissioner, 162 F.2d 184, 187 (C.A. 6, 1947), remanding 6 T.C. 773 (1946). *Compare Human Engineering Institute*, 61 T.C. at 66. But whether this situation will obtain will have to abide the event.

We conclude that petitioners' motion should be denied and that these cases should proceed to trial in due course.

An appropriate order will be entered.

Why might a taxpayer want the Tax Court to look behind the notice of deficiency? Why is it generally inappropriate for the court to do so, according to *Greenberg's Express*?

[2] "Arbitrary and Erroneous" Notices of Deficiency

The "presumption of correctness" afforded a notice of deficiency has been a powerful tool for the IRS because of the burden it places on the taxpayer to produce evidence rebutting the IRS's determination of a deficiency. What if the IRS's determination lacks any factual basis — should the notice still be presumed correct? In *United States v. Janis*, 428 U.S. 433, 440–43 (1976), the United States Supreme Court considered how the taxpayer would meet its burden of proof if all of the government's evidence were suppressed because it was obtained illegally. In *Janis*, cash and wagering records leading to an arrest for illegal bookmaking were seized pursuant to a search warrant that was later quashed. *Id.* at 435–38. The Court stated, in part:

> The policy behind the presumption of correctness and the burden of proof, *see Bull v. United States*, 295 U.S. 247, 259–260 (1935), * * * accords * * * with the burden-of-proof rule which prevails in the usual preassessment proceeding in the United States Tax Court. Lucas v. Structural Steel Co., 281 U.S. 264, 271 (1930); Welch v. Helvering, 290 U.S. 111, 115 (1933); Rule 142(a) of the Rules of Practice and Procedure of the United States Tax Court (1973). In any event, for purposes of this case, we assume that this is so and that the burden of proof may be said technically to rest with respondent Janis.

> Respondent, however, submitted no evidence tending either to demonstrate that the assessment was incorrect or to show the correct amount of wagering tax liability, if any, on his part. In the usual situation one might well argue, as the Government does, that the District Court then could not properly grant judgment for the respondent on either aspect of the suit. But the present case may well not be the usual situation. What we have is a "naked" assessment without *any* foundation whatsoever if what was seized by the Los Angeles police cannot be used in the formulation of the assessment. The determination of tax due then may be one "without rational foundation and excessive," and not properly subject to the usual rule with respect to the burden of proof in tax cases. Helvering v. Taylor, 293 U.S. 507, 514–515 (1935).[n.8] *See* 9 J. Mertens, Law of Federal Income Taxation § 50.65 (1971).
>
> * * *
>
> Certainly, proof that an assessment is utterly without foundation is proof that it is arbitrary and erroneous. For purposes of this case, we need not go so far as to accept the Government's argument that the exclusion of the evidence in issue here is insufficient to require judgment for the respondent or even to shift the burden to the Government. We are willing to assume that if the District Court was correct in ruling that the evidence seized by the Los Angeles police may not be used in formulating the assessment (on which both the levy and the counterclaim were based), then the District Court was also correct in granting judgment for Janis . . . .

Id. at 440–42.

Janis involved a refund suit, but its "naked assessment" reasoning has been applied in many deficiency suits in the Tax Court. If a notice's determination of a deficiency is based on alleged unreported income, the taxpayer's situation is analogous to a "naked assessment;" that is, the taxpayer would be in the position of proving a negative (the nonreceipt of the income). Consider the court's approach to that problem in the following case and how it may affect the burden of production and the burden of persuasion:

ANASTASATO v. COMMISSIONER

United States Court of Appeals, Third Circuit
794 F.2d 884 (1986)

Hunter, Circuit Judge:

Pano Anastasato, the taxpayer, has been involved in the travel business since 1954. In 1960, he established his own travel agency, Panmarc, Inc. ("Panmarc"), and a tour operation business, Wholesale Tours International ("WTI"). During the years 1974 through 1976, both companies were wholly owned by the taxpayer.

Panmarc purchased tickets for WTI's customers. Panmarc was licensed by the International Air Transport Association ("IATA"), a trade association of international carriers, to purchase tickets directly from the airlines. Under IATA regulations, the maximum commission that airlines could pay travel agents was ten percent of the ticket price. Compliance with these regulations was not required by law. Despite the regulations, it was common for airlines to pay excess commissions known as overrides or override commissions. Payment of overrides had to be made with strict confidentiality because IATA imposed severe sanctions for the violation of its regulations.

Panmarc did a large volume of business with KLM Royal Dutch Airlines ("KLM").

[n.8] *Taylor*, although decided more than 40 years ago, has never been cited by this Court on the burden-of-proof issue. The Courts of Appeals, the Court of Claims, the Tax Court, and the Federal District Courts, however, frequently have referred to that aspect of the case.

On April 15, 1981, the Commissioner issued statutory notices of deficiency to Anastasato totaling $633,468.00 for the years 1974, 1975, and 1976. The deficiency notice included additions to tax for fraud pursuant to I.R.C. § 6653(b) (1982). The Commissioner alleged that KLM had paid override commissions to the taxpayer by making payments into a Swiss bank account identified by the code name "GIGE." This account contains over one million dollars.

The Tax Court heard the testimony of revenue agents, employees of Panmarc, and employees of KLM. * * * In 1973, * * * Andre Luber was promoted to the position of Assistant Manager for Passenger Sales in the United States and given the responsibility for negotiating overrides.

In 1973, the taxpayer approached Luber seeking additional override commissions. From 1973 to 1975, the taxpayer and Luber engaged in negotiations. * * * From April 1974 to December 1974, override commissions were set at fifteen percent. From January 1975 to March 1975, they were set at twenty-one percent. The taxpayer often complained to his employees that KLM was not making its payments. The agreement was renegotiated and the override commissions set at eighteen percent for April 1975 through October 1975. Four million dollars worth of tickets were sold in 1974 and 1975 and were subject to the override commissions. For the period February 1976 to October 1976, override commissions were again set at eighteen percent.

* * *

In late 1979, Bohdan Huzar, a special agent with the Internal Revenue Service, began the investigation of the taxpayer. Huzar met with Paul Mifsud, general counsel to KLM in the United States, both in the United States and at the KLM headquarters in The Netherlands. Huzar also met with a Mr. Westpladt, an employee in the KLM accounting department in The Netherlands. Huzar did not take copies of any documents with him, but he recorded the contents of several in a notebook and prepared a report describing the documents. He described debit slips showing payments of approximately one million dollars from KLM to a Swiss bank account with the code name GIGE. He also saw KLM cash paid out slips totaling $26,000 signed by the taxpayer. Huzar's report stated that Westpladt had said that KLM made the payments to the Swiss bank account on behalf of the taxpayer. As hearsay, Huzar's report was admitted at trial only for the limited purpose of describing the methodology used by the Commissioner in issuing the notice of deficiency.

At trial, the taxpayer denied that he had ever received the override commissions. He admitted that he had discussed overrides with KLM officials, but he maintained that he never accepted overrides because he was worried about the IATA penalties. He seemed to imply that [an employee of KLM] was pocketing the overrides and that he merely went along with the scheme to maintain his business relationship with KLM.

On the basis of this evidence, the Tax Court upheld the Commissioner's determination of deficiencies and additions to tax in the amount of $641,288 for income tax liability for the years 1974, 1975, and 1976. However, the court held that the Commissioner had not proven fraud by the taxpayer.

The taxpayer claims that the Commissioner's deficiency determination was arbitrary and unreasonable. In addressing this contention, we first note that the government's deficiency assessment is generally afforded a presumption of correctness. *See* United States v. Janis, 428 U.S. 433, 441, 96 S. Ct. 3021, 49 L. Ed. 2d 1046 (1976); Helvering v. Taylor, 293 U.S. 507, 515, 55 S. Ct. 287, 79 L. Ed. 623 (1935); Welch v. Helvering, 290 U.S. 111, 115, 54 S. Ct. 8, 78 L. Ed. 212 (1933); Baird v. Commissioner, 438 F.2d 490, 492 (3d Cir. 1970). This presumption is a procedural device that places the burden of producing evidence to rebut the presumption on the taxpayer. *See Janis*, 428 U.S. at 441. A court usually will not look behind the Commissioner's determination, even though it may be based on hearsay or other evidence inadmissible at trial. *See* Dellacroce v. Commissioner, 83 T.C. 269, 280 (1984).

Several courts, including this one, have noted an exception to the general rule that they will not examine the basis of the deficiency determination before recognizing the Commissioner's presumption of correctness. Under this exception, a court must not give effect to the presumption of correctness in a case involving unreported income if the Commissioner cannot present "some predicate evidence connecting the taxpayer to the charged activity." Gerardo v. Commissioner, 552 F.2d 549, 554 (3d Cir. 1977). Most of the cases stating that the Commissioner is not entitled to the presumption based on a naked assessment without factual foundation have involved illegal income. *See* Weimerskirch v. Commissioner, 596 F.2d 358 (9th Cir. 1979) (drugs); Gerardo v. Commissioner, 552 F.2d 549 (3d Cir. 1977) (gambling); Pizzarello v. United States, 408 F.2d 579 (2d Cir.), *cert. denied*, 396 U.S. 986, 90 S. Ct. 481, 24 L. Ed. 2d 450 (1969) (gambling); Dellacroce v. Commissioner, 83 T.C. 269 (1984) (racketeering payoff); Llorente v. Commissioner, 74 T.C. 260 (1980), *aff'd in part and rev'd. in part*, 649 F.2d 152 (2d Cir. 1981) (drugs). Given the obvious difficulties in proving the nonreceipt of income, we believe the Commissioner should have to provide evidence linking the taxpayer to the tax-generating activity in cases involving unreported income, whether legal or illegal.

Along with other courts, we have recognized that the Commissioner's deficiency determination is entitled to a presumption of correctness and that the burden of production as well as the ultimate burden of persuasion is placed on the taxpayer. *See* Sullivan v. United States, 618 F.2d 1001, 1008 (3d Cir. 1980). The government meets its initial burden of proof in an action to collect tax merely by introducing its deficiency determination. *See* United States v. Stonehill, 702 F.2d 1288, 1293 (9th Cir. 1983), *cert. denied*, 465 U.S. 1079, 104 S. Ct. 1440, 79 L. Ed. 2d 761 (1984). The presumption of correctness establishes a prima facie case, but it arises only if supported by foundational evidence connecting the taxpayer with the tax-generating activity. *See Gerardo*, 552 F.2d at 554. The presumption shifts the burden of proof to the taxpayer. *See* DiMauro v. United States, 706 F.2d 882, 884 (8th Cir. 1983).

If the taxpayer rebuts the presumption by showing that it is arbitrary and erroneous, *see* Helvering v. Taylor, 293 U.S. at 515, the presumption disappears. Courts differ on whether the burdens of production and persuasion can be shifted to the Commissioner. Most agree that if the presumption drops out the burden of going forward shifts to the Commissioner. However, some courts have stated that at this point the ultimate burden of persuasion, or risk of nonpersuasion, remains on the taxpayer. *See* Higginbotham v. United States, 556 F.2d 1173, 1176 (4th Cir. 1977); United States v. Rexach, 482 F.2d 10 (1st Cir.), *cert. denied*, 414 U.S. 1039, 94 S. Ct. 540, 38 L. Ed. 2d 330 (1973); *Sullivan*, 618 F.2d at 1008. Other courts, however, have indicated that in unreported income cases the ultimate burden shifts to the Commissioner. *See* Keogh v. Commissioner, 713 F.2d 496, 501 (9th Cir. 1983); *United States v. Stonehill*, 702 F.2d at 1294; Stout v. Commissioner, 273 F.2d 345, 350 (4th Cir. 1959). In 1976, the Supreme Court noted, but did not reconcile, this conflict in the circuits. *See United States v. Janis*, 428 U.S. at 442.

In *Sullivan*, we stated that if the taxpayer rebuts the presumption with credible and relevant evidence sufficient to establish that the determination was erroneous, the procedural burden of going forward with the evidence shifts to the Commissioner, 618 F.2d at 1008. We further held, however, that the ultimate burden of proof or persuasion remains with the taxpayer. If the taxpayer offers evidence that the determination was incorrect and the Commissioner offers no evidence to support the assessment, the taxpayer will have met his ultimate burden "unless such evidence is specifically rejected as improbable, unreasonable, or questionable." *Id.* at 1009. *See also* Demkowicz v. Commissioner, 551 F.2d 929, 931 (3d Cir. 1977). The court can reject the taxpayer's evidence if it is contradicted by the Commissioner.

In the case before us, the Commissioner was entitled to the presumption of correctness because he introduced evidence linking the taxpayer to the tax-generating activity. The taxpayer was involved in the travel business and purchased a large volume of tickets from KLM. The taxpayer and KLM engaged in extensive negotiations regarding override commissions and the taxpayer was entitled to receive these commissions. The taxpayer has not shown that the deficiency determination was arbitrary and without factual foundation and he therefore cannot rely on *Gerardo* to dispel the presumption.

After discussing the relevant law and the facts of the case, the Tax Court properly concluded that the deficiency determination was entitled to its usual presumption of correctness. The court then should have determined whether the taxpayer had at trial, nevertheless, met his burden of ultimate persuasion and shown that the determination was incorrect. The court noted only that "petitioners herein (the taxpayer) presented no affirmative evidence to demonstrate any error in respondent's said determinations, having contented themselves throughout this trial with attacking only the basis for respondent's determinations, rather than the accuracy thereof." This statement indicates that the court believed that, once the Commissioner was granted the usual presumption of correctness, the question whether the taxpayer received the allegedly unreported income no longer remained at issue and only the amount of the assessment could be considered.

Even if the Commissioner is entitled to the initial presumption of correctness, the taxpayer must be given the opportunity to prove that the determination was incorrect. In this case, the taxpayer's evidence consisted of denials that he ever received the income in question. A general denial of liability is insufficient to meet the taxpayer's burden of nonpersuasion. *See* Avco Delta Corp. v. United States, 540 F.2d 258 (7th Cir. 1976), *cert. denied*, 429 U.S. 1040, 97 S. Ct. 739, 50 L. Ed. 2d 752 (1977). We are "not bound to accept taxpayer's testimony at face value even when it is uncontradicted if it is improbable, unreasonable, or questionable." *Baird*, 438 F.2d at 493. The Tax Court apparently rejected the taxpayer's testimony on nonreceipt of income not as "improbable, questionable, or unreasonable," *Baird*, 438 F.2d at 493, but as irrelevant once the Commissioner provided a factual foundation for the assessment and the presumption of correctness arose. The court erred since it was possible that the taxpayer could ultimately prevail by proving that while he engaged in the activity in question he never received the income in question.

It is possible that the Tax Court, on proper consideration of the taxpayer's denial of receipt of the income, will find such denials improbable. Nevertheless, because the court did not explicitly or implicitly reject the taxpayer's testimony, we will remand the case for consideration of this point.

* * *

The "arbitrary and erroneous" doctrine applied in *Anastasato* was developed in cases where the alleged unreported income was income from illegal activities. Note that it is a doctrine the taxpayer raises to rebut the presumption of correctness that typically attaches to the notice of deficiency. Was the *Anastasato* court correct in applying the doctrine in a case involving legal income? Consider the court's statement that "[t]he presumption of correctness establishes a prima facie case, but it arises only if supported by foundational evidence connecting the taxpayer with the tax-generating activity." *Anastasato*, 794 F.2d at 887. In the typical case involving allegedly unreported income from a legal source, will the taxpayer deny any connection to the tax-generating activity? What was different about the *Anastasato* case?

[3] New Matter

Reading Assignment: I.R.C. § 7522; Tax Ct. R. 142(a); skim I.R.C. §§ 6212(c)(1), 7491(a).

Tax Court Rule 142(a), the general burden of proof rule in Tax Court, provides, in part, as follows:[6]

> The burden of proof shall be upon the petitioner, except as otherwise provided by statute or determined by the Court; and except that, in respect of any *new matter, increases in deficiency*, and *affirmative defenses*, pleaded in the answer, it shall be upon the respondent. . . .

Tax Ct. R. 142(a)(1) (emphasis added). Note that this Rule places the burden of persuasion on the IRS (the respondent) "in respect of any new matter." Does the phrasing of Rule 142(a)(1) suggest that the burden of persuasion placed on the respondent only for "new matter . . . pleaded in the answer" or for all "new matter" wherever raised? Would it make sense for the IRS to bear the burden of persuasion if it raised new matter in its answer but not if it waited to raise the new matter until later — say at or shortly before trial?

The following case explains what constitutes "new matter." It may help your understanding of the case to skim Code section 482, which allows the IRS to reallocate income and deductions among two or more commonly controlled entities, if the reallocation is necessary to clearly reflect income.

ACHIRO v. COMMISSIONER

United States Tax Court

77 T.C. 881 (1981)

Achiro and Rossi each owned 50 percent of the stock of Tahoe City Disposal, and each owned 25 percent of the stock of Kings Beach Disposal. In 1974, Achiro and Rossi incorporated A & R for the purpose of rendering management services to Tahoe City Disposal and Kings Beach Disposal. Achiro and Rossi each owned 24 percent of A & R's stock, and Renato Achiro (Achiro's brother and Rossi's brother-in-law) owned the remaining 52 percent. A & R entered into management service agreements with Tahoe City Disposal and Kings Beach Disposal pursuant to which A & R provided those corporations with management services and, in exchange, received management fees. Achiro and Rossi entered into exclusive employment contracts with A & R, and, acting in their capacities as A & R's employees, rendered management services to Tahoe City Disposal and Kings Beach Disposal.

* * *

Hall, Judge.

* * *

In his notice of deficiency, respondent adjusted the income of Tahoe City Disposal by disallowing as deductions the management fees paid to A & R totaling $65,000 and $170,286 for the fiscal years ending March 31, 1975, and 1976, respectively. Respondent determined that these amounts were not expended for the purpose designated or were not ordinary and necessary business expenses. Respondent further adjusted Tahoe City

---

[6] As discussed in Chapter 11, the taxpayer may have the burden of proof shifted to the IRS if the taxpayer meets certain threshold requirements. *See* I.R.C. § 7491. If the taxpayer does not meet the requirements of Code section 7491, Rule 142(a)(1) applies. *See* Tax Ct. R. 142(a)(2).

Disposal's income by allowing it to take all the deductions for compensation, interest, depreciation, etc., originally taken by A & R, totaling $47,316 and $133,754 for the fiscal years ending March 31, 1975, and 1976, respectively. In so doing, respondent stated: "These allocations are made to you [Tahoe City Disposal] from A & R Enterprises, Inc., in order to clearly reflect your income and A & R Enterprises, Inc. income."

At trial, respondent amended his answer and asserted that all of the income and deductions of A & R should be allocated to Tahoe City Disposal and Kings Beach Disposal pursuant to section 482, section 269, or section 61 (the assignment of income doctrine or the sham corporation theory). In the alternative, respondent asserted in his amended answer that the employees of Tahoe City Disposal should be aggregated with the employees of A & R pursuant to section 414(b) for purposes of applying the antidiscrimination provisions of section 401 to A & R's pension and profit-sharing plans.

OPINION

A. Burden of Proof

As a preliminary matter it is necessary to decide which party bears the burden of proof with respect to the various issues.

At trial, respondent requested leave to file an amended answer, which this Court granted. In that amended answer, respondent alleged for the first time that section 482, section 269, or section 61 (assignment of income doctrine or the sham corporation theory) also justified the deficiency. The amended answer also contains the alternative argument that section 414(b) requires petitioners to include in their gross incomes their aliquot portions of the contributions made by A & R to its pension and profit-sharing plans.

In response to this amended answer, petitioners filed a motion to shift burden of proof with respect to the matters pleaded therein. Generally, the burden of proof is on the taxpayer. Welch v. Helvering, 290 U.S. 111 (1933); Rule 142(a), Tax Court Rules of Practice and Procedure. Rule 142(a) provides:[7]

> The burden of proof shall be upon the petitioner, except as otherwise provided by statute or determined by the Court; and except that, *in respect of any new matter*, increases in deficiency, and affirmative defenses, pleaded in his answer, *it shall be upon the respondent*. [Emphasis added.] * * *

At trial, this Court agreed with petitioners that respondent's amended answer presented new matters under Rule 142(a) and, accordingly, we shifted the burden of proof to respondent. On brief, respondent argues that the Court improperly shifted the burden of proof because his amended answer presented new theories, not new matters. He asserts that the statutory notice is sufficiently broad to encompass these theories and that petitioners knew at least as early as 5 weeks prior to trial that these theories would be relied upon by respondent and, thus, petitioners were neither surprised nor disadvantaged thereby. We are still of the view that respondent's amended answer raised new matters and that, therefore, respondent bears the burden of proof.

The assertion of a new theory which merely clarifies or develops the original determination without being inconsistent or increasing the amount of the deficiency is not a new matter requiring the shifting of the burden of proof. Estate of Jayne v. Commissioner, 61 T.C. 744, 748–749 (1974); McSpadden v. Commissioner, 50 T.C. 478, 492–493 (1968); Estate of Sharf v. Commissioner, 38 T.C. 15, 27–28 (1962). However, if the assertion in the amended answer either alters the original deficiency or requires the

---

[7] [Notice that Rule 142(a)(1), quoted above, contains essentially the same language that Rule 142(a) did before Congress enacted section 7491. — Eds.]

presentation of different evidence, then respondent has introduced a new matter. Estate of Falese v. Commissioner, 58 T.C. 895, 898–899 (1972); *McSpadden v. Commissioner, supra;* Papineau v. Commissioner, 28 T.C. 54, 57 (1957); Tauber v. Commissioner, 24 T.C. 179, 185 (1955). The factual bases and rationale required to establish that the amounts paid by Tahoe City Disposal as management fees were expended for that purpose and were ordinary and necessary business expenses are entirely different from the factual bases and rationale necessary to establish that sections 482, 269, 61, and 414(b) do not apply to the present situation. Sanderling, Inc. v. Commissioner, 66 T.C. 743, 757–758 (1976), *affd.* 571 F.2d 174 (3d Cir. 1978). Respondent's new positions raised in his amended answer require the presentation of new evidence and do not simply clarify or develop his original position.

Although we believe the general rules governing the burden of proof require the transfer of that burden to respondent with regard to his determination under section 482, we feel compelled to further comment on the specific burden of proof problems under section 482. Cases dealing with the burden of proof under section 482 have set up a three-tier approach in determining whether respondent may assert section 482, and, if so, whether respondent or petitioner bears the burden of proof thereunder.

First, if the notice of deficiency is clear that respondent is relying on section 482 in support of his deficiency, then the burden is upon the taxpayer to establish that respondent's allocation was unreasonable, arbitrary, or capricious. Brittingham v. Commissioner, 66 T.C. 373, 395 (1976), *affd.* 598 F.2d 1375 (5th Cir. 1979) (*quoting* Ach v. Commissioner, 42 T.C. 114, 125–126 (1964), *affd.* 358 F.2d 342 (6th Cir. 1966)).

Second, if respondent does not indicate in the notice of deficiency that he is relying on section 482, but alerts the taxpayer of his reliance on section 482 formally in pleadings far enough in advance of trial so as not to prejudice the taxpayer or take him by surprise at trial, then the burden of proof shifts to respondent to establish all the elements necessary to support his allocation under section 482. *See* Rubin v. Commissioner, 56 T.C. 1155, 1162-1 164 (1971), *affd.* 460 F.2d 1216 (2d Cir. 1972); Rule 142(a), Tax Court Rules of Practice and Procedure. *But see* Abatti v. Commissioner, 644 F.2d 1385 (9th Cir. 1981), *revg.* a Memorandum Opinion of this Court.

Third, if respondent raises section 482 at such a late date that the principles of fair play and justice would be abrogated by permitting him to rely on section 482, then he will not be allowed to rely on section 482 at all. United States v. First Security Bank, 334 F.2d 120, 122 n. 4 (9th Cir. 1964); Commissioner v. Chelsea Products, 197 F.2d 620, 624 (3d Cir. 1952), *affg.* 16 T.C. 840 (1951). *See Abatti v. Commissioner, supra.*

In the present case, petitioners' counsel admits that petitioners had notice of respondent's reliance on section 482 at least 5 weeks prior to the scheduled trial. Petitioners do not contend that such notice brings them within the limited circumstances which call for denying respondent the right to raise section 482, but, rather, petitioners contend they fall within the second category requiring the burden of proof to shift to respondent. We agreed at trial with petitioners, and we still agree. We note, however, that even if petitioners were to bear the burden of proof, we would find that they have met their burden of showing that respondent's section 482 allocation was arbitrary, capricious, or unreasonable.

* * *

Decisions will be entered under Rule 155.

In *Achiro*, the court stated that "if respondent raises section 482 at such a late date that the principles of fair play and justice would be abrogated by permitting him to rely on section 482, then he will not be allowed to rely on section 482 at all." This reflects the doctrine of "surprise and prejudice," which if applied, precludes the IRS from raising a new issue so late in the litigation as to surprise and prejudice the taxpayer.

Unlike in other courts, Tax Court briefs are generally filed after trial, *see* Tax Court Rule 151(a). The Tax Court will not consider issues raised for the first time in the parties' post-trial briefs if it finds surprise and prejudice. Thus, the taxpayer will not be forced to address late in the trial process an issue that was not previously raised, if doing so would put the taxpayer at a disadvantage in making his or her case. *See, e.g.*, Robertson v. Commissioner, 55 T.C. 862, 865 (1971), *acq.* 1972-2 C.B. 3 (1972); Philbrick v. Commissioner, 27 T.C. 346, 353 (1956), *acq.* 1958-2 C.B. 7 (1958); Hettler v. Commissioner, 16 T.C. 528, 535 (1951), *acq. sub nom.* Commissioner v. Crilly, 1951-2 C.B. 2 (1951). However, the court is unlikely to find surprise and prejudice if the matter is raised at or before trial, and even as to some issues raised in the IRS's post-trial briefs. *See, e.g.*, Levy v. Commissioner, 91 T.C. 838, 865 (1988) ("[A]t trial we allowed respondent to amend his answer to raise the at-risk argument under section 465(b)(3). . . . In post trial briefs, respondent also raised the at-risk argument that arises under section 465(b)(4). . . . In our opinion and on the facts of this case, petitioners are not prejudiced by our allowing respondent to rely on section 465(b)(4) in making his at-risk arguments."); Grow v. Commissioner, 80 T.C. 314, 329 (1983) ("With respect to the specific point involved here, petitioners complain that respondent first called attention to the second sentence of section 48(c)(1) in his reply brief . . . [and] that this new issue caught petitioners completely by surprise and should not, therefore, be considered by the Court. We find petitioners' objections without merit.").

Recall that the "new matter" provision of Tax Court Rule 142(a)(1) puts the burden of persuasion on the IRS on issues that were not included in the notice of deficiency if the issues constitute new matter. How does Rule 142(a)(1) affect the IRS's likelihood of including more matters up front in the notice of deficiency? If Rule 142(a)(1) applies, and the IRS has failed to include an issue in the notice of deficiency, can the IRS circumvent the Tax Court's "new matter" rule simply by sending the taxpayer a second notice of deficiency for the same tax year, raising the new issue? *See* I.R.C. § 6212(c)(1).

What other technique might the IRS use to try to avoid having late-raised issues characterized as "new matter"? Consider this excerpt from a Tax Court case:

NICHOLSON v. COMMISSIONER

United States Tax Court
T.C. Memo. 1993-183

HALPERN, JUDGE:

* * *

Normally, in this Court, a taxpayer bears the burden of proving respondent's determination to be incorrect. Rule 142(a). That burden placed upon the taxpayer is sometimes described as giving a "presumption of correctness" to respondent. In certain circumstances, however, the burden of going forward with the evidence will be placed upon respondent (depriving her of what is termed the presumption of correctness). Petitioners make two arguments for stripping respondent of her presumption of correctness and, instead, placing upon her the burden of going forward with the evidence.

* * *

1. New Matter

In the notice of deficiency, respondent determined that petitioners received unreported income of $387,055 with respect to 1980. The notice of deficiency does not state the specific basis of that determination.[n.5] Respondent's amendment to answer and brief,

---

[n.5] The "explanation" contained in the notice of deficiency is as follows: "It is determined that you received

however, demonstrate that her determination was based on a source and application of funds analysis. Subsequent to the trial, on brief, respondent formally abandoned that theory, relying instead on other theories first raised by respondent in her amendment to answer. Specifically, respondent's new theories and arguments concern: (1) Unreported income, actually or constructively received (individually), as an associate of CSN; (2) unreported income, actually or constructively received, as a dental practice owner; (3) unreported rent income, actually or constructively received, (individually) as the lessor of the dental clinics; (4) unreported income from pension plan withdrawals; and (5) unreported interest income. On account of respondent's new theories, petitioners contend that respondent has raised a "new matter", within the meaning of Rule 142(a), and therefore ought to bear the burden of proof.

We disagree. None of respondent's new theories are inconsistent with respondent's notice of deficiency, which says nothing more than that petitioners had unreported income of $387,055 in 1980, which is taxable to them inasmuch as they have failed to establish the applicability of any exclusion. We have repeatedly stated that a theory will not constitute a new matter, within the meaning of Rule 142(a), if it is consistent with the theory (or theories) advanced by respondent in the notice of deficiency. *E.g.,* Achiro v. Commissioner, 77 T.C. 881, 890 (1981) ("The assertion of a new theory which merely clarifies or develops the original determination without being inconsistent or increasing the amount of the deficiency is not a new matter requiring the shifting of the burden of proof."). Accordingly, where, as here, the theory advanced by respondent in her notice of deficiency is broadly worded, respondent is at liberty to advance in her answer (or amended answer) any argument consistent with that broad theory, without assuming the burden of proof under the new matter doctrine. Spangler v. Commissioner, 32 T.C. 782, 793 (1959), *affd.* 278 F.2d 665 (4th Cir. 1960). All of respondent's new theories deal with unreported income and therefore are consistent with respondent's extremely broad notice of deficiency, which, as discussed, does no more than charge petitioners with unreported income to which no exclusion applies. Accordingly, we find that respondent's new arguments do not constitute new matters under Rule 142(a).

* * *

What kind of problems might the court's holding in this part of the case pose for the taxpayer? Recall that the notice of deficiency forms part of the Tax Court pleadings. Under Tax Court Rule 34(b)(4), the taxpayer has to make "clear and concise assignments of each and every error which the petitioner alleges to have been committed by the Commissioner in the determination of the deficiency or liability." Look again at Code section 7522. Does it ameliorate the problem the taxpayer in *Nicholson* faced? Also recall that section 7522 states that noncompliance by the IRS will not invalidate the notice. What possible remedies might be available to enforce section 7522?

In *Shea v. Commissioner*, 112 T.C. 183 (1999), *nonacq.*, 2000-44 I.R.B. 430, the Tax Court used as its section 7522 analysis the standards under Tax Court Rule 142(a) for determining whether the IRS has raised "new matter" — the court considered whether the new issues would require the introduction of additional evidence. Specifically, the court stated, in part, "In the final analysis, we think that section 7522 makes the question of whether reliance on . . . [a particular Code section in court] is, or is not, 'inconsistent' with the notice of deficiency irrelevant, if the basis on which respondent relies was *not described in the notice of deficiency and requires different evidence.*" *Id.* at 195–196 (emphasis added). How are broadly worded notices of deficiency likely to be treated under the reasoning of *Shea*?

---

income in the amount of $387,055.00 which was not reported on your income tax return for the taxable year ended Dec. 31, 1980. This amount is determined to be taxable to you because you have failed to establish that this amount is excludable from gross income under the provisions of the Internal Revenue Code."

In *Estate of Mitchell v. Commissioner*, 250 F.3d 696 (9th Cir. 2001), the estate of hairdresser Paul Mitchell argued that the burden of proof in the Tax Court proceeding should have been shifted to the IRS because of post-notice events in the Tax Court trial. Consider the opinion of the Court of Appeals for the Ninth Circuit:[8]

ESTATE OF MITCHELL v. COMMISSIONER

United States Court of Appeals, Ninth Circuit
250 F.3d 696 (2001)

OPINION: WARDLAW, CIRCUIT JUDGE:

The Estate of Paul Mitchell (the "Estate") petitions for review of the United States Tax Court's decision allowing the Commissioner of the Internal Revenue Service (the "Commissioner") to assess an additional $2,404,571 in federal estate taxes. * * * Although we find that the Commissioner's notice was timely, we nevertheless vacate the Tax Court's judgment and remand because the Tax Court failed to shift the burden of proving the accuracy of the additional estate tax to the Commissioner and failed to provide an adequate explanation for its valuation of the JPMS stock at the time of Paul Mitchell's death.

I. BACKGROUND

Paul Mitchell, co-founder of the highly successful hair-care products company of the same name, died on April 21, 1989. * * * The IRS received the Estate's return on Monday, July 23, 1990.

On July 21, 1993, the IRS mailed to the Estate a notice of deficiency (the "Notice"), determining a deficiency in the federal estate tax in the amount of $45,117,089, and a total of $8,543,643 in penalties. The IRS asserted that the Estate had undervalued its 1,226 shares of [John Paul Mitchell Systems (JPMS)] stock. The Estate had reported the stock was worth $28.5 million based on a valuation conducted by a private accounting firm. The IRS, however, calculated the stock's value at $105 million and assessed additional taxes based on the $76.5 million discrepancy.

* * *

On June 11, 1996, the Estate filed a motion with the Tax Court disputing that it bore the burden of persuasion to show the Commissioner's assessment was inaccurate. The Estate argued that the evidence established that it owned 49.04 percent of the outstanding stock in JPMS on the valuation date and thus its interest in JPMS was a minority interest, not a controlling interest. Therefore, the Commissioner's appraisal, determining that the Estate's 49.04 percent interest was a controlling interest, was erroneous, and any additional estate taxes were excessive. The Estate contended that pursuant to *Herbert v. Commissioner*, 377 F.2d 65 (9th Cir. 1966), the burden should be placed on the Commissioner to justify the government's original assessment or to submit a more accurate figure. On July 8, 1996, the Tax Court denied the Estate's motion to shift the burden of persuasion without explanation.

The dispute over the value of the stock proceeded to trial. In addition to a substantial amount of documentary evidence, both the Estate and the Commissioner offered the testimony of expert witnesses as to the value of the 1,226 shares of JPMS stock. The experts' testimony offered a wide variety of estimates and methods for calculating the stock's value. As may be expected, the experts for the Estate minimized the stock's value, testifying that its value on the date of Paul Mitchell's death ranged from approximately $20 to $29 million, while the experts for the Commissioner maximized the stock's value in a range from $57 to $165 million. The methodology each expert used was equally varied, with some producing estimates based on the stock prices of similar

[8] *Estate of Mitchell* also raised other issues, which are discussed in Chapters 7.

companies and others using elaborate economic formulae. * * *

In 1997, the Tax Court issued its opinion as to the stock's value. Estate of Mitchell v. Commissioner, 1997 Tax Ct. Memo LEXIS 546, 74 T.C.M. (CCH) 872, 1997 T.C. Memo 461 (1997). The Tax Court found that the stock's fair market value was $41,532,600. * * *

II. DISCUSSION

* * *

B. Shifting the Burden of Proof

The Estate argues that the Tax Court erred by denying its motion to shift the burden of persuasion, leaving the burden of proof on the Estate. *See* Herbert v. Comm'r, 377 F.2d 65, 69 (9th Cir. 1967). The Tax Court denied the Estate's motion without explanation, and we will refrain from speculating as to the reasons for its decision. We nevertheless review *de novo* the Tax Court's decision to deny the Estate's motion to shift the burden. *See* Moss v. Comm'r, 831 F.2d 833, 837 (9th Cir. 1987).

In *Cohen v. Commissioner*, 266 F.2d 5 (9th Cir. 1959), we stated:

> At the outset of a Tax Court proceeding to redetermine a tax deficiency, the Commissioner's determination is presumed to be correct. The burden of proof is thus placed upon the taxpayer to show that the Commissioner's determination is invalid.
>
> When the Commissioner's determination has been shown to be invalid, the Tax Court must redetermine the deficiency. The presumption as to the correctness of the Commissioner's determination is then out of the case. The Commissioner and not the taxpayer then has the burden of proving whether any deficiency exists and if so the amount. It is not incumbent upon the taxpayer under these circumstances to prove that he owed no tax or the amount of the tax which he did owe.

Id. at 11 (citations omitted).

According to the Notice, the Commissioner concluded the value of the JPMS stock at the time of Paul Mitchell's death was $105 million. The Estate had reported the value at $28.5 million in its tax return. Due to the $76.5 million difference in value, the Commissioner asserted that the Estate owed an additional $45,117,089 in estate taxes, not including a total of $8,543,643 in penalties. At trial, Martin Hanan, a witness for the Commissioner, valued the stock at $81 million — $34 million less than the Commissioner's original valuation. Furthermore, a letter written by the Commissioner's appraiser, AIBE Valuation, dated March 18, 1993, indicates that AIBE Valuation originally appraised Mitchell's interest at $85 million as a minority interest, but increased it to $105 million, at the request of the IRS, to reflect the Estate's interest as a controlling interest. We find that Hanan's testimony and the AIBE letter support the conclusion that the Commissioner's assessment was arbitrary and excessive. United States v. Stonehill, 702 F.2d 1288, 1294 (9th Cir. 1983) (holding that "where the assessment has separable items, . . . error which demonstrates a pattern of arbitrariness or carelessness will destroy the presumption for the entire assessment"); *Cohen*, 266 F.2d at 11 (holding that when the taxpayer has shown the determination to be arbitrary and excessive, the burden of persuasion shifts to the Commissioner to prove the correct amount of tax owed and the presumption as to the correctness of the Commissioner's determination is out of the case); *see also* Helvering v. Taylor, 293 U.S. 507, 513–15, 55 S. Ct. 287, 79 L. Ed. 623 (1935).

We conclude that the Tax Court erred in denying the Estate's Motion to Shift the Burden of Persuasion. Consistent with *Cohen*, because the Commissioner's determination was demonstrated, by its own experts, to be invalid, the Commissioner — and not the Estate — had the "burden of proving whether any deficiency exists and if so the amount." *Cohen*, 266 F.2d at 11. The Tax Court treated the case as one where the burden of proof made no difference; it did not find that one party failed to carry its burden, but proceeded with its own valuation, "weighing the evidence and choosing from among conflicting inferences and conclusions those which it considers most reasonable." Tax Court Order, Docket No. 21805-93 (July 8, 1998) (*citing* Comm'r v. Scottish Am. Inv. Co., 323 U.S. 119, 123–24 (1944)). However, in responding to the petitioner's second motion for reconsideration, the Tax Court erroneously stated that valuation was a matter of approximation and judgment "on which *the petitioner* has the burden of proof." (emphasis added). Because the burden of proving the evaluation of the Estate and the commensurate deficiency shifted to the Commissioner, it was error not to put the Commissioner to its proof.

* * *

CONCLUSION

* * * We grant the Estate's petition in part, vacate, and remand for the Tax Court to shift the burden of proof to the Commissioner regarding the determination of additional taxes and explain its valuation of the stock consistent with Leonard Pipeline [Contractors v. Commissioner, 142 F.3d 1133 (9th Cir. 1998)]. In light of the foregoing, we do not reach the question whether the Tax Court correctly valued the Estate, as we are unable to conduct a meaningful review.

AFFIRMED IN PART, VACATED AND REMANDED IN PART.

Is the Court of Appeals for the Ninth Circuit saying in *Mitchell* that the IRS bears the burden of proof on deficiency amounts the IRS voluntarily decreases after the notice of deficiency was mailed? Recall that Rule 142(a)(1) provides that, the IRS bears the burden of proof on "increases in deficiency" (as well as on new matter). Is there a reason why the IRS should bear the burden of proof on decreased deficiencies as well, or are decreased deficiencies more in the nature of concessions that should be encouraged?

On remand in *Estate of Mitchell v. Commissioner*, the Tax Court stated in part:

> Pursuant to the mandate of the Court of Appeals, we shift the burden of proof to respondent. Consequently, respondent has the burden of proving by a preponderance of the evidence the existence and the amount of the deficiency. *Cohen v. Commissioner*, 266 F.2d 5, 11 (9th Cir. 1959), remanding T.C. Memo. 1957-172.
>
> The deficiency in this case is attributable to the valuation of 1,226 shares of JPMS common stock at the moment of decedent's death. On its estate tax return, the estate valued the shares at $28.5 million. Thus, respondent must prove by a preponderance of the evidence that the value of the shares at the moment of decedent's death was greater than $28.5 million.
>
> With the discussion that follows, we attempt to provide the Court of Appeals with a reasoned account of how we reach our valuation conclusion in this case, mindful that the burden of persuasion is on respondent.

Estate of Mitchell, T.C. Memo. 2002-98 at *15. After explaining its valuation, the Tax Court reentered its previous decision. The Ninth Circuit affirmed in *Fujieki v. Commissioner*, 2004-1 U.S.T.C. ¶ 60,475 (9th Cir. 2003).

[D] Invalid Notices of Deficiency

Thus far, this chapter has focused on "valid" notices of deficiency. Even notices that are "arbitrary and erroneous" are "valid" because those notices still have legal effect. As the above discussion reveals, the technical requirements for a valid notice of deficiency are relatively minimal.[9] However, the requirements that do exist are key. What are the consequences of violating section 6212's requirements? This portion of the chapter considers two major aspects of section 6212, the "last known address" aspect and the "determination" aspect.

[1] The "Last Known Address" Rule

Reading Assignment: I.R.C. § 6212(b)(1)–(2).

The Code sets forth specific procedures the IRS must follow when providing the taxpayer with notice of a deficiency. It states:

> In the absence of notice to the Secretary . . . of the existence of a fiduciary relationship, *notice of a deficiency* in respect of a tax imposed by subtitle A, chapter 12, chapter 41, chapter 42, chapter 43, or chapter 44 *if mailed to the taxpayer at his last known address, shall be sufficient* . . . even if such taxpayer is deceased, or is under a legal disability, or, in the case of a corporation, has terminated its existence.

I.R.C. § 6212(b)(1) (emphasis added).

Section 6212(b) is phrased in a noncompulsory way because mailing to the taxpayer's last known address is a safe harbor, a substitute for actual notice to the taxpayer. "If mailing results in actual notice without prejudicial delay . . . it meets the conditions of § 6212(a) no matter to what address the notice successfully was sent." Clodfelter v. Commissioner, 527 F.2d 754, 757 (9th Cir. 1975), *cert. denied*, 425 U.S. 979 (1976). What kind of delay do you think would constitute "prejudicial" delay?

Under Treasury regulations, the IRS must update its database of addresses by using the United States Postal Service National Change of Address database, which retains address changes for 36 months. Treas. Reg. § 301.6212-2(b)(2). Under the regulations, if the taxpayer's name and last known address in the IRS's records match the taxpayer's name and prior mailing address in the Postal Service database, the new address in the postal database is deemed to be the taxpayer's last known address absent "clear and concise notification of a different address." *Id.* Under the regulations, the filing of a return with a different address that the IRS properly processes requires the IRS to update the taxpayer's address. Treas. Reg. § 301.6212-2(b)(2)(ii)(A).

The following case, in which the relevant events predate the regulations, discuss what constitutes clear and concise notification to the IRS of a new address in the context of an IRS form other than a tax return filed by the taxpayer.

---

[9] Section 6212(a)(1) provides, in part: "If the Secretary determines that there is deficiency in respect of any tax imposed by subtitle A or B or chapter 41, 42, 43 or 44, he is authorized to send notice of such deficiency to the taxpayer by certified mail or registered mail." However, failure to send the notice by certified or registered mail does not invalidate the notice. *See, e.g.*, Balkissoon v. Commissioner, 995 F.2d 525, 528 (4th Cir.), *cert. denied*, 510 U.S. 978 (1993) ("Commissioner's failure to comply with the authorization in section 6212(a) inviting the use of registered or certified mail proves to be a technical, but harmless violation"); Berger v. Commissioner, 404 F.2d 668, 673 (3d Cir.), *cert. denied*, 395 U.S. 905 (1969) ("Subsection (a) [of section 6212] authorizes a notice of deficiency to be sent by registered or certified mail. In authorizing such method of notice it does not forbid any other method. If a revenue agent personally delivers by hand a notice of deficiency to the taxpayer it could not rationally be suggested that the notice was invalid because it violated a requirement of subsection (a).").

HUNTER v. COMMISSIONER

United States Tax Court
T.C. Memo. 2004-81

HOLMES, JUDGE: In September 1998, petitioner Thomas Hunter moved from Gallatin to Hendersonville, Tennessee. He knew when he moved that the IRS was auditing his tax returns. In October 1998, he hired new accountants to represent him, and filed a power-of-attorney form that both directed the IRS to send copies of all correspondence to their office in Nashville and listed his own new address in Hendersonville. In January 1999, respondent sent notices of deficiency for the tax years under audit to petitioner at his old address in Gallatin. He never received them. Respondent did not mail duplicates to him at his new address, nor did he mail duplicates to petitioner's accountants in Nashville.

The case comes to us on the parties' cross-motions to dismiss for lack of jurisdiction. The question presented is whether petitioner, by filing this power-of-attorney form, gave respondent a clear and concise notification of his change of address.

Background

This case turns on the timing of a few key events:

August 14, 1997	Petitioner files 1991–1995 returns.
July 30, 1998	Petitioner files 1996 return. The parties assume that this return listed petitioner's Gallatin address.
August 13, 1998	The revenue agent issues her findings on petitioner's 1991–1996 tax liability in a revenue agent's report that she sends to petitioner at his Gallatin address. He receives it, but doesn't respond.
September 1998	Petitioner moves to Hendersonville, Tennessee.
October 23, 1998	Petitioner signs Form 2848 ("Power of Attorney and Declaration of Representative") listing his Hendersonville address and naming three accountants as his designated representatives for the 6 tax years under audit. The form directs respondent to send copies of all correspondence to both the first and second accountants named on the form.
November 19, 1998	The IRS service center in Memphis receives and processes the Form 2848.
January 28, 1999	Respondent issues three notices of deficiency covering all 6 tax years. Respondent sends these notices to the Gallatin address. All are sent by certified mail; two are returned to the IRS as unclaimed, and there is no record of what happened to the third.
July 1999	Petitioner receives statements of account for each of the years in question from the IRS, sent to him at his Hendersonville address.
September 1999	Petitioner begins suggesting compromise to resolve all years in question.
July 2000–April 2002	Petitioner continues settlement talks, first with a revenue agent and then with the IRS Appeals office.
June 10, 2002	Petitioner files petition. (In lieu of the notices of deficiency, which he still hasn't received, he attaches the revenue agent's reports from August 1998).

Petitioner continues to be a resident of Tennessee, as he was when he filed his petition. When the case neared trial in Nashville, both parties moved to dismiss the petition for lack of jurisdiction — petitioner on the ground that respondent never sent a notice of deficiency to his last known address, and respondent on the ground that petitioner filed his petition well outside our 90-day jurisdictional limit. The parties have stipulated or not contested the key facts and documents.[n.1]

Discussion

Our jurisdiction to redetermine deficiencies exists only when the Commissioner issues a notice of deficiency and a taxpayer files a timely petition to redetermine that deficiency. * * * The Internal Revenue Code says that a notice of deficiency shall be "sufficient" if "mailed to the taxpayer at his last known address." Sec. 6212(b)(1). * * * There is no statutory definition of "last known address," and the resulting gap has been filled with a "plethora of caselaw decided by this and other courts." *Marks v. Commissioner*, T.C. Memo. 1989-575, *aff'd*, 947 F.2d 983, 292 U.S. App. D.C. 117 (D.C. Cir. 1991).[n.3]

In *Abeles v. Commissioner*, 91 T.C. 1019, 1035 (1988), we held that

> a taxpayer's last known address is that address which appears on the taxpayer's most recently filed return, unless respondent has been given clear and concise notification of a different address.

We also held in *Abeles* that once a taxpayer notifies the IRS that his address has changed, the Commissioner "must exercise reasonable care and diligence in ascertaining, and mailing the notice of deficiency to, the correct address." *Id.* at 1031. And we focus in deciding whether he's exercised reasonable care on "the information that would be available to the IRS at the time that it issued the deficiency if it had used reasonable diligence." * * * *Ward v. Commissioner*, 907 F.2d 517, 521 (5th Cir. 1990), *rev'g and remanding*, 92 T.C. 949 (1989). So the specific question to be answered is whether petitioner, by listing his new address on his power-of-attorney form, gave respondent "clear and concise notification" of his new address.

Two courts have already answered the question. In *Rizzo v. Davis*, 43 AFTR 2d 985, 79-1 USTC par. 9310 (W.D. Pa. 1979), the court found — at the Government's insistence — that the taxpayer's Form 2848 established a "last known address" different from the one appearing on the taxpayer's most recently filed return. And in *Johnson v. Commissioner*, 611 F.2d 1015, 1020 (5th Cir. 1980), *rev'g and remanding*, T.C. Memo. 1977-382, the Fifth Circuit similarly held that a Form 2848 is sufficient to change a last known address, even if the IRS later loses the form. We ourselves have repeatedly held that a power-of-attorney form directing the IRS to send all original documents to a representative is an adequate notification of a change of address: *Maranto v. Commissioner*, T.C. Memo. 1999-266; *Elgart v. Commissioner*, T.C. Memo. 1996-379; *Honts v. Commissioner*, T.C. Memo. 1995-532

This case would seem only a bit different — here petitioner directed that copies be sent to his accountants, and it is he rather than respondent who is claiming that a Form 2848 effectively makes a change of address. Petitioner suggests neither of these distinctions makes a difference. In his view, for a filing to change a "last known address," it must only be (1) clear and concise, (2) a notification, and (3) show a different address

---

[n.1] The most important fact that the parties did not stipulate is whether petitioner ever received the notice of deficiency. Petitioner testified at the short hearing held before the case was submitted that he never had. Respondent objected to the proposed finding of fact citing that testimony, but only by characterizing the testimony as "self-serving." On this crucial point, we agree with petitioner — noting especially that respondent, in his own motion to dismiss, asserted only that he sent three notices of deficiency to petitioner — the three concededly sent to petitioner's old address in January 1999.

[n.3] Respondent has issued a regulation, sec. 301.6212-2, Proced. & Admin. Regs., defining "last known address." The regulation's effective date, however, is January 29, 2001, after the events giving birth to these motions.

from the last one sent to the IRS. He then insists that his October 1998 power-of-attorney form meets all three requirements. It was "clear and concise" because the Form 2848 was the IRS's own form; it was a notification because it was sent to the appropriate IRS service center, as the IRS required, *see* Rev. Proc. 90-18, sec. 4.02 1990-13 I.R.B. 19, 1990-1 C.B. 491, 492, Rev. Proc. No. 90-18, and it definitely showed a different address. * * *

Respondent chose not to file a reply brief and so missed his chance to grapple with *Rizzo* and *Johnson*. Instead, he argues that petitioner's proposed test leaves out a critical fourth element: An express statement of intent by a taxpayer that his address of record be changed to his new address. *See* Rev. Proc. 90-18, sec. 5.04 (1), 1990-1 C.B. at 494.[n.6] This failure, which respondent strongly suggests could easily have been cured by using Form 8852 — the IRS's official change-of-address form — in his view vitiates petitioner's attempt to use a Form 2848 to effect a change of address.

Respondent finds this fourth element not in any case involving powers of attorney, but in other cases stating seemingly broad principles of "last known address" law. He begins with *Alta Sierra Vista v. Commissioner*, 62 T.C. 367, 374 (1974), a case where we noted that "Administrative realities demand that the burden fall upon the taxpayer to keep the Commissioner informed as to his proper address." *Id.* at 374 (citations omitted). *Alta Sierra Vista* spoke of respondent's "entitlement" to treat the address on a taxpayer's most recent tax return as his last known address. Respondent insists that this "entitlement" creates a presumption which simply listing a new address on a power-of-attorney form does not rebut.

* * *

Respondent * * * points to *Pyo v. Commissioner*, 83 T.C. 626 (1984), which does at least feature an IRS-designed form — Form 872, the form the IRS customarily uses to extend the statute of limitations. The IRS had itself incorrectly filled out the taxpayer-address portion of the form with the Pyos' old address before sending it to their accountant. The Pyos did not catch the mistake before returning the form to the IRS. A year later, the IRS sent a notice of deficiency to the old address, despite having traded letters with the Pyos at their new address in the meantime.

When the notice was returned as undeliverable, the IRS relied on the erroneously completed Form 872 as evidence that the Pyos' old address was their "last known address." The Court rejected this argument, holding that an "inadvertent" failure by a taxpayer to correct an IRS mistake on a form would be insufficient to establish a last known address, especially when so much time had passed since the Pyos sent back the Form 872 and the IRS had begun writing to them at their new address. Pyo does not support the proposition that a form filed for a purpose other than changing an address will not create a new "last known address"; rather, it teaches that taxpayers will not be penalized for inadvertently failing to correct IRS mistakes.

Petitioner's Form 2848, in contrast, calls upon taxpayers to fill it out themselves and include their address. "[I]t seems anomalous to permit * * * [respondent] to prescribe the medicine and then punish the patient for taking it." *Johnson*, 611 F.2d at 1019. And our caselaw — beginning at least with *Honts* — holds that a power-of-attorney form works as a change of address. Respondent tries to limit those cases' force by arguing that the Form 2848 is sufficient notice of an address change only when it directs originals of all notices and communications be sent to the taxpayer's representative instead of the taxpayer. He argues that petitioner's case is different: His form directed only copies go to his representatives, and merely informed respondent of his address, without saying that he wished the new address to supplant the old.

But we reject the assertion that a valid change-of-address notification must use

---

[n.6] Note that we have held that revenue procedures generally, and Rev. Proc. 90-18, *supra*, in particular, do not bind this Court. Westphal v. Commissioner, T.C. Memo. 1992-599

language equivalent to "please note that this is a change of address." As petitioner points out, no such glaring notification exists on a tax return, or on the power-of-attorney forms given effect in *Rizzo* and *Johnson*.

We also think that respondent's position overlooks a more general theme in the case law; namely, that the IRS is chargeable with knowing the information that it has readily available when it sends notices to taxpayers. As courts have repeatedly observed, the steady advance of technology continues to lighten the IRS's burden in searching its own records for current address information. *Union Tex. Int'l Corp. v. Commissioner*, 110 T.C. 321, 334, 110 T.C. No. 25 (1998).

Petitioner is thus right in noting that address information on the Form 2848 is not mere surplusage. The IRS asks for that information and solicits taxpayer's directions on what address should be used for original and duplicate notices. This strongly implies that respondent will actually incorporate the information on the form into its databases and use the information when sending notices to a taxpayer's "last known address."

Respondent's position is essentially that it is up to taxpayers to flag change-of-address information in a way so obvious as to be immune from occasional bureaucratic irregularities. But the minimal burden to the IRS must be balanced against the potentially serious consequences for taxpayers who rely on the IRS to process in a businesslike way the information that it receives. The *Tadros* decision itself recognized that the IRS has an "obligation" to "exercise reasonable care in determining an address." *Tadros*, 763 F.2d at 91–92 And as we announced in *Abeles*:

> the IRS's computer system was available to respondent's agent responsible for mailing the notice of deficiency, and * * * the system would have reflected the [correct address] had such agent caused a computer search of petitioner's TIN.

Abeles at 1034.[n.7] In short, the IRS should not "ignore that which it obviously knows." *United States v. Bell*, 183 Bankr. 650, 653 (S.D. Fla. 1995).

Respondent's failure to act on what he knew continued even after the notices were returned as "unclaimed." Respondent's own manual suggests that he should have kept trying to find the right address. 1 Audit, Internal Revenue Manual (CCH), sec. 4243.2(6)(b) (as in effect January 1999) (if mail is undeliverable, IRS should "check all possible sources in the case files").[n.8] Instead, the stipulated facts show no effort to redeliver the notices even after respondent began using petitioner's Hendersonville address in correspondence, and while he continued to meet with petitioner's accountants in settlement talks for several years. The caselaw calls this evidence of lack of reasonable care and due diligence. *See Pyo*, 83 T.C. at 638 (corresponding with taxpayers at new address suggests knowledge of new address); *Honts*, T.C. Memo. 1995-532 (Commissioner should verify address if in regular contact with taxpayer's representative.). And we ourselves have stressed that the Commissioner can protect himself from last-known-address problems by sending copies to each possible address. *Elgart v. Commissioner*, T.C. Memo. 1996-379; *Karosen v. Commissioner*, T.C. Memo. 1983-540. No such steps are on record here, even though petitioner had asked on his Form 2848 for copies of all correspondence to go to two of his accountants.

[n.7] The record in this case contains scant information on the procedures and database capabilities of respondent. We are guided, however, by the stipulation of the parties that the Form 2848 was processed on November 19, 1998; and by Rev. Proc. 90-18, which indicates that the IRS requires 45 days to process address information. The 45-day period, even counting from the time the Form 2848 was filed, would have ended well before January 28, 1998 — the date that the IRS sent out the notices of deficiency.

[n.8] Respondent points out that there is no record of the third notice being returned. Because we find that respondent failed to issue any of these notices to petitioner's last known address, the ambiguity surrounding the ultimate fate of this one notice is irrelevant. Respondent also argues that the house number on the Form 2848 was incorrectly listed as 2200, rather than 2220. This would only be relevant if respondent had used it to address the notices of deficiency at issue.

Nothing compels the Commissioner to ask taxpayers to list their address on a Form 2848. By doing so and by using that requested information to identify taxpayers within IRS records, respondent bears the burden of conforming his actions to the knowledge at his disposal. *See Alta Sierra Vista*, 62 T.C. at 374. This is important not only because of the statutory requirements of section 6213, but also because, as petitioner points out, taxpayers are put in the position of quite reasonably assuming that the address information they provide to the IRS will be noted and acted upon.

We agree with petitioner that listing his Hendersonville address on the Form 2848 provided respondent with "clear and concise" notification of his change of address. His Hendersonville address thus became his "last known address" under section 6213. We shall therefore grant his motion to dismiss this case for lack of jurisdiction, and deny respondent's.

To reflect the foregoing,

An order will be entered granting petitioner's, and denying respondent's, motion to dismiss for lack of jurisdiction.

As *Hunter* suggests, courts do not hesitate to invalidate notices that fail to meet the "last known address" requirement of section 6212(b). *See, e.g.*, King v. Commissioner, 857 F.2d 676 (9th Cir. 1988); Monge v. Commissioner, 93 T.C. 22 (1989); Abeles v. Commissioner, 91 T.C. 1019 (1988), *acq.*, 1989-2 C.B. 1. What is the purpose of the last known address requirement? In that regard, what should be the result if the notice is misaddressed but the taxpayer nonetheless promptly receives it? Consider what the following case says about that circumstance and the court's analysis of the actual events in that case:

MULVANIA v. COMMISSIONER

United States Court of Appeals, Ninth Circuit
769 F.2d 1376 (1985)

GOODWIN, CIRCUIT JUDGE:

The Commissioner of the Internal Revenue Service appeals a decision of the Tax Court that it lacked jurisdiction to assess a deficiency against taxpayer, Richard L. Mulvania, because he did not receive a valid notice of deficiency within the three-year statute of limitations on assessments. We affirm.

Mulvania timely filed an income tax return for 1977 showing his address as 57 Linda Isle Drive, Newport Beach, California. The return was prepared by Gerald F. Simonis Accountants, Inc. On June 13, 1979, the IRS sent a letter to Mulvania setting forth proposed adjustments to his 1974 and 1977 income tax. A copy of that letter was also forwarded to Simonis, who held a power of attorney requesting that copies of all documents sent to Mulvania also be sent to him. Mulvania received the letter.

On December 31, 1980, the IRS sent a letter to Mulvania requesting an extension of the limitations period for assessing Mulvania's 1977 tax liability, which was never executed. On April 15, 1981, the last day of the three-year statutory period in which the IRS could assess a tax deficiency, the IRS sent Mulvania a notice of deficiency with respect to the tax year 1977. The notice was sent by certified mail, addressed as "St. Linda Isle Drive," rather than "57 Linda Isle Drive," Mulvania's correct address. The postal service returned the notice to the IRS on April 21, 1984, marked "Not deliverable as addressed." The IRS placed the returned notice in Mulvania's file and, because the statutory period had expired, did not attempt to remail it.

On the same date that the misaddressed notice of deficiency was mailed to Mulvania, the IRS sent a copy of the notice by ordinary mail to Simonis, who received it on or about April 17, 1981. Expecting that Mulvania would soon call him about the notice, Simonis filed the notice and made a note to follow up. About June 1, 1981, when Simonis called Mulvania to discuss the notice of deficiency, he found out that Mulvania had never received the notice. There is no evidence in the record that Simonis discussed the contents of the notice with Mulvania.

On or about June 15, 1981, after Simonis (who is not a lawyer) advised Mulvania that Simonis' notice was not a valid notice of deficiency for 1977, Mulvania decided not to file a petition in the Tax Court for a redetermination of assessment of deficiency. Mulvania changed his mind, however, and, on April 1, 1983, filed a petition in the Tax Court requesting a redetermination of the deficiency for 1977.

Both parties then filed cross-motions to dismiss for lack of jurisdiction. The Commissioner argued that Mulvania's petition, which was filed almost two years after the notice of deficiency was mailed, was untimely pursuant to 26 U.S.C. § 6123(a). Mulvania claimed the Tax Court lacked jurisdiction to assess a deficiency for 1977 because the three-year statute of limitations had run, and Mulvania had never received a valid notice of deficiency which would have tolled the statute of limitations as provided in 26 U.S.C. § 6503(a).

The Tax Court granted Mulvania's motion to dismiss for lack of jurisdiction and denied the Commissioner's motion to dismiss. This appeal followed. * * *

Cases interpreting the interplay of * * * sections [6501(a), 6503(a), and 6212] have fallen into three broad categories.

First, a notice of deficiency actually, physically received by a taxpayer is valid under § 6212(a) if it is received in sufficient time to permit the taxpayer, without prejudice, to file a petition in the Tax Court even though the notice is erroneously addressed. Clodfelter v. Commissioner, 527 F.2d 754, 757 (9th Cir. 1975), *cert. denied*, 425 U.S. 979, 96 S. Ct. 2184, 48 L. Ed. 2d 805 (1976); Mulvania v. Commissioner, 81 T.C. 65 (1983).

Second, a notice of deficiency mailed to a taxpayer's last known address is valid under § 6212(b)(1) regardless of when the taxpayer eventually receives it. De Welles v. United States, 378 F.2d 37, 39–40 (9th Cir.), *cert. denied*, 389 U.S. 996, 88 S. Ct. 501, 19 L. Ed. 2d 494 (1967).

Third, an erroneously addressed and undelivered registered notice of deficiency is not valid under either § 6212(a) or 6212(b)(1) even if the Commissioner also sends a copy of the notice by regular mail to the taxpayer's attorney. D'Andrea v. Commissioner, 263 F.2d 904, 907, 105 U.S. App. D.C. 67 (D.C. Cir. 1959); *see* Reddock v. Commissioner, 72 T.C. 21 (1979).

In this case the actual notice of deficiency which was mailed to Mulvania became null and void when it was returned to the IRS; at that time, the IRS then knew that the notice had been misaddressed and had not been received. This is not a case in which the notice was improperly addressed, but the postal authorities nonetheless delivered the letter to the taxpayer. *Clodfelter*, 527 F.2d at 756. Mulvania has never physically received a notice of deficiency.

The Commissioner argues that because Mulvania's accountant received a courtesy copy of the notice and called Mulvania before the 90 days had expired, Mulvania therefore received valid notice and now lacks a basis for a petition in the Tax Court. Mulvania argues that a courtesy copy of a notice of deficiency cannot be transformed into a valid notice of deficiency simply because the accountant called and told the taxpayer about the notice.

With a broad power of attorney, registered notice to the attorney or accountant may also serve as notice to the taxpayer under the law of principal and agent if the taxpayer himself received some notification in time to file a petition before the tax court. Commissioner v. Stewart, 186 F.2d 239, 242 (6th Cir. 1951). *But see D'Andrea*, 263 F.2d at 907–08 (copy sent by ordinary mail insufficient where there was no evidence that taxpayer reasonably received the information contained in the notice to his attorney). A taxpayer may also designate the address of his representative as that to which any deficiency notice should be sent. Expanding Envelope and Folder Corp. v. Shotz, 385

F.2d 402, 404 (3d Cir. 1967); *see D'Andrea*, 263 F.2d at 907.

Because Simonis did not have a broad power of attorney, however, the law of principal and agent does not apply. Mulvania had only granted him a power of attorney which requests that courtesy copies of all communication be sent to his representative. The IRS clearly knew that Simonis was not to be the addressee of the official notice of deficiency; it sent him only a copy and only by ordinary, unregistered, uncertified mail. *See D'Andrea*, 263 F.2d at 905. *See also* Keeton v. Commissioner, 74 T.C. 377 (1980); Houghton v. Commissioner, 48 T.C. 656 (1967).

The Commissioner relies on two Tax Court cases for the proposition that the copy of the notice sent to Simonis sufficed to toll the three-year statute of limitations. In *Lifter v. Commissioner*, 59 T.C. 818 (1973), the notice of deficiency was sent to the taxpayers' last known address but was returned undelivered. The Commissioner then sent a copy of the notice to the taxpayers' attorney who had been appointed to handle their federal income tax matters. The taxpayers learned of the notice before the running of the statute of limitations and timely filed a petition with the Tax Court. The notice of deficiency was held valid.

Lifter may be distinguished from this case in three respects. First, the IRS sent the notice to what was reasonably believed to be petitioners' last known address, and a notice of deficiency mailed to a taxpayer's last known address is valid even if the taxpayer does not receive it. *DeWelles*, 378 F.2d at 39. Second, taxpayers invoked the jurisdiction of the Tax Court by filing a timely petition. By timely invoking Tax Court jurisdiction, taxpayers effectively waived any objection to the notice of deficiency. Finally, the attorney to whom a copy of the notice was sent apparently had a broad power of attorney, beyond mere receipt of copies of notices sent to taxpayers. The Commissioner in *Lifter* could have sent the original notice to the attorney alone. *See D'Andrea*, 263 F.2d at 905.

In *Whiting v. Commissioner*, T.C. Memo 1984-142 (1984), the notice was sent to taxpayers' previous address although the IRS had been informed of the change of address. The notice was returned undelivered. A copy of the notice was also sent to their attorney who eventually informed them of the notice. The taxpayers filed a timely petition with the Tax Court. They challenged the validity of the notice, but the Tax Court held it was valid because the petitioners became aware that the notice had been issued and timely filed a petition.

Whiting and this case differ in two critical respects. First, in *Whiting* the notice was sent to the wrong address, even after the IRS had been informed of the change of address. Here the notice was misaddressed because of a typographical error. Second, in *Whiting*, petitioners chose to invoke jurisdiction of the Tax Court after learning of the notice from their attorney. As in *Lifter*, by timely invoking Tax Court jurisdiction, taxpayers essentially acknowledged notice; the purpose of § 6212 had been satisfied. Here Mulvania has never acknowledged notice by invoking Tax Court jurisdiction in a timely manner.

In *Whiting*, the Tax Court engaged in a cursory analysis of the validity of the notice, concluding that an error in the address to which the notice of deficiency is mailed does not render the notice invalid when the petition is timely filed, citing *Mulvania*, 81 T.C. at 68. In *Mulvania*, however, the taxpayer received the actual, physical notice of deficiency although it had been mailed to his former address and had later been hand delivered by his child.

The resolution of this issue is a "least-worse" result. Mulvania argues that he never received the actual written notice of deficiency because it was misaddressed. The IRS sent the notice on the last day of the statutory period, making it impossible for the Commissioner to remail the notice within the prescribed time once the error was discovered. To decide for the Commissioner would relieve the IRS of its cumulative errors, and create uncertainty in the law. The IRS argues, however, that this is a mobile society, clerical mistakes do happen, and the taxpayer had actual knowledge of the notice even if not its contents.

The Tax Court was understandably concerned that a decision in the Commissioner's favor would result in an uncertain rule depending on whether the tax adviser happened to be a lawyer. As a lawyer, a tax adviser's call to Mulvania regarding the notice would have been privileged. The Tax Court correctly believed that a decision for the Commissioner would result in an uncertain rule, subject to manipulation by taxpayers who authorize copies to be sent to their accountant or lawyer, or by taxpayers with the most sophisticated tax advisers.

It is better for the government to lose some revenue as the result of its clerical error than to create uncertainty. If Simonis, either intentionally or unintentionally, had not informed Mulvania of the receipt of the copy of the notice of deficiency, then Mulvania would not have received any notification of the deficiency. Tax law requires more solid footings than the happenstance of a tax adviser telephoning a client to tell him of a letter from the IRS.

We conclude that, where a notice of deficiency has been misaddressed to the taxpayer or sent only to an adviser who is merely authorized to receive a copy of such a notice, actual notice is necessary but not sufficient to make the notice valid. The IRS is not forgiven for its clerical errors or for mailing notice to the wrong party unless the taxpayer, through his own actions, renders the Commissioner's errors harmless. In this case, the notice of deficiency became null and void when it was returned to the IRS undelivered. Regardless of the coincidence by which Mulvania later came to know of its existence, the taxpayer's actual knowledge did not transform the void notice into a valid one.

Had Mulvania timely petitioned the Tax Court for a redetermination of deficiency, the IRS error might have fallen into the line of harmless error cases where the taxpayer suffered no ill effects for the Commissioner's inadvertence. Such is not the case here.

Affirmed.

Was the court correct in holding that verbal notice to Mr. Mulvania by his accountant, Mr. Simonis, of receipt by Simonis of a copy of a notice directed to Mulvania did not constitute *actual notice* to Mulvania of the notice of deficiency? Simonis was an accountant but not a lawyer, so his communication to Mulvania was not privileged under then-existing law. Recall the discussion in Chapter 4 of Code section 7525, the federally authorized tax practitioner (FATP) privilege, which extends the attorney-client privilege to non-attorneys providing tax advice in civil proceedings. Would the existence of the FATP privilege affect the outcome of a case similar to *Mulvania* arising today? Would the outcome of the case likely have been different if Mr. Simonis had faxed the notice to Mr. Mulvania?

The court in *Mulvania* refers to a prior *Mulvania* decision, stating, "In *Mulvania* . . . the taxpayer received the actual, physical notice of deficiency although it had been mailed to his former address and had later been hand delivered by his child." *Mulvania*, 769 F.2d at 1380. That *Mulvania* decision was a Tax Court decision relating to the same taxpayer's 1976 tax year. *See* Mulvania v. Commissioner, 81 T.C. 65 (1983). Mr. Mulvania had timely filed a separate tax return for 1976 showing the 57 Linda Isle Drive address discussed in the opinion included in the text. Previously, he had resided at 4191 Silliman Drive. His ex-wife, Frances Mulvania, and the Mulvanias' children still resided at that address on September 16, 1981, when the IRS sent a notice of deficiency there relating to Mr. Mulvania's 1976 tax year. *Id.* at 65–66.

In that case, the following events transpired:

> On September 28, 1981, Frances Mulvania telephoned the petitioner and informed him that she had a "bill" or "statement" from the IRS for him and that he owed the IRS some money. She did not tell him what taxable year the document concerned. On October 2, 1981, the petitioner's children arrived at his residence for a custodial visit, and they brought the notice of deficiency to the petitioner from the Silliman address.
>
> On October 5 or 6, 1981, the petitioner's wife, Carol, took the notice of deficiency to the accountant's office. The accountant forwarded it to the San Francisco attorney on October 13, 1981. By April 1982, no petition had been filed with this Court, and on April 23, 1982, the Commissioner sent a notice of demand for payment of the 1976 deficiency to the petitioner at the Linda Isle address. The petitioner then retained his present counsel, and the petition was filed on June 8, 1982.

Id. at 66. The Tax Court stated:

> In the case before us, the petitioner actually received the notice of deficiency on October 2, 1981, 16 days after the Commissioner mailed it. He promptly had it delivered to his accountant, who forwarded it to the partnership attorney in San Francisco. . . . It is clear on this record that the petitioner received actual notice of the deficiency with ample time remaining to file a petition. At that time, the petitioner became responsible for filing a timely petition with this Court. There is no explanation for the failure to file such a petition, but it is apparent that inaction, after the receipt of the notice, was responsible for the late filing. Hence, the petitioner's failure to file a timely petition cannot be said to have been the direct result of any error in the address to which the notice of deficiency was mailed.

Id. at 69.

Do you agree with the Court of Appeals for the Ninth Circuit that this earlier *Mulvania* decision is distinguishable? Which set of events reflects more "happenstance" (in the language of the Ninth Circuit) in the transmission of the notice of deficiency to Mr. Mulvania — notification by Mr. Mulvania's tax adviser or delivery by Mr. Mulvania's children?

[2] Invalidating a Notice of Deficiency for IRS Failure to Make a "Determination"

Failure to send a notice to the taxpayer's last known address or provide actual notice without prejudicial delay is not the only ground on which a taxpayer has succeeded in obtaining a court decision invalidating a notice of deficiency. Section 6212(a) reads, "[i]f the Secretary *determines* that there is a deficiency. . . ." (emphasis added). One area of dispute is whether the statute requires a substantive "determination" of the taxpayer's liability by the IRS or whether the notice itself conclusively evidences a determination of a deficiency. Recall the *Greenberg's Express* case, which reflects the general proposition that courts will not "look behind" the notice of deficiency to examine the motives or methods of the IRS in determining the deficiency. *Scar v. Commissioner*, the next case, is the leading case invalidating a notice of deficiency for failure of the IRS to make a "determination." How does the court address the question of whether it is "looking behind" the notice of deficiency?

SCAR v. COMMISSIONER

United States Court of Appeals, Ninth Circuit
814 F.2d 1363 (1987)

FLETCHER, CIRCUIT JUDGE:

Taxpayers Howard and Ethel Scar petition for review of the Tax Court's denial of their motion to dismiss for lack of jurisdiction and denial of their two summary judgment motions. Taxpayers argue that the Tax Court lacked jurisdiction because the Commissioner of the Internal Revenue Service (IRS) issued an invalid notice of deficiency. Alternatively, they argue that the Tax Court incorrectly denied their motions for summary judgment and should not have granted the Commissioner's request to amend his answer. We reverse.

BACKGROUND

On September 3, 1979, petitioners Howard and Ethel Scar filed a joint return for tax year 1978.[n.1] The Scars claimed business deductions totaling $26,966 in connection with a video-tape tax shelter,[n.2] and reported total taxes due of $3,269.

On June 14, 1982, the Commissioner mailed to the Scars a letter (Form 892); it listed taxpayers' names and address, the taxable year at issue (the year ending December 31, 1978), and specified a deficiency amount ($96,600). The body of the letter stated in part:

> We have determined that there is a deficiency (increase) in your income tax as shown above. This letter is a NOTICE OF DEFICIENCY sent to you as required by the law.

It informed the taxpayers that if they wished to contest the deficiency they must file a petition with the United States Tax Court within 90 days.

Attached to the letter was a Form 5278 ("Statement — Income Tax Changes") purporting to explain how the deficiency had been determined. It showed an adjustment to income in the amount of $138,000 designated as "Partnership — Nevada Mining Project." The Form 5278 had no information in the space on the form for taxable income as shown on petitioners' return as filed. It showed as the "total corrected income tax liability" the sum of $96,600 and indicated that this sum was arrived at by multiplying 70 percent times $138,000.

Another attached document, designated as "Statement Schedule 2," with the heading "Nevada Mining Project, Explanation of Adjustments," stated as follows:

> In order to protect the government's interest and since your original income tax return is unavailable at this time, the income tax is being assessed at the maximum tax rate of 70%.
>
> The tax assessment will be corrected when we receive the original return or when you send a copy of the return to us.
>
> The increase in tax may also reflect investment credit or new jobs credit which has been disallowed.

Also attached to the letter was a document, designated as "Statement Schedule 3," with the heading "Nevada Mining Project, Explanation of Adjustments." This document explained why the Nevada Mining Project deductions were being disallowed.

On July 7, 1982, the taxpayers filed a timely petition with the Tax Court to redetermine the deficiency asserted. In their petition, they alleged that they had never

---

[n.1] The return was timely, the Scars having received an extension of time to file.

[n.2] The Scars also claimed deductions and credits with regard to this tax shelter on their 1977 returns. They received a notice of deficiency in April of 1981 and petitioned the Tax Court for a redetermination in June of 1981. In February of 1985 the Tax Court made a deficiency determination of $10,410 for the tax year 1977.

been associated with the "Nevada Mining Project Partnership" and had not claimed on their 1978 return any expenses or losses related to that venture. The Commissioner, on August 30, 1982, filed an answer denying the substantive allegations of the petition.

Sometime in September 1982, the Commissioner conceded in a telephone conversation with the taxpayers that the June 14 notice of deficiency was incorrect because it overstated the amount of disallowed deductions and wrongly connected taxpayers with a mining partnership. Nevertheless, the Commissioner maintained that the notice of deficiency was valid. The Commissioner confirmed his position in a letter dated November 29, 1982, stating "the taxpayers should not be surprised by the fact that the Commissioner means to disallow the deductions claimed in 1978 for Executive Productions, Inc." because similar objections had been made to the deductions claimed for the same tax shelter on taxpayers' 1977 return. The Commissioner enclosed with this letter a revised Form 5278, which contained the appropriate shelter explanation and decreased the amount of tax due to $10,374, and notified the taxpayers that he intended to request leave from the Tax Court to amend his answer.

On December 6, 1982 the taxpayers filed a motion to dismiss for lack of jurisdiction, claiming that the June 14 notice of deficiency was invalid because the Commissioner failed to make a "determination" of additional tax owed before issuing the notice of deficiency. The Commissioner filed a response which conceded the inaccuracy of the notice of deficiency but maintained that it was sufficient to give the Tax Court jurisdiction. On March 21, 1983, the Tax Court held a hearing on the taxpayers' motion to dismiss. At the hearing, counsel for the Commissioner attempted to explain why the Form 5278 sent to the taxpayers contained a description of the wrong tax shelter. He stated that an IRS employee transposed a code number which caused the IRS to assert the deficiency on the basis of the Nevada mining project instead of the videotape tax shelter. No witness, however, testified to this fact at the hearing,[n.3] and no explanation was ever offered for the discrepancy of over $80,000 between the deficiency notice assessment and that later conceded to be the correct amount.

Following the March 21 hearing, the taxpayers filed a motion for summary judgment based on the Commissioner's concession that they had not been involved in any mining partnerships. The Commissioner shortly thereafter filed his motion to amend his answer to correct the error made in the notice of deficiency and accompanying documents. On November 17, 1983 the Tax Court, in an opinion reviewed by the full court, ruled on these various motions. The Tax Court majority upheld the validity of the June 14 notice of deficiency, finding that it satisfied section 6212(a), which states the formal requirements for a deficiency notice. The Tax Court further ruled that the Commissioner could amend his answer as requested, and denied taxpayers' motion for summary judgment. The reviewed opinion contained several concurring and dissenting opinions. Five dissenting judges would have denied jurisdiction on the basis that the deficiency notice was invalid and four dissenting judges would not have permitted the Commissioner to amend his answer.

The Commissioner amended his answer and asserted in it, despite the patent incorrectness of the notice of deficiency and the acknowledgment of error by the Service, that the taxpayer had the burden of disproving the correctness of the Commissioner's revised determinations. The taxpayers renewed their motion for summary judgment. The Tax Court denied this second motion for summary judgment on the ground that triable issues of fact remained concerning whether the taxpayers' primary motivation for entering the videotape venture was the prospect of earning a profit or avoiding tax. On February 22, 1985, the Tax Court entered a decision, pursuant to a stipulation, that taxpayers owed $10,377 in additional tax. The stipulation afforded the taxpayers the right to file a petition for review of the Tax Court's adverse rulings.

[n.3] The Commissioner argues that a witness was present at the hearing, but since taxpayers failed to object to counsel's explanation of the IRS's mistake, the witness was never called.

DISCUSSION

In order to decide whether the Tax Court had jurisdiction we review *de novo* the Tax Court's interpretation of section 6212(a). Orvis v. Commissioner, 788 F.2d 1406, 1407 (9th Cir. 1986); Ebben v. Commissioner, 783 F.2d 906, 909 (9th Cir. 1986).

Section 6212(a) states in part: "If the Secretary determines that there is a deficiency in respect of any tax imposed . . . he is authorized to send notice of such deficiency to the taxpayer by certified mail or registered mail." Section 6213(a) provides in part: "Within 90 days . . . after the notice of deficiency authorized in section 6212 is mailed . . . taxpayer may file a petition with the Tax Court for a redetermination of the deficiency." The Tax Court has jurisdiction only when the Commissioner issues a valid deficiency notice, and the taxpayer files a timely petition for redetermination. "A valid petition is the basis of the Tax Court's jurisdiction. To be valid, a petition must be filed from a valid statutory notice." Stamm International Corp. v. Commissioner, 84 T.C. 248, 252 (1985). *See* Midland Mortgage Co. v. Commissioner, 73 T.C. 902, 907 (1980).

The taxpayers correctly note that section 6212(a) authorizes the Commissioner to send a notice of deficiency only if he first "determines that there is a deficiency." Because the deficiency notice mailed to the taxpayers contained an explanation of a tax shelter completely unrelated to their return, contained no adjustments to tax based on their return as filed, and stated affirmatively that the taxpayers's return is "unavailable at this time," taxpayers maintain that the Commissioner could not have "determined" a deficiency with respect to them. The taxpayers assert that, in the absence of a determination, the deficiency notice was invalid and therefore the Tax Court lacked jurisdiction.

The Tax Court rejected this argument, finding that "[t]he requirements of section 6212(a) are met if the notice of deficiency sets forth the amount of the deficiency and the taxable year involved." Scar v. Commissioner, 81 T.C. 855, 860-61 (1983).

We agree with the Tax Court that no particular form is required for a valid notice of deficiency, Abrams v. Commissioner, 787 F.2d 939, 941 (4th Cir.), *cert. denied*, 479 U.S. 882, 107 S. Ct. 271, 93 L. Ed. 2d 248 (1986); Benzvi v. Commissioner, 787 F.2d 1541, 1542 (11th Cir.), *cert. denied*, 479 U.S. 883, 107 S. Ct. 273, 93 L. Ed. 2d 250 (1986), and the Commissioner need not explain how the deficiencies were determined. Barnes v. Commissioner, 408 F.2d 65, 68 (7th Cir.) (*citing* Commissioner v. Stewart, 186 F.2d 239, 242 (6th Cir. 1951)), *cert. denied*, 396 U.S. 836, 90 S. Ct. 94, 24 L. Ed. 2d 86 (1969). The notice must, however, "meet certain substantial requirements." *Abrams*, 787 F.2d at 941. "The notice must at a minimum indicate that the IRS has determined the amount of the deficiency." *Benzvi*, 787 F.2d at 1542. The question confronting us is whether a form letter that asserts that a deficiency has been determined, which letter and its attachments make it patently obvious that no determination has in fact been made, satisfies the statutory mandate.

In none of the cases on which the Tax Court relied was the notice challenged on the basis that there was no determination. *See* Abatti v. Commissioner, 644 F.2d 1385, 1389 (9th Cir. 1981) (notice valid although it did not advise the taxpayer under which code section the IRS would proceed because fair warning was given before trial); *Barnes*, 408 F.2d at 68 (notice need not state the basis for the deficiency determination nor contain particulars of explanations concerning how alleged deficiencies were determined); Foster v. Commissioner, 80 T.C. 34, 229–30 (1983) (notice must advise taxpayer that Commissioner has, in fact, determined a deficiency, and must specify the year and amount), *aff'd in part and vacated in part*, 756 F.2d 1430 (9th Cir. 1985), *cert. denied*, 474 U.S. 1055, 106 S. Ct. 793, 88 L. Ed. 2d 770 (1986); Hannan v. Commissioner, 52 T.C. 787 (1969) (deficiency notice valid where record did not show that Commissioner had not assessed a deficiency even though Commissioner asserted that no deficiency existed and that the notice had been issued in error). The cases assume that the deficiency determination was made. With the exception of *Hannan*, they deal instead with the question of whether the notice imparted enough information to provide the taxpayer with fair notice.

The Tax Court asserts that it is following long-established policy not to look behind a deficiency notice to question the Commissioner's motives and procedures leading to a determination. * * *

We agree that courts should avoid oversight of the Commissioner's internal operations and the adequacy of procedures employed. This does not mean, however, that the courts cannot or should not decide the validity of a notice that can be determined solely by references to applicable statutes and review of the notice itself.

In this case, we need not look behind the notice sent to the taxpayers to determine its invalidity. The Commissioner acknowledges in the notice that the deficiency is not based on a determination of deficiency of tax reported on the taxpayers' return and that it refers to a tax shelter the Commissioner concedes has no connection to the taxpayers or their return.

Section 6212(a) "authorize[s]" the sending of a deficiency notice "if the Secretary *determines* that there is a deficiency." (emphasis added). We agree with Judge Goffe's statement in this case that "even a cursory review of this provision [section 6212(a)] discloses that Congress did not grant the Secretary unlimited and unfettered authority to issue notices of deficiency." *Scar*, 81 T.C. at 872 (Goffe, J., dissenting). In *Appeal of Terminal Wine Co.,* 1 B.T.A. 697, 701 (1925), the Board of Tax Appeals construed the meaning of the term "determine" as applied to deficiency determinations: "By its very definition and etymology the word 'determination' irresistibly connotes consideration, resolution, conclusion, and judgment."

* * * A literal reading of relevant code sections, and the absence of evidence of contrary legislative intent, leads us to conclude that the Commissioner must consider information that relates to a particular taxpayer before it can be said that the Commissioner has "determined" a "deficiency" in respect to that taxpayer. To hold otherwise would entail ignoring or judicially rewriting the plain language of the Internal Revenue Code.[n.9]

This reading of the Code is not a new one. Almost sixty years ago, the Board of Tax Appeals, while refusing to examine the intent, motive or reasoning of the Commissioner, emphasized that

> the statute clearly contemplates that before notifying a taxpayer of a deficiency and hence before the Board can be concerned, a determination must be made by the Commissioner. This must mean a thoughtful and considered determination that the United States is entitled to an amount not yet paid. If the notice of deficiency were other than the expression of a *bona fide* official determination, and were, say, a mere formal demand for an arbitrary amount as to which there were substantial doubt, the Board might easily become merely an expensive tribunal to determine moot questions and a burden might be imposed on taxpayers of litigating issues and disproving allegations for which there had never been any substantial foundation.

[n.9] The dissent, characterizing the deficiency notice as a " 'ticket' to the tax court" suggests that the majority fails "to grasp the function of the deficiency notice." Dissent at 1372. What the dissent fails to grasp, however, is that processes that may "serve their intended purposes" nonetheless may be legally insufficient. For example, notice by telephone would not suffice if written notice were required. Here, the statute requires that the Commissioner make a determination. None was made. The fact that the taxpayers received a deficiency notice does not cure the failure to make a determination.

The dissent in looking only to the fact that notice was sent skips over the Commissioner's failure to make the statutorily required determination. We readily agree with the dissent that in the usual case the sending of the notice of deficiency presumes a determination. * * * Where, however, the notice belies that presumption, it is both reasonable and necessary that the Commissioner demonstrate his compliance with the statute.

Counzens v. Commissioner, 11 B.T.A. 1040, 1159–60 (1928).

These cases inform our judgment here. They support the view that the "determination" requirement of section 6212(a) has substantive content. The Commissioner's and the dissent's contention that the issuance of a formally proper notice of deficiency[n.11] of itself establishes that the Commissioner has determined a deficiency must be rejected. To hold otherwise, would read the determination requirement out of section 6212(a).[n.12]

Finally, the Commissioner asserts that the proper remedy in this case is to eliminate the presumption of correctness that normally attaches to deficiency determinations, *see, e.g.,* Dix v. Commissioner, 392 F.2d 313 (4th Cir. 1968), not to dismiss for lack of jurisdiction. He relies, however, on cases that challenge the correctness of the determination, and not its existence. The Commissioner's belated willingness to assume the burden of proof before the Tax Court cannot cure his failure to determine a deficiency before imposing on taxpayers the obligation to defend themselves in potentially costly litigation in Tax Court. Jurisdiction is at issue here. Failure to comply with statutory requirements renders the deficiency notice null and void and leaves nothing on which Tax Court jurisdiction can rest.

Section 6212(a) of the Internal Revenue Code requires the Commissioner to determine that a deficiency exists before issuing a notice of deficiency. Because the Commissioner's purported notice of deficiency revealed on its face that no determination of tax deficiency had been made in respect to the Scars for the 1978 tax year, it did not meet the requirements of section 6212(a). Accordingly, the Tax Court should have dismissed the action for want of jurisdiction.[n.13]

Petition for review granted.

Cynthia Holcomb Hall, Circuit Judge, dissenting:

Today, the majority fortifies the impediments to tax collection on behalf of errant taxpayers seeking "no taxation without litigation." R. Jackson, Struggle for Judicial Supremacy 141 (1941). I believe the majority undermines the jurisdiction of the Tax

---

[n.11] In the case before us the Commissioner argues that, because the notice contained the Taxpayers' names, social security number, the tax year in question, and "the" amount of deficiency, it was "clearly sufficient." It is quite clear, however, that the notice did not contain the amount of deficiency, but rather contained *an* amount unrelated to any deficiency for which the Scars were responsible.

[n.12] Judge Sterrett, in dissenting, offered a sample of a valid deficiency letter under the statutory construction urged by the IRS and accepted by the Tax Court:

> Dear Taxpayer:
>
> There is a rumor afoot that you were a participant in the Amalgamated Hairpin Partnership during the year 1980. Due to the press of work we have been unable to investigate the accuracy of the rumor or to determine whether you filed a tax return for that year. However, we are concerned that the statute of limitations may be about to expire with respect to your tax liability for 1980.
>
> Our experience has shown that, as a general matter, taxpayers tend to take, on the average, excessive (unallowable) deductions, arising out of investments in partnerships comparable to Amalgamated that aggregate some $10,000. Our experience has further shown that the average investor in such partnerships has substantial taxable income and consequently has attained the top marginal tax rate.
>
> Accordingly, you are hereby notified that there is a deficiency in tax in the amount of $7,000 due from you for the year 1980 in addition to whatever amount, if any, you may have previously paid.
>
> Sincerely yours,
>
> Commissioner of Internal Revenue

Scar, 81 T.C. at 869 (Sterrett, J., dissenting).

[n.13] *Cf.* United States v. Lehigh, 201 F. Supp. 224, 234 (W.D. Ark. 1961) ("The procedures set forth in the Internal Revenue Code were prescribed for the protection of both Government and taxpayer. Neglect to comply with those procedures may entail consequences which the neglecting party must be prepared to face, whether such party be the taxpayer or the Government.").

Court by constructing a superfluous yet substantial hurdle to its jurisdiction. In reaching the conclusion that section 6212(a) of the Internal Revenue Code, 26 U.S.C. § 6212(a), imposes a substantive requirement on the Commissioner of the Internal Revenue Service to prove that he has reviewed specific data before making a determination, the majority eagerly expands jurisdictional requirements while discarding the carefully-honed and expedient jurisdictional rules that exist.

I.

The majority first turns a blind eye to reality when it finds that the incorrect explanation for the deficiency "[makes] it patently obvious that no determination has in fact been made." *See ante* at 1367. The 1978 tax return of taxpayers Howard and Ethel Scar was hardly an unlikely object of the Commissioner's suspicion. In 1977 the taxpayers participated in a videotape tax shelter, investing $6,500 in cash, signing a promissory note for $93,500, and then deducting over $15,000 in depreciation and other expenses from their 1977 tax return based on their "investment." The Commissioner audited this 1977 return and determined a deficiency of $15,875, finding that the taxpayers' "purchase of the film was lacking in profit motive and economic substance other than the avoidance of tax." The Commissioner mailed a notice of deficiency to the taxpayers, who responded by filing a petition for redetermination of the deficiency with the Tax Court on June 30, 1981.

The taxpayers' 1978 return included additional deductions totaling $27,040 based upon the now suspect videotape shelter. In all likelihood, the Commissioner's decision to issue a second deficiency notice regarding this 1978 return resulted from the continuation of the audit process which began with the previous year's tax return. This second deficiency notice, however, incorrectly explained the deficiency in terms of a Nevada mining venture in which the taxpayers had never participated. At the Tax Court hearing on March 21, 1983, counsel for the Commissioner explained that this misdescription resulted from a technical error: an IRS employee had transposed a code number, resulting in the incorrect identification of the basis of the deficiency as being the Nevada mining project instead of the videotape tax shelter. The Commissioner argues that a witness able to testify to this numerical error was present at the hearing, but was not called since the taxpayers did not object to this explanation of the IRS's mistake.

The procedural history of the taxpayers' efforts to challenge the 1978 deficiency consists largely of motions attempting to exploit this apparent mishap. These motions evince the tactics of delay employed by "every litigious man or every embarrassed man, to whom delay [is] more important than the payment of costs." Tennessee v. Sneed, 96 U.S. (6 Otto) 69, 75, 24 L. Ed. 610 (1877).

II.

The majority correctly recognizes that section 6212(a) authorizes the Commissioner to send a notice of deficiency only if he first determines that there is a deficiency. The taxpayers themselves concede that the notice of deficiency in this case satisfied section 6212(a)'s formal requirements of stating the amount of the deficiency and the taxable year involved. *See* Stamm International Corp. v. Commissioner, 84 T.C. 248, 253 (1985). *See also* Andrews, *The Use of the Injunction as a Remedy for an Invalid Federal Tax Assessment*, 40 Tax L. Rev. 653, 661 n.39 (1985).

The majority then proceeds to overload the statutory requirement of a "determination" of a deficiency with burdensome substantive content. First, the majority ignores the rule that a deficiency notice need not contain any explanation whatsoever. Abatti v. Commissioner, 644 F.2d 1385, 1389 (9th Cir. 1981); Barnes v. Commissioner, 408 F.2d 65, 69 (7th Cir.), *cert. denied*, 396 U.S. 836, 90 S. Ct. 94, 24 L. Ed. 2d 86 (1969); *Stevenson*, 43 T.C.M.(CCH) at 290. *See also B. Bittker*, Federal Taxation of Income, Estates and Gifts ¶ 115.2.2 at 115–14 (1981) ("Federal Taxation").

Second, the majority fails to grasp the function of the deficiency notice. It is nothing more than "a jurisdictional prerequisite to a taxpayer's suit seeking the Tax Court's redetermination of [the Commissioner's] determination of the tax liability." *Stamm*, 84 T.C. at 252. "The notice is only to advise the person who is to pay the deficiency that the Commissioner means to assess him; anything that does this unequivocally is good enough." Olsen v. Helvering, 88 F.2d 650, 651 (2nd Cir. 1937).[n.1] Nothing more is required as a predicate to Tax Court jurisdiction.[n.2] In fact, this Circuit has recognized that " 'it is not the *existence* of a deficiency that provides a predicate for Tax Court jurisdiction.' " Stevens v. Commissioner, 709 F.2d 12, 13 (5th Cir. 1983) (quoting Hannan v. Commissioner, 52 T.C. 787, 791 (1969) (emphasis in original)). The *Stevens* court lucidly commented:

> That seems obvious: the very purpose of the Tax Court is to adjudicate contests to deficiency notices. If the existence of an error in the determination giving rise to the notice deprived the Court of jurisdiction, the Court would lack power to perform its function.

709 F.2d at 13.

Therefore, the deficiency notice is effectively the taxpayer's "ticket" to the Tax Court. This "ticket" gives the taxpayer access to the only forum where he can litigate the relevant tax issue without first paying the tax assessed. If a properly-addressed deficiency notice states the amount of the deficiency, the taxable year involved, and notifies the taxpayer that he has 90 days from the date of mailing in which to file a petition for redetermination, then the notice is valid. The merits of the Commissioner's deficiency should not be litigated in the form of a motion to dismiss for lack of jurisdiction; once jurisdiction has been established, both sides will have the opportunity to press their views before the Tax Court.

The majority escapes from under the undesirable weight of authority requiring that the validity of a deficiency notice be determined primarily by its form by distinguishing these cases as not addressing the challenge that no determination was made by the Commissioner. In light of the emphasis of this authority on the form of the deficiency notice, I cannot agree with such a strained interpretation of these cases. *See* B. Bittker, Federal Taxation ¶ 115.2.2 at 115-12 ("the requirement of an IRS *determination* coalesces with the requirement of a *notice* of deficiency, since the usual evidence that a deficiency has been 'determined' is the notice") (emphasis in original).

For example, in *Hannan v. Commissioner*, 52 T.C. 787 (1969), the Tax Court concluded that there was a valid notice of deficiency, despite the Commissioner's

---

[n.1] The notice of deficiency mailed to the taxpayers included two forms: Form 892 and Form 5278. Form 892 is the basic deficiency notice. It includes the taxpayer's name, social security number, amount of the deficiency for the taxable year, and a short explanation of the taxpayer's options. Here, the Commissioner properly completed the Form 892. If the Commissioner had mailed only the Form 892, and nothing else, it is clear that this would have been a valid deficiency notice. *Abatti*, 644 F.2d at 1389; *Barnes*, 408 F.2d at 69; *Stevenson*, 43 T.C.M. (CCH) at 290. The Tax Court's jurisdiction would have been established, even though the Commissioner relied on the wrong tax shelter in making the determination.

[n.2] "It may well be true that the [Commissioner] erred in his determination that a deficiency existed for this period. But when he once determined that there was a deficiency, that fact gives us jurisdiction to determine whether or not it was correctly arrived at." H. Milgrim & Bros. v. Commissioner, 24 B.T.A. 853, 854 (1931).

The key question is whether the inclusion of an erroneous Form 5278, which purports to explain the deficiency in terms of an unrelated tax shelter, invalidates the deficiency notice. I believe the inclusion of the wrong Form 5278 constitutes a preparation error which does not invalidate the deficiency notice. "An error in a notice of deficiency, which otherwise fulfills its purpose, will be ignored where the taxpayer is not misled thereby and is provided by it with information sufficient for the preparation of his case for trial." Meyers v. Commissioner, 81 T.C.M. (P-H) 276, 278 (1981). Here, the taxpayers were not misled by the stray Form 5278 because they had notice from the IRS that a mistake had been made before the Tax Court had set a trial date for either the 1977 or 1978 disputes concerning the videotape tax shelter.

contentions that he neither determined a deficiency nor sought to collect one. The Tax Court rejected the Commissioner's position and found it had jurisdiction:

> Here petitioners were sent a letter which admittedly meets all the formal requirements of a statutory notice of deficiency, notifying them that "We [respondent] have determined the income tax deficiencies shown above" and listing tax deficiencies and additions to tax under section 6651(a). This was a determination of a deficiency in tax, even though, as respondent argues, on trial it may develop that there is in fact no deficiency.

Id. at 791 (footnotes omitted).

The majority misreads *Hannan* in denying that *Hannan* stands for the proposition that deficiency notices are to be judged on their face, rather than on the substance of the Commissioner's determination. * * * It is true that the Tax Court partly explained its decision by stating that there was no proof that the Commissioner was not in fact asserting a deficiency and that the taxpayers could only protect their interests by filing a petition. Although one might read this statement as implying that the Tax Court based its decision on more than a facial examination of the deficiency notice, I understand the Tax Court to mean that because the notice was ambiguous, the taxpayers had no alternative but to file a petition. This concern does not detract from the court's emphasis on the *form* of the deficiency notice.

Judging the deficiency notice in this case by the standards discussed above, I believe that the notice warned the taxpayers that the Commissioner had, rightly or wrongly, determined a deficiency and that the notice complied with the formal requirements of section 6212(a). The Commissioner clearly determined that the taxpayers had invested in a tax shelter without economic substance in order to avoid taxes. The inclusion of an erroneous explanation of the basis of the deficiency should not in itself deprive the Tax Court of jurisdiction to decide the question of whether the Commissioner can sustain the asserted deficiency.

The majority contends that here, it "need not look beyond the notice sent to the taxpayers to determine its invalidity." * * * This, however, is exactly what the majority requires when it concludes that the "determination" requirement is only satisfied where the Commissioner shows he has determined a deficiency with respect to a particular taxpayer beyond the notice itself.[n.4]

[n.4] The majority * * * makes much of the government's statement that, "In order to protect the government's interest and since your original income tax return is unavailable at this time, the income tax is being assessed at the maximum rate of 70%." The majority points to this statement as evidence supporting their conclusion that the Commissioner did not make a determination. I disagree.

Although the "unavailability" of the Scars' return may indicate that the Scars' original paper return was not before the Commissioner, it does not show that specific data on that return or relating to the video-tape tax shelter was not considered. Due to the computerization of the IRS, the Commissioner no longer operates from original paper returns. *See, e.g.,* Murphy, *Glitches and Crashes at the IRS,* TIME, Apr. 29, 1985, at 71; *New Machines Helping IRS,* Dun's Business Month, Jan. 1984, at 24; IRS, *1980 Annual Report*, 9, 14, 42–43 (1981). With well over 100 million income tax returns plus an even larger number of information returns, such as Forms W-2's and 1099's, being filed annually, it is no wonder the Commissioner has turned to the computer. *See* Klott, *Fewer IRS Workers to Process Tax Returns,* N.Y. Times, Dec. 24, 1986, at 30, col. 3; IRS, *1981 Annual Report* 5, 42–43 (Table 6) (1982). When a return is filed in a Service Center, pertinent summary data is entered into the computer system. *1980 Report* at 14; Quaglietta, *How IRS Service Centers Process Returns,* 16 Prac. Acct. 63 (1983). Such summary data includes the fact that a return was filed, whether the tax was paid or a refund check was mailed, and other data needed to match information returns with the taxpayer's return. *See 1980 Report* at 4, 14; Cloonan, *Compliance Programs,* 16 Prac. Acct. 67 (1983). This matching is done by computer. *1980 Report* at 4, 14; Walbert, *A Net Too Wide,* FORBES, Mar. 12, 1984, at 154. It is conceivable that the Commissioner had enough information on the computer to match information regarding both the tax shelter promoted by Executive Productions, Inc. and the Scars' suspect 1977 return to their 1978 income tax taxpayer's return, but not enough to determine the exact amount of a deficiency without calling up from storage the actual return. Thus, the Commissioner assessed the Scars at the 70% rate.

As a matter of tax policy, the rule against looking behind the deficiency notice appears to be well-grounded in the administrative necessities of the Commissioner's job. The Commissioner must administer tens of thousands of deficiency notices per year. A requirement that he prove the basis of his determination before the Tax Court can assert jurisdiction would unduly burden both the Commissioner and the Tax Court.

In addition, the majority's ruling that the inclusion of an erroneous explanation invalidates a deficiency notice creates an incentive for the Commissioner not to disclose his theory for asserting a deficiency when he sends the deficiency notice. If the Commissioner discloses his theory at this stage, the majority's rule invites every taxpayer to litigate whether the Commissioner has made a determination before litigating the merits. Because it is to the taxpayer's advantage that the Commissioner disclose his theory when the notice is sent, I believe it is undesirable to establish a rule which would discourage him from doing so. *See* Stewart v. Commissioner, 714 F.2d 977, 986 (9th Cir. 1983).

I view this case as presenting two related policy goals. One goal is to ensure that early in the assessment procedure each individual taxpayer receives fair notice as to the theory on which the Commissioner based his deficiency. The other goal is to encourage the Commissioner to disclose the theory on which he intends to rely in the deficiency notice whenever possible. However, because the Commissioner is not required to disclose his theory in the notice, the majority's rule that invalidates a deficiency notice accompanied with an erroneous description encourages the Commissioner to issue deficiency notices without *any* explanation. Such a rule detracts from the goal of early notice and taxpayers, on the whole, will suffer because the Commissioner is likely to use the deficiency notice solely for jurisdictional purposes and only thereafter reveal his reasons for issuing the notice. I believe that preserving the Tax Court tradition of not looking behind the deficiency notice promotes the goal of ensuring early notice to the taxpayer.

Finally, alternative remedies exist to protect the taxpayer's interests besides dismissal of the case for lack of jurisdiction. If the taxpayers are confused by the Commissioner's theory or explanation supporting the deficiency, they may seek clarification prior to trial. The Tax Court Rules "contemplate that after the case is at issue the parties will informally confer in order to exchange necessary facts, documents, and other data with a view towards defining and narrowing the areas of dispute. Rules 38, 70(a)(1), 91(a)." *Foster*, 80 T.C. at 230. *See also Stevenson*, 43 T.C.M. (CCH) at 291. Here, the informal contacts between the parties resulted in the Commissioner's disclosure of his mistake within two months of when the taxpayers filed their petition for redetermination in the Tax Court.

Furthermore, the presumed correctness of the Commissioner's deficiency notice disappears if the deficiency is arbitrary or capricious, since the burden of proof then shifts to the Commissioner. Helvering v. Taylor, 293 U.S. 507, 513–16, 55 S. Ct. 287, 79 L. Ed. 623 (1935); Weimerskirch v. Commissioner, 596 F.2d 358, 362 & n.8 (9th Cir. 1979); Jackson v. Commissioner, 73 T.C. 394, 401(1979). *See also* Rule 142(a).[10]

As of 1980, the Commissioner had identified approximately 27,000 abusive tax shelters. *1980 Report* at 3. In light of this number, the punching of the wrong computer key during an audit at the partnership level is a viable explanation for the unfortunate error of one of the 26,999 inapplicable tax shelters popping up and then being entered on the Scars' Form 5278.

So, as a result of the need to computerize information regarding the millions of filed returns and the huge number of tax shelters, we have a reasonable explanation for the two errors on the gratuitously prepared Form 5278 (the wrong shelter and the wrong tax rate of 70%). The taxpayer could have contested these errors and probably would have settled the amount of the tax due promptly. The importance of these errors is further undermined by the fact that they are found in Form 5278, which the Commissioner is not required to send with the basic deficiency notice, Form 892. *See ante* n.1.

[10] [Now Rule 142(a)(1). — Eds.]

These measures are more than adequate to prevent the Commissioner from littering the country with baseless deficiency notices. *Scar*, 81 T.C. at 869 (Sterrett, J., dissenting). The precedent holding that the validity of the deficiency notice is to be determined on its face was effective in furthering policy goals which benefit the taxpayer and the public. The majority's opinion sabotages the machinery of tax collection, thereby portending injury to the taxpayer and to the public. I therefore dissent.

Do you agree with the majority's holding in *Scar* that the word "determines" in Code section 6212(a) entails a substantive requirement with specific content? Is the dissent's approach better? Is there some other remedy the *Scar* majority could have applied to correct the errors in the notice of deficiency and/or to encourage the IRS to be more careful when sending out future notices?

In the following case, the taxpayer raised the issue of whether the notice of deficiency was invalid for failure on the part of the IRS to make a "determination." Note how his case differs from *Scar* both in terms of the facts and in terms of the result.

PORTILLO v. COMMISSIONER

United States Court of Appeals, Fifth Circuit
932 F.2d 1128 (1991)

GOLDBERG, CIRCUIT JUDGE:

Ramon Portillo appeals from the Tax Court's rejection of his challenge to a notice of deficiency from the Internal Revenue Service (the "I.R.S."). Portillo initially argues that the simple computerized matching of Portillo's employer's Form 1099 with Portillo's Form 1040 was not a "determination" as required by section 6212(a) of the Internal Revenue Code (the "Code"). We reject this argument, finding that the I.R.S. adequately linked Portillo to the alleged deficiency. We do agree with Portillo, however, that the notice of deficiency was arbitrary and erroneous because the I.R.S. failed to substantiate in any way its claim that Portillo received unreported income.

* * *

FACTS AND PROCEEDINGS BELOW

Ramon Portillo is a self-employed painting subcontractor who lived and worked in El Paso, Texas during 1984, the tax year in question. In 1984, Portillo bid for contracts to paint both residential and commercial property. According to Portillo, the general contractor he subcontracted for would pay him weekly, usually by check, for the work his crew performed. Portillo would then record his total receipts in the gross receipt portion of a ledger book he kept for his business. Since Portillo did not have a bank account, he would cash the contractor's check and then pay his workers in cash. Portillo kept a separate ledger to record his payroll expenses.

Typically, Portillo purchased all of his own supplies for his work. Portillo purchased most of these supplies from the Hanley Paint Store. Each Friday he would pay the supply store for the week's supplies and record these payments into the ledger as costs of goods sold. As a favor to Portillo, Hanley Paint Store kept copies of their invoices for these supplies, apparently with the intention that they would return them to Portillo each year end.

At the end of the year, Portillo would meet with Mrs. Rosales, a bookkeeper with Independent Businessman Bookkeeping and Tax Services, Inc., so that she could prepare his taxes. Portillo would total the gross receipts from his ledger and give them to Rosales as a basis for his Form 1040 gross income. Portillo used the Form 1099's from his various employers to confirm the gross receipts amounts. In 1984, however, Portillo had not received a 1099 from one of the contractors, Mr. Navarro, when Rosales was preparing his Form 1040. Therefore, Portillo determined his gross receipts from Navarro solely from his ledger.

On his 1984 federal income tax return, Portillo reported gross receipts in the amount of $142,108.93 and deductions of $30,917 for costs of goods sold. Included in the amount of gross receipts was $10,800 reported as the amount Navarro paid to Portillo. Sometime in mid-1985, Navarro filed a Form 1099 reporting payments to Portillo in the amount of $35,305, which was significantly more than Portillo had reported receiving from him.

In January 1987, the I.R.S. audited Portillo's 1984 tax return. At the time of the audit, Portillo could not produce any records or receipts concerning his gross receipts for 1984 because his ledger was stolen from his truck in 1985. In addition, Portillo was unable to produce invoices for materials and supplies purchased during eighteen weeks in 1984 because he had relied on Hanley Paint Store to save these for him and they apparently lost a portion of these invoices. Portillo claimed he had worked continuously during these eighteen weeks, except for holidays and during inclement weather.

Based on the discrepancy between Navarro's 1099 and Portillo's 1040 forms, I.R.S. Agent Shumate determined that Portillo had not reported $24,505 in income from Navarro. Although Portillo acknowledged that he inadvertently neglected to report $3,125 in income from Navarro, Portillo denied receiving any more than $13,925 from Navarro. Shumate contacted Navarro who could produce copies of checks paid to Portillo in the amount of $13,925, but could not produce records justifying the remaining $21,380 he claims he paid Portillo in cash.

Shumate used an indirect method of reconstructing Portillo's income and made an adjustment to incorporate the increased amount into Portillo's income for the year. An I.R.S. reviewer, Glenda Jackson, analyzed Shumate's report. She did not believe the indirect method of confirming the income supported Shumate's adjustment. Jackson stated that there appeared to be several ways to follow up to check if the taxpayer could have received the cash, and she recommended that Shumate check Navarro's tax return.

Shumate replied to this review by stating that it was Portillo's burden to prove that he did not get the payments. The I.R.S. took the position that Navarro's Form 1099 was presumed correct. Therefore the I.R.S. issued a statutory notice of deficiency for federal income taxes of $8,473 for the taxable year 1984, plus penalties assessed under Code sections 6653(a)(1), (a)(2), and 6661(a).

The Portillos filed a petition for redetermination of this alleged tax deficiency in Tax Court. The Tax Court held for the government, finding that Portillo had not met his burden of proving that he had not received the additional income from Navarro. * * *

DISCUSSION

A. Unreported Income

The Tax Court's interpretation of section 6212(a) of the Code is reviewable *de novo. See* Rutter v. Commissioner, 853 F.2d 1267 (5th Cir. 1988); Scar v. Commissioner, 814 F.2d 1363 (9th Cir. 1987). Section 6212(a) states in part: "If the Secretary determines that there is a deficiency in respect of any tax imposed . . . he is authorized to send notice of such deficiency to the taxpayer by certified mail or registered mail." Section 6213(a) provides in part: "Within 90 days . . . after the notice of deficiency authorized in section 6212 is mailed . . . taxpayer may file a petition with the Tax Court for a redetermination of the deficiency." Therefore, the Tax Court only has jurisdiction when the Commissioner issues a valid deficiency notice and the taxpayer files a timely petition for redetermination. Stamm Int'l Corp. v. Commissioner, 84 T.C. 248, 252 (1985).

Although there is no prescribed form for a deficiency notice, the notice must at a minimum (1) advise the taxpayer that the I.R.S. has determined that a deficiency exists for a particular year, and (2) specify the amount of the deficiency or provide the information necessary to compute the deficiency. Donley v. Commissioner, 791 F.2d 383

(5th Cir. 1986). As Portillo correctly points out, in order for a notice of deficiency to be valid, the I.R.S. must have made a "determination" of a tax deficiency. *See* 26 U.S.C. § 6212(a). Portillo argues that in this case the I.R.S. failed to make such a "determination" and therefore the notice was invalid and the tax court consequently lacked jurisdiction.

Remarkably few cases have considered what requirements must be met before the I.R.S. can say that it has made a "determination." The courts which have dealt with this issue have held that a determination as contemplated by section 6212(a) means "a thoughtful and considered determination that the United States is entitled to an amount not yet paid." *Scar*, 814 F.2d at 1369 (quoting Couzens v. Commissioner, 11 B.T.A. 1040, 1159–60 (1928)). In Terminal Wine Co. v. Commissioner, 1 B.T.A. 697, 701 (1925), the Board of Tax Appeals construed the meaning of the term "determine" as applied to deficiency determinations as follows: "By its very definition and etymology the word 'determination' irresistibly connotes consideration, resolution, conclusion, and judgment."

Portillo argues that in this case the I.R.S. failed to make a "determination" because the I.R.S. merely matched Navarro's Form 1099 with Portillo's Form 1040 without ever attempting to establish the reliability of Navarro's 1099 filing. According to Portillo, this lacked any indicia of a "thoughtful and considered determination" and therefore was insufficient under section 6212(a). The I.R.S. maintains, however, that all that is required for a determination is that the Commissioner consider information relating to the particular taxpayer. *See Scar,* 814 F.2d at 1368; *see also* Abrams v. Commissioner, 787 F.2d 939, 940–41 (4th Cir.), *cert. denied*, 479 U.S. 882, 107 S. Ct. 271, 93 L. Ed. 2d 248 (1986); Benzvi v. Commissioner, 787 F.2d 1541, 1543 (11th Cir.), *cert. denied,* 479 U.S. 883, 107 S. Ct. 273, 93 L. Ed. 2d 250 (1986).

In *Scar*, one of the few cases finding that the I.R.S. failed to make a determination, the Ninth Circuit held that the tax court should have dismissed the action for want of jurisdiction because the purported notice of deficiency revealed on its face that no determination of tax deficiency had been made. *Scar*, 814 F.2d at 1370. In *Scar* the Commissioner acknowledged that the notice of deficiency referred to a tax shelter that had no connection with the taxpayer's return. *Id.* at 1368. Consequently, it was apparent that the notice of deficiency was not the result of a determination based on the taxpayers' return. Therefore the court held that the Commissioner had failed to make a "determination."

In contrast to *Scar*, in this case the I.R.S. did consider information directly relating to Portillo's income tax return. The I.R.S. also investigated somewhat whether a deficiency indeed existed. Therefore, this is not a case where the I.R.S. had no basis for sending the notice of deficiency; the I.R.S. did adequately link the deficiency to Portillo.

Portillo argues that if this court should find that the Commissioner did in fact make a substantive determination, the ensuing notice of deficiency was nevertheless arbitrary and erroneous. In addressing this argument, we begin with the well settled principle that the government's deficiency assessment is generally afforded a presumption of correctness. *See* United States v. Janis, 428 U.S. 433, 441, 96 S. Ct. 3021, 3025, 49 L. Ed. 2d 1046 (1976); Helvering v. Taylor, 293 U.S. 507, 515, 55 S. Ct. 287, 290, 79 L. Ed. 623 (1935). This presumption is a procedural device that places the burden of producing evidence to rebut the presumption on the taxpayer. *See Janis*, 428 U.S. at 441, 96 S. Ct. at 3025; Anastasato v. Commissioner, 794 F.2d 884, 886 (3d Cir. 1986). In essence, the taxpayer's burden of proof and the presumption of correctness are for the most part merely opposite sides of a single coin; they combine to require the taxpayer to prove by a preponderance of the evidence that the Commissioner's determination was erroneous. Carson v. United States, 560 F.2d 693, 695–96 (5th Cir. 1977); *see also Janis*, 428 U.S. at 440, 96 S. Ct. at 3025; Bar L Ranch, Inc. v. Phinney, 426 F.2d 995, 998 (5th Cir. 1970).

In a Tax Court deficiency proceeding, like this one, once the taxpayer has established that the assessment is arbitrary and erroneous, the burden shifts to the government to prove the correct amount of any taxes owed. In a refund suit, on the other hand, the taxpayer bears the burden of proving both the excessiveness of the assessment and the correct amount of any refund to which he is entitled. *Carson*, 560 F.2d at 696; *see also Janis,* 428 U.S. at 440, 96 S. Ct. at 3025.

The presumption of correctness generally prohibits a court from looking behind the Commissioner's determination even though it may be based on hearsay or other evidence inadmissible at trial. *See* Clapp v. Commissioner, 875 F.2d 1396, 1402–03 (9th Cir. 1989); Zuhone v. Commissioner, 883 F.2d 1317, 1326 (7th Cir. 1989); Dellacroce v. Commissioner, 83 T.C. 269, 280 (1984). Justification for the presumption of correctness lies in the government's strong need to accomplish swift collection of revenues and in the need to encourage taxpayer recordkeeping. *Carson*, 560 F.2d at 696. The need for tax collection does not serve to excuse the government, however, from providing some factual foundation for its assessments. *Id.* "The tax collector's presumption of correctness has a Herculean muscularity of Goliathlike reach, but we strike an Achilles' heel when we find no muscles, no tendons, no ligaments of fact." *Id.*

In this case we find that the notice of deficiency lacks any "ligaments of fact." As the Supreme Court has held, the presumption of correctness does not apply when the government's assessment falls within a narrow but important category of a " 'naked' assessment without any foundation whatsoever. . . ." *Janis*, 428 U.S. at 442, 96 S. Ct. at 3026. Several courts, including this one, have noted that a court need not give effect to the presumption of correctness in a case involving unreported income if the Commissioner cannot present some predicate evidence supporting its determination. *Carson*, 560 F.2d at 696; *Anastasato*, 794 F.2d at 887; Weimerskirch v. Commissioner, 596 F.2d 358, 360 (9th Cir. 1979); Pizzarello v. United States, 408 F.2d 579 (2d Cir.), *cert. denied*, 396 U.S. 986, 90 S. Ct. 481, 24 L. Ed. 2d 450 (1969). Although a number of these cases involved unreported illegal income, given the obvious difficulties in proving the nonreceipt of income,[n.2] we agree with the Third Circuit that this principle should apply whether the unreported income was allegedly obtained legally or illegally. *See Anastasato,* 794 F.2d at 887.

Therefore, before we will give the Commissioner the benefit of the presumption of correctness, he must engage in one final foray for truth in order to provide the court with some indicia that the taxpayer received unreported income. The Commissioner would merely need to attempt to substantiate the charge of unreported income by some other means, such as by showing the taxpayer's net worth, bank deposits, cash expenditures, or source and application of funds. *See Weimerskirch*, 596 F.2d at 362. In these types of unreported income cases, the Commissioner would not be able to choose to rely solely upon the naked assertion that the taxpayer received a certain amount of unreported income for the tax period in question.

In this case the Commissioner's determination that Portillo had received unreported income of $24,505 from Navarro was arbitrary. The Commissioner's determination was based solely on a Form 1099 Navarro sent to the I.R.S. indicating that he paid Portillo $24,505 more than Portillo had reported on his return. The Commissioner merely matched Navarro's Form 1099 with Portillo's Form 1040 and arbitrarily decided to attribute veracity to Navarro and assume that Portillo's Form 1040 was false. Navarro, however, was not able to document $21,380 of cash payments he allegedly made to Portillo. In a situation like this, the Commissioner had some duty to investigate Navarro's bald assertion of payment and determine if Navarro's position was supported by his books, receipts, or other records.

In addition, the Commissioner failed to substantiate by any other means, such as analyzing Portillo's cash expenditures or his source and application of funds, his charge

---

[n.2] The Supreme Court has specifically noted that "as a practical matter it is never easy to prove a negative." Elkins v. United States, 364 U.S. 206, 218, 80 S. Ct. 1437, 1444, 4 L. Ed. 2d 1669 (1960); *see also Weimerskirch*, 596 F.2d at 361.

that Portillo received unreported income. Instead, the Commissioner merely chose to rely upon the presumption of correctness. We hold in situations like this involving unreported income, the presumption of correctness does not apply to the notice of deficiency.

In summary, we find that the Tax Court had jurisdiction to consider this case because the Commissioner did issue a valid deficiency notice. However, since the Commissioner failed to substantiate his charge that Portillo received cash payments from Navarro, the deficiency determination is clearly arbitrary and erroneous. Therefore, the judgment below regarding unreported income must be reversed.

* * *

What doctrine does *Portillo* draw upon in deciding how to handle the discrepancy between Navarro's 1099 Form and Portillo's Form 1040? If instead of relying on a Form 1099 to determine a deficiency, the IRS relied on the taxpayers' consent with a state government for increased state income taxes for the years in question, would that raise the same concerns? In *Sunik v. Commissioner*, T.C. Memo. 2001-195, *aff'd*, 321 F.3d 335 (2d Cir. 2003), the Tax Court distinguished *Portillo* on the ground that the IRS relied not on the statement of a third party, but on the taxpayers' agreement to an increase in their income.

In 1996, Congress added subsection (d) to section 6201. That subsection states:

> In any court proceeding, if a taxpayer asserts a reasonable dispute with respect to any item of income reported on an information return filed with the Secretary under subpart B or C of part III of subchapter A of chapter 61 by a third party and the taxpayer has fully cooperated with the Secretary (including providing, within a reasonable period of time, access to and inspection of all witnesses, information, and documents within the control of the taxpayer as reasonably requested by the Secretary), the Secretary shall have the burden of producing reasonable and probative information concerning such deficiency in addition to such information return.

I.R.C. § 6201(d). How might this section, if it had existed at the time of the *Portillo* case, have affected the proceedings?

After reading both *Scar* and *Portillo*, do you think a court would or should invalidate a notice of deficiency for failure to notify the taxpayer of the right to contact the local office of the taxpayer advocate, as is now required by section 6212? In *Morgan v. Commissioner*, T.C. Memo. 2000-231, *aff'd*, 2001 U.S. App. LEXIS 27105 (9th Cir. 2001) (unpublished op.), the taxpayer made a challenge on this basis. In *Morgan*, each notice of deficiency was mailed with a separate notice of taxpayer rights that included a toll-free number to obtain taxpayer advocate assistance, as well as the local phone numbers of taxpayer advocate offices. Holding in favor of the IRS, the Tax Court stated, "we reject without further discussion petitioners' assertion that all information required by section 6212(a) must be included on the face of the notice of deficiency in order to comply with that section." Consider also the cases discussed in Section 9.02[B], which held valid notices that omitted the deadline date to file a Tax Court petition.

PROBLEMS

1. On March 4 of this year, the IRS mailed to Peter at his home in San Diego, California a notice of deficiency dated the same day. Peter received the notice on March 8. When is the last day on which Peter can file a timely Tax Court petition?
2. Kyle recently received a notice of deficiency from the IRS. The deficiency amount was $25,000, and the only explanation was "unreported income." Kyle claims that all of his income was from wages, interest, and dividends, which he duly reported

on his return. Kyle timely petitioned the Tax Court in response to the notice. Under current law, who will bear the burden of going forward? Who will bear the burden of persuasion?

3. George received a notice of deficiency on February 20, Year 4 with respect to his Year 1 return. The notice of deficiency is based on unreported income. George timely petitioned the Tax Court on April 9, Year 4. Several months before trial, on June 1, Year 5, the IRS raised an additional issue (the disallowance of certain deductions on his Year 1 return), and moved to amend its answer to the petition. What procedural defenses or arguments can George raise with respect to the new issue?

4. On April 20, Year 4, Sheila received a notice of deficiency from the IRS with respect to her Year 1 taxable year. The notice was dated December 1, Year 3. It had been mailed to her prior address, where her former roommate still resides. Sheila filed her Year 2 and Year 3 returns after moving to her current address, and that address was on those returns. Sheila also has a forwarding order in with the Post Office, but they delivered the notice to her old address anyway. Her former roommate apparently received the envelope but did not open it. She finally put it in the mail to Sheila with some other documents; Sheila received it yesterday and brought it to you to ask what to do. She is concerned because the notice reflects an asserted deficiency of $50,000, which she cannot afford to pay in full. What do you advise?

5. Sabrina Brown, who is single, has just received a notice of deficiency from the IRS, and she is not sure how to respond to it. Sabrina would like to know the deadline, if any, for petitioning the United States Tax Court, and the likelihood that she will be able to convince the court to dismiss the case on procedural grounds. Please respond accordingly, for each of the following *alternative* scenarios:

   A. The notice of deficiency was erroneously mailed to Sabina's mother's house in another state. Sabrina has not lived there for several years and has used her own address on her tax returns since she moved out of her mother's house. Her mother received the notice, which was dated and postmarked January 3 of this year, on January 7. On February 1, her mother put the notice in the mail, and Sabrina received it on February 4.

   B. The notice was mailed to Sabrina where she currently resides, but instead of reflecting her correct apartment number, 304, the address listed apartment number 403. The error resulted in a delivery delay of several days, so that although the notice was dated January 3, Sabrina received it on January 12.

   C. The notice was mailed to Sabrina's current residence, and her address and Social Security number were completely correct. She received the notice, which was mailed on January 3, on January 6. However, the notice was addressed to "Mr. and Mrs. Gerald and Sabrina Brown," although Sabrina has never been married, and does not even know a Gerald Brown. The notice reflects a deficiency of $20,000, based on unreported income from a job as a financial consultant. Sabrina informs you that she is an electrical engineer, with no background or skill in finance. She worked full-time for a single employer during the year in question, as reflected in the sole W-2 she attached to her tax return, and did no consulting work.

6. On May 31, Year 3, the IRS mailed Gloria a notice of deficiency with respect to her Year 1 tax year. Gloria had filed her Year 1 return on April 1, Year 2. The IRS erroneously did not send the notice of deficiency to Gloria's last known address. It was ultimately forwarded to Gloria, and she received it on August 15, Year 3. Subsequently, an IRS employee who was working on Gloria's case realized that the notice had not been sent to Gloria's last known address. On

April 20, Year 4, the IRS mailed a duplicate copy of the notice to Gloria's last known address. She received it on April 25, Year 4. On June 1, Year 4, Gloria petitioned the Tax Court. In her petition, Gloria moved to dismiss the case for lack of jurisdiction on the ground that no notice of deficiency was mailed to her within the time period required by the statute of limitations on assessment.

A. Is the Year 3 notice of deficiency invalid?

B. Would your answer to Part A differ if Gloria had petitioned the Tax Court on August 20, Year 3 instead of June 1, Year 4?

C. Assume that the Year 3 notice of deficiency was invalid.

   i. Is the notice of deficiency that the IRS mailed in Year 4 invalid as a "second notice" under Code section 6212(c)?

   ii. Assume that the notice of deficiency mailed to Gloria in Year 4 is not a prohibited second notice and does not suffer from any other infirmities. Under what circumstances, if any, would the notice be timely?

Chapter 10

OVERPAYMENTS, REFUND CLAIMS, AND REFUND LITIGATION

§ 10.01 INTRODUCTION: OVERVIEW OF REFUND CLAIMS AND REFUND SUITS

Reading Assignment: I.R.C. §§ 6512(b)(1), 6532(a)(1), 7422(a); 28 U.S.C. § 1346(a)(1).

If a taxpayer overpays his or her taxes, whether through withholding or otherwise, how does he or she go about obtaining a refund of the overpayment? If the overpayment arises in connection with the taxpayer's initial income tax return for the year, the taxpayer can simply claim that overpayment as a refund on that return. If, instead, the taxpayer seeks an income tax refund after having already filed a return, but without having received a notice of deficiency from the IRS, the taxpayer must file an amended return claiming the refund. *See* I.R.C. § 7422(a).

Refund claims also arise routinely out of audits. If, in the course of an audit, the taxpayer realizes that he or she made an overpayment, the taxpayer may file a refund claim at that point. In fact, even if the IRS has already sent the taxpayer a notice of deficiency, the taxpayer can both contest the deficiency and pursue a refund of an overpayment. The notice of deficiency provides the taxpayer with a choice of responses. As you know from Chapter 9, the notice of deficiency affords the taxpayer the right to petition the Tax Court and request a review of the asserted deficiency. As explained in this chapter, the Tax Court also has jurisdiction with respect to overpayment claims arising out of the same tax year for which the taxpayer receives a notice of deficiency and files a petition. I.R.C. § 6512(b)(1). The taxpayer simply must allege in the petition that he or she made an overpayment of taxes

The taxpayer's alternative to petitioning the Tax Court is to pay the asserted deficiency and file a refund claim for both the amount paid in response to the notice and the prior overpayment. Upon disallowance of the claim, waiver of disallowance, or after waiting six months, I.R.C. § 6532(a)(1), the taxpayer can sue the government in either a federal district court or the Court of Federal Claims, I.R.C. § 7422(a); 28 U.S.C. § 1346(a)(1). The taxpayer may not file suit once two years have passed from the date of the notice of disallowance was mailed or the taxpayer's waiver was filed.

> *Example:* Sara filed her Year 1 return on April 15, Year 2. Her return showed a tax liability of $10,000, $9,000 of which was covered through withholding, and the remaining $1,000 of which she sent in with her return. The IRS mailed Sara a notice of deficiency on March 1, Year 4, alleging that she has a deficiency of $2,000 attributable to unreported income. Sara disagrees with the deficiency assertion, and upon examining her records, discovers that she failed to take an allowable deduction that would have saved her $500 in taxes. Sara has a choice. She can petition the Tax Court, contesting the $2,000 deficiency and pursuing the $500 overpayment as well. Alternatively, Sara can pay the $2,000 deficiency and claim a refund of $2,500 from the IRS, with an eye toward eventual refund litigation if the IRS denies her claim.[1]

Appeals from the district courts lie to the United States Courts of Appeals, *see* 28 U.S.C. § 1291, and appeals from Tax Court cases do, as well, *see* I.R.C. § 7482. By

[1] As indicated above, the statutes of limitations on refund suits restrict Sara to acting within certain time periods. The statutes of limitations on refund claims do too. These statutes are discussed in detail later in the chapter.

contrast, appeals from the Court of Federal Claims go to the United States Court of Appeals for the Federal Circuit. 28 U.S.C. § 1295(a)(3). Appeals from all of the circuit courts lie to the United States Supreme Court, on certiorari. 28 U.S.C. § 1254.

The remainder of this chapter considers a variety of issues that arise in connection with refund claims and refund litigation. First, the chapter discusses what constitutes an overpayment of tax (the basis for a refund claim), and in that connection, the distinction between a "payment" and a "deposit." The chapter also discusses the timing and content of refund claims, including the rules applicable to informal claims for refund; the procedural rules applicable to refund litigation in the U.S. district courts and Court of Federal Claims and to overpayment litigation in the U.S. Tax Court; how the IRS treats erroneous refunds and abatements of tax; and the statutes of limitations applicable to taxpayers' refund and overpayment claims. The final section of the chapter examines the statutory mitigation provisions and equitable recoupment, each of which allows, in certain circumstances, the recovery of otherwise barred amounts.

§ 10.02 REFUND CLAIMS

[A] Overpayments of Tax

Reading Assignment: I.R.C. § 6401(a)–(c).

In general, to obtain a refund from the IRS, a taxpayer must have made an "overpayment" of tax. What is an "overpayment"? The Code does not specifically define the term. However, Code section 6401(a) provides that an overpayment "includes" payment of tax that is assessed or collected after the applicable statute of limitations has expired. In addition, refundable credits that exceed the amount of income tax imposed for the year are "considered" overpayments of tax. I.R.C. § 6401(b). Excessive withholding tax and estimated tax payments are therefore treated as overpayments. What if a taxpayer erroneously makes a tax payment where no actual tax liability exists? Code section 6401(c) provides that the nonexistence of an actual tax liability will not preclude the payment from qualifying as an overpayment of tax.

Case law further clarifies what constitutes a tax overpayment. In *Jones v. Liberty Glass Co.*, 332 U.S. 524, 531 (1947), the United States Supreme Court considered that question, stating:

> In the absence of some contrary indication, we must assume that the framers of these statutory provisions intended to convey the ordinary meaning which is attached to the language they used. *See* Rosenman v. United States, 323 U.S. 658, 661. Hence we read the word "overpayment" in its usual sense, as meaning any payment in excess of that which is properly due. Such an excess payment may be traced to an error in mathematics or in judgment or in interpretation of facts or law. And the error may be committed by the taxpayer or by the revenue agents. Whatever the reason, the payment of more than is rightfully due is what characterizes an overpayment.

Under the Supreme Court's approach, what two items of information do you need to compute the amount of an overpayment? How does the judicial definition of an overpayment differ from the Code definition in section 6401?

[B] Which Remittances are "Payments"?

An overpayment requires that the taxpayer have made a tax "payment." Superficially, it might seem that any remittance by the taxpayer to the IRS is a tax payment. But, in fact, some remittances are mere "deposits." A deposit is refundable to the taxpayer at any time, but a payment is not. As discussed later in this chapter, a taxpayer must follow specific procedures, including filing a timely refund claim, to obtain a refund of a payment.

[1] The *Rosenman* Case

Generally, the reason a taxpayer chooses to make an early remittance is to stop the running of interest, as discussed in Chapter 13. Because both "payments" and "deposits" suspend further interest accruals, the taxpayer may not initially make clear to the IRS which he or she intended the remittance to be. For statute of limitations purposes, however, the date of "payment" is key. As a result, many cases distinguishing between payments and deposits arise in the context of the statute of limitations on refund claims. The following case is no exception. Note, however, that the length of the statute of limitations referred to in this case has since been changed.

ROSENMAN v. UNITED STATES
United States Supreme Court
323 U.S. 658 (1945)

MR. JUSTICE FRANKFURTER delivered the opinion of the Court.

* * *

Petitioners are executors of the will of Louis Rosenman, who died on December 25, 1933. Under appropriate statutory authority, the Commissioner of Internal Revenue extended the time for filing the estate tax return to February 25, 1935. But there was no extension of the time for payment of the tax which became due one year after the decedent's death, on December 25, 1934. The day before, petitioners delivered to the Collector of Internal Revenue a check for $120,000, the purpose of which was thus defined in a letter of transmittal: "We are delivering to you herewith, by messenger, an Estate check payable to your order, for $120,000, as a payment on account of the Federal Estate tax. . . . This payment is made under protest and duress, and solely for the purpose of avoiding penalties and interest, since it is contended by the executors that not all of this sum is legally or lawfully due." This amount was placed by the Collector in a suspense account to the credit of the estate. In the books of the Collector the suspense account concerns moneys received in connection with federal estate taxes and other miscellaneous taxes if, as here, no assessment for taxes is outstanding at the time. On February 25, 1935, petitioners filed their estate tax return according to which there was due from the estate $80,224.24. On March 28, 1935, the Collector advised petitioners that $80,224.24 of the $120,000 to their credit in the suspense account had been applied in satisfaction of the amount of the tax assessed under their return. On the basis of this notice, petitioners, on March 26, 1938, filed a claim for $39,775.76, the balance between the $120,000 paid by them under protest and the assessed tax of $80,224.24.

Upon completion, after nearly three years, of the audit of the return, the Commissioner determined that the total net tax due was $128,759.08. No appeal to the Board of Tax Appeals having been taken, a deficiency of $48,534.84 was assessed. The Collector thereupon applied the balance of $39,775.76 standing to the credit of petitioners in the suspense account in partial satisfaction of this deficiency, and on April 22, 1938, petitioners paid to the Collector the additional amount of $10,497.34, which covered the remainder of the deficiency plus interest. The Commissioner then rejected the petitioners' claim for refund filed in March of that year. On May 20, 1940, petitioners filed with the Collector a claim, based on additional deductions, for refund of $24,717.12. The claim was rejected on the ground, so far as now relevant, that the tax claimed to have been illegally exacted had been paid more than three years prior to the filing of the claim, except as to the amount of $10,497.34 paid by petitioners in 1938. Petitioners brought this suit in the Court of Claims which held that recovery for the amount here in dispute was barred by statute, 53 F. Supp. 722. To resolve an asserted conflict of decisions in the lower courts we brought the case here.

Claims for tax refunds must conform strictly to the requirements of Congress. A claim for refund of an estate tax "alleged to have been erroneously or illegally assessed or collected must be presented to the Commissioner within three years next after the payment of such tax." On the face of it, this requirement is couched in ordinary English, and, since no extraneous relevant aids to construction have been called to our attention, Congress has evidently meant what these words ordinarily convey. The claim is for refund of a tax "alleged to have been erroneously or illegally assessed or collected," and the claim must have been filed "after the payment of such tax," that is, within three years after payment of a tax[2] which according to the claim was erroneously or illegally collected. The crux of the matter is the alleged illegal assessment or collection, and "payment of such tax" plainly presupposes challenged action by the taxing officials.

The action here complained of was the assessment of a deficiency by the Commissioner in April 1938. Before that time there were no taxes "erroneously or illegally assessed or collected" for the collection of which petitioners could have filed a claim for refund. The amount then demanded as a deficiency by the Commissioner was, so the petitioners claimed, erroneously assessed. It is this erroneous assessment that gave rise to a claim for refund. Not until then was there such a claim as could start the time running for presenting the claim. In any responsible sense payment was then made by the application of the balance credited to the petitioners in the suspense account and by the additional payment of $10,497.34 on April 22, 1938. Both these events occurred within three years of May 20, 1940, when the petitioners' present claim was filed.

But the Government contends "payment of such tax" was made on December 24, 1934, when petitioners transferred to the Collector a check for $120,000. This stopped the running of penalties and interest, says the Government, and therefore is to be treated as a payment by the parties. But on December 24, 1934, the taxpayer did not discharge what he deemed a liability nor pay one that was asserted. There was merely an interim arrangement to cover whatever contingencies the future might define. The tax obligation did not become defined until April 1938. And this is the practical construction which the Government has placed upon such arrangements. The Government does not consider such advances of estimated taxes as tax payments. They are, as it were, payments in escrow. They are set aside, as we have noted, in special suspense accounts established for depositing money received when no assessment is then outstanding against the taxpayer. The receipt by the Government of moneys under such an arrangement carries no more significance than would the giving of a surety bond. Money in these accounts is held not as taxes duly collected are held but as a deposit made in the nature of a cash bond for the payment of taxes thereafter found to be due. *See* Ruling of the Comptroller General, A-48307, April 14, 1933, 1 (1935) Prentice-Hall Tax Service, Special Reports, paragraph 45. Accordingly, where taxpayers have sued for interest on the "overpayment" of moneys received under similar conditions, the Government has insisted that the arrangement was merely a "deposit" and not a "payment," interest on which is due from the Government if there is an excess beyond the amount of the tax eventually assessed. *See* Busser v. United States, 130 F.2d 537, 538; Atlantic Oil Producing Co. v. United States, 35 F. Supp. 766; Moses v. United States, 28 F. Supp. 817; Chicago Title & Trust Co. v. United States, 45 F. Supp. 323; Estate of Rogers v. Commissioner, 1942 Prentice-Hall B.T.A. Memorandum Decisions, paragraph 42,275. If it is not payment in order to relieve the Government from paying interest on a subsequently determined excess, it cannot be payment to bar suit by the taxpayer for its illegal retention. It will not do to treat the same transaction as payment and not as payment, whichever favors the Government. *See* United States v. Wurts, 303 U.S. 414.

* * * [B]y allowing such a deposit arrangement, the Government safeguards collection of the assessment of whatever amount tax officials may eventually find owing from a

---

[2] [Now two years under Code section 6511(a). — Eds.]

taxpayer, while the taxpayer in turn is saved the danger of penalties on an assessment made, as in this case, years after a fairly estimated return has been filed. The construction which in our view the statute compels safeguards the interests of the Government, interprets a business transaction according to its tenor, and avoids gratuitous resentment in the relations between Treasury and taxpayer.

Reversed.

[2] Post-*Rosenman* Case Law

Reading Assignment: I.R.C. § 6513(b)(1)–(2).

In response to the *Rosenman* decision, courts manifested confusion over the test for distinguishing a "payment" from a "deposit." Two circuits initially followed a "per se" test that treated a remittance as a payment only when made after the tax due had been determined by an IRS assessment, as in *Rosenman*, or the filing of a return. *See* United States v. Dubuque Packing Co., 233 F.2d 453, 460 (8th Cir. 1956); Thomas v. Mercantile Nat'l Bank, 204 F.2d 943, 944 (5th Cir. 1953). However, subsequent decisions of these courts have criticized this "per se" test or have simply failed to apply it. *See* Ford v. United States, 618 F.2d 357, 359–61 (5th Cir. 1980); Essex v. Vinal, 499 F.2d 226, 229–30 (8th Cir. 1974), *cert. denied*, 419 U.S. 1107 (1975).

Several other circuits rejected the per se test in favor of a balancing test that looks at the facts and circumstances surrounding the remittance, so that some remittances made prior to assessment are payments, and some are deposits. *See* New York Life Ins. Co. v. United States, 118 F.3d 1553, 1556–57 (Fed. Cir. 1997), *cert. denied*, 523 U.S. 1094 (1998); Moran v. United States, 63 F.3d 663, 667–68 (7th Cir. 1995), *overruled in part by* Malachinski v. Commissioner, 268 F.3d 497, 508 (7th Cir. 2001); Ewing v. United States, 914 F.2d 499, 503 (4th Cir. 1990), *cert. denied*, 500 U.S. 905 (1991); Fortugno v. Commissioner, 353 F.2d 429, 435–36 (3d Cir. 1965).

Subsequent to these decisions, in *Baral v. United States*, 528 U.S. 431, 432–35 (2000), the United States Supreme Court held that (1) withholding from the taxpayer's wages and (2) estimated taxes remitted by the taxpayer because he was concerned that the amount of withholding taxes might be less than his tax liability for the year were "paid" on the due date of the taxpayer's return for the year, under Code section 6513(b). Note that Code section 6513(b) specifically provides that withholding taxes are deemed paid "on the 15th day of the fourth month following the close of [the taxpayer's] taxable year" — which generally is April 15 for individual taxpayers. I.R.C. § 6513(b)(1). It further provides that estimated income taxes are deemed "paid" on the due date of the tax return. I.R.C. 6513(b)(2).

In *Baral*, the Supreme Court rejected the taxpayer's reliance on *Rosenman*:

> Baral contends that income tax is "paid" under § 6511(b)(2)(A) only when the income tax is assessed . . . because the concept of payment makes sense only when the liability is "defined, known, and fixed by assessment," Brief for Petitioner 9. But the Code directly contradicts the notion that payment may not occur before assessment. *See* § 6151(a) ("The person required to make [a return of tax] shall, *without assessment* or notice and demand from the Secretary, *pay* such tax . . . at the time and place fixed for filing the return" (emphasis added)); § 6213(b)(4) ("Any amount *paid* as a tax or in respect of a tax *may be assessed upon the receipt of such payment*" (emphasis added)). Nor does Baral's argument find support in our decision in *Rosenman v. United States*, 323 U.S. 658, 65 S. Ct. 536, 89 L. Ed. 535 (1945), where we applied § 6511's predecessor to a remittance of estimated estate tax. To be sure, a part of our opinion seems to endorse petitioner's view that payment only occurs at assessment. . . .

> But the remittance in *Rosenman*, unlike the ones here, was not governed by a "deemed paid" provision akin to § 6513, and we therefore had no occasion to consider the implications of such a provision for determining when a tax is "paid" under the predecessor to § 6511. *See ibid.* (noting that "no extraneous relevant aids to construction have been called to our attention"). Moreover, if the quoted passage had represented our holding, we would have broadly rejected the Government's argument that payment occurred when the remittance of estimated estate tax was made, instead of rejecting the argument . . . .

Id. at 437–38.

[3] Code Section 6603

Reading Assignment: I.R.C. § 6603.

As indicated above, tax payments and deposits both suspend the accrual of interest on underpayments. A payment can earn interest in favor of the taxpayer if it constitutes an overpayment. Can a deposit earn interest for the taxpayer? Historically, the answer was no. However, in October 2004, Congress enacted section 6603, which provides statutory authority for deposits and authorizing the payment of interest to the taxpayer on deposits made after the enactment of that section that are returned to the taxpayer and are "attributable to a disputable tax." The interest rate that applies is the federal short-term rate determined under Code section 6621(b).[3] I.R.C. § 6603(d)(4).

The term "disputable tax" is defined as "the amount of tax specified at the time of the deposit as the taxpayer's reasonable estimate of the maximum amount of any tax attributable to disputable items." I.R.C. § 6603(d)(2)(A).

> The term "disputable item" means any item of income, gain, loss, deduction, or credit if the taxpayer —
>
> (i) has a reasonable basis for its treatment of such item, and
>
> (ii) reasonably believes that the Secretary also has a reasonable basis for disallowing the taxpayer's treatment of such item.

I.R.C. § 6603(d)(3)(A). Under a safe harbor, "In the case of a taxpayer who has been issued a 30-day letter, the maximum amount of tax under subparagraph (A) shall not be less than the amount of the proposed deficiency specified in such letter." I.R.C. § 6603(d)(2)(B). Thus, section 6603 allows taxpayers to obtain interest on deposits that are attributable to a disputable tax yet avoid the time limits imposed by the statute of limitations on refund claims. This provision thus offers an attractive option to taxpayers who dispute a tax liability.

In March of 2005, the IRS issued a Revenue Procedure applicable to "remittances made to stop the running of interest on deficiencies, including remittances treated as deposits under section 6603." Rev. Proc. 2005-18, 2005-1 C.B. 798, at § 3.[4] Revenue Procedure 2005-18 details how certain undesignated remittances, as well as remittances designated as deposits under section 6603, will be treated by the IRS. Undesignated remittances generally will be treated by the IRS as payments, except in two circumstances. The more common of these circumstances occurs when an undesignated remittance is made while the taxpayer is under examination, but before a liability is proposed to the taxpayer in writing (*e.g.*, before the issuance of a revenue agent's or

---

[3] Note that this interest rate is lower than the rate applicable to overpayments, which is the federal short-term rate plus 3 percentage points for non-corporate taxpayers; plus .5 percentage point for corporate overpayments exceeding $10,000; and plus 2 percentage points for other corporate overpayments. I.R.C. § 6621(a).

[4] Revenue Procedure 2005-18 is discussed in more detail in Chapter 13.

examiner's report). Such remittance will be treated by the IRS as a deposit if the taxpayer has no outstanding liabilities. *Id.* at § 4.01(2).[5] This may be helpful to the taxpayer because a payment made before a notice of deficiency is issued, if in the full amount of the deficiency, will preclude issuance of a notice of deficiency and thus access to the Tax Court. *See id.* at § 4.03.

By contrast, an undesignated remittance made after a notice of deficiency was mailed to the taxpayer generally is treated by the IRS as a payment. *See* Rev. Proc. 2005-18, 2005-1 C.B. 798, at § 4.05(1). This will not preclude the taxpayer from accessing the Tax Court. *See* I.R.C. § 6213(b)(4).

[4] Unassessed Remittances

If a taxpayer remits an amount with the intent to pay a deficiency and the IRS fails to formally assess the tax before the statute of limitations on assessment expires, does the remittance constitute an overpayment within the meaning of section 6401? In Revenue Ruling 85-67, 1985-1 C.B. 364, the IRS stated that although it cannot assess an amount sent in after the statute of limitations on assessment has expired, *see* I.R.C. § 6401(a), the IRS does not have to return to the taxpayer a payment made while the statute of limitations was still open. The IRS reasoned that a payment made before the statute of limitations on assessment has expired does not constitute an overpayment, even though the statute subsequently expires without assessment being made.

The Court of Appeals for the Eleventh Circuit has also addressed this situation, stating:

> We must first decide whether § 6401(a) operated to create an "overpayment" of taxes. A literal reading of that statute supports [the taxpayer] WRJ's claim that an "overpayment" occurred. It provides that " 'overpayment' includes that part of the amount of the payment of any internal revenue tax which is *assessed* . . . *after* the expiration of the period of limitation," 26 U.S.C. § 6401(a) (emphasis added), which in this case is § 6501. Again, the IRS did not assess WRJ's 1993–1995 tax liability until 1999.
>
> But WRJ paid the taxes it now seeks to recover as the liabilities accrued (on a monthly basis from 1993–1995) well before the running of § 6501's limitation period. So the question, then, is whether those payments, properly owed and paid within the limitations period, somehow became "overpayments" merely because the IRS did not get around to assessing liability for them until after the limitations period expired.
>
> While this is a first impression question for our circuit, others have consistently answered it in the negative. *See Ewing*, 914 F.2d at 500–04 (4th Cir. 1990); *Moran v. United States*, 63 F.3d 663, 666 (7th Cir. 1995), *overruled in part by Malachinski v. Commissioner*, 268 F.3d 497 (7th Cir. 2001); *Crompton & Knowles Loom Works v. White*, 65 F.2d 132, 133–34 (1st Cir. 1933) (interpreting § 6401's predecessor statute). We join those circuits by holding

---

[5] The other circumstance is as follows:

> If the taxpayer has no other outstanding liabilities, an undesignated remittance made by the taxpayer after the date that the Tax Court files its decision in an amount that is greater than the amount of the deficiency determined by the Tax Court, plus any interest that has accrued on that amount at the remittance date, will be treated as a deposit, but only to the extent the amount of the remittance exceeds the amount of the deficiency determined by the Tax Court, plus interest. This excess amount will be treated as a deposit until sufficient information is obtained by the Service to apply the remittance to an outstanding liability or to determine that the amount of the remittance should be returned to the taxpayer. The amount that is less than or equal to the amount of the deficiency plus interest will be applied as a payment.

Rev. Proc. 2005-18, 2005-1 C.B. 798, at § 4.05(3).

> that, notwithstanding § 6401(a)'s language, an untimely assessment of taxes otherwise properly owed and paid within the statutory period for assessment and collection does not create an "overpayment" entitling the "late-assessed" taxpayer to a refund.

Williams-Russell & Johnson, Inc. v. United States, 371 F.3d 1350 (11th Cir.), *cert. denied*, 543 U.S. 1022 (2004). *Cf.* Cohen v. United States, 995 F.2d 205 (Fed. Cir. 1993) (remittance was a deposit and therefore was refundable); Becker Brothers, Inc. v. United States, 88-1 U.S.T.C. ¶ 9262 (C.D. Ill. 1988) (following *Goetz* in holding that "any payment prior to the assessment process, is not a 'payment,' but a 'deposit' on potential tax liability"); Estate of Goetz v. United States, 286 F. Supp. 128 (W.D. Mo. 1968) (remittance constituted deposit under *Rosenman* and therefore was refundable).

[C] Submission and Timing of the Refund Claim

Reading Assignment: I.R.C. § 6405(a).

A refund claim invites the IRS to examine the tax return that is the subject of the claim. As discussed in Chapter 3, the IRS does turn some refund claims over to an examining agent for audit. Thus, it is wise to review the underlying return before filing the claim and, if the statute of limitations on assessment remains open, consider carefully the risks and relative merits of possible claims before deciding whether to seek a refund. Note also that income, estate, gift, and certain excise tax refunds that exceed a certain dollar amount (currently $2 million) are subject to review by the Joint Committee on Taxation. *See* I.R.C. § 6405(a).

Of course, the risk that the IRS will make a deficiency adjustment in response to a refund claim is smaller where the IRS has already examined the underlying return. To reduce the risk of adjustment by the IRS even further, a claim for refund can be filed after the statute of limitations on assessment has run, assuming that the statute of limitations on refund claims has not also run. Even when the assessment limitations period has already expired, however, the IRS can still make an adjustment to a carryover or continuing item (such as a net operating loss) that affects other years for which the statute of limitations is still open. Also consider the possibility raised by the following case:

LEWIS v. REYNOLDS

United States Supreme Court
284 U.S. 281 (1932)[6]

MR. JUSTICE MCREYNOLDS delivered the opinion of the Court.

Petitioners sued the respondent Collector in the United States District Court for Wyoming, September 20, 1929, to recover $7,297.16 alleged to have been wrongfully exacted as income tax upon the estate of Cooper.

February 18, 1921, the administrator filed a return for the period January 1 to December 12, 1920, the day of final settlement. Among others, he reported deductions for attorney's fees, $20,750, and inheritance taxes paid to the State, $16,870. The amount of tax as indicated by the return was paid.

November 24, 1925, the Commissioner, having audited the return, disallowed all deductions except the one for attorney's fees and assessed a deficiency of $7,297.16. This sum was paid March 21, 1926; and on July 27, 1926, petitioners asked that it be refunded.

A letter from the Commissioner to petitioners, dated May 18, 1929, and introduced in

---

[6] *Modified*, 284 U.S. 599 (1932).

evidence by them, stated that the deduction of $20,750 for attorney's fees had been improperly allowed. He also set out a revised computation wherein he deducted the state inheritance taxes. This showed liability greater than the total sums theretofore exacted. The Commissioner further said: "Since the correct computation results in an additional tax as indicated above which is barred from assessment by the statute of limitations your claim will be rejected on the next schedule to be approved by the commissioner."

The trial court upheld the Commissioner's action and its judgment was affirmed by the Circuit Court of Appeals.

Counsel for petitioners relies upon the five year statute of limitations (Rev. Act. 1926, § 277).[7] He maintains that the Commissioner lacked authority to redetermine and reassess the tax after the statute had run.

After referring to § 284, Revenue Act of 1926, 44 Stat. 66, and § 322, Revenue Act of 1928, 45 Stat. 861, the Circuit Court of Appeals said [48 F.2d 515, 516] —

> "The above quoted provisions clearly limit refunds to overpayments. It follows that the ultimate question presented for decision, upon a claim for refund, is whether the taxpayer has overpaid his tax. This involves a redetermination of the entire tax liability. While no new assessment can be made, after the bar of the statute has fallen, the taxpayer, nevertheless, is not entitled to a refund unless he has overpaid his tax. The action to recover on a claim for refund is in the nature of an action for money had and received, and it is incumbent upon the claimant to show that the United States has money which belongs to him."

We agree with the conclusion reached by the courts below.

While the statutes authorizing refunds do not specifically empower the Commissioner to reaudit a return whenever repayment is claimed, authority therefor is necessarily implied. An overpayment must appear before refund is authorized. Although the statute of limitations may have barred the assessment and collection of any additional sum, it does not obliterate the right of the United States to retain payments already received when they do not exceed the amount which might have been properly assessed and demanded.

Bonwit Teller & Co. v. United States, 283 U.S. 258, says nothing in conflict with the view which we now approve.

Affirmed.

The *Lewis* Court applied what is known as "setoff." Specifically, what did that allow the IRS to do?

[D] Content of the Refund Claim

Reading Assignment: Treas. Reg. § 301.6402-2(b)(1).

As a general matter, a refund claim must set forth in detail each ground on which the taxpayer claims a credit or refund and include sufficient facts to inform the IRS of the basis of the claim. Treas. Reg. § 301.6402-2(b)(1). A claim for refund of an overpayment may be made on the initial return for the year, an amended return, or a special form provided by the IRS, depending on the circumstances and the type of tax involved. If an income tax return has already been filed, the claim must be submitted on the amended return appropriate for the particular type of taxpayer (for example, for individuals, the form is Form 1040X, Amended U.S. Individual Income Tax Return, and for corporations it is Form 1120X, Amended U.S. Corporation Income Tax Return). Claims for refund of

[7] [The current statute of limitations on assessment in section 6501(a) is three years. — Eds.]

taxes, penalties, and other additions relating to taxes other than income taxes must be made on Form 843, Claim for Refund and Request for Abatement. The claim must also be filed by or on behalf of the person who made the overpayment, and it must be verified.[8] For all income, gift, estate and federal unemployment tax refund claims, a separate claim must be prepared and filed for each type of tax for each taxable period.

A refund claim must include both the grounds for the claim and the supporting facts, but it need not contain any legal argument. The statement of facts need not be exhaustive, but should include the principal factual elements on which the taxpayer relies. The grounds supporting the refund claim should be listed in the explanation section of the claim. Each ground supporting the credit or refund should be set forth in detail. Treas. Reg. § 301.6402-2(b)(1). The IRS has the power to waive this requirement and consider a general claim on its merits, but it is safer not to rely on the possibility of such a waiver.

As with court pleadings, claims for refund may set forth alternative grounds for relief that are not internally consistent. However, a claim for refund may not be based on equitable grounds, although it can be advisable to add such grounds as a protective measure. After a refund claim is filed, it may be amended to add new grounds, but not after the statute of limitations on refund claims has expired.

Careful phrasing of the grounds on which the refund claim is based is critical because a subsequent refund suit is limited to the assertions raised in the claim. *See, e.g.,* United States v. Felt & Tarrant Mfg. Co., 283 U.S. 269 (1931); Hempt Bros. v. United States, 354 F. Supp. 1172, 1182 (M.D. Pa. 1973) ("a court lacks jurisdiction of an action to recover taxes except upon grounds reasonably encompassed by the claim for refund as originally filed or properly amended"). Consider the following case:

DECKER v. UNITED STATES

United States District Court, District of Connecticut
93-2 U.S.T.C. ¶ 50,408

CABRANES, CHIEF JUDGE:

* * *

BACKGROUND

The plaintiff is the former wife of Malcolm B. Decker ("Decker"). They were married in 1951. On November 29, 1969, Decker and the plaintiff were divorced in a unilateral divorce action in Juarez, Mexico where only Decker was present.

Prior to the entry of the Mexican divorce decree, the plaintiff and Decker entered into a separation agreement dated November 10, 1969, the terms of which are undisputed ("Separation Agreement"). Pursuant to the terms of the Separation Agreement, Decker was obligated to pay the plaintiff $8,000 per year plus cost-of-living escalations until the death of either party or the plaintiff's remarriage. As of September, 1976, Decker was in arrears in alimony payments due under the Separation Agreement. At that time, the plaintiff obtained a judgment against Decker in the State of New York for arrearages in the amount of $13,567. Decker did not pay that judgment and thereafter continued to fall behind in his alimony obligations.

---

[8] A federal district court found invalid a return and its accompanying refund claim because the return had an attachment and language added between the jurat and the taxpayer's signature. *See* Letscher v. United States, 2000-2 U.S.T.C. ¶ 50,723 (S.D.N.Y. 2000). The added language stated, "Without prejudice, See attachment dated 4/13/96." The attachment was a one-page document entitled "First Amendment Right for a Redress of Grievances: Attachment to 1995 Federal Tax Return." The court held that the altered jurat called into question the veracity and accuracy of the return, and violated the requirement that a return be signed under penalty of perjury. The court therefore dismissed the refund suit for lack of subject matter jurisdiction.

On January 11, 1983, the plaintiff commenced three separate proceedings in state court in Connecticut. The three separate actions sought the following relief: (1) to set aside the Mexican divorce decree; (2) to enforce the New York judgment and for arrearages following the date of that judgment; and (3) a judgment of divorce premised on the invalidity of the Mexican divorce decree. These three actions were consolidated and subsequently settled on July 8, 1985 ("Settlement").

The Settlement provided that (a) the Mexican decree is a valid and binding decree of dissolution or divorce; (b) there existed an arrearage of alimony of $126,000; (c) in exchange for a satisfaction of judgment in all three cases, Decker would pay to the plaintiff at least $100,000 in full and final satisfaction of all past debts due for alimony and/or support and all future obligations pertaining to alimony and/or support; and (d) the payment was to be made by a transfer of real property located in the Town of Fairfield, Connecticut worth approximately $100,000. Decker guaranteed that the plaintiff would receive at least $100,000 net proceeds from the sale of the property. To the extent she received proceeds in excess thereof, she was entitled to keep them.

The transfer of the property did not occur at the time provided for in the Settlement. However, on December 31, 1985 at approximately 2:30 p.m., Decker recorded a deed in the Town of Fairfield land records purporting to transfer the property to the plaintiff. In the deed of conveyance, Decker assigned the property a value of $110,000. On January 7, 1986, a court-appointed appraiser valued the property at $105,000. Thereafter, on February 27, 1986, the plaintiff sold the property to an unrelated third party for $125,000. The plaintiff's net proceeds from the sale were $113,000.

On his federal income tax return for 1985, Decker claimed an alimony deduction in the amount of $113,000. The plaintiff, though, did not include any amount of the sale proceeds as alimony income on her 1985 return. Subsequently, the Internal Revenue Service ("Service") determined that the value of the property ($113,000) should have been included in the plaintiff's gross income for the 1985 tax year. This resulted in additional tax liability of $41,117, which amount was remitted by the plaintiff in 1989. In 1990, the Service assessed $19,365.03 against the plaintiff for interest on the additional tax liability; this amount was also remitted by the plaintiff. The plaintiff filed a timely claim for a refund and, receiving no response from the Service, filed this action seeking a total refund of $60,082.03.[n.3]

DISCUSSION

* * *

In its motion, the Government contends that IRC Section 71, as in effect prior to the amendments of the Tax Reform Act of 1984 ("Old Section 71"), applies in this case and that, under that Code section, the proceeds received by the plaintiff from the sale of the property were properly included in her gross income (the so-called "taxability issue"). Moreover, the Government claims that the proceeds were appropriately applied to the 1985 tax year (the so-called "timing issue"). The plaintiff, however, contends that Old Section 71 does not apply to the transaction in question and that, under Section 71, as amended in 1984 ("New Section 71"), the proceeds in question are not properly included in her gross income. The plaintiff argues also that, even if Old Section 71 applies, she still should not be taxed because the property transfer does not constitute "alimony" under that statute. * * *

[n.3] The Service also proposed to assess a tax deficiency against Decker in order to avoid the so-called "whipsaw" effect of Decker's deduction and the plaintiff's failure to include the proceeds as income. Decker petitioned the Tax Court and, on October 30, 1990, the Tax Court entered a decision finding no income tax deficiency with respect to Decker.

A.

We turn first to the issue of the taxability of the proceeds received by the plaintiff from the sale of the property. A threshold question which must be resolved in addressing this issue is, of course, which version of IRC Section 71 applies in this case: Old Section 71 or New Section 71? If, as the plaintiff maintains, New Section 71 governs, the Government's motion must be denied. If, however, Old Section 71 applies, the plaintiff may be entitled to a refund.

(1)

In her opposition papers to the Government's motion, the plaintiff raises for the first time the issue of the applicability of New Section 71: it appears neither in her claim for a refund filed with the Service nor in her Complaint. Relying upon the so-called "variance doctrine," the Government argues that the plaintiff is barred from introducing this issue at this late juncture. The "variance doctrine" holds that "in an action for a refund . . . the law is clear that the district court is limited to those grounds which were raised in the claim for refund presented to the Commissioner." Campagna v. United States, 290 F.2d 682, 685 (2d Cir. 1961).

Before a taxpayer may sue to recover federal income taxes she must file a claim for a refund or credit with the Service setting out the material facts on which the claim is based. 26 U.S.C. § 7422(a). Moreover, "a claimant in a refund suit may not raise a wholly new factual basis for [her] claim at the later trial . . . also [she] may not shift the legal theory of [her] claim." Scovill Manufacturing Company v. Fitzpatrick, 215 F.2d 567, 569 (2d Cir. 1954) (citations omitted) (collecting cases). However, "not every minor variation between the original claim and the complaint in a civil suit thereon is fatal to recovery," Gada v. United States, 460 F. Supp. 859, 869 n.5 (D. Conn. 1978); Cities Service Company v. United States, 316 F. Supp. 61, 73 (S.D.N.Y. 1970). As our Court of Appeals stated of the predecessor statute to Section 7422 in *Scovill*: "We think that [§ 7422] goes no further than to require the taxpayer to set forth facts sufficient to enable the Commissioner of Internal Revenue to make an intelligent administrative review of the claim." *Scovill*, 215 F.2d at 569.

A review of the cases drawn to the court's attention by the Government indicates that the court may properly consider the plaintiff's claim that New Section 71 applies. In most of those cases cited by the Government, the claimants attempted to shift the fundamental nature of their cause of action or to raise significant new factual issues in their civil suits.[n.6] In other cases cited, the taxpayer's initial refund claim was so deficient that it failed to apprise the Service of any clear basis for a refund. None of these decisions is similar to the instant case. Although the plaintiff's initial claim for a refund may not have specified that, in her view, New Section 71 governs, the plaintiff has consistently maintained that she is entitled to a refund on the ground that the property transfer did not give rise to alimony income and that the characterization of the transaction as producing either income or property is to be determined by applying

---

[n.6] *See, e.g.*, Goelet v. United States, 266 F.2d 881 (2d Cir. 1959) (court refused to consider new ground for taxpayer's claim where neither that ground nor the necessary facts to support it were presented to the Commissioner); Young v. United States, 203 F.2d 686 (8th Cir. 1953) (where original claim was rejected by Commissioner, taxpayer could not "amend" claim to seek a refund for a different year); Nemours Corp. v. United States, 188 F.2d 745 (3d Cir. 1951) (taxpayer could not rely in its civil case upon a code section not stated as a basis for his claim for refund presented to Commissioner); Ronald Press Company v. Shea, 114 F.2d 453 (2d Cir. 1940) (taxpayer barred from switching basis of his claim after Commissioner had rejected the initial grounds for refund based upon a different set of facts). *See also* Mallette Brothers Construction Co. v. United States, 695 F.2d 145 (5th Cir. 1983) (taxpayer barred from raising new factual allegation that contradicted grounds set forth in claim for refund); *Campagna, supra* (court refuses to consider new issue raised involving new factual basis); Samara v. United States, 129 F.2d 594 (2d Cir. 1942) (taxpayer barred from raising facts not previously presented to the Commissioner).

Section 71. In other words, in arguing that the then-recently-amended version of Section 71 applies, the plaintiff has not altered her basic contention that the transaction is not taxable as alimony under the applicable Code section. Rather, she has simply raised the issue of which version of that Code section applies. Clearly, the Service was reasonably on notice that this issue might be raised by the plaintiff inasmuch as New Section 71 went into effect at the beginning of the very year that the Service claims the plaintiff received income from the transaction. Indeed, it is arguable that it was the Government rather than the plaintiff who first introduced this issue in this litigation. The possible applicability of New Section 71 was first formally suggested in this action in the Government's memorandum in support of its motion for summary judgment. While the record does not suggest a waiver by the Government of its right to invoke the variance doctrine in this case (as the plaintiff argues), it certainly buttresses the conclusion that the issue cannot have escaped the notice of the Service when it examined the plaintiff's claim for a refund. In sum, the court is not persuaded that the plaintiff is barred from arguing that New Section 71 applies because she did not make that specific argument in her claim for a refund.

What is the "variance doctrine" discussed in the case? How can taxpayers and their advisors plan ahead to avoid problems under this doctrine? One article advises:

> In drafting a refund claim, three rules of thumb are helpful in steering clear of legal and factual variances:
>
> • Be sure to call the IRS's attention to each specific item on the original return that is being changed.
>
> • Advance every theory (including any equitable theory, *e.g.*, estoppel) supporting a change to the original return, even if it conflicts with another theory that is offered. "Alternative pleading" in this fashion is acceptable.
>
> • Avoid patent ambiguity (*e.g.*, "The taxpayer is entitled to a refund because her return is wrong"). A claim that states only a general or "shotgun" basis for recovery is inadequate. At the same time, refrain from excessive detail, since this invites a variance defense. The stated grounds and facts need only be sufficiently definite to allow an intelligent administrative review of the claim. Stated differently, the claim "does not have to be stated with any greater particularity than is necessary to draw the Commissioner's attention to the claim [that the taxpayer] makes in his subsequent suit."[n.52] The invocation of broad language to state the grounds and facts may therefore be desirable (*e.g.*, "The taxpayer is entitled to a refund because she understated the basis of machinery sold during the year and so overstated the amount of section 1231 gain thereon"). Reference to Code Secs. can be helpful as well, but caution is advisable since citation to a specific subsection may preclude later reliance on other subsections.

Ronald Stein, *Seven Tips on Avoiding Refund Claim Pitfalls*, 4 J. TAX PRAC. & PROC. 33, 35–36 (2002/2003).[9]

As noted in *Decker*, the IRS can waive application of the variance doctrine. *See* Tucker v. Alexander, 275 U.S. 228, 231 (1927). Waiver may be found where the IRS has already investigated the merits of the newly raised claim. *See, e.g.*, Angelus Milling Co. v. Commissioner, I.R.S., 325 U.S. 293, 297 (1945); Scott Paper Co. v. United States, 943 F. Supp. 489, 494 n.4 (E.D. Pa. 1996).

---

n.52 *National Forge & Ordnance Co.*, Ct.Cl., 57-2 USTC 9839, 151 F. Supp. 937, 139 Ct. Cl. 222.

9

[E] Informal Claims for Refund

In some circumstances, the taxpayer need not file a formal refund claim, such as a claim made on a Form 1040 or Form 1040X. Following an audit, for example, if the IRS determines that the taxpayer made an overpayment, Form 870 — which is used by the IRS to reflect an agreed-upon settlement — will serve as the refund claim.

Although it is wise for a taxpayer who wishes to pursue a refund to file a formal refund claim (unless the taxpayer has signed a Form 870 that will serve as the claim), taxpayers have, at times, submitted documents that purported to claim a refund but failed to comply with all of the formal requirements for a refund claim. Case law provides that a document can be treated as an *informal* refund claim if, the following requirements are met: (1) the court determines that an informal claim was filed; (2) the claim is in writing or has a written component; and (3) the matters set forth in writing are sufficient to apprise the IRS that a refund is sought and to focus the IRS's attention on the merits of the dispute so that the IRS may commence an examination of the claim if it so desires. *See, e.g.,* Arch Engineering Co., Inc. v. United States, 783 F.2d 190, 192 (Fed. Cir. 1986); American Radiator & Standard Sanitary Corp. v. United States, 318 F.2d 915, 920 (Ct. Cl. 1963).

At a minimum, an informal claim for refund must be in writing or have a written component. The written component of the informal claim need not be in a single document, but notification is vital; the claim must be actually communicated to the IRS. Mere availability of the information is not the equivalent of notice. Moreover, it must appear from the surrounding facts, including the written element, that the taxpayer is actually requesting a refund. Consider the following case, which discusses the requirements of an informal claim in more detail.

FISHER v. UNITED STATES

United States District Court, Northern District of California
1990 U.S. Dist. LEXIS 15229

Marilyn Hall Patel, United States District Judge.

MEMORANDUM AND ORDER

Plaintiffs husband and wife, residents of Contra Costa County, California, bring this action for recovery of taxes erroneously paid to the Internal Revenue Service for the taxable years 1977 and 1978. The parties are now before the court on defendant's motion to dismiss plaintiffs' complaint for lack of subject matter jurisdiction pursuant to Federal Rule of Civil Procedure 12(b)(1). The United States argues that the court lacks jurisdiction because plaintiffs failed to timely file their claims for refund in accordance with 26 U.S.C. § 7422(a).

BACKGROUND

In connection with a series of commodities transactions on the London Metals Exchange, plaintiffs reported ordinary losses on their 1976 income tax return and capital gains on their 1977 and 1978 returns, and paid appropriate taxes for those years in full.

After being informed by the Commissioner of the Internal Revenue Service ("Commissioner") that the London Metals investments were under investigation, plaintiffs executed a series of Consents to Extend the Time to Assess Tax, the last of which extended the statute of limitations for 1976 and 1977 to December 31, 1981.

On December 31, 1981, the Commissioner mailed to plaintiffs a statutory notice of tax deficiency for 1976 and tax overassessments for 1977 and 1978, explaining that the series of London Metals transactions had been determined to be "fully integrated and constituted but a single transaction," and that the transactions were a sham. Compl. at

3–4. The statutory notice statement also provided that the overassessments would be scheduled for adjustment "provided that you protect yourself against the expiration of the statutory period of limitations by filing timely claims for refund for each year on the enclosed Forms 1040X with your District Director of Internal Revenue." Def. MTD at 7.

On March 29, 1982, plaintiffs filed a petition with the United States Tax Court challenging the deficiency in tax year 1976, to which they attached the notice of deficiency and overassessments and the explanation of adjustments. That matter is still pending before the Tax Court. On December 15, 1982, plaintiffs filed formal refund claims for the tax years 1977 and 1978.

Defendants assert that plaintiffs' Consent to Extend the Time to Assess Tax for 1977 extended the deadline for a refund claim for 1977 to June 30, 1982. They further assert that because no consent was signed for 1978, the deadline for filing a refund claim for 1978 was October 17, 1982. The United States moves to dismiss on the ground that plaintiffs did not file their claims for refund until December 1982.

Plaintiffs do not dispute these filing dates; nor do they deny that their formal refund claims were filed beyond the statute of limitations. However, they allege that by filing a petition with the Tax Court challenging the 1976 deficiency along with attachments concerning 1977 and 1978, they made an informal claim for refunds for 1977 and 1978, and that the Tax Court filing tolled the statute of limitations governing claims for the latter two years.

* * *

LEGAL STANDARD

A motion to dismiss will be denied unless it appears that the plaintiff can prove no set of facts which would entitle him or her to relief. *Conley v. Gibson*, 355 U.S. 41, 45–46 (1957); *Fidelity Fin. Corp. v. Federal Home Loan Bank of San Francisco*, 792 F.2d 1432, 1435 (9th Cir. 1986), *cert. denied*, 479 U.S. 1064 (1987). All material allegations in the complaint will be taken as true and construed in the light most favorable to the non-moving party. *NL Indus., Inc. v. Kaplan*, 792 F.2d 896, 898 (9th Cir. 1986). Although the court is generally confined to consideration of the allegations in the pleadings, when the complaint is accompanied by attached documents, such documents are deemed part of the complaint and may be considered in evaluating the merits of a motion to dismiss. *Durning v. First Boston Corp.*, 815 F.2d 1265, 1267 (9th Cir.), *cert. denied*, 484 U.S. 944 (1987).

DISCUSSION

I. *Informal Claims for 1977 and 1978*

Courts have routinely held that an informal claim for refund that is timely filed and later perfected may be treated as a valid claim. *Crocker v. United States*, 563 F. Supp. 496, 499–500 (S.D.N.Y. 1983); *American Radiator & Standard Sanitary Corp. v. United States*, 318 F.2d 915, 921–22 (Ct. Cl. 1963). Defendants contend that plaintiffs have not alleged facts sufficient to demonstrate that they filed an informal claim for refund of the overassessments for 1977 and 1978.

An informal claim must fairly advise the IRS of the nature and ground of the taxpayer's claim and intent to request a refund. *United States v. Kales*, 314 U.S. 186, 193–94 (1941). It must "set forth facts sufficient to enable the [IRS] to make an intelligent administrative review of the claim." *Crocker*, 563 F. Supp. at 500 (quoting *Scovill Mfg. Co. v. Fitzpatrick*, 215 F.2d 567, 569 (2d Cir. 1954)). Moreover, the claim must have a written component; oral claims alone are insufficient. *Gustin v. United States Internal Revenue Serv.*, 876 F.2d 485, 488 (5th Cir. 1989).

The general approach of the courts has been to examine each allegation of the informal claim on its own facts "with a view towards determining whether under those facts the Commissioner knew, or should have known, that a claim was being made." *Gustin*, 876 F.2d at 488–89 (quoting *Newton v. United States*, 163 F. Supp. 614, 619 (Ct. Cl. 1958)). Thus, although some form of written claim is required, it need not contain the entirety or every component of the claim. In addition to the written claim, the taxpayer may rely upon circumstances known to the Commissioner, or detailed knowledge of the agent investigating the claim, which would be sufficient to inform the IRS of the taxpayer's claim. *Id.* at 489.

Here, plaintiffs argue that by filing a Tax Court petition for 1976, and by attaching thereto a copy of the IRS's statutory notice statement setting forth the deficiency for 1976 and the overassessments for 1977 and 1978, they had put the IRS on notice of their intention to settle the overassessment. This settlement could have come about either by plaintiffs' receipt of an offsetting reduction in their 1976 liability based on the 1977 and 1978 overassessments, or by treating the circumstances, including the petition, attachments, and ongoing negotiations with the IRS, as an informal claim for refunds for 1977 and 1978 should the deficiency for 1976 be upheld. This informal claim was perfected by plaintiffs' filing of a formal refund claim for those years on December 15, 1982.

The court agrees that, in the overall factual context of their dealings with the IRS, plaintiffs' filing of the petition and inclusion of the statutory notice statement with the Tax Court should be treated as an informal claim for refunds for 1977 and 1978. The IRS itself had determined that the series of 1976, 1977, and 1978 London Metals Exchange transactions were to be treated as a single, integrated transaction, so that disallowing the transaction would not only result in the 1976 deficiency that plaintiffs are challenging in Tax Court, but would entitle them to refunds for the 1977 and 1978 overassessments. To the extent that the basic issue in a taxpayer's assertion of an informal claim is whether the Commissioner was on notice of the taxpayer's intent, and whether that notice was sufficiently detailed in nature, there can be no question that the IRS had notice. They knew that the validity of the 1977 and 1978 overassessments would turn on the result of plaintiff's Tax Court challenge concerning 1976, and that plaintiffs intended to seek refunds for 1977 and 1978 should the deficiency for 1976 be upheld.

The court rejects the United States' overly formalistic argument that there can be no informal claim here because the only writing prepared by plaintiffs was the Tax Court petition pertaining only to 1976 and because the attached statutory notice concerning overassessments for 1977 and 1978 had been prepared by the IRS, not plaintiffs. The underlying inquiry in determining whether an informal claim was made is not whether the taxpayer authored a statement of claim in all its particulars, but whether the Government was on notice. As the court noted in *United States v. Commercial National Bank of Peoria*:

> the written component of an informal refund request need not contain magical words or contain every fact supporting that request. A taxpayer may rely upon other documents, conversations, or correspondence to fulfill his notice obligations. Such is the case especially when taxpayers cannot claim an immediate refund because their right to a refund cannot vest until pending litigation is settled.

874 F.2d 1165, 1171 (7th Cir. 1989) (holding that informal claim had been made where IRS knew from ongoing negotiations to settle tax court litigation that taxpayers would have a right to and would request a refund pending the outcome of such negotiations).

Here, as in *Commercial National Bank*, plaintiffs are engaged in ongoing Tax Court litigation, and that litigation itself has a history of negotiations between plaintiffs and the IRS over the disputed transactions. The outcome of the Tax Court proceedings will determine the validity not only of the IRS's statutory notice of deficiency concerning 1976, but also of the overassessments concerning 1977 and 1978. Moreover, the

Government was put on notice of plaintiffs' protest, and it was the IRS itself that asserted and provided the basis for the overassessments.

Because the court finds, viewing the facts and making inferences in the light most favorable to plaintiffs, that plaintiffs have asserted facts sufficient to show that informal claims had been made for refunds for the years 1977 and 1978 and that those claims were later perfected, defendant's motion to dismiss for lack of jurisdiction is DENIED.

* * *

CONCLUSION

Plaintiffs have pled facts, including a series of negotiations, writings, and agreements, sufficient to show that the Commissioner was put on notice of the existence and basis of plaintiffs' claim for a refund for the years 1977 and 1978, conditioned upon the outcome of their Tax Court petition concerning 1976. The court finds that plaintiffs made an informal refund claim for the years 1977 and 1978, perfected by the formal claim on December 15, 1982. Defendant's motion to dismiss for lack of jurisdiction is therefore DENIED.

IT IS SO ORDERED.

Did the Tax Court petition itself suffice as a refund claim in *Fisher v. United States*? What tax year did the taxpayers' Tax Court petition address, and why was that sufficient, according to the court, to focus the IRS on other tax years, as well? Recall that an informal claim must be perfected by the taxpayer. Why might that matter?

§ 10.03 REFUND SUITS AND OVERPAYMENT SUITS

[A] Refund Suits

The United States Code provides the statutory basis for federal tax refund jurisdiction:

> The district courts shall have original jurisdiction, concurrent with the United States Claims Court [United States Court of Federal Claims], of: * * * Any civil action against the United States for the recovery of any internal-revenue tax alleged to have been erroneously or illegally assessed or collected, or any penalty claimed to have been collected without authority or any sum alleged to have been excessive or in any manner wrongfully collected under the internal-revenue laws. . . .

28 U.S.C. § 1346(a)(1). The statute provides that the federal district courts and the Court of Federal Claims are the refund fora. These fora are discussed, in turn, below, following the discussion of the limitations periods applicable to refund suits.

[1] Limitations Periods

Reading Assignment: I.R.C. § 6532(a)(1)–(3).

As with much of tax procedure, refund suits are subject to strict time limits. As stated in the introductory section of this chapter, a condition precedent to filing a refund suit is that the taxpayer file a refund claim. I.R.C. § 7422(a). Once the taxpayer files the refund claim, the taxpayer must wait until the IRS denies the claim (by mailing the taxpayer a notice of disallowance) or six months go by, whichever comes first, before the taxpayer can file suit. I.R.C. § 6532(a). The taxpayer also has the option, in many cases, of requesting an immediate notice of disallowance of the claim (a "waiver"). *Id.* Why might the taxpayer do that?

As an outside limit, the taxpayer has two years to file suit from the date the notice of disallowance is mailed or the taxpayer's waiver is "filed." I.R.C. § 6532(a)(1). The Fourth Circuit has held that a waiver of notice is "filed" when received by the IRS. Hull v. United States, 146 F.3d 235 (4th Cir. 1998). Note that the two-year period does not begin to run until the IRS mails the notice of disallowance or the taxpayer waives notice.

Code section 6532(a)(2) provides that "[t]he 2-year period prescribed in paragraph (1) shall be extended for such period as may be agreed upon in writing between the taxpayer and the Secretary." In *Kaffenberger v. United States*, 314 F.3d 944 (8th Cir. 2003), the court held "that the IRS acted within its statutory authority in entering into the Form 907 Agreement to extend the time to bring suit on the original 1989 refund claim, even though the statutory time period for bringing suit had lapsed prior to the date of the Form 907 Agreement." *Id.* at 953. The court noted, "contrary to § 6532, § 6501 expressly requires the agreement to be made 'before the expiration of the time prescribed in this section for the assessment of any tax imposed by this title.' 6501(c)(4). Congress did not include similar limiting language in § 6532(a)(2)." *Id.* The IRS has nonacquiesced on this issue, stating:

> In concluding that the taxpayers' Form 907 was validly executed, the Eighth Circuit disagreed with Rev. Rul. 71-57. The court noted that section 6501 contains a provision similar to section 6532 that allows a taxpayer and the Service to agree to extend the assessment period beyond the 3-year period of limitations, but, unlike section 6532, section 6501(c)(4)(A) expressly requires the agreement to be made "before the expiration of the time prescribed in this section for the assessment of any tax imposed by this title." The court found persuasive the fact that Congress did not include similar limiting language in section 6532(a)(2) even though sections 6501 and 6532 were enacted as part of the same tax act. The court concluded that, by including the limiting language in section 6501(c)(4)(A) but omitting it in section 6532(a)(2), Congress acted intentionally and did not intend that the Form 907 be executed within the 2-year period. We disagree with the Eighth Circuit's rationale. The focus of the inquiry, as articulated in Rev. Rul. 71-57, should be on the word "extended" in section 6532(a)(2), which means the continuation of an existing period of time with no intervening lapse. When the 2-year period expired in this case on April 28, 1997, there was no period left to extend.
>
> Although we disagree with the court's refusal to follow a published ruling, we recognize the precedential effect of the decision in the Eighth Circuit and, therefore, will follow it with respect to cases within that circuit, if the opinion cannot be meaningfully distinguished. We will continue to litigate our position in other circuits.

A.O.D. 2004-04, 2004 AOD LEXIS 4. Who do you think has the better argument on the issue of whether an agreement to extend the time to bring a refund suit must be made before the two-year period expired or after it already expired?

[2] Refund Litigation in the United States District Courts

Tax litigation in a district court is much like other litigation in that court. Because district courts are Article III courts, either party is entitled to demand a trial by jury. Applicable Court of Appeals precedent governs the case and both the Federal Rules of Civil Procedure and the Federal Rules of Evidence apply. FED. R. EVID. 101, 1101. Litigation in a district court begins when the taxpayer files a complaint. FED. R. CIV. P. 3. The fee for filing a complaint is $350. 28 U.S.C. § 1914(a). (Compare that to the $60 cost of filing a Tax Court petition. *See* TAX CT. R. 20(b).) In district court, as in Tax Court, the IRS's responsive pleading is termed an answer. FED. R. CIV. P. 7. If the answer contains a counterclaim, the taxpayer must file a reply. *See id.*

The following is a complaint filed in an actual case. (The taxpayer's complaint might instead be divided into various counts.)

LIVONIA PUBLIC SCHOOLS
SCHOOL DISTRICT
Plaintiff,

v.

UNITED STATES OF AMERICA
AND ITS DEPARTMENT OF THE TREASURY,
INTERNAL REVENUE SERVICE,
Defendants.

UNITED STATES DISTRICT COURT
FOR THE EASTERN DISTRICT OF MICHIGAN
SOUTHERN DIVISION

* * *

JUDGE: Cleland, Robert H.

COMPLAINT

NOW COMES Plaintiff, LIVONIA PUBLIC SCHOOLS, by and through its attorneys, KELLER THOMA, A Professional Corporation, and for its Complaint, it states as follows:

1. This Court has jurisdiction over the parties and the subject matter of this action pursuant to 28 U.S.C. section 1346(a)(1). Venue is proper pursuant to 28 U.S.C. section 1391(e).

2. Plaintiff is a Michigan public school district organized and operated pursuant to the Michigan School Code, MCLA 380.1 *et seq.*, with its central offices located in Livonia, Michigan.

3. Plaintiff offered a Retirement/Severance Program to its teachers and administrators in 2000. This program involved the payment of a Twenty-Five Thousand Dollar ($25,000) lump sum to eligible employees in exchange for their resignations, as well as a complete release and waiver of, inter alia, all tenure rights under Michigan Teacher Tenure Act. Many employees afforded themselves of this program, and voluntarily resigned from their employment with Plaintiff in June of 2000.

4. Plaintiff paid the employer's portion of the FICA tax for each of these payments.

5. On April 15, 2003, Plaintiff filed a Form 843 with the United States of America, Department of Treasury, Internal Revenue Service, seeking reimbursement for the employer's portion of the FICA taxes paid relative to the program in June of 2000, on the grounds that these payments to employees who relinquished their tenure rights are not wages. Plaintiff cited the case of North Dakota State University v. United States of America, 255 F.3d 599 (8th Cir. 2001) as support for its position. (See Exhibit A, Plaintiffs Form 843 Submission).

6. On July 2, 2003, the United States of America, Department of Treasury, Internal Revenue Service, sent a notice to Plaintiff denying its request for refund of the taxes paid. (See Exhibit B).

7. Plaintiff again offered a Retirement/Severance Program to its teachers and administrators in 2003. This program involved the payment of Thirty Thousand Dollars ($30,000) to eligible employees in exchange for their resignations, as well as a complete release and waiver of, inter alia, all tenure rights under Michigan's Teacher Tenure Act. Plaintiff agreed to pay the Thirty Thousand Dollars ($30,000) in three (3) equal installments made at the end of the 2002–2003, 2003–2004, 2004–2005 school years. Many employees afforded themselves of this program, and voluntarily resigned from their employment with Plaintiff in June of 2003.

8. Plaintiff paid the employer's portion of the FICA tax for the first and second of these installments.

9. On February 1, 2005, Plaintiff filed Forms 843 with the United States of America, Department of Treasury, Internal Revenue Service, seeking reimbursement for the employer's portion of the FICA taxes paid relative to the program on the grounds that these payments to employees who relinquished their tenure rights are not wages. Plaintiff again cited the case of North Dakota State University v. United States of America, 255 F.3d 599 (8th Cir. 2001) as support for its position. (See Exhibit C, Plaintiffs Form 843 Submission).

9. [sic] On April 5, 2005, the United States of America, Department of Treasury, Internal Revenue Service, sent a notice to Plaintiff denying its request for refund of the taxes paid. (See Exhibit D).

10. On August 2, 2004, Judge David M. Lawson of the United States District Court, Eastern District of Michigan, Northern Division, entered an Order in the matter of Phyllis F. Klender, et. al., v. United States of America, 328 F. Supp. 2d 754 (E. D. Mich. 2004), granting Summary Judgment to the Plaintiffs. Judge Lawson's decision adopts the reasoning of the Eighth Circuit Court of Appeals in the case of North Dakota State University v. United States of America, which was cited by Plaintiff in its Form 843 submission. In the Klender case, Judge Lawson held that "the payments made to the public school teachers in exchange for their tenure rights . . . pursuant to the early retirement incentive plans outlined earlier, were not 'wages' within the meaning of FICA, 26 U.S.C. section 3121(a)." The Court determined that the "tax should not have been assessed on those payments, and the plaintiff's [sic] claim for a refund should have been allowed." (See Exhibit E, Opinion).

11. Despite the fact that Appoloni v. United States of America, 333 F. Supp. 2d 624 (W.D. Mich. 2004), reaches a contrary result, and that both the Klender and Appoloni cases are on appeal to the United States Court of Appeals for the Sixth Circuit, these payments referenced above by the Plaintiff were not paid as a result of "wages," within the meaning of 26 U.S.C. section 3111. Accordingly, no taxes should have been assessed on those payments, and Plaintiffs requests for refunds should have been granted.

WHEREFORE, Plaintiff respectfully requests that this Court award it a refund of the FICA taxes paid, together with interest, attorneys fees, and any other relief this Court may deem proper.

Respectfully submitted,

Keller Thoma, P.C.

By: Gary P. King (P32640)
Karin M. Young (P55808)
Attorneys for Plaintiff,
Livonia Public Schools
440 East Congress, 5th Floor
Detroit, Michigan 48226
(313) 965-7610

Dated: June 28, 2005

[3] Refund Litigation in the Court of Federal Claims

Tax litigation in the United States Court of Federal Claims begins when the taxpayer files a complaint. U.S. Ct. Fed. Cl. R. 3. The complaint will resemble the District Court complaint reproduced above. The IRS then files an answer. U.S. Ct. Fed. Cl. R. 7. "[I]f the answer contains a counterclaim or offset or a plea of fraud, there shall be a reply thereto." *Id.* Like the Tax Court, the Court of Federal Claims is an Article I court. *See* 28 U.S.C. § 171. The court has sixteen judges, who are appointed by the President with the advice and consent of the Senate. *Id.* The judges each have a 15-year term. 28 U.S.C. § 172. Each trial is heard by a single judge. U.S. Ct. Fed. Cl. R. 77(e).

The Court of Federal Claims is based in Washington, D.C., but the judges travel to hear cases in other cities. 28 U.S.C. § 173. The Court of Federal Claims' rules are particularly flexible about the place of trial, so that some trials consist of sessions in various parts of the country, for the convenience of witnesses. The Federal Rules of Evidence apply. FED. R. EVID. 101, 1101. Decisions are appealable to the Court of Appeals for the Federal Circuit, and its precedent applies.[10] 28 U.S.C. § 1295(a)(3).

[4] The "Full Payment" Rule

As discussed above, a refund suit must be based on the same "grounds" as those stated in the refund claim. *See* I.R.C. § 7422(a); Treas. Reg. § 301.6402-2(b)(1). Refund suits have another jurisdictional prerequisite: "full payment" of the tax. This United States Supreme Court case established the "full payment" requirement.

FLORA v. UNITED STATES
United States Supreme Court
362 U.S. 145 (1960)[11]

MR. CHIEF JUSTICE WARREN delivered the opinion of the Court.

The question presented is whether a Federal District Court has jurisdiction under 28 U.S C. § 1346(a)(1) of a suit by a taxpayer for the refund of income tax payments which did not discharge the entire amount of his assessment.

This is our second consideration of the case. In the 1957 Term, we decided that full payment of the assessment is a jurisdictional prerequisite to suit, 357 U.S. 63. Subsequently the Court granted a petition for rehearing. 360 U.S. 922. The case has been exhaustively briefed and ably argued. After giving the problem our most careful attention, we have concluded that our original disposition of the case was correct.

* * *

THE FACTS

The relevant facts are undisputed and uncomplicated. This litigation had its source in a dispute between petitioner and the Commissioner of Internal Revenue concerning the proper characterization of certain losses which petitioner suffered during 1950. Petitioner reported them as ordinary losses, but the Commissioner treated them as capital losses and levied a deficiency assessment in the amount of $28,908.60, including interest. Petitioner paid $5,058.54 and then filed with the Commissioner a claim for refund of that amount. After the claim was disallowed, petitioner sued for refund in a District Court. The Government moved to dismiss, and the judge decided that the petitioner "should not maintain" the action because he had not paid the full amount of the assessment. But since there was a conflict among the Courts of Appeals on this jurisdictional question, and since the Tenth Circuit had not yet passed upon it, the judge believed it desirable to determine the merits of the claim. He thereupon concluded that the losses were capital in nature and entered judgment in favor of the Government. 142 F. Supp. 602. The Court of Appeals for the Tenth Circuit agreed with the district judge upon the jurisdictional issue, and consequently remanded with directions to vacate the judgment and dismiss the complaint. 246 F.2d 929. We granted certiorari because the Courts of Appeals were in conflict with respect to a question which is of considerable importance in the administration of the tax laws.

---

[10] Decisions of the United States Court of Claims, the predecessor to the Court of Federal Claims, entered prior to September 30, 1982, also apply as precedent. South Corp. v. United States, 690 F.2d 1368, 1370–71 (Fed. Cir. 1982).

[11] *Reh'g denied*, 362 U.S. 972 (1960).

THE STATUTE

The question raised in this case has not only raised a conflict in the federal decisions, but has also in recent years provoked controversy among legal commentators. In view of this divergence of expert opinion, it would be surprising if the words of the statute inexorably dictated but a single reasonable conclusion. Nevertheless, one of the arguments which has been most strenuously urged is that the plain language of the statute precludes, or at the very least strongly militates against, a decision that full payment of the income tax assessment is a jurisdictional condition precedent to maintenance of a refund suit in a District Court. If this were true, presumably we could but recite the statute and enter judgment for petitioner — though we might be pardoned some perplexity as to how such a simple matter could have caused so much confusion. Regrettably, this facile an approach will not serve.

Section 1346(a)(1) provides that the District Courts shall have jurisdiction, concurrent with the Court of Claims, of

> "(1) Any civil action against the United States for the recovery of *any internal-revenue tax* alleged to have been erroneously or illegally assessed or collected, or *any penalty* claimed to have been collected without authority or *any sum* alleged to have been excessive or in any manner wrongfully collected under the internal-revenue laws. . . ." (Emphasis added.)

It is clear enough that the phrase "any internal-revenue tax" can readily be construed to refer to payment of the entire amount of an assessment. Such an interpretation is suggested by the nature of the income tax, which is "*A* tax . . . imposed for each taxable year," with the "amount of *the* tax" determined in accordance with prescribed schedules. (Emphasis added.) But it is argued that this reading of the statute is foreclosed by the presence in § 1346(a)(1) of the phrase "any sum." This contention appears to be based upon the notion that "any sum" is a catchall which confers jurisdiction to adjudicate suits for refund of part of a tax. A catchall the phrase surely is; but to say this is not to define what it catches. The sweeping role which petitioner assigns these words is based upon a conjunctive reading of "any internal-revenue tax," "any penalty," and "any sum." But we believe that the statute more readily lends itself to the disjunctive reading which is suggested by the connective "or." That is, "any sum," instead of being related to "any internal-revenue tax" and "any penalty," may refer to amounts which are neither taxes nor penalties. Under this interpretation, the function of the phrase is to permit suit for recovery of items which might not be designated as either "taxes" or "penalties" by Congress or the courts. One obvious example of such a "sum" is interest. And it is significant that many old tax statutes described the amount which was to be assessed under certain circumstances as a "sum" to be added to the tax, simply as a "sum," as a "percentum," or as "costs." Such a rendition of the statute, which is supported by precedent, frees the phrase "any internal-revenue tax" from the qualifications imposed upon it by petitioner and permits it to be given what we regard as its more natural reading — the full tax. Moreover, this construction, under which each phrase is assigned a distinct meaning, imputes to Congress a surer grammatical touch than does the alternative interpretation, under which the "any sum" phrase completely assimilates the other two. Surely a much clearer statute could have been written to authorize suits for refund of any part of a tax merely by use of the phrase "a tax or any portion thereof," or simply "any sum paid under the internal revenue laws." This Court naturally does not review congressional enactments as a panel of grammarians; but neither do we regard ordinary principles of English prose as irrelevant to a construction of those enactments. *Cf.* Commissioner v. Acker, 361 U.S. 87.

We conclude that the language of § 1346(a)(1) can be more readily construed to require payment of the full tax before suit than to permit suit for recovery of a part payment. But, as we recognized in the prior opinion, the statutory language is not absolutely controlling, and consequently resort must be had to whatever other materials might be relevant.

LEGISLATIVE HISTORY AND HISTORICAL BACKGROUND

Although frequently the legislative history of a statute is the most fruitful source of instruction as to its proper interpretation, in this case that history is barren of any clue to congressional intent.

* * *

We are not here concerned with a single sentence in an isolated statute, but rather with a jurisdictional provision which is a keystone in a carefully articulated and quite complicated structure of tax laws. From * * * related statutes, all of which were passed after 1921, it is apparent that Congress has several times acted upon the assumption that § 1346(a)(1) requires full payment before suit. Of course, if the clear purpose of Congress at any time had been to permit suit to recover a part payment, this subsequent legislation would have to be disregarded. But, as we have stated, the evidence pertaining to this intent is extremely weak, and we are convinced that it is entirely too insubstantial to justify destroying the existing harmony of the tax statutes. The laws which we consider especially pertinent are the statute establishing the Board of Tax Appeals (now the Tax Court), the Declaratory Judgment Act, and § 7422(e) of the Internal Revenue Code of 1954.

THE BOARD OF TAX APPEALS

The Board of Tax Appeals was established by Congress in 1924 to permit taxpayers to secure a determination of tax liability before payment of the deficiency. The Government argues that the Congress which passed this 1924 legislation thought full payment of the tax assessed was a condition for bringing suit in a District Court; that Congress believed this sometimes caused hardship; and that Congress set up the Board to alleviate that hardship. Petitioner denies this, and contends that Congress's sole purpose was to enable taxpayers to prevent the Government from collecting taxes by exercise of its power of distraint.

We believe that the legislative history surrounding both the creation of the Board and the subsequent revisions of the basic statute supports the Government. The House Committee Report, for example, explained the purpose of the bill as follows:

> "The committee recommends the establishment of a Board of Tax Appeals to which a taxpayer may appeal *prior to the payment* of an additional assessment of income, excess-profits, war-profits, or estate taxes. *Although a taxpayer may, after payment of his tax, bring suit for the recovery thereof* and thus secure a judicial determination on the questions involved, he can not, in view of section 3224 of the Revised Statutes, which prohibits suits to enjoin the collection of taxes, secure such a determination prior to the payment of the tax. The right of appeal after payment of the tax is an incomplete remedy, and does little to remove the hardship occasioned by an incorrect assessment. The payment of a large additional tax on income received several years previous and which may have, since its receipt, been either wiped out by subsequent losses, invested in nonliquid assets, or spent, sometimes forces taxpayers into bankruptcy, and often causes great financial hardship and sacrifice. These results are not remedied by permitting the taxpayer *to sue for the recovery of the tax after this payment.* He is entitled to an appeal and to a determination of his liability for the tax prior to its payment." (Emphasis added.)

Moreover, throughout the congressional debates are to be found frequent expressions of the principle that payment of the full tax was a precondition to suit: "pay his tax . . . then . . . file a claim for refund"; "pay the tax and then sue"; "a review in the courts after payment of the tax"; "he may still seek court review, but he must first pay the tax assessed"; "in order to go to court he must pay his assessment"; "he must pay it [his assessment] before he can have a trial in court"; "pay the taxes adjudicated against him, and then commence a suit in a court"; "pay the tax . . . then . . . sue to get it back"; "paying his tax and bringing his suit"; "first pay his tax and then sue to get it back"; "take his case to the district court — conditioned, of course, upon his paying the assessment."

Petitioner's argument falls under the weight of this evidence. It is true, of course, that the Board of Tax Appeals procedure has the effect of staying collection, and it may well be that Congress so provided in order to alleviate hardships caused by the long-standing bar against suits to enjoin the collection of taxes. But it is a considerable leap to the further conclusion that amelioration of the hardship of prelitigation payment as a jurisdictional requirement was not another important motivation for Congress's action. * * *

In sum, even assuming that one purpose of Congress in establishing the Board was to permit taxpayers to avoid distraint, it seems evident that another purpose was to furnish a forum where full payment of the assessment would not be a condition precedent to suit. The result is a system in which there is one tribunal for prepayment litigation and another for post-payment litigation, with no room contemplated for a hybrid of the type proposed by petitioner.

* * *

SECTION 7422(e) OF THE 1954 CODE[12]

One distinct possibility which would emerge from a decision in favor of petitioner would be that a taxpayer might be able to split his cause of action, bringing suit for refund of part of the tax in a Federal District Court and litigating in the Tax Court with respect to the remainder. In such a situation the first decision would, of course, control. Thus if for any reason a litigant would prefer a District Court adjudication, he might sue for a small portion of the tax in that tribunal while at the same time protecting the balance from distraint by invoking the protection of the Tax Court procedure. On the other hand, different questions would arise if this device were not employed. For example, would the Government be required to file a compulsory counterclaim for the unpaid balance in District Court under Rule 13 of the Federal Rules of Civil Procedure? If so, which party would have the burden of proof?

Section 7422(e) makes it apparent that Congress has assumed these problems are nonexistent except in the rare case where the taxpayer brings suit in a District Court and the Commissioner then notifies him of an additional deficiency. Under § 7422(e) such a claimant is given the option of pursuing his suit in the District Court or in the Tax Court, but he cannot litigate in both. Moreover, if he decides to remain in the District Court, the Government may — but seemingly is not required to — bring a counterclaim; and if it does, the taxpayer has the burden of proof. If we were to overturn the assumption upon which Congress has acted, we would generate upon a broad scale the very problems Congress believed it had solved.

These, then, are the basic reasons for our decision, and our views would be unaffected by the constancy or inconstancy of administrative practice. However, because the petition for rehearing in this case focused almost exclusively upon a single clause in the prior opinion — "there does not appear to be a single case before 1940 in which a taxpayer attempted a suit for refund of income taxes without paying the full amount the Government alleged to be due," 357 U.S., at 69 — we feel obliged to comment upon the material introduced upon reargument. The reargument has, if anything, strengthened, rather than weakened, the substance of this statement, which was directed to the question whether there has been a consistent understanding of the "pay first and litigate later" principle by the interested government agencies and by the bar.

---

[12] [Section 7422(e) is discussed in § 11.07[B] of Chapter 11. — Eds.]

* * *

There is strong circumstantial evidence that this view of the jurisdiction of the courts was shared by the bar at least until 1940, when the Second Circuit Court of Appeals rejected the Government's position in *Coates v. United States*, 111 F.2d 609. Out of the many thousands of refund cases litigated in the pre-1940 period — the Government reports that there have been approximately 40,000 such suits in the past 40 years — exhaustive research has uncovered only nine suits in which the issue was present, in six of which the Government contested jurisdiction on part-payment grounds.[n.37] The Government's failure to raise the issue in the other three is obviously entirely without significance. Considerations of litigation strategy may have been thought to militate against resting upon such a defense in those cases. Moreover, where only nine lawsuits involving a particular issue arise over a period of many decades, the policy of the Executive Department on that issue can hardly be expected to become familiar to every government attorney. But most important, the number of cases before 1940 in which the issue was present is simply so inconsequential that it reinforces the conclusion of the prior opinion with respect to the uniformity of the pre-1940 belief that full payment had to precede suit.

A word should also be said about the argument that requiring taxpayers to pay the full assessments before bringing suits will subject some of them to great hardship. This contention seems to ignore entirely the right of the taxpayer to appeal the deficiency to the Tax Court without paying a cent.[n.38] If he permits his time for filing such an appeal to expire, he can hardly complain that he has been unjustly treated, for he is in precisely the same position as any other person who is barred by a statute of limitations. On the other hand, the Government has a substantial interest in protecting the public purse, an interest which would be substantially impaired if a taxpayer could sue in a District Court without paying his tax in full. * * *

In sum, if we were to accept petitioner's argument, we would sacrifice the harmony of our carefully structured twentieth century system of tax litigation, and all that would be achieved would be a supposed harmony of § 1346(a)(1) with what might have been the nineteenth century law had the issue ever been raised. Reargument has but fortified our view that § 1346(a)(1), correctly construed, requires full payment of the assessment before an income tax refund suit can be maintained in a Federal District Court.

Affirmed.

Does federal income tax withheld from a taxpayer's wages constitute tax "paid" within the meaning of *Flora*?

If the amount sought to be refunded includes interest and penalties, does *Flora* require the taxpayer to pay those amounts before jurisdiction will be granted? The

---

[n.37] Petitioner cites a number of cases in support of his argument that neither the bar nor the Government has ever assumed that full payment of the tax is a jurisdictional prerequisite to suit for recovery. The following factors rob these cases of the significance attributed to them by the petitioner:

. . .

(b) A number of the cited cases involved excise taxes. The Government suggests — and we agree — that excise tax deficiencies may be divisible into a tax on each transaction or event, and therefore present an entirely different problem with respect to the full-payment rule.

. . .

[n.38] Petitioner points out that the Tax Court has no jurisdiction over excise tax cases. *See* 9 Mertens, Law of Federal Income Taxation (Zimet Rev. 1958), § 50.08. But this fact provides no policy support for his position, since, as we have noted, excise tax assessments may be divisible into a tax on each transaction or event, so that the full-payment rule would probably require no more than payment of a small amount. *See* note 37, *supra*.

answer is unclear. However, some courts have held that whether "full payment" requires the payment of interest and penalties depends on whether those amounts were part of the assessment and whether they are at issue in the litigation. *Compare* Shore v. United States, 9 F.3d 1524, 1527–1528 (Fed. Cir. 1993) ("Only if the taxpayers assert a claim over assessed interest or penalties on grounds not fully determined by the claim for recovery of principal must they prepay such interest and penalties as well as the assessed tax principal."), *with* Magnone v. United States, 902 F.2d 192, 193 (2d Cir.), *cert. denied*, 498 U.S. 853 (1990) ("[T]he full payment rule requires as a prerequisite for federal court jurisdiction over a tax refund suit, that the taxpayer make full payment of the assessment, including penalties and interest."); *and* Greenhouse v. United States, 738 F. Supp. 709, 713 (S.D.N.Y. 1990) ("It is well settled that, under the full payment rule, a federal court has jurisdiction over a tax refund suit only after the taxpayer has made full payment of the assessment, including penalties and interest.").

There is no "hardship" exception to *Flora. See, e.g.*, Curry v. United States, 774 F.2d 852 (7th Cir. 1985). Thus, in responding to a notice of deficiency, the "full payment" rule is an important consideration in deciding whether to pursue the matter as a deficiency case in the Tax Court or as a refund action.

With respect to disputes involving certain types of taxes, such as excise taxes, the Tax Court has no jurisdiction whatsoever. In those cases, the "divisible tax" rule mitigates the hardship that might accompany the full payment rule by providing that payment of a single "divisible" tax, such as an excise or employment tax, constitutes full payment. *See* Steele v. United States, 280 F.2d 89, 90–91 (8th Cir. 1960) (full payment rule is not applicable to employment taxes because they are divisible into separate taxes for each employee); *see also Flora*, 362 U.S. at 174 n.37 ("The Government suggests — and we agree — that excise tax deficiencies may be divisible into a tax on each transaction or event, and therefore present an entirely different problem with respect to the full-payment rule.").

[B] Overpayment Litigation in Tax Court

As you learned in Chapter 9, Tax Court subject matter jurisdiction requires a notice of deficiency and timely responsive petition. Therefore, to pursue in Tax Court a refund of an overpayment, a taxpayer must have received a notice of deficiency and timely petitioned the court. When that occurs, the Tax Court has jurisdiction to find an overpayment, I.R.C. § 6512(b)(1), and jurisdiction to enforce payment by the IRS, I.R.C. § 6512(b)(2). Overpayment jurisdiction also includes jurisdiction over overpayments of interest. *See* Winn-Dixie v. Commissioner, 110 T.C. 291 (1998).

A taxpayer need not file a claim for refund with the IRS to pursue overpayment litigation in Tax Court. Because of the absence of a refund claim requirement, the statute of limitations for claiming a refund in Tax Court has an additional layer of complexity. The statute of limitations issues that arise in Tax Court cases are discussed below, in Sections 10.05[C] and [D].

§ 10.04 ERRONEOUS REFUNDS AND ABATEMENTS OF TAX

Reading Assignment: I.R.C. §§ 6211(a), 6404(a), 7405(a)–(b).

Code section 7405 allows an action for recovery of refunds erroneously made by the IRS.[13] Code section 6532(b) grants the IRS a two-year statute of limitations for suing for recovery of an erroneous refund, unless the refund, or any part of it, was induced by fraud or the taxpayer's misrepresentation of a material fact. In either case, the period

---

[13] Section 7405 does not create the right to recover erroneous refunds, but merely declares it; the government's right to sue exists independent of the statute. United States v. Wurts, 303 U.S. 414, 415 (1938); *see also* Marshall v. United States, 158 F. Supp. 793, 795 (E.D. Tex. 1958).

starts to run from issuance of the refund. What the language of section 7405 does not reflect is the fact that there are two types of erroneous refunds, "rebate refunds" and "non-rebate refunds."

Recall that the definition of a deficiency in Code section 6211(a) refers to "rebates." In general, ignoring prior rebates, a rebate is any portion of a repayment made by the IRS to a taxpayer on the ground that the tax imposed was less than the amounts admitted by the taxpayer on his return plus assessments previously made. Professor Bryan Camp explains:

> A rebate refund occurs when the taxpayer gets money back because the amount paid or credited is greater than the true liability properly reflected in the IRS books. My yearly refund that I love so much is a rebate refund because my amount paid is greater than my true tax. Erroneous earned income tax credit refunds are rebate refunds because the refundable credit is greater than the true tax liability. Likewise, the IRS sometimes determines the previous assessment was excessive because a taxpayer files an amended return that is accepted by the IRS, or because an audit results in a lower tax liability. In those cases, the assessment is abated under section 6404(a) and any resulting refund becomes a rebate within the meaning of section 6213(b).

Bryan Camp, *The Mysteries of Erroneous Refunds*, 114 Tax Notes 231, 237 (2007) (footnote omitted).

If the IRS later reevaluates the merits of the tax and determines that the rebate refund was in error, the payment of the rebate will have created a deficiency within the meaning of section 6211. That is because, in this context, the determination will be based on a substantive redetermination of tax liability. Accordingly, the deficiency procedures of section 6212 and 6213 apply. *See id.* at 237–38.

A refund made for any other reason is a non-rebate refund. This type of refund may be made erroneously for such reasons as a mathematical, clerical, or computer error. Such a refund does not create a deficiency within the meaning of section 6211(a) because it is not a "rebate" within the meaning of Code section 6211(b)(2). *See* Groetzinger v. Commissioner, 69 T.C. 309, 314 (1977). Instead, the refund creates an underpayment of tax that is based on the original assessment, which the taxpayer already had the opportunity to contest. For example, if a taxpayer files a return showing a tax liability of $5,000 and pays that $5,000 in full, the IRS will assess the $5,000. If the taxpayer then receives a non-rebate erroneous refund of $1,000 for the same tax year (because, for example, the IRS erroneously credited someone else's payment to the taxpayer's account), the IRS may use its administrative collection procedures, rather than deficiency procedures, to recover the $1,000. *See* General Counsel Memorandum 36624 (Mar. 11, 1976).

Note that if a tax liability has not yet been paid when the IRS determines that it is too high, the IRS will not make a refund, but rather will abate the tax. *See* I.R.C. § 6404(a). If the abatement is in error, it will constitute an erroneous abatement. As above, if the error was on the merits, then the IRS must reassess the tax liability within the limitations period under section 6501 in order to reverse the abatement. *See* Notice CC-2001-014, *reprinted at* 2001 TNT 40-22 (Feb. 28, 2001). However, if the abatement was based on a mathematical or clerical error, the IRS may simply reverse the abatement and reinstate the original assessment, regardless of whether the limitations period for assessments has run, as long as the limitations period for collection is still open. *See id.*

§ 10.05 STATUTES OF LIMITATIONS ON REFUND CLAIMS

[A] Overview

Reading Assignment: I.R.C. §§ 6511(a), 6513(a)–(b), 7503; skim I.R.C. § 7502(a).

In general, a claim for refund or credit of an overpayment is timely if it is filed within three years from the date the return was filed or within two years of when the claimed tax was paid, whichever is later. I.R.C. § 6511(a). (Why isn't just the three-year rule sufficient? Without a period stemming from payment of the tax, a taxpayer who received a notice of deficiency three or more years after filing the return (such as in a case of substantial omission of items, which has a six-year period of limitations on assessment under section 6501(e)) would not have the opportunity to claim a refund of tax paid in response to the notice, as a prerequisite to refund litigation.) If no return was filed, the statutory period is two years from when the tax was paid. I.R.C. § 6511(a).

Recall that Code section 7502 establishes that a return timely mailed is timely filed. Because late-mailed returns or claims are not filed until actually received, it is important to determine, when filing a refund claim, if it was timely mailed.[14] When calculating these time periods under section 6511, it is also helpful to know that an early return is deemed filed on the due date of the return. I.R.C. § 6513(a). Similarly, any portion of tax paid before the last day prescribed for payment is considered paid on the last day. I.R.C. § 6513(a). The same is true for withholding taxes. I.R.C. § 6513(b).

Because of the two-years-from-payment rule, theoretically at least, a taxpayer could pay to the IRS $1 on a date more than three years after filing the return, and soon thereafter file a refund claim for not only the $1 paid but also for all taxes paid with the return. Section 6511 contains a "limitation on amount" that precludes that approach. Where the refund claim is not filed within the three-year period, the amount recoverable as a refund is measured by and limited to the tax paid within two years before the taxpayer filed the claim. Therefore, in the hypothetical situation involving a $1 payment more than three years after the return was filed, the statute of limitations would allow the taxpayer only to claim a refund of $1, not any additional amount paid with the return.

Similarly, in cases in which the three-year period applies, the refund amount is measured by and limited to the tax paid within three years before the taxpayer filed the claim, plus any extension of time the taxpayer had for filing the return. I.R.C. § 6511(b)(2)(A). If the taxpayer has not filed a claim but the IRS allows a refund, the refund amount is measured by the amount that would be allowed or made if a claim had been filed on the date the credit or refund is allowed. I.R.C. § 6511(b)(2).

> *Example:* Teresa timely filed her Year 1 return on March 21, Year 2. Her return accurately reflected a tax liability of $7,000, and withholding of $6,000. She mailed a check for $1,000 to the IRS with the return. All $7,000 of tax is considered paid on April 15, Year 2, and her return is deemed filed on that date as well. I.R.C. § 6513(a), (b). The latest date on which Teresa can file for refund of any of the $7,000 is April 15, Year 5, three years from when she filed her Year 1 return.
>
> Assume that the IRS mails Teresa a notice of deficiency in the amount of $2,000 on March 1, Year 4, and Teresa pays the $2,000 on April 1, Year 4. Under section 6511, Teresa has until April 1, Year 6 (2 years from payment of the $2,000, invoking a 2-year look-back) to claim a refund for Year 1 of up to $2,000 on any issue. To claim a refund up to a maximum of $9,000 (the $7,000 she previously

[14] Does an initial return mailed after its due date benefit from section 7502 if it contains a refund claim that would be timely if measured by the date the document was mailed? *See* Treas. Reg. § 301.7502-1(f).

paid, plus the $2,000 paid in response to the notice of deficiency), she only has until April 15, Year 5 (3 years from the date the return was filed, invoking a 3-year look-back). That is the last date on which a refund claim would be timely with respect to all of Teresa's Year 1 taxes.

What happens if the last day to file a return falls on a non-business day? Code section 7503 provides that "when the last day . . . for performing any act falls on Saturday, Sunday, or a legal holiday, the performance of such act shall be considered timely if it is performed on the next succeeding day which is not a Saturday, Sunday, or a legal holiday." I.R.C. § 7503.[15] In general, the application of this section is relatively clear. However, it is not as clear how this section applies if the act in question is not actually performed on the "next succeeding day."

For example, if a return is due on Monday, April 17 of Year 1 because April 15 was a Saturday, does a taxpayer have until April 17 of Year 4 (assuming a three-year period applies) to claim a refund on the taxpayer's first return for the year? In Revenue Ruling 2003-41, 2003-1 C.B. 814, the IRS ruled that Code section 7503 does not extend the time to file a refund claim when the deadline for filing the return to which the claim relates fell on a Saturday, Sunday, or legal holiday, but the taxpayer did not actually take advantage of the section 7503 extension (that is, the taxpayer filed earlier or later than the extended due date). In *Weisbart v. IRS*, 2004-1 U.S.T.C. ¶ 50,230 (E.D.N.Y. 2004), the District Court applied that ruling to bar a return containing a refund claim for 1992 that the taxpayer argued was mailed on Friday, August 16, 1996, under an extension of time to file until August 15, 1993 (which fell on a Sunday).

The taxpayer in *Weisbart* is the same taxpayer who prevailed in *Weisbart v. U.S. Dep't of Treas.*, 222 F.3d 93 (2d Cir. 2000). The latter case involved his 1991 return, which was due, under an extension of time to file, on August 17, 1992. *Id.* at 94. He actually mailed it to the IRS on August 17, 1995. *Id.* The principal issue in that case was the application of the "mailbox rule" of section 7502. That case apparently did not involve an application of Code section 7503 because, although August 17, 1992 was a Monday, suggesting that the four-month extension obtained by Mr. Weisbart might have expired Saturday, August 15, 1992, it appears from the District Court opinion that the original extension granted was in fact until August 17, 1992. *See* Weisbart v. U.S. Dep't of Treas., 99-1 U.S.T.C. ¶ 50,549 (E.D.N.Y. 1999), *aff'd*, 222 F.3d 93 (2d Cir. 2000) ("Plaintiff asked for this extension by filing I.R.S. Form 4868 entitled "Application for Automatic Extension of Time to File U.S. Individual Income Tax Return which states that the plaintiff requested an extension until August 17, 1992. By its terms, such an extension is automatically granted, and there is no dispute that plaintiff's tax return was due on August 17, 1992."). Note that if, in *Weisbart v. IRS*, Mr. Weisbart had requested and obtained an extension for his 1992 tax year until Monday, August 16, 1993, then a refund claim mailed on Friday, August 16, 1996 would have been timely.

[B] Statutory Period Applicable When the Taxpayer Extended the Statute of Limitations on Assessment

Reading Assignment: I.R.C. § 6511(c).

If the taxpayer agrees to extend the statute of limitations on assessment of tax for any taxable year, the statute of limitations on filing a refund claim for that year is also extended, subject to certain exceptions explained below. In the usual case, the taxpayer is permitted to file a claim for credit or refund of an overpayment at any time within the

---

[15] Section 7503 applies not only to taxpayer documents such as returns and refund claims, but also to IRS documents such as the notice of deficiency. Its application to a notice of deficiency is discussed in Chapter 7 in the context of *Estate of Mitchell v. Commissioner*, 250 F.3d 696 (9th Cir. 2001), a case that is excerpted in Chapter 9.

extended period provided in the agreement plus an additional six months. I.R.C. § 6511(c)(1). If the taxpayer files a claim within that time, the amount of the credit or refund may include not only the portion of the tax paid after the agreement was executed, but the amount of tax that could have been refunded if a claim had been filed on the date the extension agreement was executed. I.R.C. § 6511(c)(2). These special rules do not apply if the taxpayer filed a claim (or a refund was made) either before the extension agreement was executed or more than six months after the expiration of the extended assessment period. I.R.C. § 6511(c)(3).

Example: Michael filed his Year 1 return on April 15, Year 2. His return showed a tax liability of $20,000, all of which was covered by withholding from his salary. The IRS audits Michael's Year 1 return, and, on April 1, Year 5, Michael agrees to extend the statute of limitations until April 15, Year 6. Assume that the IRS subsequently determines that Michael's tax treatment of the issues it was auditing was correct and does not issue a notice of deficiency. However, during the course of the audit, Michael determines that he has an argument that entitles him to a refund of $5,000 of the taxes previously paid. The last date on which Michael can file a refund claim for Year 1 is six months from the expiration of the extended assessment period — October 15, Year 6. In a claim made by that date, Michael is entitled to claim a refund of the $5,000 (in fact, up to the full $20,000 of taxes he paid for Year 1, all deemed paid on April 15, Year 2, under Code section 6513(b)(1)). That is because if, hypothetically, Michael had filed a refund claim on the date that the agreement extending the statute of limitations on assessment was executed (April 1, Year 5), Michael would have been able to claim a refund of up to $20,000 under the 3-year period of Code section 6511(a).

[C] Statutes of Limitations on Refund Claims Applicable in Tax Court Cases

Reading Assignment: I.R.C. § 6512(b)(3).

Because taxpayers are authorized to assert in a Tax Court petition the refund of an overpayment, without ever filing a refund claim, a special statute of limitations applies in Tax Court cases. Read section 6512(b)(3) carefully. It has three parts. Section 6512(b)(3)(A) allows a refund of any amount paid after the notice of deficiency was mailed. Because the taxpayer could have claimed a refund of that amount and pursued the refund method at that time, the treatment in Tax Court is parallel to the treatment under the refund procedures. Section 6512(b)(3)(C) entitles the taxpayer to a refund for which the taxpayer already filed a timely refund claim before the notice of deficiency was mailed, and with respect to which the taxpayer had not already been time-barred under the refund method. Again, this makes the Tax Court treatment of overpayment claims parallel to the refund method.

The hardest provision to follow is section 6512(b)(3)(B). What it does, particularly in a situation in which the taxpayer did *not* file a refund claim *before* the notice of deficiency was mailed, and the payment in question was not made after the notice was mailed, is, for purposes of the limitations period of section 6511 to *deem* the date the IRS mailed the notice of deficiency to be the date the taxpayer made a hypothetical refund claim for the full amount that the taxpayer seeks as an overpayment. As a result, under section 6512(b)(3)(B), the taxpayer can obtain a refund in Tax Court only of amounts that would have been recoverable in the time period applicable under section 6511. The intent seems to be to make both the time limitation and limitation on amount restrictions applicable to an overpayment claimed in Tax Court comparable to the restrictions that would apply when simply claiming a refund directly. Because a refund claim is not required in Tax Court cases, but a notice of deficiency is a prerequisite for all Tax Court overpayment litigation, section 6512 uses the date the notice of deficiency was mailed —

rather than the date of a refund claim filing — as the benchmark date for applying section 6511 in the Tax Court overpayment context.

Example: Jim filed his Year 1 return on April 15, Year 2. His return showed a tax liability of $10,000, all of which was covered by withholding from his salary. The IRS mailed Jim a notice of deficiency on April 1, Year 5, alleging that he has a deficiency of $5,000 attributable to unreported income. Jim timely petitions the Tax Court on June 1, Year 5. In his petition, he claims both that the deficiency is in error and that he made an overpayment of $3,000 attributable to unclaimed deductions. Jim is deemed to have made a refund claim on April 1, Year 5, the date the notice of deficiency was mailed. Because that is within 3 years of the date he filed his return, he can claim a refund up to the amount he paid within that 3-year look-back period. The $10,000 of withholding is deemed paid on April 15, Year 2 under section 6513(b)(1), so Jim's overpayment claim for $3,000 is timely.

[D] Application of the Statutes of Limitations to Delinquent Returns

[1] Applying Sections 6511 and 6512 to Delinquent Returns

Reading Assignment: Review I.R.C. §§ 6511(a), 6512(b)(3)(B).

The application of the limitations periods in Code sections 6511 and 6512 becomes more complicated in the case of late-filed returns. If a taxpayer files a return late, does that mean "no return was filed" so that a two-year statute of limitations applies? As discussed in the Supreme Court's opinion in *Commissioner v. Lundy*, 516 U.S. 235 (1996), numerous cases had arisen in which the taxpayer did not file a return, received a notice of deficiency from the IRS, and petitioned the Tax Court to both contest the deficiency and make an overpayment claim. This situation commonly arises because a taxpayer entitled to a refund might not feel time-pressed to file a return. However, in the absence of a return showing the taxpayer's filing status, deductions, exemptions, and credits, the IRS will not know the taxpayer's situation and may instead find a deficiency.

In its lengthy opinion in *Lundy*, the Supreme Court stated:

> In this case, we must determine which of these two look-back periods to apply when the taxpayer fails to file a tax return when it is due, and the Commissioner mails the taxpayer a notice of deficiency before the taxpayer gets around to filing a late return. The Fourth Circuit held that a taxpayer in this situation is entitled to a 3-year look-back period if the taxpayer actually files a timely claim at some point in the litigation, 516 U.S. at 246, and respondent offers additional reasons for applying a 3-year look-back period, 516 U.S. at 249–252. We think the proper application of § 6512(b)(3)(B) instead requires that a 2-year look-back period be applied.
>
> We reach this conclusion by following the instructions set out in § 6512(b)(3)(B). The operative question is whether a claim filed "on the date of the mailing of the notice of deficiency" would be filed "within 3 years from the time the return was filed." *See* § 6512(b)(3)(B) (incorporating §§ 6511(b)(2) and 6511(a)). In the case of a taxpayer who does not file a return before the notice of deficiency is mailed, the claim described in § 6512(b)(3)(B) could not be filed "within 3 years from the time the return was filed." No return having been filed, there is no date from which to measure the 3-year filing period described in § 6511(a). Consequently, the claim contemplated in § 6512(b)(3)(B) would not be filed within the 3-year window described in § 6511(a), and the 3-year look-back period set out in § 6511(b)(2)(A) would not apply. The applicable look-back period is instead the default 2-year period described in § 6511(b)(2)(B), which is

> measured from the date of the mailing of the notice of deficiency, *see* § 6512(b)(3)(B). The taxpayer is entitled to a refund of any taxes paid within two years prior to the date of the mailing of the notice of deficiency.

Lundy, 516 U.S. at 243.

Subsequent to *Lundy*, Congress amended section 6512(b)(3), adding the following language: "In a case described in subparagraph (B) where the date of the mailing of the notice of deficiency is during the third year after the due date (with extensions) for filing the return of tax and no return was filed before such date, the applicable period under subsections (a) and (b)(2) of section 6511 shall be 3 years." Does this provide for a different result in cases like *Lundy*? Does it put a nonfiler who receives a notice of deficiency within three years after the due date of the return in a better position with respect to an overpayment claim than one who does not? Consider the following case, which applies the amendment to section 6512(b)(3) quoted above.

ZARKY v. COMMISSIONER

United States Tax Court
123 T.C. 132 (2004)

LARO, JUDGE: Petitioner petitioned the Court to redetermine respondent's determinations as to petitioner's 1999 taxable year. Respondent determined that petitioner is liable for a $63,066 deficiency and additions thereto of $14,129.10, $9,105.42, and $3,014.25 under sections 6651(a)(1) and (2) and 6654(a), respectively. Petitioner asserted in his petition that he is entitled to a $270 overpayment.

Following respondent's concession that petitioner overpaid his 1999 Federal income tax by $270, we are left to decide whether petitioner is entitled to that overpayment. We hold he is.

FINDINGS OF FACT

The parties have filed with the Court certain stipulations of fact and an exhibit related thereto. We incorporate herein the stipulated facts and exhibit and find the stipulated facts accordingly. Petitioner resided in Moorpark, California, when his petition was filed.

Petitioner did not file a 1999 Federal income tax return. His taxable income for that year totaled $874, all from interest earned on his savings accounts. The payors of that interest notified respondent that they had paid this interest to petitioner as income and that they had withheld $270 of it as Federal income tax. Respondent was also notified by a brokerage firm that petitioner had during 1999 received $212,029 from brokerage sales.

Respondent determined in the relevant notice of deficiency mailed to petitioner on February 27, 2003, that petitioner's 1999 gross income included both the $212,029 and the $874. Respondent has since conceded that none of the $212,029 was so includable and that petitioner has overpaid his 1999 Federal income tax by the withheld amount of $270.

OPINION

Petitioner seeks the $270 that he overpaid for 1999. Respondent argues that petitioner is not entitled to that amount because, respondent states, none of it was paid within the 2-year period of section 6511(a).

We conclude that petitioner is entitled to the $270 overpayment. Section 6512(b)(1) empowers this Court to determine the existence and amount of any overpayment of tax to be refunded for a year before us. Under section 6512(b)(3)(B), however, we may not award a refund in a case such as this unless we determine that the refunded amount was paid "within the period which would be applicable under section 6511(b)(2) * * *, if on the date of the mailing of the notice of deficiency a claim had been filed (whether or not filed) stating the grounds upon which the Tax Court finds that there is an overpayment."

For taxable years ended before August 6, 1997, the period of section 6511(b)(2) that was applicable in a case such as this was the 2-year period of section 6511(b)(2)(B). *Commissioner v. Lundy*, 516 U.S. 235, 116 S. Ct. 647, 133 L. Ed. 2d 611 (1996); *see also Healer v. Commissioner*, 115 T.C. 316 (2000). For taxable years ended after August 5, 1997, however, the Taxpayer Relief Act of 1997, Pub. L. 105-34, sec. 1282(a) and (b), 111 Stat. 1037, added to section 6512(b) flush language that in certain cases lengthened this 2-year period. That language provides that the applicable period under section 6511(a) and (b)(2) is 3 years "In a case described in subparagraph (B) [of section 6512(b)(3)] where the date of the mailing of the notice of deficiency is during the third year after the due date (with extensions) for filing the return of tax and no return was filed before such date." Thus, in a case of a taxpayer such as petitioner who as of the date of the mailing of a notice of deficiency had not filed a Federal income tax return for a taxable year ended after August 5, 1997, but who has petitioned this Court seeking an overpayment for that year, section 6512(b) allows the taxpayer to receive that overpayment to the extent that it relates to amounts paid within 3 years of the notice of deficiency. *See also* H. Conf. Rept. 105-220, at 701 (1997), 1997-4 C.B. (Vol. 2) 1457, 2171:

> The House bill permits taxpayers who initially fail to file a return, but who receive a notice of deficiency and file suit to contest it in Tax Court during the third year after the return due date, to obtain a refund of excessive amounts paid within the 3-year period prior to the date of the deficiency notice.

Pursuant to section 6513(b)(1), the $270 that was withheld from petitioner's interest income was considered paid to the Commissioner by petitioner on April 15, 2000. Accordingly, in order for petitioner to prevail as to his 1999 overpayment, (1) the relevant notice of deficiency must have been mailed to him during the third year after the due date of his 1999 return and (2) he must have paid the $270 within 3 years of the mailing of the notice of deficiency. Given that the notice of deficiency was in fact mailed within the applicable period and that petitioner was considered during the applicable period to have paid the $270 to the Commissioner, we hold that petitioner is entitled to the $270 overpayment.

All of the parties' arguments have been considered, and those arguments not discussed herein have been found to be without merit. Accordingly,

Decision will be entered stating that there is no deficiency or addition to tax due from petitioner and that there is a $270 overpayment due to petitioner for 1999.

Recall that the Supreme Court's decision in *Lundy* involved a Tax Court overpayment claim. Prior to *Lundy*, courts decided a few cases in which the taxpayer did not file a timely return; subsequently filed a first return for the year claiming a refund; and upon denial of the claim, litigated the issue of timeliness of the claim in a refund court. *See, e.g.,* Miller v. United States, 38 F.3d 473 (9th Cir. 1994); Musser v. United States, 92-1 U.S.T.C. ¶ 50,245 (D. Alaska 1991) (unpublished), *aff'd*, 8 F.3d 28 (9th Cir. 1993) (unpublished); Arnzen v. IRS, 91-1 U.S.T.C. ¶ 50,020 (W.D. Wash. 1990). Does *Lundy*, coupled with the amendment to section 6512 discussed above, provide the limitations period applicable in those cases? What *should* the statutory period be in those cases, two years or three years?

For a while, the IRS had argued for a two-year period, and *Miller*, cited above, supported that view. The IRS subsequently reversed course, issuing a Chief Counsel Notice stating that it disagreed with *Miller* and would no longer rely on it to deny refund claims. *See* Chief Counsel Notice 2001-19, *reprinted at* 2003 TNT 126-13 (July 1, 2003). In a subsequent Ninth Circuit case, in line with the Chief Counsel Notice, both the government and the taxpayer argued to the Ninth Circuit that the court should not follow *Miller*. Omohundro v. United States, 300 F.3d 1065, 1067 (9th Cir. 2002) (*per curiam*). Thus, an important issue on appeal was the binding effect of *Miller* on the *Omohundro* panel.

In *Omohundro*, the court stated, "[w]e are not bound by the decision of a prior panel if a subsequent en banc decision, Supreme Court decision, or legislation has undermined it." *Id.* at 1067. There might not seem to have been such intervening activity with respect to Code section 6511, the limitations period on refund claims. However, in *Miller*, the Ninth Circuit had not addressed Revenue Ruling 76-511, 1976-2 C.B. 428, which provided for a three-year period of limitations on a refund claim made on a delinquent return. In *Omohundro*, the court found that the post-*Miller* United States Supreme Court decision in *United States v. Mead Corp.*, 533 U.S. 218 (2001), which held that courts must provide the level of deference set forth in *Skidmore v. Swift & Co.*, 323 U.S. 134 (1944), to a Customs Service tariff ruling, which the Ninth Circuit found "closely akin to an IRS revenue ruling," justified reconsideration of *Miller*.[16] *Omohundro*, 300 F.3d at 1067. The court therefore ruled in favor of Mrs. Omohundro, applying a three-year statute of limitations to the delinquent return claiming a refund.

[2] Applying Section 7502 to Delinquent Returns

Reading Assignment: I.R.C. § 7502(a).

If a return is filed late but the refund claim on it is arguably timely (because its deadline is so much later), can the mailbox rule in section 7502 apply to only the claim? During 2000, the Second and Eighth Circuits split on this issue. *Compare* Weisbart v. U.S. Dept. of Treasury, 222 F.3d 93 (2d Cir. 2000), *acq.*, AOD CC-2000-09 (applying section 7502), *with* Anastasoff v. United States, 223 F.3d 898 (8th Cir. 2000) (refusing to apply section 7502). *Anastasoff* was vacated as moot because the IRS conceded the issue. *See* Anastasoff v. United States, 235 F.3d 1054 (8th Cir. 2000). Subsequently, the IRS issued new, final regulations under section 7502 that treat a claim for refund made on a late-filed income tax return as timely made if the postmark date is timely. An example provides:

> (i) Taxpayer A, an individual, mailed his 2001 Form 1040, "U.S. Individual Income Tax Return," on April 15, 2005, claiming a refund of amounts paid through withholding during 2001. The date of the postmark on the envelope containing the return and claim for refund is April 15, 2005. The return and claim for refund are received by the Internal Revenue Service (IRS) on April 18, 2005. Amounts withheld in 2001 exceeded A's tax liability for 2001 and are treated as paid on April 15, 2002, pursuant to section 6513.
>
> (ii) Even though the date of the postmark on the envelope is after the due date of the return, the claim for refund and the late filed return are treated as filed on the postmark date. . . . Accordingly, the return will be treated as filed on April 15, 2005. In addition, the claim for refund will be treated as timely filed on April 15, 2005. *Further, the entire amount of the refund attributable to withholding is allowable as a refund under section 6511(b)(2)(A).*

Treas. Reg. § 301.7502-1(f)(3) (emphasis added).[17]

---

[16] The level of deference courts accord to Revenue Rulings is discussed in Chapter 2.

[17] The last sentence in (ii) implied that the IRS might no longer argue that a two-year limitations period applies to refund claims made on delinquent returns under *Miller v. United States*, 38 F.3d 473 (9th Cir. 1994). As discussed above, the IRS confirmed that in early 2001 (shortly after issuing the section 7502 regulations), in Chief Counsel Notice 2001-19.

[E] Tolling of Statutes of Limitations on Refund Claims

Reading Assignment: I.R.C. § 6511(h).

The refund statutes of limitations are applied fairly strictly to cut off untimely claims. That can create difficulties in circumstances in which taxpayers are incapacitated or otherwise unable to act within the requisite time period. Prior to the United States Supreme Court's decision in *United States v. Brockamp*, 519 U.S. 347 (1997), and Congress's subsequent enactment of Code section 6511(h), it was unclear whether the statute of limitations on refund claims could be tolled for equitable reasons where the taxpayer had a disability that prevented the filing of a timely refund claim. In *Brockamp*, the Court addressed the situations of two different taxpayers. One of the situations was as follows:

> In April 1984, Mr. McGill, who was 93 years old at the time, mailed a check to the Internal Revenue Service ("IRS") for $7,000, along with an application for an automatic extension of time to file his 1983 income tax return. He made no indication of his reason for sending the $7,000. Despite his extension request, Mr. McGill never filed an income tax return for 1983. * * * Mr. McGill died intestate on November 7, 1988 at the age of 98. During the administration of his estate, Mrs. Brockamp discovered the $7,000 payment and requested a refund. In a letter to the IRS, Mrs. Brockamp characterized her father as "senile" and stated that he had mistakenly sent the check for $7,000 rather than $700."

Brockamp v. United States, 67 F.3d 260 (9th Cir. 1995), *rev'd*, 519 U.S. 347 (1997).

The basic facts of *Scott*, the companion case, are these:

> In the early 1980s, Nicholas Scott began to experience severe difficulties resulting from his alcohol abuse, including multiple citations for driving under the influence of alcohol and the loss of his job. He turned over power of attorney for his financial affairs to his father. In 1984, pursuant to the power of attorney, Mr. Scott's father made a number of federal tax deposits on Mr. Scott's behalf. Then, after Mr. Scott revoked the power of attorney, he himself made a final estimated tax payment in January 1985. Altogether, the payments made toward Mr. Scott's 1984 taxes totalled $30,096. In actuality, Mr. Scott had no tax liability that year. Mr. Scott filed tax returns for the 1984–88 tax years on November 29, 1989 and claimed a refund of $30,096 plus interest.

Scott v. United States, 95-2 U.S.T.C. ¶ 50,557 (9th Cir. 1995), *rev'd sub nom.* United States v. Brockamp, 519 U.S. 347 (1997).

In the consolidated cases, the Supreme Court considered whether equitable tolling applied to the statute of limitations on refund claims under Code section 6511. The Court concluded that it did not, explaining, in part:

> Section 6511 sets forth its time limitations in unusually emphatic form. Ordinarily limitations statutes use fairly simple language, which one can often plausibly read as containing an implied "equitable tolling" exception. *See, e.g.,* 42 U.S.C. § 2000e-16(c) (requiring suit for employment discrimination to be filed "within 90 days of receipt of notice of final [EEOC] action . . . "). But § 6511 uses language that is not simple. It sets forth its limitations in a highly detailed technical manner, that, linguistically speaking, cannot easily be read as containing implicit exceptions. Moreover, § 6511 reiterates its limitations several times in several different ways. * * *
>
> The Tax Code reemphasizes the point when it says that refunds that do not comply with these limitations "shall be considered erroneous," § 6514, and specifies procedures for the Government's recovery of any such "erroneous" refund payment. §§ 6532(b), 7405. In addition, § 6511 sets forth explicit excep-

> tions to its basic time limits, and those very specific exceptions do not include "equitable tolling." * * *
>
> To read an "equitable tolling" provision into these provisions, one would have to assume an implied exception for tolling virtually every time a number appears. To do so would work a kind of linguistic havoc. Moreover, such an interpretation would require tolling, not only procedural limitations, but also substantive limitations on the amount of recovery — a kind of tolling for which we have found no direct precedent. Section 6511's detail, its technical language, the iteration of the limitations in both procedural and substantive forms, and the explicit listing of exceptions, taken together, indicate to us that Congress did not intend courts to read other unmentioned, open-ended, "equitable" exceptions into the statute that it wrote. There are no counter-indications. Tax law, after all, is not normally characterized by case-specific exceptions reflecting individualized equities.

Brockamp, 519 U.S. at 350–52.

After *Brockamp* was decided, Congress enacted Code section 6511(h) as part of the IRS Reform Act. What is the policy behind section 6511(h)? What effects might it have on refund litigation?

In Revenue Procedure 99-21, 1999-1 C.B. 786, the IRS explained how a taxpayer may obtain "equitable tolling" of the statute of limitations on refund claims under section 6511(h) based on a financial disability. It provides, in part:

> Unless otherwise provided in IRS forms and instructions, the following statements are to be submitted with a claim for credit or refund of tax to claim financial disability for purposes of § 6511(h).
>
> (1) a written statement by a physician (as defined in § 1861(r)(1) of the Social Security Act, 42 U.S.C. § 1395x), qualified to make the determination, that sets forth:
>
> (a) the name and a description of the taxpayer's physical or mental impairment;
>
> (b) the physician's medical opinion that the physical or mental impairment prevented the taxpayer from managing the taxpayer's financial affairs;
>
> (c) the physician's medical opinion that the physical or mental impairment was or can be expected to result in death, or that it has lasted (or can be expected to last) for a continuous period of not less than 12 months;
>
> (d) to the best of the physician's knowledge, the specific time period during which the taxpayer was prevented by such physical or mental impairment from managing the taxpayer's financial affairs; and
>
> (e) the following certification, signed by the physician:
>
> I hereby certify that, to the best of my knowledge and belief, the above representations are true, correct, and complete.
>
> (2) A written statement by the person signing the claim for credit or refund that no person, including the taxpayer's spouse, was authorized to act on behalf of the taxpayer in financial matters during the period described in paragraph (1)(d) of this section. Alternatively, if a person was authorized to act on behalf of the taxpayer in financial matters during any part of the period described in paragraph (1)(d), the beginning and ending dates of the period of time the person was so authorized.

Id. at § 4. What do you think the purpose of these requirements is?

Based on the language of section 6511(h) and Revenue Procedure 99-21, in what kinds of cases will equitable tolling apply? In *Brosi v. Commissioner*, 120 T.C. 5 (2003), the Tax Court refused to allow equitable tolling of the statute of limitations on refund claims under Code section 6511(h) where the taxpayer had not been financially disabled but rather was caring for his mother as well as working full-time as a pilot. In *Henry v. United States*, 2007-1 U.S.T.C. ¶ 50,359 (N.D. Tex. 2006), a district court denied relief under section 6511(h) where the taxpayer produced letters from two doctors, neither of whom had treated her during the relevant time period, and neither of which contained a medical opinion that the taxpayer's illness prevented her from managing her financial affairs during the period in question. The court found affidavits from herself, her children, and her accountant insufficient to comply with the physician's opinion requirement of the Revenue Procedure.

By contrast, the IRS upheld equitable tolling in Chief Counsel Advice 200210015, where the taxpayer-husband, who suffered from cancer, "provided statements from two doctors who stated that [he] was physically and mentally incapable of handling his financial affairs between 1996 and 2000. He also provided his own statement that during his disability, no person, including [his wife], was authorized to act on his behalf in financial matters." *Id.* The IRS further found that "The IRS cannot deny section 6511(h) relief to [taxpayer-husband] merely because the spouses filed a joint return and no relief is available to [taxpayer-wife]. Each spouse's claim must be separately considered." *Id.*

[F] The Statutory Mitigation Provisions and Equitable Recoupment

[1] Statutory Mitigation of the Statute of Limitations

Reading Assignment: I.R.C. §§ 1311, 1312(1), 1313(a)(1), 1314(b).

Under limited circumstances, the expiration of the statute of limitations on refund claims may not bar the claim. For example, what if, in Year 6, the taxpayer loses a court case and is required by the court to include in income for Year 1 an amount that the taxpayer had already included in Year 2: Can the taxpayer claim a refund of the amount paid with respect to Year 2 if the statute of limitations on refund claims for that year has already expired? Recall the statutory mitigation provisions discussed in Chapter 7. In Chapter 7, the discussion focused on the *IRS's* reliance on these provisions to reopen a barred year to *make an assessment.* The mitigation provisions also apply to allow the *taxpayer* to reopen a barred year to *claim a refund* in order to avoid, for example, inclusion of the same income amount in two different tax years.

What is the time limit that the taxpayer has to file a refund claim in the circumstance described above? Code section 1314(b) provides, in part "The adjustment authorized in section 1311(a) . . . shall be made by . . . refunding or crediting[] the amount thereof in the same manner as if it were . . . an overpayment claimed by such taxpayer . . . for the taxable year or years with respect to which an amount is ascertained under subsection (a), and as if on the date of the determination, one year remained before the expiration of the periods of limitation upon . . . filing claim for refund for such taxable year or years."

One commentator provides the following example:

> [A]ssume that a cash basis taxpayer's last paycheck from his employer for 1995 is lost in the mail. The taxpayer receives a replacement in March 1996, after she has received her W-2 statement of wages for 1995. The W-2 statement was promptly sent to her accountant in 1995 without telling the accountant of her failure to receive the lost check that year. The taxpayer's return for 1995 thus includes an amount that she did not receive and which has thus been erroneously reported. When the taxpayer files her own return for 1996, she does

> not report the amount of the replacement check for 1995. Because the check was received in 1996, however, it is income for 1996. Her failure to report this amount is discovered by the IRS before April 15, 2000 — a timely discovery as to 1996, but too late for the taxpayer to file a claim for a refund of the same amount reported in 1995. Once there has been a determination of the inconsistent tax treatment of the same item in two different tax years, the taxpayer has one year to seek a reopening of 1995 to claim a refund for the amount of tax she erroneously overpaid.

John A. Lynch, Jr., *Income Tax Statute of Limitations: Sixty Years of Mitigation — Enough, Already!!*, 51 S.C. L. Rev. 62, 70 (1999).

[2] Equitable Recoupment

In situations in which the statutory mitigation provisions do not afford the taxpayer relief, a doctrine known as "equitable recoupment," discussed in Chapter 7, might help the taxpayer.

> "Equitable recoupment" has been utilized in tax cases to allow one party to recover a time-barred claim by offsetting it against an amount owed to the other party. It is based upon the concept that "one taxable event should not be taxed twice, once on a correct theory and once on an incorrect theory . . . and that to avoid this happening the statute of limitations will be waived."

Mann v. United States, 552 F. Supp. 1132, 1135 (N.D. Tex. 1982) (*quoting* Minskoff v. United States, 490 F.2d 1283, 1285 (6th Cir. 1974)). In 2006, Congress amended Code section 6214 to provide that "the Tax Court may apply the doctrine of equitable recoupment to the same extent that it is available in civil tax cases before the district courts of the United States and the United States Court of Federal Claims." I.R.C. § 6214(b).

In a refund action, it would generally be the IRS that would assert the defense of equitable recoupment to reduce or eliminate the taxpayer's refund. The IRS would argue that a time-barred deficiency arose out of the same transaction. For example, the amount recoverable by an estate in a suit for refund of income taxes might be subject to offset by an amount of additional estate tax, otherwise barred by the statute of limitations on assessment, based on the theory adopted in the income tax suit.

Dalm v. United States, 494 U.S. 596, 598 (1990), held that equitable recoupment cannot serve as an independent basis for a refund suit. The Court explained its holding as follows, drawing on its prior equitable recoupment decisions, which help explain the operation of the doctrine:

> In her complaint, Dalm invoked 28 U.S.C. § 1346(a)(1) (1982 ed.), under which a district court has jurisdiction over a "civil action against the United States for the recovery of any internal-revenue tax alleged to have been erroneously or illegally assessed or collected, or any penalty claimed to have been collected without authority or any sum alleged to have been excessive or in any manner wrongfully collected under the internal-revenue laws." * * *
>
> There is no doubt that Dalm failed to comply with the[] statutory requirements [for refund suits]. The Schriers [who gave Dalm the gift] filed their gift tax return and Dalm paid the gift tax on the 1976 transfer in December 1976. She paid the penalties and interest on that tax in March 1977. Dalm did not file her claim for refund of the gift tax until November 1984, long after the limitations period expired. Under the plain language of §§ 6511(a) and 7422(a), the District Court was barred from entertaining her suit for a refund of the tax.

B

The Court of Appeals did not contest this analysis; indeed, it recognized that "[t]here is no statutory basis for permitting the recovery of a tax overpayment after the statute of limitations has expired." 867 F.2d, at 308. Despite the lack of a statutory basis for recovery, the court concluded that the doctrine of equitable recoupment permits Dalm to maintain an action to recover the overpaid gift tax. We disagree.

The doctrine of equitable recoupment was first addressed by us in our opinion in *Bull v. United States*, [295 U.S. 247 (1935)]. There, the dispute centered on whether partnership distributions received by a decedent's estate after his death were subject to estate tax or income tax. After an audit, the executor of the estate included the sums in the estate tax return and paid the estate tax in 1920 and 1921. In 1925, the Commissioner of Internal Revenue notified the estate of a deficiency in the estate's income tax for the 1920 tax year, contending that the same distributions upon which estate tax had been paid should have been treated as income. The Commissioner, however, did not give credit for the estate tax earlier paid on the value of the distributions.

That same year, the estate petitioned to the Board of Tax Appeals for a redetermination of the deficiency. After the Board sustained the Commissioner's determination, the estate paid the additional income tax and filed a claim for refund of the income tax paid. The Commissioner rejected the claim, and, in September 1930, the executor sued in the Court of Claims for a refund of the income tax.[n.4] In his petition to the Court of Claims, the executor argued (1) that the amount taxed was not income, so that the estate was entitled to a refund of the entire amount of income tax paid; and (2) alternatively, if the amount taxed was income, the Government should credit against the income tax due the overpayment of estate tax, plus interest, attributable to the inclusion of the amount in the taxable estate. The Court of Claims rejected both arguments.

We reversed, holding that the executor was entitled to a credit against the income tax deficiency in the amount of the overpayment of estate tax, with interest. 295 U.S., at 263. We began by acknowledging that the executor had not filed a claim for refund of the estate tax within the limitations period, and that any action for refund of the tax was now barred. *Id.*, at 259, 260–61. "If nothing further had occurred, Congressional action would have been the sole avenue of redress." *Id.*, at 261.

What did occur, however, was that after the limitations period on the estate tax had run, the Government assessed a deficiency in the estate's income tax based upon the same taxable event, and the deficiency became the subject of litigation between the estate and the Government. We reasoned that a tax assessment is in essence an assertion by the sovereign that the taxpayer owes a debt to it; but that, because "taxes are the life-blood of government," it was necessary for the tax assessed to be collected prior to adjudication of whether the assessment was erroneous or unlawful. As a result,

> "the usual procedure for the recovery of debts is reversed in the field of taxation. Payment precedes defense, and the burden of proof, normally on the claimant, is shifted to the taxpayer. . . . But these reversals of the

---

[n.4] Before the enactment of the Revenue Act of 1926, there was no direct review of Board of Tax Appeals decisions. As a result, a taxpayer who lost in proceedings before the Board was permitted to sue in district court or the Court of Claims for a refund after payment of the deficiency. In effect, the refund suit, although nominally a separate proceeding, was a mechanism by which taxpayers could obtain review of Board decisions. *See Old Colony Trust Co.*, *supra*, at 721–22; Ferguson, *Jurisdictional Problems in Federal Tax Controversies*, 48 Iowa L. Rev. 312, 350–351 (1963). The Revenue Act of 1926 put an end to this circuitous process. * * *

normal process of collecting a claim cannot obscure the fact that after all what is being accomplished is the recovery of a just debt owed the sovereign."

Id., at 260.

Under our reasoning, the proceeding between the executor and the Government was in substance an attempt by the Government to recover a debt from the estate. The debt was the income tax that was owed, even though in fact it already had been paid. Had the Government followed the "usual procedure" of recovering debts by instituting an action at law for the income tax owed, the executor would have been able to defend against the suit by "demanding recoupment of the amount mistakenly collected as estate tax and wrongfully retained." *Id.*, at 261 (citing United States v. State Bank, 96 U.S. 30 (1878)).

> "If the claim for income tax deficiency had been the subject of a suit, any counter demand for recoupment of the overpayment of estate tax could have been asserted by way of defense and credit obtained notwithstanding the statute of limitations had barred an independent suit against the Government therefor. This is because recoupment is in the nature of a defense arising out of some feature of the transaction upon which the plaintiff's action is grounded. Such a defense is never barred by the statute of limitations so long as the main action itself is timely." 295 U.S. at 262.

We found it immaterial that, rather than the Government having to sue to collect the income tax, the executor was required first to pay it and then seek a refund. "This procedural requirement does not obliterate his substantial right to rely on his cross-demand for credit of the amount which if the United States had sued him for income tax he could have recouped against his liability on that score." *Id.* at 263.[n.5]

Dalm contends that the only distinction between her case and *Bull* is the "meaningless procedural distinction" that her claim of equitable recoupment is raised in a separate suit for refund of gift tax, after she had litigated the income tax deficiency, while in *Bull* the claim of equitable recoupment of the estate tax was litigated as part of a suit for refund of that tax alleged to be inconsistent with the estate tax. A distinction that has jurisdiction as its central concept is not meaningless. In *Bull*, the executor sought equitable recoupment of the estate tax in an action for refund of income tax, over which it was undisputed that the Court of Claims had jurisdiction. *See* n.4, *supra*. All that was at issue was whether the Court of Claims, in the interests of equity, could adjust the income tax owed to the Government to take account of an estate tax paid in error but which the executor could not recover in a separate refund action. Here, Dalm does not seek to invoke equitable recoupment in determining her income tax liability; she has already litigated that liability without raising a claim of equitable recoupment and is foreclosed from relitigating it now. *See* § 6512(a). She seeks to invoke equitable recoupment only in a separate action for refund of gift tax, an action for which there is no statutory authorization by reason of the bar of the limitations statute.

It is instructive to consider what the facts in *Bull* would have to be if Dalm's contention is correct that her case is identical to *Bull* in all material respects. The executor in *Bull* would have litigated the income tax liability, without raising a claim of equitable recoupment in the Board of Tax Appeals and/or in

---

[n.5] Since *Bull*, we have emphasized that a claim of equitable recoupment will lie only where the Government has taxed a single transaction, item, or taxable event under two inconsistent theories. *See Rothensies v. Electric Storage Battery Co.*, 329 U.S. 296, 299–300 (1946); *cf. Stone v. White*, 301 U.S. 532 (1937) (permitting the Government to invoke equitable recoupment as a defense against a claim for refund of income tax paid by a trust where there was a complete identity of interest between the trust and the beneficiary who had received the income, and a claim against the beneficiary for the income tax was then barred).

> the Court of Claims, with the Government winning in each forum. Then, having exhausted his avenues of litigating the income tax liability and paid the tax, the executor would have filed a claim for refund of the estate tax with the Commissioner, asserting equitable recoupment, as the basis for the refund, with the Commissioner rejecting it as untimely. At that point, the executor would have brought suit for refund of the estate tax in the Court of Claims after the statute of limitations had run. Had the case come to us with those facts, we would have faced the issue presented here whether the court in which the taxpayer was seeking a refund was barred from entertaining the suit. We can say with assurance that we were not presented with this issue in *Bull* and did not consider it. Even had the issue been raised, *Bull* itself suggests that we would have rejected Dalm's argument out of hand. *See Bull*, 295 U.S. at 259 ("The fact that the petitioner relied on the Commissioner's assessment for estate tax, and believed the inconsistent claim of deficiency of income tax was of no force, cannot avail to toll the statute of limitations, which forbade the bringing of any action in 1930 for refund of estate tax payments made in 1921.").
>
> The only other decision in which we have upheld a claim or defense premised upon the doctrine of equitable recoupment is consistent with our analysis today. In *Stone v. White*, 301 U.S. 532 (1937), a trust had paid the income it received from the corpus to its sole beneficiary and also paid the tax due on the income. After the statute of limitations governing the Government's right to collect the income tax from the beneficiary had run, the trust filed a timely suit seeking a refund of the income tax paid on the theory that the beneficiary, not the trust, was liable for the tax. We held that, given the identity of interest between the beneficiary and the trust, the Government could invoke equitable recoupment to assert its now-barred claim against the beneficiary as a defense to the trust's timely claim for a refund. *Id.*, at 537–539. As in *Bull*, there was no dispute that the court in which we allowed the doctrine of equitable recoupment to be raised had jurisdiction over the underlying action: the trust's timely action for a refund of income tax.
>
> In sum, our decisions in *Bull* and *Stone* stand only for the proposition that a party litigating a tax claim in a timely proceeding may, in that proceeding, seek recoupment of a related, and inconsistent, but now time-barred tax claim relating to the same transaction. In both cases, there was no question but that the courts in which the refund actions were brought had jurisdiction. To date, we have not allowed equitable recoupment to be the sole basis for jurisdiction.

Dalm, 494 U.S. at 601–08.

Justice Stevens, joined by Justices Brennan and Marshall, dissented in *Dalm*, finding the case indistinguishable from *Bull*. The dissent argued:

> Ignoring both the policies underlying the statute of limitations and the principles of just conduct underlying *Bull*, the Court confronts respondent with the majestic voices of "jurisdiction" and "sovereign immunity" — voices that seem to have a haunting charm for this Court's current majority.
>
> The Court that decided the *Bull* case reasoned not in obeisance to these siren-like voices but rather under the reliable guidance of a bright star in our jurisprudence: the presumption that for every right, there should be a remedy. *See Marbury v. Madison*, 1 Cranch 137, 162–63 (1803). Without any sacrifice of technical propriety, the *Bull* Court could have found that the lapse of time had divested the Court of Claims of jurisdiction to allow the taxpayer credit for the previously paid estate tax. It easily avoided that unjust result, however, by relying on the special features of the tax collection procedures that impose burdens on the taxpayer unlike those imposed on ordinary litigants. The net effect of its analysis was to hold that in a refund action based on the multiple and inconsistent taxation of a single transaction, the taxpayer is to be treated as

> though she were the defendant even though she is actually the plaintiff.

Id. at 616–17 (Stevens, J., dissenting).

How does the doctrine of equitable recoupment described in *Dalm* differ from the doctrine of setoff, which was applied by the Supreme Court in *Lewis v. Reynolds*, reproduced above in Section 10.02[C]?

PROBLEMS

1. Bob mailed his Year 1 return to the IRS on April 3, Year 2, along with a payment of $2,000. On March 1, Year 4, Bob filed a refund claim for $1,000, specifying that the reason for the claim is that he erroneously included excludable damages from an age discrimination lawsuit in gross income. On November 1, Year 4, the IRS denied the claim, and Bob plans to bring suit in the local U.S. District Court. However, Bob has since realized that the damages were includible in gross income because they were not received on account of physical injury. However, he believes that he is nonetheless entitled to a $700 refund as a result of medical expenses relating to psychiatric treatment. Assuming that Bob's suit would be timely, is there any procedural barrier to Bob's litigation of this issue in order to prove his entitlement to a refund?

2. Adrian has received a notice of deficiency from the IRS in the amount of $5,000 with respect to his Year 1 tax year. After receiving the notice, and within 45 days of the date on the notice, Adrian mailed the IRS a $5,000 check with only the notation "Year 1 taxes" on the memo line of the check.
    A. Is Adrian still entitled to petition the Tax Court in response to the notice of deficiency?
    B. How would it affect Adrian's rights if instead he had printed "deposit — Year 1 taxes" on the memo line of his check?
    C. Would your answer to Part A differ if Adrian had mailed in $5,000 after receiving a 30-day letter but before receiving the notice of deficiency?
    D. Assume that Adrian does not petition the Tax Court. If the statute of limitations on assessment expires after Adrian's remittance of the $5,000 without an assessment by the IRS, is the IRS obligated to refund the $5,000 to Adrian?

3. Joanne filed her Year 1 return on April 1, Year 2. She owed $500, which she mailed with her return. The rest of her tax liability, $7,000, was covered by withholding. After examining her return a few months later, she realized that she made an error that may entitle her to a refund of $1,000.
    A. How can Joanne claim a refund of the $1,000?
    B. When is the last day she can claim a refund?
    C. How, if at all, would your answer to Part B change if Joanne had filed her return on April 15, Year 2 instead?
    D. How, if at all, would your answer to Part B change if Joanne had granted the IRS a one-year extension of the statute of limitations on assessment with respect to Year 1?
    E. Assume that Joanne filed a timely refund claim on July 8, Year 3.
        i. If the IRS never responds to her claim, when is the first day she can file a refund suit? When is the last day?
        ii. Assume the IRS denied Joanne's refund claim on January 3, Year 4. When is the first day she can file a refund suit? When is the last day?

4. Mary filed her Year 1 tax return on May 1, Year 2, without having obtained an extension of time to file. $10,000 of tax had been withheld from her wages. She computed a tax liability of $11,000, so she mailed a check for $1,000 with the Year

1 return. On April 20, Year 5, the IRS mailed Mary a notice of deficiency, which she received on April 25, Year 5, reflecting the Commissioner's determination of a deficiency of $500. The $500 deficiency is attributable to income allegedly received by Mary and not reported on the return. Mary believes that she does not owe the $500 and that she is in fact entitled to a refund of $700 of the amounts already paid.

A. Assume that Mary filed a Tax Court petition on May 1, Year 5, contesting the notice of deficiency and claiming that she made an overpayment of $700. Can the Tax Court order the IRS to refund $700 to Mary if the court agrees with her on the merits?

B. Assume Mary paid the $500 deficiency on May 1, Year 5.

i. If Mary wishes to pursue a refund in federal district court of the $1,200 (the $500 paid in response to the notice plus the $700 alleged overpayment), when is the last day on which she can file a timely refund claim with the IRS to be entitled to pursue a refund of at least some of the $1,200?

ii. Assume that Mary filed a timely claim for refund only of the $500, and, after receiving a notice of disallowance of her claim, filed a timely suit for refund of the $500 on June 1, Year 6. The IRS has not only contested Mary's entitlement to a refund of the $500, but also has counterclaimed for $800 based on the disallowance of certain deductions. If the court enters a decision on May 5, Year 7 in Mary's favor on the $500 issue and in the IRS's favor on the $800 issue, what amount, if any, may each side collect from the other?

5. Dan negligently failed to mail his Year 1 return until May 10, Year 4. When filed, the return reflected a tax liability of $3,000 for Year 1, and wage withholding credits of $2,500 (consistent with the Form W-2 included with the return). Accordingly, he mailed a $500 payment in with the return, which the IRS received with the return on May 13, Year 4. On April 1, Year 7, the IRS mailed Dan a notice of deficiency in the amount of $1,000 based on income Dan allegedly received but did not report.

A. Assume that Dan failed to respond in any way to the notice of deficiency, and the IRS assesses the $1,000 deficiency on July 15, Year 7. Is the assessment timely?

B. Alternatively, assume instead that Dan responded to the notice by filing a petition in the United States Tax Court on April 30, Year 7. He alleges never having received the income referenced in the notice of deficiency. In addition, he alleges that he is entitled to additional deductions entitling him to a refund of $700. Assuming that the Tax Court agrees with Dan on the merits, does the Tax Court have jurisdiction to order the IRS to award Dan a $700 refund?

C. Do both the statute of limitations on assessment of a $1,000 deficiency for Dan's Year 1 tax year and the statute of limitations for Dan to claim a refund of $700 with respect to his Year 1 tax year expire on the same day? Is your answer affected by whether or not Dan petitions the Tax Court?

6. June is a recovering addict who, over the past few years, has been through several outpatient treatment programs designed to help those with substance abuse problems. She has refrained from using illegal drugs since January 1 of this year. June recently realized that she had neglected to file her tax returns for 1997 through last year, although she was employed for portions of each year and is owed a refund for each year. She explains that she was unable to timely file those returns because she was incapacitated by her drug addiction. No one was authorized to act on her behalf with respect to her financial matters. June has

never been contacted by the IRS. Can she claim a refund for any of those years, or has the statute of limitations expired on all of them?

7. Tara Green asks your assistance in claiming a refund from the IRS. After timely filing her Year 1 Form 1040 by mail in March of Year 2, she realized that she had forgotten to deduct $6,000 in home mortgage interest, real property taxes of $2,000, and state income taxes of $4,000 she had paid in Year 1. (She had not itemized her deductions on her original return, but instead took the standard deduction. She also correctly claimed one personal exemption.) She has no other deductions or income items. Tara is single, has no dependents, and had adjusted gross income of $80,000 in Year 1, consisting entirely of salary. $10,000 had been withheld from Tara's wages for federal income tax purposes, and she had paid the remainder of her tax liability with her return. She still resides at 125 Main St., Wayne, NJ 07470, where she lived when she filed the return in question. Her Social Security number is 222-33-4444 and her telephone number is (973) 264-9872. She did not and does not wish to make a Presidential Election Campaign Fund designation. Draft Tara's refund claim.

Chapter 11

TAX LITIGATION AND SETTLEMENT OF TAX CASES

§ 11.01 INTRODUCTION

Chapters 8 through 10 discussed litigation in the U.S. Tax Court, the federal district courts, and the Court of Federal Claims, which are the three principal courts that have trial-level jurisdiction over most federal tax cases. *See* I.R.C. § 6213; 28 U.S.C. §§ 1346(a)(1), 1491(a)(1). The Tax Court has jurisdiction over both tax "deficiencies" and overpayment claims that arise out of the same tax year for which the taxpayer received a notice of deficiency. I.R.C. §§ 6213(a); 6512(b)(1). The district courts and Court of Federal Claims share jurisdiction over "refund" actions. 28 U.S.C. § 1346(a)(1). As explained below, the United States Bankruptcy Courts can also consider tax claims that arise in the context of a bankruptcy proceeding.

Although Chapters 8 through 10 focused on tax litigation concerning deficiencies and refunds, it is important to note that the Tax Court, Court of Federal Claims, and district courts also have jurisdiction over certain other types of tax claims. For example, the Tax Court has jurisdiction over all Collection Due Process litigation, as discussed in Chapter 16. *See* I.R.C. § 6330(d)(1). The Tax Court and the District Court for the District of Columbia all have jurisdiction over disclosure actions under section 6110 of the Code, discussed in Chapter 6. *See* I.R.C. § 6110(f)(4)(A). The Tax Court, Court of Federal Claims, and the District Court for the District of Columbia all have declaratory judgment jurisdiction over cases involving a determination by the IRS with respect to the tax-exempt status of various types of organizations. *See* I.R.C. § 7428(a).

After discussing the bankruptcy courts' jurisdiction over federal tax issues, the chapter considers the differences in the litigation fora from a strategic perspective, as the taxpayer often will have a choice of forum. The chapter then considers various procedural issues that are not necessarily specific to a particular forum: the burden of proof in tax cases; settlement of litigated tax cases; awards of administrative fees and litigation costs; the treatment of issues arising in multiple tax cases; the government's use of summonses during discovery; litigation sanctions; and the controversy over unpublished opinions.

§ 11.02 BANKRUPTCY COURT JURISDICTION OVER FEDERAL TAX CLAIMS

Under the Bankruptcy Code, 11 U.S.C. § 101 *et seq.*, the filing of a bankruptcy petition by a debtor creates an "estate" of the debtor's property. *Id.* § 541(a). The bankruptcy petition also triggers an automatic stay prohibiting a wide variety of acts, including collection of taxes, *id.* § 362(a)(6), and "the commencement or continuation of a proceeding before the United States Tax Court concerning" the debtor, *id.* § 362(a)(8). The automatic stay remains in effect until the earliest of three events: (1) the case is closed; (2) the case is dismissed; or (3) if the case concerns an individual and is under Chapter 7 of the Bankruptcy Code, or is under Chapters 11 or 13 of the Bankruptcy Code, the time a discharge is granted or denied. *Id.* § 362(c)(2).

Once the taxpayer files a bankruptcy petition, the bankruptcy court has jurisdiction to "determine the amount or legality of any tax, any fine or penalty relating to a tax, or any addition to tax, . . . whether or not previously assessed, whether or not paid, and whether or not contested before and adjudicated by a judicial or administrative tribunal of competent jurisdiction." *Id.* § 505(a)(1). However, the bankruptcy court may not determine a tax which was "contested before and adjudicated by a judicial or administrative tribunal of competent jurisdiction before the commencement of the case under this title," *id.* § 505(a)(2)(A).[1]

Although the IRS may issue a notice of deficiency during the automatic stay,[2] a taxpayer cannot file a Tax Court petition during the pendency of the stay. *See* Moody v. Commissioner, 95 T.C. 655 (1990); McClamma v. Commissioner, 76 T.C. 754, 757 (1981). However, a party in interest can file a motion in the bankruptcy court to lift the stay to allow litigation in another court to go forward. 11 U.S.C. § 362(d). On such a petition by the taxpayer-debtor or the IRS, the bankruptcy court determines whether to decide the tax issues itself or to release the stay to allow the taxpayer to petition the Tax Court. "While both a bankruptcy court and a tax court may have jurisdiction to determine tax matters, the bankruptcy court acts as 'traffic cop,' determining which of the courts with jurisdiction ultimately will decide the claim." Stephen W. Sather, *Tax Issues in Bankruptcy*, 25 St. Mary's L.J. 1364, 1400 (1994). As a result, the bankruptcy court has decided many complex federal tax issues.[3] Therefore, in a sense, the bankruptcy courts provide a fourth trial-level forum for federal tax cases, albeit not a forum a taxpayer chooses for that purpose.

§ 11.03 CHOICE OF FORUM

A taxpayer who receives a notice of deficiency and wishes to litigate can choose either (1) to timely petition the Tax Court or (2) to pay the deficiency, claim a refund, and follow up the claim with a timely suit in a federal district court or the Court of Federal Claims. If the taxpayer did not receive a notice of deficiency but wishes to litigate a refund claim, the taxpayer can choose between district court and the Court of Federal Claims. The following article highlights several of the differences among the fora:

David B. Porter, *Where Can You Litigate Your Federal Tax Case?*[4]

98 Tax Notes 558 (2003)

Historically, when a taxpayer had a controversy with the Internal Revenue Service that could not be resolved at the examination level, the taxpayer nearly always went to the Tax Court to seek relief. However, there have always been different options available to litigate a tax controversy. Today, those options are more important to examine and evaluate than in the past. This article explores the aspects of each of those options.

* * *

I. Alternatives for Tax Litigation

There are three places to litigate a tax controversy against the IRS: the U.S. Tax Court, U.S. District Court, and the Court of Federal Claims. Each has advantages and disadvantages.

---

[1] The bankruptcy court also may not determine entitlement to a tax refund until 120 days after the bankruptcy trustee properly requests the refund or the governmental unit makes a determination on the request. 11 U.S.C. § 505(a)(2)(B).

[2] The IRS uses a slightly different form for a notice of deficiency issued in bankruptcy than the sample notice included in Chapter 9.

[3] *See* Steve R. Johnson, *The Pheonix and the Perils of the Second Best: Why Heightened Appellate Deference to Tax Court Decisions is Undesirable*, 77 Or. L. Rev. 235, 241 & nn.22, 23 (1998).

[4]

A. U.S. Tax Court

Most tax disputes are resolved in the U.S. Tax Court. Located in Washington, it is composed of 19 judges, each appointed for a 15-year term. The judges hear only tax cases, and therefore they are presumed to be experts in the tax law. The court rides a "circuit," and judges regularly travel to major cities throughout the country where they conduct their trials. The taxpayer has the opportunity to designate a place of trial in whatever major city he or she chooses. The court will then come to the designated city and hold a trial session where a calendar of cases will be heard generally over a two-week period.

* * *

The pretrial discovery procedures in Tax Court are rather informal, and depositions are extraordinary. Settlement of a Tax Court case is negotiated with an IRS Appeals Officer, or closer to trial with the Area Counsel trial lawyer. A Tax Court trial is held before one judge without a jury. Before trial, the court requires the parties to stipulate or agree to all facts not in dispute. This process speeds up the trial and assists in the settlement of many cases prior to trial.

The Tax Court follows the Federal Rules of Evidence (applicable to trials without a jury in the District of Columbia). Some Tax Court judges are lenient in enforcing the rules and allowing the admission of evidence, presumably because the judge, not a jury, is the decisionmaker regarding both the facts and the law. The judge may allow evidence into the record, yet later rule that the evidence does not have much weight or is not credible, and the judge may therefore choose not to rely on it in the court's determination.

After trial, the Tax Court sets a briefing schedule, usually 90 days, and requires the parties to file briefs containing proposed findings of fact with citations to the record, and a legal argument. Thereafter, the court usually issues an opinion within a year of the trial. The Tax Court attempts to apply the tax law consistently throughout the country, regardless of the circuit or region where the trial occurs or the taxpayer lives. The losing party has the right to appeal to the Court of Appeals for the circuit where the taxpayer resides. (Further, the Golsen rule[5] requires the Tax Court to follow a Court of Appeals decision that is squarely on point and where the Tax Court decision will be appealed to that same Court of Appeals.)

B. U.S. District Court

As an alternative to filing in Tax Court, the taxpayer has the choice of suing in U.S. District Court. Significantly, the taxpayer must pay the tax first and then file a refund claim, while in Tax Court the tax need not be paid until after the case is concluded. This practical difference eliminates the U.S. District Court for many tax disputes.

The U.S. District Court is the general trial court for the federal judicial system. The district court is located in a certain geographic region and hears cases only from within that district. District judges are appointed to the bench for life. They hear a wide variety of cases that may range from civil employment law to criminal drug conspiracies. The district judge may or may not be a specialist in tax law.

Again, the taxpayer must pay the proposed tax deficiency first, before going to court. * * *

Pretrial discovery is conducted pursuant to the Federal Rules of Civil Procedure. Depositions and other discovery tools, such as interrogatories and requests for admission, are common. Before trial there may be a summary judgment motion filed by either side that requests the court to rule as a matter of law that the claim should (or

---

[5] [Golsen v. Commissioner, 54 T.C. 742 (1970), *aff'd*, 445 F.2d 985 (10th Cir. 1971). — Eds.]

should not) be allowed. This motion is significant, as the case may be decided on this motion if the judge, considering all of the undisputed facts, determines that there can only be one outcome as a matter of law.

In a district court case, the IRS will be represented by the Tax Division of the Department of Justice in Washington or the Tax Division of the U.S. Attorney's Office in the few cities in the country that have such a division. Settlement authority is vested in the trial attorney assigned to the case.

Significantly, the district court is the only court for tax matters in which a jury is available. The facts of the case will be decided by laypersons, not tax experts. The rules of evidence are governed by the Federal Rules of Evidence and strictly enforced since a jury is present. Once the jury returns a verdict, the case is completed. There is no further delay with a briefing schedule or decision by the court.

The district courts are bound by the decisions of the court of appeals for the circuit in which the district is located and by the U.S. Supreme Court. Following a verdict by the jury, and possibly post-trial motions, the case is concluded. Decisions of the district court are appealed to the court of appeals where the district is located.

C. United States Court of Federal Claims

The third choice for litigating federal tax disputes is the U.S. Court of Federal Claims. The U.S. Court of Federal Claims, like the Tax Court, sits in Washington and travels on a circuit to various cities to hold its trials. The court consists of 16 judges appointed for 15-year terms like Tax Court judges, and the court hears various claims brought against governmental agencies. The court has equitable jurisdiction, since it was founded in 1982 (from 1982 to 1992 the court was named the Claims Court) and hears primarily money cases founded upon the Constitution, federal statutes, or contracts with the U.S.

As in district court, the taxpayer must pay the tax deficiency and file a claim for refund before the tax assessment may be contested in court. The discovery procedures available in the Court of Federal Claims are almost the same as those in the district court, as the rules were patterned after the Federal Rules of Civil Procedure. The government in such cases is represented by the Tax Division of the Department of Justice, Claims Court Section, in Washington. The attorney will have settlement authority, but will consult on all matters with the client, the IRS.

A trial is held before one judge without a jury. Following a trial, the court will issue a briefing schedule like the Tax Court for the parties to submit proposed findings of fact and legal argument. Thereafter, the court will render an opinion months later. An appeal from a Court of Federal Claims decision is taken to the Court of Appeals for the Federal Circuit, not the circuit where the taxpayer resides, as in the other two courts.

II. The Bond Procedure

One practical problem with choosing to go to Tax Court is that if the deficiency is upheld, then interest will have run on the tax during the entire controversy. Interest is always a large factor to consider. (Sometimes it reaches the same amount as the deficiency itself after five or six years.) A procedure that is not used often (I've only used it once), as an alternative to either paying or not paying the tax, is to make a remittance to the IRS under the cash bond procedure.

Revenue Procedures . . .[6] provide procedures for taxpayers to make remittances to stop the running of interest on deficiencies. A deposit in the nature of a cash bond is not

[6] [The Revenue Procedures the article cited subsequently were superseded by Revenue Procedure 2005-18, 2005-1 C.B. 798. Revenue Procedure 2005-18 is discussed in Chapters 10 and 13. — Eds.]

a payment of tax, is not subject to a claim for credit or refund, and, if returned to the taxpayer, does not bear interest.

* * *

III. Weighing Alternatives

An emerging consensus among some tax practitioners today is that if a taxpayer has the ability to pay the tax, the district court is frequently the best choice. The Tax Court has acquired a reputation for being pro-government.[7] Furthermore, paying the tax assessment will stop the running of interest on the deficiency.

There is also a difference in personnel depending on where the case is pursued. The revenue agent, Appeals Officer, and Area Counsel Attorney are all IRS personnel. If the taxpayer files a refund suit he or she will be dealing with a U.S. Department of Justice Tax Division Trial Attorney or an Assistant United States Attorney (Tax Division). * * * The vast majority of cases in both Tax Court and district court settle for a percentage of the proposed deficiency prior to trial.

An advantage to district court is that a jury is available, while a Tax Court case is decided by a judge. A Tax Court judge is, by definition, trained in the tax law, which can be helpful or hurtful, depending on the case. A disadvantage in the district court is that motions for summary judgment are common. It is likely that the government would file such a motion before trial, and ask the judge to rule that the taxpayer cannot prevail as a matter of law.

If the government's motion is successful, then judgment is entered in its favor. However, if the government's motion is denied, then the likelihood of settlement increases dramatically. The government may not wish to risk allowing the case to go to a jury, especially a case that may generate significant sympathy and feelings of injustice about the tax system.

Another advantage to the district court is that the resolution is much swifter than in Tax Court. In district court, the jury returns a verdict and a judgment is entered. In Tax Court, following the trial the parties must file post-trial briefs (opening and answering briefs) citing the trial transcript and record.

A significant factor in selecting the forum for a tax case is whether the substantive law on the particular tax question involved is different in each of the trial courts and appellate courts. In some cases, this can be a determining factor.

As with so many things these days, much of this comes down to a question of money. If the taxpayer has the financial resources, then litigating a tax case in district court (or the Court of Federal Claims) is a real option. A jury will be the trier of fact in the district court (but not the Court of Federal Claims) and may be more sympathetic to the taxpayer than a judge. Furthermore, there will be no delay in issuing a final determination at the end of the trial, while in Tax Court the delay can be up to one or two years. These delays bring to mind the adage about justice delayed is justice denied. Today, more than ever, a taxpayer must carefully consider all alternatives before automatically going straight to Tax Court.

The excerpt above covers many of the issues relevant to choice of forum. There are others, as well. For example, recall that the Tax Court allows nonlawyers to become members of its bar. Also, recall that the Tax Court offers informal procedures for small tax cases, as discussed in Section 8.06 of Chapter 8. Based on the above discussion, which factors do you think are most determinative of where a federal tax case will be brought?

---

[7] [The issue of whether the Tax Court is biased in favor of the government is discussed in § 8.07 of Chapter 8. — Eds.]

Some commentators have argued that the choice of fora in federal tax cases is inappropriate. According to one view, the multiplicity of trial-level fora in federal tax cases breeds inconsistency. In addition, the review of federal tax cases by thirteen different Courts of Appeals only exacerbates this problem. Does the *Golsen* rule eliminate inconsistency in the precedent that applies to cases in each of the three courts? Consider the following argument in favor of a single trial-level court and a single appellate court for all federal tax cases. Do you agree?

Judge Howard A. Dawson, Jr., *Should the Federal Civil Tax Litigation System Be Restructured?*[8]

40 Tax Notes 1427 (1988)

* * * Hasn't the time come for us to make a careful and critical examination of our trial and appellate systems for litigating Federal civil tax controversies? Now that some degree of *substantive* tax reform has been achieved, why not turn our attention to *procedural* tax reform in the judicial system? The present litigation system for civil tax cases is severely flawed at both the trial level and the appellate level. To put it bluntly — I think it is an unsatisfactory system — one that promotes unfairness, inefficiency, and uncertainty. As Roswell Magill, a Columbia University law professor and a former Treasury Department official, said 45 years ago: "If we were seeking to secure a state of complete uncertainty in tax jurisprudence, we could hardly do better than the system now in place." Generally the difficulty with any system lies not in formulating new ideas but in escaping from the old ones. It seems to me, as Justice Cardozo once commented, that there comes a time in the course of substantive and procedural law when it becomes necessary to pick up the driftwood and leave the waters pure.

Our system for resolving tax disputes is structured to allow three trial courts — the Tax Court, the Claims Court, and the Federal district courts — 12 circuit courts of appeals, and the court of appeals for the Federal Circuit to express their disparate views freely on tax issues. Inevitably, conflicts arise at the trial and appellate levels and, sooner or later — usually years later — the Supreme Court must resolve the conflicts. In the interim there is uncertainty; there is inconsistency; and there is unpredictability. It is very costly to taxpayers and the Federal government alike. Even when the Supreme Court speaks, while there is a "final" answer, we cannot always be sure we have been blessed with the "right" answer.

The greatest oddity of our Federal system for adjudicating tax disputes lies in the area of forum selection. Trial court jurisdiction is trifurcated. Which of the three courts will you choose? Each court has different rules and procedures; each court has judges of different backgrounds and expertise; and each court is governed by a different body of precedents. If you choose not to pay the asserted tax, you are in a deficiency posture and off to the Tax Court. Alternatively, if you choose to pay the asserted tax, assuming you can afford to pay *all* of it, and are not given a refund after you claim it, then you have two choices. You can go to the Federal district court in your home area and get a jury trial if you want one. Or you can take your case to the Claims Court in Washington. This is delightful if you see any merit in forum shopping, and I guess a lot of tax lawyers do. My own view is that it is better to promote the development of a coherent body of case law and that can be done by restructuring the civil tax litigation system in a way that will eliminate forum shopping. It is very unfortunate and unfair that a taxpayer's financial condition is an important aspect of forum selection. It is obviously inequitable to have a procedure where the doors of certain courts are open to those with the financial resources to pay their putative tax liability in advance and closed to those who cannot raise the money required. This is an aberration in the system that is indefensible. It clearly favors rich individuals and wealthy corporations over low- and middle-income persons and small corporations. I am too much of a populist to believe

---

[8] Copyright © 1988 Tax Analysts. All rights reserved. Reprinted by permission.

that this is good for the tax litigation system. Why should a select group of taxpayers be able to utilize differences in court procedures to gain a significant advantage? Why should some taxpayers be able to select a forum where the trend of prior decisions seems more conducive to success while others for financial reasons do not have that choice? Perhaps the major objection to forum shopping is the undue delay in obtaining certainty in tax results — a plague on all taxpayers and the government.

As I see it, the present litigation system at the trial level cannot be improved simply by some tinkering or minor modifications. I think consideration should be given to its replacement or restructure. I speak only for myself and not for the Chief Judge or any judges of the Tax Court.* * *

In short, the tax litigation system at the trial level would be improved by removing Federal tax refund jurisdiction from the Federal district courts and the Claims Court and placing it entirely in the Tax Court — the premier court of tax specialists. It is capable of handling all tax refund litigation. . . . I also think it would be advisable to eliminate jury trials in civil tax cases, particularly if jurisdiction over all tax refund suits is given to the Tax Court. These suggestions would eradicate forum shopping and provide consistency and uniformity of treatment for all taxpayers at the trial level by a single court of tax specialists. It is also possible that with all deficiency and refund jurisdiction in the Tax Court, the present IRS system of acquiescence and nonacquiescence in Tax Court opinions could be modified or eliminated if an appeal could be taken to a single National Court of Tax Appeals rather than to 12 different courts of appeals.

That brings me to the second prong of my suggestions for restructuring the Federal civil tax litigation system. Would it improve the system to have a single court of tax appeals? The concept is not new and it has generated different views. In 1944, Dean Erwin Griswold of Harvard first advocated a National Court of Tax Appeals and in 1973, Judge Henry Friendly of the Second Circuit Court of Appeals also proposed it. In 1978, in hearings before a Senate Judiciary Subcommittee, Dean Griswold, three former Commissioners of Internal Revenue — Mortimer Caplin, Sheldon Cohen, and Donald Alexander — as well as officials of the Treasury Department and some members of the tax bar testified in favor of creating a National Court of Tax Appeals. At that time, most Tax Court judges opposed the idea and almost all of them still oppose it. I disagreed with the Tax Court's view in 1978 and I disagree with it now. In these times when our Federal tax laws are so complicated that they often defy comprehension, we continue to operate under a cumbersome and complex litigation system for resolving civil tax disputes. A major criticism of the present system is that, absent a controlling Supreme Court decision, it lacks a practical and reliable method for permanently resolving tax disputes. The Tax Court has done an incredibly effective job of attempting to provide uniformity and consistency at the trial level. But that effort alone does not solve the problems of conflicting decisions by the courts of appeals, which review its decisions. * * * Since the Supreme Court seldom grants *certiorari* in tax cases, we have 13 courts of appeals engaged in deciding tax issues. The system creates substantial problems for taxpayers and for the government. Delay and uncertainty in the resolution of tax issues, in defining judicial interpretation of ambiguous statutory terms, and in the application of the law exacerbate difficulties faced by taxpayers who want to meet their responsibilities and also by the Internal Revenue Service, which must inform taxpayers of their rights and duties and how to comply with the law.

It has been argued that the present system results in a better final product — a more ideal set of ultimate tax decisions — than a system in which a single court of appeals would resolve issues at an earlier stage and without extended debate and ferment. In reply to this argument, former Commissioner Donald Alexander said:

> I think this suggestion has more validity in theory than in reality. If it were correct, then one would think the government should reject any two-Circuit or

> three-Circuit rule and litigate to the bitter end. Moreover, this theory apparently assumes that the final decision must be better than and differs in material respects from the first decision, and I doubt that this is so. And even if the final product of 10 years or more judicial consideration of a tax issue of broad application were different and were better, is such benefit worth the cost? As a former tax administrator and as a long-time tax practitioner, I think not.

The real defect in today's system of Federal tax litigation is the long period of uncertainty engendered by the delay in getting a final decision on a particular issue. We should be able to find a way to achieve finality in tax litigation in a more rapid fashion.

Because decisions of no court, except the Supreme Court, are final, both the Internal Revenue Service and taxpayers continue to assert positions contrary to existing precedents. For example, just look at *Commissioner v. Kowalski*, 434 U.S. 77 (1977), which involved cash meal allowances for state highway police. That issue was in litigation for more than 20 years. The fundamental goal of the Federal tax litigation process should be the development of authoritative rules to guide the administrative disposition of tax controversies.

The creation of a National Court of Tax Appeals would make our tax system fairer and more efficient. It would eliminate situations in which different Federal tax obligations are imposed on taxpayers located in different parts of the country. It would eliminate repetitious litigation that is burdensome to the judicial system and requires an inordinate amount of judicial resources. It would place a less heavy burden on the administrative process through which the vast majority of tax disputes are settled. And it surely would make it less difficult and less expensive for lawyers to give advice. Advice in grey areas of the tax law often does not provide the clear guidance a client seeks.

After many years of proposals and criticisms of the present system, isn't it in the public interest to adopt a workable solution to the horrendous tax litigation problems that now exist? I certainly think so.

In summary, I advocate a single trial court — the Tax Court — for all deficiency and refund actions and a single appellate court — a United States Court of Tax Appeals. It would be a giant step forward. I call for the resurrection and serious consideration of these suggestions for the improvement of our Federal civil tax litigation system. It should be given its long-needed overall revision. Let us join together — tax academicians, tax lawyers, and accountants, the Treasury and Justice Departments, the Judiciary and Congress — to create a better system for all of our people.

In 1997, Congress established the Commission on Structural Alternatives for the Federal Courts of Appeals, chaired by retired Supreme Court Justice Byron White, to study the circuit courts and make recommendations for change. The Commission's final report, released on December 18, 1998, noted the possibility of centralizing appellate tax jurisdiction in the Court of Appeals for the Federal Circuit, but did not make a recommendation on this point. *See* David Lupi-Sher, *National Court of Tax Appeals: An Idea That Never Quite Goes Away*, 81 Tax Notes 1159 (1998). What objections do you see to the proposal to have all appellate tax cases heard by the Court of Appeals for the Federal Circuit?

§ 11.04 THE BURDEN OF PROOF IN TAX CASES

Reading Assignment: I.R.C. §§ 7454(a), 7491(a); Tax Ct. R. 142(a).

The "burden of proof" in a court case has two components: The burden of going forward (or "burden of production") and the burden of persuasion. The burden of going forward requires the party who bears the burden to produce sufficient evidence to make a *prima facie* case, or the case may be dismissed. Once one party makes a *prima facie* case, the action goes forward. The party who bears the burden of persuasion must persuade the court by whatever standard applies (such as "preponderance of the evidence" or "clear and convincing evidence") that its version of the relevant facts is the correct version. Note that burden of proof applies only to factual questions. The court decides the legal questions without regard to the burden of proof.

Prior to the IRS Reform Act, the general burden of proof rules in tax cases were established by judicial decision, and in the Tax Court, by Tax Court Rule 142(a). In 1998, the IRS Reform Act created the first generally applicable statutory burden of proof rule for tax cases, effective for court proceedings arising in connection with examinations begun after July 22, 1998. *See* I.R.C. § 7491. Section 7491(a) has several threshold requirements, discussed below, that make eligibility quite difficult. If the taxpayer fails to meet these requirements or chooses not to present evidence on these requirements, the default rule is that the burden of proof remains on the taxpayer. Jurisprudence developed under prior law still applies when the burden does not shift under section 7491(a).

In general, assuming that Code section 7491 does not apply, the taxpayer bears the burden of persuasion. The allocation of the burden of persuasion to the taxpayer derives in part from the practical reality that the taxpayer holds all the evidence that can prove the existence (or nonexistence) of the deficiency or overpayment. In most instances, the burden that applies is the preponderance of the evidence standard, meaning that the majority of the evidence supports a particular position.

In some instances outside the context of 7491(a), the IRS will bear the burden of proof. Most notably, the IRS bears the burden of proving fraud by clear and convincing evidence. I.R.C. § 7454(a).

> Fraud cases involve a split burden of proof. The taxpayer must prove any error in the deficiency determination by a preponderance of the evidence, and the Commissioner must prove fraud by clear and convincing evidence. Sec. 7454(a); Rule 142(a) and (b); *Zack v. Commissioner*, 692 F.2d 28 (6th Cir. 1982), affg. T.C. Memo. 1981-700. However, respondent may not rely solely on the taxpayer's failure to prove error in respondent's deficiency determination to satisfy respondent's burden of proof as to fraud.

Thorne v. Commissioner, 99 T.C. 67, 87 (1992). "To carry the burden of proof on the issue of fraud, the Commissioner must show, for each year at issue, that (1) an underpayment of tax exists and (2) some portion of the underpayment is due to fraud. Petzoldt v. Commissioner, [92 T.C. 661] *supra* at 699." Vogt v. Commissioner, T.C. Memo. 2007-2.

Although analysis of the burden of proof in refund suits and deficiency suits is similar, the issues are not always identical. In Tax Court cases, the notice of deficiency plays an important role in allocating the burden of proof, as discussed in Chapter 9. In a refund suit, the taxpayer may not have ever received a notice of deficiency. Instead, the refund suit is premised on the refund claim the taxpayer must first have made with the IRS. In refund suits, unlike in Tax Court cases, the taxpayer traditionally has borne the additional burden of establishing the *correct amount of the tax. See* Helvering v. Taylor, 293 U.S. 507, 513 (1935) ("Obviously the burden was on the plaintiff, in order to establish a basis for judgment in his favor, specifically to show not merely that the assessment was erroneous but also the amount to which he was entitled.") (dictum); *see also* Lewis v. Reynolds, 284 U.S. 281, *modified*, 284 U.S. 599 (1932). By contrast, in Tax Court, the taxpayer need only rebut the assertions in the notice of deficiency; the taxpayer need not prove what the correct liability is for the tax year.

[A] Code Section 7491

Section 7491(a) of the Code generally provides that the burden of proof with respect to a factual issue shifts from the taxpayer to the IRS where the taxpayer meets five requirements: (1) the taxpayer has complied with all substantiation requirements; (2)

the taxpayer has maintained all required records; (3) the taxpayer has cooperated with the IRS's reasonable requests for witnesses, information, documents, meetings, and interviews; (4) the taxpayer produces "credible evidence" on the factual issue; and (5) if the taxpayer is a partnership, corporation or trust, it meets a net worth limitation.[9]

One article explains the first three requirements as follows:

> [The requirement that] [t]he taxpayer kept records that meet the substantiation requirements of the Code . . . may apply to the substantiation requirements of a particular Code section, or it may apply to the general requirement of Section 6001 that taxpayers must maintain adequate books and records. . . .
>
> [With respect to the requirement that] [t]he taxpayer cooperated with IRS requests for information, including documents, witness interviews, and meetings[,] [t]he committee reports clarify that this provision requires that the taxpayer have exhausted any available administrative remedies within the IRS, including any appeal rights. The committee reports also indicate, however, that the taxpayer need not consent to an extension of the statute of limitations in order to be considered to have exhausted administrative remedies.
>
> Although this requirement may be relatively easy to satisfy, it also may have its disadvantages. The requirement of witness interviews, for example, could be a significant detriment to a taxpayer in some situations. In the Tax Court, depositions are generally not permitted without the consent of the parties or an order from the court, and taxpayers usually have greater knowledge of the facts than the Service. A taxpayer wishing to preserve that advantage will be reluctant to grant interviews.

Philip N. Jones, *The Eighth Circuit Weighs in on the Burden of Proof— Will it Change the Outcome After All?*, 98 J. TAX'N 226, 226–27 (2003) (footnotes omitted).

What does the "credible evidence" requirement call for? The Senate Finance Committee stated, "[c]redible evidence is the quality of evidence which, after critical analysis, the court would find sufficient upon which to base a decision on the issue if no contrary evidence were submitted (without regard to the judicial presumption of IRS correctness)." S. Rep. 105-174, at 45–46 (1998), 1998-3 C.B. 537, 581–582. What does that mean? In *Blodgett v. Commissioner*, 394 F.3d 1030 (8th Cir. 2005), the Court of Appeals for the Eighth Circuit addressed that issue. On the issue of what constitutes credible evidence, the court stated:

> In *Griffin*, we defined "credible evidence" for purposes of § 7491 as "the quality of evidence, which after critical analysis, the court would find sufficient upon which to base a decision on the issue *if no contrary evidence were submitted* (without regard to the judicial presumption of IRS correctness)." 315 F.3d at 1021. Ms. Blodgett contends the tax court ignored § 7491 by failing to shift the burden of disproving her loss to the Commissioner after she introduced uncontroverted testimony, which she alleges was thoroughly corroborated by documentary evidence, that, as part of the settlement agreement, she irrevocably lost millions of dollars in assets when she turned over the assets to the FTC receiver. Ms. Blodgett's argument, however, fails to the extent she relies on Griffin for the proposition any testimony offered by the taxpayer tending to support a claimed deduction is sufficient to shift the burden of proof to the I.R.S. While a tax court must consider the testimony as "if no contrary evidence were submitted (without regard to the judicial presumption of IRS correctness)," a

[9] The text focuses on section 7491(a). Section 7491(b) provides: "In the case of an individual taxpayer, the Secretary shall have the burden of proof in any court proceeding with respect to any item of income which was reconstructed by the Secretary solely through the use of statistical information on unrelated taxpayers." Section 7491(c) provides that, "[n]otwithstanding any other provision of this title, the Secretary shall have the burden of production in any court proceeding with respect to the liability of any individual for any penalty, addition to tax, or additional amount imposed by this title." Section 7491(c) is discussed in Chapter 12.

tax court has the right in the first instance to reject the testimony as incredible. *See* Marcella v. C.I.R., 222 F.2d 878, 883 (8th Cir. 1955) (stating a tax court "is not compelled to believe evidence which to it seems improbable, or to accept as true uncorroborated evidence of interested witnesses even though uncontradicted"); . . . . A fact finder may choose to disbelieve evidence on its face even without evidence to the contrary. *See* Steel v. Downs, 438 F.2d 310, 312 (8th Cir. 1971) (stating "the trier of the facts is not required to accept the uncontradicted testimony of an uncorroborated interested party, although such testimony is not contradicted by other testimony."); . . . . This concept is not only fundamental since incredible testimony, axiomatically, cannot constitute credible evidence, but this concept is contained within the definition of credible evidence. Ms. Blodgett conveniently disregards the portion of the credible evidence definition requiring a tax court to conduct a "critical analysis" of the evidence. If a critical analysis requires nothing else, it requires a tax court to conduct a credibility determination before labeling evidence "credible." With this qualification on her interpretation of *Griffin*, we will now analyze each claimed deduction.

* * *

4. Loss of Condominium

Ms. Blodgett testified to the purchase of a condominium in Florida for the purpose of renting it out and sustained a $142,482 investment loss when the property was transferred to the settlement estate and later the bankruptcy trustee. The Tax Code allows a deduction for a loss incurred in connection with a transaction conducted for profit, but does not allow a deduction for a personal, living or family expense. 26 U.S.C. § 165(c)(2). Ms. Blodgett testified she and her husband bought the property as an investment. She argues her testimony is sufficient to shift the burden of proof. The tax court, however, found her testimony lacked credibility at trial. Incredible testimony is not sufficient to shift the burden of proof. *Griffin*, 315 F.3d at 1021. In any event, the tax court ultimately found the objective evidence, namely, the evidence of the Blodgetts' lack of expertise in the real estate business, lack of market analysis prior to purchase, and the failure to actually rent out the property, outweighed any incredible statements supporting the deduction. The tax court concluded the Blodgetts purchased the property for personal, living and family purposes.

* * *

6. Loss on Rare Coins and Historical Documents

Ms. Blodgett testified she suffered deductible carryforward business or investment losses on $561,375 in rare coins and $125,403 in historical documents. The tax court, however, found her self-serving testimony incredible. She produced no other specific evidence regarding the ownership, value and transfer of the rare coins and historical documents claimed as carryforward business or investment losses. Accordingly, the tax court found she did not meet her burden of proof with respect to the ownership, value, and transfer of the rare coins and historical documents. Considerable evidence existed showing the Blodgetts did not own the coins and documents, rather T.G. Morgan and its customers did. Moreover, if she claimed the losses as theft losses, such are only deductible in the year discovered, and she did not show when she discovered them. 26 U.S.C. § 165(e).

Id. at 1035–40.

As the discussion in *Blodgett* shows, to constitute credible evidence, evidence must be believable. The Conference Committee Report quoted in part above further states, "[a] taxpayer has not produced credible evidence for these purposes if the taxpayer merely makes implausible factual assertions, frivolous claims, or tax protestor-type arguments. *The introduction of evidence will not meet this standard if the court is not convinced that it is worthy of belief.* . . . " H. Conf. Rept. 105-599, at 240–241 (1998), 1998-3 C.B. 747, 994–995 (emphasis added). Thus, it seems as if the "quality" referred to is *believability*.

The Tax Court, citing the legislative history, has held that the taxpayer bears the burden of proving that section 7491 applies. *See* Gutierrez v. Commissioner, T.C. Memo. 2003-321; O'Toole Commissioner, T.C. Memo. 2002-265. In addition, the Tax Court has held that a request to shift the burden made for the first time in a post-trial brief is untimely. *See* Deputy v. Commissioner, T.C. Memo. 2003-176. The Court of Appeals for the Tenth Circuit recently held that section 7491 could not be raised for the first time on appeal. *See* Williams v. Commissioner, 2005 U.S. App. LEXIS 1279 (10th Cir. 2005) (unpublished). In that case, counsel for the taxpayer had mentioned section 7491 in his opening statement but not subsequently. The Court of Appeals stated, "The matter was never mentioned again during the ensuing trial, nor was it raised or referred to in any post-trial proceeding. It is on this basis that the Commissioner argues in this Court that the issue was not raised in the Tax Court, and therefore cannot be raised in this Court for the first time. We agree with the Commissioner." *Id.*

Having read section 7491 and the brief discussion above about the law that applies if the taxpayer does not meet the section 7491 requirements, consider how you might advise a client in a dispute with the IRS. The IRS, one presumes, will need to prepare for the possibility that it will bear the burden of persuasion.[10] How might the IRS obtain the evidence necessary to meet that burden? Which party controls that evidence? How should a taxpayer prepare for litigation if he or she hopes to shift the burden of proof to the IRS? At the audit stage, what might you advise your client to consider in planning a strategy that contemplates possible litigation of the controversy?

[B] Does the Burden of Proof Matter?

Does the placement of the burden of proof actually affect case outcomes? A series of decisions in the Court of Appeals for the Eighth Circuit provide a window into that question. In *Griffin v. Commissioner*, T.C. Memo. 2002-6, *rev'd & remanded*, 315 F.3d 1017 (8th Cir. 2003), the taxpayers were the sole owners of an S corporation that in turn was a 60 percent partner in two partnerships. The taxpayer-husband had personally paid delinquent real property taxes with respect to certain property owned by the partnerships, and the taxpayers argued that the payments were deductible. One of the taxpayers' arguments was that they were entitled to the deduction under Code section 162, even though the taxpayers did not directly own the property in question.

The taxpayers argued that the IRS bore the burden of proof under section 7491. The IRS countered that the taxpayers had failed to present "credible evidence" that they were engaged in a trade or business of their own — separate from the trade or business of the taxpayers' S corporation or the partnerships in which the S corporation was a partner — as required by applicable case law. The Tax Court described Mr. Griffin's testimony on the trade or business issue as "summary and uncorroborated." *Griffin*, T.C. Memo. 2002-6. The court further found that, even if the taxpayers were engaged in a trade or business, there was no credible evidence that the payments constituted ordinary and necessary expenses of such a trade or business. In addition, as is often the case, the court stated, in a footnote, that it would have ruled for the IRS on the issue even if the IRS had borne the burden of proof. *Id.* at n.4. *Cf.* Payne v. Commissioner,

---

[10] The IRS generally will not know during the audit or Appeals stage which cases will go to trial, and in which of those trials the taxpayer will meet the requirements of section 7491.

T.C. Memo. 2003-90; Deputy v. Commissioner, T.C. Memo. 2003-176 (because facts were not disputed, "[i]n these circumstances, the question of which party has or had the burden of proof has become wholly academic.").

On appeal, the Court of Appeals for the Eighth Circuit reversed and remanded. *See Griffin*, 315 F.3d 1017 (8th Cir. 2003). It found that, "[v]iewing Robert Griffin's testimony in the absence of any evidence or presumptions to the contrary, we conclude that appellants did produce sufficient 'credible evidence' to support their personal deductions of the real property tax payments at issue." *Id.* at 1021 (emphasis in original). It noted that Mr. Griffin had testified, "I had to pay [the real property taxes] to preserve my integrity and my standing with the bank, and my good name, my good will. And in order to stay in business, I had to pay the taxes." However, the IRS had argued, in part, " . . . that Robert Griffin's testimony was not credible because the 1995 and 1996 returns and the testimony of appellants' own accountant, William LaRue, established that the real property tax payments in question were *made in connection with the business of their subchapter S corporations*, which were listed on their Schedules E." *Id.* at 1021 (emphasis added).

Why did the Eighth Circuit reach a different conclusion than that of the Tax Court? Among other things, the Court of Appeals seemed to believe that the question was one of statutory interpretation (rather than fact-finding); the court applied a *de novo* standard of review on that basis. *See id.* at 1021. It remanded the case, seemingly challenging the Tax Court to justify its holding:

> On the record before us, we cannot determine whether the Commissioner has met his burden of proof. It is not sufficient to summarily conclude that the outcome is the same regardless of who bears the burden of proof; if that were the case, § 7491(a) would have no meaning. We therefore remand the case to the tax court for further proceedings on the merits. On remand, the tax court may reconsider all of the evidence properly before it or hold a new hearing. In either case, the tax court is instructed to make new findings of fact in light of the shifted burden of proof. If the same conclusion is reached by the tax court without a new hearing, an explanation is warranted as to how the existing record justifies the conclusion that the Commissioner has met his burden of proof.

Griffin, 315 F.3d at 1022.

On remand, the Tax Court reversed its original holding, seemingly out of a sense of compulsion. However, it justified its statement that the placement of the burden of proof did not matter:

> In our original opinion, we noted: "Even if the burden of proof were placed on respondent, we would decide the issue [as to the deductibility of the tax payments] in his favor based on the preponderance of the evidence." T.C. Memo. 2002-6 n.4. This statement reflected this Court's conclusion that *Mr. Griffin's testimony was not only insufficient to support petitioners' claim to ordinary and necessary business deductions but indeed undermined their claim*, insofar as Mr. Griffin's testimony convinced us that his relevant business activities were conducted entirely through S corporations. In light of the Court of Appeals' conclusion that Mr. Griffin's testimony was sufficient to support the claimed deductions, the preponderance of the evidence, thus evaluated, is no longer in respondent's favor.

Id. n.7 (emphasis added).

In contrast with *Griffin*, another panel of the Eighth Circuit affirmed the Tax Court's refusal to shift the burden of proof, finding that the burden of proof rarely matters. *See* Polack v. Commissioner, 366 F.3d 608 (8th Cir. 2004) (*citing* Cigaran v. Heston, 159 F.3d 355, 357 (8th Cir. 1998)). This created an intra-circuit conflict. The *Blodgett* panel addressed this issue:

> According to Ms. Blodgett, any failure to shift the burden of proof would require us to reverse the decision of the tax court and remand the case with instructions to retry it with the burden assigned to the I.R.S. Once again, she relies on *Griffin. See* 315 F.3d at 1022 (reversing and remanding for failure to shift the burden of proof). In *Griffin*, like the instant case, the tax court declined to shift the burden of proof to the I.R.S. under § 7491 because the taxpayer's "uncorroborated and self-serving testimony was not enough to overcome the clear evidence of nondeductibility." *Id.* at 1021. On appeal, the taxpayer claimed he produced sufficient "credible evidence" within the meaning of § 7491 to shift the burden of proving the issue of non-deductibility to the I.R.S. *Id.* at 1020–21. The court agreed. Upon reviewing the taxpayer's testimony in absence of any evidence or presumptions to the contrary, the court determined the taxpayer produced enough credible evidence to support the claimed deductions. *Id.* The court remanded the case to the tax court for further proceedings despite the tax court's statement in its opinion the burden of proof was irrelevant because the weight of the evidence supported a finding for the I.R.S. *Id.* at 1022. Rebuking the tax court, the court declared "it is not sufficient to summarily conclude that the outcome is the same regardless of who bears the burden of proof; if that were the case, § 7491 would have no meaning." *Id.*
>
> In contrast to *Griffin*, another panel of this Court has found a tax court does not commit error in not addressing the burden of proof because " 'the shifting of the evidentiary burden of preponderance is of practical consequence only in the rare event of an evidentiary tie.' " Polack v. C.I.R., 366 F.3d 608, 613 (8th Cir. 2004) (quoting Cigaran v. Heston, 159 F.3d 355, 357 (8th Cir. 1998)). While the *Polack* panel addressed the burden shift in the context of a new matter rather than under § 7491, *id.*, the significance of a burden shift is of general application. The circumstances of *Griffin* and *Polack* are remarkably similar in that the tax court in both cases did not decide the burden of proof question because the weight of the evidence supported a finding for the I.R.S. *Compare Griffin*, 315 F.3d at 1020, *with Polack*, 366 F.3d at 613. We are thus faced with an apparent conflict in precedents on the significance of the shifting burden of proof.
>
> "When faced with conflicting precedents we are free to choose which line of cases to follow." Graham v. Contract Transp., Inc., 220 F.3d 910, 914 (8th Cir. 2000). We choose to follow the guidance of *Polack*. There is a simple reason for our choice. In a situation in which both parties have satisfied their burden of production by offering some evidence, then the party supported by the weight of the evidence will prevail regardless of which party bore the burden of persuasion, proof or preponderance. *See* Philip N. Jones, *The Eighth Circuit Weighs In on the Burden of Proof— Will It Change the Outcome After All?*, 98 J. Tax'n 226, 230 (2003). Therefore, a shift in the burden of preponderance has real significance only in the rare event of an evidentiary tie. *Id.* Here, the record is clear, if the tax court did err in failing to shift the burden of proof, any error was harmless because the weight of the evidence supported a decision for the Commissioner.

Blodgett, 394 F.3d at 1039.

In *Forste v. Commissioner*, T.C. Memo. 2003-103, by contrast, the Tax Court found that, based on stipulations, Code section 7491 applied to any issue on which the taxpayers presented credible evidence. The case involved a claim for exclusion of certain payments under Code section 104(a)(2) as compensation for personal injuries. Construing the settlement agreement between the taxpayer and the payor, the Tax Court stated, "[a]lthough this case is very close, we find that petitioners have presented credible evidence; i.e., sufficient evidence upon which to base a decision that the payment of $25,130 pursuant to paragraph 1 of the settlement agreement was made in settlement of Mr. Forste's tort or tort type claims for personal injury." *Id.* The burden shift seems to have made a difference in the outcome on this issue. The court explained that the lone IRS witness could not recall whether the taxpayer's former employer intended to compensate Mr. Forste for personal injury claims. The court suggested that that failure might raise an inference that would detract from the taxpayers' evidence, but, since the burden of proof was on the IRS, it was not sufficient to prevail on this issue.

Based on this discussion, how likely is it that the burden of proof under a preponderance of the evidence standard will affect who wins a case? Does it matter whether the case involves a highly fact-sensitive issue, such as valuation?

One area in which the burden of proof it might play a role is in settlement negotiations:

> [O]ur experience is that very few tax cases hinge on who has the burden of proof. . . .
>
> As a result, even with the aggressive interpretation given section 7491(a) by the Eighth Circuit in *Griffin*, we do not see litigation as being where tax practitioners can get the most mileage out of section 7491. Most cases are settled before trial, and section 7491 has already proven of some help in settlement negotiations. Settlements at the appeals office level or after cases have been docketed with the Tax Court reflect the hazards of litigation. Our experience, and that of other practitioners with whom we have discussed the question, has generally been that appeals officers give more weight to the section 7491 burden of proof than do IRS litigators or Tax Court judges. Where it is plausible to believe that section 7491(a) can help the taxpayer in the event of trial, that possibility is useful in creating a more positive settlement climate.

Burgess J.W. Raby & William L. Raby, *Credible Evidence Shifts Burden of Proof*, 98 Tax Notes 725, 727 (2003).

§ 11.05 SETTLEMENT OF LITIGATED TAX CASES

Many cases settle after being docketed in court. Post-docketing settlements raise additional issues, such as when a case actually is settled, and what obligations, if any, the IRS has to offer consistent settlements to litigants in related cases. This part of the chapter addresses those issues.

In an Article III court such as a United States district court, a mutually agreed-upon settlement moots a case, requiring its dismissal. That is because the United States Supreme Court has interpreted the "cases or controversies" clause of Article III of the United States Constitution as prohibiting decision in any "non-justiciable" case. *See, e.g.*, Honig v. Doe, 484 U.S. 305, 317 (1988). Article I courts (such as the Tax Court and the Court of Federal Claims) are subject to no such Constitutional restriction.

A Tax Court case that is settled by agreement of the parties is entered by the judge as a "stipulated decision." However, an offer of full concession by one party to a Tax Court case is not the same as a settlement. If a party offered a full concession by the other side rejects the offer, the Tax Court has the option to choose to treat the unilateral concession as a settlement and enter a stipulated decision. In making that determination, the court considers not only the interests of the parties but also the interests of non-parties in the potential precedential value of the case. *See* Leandra Lederman, *Precedent Lost: Why Encourage Settlement, and Why Allow Non-Party Involvement in Settlement*?, 75 Notre Dame L. Rev. 221 (1999). Similarly, if one party accepts the other's offer of full concession but reneges prior to executing a decision document, the Tax Court treats the situation like a rejected offer of full concession with the additional factor of the reneging party's prior acceptance of the concession. *See, e.g.*, Greenlee v. Commissioner, T.C. Memo. 1985-218; Smith v. Commissioner, T.C. Memo. 1965-224.

The Tax Court's jurisprudence on full concessions should be contrasted with its jurisprudence on repudiation of settlement agreements. If one party seeks to be relieved of a settlement made in a case docketed in Tax Court, the Tax Court sets a high threshold for relief from that agreement. *See* Dorchester Indus., Inc. v. Commissioner, 108 T.C. 320, 337 (1997) (reviewed by the court). Under current law:

> The party seeking modification . . . must show that the failure to allow the modification might prejudice him. . . . Discretion should be exercised to allow modification where no substantial injury will be occasioned to the opposing party; refusal to allow modification might result in injustice to the moving party; and the inconvenience to the Court is slight. . . .

Adams v. Commissioner, 85 T.C. 359, 375 (1985) (citations omitted).[11]

If the Tax Court has cancelled the trial date in reliance on a purported settlement agreement, and a party makes a motion to be relieved of that agreement on the eve of trial, the Tax Court will hold the parties to their agreement absent fraud, mistake, or some other factor that vitiates the consent on which the settlement agreement was based. *See* Dorchester Indus., *supra*; *see also* Mearkle v. Commissioner, 87 T.C. 527, 528 (1986), *rev'd and remanded*, 838 F.2d 880 (6th Cir. 1988). Why might the Tax Court, which exercises discretion to enter a settlement in the context of a unilateral offer of full concession, be so strict in its refusal to relieve a party of a settlement agreement in this context? Does a unilateral offer of full concession differ from a bilateral settlement agreement in such a way that the Tax Court should engage in different tests in deciding whether to enter a stipulated decision in each of these situations?

Issues about the finality of settlement also arise when a taxpayer seeks to repudiate a settlement with the IRS and to force the IRS to settle the taxpayer's case on terms the IRS has offered others. In *Slovacek v. United States*, 40 Fed. Cl. 828 (1998), the taxpayers executed a Form 870-L(AD), Settlement Agreement for Partnership Adjustment and Affected Items, that disallowed all losses flowing through from a partnership, and imposed penalties on them. The taxpayers then filed a refund suit on the basis that the statute of limitations had expired before their settlement was executed. As you might expect after reading *Kretchmar v. United States*, 9 Cl. Ct. 191 (1985), in Chapter 5, the court ruled against the taxpayers on that issue, finding, in part, that the taxpayers had waived their right to a refund by signing the Form 870-L(AD). Slovacek v. United States, 36 Fed. Cl. 250, 256 (1996). Subsequently, the IRS offered to the partners in the partnership who had not pursued refund claims a more favorable settlement agreement, allowing the deduction of seventeen percent of the partnership losses, and abating the penalties. The Slovaceks formally requested settlement of their case on the same terms the IRS extended to the other partners, but the Department of Justice, handling the case because it had been filed as a refund suit, rejected the offer and refused to settle. The Court of Federal Claims agreed with the government, stating that settlement discretion includes discretion to treat similarly situated cases differently. *Slovacek*, 40 Fed. Cl. at 832 (*citing* Bunce v. United States, 28 Fed. Cl. 500, 509–510 (1993), *aff'd*, 26 F.3d 138 (Fed. Cir. 1994)).

Another issue that may arise regarding settlement of docketed cases involves settlement of test cases. The Tax Court may use test cases when numerous cases are

---

[11] However, note that three Tax Court judges joined in a 1997 concurrence by Judge Parr that expressed the view that the Tax Court has a right to reject a bilateral settlement agreement:

> I write separately . . . to emphasize that nothing in the majority opinion should be understood to limit the sound discretion of the Court to reject an agreement between the parties, where good cause is shown and the interests of justice require it.
>
> It is easy to imagine a situation, not here present, where an agreement between the parties may not be in the interests of justice. For instance, agreements that would abuse the process of this Court, would usurp the Court's control over its calendar, or that would be contrary to sound public policy should not be enforced.

Dorchester Indus., Inc v. Commissioner, 108 T.C. 320, 343 (1997) (reviewed by the court) (Parr, J., concurring).

pending that involve the same legal issue or issues, on similar facts. The parties and the court agree to designate certain cases as test cases. The petitioners in the other cases are encouraged to sign stipulations to be bound by the outcome of the test cases ("piggyback agreements"). *See* Dixon v. Commissioner, T.C. Memo. 1999-101, *rev'd and remanded*, 316 F.3d 1041 (9th Cir. 2003). *Dixon* involved a group of over a thousand cases involving the IRS's disallowance of interest deductions with respect to various tax shelters promoted by Henry F.K. Kersting (Kersting). *See id.* Fourteen docketed cases of eight petitioners were designated by the parties as test cases. *Id.* A problem arose in *Dixon* because IRS trial counsel Kenneth W. McWade (McWade) and his supervisor, Honolulu District Counsel William A. Sims (Sims) entered into favorable settlement agreements regarding the test case of John R. and Maydee Thompson (the Thompsons) without disclosure to the court or to the parties to the other test cases or their counsel. The settlement required the Thompsons to maintain their case until after trial.

In *Dixon*, the Tax Court found that neither the settlement agreement, nor its nondisclosure, was material to the outcome of the case, so that the court's holding for the government would stand. The court commented, "[s]tated differently, although we disapprove Messrs. Sims' and McWade's misconduct, as well as the misconduct of Mr. Kersting and [the Thompsons' attorney] Mr. DeCastro, we do not conclude that their misconduct resulted in a structural defect in the trial of the test cases mandating either a new trial or entry of decisions in petitioners' favor." *Dixon, supra*. The court also concluded that the error constituted "harmless error." *Id.*

On appeal, the Court of Appeals for the Ninth Circuit disagreed. After detailing the extent of the IRS attorneys' deception, which the court found included "a cover-up, which was carefully designed to prevent the Tax Court and other taxpayers from learning of the secret settlement agreements," Dixon v. Commissioner, 316 F.3d 1041 (9th Cir. 2003), the court found:

> [T]he factual findings of the Tax Court support the conclusion that a fraud, plainly designed to corrupt the legitimacy of the truth-seeking process, was perpetrated on the trial court by McWade and Sims. The Tax Court, however, applied the wrong law when it imposed a requirement that taxpayers show prejudice as a result of the misconduct.
>
> Prejudice is not an element of fraud on the court. *Hazel-Atlas*, 322 U.S. at 238; *Pumphrey v. K.W. Thompson Tool Co.*, 62 F.3d 1128, 1132–33 (9th Cir. 1995). Fraud on the court occurs when the misconduct harms the integrity of the judicial process, regardless of whether the opposing party is prejudiced. *Alexander v. Robertson*, 882 F.2d 421, 424 (9th Cir. 1989). Furthermore, the perpetrator of the fraud should not be allowed to dispute the effectiveness of the fraud after the fact. *Hazel Atlas*, 322 U.S. at 247; *Pumphrey*, 62 F.3d at 1133. Because the Tax Court applied the wrong legal standard, it abused its discretion. *See Paulson v. City of San Diego*, 294 F.3d 1124, 1128 (9th Cir. 2002) (en banc).

Id. at 1046–47.

In devising a remedy, the court explained:

> We have the inherent power to vacate the judgment of the Tax Court, fashion an appropriate remedy, . . . and sanction a party or its lawyers for willful abuse of the judicial process, particularly when the party or its lawyers have intentionally practiced a fraud upon the court. . . .
>
> Here, it plainly would be unjust to remand for a new, third trial. The IRS had an opportunity to present its case fairly and properly. Instead its lawyers intentionally defrauded the Tax Court. The Tax Court had two opportunities to equitably resolve this situation and failed. Enormous amounts of time and judicial resources have been wasted. In addition, the IRS has done little to

> punish the misconduct[n.10] and even less to dissuade future abuse. The taxpayers should not be forced to endure another trial and the IRS should be sanctioned for this extreme misconduct.
>
> Conversely, we will not enter judgment eradicating all tax liability of these taxpayers. Such an extreme sanction, while within the court's power, is not warranted under these facts. . . . Instead, we remand to the trial court with directions to enter judgment in favor of Appellants and all other taxpayers properly before this Court on terms equivalent to those provided in the settlement agreement with Thompson and the IRS.

Id. at 1047–48. The Tax Court subsequently did so. *See* Hartman v. Commissioner, T.C. Memo. 2008-124; Dixon v. Commissioner, T.C. Memo. 2006-190. What do you think of the Ninth Circuit's remedy in *Dixon*?

§ 11.06 AWARDS OF ADMINISTRATIVE AND LITIGATION COSTS AND FEES TO TAXPAYERS

Reading Assignment: I.R.C. § 7430(a)–(c), (f); Treas. Reg. § 301.7430-1(b), -2(c), -4(c), -5.

The Code permits a prevailing party to recover, in limited circumstances, (1) reasonable administrative costs in connection with proceedings before the IRS, and (2) reasonable litigation costs in connection with civil actions in a federal court, including deficiency proceedings before the Tax Court and refund actions before a U.S. district court or the Court of Federal Claims. *See* I.R.C. § 7430(a), (c)(6). Among other requirements, a party who seeks to recover costs under section 7430 must qualify as a "prevailing party," must exhaust available administrative remedies within the IRS, and must meet financial eligibility requirements.[12] The types of costs recoverable are specified by statute and are limited in amount.

[A] Qualification Requirements

To qualify as a prevailing party, the taxpayer must "substantially prevail" with respect to either the amount in controversy or with respect to the most significant issue or set of issues presented. *See* I.R.C. § 7430(c)(4)(A). In *refund* cases, the taxpayer substantially prevails with respect to the amount in controversy when he or she recovers a substantial amount of the claimed refund. The determination of whether the taxpayer recovers a substantial amount is made on a case-by-case basis; no particular recovery percentage is determinative. For example, a taxpayer was considered to have substantially prevailed although he recovered less than half of the amounts requested when the IRS conceded two out of three of the taxpayer's claims. Keeter v. United States, 98-1 U.S.T.C. ¶ 50,481 (E.D. Cal. 1998), *order vacated in part on other grounds on denial of reconsideration*, 82 A.F.T.R.2d 98-5943 (E.D. Cal. 1998).

[n.10] McWade and Sims were both suspended for two weeks without pay and transferred out of the Honolulu division. Sims accepted this censure and was transferred to the San Francisco Regional Counsel Office, where he was assigned nonsupervisory duties. McWade retired from the IRS, choosing not to accept the terms of the proposed disciplinary action but keeping the $1,000 bonus earlier paid him for his performance in the original Tax Court proceedings. We note that counsel for the Hongsermeier test case petitioners recently filed a grievance against McWade and Sims with the attorneys' respective Bars.

[12] The ability to recover costs and fees under section 7430 is not limited to taxpayers. Others, typically owners of levied or encumbered property, may also recover awards if they satisfy the qualification requirements. A creditor of the taxpayer, however, is not entitled to an award under section 7430. *See* Bermensolo v. United States, 883 F.2d 58 (9th Cir. 1989). For convenience, the party requesting an award under section 7430 is referred to as the taxpayer.

In *deficiency* cases, a party substantially prevails with respect to the amount in controversy when the Tax Court decision shows that no deficiency existed or the amount of the deficiency is small in relation to the deficiency originally proposed by the IRS. Treas. Reg. § 301.7430-5(d). This determination is also made on a case-by-case basis. *See, e.g.*, Hall v. Commissioner, T.C. Memo. 1989-187 (finding that taxpayer did substantially prevail when the final settlement was for 17 percent of the deficiency amount determined by the IRS); Bragg v. Commissioner, 102 T.C. 715 (1994) (finding that taxpayer did not substantially prevail when the Tax Court upheld more than 70 percent of the amount of the IRS's asserted deficiency).

If the taxpayer does not substantially prevail with respect to the amount in controversy, the taxpayer may still qualify as a prevailing party if the taxpayer substantially prevails with respect to the most significant issue or set of issues presented, as indicated above. The determination of what is the most significant issue in a case is made using an objective standard. The most significant issue is not necessarily the one involving the largest dollar amount. *See* Huckaby v. United States, 804 F.2d 297 (5th Cir. 1986) (finding that most significant issue in a wrongful disclosure case is whether IRS agent violated section 6103, not the amount of the recoverable damages). In a case involving the taxpayer's request that the IRS abate interest on a tax deficiency, Goettee v. Commissioner, 124 T.C. 286 (2005), the taxpayer was not considered to have substantially prevailed on the most significant issue when the court allowed interest abatement for only a short period of time. If the case does not involve multiple issues (and thus does not have any issue or set of issues that is more significant than the others), the taxpayer can recover costs only if he or she substantially prevails with respect to the amount in controversy. *See* Treas. Reg. § 301.7430-5(e).[13]

The taxpayer will not be treated as the prevailing party if the government establishes that the position it maintained during the administrative or court proceedings was "substantially justified." *See* I.R.C. § 7430(c)(4)(B)(i). Note that the burden of proof falls on the Government, not the requesting party, to establish that its position was substantially justified. *Id.*

In administrative proceedings before the IRS, the position that the government must substantially justify is determined as of the earlier of (1) the date the taxpayer receives the decision of the Appeals Division or (2) the date the IRS issues the notice of deficiency. *See* Fla. Country Clubs, Inc. v. Commissioner, 122 T.C. 73 (2005) (IRS is not considered to have taken a position as early as the 30-day letter), *aff'd*, 404 F.3d 1291 (11th Cir. 2005). In court proceedings, the relevant position is the one that the government asserts in the judicial proceeding. I.R.C. § 7430(c)(7). *See* Huffman v. Commissioner, 978 F.2d 1139 (9th Cir. 1992) (holding that government's position was the one asserted in the answer). The government's position is substantially justified if, based on all the facts and circumstances surrounding the proceedings, the position has a reasonable basis in law and in fact. *See, e.g.*, Cox v. Commissioner, 121 F.3d 390 (8th Cir. 1997). In making this determination, the statute instructs the court to take into account whether the government has won or lost in the past on substantially similar issues in Courts of Appeals for other circuits. I.R.C. § 7430(c)(4)(B)(iii).

Just because the IRS ultimately loses on the underlying issue at trial or the IRS ultimately concedes the issue does not necessarily mean that the government's position was not substantially justified. *See, e.g.*, Wilfong v. United States, 991 F.2d 359 (7th Cir. 1993); Favret v. United States, 341 F. Supp. 2d 613 (E.D. La. 2004). A jury verdict in the taxpayer's favor on the underlying tax issue also is not dispositive on the question of whether the IRS's position was substantially justified. *See, e.g.*, *Wilfong*, *supra*. However, a rebuttable presumption exists that the government's position is not substantially justified if the IRS fails to follow current regulations, Revenue Rulings,

---

[13] The taxpayer and the government may also simply agree that the taxpayer is a prevailing party. I.R.C. § 7430(c)(4)(C).

Notices, or Information Releases. The rebuttable presumption also applies if the IRS fails to comply with letter rulings or determination letters issued to the taxpayer. I.R.C. § 7430(c)(4)(B)(ii); *see also* Treas. Reg. § 301.7430-5(c).[14]

As a general rule, section 7430 requires that the requesting party must exhaust available administrative remedies within the IRS. I.R.C. § 7430(b)(1). In *refund* cases, the requesting party must participate, either in person or through a qualified representative, in an Appeals conference before the party files a refund suit in court. If the IRS does not offer an Appeals conference, the requesting party must, before the IRS issues a notice disallowing the party's refund claim, request an Appeals conference and file all necessary papers required to obtain the conference. Treas. Reg. § 301.7430-1(b)(1). In *deficiency* cases, the requesting party (or his or her representative) must request Appeals consideration before the IRS issues the notice of deficiency (the 90-day letter) and must file a written protest, if necessary to obtain Appeals consideration. Treas. Reg. § 301.7430-1(b)(1).[15]

Recovery of costs under section 7430 also hinges upon the taxpayer's satisfaction of the net worth requirements of the Equal Access to Justice Act. I.R.C. § 7430(c)(4)(A)(ii) (referencing 28 U.S.C. § 2412(d)(2)(B)). The net worth of an individual requesting an award of costs and fees must not exceed $2 million. Individuals who file joint returns are treated separately and are subject to a combined net worth limitation of $4 million. I.R.C. § 7430(c)(4)(D)(i); 28 U.S.C. § 2412(d)(2)(B)(i). Businesses and other organizations are eligible for an award of costs and fees only if the net worth of the organization is $7 million or less. In addition, the organization may not have more than 500 employees at the time the organization filed the request for recovery of costs and fees. 28 U.S.C. § 2412(d)(2)(B)(ii).

Finally, even if the taxpayer qualifies as a prevailing party and satisfies the other requirements, the taxpayer may not recover costs and fees under section 7430 if he or she unreasonably protracted the proceedings. I.R.C. § 7430(b)(3). The Tax Court, for example, has denied recovery on this basis when the taxpayer's attorney failed to respond to interrogatories, delayed providing documents to the IRS, and filed an incomplete offer in compromise. Gaskins v. Commissioner, T.C. Memo. 1996-268.

[B] Measure of Recovery

If section 7430 otherwise applies, the award allowed to a prevailing party is for (1) "reasonable administrative costs" incurred in connection with administrative proceedings before the IRS, and (2) "reasonable litigation costs" incurred in connection with court proceedings. Reasonable administrative costs include administrative fees or charges imposed by the IRS; reasonable expert witness fees; reasonable costs of studies, tests, and engineering reports; and reasonable attorney's fees (subject to the same statutory cap that applies to litigation costs, which is discussed below). *See* I.R.C. § 7430(c)(2). The award, however, can only include such costs incurred after the earliest of the date the taxpayer receives the notice of the Appeals decision in the case, the date

[14] As explained in more detail in Chapter 5, a requesting party who does not otherwise qualify as a prevailing party by virtue of having substantially prevailed may be treated as a prevailing party if the party makes a "qualified offer," the IRS rejects the qualified offer, and the IRS later obtains a judgment against the taxpayer in an amount that is equal to or less than the taxpayer's offer. I.R.C. § 7430(c)(4)(E); Treas. Reg. § 301.7430-7(b).

[15] A taxpayer's failure to agree to extend the statute of limitations on assessment cannot be taken into account when determining whether the taxpayer exhausted his or her administrative remedies. I.R.C. § 7430(b)(1); Treas. Reg. § 301.7430-1(b)(4). The regulations also specify instances in which the taxpayer will be deemed to have exhausted administrative remedies. For example, if the taxpayer did not receive a 30-day letter before the IRS issued the notice of deficiency and the taxpayer did not refuse to participate in an Appeals conference while the case was docketed before the Tax Court, the taxpayer will be treated as having met the administrative remedies requirement. Treas. Reg. § 301.7430-1(f)(2).

of the notice of deficiency, or the date of the 30-day letter. *Id.* As a result of these limitations, if the parties settle the case before the IRS issues a notice of deficiency or other decision notice in the case, the costs the taxpayer incurs while negotiating with the revenue agent are not recoverable. Costs incurred in connection with preparing for and filing a refund action in U.S. district court or the Court of Federal Claims, as well as costs incurred after the commencement of the refund case, are recoverable as litigation costs, not administrative costs. Similarly, preparation costs associated with a Tax Court petition constitute litigation, rather than administrative costs. Treas. Reg. § 301.7430-4(c)(3).

To obtain a recovery of administrative costs in a nondocketed case, the taxpayer generally must file a written request with the IRS that includes information establishing that the taxpayer met all the section 7430 requirements, as well as detailed affidavits setting forth the nature and the amount of the requested administrative fees. Treas. Reg. § 301.7430-2(c)(1). The taxpayer must submit the request for administrative fees and costs to the IRS within 90 days after the date that the IRS mails or otherwise furnishes to the taxpayer the IRS's final decision with respect to the tax and additions (including penalties). I.R.C. § 7430(b)(4). A settlement agreement (Form 870), closing agreement, Notice and Demand for Payment, and statutory notice of deficiency all qualify as final decision notices. Treas. Reg. § 301.7430-2(c)(5). A revenue agent's report issued at the conclusion of an examination, even if the taxpayer resolves the issues with the revenue agent, does not constitute a final decision. *Id.* An IRS denial of administrative costs is subject to appeal to the Tax Court. *See* I.R.C. § 7430(f)(2). The Tax Court's disposition of the petition is then subject to appeal in the same manner as any other Tax Court decision. I.R.C. § 7430(f)(3). However, if a taxpayer negotiates with the Appeals Division after having received a notice of deficiency and after having filed a Tax Court petition, and the Tax Court ultimately decides the underlying issues in favor of the taxpayer, the motion for recovery of administrative fees incurred while negotiating with Appeals is properly made to the Tax Court, not the IRS. *See* Treas. Reg. § 301.7430-2(e) Ex. 2.

Litigation costs include court costs, expenses of expert witnesses, costs of studies, tests, and engineering reports, and attorney's fees. I.R.C. § 7430(c)(1). The recovery for attorney's fees is generally limited to a specified hourly rate, which is subject to an adjustment for inflation. *See, e.g.*, Rev. Proc. 2007-66, 2007-45 I.R.B. 970 (setting $170 per hour inflation-adjusted limit for 2008). Courts do have the discretion to award attorney's fees in excess of the statutory cap when special factors exist. I.R.C. § 7430(c)(1)(B)(iii). Special factors include the limited availability of qualified attorneys, the difficulty of the issues, and the local availability of tax expertise. *Id.* Does specialized expertise in tax matters justify an award above the statutory cap?

> Federal courts have consistently noted that tax expertise itself is not a special factor requiring an upward departure from the statutory rate. *See, e.g., Huffman v. CIR*, 978 F.2d 1139, 1150 (9th Cir. 1992); *Cassuto v. CIR*, 936 F.2d 736, 743 (2d. Cir. 1991); *JJR, Inc. v. United States*, 36 F. Supp. 2d 1259, 1263 (W.D. Wash. 1999); *United States v. Guess*, 425 F. Supp. 2d 1143, 1151 (S.D. Cal. 2006). In *Pierce v. Underwood*, the U.S. Supreme Court found that the special factor formulation suggests that tax expertise is not "special." 487 U.S. at 572. This Court recognizes that section 7430 was amended to include the example "local availability of tax expertise," however, this does not change the Court's conclusion. Courts have construed that language to pertain specifically to mean "an actual shortage of qualified attorneys who could handle the case rather than an inability to retain qualified counsel willing to take on the representation at the statutory maximum hourly rate." *Guess*, 425 F. Supp. 2d at 1155.

Cheung Inc. v. United States, 2007 U.S. Dist. LEXIS 85488. Attorney's fees also include fees paid to a non-attorney authorized to practice before the IRS or the Tax Court. I.R.C. § 7430(c)(3)(A).

To obtain a recovery of administrative and litigation costs in a docketed case, the taxpayer must apply to the judicial body that heard the underlying issues. *See* I.R.C. § 7430(f)(1). Rules 230 through 233 of the Tax Court Rules of Practice and Procedure set forth guidelines for claiming costs. The taxpayer must make a motion to the court that contains representations speaking to the qualification requirements under section 7430. The moving party must file the motion for costs and fees within 30 days after service of a written opinion determining the issues in the case. In the case of a bench opinion, the taxpayer must file the motion within 30 days after service of the transcript containing the judge's determination. TAX CT. R. 231.

In the typical case, the Tax Court will dispose of the motion for fees without a separate hearing. If the court grants the taxpayer's motion, the Tax Court will determine the amount of the recoverable fees. In other cases, the Tax Court will direct IRS counsel to file a response to the taxpayer's motion. If, after consultation between the parties, the parties cannot agree upon the recoverable fee amount, the taxpayer may be required to file an affidavit detailing the services rendered and the fees incurred. *See* TAX CT. R. 232(a), (b), (d). If the parties have settled all issues in the case other than the recovery of fees, a motion for fees may be made after the settlement is finalized. If the parties settle the entire case, including the claim for fees and costs, the award of costs must be included as part of a stipulated decision submitted to the Tax Court. *See* Chief Counsel Notice CC-2003-013, *available at* 2003 TNT 80-13 (Apr. 25, 2003).

If the underlying issue is decided by a court other than the Tax Court, the requesting party must file a claim for administrative and litigation costs that conforms to the local court rules relating to content and timing. These rules vary. For refund actions brought in U.S. district courts, for example, the requesting party typically must file a motion for recovery of attorney's fees no later than 14 days after the judgment is entered by the court. *See* FED. R. CIV. P. 54(d)(2)(B); *see also* 28 U.S.C. § 2412(d)(1)(B) (requiring party to submit application for fees within 30 days of the final judgment in the action). A requesting party may appeal a court determination regarding administrative and litigation fees in the same manner as the party would appeal the underlying decision. I.R.C. § 7430(f)(1). Most courts have held that the appropriate standard for reviewing a decision relating to fees and costs under section 7430 is an abuse of discretion standard. *See, e.g.*, In re Rasbury, 24 F.3d 159 (11th Cir. 1994); TKB Int'l, Inc. v. United States, 995 F.2d 1460 (9th Cir. 1993); Pate v. United States, 982 F.2d 457 (10th Cir. 1993).

§ 11.07 ISSUES IN MULTIPLE TAX CASES

If the taxpayer faces the same tax issue in more than one case, can it be litigated twice? That question is answered by reference to the principles of collateral estoppel and res judicata (or issue preclusion and claim preclusion), which are discussed below in Section A. Can a taxpayer bifurcate litigation of a single taxpayer, litigating some issues in one forum, such as a refund court, and the rest in another, such as the Tax Court? That issue is discussed below in Section B.

[A] Collateral Estoppel and Res Judicata

Both collateral estoppel and res judicata can apply in tax cases. Collateral estoppel or "issue preclusion" generally bars relitigation of substantially the same issue. It applies to the parties and their privies. "[F]or collateral estoppel to apply the issue in the second action must be identical and have been raised and necessarily decided in the first action." Danshera Cords, *Collection Due Process: The Scope and Nature of Judicial Review*, 73 U. CIN. L. REV. 1021, 1047 (2005) (*citing* Commissioner v. Sunnen, 333 U.S. 591, 599–600 (1948)).

Collateral estoppel may be used by a party offensively or defensively.

> Offensive use of collateral estoppel occurs when a plaintiff seeks to foreclose a defendant from relitigating an issue the defendant has previously litigated

> unsuccessfully in another action against the same or a different party. Defensive use of collateral estoppel occurs when a defendant seeks to prevent a plaintiff from relitigating an issue the plaintiff has previously litigated unsuccessfully in another action against the same or a different party.

United States v. Mendoza, 464 U.S. 154, 159 n.4 (1984).

> In the context of federal civil litigation, the Supreme Court abandoned the requirement of mutuality in cases involving defensive issue preclusion. As a result, only the party against whom issue preclusion is sought to be used must have been a party in the first action. Eight years later, in Parklane Hosiery Co. v. Shore, Inc., the Supreme Court held that in the federal civil context, trial courts should have broad discretion in allowing offensive issue preclusion. Therefore, in federal civil cases, issue preclusion can be used in the second lawsuit by either the defendant or the plaintiff and can bind a party who was not a party in the first action.

Michelle S. Simon, *Offensive Issue Preclusion in the Criminal Context: Two Steps Forward, One Step Back*, 34 U. Mem. L. Rev. 753, 754–56 (2004) (footnotes omitted).

The IRS's interpretation of the application of collateral estoppel to federal tax cases is reflected in the following examples from a Litigation Guideline Memorandum:

> Ex. 1: The Government loses against shareholder #1. Shareholder #2 cannot collaterally estop the Government from relitigating the same issue. The shareholder's attempted use of estoppel would be nonmutual and not allowable under [United States v. Mendoza, 464 U.S. 154 (1984)] and [Divine v. Commissioner, 59 T.C. 152 (1972), *rev'd on other grounds*, 500 F.2d 1041 (2d Cir. 1974)].
>
> Ex. 2: The Government wins against shareholder #1. The Government cannot collaterally estop shareholder #2 from relitigating the same issue because shareholder #2 was not a party to the earlier suit. Estoppel can only be used against an entity which was a party or a privy to the earlier suit.
>
> Ex. 3: Taxpayer loses an issue in state court. The Government can apply estoppel on this issue against taxpayer in tax litigation involving the same issue. [Kurlan v. Commissioner, 343 F.2d 625 (2d Cir. 1965)] and [Baily v. United States, 355 F. Supp. 325 (E.D. Pa. 1973)].
>
> Ex. 4: Taxpayer wins an issue in state court. Taxpayer cannot apply estoppel against the Government on this issue in a later tax suit. The Government was not a party to the earlier proceeding and nonmutual estoppel cannot be applied against it. *Mendoza*.
>
> Ex. 5: The Government loses against taxpayer in year 1. If the same issue and the same facts arise regarding taxpayer in year 2, taxpayer can use mutual collateral estoppel against the Government unless the year 2 litigation is in a circuit that has adopted the Government's position on that issue.
>
> Ex. 6: The Government loses against taxpayer in year 1. In year 2 there is an intervening change in law with respect to this issue. In year 3 taxpayer cannot use collateral estoppel against the Government on this issue. [Commissioner v. Sunnen, 333 U.S. 591 (1948)] and [Limbach v. Hooven & Allison Co., 466 U.S. 353 (1984)].

Litigation Guideline Memorandum TL-28 (Jan. 22, 1988), *available at* 2000 TNT 121-110 (June 22, 2000).

Res judicata or "claim preclusion" provides a broader bar to litigation of any issues that were or could have been raised in a prior proceeding, so long as the judgment in the prior proceeding was on the merits.[16] Gerald A. Kafka & Rita A. Cavanagh, Litigation

---

[16] There is an exception for jeopardy and termination assessments. *See* Gerald A. Kafka & Rita A. Cavanagh, Litigation of Federal Civil Tax Controversies ¶ 22.02 (1996).

OF FEDERAL CIVIL TAX CONTROVERSIES ¶ 22.02 (1996). Res judicata, like collateral estoppel, applies to the parties and their privies. It reflects a policy of finality of court decisions. *Id.*

The Supreme Court has explained how res judicata applies in the tax case context, as follows:

> Income taxes are levied on an annual basis. Each year is the origin of a new liability and of a separate cause of action. Thus if a claim of liability or non-liability relating to a particular tax year is litigated, a judgment on the merits is *res judicata* as to any subsequent proceeding involving the same claim and the same tax year. But if the later proceeding is concerned with a similar or unlike claim relating to a different tax year, the prior judgment acts as a collateral estoppel only as to those matters in the second proceeding which were actually presented and determined in the first suit. . . .

Commissioner v. Sunnen, 333 U.S. 591, 598 (1948).

The following case involves an application of res judicata. In which court was the previous case litigated?

UNITED STATES v. DAVENPORT

United States Court of Appeals, Fifth Circuit
484 F.3d 321 (2007)

KING, CIRCUIT JUDGE:

In an action to determine the federal tax liability of the estate of Birnie Davenport, the tax court held that the estate was liable for the unpaid gift tax on inter-vivos gifts of stock made by Birnie Davenport to her two nephews, Gordon Davenport and Charles Botefuhr, and her niece, Patricia Vestal. Because the estate did not pay the tax, the government now seeks to collect it from Gordon Davenport under the provisions of the Internal Revenue Code imposing liability for an unpaid gift tax on the transferee of the gift. The district court held that Gordon Davenport was not bound by the doctrine of res judicata to certain key determinations made by the tax court. Because we agree with the government that this case involves the same nucleus of operative facts as the proceeding in the tax court, and that as a result res judicata applies, the district court's judgment is REVERSED.

I. FACTUAL AND PROCEDURAL BACKGROUND

Birnie and Elizabeth Davenport, who were sisters, lived together much of their adult lives. Over many years, the two sisters commingled all of their earnings and assets. Pursuant to a long-standing oral agreement between the two, Elizabeth Davenport held legal title to the assets, but the sisters shared equally in the profits and losses of their investments. They considered all of their assets to be jointly owned, and their income tax returns filed over many years reflected this belief. Each of the sisters filed a separate income tax return in which she reported her earnings from her job and an equal share of profits and losses from the joint investments. The IRS accepted this split of investment income and expenses throughout numerous audits between 1965 and 1979.

The sisters' investments included stock in Hondo Drilling Company. At the time of Elizabeth Davenport's death in 1979, the sisters owned 3220 shares of Hondo stock. The sisters had two nephews, Gordon Davenport and Charles Botefuhr, and one niece, Patricia Vestal. Gordon Davenport, Botefuhr, and Vestal were appointed co-executors of Elizabeth Davenport's estate.

In July 1980, slightly more than six months after her sister's death, using two conveyance methods, Birnie Davenport transferred half (1610 shares) of the Hondo stock to her niece and nephews. First, she transferred 537 shares to Gordon Davenport and 536 shares to Vestal through installment sale agreements, with the stock being valued in the agreements at $804 per share. Birnie Davenport reported the installment sales on her 1980 income tax return and indicated on that form that the sales were to related parties. Second, Birnie Davenport transferred 537 shares to Botefuhr as an outright gift. In a signed "Family Agreement," Botefuhr promised to file the appropriate gift tax return that would report the gift made by Birnie Davenport and to pay on her behalf the gift taxes associated with his gift. Botefuhr did not fulfill this responsibility. In July 1981, Hondo Drilling Company redeemed Botefuhr's shares at $2190 per share.[n.4]

Birnie Davenport died in 1991. Gordon Davenport, Vestal, and Botefuhr were appointed as personal representatives of her estate. While preparing Birnie Davenport's estate tax return in 1991, Corrine Childs, the Davenport sisters' long-time tax attorney, learned that Botefuhr had not filed the 1980 gift tax return or paid the taxes as promised. When Vestal and Gordon Davenport filed the estate tax return, they filed a gift tax return reporting the 1980 gift to Botefuhr at $804 per share. The estate paid a gift tax of $95,322 with the return. Botefuhr did not sign either the gift tax return or the estate tax return.

In 1992 the IRS initiated an audit of Birnie Davenport's estate tax return and 1980 gift tax return and ultimately determined that Birnie Davenport's gift of Hondo stock to Botefuhr should have been valued at $2730 per share rather than $804 per share. The large discrepancy in values created a correspondingly large gift tax deficiency, which Birnie Davenport's estate contested in tax court. *See Estate of Davenport v. Comm'r*, 74 T.C.M. (CCH) 405, T.C. Memo 1997-390 (1997). One issue before the tax court was whether Birnie Davenport made a completed gift to Gordon Davenport, Vestal, and Botefuhr. *Id.* at 411. The tax court held that even though Birnie Davenport did not have legal title at the time of the transfers, she did effect inter vivos gifts to Gordon Davenport, Vestal, and Botefuhr of the Hondo stock, which the tax court valued at $2000 per share.[n.5] *Id.* at 407, 412. A second issue before the tax court was whether the statute of limitations barred the government from recovering the gift tax due. The tax court held that the statute of limitations did not bar assessment of gift tax liability because with respect to each of the transfers, the limitations period started running on November 7, 1991, when Vestal and Gordon Davenport filed Birnie Davenport's 1980 gift tax return. *Id.* at 412. In accordance with its findings, the court calculated the tax deficiency owed by the estate. The Tenth Circuit affirmed the tax court's decision. * * *

Despite the tax court's decision, the estate did not pay the taxes owed. Because the tax court lacks the authority to enforce its judgments, the government filed the current action in the Northern District of Oklahoma against the estate and all three cousins to reduce to judgment the estate's liability and the donees' liability as transferees pursuant to I.R.C. § 6324(b). *See United States v. Estate of Davenport*, 159 F. Supp. 2d 1330, 1332 (N.D. Okla. 2001). The estate conceded liability. *Id.* The government also

---

[n.4] During this time, the IRS investigated the estate tax owed by Elizabeth Davenport. The investigation culminated late in 1982. The report concluded that: (1) all of the property held in Elizabeth Davenport's name, including all of the Hondo stock, should be included in her estate and (2) that Birnie Davenport's prior conveyances were ineffective. The estate settled the claim at a valuation of $2,400 per share of Hondo stock so that the IRS would abandon its claim that all of the property recorded in Elizabeth Davenport's name belonged only to her. Thus, the settlement cleared up title concerns on Birnie Davenport's half of the property.

[n.5] The tax court decided this value and incorporated by reference the parties' stipulation of fact which read:

> 38. For the purposes of this litigation, if the Court finds that Birnie Davenport transferred Hondo stock to Patricia Vestal, Gordon Davenport, and Charles Botefuhr in the calendar quarter ending September 30, 1980, the parties agree that the fair market value of such Hondo stock was $2,000.00 per share at the time of the transfers.

sought individual liability against the three cousins in their capacity as co-executors pursuant to 31 U.S.C. § 3713 for allegedly making improper distributions from the estate before paying the federal tax liabilities. *Id.* The district court dismissed the § 3713 claim pre-trial. *Id.*

Although Gordon Davenport and Botefuhr contested jurisdiction, the district court overruled their motions to dismiss for lack of personal jurisdiction. *Id.* at 1335. On appeal, the Tenth Circuit held that the Oklahoma district court did not have jurisdiction over Botefuhr and Gordon Davenport after dismissing the § 3713 claim. *United States v. Botefuhr*, 309 F.3d 1263, 1274 (10th Cir. 2002).

The case was remanded to the Oklahoma district court, which transferred Botefuhr's case to the Western District of Texas and Gordon Davenport's case to the Southern District of Texas. The case before this panel involves solely Gordon Davenport's appeal.

The Southern District of Texas ruled on multiple motions for summary judgment by Gordon Davenport and the government. First it determined that the statute of limitations barred assessment of the gift tax on the imputed gift arising from the July 1980 installment sale, but that the statute of limitations did not bar assessment of the gift to Botefuhr. Second, it held that although res judicata and collateral estoppel bound Gordon Davenport to the tax court's finding that he was a donee, neither doctrine established the value of the gift to him (the Hondo stock) or the amount of his liability. Finally, the district court held that the government failed to provide any evidence on damages, an essential element of its claim, and it granted summary judgment against the government. The government now appeals.

II. DISCUSSION

The Internal Revenue Code imposes tax liability "on the transfer of property by gift." I.R.C. § 2501(a). The definition of a gift includes transfers of property for "less than an adequate and full consideration in money or money's worth." I.R.C. § 2512. The donor, as the party who makes the gift, bears the primary responsibility for paying the gift tax. *See* I.R.C. § 2502(c) ("The tax imposed by 2501 shall be paid by the donor."). When, as here, the donor dies before paying the gift tax owed, the personal representative of the estate is responsible for paying the tax out of the estate, as a debt against the donor's estate. Treas. Reg. § 25.2502-2. The donee may also be held personally liable for the full amount of any unpaid gift tax pursuant to 26 U.S.C. § 6324(b). Although the donee's liability is limited to the value of the gift he received from the donor, he may be forced to pay more than the gift tax attributable to his gift. § 6324(b); *see also* 14 EDWARD J. SMITH, MERTENS LAW OF FEDERAL INCOME TAXATION § 53:42 (2004). Thus, Gordon Davenport is liable for all the gift tax owed by the estate for 1980, up to the value of the gift he received.

The government seeks to collect unpaid gift taxes owed by the Birnie Davenport estate from Gordon Davenport pursuant to the transferee liability provision of I.R.C. § 6324(b). The government argues that the tax court's decision is res judicata as to the liability of Gordon Davenport, and that accordingly, Gordon Davenport may not relitigate the value of the Hondo stock or whether the statute of limitations expired on the gifts to Gordon Davenport, Vestal, and Botefuhr.

The term "res judicata" is often used to describe two discrete preclusive doctrines: res judicata and collateral estoppel. *Baker by Thomas v. GMC*, 522 U.S. 222, 233 n.5, 118 S. Ct. 657, 139 L. Ed. 2d 580 (1998). These doctrines "relieve parties of the cost and vexation of multiple lawsuits, conserve judicial resources, and, by preventing inconsistent decisions, encourage reliance on adjudication." *Allen v. McCurry*, 449 U.S. 90, 94, 101 S. Ct. 411, 66 L. Ed. 2d 308 (1980). Under the doctrine of res judicata, "a final judgment on the merits bars further claims by parties or their privies based on the same cause of action." *Montana v. United States*, 440 U.S. 147, 153, 99 S. Ct. 970, 59 L. Ed. 2d 210 (1979). The bar prevents relitigation of all "issues that were or could have been raised in [the previous] action." *Federated Dep't Stores, Inc. v. Moitie*, 452 U.S. 394, 398, 101 S. Ct. 2424, 69 L. Ed. 2d 103 (1981). In contrast, under the doctrine of collateral estoppel, "the second action is upon a different cause of action and the judgment in the prior suit precludes relitigation of issues actually litigated and necessary to the outcome of the first action." *Parklane Hosiery Co. v. Shore*, 439 U.S. 322, 327 n.5, 99 S. Ct. 645, 58 L. Ed. 2d 552 (1979).

This court reviews the res judicata effect of a prior judgment de novo because it is a question of law. *Test Masters Educ. Servs., Inc. v. Singh*, 428 F.3d 559, 571 (5th Cir. 2005). For res judicata to apply, the following four-part test must be satisfied: (1) the parties must be either "identical or in privity; (2) the judgment in the prior action [must have been] rendered by a court of competent jurisdiction; (3) the prior action must have been concluded to a final judgment on the merits; and (4) the same claim or cause of action [must have been] involved in both actions." *In re Southmark Corp.*, 163 F.3d 925, 934 (5th Cir. 1999); *see also* 15 Elizabeth K. Berman, Mertens Law of Federal Income Taxation § 60:32 (2000).

This court determines whether two suits involve the same claim or cause of action by applying the transactional test of the Restatement (Second) of Judgments, § 24. *Petro-Hunt, L.L.C. v. United States*, 365 F.3d 385, 395 (5th Cir. 2004). Under the transactional test, our inquiry focuses on whether the two cases under consideration are based on "the same nucleus of operative facts." *In re Southmark Corp.*, 163 F.3d at 934 (quoting *In re Baudoin*, 981 F.2d 736, 743 (5th Cir. 1993)). The nucleus of operative facts, rather than the type of relief requested, substantive theories advanced, or types of rights asserted, defines the claim. *Agrilectric Power Partners, Ltd. v. Gen. Elec. Co.*, 20 F.3d 663, 665 (5th Cir. 1994). If the cases are based on the same nucleus of operative facts, the prior judgment's preclusive effect "extends to all rights the original plaintiff had 'with respect to all or any part of the transaction, or series of connected transactions, out of which the [original] action arose.' " *Petro-Hunt*, 365 F.3d at 395 (citing Restatement (Second) of Judgments § 24(1)). Generally, "[t]he tax liability of a particular tax for a particular taxable year" is a single cause of action. 15 Elizabeth K. Berman, Mertens Law of Federal Income Taxation § 60:33 (2000).

The first three elements of res judicata are not contested by the parties. As transferee, Gordon Davenport was in privity with a party to the tax court proceeding, Birnie Davenport's estate, the transferor. *See Baptiste v. Comm'r*, 29 F.3d 1533, 1539 (11th Cir. 1994) ("[I]t is well settled that a transferee is in privity with his transferor for purposes of the Internal Revenue Code."); *First Nat'l Bank of Chicago v. Comm'r*, 112 F.2d 260, 262 (7th Cir. 1940) (same). Indeed, the tax liability of the donor and donee are inseparable. A prior decision determining the liability of the donor binds the donee. 14 Edward J. Smith, Mertens Law of Federal Income Taxation § 53:6 (2004). And the tax court, a court of competent jurisdiction, rendered final judgment on the merits.[n.10]

The parties differ as to whether the fourth element of res judicata is satisfied: whether this case involves the same cause of action as the tax court proceeding. The district court, in its res judicata analysis, held that the tax court proceeding involved different operative facts than this case. The district court determined that the tax court case involved a deficiency notice against the estate itself and involved distinct facts relating to Birnie Davenport's ownership interests, donative intent, and the estate's ultimate gift tax liability, but that this case involves facts relating to donee liability and the statute of limitations under § 6324(b). The government contends, however, that the

[n.10] The final judgment element does not require contested litigation. "An agreed judgment is entitled to full res judicata effect." *United States v. Shanbaum*, 10 F.3d 305, 313 (5th Cir. 1994) (holding that an agreed decision in the tax court prevented the application of the innocent spouse rule in an action to enforce the tax court judgment under res judicata); *see also Matter of W. Tex. Mktg Corp.*, 12 F.3d 497, 500–01 (5th Cir. 1994) (stating that a settlement agreement between the IRS and the taxpayer incorporated into a judgment must be given full res judicata effect).

district court improperly focused on the facts litigated, as would be proper under the doctrine of collateral estoppel, rather than the operative facts of the case.

The district court's focus was improper because it looked to the legal theories advanced, forms of relief requested, and types of rights asserted. *See Agrilectric Power Partners, Ltd.*, 20 F.3d at 665. The operative facts in this case and the tax court case are identical. Both cases are based on the same two transactions and factual events: (1) the July 1980 installment sale of the Hondo stock from Birnie Davenport to Vestal and Gordon Davenport and (2) the July 1980 gift of the Hondo stock to Botefuhr. The tax court was required to decide the value of the stock to calculate the tax owed by the estate. Accordingly, under the transactional test the same cause of action is involved in both cases, and the district court improperly focused on what was actually litigated rather than the operative facts.

Our decision that the same cause of action is involved is consistent with the decisions of the Eighth and Eleventh Circuits that a transferee cannot relitigate the tax due after a prior court had already determined the estate's tax liability. *See Baptiste v. Comm'r*, 29 F.3d 1533, 1539 (11th Cir. 1994); *Baptiste v. Comm'r*, 29 F.3d 433, 436 (8th Cir. 1994). The *Baptiste* cases involved two brothers; Gabriel, residing in Nebraska, and Richard, residing in Florida. *See id.* Each brother received $50,000 as a beneficiary of his father's life insurance policy. *Baptiste*, 29 F.3d at 434. The IRS determined that the estate owed a deficiency in estate tax, and after the estate contested that deficiency, the IRS and the estate agreed to the estate tax owed. *Id.* The tax court entered a stipulated decision of the tax due from the estate, but the estate never paid the tax, prompting the government to attempt to collect the tax from the Baptiste brothers as transferees. *Id.*

Although Gabriel Baptiste did not contest that he was personally liable as a transferee under I.R.C. § 6324(a)(2), he attempted to contest the amount of the underlying estate tax liability in a separate proceeding in the tax court. The effort was unsuccessful, the tax court holding that res judicata applied to bar him from contesting the amount of the estate tax liability. *Id.* at 435. On appeal, Gabriel Baptiste argued that res judicata did not apply to bind him to the tax court's decision regarding the existence and amount of estate tax imposed for purposes of determining his transferee liability pursuant to § 6324(a)(2). *Id.* The Eighth Circuit held that the causes of action in the two cases were identical, that is "the transferor and Gabriel[] [Baptiste's] respective obligation to pay the estate tax imposed on the transfer of the decedent's estate." *Id.* at 436. Because the causes of action were identical, res judicata bound Gabriel Baptiste to the tax court's decision for purposes of determining both the transferee's obligation to pay the estate tax and the amount of the transferee's liability. *Id.* The court reasoned that the donee's liability was determined by the amount of the estate's tax. *See id.*

The Eleventh Circuit ruled similarly in the challenge brought by Richard Baptiste. *Baptiste*, 29 F.3d at 1539. Richard Baptiste wanted to relitigate the valuation of the property, but the court of appeals denied him that opportunity. *Id.* The Eleventh Circuit held that "[t]he fact that his purpose is to decrease his personal liability, rather than in the interest of the estate, is of no moment. The estate's liability under section 2002 and Baptiste's liability under section 6324(a)(2) both embrace the same determination — the amount of estate tax imposed by chapter 11." *Id.*

Gordon Davenport argues that his case can be distinguished from the Eighth and Eleventh Circuits' decisions because unlike the Baptistes, who challenged the estate's liability, he contests the extent of his own transferee liability. He contends that because the Baptiste brothers received cash, the extent of the donee's liability was fixed at the amount of the cash received and that the value of cash cannot be questioned in the way that a stock's value can be. He argues that because the Baptiste brothers could not relitigate the value of the cash (and thus the extent of their liability), they attempted to relitigate the underlying estate's liability as a means of reducing their own transferee liability.

This argument does not succeed because the value of the Hondo stock was a fundamental part of calculating the tax due in this case. The tax court's determinations of the value of the stock and the tax due are not separable. Once a court determines the tax liability of the transferor, "the decision is res judicata of the liability with regard to the transferee for the same tax if transferee status can be established." 14 EDWARD J. SMITH, MERTENS LAW OF FEDERAL INCOME TAXATION § 53:31 (2004). The tax court concluded Gordon Davenport was a transferee, and the Tenth Circuit affirmed that decision.

Gordon Davenport also argues that we should follow the lead of the Tenth Circuit in *Botefuhr*, a case in which the facts were identical to those in this case. In *Botefuhr*, the government attempted to assert transferee liability against Vestal to collect the tax owed by Birnie Davenport's estate. 309 F.3d at 1275. The question before the Tenth Circuit was whether Vestal was bound by the estate's stipulation during the tax court proceedings that the value of the Hondo stock was $2000 per share. *Id.* at 1281. Vestal argued that the stipulation was limited to the tax court proceeding and did not preclude litigation of that issue in the subsequent proceeding. *Id.* The Tenth Circuit acknowledged that confusion existed regarding whether the preclusion issue should be analyzed under the principles of collateral estoppel or res judicata. *Id.* at 1281–82. It concluded that "this matter must be evaluated as an assertion of [collateral estoppel], rather than [res judicata]. [Res judicata] is inapplicable to the situation here presented." *Id.* The Tenth Circuit offered no other insight into its conclusion that res judicata did not apply.[n.12]

Although we have the utmost respect for the Tenth Circuit, we decline to follow its decision in *Botefuhr* that res judicata does not apply; instead, we side with the Eighth and Eleventh Circuits in the *Baptiste* cases. As discussed above, each element of res judicata has been satisfied in the instant case. Accordingly, the doctrine of res judicata applies to preclude Gordon Davenport and the government from litigating matters arising from the same nucleus of operative facts that were or could have been raised in the previous proceeding. *See Moitie*, 452 U.S. at 398.

Finally, Gordon Davenport argues that the language of the stipulation concerning the stock value was limited to the tax court proceeding and in effect the government waived res judicata with regard to that issue. His argument fails because the language does not expressly waive res judicata or express any intent regarding future proceedings. The stipulation merely states the parties' intent with regard to the proceeding in the tax court: that the Hondo stock should be valued at $2000 per share.

In conclusion, we hold that all elements of res judicata have been satisfied. Accordingly, res judicata binds Gordon Davenport to the value of the Hondo stock established in the tax court proceeding. The doctrine also precludes him from relitigating other issues that were or could have been litigated in that suit, such as whether the statute of limitations barred assessment of the gift tax on either the gift to Botefuhr or the gifts involved in the installment sale transactions. Because we hold that res judicata applies, we do not address the government's remaining arguments.

* * *

In the *Davenport* case, what test does the court apply to determine whether res judicata applies? The Court of Appeals reversed the district court, finding that the cause of action in the prior litigation was the same, contrary to the district court's holding. What did the Court of Appeals examine in making the determination that led to a different outcome? And what is the nature of the disagreement between the Court of

---

[n.12] Under the doctrine of collateral estoppel, the Tenth Circuit ultimately held that Vestal was not precluded from relitigating the value of the Hondo stock because it had never been litigated on the merits. *United States v. Botefuhr*, 309 F.3d 1263, 1283 (2002).

Appeals for the Fifth Circuit and the Court of Appeals for the Tenth Circuit as to whether res judicata applies? Finally, what does this case suggest about the effect of stipulations, and does it depend on the court's finding that res judicata, not collateral estoppel, applied?

The *Davenport* case involved a prior civil proceeding. Can an acquittal or conviction in a prior criminal proceeding provide estoppel in a subsequent civil proceeding? One commentator explains the relationship between the two types of proceedings as follows:

> [I]n the Supreme Court's analysis in *Helvering v. Mitchell*, 303 U.S 391 (1938)[,] [t]he issues were (1) whether the taxpayer's acquittal of a charge of tax evasion was preclusive as to his nonliability for the civil fraud penalty and (2) whether civil fraud the penalty violated the constitutional prohibition of double jeopardy. Only the first issue concerns us here. The Court held that the acquittal was not preclusive. The Court reasoned that all that had been determined in the verdict of acquittal for tax evasion was that the Government had not proved beyond a reasonable doubt that the taxpayer was guilty of tax evasion. The verdict of acquittal "did not determine that Mitchell had not wilfully attempted to evade the tax." Since, the issue for civil fraud purposes is resolved by a lesser standard of proof (now clear and convincing under section 7454(a) in civil tax cases), the verdict of acquittal is not preclusive as to nonliability for the civil fraud penalty.
>
> This analysis means that a verdict of guilt of tax evasion — because it does affirmatively find the presence of the key fraud element by a higher standard of proof — would be preclusive as to the key fraud element the civil fraud penalty.

John A. Townsend, *Collateral Estoppel in Civil Cases Following Criminal Convictions*, 2005 TNT 4-28 (Jan. 6, 2005) (footnote omitted). This issue is discussed further in Chapter 12, which discusses civil penalties.

[B] Coordination of Deficiency and Refund Suits

Reading Assignment: I.R.C. § 7422(e).

As discussed in Chapter 9, IRS mailing of a notice of deficiency is a prerequisite for the taxpayer to litigate a deficiency matter in Tax Court. The "full payment" rule of *Flora v. United States* ensures that the taxpayer cannot respond to the notice of deficiency by paying a portion of the deficiency and litigating just that portion in refund court while litigating the remainder in Tax Court. *See* Flora v. United States, 362 U.S. 145, 165 (1960). However, it is possible that a taxpayer pursuing refund litigation for a particular tax year could receive a notice of deficiency for the same year. That could occur, for example, if the taxpayer pursued the refund court option in response to an initial notice of deficiency and the IRS later sent another notice asserting an additional deficiency. Similarly, the taxpayer could initiate a refund action after filing an original return or amended return claiming a refund, and the IRS could both deny the refund and issue a notice of deficiency.

Code section 7422(e) provides the procedure for such situations:

> If the Secretary prior to the hearing of a suit brought by a taxpayer in a district court or the United States Claims Court for the recovery of any income tax, estate tax, gift tax, or tax imposed by chapter 41, 42, 43, or 44 (or any penalty relating to such taxes) mails to the taxpayer a notice that a deficiency has been determined in respect of the tax which is the subject matter of taxpayer's suit, the proceedings in taxpayer's suit shall be stayed during the period of time in which the taxpayer may file a petition with the Tax Court for a redetermination of the asserted deficiency, and for 60 days thereafter. If the taxpayer files a petition with the Tax Court, the district court or the United States Claims Court, as the case may be, shall lose jurisdiction of taxpayer's suit to whatever

> extent jurisdiction is acquired by the Tax Court of the subject matter of taxpayer's suit for refund. If the taxpayer does not file a petition with the Tax Court for a redetermination of the asserted deficiency, the United States may counterclaim in the taxpayer's suit . . . within the period of the stay of proceedings notwithstanding that the time for such pleading may have otherwise expired. . . .

I.R.C. § 7422(e).

Note that section 7422(e) provides the taxpayer with the option to petition the Tax Court in this scenario only if the IRS mails the notice of deficiency "prior to the hearing of" the refund court case, and that the refund court "shall lose jurisdiction of taxpayer's suit to whatever extent jurisdiction is acquired by the Tax Court of the subject matter of taxpayer's suit for refund. . . ." The following case considers the meaning of these provisions.

STATLAND v. UNITED STATES

United States Court of Appeals, Seventh Circuit

178 F.3d 465 (1999)

Coffey, Circuit Judge. Plaintiffs-Appellants Donald and Iris Statland ("the Statlands") allege that they overpaid their federal income tax for the tax year of 1976, and are entitled to be reimbursed for the overpayment in the amount of $8,929. In December, 1991, the Plaintiffs filed a "taxpayer's refund suit" against the government in the United States District Court. Thereafter, the IRS issued a Notice of Deficiency to the Statlands, alleging that they had actually *underpaid* their 1976 income tax and owed a total of $4,023 as a result of the underpayment. The Plaintiffs-Appellants responded with the filing of a petition in the United States Tax Court asking for a redetermination of their 1976 tax liability.

After the Statlands filed their petition in the tax court requesting a redetermination of the IRS's assessment, the government filed a motion to dismiss the case (the taxpayer's refund suit) for lack of jurisdiction pursuant to Fed. R. Civ. P. 12(b)(1). Magistrate Judge Ronald A. Guzman granted the motion and dismissed the case for lack of jurisdiction pursuant to 26 U.S.C. § 7422(e). The magistrate found that under the statute, the district court lost jurisdiction once the Statlands filed a petition with the tax court requesting a redetermination of the IRS's assessment. The Plaintiffs appeal. We AFFIRM.

BACKGROUND

On December 1, 1992, Donald and Iris Statland filed a complaint in the United States District Court alleging that they overpaid their federal income taxes for tax year 1976 and thus were entitled to be reimbursed as a result of their overpayment of $8,929.26. The alleged overpayment resulted from two adjustments that the Statlands contend should be made to their 1976 income tax return: lessening their share of income from a business in which the Statlands possessed a partnership interest; and the Statlands' entitlement to an additional exemption for a dependant that they had originally been unable to claim.

Three months after the Statlands filed suit, on February 12, 1993, the district judge held the first of three status hearings. Over the course of these three meetings, the parties entered their initial appearances, consented to have Magistrate Judge Ronald A. Guzman preside over the case, discussed the potential avenues of appeal for the Statlands if they lost their case before the magistrate judge, and set dates for the end of discovery. The substantive issues in the Statlands' taxpayer relief suit were not discussed in any of these status conferences, though at one point during the third meeting the parties did briefly refer to a separate proceeding involving the Statlands in the tax court.

On June 4, 1993, the IRS mailed a Notice of Deficiency to the Statlands which explained that, according to the IRS's determination, there existed a $4,023 deficiency in their 1976 federal tax payment. According to the Internal Revenue Service, the Statlands' district court complaint, alleging that the government owed them $8,929.26 for tax year 1976, was in error. Rather, the IRS had determined that the Statlands actually owed the government $4,023 as a result of miscalculations in the Statlands' 1976 tax return documents. The IRS notice alleged that an adjustment was required to be made to the Statlands' 1979 tax return, and the change reduced a net operating loss that the Statlands had attempted to claim as investment credit and carry back to their 1976 return. According to the IRS, as a result of the adjustment there was *in fact* no investment credit available to be carried back to 1976, thus the Statlands erroneously carried back credit to their 1976 tax return that never existed. The IRS made the proper adjustments necessary to compensate for this oversight, and determined that the Statlands' tax liability for 1976 increased by $4,023, the amount of the alleged deficiency.

On June 7, 1993, the IRS sent a letter to the Statlands which referenced the Internal Revenue Code, 26 U.S.C. § 7421 et seq., and stated that proceedings in the Statlands' court case before Magistrate Judge Guzman would be effectively stayed pursuant to 26 U.S.C. § 7422(e), since the IRS mailed the Notice of Deficiency to the Statlands on June 4, 1993. The IRS specifically cited to § 7422(e). . . .

On June 22, 1993, the government filed a motion to stay the proceedings in the district court pursuant to § 7422(e). The Statlands argued that § 7422 did not require the district court to stay proceedings and noted that the initial sentence of § 7422(e) requires the IRS to mail the Notice of Deficiency "prior to the hearing of [the taxpayer suit]." They proceeded to argue that the term "hearing" should be broadly construed, and that the three status conferences constituted "hearings" of their taxpayer suit. The Statlands concluded that since the "hearings" occurred before the IRS mailed the Notice of Deficiency on June 4, 1993, § 7422(e) was inapplicable and did not require the district court to stay proceedings.

On August 23, 1993, before the magistrate judge had ruled upon the government's motion to stay proceedings, the Statlands also filed a petition in the tax court pursuant to § 7422(e). In the petition, they requested a redetermination of the IRS's conclusion that the Statlands owed $4,023 to the IRS for tax year 1976.

On September 13, 1993, the district judge issued a memorandum and order in which he rejected the Statlands' argument that § 7422(e) did not apply, and proceeded to grant the government's motion to stay proceedings pursuant to § 7422(e). The magistrate judge found that "the hearing of the [taxpayer's suit]" had not yet occurred, specifically noting that "in the instant case it cannot be concluded that any type of substantive hearing has taken place with respect to the merits of the Statlands' case . . . . None of the [three status conferences] could be argued to have substantively determined any of the issues in the pending litigation or raised any arguments as to *res judicata*. Thus I have concluded that a hearing has not taken place for purposes of [§ 7422(e)]." Pursuant to the magistrate judge's order, the stay remained in effect until November 1, 1993.

On June 27, 1994, before the tax court had ruled on the Statlands' petition for a redetermination of the IRS assessment, the government moved to dismiss the Statlands' district court case for lack of jurisdiction, and the Statlands opposed the motion. Both parties relied upon the language of § 7422(e), and in particular both parties relied on the provision (cited earlier) which states as follows:

> if the taxpayer files a petition with the Tax Court, the district court . . . shall lose jurisdiction of taxpayer's suit to whatever extent jurisdiction is acquired by the Tax Court of the subject matter of taxpayer's suit for refund.

In support of their request for dismissal, the government alleged that because the

Statlands filed their August 23, 1993, petition in the tax court (requesting a redetermination of the IRS's asserted deficiency in the 1976 tax payment), the Statlands had chosen to litigate in the tax court, and § 7422(e) mandated that the district court had lost jurisdiction over the Statlands' lawsuit.

The Statlands argued that the district court lost jurisdiction over their suit *only* to the extent jurisdiction was acquired by the tax court over the subject matter of the district court case. Specifically, the Statlands claimed that they petitioned the tax court to determine issues relating solely to the IRS's adjustment reducing the 1979 investment tax credit which the Statlands had credited toward the 1976 tax year. Their district court case, on the other hand, contemplated an entirely different subject matter; namely, the adjustment to the Statlands' share of partnership income as well as their entitlement to an additional exemption for a dependant. The Statlands claimed that the tax court case and the district court case were separate and distinct and dealt with a different "subject matter" under § 7422(e), thus the district court was not divested of jurisdiction over their district court case.

The magistrate judge disagreed with the Statlands' attempt to distinguish the cases and granted the government's motion to dismiss. The judge found that "despite the Statlands' attempts to separate the various components of their federal income tax liability for 1976, the primary issue is whether these components combine to realize a loss or instead establish that a deficiency was due that year." The court further noted that the Statlands' district court complaint demonstrated that they had attempted to carry their 1979 unused investment tax credit back to 1976, and thus the issues surrounding the 1979 credit actually bore upon whether the Statlands owed taxes for tax year 1976. Finally, the magistrate judge found that "the Statlands may pursue their suit as to such a single claim in the District Court or the Tax Court, but they cannot litigate in both. *Flora v. United States*, 362 U.S. 145, 166, 80 S. Ct. 630, 4 L. Ed. 2d 623 (1960)." The judge concluded that when the Statlands chose to petition the tax court for a redetermination of the IRS's asserted deficiency, the clear language of § 7422(e) effectively divested the district court of jurisdiction over "all possible issues controlling the determination of the amount of tax liability for [1976]." Based on these findings, the magistrate judge granted the government's motion to dismiss the Statlands' court case in its entirety, and the case proceeded in the tax court. The Statlands now appeal the dismissal of their district court case.

ISSUES

On appeal, the Statlands raise three issues:

(1) whether the magistrate judge properly found that the three status conferences before the district court and the magistrate judge did not constitute "the hearing" of the Statlands' taxpayer refund suit for purposes of 26 U.S.C. § 7422(e);

(2) whether the magistrate judge correctly determined that the tax court had acquired jurisdiction over the entire subject matter of the Statlands' district court taxpayer refund suit for purposes of 26 U.S.C. § 7422(e); and

(3) whether the dismissal of the Statlands' lawsuit unconstitutionally deprived them of their Seventh Amendment right to a jury trial.

DISCUSSION

This Court reviews *de novo* the district court's dismissal for lack of jurisdiction. *See Deveraux v. City of Chicago*, 14 F.3d 328, 330 (7th Cir. 1994). The court must take all well-pleaded allegations in the plaintiffs' complaint as true and draw all reasonable inferences in favor of the plaintiffs. *See Rueth v. United States Envtl. Protection Agency*, 13 F.3d 227, 229 (7th Cir. 1993).

I. *Whether the magistrate judge properly found that the three status conferences before the district court and the magistrate judge did not constitute "the hearing" of the Statlands' taxpayer refund suit for purposes of 26 U.S.C. § 7422(e).*

Section 7422(e) requires the district court to stay proceedings in a taxpayer refund suit only if the IRS mails to the taxpayer a Notice of Deficiency "*prior to* the hearing of [the taxpayer's district court suit]. . . ." (Emphasis supplied.) The Statlands allege that the IRS's June 4, 1993, Notice of Deficiency was mailed following, *not prior to*, the three "hearings" that occurred in the district court. The Statlands contend that because the Notice of Deficiency was not mailed until *after* these three hearings were conducted, the provisions of § 7422(e) are totally inapplicable to this case. If § 7422(e) is inapplicable, then the trial court was not divested of jurisdiction over the case, and dismissal was improper.

It is undisputed that between the time that the Statlands filed their district court complaint and the time the IRS mailed the Notice of Deficiency on June 3, 1993, the parties engaged in a total of three meetings. * * *

In finding that § 7422(e) required a stay of proceedings in the Statlands' district court case, Magistrate Judge Guzman found that "none of these three appearances substantively determined any of the issues in the pending litigation or raised any arguments as to *res judicata*. Thus I have concluded that a hearing has not taken place for purposes of 26 U.S.C. § 7422(e)." After reviewing the transcripts contained in the record, we agree with the magistrate judge's conclusion that as a factual matter, none of the three meetings even explored, much less determined, any of the substantive issues being disputed in the Statlands' refund suit. Moreover, the record does not reflect that either the district judge or the magistrate judge entered any judgments which could constitute *res judicata* as to other issues in the controversy.

The key to ruling upon the Statlands' claim is to decipher what exactly Congress meant by the phrase "*prior to the hearing of* [the taxpayer's district court suit]" as contained in § 7422(e). The Statlands argue that the term "hearing" is broadly construed and does not require that a trial occur. The government, on the other hand, alleges that "the hearing" of the case is equivalent to "the trial" of the case. The proper interpretation of the phrase "the hearing" as used in § 7422(e) was recently addressed in *Brown v. Commissioner*, 1996 Tax Ct. Memo LEXIS 95, 71 T.C.M. (CCH) 2301, 1996 T.C. Memo 100 (1996). In that case, petitioner Brown filed a complaint with the United States Court of Federal Claims concerning his tax liabilities for the tax years 1990 and 1991. The IRS then sent the petitioner a Notice of Deficiency, alleging that he failed to report income for tax years 1990 and 1991. Brown wanted to contest the determinations made by the IRS, and filed a petition for a redetermination with the United States tax court pursuant to § 7422(e). Thereafter, petitioner Brown argued that the tax court was without jurisdiction to hear the case. The tax court judge disagreed, and found that:

> To avoid concurrent jurisdiction over cases involving the same taxable year, Congress enacted section 7422(e). . . . Subsection (e) does not apply if the case in the Court of Federal Claims or the District Court . . . has already proceeded to a hearing, that is, to actual trial. (Citations omitted). The main thrust of section 7422(e) is to prevent two courts from having jurisdiction of the same taxable year at the same time. *Flora v. United States*, 362 U.S. 145, 166, 80 S. Ct. 630, 4 L. Ed. 2d 623 (1960). . . . If the taxpayer files a petition with the Tax Court before a hearing takes place in the refund suit, then the refund suit is stayed. Since [the IRS] filed a notice of deficiency *prior to the actual trial in the case* before the Court of Federal Claims, . . . this Court does have jurisdiction over petitioner's 1990 and 1991 taxes as determined in the notice of deficiency.

(Emphasis added.)

In the case under consideration, the Statlands' district court case has not proceeded to an actual trial as is required by the *Brown* decision. The three district court meetings could not even remotely be interpreted as "actual trials"; rather, the transcripts of proceedings reveal that these meetings were mere status conferences wherein none of the issues which would be disputed at trial were even touched upon. Where the case has not proceeded to actual trial, "a claimant is given the option of pursuing his suit in the District Court or in the tax court, but he cannot litigate in both." *Flora*, 362 U.S. at 166. We agree with the *Brown* court's reasoning, and hold that once the Statlands opted to litigate in tax court, the magistrate judge was bound to apply § 7422(e). We further hold that the magistrate judge followed the clear mandate of § 7422(e) when he stayed the district court proceedings and later dismissed the case.

II. *Whether the magistrate judge correctly determined that the tax court had acquired jurisdiction over the entire subject matter of the Statlands' district court taxpayer refund suit for purposes of 26 U.S.C. § 7422(e).*

Section 7422(e) specifies that where a taxpayer has filed a petition with the tax court, the district court in which the action is pending loses jurisdiction over the taxpayer's suit "*to whatever extent* jurisdiction is acquired by the tax court *of the subject matter* of the taxpayer's suit for a refund." 26 U.S.C. § 7422(e) (emphasis added). The magistrate judge found that the tax court acquired jurisdiction over "all possible issues controlling the determination of the amount of tax liability for the year in question [1976]. . . ."

The Statlands argue that under § 7422(e), the tax court does not simply usurp jurisdiction *over the entire subject matter* of the Statlands' district court claim. Rather, they contend that § 7422(e) permits them to proceed in both the United States District Court for the Northern District of Illinois and the United States Tax Court because each court is examining *a different subject matter* affecting the Statlands' 1976 tax situation. Specifically, the Plaintiffs-Appellants contend that the tax court is dealing with the narrow issue of whether a tax investment credit from 1979 was properly carried back to their 1976 taxes. The district court, on the other hand, is primarily concerned with the Statlands' refund action claims concerning their distributive share of partnership income and their entitlement to an additional exemption for a dependant in 1976.

We disagree with the Statlands' argument that they are permitted to litigate these issues in separate fora. The Statlands admit that the taxpayer refund suit they initiated in district court, as well as the petition (for a redetermination of the IRS assessment) that they filed with the tax court, center around whether or not they are entitled to a refund from the federal government for overpayment of their income taxes for tax year 1976. The Notice of Deficiency sent by the IRS stated that the Statlands owed $4,023 for tax year 1976. The Statlands' original district court action alleged that they had overpaid for the tax year 1976. Thus, both the Notice of Deficiency (which the Statlands challenged in tax court), and the Statlands' complaint (which they filed in the district court), involved only tax year 1976. It is a well-established principle that each tax year is the origin of a new liability and, more importantly for purposes of the instant case, a separate cause of action. *See Commissioner of Internal Revenue v. Sunnen*, 333 U.S. 591, 598, 92 L. Ed. 898, 68 S. Ct. 715 (1948). Thus, "in federal tax litigation, one's total income tax liability for each taxable year constitutes a single, unified cause of action, regardless of the variety of contested issues and points that may bear on the final computation." *Finley v. United States*, 612 F.2d 166, 170 (5th Cir. 1980). We agree with the magistrate's conclusion that:

> the Tax Court acquired jurisdiction . . . over the subject matter of the refund as it referred to the cause . . . of action involved in the deficiency notice. This included all possible issues controlling the determination of the amount of tax liability for [1976] whether or not raised by the deficiency notice. The Tax Court therefore acquired jurisdiction over any matter concerning an adjustment to the Statlands' 1976 tax liability.

Under § 7422(e), the Statlands were authorized to pursue the suit surrounding the

1976 tax payments in either the district court or the tax court, but not both. *See Flora*, 362 U.S. at 166. Once the Statlands chose to file a petition in the tax court for a redetermination of the 1976 deficiency alleged by the IRS, the Statlands effectively opted to litigate all issues surrounding their 1976 taxes in the tax court instead of the district court, not in two separate venues at the same time. Section 7422(e) was enacted precisely to avoid concurrent jurisdiction over cases involving the same taxable year. *See Brown*, 1996 Tax Ct. Memo LEXIS 95, 71 T.C.M. (CCH) 2301, 1996 T.C. Memo 100 (1996). Congress's goal in enacting § 7422(e) was laudable, for as we have often noted, the federal courts are overburdened enough without affording parties the luxury of litigating the same case in two different courts. *See, e.g., Dunn v. Peabody Coal Co.*, 855 F.2d 426, 429 (7th Cir. 1988) (praising legislation which limited plaintiff's remedy to a single proceeding and thus "cuts down on the already heavy caseload of our overburdened court system.").

We hold that the clear language of § 7422(e) should have made the Statlands aware of the consequences of their decision to file the petition for a redetermination, and the magistrate judge correctly concluded that once the Plaintiffs chose the tax court venue, the district court was deprived of jurisdiction over the case.

III. *Whether the dismissal of the Statlands' lawsuit unconstitutionally deprived them of their Seventh Amendment right to a jury trial.*

The Statlands' last point of contention is that the district court's dismissal of the Statlands' district court lawsuit unconstitutionally deprives them of their Seventh Amendment right to trial by jury. When the Statlands filed their complaint in the district court, they demanded a jury trial. However, when they filed a petition in the tax court and divested the district court of jurisdiction, their case was dismissed and their request for a trial before a jury was extinguished. The Statlands allege the dismissal thus infringes their Seventh Amendment right to a jury trial. We disagree.

Initially, we note that the Statlands could have had a jury trial by opting not to file a tax court petition. * * * But once the Statlands elected to litigate their case in the tax court, the district court was without jurisdiction, and thus there could be no trial in the district court, whether before a judge or a jury. The question, then, is whether the Statlands were entitled to a jury trial in the tax court. We note that the right to a jury trial does not apply to civil actions against the United States. * * * Our Circuit and others have held that there is no right to a jury trial in the tax court. * * * The Statlands were not unconstitutionally deprived of their Seventh Amendment right to trial by jury.

AFFIRMED.

According to the Court of Appeals for the Seventh Circuit, what constitutes a "hearing" for purposes of Code section 7422(e)? What was the "subject matter" of the Statlands' lawsuit?

§ 11.08 IRS USE OF SUMMONSES IN DISCOVERY

In a litigated tax case, a method the IRS can use to compel a taxpayer to produce documents is the discovery process. As discussed in Chapter 8, the Tax Court does not allow open-ended discovery by either the taxpayer or the IRS when preparing for Tax Court trial. The use by the IRS of its summons power could undermine Tax Court discovery by providing a one-sided tool broader than that generally available. In certain circumstances, the Tax Court will issue a protective order to prevent the IRS from using information obtained through a summons in a pending case. The Tax Court set forth guidelines in the following case:

ASH v. COMMISSIONER

United States Tax Court

96 T.C. 459 (1991)

OPINION

WRIGHT, JUDGE:

This matter is before the Court on petitioner's motion for protective order filed on July 6, 1990. Petitioner [Mary Kay Ash] seeks a protective order under Rule 103 to restrict respondent's use of information obtained through administrative summonses.

* * *

In a petition filed on December 29, 1989, petitioner seeks a redetermination of the deficiencies for . . . taxable years [1983 and 1985]. Petitioner resided in Dallas, Texas, when she filed her petition. In her petition, petitioner states that on November 29, 1985, petitioner, along with certain other individuals and trusts (the transferors), exchanged Mary Kay Cosmetics, Inc., common stock for: (1) Common or preferred stock of Mary Kay Holding Corp.; and (2) long-term notes of Mary Kay Holding Corp. . . .

* * *

During June of 1989, respondent began an examination of Mary Kay Corp.'s Federal income tax return for taxable year 1985. As of the date petitioner's motion for protective order was filed, no notice of deficiency had been issued to Mary Kay Corp.

During August of 1989, respondent began an examination of petitioner's Federal income tax return for taxable year 1985. In his notice of deficiency for taxable year 1985, respondent determined that petitioner had received dividends in the amount of the distributed Mary Kay Holding Corp. notes, or $10,669,951. Respondent also determined that petitioner had received constructive dividends with respect to $2,626,061 of the MKCI leveraged buyout expenses. With respect to taxable year 1983, respondent determined that as a result of adjustments to taxable year 1985, there was no investment credit carryback to taxable year 1983 as claimed by petitioner on her Federal income tax return for that year.

THE SUMMONSES

On September 20, 1989, respondent issued an administrative summons pursuant to section 7602 to Lawrence Cox, treasurer of Mary Kay Corp., seeking certain information, testimony, and documents (the MKC summons). The MKC summons relates to the 1985 and 1986 taxable years of Mary Kay Corp. and its subsidiaries. The return date of the summons was October 18, 1989.

On October 3, 1989, respondent issued a third-party recordkeeper summons (see section 7609(a)) to Jack Morris, a partner with the accounting firm of Ernst & Young, seeking certain information, testimony, and documents (the petitioner/Morris summons). The petitioner/Morris summons relates to petitioner's 1985 and 1986 taxable years. The return date of the summons was November 3, 1989.

Also on October 3, 1989, respondent issued another third-party recordkeeper summons to Jack Morris (the Rogers/Morris summons). * * *

During May and June 1990, respondent issued third-party recordkeeper summonses to officials of Morgan, Stanley & Co., Inc., Merrill Lynch Capital Markets, and Rothchild, Inc. (the adviser summonses), seeking certain testimony, information, and documents relating to Mary Kay Corp.'s 1985 and 1986 taxable years.

On October 18, 1989, the return date of the MKC summons, the treasurer of MKC provided certain documents to respondent, but withheld other documents that MKC concluded are subject to the attorney-client privilege. On November 3, 1989, the return date of both the petitioner/Morris summons and the Rogers/Morris summons, Jack Morris provided to respondent the information requested in the summonses and some of the requested documents. Morris withheld other documents on advice of counsel that such documents are subject to the attorney-client privilege.

On April 12, 1990, respondent commenced an action in the U.S. District Court for the Northern District of Texas to enforce the petitioner/Morris summons and the MKC summons. As of the date of petitioner's motion, no action had been taken to enforce the Rogers/Morris summons or the adviser summonses.

In her motion for protective order petitioner seeks an order prohibiting respondent's attorneys, agents, and employees engaged in representing him before this Court from obtaining access to, reviewing, or using any testimony, documents, or other information obtained pursuant to the MKC summons, the petitioner/Morris summons, the Rogers/Morris summons, and the adviser summonses after December 29, 1989, the date her petition was filed.

DISCUSSION

As a preliminary matter we note that the enforceability of the summonses is not at issue. The parties agree that the District Court, not this Court, has jurisdiction to decide such issue. Sec. 7604. We therefore do not address the issue of whether the summonses are enforceable.

I. Tax Court Rules of Practice and Procedure

Section 7453 provides that proceedings of the Tax Court shall be conducted in accordance with such rules of practice and procedure as the Court may prescribe. Petitioner argues that respondent's use of administrative summonses to obtain information related to the case pending before this Court allows respondent to undermine the discovery rules contained in title VII of our Rules of Practice and Procedure (Rules 70 through 76) and gives him an unfair advantage. Title VII provides rules addressing interrogatories, production of documents and things, examination by transferees, depositions upon consent of the parties, depositions without the consent of the parties, and deposition of expert witnesses.

The purpose of discovery in the Tax Court is to ascertain facts which have a direct bearing on the issues before the Court. *Penn-Field Industries, Inc. v. Commissioner*, 74 T.C. 720, 722 (1980). Discovery is not as broad in the Tax Court as it is in the Federal District Courts. *Estate of Woodard v. Commissioner*, 64 T.C. 457, 459 (1975). The discovery procedures established by our Rules in essence follow the Federal Rules of Civil Procedure (Federal Rules), but are not identical. *See* 60 T.C. 1097 (1973) (note accompanying Rule 70(a) (1974), which, for the first time, permitted interrogatories and requests for production and inspection of papers and other things). * * *

II. Authorization to Issue Summonses

Respondent is authorized by sections 7602 and 7609 to issue summonses and to utilize the information obtained through them. In relevant part section 7602(a) provides that for the purpose of determining the liability of any person for any internal revenue tax the Secretary is authorized: (1) To examine any books, papers, records, or other data which may be relevant or material to such inquiry; (2) to summon the person liable for tax, any officer or employee of such person, or the person having possession, custody, or care of books of account containing entries relating to the business of the person liable for tax, or any other person the Secretary may deem proper, to appear before the Secretary and to produce such books, papers, records, or other data, and to give such testimony, under oath, as may be relevant or material to such inquiry; and (3) to take such testimony of the person concerned, under oath, as may be relevant or material to such inquiry. Section 7609(a) provides for special procedures when a summons is served on any person who is a third-party recordkeeper.

III. Prior Opinions of This Court

A. *Universal Manufacturing Co. v. Commissioner*

* * *

In *Universal Manufacturing Co.* [*v. Commissioner*, 93 T.C. 589 (1989),] an agent of the Commissioner's Criminal Investigation Division served summonses on or about January 10, 1989, on two employees of WNC and third-party recordkeeper summonses upon two accountants for WNC. The testimony and documents sought by the Commissioner under those summonses were directly related to the matters at issue in the pending civil cases. The taxpayers moved for a protective order under Rule 103, asserting that the Commissioner's use of administrative summonses to obtain information directly related to the issues of civil cases pending before this Court allowed him to circumvent the discovery rules contained in title VII of our Rules of Practice and Procedure and gave him an unfair advantage in the prosecution of litigation before this Court. The taxpayers urged the Court to exercise its inherent authority over the proceedings to prevent the Commissioner from utilizing in the Tax Court proceedings any information obtained pursuant to those administrative summonses.

In *Universal Manufacturing Co.*, respondent argued that he was entitled to free and unfettered use of information developed through the administrative summonses in question. We noted that respondent chose to issue the notices of deficiency at issue and, in effect, chose to give the taxpayers the opportunity to come to this Court and invoke our Rules before his criminal investigation was completed, even though his internal administrative guidelines seemed to provide that a notice of deficiency normally would not be issued in such a situation. *Universal Manufacturing Co. v. Commissioner*, *supra* at 594. We went on to reason that the subject motion required us to reconcile two competing considerations. First, this Court has no desire to interfere in any way with respondent's investigations into violations of the internal revenue laws. We noted that respondent has the obligation to initiate such investigations and to pursue them to completion. Second, respondent's use of administrative summonses in a criminal case to interview third-party witnesses and obtain relevant documents concerning the issues in civil cases pending before the Court circumvents our discovery rules. *Universal Manufacturing Co. v. Commissioner*, *supra* at 594.

After balancing both considerations, the Court found that the Commissioner's use of administrative summonses to interview third-party witnesses and obtain relevant documents concerning the issues in cases pending before the Court impermissibly undermined the Court's discovery rules. The Court held that this was so even if the Commissioner's motives were fully proper. The Court stated its objective in so holding was to "require respondent to present his position in the civil cases pending before us without utilizing any information obtained pursuant to an administrative summons served after the cases were docketed in this Court." 93 T.C. at 595. The Court issued an order providing that the Commissioner was not to "obtain or use any testimony, documents or other information obtained pursuant to an administrative summons served after September 2, 1988," the date the petition to this Court was filed. *Universal Manufacturing Co. v. Commissioner*, *supra* at 595.

* * *

IV. Summonses Issued Prior to Filing of Petition

With regard to the summonses issued in the instant case before petitioner filed her petition with this Court (MKC summons, petitioner/Morris summons, and Rogers/Morris summons), we find that *Universal Manufacturing Co. v. Commissioner*, *supra*, is inapplicable. That case involved a summons issued after the filing of the petition.

Petitioner argues that we should extend our holding in *Universal Manufacturing Co.* to information obtained after the filing of her petition through the MKC summons, petitioner/Morris summons, and Rogers/Morris summons, which were issued before her petition was filed, because respondent's purpose in issuing them was to undermine this Court's discovery rules. First, we note that relatively few notices of deficiency result in the filing of a petition in this Court. Respondent had no way of knowing whether petitioner would file a petition. In addition, until a petition is filed, we have no basis on which to impose the rules provided for in title VII of our Rules of Practice and Procedure, and any administrative summonses issued by respondent prior thereto do not pose a threat to the integrity of our Rules. Nor will the summonses pose a threat to the administration or effectiveness of our Rules of Practice and Procedure. When the petition was filed, the parties on whom summonses were served were already under an obligation to provide the information called for pursuant to sections 7602 and 7609. Therefore, the competing considerations addressed in *Universal Manufacturing Co.* are not present here. If the summonses are for any reason invalid, petitioner's remedy lies with the U.S. District Court, not here.

We deny petitioner's motion for protective order with respect to the MKC summons, petitioner/Morris summons, and Rogers/Morris summons, which were all served prior to the filing of the petition in this case.

V. Summonses Issued After Filing of Petition

With respect to the adviser summonses, petitioner asks that we grant her motion pursuant to Rule 103. Rule 103 authorizes this Court to restrict the use of discovery procedures or information obtained through discovery when required to protect a party or other person against "annoyance, embarrassment, oppression, or undue burden or expense." As an initial matter, we must address the issue of whether this Rule may be used to restrict a party's use of information which is obtained through means *other than* our discovery rules.

Rule 103 is derived from, and for all practical purposes is identical to, Rule 26(c) of the Federal Rules. 60 T.C. 1057, 1122 (1973). Accordingly, we look to cases construing Rule 26(c) of the Federal Rules for guidance on the breadth of application of Rule 103. *Willie Nelson Music Co. v. Commissioner*, 85 T.C. 914, 917 (1985). Those cases uniformly hold that Rule 26(c) provides no authority for the issuance of protective orders to regulate the use of information or documents obtained through means other than discovery in the proceedings before the Court. * * * Thus, based on these cases we could conclude that this Court does not have the authority to issue protective orders under such Rule restricting the use of information *which was not obtained through the use of the Court's discovery procedures*, but was obtained through other legal procedures. To the extent that *Universal Manufacturing Co. v. Commissioner*, 93 T.C. 589 (1989), may be read as applying Rule 103 more broadly, we reject such a reading. Because a ruling under Rule 103 would not be definitive here, we do not express a conclusion as to the application of that Rule to the question before us.

That is not to say, however, that this Court is powerless to regulate the processes of this Court, viz, the use in this Court of information obtained by administrative summons. It is undisputed that courts have inherent powers vested in the courts upon their creation and not derived from any statute. *Eash v. Riggins Trucking, Inc.*, 757 F.2d 557, 561 (3d Cir. 1985) (and cases cited thereat). * * *

Moreover, our own rules contemplate questions of practice and procedure for which there is no applicable rule of procedure and direct the Judge before whom the matter is pending to prescribe an appropriate procedure. Rule 1(a).

As we have already stated, *supra*, our Rules of discovery in essence follow the Federal Rules but are not identical. Rule 26(a) of the Federal Rules (Rule 26(a)) allows, generally, nonconsensual discovery by deposition; our Rules do not. To give respondent carte blanche with regard to the admission of evidence obtained by administrative summons would, in effect, give him the full advantage of Rule 26(a), an advantage that we have withheld. We need not do so; we have the power to uphold the integrity of the Court's process by enforcing the limited discovery that, by rule, we have adopted. Where litigation in this Court has commenced, and an administrative summons is issued with regard to the same taxpayer and taxable year, we will exercise our inherent power to enforce the limited discovery contained in our Rules. We will do so unless respondent can show that the summons has been issued for a sufficient reason, independent of that litigation. Where litigation in this Court has commenced, and an administrative summons is issued not with regard both to the same taxpayer and taxable year (for instance where the summons concerns another taxpayer or a different taxable year), *normally* we will not exercise our inherent power. We will exercise that power, however, when petitioner can show lack of an independent and sufficient reason for the summons. In the instant case, only the adviser summonses were issued after litigation commenced. Those summonses fall within that situation where normally we will not exercise our inherent power. Since petitioner has not shown a lack of independent and sufficient reason for the adviser summonses, we need not exercise our inherent power nor detail how that power could be exercised. Rule 1 authorizes the Judge before whom a matter is pending to prescribe an appropriate procedure. What would be appropriate would depend on how best to maintain control "over [our] own process, to prevent abuse, oppression and injustice." *Gumbul v. Pitkin*, [124 U.S. 131, 146 (1888).]

Universal Manufacturing Co. presents the first situation (post-petition summons, same taxpayer, same year), and, we believe, the Court there may have concluded that there was no real prospect of a criminal investigation, although the Court did not make such a finding. *Westreco, Inc.* [*v. Commissioner*, T.C. Memo. 1990-501] presents a different situation. The Court there stated that it found compelling facts that justified its protective order but cautioned that no implication was to be drawn that all activities of respondent's trial counsel in an audit would justify a similar order.

* * *

We next consider petitioner's argument that this Court's power to exclude the evidence in question is inherent in its obligation as a judicial body to protect the integrity of its processes and to regulate the proceedings and parties that appear before it. We already have discussed the circumstances that would allow us to regulate the proceedings as requested by petitioner and, based on the record before us, we find that the summonses *in issue* are not a threat to the integrity of this Court's processes. The development of additional evidence through the summonses *in issue* will in fact benefit this Court's processes because it will result in a more fully developed factual background in which to consider petitioner's case. The additional evidence may also lead to the settlement of the case.

We also find that we are not compelled to grant petitioner's motion in order to regulate the proceedings and parties that appear before us. Our holding in this case that a protective order is not appropriate involves legitimate and good faith summonses with respect to other years, to related taxpayers, and to related tax liabilities, and involves the absence of any other underlying facts or circumstances that would justify the issuance of a protective order in this case. Petitioner has failed to show respondent's lack of an independent and sufficient reason for the summonses. The rule we announce herein in no way limits this Court's exercise of its power to issue protective orders or to impose other appropriate sanctions where the underlying facts and circumstances of a particular case establish an abusive or prejudicial situation that warrants relief. If, as we proceed, an abusive or prejudicial situation becomes apparent (which petitioner has so far not shown), we will be able to regulate the proceedings regardless of the rule we announce herein.

* * *

In conclusion, we deny petitioner's motion for protective order. With regard to each of the summonses other than the adviser summonses, we do so since all were issued prior to commencement of the litigation herein. With regard to the adviser summonses, we do so since petitioner has not shown a lack of a sufficient, independent reason for their issuance.

What standards does the *Ash* court set forth to address situations in which a taxpayer has petitioned the Tax Court and the IRS issues a summons relating to the same taxpayer and tax year or the same taxpayer but a different tax year? Does the Tax Court have discretion in such situations?

Compare *Ash* with *United States v. Admin. Enters., Inc.*, 46 F.3d 670 (7th Cir. 1995). In that case, the IRS issued a summons to a tax preparer in 1990 with respect to Burton and Naomi Kanter.[17] The IRS did not request an order from the District Court to enforce the summons until three and a half years later, at which time a Tax Court case to determine the Kanters' tax liability was pending. In an opinion focusing primarily on the delay between the issuance of the summons and the request for an order enforcing it, Judge Posner found the summons enforceable, finding that laches did not apply and that "[t]here is no defense of 'staleness,' despite a dictum in *United States v. Gimbel*, 782 F.2d 89, 93 (7th Cir. 1986), on which the appellants rely." *Id.* at 672. Is the *Admin. Enters.* decision consistent with *Ash*?

§ 11.09 LITIGATION SANCTIONS

[A] Tax Court

Reading Assignment: I.R.C. § 6673(a).

Taxpayers and others who abuse the litigation process may be subject to sanctions. In Tax Court, Code section 6673(a) may apply. It provides, in part:

(a) Tax court proceedings.

(1) Procedures instituted primarily for delay, etc. — Whenever it appears to the Tax Court that —

(A) proceedings before it have been instituted or maintained by the taxpayer primarily for delay,

(B) the taxpayer's position in such proceeding is frivolous or groundless, or

(C) the taxpayer unreasonably failed to pursue available administrative remedies,

the Tax Court, in its decision, may require the taxpayer to pay to the United States a penalty not in excess of $25,000.

A position is frivolous "if it is contrary to established law and unsupported by a reasoned, colorable argument for change in the law." Coleman v. Commissioner, 791 F.2d 68, 71 (7th Cir. 1986). Furthermore, if the Tax Court finds that someone admitted to practice before it has "multiplied the proceedings in any case unreasonably and vexatiously," the court can require that person, or, if an IRS representative, the United States, to pay "the excess costs, expenses, and attorneys' fees reasonably incurred because of such conduct. . . ." I.R.C. § 6673(a)(2).

One scholar notes:

---

[17] Burton Kanter was also involved in *Ballard v. Commissioner*, 544 U.S. 40 (2005), discussed in Chapter 8.

> These penalties have been regularly imposed on tax protestors. Before imposing a section 6673(a) sanction in a particular context, the Tax Court often warns future litigants that it will impose penalties. Even when a court dismisses a case for lack of jurisdiction, the court can impose penalties, which may be important when a tax protestor institutes proceedings for purposes of delay.
>
> While this penalty is substantial, it is discretionary in both application and amount. Such discretion means that similarly situated taxpayers may ultimately receive different results. More uniform application could increase the perception of fairness.

Danshera Cords, *Tax Protestors and Penalties: Ensuring Perceived Fairness and Mitigating Systemic Costs*, 2005 B.Y.U. L. Rev. 1515, 1561.

In *The Nis Family Trust v. Commissioner*, 115 T.C. 523 (2000), the Tax Court imposed penalties not only on the taxpayers, but also on their attorney. In that case, when the taxpayers brought in an attorney, she echoed their tax-protestor type arguments and added similar ones of her own. Neither the taxpayers nor their attorney, whom the court found acted in bad faith, responded to orders to show cause why they should not pay costs or sanctions. As that case reflects, the Tax Court is quite unsympathetic to tax protestors who allege, for example, that the income tax is unconstitutional or that they are not subject to tax. Consider the following case:

PHILIPS v. COMMISSIONER

United States Tax Court
T.C. Memo. 1995-540[18]

Foley, Judge: * * *

This case presents the following issues:

1. Whether petitioner is liable for the deficiencies determined by respondent. We hold that petitioner is liable.

* * *

4. Whether petitioner has asserted frivolous and groundless arguments that warrant the imposition of a penalty pursuant to section 6673. We hold that petitioner has asserted frivolous and groundless arguments, and the Court shall impose a penalty.

FINDINGS OF FACT

The parties have stipulated all relevant facts, and these facts are so found.

Petitioner resided in San Clemente, California, at the time he filed his petition. Petitioner has acknowledged that he received income from several sources in taxable years 1987 through 1991 yet did not file individual income tax returns for those years. . . .

In answering respondent's notice of deficiency, petitioner on June 9, 1994, filed a defective petition with this Court. The petition submitted did not comply with the form and content rules set forth in Rule 34(b). Petitioner presented typical tax protester arguments and claimed that he is not subject to the income tax. He also challenged respondent's "SUBJECT MATTER JURISDICTION", questioned whether he could "BE LIABLE FOR AN INCOME TAX" on his wages, and asserted that wages "ARE NOT A REVENUE TAXABLE EVENT WITHIN THE PURVIEW OF THE INTERNAL REVENUE CODE."

On June 14, 1994, the Court ordered petitioner to file an amended petition by August

---

[18] *Aff'd*, 99 F.3d 1146 (9th Cir. 1996).

15, 1994. In response, petitioner submitted on August 11, 1994, the same defective petition that had been rejected by the Court on June 14, 1994 (except that it bore a new date). On October 13, 1994, respondent filed a Motion to Dismiss for Failure to State a Claim upon Which Relief Can Be Granted. In her motion, respondent also asked the Court to impose a penalty pursuant to section 6673.

On October 14, 1994, the Court issued an order directing petitioner to file a written objection setting forth clear and concise reasons why respondent's motion to dismiss should not be granted or, in the alternative, setting forth clear and concise allegations of error and facts concerning the merits of the specific adjustments contained in the notices of deficiency. In its order, the Court also advised petitioner that penalties have been imposed under section 6673 in similar cases.

On November 14, 1994, petitioner filed a second amended petition that complied with the Court's form and content requirements. Accordingly, the Court denied respondent's motion to dismiss on November 21, 1994.

On September 11, 1995, respondent filed a Motion for Sanctions Pursuant to I.R.C. § 6673. A trial was held in Los Angeles, California, on September 12, 1995.

OPINION

The Internal Revenue Code provides that gross income means all income from whatever source derived. Sec. 61(a). The Supreme Court has held that income includes "gain derived from capital, from labor, or from both combined." Eisner v. Macomber, 252 U.S. 189, 207 (1920). The Court of Appeals for the Ninth Circuit, to which any appeal in this case would lie, has expressly held that wages are income and are subject to taxation. United States v. Romero, 640 F.2d 1014, 1016 (9th Cir. 1981).

In affirming this Court's decision in a tax protester case, the Court of Appeals for the Seventh Circuit aptly noted: "Some people believe with great fervor preposterous things that just happen to coincide with their self-interest. 'Tax protesters' have convinced themselves that wages are not income, that only gold is money, that the Sixteenth Amendment is unconstitutional, and so on." Coleman v. Commissioner, 791 F.2d 68, 69 (7th Cir. 1986).

In this case, petitioner advanced a variety of constitutional arguments that the courts have uniformly rejected. Generally, he argued that: (1) He is not a "taxpayer" as defined in the Internal Revenue Code; (2) the Tax Court lacks jurisdiction to decide this case; and (3) an income tax violates the Sixteenth Amendment because it is an impermissible "direct tax". We see no need to fully describe each of petitioner's constitutional arguments or to address them individually. To do so might imply that the arguments have some colorable merit when in fact they are groundless.

It is sufficient to note that petitioner readily acknowledges that he received income yet refuses to pay tax on it. Accordingly, we hold that petitioner is liable for the deficiencies determined by respondent.

* * *

Finally, we consider whether a penalty should be imposed under section 6673. Section 6673(a)(1) provides that, whenever it appears to the Tax Court that the taxpayer's position in a proceeding is frivolous or groundless, the Court may impose a penalty not in excess of $25,000. This Court has often imposed such penalties on taxpayers who make frivolous tax protester arguments. *See, e.g.*, Coulter v. Commissioner, 82 T.C. 580, 584–586 (1984); Abrams v. Commissioner, 82 T.C. 403, 408–413 (1984); Wilkinson v. Commissioner, 71 T.C. 633, 639–643 (1979); Santangelo v. Commissioner, T.C. Memo. 1995-468; McNeel v. Commissioner, T.C. Memo. 1995-211; Devon v. Commissioner, T.C. Memo. 1995-206; Carr v. Commissioner, T.C. Memo. 1995-138; *cf.* Connor v. Commissioner, 770 F.2d 17, 20 (2d Cir. 1985) (noting that the argument that wages are not income "has been rejected so frequently that the very raising of it justifies the imposition of sanctions").

In this case, petitioner knew that courts have repeatedly rejected his constitutional arguments and repeatedly imposed the section 6673 penalty on taxpayers who have made such arguments. Indeed, the Court so advised petitioner in its October 14, 1994, order.

In his trial memorandum, however, petitioner continued to assert the same groundless claims. Petitioner stated, for example, that "the free exercise and enjoyment of the God-given and *constitutionally secured right* to lawfully acquire property or compensatory income, by lawfully contracting one's own labor in innocent and harmless activities, for lawful compensation, cannot be (and therefore has not been) taxed for *revenue purposes*." Petitioner made similar assertions in his request for admissions, in his proposed joint stipulation of facts, and in a list of 21 "Special Questions for the Tax Court" that served no function but to restate petitioner's antitax views.

At the beginning of the trial, the Court warned petitioner that it would impose a penalty, up to $25,000, if it found his position to be frivolous and groundless. During the trial, the Court admonished petitioner several times to set forth a legitimate argument for not paying the taxes due. Ignoring these admonitions, petitioner consumed all of his trial time asserting that his income is not subject to taxation, contending that this Court did not have jurisdiction, and asking extraneous questions. Among his inquiries, he asked: "Am I here under common law?", "Is this a Court of Admiralty?", and "Does this Court have anything to do with the Uniform Commercial Code?" He also stated that he did not "see a corpus delicti" in this case.

In sum, petitioner has advanced trite constitutional arguments in his submissions to this Court and at trial. Petitioner has received $412,221 during the tax years in issue yet has steadfastly refused to honor his obligation to pay taxes. Indeed, his actions have wasted the time and resources of the Internal Revenue Service and this Court. Accordingly, we hold that petitioner's position in these proceedings is frivolous and groundless, and the Court shall impose a penalty of $10,000.

Respondent's motion for sanctions will be granted, and decision will be entered for respondent.

[B] Other Courts

Reading Assignment: Fed. R. Civ. P. 11(b)–(c).

The frivolous litigation penalty of Code section 6673(a)(1) can only be imposed by the Tax Court. The sanctions regime applicable in the other federal courts is different. Courts have applied Federal Rule of Civil Procedure 11[19] in some tax protestor cases. *See, e.g.*, Cheek v. Doe, 828 F.2d 395 (7th Cir.), *cert. denied*, 484 U.S. 955 (1987); In re Busby, 1998 U.S. Dist. LEXIS 16674 (M.D. Fla. 1988); LaRue v. United States, 959 F. Supp. 959 (C.D. Ill. 1997); *see also* Shrock v. United States, 907 F. Supp. 1241 (N.D. Ind. 1995), *aff'd*, 92 F.3d 1187 (7th Cir.), *cert. denied*, 519 U.S. 994 (1996). The Court of Federal Claims can similarly impose sanctions under its Rule 11, as well as its Rule 16(f).[20] *See* Lonsberry v. United States, 97-2 U.S.T.C. ¶ 50,888 (Ct. Fed. Cl. 1997).

---

[19] That Rule provides, in part, "[i]f, after notice and a reasonable opportunity to respond, the court determines that Rule 11(b) has been violated, the court may impose an appropriate sanction on any attorney, law firm, or party that violated the rule or is responsible for the violation." Fed. R. Civ. P. 11(c).

[20] Court of Federal Claims Rule 16(f) provides:

> If a party or party's attorney fails to obey a scheduling or pretrial order, or if no appearance is made on behalf of a party at a scheduling or pretrial conference, or if a party or party's attorney is substantially unprepared to participate in the conference, or if a party or party's attorney fails to participate in good faith, the court, upon motion or its own initiative, may make such orders with

Professor Cords comments:

> Because many tax protestors are pro se litigants, the courts may be hesitant to impose Rule 11 sanctions. This is particularly the case where the government fails to ask the court to impose Rule 11 sanctions. As with I.R.C. section 6673 penalties, Rule 11 sanctions can be imposed even if a case is later dismissed for lack of jurisdiction.
>
> It is important that the district courts and the federal court of claims have the ability to impose significant penalties on tax protestors even though these courts' jurisdiction over tax litigation is generally limited to refund jurisdiction. In addition to refund claims, tax protestors often file suit in district courts when the IRS asserts a deficiency, claiming that the United States Tax Court is not a legitimate court. The burden on the judicial system is also increased by claims filed by tax protestors seeking to enjoin tax collection, which are often filed despite the Anti-Injunction Act's prohibition against such suits.
>
> Because I.R.C. section 6673(a)(1) penalties cannot be imposed by the district courts or the court of claims,[n.242] the amount and nature of the penalties imposed by the court may depend on whether a taxpayer brings a prepayment suit in the Tax Court or a refund claim in the district court or court of claims. Since the jurisdiction of these courts is not coextensive, this difference in treatment, based entirely on the court in which the case is brought, may result in the perception that taxpayers are treated differently. This may seem unfair to some taxpayers.

Cords, *supra*, at 1562 (footnotes omitted).

The Courts of Appeals can impose sanctions for the filing of frivolous appeals under 28 U.S.C. sections 1912 and 1927.[21] The sanction under section 1912 consists of "just damages for [the] delay, and single or double costs." *Id.* at § 1912. Section 1927 provides that

> Any attorney or other person admitted to conduct cases in any court of the United States or any Territory thereof who so multiplies the proceedings in any case unreasonably and vexatiously may be required by the court to satisfy personally the excess costs, expenses, and attorneys' fees reasonably incurred because of such conduct.

Id. § 1927. Furthermore, Federal Rule of Appellate Procedure 38 provides: "If a court of appeals determines that an appeal is frivolous, it may, after a separately filed motion or notice from the court and reasonable opportunity to respond, award just damages and single or double costs to the appellee."

The following cases are among those that have been publicized by the IRS:

> On Feb. 2, [2001], the Tenth Circuit Court of Appeals imposed an $8,000 penalty on Larry and Sandee Gass of Capulin, Col., for appealing district court decisions which rejected their contentions that taxes on income from real property are

---

regard thereto as are just, and among others any of the orders provided in Rule 37(b)(2)(B), (C), (D). In lieu of or in addition to any other sanction, the court shall require the party or the attorney representing the party or both to pay the reasonable expenses incurred because of any noncompliance with this rule, including attorneys' fees, unless the court finds that the noncompliance was substantially justified or that other circumstances make an award of expenses unjust.

[n.242] I.R.C. section 6673 has limited application outside the Tax Court. Other courts may assess an I.R.C. section 6673 penalty of up to $10,000 only for frivolous or groundless proceedings under I.R.C. section 7433, which permits actions for certain unauthorized collection actions. I.R.C. 6673(b)(1) (2000).

[21] Monetary sanctions, penalties, and court costs awarded to the United States with respect to a tax case in District Court, the Court of Federal Claims, or the Courts of Appeals may be assessed by the IRS and collected in the same manner as a tax following notice and demand for payment. I.R.C. § 6673(b)(2), (3).

> unconstitutional. The Appeals Court had earlier fined them $2,000 for using the same arguments in another case. (Gass v. U.S.)
>
> Michele Brashier and Richard Hembree, of Tulsa, Okla., each drew $1,000 penalties on April 13 for arguing that requiring them to file sworn income tax returns violated their Fifth Amendment right against self-incrimination. The Tenth Circuit Court of Appeals noted that sanctions were warranted because the Tax Court had warned them that their argument — rejected consistently for more than seventy years — was frivolous. (Brashier v. Commissioner)

IR-2001-59. Consider the following case, as well.

CHRISTENSEN v. WARD

United States Court of Appeals, Tenth Circuit
916 F.2d 1462 (1990)[22]

STEPHEN H. ANDERSON, CIRCUIT JUDGE.

These cases are another chapter in Mr. Christensen's quarrel with the government over federal taxes, including his conviction and imprisonment for failure to file returns beginning in 1972, the subsequent assessment of taxes against him, and the collection of his liabilities through the seizure and sale of property. Having had or, in some instances, having waived his day in court on the merits of both civil and criminal proceedings against him, all without success, Mr. Christensen has now sued almost everyone in the government who has disagreed with him, from the Supreme Court to IRS agents. One suit was filed in state court and removed to federal court. The other suit was filed in federal court. The district court opinions filed on May 8 and June 2, 1989, copies of which are attached hereto, identify the parties sued and describe and address Mr. Christensen's contentions in detail. For the reasons set forth in the district court's opinion of June 2, 1989, the court granted the respective defendants' motions to dismiss pursuant to Fed. R. Civ. P. 12(b) and 56.

Mr. Christensen believes that he has no obligation to file income tax returns, that federal employees have no authority to pursue collection of the tax, and that federal courts have no constitutional grant of jurisdiction relating to such matters. Examples of his arguments in the cases before us are illustrative:

> A law requiring individuals to file returns of their income, private financial information, with public employees would be in conflict with both the Fourth and Thirteenth Amendments of the U.S. Constitution.

Reply Brief of Appellant at 6.

> Those who would cite the Sixteenth Amendment are destitute of mentality because the power to lay and collect Taxes, as provided in the Sixteenth Amendment, is totally different from the power to require individuals to report their private financial information to government employees.

Id. at 5.

> Defendant Sam violated the liberty provision of the Constitution . . . by finding a liability without citing a law making Plaintiff liable for the income Tax, which there is none.

Memorandum in Support of Motion to Vacate Memorandum Opinion, Order and Judgment, R. Vol. II, Tab 26 at 6–7.

> The power to require Edward D. Christensen to make income Tax returns is not delegated to the United States by the Constitution, nor is it reasonably to be

---

[22] Later proceeding, 916 F.2d 1485 (10th Cir.), *cert. denied*, 498 U.S. 999 (1990), *reh'g denied*, 498 U.S. 1075 (1991), *appeal dismissed sub nom.* United States v. Christensen, 1992 U.S. App. LEXIS 7250 (10th Cir. 1992).

implied from the power to lay and collect Taxes, an entirely different subject.

Memorandum and Conclusions of Law in Support of Motion to Vacate Sentence, January 9, 1986, R. Vol. I, Tab 12 at 13.

> Further, this Court must have jurisdiction over the persons. Neither the Plaintiff nor any of the Defendants live on a federal enclave in the State of Utah where the United States has exclusive territorial jurisdiction, therefore this Court lacks jurisdiction over all persons.

Id. at 3.

As indicated above, Mr. Christensen had an opportunity to test those or similar arguments on the merits in his criminal case, Tax Court case and collection cases. The problem is that he refuses to accept the finality of the decisions against him in those cases. The history of his litigiousness on the point includes the following.

With respect to his criminal conviction, Mr. Christensen knowingly waived his right to a direct appeal. Transcript of Proceedings in No. CR77-276S, R. Vol. I, Tab 12, at pp. 2, 4. Thereafter, he pursued collateral challenges to that conviction on three separate occasions. * * *

The Tax Court filed its decision upholding taxes and penalties against Mr. Christensen on November 22, 1982. Christensen appealed to this court which dismissed the appeal for failure to prosecute. Christensen v. Commissioner, No. 83-1227, slip. op. (10th Cir. Aug. 17, 1983). Christensen then petitioned for a writ of certiorari to the United States Supreme Court which denied the petition. 465 U.S. 1037, 104 S. Ct. 1313, 79 L. Ed. 2d 710 (1984). Thus, the Tax Court decision became final and unreviewable. Yet, almost four years after the judgment was entered, Christensen filed a motion [with] the Tax Court to vacate the judgment. In his motion he reasserted his original claims. The Tax Court denied the petition. Christensen then appealed once again to this court which affirmed the Tax Court and imposed sanctions against Christensen in the amount of $3,383.79 for filing a legally frivolous appeal. Christensen v. Commissioner, No. 86-2788, slip. op. (10th Cir. Dec. 23, 1987). To date those sanctions remain unpaid.

In addition to the appeals just listed, Mr. Christensen has filed five other appeals in this court, and one in the Ninth Circuit, all relating to his federal income tax controversy: United States v. Christensen, No. 87-2158, slip op. (10th Cir. Feb. 24, 1988) (appeal dismissed for lack of jurisdiction); United States v. Christensen, No. 84-2459, slip op. (10th Cir. March 4, 1985) (affirming judgment of the district court directing the sale of 1,293 silver dollars in partial satisfaction of Christensen's tax liabilities), *cert. denied*, 475 U.S. 1018, 106 S. Ct. 1203, 89 L. Ed. 2d 316 (1986); Christensen v. United States, No. 84-2503, slip op. (10th Cir. March 4, 1985) (affirming judgment of the district court denying Christensen's motion to vacate two writs of entry pursuant to which IRS Agents seized personal property in partial satisfaction of Christensen's tax liability), *cert. denied*, 475 U.S. 1018, 106 S. Ct. 1203, 89 L. Ed. 2d 316 (1986); Christensen v. Commissioner, No. 80-2302, slip op. (10th Cir. May 7, 1981) (denying Christensen's Petition for a Writ of Mandamus against the Commissioner of Internal Revenue and the Chief Judge of the Tax Court); Christensen v. Commissioner, No. 80-1065, slip op. (10th Cir. Jan. 26, 1981) (dismissing an appeal from the Tax Court); and United States v. Christensen, 831 F.2d 303 (9th Cir. 1987), *cert. denied*, 485 U.S. 1035, 108 S. Ct. 1595, 99 L. Ed. 2d 910 (1988).

Now we have before us yet again Mr. Christensen's persistent attack on these final judgments, using the same arguments he lost on originally to support a claim that judges and employees in the executive branch were wrong on the law. * * *

It is apparent from the history of this litigation that Mr. Christensen will not accept the judgment of the courts. The cases before us are not only another example of that fact, they yield insight into Mr. Christensen's thinking. The district court patiently explained its reasoning, with supporting authority, in two opinions running thirty pages in length. In response, Mr. Christensen characterizes the cases cited against him as "garbage decisions" and with respect to the laws in question he states: "Such laws, for lack of a better term, are 'garbage laws' which corrupt the law books and undermine those laws which are pursuant to the Constitution. The same is true of Rules and court decisions which are not pursuant to the Constitution." Brief of Appellant at 15, 17.

The district court did not impose sanctions against Mr. Christensen, but warned him that he is "edging toward the line where sanctions are warranted for frivolous, insupportable suits." R. Vol. II, Tab 24 at 23. We think Mr. Christensen has crossed that line, especially since he is reurging positions which we have previously determined to be frivolous, and for which we imposed sanctions. He is clearly determined to continue to litigate the same arguments which have been repeatedly rejected, by simply repackaging those arguments and adding new defendants. This court has the power to impose sanctions such as costs, attorneys fees and double costs for the filing of frivolous appeals, Fed. R. App. P. 38, and the inherent power to impose sanctions that are necessary to regulate the docket, promote judicial efficiency, and most importantly in this case, to deter frivolous filings. Van Sickle v. Holloway, 791 F.2d 1431, 1437 (10th Cir. 1986). *See also* Tripati v. Beaman, 878 F.2d 351, 353 (10th Cir. 1989). As in *Van Sickle v. Holloway*, we think that the following sanctions are appropriate: (1) Double costs are imposed against Mr. Christensen; (2) Mr. Christensen is prohibited from filing any further complaints in the United States District Court for the District of Utah, or any appeals in this court, that contain the same or similar allegations as those set forth in his complaints and other pleadings in the cases at bar (including any direct or indirect challenge to the previous court proceedings or judgments referred to herein), and the clerks of those courts are directed to return any such complaints or appeals to Mr. Christensen without filing; and (3) Mr. Christensen shall pay to the Clerk of the United States Court of Appeals for the Tenth Circuit $500.00 as a limited contribution to the United States for the cost and expenses of this action.

Although Mr. Christensen has already had an opportunity to respond to a request for sanctions, he has not been able to address the specific sanctions proposed herein. *See* Braley v. Campbell, 832 F.2d 1504 (10th Cir. 1987).

Accordingly, the clerk is directed to issue an order requiring Mr. Christensen to show cause why the above sanctions should not be imposed. Mr. Christensen's response will be limited to five pages. If the response is not received by the clerk within ten days from the filing of this opinion, the sanctions will be imposed. *See Van Sickle v. Holloway*, 791 F.2d at 1437.[23]

What do you think of the sanctions the court imposed in *Christensen v. Ward*? Do you think they were likely to be effective in deterring the sanctioned behavior?

§ 11.10 UNPUBLISHED OPINIONS

The citation to and precedential value of "unpublished" or "nonprecedential" court opinions rose to prominence following the Eight Circuit's decision in *Anastasoff v. United States*, 223 F.3d 898 (8th Cir. 2000). In *Anastasoff*, the Eighth Circuit not only followed its prior unpublished decision in *Christie v. United States*, No. 91-2375MN (8th Cir. 1992) (unpublished), but also stated that it considered *Christie* binding precedent. The court held that "the portion of [the Eighth Circuit's local rule,] Rule 28A(i) that declares that unpublished opinions are not precedent is unconstitutional under Article III, because it purports to confer on the federal courts a power that goes beyond the 'judicial.' " *Id.* at 899. In an *en banc* decision, the Court of Appeals for the Eight Circuit

---

[23] [The court subsequently imposed this sanction. *See* Christensen v. Ward, 916 F.2d 1485 (10th Cir. 1990). — Eds.]

vacated the panel's decision in *Anastasoff*, leaving the issue of the citation to unpublished opinions unresolved. *See* Anastasoff v. Commissioner, 235 F.3d 1054 (8th Cir. 2000).

Subsequently, the Court of Appeals for the Ninth Circuit, in *Hart v. Massanari*, 266 F.3d 1155 (9th Cir. 2001), disagreed with *Anastasoff*, stating, "We believe *Anastasoff* erred in holding that, as a constitutional matter, courts of appeals may not decide which of their opinions will be deemed binding on themselves and the courts below them." *Id.* at 1175. The court thus upheld as constitutional the Ninth Circuit's rule prohibiting citation of its unpublished opinions. *Id.* at 1180. The Court of Appeals for the Federal Circuit also refused to follow *Anastasoff*, stating that it agreed with *Hart*. *See* Symbol Techs. Inc. v. Lemelson Med., 277 F.3d 1361, 1366–68 (Fed. Cir. 2002).

In response to this controversy, the following rule was added to the Federal Rules of Appellate Procedure:

> (a) Citation Permitted. A court may not prohibit or restrict the citation of federal judicial opinions, orders, judgments, or other written dispositions that have been:
>
> (i) designated as "unpublished," "not for publication," "non-precedential," "not precedent," or the like; and
>
> (ii) issued on or after January 1, 2007.
>
> (b) Copies Required. If a party cites a federal judicial opinion, order, judgment, or other written disposition that is not available in a publicly accessible electronic database, the party must file and serve a copy of that opinion, order, judgment, or disposition with the brief or other paper in which it is cited.

Fed. R. App. P. 32.1.

The rule addresses parties' citation to unpublished opinions and what is required if the opinion is not readily available. Does it resolve the issue of the precedential value of such opinions? One commentator explains:

> The Rule's enactment (in which both Chief Justice Roberts and Justice Alito played significant roles) follows several years of vigorous debate not ordinarily associated with consideration of a rule of procedure, let alone the typically quiet rulemaking process for the federal courts of appeals.
>
> Unfortunately, the furor over the new citation rule has overshadowed a more important and divisive issue — whether it is appropriate for appeals courts to designate some (in fact, most) of their decisions as nonprecedential. The sponsors of Rule 32.1 were aware of the controversy that has emerged during the past decade regarding the wisdom and constitutionality of this practice, but they steered clear of it, emphasizing early on that the Rule is "extremely limited" and avoids taking any position on this highly-charged question.

Scott E. Gant, *Missing the Forest for a Tree: Unpublished Opinions and New Federal Rule of Appellate Procedure 32.1*, 47 B.C. L. Rev. 705, 705–06 (2006).

Why are some opinions unpublished? A report of the American College of Trial Lawyers explains:

> The anti-citation circuits use two main arguments to justify the wholesale quarantine of their own decisions. One, of course, is the rationale articulated in the rules of the various circuits — that these cases add nothing to the body of law: We put the important decisions in the "A" pile and the unimportant ones in the "B" pile and you shouldn't even look at the "B" pile decisions, much less talk about them. The prior restraint will not hurt you or your client because you really have no use for those "B" pile decisions. Everything you will ever need is over here in the "A" pile. The second rationale is articulated by Judge Kozinski in *Hart*, and by Judges Kozinski and Reinhardt in their article, *Please Don't*

> *Cite This!* — that the nonbinding decisions are correct (of course), but are not written for the ages, or calculated to lay down principles for all cases; that the judges are too busy to write better or more universally applicable nonbinding opinions; that, if lawyers start citing these "B" pile opinions, the judges will work harder to write better ones; and that this, in turn, will lead to a degradation in the quality of the "A" pile opinions, the circuit binding ones, because the judges will not have time to do them justice.

William T. Hangley, *Opinions Hidden, Citations Forbidden: Report and Recommendations of the American College of Trial Lawyers on the Publication and Citation of Nonbinding Federal Circuit Court Opinions*, 208 F.R.D. 645, 673 (2002) (footnote omitted). He goes on to argue:

> Neither argument is persuasive.
>
> The fundamental problem with the first thesis is that it is wrong: The judges and their screening clerks are not and never will be infallible in determining what is or is not a novel holding or a helpful discussion, or what will be one when considered in the context of a legal dispute that hasn't happened yet, and the functions for which past decisions may or must be cited are infinitely variable and largely unpredictable.
>
> A recent article points out that
>
> > [a]s an empirical matter, plenty of unpublished decisions have been accepted for review and reversed by the Supreme Court, demonstrating that it is difficult to make prospective judgments about which legal issues are "easy" in the abstract. . . . Consider [also] the number of unpublished opinions that involve lengthy dissents.

Id. at 674.

Once a nonprecedential category of opinion exists, is there no temptation to use that categorization on cases where the judges are simply not ready to create precedent, although the issue is one of first impression? The report of the American College of Trial Lawyers argues:

> Instead of making their "B" pile designations on the basis of a case's unimportance or lack of factual or legal novelty, the judges are sometimes denying binding precedential status to a case when they aren't absolutely sure that their logic is unassailable, or that they can persuade another panel member to reach the same result for the same reason if that reasoning is to have circuit binding power. In short, cases are sometimes consigned to the "B" pile not because they are too easy but because they are too *hard*. One might argue that, for busy courts, these are valid reasons for refusing circuit binding stature to such an opinion, but there is *no* principled argument for the proposition that its reasoning cannot be discussed.

Id. at 683.

The arguments for and against publication also arise in the Tax Court context. Although the Tax Court is an Article I court, and the status of its opinions therefore does not raise the same constitutional issues, the publication/nonpublication question arises there in connection with opinions that the Tax Court considers to have no precedential value, such as Memorandum Opinions. *See* Nico v. Commissioner, 67 T.C. 647, 654, *aff'd in part and rev'd in part*, 565 F.2d 1234 (2d Cir. 1977); McGah v. Commissioner, 17 T.C. 1458 (1952), *rev'd on other grounds*, 210 F.2d 769 (9th Cir. 1954). Accordingly, every decision to release an opinion as a Memorandum Opinion instead of a Division (T.C.) Opinion is both a predictive decision about the precedential value of the case and a decision as to whether others should be allowed to rely on it in the future.

Tax Court bench opinions (those rendered orally from the bench) raise similar issues. In 2008, in conjunction with the announcement that, after March 1, 2008, bench opinions would become available on its website,[24] the Tax Court amended Rule 152 to state:[25] "Opinions stated orally in accordance with paragraph (a) of this Rule shall not be relied upon as precedent, except as may be relevant for purposes of establishing the law of the case, res judicata, collateral estoppel, or other similar doctrine." TAX CT. R. 152(c). Accordingly, citation to bench opinions will be permitted, but they are treated as nonprecedential.

Do you agree with the arguments advanced in favor of unpublished opinions or with the arguments against them advanced by the author of the report of the American College of Trial Lawyers? Does the Article I or Article III status of a particular court affect your view on this issue?

PROBLEMS

1. If tax litigation were to be reformed, would you advocate a single trial-level court for all federal tax cases, a single appellate court, or both? Why?
2. What effects on tax litigation would the creation of a Court of Tax Appeals that heard all appeals from the Tax Court likely have? Would you support or oppose such a proposal, and why?
3. Dawn has received a preliminary notice (30-day letter) from the IRS reflecting adjustments to her Year 1 tax return that would increase her tax liability for Year 1 by $25,000. The adjustments relate to a large deduction Dawn took on her return. Dawn feels that the IRS's position is completely wrong, and although she will consider settling, she is willing to litigate the issue if necessary. Dawn's attorney has informed Dawn that there is a possibility that Dawn might obtain a shift to the IRS of the burden of proof under Code section 7491 if the matter is litigated.
    - A. Will the possible shift in the burden of proof if the matter is litigated likely affect negotiations with the Appeals Division if Dawn's attorney files a tax protest on her behalf in response to the 30-day letter?
    - B. Do you advise that Dawn and her attorney prepare to try to shift the burden of proof to the IRS under section 7491? Does your answer depend at all on whether the dispute between Dawn and the IRS is primarily factual or primarily legal?
    - C. Assume that Dawn is interested in preparing for the possibility of shifting the burden of proof to the IRS in eventual litigation.
        - i. What can Dawn and her attorney do to prepare to request a shift of the burden of proof to the IRS under section 7491?
        - ii. If Dawn were Dawn, Inc., a Subchapter C corporation (instead of an individual), what additional requirement(s) would it have to meet in order to be eligible for a burden of proof shift under section 7491?
4. Marisol mailed her Year 1 return to the IRS on April 1, Year 2. The return reflected her $40,000 wages, a tax liability of $5,000, and her wage withholding

---

[24] *See* Tax Court Press Release (Jan. 15, 2008), *available at* http://www.ustaxcourt.gov/press/011508.pdf, at 1.

[25] The accompanying press release explained:

> New rule 32.1 of the Federal Rules of Appellate Procedure, effective December 1, 2006, provides that a court may not prohibit or restrict the citation of Federal judicial opinions, orders, judgments, or other written dispositions that have been designated as nonprecedential. Although the Court is not bound by rule 32.1, *paragraph (c) is amended to remove any restriction on the citation of bench opinions*.

Tax Court Press Release (Jan. 15, 2008), *available at* http://www.ustaxcourt.gov/press/011508.pdf, at 17 (emphasis added).

credits of $4,000. Accordingly, she mailed a $1,000 payment in with the return. The IRS began examining Marisol's Year 1 return in 2005. On February 20, Year 4, the IRS mailed Marisol a notice of deficiency in the amount of $4,000 based on lottery winnings Marisol allegedly received but did not report. Marisol responded to the notice by paying in full the $4,000 deficiency and filing a timely refund claim on June 21, Year 4 for the $4,000. The IRS denied the refund claim, sending Marisol a notice of disallowance on October 1, Year 4, in response to which Marisol filed a timely refund suit in District Court.

A. On April 5, Year 5, the IRS counterclaimed in District Court for an additional deficiency of $2,000 based on deductions claimed on Marisol's return that the IRS alleges are erroneous. Assuming that the IRS is entitled to pursue the counterclaim, who will bear the burden of persuasion on it?

B. Assume instead that, three weeks prior to trial, but after a pretrial conference, the IRS sent Marisol a notice of deficiency in the amount of $2,000 based on deductions claimed on Marisol's Year 1 return that the IRS alleges are erroneous and fraudulent. Can Marisol petition the Tax Court? What will the consequences be if she does?

5. You represent Ruby, a calendar-year taxpayer, in connection with the audit of her Year 1 tax return. In response to a 30-day letter proposing a $40,000 deficiency in her Year 1 tax arising out of the disallowance of trade or business expense deductions, Ruby decides to appeal the IRS's asserted deficiency on a nondocketed basis. After settlement negotiations with the IRS fail, you file a Tax Court petition on Ruby's behalf contesting the disallowance of the deductions. The Tax Court ultimately rules that Ruby was entitled to deduct her Year 1 trade or business expenses, resulting in no deficiency. As the basis for its decision, the Tax Court ruled that the IRS had ignored applicable Treasury regulations that permitted the deduction. Assume that Ruby incurred the following expenses in connection with her case: (1) $2,000 in attorney's fees (8 hours at $250 per hour) for legal services provided during the audit stage of the controversy (before the IRS issued the 30-day letter); (2) $4,000 in attorney's fees (16 hours at $250 per hour) for legal services provided during the Appeals stage of the controversy; (3) $6,000 in attorney's fees (24 hours at $250 per hour), for legal services provided during the Tax Court proceedings, and (4) $500 in court costs.

A. Are any of the administrative and legal expenses recoverable by Ruby under section 7430? If so, which ones?

B. Procedurally, how does Ruby request a recovery of fees? How would your answer change if the IRS had settled the case during the Appeals stage of the controversy, before Ruby filed a Tax Court petition?

6. Travis conducts a software business as a sole proprietorship. In Year 1, he deducted certain business expenses. In Year 3, he incurred similar expenses and deducted them. The IRS audited Travis's Year 1 return and sent him a notice of deficiency in Year 4 asserting that the business expenses should be capitalized rather than deducted. Travis petitioned the Tax Court. While the suit was pending, the IRS sent Travis a notice of deficiency for Year 3, raising the business expense/capitalization issue and also raising an unreported income issue. Travis petitions the Tax Court in response to the notice of deficiency for Year 3. Soon after, the Tax Court decides the suit regarding Year 1 in Travis's favor, finding that the business expense is in fact deductible. Does res judicata or collateral estoppel apply to the Year 3 suit?

7. Meta Corp.'s Year 1 and Year 2 returns were audited by the IRS. During the course of the audit, on September 5, Year 3, the IRS served Meta Corp.'s accountant with a summons relating to Meta Corp.'s Year 1 and Year 2 taxable years. In December of Year 4, the IRS issued a notice of deficiency relating to

Meta Corp.'s Year 1 taxable year, and Meta Corp. petitioned the Tax Court. In February of Year 5, the IRS served Meta Corp.'s President, Arlette Spencer, with a summons seeking testimony and documents relating to Meta Corp.'s Year 1 taxable year. Can Meta Corp. obtain any protection from the IRS's use in the Tax Court case of the information obtained from the two summonses?

8. On April 15, Year 2, Paul, who is single and has no dependents, filed a Year 1 tax return reflecting zero tax liability. He reported wages of $50,000, in accordance with the W-2 he attached, and took a deduction for $50,000 which he labeled "value of labor expended." On the bottom of the return, below his signature, he wrote "It is unconstitutional to tax wages without allowing a deduction for labor." Paul claimed a refund of all of the withholding tax reflected in his W-2 (a small amount because Paul had claimed nine personal exemptions on his W-4 form). On September 1, Year 4, the IRS mailed Paul a notice of deficiency reflecting gross income of $50,000, the standard deduction, and one personal exemption. Paul timely petitioned the Tax Court. In his petition, he asserted the alternative arguments that (1) wages are not income within the meaning of the Sixteenth Amendment to the Constitution; and (2) if wages are income, the Sixteenth Amendment requires that the value of labor be allowed as a deduction. The IRS denied the allegations in the petition and made a motion for sanctions under section 6673. Are sanctions available? If so, what is the maximum amount of any sanction that may be imposed against Paul?

Chapter 12
CIVIL TAX PENALTIES

§ 12.01 INTRODUCTION: THE ROLE OF PENALTIES

The Code contains monetary penalties designed to discourage the three primary types of taxpayer noncompliance: Failure to timely file a return; failure to timely pay the amount of tax liability owed; and failure to determine and report on the return the correct amount of tax liability. The IRS prefers to speak of penalties not as punishment for wrongdoing (or as a source of revenue) but as a means of encouraging compliant conduct.

The following policy statement reflects the IRS's philosophy on the imposition of penalties:

INTERNAL REVENUE MANUAL
PART 20
Policy Statement 20-1

1. Penalties are used to enhance voluntary compliance.
2. The Internal Revenue Service has a responsibility to collect the proper amount of tax revenue in the most efficient manner. Penalties provide the Service with an important tool to achieve that goal because they enhance voluntary compliance by taxpayers. In order to make the most efficient use of penalties, the Service will design, administer, and evaluate penalty programs based on how those programs can most efficiently encourage voluntary compliance.
3. Penalties encourage voluntary compliance by: (1) demonstrating the fairness of the tax system to compliant taxpayers; and (2) increasing the cost of noncompliance.

* * *

9. The Service will demonstrate the fairness of the tax system to all taxpayers by:
   a. Providing every taxpayer against whom the Service proposes to assess penalties with a reasonable opportunity to provide evidence that the penalty should not apply;
   b. Giving full and fair consideration to evidence in favor of not imposing the penalty, even after the Service's initial consideration supports imposition of a penalty; and
   c. Determining penalties when a full and fair consideration of the facts and the law support doing so.

   This means that penalties are not a "bargaining point" in resolving the taxpayer's other tax adjustments. Rather, the imposition of penalties in appropriate cases serves as an incentive for taxpayers to avoid careless or overly aggressive tax reporting positions.

I.R.M. 20.1.1-1.

The IRS's view of penalties as a means of encouraging compliant conduct is consistent with economic and behavioral theories of tax compliance discussed in Chapter 1. Along with the audit rate, penalties largely determine the expected value of the taxpayer's punishment for noncompliance. Penalties also strengthen compliance norms among otherwise compliant taxpayers by assuring them that those who do not comply will be punished.

If penalties are to have any deterrent effect, taxpayers and their advisors must be aware of when they apply and when they do not. Over the years, Congress has sought to consolidate the tax penalty structure, reduce complexity, and establish precise standards for when penalties apply. *See, e.g.*, Improved Penalty Administration and Compliance Act of 1989 ("IMPACT"), Pub. L. No. 101-239, 103 Stat. 2106. And while some progress has been made, the Code still contains over 100 civil tax penalties. As you read through the chapter, reflect upon the IRS's Policy Statement and judge for yourself whether the current structure achieves its goal of enhancing voluntary compliance.

Although Code section 6751 requires that notices asserting a penalty contain an explanation and a computation of the penalty being asserted, a practitioner's understanding of when these additions to tax can apply remains important for purposes of advising clients of their obligations under the Code, formulating return positions, and planning transactions. This chapter focuses primarily on taxpayer-related penalties — those imposed upon taxpayers for delinquent filing or payment and for reporting positions leading to tax understatements. These taxpayer-related penalties represent the type most frequently asserted by the IRS and most frequently litigated by taxpayers. In addition, the chapter covers return-preparer penalties and penalties aimed specifically at tax shelter-type transactions.

§ 12.02 CIVIL PENALTIES APPLICABLE TO TAXPAYERS AND DEFENSES TO THOSE PENALTIES

[A] The Delinquency Penalty — Code Section 6651

Reading Assignment: I.R.C. §§ 6651, 7502(a); Treas. Reg. § 301.6651-1(a), (c).

The delinquency penalty in Code section 6651 seeks to encourage timely reporting and timely payment of tax. Both the late filing and late payment portions of the penalty apply to all types of taxes for which a taxpayer is required to file a return, including individual and corporate income taxes, gift and estate taxes, and most excise taxes. A separate failure to file penalty applies to information returns, and is discussed below.

Establishing whether the taxpayer timely filed a return and timely paid the tax liability implicates some of the issues addressed in Chapter 3, particularly those relating to due dates, filing extensions, and the sufficiency of a return.[1] Thus, for example, if the taxpayer submits a form or document that does not satisfy the formal requirements of an income tax return, the taxpayer may be subject to the failure to file penalty. *See* Beard v. Commissioner, 82 T.C. 766 (1984). Keep in mind, as well, that the taxpayer cannot use the "mailbox rule" in section 7502 to determine the date on which the taxpayer filed the return or paid the tax if the return or tax payment was mailed after the prescribed due date. I.R.C. § 7502(a)(2)(A).

[1] The Failure to File Penalty

The penalty under Code section 6651(a)(1) for failure to timely file a return applies on a graduated basis. The late filing penalty equals five percent of the amount of tax required to be shown on the return for each month (or fraction of a month) during which the failure to file continues, up to a maximum of 25 percent. If the taxpayer's

---

[1] As a general matter, the penalties discussed in this chapter can apply to an amended return, just as they can to an original return. *See, e.g.*, Colton v. Gibbs, 902 F.2d 1462, 1463 (9th Cir. 1990) (frivolous return penalty can apply to amended return); Mattingly v. United States, 722 F. Supp. 568 (E.D. Mo. 1989) (penalty for aiding and abetting understatement of tax liability can apply to amended return). Also, in most cases, a correct amended return does not preclude the application of a penalty to an incorrect original return. *See, e.g.*, Evans Cooperage Co. v. United States, 712 F.2d 199, 201 (5th Cir. 1983); (estimated tax penalty). *Cf.* Toronto v. Commissioner, 202 F.3d 255 (3d Cir. 1999) (filing of amended return does not prove absence of fraud in original return; amended return was filed after taxpayer pled guilty to a criminal charge); Shah v. Commissioner, T.C. Memo. 1999-71 (fraud penalty applied to original returns; amended returns were admissions of underpayment).

failure to file is fraudulent, the penalty rate increases to 15 percent per month, up to a maximum of 75 percent. I.R.C. § 6651(f). The penalty period commences the first day after the return is due (taking into account extensions of time to file) and ends once the IRS actually receives the delinquent return. Rev. Rul. 73-133, 1973-1 C.B. 605. The late filing penalty is computed based on the *net* amount of tax required to be shown on the return. For this purpose, the liability shown on the return is reduced by tax prepayments, estimated tax payments, and allowable credits (including the wage withholding credit under Code section 31). I.R.C. § 6651(b)(1).

The flush language in section 6651(a) contains a minimum penalty amount that applies specifically to income tax returns. If the taxpayer files the income tax return more than 60 days late, the late filing penalty cannot be less than the lesser of $100 or the amount required to be shown on the return. Under this formulation, would a delinquent return showing no net tax due still incur a $100 penalty? The Tax Court takes the position, supported by legislative history, that unless the delinquent return reflects some net tax due, no late filing penalty, not even the $100 minimum penalty amount, applies. *See* Patronik-Holder v. Commissioner, 100 T.C. 374 (1993) (*citing* H.R. Conf. Rep. No. 97-760, at 571 (1982)), *acq.* 1993-2 C.B. 1.

[2] The Failure to Pay Penalty

As you learned in Chapter 3, the due date for a tax payment is normally the date on which the tax return is required to be filed. I.R.C. § 6151(a). Failure to timely pay tax liability shown on the return triggers the late payment portion of the delinquency penalty in section 6651(a)(2). The late payment penalty also applies on a graduated basis, starting at .5 percent for the first month during which the tax remains unpaid and increasing an additional .5 percent for each month (or fraction thereof) during which the tax remains outstanding, up to a maximum of 25 percent. The penalty stops accruing on the date the IRS receives payment.[2] As with the late filing penalty, the late payment penalty in section 6651(a)(2) is calculated based on the net amount due. Moreover, if the amount of tax liability the taxpayer reports on the return is greater than the amount of tax required to be shown on the return (that is, the taxpayer over-reports), the lower amount is used to calculate the penalty. I.R.C. § 6651(c)(2).

The late payment penalty may also be triggered by the taxpayer's failure to timely pay a tax deficiency after it has been assessed by the IRS. I.R.C. § 6651(a)(3). For deficiencies of less than $100,000, the taxpayer has 21 calendar days after notice and demand is made to pay before a late payment penalty begins to accrue. If the amount of the assessed deficiency is $100,000 or more, the allotted time period drops to ten business days after the date of the notice and demand. *See* Treas. Reg. § 301.6651-1(a)(3). The penalty rate for failing to timely pay an assessed deficiency after notice and demand is also .5 percent per month or fraction of a month that the amount remains unpaid, but it increases to 1 percent per month or fraction of a month for the period after the IRS issues a Notice of Intent to Levy. I.R.C. § 6651(d). The maximum rate is 25 percent. I.R.C. § 6651(a)(3).

Under section 6651(c)(1), if both the late filing and late payment penalties apply during the same time period, the taxpayer may offset the late payment portion of the penalty against the late filing portion. As a result, during the period of time in which both additions apply, the combined penalty amount may not exceed 5 percent per month (composed of a 4.5 percent penalty for filing late and a .5 percent penalty for paying late). Consider the following example.

---

[2] The failure to pay penalty is reduced for individuals who timely file their returns and enter into installment agreements with the IRS to pay their tax liability over time. *See* I.R.C. § 6651(h). The penalty is reduced from .5 percent per month to .25 percent per month during the period of the installment agreement. Installment agreements are discussed in Chapter 15.

Example: Mary mails her calendar-year income tax return on August 14, without having obtained an extension of time to file. The return is received by the IRS on August 19. Mary's return reflects $33,000 of tax liability, of which $28,000 has been paid through wage withholding. Mary pays the balance due as shown on the return ($5,000) on August 31. The late payment penalty under section 6651(a)(2) totals $125 ($5,000 multiplied by 2.5 percent: .5 percent per month for the 4 full months from April 16 through August 15, and .5 percent for the fractional part of the month from August 16 through August 31). In addition, Mary is subject to a late filing penalty under section 6651(a)(1) totaling $1,125 ($5,000 multiplied by 25 percent — 5 percent per month for the 4 full months from April 16 through August 15 and an additional 5 percent for the fractional part of the month from August 16 through August 18 — reduced by $125, the late filing penalty that accrued during that same time period).

Notice that the 25 percent maximum rate applicable to each of the late filing and late payment additions applies separately. As a result, the late payment penalty may continue to accrue beyond the 5-month period after which the late filing penalty reaches its maximum. The combined delinquency penalty, therefore, can reach as high as 47.5 percent. Note also that the late payment portion of the delinquency penalty applies only if the taxpayer files a return. Would a taxpayer be well advised to avoid the late payment penalty by not filing a return for the year?

The number of months during which the late filing penalty and the late payment penalty in section 6651(a)(2) accrue is determined by taking into account extensions of time to file and extensions of time to pay. Recall from Chapter 3 that an extension of time to file a return does *not* extend the date prescribed for payment. Under the section 6651 regulations, however, obtaining an automatic extension of time to file an individual income tax return is treated as an extension of time to pay the tax if (1) at least 90 percent of the tax shown on the return is paid on or before the regular due date for the return and (2) the balance of the tax due is paid with the return. Treas. Reg. § 301.6651-1(c)(3). A similar rule applies to an automatic extension of time to file a corporate income tax return obtained by filing Form 7004. Treas. Reg. § 301.6651-1(c)(4).

[3] The Reasonable Cause Defense

Neither the late filing nor late payment addition applies if the delinquency is due to reasonable cause and not willful neglect. According to the section 6651 regulations, reasonable cause exists when the taxpayer exercises ordinary business care and prudence, but is still unable to file or pay on time. *See* Treas. Reg. § 301.6651-1(c). The Penalty Handbook portion of the Internal Revenue Manual includes a summary of the pertinent facts and circumstances that IRS agents should consider when deciding whether reasonable cause exists.

INTERNAL REVENUE MANUAL
PART 20 — Penalties and Interest

20.1.1.3.1

Reasonable Cause

(1) Reasonable cause is based on all facts and circumstances in each situation and allows the Service to provide relief from a penalty that would otherwise be assessed. Reasonable cause relief is generally granted when the taxpayer exercises ordinary business care and prudence in determining their tax obligations but is unable to comply with those obligations.

* * *

(5) Taxpayers have reasonable cause when their conduct justifies the nonassertion or abatement of a penalty. Each case must be judged individually based on the facts and circumstances at hand. Consider the following in conjunction with specific criteria identified in the remainder of IRM 20.1.1.3.

- What happened and when did it happen?
- During the period of time the taxpayer was noncompliant, what facts and circumstances prevented the taxpayer from filing a return, paying a tax, or otherwise complying with the tax law?
- How did the facts and circumstances prevent the taxpayer from complying?
- How did the taxpayer handle the remainder of their affairs during this time?
- Once the facts and circumstances changed, what attempt did the taxpayer make to comply?

(6) Reasonable cause **does not exist** if, after the facts and circumstances that explain the taxpayer's noncompliant behavior cease to exist, the taxpayer fails to comply with the tax obligation within a reasonable period of time.

* * *

Ordinary Business Care and Prudence

20.1.1.3.1.2

(1) Ordinary business care and prudence includes making provision for business obligations to be met when reasonably foreseeable events occur. A taxpayer may establish reasonable cause by providing facts and circumstances showing the taxpayer executed ordinary business care and prudence (taking that degree of care that a reasonably prudent person would exercise), but nevertheless was unable to comply with the law.

(2) In determining if the taxpayer exercised ordinary business care and prudence, review available information including the following:

a. **Taxpayer's Reason.** The taxpayer's reason should address the penalty imposed. To show reasonable cause, the dates and explanations should clearly correspond with events on which the penalties are based. If the dates and explanations do not correspond to the events on which the penalties are based, request additional information from the taxpayer that may clarify the explanation (*See* IRM 20.1.1.3.1).

b. **Compliance History.** Check the preceding tax years (at least 2) for payment patterns and the taxpayer's overall compliance history. The same penalty, previously assessed or abated, may indicate that the taxpayer is not exercising ordinary business care. If this is the taxpayer's first incident of noncompliant behavior, weigh this factor with other reasons the taxpayer gives for reasonable cause, since a first time failure to comply does not by itself establish reasonable cause.

c. **Length of Time.** Consider the length of time between the event cited as a reason for noncompliance and subsequent compliance. *See* IRM 20.1.1.3.1. Consider (1) when the act was required by law, (2) the period of time during which the taxpayer was unable to comply with the law due to circumstances beyond the taxpayer's control, and (3) when the taxpayer complied with the law.

d. **Circumstances Beyond the Taxpayer's Control.** Consider whether or not the taxpayer could have anticipated the event that caused the noncompliance. Reasonable cause is **generally** established when the taxpayer exercises ordinary business care and prudence but, due to circumstances beyond the taxpayer's control, the taxpayer was unable to timely meet the tax obligation. The taxpayer's obligation to meet the tax law requirements is ongoing. Ordinary business care and prudence requires that the taxpayer continue to attempt to meet the requirements, even though late.

* * *

Ignorance of the Law

20.1.1.3.1.2.1

(1) In some instances taxpayers may not be aware of specific obligations to file and/or pay taxes. The **ordinary business care and prudence standard** requires that taxpayers make reasonable efforts to determine their tax obligations. Reasonable cause may be established if the taxpayer shows ignorance of the law in conjunction with other facts and circumstances.

(2) For example, consider:

a. The taxpayer's education,

b. If the taxpayer has been subject to the tax,

c. If the taxpayer has been penalized, or

d. If there were recent changes in the tax forms or law which a taxpayer could not reasonably be expected to know.

(3) The level of complexity of a tax or compliance issue is another factor that should be considered in evaluating reasonable cause because of ignorance of the law.

(4) Reasonable cause should never be presumed, even in cases where ignorance of the law is claimed.

* * *

Death, Serious Illness, or Unavoidable Absence

20.1.1.3.1.2.4

(1) Death, serious illness, or unavoidable absence of the taxpayer may establish reasonable cause for late filing, payment, or deposit, for the following:

a. An **individual**: If there was a death, serious illness, or unavoidable absence of the taxpayer or a death or serious illness in that taxpayer's immediate family (i.e., spouse, sibling, parents, grandparents, children).

* * *

(2) If someone, other than the taxpayer or the person responsible, is authorized to meet the obligation, consider the reasons why that person did not meet the obligation when evaluating the request for relief. In the case of a business, if only one person was authorized, determine whether this was in keeping with ordinary business care and prudence.

(3) Information to consider when evaluating a request for penalty relief based on reasonable cause due to death, serious illness or unavoidable absence includes, but is not limited to, the following:

a. The relationship of the taxpayer to the other parties involved.

b. The date of death.

c. The dates, duration, and severity of illness.

d. The dates and reasons for absence.

e. How the event prevented compliance.

f. If other business obligations were impaired.

g. If tax duties were attended to promptly when the illness passed, or within a reasonable period of time after a death or absence.

Unable to Obtain Records

20.1.1.3.1.2.5

(1) Explanations relating to the inability to obtain the necessary records may constitute reasonable cause in some instances, but may not in others.

(2) Consider the facts and circumstances relevant to each case and evaluate the request for penalty relief.

(3) If the taxpayer was unable to obtain records necessary to comply with a tax obligation, the taxpayer may or may not be able to establish reasonable cause. Reasonable cause may be established if **the taxpayer exercised ordinary business care and prudence, but due to circumstances beyond the taxpayer's control they were unable to comply**.

(4) Information to consider when evaluating such a request includes, but is not limited to, an explanation as to:

- Why the records were needed to comply;
- Why the records were unavailable and what steps were taken to secure the records;
- When and how the taxpayer became aware that they did not have the necessary records;
- If other means were explored to secure needed information;
- Why the taxpayer did not estimate the information;
- If the taxpayer contacted the Service for instructions on what to do about the missing information;
- If the taxpayer promptly complied once the missing information was received; and
- Supporting documentation such as copies of letters written and responses received in an effort to get the needed information.

* * *

May a taxpayer avoid a delinquency penalty by relying on a third party to file or pay on the taxpayer's behalf? The following case considers the circumstances under which, if any, a taxpayer may delegate to another party the duty to file or pay taxes.

UNITED STATES v. BOYLE

United States Supreme Court
469 U.S. 241 (1985)

CHIEF JUSTICE BURGER delivered the opinion of the Court.

We granted certiorari to resolve a conflict among the Circuits on whether a taxpayer's reliance on an attorney to prepare and file a tax return constitutes "reasonable cause" under § 6651(a)(1) of the Internal Revenue Code, so as to defeat a statutory penalty incurred because of a late filing.

I.

A.

Respondent, Robert W. Boyle, was appointed executor of the will of his mother, Myra Boyle, who died on September 14, 1978; respondent retained Ronald Keyser to serve as attorney for the estate. Keyser informed respondent that the estate must file a federal estate tax return, but he did not mention the deadline for filing this return. Under § 6075(a), the return was due within nine months of the decedent's death, *i.e.*, not later than June 14, 1979. Although a businessman, respondent was not experienced in the field of federal estate taxation, other than having been executor of his father's will 20 years earlier. It is undisputed that he relied on Keyser for instruction and guidance. He cooperated fully with his attorney and provided Keyser with all relevant information and records. Respondent and his wife contacted Keyser a number of times during the spring and summer of 1979 to inquire about the progress of the proceedings and the preparation of the tax return; they were assured that they would be notified when the return was due and that the return would be filed "in plenty of time." App. 39. When respondent called Keyser on September 6, 1979, he learned for the first time that the return was by then overdue. Apparently, Keyser had overlooked the matter because of a clerical oversight in omitting the filing date from Keyser's master calendar. Respondent met with Keyser on September 11, and the return was filed on September 13, three months late.

B.

Acting pursuant to 26 U.S.C. § 6651(a)(1), the Internal Revenue Service assessed against the estate an additional tax of $17,124.45 as a penalty for the late filing, with $1,326.56 in interest. Section 6651(a)(1) reads in pertinent part:

> "In case of failure . . . to file any return . . . on the date prescribed therefor . . . , *unless it is shown that such failure is due to reasonable cause and not due to willful neglect,* there shall be added to the amount required to be shown as tax on such return 5 percent of the amount of such tax if the failure is for not more than 1 month, with an additional 5 percent for each additional month or fraction thereof during which such failure continues, not exceeding 25 percent in the aggregate . . . ." (Emphasis added.)

A Treasury Regulation provides that, to demonstrate "reasonable cause," a taxpayer filing a late return must show that he "exercised ordinary business care and prudence and was nevertheless unable to file the return within the prescribed time." 26 CFR § 301.6651-1(c)(1) (1984).[n.1]

Respondent paid the penalty and filed a claim for a refund. He conceded that the assessment for interest was proper, but contended that the penalty was unjustified

[n.1] The Internal Revenue Service has articulated eight reasons for a late filing that it considers to constitute "reasonable cause." These reasons include unavoidable postal delays, the taxpayer's timely filing of a return with the wrong IRS office, the taxpayer's reliance on the erroneous advice of an IRS officer or employee, the death or series illness of the taxpayer or a member of his immediate family, the taxpayer's unavoidable absence, destruction by casualty of the taxpayer's records or place of business, failure of the IRS to furnish the taxpayer with the necessary forms in a timely fashion, and the inability of an IRS representative to meet with the taxpayer when the taxpayer makes a timely visit to an IRS office in an attempt to secure information or aid in the preparation of a return. Internal Revenue Manual (CCH) § 4350, (24) ¶ 22.2(2) (Mar. 20, 1980) (Audit Technique Manual for Estate Tax Examiners). If the cause asserted by the taxpayer does not implicate any of these right reasons, the district director determines whether the asserted cause is reasonable. "A cause for delinquency which appears to a person of ordinary prudence and intelligence as a reasonable cause for delay in filing a return and which clearly negatives willful neglect will be acceptable as reasonable." *Id.* ¶ 22.2(3).

because his failure to file the return on time was "due to reasonable cause," *i.e.*, reliance on his attorney. Respondent brought suit in the United States District Court, which concluded that the claim was controlled by the Court of Appeals' holding in *Rohrabaugh v. United States*, 611 F.2d 211 (CA7 1979). In *Rohrabaugh*, the United States Court of Appeals for the Seventh Circuit held that reliance upon counsel constitutes "reasonable cause" under § 6651(a)(1) when: (1) the taxpayer is unfamiliar with the tax law; (2) the taxpayer makes full disclosure of all relevant facts to the attorney that he relies upon, and maintains contact with the attorney from time to time during the administration of the estate; and (3) the taxpayer has otherwise exercised ordinary business care and prudence. 611 F.2d at 215, 219. The District Court held that, under *Rohrabaugh*, respondent had established "reasonable cause" for the late filing of his tax return; accordingly, it granted summary judgment for respondent and ordered refund of the penalty. A divided panel of the Seventh Circuit, with three opinions, affirmed. 710 F.2d 1251 (1983).

We granted certiorari, 466 U.S. 903 (1984), and we reverse.

II.

A.

Congress' purpose in the prescribed civil penalty was to ensure timely filing of tax returns to the end that tax liability will be ascertained and paid promptly. The relevant statutory deadline provision is clear; it mandates that all federal estate tax returns be filed within nine months from the decedent's death, 26 U.S.C. § 6075(a). Failure to comply incurs a penalty of 5 percent of the ultimately determined tax for each month the return is late, with a maximum of 25 percent of the base tax. To escape the penalty, the taxpayer bears the heavy burden of proving both (1) that the failure did not result from "willful neglect," and (2) that the failure was "due to reasonable cause." 26 U.S.C. § 6651(a)(1).

The meaning of these two standards has become clear over the near-70 years of their presence in the statutes. As used here, the term "willful neglect" may be read as meaning a conscious, intentional failure or reckless indifference. *See* Orient Investment & Finance Co. v. Commissioner, 166 F.2d 601, 602, 83 U.S. App. D.C. 74, 75 (1948) * * * . Like "willful neglect," the term "reasonable cause" is not defined in the Code, but the relevant Treasury Regulation calls on the taxpayer to demonstrate that he exercised "ordinary business care and prudence" but nevertheless was "unable to file the return within the prescribed time." 26 CFR § 301.6651-1 (c)(1) (1984); *accord, e.g.*, Fleming v. United States, 648 F.2d 1122, 1124 (CA7 1981) * * * . The Commissioner does not contend that respondent's failure to file the estate tax return on time was willful or reckless. The question to be resolved is whether, under the statute, reliance on an attorney in the instant circumstances is a "reasonable cause" for failure to meet the deadline.

B.

In affirming the District Court, the Court of Appeals recognized the difficulties presented by its formulation but concluded that it was bound by *Rohrabaugh v. United States*, 611 F.2d 211 (CA7 1979). The Court of Appeals placed great importance on the fact that respondent engaged the services of an experienced attorney specializing in probate matters and that he duly inquired from time to time as to the progress of the proceedings. As in *Rohrabaugh*, *see id.*, at 219, the Court of Appeals in this case emphasized that its holding was narrowly drawn and closely tailored to the facts before it. The court stressed that the question of "reasonable cause" was an issue to be determined on a case-by-case basis. *See* 710 F.2d at 1253–1254; *id.*, at 1254 (Coffey, J., concurring).

Other Courts of Appeals have dealt with the issue of "reasonable cause" for a late filing and reached contrary conclusions. In *Ferrando v. United States*, 245 F.2d 582 (CA9 1957), the court held that taxpayers have a personal and nondelegable duty to file a return on time, and that reliance on an attorney to fulfill this obligation does not constitute "reasonable cause" for a tardy filing. *Id.*, at 589. The Fifth Circuit has similarly held that the responsibility for ensuring a timely filing is the taxpayer's alone, and that the taxpayer's reliance on his tax advisers — accountants or attorneys — is not a "reasonable cause." Millette & Associates v. Commissioner, 594 F.2d 121, 124–125 (per curiam), *cert. denied*, 444 U.S. 899 (1979); Logan Lumber Co. v. Commissioner, 365 F.2d 846, 854 (1966). The Eighth Circuit also has concluded that reliance on counsel does not constitute "reasonable cause." Smith v. United States, 702 F.2d 741, 743 (1983) (*per curiam*) * * * .

III.

We need not dwell on the similarities or differences in the facts presented by the conflicting holdings. The time has come for a rule with as "bright" a line as can be drawn consistent with the statute and implementing regulations. Deadlines are inherently arbitrary; fixed dates, however, are often essential to accomplish necessary results. The Government has millions of taxpayers to monitor, and our system of self-assessment in the initial calculation of a tax simply cannot work on any basis other than one of strict filing standards. Any less rigid standard would risk encouraging a lax attitude toward filing dates. Prompt payment of taxes is imperative to the Government, which should not have to assume the burden of unnecessary ad hoc determinations.

Congress has placed the burden of prompt filing on the executor, not on some agent or employee of the executor. The duty is fixed and clear; Congress intended to place upon the taxpayer an obligation to ascertain the statutory deadline and then to meet that deadline, except in a very narrow range of situations. Engaging an attorney to assist in the probate proceedings is plainly an exercise of the "ordinary business care and prudence" prescribed by the regulations, 26 CFR § 301.6651-1(c)(1) (1984), but that does not provide an answer to the question we face here. To say that it was "reasonable" for the executor to *assume* that the attorney would comply with the statute may resolve the matter as between them, but not with respect to the executor's obligations under the statute. Congress has charged the executor with an unambiguous, precisely defined duty to file the return within nine months; extensions are granted fairly routinely. That the attorney, as the executor's agent, was expected to attend to the matter does not relieve the principal of his duty to comply with the statute.

This case is not one in which a taxpayer has relied on the erroneous advice of counsel concerning a question of law. Courts have frequently held that "reasonable cause" is established when a taxpayer shows that he reasonably relied on the advice of an accountant or attorney that it was unnecessary to file a return, even when such advice turned out to have been mistaken. *See, e.g.,* United States v. Kroll, 547 F.2d 393, 395–396 (CA7 1977) * * * . This Court also has implied that, in such a situation, reliance on the opinion of a tax adviser may constitute reasonable cause for failure to file a return. *See* Commissioner v. Lane-Wells Co., 321 U.S. 219, 64 S. Ct. 511, 88 L. Ed. 684 (1944) (remanding for determination whether failure to file return was due to reasonable cause, when taxpayer was advised that filing was not required).

When an accountant or attorney *advises* a taxpayer on a matter of tax law, such as whether a liability exists, it is reasonable for the taxpayer to rely on that advice. Most taxpayers are not competent to discern error in the substantive advice of an accountant or attorney. To require the taxpayer to challenge the attorney, to seek a "second opinion," or to try to monitor counsel on the provisions of the Code himself would nullify the very purpose of seeking the advice of a presumed expert in the first place. *See Haywood Lumber, supra*, at 771. "Ordinary business care and prudence" do not demand such actions.

By contrast, one does not have to be a tax expert to know that tax returns have fixed filing dates and that taxes must be paid when they are due. In short, tax returns imply deadlines. Reliance by a lay person on a lawyer is of course common; but that reliance cannot function as a substitute for compliance with an unambiguous statute. Among the first duties of the representative of a decedent's estate is to identify and assemble the assets of the decedent and to ascertain tax obligations. Although it is common practice for an executor to engage a professional to prepare and file an estate tax return, a person experienced in business matters can perform that task personally. It is not unknown for an executor to prepare tax returns, take inventories, and carry out other significant steps in the probate of an estate. It is even not uncommon for an executor to conduct probate proceedings without counsel.

It requires no special training or effort to ascertain a deadline and make sure that it is met. The failure to make a timely filing of a tax return is not excused by the taxpayer's reliance on an agent, and such reliance is not "reasonable cause" for a late filing under § 6651(a)(1). The judgment of the Court of Appeals is reversed.

It is so ordered.

After *Boyle*, what do you think the outcome should be in a case in which a taxpayer has a return prepared, signed, and delivered to the company comptroller with instructions to "file" it, and the comptroller files it in the company's files (rather than with the IRS), believing it is a copy? In *Henry v. United States*, 73 F. Supp. 2d 1303 (N.D. Fla. 1999), the court held that under *Boyle*, as a matter of law, this mistake could not constitute "reasonable cause" so as to avoid the late-filing penalty. Compare *Boyle* with *Brown v. United States*, 630 F. Supp. 57 (M.D. Tenn. 1985), a case decided about 9 months after *Boyle*, in which a federal district court found reasonable cause for late filing of an estate tax return by the administrator of the estate where he was elderly, high-school educated, had no experience with tax matters, was in poor health, had not been told the deadline for filing, and the accountant who was supposed to file the return became ill and was hospitalized.

In applying the reasonable cause standard, the Supreme Court in *Boyle* drew a distinction between reliance on an expert's advice relating to a substantive matter of law and reliance on an expert's advice relating to a procedural matter. Would the reasonable cause exception apply to a taxpayer who relied on an attorney's advice that, on the facts presented to the attorney, no tax return was required to be filed?

[B] The Estimated Tax Penalty — Code Section 6654

Reading Assignment: I.R.C. § 6654.

Because the tax system entitles the government to collect taxes throughout the year, section 6654 provides a penalty that applies when a taxpayer owes too much tax with the return, which can happen when the taxpayer's liability is not sufficiently covered by withholding and the taxpayer has failed to make quarterly estimated tax payments. For purposes of section 6654, withholding payments are deemed estimated tax payments, and are deemed paid equally through the year, I.R.C. § 6654(g). Because of this, most taxpayers with wage income are not required to make estimated tax payments. Estimated taxes are discussed in more detail in Chapter 3.

Under section 6654, if the taxpayer, after taking into account withholding tax, *see* I.R.C. § 6654(e)(1), owes $1,000 or more in taxes with the return, the taxpayer is liable for a penalty unless he or she has already paid either 90 percent of the tax due for the year or 100 percent of his or her tax liability for the prior year,[3] I.R.C. § 6654(d)(1)(B),

---

[3] If the taxpayer's adjusted gross income was more than $150,000 during the preceding year, the 100

or, under certain circumstances, had no tax liability for the preceding year, I.R.C. § 6654(e)(2). The penalty is computed by applying the interest rate for tax underpayments to the amount of the underpayment for the period of the underpayment. I.R.C. § 6654(a). For amounts due with the return, the period runs from January 15 of the year the return is due until April 15 of that year or until the amount is paid, whichever is earlier. I.R.C. § 6654(b)(2), (c)(2).

[C] Accuracy-Related Penalties — Code Section 6662

Reading Assignment: I.R.C. §§ 6662(a)–(b), 6664(a). Skim I.R.C. § 6663.

The delinquency penalty in section 6651 addresses only one aspect of taxpayer noncompliance. As important as timely filing and payment are, ensuring that taxpayers accurately report their tax liabilities on their returns is essential and, from a compliance standpoint, presents a greater challenge for the IRS. Prior to legislation in 1989, the Code contained separate penalty provisions relating to negligence, substantial understatements of tax liability, and inaccuracies resulting from valuation overstatements and understatements. Current section 6662, applicable to tax returns due after December 31, 1989, imposes a single accuracy-related penalty, accompanied by uniform definitions. The amount of the penalty is 20 percent of the portion of the underpayment of tax attributable to one or more of the following types of misconduct: (1) negligence or disregard of rules and regulations; (2) any substantial understatement of tax; (3) any substantial valuation misstatement; (4) any substantial overstatement of pension liabilities; and (5) any substantial estate or gift tax valuation understatement. I.R.C. § 6662(b).

Notice that the maximum accuracy-related penalty that may be imposed on any portion of a tax underpayment is 20 percent, even if the underpayment is attributable to more than one type of misconduct. Thus, if a portion of the tax underpayment results from both negligence and a substantial valuation misstatement, only one 20-percent accuracy-related penalty may be applied. Although section 6662(a) itself does not permit penalty "stacking," if the taxpayer files the return after the prescribed due date, both the accuracy-related penalty and the late filing penalty in section 6651 may apply to the same portion of a tax underpayment. However, the accuracy-related penalty does not apply to any portion of an underpayment subject to the civil fraud penalty, discussed below.[4] I.R.C. § 6662(b).

The base to which the accuracy-related penalty applies is the "portion of an underpayment of tax required to be shown" on the return. The term underpayment is defined in section 6664(a) as the amount by which the "correct tax" exceeds the amount of tax shown on the return (plus amounts not shown on the return but which have been previously assessed or collected without assessment), reduced by the amount of any rebates. Amounts collected without assessment include both withholding credits and estimated tax payments. As a general rule, the amount of the underpayment will normally equal the balance due as shown in the revenue agent's report issued at the conclusion of the audit.

---

percent minimum installment amount rises to 110 percent of the tax liability for the prior year. I.R.C. § 6654(d)(1)(C)(i).

[4] Does this mean that fraud is a defense to application of the negligence portion of the accuracy-related penalty? In *Ames v. Commissioner*, 112 T.C. 304 (1999), the Tax Court found CIA employee Aldrich Ames liable for the negligence penalty with respect to unreported income from espionage, although he argued that his conduct had been fraudulent, not negligent. The court stated, "It is rather obvious that fraudulent concealment goes far beyond and is inclusive of 'negligence or disregard of rules or regulations.' " *Id.* at 315.

[1] Negligence or Disregard of Rules or Regulations

Reading Assignment: I.R.C. §§ 6662(b)(1), (c), 6664; Treas. Reg. §§ 1.6662-3(b)(3), (c), 1.6664-4(b)–(c).

Section 6662(b)(1) imposes the 20 percent accuracy-related penalty for negligence or disregard of rules or regulations. The statute defines negligence "as any failure to make a reasonable attempt to comply with" the Code, while a taxpayer's "disregard" of rules or regulations must be careless, reckless, or intentional. I.R.C. § 6662(c). The regulations expand upon these basic definitions and provide more concrete examples — some more helpful than others — of the type of conduct prohibited. Read carefully the applicable portion of regulation section 1.6662-3. Would you describe the standards set forth in the regulations as objective or subjective?

Section 6664 creates a reasonable cause exception that applies to all prongs of the accuracy-related penalty in section 6662, including the negligence prong, as well as the civil fraud penalty in section 6663, among others. I.R.C. § 6664(c).[5] To qualify for the exception, the taxpayer must establish that there was reasonable cause for the tax underpayment and that the taxpayer acted in good faith. Most reasonable cause exception claims are based on the argument that the taxpayer reasonably relied on the opinion or advice of a tax professional. Yet not all professional advice protects the taxpayer against a penalty. Consider the following case in connection with the regulation in section 1.6664-4(c):

ORIA v. COMMISSIONER

United States Tax Court
T.C. Memo 2007-226

HALPERN, JUDGE:

[The basic facts of *Oria* are as follows: The petitioner-husband, Mr. Oria, was the president and sole shareholder of Medico Medical Services, Inc. (Medico). Mr. Oria signed all of Medico's checks issued in 2000 and generally performed all duties connected with its business. He hired Mr. Loeser, an experienced certified public accountant, to prepare individual and corporate income tax returns, as well as employment tax returns for himself and Medico. The petitioners stipulated as part of the case that they understated their taxable income during 2000 by failing to report on their income tax return personal expenses charged to the corporations' credit card, receipts belonging to Medico that Mr. Oria deposited in his personal account, and personal expenses paid by Medico on Mr. Oria's behalf.

In addition, the petitioners stipulated that Mr. Oria understated his salary income during 2000 in the amount of $248,524. Although Mr. Oria reported the entire amount reflected on his W-2 from Medico, the W-2, which was prepared by Mr. Loeser, understated Mr. Oria's income. The method by which Mr. Loeser calculated Mr. Oria's income is not entirely clear. Medico's general ledger records recorded numerous transactions in which Medico paid amounts to Mr. Loeser, as well as entities, incorporated and unincorporated, owned by Mr. Loeser. The actual checks written by Medico, however, were in amounts less than the amounts recorded as expenses. The difference was then credited to Mr. Oria's own drawing account. Mr. Loeser reduced Mr. Oria's 2000 salary figure by the amounts credited to the drawing account. Having stipulated the existence and amount of the 2000 deficiency, the issue before the Tax

---

[5] Notice the overlap between the uniform reasonable cause exception in section 6664(c) and the reasonable cause condition inherent in section 6651, discussed above. Although the two standards differ somewhat (the 6664(c) exception requires a showing of good faith while the 6651 condition requires that the taxpayer establish that the failure to file or pay was not due to willful neglect), the same facts and circumstances are taken into account in both situations.

Court was whether the negligence prong of the accuracy-related penalty applied. — Eds.]

Opinion

Section 6662 imposes an accuracy-related penalty in the amount of 20 percent of the portion of any underpayment attributable to, among other things, negligence. Sec. 6662(a) and (b)(1). Negligence has been defined as the failure to exercise the due care of a reasonable and ordinarily prudent person under like circumstances. *Nis Family Trust v. Commissioner*, 115 T.C. 523, 542 (2000). Negligence includes any failure to make a reasonable attempt to comply with the provisions of the internal revenue laws or to exercise ordinary and reasonable care in the preparation of a tax return. Sec. 1.6662-3(b)(1), Income Tax Regs.

The Commissioner bears the burden of production with respect to the accuracy-related penalty. Sec. 7491(c). In order to meet that burden, the Commissioner must produce sufficient evidence that it is appropriate to impose the penalty. *Higbee v. Comm'r*, 116 T.C. 438, 446 (2001). We may take a taxpayer's concession into account in determining whether the Commissioner has carried his burden. *See, e.g., Rogers v. Comm'r*, T.C. Memo 2005-248. Petitioners have conceded that they understated their taxable income on account of: (1) erroneous credits to Mr. Oria's drawing account resulting from fictitious payments to Mr. Loeser or one of his affiliates, (2) Mr. Oria's personal expenses charged on Medico's American Express card, (3) Mr. Oria depositing Medico's receipts into his personal account, and (4) Medico's payment of Mr. Oria's golf club and other personal expenses. Petitioners' concessions are sufficient for us to conclude that respondent has carried his burden. Mr. Oria signed all of Medico's checks issued in 2000, and he generally performed all duties connected with its business. Given Mr. Oria's business degree, his experience in business, and his knowledge of both Medico's and his own affairs, petitioners' tax treatment of the conceded items is not plausible. Mr. Oria failed to use the due care of a reasonable and ordinarily prudent person under like circumstances to insure that his own compensation from Medico was properly accounted for and reported.

The accuracy-related penalty does not apply to any part of an underpayment of tax if it is shown the taxpayer acted with reasonable cause and in good faith. Sec. 6664(c)(1). The determination of whether a taxpayer acted in good faith is made on a case-by-case basis, taking into account all the pertinent facts and circumstances. Sec. 1.6664-4(b)(1), Income Tax Regs. Generally, the most important factor is the extent of the taxpayer's effort to assess his proper tax liability. *Id.* The taxpayer bears the burden of proof that he had reasonable cause and acted in good faith with respect to the underpayment. *Higbee v. Comm'r, supra* at 447.

Petitioners defend against the accuracy-related penalty on the ground that they acted with reasonable cause and in good faith. They argue that the penalty should not apply because they relied on the advice of Mr. Loeser, a certified public accountant with extensive experience in preparing tax returns.

The general rule is that a taxpayer has a duty to file a complete and accurate tax return and cannot avoid that duty by placing responsibility with an agent. *United States v. Boyle*, 469 U.S. 241, 252, 105 S. Ct. 687, 83 L. Ed. 2d 622 (1985); *Metra Chem Corp. v. Commissioner*, 88 T.C. 654, 662 (1987). In limited situations, the good faith reliance on the advice of an independent, competent professional in the preparation of the tax return can satisfy the reasonable cause and good faith exception. *United States v. Boyle, supra* at 250–251; *Weis v. Commissioner*, 94 T.C. 473, 487 (1990). However, reliance on the advice of a professional tax adviser does not necessarily demonstrate reasonable cause and good faith. Sec. 1.6664-4(b)(1), Income Tax Regs. All facts and circumstances must be taken into account. Sec. 1.6664-4(c)(1), Income Tax Regs. The advice must be based upon all pertinent facts and the applicable law. Sec. 1.6664-4(c)(1)(i), Income Tax Regs. The advice must not be based on unreasonable factual or legal assumptions. Sec. 1.6664-4(c)(1)(ii), Income Tax Regs. The advice cannot be based on an assumption that the taxpayer knows, or has reason to know, is unlikely to be true. *Id.*

* * *

Petitioners concede that they underreported their 2000 taxable income in the amount of $248,524 by failing to report the total of the checks Mr. Oria received from Medico in that year. They claim that they did so on the advice of Mr. Loeser. They do not claim that Mr. Oria was not aware of the total of salary checks that, during 2000, he had signed on behalf of, and received from, Medico. They claim that they relied on Mr. Loeser to prepare a correct income tax return for them. Mr. Oria was aware that Medico was participating in a plan designed by Mr. Loeser under which Medico was paying Mr. Loeser money so that, Mr. Loeser claimed, Mr. Oria could save on taxes. A reasonably prudent person would not rely on an adviser having an interest in the subject of the advice. *Neonatology Assocs., P.A. v. Comm'r*, 115 T.C. 43, 99 (2000), *aff'd*, 299 F.3d 221 (3d Cir. 2002). Moreover, Mr. Oria made no attempt to understand the transactions Medico was engaging in to implement Mr. Loeser's plan. The detail of those transactions was spelled out in Medico's tax returns and the general ledger, yet Mr. Oria was uninterested in Mr. Loeser's explanation of those documents, regarding their contents as "mumbo jumbo numbers". The assumption underlying the erroneous credits posted to his drawing account was either that he had paid Mr. Loeser or one of his affiliates directly on Medico's behalf or that he had reimbursed Medico, which had paid Mr. Loeser or one of his affiliates. Had he paid attention to Mr. Loeser's explanations, Mr. Oria would have realized that the factual premises relied on by Mr. Loeser were incorrect, since he had neither paid Mr. Loeser or one of his affiliates directly nor had he reimbursed Medico. A taxpayer cannot stick his head in the sand while an adviser explains the basis of his advice and pop it out only to hear the favorable conclusion. Considering all the facts and circumstances, we conclude, and find, that petitioners did not act with reasonable cause and in good faith in relying on Mr. Loeser to prepare a correct income tax return for them. The underpayment in tax attributable to the $248,524 in checks received from Medico and not reported on the Form 1040 is due to negligence, and there is not reasonable cause, nor did petitioners act in good faith, with respect to that portion of the underpayment.

We sustain the accuracy-related penalty determined by respondent with respect to petitioners' underpayment of tax for 2000.

The decision in *Oria* illustrates some of the limitations set forth in the section 1.6664-4(c) regulations relating to reliance on professional advice as a basis for the reasonable cause exception. In addition, a taxpayer who relies on the advice of a practitioner for "penalty insurance" must establish that (1) the adviser was a competent professional with sufficient expertise to justify the taxpayer's reliance on the adviser; (2) the taxpayer provided accurate and necessary information to the adviser; and (3) the taxpayer actually relied in good faith on the adviser's judgment. Baldwin v. Commissioner, T.C. Memo 2002-162.

The "disregard of rules or regulations" component of the accuracy-related penalty may be avoided if the taxpayer adequately discloses to the IRS the relevant facts affecting the items' tax treatment. Treas. Reg. § 1.6662-3(c)(1). The disclosure exception applies only if the position has a "reasonable basis" and the taxpayer maintains adequate books and records to substantiate the items properly. Review regulation section 1.6662-3(b)(3), which explains the reasonable basis standard. Disclosure is discussed further in the next section, in connection with the substantial understatement penalty.

[2] Substantial Understatement of Tax and its Defenses

[a] Substantial Understatement of Tax

Reading Assignment: I.R.C. § 6662(b)(2), (d).

As any student of tax law knows, the complexity surrounding the Code's substantive rules leads to "gray areas" — arguable positions with varying degrees of uncertainty. Within these gray areas of the law, the negligence standard may prove to be an insufficient check on noncompliant behavior. The second prong of the accuracy-related penalty imposes a cost on taxpayers who take aggressive return positions (although not necessarily negligently) that do not have adequate legal support.

Section 6662(b)(2) imposes the 20 percent accuracy-related penalty on any portion of an underpayment attributable to a "substantial understatement" of income tax. An understatement of tax is considered substantial if the understatement exceeds the greater of 10 percent of the tax required to be shown on the return, or $5,000 ($10,000 for corporations other than S corporations and personal holding companies).

> *Example:* Miranda filed an income tax return showing taxable income of $35,000 and a corresponding tax liability of $12,150. An audit reveals that Miranda failed to report on the return additional gross income of $25,000. Miranda's total tax liability, including the tax on the unreported income, equals $20,000. Because the resulting $7,850 understatement of tax ($20,000 – $12,150 = $7,850) is greater than $5,000 and greater than 10 percent of the correct tax ($20,000 x .10 = $2,000), the substantial understatement penalty applies.

In this example, is the correct amount of the penalty 20 percent of $25,000 or 20 percent of $7,850?

[b] Defenses to the Penalty

[i] Substantial Authority

Reading Assignment: Treas. Reg. § 1.6662-4(d).

For purposes of determining whether the difference between the tax liability reported on the return and the correct liability is "substantial," the amount of the tax understatement is reduced by items supported by substantial authority. The regulations at section 1.6662-4(d) define in some detail the substantial authority standard and the process for determining whether substantial authority exists. How would you describe the substantial authority standard in percentage terms given the language of section 1.6662-4(d)(2)?

The regulations also specify the types of sources that are considered for purposes of establishing whether a position is or is not supported by substantial authority. The sources are intended to reflect the types of authorities used by practitioners and courts. They include the Code, Treasury Regulations, court decisions, Revenue Rulings and Procedures, certain legislative history sources, and private letter rulings. Treatises, legal periodicals and tax opinions, however, are specifically excluded from the list of sources that may be considered. Treas. Reg. § 1.6662-4(d)(3)(iii).

Substantial authority exists for the tax treatment of a particular item only if "the weight of authorities supporting the treatment is substantial in relation to the weight of authorities supporting contrary treatment." Treas. Reg. § 1.6662-4(d)(3)(i). Balancing the weight of authorities requires a careful consideration of the relevance and persuasiveness of the cited authority and an understanding of the precedential value of a particular source. The substantial authority standard does not require that the taxpayer actually "prevail" on the underlying substantive issue in order to avoid a substantial understatement penalty. If it did, taxpayers whose understatements exceeded the minimum thresholds could be subject to a penalty anytime they lost in Tax Court.

When the court considers whether substantial authority exists, is this a question of fact or law? Consider *Osteen.*

OSTEEN v. COMMISSIONER

United States Court of Appeals, Eleventh Circuit
62 F.3d 356 (1995)

RONEY, SENIOR CIRCUIT JUDGE:

Harry and Gail Osteen (taxpayers) appeal the United States Tax Court's decision disallowing certain tax deductions attributable to their farming and horse breeding operation on the grounds that this activity was not engaged in for profit and assessing tax deficiencies and penalties for a substantial tax understatement.

We hold that the Tax Court's factual findings that the Osteens lacked a profit objective are not clearly erroneous and affirm its decision on that issue. We reverse the Tax Court, however, on its assessment of the understatement penalty because there was substantial authority for the taxpayers' position.

The facts of this case are discussed in detail in the Tax Court's memorandum opinion, 66 T.C.M. (CCH) 1237, T.C. Memo 1993-519, and will not be repeated here. During the years at issue, Harry Osteen was employed full-time as a bank executive. His wife, Gail Osteen, was a full-time registered nurse. The Osteens became interested in breeding and raising Percheron horses in Florida. Percherons are a breed of large draft horses that originally were bred for moving or towing heavy objects before the advent of tractors. There were no Percheron horse breeders nor was there an established market for Percherons in Florida at the time. The Osteens' intent was to breed the horses, train them by showing them and using them to operate a horse-powered farm, and then to sell the horses. For several consecutive years, the Osteens generated losses from the horse breeding activity.

PROFIT OBJECTIVE

A taxpayer who is carrying on a trade or business may deduct ordinary and necessary expenses incurred in connection with the operation of the business. I.R.C. § 162. An activity constitutes a "trade or business" within the meaning of section 162 if the taxpayer's actual and honest objective is to realize a profit. Dreicer v. Commissioner, 78 T.C. 642, 645, *aff'd*, 702 F.2d 1205 (D.C. Cir.1983). The courts have relied on factors set forth in section 183 in making the requisite profit motive analysis under section 162. Brannen v. Commissioner, 722 F.2d 695, 704 (11th Cir.1984).

Section 183 specifically precludes deductions for activities "not engaged in for profit," such as pursuing hobbies or generating losses to shelter unrelated income. I.R.C. § 183(a); S. Rep. No. 552, 91st Cong., 1st Sess. (1969), reprinted in 1969 U.S.C.C.A.N. 1645, 2133 (legislative history of § 183). Although the taxpayer's expectation of profit does not have to be reasonable, objective facts and circumstances must indicate that the taxpayer's intent was to make a profit. A taxpayer's subjective statements of intent to make a profit are not sufficient. Treas. Reg. § 1.183-2(a) (1972). The regulations list nine factors to guide courts in determining whether an activity is engaged in for profit. These are not exclusive considerations, however, and no single factor or mathematical preponderance of factors is determinative. Treas. Reg. § 1.183-2(b) (1972).

* * *

A review of the record reveals that the Tax Court properly followed the nine factors listed in the regulations, viewed all facts and circumstances of the case, and was not clearly erroneous in determining that the Osteens engaged in the Percheron breeding business without a bona fide profit motive. The Tax Court relied on facts such as the taxpayers' inexperience in breeding Percheron horses and their failure to hire experienced assistants or bring in experienced partners, the lack of any profitability assessment of breeding Percherons in Florida, the limited time spent managing the operation, the string of consistent losses, and the significant income Osteen earned as a bank executive which allowed him to tolerate such losses.

SUBSTANTIAL UNDERSTATEMENT PENALTY

The Osteens appeal the Tax Court's assessment of section 6661 [currently I.R.C. § 6662. Eds.] understatement penalties. The Osteens do not dispute that their tax understatements for the two years in question met the definition of "substantial understatements" under this provision. The Osteens contend, however, that they had substantial authority to believe they could claim the farming and horse breeding losses, an exception to the imposition of understatement penalties.

* * *

For our purposes, section 6661(b)(2)(A) defines the "understatement" as the excess of:

(i) the amount of the tax required to be shown on the return for the taxable year, over

(ii) the amount of the tax imposed which is shown on the return. . . .

The understatement, for the purposes of imposing the addition, *shall* be reduced "by that portion of the understatement which is attributable to the tax treatment of any item by the taxpayer if there is or was *substantial authority* for such treatment. . . ." * * *

The application of a substantial authority test is confusing in a case of this kind. If the horse breeding enterprise was carried on for profit, all of the deductions claimed by the Osteens would be allowed. There is no authority to the contrary. If the enterprise was not for profit, none of the deductions would be allowed. There is no authority to the contrary. Nobody argues, however, not even the Government, that because the taxpayers lose on the factual issue, they also must lose on what would seem to be a legal issue.

The Tax Court in this case, as it seems to do in most of the cases, gives little explanation as to why there is substantial authority in one case, but not in another: "Based on the discussion above, we are convinced that there was not substantial authority for petitioners' position." Order at 15. *Cf.* Harston v. Commissioner, 60 T.C.M. (CCH) 1008, T.C. Memo. 1990-538 (1990) ("Although [the taxpayers] were not successful enough to show that they were entitled to the [§ 183] losses claimed, petitioners have convinced us that they had substantial authority for their position.").

There are no court decisions that give us guidance, and the regulations themselves, although speaking in terms of a test, are unsatisfactory in application to an all or nothing case of this kind.

If the Tax Court was deciding that there was no substantial authority because of the weakness of the taxpayers' *evidence* to establish a profit motive, we reverse because a review of the record reveals there was evidence both ways. In our judgment, under the clearly erroneous standard of review, the Tax Court would be due to be affirmed even if it had decided this case for the taxpayers. With that state of the record, there is substantial authority from a factual standpoint for the taxpayer's position. Only if there was a record upon which the Government could obtain a reversal under the clearly erroneous standard could it be argued that from an evidentiary standpoint, there was not substantial authority for the taxpayer's position.

If the Tax Court was deciding there was not substantial *legal* authority for the deductions, we reverse because of the plethora of cases in which the Tax Court has found a profit motive in the horse breeding activities of taxpayers that were similar to those at hand. *E.g.*, Engdahl v. Commissioner, 72 T.C. 659, 1979 WL 3705 (1979) (profit motive found; taxpayer had businesslike operation, consulted experts, kept quarterly records, showed horses, and did physical labor and menial chores); Holbrook v. Commissioner, T.C. Memo. 1993-383, 66 T.C.M. (CCH) 484, 1993 WL 325083 (1993) (husband and wife engaged in horse breeding for profit; activities conducted in businesslike manner; wife kept detailed records while husband developed expertise in horse breeding); * * * .

Although it can be properly argued that those cases are distinguishable from the case at hand, as well they are because the ultimate facts were found for the taxpayer rather than against the taxpayer as in this case, they are not so dissimilar that they must be discarded as providing no substantial authority for the tax returns filed in this case.

As a bottom line, we find little distinction between this case and the Tax Court case of *Harston*. The imposition of additions to the tax under § 6661 must turn on some analysis other than the conclusory decision of the Tax Court. The Tax Court should articulate some consistent and workable test to justify the imposition of additions in all or nothing situations of this kind, otherwise the imposition of the addition is left to the educated reaction of the particular Tax Court judge hearing the case.

We affirm the Tax Court's finding of tax deficiencies for lack of a profit motive, but we reverse the Tax Court's imposition of a penalty for substantial understatement.

Affirmed in part, reversed in part.

Does the Eleventh Circuit in *Osteen* resolve the issue of whether substantial authority involves the question of whether the factual evidence could support the taxpayer's position, as opposed to whether the taxpayer's position is supported by legal authority? What do the regulations in section 1.6662-4 (d)(2) have to say about this issue? In another horse breeding case, the Sixth Circuit held that whether the taxpayer's deductions were supported by substantial authority includes factual evidence as well as legal sources. Estate of Kluener v. Commissioner, 154 F.3d 630 (6th Cir. 1998).

[ii] Disclosure

Reading Assignment: I.R.C. § 6662(d)(2)(B); Treas. Reg. § 1.6662-4(e).

For purposes of determining whether an understatement of tax is substantial, the amount of the understatement is also reduced by amounts attributable to an item if the relevant facts relating to the tax treatment of the item are "adequately disclosed" on the return or in a statement attached to the return and there is a "reasonable basis" for the taxpayer's tax treatment of the item. I.R.C. § 6662(d)(2)(B)(ii). A taxpayer may use Form 8275, Disclosure Statement, to disclose a return position.[6] The IRS issues a Revenue Procedure each year that identifies those items for which disclosure on the return is adequate for the purpose of reducing the substantial understatement portion of the accuracy-related penalty. These items include deductions for medical expenses, taxes, interest, certain charitable contributions, casualty and theft losses, and legal fees. As long as the taxpayer can substantiate these claimed deductions and has maintained all the necessary books and records with respect to the items or positions in issue, the taxpayer need not make any additional disclosures. *See, e.g.*, Revenue Procedure 2008-14, 2008-7 I.R.B. 435.[7]

---

[6] The disclosure exception does not apply to tax shelter items. *See* I.R.C. § 6662(d)(2)(c).

[7] The Revenue Procedure does not apply with respect to the disregard of rules and regulations portion of the section 6662 accuracy-related penalty, which, as noted above, is also subject to an exception for adequate disclosure. Rev. Proc. 2008-14, 2008-7 I.R.B. 435.

As indicated above, for the disclosure exception to apply, the taxpayer's treatment of the item giving rise to the understatement also must have a reasonable basis. *See* I.R.C. § 6662(d)(2)(B)(ii)(II); Treas Reg. § 1.6662-4(e)(2)(i). Note that the "reasonable basis" standard is defined by reference to Treasury Regulation section 1.6662-3(b)(3), which also applies to the disregard of rules or regulations portion of the accuracy-related penalty. How would you describe the reasonable basis standard in percentage terms? How useful do you think the disclosure exception is to the taxpayer?

[3] Valuation Misstatements

Reading Assignment: I.R.C. § 6662(b)(3), (e).

The remaining prongs of the accuracy-related penalty single out specific types of taxpayer misconduct relating to valuation misstatements. Under section 6662(b)(3), the 20 percent addition to tax applies to an underpayment of tax attributable to a "substantial valuation misstatement." The substantial valuation misstatement penalty applies most commonly to a taxpayer who, in an attempt to inflate a charitable contribution deduction, overstates the value of property, or to a taxpayer who, in an attempt to increase depreciation deductions or reduce the amount of realized gain, overstates the adjusted basis of property reported on the return. In order to trigger the penalty, the overstatement of value or basis must be at least 150 percent of the correct value or the correct adjusted basis, as the case may be, and the tax underpayment attributable to the valuation misstatement must exceed $5,000 ($10,000 in the case of a corporation other than an S corporation or a personal holding company). I.R.C. § 6662(e)(1)(A). If the value or adjusted basis of any property claimed on a return is 200 percent or more of the amount determined to be the correct valuation or adjusted basis, the penalty rate increases to 40 percent of the resulting underpayment.[8] I.R.C. § 6662(h). Does the valuation misstatement penalty apply to valuation *under*statements? In what circumstances might a valuation understatement occur?

If the IRS denies a deduction resulting from a valuation misstatement, for purposes of the valuation misstatement penalty, is the underpayment of tax attributable to the valuation misstatement or to the improper deduction? Consider the following case.

HEASLEY v. COMMISSIONER

United States Court of Appeals, Fifth Circuit

902 F.2d 380 (1990)

GOLDBERG, CIRCUIT JUDGE:

STATEMENT OF FACTS

Between 1981 and 1983, Gaylen Danner, a self-styled economic and financial consultant and securities dealer, introduced Kathleen and Dennis Heasley to numerous investment plans. Before meeting Danner, the Heasleys invested in a mutual fund plan and held $3,000 in stocks as part of Mr. Heasley's job benefit plan. They had no other investment experience. Both held blue collar jobs. Neither Heasley graduated from high school, although Ms. Heasley earned a G.E.D. and 18 college credits, one course at a time. Worried about their future and that of their four children, but not knowledgeable enough to invest on their own, the Heasleys accepted Danner's investment advice.

---

[8] The Pension Protection Act of 2006, Pub. L. No. 109-280, reduced the thresholds for imposing the accuracy-related penalty for substantial and gross valuation misstatements. For returns filed on or before August 17, 2006, the threshhold for the 20-percent penalty was 200 percent (rather than 150), and for the 40-percent penalty was 400 percent (rather than 200).

In December 1983, Danner introduced the Heasleys to the investment that generated this lawsuit. Danner told the Heasleys that the O.E.C. Leasing Corporation ("O.E.C.") had an energy conservation program ("the plan") that would generate the future income they sought. The plan required the Heasleys to lease energy savings units ("units") from O.E.C. at $5,000 per unit per year. O.E.C. valued the units at $100,000 each. A service company then installed the units in businesses ("end users"). The units reduce energy consumption, thus reducing end users' energy bills. The end users would pay a percentage of their utility savings to investors such as the Heasleys. The higher the price of energy, the more money saved, and the greater the return on the investment.

Danner reviewed the O.E.C. prospectus with the Heasleys. They focused on the cash flow charts, which showed a positive cash flow of $2,000 in 1984 increasing to $11,876 in 1992. Danner also discussed the investment's tax advantages. Already somewhat familiar with the home version of the energy savings unit, the Heasleys believed the O.E.C. investment would generate future income.

The Heasleys invested $10,000 to buy two units and $4,161 for startup costs, including installation, telephone hookups, and insurance. In a late December closing, they signed documents Danner prepared, including service agreements for the two units. The manufacturer of the units later sent the Heasleys warranty cards, unit serial numbers, and photographs of the units. The servicing agent sent them photographs and addresses of the businesses where the servicing agent installed the two units.

In the past, the Heasleys always prepared their own tax returns. However, they did not know how to report the O.E.C. investment. At Danner's suggestion, the Heasleys employed Gene Smith, a C.P.A., to prepare their 1983 tax return. Smith reviewed the O.E.C. prospectus and the accompanying tax and legal opinions and found everything in order. He then deducted the $10,000 advance rents for the two units and claimed a $20,000 investment tax credit. Because the investment generated a larger investment tax credit than the Heasleys could use in 1983, Smith carried the investment tax credit back to 1980 and 1981. As a result of the O.E.C. generated deduction and investment tax credit, the Heasleys received more than $23,000 in refunds for the three years from the Internal Revenue Service ("I.R.S."). The Heasleys used the refunds to recoup the money they invested in the plan. They also invested $3,000 of the refunds in a time share plan recommended by Danner. They put $10,000 of the money into a certificate of deposit as collateral for one of Danner's business loans.

Despite Danner's rosy predictions and the Heasleys' high hopes, the Heasleys earned not one penny off of the units or any other of Danner's suggested investments. Even worse, they lost every penny they invested with Danner (more than $25,000). Their loss exceeded the tax refund generated by the plan.

In 1986, the I.R.S. sent the Heasleys a pre-filing notification letter. The Heasleys contacted Danner. He assured them that their investment would pass muster with the I.R.S. Danner was wrong. In September 1986, the I.R.S. totally disallowed the $10,000 advance rental payments and the $20,000 investment tax credit. As a result, the Heasleys' income tax liability increased by approximately $23,000 plus interest. The I.R.S. also assessed penalties totaling $7,419.75: a $1,153.05 negligence penalty * * * ; a $5,940.90 valuation overstatement penalty * * * ; and a $325.80 substantial understatement penalty * * * . The I.R.S. also increased the interest due on the disallowed investment tax credit under 26 U.S.C. § 6621(c).

After exhausting their administrative remedies, the Heasleys sued the I.R.S. They do not dispute the tax deficiency but instead challenge the I.R.S.'s assessment of penalties. The tax court found for the I.R.S. The Heasleys appealed. We must decide whether the tax court erred in upholding the I.R.S.'s assessment of the penalties and interest. We need not decide, nor did the tax court decide, the Heasleys' tax liability.

* * *

THE VALUATION OVERSTATEMENT PENALTY

The I.R.S. may impose a valuation overstatement penalty for any underpayment of tax "attributable to a valuation overstatement." The Heasleys overvalued each unit by $95,000. Because the Heasleys overvalued the units, the I.R.S. imposed the valuation overstatement penalty. The tax court upheld the penalty. The court reasoned that the Heasleys's $10,000 investment tax credit depended upon the value of the units. "Thus," the court concluded, "to the extent the underpayment is due to the disallowed credits, the underpayment is attributable to a valuation overstatement." Mem. Op. at 21.

After the Tax Court issued its opinion in this case, we interpreted the meaning of "attributable to a valuation overstatement" in *Todd v. I.R.S.*, 862 F.2d 540 (5th Cir. 1988). In *Todd*, as in this case, the I.R.S. completely disallowed the taxpayer's deductions and credits. On appeal, we compared Todd's actual tax liability (without the improperly claimed deductions and credits) with his actual tax liability including the valuation overstatement. *Todd*, 862 F.2d at 542–543. We arrived at the same figure for both calculations because the I.R.S. completely disallowed the deductions and credits containing the valuation overstatement. Because we arrived at the same figure, we concluded that Todd's valuation overstatement did not attribute to the underpayment. Therefore, the I.R.S. could not assess a valuation overstatement penalty.

We see no reason to treat this case any differently than *Todd*. Whenever the I.R.S. totally disallows a deduction or credit, the I.R.S. may not penalize the taxpayer for a valuation overstatement included in that deduction or credit. In such a case, the underpayment is not attributable to a valuation overstatement. Instead, it is attributable to claiming an improper deduction or credit. In this case, the Heasleys' actual tax liability does not differ one cent from their tax liability with the valuation overstatement included. In other words, the Heasleys' valuation overstatement does not change the amount of tax actually owed. Therefore, the I.R.S. erred when it assessed the valuation overstatement penalty and the Tax Court erred as a matter of law by upholding that assessment.

* * *

CONCLUSION

The I.R.S. should not exact every penalty possible in every case where taxpayers pay less than the full amount of tax due. Here, on rather questionable facts, the I.R.S. did just that. This case simply does not support such draconian efforts. Therefore, we REVERSE the decision of the Tax Court and the I.R.S.'s assessment of penalties and interest.

Do you find the reasoning in *Heasley* persuasive? There is currently a split in the circuits on the issue of whether the valuation misstatement penalty applies in the context of a deduction disallowed as a result of an erroneous valuation. *Heasley* reflects the minority view. *Compare Heasley*, *supra* (penalty does not apply), *and* Gainer v. Commissioner, 893 F.2d 225, 226–228 (9th Cir. 1990) (same), *with* Merino v. Commissioner, 196 F.3d 147, 158 (3d Cir. 1999) (penalty applied; *Heasley* is distinguishable); Zfass v. Commissioner, 118 F.3d 184, 190–191 (4th Cir. 1997) (penalty does apply); Massengill v. Commissioner, 876 F.2d 616, 619–20 (8th Cir. 1989) (same); Illes v. Commissioner, 982 F.2d 163, 167 & n.2 (6th Cir. 1992) (penalty applied; *Heasley* is distinguishable), *cert. denied*, 507 U.S. 984 (1993), *and* Gilman v. Commissioner, 933 F.2d 143, 151 (2d Cir. 1991) (penalty does apply), *cert. denied*, 502 U.S. 1031 (1992).

How would you explain the weight of authority contrary to *Heasley*? Does the exceptional holding in *Heasley* hinge on the fact that the court found that the Heasleys' valuation overstatement did not affect the amount of their underpayment because their deduction would have been disallowed regardless of any overstatement? *Cf.* McCrary v. Commissioner, 92 T.C. 827, 859–60 (1989) (distinguishing, in determining whether a transaction was tax-motivated, valuation overstatements that are inseparable from the ground for disallowing a deduction from those that are separable). *But see, e.g., Massengill*, 876 F.2d at 619–20 ("when an underpayment stems from disallowed depreciation deductions or investment credits due to lack of economic substance, the deficiency is attributable to overstatement of value, and subject to the [overstatement] penalty."). Is *Heasley* distinguishable from many other cases involving valuation misstatements because the Heasleys had a genuine (though uninformed) profit motive? *See, e.g.*, Donahue v. Commissioner, 1992 U.S. App. LEXIS 7139 (6th Cir. 1992) ("[in *Heasley*,] the taxpayers, unlike Donahue, were found to have operated with a profit motive."). Was the Court of Appeals for the Fifth Circuit simply overly sympathetic to the Heasleys because of their apparent victimization by Gaylen Danner? *See, e.g., Merino*, 196 F.3d at 158 ("we do not find the *Heasley* rationale persuasive here because the court's decision appears to have been driven by understandable sympathy for the Heasleys rather than by a technical analysis of the statute."); *Zfass*, 118 F.3d at 190 n.8 ("the Heasleys were indeed scammed out of a considerable sum of money."). Or do different courts reasonably differ on the interpretation of the applicable Code section? *See Gainer*, 893 F.2d at 226–228 (agreeing with *Todd*, 862 F.2d 540 (5th Cir. 1988), followed in *Heasley*, on the interpretation of the language of the valuation overstatement penalty, based in part on legislative history).

As with the other prongs of the accuracy-related penalty, a taxpayer can avoid the valuation misstatement penalty if the reasonable cause exception in section 6664 applies. In a high-profile case, *Long Term Capital Holdings v. United States*, 330 F. Supp. 2d 122 (D. Conn. 2004), a federal district court disallowed the taxpayer's claimed $100 million loss arising from a cross-border lease stripping transaction on the basis that the transaction lacked economic substance. *Id.* at 171–90. The judge also sustained a 40-percent gross valuation misstatement penalty for inflating stock basis and, in the alternative, a substantial understatement penalty attributable to the same tax understatement. *Id.* at 199–205. The court upheld the imposition of the penalties notwithstanding the fact that the taxpayer had received opinion letters from two of the largest law firms in the country, including King & Spalding. The judge ruled that the taxpayer's reliance on the opinion letters could not establish a reasonable cause defense to the accuracy-related penalties because the taxpayer's reliance was not reasonable. In its 90-page opinion, the District Court found that (1) no evidence existed to show that the King & Spalding opinion was received before the taxpayer filed the return reporting the losses, so the taxpayer could not be said to have relied on the legal advice; (2) the opinion was based on unreasonable and unsupportable factual assumptions; and (3) the opinion did not cite relevant authority. *Id.* at 206–211.

The Second Circuit Court of Appeals, in an unpublished summary order, affirmed the district court's holding that the taxpayers in *Long-Term Capital Holdings* were subject to a 40-percent gross valuation misstatement penalty. Long-Term Capital Holdings, LP v. United States, 2005-2 U.S.T.C. ¶ 50575 (2d Cir. 2005). The Second Circuit rejected the taxpayers' argument that the district court's holding required the taxpayers to "second guess" the advice of its tax advisor at a major law firm. Instead, the court stated that the district court "made a series of factual findings and determined on the basis of those findings that Long-Term did not meet the threshold requirements of the reasonable cause exception" in section 6664. *Id.* The court further held:

> The district court found no credible evidence that Long-Term received the tax advice from [King & Spalding] on which it claimed to have relied in reporting the $106 million loss on its tax return because [the attorney]'s memo addressed only the allocation of the loss and [the attorney]'s testimony concerning his April 14, 1998 conversation with [the taxpayer's representative] was "vague" and "inconsistent." . . . The court also found that even assuming, *arguendo*, that Long-Term had received relevant tax advice prior to filing its

> return, it had failed to demonstrate that [King & Spaldings]'s advice was based upon all pertinent facts and circumstances and did not unreasonably rely on statements that the taxpayer knew were unlikely to be true. *See* Treas. Reg. § 1.6664-4(c)(1) (stating the two threshold requirements a taxpayer must satisfy in order to show that it relied on advice reasonably and in good faith). Long-Term directed [King & Spalding] to assume that Long-Term entered into the transaction . . . for a valid and substantial business purpose independent of federal income tax considerations, that it reasonably expected to derive a material pre-tax profit from this transaction, and that there was no preexisting agreement . . . to sell its partnership interest to Long-Term Capital Management ("LTCM"). The record provides ample support for the district court's finding that Long-Term knew these assumptions to be false and that it was unreasonable for [King & Spalding] to rely on these assumptions when a reasonably diligent review of the pertinent facts and circumstances would have revealed them to be false.

Id. Commentators view *Long-Term Capital Holdings* as a cautionary tale for taxpayers who rely too heavily on professional advice for penalty protection. *See, e.g.*, Burgess J.W. Raby & William L. Raby, *Practitioner Advice as a Defense Against Penalties*, 109 TAX NOTES 329 (2005); Sheryl Stratton, *Long-Term Capital Loses on Merits, Gets Hit with Penalties*, 104 TAX NOTES 1003 (2004).[9]

The substantial valuation misstatement penalty applies to a section 482 valuation misstatement as well, a topic best discussed as part of an international tax course. Separate prongs of the accuracy-related penalty may also apply to an employer who attempts to inflate pension contribution deductions, I.R.C. § 6662(b)(4), or to a taxpayer who understates the value of property reported on a gift or estate tax return, I.R.C. § 6662(b)(5).

[4] Erroneous Refund Claims

Reading Assignment: I.R.C. § 6676.

The accuracy-related penalty in section 6662 is calculated based on the amount of the tax underpayment attributable to the types of conduct listed in section 6662. As a result, if a taxpayer files an erroneous claim for refund, no penalty applies if there was no additional tax liability attributable to the erroneous refund claim. In order to deter taxpayers from filing wrongful claims for refund, Congress enacted section 6676 as part of the Small Business and Work Opportunity Act of 2007, Pub. L. No. 110-28, 121 Stat. 112. Section 6676(a) provides, "If a claim for refund or credit with respect to income tax (other than a claim for a refund or credit relating to the earned income credit under section 32) is made for an excessive amount, unless it is shown that the claim for such excessive amount has a reasonable basis, the person making such claim shall be liable for a penalty in an amount equal to 20 percent of the excessive amount." An "excessive amount" is the amount by which the taxpayer's claim for refund or credit exceeds the allowable amount of the claim. I.R.C. § 6676(b). The erroneous refund penalty does not apply to any portion of the excessive amount that is also subject to either the

---

[9] The case is also a cautionary tale for practitioners who draft tax opinions. Chapter 18 explores some of the implications of the *Long-Term Capital Holdings* case from the tax practitioner's perspective.

The district judge in *Long-Term Capital Holdings* determined that the transaction at issue was a tax shelter within the meaning of section 6662(d)(2)(C)(ii). *Long-Term Capital Holdings*, 330 F. Supp. 2d at 201. Shortly after the case was decided, Congress enacted legislation that limits situations in which a taxpayer may rely on practitioner advice to establish reasonable cause. *See* I.R.C. § 6664(d). These limitations are discussed in Section 12.04, below.

accuracy-related penalty in section 6662 or the civil fraud penalty in section 6663. I.R.C. § 6676(c). The penalty can apply to any refund claim filed or submitted after May 25, 2007.

[D] The Civil Fraud Penalty

Reading Assignment: I.R.C. § 6663.

The civil fraud penalty in section 6663 applies when the taxpayer's behavior extends substantially beyond a failure to exercise reasonable care and evidences an intentional effort to underpay taxes. The increased penalty rate, 75 percent of the portion of an underpayment attributable to fraud, reflects the higher level of culpability that must exist in order to trigger the addition to tax. The civil fraud penalty applies only if a tax return has been filed. If the taxpayer's failure to file a return is fraudulent, this triggers a 75 percent delinquency penalty under section 6651(f) instead, as discussed in Section 12.02[A]. While under prior law, the accuracy-related penalties and the civil fraud penalty could be asserted simultaneously with respect to the same underpayment, current law confirms that the accuracy-related penalties apply only to that portion of an underpayment not attributable to fraud. I.R.C. § 6662(b).

The initial burden of proving fraud on the part of the taxpayer rests with the IRS. *See* I.R.C. § 7454(a). If the IRS can establish by clear and convincing evidence that any portion of an underpayment is attributable to fraud, the statute presumes the entire underpayment is attributable to fraud. The burden of proof then shifts to the taxpayer to establish, by a preponderance of the evidence, the portion of the underpayment *not* attributable to fraud. I.R.C. § 6663(b).

Proof of fraud requires a showing that the taxpayer engaged in intentional wrongdoing with the specific intent to avoid a tax known or believed to be owing. Stoltzfus v. United States, 398 F.2d 1002 (3d Cir. 1968), *cert. denied*, 393 U.S. 1020. The IRS normally seeks to prove fraud based on circumstantial evidence. The *Morse* case, which is reproduced below, lists some of the badges of fraud. Notice also the IRS's use of a prior criminal conviction under Code section 7206(1) for filing false tax returns to help meet its burden of proof under section 6663.

MORSE v. COMMISSIONER

United States Tax Court
T.C. Memo. 2003-332[10]

Jacobs, Judge:

Respondent determined deficiencies in petitioner's Federal income taxes, as well as fraud penalties pursuant to section 6663, for 1991–94. . . .

[The issue to be decided is:]

(1) Whether petitioner is liable for the fraud penalty for each of the years at issue; . . . .

FINDINGS OF FACT

Some of the facts have been stipulated and are so found. The stipulation of facts and the exhibits attached thereto are incorporated herein by this reference.

Petitioner resided in Austin, Minnesota, on the date the petition in this case was filed. During the years at issue, petitioner farmed approximately 700 to 800 acres. He grew soybeans, corn, and other crops. These crops were then sold to various grain elevator companies and canneries in the area. In addition, petitioner worked between

[10] *Aff'd*, 419 F.3d 829 (8th Cir. 2005).

25 and 30 hours a week as a theater manager/projectionist.

* * *

In April 1998, petitioner was indicted in the U.S. District Court for the District of Minnesota on four counts of filing false tax returns in violation of section 7206(1). The indictment charged that for 4 separate years (1991–94), petitioner willfully made and subscribed to Federal income tax returns (verified by petitioner's written declaration made under penalties of perjury) which he did not believe to be true and correct as to every material matter. . . .

Petitioner was tried and convicted on all four counts. His conviction was affirmed by the U.S. Court of Appeals for the Eighth Circuit, United States v. Morse, 210 F.3d 380 (8th Cir. 2000), and his petition for certiorari was denied, 531 U.S. 1079 (2001). Petitioner was sentenced to imprisonment for a term of 18 months and ordered to pay a fine of $10,000 and to make restitution of $61,700 to the Internal Revenue Service (IRS). . . . Petitioner paid the fine and restitution on or before September 14, 1999.

On August 17, 2000, respondent sent to petitioner a statutory notice of deficiency, determining deficiencies in Federal income tax and fraud penalties for 1991–94. The deficiencies were based in large part upon respondent's reconstruction of petitioner's income using the bank deposits method. Respondent determined that petitioner received unreported income from crop sales (which he deposited into his checking account at Farmer's State Bank). . . .

On November 16, 2000, petitioner filed a petition with this Court, disputing the full amount of the deficiencies and penalties. Petitioner now concedes that, on his 1991–94 returns, he omitted grain sale receipts of $75,799 in 1991, $39,900 in 1992, $24,481 in 1993, and $68,713 in 1994. Respondent concedes all other adjustments to Schedule F. . . .

OPINION

Issue 1. Whether Petitioner Is Liable for the Fraud Penalty Pursuant to Section 6663(a)

Respondent contends that petitioner is liable for the fraud penalty under section 6663(a) for 1991–94. Section 6663(a) imposes a penalty in an amount equal to 75 percent of the portion of any underpayment of tax (required to be shown on a return) that is attributable to fraud. In addition, if respondent establishes that any portion of the underpayment is attributable to fraud, the entire underpayment is treated as attributable thereto, except to the extent that petitioner establishes otherwise. Sec. 6663(b).

Respondent bears the burden of proving the applicability of the civil fraud penalty by clear and convincing evidence. Sec. 7454(a); Rule 142(b). To sustain this burden, respondent must establish both (1) that there was an underpayment of tax for each taxable year in issue and (2) that at least some portion of the underpayment for each year was due to fraud. DiLeo v. Commissioner, 96 T.C. 858, 873 (1991), *aff'd* 959 F.2d 16 (2d Cir. 1992); . . .

1. Underpayments of Tax

An underpayment of tax will exist where unreported gross receipts exceed the costs of goods sold and deductible expenses. Where the Commissioner provides clear proof of unreported receipts, the burden of coming forward with offsetting costs or expenses generally shifts to the taxpayer. Siravo v. United States, 377 F.2d 469, 473–474 (1st Cir. 1967); Elwert v. United States, 231 F.2d 928, 933 (9th Cir. 1956); . . . .

Petitioner has stipulated that he omitted from his Federal tax returns grain sale receipts of $75,799 in 1991, $39,900 in 1992, $24,481 in 1993, and $68,713 in 1994.

Furthermore, petitioner's conviction under section 7206(1) is highly probative that he received unreported receipts from the sale of crops. . . . Thus, respondent has carried the burden of establishing underpayments by clear and convincing evidence.

2. Fraudulent Intent

Respondent must also prove fraudulent intent. This burden is met if it is shown that petitioner intended to evade taxes known to be owing by conduct intended to conceal, mislead, or otherwise prevent the collection of such taxes. Webb v. Commissioner, 394 F.2d 366, 377 (5th Cir. 1968), *aff'g*, T.C. Memo 1966-81. Fraud is never presumed; it must be established by affirmative evidence. Beaver v. Commissioner, 55 T.C. 85, 92 (1970). Since direct evidence of fraud rarely is available, respondent may prove petitioner's fraud by circumstantial evidence. Scallen v. Commissioner, 877 F.2d 1364, 1370 (8th Cir. 1989), *aff'g* T.C. Memo 1987-412; Klassie v. United States, 289 F.2d 96, 101 (8th Cir. 1961).

Conduct that may indicate fraudulent intent, commonly referred to as "badges of fraud", includes, but is not limited to: (1) understating income; (2) maintaining inadequate records; (3) giving implausible or inconsistent explanations of behavior,(4) concealing income or assets, (5) failing to cooperate with tax authorities, (6) engaging in illegal activities, (7) providing incomplete or misleading information to one's tax preparer, (8) lack of credibility of the taxpayer's testimony, (9) filing false documents, including filing false income tax returns, (10) failing to file tax returns, and (11) dealing in cash. Spies v. United States, 317 U.S. 492 (1943); . . . Bradford v. Commissioner, 796 F.2d 303, 307–308 (9th Cir. 1986), *aff'g*, T.C. Memo 1984-601; . . . . Although no single factor is necessarily sufficient to establish fraud, a combination of several factors is persuasive circumstantial evidence of fraud. Bradford v. Commissioner, *supra* at 307; . . . . An intent to mislead may be inferred from a pattern of conduct. Webb v. Commissioner, *supra* at 379.

The following badges of fraud are present in this case: (1) Substantially understating income for several years, (2) providing incomplete or misleading information to his tax preparer, and (3) being convicted of filing false returns under section 7206(1). Bradford v. Commissioner, *supra* at 307–308; Korecky v. Commissioner, 781 F.2d 1566, 1569 (11th Cir. 1986), *aff'g* T.C. Memo 1985-63; . . . Wright v. Commissioner, 84 T.C. 636, 643–644 (1985); Farber v. Commissioner, 43 T.C. 407, 420 (1965), *modified* 44 T.C. 408 (1965); . . . .

Over a 4-year period, petitioner consistently underreported large amounts of gross receipts and net income. Petitioner provided no explanation for underreporting his gross receipts. A consistent pattern of underreporting large amounts of income over a period of years is substantial evidence bearing upon an intent to defraud, particularly where the reason for such understatement is not satisfactorily explained or shown to be due to innocent mistake. Holland v. United States, 348 U.S. 121, 137, 75 S. Ct. 127, 99 L. Ed. 150 (1954); Webb v. Commissioner, *supra* at 379; . . . . Petitioner did not advise his tax preparer of the income omitted from his returns. Concealing income from one's return preparer can be evidence of fraud. Korecky v. Commissioner, *supra* at 1569; Farber v. Commissioner, *supra* at 420; . . . .

Moreover, petitioner was convicted of filing false Federal income tax returns under section 7206(1) for each of the years at issue. Section 7206(1) makes it a crime for a taxpayer to willfully make and submit any return verified by a written declaration that it is made under the penalties of perjury which he does not believe to be true and correct as to every material matter. Wright v. Commissioner, *supra* at 639. A taxpayer who has been convicted of willfully and knowingly subscribing to a false income tax return under section 7206(1) is not collaterally estopped from contesting that he or she is liable for the addition to tax for fraud because a conviction under section 7206(1) does not require a showing that the taxpayer willfully attempted to evade tax. However, a conviction for filing false Federal income tax returns under section 7206(1) is highly persuasive evidence that the taxpayer intended to evade tax. Stefansson v. Commissioner, T.C. Memo 1994-162; Avery v. Commissioner, T.C. Memo 1993-344; Miller v. Commissioner, T.C. Memo 1989-461. In *First Trust & Sav. Bank v. United States*, 206 F.2d 97, 100 (8th Cir. 1953), the U.S. Court of Appeals for the Eighth Circuit, the court to which an appeal in this case would lie, cited with approval *United States v. Croessant*, 178 F.2d 96, 97 (3d Cir. 1949), wherein the U.S. Court of Appeals for the Third Circuit stated

> the man who files a willfully false return has endeavored to mislead his government. He creates the appearance of having complied with the law, whereas his neighbor who has filed no return does no such thing. Not only has he created the appearance of complying, but that apparent compliance stands a good chance of remaining unattacked, for the tax authorities cannot possibly audit every taxpayer's return every year. * * * The law has always distinguished between failing to disclose useful information and making a disclosure which is a lie.

Petitioner's intentional filing of a false tax return each year from 1991 to 1994, reporting amounts of income which he knew to be false, is a strong indicium of fraudulent intent with respect to those years. Klassie v. United States, *supra* at 102. Absent some credible evidence that knowingly filing a false return should not be considered indicative of fraud, a section 7206(1) conviction is highly persuasive of fraud. *Id.* at 101; Biaggi v. Commissioner, T.C. Memo 2000-48, *aff'd.* 8 Fed. App'x 66 (2001); . . . . Petitioner has failed to submit credible evidence that he knowingly filed the false returns for any reason other than to evade taxes he knew to be owing. Thus, we conclude that petitioner fraudulently intended to underpay his tax for each of the years at issue.

Further, petitioner has failed to submit credible evidence showing that any part of the underpayment attributable to the omitted income is not due to fraud. To the contrary, the record establishes by clear and convincing evidence that the entire underpayment for each year is due to fraud. Accordingly, we hold that petitioner is liable for the section 6663 civil fraud penalty on the entire underpayment for each year at issue. Sec. 6663(b).

* * *

To reflect the foregoing and concessions by respondent, Decision will be entered under Rule 155.

As the court in *Morse* notes, a criminal conviction for making false statements on a return under Code section 7206(1) does not collaterally estop the taxpayer from asserting a defense to civil tax fraud. By contrast, as discussed in Section 11.07[A] of Chapter 11, a criminal conviction under Code section 7201 for criminal tax evasion, which has as one of its elements an affirmative act of tax evasion or attempted evasion, typically does estop the taxpayer from denying the fraud in a subsequent civil tax proceeding. *See, e.g.*, Rodney v. Commissioner, 53 T.C. 287 (1969); *see also* Chief Counsel Notice CC-2005-012. What if the taxpayer is acquitted on a charge of criminal tax evasion under Code section 7201 — is the IRS collaterally estopped from imposing the civil fraud penalty?

[E] Information Reporting Penalties

Reading Assignment: I.R.C. §§ 6721(a)–(c), 6722, 6724(a).

One of the most important tools the IRS has to combat underreporting and nonreporting of income is its Information Returns Program (IRP). The IRP verifies whether taxpayers fully reported their income by digitally matching data on information returns filed by employers and other payors with the recipients' income tax returns.

Failure by the taxpayer to include income reported on an information return will normally cause the IRS to send the taxpayer a notice explaining the discrepancy and requesting payment of any resulting tax adjustment. Under current law, information returns are required for numerous types of payments, including wages (Form W-2), interest (Form 1099-INT), dividends (Form 1099-DIV), and broker transactions (Form 1099-B). In addition to reporting these amounts to the IRS, the payor must also send a copy of the return to the payee (a "payee statement") so that the recipient can accurately and timely complete his or her own return. I.R.C. §§ 6041–6053.

The effectiveness of the IRP hinges upon information returns and payee statements being timely filed and correctly completed. To ensure that this occurs, the Code applies a series of information reporting penalties to those who fail to meet their reporting obligations. A payor who fails to timely file an information return or to properly include all the required information on the return is subject to a penalty of $50 per return, up to a maximum of $250,000 per calendar year. I.R.C. § 6721 (a). Although a single return may contain more than one reporting error, only one penalty is imposed with respect to a single information return. Treas. Reg. § 301.6721-1. To encourage payors to correct errors as soon as possible, the per-return and maximum annual penalty amounts decrease based upon when the filer rectifies the errors. If the reporting failures are corrected within 30 days after the due date of the return (normally March 30), the penalty amount is reduced to $15 per return, with a maximum annual penalty of $75,000. I.R.C. § 6721(b). Reporting failures corrected after March 30 but before August 1 carry a $30 per return penalty, not to exceed $150,000 per year. I.R.C. § 6721(b). Errors or omissions that are "inconsequential" and do not prevent the IRS from matching the information return to the corresponding payee statement are ignored. Treas. Reg. § 301.6721-1(c)(1).

A similar set of penalties applies to a payor's failure to timely furnish a required payee statement or to include in the payee statement all the correct information. I.R.C. § 6722(a). The penalty is $50 for each statement with respect to which the failure occurs, up to a maximum penalty amount of $100,000 per year. The exception for inconsequential errors also applies to payee statements but, unlike the information reporting penalty in section 6721, the 6722 penalty amount is not reduced for prompt corrections. This reflects Congress' concern that payee statements be provided early enough in the process (normally by February 28) so that taxpayers can carry out their own filing requirements on time. *See* H.R. Rep. No. 101-386, at 1385 (1989).

The reporting penalties in sections 6721 and 6722 may both be waived if the filer shows that the failure was due to reasonable cause and that the filer acted in a responsible manner. I.R.C. § 6724(a). In this context, reasonable cause may be established by a showing that (1) there are significant mitigating factors for the failure (for example, the filer has an established history of complying with the reporting requirements with respect to which the failure occurred), or (2) the failure arose from events beyond the filer's control. Treas. Reg. § 301.6724-1(a), (b). Events beyond the filer's control include the unavailability of relevant business records caused by unforeseen circumstances; reasonable and good faith reliance on erroneous information supplied by the IRS; failure by the payee to furnish correct information; or reasonable reliance on a third party agent to file the returns. Treas. Reg. § 301.6724-1(c).

§ 12.03 PREPARER PENALTIES

Reading Assignment: I.R.C. §§ 6694(a)–(b), 6695A, 7701(a)(36).

Tax return preparer penalties are designed to buttress the penalty structure that applies to taxpayers. In particular, the rules seek to discourage practitioners from cooperating with taxpayers who seek to underreport their liabilities and to prevent practitioners from encouraging inaccurate reporting. If a tax return preparer knows (or reasonably should know) that an understatement on the taxpayer's return is due to an "unrealistic position," the preparer is subject to a penalty equal to the greater of $1,000 or 50 percent of advisor's fees derived from preparing the return. I.R.C. § 6694(a)(1).

Prior to amendments to section 6694 in 2007, an unrealistic position, if not disclosed by the taxpayer, was one that had no realistic possibility of being sustained on the merits. A position was considered to have a realistic possibility of being sustained on its merits "if a reasonable and well-informed analysis by a person knowledgeable in the tax law would lead such a person to conclude that the position has approximately a one in three, or greater, likelihood of being sustained on its merits (realistic possibility standard)." Treas. Reg. § 1.6694-2(b). In applying this 1-in-3 standard, the possibility that the return would not be audited or, if audited, the issue would not be raised, was not taken into account. *Id.*[11]

The 2007 amendments raised the expected standards of conduct on the part of tax return preparers. The standards differ somewhat based on whether the position is disclosed or undisclosed. The tax return preparer may be subject to a penalty if the position that creates the tax understatement *is not disclosed*; the preparer "knew (or reasonably should have known) of the position"; and the preparer did not reasonably believe that the position would "more likely than not" be sustained on its merits. If the position that creates the tax understatement *is disclosed*, the preparer may be penalized if the preparer knew, or reasonably should have known of the position, and "there was no reasonable basis for the position." I.R.C. § 6694(a)(2).

Proposed regulations attempt to quantify the more-likely-than-not standard:

> A tax return preparer may "reasonably believe that a position would more likely than not be sustained on its merits" if the tax return preparer analyzes the pertinent facts and authorities, and in reliance upon that analysis, reasonably concludes in good faith that the position has a greater than 50 percent likelihood of being sustained on its merits. In reaching this conclusion, the possibility that the position will not be challenged by the Internal Revenue Service (IRS) (for example, because the taxpayer's return may not be audited or because the issue may not be raised on audit) is not to be taken into account. . . . Whether a tax return preparer meets this standard will be determined based on all facts and circumstances, including the tax return preparer's diligence. In determining the level of diligence in a particular situation, the tax return preparer's experience with the area of Federal tax law and familiarity with the taxpayer's affairs, as well as the complexity of the issues and facts, will be taken into account.

Prop. Reg. § 1.6694-2(b)(1). For purposes of applying the more-likely-than-not standard, the preparer employs the same type of analysis (and may consider the same type of authorities) as that used to determine whether "substantial authority" exists for purposes of the substantial understatement penalty in section 6662(d). *See id.* (referring to regulation section 1.6662-4(d)(3)(ii)).

Increasing the expected standard of conduct from a 1-in-3 likelihood of success to a greater than 50-percent likelihood of success sparked extensive criticism among policymakers and practitioners. Some practitioners maintain that the more-likely-than-not standard creates a conflict of interest between the return preparer and the client. For example, assume that the return preparer determines that a return position has a 50-percent likelihood of success. If the position were not disclosed, the preparer could be subject to the section 6694 penalty even though, with a 50-percent likelihood of success, the taxpayer would not be subjected to either the negligence prong of the accuracy-related penalty in section 6662 or substantial understatement prong of the penalty because, with a 50-percent likelihood of success, the position would be supported by

[11] An individual who consistently engages in the type of conduct giving rise to the section 6694 penalty may be enjoined by the IRS from acting as an income tax return preparer. I.R.C. § 7407.

substantial authority.[12] What would you suggest the practitioner do if faced with this dilemma? Proposed regulations indicate that as long as the tax return preparer advises the taxpayer of all the penalty standards applicable to the taxpayer under section 6662 (the accuracy-related penalty) and documents the advice in the preparer's file, the return preparer will not be subject to a penalty. Prop. Reg. § 1.6694-2(c)(3). Why might the regulations not counsel the preparer simply to advise the taxpayer to disclose the position, thereby protecting the return preparer against the penalty?

In assessing exposure to these penalties, to what extent must the return preparer verify the information provided by the taxpayer? As a general rule, a preparer may rely in good faith on information furnished by the taxpayer, and need not review the taxpayer's books and records for accuracy and completeness. Also, a return preparer may rely in good faith and without verification upon information furnished by another advisor, tax return preparer, or other third party. Prop. Reg. § 1.6694-1(e)(1). Although a return preparer is not required to independently verify information provided by the taxpayer or a third party, the penalty may apply where the preparer fails to inquire as to furnished information that appears, based upon facts actually known to the preparer, to be incomplete or incorrect. Moreover, if a Code provision requires that the taxpayer maintain specific documents to substantiate a deduction or credit, the return preparer must make appropriate inquiries to determine whether those documents exist. *Id.* IRS guidance provides the following two examples:

> *Example 1*: During an interview conducted by Preparer E, a taxpayer stated that he had made a charitable contribution of real estate in the amount of $50,000 during the tax year, when in fact he had not made this charitable contribution. E did not inquire about the existence of a qualified appraisal or complete a Form 8283, Noncash Charitable Contributions, in accordance with the reporting and substantiation requirements under section 170(f)(11). E reported deductions on the tax return for the charitable contribution which resulted in an understatement of liability for tax, and signed the tax return as the tax return preparer. E is subject to a penalty under section 6694.
>
> *Example 2*: While preparing the 2008 tax return for an individual taxpayer, Preparer F realizes that the taxpayer did not provide a Form 1099 for a bank account that produced significant taxable income in 2008. When F inquired about any other income, the taxpayer furnished the Form 1099 for F to use in preparation of the 2008 tax return. F did not know that the taxpayer owned an additional bank account that generated taxable income for 2008 and the taxpayer did not reveal this information to the tax return preparer notwithstanding F's general inquiry about any other income. F signed the taxpayer's return as the tax return preparer. Preparer F is not subject to a penalty under section 6694.

Prop. Reg. § 1.6694-1(e)(3) Ex. 1 & 2.

As a result of amendments made in 2007 that generally are effective as of the beginning of 2008,[13] the penalty in section 6694 applies not just to those who prepare income tax returns, but also to preparers of amended returns and claims for refund; estate and gift tax returns; excise tax returns; and employment tax returns. A person

---

[12] Although the regulations do not define negligence or substantial authority in percentage terms, the two concepts are generally considered to be lower standards of conduct than the more-likely-than-not standard requires. *See* Cherie J. Hennig et al., *Small Business Tax Act: Analysis and Tax Planning Opportunities*, 85 Taxes 45, 50–51 (2007) (describing a position that has a 40% likelihood of success as satisfying the substantial authority standard).

[13] *See* Small Business and Work Opportunity Act of 2007, Pub. L. No. 110-28 (amending sections 6694(a) and (b)); 2007-27 I.R.B. 12, Notice 2007-54 (effective date). Increased penalty amounts (the greater of $5,000 or 50 percent of the income derived or to be derived) apply to preparer conduct that is willful or reckless. I.R.C. § 6694(b).

may qualify as a tax return preparer even if the person does not sign the return and even if he or she renders advice with respect to only one entry on the return if the entry constitutes a "substantial portion" of the return.[14] *See* Prop. Reg. § 301.7701-15(b)(2), (3). Someone who provides tax planning advice, however, generally will not be subject to the penalty. According to proposed Treasury regulations, a person who gives advice but who does not sign the return is considered a tax return preparer only if the advice is given with respect to events that have already occurred at the time the advice is rendered. *See id.* The regulations include the following examples.

> *Example 1*: Attorney A, an attorney in a law firm, provides legal advice to a large corporate taxpayer regarding a completed corporate transaction. The advice provided by A is directly relevant to the determination of an entry on the taxpayer's return and this advice constitutes a substantial portion of the return. A, however, does not prepare any other portion of the taxpayer's return and is not the signing tax return preparer of this return. A is considered a tax return preparer.
>
> *Example 2*: Attorney B, an attorney in a law firm, provides legal advice to a large corporate taxpayer regarding the tax consequences of a proposed corporate transaction. Based upon this advice, the corporate taxpayer enters into the transaction. Once the transaction is completed, the corporate taxpayer does not receive any additional advice from B with respect to the transaction. B did not provide advice with respect to events that have occurred and is not considered a tax return preparer.

Prop. Reg. § 301.7701-15(b)(2)(ii) Ex. 1 & 2.

A person's status as a tax return preparer does not take into account educational qualifications or professional status. I.R.C. § 7701(a)(36); Prop. Reg. § 301.7701-15(d). In Revenue Ruling 86-55, 1986-1 C.B. 373, for example, the IRS ruled that a used car dealership that offered to prepare returns free of charge to customers who purchased an automobile from the dealership with the resulting refund was an income tax return preparer. Chapter 18 discusses in more detail the relationship among the return preparer penalty, the ethical standards for tax practitioners set forth in American Bar Association guidance, and the standards of conduct for those practicing before the IRS in Treasury Circular 230.

In 2006, Congress created a separate civil penalty that applies to appraisers who prepare a valuation appraisal if: (1) the appraiser knows, or reasonably should have known, that the appraisal would be used in connection with a federal tax return or refund claim; and (2) the claimed value of the appraised property results in a substantial valuation misstatement related to income tax under section 6662(e) or a gross valuation misstatement under section 6662(h). I.R.C. § 6695A(a) (applicable to appraisals prepared with respect to returns filed after August 17, 2006). The section 6695A penalty is the lesser of two amounts: (1) the greater of $1,000 or 10 percent of the tax underpayment attributable to the valuation misstatement; or (2) 125 percent of the gross income received by the appraiser for preparing the appraisal. I.R.C. § 6695A(b). The appraiser may avoid liability for the penalty if he or she can establish that the appraised value was more likely than not the proper valuation. I.R.C. § 6695A(c).

---

[14] For a person who does not sign the return, whether an entry or portion of a return is a substantial portion depends on all the surrounding facts and circumstances. An entry or portion of a return is not considered substantial if the entry involves amounts of gross income or deductions that are (1) less than $10,000, or (2) less than $400,000 and also less than 20 percent of the gross income (adjusted gross income if the taxpayer is an individual) shown on the return. Prop. Reg. § 301.7701-15(b)(3).

§ 12.04 PENALTIES AIMED AT TAX SHELTER TRANSACTIONS

Since the mid-1990s, the IRS has waged an aggressive campaign against abusive tax shelter transactions involving both individual and corporate taxpayers. For individuals, the principal focus has been off-shore and trust arrangements used by wealthy taxpayers to hide income, and transactions designed to generate artificial losses. *See, e.g.*, 2004-2 C.B. 600, Notice 2004-67. In the corporate and partnership area, the IRS has identified varied, complex transactions with titles such as "LILO," "BOSS," and "Son of BOSS" that produce tax benefits with little economic risk for the parties who participate in the transaction. *See id.* The following discussion, while not exhaustive, examines penalty provisions specifically aimed at tax-avoidance transactions.

[A] Tax Shelter Organizers and Promoters

Reading Assignment: I.R.C. §§ 6700(a), 6707, 6708; skim I.R.C. §§ 6111(a), 6112.

Section 6700 contains a series of penalties for promoting abusive tax shelters. First, a 50-percent penalty applies to any person who organizes or sells an interest in a partnership, entity, or other arrangement, and in connection with the arrangement makes or furnishes a statement concerning the allowance of any tax benefit (*e.g.*, a deduction, credit, or exclusion), if the person knows or has reason to know that the tax benefit statement is false or fraudulent. I.R.C. § 6700(a). The penalty amount is calculated based on the gross income derived from the tax shelter arrangement. *Id.* The IRS may also impose a penalty under section 6700 on a person who makes a gross valuation overstatement in connection with a tax shelter arrangement. I.R.C. § 6700(a), (b). The penalty for a gross valuation overstatement (a statement of value that exceeds 200 percent of the correct value) is $1,000 or 100 percent of the gross income derived from arrangement, whichever is less. *Id.*

The penalty in section 6700 was enacted originally to combat tax shelter transactions popular in the 1970s and early 1980s, most involving generous tax credits, nonrecourse debt, and passive losses. Substantive tax legislation in 1986 did away with most of the incentives for engaging in these earlier shelters, *see, e.g.*, I.R.C. §§ 465 (at risk limitation on loss deductions), 469 (passive activity loss limitations). Section 6700 has proven to be a relatively ineffective deterrent against the more recent types of tax shelters because it applies only after the IRS discovers the shelter activity. One of the most challenging hurdles for the IRS when combating the new wave of shelter activity has been identifying shelter investments in the first instance. In fact, the IRS usually learns of newer varieties of tax shelters from third-party sources such as informants and newspaper articles, rather than from auditing investors and promoters. In response, the IRS and Treasury have over the past several years expanded existing procedures requiring tax shelter promoters to disclose to the IRS the existence of shelter investments and the identities of those who invest in them. *See* 2007-38 I.R.B. 607, T.D. 9350 (final regulations on disclosure of reportable transactions). Congress has also stiffened penalties on those who fail to comply with applicable disclosure and list-maintenance requirements.

Section 6111 requires some tax shelter organizers, managers, and promoters (termed "material advisors" in the statute) to file an information return with the IRS identifying the shelter transaction and describing the expected tax benefits. I.R.C. § 6111(a). The types of shelter transactions subject to the disclosure requirement in section 6111 are identified as "reportable transactions" and include tax shelter investments (1) marketed under conditions of confidentiality and (2) those that promise a full or partial refund of fees if the promised tax benefits are not sustained. *See* I.R.C. § 6111(b)(2) (referring to transactions described in I.R.C. § 6707A(c), which, in turn, refers to regulations under section 6011); *see also* Treas. Reg. § 1.6011-4(b). Reportable transactions also include sub-categories for (1) "listed transactions," which encompasses specific transactions that the IRS has identified by notice or other pronouncement as having a tax avoidance purpose, and (2) "transactions of interest," which encompasses transactions that the IRS has identified by notice or other pronouncement as having the potential for tax avoidance or evasion. Treas. Reg. § 1.6011-4(b)(2), (6). A material advisor who fails to file, or files an incomplete or false, information return is subject to a penalty of $50,000. I.R.C. § 6707(a), (b)(1). If the shelter arrangement at issue is a listed transaction, the penalty amount increases to $200,000 (or, if greater, 50 percent of the gross income derived with respect to advice provided in connection with the transaction). I.R.C. § 6707(b)(2).

A material advisor must also maintain a list of investors in any reportable transaction. I.R.C. § 6112(a). Upon written request from the IRS, the advisor must make the list available for inspection by the agency. I.R.C. § 6112(b). If the advisor fails to make the list available within 20 business days after the request, the IRS may assess a penalty of $10,000 per day, with no maximum. I.R.C. § 6708(a)(1). Although a reasonable cause exception to the section 6708 penalty exists, I.R.C. § 6708(a)(2), the legislative history confirms that an advisor's failure to maintain a list will not be considered reasonable cause for failing to make the list available to the IRS. H.R. Rep. No. 108-548

[B] Tax Shelter Investors

Reading Assignment: I.R.C. §§ 6662A(a)–(c), 6707A(a)–(c).

As a general matter, the accuracy-related penalties in section 6662 for negligence and substantial understatements apply to taxpayers who report tax-avoidance and shelter transactions the same way they do in any other context. In some instances, however, the Code and regulations impose more stringent standards in the case of tax shelter transactions and, in limited instances, higher penalty amounts.

For example, a taxpayer may not avoid the substantial understatement penalty by disclosing the transaction if the transaction constitutes a tax shelter. I.R.C. § 6662(d)(2)(C). Moreover, a separate accuracy-related penalty applies to understatements attributable to listed and reportable transactions that have a significant tax avoidance purpose. I.R.C. § 6662A(a). For these purposes, listed and reportable transactions are defined with reference to the regulations under 6011 and include the same types of transactions that are the object of the disclosure and list-maintenance requirements in sections 6111 and 6112. I.R.C. § 6662A(d). The penalty is generally 20 percent of the tax understatement if the taxpayer discloses the transaction, and 30 percent if the taxpayer does not. I.R.C. § 6662A(a), (c). *See* 2005-7 I.R.B. 494, Notice 2005-12 (providing interim guidance relating to the reportable transaction understatement penalty in section 6662A).

While Congress created a limited reasonable cause exception aimed at understatements otherwise subject to section 6662A, the 30-percent penalty that applies where the taxpayer failed to disclose the transaction properly cannot be waived under any circumstance. I.R.C. § 6664(d). Moreover, a taxpayer seeking to qualify for the reasonable cause exception cannot rely upon a "disqualified opinion" or the advice of a "disqualified tax advisor." A disqualified opinion includes one that is based on unreasonable factual or legal assumptions or that does not identify and consider all the relevant facts. I.R.C. § 6664(d)(3)(B)(iii). A disqualified tax advisor includes a material advisor with respect to the transaction (defined with reference to section 6111(b)) or a person who has a financial interest in the transaction that is contingent upon the promised tax benefits being sustained. I.R.C. § 6664(d)(3)(B)(ii).

Just as shelter promoters and organizers must disclose tax avoidance transactions to the IRS, taxpayers who invest in reportable transactions (defined with reference to the section 6011 regulations) are also subject to mandatory disclosure rules. Treas. Reg. § 1.6011-4. An individual taxpayer who fails to disclose his or her participation in a reportable transaction in accordance with application regulations is subject to a $10,000 penalty ($100,000 in the case of a listed transaction). The penalty amount for all other types of taxpayers is $50,000 ($200,000 in the case of a listed transaction). I.R.C. § 6707A(a). The investor penalties in section 6707A do not depend upon whether an understatement of tax is ultimately determined to exist, but rather upon whether the transaction at issue is a reportable transaction. Moreover, no reasonable cause exception for failing to disclose exists, although the IRS has discretion to abate penalties. I.R.C. § 6707A(d); *see also* Rev. Proc. 2007-21, 2007-9 I.R.B. 613 (providing procedures for requesting rescission of the failure to disclose penalty in section 6707A). The Code also extends the statute of limitations on assessment in the case of tax liability arising from a listed transaction that the taxpayer fails to report in accordance with section 6011, I.R.C. § 6501(c)(10), and denies an interest deduction to a corporate taxpayer if the interest is attributable to a deficiency arising from an undisclosed listed transaction, I.R.C. § 163(m).

§ 12.05 ASSESSMENT, ABATEMENT, AND SUSPENSION OF PENALTIES

Reading Assignment: I.R.C. §§ 6404(g), 6665, 6671.

The procedural rules that address when and how the IRS may assess penalties are somewhat confusing. While relatively few penalties are explicitly subject to the deficiency assessment procedures described in Chapter 7, if a penalty is based on liability determined under those procedures, the penalty itself will be assessed in the same manner. *See* I.R.C. § 6665. As a practical matter, therefore, because the accuracy-related and civil fraud penalties hinge upon an underpayment of tax (which must be assessed as a deficiency), the penalties themselves must also be included in the notice of deficiency, and may be reviewed by the Tax Court, before they can be formally assessed. Moreover, the Appeals Division will consider the penalty at the same time it considers the underlying tax liability.

With respect to the delinquency penalty in section 6651, in most cases, the IRS need only notify the taxpayer of a penalty assessment resulting from a failure to file or pay and make a demand for payment. After notice and demand, the IRS may collect the resulting amount. I.R.C. § 6665(b). Subject to the abatement procedures described below, the taxpayer's only recourse at that point is to file a refund claim and, if the claim is rejected, file a suit in a district court or the Court of Federal Claims for a refund of the penalty amount.

Neither the information reporting nor the preparer penalties are subject to the deficiency assessment procedures. I.R.C. § 6671(a). Nevertheless, the IRS has created a pre-assessment appeals procedure for preparer penalty cases that is similar to that followed in deficiency cases. Under this procedure, the IRS issues the preparer a 30-day letter and provides an opportunity for the preparer to protest the penalty before it is assessed. Treas. Reg. § 1.6694-4(a). Once the section 6694 penalty is assessed, the preparer can delay collection of the full amount by paying 15 percent of the assessed penalty and filing a claim for refund. If the refund claim is denied, the preparer can maintain a refund suit in district court to recover the previously paid amount. I.R.C. § 6694(c).

The IRS has authority to waive or abate an asserted penalty under specified circumstances. The Code itself, for example, allows the return preparer penalty to be abated if it is later established as part of a final administrative determination or judicial proceeding that the return on which the penalty was based contained no understatement of tax. I.R.C. § 6694(d). The IRS has also established an administrative appeals procedure under which a taxpayer may request waiver of the penalty after it has already been assessed. I.R.M. 20.1.1.4. The post-assessment appeals procedure applies to most penalties that may be waived based on a reasonable cause, due diligence, good conscience, or other similar exception. Taxpayers most commonly utilize these appeals procedures to protest delinquency penalties. If the abatement request is denied, the taxpayer can protest that denial to the Appeals Division. If the Appeals Division refuses to abate the penalty, the taxpayer may file a claim for refund and then a refund suit. I.R.M. 20.1.1.4.1.2.

Prior to the IRS Reform Act, the IRS generally did not abate a penalty simply because it had delayed contacting the taxpayer about an asserted deficiency. Code section 6404(g) now requires the IRS to suspend the imposition of a penalty in cases where the IRS does not properly notify the taxpayer of additional liability within the 36-month period after the taxpayer files his return.[15] If the IRS does not act timely, penalties are suspended beginning on the day after the close of the 36-month period.

The suspension rule applies to any penalty "which is computed by reference to the period of time the failure continues to exist." I.R.C. § 6404(g)(1)(A). This provision specifically excludes the delinquency penalty under section 6651 and the fraud penalty under 6663 from qualifying for relief. I.R.C. § 6404(g)(2). What types of penalties discussed in this chapter would qualify for suspension under this rule? The application of section 6404(g) is discussed in more detail in Chapter 13, in the context of underpayment interest.

§ 12.06 BURDEN OF PROOF WITH RESPECT TO PENALTIES

Reading Assignment: I.R.C. § 7491(c).

Code section 7491, which is discussed in Chapter 11, provides a special rule for penalties, placing an initial burden of production on the IRS in any court proceeding relating to an individual's liability for penalties. In *Higbee v. Commissioner*, 116 T.C. 438 (2001), the Tax Court held that the Commissioner had carried the burden of production with regard to the late filing penalty in section 6651 and the accuracy-related penalty in section 6662:

> Although the statute does not provide a definition of the phrase "burden of production", we conclude that Congress' intent as to the meaning of the burden of production is evident from the legislative history. The legislative history of section 7491(c) sets forth: [I]n any court proceeding, the Secretary must initially come forward with evidence that it is appropriate to apply a particular penalty to the taxpayer before the court can impose the penalty. This provision is not intended to require the Secretary to introduce evidence of elements such as reasonable cause or substantial authority. Rather, the Secretary must come forward initially with evidence regarding the appropriateness of applying a particular penalty to the taxpayer; if the taxpayer believes that, because of reasonable cause, substantial authority, or a similar provision, it is inappropriate to impose the penalty, it is the taxpayer's responsibility (and not the Secretary's obligation) to raise those issues. [H. Conf. Rept. 105-599, 1998-3 C.B. at 995.]
>
> Therefore, with regard to section 7491(c), we conclude that for the Commissioner to meet his burden of production, the Commissioner must come forward with sufficient evidence indicating that it is appropriate to impose the relevant penalty.

[15] The 36-month period generally applies to notices issued after November 25, 2007. An 18-month period applied under prior law. See Section 13.02[B] for a complete discussion of the effective date associated with the 36-month period.

* * *

Finally, we note that Congress placed only the burden of production on the Commissioner pursuant to section 7491(c). Congress' use of the phrase "burden of production" and not the more general phrase "burden of proof" as used in section 7491(a) indicates to us that Congress did not desire that the burden of proof be placed on the Commissioner with regard to penalties.[n.6] *See* sec. 7491(c). Therefore, once the Commissioner meets his burden of production, the taxpayer must come forward with evidence sufficient to persuade a Court that the Commissioner's determination is incorrect.

Having described the framework of section 7491(c), we evaluate whether respondent has met his burden of production with regard to the section 6651(a)(1) addition to tax and the section 6662 accuracy-related penalty. We also discuss whether petitioners have presented any evidence which would cause us not to sustain respondent's determinations with regard to the addition to tax and the accuracy-related penalty.

Section 6651(a)(1) imposes an addition to tax for a taxpayer's failure to file a required return on or before the specified filing date, including extensions. The amount of the liability is based upon a percentage of the tax required to be shown on the return. *See* sec. 6651(a)(1). The addition to tax is inapplicable, however, if the taxpayer's failure to file the return was due to reasonable cause and not to willful neglect. *See* sec. 6651(a)(1). Under section 7491(c), . . . ; the Commissioner bears the burden of production with regard to whether the section 6651(a)(1) addition to tax is appropriate, but he does not bear the burden of proof with regard to the "reasonable cause" exception of section 6651(a).

Respondent determined that petitioners are liable for a section 6651(a)(1) addition to tax with regard to their 1996 tax return. The parties have stipulated that petitioners filed their 1996 return on April 18, 1998, approximately 1 year after it was due. Accordingly, we conclude that respondent has produced sufficient evidence to show that the section 6651(a)(1) addition to tax is appropriate, unless petitioners prove that their failure to file was due to reasonable cause.

Petitioners have not provided any evidence indicating that their failure to file was due to reasonable cause. Therefore, an addition to tax is sustained in the instant case. * * *.

Pursuant to section 6662(a), a taxpayer may be liable for a penalty of 20 percent on the portion of an underpayment of tax (1) attributable to a substantial understatement of tax or (2) due to negligence or disregard of rules or regulations. *See* sec. 6662(b). A substantial understatement of tax is defined as an understatement of tax that exceeds the greater of 10 percent of the tax required to be shown on the tax return or $5,000. *See* sec. 6662(d)(1)(A). The understatement is reduced to the extent that the taxpayer has (1) adequately disclosed his or her position and has a reasonable basis for such position or (2) has substantial authority for the tax treatment of the item. *See* sec. 6662(d)(2)(B). In addition, section 6662(c) defines "negligence" as any failure to make a reasonable attempt to comply with the provisions of the Internal Revenue Code, and "disregard" means any careless, reckless, or intentional disregard.

[n.6] We note that sec. 6665(a)(2) provides that any reference to tax shall be deemed also to refer to penalties. However, the application of sec. 6665(a)(2) is limited by the language "Except as otherwise provided in this title". Considering that limiting language of sec. 6665(a)(2), the reference in sec. 7491(a) to tax liabilities imposed by subtitle A or B (whereas penalties are imposed by subtitle F), and the structure of sec. 7491 as a whole, we believe that Congress intended for sec. 7491(c) (and not sec. 7491(a)) to apply to penalties.

> Whether applied because of a substantial understatement of tax or negligence or disregard of the rules or regulations, the accuracy-related penalty is not imposed with respect to any portion of the understatement as to which the taxpayer acted with reasonable cause and in good faith. *See* sec. 6664(c)(1). The decision as to whether the taxpayer acted with reasonable cause and in good faith depends upon all the pertinent facts and circumstances. *See* sec. 1.6664-4(b)(1), Income Tax Regs. Relevant factors include the taxpayer's efforts to assess his proper tax liability, including the taxpayer's reasonable and good faith reliance on the advice of a professional such as an accountant. *See id.* Further, an honest misunderstanding of fact or law that is reasonable in light of the experience, knowledge, and education of the taxpayer may indicate reasonable cause and good faith. *See* Remy v. Commissioner, T.C. Memo 1997-72.
>
> For the 1997 tax year, respondent determined that petitioners are liable for an accuracy-related penalty attributable to a substantial understatement of tax or, in the alternative, due to negligence or disregard of rules or regulations. Petitioners have conceded that they are not entitled to $30,245 in itemized deductions relating to NOL carryovers ($28,036) and certain taxes ($2,209) claimed on Schedule A of their 1997 tax return. With regard to respondent's determination that petitioners were negligent and disregarded rules and regulations, respondent argues that he has met his burden of production under section 7491(c) through petitioners' above concessions, along with evidence in the record indicating that petitioners were experienced in business affairs. Further, respondent contends that because petitioners have failed to introduce any evidence to indicate that they were not negligent, petitioners have failed to meet their burden of proof, which they retain despite the application of section 7491(c).
>
> Respondent has shown that petitioners have failed to keep adequate books and records or to substantiate properly the items in question. Such a failure in the instant case is evidence of negligence. *See* sec. 1.6662-3(b), Income Tax Regs. Consequently, we conclude that respondent has met his burden of production for his determination of the accuracy-related penalty based on negligence or disregard of rules or regulations. Additionally, with regard to that determination, petitioners have failed to meet their burden of proving that they acted with reasonable cause and in good faith. We therefore sustain respondent's determination that petitioners are liable for the accuracy-related penalty on the underpayment associated with the disallowed itemized deductions conceded by petitioners.

Id. at 446–49.

In *Higbee*, the Commissioner relied largely on the taxpayers' own stipulations and concessions to carry the burden of production. If the taxpayers had not made these concessions, what sort of evidence might the IRS have introduced to sustain its burden? The taxpayers also helped the government's case by failing to introduce any evidence to support a penalty defense. What if the taxpayer fails to contest the IRS's penalty determination in the Tax Court petition? In *Swain v. Commissioner*, 118 T.C. 358 (2002), the Tax Court ruled that if a taxpayer fails to challenge a penalty by assigning error to it pursuant to Tax Court Rule 34(b), the taxpayer has conceded the penalty, and, consequently, the IRS has no obligation under section 7491(c) to produce evidence establishing that the penalty is appropriate.

PROBLEMS

1. Elaine mailed in her Year 1 income tax return on June 9, Year 2, showing a total tax liability of $25,000. It was received by the IRS on June 14. Elaine's employer had withheld from her wages during the year a total of $15,000 in tax. Elaine paid the entire balance due ($10,000) at the time she filed her return.

A. Assume that the reason Elaine mailed her return on June 9 is because, on April 14, she gave the return to her friend Newman, who works at the Post Office, and asked him to mail it for her. He left the envelope in his jacket and did not remember or discover it until June 9, when he promptly mailed it (with an attached note explaining that the delay was entirely his fault). Is Elaine liable for a delinquency penalty under section 6651 and, if so, in what amount?

B. Assume instead that Elaine had obtained an automatic extension of time to file her return by timely filing Form 4868.

  i. Is Elaine liable for a delinquency penalty under section 6651 and, if so, in what amount?

  ii. Upon audit, the IRS determined, much to Elaine's satisfaction, that her total tax liability for Year 1 was only $23,000. What, if anything, is the amount of the delinquency penalty she will owe?

2. At his employer's annual picnic, Carlos won as part of a grand prize drawing a vintage 1967 Chevrolet Camaro. Although it was announced at the picnic that the car had a value of $35,000, the 1099-MISC information return that Carlos received from his employer showed the value of the Camaro at $1,000. Carlos had his return prepared by a paid tax preparer, Mr. Price. At the time Carlos showed the 1099-MISC to Mr. Price, Carlos explained that he had won the car at a company picnic, but he did not explain that the actual fair market value of the car was $35,000. Mr. Price did not inquire about the value of the car. Instead, he reported $1,000 of income on Carlos's return, reflecting the receipt of the car. Assume that Carlos's failure to report $35,000 of income from winning the car (rather than just $1,000) resulted in an $8,000 tax understatement and a corresponding underpayment of the same amount.

  A. Assuming the IRS can establish that the Camaro's actual fair market value on the date of the drawing was $35,000, on what basis might the IRS impose an accuracy-related penalty with respect to Carlos's return? Describe how the potential penalty amount would be calculated.

  B. What defenses might Carlos assert to avoid the penalty amount?

  C. Describe the potential penalty applicable to Carlos's employer based upon the Form 1099-MISC.

3. Jill, who is self-employed, owns and operates Mountain Crafts Center, a retail outlet selling souvenirs in Monteagle, Tennessee. Jill incurred some business-related expenses but was uncertain about whether the expenses were deductible under section 162. Jill consulted a tax attorney, who, after careful consideration, concluded that, given Jill's fact situation and applicable case and statutory law, approximately a 40-percent likelihood exists that the IRS would allow the deductions. Jill insisted that the costs be deducted. Reluctantly, the attorney prepared Jill's return and reported the business deductions. The attorney did not counsel Jill to disclose the existence of the deductions on Form 8275, nor did the attorney explain to Jill the possibility that the IRS might impose a penalty should the IRS seek to deny the deductions.

  A. Can Jill be liable for the substantial understatement portion of the accuracy-related penalty in this case? Assume that the tax understatement attributable to the deductions would be substantial within the meaning of section 6662(d).

  B. Is there any potential penalty liability for the attorney? What might the attorney have done to avoid potential penalty liability?

4. Matt is planning a transaction that will lower his total tax liability for the year if his tax position is respected by the IRS. His primary concern is that, if he is audited and the IRS does not respect his characterization of the transaction, the

IRS will add penalties to the tax deficiency. What type of sources may Matt consult to try to determine the IRS's tax treatment of similar transactions?

5. Lucinda filed her Year 1 return on June 17, Year 2. The IRS has sent Lucinda a notice of deficiency that includes a fraud penalty, and Lucinda has timely petitioned the Tax Court.

   A. Which party bears the burden of proving fraud on Lucinda's part?

   B. Can the IRS assert for the first time in its answer that Lucinda's return was not timely filed?

      i. Assuming that the IRS can raise the late-filing issue in its answer, can the IRS assert a delinquency penalty in addition to the fraud penalty?

      ii. Assuming that the IRS can raise the late-filing issue in its answer, and that if Lucinda's return is late it will affect the amount of the penalties that Lucinda may owe, who will bear the burden of proof on this issue?

   C. Can a negligence penalty automatically apply in either of the following circumstances?

      i. Lucinda prevails on the issue of fraud.

      ii. Lucinda loses on the issue of fraud.

   D. If the IRS loses on the fraud issue, does that outcome affect the deadline for assessing any tax that may be due for Lucinda's Year 1 tax year?

6. Dylan is representing a client who recently received a 30-day letter from the IRS. The client is eager to settle the case. Dylan has explained to the client the IRS Appeals process, and the advantages and disadvantages of a nondocketed IRS Appeal, which Dylan is inclined to pursue. The client fears that if Dylan tries to negotiate a settlement with the Appeals Division, the IRS will assert additional civil penalties. How realistic is that fear?

Chapter 13

INTEREST ON TAX UNDERPAYMENTS AND OVERPAYMENTS

§ 13.01 INTRODUCTION

A taxpayer who fails to report his or her tax liability correctly and on time is subject to another addition to that liability in the form of interest. Conversely, in some instances in which a taxpayer overpays taxes either by mistake or as a result of an erroneous IRS determination, the taxpayer is entitled to receive interest from the government. Consider the role that interest charges play in encouraging prompt payment by both the taxpayer and the government:

> Interest is not a penalty, although it may be perceived by some taxpayers as tantamount to a penalty. Interest is a charge or compensation for the use or forbearance of money. Compensation for the use of money has been the principal, and at times the only, rationale for charging interest with respect to tax deficiencies or overpayments. . . . [T]he broad principle of interest as a charge for the use of money subsumes a number of different, related theories that individually may justify charging interest — that interest reflects the time value of money, that it provides incentives for prompt satisfaction of debts, or that it is compensation for the credit risk of lending money and collecting unpaid debt.
>
> With respect to the time value of money rationale, a fundamental premise underlying financial markets is that a dollar receivable in the future is worth less than a dollar received today. The discount may be attributable to the opportunity cost of alternative investments (*e.g.*, prevailing rates of return, including interest rates) as well as inflation and the lenders' expectation concerning risk and the creditworthiness of the borrower. In the commercial context, therefore, interest must be charged to render the lender whole (apart from any profit derived from the service of lending). The failure to charge interest on a tax debt (underpayment or overpayment) for which payment is long-delayed would leave the creditor (either the government or the taxpayer) worse off for having the right to be paid than if that party had been paid immediately.
>
> Interest provides an incentive for prompt payment of debts. Relative interest rates on different borrowings can affect which creditors a taxpayer with limited resources will prefer to pay. If taxpayers were not charged interest on a tax debt, they would have an incentive to defer payment of their tax debt and to utilize the funds either for other investment purposes on which a positive rate of return would be earned or to pay other creditors who charged interest. The government would have a similar incentive if it were not charged interest on its tax refunds. . . . Providing that a tax debt bears a market-related interest charge neutralizes (or at least reduces) the advantages that otherwise could be obtained by avoiding payment and investing elsewhere or paying off other creditors. Consequently, interest charges are necessary in both directions to prevent either taxpayers or the government from receiving perverse incentives to fail to settle their tax accounts.

Department of the Treasury, Report to the Congress on Penalty and Interest Provisions of the Internal Revenue Code (Oct. 1999) (footnotes omitted); *see also* Avon Products v. United States, 588 F.2d 342, 343 (2d Cir. 1978) ("[I]t is a clearly established principle that underpayment] interest is . . . intended only to compensate the Government for delay in payment of tax.").

Understanding how interest on overpayments and underpayments encourages taxpayers and the government to pay their obligations to one another in a timely manner is only one piece of the interest puzzle. It is also important to understand how the IRS computes interest on tax overpayments and underpayments, including what the applicable rates and accrual periods are. This chapter discusses those mechanics, and also examines how interest charges may be minimized through proper planning and the use of administrative remedies. Finally, the chapter discusses the technical rules for netting interest on underpayments and overpayments.

§ 13.02 INTEREST ON UNDERPAYMENTS

Reading Assignment: I.R.C. §§ 6601(e), (g), 6631.

As explained above, without an interest charge on unpaid taxes, taxpayers might have an incentive to defer payment of their tax liabilities, in effect obtaining from the government an interest-free loan. Under current law, interest charges can amount to a significant portion of the total figure assessed against the taxpayer. The Code requires the IRS to include with each notice to an individual taxpayer that contains an interest charge (1) the Code section under which the interest is imposed and (2) a detailed computation of the interest charged. I.R.C. § 6631. Notwithstanding this requirement, a practitioner should verify the interest rate applied and the period during which it is due in order to confirm that the IRS's calculations are correct. Specialized software is available to facilitate this calculation.

Interest is payable by the taxpayer on notice and demand and is assessed and collected in the same manner as tax. I.R.C. § 6601(e)(1). Interest on a tax underpayment is not, however, subject to deficiency procedures. *Id.*; *see also* Section 13.05, below. Furthermore, the statute of limitations on assessing and collecting interest on tax underpayments is different from the limitations period for assessing the underlying tax liability. Interest on a tax underpayment may be assessed and collected during the same period in which the related tax liability could be *collected* (generally 10 years from the date of assessment). I.R.C. § 6601(g).

[A] Applicable Interest Rates

Reading Assignment: I.R.C. §§ 6621, 6622; Treas. Reg. § 301.6621-3(b).

Historically, the interest rate applicable to tax underpayments (deficiencies) was significantly higher than prevailing market interest rates, thereby helping to ensure that taxpayers would pay their tax liabilities promptly. During the 1970s, due to high levels of inflation, the underpayment rate, which was a flat six percent, fell below commercial rates. Concerned that taxpayers would find it more profitable to "borrow" tax funds at the relatively lower underpayment rate than to pay their correct tax liabilities when due, Congress introduced a regime under which the underpayment (and overpayment) rates were tied directly to the prime rate of interest charged by commercial banks. S. Rep. No. 1357, 93d Cong., 2d Sess. 12-18 (1974). This regime was further refined by the Tax Reform Act of 1986, which based the applicable rate on a fluctuating federal short-term rate. *See* Pub. L. No. 99-514, § 1511(a), 100 Stat. 2085.

Underpayment interest compounds on a daily basis. I.R.C. § 6662. Currently, the interest rate on tax underpayments (commonly called "deficiency interest") is computed based on the federal short-term rate specified in section 1274(d), increased by three percentage points. I.R.C. § 6621(a). The federal short-term rate is based on the average yield on marketable United States obligations with remaining maturity dates of three years or less. *See* I.R.C. § 6621(b). Most penalties also bear interest at the same rates as tax underpayments. The IRS publishes the applicable underpayment rate in a quarterly Revenue Ruling, *see, e.g.*, Rev. Rul. 2008-10, 2008 I.R.B. LEXIS 158, which keys the prevailing rate to a series of factor tables in Revenue Procedure 95-17, 1995-1 C.B. 556. The tables permit the taxpayer to calculate the specific dollar amount of interest owed.[1]

The underpayment rate increases to five percentage points above the federal short-term rate for large corporate underpayments owed by a Subchapter C corporation (commonly referred to as "hot interest"). The Code defines a large corporate underpayment as "any underpayment of a tax by a C corporation for any taxable period if the amount of such underpayment for such period exceeds $100,000." I.R.C. § 6621(c)(3)(A). Although the increased interest rate may also apply to penalties, interest, and additions to the underlying tax, the $100,000 underpayment threshold is computed without regard to these additional amounts. Treas. Reg. § 301.6621-3(b)(2). Assuming a large corporate underpayment exists for a particular year, the increased interest rate applies only if the taxpayer does not pay the deficiency within 30 days after the date of a 30-day letter or notice of deficiency reflecting a deficiency greater than $100,000. I.R.C. § 6621(c)(2). If the corporation pays the tax within 30 days after the date of the letter or notice that triggers the higher rate, the increased interest rate will not apply. I.R.C. § 6621(c)(2)(B)(ii).

> *Example:* Zylar, Inc., a C corporation, timely filed its Year 1 return on March 15 of Year 2 and included payment of the entire amount of tax shown to be due. On June 1, Year 3, the IRS mails to Zylar a 30-day letter proposing a $110,000 tax deficiency, along with penalty and interest additions totaling $60,000. Zylar's threshold underpayment for Year 1 is $110,000, thereby triggering the section 6621(c) rate. The "applicable date" is July 1, Year 3, the 30th day after the IRS sent to Zylar the 30-day letter containing the greater than $100,000 asserted deficiency. During the period of March 16, Year 2 through July 1, Year 3, the interest rate applicable to the $110,000 underpayment, as well as any penalty and interest accruals (including the $60,000), is three percentage points above the federal short-term rate. The underpayment rate for the period after July 1, Year 3 is five percentage points above the short-term rate.

If underpayment interest is imposed in order to compensate the government for periods during which tax liability is deferred, why apply a higher interest rate to large corporate underpayments? Is the section 6621(c) rate more in the nature of a penalty than a remedial measure?

[B] Accrual and Suspension Periods

Reading Assignment: I.R.C. §§ 6404(g), 6601; Treas. Reg. § 301.6601-1(a), (d), (f).

[1] Beginning and Ending Dates

Interest on a tax deficiency normally begins to run from the last date prescribed for payment of the tax (generally the same date that the underlying return is due). I.R.C. §§ 6601(a), 6151(a). Even when the taxpayer obtains a valid extension of time either to file the return or to pay the tax, underpayment interest accrues from the unextended due date of the return. Underpayment interest ceases to accumulate in favor of the government on the date the tax is paid, which is normally considered the date on which the IRS receives the payment, rather than the date the payment is mailed. I.R.C. § 6601(a); Treas. Reg. § 301.6601-1(a)(1).[2]

---

[1] Interest rates on tax claims in bankruptcy cases, including interest payable on claims under a confirmed plan, are determined under applicable provisions of the Internal Revenue Code. 11 U.S.C. § 511.

[2] As indicated above, the IRS must assess and collect underpayment interest within the period that the underlying tax may be collected. I.R.C. § 6601(g). The deadline, therefore, is measured with reference to the last day for collecting the tax under section 6502, rather than the last day for assessing the related tax under

A rule of administrative convenience allows interest to stop accruing on the date the IRS issues a notice and demand for the underpayment if the taxpayer submits payment within 21 calendar days of the notice and demand (10 business days if the amount demanded exceeds $100,000). I.R.C. § 6601(e)(3). Without this statutory grace period, a taxpayer would otherwise have to estimate when payment would be received by the IRS and calculate interest accordingly.

As in the case of a tax deficiency, interest accrues on the failure to file penalty in section 6651(a)(1) and the accuracy-related and civil fraud penalties (imposed under "part II of subchapter A of chapter 68") from the due date for the underlying return (including extensions) to the date the penalty is paid. I.R.C. § 6601(e)(2)(B). In addition, prompt payment of these three penalties within the 21 or 10-day window after notice and demand for their payment prevents any further accrual of interest during the period after the date of the notice and demand. I.R.C. § 6601(e)(3); Treas. Reg. § 301.6601-1(f)(4). For most other penalties and additions to tax, a special rule in Code section 6601(e)(2)(A) affords the taxpayer an opportunity to *prevent* any interest from accruing if those amounts are paid within 21 days after notice and demand for their payment (10 days if the amount in issue equals or exceeds $100,000). Even if the taxpayer does not promptly pay the penalty within these specified time periods, interest accrues only from the date the IRS issues the notice and demand. I.R.C. § 6601(e)(2)(A).

[2] Possible Suspension Periods

The Code provides several instances in which interest accruals may be suspended because of inaction or delay on the part of the IRS. For example, if a taxpayer who decides not to contest the results of an IRS examination executes a waiver of restrictions on assessment (Form 870)[3] and the IRS does not issue a Notice and Demand for Payment within 30 days after the taxpayer files the waiver, underpayment interest is suspended from the 30th day after the taxpayer files the waiver. Interest starts to accrue again on the date after the IRS issues a notice and demand. I.R.C. § 6601(c); Treas. Reg. § 301.6601-1(d).

Also, as noted in Chapter 12, section 6404(g) suspends the accrual of both interest and certain time-sensitive penalties in cases in which the IRS delays notifying the taxpayer that additional tax may be due. *See* I.R.C. § 6404(g). Under current law, interest ceases to accrue if the IRS does not send the taxpayer a notice specifically stating the taxpayer's liability and the basis for the liability within the 36-month period following the later of the due date of the return (without regard to extensions) or the date on which the taxpayer timely filed the return. I.R.C. § 6404(g)(1)(A). Interest accrual resumes 21 days after the IRS sends the required notice to the taxpayer. I.R.C. § 6404(g)(3). The interest suspension period in section 6404(g) applies only to individual taxpayers and only with respect to income tax liability. Moreover, the suspension only applies to a taxpayer who timely filed a tax return (taking into account extensions of time to file). I.R.C. § 6404(g)(1)(A).

As originally enacted, the suspension period in section 6404(g) began if the IRS failed to send the taxpayer the required notice within 18 months after the taxpayer filed the return. That period was extended to 36 months as a result of legislation in 2007.[4] According to IRS guidance, if the taxpayer files the return on or after November 25, 2007, the 36-month period applies. If the taxpayer filed the return before November 25, 2007, and, as of that date, a full 18-month period had passed without the IRS issuing the

---

section 6501. Underpayment interest is assessed and collected in the same manner as taxes. I.R.C. § 6601(e).

[3] The same rules also apply to waivers executed on a Form 870-AD. Waivers of restriction on assessment and a waiver's effect on the running of the statute of limitations on deficiency assessments are discussed in more detail in Chapter 7.

[4] Small Business and Work Opportunity Tax Act of 2007, Pub. L. No. 110-28.

required notice, then the 18-month period applies. Otherwise, the 36-month period applies to returns filed before November 25, 2007. 2007-48 I.R.B. 1072, Notice 2007-93. The following examples illustrate how the suspension period operates, as well as the effective date of the 2007 legislation that extended the period from 18 months to 36 months:

> *Example 1:* Barbara timely filed her 2005 income tax return on April 15, 2006. The return reflects a $1,000 deficiency. On December 26, 2007, the IRS sends to Barbara a notice that specifically states the basis for the $1,000 deficiency. Because 18 months have passed as of November 25, 2007 without the IRS having provided the required notice, interest will be suspended with respect to Barbara's return beginning on October 15, 2007 (the day after the close of the 18-month period) and ending on January 16, 2008 (the day that is 21 days after the notice was provided). Barbara owes interest on the deficiency from April 15, 2006 through October 14, 2007 (the 18-month period following the filing of her return). Interest also accrues on the deficiency from January 17, 2008 until Barbara pays the deficiency.
>
> *Example 2:* Ricky mailed his 2006 income tax return on April 13, 2007. The return reflects a $5,000 deficiency. On January 2, 2009, the IRS sends to Ricky a notice that specifically states the basis for the $5,000 deficiency. On March 17, 2010, the IRS sends Ricky a Notice and Demand for Payment of the deficiency. Ricky pays the entire amount requested in the notice and demand on April 1, 2010. Because the 18-month period had not expired as of November 25, 2007, the 36-month period applies for purposes of section 6404(g). Given that the IRS issued the required notice to Ricky within 36 months after the due date of the return, the suspension period in section 6404(g) does not apply. Under section 6601(a), Ricky owes interest on the deficiency from April 15, 2007 (the due date of the return) until March 17, 2010 (the date of the notice and demand). *See* I.R.C. § 6601(e)(3).

What type of notification from the IRS "specifically stat[es] the taxpayer's liability and the basis for the liability"? Proposed regulations provide:

> The notice must provide the taxpayer with sufficient information to identify which items of income, deduction, loss, or credit the IRS has adjusted or proposes to adjust, and the reason for that adjustment. Notice of the reason for the adjustment does not require a detailed explanation or a citation to any Internal Revenue Code section or other legal authority. The IRS does not have to incorporate all the information necessary to satisfy the notice requirement within a single document or provide all the information at the same time. Documents that may contain information sufficient to qualify as notice, either alone or in conjunction with other documents, include, but are not limited to statutory notices of deficiency, examination reports . . . , notices of proposed deficiency that allow the taxpayer the opportunity for review in the Office of Appeals (30-day letters), notices pursuant to section 6213(b) (mathematical error or clerical errors), and Notice and Demand for Payment of a jeopardy assessment under section 6861.

Prop. Reg. § 301.6404-4(a)(6).

If the taxpayer timely files his or her income tax return and then files an amended return showing an additional amount of tax for the taxable year, when does the 36-month (or 18-month) notification period begin? Legislation passed in 2005 amended section 6404(g)(1) to provide that, in such a case, the period within which the IRS must provide the required notification begins to run from the date that the amended return is filed, not the date on which the original return was filed.[5] As a result, an amended return is

[5] Gulf Opportunity Zone Act of 2005, Pub. L. No. 109-135 (applicable to documents provided on or after

considered a "return" for purposes of determining when the 36-month (or 18-month) notification period begins.

What is the purpose of the interest suspension period in section 6404(g)? Is it consistent with the use-of-money principles underlying the interest rules? According to its legislative history, section 6404(g) was intended to motivate the IRS to notify taxpayers of pending liabilities more expeditiously. Drafters also noted their concern that "accrual of interest and penalties absent prompt resolution of tax deficiencies may lead to the perception that the IRS is more concerned about collecting revenue than in resolving taxpayer problems." H.R. Conf. Rep. No. 105-599 (1998). Given that Congress has extended the period within which the IRS must provide the required notice to 36 months, does section 6404(g) have much of a role left to play? Bearing in mind that 36 months is the same period of time as the general statute of limitations on deficiency assessments in section 6501, as well as the fact that the suspension period in section 6404(g) does not apply in cases involving fraud or gross misstatements, I.R.C. § 6404(g)(2), which might otherwise extend the statute of limitations on deficiency assessments beyond the general 3-year limitations period, under what circumstance might the suspension period apply with respect to an income tax return filed after November 25, 2007? Consider the following example:

> *Example:* Mindy timely files her 2007 income tax return on April 15, 2008. At the IRS's request, Mindy subsequently consents to extend the statute of limitations within which the IRS may assess tax until June 30, 2012. On December 20, 2011, the IRS provides Mindy a notice stating the basis for a tax deficiency arising from her 2007 return. Interest will be suspended beginning on April 15, 2011 (the date after the close of the 36-month period) and ending on January 10, 2012 (21 days after the notice was provided).[6]

[C] Deductibility of Interest on Underpayments

In considering the actual economic cost of an amount owned to the IRS, taxpayers should consider not the pre-tax interest cost, but its after-tax cost. This raises the question of whether interest on a tax underpayment is deductible. As you may recall from your income tax class, Code section 163(a) permits individuals to claim an above-the-line deduction for interest on indebtedness properly allocable to a trade or business activity. In contrast, personal interest (defined by exclusion in section 163(h)), is not deductible. If an individual taxpayer incurs interest on an underpayment of tax liability, is that underpayment interest properly characterized as nondeductible personal interest?

Temporary Treasury Regulation section 1.163-9T specifically provides that personal interest includes interest "[p]aid on underpayments of individual Federal, State or local income taxes and on indebtedness used to pay such taxes." The Tax Court initially issued several opinions invalidating the temporary regulation, ruling that interest on a tax deficiency was not necessarily nondeductible personal interest. The Tax Court's position on this issue was reversed twice, however. *See* Redlark v. Commissioner, 106

December 21, 2005). The legislative change reverses pro-taxpayer guidance issued by the IRS earlier in 2005. *See* Rev. Rul. 2005-4, 2005-4 I.R.B. 366 (holding that the 18-month period began to run from the date the original return was filed even if the taxpayer filed an amended return).

[6] Because section 6404(g) provides for interest "suspension" rather than interest "abatement," a claim by the taxpayer that the IRS assessed interest that was actually suspended under section 6404(g) is not available via the Code. Nevertheless, the IRS has issued a procedure by which a taxpayer can submit Form 843, Claim for Refund and Request for Abatement, and notify the IRS that it assessed interest that should have been suspended. Revenue Procedure 2005-38, 2005-28 I.R.B. 81. If the IRS denies the request, the denial is not appealable. The taxpayer could, however, pay the disputed interest assessment, file a claim for refund, and, if necessary, file a suit for refund to recover the disputed amount. *Id.*

T.C. 31 (1996), *rev'd*, 141 F.3d 936 (9th Cir. 1998), Kikalos v. Commissioner, T.C. Memo. 1998–92, *rev'd*, 190 F. 3d 791 (7th Cir. 1999).

In *Robinson v. Commissioner*, 119 T.C. 44 (2002) (reviewed by the court), a plurality of the Tax Court's judges, applying a *Chevron*-type analysis,[7] reassessed the court's position and validated temporary regulation section 1.163-9T as a reasonable interpretation of an ambiguous statute. But what if the tax deficiency that produced the liability for interest was the result of an underpayment attributable to income generated in the course of the taxpayer's trade or business activities. Is the resulting deficiency interest still nondeductible personal interest? Consider the following case:

ALFARO v. COMMISSIONER

United States Court of Appeals, Fifth Circuit
349 F.3d 225 (2003)

Wiener, Circuit Judge:

Petitioners-Appellants Daniel V. Alfaro and Irma L. Alfaro, husband and wife ("Taxpayers") appeal the ruling of the United States Tax Court ("Tax Court") in its Memorandum Opinion, upholding the notice of deficiency issued by the Internal Revenue Service ("IRS") on behalf of Respondent-Appellee Commissioner of Internal Revenue ("CIR"). That notice of deficiency disallowed the Taxpayers' claim of a 1996 interest expense deduction of $1,527,695, the amount that they paid in accrued statutory interest that year on an income tax deficiency for a prior year. None dispute that the interest had been paid in 1996 in connection with a compromise between the parties under which the Taxpayers remitted additional taxes on income earned by Daniel Alfaro in his law practice during prior years. Neither is it disputed that this law practice was Mr. Alfaro's principal trade or business. In this issue of first impression in this circuit,[n.2] we affirm the Tax Court's validation of the Treasury regulation relied on by the Commissioner for the proposition that statutory interest paid by an individual taxpayer on prior income tax deficiencies is not the kind of interest that is deductible. We do so even though the tax deficiency that produced the liability for statutory interest was the result of underpayment of tax on income generated by the principal trade or business of one of the individual taxpayers.

FACTS AND PROCEEDINGS

Based entirely on stipulations, the Tax Court found that, from at least 1982 through 1996, Attorney Alfaro was the sole proprietor of his law practice. The IRS audited the Taxpayers' joint income tax returns for the years 1982–88 and assessed deficiencies related entirely to Taxpayers' income from that law practice. In 1995 the Taxpayers and the IRS settled all matters related to the years in question; and in 1996, the Taxpayers paid $1,527,695 in accrued statutory interest on their agreed income tax deficiencies for the subject years. The income that was the subject of the tax deficiency and in turn gave rise to the statutory interest at issue here was produced by Mr. Alfaro's law practice and thus arose from his principal trade or business for purposes of reporting on Schedule C. For 1996, the year in which the Taxpayers paid the statutory interest, they claimed an interest expense deduction on Schedule C of their joint return.

As reflected in a notice of deficiency issued to the Taxpayers in 2000 as a result of an audit of their 1996 return, the IRS disallowed that interest expense deduction. The Taxpayers challenged the deficiency determination in the Tax Court, arguing that the

---

[7] Chevron U.S.A., Inc. v. Natural Resources Defense Council, Inc., 467 U.S. 837 (1984). Courts' use of the analysis set forth in *Chevron* to determine the validity or invalidity of Treasury Regulations is discussed in detail in Chapter 3.

[n.2] Five other circuits have addressed this issue previously, however, and all have held as we do today. *See infra* n.7.

interest was deductible because the underlying income on which the taxes had been owed was from Mr. Alfaro's trade or business in the practice of law and thus not "personal interest" for purposes of § 163(h) of the Internal Revenue Code ("I.R.C."). The gravamen of the Taxpayers' argument in the Tax Court was that the Commissioner's reliance on Temporary Treasury Regulation § 1.163-9T(b)(2)(i)(A), the "Regulation") was misplaced. They insist that the Regulation is invalid because, according to Taxpayers, it conflicts with I.R.C. § 163(h). In rejecting the Taxpayers' argument, the Tax Court relied in large part on its recent opinion in *Robinson v. Commissioner*[n.3] which held this kind of interest to be non-deductible personal interest, relying on the Regulation as authority. Taxpayers timely filed a notice of appeal.

II.

ANALYSIS

* * *

B. *Contentions of Taxpayers*

In their appellate brief, counsel for Taxpayers present a strong and cogent argument for reversing the Tax Court. As summarized in that brief, Taxpayers begin by noting that Congress is presumed to have known the case law that was in existence when it enacted the Tax Reform Act of 1986, adding I.R.C. § 163(h) to the Code to abolish the deductibility of specified types of interest. The Taxpayers advance that the prior jurisprudence made clear that interest paid on an individual taxpayer's income tax deficiency is deductible when the underlying deficiency was on income from the trade or business of such taxpayer. And, urge the Taxpayers, given the absence of an unmistakable showing of congressional intent to reverse or depart from such pre-existing case law, it must be presumed to continue in effect. Furthermore, argue the Taxpayers, the language of the 1986 Tax Reform Act reflects a congressional intent for this species of interest to remain deductible.

The Taxpayers continue by insisting that, by characterizing all interest payments on an income tax deficiency of an individual as non-deductible, without excepting interest on a deficiency properly allocable to income from a trade or business, the Regulation is inconsistent with the plain wording of I.R.C. § 163(h). And a regulation that contradicts the plain meaning of the statute that it addresses, assert the Taxpayers, is invalid. Taxpayers further contend that the Treasury's issuance of the Regulation without following routine notice and comment procedures eschews the usual deference to which regulations promulgated by a federal agency are entitled under *Chevron U.S.A., Inc. v. Natural Resources Defense Council, Inc.*[n.5] Finally, Taxpayers urge that it would be bad policy to allow a corporation to deduct interest paid on tax deficiencies related to income from a trade or business without affording non-corporate taxpayers the same privilege.

C. *Contentions of the Commissioner*

The Commissioner supports the Tax Court's ruling in reliance on its own opinion in *Robinson*,[n.6] in which that court upheld the validity of the Regulation. The Commissioner first notes that all five courts of appeals that have addressed the Regulation have upheld it.[n.7] Next, the Commissioner takes issue with the Taxpayers' position on

---

n.3 119 T.C. 44 (2002).

n.5 467 U.S. 837, 104 S. Ct. 2778, 81 L. Ed. 2d 694 (1984).

n.6 119 T.C. 44 (2002).

n.7 *Allen v. United States*, 173 F.3d 533 (4th Cir. 1999); *McDonnell v. United States*, 180 F.3d 721 (6th Cir.

deference. The Commissioner reiterates the well-known *Chevron* maxim that agency regulations are valid and must be upheld if they implement the related statute in some reasonable way or if they are "based on a permissible construction of the statute."[n.8] . . .

The Commissioner notes that I.R.C. § 163(h) eliminates deductions of "personal interest" by non-corporate taxpayers, emphasizing that non-deductible "personal interest" includes "interest paid or accrued on indebtedness *properly allocable* to a trade or business."[n.12] The Commissioner observes that I.R.C. § 163(h) fails to specify a method of "properly" allocating interest and does not purport to answer the question whether interest paid on an underpayment of individual income tax is deemed to be "properly allocable to a trade or business" when the interest is paid on tax liability arising from adjustments to reported income from an individual's non-corporate trade or business. Thus, concludes the Commissioner, I.R.C. § 163(h) is ambiguous because the undefined term "properly allocable to a trade or business" is susceptible of more than one reasonable interpretation.

In contrast, notes the Commissioner, the regulations implementing I.R.C. § 163(h) do address the precise issue now before us. The Regulation provides that interest "paid on underpayments of individual Federal, State, or local income taxes . . . regardless of the source of the income generating the tax liability" is included in the category of non-deductible personal interest.[n.13] The Commissioner asserts that the Regulation does not conflict with the language of the Code section; on the contrary, the Regulation constitutes a reasonable position, because the duty to pay one's individual income tax is not a business obligation but a personal one. As such, reasons the Commissioner, the payment of interest resulting from a failure to pay such taxes in full when due is likewise personal, regardless of the origin of the underlying income.

As for pre-1986 jurisprudence, the Commissioner points out that the cases cited by the Taxpayers did not address whether an item of interest was deductible *per se*. In addition, urges the Commissioner, the pre-§ 163(h) case law did not contain any reasoned, persuasive analysis that would support the Taxpayers' position that interest on underpayments of personal income tax is a business expense when the individual taxpayer's income tax liability arose from income derived from his principal trade or business. And, not surprisingly, the Commissioner finds comfort in *Robinson* and all prior federal appellate cases on point.

The Commissioner's argument that we perceive to be most compelling is grounded in the General Explanation of the Tax Reform Act of 1986, the so-called "Blue Book," which was prepared by the staff of Congress's Joint Committee on Taxation. This publication states unequivocally that interest on underpayments of federal and state income taxes constitute personal interest (and are therefore not deductible), even when the income on which the tax is imposed was generated by a trade or business. The Tax Court in *Robinson* and the five courts of appeals that have validated the Regulation relied heavily on this statement in the Blue Book.

D. *Validity of the Regulation*

Despite the forceful case advanced by counsel for the Taxpayers, we begin with trepidation in the face of the solid array of five federal courts of appeals that have validated the Regulation and none that has held to the contrary: We are always chary to create a circuit split. Adding to this daunting prospect is the Tax Court's *Robinson*

1999); *Kikalos v. Comm'r*, 190 F.3d 791 (7th Cir. 1999); *Miller v. United States*, 65 F.3d 687 (8th Cir. 1995); *Redlark v. Comm'r*, 141 F.3d 936 (9th Cir. 1998).

[n.8] *Chevron USA, Inc.*, 467 U.S. at 843.

[n.12] I.R.C. § 163(h)(2)(A) (emphasis added).

[n.13] Temp. Treas. Reg. § 1.163-9T(b)(2)(i)(A).

decision to the same effect. It is in the context of that high hurdle that we read the Joint Tax Committee's explanation:

> Under the Act, personal interest is not deductible. Personal interest is any interest, other than interest incurred or continued in connection with the conduct of a trade or business (other than the trade or business of performing services as an employee), investment interest, or interest taken into account in computing the taxpayer's income or loss from passive activities for the year. Thus, personal interest includes, for example, interest on a loan to purchase an automobile, interest on a loan to purchase a life insurance policy, and credit card interest, where such interest is not incurred or continued in connection with the conduct of a trade or business. *Personal interest also includes interest on underpayments of individual Federal, State or local income taxes notwithstanding that all or a portion of the income may have arisen in a trade or business, because such taxes are not considered derived from the conduct of a trade or business.*[n.17]

We agree with the Commissioner's position that the Blue Book directly supports the Regulation: Interest paid on an underpayment of an individual's income tax is personal interest, notwithstanding that the tax liability that generated the interest is owed on income from the Taxpayer's trade or business.

The Taxpayers are correct that, inasmuch as the Blue Book was prepared following the adoption of the statute that it explains, this publication is not binding authority. As the Eleventh Circuit said in *Estate of Wallace v. Commissioner*, however, the Blue Book provides "a valuable aid to understanding the statute."[n.18] The Commissioner properly reminds us that, in the absence of definitive legislative history — as is the situation here — substantial weight should be given to the Blue Book.[n.19] Importantly, the Regulation tracks the Blue Book, and must be sustained if it is "based on a permissible construction of the statute."[n.20]

* * *

Finally, we perceive logical support for concluding that the Regulation's augmentation of I.R.C. § 163(h) is reasonable — and thus valid — when it proscribes the deductibility of statutory interest paid by an individual taxpayer for prior delinquent or deficient payments of income tax. These and other statutory interest provisions of the I.R.C. and the Treasury regulations presumably serve the dual purpose of (1) encouraging full and timely payment of taxes, and (2) making the Treasury whole by replacing the value of the lost use of the funds between their due date and their subsequent receipt. If amounts paid by individual taxpayers as statutory interest on delinquencies were then allowed to be deducted against income in the year such interest is paid — thereby reducing taxes due to the Treasury for that year — the taxpayer's incentive to pay promptly and fully would be reduced by the amount of the tax benefit provided to the taxpayer by such a deduction. Likewise, the value of the amount

---

n.17 Staff of the Joint Comm. on Taxation, 100th Cong., 1st Sess., *General Explanation of the Tax Reform Act of 1986* 266 (Comm. Print 1987) (emphasis added) (footnote omitted).

n.18 965 F.2d 1038, 1050 n.15 (11th Cir. 1992). *See also McDonald v. Comm'r*, 764 F.2d 322, 336 n.25 (5th Cir. 1985) (stating that the Blue Book is "entitled to great respect").

n.19 *See, e.g., Federal Power Comm'n v. Memphis Light, Gas & Water Div.*, 411 U.S. 458, 472, 93 S. Ct. 1723, 36 L. Ed. 2d 426 (1973) (describing General Explanation of Tax Reform Act of 1965 as "compelling contemporary indication" of the effect of a provision). *See also Estate of Hutchinson v. Comm'r*, 765 F.2d 665, 670 (7th Cir. 1985) (concluding that Blue Book explanations are "highly indicative of what Congress did, in fact, intend" particularly when consistent with other evidence of legislative intent).

n.20 *NationsBank of N.C., N.A. v. Variable Annuity Life Ins. Co.*, 513 U.S. 251, 257, 115 S. Ct. 810, 130 L. Ed. 2d 740 (1995) (quoting *Chevron U.S.A., Inc. v. Natural Resources Defense Council*, 467 U.S. 837, 843, 81 L. Ed. 2d 694, 104 S. Ct. 2778 (1984)).

recouped through statutory interest to cover the Treasury's lost use of these tax dollars during the period that the deficiency subsisted would be diminished by the deduction of that interest and the concomitant reduction in taxes collected by the Commissioner for the year of the interest payment. When we assume (as we must) that rates of statutory interest are reasonable, the *effective* rate that would result from allowing a subsequent deduction in the amount of the statutory interest paid would, *per force*, be less than reasonable. The fact that a different treatment appertains to corporate taxpayers is of no moment, given the innumerable differences in the taxation of individuals and corporations.

In sum, after carefully considering these and the other arguments advanced, on the one hand, by Taxpayers and, on the other hand, by the Commissioner, we are satisfied that the Regulation is valid, and that its rule — that an individual's income tax liability, regardless of the nature of the income giving rise to the liability, is a personal, non-business obligation so that interest owed by the individual for failing timely and fully to pay his tax obligations is also personal — is reasonable. This result is not affected by the fact that the interest obligation arises from the individual taxpayer's deficiency for taxes owed on income that happens to have been derived from his trade or business.

III.

CONCLUSION

The Taxpayers' income from the prior years in question was derived from Attorney Alfaro's law practice, which is his principal trade or business. His obligation to pay taxes on that income, however, and thus the deficiency for failing to pay them in a full and timely manner, were personal. Consequently, the interest that Taxpayers paid on that personal tax deficiency was itself personal and thus not deductible under I.R.C. § 163(h), as reasonably interpreted by Temporary Treasury Regulation § 1.163-9T(b)(2)(i)(A). The Tax Court's ruling, validating the Regulation and upholding the deficiency assessed to the Taxpayers, is therefore

AFFIRMED.

Do you accept the Fifth Circuit's conclusion that the disparity between corporate taxpayers (which may be entitled to deduct deficiency interest) and individual taxpayers who operate businesses in a noncorporate form (who are not entitled to deduct deficiency interest) is "of no moment"?

[D] Limiting the Accrual of Deficiency Interest

Reading Assignment: I.R.C. § 6603(c), (d).

[1] Advance Remittances

A taxpayer under examination faces the prospect of interest accruing on a subsequently determined tax deficiency from the date the underlying tax return was due. If the taxpayer expects a protracted dispute with the IRS and is not certain of prevailing on the merits, the resulting interest amount can be significant. Once the taxpayer has received from the IRS a 30-day letter proposing a deficiency, the taxpayer has several options available to avoid further accrual of underpayment interest. As discussed in Chapter 10, the taxpayer can pay the disputed tax liability and file a claim for refund. Even if the taxpayer fails to obtain the refund, the payment stops the running of underpayment interest from the date the IRS receives the payment. *See* Rev. Proc. 2005-18, 2005-13 I.R.B. 798 § 4.01(2) (superseding Revenue Procedure 84-58,

1984-2 C.B. 501). If the taxpayer prevails on the refund claim, the taxpayer generally can obtain interest from the government on the amount that is ultimately refunded to the taxpayer. *See* Section 13.03, below.

A second option for the taxpayer to stop the running of interest on a potential underpayment is to remit a deposit to the IRS. Like a payment, a remittance in the nature of a deposit suspends the running of underpayment interest from the date it is received by the IRS. Moreover, to the extent the IRS uses the deposit to satisfy tax liability, the tax is treated as having been *paid* as of the date the taxpayer made the deposit. I.R.C. § 6603(b).

Section 6603(d) also allows certain deposits attributable to a "disputable tax" to earn *overpayment* interest in favor of the taxpayer. If, for example, an asserted deficiency is resolved in favor of the taxpayer (or the taxpayer withdraws the deposited amount before the dispute is resolved), interest may be payable to the taxpayer on the deposit at the federal short-term rate. I.R.C. § 6603(d) (effective for deposits made after October 22, 2004).[8] Prior to the enactment of section 6603, if the taxpayer requested a return of a deposit prior to assessment (or the deposited amount exceeded the assessed amount), the taxpayer was not entitled to any overpayment interest on the deposit while it was held in the government's possession. Rev. Proc. 84-58, at § 5.01 (superseded).

As indicated above, a taxpayer is entitled to receive interest on a returned deposit only if the deposit is attributable to a "disputable tax," I.R.C. § 6603(d)(1), and interest accrues only during the period that the tax was disputable, I.R.C. § 6603(d)(2). A disputable tax is the amount of tax specified at the time of the deposit that is the taxpayer's reasonable estimate of the maximum amount of tax attributable to "disputable items." I.R.C. § 6603(d)(2)(A). A disputable item for any taxpayer is an item of income, gain, loss, deduction, or credit if the taxpayer has a reasonable basis for its treatment and reasonably believes that the IRS also has a reasonable basis for disallowing the taxpayer's treatment of the item. I.R.C. § 6603(d)(3)(A). The tax treatment of all items that the IRS agent raises in a 30-day letter are automatically considered to be disputable items. I.R.C. § 6603(d)(2)(B). Revenue Procedure 2005-18 provides procedures for making deposits under section 6603.

> *Example:* The IRS sends Mary a 30-day letter asserting a $50,000 deficiency arising out of her Year 1 taxable year. Mary remits a $50,000 section 6603 deposit on June 15, Year 3, following all applicable procedures. The $50,000 asserted deficiency constitutes a disputable tax because it is attributable to a proposed deficiency made by the IRS in a 30-day letter. On April 15, Year 4, Mary and the IRS agree that Mary's Year 1 deficiency was only $30,000. Mary requests a return of the $20,000 excess deposit on that date. Mary owes underpayment interest on the $30,000 agreed deficiency from April 15, Year 2 (the due date of Mary's Year 1 return) to June 15, Year 3 (the date of the $50,000 deposit). Under section 6603, Mary is entitled to receive interest on $20,000 from June 15, Year 3 until a date not more than 30 days preceding the date of the check repaying the excess deposit.

The purpose of the "disputable tax" limitation is to prevent taxpayers who do not have controversies with the IRS from transferring funds to the IRS as, in effect, an investment opportunity.

While, as a result of section 6603, deposits, like payment, can suspend the accrual of underpayment interest and entitle the taxpayer to overpayment interest on the returned

[8] Revenue Procedure 2005-18 contains a series of transitional rules for remittances made and designated as deposits before October 23, 2004. *See* Rev. Proc. 2005-18, at § 10. The American Jobs Creation Act of 2004 (AJCA) that enacted section 6603 also contains an off-Code provision that allows a taxpayer who made a deposit pursuant to Revenue Procedure 84-58 before the enactment of section 6603 to designate the deposit as one made under section 6603. AJCA § 842(c)(2).

amounts, characterizing a remittance to the IRS as a payment versus a deposit can have important consequences. For example, unless the IRS has already applied the deposited amount against an outstanding liability of the taxpayer, the IRS must return a deposit to the taxpayer if the taxpayer merely requests that in writing. *See* I.R.C. § 6603(c). In contrast, to obtain a refund of a payment, the taxpayer must comply with the formal refund procedures discussed in Chapter 10. The applicable interest rates on returned deposits and refunded payments also differ. The interest rate payable on returned deposits equals the federal short-term rate, while the overpayment interest rate under section 6621(a)(2) payable on overpayments is three percentage points higher. I.R.C. § 6621(a)(1).

Revenue Procedure 2005-18, which addresses section 6603, also clarifies some of the rules for characterizing advance remittances as either payments or deposits.

SECTION 4. PROCEDURES FOR MAKING DEPOSITS UNDER SECTION 6603; TREATMENT OF OTHER REMITTANCES

.01 *In General.*

(1) A taxpayer may make a deposit under section 6603 by remitting to the Internal Revenue Service Center at which the taxpayer is required to file its return, or to the appropriate office at which the taxpayer's return is under examination, a check or a money order accompanied by a written statement designating the remittance as a deposit. The written statement also must include:

(a) The type(s) of tax;

(b) The tax year(s); and

(c) The statement described in section 7.02 identifying the amount of and basis for the disputable tax.

(2) Except as provided [below], a remittance that is not designated as a deposit (an "undesignated remittance") will be treated as a payment and applied by the Service against any outstanding liability for taxes, penalties or interest. Undesignated remittances treated as payments will be applied to the earliest taxable year for which there is a liability, and will be applied first to tax, then penalties and finally to interest. An undesignated remittance treated as a payment of tax will be posted to the taxpayer's account as a payment upon receipt, or as soon as possible thereafter, and may be assessed, provided that assessment will not imperil a criminal investigation or prosecution. The amount of an undesignated remittance treated as a payment will be taken into account by the Service in determining the existence of a deficiency and whether a notice of deficiency is required to be issued.

.02 *Treatment of deposits made during an examination upon the completion of such examination by the Service.*

(1) Upon completion of an examination, if a taxpayer who has made a deposit executes a waiver of restrictions on assessment and collection of the deficiency or otherwise agrees to the full amount of the deficiency, an assessment will be made and any deposit will be applied against the assessed liability as a payment of tax as of the date the assessment was made. Interest on an underpayment for which a deposit is applied as a payment will be determined as provided under section 8. If the deposit satisfies the assessed liability, no notice of deficiency will be mailed and the taxpayer will not have the right to petition the Tax Court for a redetermination of the deficiency.

(2) Upon completion of an examination, if a taxpayer who has made a deposit does not execute a waiver of restrictions on assessment and collection or otherwise agree to the full amount of the deficiency, the Service will mail a

notice of deficiency and the taxpayer will have the right to petition the Tax Court. The portion of the deposit that is not greater than the determined deficiency plus any interest that has accrued on that deficiency will be posted to the taxpayer's account as a payment of tax upon the expiration of the 90 or 150-day period during which assessment is stayed, unless the taxpayer files a petition with the Tax Court and requests in writing before the expiration of that period that the deposit continue to be treated as a deposit during the applicable Tax Court proceeding. If a petition is filed, but no written request is submitted to continue the treatment as a deposit before the expiration of the 90 or 150-day period, the tax will be assessed subject to the restrictions imposed by section 6213 and the deposit will be applied as payment of the tax upon the expiration of the 90 or 150-day period. Interest on an underpayment for which a deposit is applied as a payment will be determined as provided under section 8.

(3) A taxpayer may elect to have a deposit that exceeds the amount of tax ultimately determined to be due applied against another assessed or unassessed liability. For example, a taxpayer under examination for several different years may request that a deposit made for one type of tax in one year be applied to another type of tax in another year. The request must be in writing and must be directed to the same office where the original deposit was made.

.03 *Treatment of an undesignated remittance in the full amount of a proposed liability.*

If an undesignated remittance is made in the full amount of a proposed liability, such as an amount proposed in a revenue agent's or examiner's report, the undesignated remittance will be treated as a payment of tax, a notice of deficiency will not be mailed and the taxpayer will not have the right to petition the Tax Court for a redetermination of the deficiency.

.04 *Treatment of remittances that are made during an examination, but prior to the time the Service proposes a liability.*

(1) Any undesignated remittance that is made while the taxpayer is under examination, but before a liability is proposed to the taxpayer in writing (*e.g.*, before the issuance of a revenue agent's or examiner's report), will be treated by the Service as a deposit if the taxpayer has no outstanding liabilities. The taxpayer will be notified concerning the status of the remittance as a deposit, and may elect to have the deposit returned prior to the issuance of a revenue agent's or examiner's report.

(2) If the taxpayer leaves an undesignated remittance on deposit until completion of the examination, the Service will follow the procedures described in section 4.02.

.05 *Post statutory notice remittances.*

(1) An undesignated remittance made after the mailing of a notice of deficiency in complete or partial satisfaction of the deficiency will be considered a payment of tax, will be posted to the taxpayer's account as soon as possible, and will not deprive the Tax Court of jurisdiction over the deficiency.

(2) A remittance that is made before the decision of the Tax Court is final and specifically designated by the taxpayer in writing as a deposit, is not a substitute for a bond to stay assessment and collection described in section 7485.

(3) If the taxpayer has no other outstanding liabilities, an undesignated remittance made by the taxpayer after the date that the Tax Court files its decision in an amount that is greater than the amount of the deficiency determined by the Tax Court, plus any interest that has accrued on that amount at the remittance date, will be treated as a deposit, but only to the extent the amount of the remittance exceeds the amount of the deficiency determined by the Tax Court, plus interest. This excess amount will be treated as a deposit

> until sufficient information is obtained by the Service to apply the remittance to an outstanding liability or to determine that the amount of the remittance should be returned to the taxpayer. The amount that is less than or equal to the amount of the deficiency plus interest will be applied as a payment.

Revenue Procedure 2005-18, 2005-13 I.R.B. 798.

As Revenue Procedure 2005-18 makes clear, if the taxpayer makes an *undesignated remittance* in response to a liability proposed *before* the IRS issues a notice of deficiency — in response to a 30-day letter, for example — the taxpayer may have given up the right to contest the liability in Tax Court. In such a case, the undesignated remittance is treated as a payment, and if the payment satisfies the asserted liability in full, no deficiency exists and thus the IRS will not issue a notice of deficiency to the taxpayer. *Id.* at § 4.03. An undesignated remittance made *in response* to a valid notice of deficiency, however, will not deprive the Tax Court of jurisdiction over the proposed deficiency. I.R.C. § 6213(b)(4); Rev. Proc. 2005-18, at § 4.05. A remittance in the nature of a deposit, as a general rule, does not impair a taxpayer's right to petition and contest the proposed deficiency determination in Tax Court.

[2] Interest Abatement

Reading Assignment: I.R.C. § 6404(e), (h); Treas. Reg. § 301.6404-2.

Under most circumstances, the IRS views the application of interest as nothing more than a mathematical computation based on the rate of interest and the appropriate accrual period. Consequently, the interest portion of an amount owed the government normally may not be reduced except where the underlying tax liability is reduced as well. Over the years, however, Congress has identified situations where, in the interests of fairness, the IRS should consider abating a taxpayer's interest charge on an otherwise unchanged liability.

Under Code section 6404(e), the IRS has discretionary authority to abate interest accruing on tax deficiencies where an IRS official fails to perform a ministerial or managerial act in a timely manner or makes an error in the performance of such an act. The authority to abate interest applies to interest that accrued during the period attributable to the unreasonable error or delay and only if no significant aspect of the delay or error is attributable to the actions of the taxpayer.[9] According to Treasury Regulation section 301.6404-2(b)(2), a ministerial act is a procedural or mechanical act occurring during the processing of a taxpayer's case that does not involve the exercise of judgment or discretion on the part of the IRS representative. Examples include: (1) a failure to timely transfer a case to another IRS office after the taxpayer's transfer request has been approved, and (2) an untimely issuance of a notice of deficiency after the examination of a taxpayer's return has been completed and the notice prepared. *See* Treas. Reg. § 301.6404-2(c).

The IRS's abatement discretion was expanded in 1996 to take into account unreasonable errors or delays by the IRS while performing a managerial act, defined as "an administrative act that occurs during the processing of a taxpayer's case involving a temporary or permanent loss of records or the exercise of judgment or discretion relating to management of personnel." Treas. Reg. § 301.6404-2(b)(1). Managerial acts also include delays that might occur when an IRS employee is transferred or the employee suffers an extended absence due to illness, leave, or retraining. *See* Treas.

---

[9] *See also* I.R.C. § 6404(d) (authorizing IRS to abate interest on a deficiency attributable to a mathematical error made by an IRS employee while assisting a taxpayer in preparing a return), (e)(2) (authorizing IRS to abate underpayment interest on an erroneous refund until such time as the IRS demands repayment of the erroneous refund).

Reg. § 301.6404-2(c) Ex. 3-5. An IRS representative's interpretation of substantive federal tax law does not constitute either a ministerial or managerial act.

Procedurally, a taxpayer requests interest abatement by filing Form 843, Claim for Refund and Request for Abatement. If the IRS denies the request, the taxpayer can seek judicial review of the decision by filing an action within 180 days after the IRS mails the notice denying the abatement request. Judicial review is only available to an individual taxpayer whose net worth does not exceed $2 million at the time the action is filed, and to a business, corporation, or partnership of less than 500 employees with a net worth not exceeding $7 million at the time the action is filed. I.R.C. §§ 6404(h)(1), (2), 7430(c)(4)(A)(ii).

The Supreme Court recently ruled that the Tax Court has exclusive jurisdiction to review a determination by the IRS that the taxpayer is not entitled to abatement. Hinck v. United States, 127 S. Ct. 2011 (2007). The Supreme Court's decision overrules *Beall v. United States*, 336 F.3d 419 (5th Cir. 2003), in which the Fifth Circuit held that the grant of jurisdiction to the Tax Court in section 6404(h) was not exclusive and that a district court also had jurisdiction to review the IRS's refusal to abatement interest. The Tax Court applies an abuse of discretion standard when exercising its newly confirmed exclusive jurisdiction to review abatement requests. Consider the following case.

KRUGMAN v. COMMISSIONER

United States Tax Court
112 T.C. 230 (1999)

COLVIN, JUDGE:

On April 10, 1997, respondent issued a final determination partially disallowing petitioner's claim to abate interest. Petitioner timely filed a petition under section 6404(g)[10] and Rule 280.

* * *

FINDINGS OF FACT

Some of the facts have been stipulated and are so found.

A. Petitioner

Petitioner lived in Grand Junction, Colorado, when he filed the petition to abate interest. He graduated from the University of Nebraska with degrees in architecture and construction management. He worked in energy conservation before 1995 and in home construction after 1995.

B. Petitioner's Returns For 1985–91

On July 21, 1992, petitioner read an article in the Rocky Mountain News which said that respondent had designed a program to encourage nonfilers to file late returns without being subject to criminal penalties. The program required nonfilers to pay back taxes and penalties. The program offered a payment plan for payment of taxes and penalties. The article did not mention interest payments. On October 27, 1992, in response to the article, petitioner filed Federal income tax returns for 1985 to 1991.

Petitioner reported on his 1985 return that he owed $3,199 in tax and that he had not paid any of that amount. He did not make any payment with his 1985 return.

---

[10] [This was redesignated as section 6404(i) by the IRS Reform Act, Pub. L. 105-206, secs. 3305(a), 3309(a), 112 Stat. 685, 743, 745, and redesignated again as section 6404(h)(1) by the Victims of Terrorism Tax Relief Act of 2001, Pub. L. 107-134. — Eds.]

C. Respondent's Notices in 1993

On April 12, 1993, respondent sent petitioner a notice stating that petitioner owed tax of $3,416.31 and a penalty of $854.08 for filing late, for a total of $4,270.39. The notice said:

> We changed your 1985 return because: an error was made on your return when the amount of your social security self employment was transferred from Schedule SE (Form 1040).
>
> As a result of these changes, you owe $4,270.39. Please pay the amount you owe by April 22, 1993, to avoid more interest and penalties. * * *

On June 21, 1993, respondent notified petitioner that he had an unpaid tax balance of $3,695.34. Respondent calculated this amount by subtracting from $4,270.39 (balance shown on the April 12, 1993, notice), overpayments from petitioner's returns of $238 for 1989 and $337.05 for 1990. This notice stated that petitioner did not owe a late payment penalty or interest. The notice said: "To avoid additional penalties and interest, send your payment for the amount you owe by 07-01-93."

D. The Installment Agreement Form and Petitioner's Payments

In July 1993, petitioner signed a preprinted installment agreement (Form 433-D), which had no dollar amounts written on it, and sent it to respondent. The Form 433-D that respondent used in 1993 states in part:

> I/We agree that the Federal taxes shown above, *PLUS ALL PENALTIES AND INTEREST PROVIDED BY LAW*, will be paid as follows: [Emphasis in original.]
>
> $__________ will be paid on ____________________ and $__________ will be paid no later than the __________ of each month thereafter until the total liability is paid in full. I/we also agree that the above installment payment will be increased or decreased as follows:

Date of increase (or decrease)	/ /
Amount of increase (or decrease)	$
New installment amount	$

In July 1993, petitioner paid respondent $1,000 to be applied to his 1985 tax liability. On August 16, 1993, respondent sent petitioner a letter stating in pertinent part the following:

> We have set up an installment agreement to help you pay the amount you owe for the tax period(s) shown above. Your payments are $74.87, due on the 15th of each month, beginning on Sep. 15, 1993.
>
> * * *
>
> In about six weeks, we will send you a notice showing the amount of tax, penalty, and interest you owe. You do not have to answer that notice.

Petitioner did not receive any other correspondence relating to his 1985 tax liability until around September 1, 1993, when he received a payment notice which said that he had a monthly payment of $74.87 due by September 15, 1993. It said: "Total balance owed including penalties and interest: $2,695.34."

Respondent sent petitioner a statement each month for 19 months which stated the amount of the payment due ($74.87), the due date of the next installment, and erroneously stated the "Total balance owed including penalties and interest", with an amount that declined with each payment. None of the notices included interest.

Petitioner timely paid at least $100 per month, which was more than respondent's notices said was due. Respondent's notice dated March 1, 1995, said that "total balance owed including penalties and interest" was $180.24. On March 9, 1995, petitioner paid $180.24 to respondent.

E. Respondent's August 9, 1995, Notice of Interest Due and Events Thereafter

On August 7, 1995, respondent assessed interest of $5,284.44 that had accrued for petitioner's 1985 tax year from April 15, 1986, to August 7, 1995.

Respondent sent petitioner a notice on August 9, 1995, which stated in part as follows:

> YOUR NEXT PAYMENT IS DUE SOON
>
> Your next payment of $74.87 is due on 08-15-95.
>
> The current status of your account is shown below. We apply installment payments to tax periods in the order they are assessed.

FORM NUMBER	CAF	TAX PERIOD ENDED	AMOUNT
1040	0	12-31-85	$6,019.10
Payment due	—	—	$74.87

> The amount shown doesn't include accumulated penalty and interest. Please contact us for the total amount due.

On September 14, 1995, petitioner wrote a letter to respondent in which he stated that he had made his final payment of $180.24 for his 1985 tax liability and asked respondent to abate the $6,019.10 claim. On April 21, 1996, petitioner filed a Claim for Refund and Request for Abatement (Form 843) for his 1985 tax year, in which he asked respondent to abate interest that had accrued because of respondent's errors and delays and additional but unspecified, penalties. Petitioner contacted respondent's Problem Resolution Office in August 1996. The case was assigned to the Problem Resolution Office by August 29, 1996.

On September 12, 1996, respondent abated $352.11 of interest that had accrued from March 1, 1995, to August 7, 1995, but otherwise rejected petitioner's request without providing any helpful explanation. In that letter, respondent's Problem Resolution Program[11] staff said:

> We are sorry, but we cannot allow your request to remove all of the interest charged for the tax period shown above [ending December 31, 1985]. This letter is your notice that your request is partially disallowed. We allowed only $352.11 of the request for the following reasons:
>
> Interest waiver applies from March 1, 1995, through August 7, 1995. A notice was issued on March 1, 1995, giving you an erroneous payoff amount which you paid. The prior notices issued cannot be considered because the total payoff amounts were not paid. On August 7, 1995 a notice was issued giving you a correct payoff amount. For your information, enclosed is a detailed interest computation of your tax account for 1985.
>
> The current balance due for the tax period ended December 31, 1985, is $5,159.23, which includes interest computed to October 7, 1996. Interest will continue to accrue until the balance due is paid in full.

On October 10, 1996, petitioner wrote to ask respondent's Appeals Office to consider

---

[11] [The IRS Reform Act replaced the Problem Resolution Program with local Taxpayer Advocates who coordinate with the National Taxpayer Advocate to resolve taxpayer-specific problems. *See* Section 1.02 of Chapter 1. — Eds.]

his case. On March 4, 1997, an Appeals officer for respondent wrote to petitioner to acknowledge that respondent's 19 erroneous notices were "misleading", and explained that, despite those notices, petitioner was liable for interest for 1985:

> I received your claim for abatement of interest for 1985 in Appeals. The installment agreement states the balance owed as of a certain date. The installment agreement also states *plus all penalties and interest provided by law*. Thus, interest continues to accrue on the unpaid balance during the installment period until paid in full. However, the additional interest which accrues on the unpaid balance during the installment period is not recalculated until the end of the installment period. I will agree that the statement on your monthly bills "including penalties and interest" is misleading and I will attempt to get this language revised. However, since you did not pay off the stated balance due until March, 1995, I cannot recommend abatement of interest in excess of what Examination Division has already recommended.

On April 10, 1997, one of respondent's Appeals officers issued a final determination of petitioner's claim to abate interest under section 6404(e).

On August 17, 1997, respondent issued a levy to petitioner's bank which stated that he had an unpaid assessment for 1985 of $5,426.38 and statutory additions of $147.21, for a total of $5,573.59. On September 18, 1997, respondent collected $127.96 from the levy.

Interest accrued on petitioner's tax liability for 1985 as follows:

Period	Interest
Apr. 15, 1986 – Apr. 11, 1993	$4,022.76
Apr. 12, 1993 – Aug. 8, 1995	1,106.81
Aug. 9, 1995 – date of trial	1,354.30

Petitioner meets the net worth requirements under 28 U.S.C. section 2412(d)(2)(B) (1994).

Petitioner petitioned this Court to review respondent's refusal to abate interest in the amount of $5,426.38. Petitioner also alleged in the petition that he is not liable for additions to tax (other than that which he already paid in installments), that respondent improperly levied his bank account, and that he may offset his 1985 income tax liability with a refund from 1995. Respondent filed an answer generally denying the contentions in the petition.

At trial, respondent filed a motion to dismiss for lack of jurisdiction over the part of the case with respect to petitioner's claim for abatement of penalties and wrongful levy.

OPINION

[The Tax Court first concluded that it did not have jurisdiction to decide the Petitioner's contentions about a wrongful levy, refund offset, and liabilities for additions to tax or penalties. — Eds.]

* * *

B. Abatement of Interest

1. Contentions of the Parties

The parties agree that respondent's monthly payment notices had incorrect payoff figures, but they disagree about the effect of respondent's error.

Petitioner contends that he is not liable for interest for 1985 because he fully complied with respondent's payment notices, in which respondent repeatedly said the payments included interest. He contends that respondent should not charge interest after establishing payment terms which he fully met. Petitioner contends that respondent's failure to abate interest that accrued from April 15, 1986, to April 11, 1993, is an abuse of discretion.

Respondent concedes that petitioner is entitled to an abatement of interest which accrued on his deficiency and addition to tax from April 12, 1993 (the date that respondent first told petitioner that he owed tax and an addition to tax, but incorrectly failed to notify him that he owed interest), to August 9, 1995 (the day respondent corrected the error and first told petitioner how much interest he owed for 1985). Respondent contends that petitioner is not entitled to further abatement of interest under section 6404(e).

2. The Commissioner's Authority to Abate Interest

Under section 6404(e)(1), the Commissioner may abate part or all of an assessment of interest on any deficiency or payment of income, gift, estate, and certain excise tax to the extent that any error or delay in payment is attributable to erroneous or dilatory performance of a ministerial act by an officer or employee of the Commissioner if (a) the Commissioner notified the taxpayer in writing about the deficiency or payment, and (b) the taxpayer did not contribute significantly to the error or delay. Congress intended for the Commissioner to abate interest under section 6404(e) "where failure to abate interest would be widely perceived as grossly unfair" but not that it "be used routinely to avoid payment of interest". H. Rept. 99-426, at 844 (1985), 1986-3 C.B. (Vol. 2) 1, 844; S. Rept. 99-313, at 208 (1986), 1986-3 C.B. (Vol. 3) 1, 208.

3. Jurisdiction of the Tax Court

We have jurisdiction to decide whether respondent's failure to abate interest under section 6404(e)(1)(B) is an abuse of discretion because (a) petitioner made a claim under section 6404(e) to abate interest on unpaid tax, (b) after July 30, 1996, respondent issued a final determination which disallowed a part of petitioner's claim to abate interest, and (c) petitioner timely filed a petition to review the failure to abate interest. Sec. 6404(g)(1).

4. Whether Respondent's Refusal to Abate Interest from April 15, 1986, to April 11, 1993, was an Abuse of Discretion

a. April 15, 1986, to April 11, 1993

Petitioner's 1985 return was due on April 15, 1986. He filed that return on October 27, 1992. Respondent issued a notice on April 12, 1993. Petitioner contends that respondent's refusal to abate interest from April 15, 1986, to April 11, 1993, was an abuse of discretion under section 6404(e).

We disagree with petitioner. Section 6404(e) applies only after respondent has contacted the taxpayer in writing about the deficiency or payment of tax. Sec. 6404(e)(1) (flush language); H. Rept. 99-426, *supra*, 1986-3 C.B. (Vol. 2) at 844 ("This provision does not therefore permit the abatement of interest for the period of time between the date the taxpayer files a return and the date the IRS commences an audit, regardless of the length of that time period."). Thus, petitioner is not entitled to relief under section 6404 for the period from April 15, 1986, to April 11, 1993.

b. April 12, 1993, to August 9, 1995

Respondent concedes that the failure to include interest on the notice dated April 12, 1993, was an error, that petitioner is not liable for interest from April 12, 1993, to August 9, 1995, and that interest for that period should be abated.

To reflect the foregoing and concessions, an appropriate order will be issued.

Given that the IRS conceded that the taxpayer in *Krugman* was entitled to interest abatement for the period beginning on April 12, 1993, why was the taxpayer not entitled to abatement for the nearly seven-year period before that?

For an example of a case in which the IRS did abuse its discretion by failing to abate interest, see *Douponce v. Commissioner*, T.C. Memo. 1999-398. In *Douponce*, the taxpayer asked an IRS employee for his "total amount due" for three previous years. The employee responded with specific figures, and the taxpayer promptly paid those amounts. The taxpayer understood that the figures given him included all the tax due, plus interest and penalties. In fact, the IRS employee did not include in the amounts reported to the taxpayer all of the accrued but unassessed interest. Given that the taxpayer promptly paid his liability when he was notified, the court assumed that "the only reasons for the delay [in payment of the full amount] was caused by respondent's failure to tell petitioner the correct amounts due when the petitioner requested the information." *Id.* Under the circumstances, the IRS's failure to abate interest that accrued from the date the taxpayer paid the total amount he was told was due constituted an abuse of discretion.

Several other subsections in section 6404 either require abatement of interest or give the IRS discretionary abatement authority. Section 6404(c), for example, grants the IRS the authority to abate interest if the amount is so small that administration costs would not warrant collection of the amounts due. Section 6404(f) requires the IRS to abate interest in a case in which an IRS employee provides erroneous written advice to the taxpayer. The taxpayer must have reasonably relied on the advice and have made the request in writing. The written request for advice must include adequate and accurate information. *See* Treas. Reg. § 301.6404–3. Abatement attributable to erroneous written advice also applies to most penalties as well. Another abatement provision, section 6404(g), is discussed in Section 13.02[B][2], above.

§ 13.03 INTEREST ON OVERPAYMENTS

Reading Assignment: I.R.C. § 6611(b)(2), (e).

Just as a taxpayer must reimburse the government for using its money to fund an underpayment, the government must reimburse a taxpayer for the period of time, subject to several grace periods, that it held a payment that exceeded the taxpayer's correct liability. For an analysis of when an overpayment exists, see Chapter 10. In most cases in which the IRS pays overpayment interest, it is in connection with the allowance of a refund or credit. If the IRS grants the taxpayer's administrative claim for refund of a tax overpayment but does not include overpayment interest that is due, the taxpayer can simply request that the IRS pay the interest owed. The request for overpayment interest need not be accompanied by a separate formal claim for refund because the taxpayer is not seeking a refund of an amount previously paid. Section 13.05, below, contains a more extensive discussion of procedural issues surrounding recoveries of overpayment interest.

When the IRS refunds an overpayment, interest ceases to accrue in favor of the taxpayer on a date (determined within the IRS's discretion) not more than 30 days preceding the date of the refund check. I.R.C. § 6611(b)(2). Like the 10 or 21-day grace period allowed the taxpayer for paying underpayment interest, the 30-day interval permits the IRS an interest-free time period in which to process and deliver the refund check to the taxpayer. This general rule is subject to an exception in section 6611(e), which grants the IRS a specified time period in which to refund an overpayment without having to pay the taxpayer any interest at all. *See* I.R.C. § 6611(e). If the IRS issues a refund within 45 days after the due date of the return reflecting the overpayment (without regard to extensions of time to file the return), no interest accrues in favor of the taxpayer. If the return is filed late, the 45-day interest-free period runs from the date the return was actually filed. This provision explains why most taxpayers who file a return that reflects an overpayment due to excessive withholding credits receive no interest on the resulting refund. *See* I.R.C. § 6611(e)(1).

The 45-day period also applies when the taxpayer files an amended return in order to claim a refund of the overpayment. If the IRS refunds an overpayment within 45 days after the taxpayer filed the refund claim, no interest accrues from the date the claim is filed to the date the refund is made. I.R.C. § 6611(e)(2). Under those circumstances, however, interest would accrue from the date of overpayment to the date the refund claim was filed.

[A] Applicable Interest Rates

Reading Assignment: I.R.C. §§ 6621(a), 6622.

Prior to 1998, the interest rate on tax overpayments equaled the federal short-term rate plus two percentage points — one percentage point below the then-existing interest rate on tax underpayments. The one-percent differential applied to refunds owing to both corporate and noncorporate taxpayers. The IRS Reform Act increased the overpayment rate payable to noncorporate taxpayers to three percentage points above the federal short-term rate, thereby equalizing the before-tax overpayment and underpayment rates.[12] For corporate taxpayers, however, the overpayment rate remains at its prior level of two percentage points above the federal rate, and drops to one-half a percentage point above the federal short-term rate for "large corporate overpayments" — those exceeding $10,000. *See* I.R.C. § 6621(a)(1). As in the case of tax underpayments, interest on overpayments compounds on a daily basis. I.R.C. § 6622.[13]

Is an S corporation entitled to recover overpayment interest at the higher rate that applies to noncorporate taxpayers or the lower rate that applies to corporate taxpayers? In *Garwood Irrigation Co. v. Commissioner*, 126 T.C. 233 (2006), the Tax Court held that an S corporation was a "corporation" within the meaning of section 6621(a)(1)(B), so the applicable overpayment rate was two percentage points above the federal short-term rate. On the issue of whether the S corporation could be subjected to the reduced overpayment interest rate for large corporate overpayments, the Tax Court concluded, based in part on legislative history, that the types of overpayments subject to the lower rate of overpayment interest are those of C corporations. As a result, the Tax Court did not limit the S corporation to the .5 percent addition to the federal short-term rate. *Id.* at 236.

---

[12] Given that overpayment interest is fully includible in gross income, while individuals' underpayment interest generally is not deductible, the *effective* interest rate on underpayments payable by a noncorporate taxpayer remains above the overpayment rate, despite the elimination in 1998 of the difference in the *nominal* rates applied to noncorporate taxpayers' underpayments and overpayments. Assuming a federal short-term rate of 6 percent and a 35 percent marginal tax rate, the after-tax rate of interest on deficiencies is 9 percent, while the after-tax rate applicable to refunds is only 5.85 percent. *See* Marvin J. Garbis & Miriam L. Fischer, *The Tilted Table: Penalties and Interest on Federal Tax Deficiencies*, 7 VA. TAX REV. 485 (1988).

[13] Revenue Procedure 95-17, 1995-1 C.B. 556, also includes tables allowing interest computations for overpayments.

[B] Accrual and Suspension Periods

Reading Assignment: I.R.C. §§ 6402, 6601(f), 6611(b), (d); Prop. Reg. § 301.6611-1(b)–(d).

An overpayment may be refunded directly to the taxpayer or credited by the IRS against any unpaid assessment of other tax liability. *See* I.R.C. § 6402. In either case, overpayment interest begins to accrue from the "date of the overpayment." I.R.C. § 6611(b)(1), (2). According to the regulations, the date of overpayment of any tax is the date of payment of the first amount which (when added to previous payments) is in excess of the taxpayer's correct liability (including any interest, addition to the tax, or additional amount). Prop. Reg. § 301.6611-1(b). When applying this formulation, payments made before the return's due date, estimated tax payments, and income taxes withheld from wages are all deemed to be paid on the due date of the return. I.R.C. § 6611(d); Prop. Reg. § 301.6611-1(d). Moreover, the section 7502 "mailbox rule" may cause the date the taxpayer mails the payment to be deemed the payment date.

> *Example:* Ken timely mails, by certified mail, his income tax return for Year 1 on April 15, Year 2. The return reflects a tax liability of $40,000, $35,000 of which was prepaid by Ken through wage withholding, and the remaining $5,000 of which was submitted by him with the return. On October 5, Year 4, the IRS assesses an additional $10,000 tax deficiency, which Ken pays on November 1 of the same year. It is ultimately determined, in February of Year 5, that Ken's correct liability for Year 1 is only $38,000. The amounts withheld from Ken's wages during Year 1 and the $5,000 payment submitted with the return are deemed paid by him on April 15, Year 2. As a result, the entire tax liability of $38,000 was satisfied on that date. The balance of the payment deemed to have been made on April 15, Year 2 ($2,000) and the amount paid on November 1, Year 4 in response to the assessment ($10,000) constitute the amount of the overpayment. The date of the $2,000 overpayment is April 15, Year 2, while the date of the $10,000 overpayment is November 1, Year 4.

See Prop. Reg. § 301.6611-1(c) Ex. 2. Not surprisingly, if a taxpayer files his or her return after the required due date (taking into account extensions), overpayment interest does not accrue during the period before the return is filed. I.R.C. § 6611(b)(3).

If instead of refunding the overpayment to the taxpayer, the IRS credits the amount against an outstanding liability, overpayment interest runs from the date of the overpayment to the original due date of the return against which the overpayment is credited. I.R.C. § 6611(b)(1). Thus, for example, if the overpayment is credited against an underpayment in a subsequent taxable year, interest accrues from the date of the overpayment in the earlier year to the due date of the subsequent year's return.

> *Example:* Julie timely files her Year 1 and Year 2 income tax returns. A subsequent examination reveals that the Year 1 return reflects a $1,000 overpayment while the Year 2 return reflects a $600 underpayment. On April 15, Year 4, the IRS credits the $1,000 overpayment against the $600 underpayment. Interest accrues on the $1,000 overpayment from April 15, Year 2 (the date of the Year 1 overpayment) to April 15, Year 3 (the due date of the amount against which the overpayment is credited). Overpayment interest accrues on the $400 balance ($1,000 overpayment less $600 underpayment) from April 15, Year 3 to a date not more than 30 days prior to the date of the refund check.

See Treas. Reg. § 301.6601-1(b) Ex. 2. *See also* Marsh & McLennan Co. Inc. v. United States, 50 Fed. Cl. 140 (2001) (ending date for the calculation of overpayment interest credited against a later-arising liability is the original due date of the return for the period to which the overpayment amount was credited, not the date the IRS actually applied the overpayment against the later-arising liability). If the IRS credits an overpayment against an underpayment from an earlier taxable year, no overpayment interest accrues. What explains this result?

Crediting an overpayment against an underpayment affects also the period during which underpayment interest accrues in favor of the government. According to Code section 6601(f), if any part of an underpayment for one taxable year is satisfied by credit of any overpayment for another year, underpayment interest does not accrue on the portion of the underpayment so satisfied for any period during which interest would have been allowed on the overpayment if it had been refunded to the taxpayer instead of credited. Although the formulation in 6601(f) may sound complicated, it merely serves to offset overpayment and underpayment interest against one another during any period for which both amounts are outstanding. In the example above, for instance, because a refund of the $600 portion of the Year 1 overpayment credited against the Year 2 underpayment would have resulted in overpayment interest accruing on such amount from April 15, Year 2, no interest is imposed on the Year 2 underpayment. *See* Treas. Reg. § 301.6601-1(b) Ex. 2. Revenue Ruling 88–97 further clarifies the application of § 6601(f) and provides some helpful examples.

REVENUE RULING 88–97

1988-2 C.B. 355

ISSUE

If a liability for one tax year is satisfied by the credit of an overpayment for a subsequent year, to what date does interest run on the underpayment?

FACTS

Situation 1. A, an individual who files income tax returns on a calendar year basis, timely filed Form 1040, U.S. Individual Income Tax Return, for 1984 showing tax due of 10x dollars. A did not pay the amount due. On February 15, 1986, A filed Form 1040 for 1985 showing tax of 20x dollars and income tax withholding of 40x dollars.

Situation 2. The facts are the same as in *Situation 1*, except that A filed Form 1040 for 1985 on August 15, 1986, after having filed a timely application for an automatic four month extension of time to file.

Situation 3. The facts are the same as in *Situation 1*, except that A filed Form 1040 for 1985 on December 15, 1986.

LAW AND ANALYSIS

Section 6601(a) of the Internal Revenue Code provides that if any amount of tax is not paid on or before the last date prescribed for payment, interest is payable for the period running from that date to the date paid.

Section 6601(f) of the Code provides that if any portion of a tax is satisfied by credit of an overpayment, then no interest shall be imposed under section 6601 on the portion of the tax so satisfied for any period during which, if the credit had not been made, interest would have been allowable with respect to the overpayment.

Section 6611 of the Code sets forth rules for determining the period for which interest is allowed on overpayments. Section 6611(b)(1) provides that, in the case of a credit, interest is allowable from the date of overpayment. In the case of a refund, section 6611(b)(2) provides that interest is allowable from the date of the overpayment.

Section 301.6611-1(d) of the Regulations on Procedure and Administration provides that in the case of advance payment of tax, payment of estimated tax, or credit for income tax withholding, the provisions of section 6513 (except for section 6513(c)) of the Code are applicable in determining the date of overpayment for purposes of computing interest.

Under section 6513(b) of the Code [now 6611(d) — Eds.], taxes withheld at the source or paid as estimated taxes are deemed paid on the due date of the return (determined without regard to any extension of time for filing).

For returns filed after October 3, 1982, section 6611(b)(3) of the Code, as enacted by the Tax Equity and Fiscal Responsibility Act of 1982 (TEFRA), section 346(a), 1982-2 C.B. 462, 579, provides that, notwithstanding section 6611(b)(1) or (2), in the case of a return of tax that is filed after the last date prescribed for filing (determined with regard to extensions), no interest shall be allowed or paid for any day before the date the return is filed.

Section 6601(f) of the Code is intended to prevent the imposition of interest on any portion of an underpayment relating to one taxable year that is satisfied by credit of an overpayment relating to a subsequent taxable year for the period during which interest would run on the overpayment so credited if the credit had not been made (e.g., if the overpayment had instead been refunded). *See* S. Rep. No. 1983, 85th Cong., 2d Sess. 99 (1958), 1958-3 C.B. 922, 1155.

In *Situation 1* and *Situation 2*, if there had been no outstanding liability for 1984 and A's 1985 overpayment had therefore been refunded, interest would not have been allowable for any period before the due date for filing the 1985 return (determined without regard to extensions) because section 301.6611-1(d) of the regulations and section 6513(b) of the Code [now 6611(d) — Eds.] establish the due date as the date of overpayment. Under section 6601(f), therefore, the due date for the 1985 return is the date to which interest on the 1984 underpayment is imposed in both situations. *See* sections 3.02(3) and 3.02(5)c. of Rev. Proc. 60-17, 1960-2 C.B. 942.

In *Situation 3*, if the overpayment had been refunded, interest would only have been allowable from the date the return was filed, because section 6611(b)(3) of the Code does not allow interest for any period prior to the filing date. The date the return was filed is therefore the date to which interest on the 1984 underpayment is imposed under section 6601(f).

HOLDINGS

Situation 1. Interest on a liability for one year that is satisfied by the credit of an overpayment from a return for a subsequent year filed on or before the original due date runs from the due date of the return for the earlier year to the due date of the subsequent year's return. A owes interest for the period from April 15, 1985, to April 15, 1986.

Situation 2. Interest on a liability for one year that is satisfied by the credit of an overpayment from a subsequent year's return filed after the original due date but within a valid extension period also runs to the due date of the subsequent year's return (determined without regard to extensions). A owes interest for the period from April 15, 1985, to April 15, 1986.

Situation 3. Interest on a liability for one year that is satisfied by the credit of an overpayment claimed on a delinquent return for a subsequent year runs from the due date of the return for the earlier year to the date the return for the subsequent year is filed. A owes interest for the period from April 15, 1985, to December 15, 1986, the date on which the late return was filed.

Rules for determining when the IRS will credit a claimed overpayment against a succeeding year's estimated taxes (which also serve to determine when interest begins to run on a subsequently determined deficiency) are found in Revenue Ruling 99-40, 1999-40 I.R.B. 441. *See also* I.R.C. § 6402(b) (authorizing IRS to credit overpayments against estimated taxes).

§ 13.04 NETTING UNDERPAYMENT AND OVERPAYMENT INTEREST

Reading Assignment: I.R.C. §§ 6402(a), 6601(f), 6621(d).

As the discussion above of Code section 6601(f) may suggest, calculating the correct amount of interest owed by and to the government when a taxpayer has outstanding both an underpayment and an overpayment has long been a source of controversy. If a taxpayer simultaneously owes tax liability for one year and is due a refund for a separate year, should the taxpayer be able to net the overlapping overpayment and underpayment before calculating the appropriate amount of interest due or payable?[14]

During periods when the underpayment rate payable by the taxpayer exceeded the overpayment rate payable by the government, a failure to net the underlying amounts allowed the IRS to collect a net interest charge on the underpayment even though an offsetting overpayment existed. Congress responded to this perceived inequity initially by enacting Code section 6402(a), which authorizes the IRS to credit an overpayment for one taxable year against an assessed liability arising in a different taxable year. As noted above, if the IRS credits an underpayment against an overpayment, this has the ultimate effect of applying a zero rate of interest during the period of time that the taxpayer's overpayments and underpayments overlap. *See* I.R.C. § 6601(f).

Prior to 1998, the IRS interpreted its grant of authority under section 6402(a) as permitting credit of an overpayment only against an "outstanding" or unpaid underpayment liability. *See* Northern States Power Co. v. United States, 73 F.3d 764 (8th Cir.), *cert. denied*, 519 U.S. 862 (1996). If the taxpayer had already paid an asserted liability at the time of the netting request, no netting computation took place.

> *Example:* Xena, Inc. is a calendar year corporation. As a result of an audit of Xena, Inc.'s Year 2 income tax return, the IRS determined that Xena, Inc. underpaid its income tax by $500,000. Xena, Inc. paid the $500,000 underpayment, along with interest calculated under section 6601, on June 1, Year 3. During the same year, Xena, Inc. filed an amended return for its Year 1 taxable year showing a tax overpayment of $500,000. The IRS paid the refund on August 1, Year 3, with overpayment interest calculated under section 6611 for the period from March 15, Year 2, the date of the overpayment, to July 8, Year 3, a date within 30 days prior to the date of the refund check.
>
> From March 15, Year 3, the due date of the Year 2 return, until June 1, Year 3, the date the underpayment was paid, a period of mutual indebtedness exists. In other words, during this time period, Xena, Inc. owed the government $500,000 and the government owed Xena, Inc. an equal amount. Under prior law, the IRS would have resisted any request made after June 1, Year 3 to net the underpayment and overpayment during the period of mutual indebtedness because Xena, Inc. had already satisfied the $500,000 underpayment at that time. If no netting took place, Xena, Inc. would owe the government interest on that portion of the underpayment in excess of $100,000 calculated at a rate that is 4.5 percentage points higher than the interest rate that the government would have to use when calculating underpayment interest payable to Xena, Inc.

The failure of the IRS to credit an overpayment against an underpayment when the underpayment was no longer outstanding produced an incentive, at least according to some practitioners, for taxpayers to postpone paying outstanding tax deficiencies in the

[14] The IRS will net all increases or decreases in a taxpayer's liability arising in the *same* taxable year. *See* Rev. Proc. 94-60, 1994-2 C.B. 774. For any one taxable year, therefore, the taxpayer will have either a net underpayment or a net overpayment.

hopes of using those amounts in the netting computation. *Cf.* Mecom v. Commissioner, 101 T.C. 374, 392 (1993) ("petitioner contributed to the delay by asking respondent to close his 1976 year contemporaneously with other years to offset his refunds and deficiencies."), *aff'd without op.*, 40 F.3d 385 (5th Cir. 1994).

As part of the IRS Reform Act, Congress mandated a net zero rate of interest to the extent overpayments and underpayments exist for any period, regardless of whether the overpayment or underpayment is currently outstanding. *See* I.R.C. § 6621(d); H.R. Conf. Rep. No. 105-599 (1998). In other words, in determining the applicable interest rate, the IRS must take into account previously determined overpayments and underpayments, even if interest on these amounts has already been paid. This concept is referred to as "global" interest netting.

Revenue Procedure 2000-26, 2000-1 C.B. 1257, provides guidance on the application of the zero net interest rate under section 6621(d) for interest accruing on or after October 1, 1998. Admitting that it does not have the technology necessary to automatically apply the netting computation under Revenue Procedure 2000-26, the IRS advises taxpayers to request the net zero rate. Taxpayers are asked to file Form 843, Claim for Refund and Request for Abatement, and label the top of the form, "Request for Net Interest Rate of Zero Under Rev. Proc. 2000-26." As part of the request, the taxpayer must identify the periods for which the taxpayer overpaid and underpaid taxes and, if applicable, when the underpayment was paid or the refund received. The taxpayer is also requested to calculate the amount of interest the taxpayer believes should be refunded or abated in order to generate a net interest rate of zero.[15]

Revenue Procedure 2000-26 also details how the IRS will apply the zero net rate. If the statute of limitations for refunding underpayment (deficiency) interest (generally, three years from the time the return was filed or two years from the time the interest was paid, whichever expires later, I.R.C. § 6511(a)) is open at the time a claim is filed, the IRS will apply the net rate of zero by *decreasing* underpayment interest owed *by* the taxpayer. (Note that if the taxpayer has already paid the underpayment interest, the decrease in interest owed by the taxpayer may be reflected as a refund to the taxpayer of the interest differential for the overlapping period.)[16] If, however, the period of limitations for refunding underpayment interest has expired at the time the claim is filed, but the period for paying additional overpayment interest remains open (generally, the six-year period beginning on the date the refund is allowed and within which a suit must be filed against the government, *see* 28 U.S.C. §§ 2401 & 2501), the IRS will apply the net rate of zero by *increasing* overpayment interest owed *to* the taxpayer. If both periods of limitation have expired, no interest netting takes place.[17]

> *Example:* Assume the same basic facts as in the previous Example involving Xena, Inc. That is, in Year 3, Xena, Inc. files an amended return for Year 1 and also paid underpayment interest with respect to its Year 2 taxable year. Assume also that the 6-year period of limitation for claiming additional overpayment interest on Xena's Year 1 refund and the 2-year period of limitation for claiming a refund of underpayment interest paid in Year 3 are open. Notwithstanding the

---

[15] The idea of a net zero rate of interest is a bit of a misnomer because, in practice, global interest netting does not involve interest being paid or allowed at a zero rate. Instead, the IRS eliminates the interest rate differential on overlapping overpayments and underpayments.

[16] If the netting computation requires a decrease in underpayment interest owed by the taxpayer, but the taxpayer has not yet paid the interest previously assessed, the taxpayer can request an interest abatement, rather than a refund, to reflect the decrease.

[17] Because a designated deposit under section 6603 is not a tax payment, an excess deposit, although it bears interest at the federal short-term rate, is not available for netting against a tax underpayment. Moreover, a tax underpayment that is covered by a section 6603 deposit would not be netted against an outstanding tax overpayment because, even though the underpayment exists, the deposit eliminates liability for interest on the underpayment.

fact that the underpayment has already been paid by Xena, Inc., the zero net rate for the period during which the underpayment and overpayment overlap (March 15, Year 3, the due date of the Year 2 return, until June 1, Year 3, the date the deficiency was paid) is applied by having the IRS refund to Xena, Inc. a portion of the previously paid underpayment interest in an amount equal to the difference between the underpayment interest paid on $500,000 for that period and the overpayment interest computed and paid on $500,000 for the same period.

Global interest netting under Code section 6621(d) applies to all types of taxes imposed by the Code, meaning that interest on income taxes may be offset against interest on estate taxes, interest on estate taxes may be offset against interest on excise taxes, and the like. To what extent does this netting benefit individual taxpayers? Initially it might seem that the equalization of interest rates applicable to overpayments and underpayments, which was discussed above in Section 13.03[A], renders the expanded interest netting rules somewhat less important for individual taxpayers. However, recall that, because of the inclusion of interest income in gross income and the general nondeductibility of interest paid, even individual taxpayers experience different *effective* tax rates on interest overpayments and underpayments. Interest netting eliminates that discrepancy for netted amounts. Nonetheless, the IRS takes the position that it will not apply global netting computations for individual taxpayers with respect to interest accruing on or after January 1, 1999 (the period after which the interest rates on underpayments and overpayments are equal). *See* Rev. Proc. 2000-26, 2000-24 I.R.B. 1257.[18]

Corporate taxpayers particularly benefit from interest netting, not only because of the continued rate differential applicable to corporate taxpayers, but also because the net zero rate can apply even when the underpayment would otherwise be subject to the increased interest rate on large corporate underpayments and the overpayment would otherwise be subject to a reduced interest rate because it was in excess of $10,000. This benefit is illustrated in the Xena, Inc. Example above.

§ 13.05 PROCEDURAL ISSUES

Reading Assignment: I.R.C. §§ 6511, 6512(b), 6532(a), 7481(c); Tax Ct. R. 260, 261.

Given the complications associated with calculating overpayment and underpayment interest, it is not surprising that disputes between taxpayers and the IRS over interest computations frequently arise. The processes through which a taxpayer may contest the IRS's calculation of interest raise some fairly complicated procedural issues.

[A] Tax Court Jurisdiction

Because interest on a tax deficiency is not included within the definition of a deficiency, as a general matter, the Tax Court does not have jurisdiction to consider the question of interest in a deficiency proceeding. Once a decision has been entered by the court, however, section 7481(c) grants the Tax Court jurisdiction to resolve post-decisional disputes involving underpayment and overpayment interest. To carry out its jurisdictional grant under section 7481, the Tax Court promulgated Tax Court Rule 261, which provides for a post-decision supplemental proceeding during which the taxpayer can raise disputes concerning whether the taxpayer overpaid or underpaid

[18] For guidance regarding interest accruing before October 1, 1998, see Revenue Procedure 99-43, 1999-2 C.B. 579.

interest. Before the Tax Court will consider the issue, however, the taxpayer must pay the deficiency and any underpayment interest assessed by the IRS.[19] I.R.C. § 7481(c)(2)(A)(ii).

The Tax Court also has jurisdiction, in certain cases, to determine overpayments of interest as part of its supplemental jurisdiction under section 6512. As discussed in Chapter 8, once the IRS issues a notice of deficiency and the taxpayer invokes the Tax Court's jurisdiction by filing a petition, the Tax Court also has jurisdiction to determine that the taxpayer made a tax overpayment. I.R.C. § 6512(b)(1). If the court finds that an overpayment exists, the court has jurisdiction to force the IRS to refund the overpayment "together with interest thereon." I.R.C. § 6512(b)(2). Once the Tax Court determines the amount of the overpayment, Tax Court Rule 260 provides for a post-decisional supplemental proceeding during which the taxpayer can resolve disputes concerning accrued interest on the overpayment. *See* Estate of Smith v. Commissioner, 429 F.3d 533 (5th Cir. 2005) (holding that the Tax Court exceeded its section 6512(b) jurisdiction when it ruled that its determination of the amount of the taxpayer's overpayment necessarily decided the extent of the taxpayer's liability for underpayment interest).

While these post-decisional methods of resolving interest disputes may seem odd, bear in mind that, if the Tax Court determines that the taxpayer made an overpayment, the amount of interest that the IRS pays on the overpayment, if any, will be determined based on whether the amount is refunded to the taxpayer or credited against outstanding liabilities. As the Tax Court will not know at the time it enters its decision how the IRS will treat the overpayment, any attempts to compute interest would likely be a waste of the court's time. *See Estate of Smith, supra* (holding that underpayment interest need not be included in Tax Court decisions entered in overpayment cases, and that such interest may still be collected by the IRS even though decision is silent on the issue).

[B] Refunds of Underpayment Interest

As noted above, if the taxpayer seeks recovery of a tax overpayment by making a claim for refund, the taxpayer typically does not need to file a separate refund claim for interest on the overpayment. In that case, the claim for refund of the tax overpayment is treated as an implicit claim for any interest assessed and paid on the overpayment, even if the claim for refund does not include words such as "plus associated interest." *See* TAM 9643001. In fact, as discussed in Chapter 10, if the only substantive ground for recovery of interest is based on the contention that the underlying tax was overpaid, the taxpayer may or may not need to make full payment of the interest assessment in order to satisfy the jurisdictional prerequisite of full payment as provided in *Flora v. United States*. *Compare* Shore v. United States, 9 F.3d 1524, 1527–28 (Fed. Cir. 1993), *with* Magnone v. United States, 902 F.2d 192, 193 (2d Cir.), *cert. denied*, 498 U.S. 853 (1990).

If the taxpayer files suit in order to recover a tax overpayment, the district court or Court of Federal Claims will also typically consider whether the taxpayer is entitled to overpayment interest. The taxpayer may also file suit in either of these courts to recover overpayment interest alone. *See* 28 U.S.C. §§ 1346(a)(2) (district court action limited to a $10,000 recovery), 1491(a)(1) (no dollar limitation on recovery in Court of Federal Claims action). The statute of limitations on a suit for overpayment interest is six years from the date the right of action first accrues, 28 U.S.C. §§ 2401 (district court), 2501 (Court of Federal Claims). The right of action first accrues on the date the refund or credit of the overpayment is allowed. *See* 28 U.S.C. 6407.

---

[19] In addition, the Tax Court has jurisdiction to review a taxpayer's request for interest abatement, a topic discussed in Section 13.02[D][2]. As discussed below, it also has jurisdiction to determine overpayment interest, in certain cases.

If the taxpayer seeks to recover an alleged overpayment of interest on a tax deficiency because, for example, the IRS failed to suspend the running of underpayment interest or misapplied the interest netting rules, the taxpayer must file a timely claim for refund that specifically alleges the grounds for recovery. *See* Field Service Advice 199939003; Computervision Corp. v. United States, 62 Fed. Cl. 299 (2004) (holding that doctrine of substantial variance barred taxpayer's interest suspension theory because theory not raised in a timely filed refund claim). If the taxpayer is also claiming a refund for a tax overpayment, the taxpayer can include the grounds for recovery of deficiency interest in the same claim, or the taxpayer can file a stand-alone claim for just the interest. In cases in which the taxpayer seeks to recover underpayment interest previously paid, the refund claim generally must be filed within three years from the date the underlying tax return was filed or within two years from the date the interest that is the subject of the refund claim was paid. I.R.C. § 6511. The taxpayer may file a suit for refund six months after filing the refund claim and no later than two years from the date the IRS denies the claim. I.R.C. § 6532(a).

PROBLEMS

1. Daniel, an individual, timely filed his Year 1 income tax return on April 15, Year 2. On August 1, Year 3, the IRS mailed to Daniel a 30-day letter (arising from an audit commenced early in Year 3), reflecting the revenue agent's disallowance of $15,000 of claimed deductions. The proposed adjustment resulted in a $4,200 asserted tax deficiency, along with a negligence penalty equal to $840 (20 percent of $4,200). On August 10, Year 4, Daniel filed a Form 870 agreeing to the proposed adjustment. Two weeks later, on August 28, the IRS issued a Notice and Demand for Payment. Daniel mailed a check to the IRS on September 10, and it was received on September 15. Assuming that the federal short-term rate in effect throughout the time periods involved is 6 percent, specify the applicable underpayment rate and the inclusive time periods during which interest accrues.
   A. Assume the same facts as in Problem 1 except that the 30-day letter (the first official notice that Daniel received in connection with his Year 1 return) was not issued by the IRS until December 15, Year 3. Assuming that the section 6404(g) required notice period is 18 months, what is the applicable time period during which interest accrues? What is the applicable time period during which interest accrues if the section 6404(g) required notice period is 36 months?
   B. Assume the same facts as in Problem 1 except that, in response to Daniel's Form 870, the IRS issued the Notice and Demand for Payment on October 1, Year 4. Daniel mailed payment to the IRS on October 5, Year 4, and it was received by the IRS on October 10. What is the applicable underpayment rate and the time period during which interest accrues?
   C. Assume the same facts as in Problem 1 except that instead of filing a Form 870, Daniel appealed the proposed deficiency set forth in the 30-day letter. Unable to reach a settlement with the Appeals Division, and having received a notice of deficiency asserting a $4,200 tax deficiency and an $840 negligence penalty, Daniel timely filed a petition in Tax Court to challenge the proposed amounts. When will interest stop accruing?
   D. Assume the same facts as in Problem 1, except (1) Daniel is Daniel, Inc., a corporation taxable under Subchapter C of the Code; (2) Daniel, Inc. timely filed its Year 1 return on March 15, Year 2; and (3) the deficiency proposed in the 30-day letter amounts to $125,000 (not including interest and penalties). What is the applicable underpayment rate and the time period during which interest accrues?
2. Ruth is the sole proprietor of a local grocery store. Accordingly, she reports all of the income and expenses of the store on her Form 1040, Schedule C. As a

result of a recent audit by the IRS, Ruth has been assessed a deficiency resulting from the recharacterization of certain renovation costs as capital expenditures rather than currently deductible repair expenses. The interest on the tax deficiency amounts to $2,000. Is the interest paid by Ruth on the deficiency deductible for federal income tax purposes?

3. Jaime filed his Year 1 return on Wednesday, April 17, Year 2, two days after the required filing date. The return reflects a refund of $500, representing amounts previously withheld by Jamie's employer during Year 1. The IRS mailed the refund check on June 28, Year 2 and Jaime received the check on July 1, Year 2. Is Jaime entitled to interest on his refund and, if so, during what period does the interest accrue?

4. In June of Year 3, Domestic, Inc. (D Corporation) filed an amended return for its Year 1 taxable year, showing an overpayment of $10,000. Later in Year 3, the IRS audited D Corporation's Year 2 income tax return and determined that it had made a $30,000 underpayment for Year 2. On December 1, Year 3, D Corporation paid the $30,000 underpayment along with interest determined at the underpayment rate. Assume that both the statute of limitations for claiming additional overpayment interest with respect to the $10,000 overpayment made during Year 1 and the statute of limitations for claiming a refund of underpayment interest paid during Year 3 are open.

   A. Is the IRS obligated to engage in global interest netting under section 6621(d) for any period of time on these facts?

   B. If the IRS is obligated to pay interest to D Corporation, on what dollar amount does it apply, and for what period of time?

5. On March 5, Year 3, No Dice, Inc., a manufacturer of children's board games, received a 30-day letter from the IRS asserting a $150,000 deficiency with respect to its Year 1 tax year. Assume that No Dice timely filed its income tax return for Year 1 on March 15, Year 2.

   A. If No Dice wishes to suspend the accrual of underpayment interest on the potential tax deficiency by remitting $150,000 to the IRS, should No Dice designate the remittance as a payment or a deposit under section 6603?

   B. Assume that No Dice does not designate the remittance as either a payment or deposit.

      i. How will the remittance be treated by the IRS?

      ii. What effect will the undesignated remittance have on No Dice's ability to ultimately contest the $150,000 asserted deficiency arising from Year 1 in Tax Court?

   C. Assume that, instead of receiving a 30-day letter, on March 1, Year 4, No Dice received a notice of deficiency from the IRS in the amount of $150,000 with respect to its Year 1 taxable year. In response, No Dice mailed to the IRS a check for $150,000 with no designation or explanation. The check was received by the IRS on May 1, Year 4. Shortly thereafter, No Dice timely filed a Tax Court petition in response to the notice. The Tax Court conducted a trial in the case, and entered a decision that became final on August 5, Year 6. The decision found that No Dice was liable for a tax deficiency of $60,000. The IRS assessed the $60,000 on September 1, Year 6.

      i. Does the IRS owe No Dice interest for the period of time it held the $150,000 prior to assessment?

      ii. If the IRS does owe No Dice interest, on what amount does it owe interest and for what time period?

Chapter 14
LIENS, LEVIES, AND OTHER COLLECTION PROCEDURES

§ 14.01 INTRODUCTION

Having examined how the IRS properly assesses taxes, penalties, and interest, the next two chapters consider the final step in the administrative process — collection of these amounts. As you may recall from Chapter 7, a valid assessment of the underlying tax liability is a prerequisite to administrative collection efforts on the part of the IRS.[1] There are two different procedures the IRS generally utilizes to collect an unpaid assessment: administrative collection procedures and judicial collection procedures. The more important of the two, and more often utilized, are the administrative collection procedures, which usually allow the IRS to collect tax without recourse to the court system. These procedures are the primary focus of this chapter. Section 14.02 discusses the collection process generally and the statute of limitations on collection actions. Section 14.03 examines the role of the federal tax lien, which forms the foundation of the IRS's administrative collection processes. In that section, issues relating the attachment of the lien and lien priorities are discussed, followed by a review of the IRS's levy and administrative sale procedures.

The IRS does not use judicial collection procedures as frequently as administrative collection procedures. The reluctance on the part of the government to use the judicial process to collect tax reflects the expensive and time-consuming nature of litigation. However, if the government is unable to levy on the taxpayer's property, or to do so is not administratively feasible, the government can protect its lien rights by filing suit. The two most common types of collection-related lawsuits instituted by the government are suits to foreclose a federal tax lien and suits to reduce a tax lien to a personal judgment. *See* I.R.C. §§ 7401, 7402, 7403. In a foreclosure action under section 7403, the government petitions a U.S. district court to force a judicial sale of the entire property in which the delinquent taxpayer has an interest and then divide the sales proceeds among the lien holders, including the IRS. A suit to reduce an assessment to personal judgment generally is utilized to extend the statute of limitations on collection. Although this chapter focuses primarily on administrative collection procedures, the operation of judicial procedures, both in cases in which the government institutes the proceedings and in which the taxpayer institutes the proceedings, is discussed in Section 14.04.

The tax collection area was heavily affected by the IRS Reform Act. In an effort to increase taxpayers' process rights during collection proceedings, the IRS Reform Act placed limitations on the use of many of the IRS's enforcement tools and added additional procedures to the collection process. For example, Code section 6304 now requires the IRS to comply with certain provisions of the Fair Debt Collection Practices Act, 15 U.S.C. § 1692. Among other restrictions, the IRS is prohibited from communicating with a taxpayer at a time or place inconvenient to the taxpayer, and from attempting to contact the taxpayer at his or her place of employment if the IRS has reason to know that the taxpayer's employer prohibits such communications. I.R.C. § 6304(a). Furthermore, the IRS may not engage in any conduct intended to harass or abuse the taxpayer, including threats of violence or use of obscene language. I.R.C. § 6304(b). If the IRS violates any of these provisions, the taxpayer may bring a civil action against the United States in district court under section 7433 to recover damages. I.R.C. § 6304(c).

---

[1] As discussed in Chapter 7, the types of assessments include summary, deficiency, jeopardy, and termination assessments. Assessment occurs once the IRS records the taxpayer's name and liability on a list of debts owed to the IRS.

The IRS Reform Act also instituted procedures, some discussed in this chapter, that require the IRS to obtain prior judicial approval before taking enforced collection action with respect to certain taxpayer assets. The most important of the new procedures added by the IRS Reform Act is the opportunity afforded most taxpayers to obtain review from the IRS Appeals Division of their collection cases through the Collection Due Process (CDP) procedures before the IRS levies on the taxpayer's property. *See* I.R.C. §§ 6320, 6330. The CDP procedures are mentioned briefly in this chapter, and are discussed in more detail in Chapter 16.

Whatever method the government uses to collect tax, does the prospect of enforced collection action substantially affect voluntary compliance on the part of taxpayers? As explained in Chapter 1, the number of enforced collection cases (liens, levies and seizures) declined dramatically after the enactment of the IRS Reform Act, as the IRS attempted to implement the newly enacted taxpayer rights provisions. Although enforced collection activity has rebounded somewhat since then, what impact do you think the drop in enforcement cases had on taxpayers' willingness to comply with their filing and payment obligations? Attempting to answer these questions might be premature at this point, but consider these issues as you read the remainder of this chapter.

§ 14.02 COLLECTION PROCEDURES IN GENERAL

Reading Assignment: I.R.C. §§ 6303, 6306, 6322, 6502, 6503.

[A] The IRS's Collection Operation

If a taxpayer's account remains unpaid after the IRS makes an assessment, the taxpayer will begin receiving a series of computer-generated bills notifying the taxpayer of the delinquency. If the taxpayer ignores the bills, the IRS will send subsequent notices that become increasingly more insistent in their payment demands. As explained below, some of these notices are required by statute and serve the function of satisfying notification requirements that the IRS must meet before it can properly take enforced collection action against the taxpayer's property. If these notices prove unsuccessful, the account is then usually assigned to the IRS's Automated Collection System ("ACS"). ACS is a computerized collection system that prompts IRS personnel to contact taxpayers by phone in an effort to collect unpaid amounts.

In 2004, Congress authorized the IRS to begin using private debt collection agencies, rather than IRS employees, to collect outstanding tax liabilities from certain delinquent taxpayers. *See* I.R.C. § 6306. The private agencies are paid for their work based on a percentage of the amounts they collect. I.R.C. § 6306(c). The scope of the activities that the private firms can perform is limited. The firms are authorized to collect tax only in cases in which the taxpayer has not disputed the tax liability. Moreover, the firms may not engage in enforced collections actions such as levies and seizures. *See* I.R.C. § 6306(b). The private debt collection program began in 2006, and while the firms must comply with specified fair debt collection practices, critics of the program have expressed concerns about the potential for taxpayer abuse and privacy risks. *See* Diane Freda, *Service Issues Publication Telling Taxpayers What to Expect from Private Debt Collection*, 159 Daily Tax Rep. (BNA) (Aug. 17, 2006), at G-5.

If initial efforts to collect an outstanding payment, whether performed by IRS personnel or a private agency, prove unsuccessful, the delinquent account normally is transferred to an IRS revenue officer for a field investigation. Once assigned to a case, a revenue officer will contact the taxpayer to determine the current status of the taxpayer's account and will again demand immediate and full payment of all delinquent amounts. If the taxpayer fails to appear at the interview or otherwise refuses to cooperate, the revenue officer can issue a summons requiring the taxpayer to appear and provide financial information. If the outstanding liability cannot be collected by the revenue officer at the initial meeting, the revenue officer will attempt to ascertain information about the taxpayer's assets and will eventually decide whether enforced collection activity, discussed below, is necessary and how is should proceed. *See* I.R.M. 5.1.10.3.2.

[B] The Notice and Demand for Payment

Once the IRS makes a valid assessment, the billing process described above begins. The first computer-generated notice the taxpayer receives is the Notice and Demand for Payment (also called a "Request for Payment"). Section 6303 mandates that the IRS send the notice and demand within 60 days after tax is assessed. The notice sets forth the amount of the unpaid liability and demands payment within 10 days. A taxpayer's failure to pay the amount owed within 21 days after notice and demand (10 days in the case of liabilities of $100,000 or more) triggers the failure to pay penalties under section 6651(a)(3), discussed in Chapter 12.

The notice and demand may be left at the taxpayer's dwelling or usual place of business, or mailed to the taxpayer's last known address.[2] In the case of a jointly filed return, a joint notice and demand is usually sufficient for both spouses. Similarly, if an agency relationship exists among two or more taxpayers, a single notice to one taxpayer is generally considered notice to all. Section 6303 incorporates no other formal requirements for the notice and demand, and unlike the treatment afforded a notice of deficiency, courts have been lenient towards the IRS in accepting evidence that a valid notice and demand has been made.[3]

Because the administrative collection procedures are expressly conditioned upon the section 6303 notice, the IRS's failure to provide a valid notice and demand to the delinquent taxpayer precludes the IRS from using the lien and levy procedures to collect the unpaid amount. I.R.C. §§ 6321; 6311. Failure by the IRS to issue a notice and demand does not, however, invalidate the underlying tax assessment, *see* Blackston v. United States, 91-2 U.S.T.C. ¶ 50,507 (D. Md. 1991), nor does it prevent the IRS from suing the taxpayer to collect the amount owed under the judicial collection procedures. *See* United States v. Berman, 825 F.2d 1053 (6th Cir. 1987).

[C] Statutes of Limitations on Collection

Once the IRS assesses tax liability, it generally has ten years from the date of the assessment to collect the tax by levy or through a judicial proceeding. I.R.C. § 6502(a). Prior to the IRS Reform Act, section 6502 permitted the IRS to request that the taxpayer agree to extend the limitations period on collection. Believing that the IRS should collect all taxes within ten years, Congress amended section 6502 to prohibit the IRS from requesting an extension, except in limited circumstances. *Cf.* I.R.C. § 6501 (allowing for extension of the statute of limitations on assessments). If, for example, the taxpayer enters into an installment agreement to pay the outstanding liability over a period of time, the IRS is permitted to request an extension of the statute of limitations to cover the period during which payment is to take place. In that case, the limitations period expires after the agreed-upon date, plus 90 days. I.R.C. § 6502(a)(2)(A); *see generally* Treas. Reg. § 301.6502-1.[4]

---

[2] The same "last known address" issues applicable to notices of deficiency, discussed in Chapter 9, arise in this context as well.

[3] Code section 7522(a) requires that IRS notices, such as a notice and demand, describe the basis for and identify the amount of the tax due, along with interest and any assessable penalties. An inadequate description of the amount due, however, will not invalidate a notice and demand. I.R.C. § 7522(a).

[4] Another exception extends the limitations period if there has been a levy on any part of the taxpayer's property before the 10-year period expired, and the extension is agreed upon in writing before a release of levy

Section 6503 also specifies circumstances in which the limitations period may be suspended or tolled. As in the case of the statute of limitations on assessment, the limitations period in section 6502 is tolled during the prohibited period set forth in section 6213(a) (that is, for 90 or 150 days after the mailing of the notice of deficiency, or, if the taxpayer files a Tax Court petition, until the decision of the Tax Court becomes final), plus an additional 60 days. I.R.C. § 6503(a)(1). If the taxpayer files for bankruptcy, the limitations period is tolled during the period of time that the IRS is prohibited from collecting the tax because of the bankruptcy proceeding, plus 6 months. I.R.C. § 6503(h). The period may also be suspended during the time the taxpayer is out of the country, I.R.C. § 6503(c), or during any period in which the taxpayer's property is in the custody or control of a federal or state court, I.R.C. § 6503(b).

Finally, commencement by the government of a personal judgment suit against the taxpayer tolls the limitations period. I.R.C. § 6322. Should the government prevail in the suit, this creates a judgment lien that remains enforceable for the life of the judgment as determined by state law. *Id.* In some cases, the judgment may remain enforceable far beyond the limitations period in the Code, which is the typical reason that the government would file one of these suits.

§ 14.03 ADMINISTRATIVE COLLECTION PROCEDURES

As noted above, administrative collection cases normally begin with a written demand for payment by the IRS. Unless the taxpayer or the taxpayer's representative intervenes to negotiate a compromise or deferred payment schedule, or the IRS determines that the unpaid liability is uncollectible, the process may lead to seizure and sale of the taxpayer's assets to satisfy the amounts owed. Because of the statutory federal tax lien, the IRS can collect an outstanding liability pursuant to these administrative collection procedures without seeking judicial intervention. Each step in the administrative collection process is discussed below, with particular emphasis on the role of the federal tax lien. The special procedures that apply to amounts immediately assessed under the jeopardy assessment procedures are also discussed.

[A] The Statutory Federal Tax Lien

Reading Assignment: I.R.C. §§ 6321, 6322.

If a taxpayer neglects or refuses to pay the entire assessed amount after notice and demand, a lien in favor of the IRS automatically attaches to all of the taxpayer's property. I.R.C. § 6321. The federal tax lien is retroactive to the date of assessment.[5] I.R.C. § 6322. In the case of a jeopardy assessment, the federal tax lien arises automatically upon assessment, with no notice and demand required. Although a federal tax lien represents nothing more than a claim or encumbrance against the taxpayer's

under section 6343. In addition, if the taxpayer requests an installment agreement or offer in compromise and the request is denied, the statute of limitations on collection is tolled during the period in which the request is pending (plus 30 days) and while any appeal of the denial is pending. I.R.C. § 6331(k). Moreover, if the taxpayer requests a Collection Due Process (CDP) hearing, the limitations period in section 6502 with respect to taxes listed in the CDP notice is suspended beginning on the date the IRS receives the taxpayer's hearing request and ending on the date the taxpayer has exhausted the right to appeal an adverse determination. I.R.C. § 6330(e).

[5] While the Code provides for no express time delay before the lien arises, the initial notice and demand allows the taxpayer ten days in which to pay. Moreover, section 6331(d) requires the IRS to wait 30 days, in most cases, after providing the taxpayer with a Notice of Intent to Levy before the taxpayer's property may be levied upon. This time delay affords the taxpayer an opportunity to pay the tax before levy proceedings may be instituted.

property, the lien is important because it is a necessary step down a path that eventually allows the IRS to seize the taxpayer's property, which may then be sold to generate funds to pay the tax.

[1] Attachment of the Federal Tax Lien

The federal tax lien arises at the time the underlying tax liability is assessed and continues until the amount assessed is paid or becomes unenforceable because of a lapse of time. The tax lien attaches (encumbers) "all property and rights to property, whether real or personal, tangible or intangible, belonging to" the delinquent taxpayer. Treas. Reg. § 301.6321-1. Importantly, the tax lien also attaches to assets that the delinquent taxpayer acquires after the lien arises, provided that the lien is still in effect. *Id.* For most property interests the taxpayer holds — fee simple ownership in real estate, bank accounts, personal property, etc. — the answer to the question of whether the tax lien attaches is simple — yes. For certain joint interests, as well as property interests subject to restrictions on alienation and state law protections against the claims of creditors, the question is somewhat more difficult to answer. The ultimate determination of whether the section 6321 lien encumbers the delinquent taxpayer's interest in property requires a consideration of both state and federal law. The following case illustrates the analysis.

DRYE v. UNITED STATES
United States Supreme Court
528 U.S. 49 (1999)

Justice Ginsburg delivered the opinion of the Court.

This case concerns the respective provinces of state and federal law in determining what is property for purposes of federal tax lien legislation. At the time of his mother's death, petitioner Rohn F. Drye, Jr., was insolvent and owed the Federal Government some $325,000 on unpaid tax assessments for which notices of federal tax liens had been filed. His mother died intestate, leaving an estate with a total value of approximately $233,000 to which he was sole heir. After the passage of several months, Drye disclaimed his interest in his mother's estate, which then passed by operation of state law to his daughter. This case presents the question whether Drye's interest as heir to his mother's estate constituted "property" or a "right to property" to which the federal tax liens attached under 26 U.S.C. § 6321, despite Drye's exercise of the prerogative state law accorded him to disclaim the interest retroactively.

We hold that the disclaimer did not defeat the federal tax liens. The Internal Revenue Code's prescriptions are most sensibly read to look to state law for delineation of the taxpayer's rights or interests, but to leave to federal law the determination whether those rights or interests constitute "property" or "rights to property" within the meaning of § 6321. "Once it has been determined that state law creates sufficient interests in the [taxpayer] to satisfy the requirements of [the federal tax lien provision], state law is inoperative to prevent the attachment of liens created by federal statutes in favor of the United States." *United States v. Bess*, 357 U.S. 51, 56–57, 78 S. Ct. 1054, 2 L. Ed. 2d 1135 (1958).

I.

A.

The relevant facts are not in dispute. On August 3, 1994, Irma Deliah Drye died intestate, leaving an estate worth approximately $233,000, of which $158,000 was personalty and $75,000 was realty located in Pulaski County, Arkansas. Petitioner Rohn F. Drye, Jr., her son, was sole heir to the estate under Arkansas law. *See* Ark. Code

Ann. § 28-9-214 (1987) (intestate interest passes "first, to the children of the intestate"). On the date of his mother's death, Drye was insolvent and owed the Government approximately $325,000, representing assessments for tax deficiencies in years 1988, 1989, and 1990. The Internal Revenue Service (IRS or Service) had made assessments against Drye in November 1990 and May 1991 and had valid tax liens against all of Drye's "property and rights to property" pursuant to 26 U.S.C. § 6321.

Drye petitioned the Pulaski County Probate Court for appointment as administrator of his mother's estate and was so appointed on August 17, 1994. Almost six months later, on February 4, 1995, Drye filed in the Probate Court and land records of Pulaski County a written disclaimer of all interests in his mother's estate. Two days later, Drye resigned as administrator of the estate.

Under Arkansas law, an heir may disavow his inheritance by filing a written disclaimer no later than nine months after the death of the decedent. Ark. Code Ann. §§ 28-2-101, 28-2-107 (1987). The disclaimer creates the legal fiction that the disclaimant predeceased the decedent; consequently, the disclaimant's share of the estate passes to the person next in line to receive that share. The disavowing heir's creditors, Arkansas law provides, may not reach property thus disclaimed. § 28-2-108. In the case at hand, Drye's disclaimer caused the estate to pass to his daughter, Theresa Drye, who succeeded her father as administrator and promptly established the Drye Family 1995 Trust (Trust).

On March 10, 1995, the Probate Court declared valid Drye's disclaimer of all interest in his mother's estate and accordingly ordered final distribution of the estate to Theresa Drye. Theresa Drye then used the estate's proceeds to fund the Trust, of which she and, during their lifetimes, her parents are the beneficiaries. Under the Trust's terms, distributions are at the discretion of the trustee, Drye's counsel Daniel M. Traylor, and may be made only for the health, maintenance, and support of the beneficiaries. The Trust is spendthrift, and under state law, its assets are therefore shielded from creditors seeking to satisfy the debts of the Trust's beneficiaries.

Also in 1995, the IRS and Drye began negotiations regarding Drye's tax liabilities. During the course of the negotiations, Drye revealed to the Service his beneficial interest in the Trust. Thereafter, on April 11, 1996, the IRS filed with the Pulaski County Circuit Clerk and Recorder a notice of federal tax lien against the Trust as Drye's nominee. The Service also served a notice of levy on accounts held in the Trust's name by an investment bank and notified the Trust of the levy.

B.

On May 1, 1996, invoking 26 U.S.C. § 7426(a)(1), the Trust filed a wrongful levy action against the United States in the United States District Court for the Eastern District of Arkansas. The Government counterclaimed against the Trust, the trustee, and the trust beneficiaries, seeking to reduce to judgment the tax assessments against Drye, confirm its right to seize the Trust's assets in collection of those debts, foreclose on its liens, and sell the Trust property. On cross-motions for summary judgment, the District Court ruled in the Government's favor.

The United States Court of Appeals for the Eighth Circuit affirmed the District Court's judgment. Drye Family 1995 Trust v. United States, 152 F.3d 892 (1998). The Court of Appeals understood our precedents to convey that "state law determines whether a given set of circumstances creates a right or interest; federal law then dictates whether that right or interest constitutes 'property' or the 'right to property' under § 6321." 152 F.3d at 898.

We granted certiorari, 526 U.S. 1063 (1999), to resolve a conflict between the Eighth Circuit's holding and decisions of the Fifth and Ninth Circuits.[n.1] We now affirm.

[n.1] In the view of those courts, state law holds sway. Under their approach, in a State adhering to an

II.

Under the relevant provisions of the Internal Revenue Code, to satisfy a tax deficiency, the Government may impose a lien on any "property" or "rights to property" belonging to the taxpayer. Section 6321 provides: "If any person liable to pay any tax neglects or refuses to pay the same after demand, the amount . . . shall be a lien in favor of the United States upon all property and rights to property, whether real or personal, belonging to such person." 26 U.S.C. § 6321. A complementary provision, § 6331(a), states:

> "If any person liable to pay any tax neglects or refuses to pay the same within 10 days after notice and demand, it shall be lawful for the Secretary to collect such tax . . . by levy upon all property and rights to property (except such property as is exempt under section 6334) belonging to such person or on which there is a lien provided in this chapter for the payment of such tax."

The language in §§ 6321 and 6331(a), this Court has observed, "is broad and reveals on its face that Congress meant to reach every interest in property that a taxpayer might have." United States v. National Bank of Commerce, 472 U.S. 713, 719–720, 105 S. Ct. 2919, 86 L. Ed. 2d 565 (1985) (*citing* 4 B. Bittker, Federal Taxation of Income, Estates and Gifts ¶ 111.5.4, p. 111-100 (1981)); *see also* Glass City Bank v. United States, 326 U.S. 265, 267, 66 S. Ct. 108, 90 L. Ed. 56 (1945) ("Stronger language could hardly have been selected to reveal a purpose to assure the collection of taxes."). When Congress so broadly uses the term "property," we recognize, as we did in the context of the gift tax, that the Legislature aims to reach " 'every species of right or interest protected by law and having an exchangeable value.' " Jewett v. Commissioner, 455 U.S. 305, 309, 102 S. Ct. 1082, 71 L. Ed. 2d 170 (1982) (*quoting* S. Rep. No. 665, 72d Cong., 1st Sess., 39 (1932); H. R. Rep. No. 708, 72d Cong., 1st Sess., 27 (1932)).

Section 6334(a) of the Code is corroborative. That provision lists property exempt from levy. The list includes 13 categories of items; among the enumerated exemptions are certain items necessary to clothe and care for one's family, unemployment compensation, and workers' compensation benefits. §§ 6334(a)(1), (2), (4), (7). The enumeration contained in § 6334(a), Congress directed, is exclusive: "Notwithstanding any other law of the United States . . . , no property or rights to property shall be exempt from levy other than the property specifically made exempt by subsection (a)." § 6334(c). Inheritances or devises disclaimed under state law are not included in § 6334(a)'s catalog of property exempt from levy. *See Bess*, 357 U.S. at 57 ("The fact that . . . Congress provided specific exemptions from distraint is evidence that Congress did not intend to recognize further exemptions which would prevent attachment of [federal tax] liens[.]"); United States v. Mitchell, 403 U.S. 190, 205, 91 S. Ct. 1763, 29 L. Ed. 2d 406 (1971) ("The language [of § 6334] is specific and it is clear and there is no room in it for automatic exemption of property that happens to be exempt from state levy under state law."). The absence of any recognition of disclaimers in §§ 6321, 6322, 6331(a), and 6334(a) and (c), the relevant tax collection provisions, contrasts with § 2518(a) of the Code, which renders qualifying state-law disclaimers "with respect to any interest in property" effective for federal wealth-transfer tax purposes and for those purposes only.

Drye nevertheless refers to cases indicating that state law is the proper guide to the critical determination whether his interest in his mother's estate constituted "property"

---

acceptance-rejection theory, under which a property interest vests only when the beneficiary accepts the inheritance or devise, the disclaiming taxpayer prevails and the federal liens do not attach. If, instead, the State holds to a transfer theory, under which the property is deemed to vest in the beneficiary immediately upon the death of the testator or intestate, the taxpayer loses and the federal lien runs with the property. *See* Leggett v. United States, 120 F.3d 592, 594 (CA5 1997); Mapes v. United States, 15 F.3d 138, 140 (CA9 1994); *accord*, United States v. Davidson, 55 F. Supp. 2d 1152, 1155 (Colo. 1999). Drye maintains that Arkansas adheres to the acceptance-rejection theory.

or "rights to property" under § 6321. His position draws support from two recent appellate opinions: Leggett v. United States, 120 F.3d 592, 597 (CA5 1997) ("Section 6321 adopts the state's definition of property interest."); and Mapes v. United States, 15 F.3d 138, 140 (CA9 1994) ("For the answer to the question [whether taxpayer had the requisite interest in property], we must look to state law, not federal law."). Although our decisions in point have not been phrased so meticulously as to preclude Drye's argument,[n.4] we are satisfied that the Code and interpretive case law place under federal, not state, control the ultimate issue whether a taxpayer has a beneficial interest in any property subject to levy for unpaid federal taxes.

III.

As restated in *National Bank of Commerce*: "The question whether a state-law right constitutes 'property' or 'rights to property' is a matter of federal law." 472 U.S. at 727. We look initially to state law to determine what rights the taxpayer has in the property the Government seeks to reach, then to federal law to determine whether the taxpayer's state-delineated rights qualify as "property" or "rights to property" within the compass of the federal tax lien legislation. *Cf.* Morgan v. Commissioner, 309 U.S. 78, 80, 60 S. Ct. 424, 84 L. Ed. 585 (1940) ("State law creates legal interests and rights. The federal revenue acts designate what interests or rights, so created, shall be taxed.").

In line with this division of competence, we held that a taxpayer's right under state law to withdraw the whole of the proceeds from a joint bank account constitutes "property" or the "right to property" subject to levy for unpaid federal taxes, although state law would not allow ordinary creditors similarly to deplete the account. *National Bank of Commerce*, 472 U.S. at 723–727. And we earlier held that a taxpayer's right under a life insurance policy to compel his insurer to pay him the cash surrender value qualifies as "property" or a "right to property" subject to attachment for unpaid federal taxes, although state law shielded the cash surrender value from creditors' liens. *Bess*, 357 U.S. at 56–57. By contrast, we also concluded, again as a matter of federal law, that no federal tax lien could attach to policy proceeds unavailable to the insured in his lifetime. 357 U.S. at 55–56 ("It would be anomalous to view as 'property' subject to lien proceeds never within the insured's reach to enjoy.").

Just as "exempt status under state law does not bind the federal collector," *Mitchell*, 403 U.S. at 204, so federal tax law "is not struck blind by a disclaimer," United States v. Irvine, 511 U.S. 224, 240, 114 S. Ct. 1473, 128 L. Ed. 2d 168 (1994). Thus, in *Mitchell*, the Court held that, although a wife's renunciation of a marital interest was treated as retroactive under state law, that state-law disclaimer did not determine the wife's liability for federal tax on her share of the community income realized before the renunciation. *See* 403 U.S. at 204 (right to renounce does not indicate that taxpayer never had a right to property).

IV.

The Eighth Circuit, with fidelity to the relevant Code provisions and our case law, determined first what rights state law accorded Drye in his mother's estate. It is beyond debate, the Court of Appeals observed, that under Arkansas law Drye had, at his mother's death, a valuable, transferable, legally protected right to the property at issue. *See* 152 F.3d at 895 (although Code does not define "property" or "rights to property," appellate courts read those terms to encompass "state-law rights or interests that have pecuniary value and are transferable"). The court noted, for example, that a prospective

---

n.4 *See, e.g.*, United States v. National Bank of Commerce, 472 U.S. 713, 722, 105 S. Ct. 2919, 86 L. Ed. 2d 565 (1985) ("The federal statute 'creates no property rights but merely attaches consequences, federally defined, to rights created under state law.' ") (*quoting* United States v. Bess, 357 U.S. 51, 55, 78 S. Ct. 1054, 2 L. Ed. 2d 1135 (1958)).

heir may effectively assign his expectancy in an estate under Arkansas law, and the assignment will be enforced when the expectancy ripens into a present estate. *See* 152 F.3d at 895–896 (citing several Arkansas Supreme Court decisions, including: Clark v. Rutherford, 227 Ark. 270, 270–271, 298 S.W.2d 327, 330 (1957); Bradley Lumber Co. of Ark. v. Burbridge, 213 Ark. 165, 172, 210 S.W.2d 284, 288 (1948); Leggett v. Martin, 203 Ark. 88, 94, 156 S.W.2d 71, 74–75 (1941)).[n.7]

Drye emphasizes his undoubted right under Arkansas law to disclaim the inheritance, *see* Ark. Code Ann. § 28-2-101 (1987), a right that is indeed personal and not marketable. *See* Brief for Petitioners 13 (right to disclaim is not transferable and has no pecuniary value). But Arkansas law primarily gave Drye a right of considerable value — the right either to inherit or to channel the inheritance to a close family member (the next lineal descendant). That right simply cannot be written off as a mere "personal right . . . to accept or reject [a] gift." Brief for Petitioners 13.

In pressing the analogy to a rejected gift, Drye overlooks this crucial distinction. A donee who declines an inter vivos gift generally restores the status quo ante, leaving the donor to do with the gift what she will. The disclaiming heir or devisee, in contrast, does not restore the status quo, for the decedent cannot be revived. Thus the heir inevitably exercises dominion over the property. He determines who will receive the property — himself if he does not disclaim, a known other if he does. *See* Hirsch, "The Problem of the Insolvent Heir," 74 Cornell L. Rev. 587, 607–608 (1989). This power to channel the estate's assets warrants the conclusion that Drye held "property" or a "right to property" subject to the Government's liens.

* * *

In sum, in determining whether a federal taxpayer's state-law rights constitute "property" or "rights to property," "the important consideration is the breadth of the control the [taxpayer] could exercise over the property." *Morgan*, 309 U.S. at 83, 84 L. Ed. 2d 585, 60 S. Ct. 424. Drye had the unqualified right to receive the entire value of his mother's estate (less administrative expenses), *see National Bank of Commerce*, 472 U.S. at 725 (confirming that unqualified "right to receive property is itself a property right" subject to the tax collector's levy), or to channel that value to his daughter. The control rein he held under state law, we hold, rendered the inheritance "property" or "rights to property" belonging to him within the meaning of § 6321, and hence subject to the federal tax liens that sparked this controversy.

For the reasons stated, the judgment of the Court of Appeals for the Eighth Circuit is

Affirmed.

Note that the *Drye* Court did not specifically identify what type of property interest under state law (fee simple, remainder, or leasehold) Drye held in the assets comprising his mother's estate. The closest the Court came to characterizing Drye's state law right to the assets is his "control rein" over them. What does control rein entail?

A few years after the Supreme Court decided *Drye*, the Court had the opportunity to expand upon its analysis in the case of *United States v. Craft*, 535 U.S. 274 (2002), which involved the question of whether the tax lien attached to a delinquent taxpayer's tenancy

---

n.7 In recognizing that state-law rights that have pecuniary value and are transferable fall within § 6321, we do not mean to suggest that transferability is essential to the existence of "property" or "rights to property" under that section. For example, although we do not here decide the matter, we note that an interest in a spendthrift trust has been held to constitute " 'property' for purposes of § 6321" even though the beneficiary may not transfer that interest to third parties. *See Bank One*, 80 F.3d at 176. Nor do we mean to suggest that an expectancy that has pecuniary value and is transferable under state law would fall within § 6321 prior to the time it ripens into a present estate.

by the entireties interest in property. A tenancy by the entireties interest is a type of unitary property interest limited to married individuals that carries with it rights of survivorship (the surviving spouse becomes the fee simple owner of the property) and shared rights of use and possession, much like a joint tenancy interest. In those states that recognize tenancies by the entireties, neither spouse is considered to hold a separate interest in the property; instead, the property is held by the marital unit. In most states that recognize this type of interest — including Michigan, the state in which the property owned by the Crafts was located — liens held by separate creditors do not attach to the entireties property. In others, liens of separate creditors can attach, but they are subject to the rights of the nondebtor spouse.

In *Craft*, the debtor-husband, after the IRS filed a Notice of Federal Tax Lien against the couple's property, transferred his interest in the property to his wife for $1.[6] With the consent of the IRS, the wife sold the property to a third party after having agreed to put half the sales proceeds in an escrow account. As part of a quiet title action filed by the wife contesting the IRS's claim to the funds,[7] the U.S. District Court for the Western District of Michigan held that the tax lien attached to the husband's interest in the property, based on a view that the tenancy ceased under state law when the property was sold to Mrs. Craft, and, at the time of that transfer, each spouse held a separate one-half interest in the property. Craft v. United States, 1994 U.S. Dist. LEXIS 13310 (W.D. Mich. 1994). The Sixth Circuit reversed the District Court, 140 F.3d 638 (6th Cir. 1998) (*Craft I*), finding that there was no property interest to which the lien could attach.[8]

Subsequently, the Supreme Court, in a 6 to 3 decision, reversed the Sixth Circuit. United States v. Craft, 535 U.S. 274 (2002). Writing for the majority, Justice O'Connor stated:

> Whether the interests of [the delinquent taxpayer] husband in the property he held as a tenant by the entirety constitutes "property and rights to property" for the purposes of the federal tax lien statute, 26 U.S.C. § 6321, is ultimately a question of federal law. The answer to this federal question, however, largely depends upon state law. . . . Accordingly, "we look initially to state law to determine what rights the taxpayer has in the property the Government seeks to reach, then to federal law to determine whether the taxpayer's state-delineated rights qualify as 'property' or 'rights to property' within the compass of the federal tax lien legislation." Drye v. United States, 528 U.S. 49, 58, 120 S. Ct. 474, 145 L. Ed. 2d 466 (1999).
>
> A common idiom describes property as a "bundle of sticks" — a collection of individual rights which, in certain combinations, constitute property. *See* B. Cardozo, Paradoxes of Legal Science 129 (1928) (reprint 2000); *see also* Dickman v. Commissioner, 465 U.S. 330, 336, 104 S. Ct. 1086, 79 L. Ed. 2d 343 (1984). State law determines only which sticks are in a person's bundle. Whether those sticks qualify as "property" for purposes of the federal tax lien statute is a question of federal law.

Id. at 278–79.

Justice O'Connor then proceeded to apply the multi-stage analysis established in *Drye*. On the state law question, the majority opinion states:

> In determining whether respondent's husband possessed "property" or "rights to property" within the meaning of 26 U.S.C. § 6321, we look to the

[6] The wife was not jointly liable for the unpaid tax.

[7] Quiet title actions are discussed in Section 14.04, below, in connection with *Robinson v. United States*.

[8] *Craft I* was decided before the Supreme Court released its opinion in *Drye*. In a subsequent decision, 233 F.3d 358 (6th Cir. 2000) (*Craft II*), the Sixth Circuit rejected the IRS's request to reconsider its earlier holding in light of *Drye*.

> individual rights created by these state law rules. According to Michigan law, respondent's husband had, among other rights, the following rights with respect to the entireties property: the right to use the property, the right to exclude third parties from it, the right to a share of income produced from it, the right of survivorship, the right to become a tenant in common with equal shares upon divorce, the right to sell the property with the respondent's consent and to receive half the proceeds from such a sale, the right to place an encumbrance on the property with the respondent's consent, and the right to block respondent from selling or encumbering the property unilaterally.

Id. at 282.

With respect to the second stage of the analysis, that is, whether the rights Michigan law granted to the husband as a tenant by the entireties qualify as "property" or "rights to property" under Code section 6321, the opinion states:

> Michigan law grants a tenant by the entirety some of the most essential property rights: the right to use the property, to receive income produced by it, and to exclude others from it. *See* Dolan v. City of Tigard, 512 U.S. 374, 384, 114 S. Ct. 2309, 129 L. Ed. 2d 304 (1994) ("The right to exclude others" is " 'one of the most essential sticks in the bundle of rights that are commonly characterized as property' ") (*quoting* Kaiser Aetna v. United States, 444 U.S. 164, 176, 100 S. Ct. 383, 62 L. Ed. 2d 332 (1979)); Loretto v. Teleprompter Manhattan CATV Corp., 458 U.S. 419, 435, 102 S. Ct. 3164, 73 L. Ed. 2d 868 (1982) (including "use" as one of the "property rights in a physical thing"). These rights alone may be sufficient to subject the husband's interest in the entireties property to the federal tax lien. They gave him a substantial degree of control over the entireties property, and, as we noted in *Drye*, "in determining whether a federal taxpayer's state-law rights constitute 'property' or 'rights to property,' the important consideration is the breadth of the control the [taxpayer] could exercise over the property." 528 U.S. at 61 (internal quotation marks omitted).

Id. at 283.

In support of its conclusion that Mr. Craft's property interest was subject to the federal tax lien, the majority opinion then comments on his rights to alienate the property interest:

> The husband's rights in the estate, however, went beyond use, exclusion, and income. He also possessed the right to alienate (or otherwise encumber) the property with the consent of respondent, his wife. *Loretto, supra*, at 435 (the right to "dispose" of an item is a property right). It is true, as respondent notes, that he lacked the right to unilaterally alienate the property, a right that is often in the bundle of property rights. . . . There is no reason to believe, however, that this one stick — the right of unilateral alienation — is essential to the category of "property." This Court has already stated that federal tax liens may attach to property that cannot be unilaterally alienated. In *United States v. Rodgers*, 461 U.S. 677, 103 S. Ct. 2132, 76 L. Ed. 2d 236 (1983), we considered the Federal Government's power to foreclose homestead property attached by a federal tax lien. Texas law provided that " 'the owner or claimant of the property claimed as homestead [may not], if married, sell or abandon the homestead without the consent of the other spouse.' " *Id.* at 684–685 (quoting Tex. Const., Art. 16, § 50). We nonetheless stated that "in the homestead context . . . , there is no doubt . . . that not only do both spouses (rather than neither) have an independent interest in the homestead property, but that a federal tax lien can at least attach to each of those interests." 461 U.S. at 703 n. 31; *cf. Drye, supra*, at 60, n.7 (noting that "an interest in a spendthrift trust has been held to constitute 'property for purposes of § 6321' even though the beneficiary may not transfer that interest to third parties").

> Excluding property from a federal tax lien simply because the taxpayer does not have the power to unilaterally alienate it would, moreover, exempt a rather large amount of what is commonly thought of as property. It would exempt not only the type of property discussed in *Rodgers*, but also some community property. Community property states often provide that real community property cannot be alienated without the consent of both spouses. *See, e.g.*, Ariz. Rev. Stat. Ann. § 25-214(C) (2000); Cal. Fam. Code Ann. § 1102 (West 1994); Idaho Code § 32-912 (1996); La. Civ. Code Ann., Art. 2347 (West Supp. 2002); Nev. Rev. Stat. § 123.230(3) (1995); N.M. Stat. Ann. § 40-3-13 (1999); Wash. Rev. Code § 26.16.030(3) (1994). Accordingly, the fact that respondent's husband could not unilaterally alienate the property does not preclude him from possessing "property and rights to property" for the purposes of § 6321.

Id. at 283–85.

The question in *Craft* arose because only one of the joint owners was responsible for the tax liability. Had Mr. and Mrs. Craft been jointly liable, the entire property would have been subject to the federal tax lien. *See* Tony Thornton Auction Service, Inc. v. United States, 791 F.2d 635 (8th Cir. 1986). Notice that the Supreme Court in *Craft* cites several times to *United States v. Rodgers*, 461 U.S. 677 (1983), a case that is excerpted later in the chapter. *Rodgers* confirms that the federal tax lien attaches to property even though a nondelinquent spouse holds a homestead interest in the property. The Court in *Rodgers*, however, deals primarily with a different issue: What action the IRS can take against the property interest subject to the federal tax lien to enforce collection of the unpaid liability. That question is taken up later in the chapter.

Because of the importance of state law principles to the application of Code section 6321, drawing broad conclusions as to which property interests are subject to attachment can be difficult. In virtually all cases, however, the delinquent taxpayer's separate interest in property held as tenants in common is subject to the federal tax lien, *see, e.g.*, United States v. Kocher, 468 F.2d 503 (2d Cir. 1972), *cert. denied*, 411 U.S. 931 (1973), as are partial interests in property such as life estates, *see, e.g.*, United States v. United Banks of Denver, 542 F.2d 819 (10th Cir. 1976), and future interests such as contingent remainders, *see, e.g.*, Dominion Trust v. United States, 7 F.3d 233 (6th Cir. 1993). While it also clear that the federal tax lien attaches to the delinquent taxpayer's interest in property held with a non-delinquent co-owner as joint tenants with rights of survivorship, *see, e.g.*, Shaw v. United States, 331 F.2d 493 (9th Cir. 1964), whether the tax lien survives the delinquent taxpayer's death depends upon state law. *Compare* Fecarotta v. United States, 154 F. Supp. 592 (D. Ariz. 1956) (applying Arizona law, death of delinquent taxpayer terminates delinquent taxpayer's interest in joint tenancy, thus lien expires), *with* United States v. Librizzi, 108 F.3d 136 (7th Cir. 1997) (applying Wisconsin law, surviving joint tenant takes property subject to lien arising from liability of deceased joint tenant). For the lien attachment rules relating to community property interests, see David A. Schmudde, *Federal Tax Liens* (4th ed. 2001).

As further illustration of the breadth of the federal tax lien, the lien may attach to property interests that are conditioned upon future action of the taxpayer, *see* United States v. Kogan, 257 B.R. 1 (C.D. Cal. 2000) (under California law, attorney's work in progress, even with respect to cases covered by contingent fee arrangements, constitutes property to which federal tax lien can attach); In re Jeffrey, 261 B.R. 396 (W.D. Pa. 2001) (under Pennsylvania law, taxpayer/debtor's medical malpractice cause of action against third party is property in which taxpayer/debtor has an interest; as a result, tax lien attaches to cause of action and will attach to damage award should taxpayer prevail on the malpractice claim), as well as those conditioned upon the future action of a third party, *see* United States v. Murray, 217 F.3d 59 (1st Cir. 2000) (federal tax lien attaches to taxpayer's interest in a trust holding marital home in which taxpayer had a one-half interest even though trustees could divest taxpayer's interest under a separation agreement). State-created exemptions generally do not affect a federal tax lien that has attached to the subject property. For example, the tax lien can attach to a delinquent taxpayer's property interest despite another party's homestead interest in the same property, *see* United States v. Rodgers, 461 U.S. 677 (1983), as well as to assets held in a "spendthrift" trust that are otherwise protected against the claims of most creditors, *see* C.C.A. 200614006.

[2] Lien Priorities in the Internal Revenue Code

Reading Assignment: I.R.C. § 6323(a)–(c); Treas. Reg. §§ 301.6323(b)-1, 301.6323(h)-1.

Once a federal tax lien attaches, no additional action on the part of the IRS or a court is required to establish the government's interest in the taxpayer's property. For this reason, the federal tax lien is often referred to as a "secret lien." Although the existence of the tax lien may be known only to the taxpayer and the IRS, the government may still have priority against third-party creditors asserting an interest in the taxpayer's property.

Priority conflicts between a federal tax lien and the interests of competing creditors are common. Under prior law, in order for a competing creditor to retain priority over a federal tax lien, the creditor's lien must have arisen prior to assessment of the underlying tax liability, and must have been "choate" prior to the time the tax was assessed. *See, e.g.*, United States v. City of New Britain, 347 U.S. 81 (1954). In order to satisfy this choateness standard, the competing creditor had to establish the specific identity of the lienor, the amount of the lien, and the identity of the property to which the lien attached. *Id.* Although the choateness standard still exists, lien priorities are now determined primarily under section 6323.[9] Section 6323 sets forth a series of rules that provide protection for classes of creditors who might otherwise acquire property subject to the federal tax lien without knowledge of the lien's existence. Congress amended section 6323 in 1966 to further clarify its application and to better conform the treatment of priority rights relating to federal tax liens to those that exist under the Uniform Commercial Code. *See* S. Rep. No. 89-1708, at 2 (1966).

Section 6323(a) provides that the federal tax lien is not valid (perfected) against certain classes of creditors until the Secretary files (records) a Notice of Federal Tax Lien, Form 668, in accordance with the Code. The formalities the IRS must follow when filing a Notice of Federal Tax Lien are contained in section 6323(f), which generally refers to state law procedures.[10] Section 6320 requires the IRS to notify the delinquent taxpayer, in writing, of the existence of the lien within five days after it files the notice. I.R.C. § 6320(a). The taxpayer is then afforded an opportunity to request a hearing with an IRS Appeals Officer (the "Collection Due Process" or "CDP" hearing) within a 30-day period beginning on the date after the five-day period expires. I.R.C. § 6320(b). The CDP hearing and the issues that may be discussed at the hearing are explored in Chapter 16.

Once the Secretary properly records the notice, the lien normally takes priority over *subsequent* purchasers, security interest holders, mechanic's lienors, and judgment

---

[9] In addition to these procedures relating to release and discharge, Code section 6323(j) and regulation section 301.6323(j)-1(b) set forth circumstances in which the IRS may be willing to withdraw a Notice of Federal Tax Lien, including where: (1) the filing of the notice was premature or otherwise not in accordance with administrative procedures; (2) the taxpayer has entered into an installment agreement to satisfy the liability for which the lien was imposed; (3) the withdrawal notice will facilitate collection of the tax liability; or (4) the withdrawal notice would be in the best interests of both the taxpayer and the government.

[10] For example, in Kansas, the Notice of Federal Tax Lien is required to be filed with the Secretary of State's office in the case of most personal property and, in the case of real property, in the register of deeds office in the county in which the real property is located. *See* Kan. Stat. Ann. § 79-2614 (1997).

creditors.[11] Section 6323(a) is intended, therefore, to provide protection for certain interests transferred or created between the time the federal tax lien arose and the time the IRS files notice of the lien.

> *Example:* On May 1, Year 3, the IRS assessed against Sally a $1,000 deficiency arising from her failure to pay income taxes for Year 1. At the time of assessment, Sally owned $10,000 worth of stock in X Corporation. On May 20, Year 3, Sally obtained a loan from her bank for $5,000, transferring the X Corporation stock to the bank as collateral. On June 30, Year 3, the IRS properly files a Notice of Federal Tax Lien with respect to Sally's delinquent tax liability. Because Sally's bank acquired and perfected a security interest in the stock before the IRS recorded the tax lien, the tax lien does not have priority as against the bank's security interest. Had the bank loaned funds to Sally and acquired its security interest in the X Corporation stock after June 30, Year 3, the security interest held by the bank would not be entitled to priority over the government's tax lien.

The Code and regulations detail the types of creditors who may fall within the protection of the four categories listed in section 6323(a). In each of the four cases, the Code and regulations not only define the nature of the creditor interest, but also attach prerequisites that must be satisfied before the creditor is protected. As a general rule, the creditor must "perfect" its interest under state law before the IRS files a Notice of Federal Tax Lien in order to obtain priority over the tax lien. Read section 6323(h)(1), which defines a security interest in much the same manner as the Uniform Commercial Code. A security interest is considered to exist for purposes of section 6323 only if (1) the property subject to the security interest is in existence and the security interest has become protected under local law against a subsequent judgment lien arising out of an unsecured obligation (another way of saying that the security interest must be perfected under local law) and (2) the security holder parts with money or money's worth. *See* Treas. Reg. § 301.6323(h)-1(a)(2). Only if the security holder satisfies these requirements before the IRS files its Notice of Federal Tax Lien does the security holder's interest become protected against a subsequently filed lien.[12] Similarly, a judgment lien does not arise for purposes of section 6323(a) until the judgment lien creditor perfects the lien on the property that it affects. If, under local law, the judgment lien is not perfected until the judgment creditor dockets the judgment in the county where the debtor is located, the creditor must do so in order to retain priority. Treas. Reg. § 301.6323(h)-1(g); *see also* Richards v. Richards, 368 F. Supp. 2d 817 (W.D. Mich. 2005) (holding that federal tax lien trumps judicial lien on sales proceeds awarded to taxpayer as part of a divorce proceeding, even though judicial lien arose first in time, because judicial lien was not properly perfected under state law).

Even timely filing a Notice of Federal Tax Lien does not assure the IRS's priority in all cases. Section 6323(b) describes classes of purchasers and lien holders who are afforded a "superpriority," protecting the party's interest despite the fact that the IRS may have previously filed a Notice of Federal Tax Lien. As a general matter, section 6323(b) establishes priority for these third parties in cases in which it may be unreasonable to assume that the third-party purchaser would check for federal tax liens and in situations where a third-party lender or service provider increases the value of the taxpayer's property and thereby increases the likelihood that the IRS will collect

---

[11] Actual knowledge of the tax lien does not displace the creditor's priority with respect to the IRS if the IRS has not filed a Notice of Federal Tax Lien. Revenue Ruling 2003-108, 2003-44 I.R.B. 963. Thus, "a purchaser, holder of a security interest, mechanic's lienor, or judgment lien creditor is protected against a statutory tax lien for which a notice of federal tax lien has not been filed notwithstanding actual knowledge of the statutory tax lien." *Id.*

[12] Because of these prerequisites, a security interest for section 6323 purposes is more limited in scope than a security interest under the Uniform Commercial Code.

against the property by levy. This preferred status is granted with respect to ten separate interests, including (1) securities purchased without actual notice or knowledge of the tax lien; (2) motor vehicles purchased without prior knowledge of the federal tax lien; (3) tangible personal property purchased at retail in the ordinary course of the seller's business; and (4) personal property, such as household furnishings and personal effects, purchased in a casual sale. Liens covering real property taxes, payments for repairs and improvements of the taxpayer's personal residence, and attorneys' fees are also accorded priority status if the specific requirements of the statute are met. *See* Treas. Reg. § 301.6323(b)-1.

> *Example:* Marshall, a delinquent taxpayer against whom a Notice of Federal Tax Lien has been filed, sells his automobile to Fred, an automobile dealer. Subsequent to his purchase, Fred learns of the existence of the tax lien. Even though the Notice of Federal Tax Lien was filed prior to Fred's purchase, the lien is not valid against Fred because he did not know of the existence of the lien before the purchase and before actually taking possession of the car.

See Treas. Reg. § 301.6323(b)-1(b)(2) Ex. (2). To facilitate the use of common financing techniques, section 6323(c) also confers priority status on certain security interests resulting from commercial transaction financing agreements. *See* I.R.C. § 6323(c)(2); Treas. Reg. § 301.6323(c)-1.

Although the Code and regulations provide detailed descriptions and examples of how section 6323 is intended to operate, it leaves some priority questions unanswered. Recall that a federal tax lien also attaches to *after-acquired* property of the taxpayer. The issue presented in the *McDermott* case, reproduced below, is how priority should be determined when a judgment creditor first dockets a judgment, the government subsequently files its Notice of Federal Tax Lien, and later still, the debtor/taxpayer acquires the property in question. Notice the Court's reliance on the choateness principles mentioned above.

UNITED STATES v. McDERMOTT

United States Supreme Court
507 U.S. 447 (1993)

Justice Scalia delivered the opinion of the Court.

We granted certiorari to resolve the competing priorities of a federal tax lien and a private creditor's judgment lien as to a delinquent taxpayer's after-acquired real property.

I.

On December 9, 1986, the United States assessed Mr. and Mrs. McDermott for unpaid federal taxes due for the tax years 1977 through 1981. Upon that assessment, the law created a lien in favor of the United States on all real and personal property belonging to the McDermotts, 26 U.S.C. §§ 6321 and 6322, including after-acquired property, Glass City Bank v. United States, 326 U.S. 265, 66 S. Ct. 108, 90 L. Ed. 56 (1945). Pursuant to 26 U.S.C. § 6323(a), however, that lien could "not be valid as against any purchaser, holder of a security interest, mechanic's lienor, or *judgment lien creditor* until notice thereof . . . has been filed." (Emphasis added.) The United States did not file this lien in the Salt Lake County Recorder's Office until September 9, 1987. Before that occurred, however — specifically, on July 6, 1987 — Zions First National Bank, N. A. (Bank), docketed with the Salt Lake County Clerk a state-court judgment it had won against the McDermotts. Under Utah law, that created a judgment lien on all of the McDermotts' real property in Salt Lake County, "owned . . . at the time or . . . thereafter acquired during the existence of said lien." Utah Code Ann. § 78-22-1 (1953).

On September 23, 1987, the McDermotts acquired title to certain real property in

Salt Lake County. To facilitate later sale of that property, the parties entered into an escrow agreement whereby the United States and the Bank released their claims to the real property itself but reserved their rights to the cash proceeds of the sale, based on their priorities in the property as of September 23, 1987. Pursuant to the escrow agreement, the McDermotts brought this interpleader action in state court to establish which lien was entitled to priority; the United States removed to the United States District Court for the District of Utah.

On cross-motions for partial summary judgment, the District Court awarded priority to the Bank's judgment lien. The United States Court of Appeals for the Tenth Circuit affirmed. McDermott v. Zions First Nat. Bank, N. A., 945 F.2d 1475 (1991). We granted certiorari. 504 U.S. 939 (1992).

II.

Federal tax liens do not automatically have priority over all other liens. Absent provision to the contrary, priority for purposes of federal law is governed by the common-law principle that " 'the first in time is the first in right.' " United States v. New Britain, 347 U.S. 81, 85, 74 S. Ct. 367, 98 L. Ed. 520 (1954); *cf.* Rankin v. Scott, 25 U.S. 177, 6 L. Ed. 592, 12 Wheat. 177, 179 (1827) (Marshall, C. J.). For purposes of applying that doctrine in the present case — in which the competing state lien (that of a judgment creditor) benefits from the provision of § 6323(a) that the federal lien shall "not be valid . . . until notice thereof . . . has been filed" — we must deem the United States' lien to have commenced no sooner than the filing of notice. As for the Bank's lien: Our cases deem a competing state lien to be in existence for "first in time" purposes only when it has been "perfected" in the sense that "the identity of the lienor, *the property subject to the lien*, and the amount of the lien are established." *United States v. New Britain*, 347 U.S. at 84 (emphasis added); *see also id.*, at 86; United States v. Pioneer American Ins. Co., 374 U.S. 84, 83 S. Ct. 1651, 10 L. Ed. 2d 770 (1963).

The first question we must answer, then, is whether the Bank's judgment lien was perfected in this sense before the United States filed its tax lien on September 9, 1987. If so, that is the end of the matter; the Bank's lien prevails. The Court of Appeals was of the view that this question was answered (or rendered irrelevant) by our decision in *United States v. Vermont*, 377 U.S. 351, 84 S. Ct. 1267, 12 L. Ed. 2d 370 (1964), which it took to "stand for the proposition that a noncontingent . . . lien on all of a person's real property, perfected prior to the federal tax lien, will take priority over the federal lien, regardless of whether after-acquired property is involved."[n.1] 945 F.2d at 1480. That is too expansive a reading. Our opinion in *Vermont* gives no indication that the property at issue had become subject to the state lien only by application of an after-acquired-property clause to property that the debtor acquired after the federal lien arose. To the contrary, the opinion says that the state lien met (presumably at the critical time when the federal lien arose) "the test laid down in *New Britain* that . . . 'the property subject to the lien . . . [be] established.' " 377 U.S. at 358 (citation omitted). The argument of the United States that we rejected in *Vermont* was the contention that a state lien is not perfected within the meaning of *New Britain* if it "attach[es] to *all* of the taxpayer's property," rather than "to specifically identified portions of that property." 377 U.S. at 355 (emphasis added). We did not consider, and the facts as recited did not implicate, the quite different argument made by the United States in the present case: that a lien in after-acquired property is not "perfected" as to property yet to be acquired.

[n.1] As our later discussion will show, we think it contradictory to say that the state lien was "perfected" before the federal lien was filed, insofar as it applies to after-acquired property not acquired by the debtor until after the federal lien was filed. The Court of Appeals was evidently using the term "perfected" (as the Bank would) in a sense not requiring attachment of the lien to the property in question; our discussion of the Court of Appeals' opinion assumes that usage.

The Bank argues that, as of July 6, 1987, the date it docketed its judgment lien, the lien was "perfected as to all real property then and thereafter owned by" the McDermotts, since "nothing further was required of [the Bank] to attach the noncontingent lien on after-acquired property." Brief for Respondent 21. That reflects an unusual notion of what it takes to "perfect" a lien.[n.4] Under the Uniform Commercial Code, for example, a security interest in after-acquired property is generally not considered perfected when the financing statement is filed, but only when the security interest has attached to particular property upon the debtor's acquisition of that property. §§ 9-203(1) and (2), 3 U.L.A. 363 (1992); § 9-303(1), 3A U.L.A. 117 (1992). And attachment to particular property was also an element of what we meant by "perfection" in *New Britain. See* 347 U.S. at 84 ("when . . . the property subject to the lien . . . [is] established"); *id.,* at 86 ("The priority of each statutory lien contested here must depend on the time it attached to the property in question and became [no longer inchoate]").[n.5] The Bank concedes that its lien did not actually attach to the property at issue here until the McDermotts acquired rights in that property. Brief for Respondent 16, 21. Since that occurred *after* filing of the federal tax lien, the state lien was not first in time.

But that does not complete our inquiry: Though the state lien was not first in time, the federal tax lien was not necessarily first in time either. Like the state lien, it applied to the property at issue here by virtue of a (judicially inferred) after-acquired-property provision, which means that it did not attach until the same instant the state lien attached, viz., when the McDermotts acquired the property; and, like the state lien, it did not become "perfected" until that time. We think, however, that under the language of § 6323(a) ("shall not be valid as against any . . . judgment lien creditor until notice . . . has been filed"), the filing of notice renders the federal tax lien extant for "first in time" priority purposes regardless of whether it has yet attached to identifiable property. That result is also indicated by the provision, two subsections later, which accords priority, even against *filed* federal tax liens, to security interests arising out of certain agreements, including "commercial transactions financing agreement[s]," entered into before filing of the tax lien. 26 U.S.C. § 6323(c)(1). That provision protects certain security interests that, like the after-acquired-property judgment lien here, will have been recorded before the filing of the tax lien, and will attach to the encumbered property after the filing of the tax lien, and simultaneously with the attachment of the tax lien (*i.e.,* upon the debtor's acquisition of the subject property). According *special*

[n.4] The dissent accepts the Bank's central argument that perfection occurred when "there was 'nothing more to be done' by the Bank 'to have a choate lien' on any real property the McDermotts might acquire." (*quoting United States v. New Britain, supra*). This unusual definition of perfection has been achieved by making a small but substantively important addition to the language of *New Britain.* " 'Nothing more to be done . . . to have a choate lien' " (the language of *New Britain*) becomes "nothing more to be done *by the Bank* to have a choate lien." Once one recognizes that the dissent's concept of a lien's "becoming certain as to the property subject thereto," is meaningless, it becomes apparent that the dissent, like the Bank, would simply have us substitute the concept of "best efforts" for the concept of perfection.

[n.5] The dissent refuses to acknowledge the unavoidable realities that the property subject to a lien is not "established" until one knows what specific property that is, and that a lien cannot be anything other than "inchoate" with respect to property that is not yet subject to the lien. Hence the dissent says that, upon its filing, the lien at issue here "was perfected, even as to the real property later acquired by the McDermotts, in the sense that it was definite as to the property in question, noncontingent, and summarily enforceable." * * * But how could it have been, at that time, "definite" as to this property, when the identity of this property (established by the McDermotts' later acquisition) was yet unknown? Or "noncontingent" as to this property, when the property would have remained entirely free of the judgment lien had the McDermotts not later decided to buy it? Or "summarily enforceable" against this property when the McDermotts did not own, and had never owned, it? The dissent also says that "the lien was *immediately enforceable* through levy and execution against all the debtors' property, *whenever acquired.*" *Ibid.* (emphasis added.) But of course it was *not* "immediately enforceable" (as of its filing date, which is the relevant time) against property that the McDermotts had not yet acquired.

priority to certain state security interests in these circumstances obviously presumes that otherwise the federal tax lien would prevail — *i.e.*, that the federal tax lien is ordinarily dated, for purposes of "first in time" priority against § 6323(a) competing interests, from the time of its filing, regardless of when it attaches to the subject property.[n.7]

The Bank argues that "by common law, the first lien of record against a debtor's property has priority over those subsequently filed unless a lien-creating statute clearly shows or declares an intention to cause the statutory lien to override." Brief for Respondent Zions First National Bank, N. A., 11. Such a strong "first-to-record" presumption may be appropriate for simultaneously perfected liens under ordinary statutes creating private liens, which ordinarily arise out of voluntary transactions. When two private lenders both exact from the same debtor security agreements with after-acquired-property clauses, the second lender knows, by reason of the earlier recording, that that category of property will be subject to another claim, and if the remaining security is inadequate he may avoid the difficulty by declining to extend credit. The Government, by contrast, cannot indulge the luxury of declining to hold the taxpayer liable for his taxes; notice of a previously filed security agreement covering after-acquired property does *not* enable the Government to protect itself. A strong "first-to-record" presumption is particularly out of place under the present tax-lien statute, whose *general rule* is that the tax collector prevails even if he has not recorded *at all.* 26 U.S.C. §§ 6321 and 6322; United States v. Snyder, 149 U.S. 210, 13 S. Ct. 846, 37 L. Ed. 705 (1893). Thus, while we would hardly proclaim the statutory meaning we have discerned in this opinion to be "clear," it is evident enough for the purpose at hand. The federal tax lien must be given priority.

The judgment of the Court of Appeals is reversed, and the case is remanded for further proceedings consistent with this opinion.

So ordered.

JUSTICE THOMAS, with whom JUSTICE STEVENS and JUSTICE O'CONNOR join, dissenting.

I agree with the Court that under 26 U.S.C. § 6323(a) we generally look to the filing of notice of the federal tax lien to determine the federal lien's priority as against a competing state-law judgment lien. I cannot agree, however, that a federal tax lien trumps a judgment creditor's claim to after-acquired property whenever notice of the federal lien is filed before the judgment lien has "attached" to the property. In my view, the Bank's antecedent judgment lien "had [already] acquired sufficient substance and had become so perfected," with respect to the McDermotts' after-acquired real property, "as to defeat [the] later-filed federal tax lien." United States v. Pioneer American Ins. Co., 374 U.S. 84, 88, 83 S. Ct. 1651, 10 L. Ed. 2d 770 (1963).

Applying the governing "first in time" rule, the Court recognizes — as it must — that if the Bank's interest in the property was "perfected in the sense that there [was] nothing more to be done to have a choate lien" before September 9, 1987 (the date the federal notice was filed), United States v. New Britain, 347 U.S. 81, 84, 74 S. Ct. 367, 98 L. Ed. 520 (1954), "that is the end of the matter; the Bank's lien

---

[n.7] The dissent contends that "there is no persuasive reason for not adopting as a matter of federal law the well-recognized common-law rule of parity and giving the Bank an equal interest in the property." As we have explained, the persuasive reason is the existence of § 6323(c), which displays the assumption that all perfected security interests are defeated by the federal tax lien. There is no reason why this assumption should not extend to judgment liens as well. A "security interest," as defined in § 6323, is not an insignificant creditor's preference. The term includes only interests protected against subsequent judgment liens. *See* 26 U.S.C. §§ 6323(h)(1) and 6323(c)(1)(B). Moreover, the text of § 6323(a) ("The lien . . . shall not be valid as against any purchaser, holder of a security interest, mechanic's lienor, or judgment lien creditor") treats security interests and judgment liens alike. Parity may be, as the dissent says, a "well-recognized common-law rule," * * * but we have not hitherto adopted it as the federal law of tax liens in 127 years of tax lien enforcement.

prevails." * * * Because the Bank's identity as lienor and the amount of its judgment lien are undisputed, the choateness question here reduces to whether "the property subject to the lien" was sufficiently "established" as of that date. *New Britain, supra,* at 84. *Accord, Pioneer American, supra,* at 89. *See* 26 CFR § 301.6323(h)-1(g) (1992). The majority is quick to conclude that "establish[ment]" cannot precede attachment, and that a lien in after-acquired property therefore cannot be sufficiently perfected until the debtor has acquired rights in the property. * * * That holding does not follow from, and I believe it is inconsistent with, our precedents.

We have not (before today) prescribed any rigid criteria for "establishing" the property subject to a competing lien; we have required only that the lien "become certain as to . . . the property subject thereto." *New Britain, supra,* at 86 (emphasis added). Our cases indicate that "certain" means nothing more than "determined and definite," *Pioneer American, supra,* at 90, and that the proper focus is on whether the lien is free from "contingencies" that stand in the way of its execution, United States v. Security Trust & Savings Bank, 340 U.S. 47, 50, 71 S. Ct. 111, 95 L. Ed. 53 (1950). In *Security Trust,* for example, we refused to accord priority to a mere attachment lien that "had not ripened into a judgment," *New Britain, supra,* at 86, and was therefore "contingent upon taking subsequent steps for enforcing it," 340 U.S. at 51. And in *United States v. Vermont,* 377 U.S. 351, 84 S. Ct. 1267, 12 L. Ed. 2d 370 (1964), we recognized the complete superiority of a general tax lien held by the State of Vermont upon all property rights belonging to the debtor, even though the lien had not "attached to [the] specifically identified portions of that property" in which the Federal Government claimed a competing tax lien. *Id.,* at 355. With or without specific attachment, Vermont's general lien was "sufficiently choate to obtain priority over the later federal lien," because it was "summarily enforceable" upon assessment and demand. *Id.,* at 359, and n.12.

Although the choateness of a state-law lien under § 6323(a) is a federal question, that question is answered in part by reference to state law, and we therefore give due weight to the State's "'classification of [its] lien as specific and perfected.'" *Pioneer American, supra,* at 88, n.7 (quoting *Security Trust, supra,* at 49). Here, state law establishes that upon filing, the Bank's judgment lien was perfected, even as to the real property later acquired by the McDermotts, in the sense that it was definite as to the property in question, noncontingent, and summarily enforceable. Pursuant to Utah statute, from the moment the Bank had docketed and filed its judgment with the Clerk of the state court on July 6, 1987, it held an enforceable lien upon all nonexempt real property owned by the McDermotts or thereafter acquired by them during the existence of the lien. *See* Utah Code Ann. § 78-22-1 (1953). The lien was immediately enforceable through levy and execution against all the debtors' property, whenever acquired. *See* Belnap v. Blain, 575 P.2d 696, 700 (Utah 1978). *See also* Utah Rule Civ. Proc. 69. And it was "unconditional and not subject to alteration by a court on equitable grounds." Taylor National, Inc. v. Jensen Brothers Constr. Co., 641 P.2d 150, 155 (Utah 1982). Thus, the Bank's lien had become certain as to the property subject thereto, whether then existing or thereafter acquired, and all competing creditors were on notice that there was "nothing more to be done" by the Bank "to have a choate lien" on any real property the McDermotts might acquire. *New Britain, supra,* at 84. *See Vermont, supra,* at 355.

The Court brushes aside the relevance of our *Vermont* opinion with the simple observation that that case did not involve a lien in after-acquired property. * * * This is a wooden distinction. In truth, the Government's "specificity" claim rejected in *Vermont* is analytically indistinguishable from the "attachment" argument the Court accepts today. Vermont's general lien applied to all of the debtor's rights in property, with no limitation on when those rights were acquired, and remained valid until the debt was satisfied or became unenforceable. *See* 377 U.S. at 352. The United States claimed that its later-filed tax lien took priority over Vermont's as to the debtor's interest in a particular bank account, because the State had not taken "steps to perfect its lien by attaching the bank account in question" until after the federal lien had been recorded. Brief for United States in United States v. Vermont, O. T. 1963, No. 509, p. 12. "Thus," the Government asserted, "when the federal lien arose, the State lien did not meet one of the three essential elements of a choate lien: that it attach to specific property." *Ibid.* In rejecting the federal claim of priority, we found no need even to mention whether the debtor had acquired its property interest in the deposited funds before or after notice of the federal lien. If specific attachment is not required for the state lien to be "sufficiently choate," 377 U.S. at 359, then neither is specific acquisition.

* * *

I acknowledge that our precedents do not provide the clearest answer to the question of after-acquired property. * * * But the Court's parsimonious reading of *Vermont* undercuts the congressional purpose — expressed through repeated amendments to the tax lien provisions in the century since *United States v. Snyder*, 149 U.S. 210, 37 L. Ed. 705, 13 S. Ct. 846 (1893) — of "protecting third persons against harsh application of the federal tax lien," Kennedy, *The Relative Priority of the Federal Government: The Pernicious Career of the Inchoate and General Lien*, 63 Yale L. J. 905, 922 (1954). The attachment requirement erodes the "preferred status" granted to judgment creditors by § 6323(a), and renders a choate judgment lien in after-acquired property subordinate to a "secret lien for assessed taxes." *Pioneer American*, 374 U.S. at 89. I would adhere to a more flexible choateness principle, which would protect the priority of validly docketed judgment liens.

Accordingly, I respectfully dissent.

Is the majority's holding that priority questions should be determined with reference to the date the federal tax lien was filed by the IRS consistent with its holding that the federal tax lien was not perfected until the taxpayer obtained an interest in the after-acquired property? Is the holding consistent with the purpose of section 6323(a) to provide protection to preexisting creditors against a nonfiled (secret) federal tax lien? *See generally* William H. Baker, *The* McDermott *Tax Lien Case: And the First Shall Be Last*, 55 La. L. Rev. 879 (1995).

[3] Lien Priorities in Bankruptcy

The taxpayer's filing of a bankruptcy petition automatically stays most collection proceedings, including attempts by the IRS to levy against the debtor/taxpayer's assets. 11 U.S.C. § 362. The petition in bankruptcy also creates a bankruptcy estate, into which flows all assets (if not otherwise exempt) in which the debtor has a legal or equitable interest. If the IRS has already seized the debtor's assets in order to satisfy a tax liability but has not yet sold the assets, the IRS may be required to turn the seized assets back over to the bankruptcy estate. *See* United States v. Whiting Pools, Inc., 462 U.S. 198 (1983). Like most other creditors, the IRS generally must file a claim with the bankruptcy court in order to collect any unpaid liability. That is true even if either (1) the IRS already assessed the liability or (2) the liability is the subject of an ongoing Tax Court proceeding.

Once the bankruptcy estate is created and the debtor's assets are retrieved, the bankruptcy court determines which of the IRS's tax claims are allowed, as well as the order and amount of payment. Tax claims arising out of a taxable year ending before the taxpayer/debtor files a bankruptcy petition (a pre-petition claim) are initially divided into secured and unsecured claims. As a general rule, the IRS has a secured claim if it filed a Notice of Federal Tax Lien prior to the commencement of the bankruptcy proceeding. 11 U.S.C. § 506. Tax claims not supported by a timely filed notice are considered unsecured claims, which are further categorized into general and priority claims. Priority unsecured tax claims include those relating to income taxes for which a return was due within three years before the bankruptcy petition was filed, income taxes assessed not more than 240 days before the petition was filed (even if the due date for the underlying return was beyond the three year period), and withholding and other employment taxes paid by an employer on behalf of an employee (commonly called "trust fund" taxes). 11 U.S.C. § 507. Post-petition tax claims relating to the operation of the debtor/taxpayer's business during the bankruptcy proceeding are treated as administrative expenses and also afforded priority. *Id.* § 507(a)(1).

Tax claims not qualifying for priority are treated as general unsecured claims. Both the order in which creditors' claims are satisfied out of the bankruptcy estate and the manner in which they may be paid (lump sum versus deferred payment) differ based on the type of proceeding involved — Chapter 7, Chapter 11, or Chapter 13. In a Chapter 7 liquidation proceeding, for example, the IRS's secured tax claims are subordinated to non-tax claims that were filed prior to the Notice of Federal Tax Lien, as well as to certain other unsecured non-tax priority claims (up to the value of the IRS's secured tax claims). After paying off other general secured claims, unsecured priority claims, including the IRS's, are satisfied, with the remainder of the bankruptcy estate distributed to satisfy general unsecured claims. *See* 11 U.S.C. § 724. In both Chapter 11 and Chapter 13 bankruptcies, the amount recoverable by the IRS for its tax claims depends upon whether the claims are secured or unsecured, and the priority of the unsecured claims.[13]

[B] Effect of the Federal Tax Lien

Reading Assignment: I.R.C. §§ 6320(a), (b), 6323, 6325, 6326.

As noted above, the IRS typically files the Notice of Federal Tax Lien to preserve its priority as against certain classes of creditors. Because a Notice of Federal Tax Lien filed against a taxpayer's property may result in a significant hardship for the taxpayer and may prevent the taxpayer from borrowing funds to pay the assessed liability, revenue officers do not automatically file the notice immediately upon the taxpayer's failure to pay in response to the notice and demand. The Internal Revenue Manual instructs revenue officers, before filing a Notice of Federal Tax Lien, to provide the taxpayer with an opportunity to pay the assessment or to work out a security or deferred payment arrangement. Officers must also explain to the taxpayer the negative effects a Notice of Federal Tax Lien may have on the taxpayer's normal business operations and credit rating. I.R.M. 5.12.2.3. In cases in which the outstanding unpaid balance is $5,000 or more, or the taxpayer indicates that he or she is intending to file a bankruptcy proceeding, the Internal Revenue Manual instructs the revenue officer to file notice of the lien. *Id.* 5.12.2.4.1. The IRS will typically not file a Notice of Federal Tax Lien in cases in which the unpaid balance is less than $5,000, the taxpayer is deceased and no estate assets exist, or when there are indications that the taxpayer's liability has already been paid, is incorrect, or will be offset with existing tax credits. *See id.*

[1] Release and Discharge

Section 6325 specifies the circumstances under which the IRS will release a federal tax lien or discharge property from the lien. A lien must be released no later than 30 days after the day on which the lien has been satisfied in full or becomes legally unenforceable. The lien must also be released if the taxpayer posts an acceptable bond that is conditioned upon payment of the assessed amount plus interest. I.R.C. § 6325(a). In addition, the IRS has expressed its willingness to release a lien once an offer in compromise, discussed in Chapter 15, is accepted, provided the taxpayer pays the

[13] Section 15.05 discusses in more detail those tax liabilities that may be discharged as part of a bankruptcy proceeding.

offered amount and otherwise complies with the offer agreement. I.R.M. 5.12.2.4.2. A release occurs when the IRS files a Certificate of Release of Federal Tax Lien. Although the statute specifies the time period in which the release must take place, as a practical matter taxpayers usually must request a release from the IRS to ensure prompt action. *See* Treas. Reg. § 301.6325-1(f) (procedures for requesting release).

Unlike a release, which frees up all the taxpayer's property from the tax lien, a discharge applies only to a specific item of property. The IRS has discretionary authority to discharge property from a tax lien, without the necessity of payment or bond, if the remaining property covered by the tax lien has a fair market value at least twice the amount of the sum of the tax lien and any other liens that have priority over the tax lien. *See* I.R.C. § 6325(b)(1). For example, if the taxpayer owes $2,000 in unpaid taxes and also owns a parcel of real property with a fair market value of $20,000, the IRS may discharge the taxpayer's other property from the lien as long as any other prior liens on the real property do not exceed $8,000. *See* Treas. Reg. § 301.6325-1(b)(1)(ii) Ex. Form 669A, *Certificate of Discharge of Property from Federal Tax Lien*, is used for this purpose. The IRS may also issue a certificate of discharge with respect to a specific item of property if the taxpayer pays the government an amount equal to its equity interest in that property. Form 669B is used for these purposes.[14]

Finally, the tax lien encumbering property may be discharged in order to permit the delinquent taxpayer to sell the subject property. In that case, the IRS substitutes its lien on the property for one on the proceeds derived from the sale. I.R.C. § 6325(b)(3); Treas. Reg. § 301.6325-1(b)(3). Such a procedure is common when a dispute arises among competing claimants and the property is sold to facilitate a resolution. Instructions relating to an application for a lien discharge, including a list of all supporting documents required, are contained in Publication 783, *How to Apply for Certificate of Discharge of Property from Federal Tax Lien*.[15]

[2] Erroneously Filed Liens

A taxpayer who believes that the IRS has erroneously filed a Notice of Federal Tax Lien against the taxpayer's property may file an administrative appeal with the IRS under section 6326 to release the lien. A lien notice is considered to have been erroneously filed where the liability was already satisfied at the time of filing; the liability was assessed in violation of the section 6213 deficiency procedures; or the statute of limitations on collection had expired prior to filing the notice of lien. Treas. Reg. § 301.6326-1(b). This appeal procedure does not permit the taxpayer to contest the merits of the underlying assessment. *Id.* The regulations accompanying section 6326 specify the applicable procedures and methods of proof required to establish that the lien was erroneously filed. If the taxpayer prevails, the IRS will provide a copy of the release and a letter of apology to the taxpayer's creditors. I.R.M. 5.12.3.5.

In the situation in which the IRS mistakenly files a Notice of Federal Tax Lien with respect to property not owned by the delinquent taxpayer, the actual owner may suffer serious damage from having the property encumbered by the lien. The Code provides a third party a number of avenues of relief in the case of an erroneously filed lien. Section

---

[14] If the IRS determines that the government's interest in certain property has no value (because, for example, the amount of prior encumbrances exceeds the total value of the property), the IRS may issue a certificate releasing the property from the tax lien. I.R.C. § 6325(b)(2)(B). A request for release may be made by the taxpayer on Form 669C.

[15] In addition to these procedures relating to release and discharge, Code section 6323(j) and Treasury regulation section 301.6323(j)-1(b) set forth circumstances in which the IRS may be willing to withdraw a Notice of Federal Tax Lien, including where: (1) the filing of the notice was premature or otherwise not in accordance with administrative procedures; (2) the taxpayer has entered into an installment agreement to satisfy the liability for which the lien was imposed; (3) the withdrawal notice will facilitate collection of the tax liability; or (4) the withdrawal notice would be in the best interests of both the taxpayer and the government.

6325(b)(4), for example, permits a third-party owner of property against which a federal tax lien has been filed to obtain a certificate discharging the property from the tax lien if the third party deposits with the IRS funds equal to the value of the government's interest in the property or provides a bond in a like amount. After receiving the certificate of discharge, the third party may file a civil action in federal district court in order to determine whether and to what extent the property was properly encumbered by the tax lien. I.R.C. § 7426(a)(4). If the IRS does not have a valid interest in the property, or the IRS interest turns out to be valued at an amount less than the deposited or bonded amount, the district court can order a refund of the deposited amount, with interest, and a release of the bond. Relief may also be afforded third parties under section 6325(e), which authorizes the IRS to issue a certificate of nonattachment specifying that the tax lien does not attach to the property of the third party. Nonattachment usually occurs when, because of similarities in names, the IRS files the tax lien with respect to the wrong taxpayer's property.

[C] Levy and Sale

Reading Assignment: I.R.C. §§ 6330(a)–(b), 6331(a)–(e), 6332(a), (d), 6334(a), (d), (e), 6335, 6337, 6343(a), (d).

A federal tax lien is merely an encumbrance against the taxpayer's property. While its existence may prevent the taxpayer from acquiring a buyer for his or her property, the lien does not result in the IRS obtaining possession of the taxpayer's property or funds until the IRS enforces or executes the lien. The primary method used by the IRS to enforce the tax lien is the administrative procedure of levy (or seizure). Section 6331 permits the IRS to levy upon the taxpayer's property and, if necessary, sell the property at public auction in order to generate proceeds to satisfy the unpaid liability.[16] I.R.C. § 6331(b). In most cases, no judicial intervention is required. In cases not involving a jeopardy assessment, the IRS must wait to levy against the taxpayer's property until after the expiration of a ten-day period following the issuance of a Notice and Demand for Payment. In the usual case, the IRS will issue one or two additional demands for payment before resorting to levy. If the taxpayer can convince the IRS that he or she is making a sincere effort to pay the liability, the levy may be postponed. Other collection alternatives, such as installment agreements and offers in compromise, may also postpone a levy. These procedures are discussed in Chapter 15.

[1] Notice of Intent to Levy

Before seizing the taxpayer's property, the IRS must mail or deliver a written statement (the Notice of Intent to Levy) notifying the taxpayer of its intent to levy and describing both (1) the statutory and administrative procedures relating to levy and sale and (2) the alternatives that may be available to the taxpayer to prevent a levy. I.R.C. § 6331(d). The IRS must provide the Notice of Intent to Levy at least 30 days prior to levying on the taxpayer's property.[17] *Id.* The revenue officer typically must obtain supervisor approval before issuing a levy notice and seizing the taxpayer's property. IRS Reform Act § 3421; I.R.M. 5.10.2.14. In the case of a jeopardy assessment, the Code permits the IRS to levy and seize a delinquent taxpayer's property immediately after making notice and demand, with no prior notice required. I.R.C. § 6331(a).

---

[16] A levy normally is followed by seizure of the property. However, for intangible property not represented by a document or other physical asset, the levy itself generally suffices. *See* United States v. Donahue Indus., 905 F.2d 1325, 1329 (9th Cir. 1990).

[17] Code section 6213 also prohibits the IRS from making a levy until 90 days after mailing a notice of deficiency or, if a petition is filed in the Tax Court, until the Tax Court's decision becomes final.

The notice of levy that the IRS now uses also typically fulfills the IRS's obligation under section 6330 to notify the taxpayer of the right to protest the proposed levy with the Appeals Division as part of a Collection Due Process (CDP) hearing. I.R.C. § 6330. The procedures under section 6330 are similar to the procedures in section 6320 relating to the post-lien CDP notice. The issues that taxpayers may raise in the CDP hearing are discussed in Chapter 16. A delinquent taxpayer in a jeopardy case is not entitled to a CDP notice prior to levy, but still has a right to request a CDP hearing within a reasonable amount of time after the levy occurs. I.R.C. § 6330(f)(1). Similarly, section 6330 does not require that the taxpayer be granted a pre-levy CDP hearing before issuing a levy to collect a state tax refund owed the taxpayer. As in a jeopardy case, a post-levy hearing is all that is required. Treas. Reg. § 301.6330-1(a)(2).

[2] Property Subject to Levy

A levy may be made on all of the delinquent taxpayer's property or rights to property — real or personal, tangible or intangible — unless specifically exempted. In addition, property that is encumbered by the federal tax lien is subject to levy whether the property is in the taxpayer's or someone else's possession. I.R.C. § 6331(a). Unlike the federal tax lien, which automatically attaches to after-acquired property, a levy does not operate prospectively to subject after-acquired property to levy or seizure. In other words, the IRS may impose a levy only on the taxpayer's property or rights to property (including future interests and obligations owed the taxpayer) existing at the time of levy. *See, e.g.,* Tull v. United States, 69 F.3d 394 (9th Cir. 1995). As discussed below, an exception is made in the case of wages, salaries, and certain other periodic payments. In these specific cases, the levy is deemed to be continuous, thereby permitting the IRS to collect amounts accruing after the date of levy so long as the liability remains unpaid. I.R.C. § 6331(e), (h). Outside these special cases, if the value of the taxpayer's property levied upon is insufficient to cover the entire outstanding debt, the IRS can reach additional or after-acquired property only by making an additional levy. I.R.C. § 6331(c). These successive levies must satisfy the notice requirements applicable to all levies.

Section 6334(a) enumerates classes of property that are exempt from levy. Among other items, property exempt from levy includes ordinary clothing and schoolbooks necessary for the taxpayer or members of the taxpayer's family; certain household and personal effects; certain books and tools necessary for a trade or business; salary and wages that must be paid under a child support order; and minimum amounts of wages and other income, which are determined in part based on the number of the taxpayer's dependents. I.R.C. § 6334(a), (d). Exemptions from levy are specifically limited to those types of property listed in section 6334. As a result, state laws that may exempt property from levy do not protect against federal tax collection efforts.

[3] Levy and Seizure

Once a valid levy is made, the IRS will seek to obtain possession of the levied property either from the taxpayer or a third party. In most cases, the IRS will first seek to levy upon the delinquent taxpayer's bank deposits, if any, and wages owing from an employer. In the case of a wage levy, the employer must withhold the nonexempt portion of the taxpayer's wages and remit the amount directly to the IRS. Because a levy on wages and salaries is continuous, the employer must continue to remit portions of the taxpayer's salary to the IRS until the liability is satisfied in full. In the case of a bank levy, the financial institution is required to hold the taxpayer's accounts for 21 days after receiving notice of the levy in order to permit the taxpayer time to seek a release of the levy. After the 21-day period, the bank must remit the entire account balance to the IRS. I.R.C. § 6332(c). The IRS uses Form 668W in the case of wage levies and Form 668A in the case of bank or other third party levies.

Example: Acme Bank is served with a Notice of Levy, Form 668A, for an unpaid tax liability due from Jim Smith in the amount of $2,000. Acme Bank holds $1,000 in a checking account in Jim's name at the time the notice is issued. Acme Bank must hold the funds for a period of 21 days, at which time it must remit the entire $1,000 to the IRS if the levy has not been released. If Jim deposits an additional amount in the checking account after the initial Notice of Levy is issued, Acme Bank is not required to remit that additional deposit to the IRS. However, the IRS may issue a successive bank levy in order to obtain possession of the later deposit.

If the property sought to be levied upon is in the hands of the taxpayer, the IRS uses Form 668B to demand possession. Since 2002, the IRS also imposes a continuous levy on the taxpayer's social security benefits in an effort to collect unpaid taxes. *See* IR-2001-89.

The IRS Reform Act imposed significant restrictions on the IRS's ability to seize the taxpayer's personal residence and business-related assets in an effort to ensure that these assets are seized only as a last resort. If the IRS wishes to seize the taxpayer's principal residence, the IRS must obtain prior written approval of a United States district court. I.R.C. § 6334(e)(1). Moreover, the IRS may not seize any residence used by the taxpayer, or any non-rental real property of the taxpayer that is used as a residence by someone else, for a deficiency (including taxes, interest, and penalties) of $5,000 or less. I.R.C. § 6334(a)(13). Treasury regulations under section 6334 outline the notice requirements and other limitations the IRS must abide by if it seeks to seize a personal residence. *See* Treas. Reg. § 301.6334-1(d).

Congress was also concerned that a seizure of property used by the taxpayer to carry out a trade or business could adversely affect the taxpayer's ability to pay the tax liability. As a result, the Code now requires prior written approval from an IRS official before such assets may be seized. Levy approval may be granted only if the IRS official determines that the taxpayer's other assets are insufficient to cover the unpaid assessment. I.R.C. § 6334(a)(13)(B), (e)(2). As a practical matter, therefore, the IRS must exhaust all other payment options before seizing the taxpayer's business assets.

The taxpayer or third party in possession of the property subject to levy normally must surrender the property to the IRS on demand. I.R.C. § 6332(a). Once a third party surrenders an asset or payment to the IRS in response to a levy notice, that party is discharged from any liability to the delinquent taxpayer regarding the surrendered amount. I.R.C. § 6332(e). If the party in possession does not surrender the levied property upon demand, that party becomes personally liable to the United States in an amount equal to the value of the property not surrendered. I.R.C. § 6332(d). In addition, if the person who is required to surrender the levied property fails to do so without reasonable cause, he or she becomes liable for a penalty equal to 50 percent of the amount of the liability. *Id.*

In cases where the property is not voluntarily turned over, the IRS may forcibly seize the property from the taxpayer or the party in possession. Depending upon the type of property involved, the revenue officer will remove the property to a storage area or padlock it to prevent the taxpayer from retaking possession. As soon as practical after the property is seized, the IRS must provide the owner or possessor of the seized property with a notice describing the property and the amount demanded by the IRS for its release. Treas. Reg. § 301.6335-1(a). The IRS uses Form 2433, Notice of Seizure, for this purpose. Other restrictions relating to the seizure of property are described in section 6335.

Before the IRS attempts to sell a seized asset, the taxpayer normally is given a last opportunity to come to some payment arrangement with the IRS. If the taxpayer and the IRS agree upon a final payment and such payment is made, the IRS will release the levy and, if necessary, return the seized property to the owner. *See* I.R.C. § 6337(a). The IRS is also required to release a levy if (1) the underlying liability for which the levy was made becomes unenforceable due to a lapse of time; (2) the release will facilitate collection of the tax liability; (3) the levy causes economic hardship for the taxpayer (by, for example, preventing the taxpayer from meeting basic living expenses); or (4) the taxpayer enters into an agreement for paying the tax in installments. I.R.C. § 6343; Treas. Reg. § 301.6343-1(b). The IRS may find that a release facilitates collection if the taxpayer is willing to place the property in escrow to secure payment or to provide an acceptable bond conditioned upon payment. Treas. Reg. § 301.6343-1(b)(2). Procedures for requesting a levy release are contained in Treas. Reg. § 301.6343-1(c).

If the property owner can prove that the property has been wrongfully levied upon (because the IRS failed to satisfy the procedural requirements before seizure, for instance), the owner can seek a return of the levied property or payment of an amount of money equal to the amount realized on the sale of the property. I.R.C. § 6343(b), (d). In addition, an owner other than the delinquent taxpayer may bring a wrongful levy action in district court seeking similar relief, as well as an injunction prohibiting the IRS from levying upon or selling the subject property. *See* I.R.C. § 7426; Sessler v. United States, 7 F.3d 1449 (9th Cir. 1993).[18]

[4] Sale Following Seizure

If the taxpayer is unable to obtain a release of the levy, the IRS can sell the taxpayer's interest in the property subject to the federal tax lien at an administrative sale. Before doing so, however, the IRS must provide the delinquent taxpayer with a Notice of Sale, which specifies the property to be sold and the time, place, and manner of the sale. The Notice of Sale must also be published locally in a newspaper of general circulation. I.R.C. § 6335(b). As an additional prerequisite before sale, the IRS must conduct a pre-sale investigation that confirms the taxpayer's liability, assures that the levy will yield a meaningful sum for the IRS (beyond levy expenses), and considers (or reconsiders) the possibility of alterative means of collection. I.R.C. § 6331(j). If the IRS proceeds with the sale, the property will be sold to the highest bidder at a public auction not less than ten days or more than 40 days following the Notice of Sale. I.R.C. § 6335(d), (e). Only the delinquent taxpayer's right, title, and interest is offered for sale, and such interest is sold subject to all encumbrances and liens that are superior to the government's tax lien.[19] Treas. Reg. § 301.6335-1(c)(5)(iii). See generally I.R.C. § 6335(e) for procedures relating to the sale of seized property.

Proceeds from the sale are first applied to reimburse the IRS for levy and sale expenses, then to the delinquent taxpayer's liability. I.R.C. § 6342(a). Any surplus is paid to the person or persons (including the taxpayer) who make an application and provide satisfactory proof that they are entitled to the remaining amounts. I.R.C. § 6342(b); Treas. Reg. § 301.6342-1(b). If competing claimants exist, the government may institute an interpleader action to determine who is legally entitled to the surplus sales proceeds. In the case of real estate, even though the property has been sold, the taxpayer is given a final opportunity to redeem (buy back) the real property within 180 days of the sale. The taxpayer must pay the purchaser the amount paid at auction plus interest calculated at a rate of 20 percent per annum. I.R.C. § 6337(b). This post-sale right of redemption does not apply to personal property.

---

[18] The Supreme Court ruled in *EC Term of Years Trust v. United States*, 127 S. Ct. 1763 (2007), that a third party whose property has been levied upon in order to satisfy a claim against the taxpayer must seek relief under the wrongful levy procedures in Code section 7426. The third party may not challenge the levy under the general refund procedures of 28 U.S.C. section 1346. As a result, claimants are subject to the nine-month statute of limitations in section 7426, I.R.C. § 6532(c), rather than the longer limitations period associated with actions brought under the general refund statute discussed in Chapter 10. *See* I.R.C. § 6532(a).

[19] Sale of the levied property extinguishes the government's tax lien on that property, as well as all liens inferior to the tax lien. The sale does not extinguish liens that are superior to or have priority over the federal tax lien.

§ 14.04 JUDICIAL COLLECTION PROCEEDINGS

[A] Judicial Proceedings Instituted by the Government

Reading Assignment: I.R.C. §§ 7401, 7403.

As discussed above, the federal tax lien attaches to all the delinquent taxpayer's property interests. I.R.C. § 6321. After satisfying the necessary conditions, the IRS can administratively seize and sell the delinquent taxpayer's interest in the encumbered property. If the delinquent taxpayer holds an undivided interest in property with another party who is not liable for the unpaid tax liability, only the delinquent taxpayer's interest is subject to the IRS's administrative collection procedures. Efforts by the IRS to sell the delinquent taxpayer's undivided interest are likely to attract few buyers, and thus little sales proceeds with which to discharge the taxpayer's liability. In these cases, the IRS may resort to judicial collection procedures, which may allow the IRS to sell the entire property and then compensate the nondelinquent co-owners out of the proceeds.

The following case, which involves a suit to judicially enforce a lien under section 7403 (also known as a lien foreclosure suit), illustrates the hardship that may be caused to the nondelinquent party who also owns an interest in the property sought to be sold. The case also contrasts the section 7403 judicial collection procedures with administrative collection procedures.

UNITED STATES v. RODGERS
United States Supreme Court
461 U.S. 677 (1983)

Justice Brennan delivered the opinion of the Court.

These consolidated cases involve the relationship between the imperatives of federal tax collection and rights accorded by state property laws. Section 7403 of the Internal Revenue Code of 1954, 26 U. S. C. § 7403 (1976 ed. and Supp. V), authorizes the judicial sale of certain properties to satisfy the tax indebtedness of delinquent taxpayers. The issue in both cases is whether § 7403 empowers a federal district court to order the sale of a family home in which a delinquent taxpayer had an interest at the time he incurred his indebtedness, but in which the taxpayer's spouse, who does not owe any of that indebtedness, also has a separate "homestead" right as defined by Texas law. We hold that the statute does grant power to order the sale, but that its exercise is limited to some degree by equitable discretion. We also hold that, if the home is sold, the nondelinquent spouse is entitled, as part of the distribution of proceeds required under § 7403, to so much of the proceeds as represents complete compensation for the loss of the homestead estate.

* * *

B.

The substance of Texas law related to the homestead right may usefully be divided into two categories. *Cf.* Woods v. Alvarado State Bank, 19 S.W. 2d 35, 35, 118 Tex. 586, 590 (1929). First, in common with a large number of States, Texas establishes the family home or place of business as an enclave exempted from the reach of most creditors. Thus, under Tex. Const., Art. 16, § 50:

> "The homestead of a family, or of a single adult person, shall be, and is hereby protected from forced sale, for the payment of all debts except for [certain exceptions not relevant here]. . . . No mortgage, trust deed, or other lien on

the homestead shall ever be valid, except for [certain exceptions not relevant here]."

Second, in common with a somewhat smaller number of States, Texas gives members of the family unit additional rights in the homestead property itself. Thus, in a clause not included in the above quotation, Tex. Const., Art 16, § 50, also provides that "the owner or claimant of the property claimed as homestead [may not], if married, sell or abandon the homestead without the consent of the other spouse, given in such manner as may be prescribed by law." Equally important, Art. 16, § 52, provides:

> "On the death of the husband or wife, or both, the homestead shall descend and vest in like manner as other real property of the deceased, and shall be governed by the same laws of descent and distribution, but it shall not be partitioned among the heirs of the deceased during the lifetime of the surviving husband or wife, or so long as the survivor may elect to use or occupy the same as a homestead, or so long as the guardian of the minor children of the deceased may be permitted, under the order of the proper court having the jurisdiction, to use and occupy the same."

The effect of these provisions in the Texas Constitution is to give each spouse in a marriage a separate and undivided possessory interest in the homestead, which is only lost by death or abandonment, and which may not be compromised either by the other spouse or by his or her heirs.[n.10] It bears emphasis that the rights accorded by the homestead laws vest independently in each spouse regardless of whether one spouse, or both, actually owns the fee interest in the homestead. Thus, although analogy is somewhat hazardous in this area, it may be said that the homestead laws have the effect of reducing the underlying ownership rights in a homestead property to something akin to remainder interests and vesting in each spouse an interest akin to an undivided life estate in the property. *See* Williams v. Williams, 569 S.W. 2d 867, 869 (Tex. 1978), and cases cited; Paddock v. Siemoneit, 218 S.W. 2d 428, 436, 147 Tex. 571, 585 (1949), and cases cited; Hill v. Hill, 623 S.W. 2d 779, 780 (Tex. App. 1981), and cases cited. This analogy, although it does some injustice to the nuances present in the Texas homestead statute, also serves to bring to the fore something that has been repeatedly emphasized by the Texas courts, and that was reaffirmed by the Court of Appeals in these cases: that the Texas homestead right is not a mere statutory entitlement, but a vested property right. * * * As the Supreme Court of Texas put it, a spouse "has a vested estate in the land of which she cannot be divested during her life except by abandonment or a voluntary conveyance in the manner prescribed by law." * * * .

II.

The two cases before us were consolidated for oral argument before the United States Court of Appeals for the Fifth Circuit, and resulted in opinions issued on the same day. *United States v. Rogers*, *supra*; Ingram v. Dallas Dept. of Housing & Urban Rehabilitation, 649 F.2d 1128 (1981). They arise out of legally comparable, but quite distinct, sets of facts.

A.

Lucille Mitzi Bosco Rodgers is the widow of Philip S. Bosco, whom she married in 1937. She and Mr. Bosco acquired, as community property, a residence in Dallas, Texas,

---

[n.10] The homestead character of property is not destroyed even by divorce, if one of the parties to the divorce continues to maintain the property as a proper homestead. *See* Renaldo v. Bank of San Antonio, 630 S.W. 2d 638, 639 (Tex. 1982); Wierzchula v. Wierzchula, 623 S.W. 2d 730, 732 (Tex. Civ. App. 1981). The courts may, however, partition the property, award it to one or the other spouse, or require one spouse to compensate the other, as part of the disposition of marital property attendant to the divorce proceedings. *See* Hedtke v. Hedtke, 248 S.W. 21, 112 Tex. 404 (1923); Brunell v. Brunell, 494 S.W. 2d 621, 622–623 (Tex. Civ. App. 1973).

and occupied it as their homestead. Subsequently, in 1971 and 1972, the Internal Revenue Service issued assessments totaling more than $900,000 for federal wagering taxes, penalties, and interest, against Philip for the taxable years 1966 through 1971. These taxes remained unpaid at the time of Philip's death in 1974. Since Philip's death, Lucille has continued to occupy the property as her homestead, and now lives there with her present husband.

On September 23, 1977, the Government filed suit under 26 U. S. C. §§ 7402 and 7403 in the United States District Court for the Northern District of Texas against Mrs. Rodgers and Philip's son, daughter, and executor. The suit sought to reduce to judgment the assessments against Philip, to enforce the Government's tax liens, including the one that had attached to Philip's interest in the residence, and to obtain a deficiency judgment in the amount of any unsatisfied part of the liability. On cross-motions for summary judgment, the District Court granted partial summary judgment on, among other things, the defendants' claim that the federal tax liens could not defeat Mrs. Rodgers' state-created right not to have her homestead subjected to a forced sale. Fed. Rule Civ. Proc. 54(b).

The Court of Appeals affirmed on the homestead issue, holding that if "a homestead interest is, under state law, a property right, possessed by the nontaxpayer spouse at the time the lien attaches to the taxpayer spouse's interest, then the federal tax lien may not be foreclosed against the homestead property for as long as the nontaxpayer spouse maintains his or her homestead interest under state law." 649 F.2d, at 1125 (footnotes omitted). The court implied that the Government had the choice of either waiting until Mrs. Rodgers' homestead interest lapsed, or satisfying itself with a forced sale of only Philip Bosco's interest in the property.

B.

Joerene Ingram is the divorced wife of Donald Ingram. During their marriage, Joerene and Donald acquired, as community property, a residence in Dallas, Texas, and occupied it as their homestead. Subsequently, in 1972 and 1973, the Internal Revenue Service issued assessments against Donald Ingram relating to unpaid taxes withheld from wages of employees of a company of which he was president. Deducting payments made on account of these liabilities, there remains unpaid approximately $9,000, plus interest. In addition, in 1973, the Service made an assessment against both Donald and Joerene in the amount of $283.33, plus interest, relating to their joint income tax liability for 1971. These amounts also remain unpaid.

In March 1975, at about the time the Ingrams were seeking a divorce, their residence was destroyed by fire. In September 1975, the Ingrams obtained a divorce. In connection with the divorce, they entered into a property settlement agreement, one provision of which was that Donald would convey to Joerene his interest in the real property involved in this case in exchange for $1,500, to be paid from the proceeds of the sale of the property. Joerene tried to sell the property, through a trustee, but was unsuccessful in those efforts, apparently because of the federal tax liens encumbering the property. To make matters worse, she then received notice from the City of Dallas Department of Housing and Urban Rehabilitation (Department) that unless she complied with local ordinances, the remains of the fire-damaged residence would be demolished. Following a hearing, the Department issued a final notice and a work order to demolish. Joerene Ingram and the trustee then filed suit in Texas state court to quiet title to the property, to remove the federal tax liens, and to enjoin demolition. The defendants were the United States, the Department, and several creditors claiming an interest in the property.

The United States removed the suit to the District Court for the Northern District of Texas. It then filed a counterclaim against Joerene Ingram and Donald Ingram (who was added as a defendant on the counterclaim) for both the unpaid withholding taxes and the joint liability for unpaid income taxes. In its prayer for relief, the Government sought, among other things, judicial sale of the property under § 7403. Pursuant to a stipulation of the parties, the property was sold unencumbered and the proceeds (approximately $16,250) were deposited into the registry of the District Court pending the outcome of the suit. The parties agreed that their rights, claims, and priorities would be determined as if the sale had not taken place, and that the proceeds would be divided according to their respective interests. On cross-motions for summary judgment, the District Court granted summary judgment on the Government's counterclaims.

The Court of Appeals affirmed in part, and reversed and remanded in part. It agreed that the Government could foreclose its lien on the proceeds from the sale of the property to collect the $283.33, plus interest, for the unpaid income tax owed by Joerene and Donald Ingram jointly. Applying its decision in *Rodgers,* however, it also held that the Government could not reach the proceeds of the sale of the property to collect the individual liability of Donald Ingram, assuming Joerene Ingram had maintained her homestead interest in the property. The court remanded, however, for a factual determination of whether Joerene had "abandoned" the homestead by dividing the insurance proceeds with Donald and by attempting — even before the stipulation entered into with the Government — to sell the property and divide the proceeds of that sale with Donald.[n.15]

C.

The Government filed a single petition for certiorari in both these cases. See this Court's Rule 19.4. We granted certiorari, 456 U.S. 904 (1982), in order to resolve a conflict among the Courts of Appeals as to the proper interpretation of § 7403.

III.

A.

The basic holding underlying the Court of Appeals' view that the Government was not authorized to seek a sale of the homes in which respondents held a homestead interest is that "when a delinquent taxpayer shares his ownership interest in property jointly with other persons rather than being the sole owner, his 'property' and 'rights to property' to which the federal tax lien attaches under 26 U.S.C. § 6321, and on which federal levy may be had under 26 U.S.C. § 7403(a), involve only his *interest* in the property, and not the entire property." 649 F.2d, at 1125 (emphasis in original). According to the Court of Appeals, this principle applies, not only in the homestead context, but in any co-tenancy in which unindebted third parties share an ownership interest with a delinquent taxpayer. *See* Folsom v. United States, 306 F.2d 361 (CA5 1962).

We agree with the Court of Appeals that the Government's lien under § 6321 cannot extend beyond the property interests held by the delinquent taxpayer. We also agree that the Government may not ultimately collect, as satisfaction for the indebtedness owed to it, more than the value of the property interests that are actually liable for that debt. But, in this context at least, the right to collect and the right to seek a forced sale are two quite different things.

The Court of Appeals for the Fifth Circuit recognized that it was the only Court of Appeals that had adopted the view that the Government could seek the sale, under § 7403, of only the delinquent taxpayer's "*interest* in the property, and not the entire property." 649 F.2d, at 1125, and n.12. We agree with the prevailing view that such a restrictive reading of § 7403 flies in the face of the plain meaning of the statute. *See, e.g.,*

[n.15] The Court of Appeals did suggest that neither the fire nor the intention to sell the house would, in and of themselves, necessarily indicate an abandonment of the homestead. 649 F.2d, at 1132, and n.6. * * *

United States v. Trilling, 328 F.2d 699, 702–703 (CA7 1964); Washington v. United States, 402 F.2d 3, 6–7 (CA4 1968); United States v. Overman, 424 F.2d 1142, 1146 (CA9 1970); United States v. Kocher, 468 F.2d 503, 506–507 (CA2 1972); *see also* Mansfield v. Excelsior Refining Co., 135 U.S. 326, 339–341 (1890).

Section 7403(a) provides not only that the Government may "enforce [its] lien," but also that it may seek to "subject *any property,* of whatever nature, of the delinquent, or *in which he has any right, title, or interest,* to the payment of such tax or liability" (emphasis added). This clause in and of itself defeats the reading proposed by the Court of Appeals. Section 7403(b) then provides that "[all] persons having liens upon *or claiming any interest in the property involved in such action* shall be made parties thereto" (emphasis added). Obviously, no joinder of persons claiming independent interests in the property would be necessary if the Government were only authorized to seek the sale of the delinquent taxpayer's own interests. Finally, § 7403(c) provides that the district court should "determine the merits of all claims to and liens upon the property, and, in all cases where a claim or interest of the United States therein is established, may decree a sale *of such property . . . and a distribution of the proceeds of such sale according to the findings of the court in respect to the interests of the parties and of the United States*" (emphasis added). Again, we must read the statute to contemplate, not merely the sale of the delinquent taxpayer's own interest, but the sale of the entire property (as long as the United States has any "claim or interest" in it), and the recognition of third-party interests through the mechanism of judicial valuation and distribution. * * *

Our reading of § 7403 is consistent with the policy inherent in the tax statutes in favor of the prompt and certain collection of delinquent taxes. * * * It requires no citation to point out that interests in property, when sold separately, may be worth either significantly more or significantly less than the sum of their parts. When the latter is the case, it makes considerable sense to allow the Government to seek the sale of the whole, and obtain its fair share of the proceeds, rather than satisfy itself with a mere sale of the part.

* * *

Finally, our reading of the statute is significantly bolstered by a comparison with the statutory language setting out the administrative levy remedy also available to the Government. Under 26 U.S.C. § 6331(a), the Government may sell for the collection of unpaid taxes all nonexempt "property and rights to property . . . *belonging to such person* [*i.e.*, the delinquent taxpayer] or on which there is a lien provided in this chapter for the payment of such tax" (emphasis added). This language clearly embodies the limitation that the Court of Appeals thought was present in § 7403, and it has been so interpreted by the courts. Section 6331, unlike § 7403, does not require notice and hearing for third parties, because no rights of third parties are intended to be implicated by § 6331. Indeed, third parties whose property or interests in property have been seized inadvertently are entitled to claim that the property has been "wrongfully levied upon," and may apply for its return either through administrative channels, 26 U.S.C. § 6343(b), or through a civil action filed in a federal district court, § 7426(a)(1); *see* §§ 7426(b)(1), 7426(b)(2)(A). In the absence of such "wrongful levy," the entire proceeds of a sale conducted pursuant to administrative levy may be applied, without any prior distribution of the sort required by § 7403, to the expenses of the levy and sale, the specific tax liability on the seized property, and the general tax liability of the delinquent taxpayer. 26 U.S.C. § 6342.

We are not entirely unmoved by the force of the basic intuition underlying the Court of Appeals' view of § 7403 — that the Government, though it has the "right to pursue the property of the [delinquent] taxpayer with all the force and fury at its command," should not have any right, superior to that of other creditors, to disturb the settled expectations of innocent third parties. *Folsom v. United States*, 306 F.2d, at 367–368. In fact, however, the Government's right to seek a forced sale of the entire property in which a delinquent taxpayer had an interest does not arise out of its privileges as an ordinary creditor, but out of the express terms of § 7403. Moreover, the use of the power granted by § 7403 is not the act of an ordinary creditor, but the exercise of a sovereign prerogative, incident to the power to enforce the obligations of the delinquent taxpayer himself, and ultimately grounded in the constitutional mandate to "lay and collect taxes." *Cf. Bull v. United States*, 295 U.S., at 259–260; Phillips v. Commissioner, 283 U.S. 589, 595–597 (1931); United States v. Snyder, 149 U.S. 210, 214–215 (1893).

Admittedly, if § 7403 allowed for the gratuitous confiscation of one person's property interests in order to satisfy another person's tax indebtedness, such a provision might pose significant difficulties under the Due Process Clause of the Fifth Amendment. But, as we have already indicated, § 7403 makes no further use of third-party property interests than to facilitate the extraction of value from those concurrent property interests that *are* properly liable for the taxpayer's debt. To the extent that third-party property interests are "taken" in the process, § 7403 provides compensation for that "taking" by requiring that the court distribute the proceeds of the sale "according to the findings of the court in respect to the interests of the parties and of the United States." *Cf. United States v. Overman*, 424 F.2d, at 1146. Moreover, we hold, on the basis of what we are informed about the nature of the homestead estate in Texas, that it is the sort of property interest for whose loss an innocent third party must be compensated under § 7403. *Cf.* United States v. General Motors Corp., 323 U.S. 373, 377–378 (1945). We therefore see no contradiction, at least at the level of basic principle, between the enforcement powers granted to the Government under § 7403 and the recognition of vested property interests granted to innocent third parties under state law.

The exact method for the distribution required by § 7403 is not before us at this time. But we can get a rough idea of the practical consequences of the principles we have just set out. For example, if we assume, *only for the sake of illustration*, that a homestead estate is the exact economic equivalent of a life estate, and that the use of a standard statutory or commercial table and an 8% discount rate is appropriate in calculating the value of that estate, then three nondelinquent surviving or remaining spouses, aged 30, 50, and 70 years, each holding a homestead estate, would be entitled to approximately 97%, 89%, and 64%, respectively, of the proceeds of the sale of their homes as compensation for that estate. In addition, if we assume that each of these hypothetical nondelinquent spouses also has a protected half-interest in the underlying ownership rights to the property being sold, then their total compensation would be approximately 99%, 95%, and 82%, respectively, of the proceeds from such sale.

In sum, the Internal Revenue Code, seen as a whole, contains a number of cumulative collection devices, each with its own advantages and disadvantages for the tax collector. Among the advantages of administrative levy is that it is quick and relatively inexpensive. Among the advantages of a § 7403 proceeding is that it gives the Federal Government the opportunity to seek the highest return possible on the forced sale of property interests liable for the payment of federal taxes. The provisions of § 7403 are broad and profound. Nevertheless, § 7403 is punctilious in protecting the vested rights of third parties caught in the Government's collection effort, and in ensuring that the Government not receive out of the proceeds of the sale any more than that to which it is properly entitled. Of course, the exercise in any particular case of the power granted under § 7403 to seek the forced sale of property interests other than those of the delinquent taxpayer is left in the first instance to the good sense and common decency of the collecting authorities. 26 U.S.C. § 7403(a). We also explore in Part IV of this opinion the nature of the limited discretion left to the courts in proceedings brought under § 7403. But that the power exists, and that it is necessary to the prompt and certain enforcement of the tax laws, we have no doubt.

B.

There is another, intermeshed but analytically distinguishable, ground advanced by the Court of Appeals and the respondents — and reiterated by the dissent — for denying the Government the right to seek the forced sale of property held as a homestead by a nondelinquent third party. Taken in itself, this view would hold that, even if § 7403 normally allows for the forced sale of property interests other than those directly liable for the indebtedness of the delinquent taxpayer, the special protections accorded by the exemption aspect of Texas homestead law, *see supra*, should immunize it from the reach of § 7403.

The Court of Appeals conceded that "the homestead interest of a *taxpayer* spouse, *i.e.*, that of one who himself has tax liability, clearly cannot by itself defeat [the enforcement under § 7403 of] a federal tax lien." 649 F.2d, at 1121 (emphasis in original); *see also* 649 F.2d, at 1132 (authorizing levy on proceeds in *Ingram* case to the extent of the $283.33 liability jointly owed by Mr. and Mrs. Ingram). This proposition, although not explicit in the Code, is clearly implicit in 26 U.S.C. § 6334(c) (relating to exemptions from levy), and in our decisions in *United States v. Mitchell*, 403 U.S., at 204–205; *Aquilino v. United States*, 363 U.S., at 513–514; and *United States v. Bess*, 357 U.S., at 56–57, * * * . The Court of Appeals also held that, if the homestead interest under Texas law were "merely an exemption" without accompanying vested property rights, it would not be effective against the Federal Government in a § 7403 proceeding, even in the case of a nondelinquent spouse. 649 F.2d, at 1125. Nevertheless, the court concluded that, if the homestead estate both was claimed by a nondelinquent spouse and constituted a property right under state law, then it would bar the Federal Government from pursuing a forced sale of the entire property.

We disagree. If § 7403 is intended, as we believe it is, to reach the entire property in which a delinquent taxpayer has or had any "right, title, or interest," then state-created exemptions against forced sale should be no more effective with regard to the entire property than with regard to the "right, title, or interest" itself. *Accord*, *United States v. Overman*, 424 F.2d, at 1145–1147; Herndon v. United States, 501 F.2d 1219, 1223–1224 (CA8 1974) (Ross, J., concurring). No exception of the sort carved out by the Court of Appeals appears on the face of the statute, and we decline to frustrate the policy of the statute by reading such an exception into it. *Cf.* Hisquierdo v. Hisquierdo, 439 U.S. 572, 586–587 (1979); *United States v. Mitchell*, *supra*, at 205–206. Moreover, the Supremacy Clause which provides the underpinning for the Federal Government's right to sweep aside state-created exemptions in the first place — is as potent in its application to innocent bystanders as in its application to delinquent debtors. *See United States v. Union Central Life Insurance Co.*, 368 U.S., at 293–295 (federal tax lien good against bona fide purchaser, even though lien not filed in accordance with provisions of state law); *cf. Hisquierdo v. Hisquierdo*, *supra*, at 585–586; United States v. Carmack, 329 U.S. 230, 236–240 (1946). Whatever property rights attach to a homestead under Texas law are adequately discharged by the payment of compensation, and no further deference to state law is required, either by § 7403 or by the Constitution.

The dissent urges us to carve out an exception from the plain language of § 7403 in that "small number of joint-ownership situations . . . [in which] the delinquent taxpayer has no right to force partition or otherwise to alienate the entire property without the consent of the coowner." * * * Its primary argument in favor of such an exception is that it would be consistent with traditional limitations on the rights of a lienholder. * * * If § 7403 truly embodied traditional limitations on the rights of lienholders, however, then we would have to conclude that *Folsom v. United States*, 306 F.2d 361 (CA5 1962), discussed *supra*, was correctly decided, a proposition that even the dissent is not willing to advance. * * * More importantly, we believe that the better analogy in this case is not to the traditional rights of lienholders, but to the traditional powers of a taxing authority in an *in rem* enforcement proceeding. * * *

IV.

A.

Although we have held that the Supremacy Clause allows the federal tax collector to convert a nondelinquent spouse's homestead estate into its fair cash value, and that such a conversion satisfies the requirements of due process, we are not blind to the fact that in practical terms financial compensation may not always be a completely adequate substitute for a roof over one's head. *Cf.* United States v. 564.54 Acres of Land, 441 U.S. 506, 510–513 (1979). This problem seems particularly acute in the case of a homestead interest. First, the nature of the market for life estates or the market for rental property may be such that the value of a homestead interest, calculated as some fraction of the total value of a home, would be less than the price demanded by the market for a lifetime's interest in an equivalent home. Second, any calculation of the cash value of a homestead interest must of necessity be based on actuarial statistics, and will unavoidably under-compensate persons who end up living longer than the average. Indeed, it is precisely because of problems such as these that a number of courts, in eminent domain cases involving property divided between a homestead interest and underlying ownership rights or between a life estate and a remainder interest, have refused to distribute the proceeds according to an actuarial formula, and have instead placed the entire award in trust (or reinvested it in a new parcel of property) with the income (or use) going to the life-estate holder during his or her lifetime, and the corpus vesting in the holder of the remainder interest upon the death of the life-estate holder.

If the sale and distribution provided for in § 7403 were mandatory, the practical problems we have just described would be of little legal consequence. The statute provides, however, that the court in a § 7403 proceeding "*shall* . . . proceed to adjudicate all matters involved therein and finally determine the merits of all claims to and liens upon the property, and, in all cases where a claim or interest of the United States therein is established, *may* decree a sale of such property . . . " (emphasis added), and respondents argue that this language allows a district court hearing a § 7403 proceeding to exercise a degree of equitable discretion and refuse to authorize a forced sale in a particular case. *See* Tillery v. Parks, 630 F.2d 775 (CA10 1980); United States v. Eaves, 499 F.2d 869, 870–871 (CA10 1974); *United States v. Hershberger*, 475 F.2d, at 679–680; *United States v. Overman*, 424 F.2d, at 1146; United States v. Morrison, 247 F.2d 285, 289–291 (CA5 1957). The Court of Appeals agreed with this interpretation of the statute, although it does not appear to have relied on it, 649 F.2d, at 1125, and in any event neither it nor the District Court undertook any particularized equitable assessment of the cases now before us. We find the question to be close, but on balance, we too conclude that § 7403 does not require a district court to authorize a forced sale under absolutely all circumstances, and that some limited room is left in the statute for the exercise of reasoned discretion.

B.

* * *

Finally, we are convinced that recognizing that district courts may exercise a degree of equitable discretion in § 7403 proceedings is consistent with the policies of the statute: unlike an absolute exception, which we rejected above, the exercise of limited equitable discretion in individual cases can take into account both the Government's interest in prompt and certain collection of delinquent taxes and the possibility that innocent third parties will be unduly harmed by that effort.

C.

To say that district courts need not always go ahead with a forced sale authorized by § 7403 is not to say that they have unbridled discretion. We can think of virtually no circumstances, for example, in which it would be permissible to refuse to authorize a sale simply to protect the interests of the delinquent taxpayer himself or herself. And even when the interests of third parties are involved, we think that a certain fairly limited set of considerations will almost always be paramount.

First, a court should consider the extent to which the Government's financial interests would be prejudiced if it were relegated to a forced sale of the partial interest actually liable for the delinquent taxes. Even the Government seems to concede that, if such a partial sale would not prejudice it at all (because the separate market value of the partial interest is likely to be equal to or greater than its value as a fraction of the total value of the entire property) then there would be no reason at all to authorize a sale of the entire property. Tr. of Oral Arg. 7, 13; Reply Brief for United States 8, n.5. We think that a natural extension of this principle, however, is that, even when the partial interest would be worth *less* sold separately than sold as part of the entire property, the possibility of prejudice to the Government can still be measured as a matter of degree. Simply put, the higher the expected market price, the less the prejudice, and the less weighty the Government's interest in going ahead with a sale of the entire property.

Second, a court should consider whether the third party with a nonliable separate interest in the property would, in the normal course of events (leaving aside § 7403 and eminent domain proceedings, of course), have a legally recognized expectation that that separate property would not be subject to forced sale by the delinquent taxpayer or his or her creditors. If there is no such expectation, then there would seem to be little reason not to authorize the sale. Again, however, this factor is amenable to considerations of degree. The Texas homestead laws are almost absolute in their protections against forced sale. The usual cotenancy arrangement, which allows any cotenant to seek a judicial sale of the property and distribution of the proceeds, but which also allows the other cotenants to resist the sale and apply instead for a partition in kind, is further along the continuum. And a host of other types of property interests are arrayed between and beyond.

Third, a court should consider the likely prejudice to the third party, both in personal dislocation costs and in the sort of practical undercompensation described *supra* [Part IV.A. of the Opinion. — Eds.].

Fourth, a court should consider the relative character and value of the nonliable and liable interests held in the property: if, for example, in the case of real property, the third party has no present possessory interest or fee interest in the property, there may be little reason not to allow the sale; if, on the other hand, the third party not only has a possessory interest or fee interest, but that interest is worth 99% of the value of the property, then there might well be virtually no reason to allow the sale to proceed.

We do not pretend that the factors we have just outlined constitute an exhaustive list; we certainly do not contemplate that they be used as a "mechanical checklist" to the exclusion of common sense and consideration of special circumstances. *Cf.* Moses H. Cone Hospital v. Mercury Construction Corp., 460 U.S. 1, 16 (1983). We do emphasize, however, that the limited discretion accorded by § 7403 should be exercised rigorously and sparingly, keeping in mind the Government's paramount interest in prompt and certain collection of delinquent taxes.

V.

In these cases, no individualized equitable balance of the sort we have just outlined has yet been attempted. In the *Rodgers* case, the record before us, although it is quite clear as to the legal issues relevant to the second consideration noted above, affords us little guidance otherwise. In any event, we think that the task of exercising equitable discretion should be left to the District Court in the first instance.

The *Ingram* case is a bit more complicated, even leaving aside the fact of the stipulated sale by which we are constrained to treat the escrow fund now sitting in the registry of the District Court as if it were a house. First, as the Court of Appeals pointed out, there remains a question under Texas law as to whether Joerene Ingram abandoned the homestead by the time of the stipulated sale. Second, the Government, in addition to its lien for the individual debt of Donald Ingram, has a further lien for $283.33, plus interest, on the house, representing the joint liability of Donald and Joerene Ingram. Because Joerene Ingram is not a "third party" as to that joint liability, we can see no reason, as long as that amount remains unpaid, not to allow a "sale" of the "house" (*i.e.,* a levy on the proceeds of the stipulated sale) for satisfaction of the debt. Moreover, once the dam is broken, there is no reason, under our interpretation of § 7403, not to allow the Government also to collect on the individual debt of Donald Ingram *out of that portion of the proceeds of the sale representing property interests properly liable for the debt.* On the other hand, it would certainly be to Mrs. Ingram's advantage to discharge her personal liability before the Government can proceed with its "sale," in which event, assuming that she has not abandoned the homestead, the District Court will be obliged to strike an equitable balance on the same general principles as those that govern the *Rodgers* case.

The judgment of the Court of Appeals in *Rodgers* is reversed, its judgment in *Ingram* is vacated, and both cases are remanded with directions that they be remanded to the District Court for further proceedings consistent with this opinion.

So ordered.

JUSTICE BLACKMUN, with whom JUSTICE REHNQUIST, JUSTICE STEVENS, and JUSTICE O'CONNOR join, concurring in the result in part and dissenting in part.

The Court today properly rejects the broad legal principle concerning 26 U.S.C. § 7403 that was announced by the Court of Appeals. * * * I agree that, in some situations, § 7403 gives the Government the power to sell property *not* belonging to the taxpayer. Our task, however, is to ascertain how far Congress intended that power to extend. In my view, § 7403 confers on the Government the power to sell or force the sale of jointly owned property only insofar as the *tax debtor's* interest in that property would permit *him* to do so; it does not confer on the Government the power to sell jointly owned property if an unindebted co-owner enjoys an *indestructible* right to bar a sale and to continue in possession. Because Mrs. Rodgers had such a right, and because she is not herself indebted to the Government, I dissent from the Court's disposition of her case.

I.

It is basic in the common law that a lienholder enjoys rights in property no greater than those of the debtor himself; that is, the lienholder does no more than step into the debtor's shoes. 1 L. Jones, LAW OF LIENS § 9, pp. 9–10 (1914). * * *

In most situations in which a delinquent taxpayer shares property with an unindebted third party, it does no violence to this principle to order a sale of the entire property so long as the third party is fully compensated. A joint owner usually has at his disposal the power to convey the property or force its conveyance. Thus, for example, a joint tenant or tenant in common may seek partition. *See generally* W. Plumb, FEDERAL TAX LIENS 35 (3d ed. 1972). If a joint tenant is delinquent in his taxes, the United States does no more than step into the delinquent taxpayer's shoes when it compels a sale.

In a small number of joint-ownership situations, however, the delinquent taxpayer has no right to force partition or otherwise to alienate the entire property without the consent of the co-owner. These include tenancies by the entirety and certain homestead estates. *See* Plumb, "Federal Liens and Priorities — Agenda for the Next Decade II," 77 Yale L. J. 605, 634 (1968). In this case, the homestead estate owned by the delinquent taxpayer — Mrs. Rodgers' deceased husband — did not include the right to sell or force the sale of the homestead during Mrs. Rodgers' lifetime without her consent. Mrs. Rodgers had, and still has, an indefeasible right to possession, an interest, as the Court recognizes, "akin to an undivided life estate." * * * A lienholder stepping into the shoes of the delinquent taxpayer would not be able to force a sale.

II.

By holding that the District Court has the discretion to order a sale of Mrs. Rodgers' property, the Court necessarily finds in the general language of § 7403 a congressional intent to abrogate the rule that the tax collector's lien does not afford him rights in property in excess of the rights of the delinquent taxpayer. I do not dispute that the general language of § 7403, standing alone, is subject to the interpretation the Court gives it. From its enactment in 1868 to the present day, the language of this statute has been sweeping; read literally, it admits of no exceptions. But when broadly worded statutes, particularly those of some antiquity, are in derogation of common-law principles, this Court has hesitated to heed arguments that they should be applied literally. *See* Imbler v. Pachtman, 424 U.S. 409, 417 (1976). In such cases, the Court has presumed in the absence of a clear indication to the contrary that Congress did not mean by its use of general language to contravene fundamental precepts of the common law.

A.

Apart from the general language of the statute, the Court points to nothing indicating a congressional intent to abrogate the traditional rule. It seems to me, indeed, that the evidence definitely points the other way. Scholarly comment on § 7403, and on § 6321, the tax lien provision, consistently has maintained that, in States such as Texas that confer on each spouse absolute rights to full use and possession of the homestead for life, the homestead property rights of an unindebted spouse may not be sold by the tax collector to satisfy the other spouse's tax debt. Court decisions addressing this point have been to the same effect. * * *

* * *

III.

Without direct evidence of congressional intent to contravene the traditional — and sensible — common-law rule, the Court advances three arguments purporting to lend indirect support for its construction of § 7403.

A.

First, the Court claims that its construction is consistent with the policy favoring "the prompt and certain collection of delinquent taxes." * * * This rationale would support any exercise of governmental power to secure tax payments. Were there two equally plausible suppositions of congressional intent, this policy might counsel in favor of choosing the construction more favorable to the Government. But when one interpretation contravenes both traditional rules of law and the common sense and common values on which they are built, the fact that it favors the Government's interests cannot be dispositive.

Moreover, the Government's interest would not be compromised substantially by a rule permitting it to sell property only when the delinquent taxpayer could have done so. In this case, the delinquent taxpayer's homestead interest, it is assumed, gave him a "half-interest in the underlying ownership rights to the property being sold." * * * An immediate forced sale of the entire property would yield for the Government no more than half the present value of the remainder interest, the residue left after the present values of the nondelinquent spouse's life estate and half-interest in the remainder are subtracted. As the Court notes, the Government can expect to receive only a small fraction of the proceeds. * * * An immediate sale of the delinquent taxpayer's future interest in the property might well command a commensurate price.

Alternatively, the Government could maintain its lien on the property until Mrs. Rodgers dies and then could force a sale. Because the delinquent taxpayer's estate retains a half-interest in the remainder, the Government would be entitled to half of the proceeds at that time. The Government's yield from this future sale, discounted to its present value, should not differ significantly from its yield under the Court's approach. The principal difference is that, following the common-law rule, Mrs. Rodgers' entitlement to live out her life on her homestead would be respected.

* * *

B.

The Court also would support its construction by contrasting § 7403 with the more restrictive language of § 6331, the administrative tax levy provision. * * * It is true that § 6331 permits the sale only of "property and rights to property . . . belonging to" the taxpayer, while § 7403 generally authorizes the sale of property in which the taxpayer has an interest. But the greater power conferred by § 7403 is needed to enable the Government to seek the sale of jointly owned property whenever the tax debtor's rights in the property would have permitted *him* to seek a forced sale. Section 7403 certainly permits the Government, in such circumstances, to seek partition of the property in federal, rather than state, court, to seek authority to sell the tax debtor's part or the whole, and, in the same proceeding, to have determined the entitlements of the various claimants, including competing lienholders, to the proceeds of the property sold. *See generally* Plumb, 77 Yale L. J., at 628–629. Absent the more expansive language of § 7403, this would not be possible. That language, however, does not manifest congressional intent to produce the extraordinary consequences yielded by the Court's interpretation.

C.

* * *

IV.

The Court recognizes that Mrs. Rodgers has an indestructible property right under Texas law to use, possess, and enjoy her homestead during her lifetime, and that the delinquent taxpayer's property interests would not have enabled him to disturb that right against her will. The Court recognizes that Mrs. Rodgers has no outstanding tax liability and that the Government has no lien on Mrs. Rodgers' property or property rights. Because I conclude that Congress did not intend § 7403 to permit federal courts to grant property rights to the Government greater than those enjoyed by the tax debtor, I would hold that the Government may not sell Mrs. Rodgers' homestead without her consent. To the extent the Court holds to the contrary, I respectfully dissent.

V.

Mrs. Ingram's case, however, is materially different. Like her husband, Mrs. Ingram was liable for back taxes, and consequently the Government had a lien on her interests in property as well as on her husband's interests. Exercising both spouses' rights in the homestead, the Government is entitled to force a sale, Plumb, 13 Tax L. Rev., at 263; *see* Shambaugh v. Scofield, 132 F.2d 345 (CA5 1942), subject only to the discretion of the District Court. * * * Second, when Mrs. Ingram and her former husband were divorced, the homestead became subject to partition under Texas law. * * * In Mrs. Ingram's case, therefore, I concur in the result.

In *Rodgers*, the majority and dissent agreed that the government could force a sale of the property in which Mrs. Ingram held an interest but disagreed over the government's authority to force a sale of the property in which Mrs. Rodgers held her homestead interest. Why was the dissent reluctant to allow a forced sale to go forward in Mrs. Rodgers' situation?

Recall the discussion of the Supreme Court's opinion in *United States v. Craft*, discussed above in connection with the federal tax lien. Once the Court confirmed that the federal tax lien could attach to an interest in property held as a tenant by the entireties, the question then arose as to what type of enforced collection action the IRS could take with respect to the property. That particular issue did not create much of a problem on the facts of the *Craft* case because the IRS had already agreed to allow the wife to sell the property to a third party on the condition that she set aside half the sales proceeds in an escrow account for the IRS.[20] Anticipating difficulties in other cases, however, the IRS issued 2003-39 I.R.B. 643, Notice 2003-60, which provides guidance on the application of *Craft* in the form of a series of questions and answers. In the excerpt from Notice 2003-60 set forth below, notice particularly the distinction between the IRS's administrative collection procedure (an administrative sale of the delinquent taxpayer's interest in the entireties property) and the judicially enforced collection alternative (a judicial action to foreclose the lien encumbering the property by forcing a sale of the entire property):

> Q7. Will the Service administratively seize and sell the taxpayer's interest in entireties property?
>
> A7. The Service can administratively seize and sell a taxpayer's interest in real and personal property held in a tenancy by the entirety. Because of the nature of entireties property, it would be very difficult to gauge what market there would be for the taxpayer's interest in the property. The amount of any bid would in all likelihood be depressed to the extent that the prospective purchaser, given the rights of survivorship, would take the risk that the taxpayer may not outlive his or her spouse. In addition, a prospective purchaser would not know with any certainty if, how, and the extent to which the rights acquired in an administrative sale could be enforced. For example, rights acquired would include the right to use the property and the right to exclude others from the property. It is not clear how the rights of a prospective purchaser ultimately would be balanced with the co-existing rights of the spouse of the taxpayer. Therefore, the Service has determined that an administrative sale is not a preferable method of collection with respect to entireties property.
>
> Levying on cash and cash equivalents held as entireties property does not present the same impediments as seizing and selling entireties property. For example, where the Service levies on a bank account that a taxpayer holds as entireties property and has the right to withdraw the funds in the account, the bank is obligated to turn over the funds in response to the levy. While the taxpayer's spouse, as the other account holder, may have an administrative or judicial claim under sections 6343(b) or 7426, respectively, *see* United States v. National Bank of Commerce, 472 U.S. 713 (1985), the amount realizable by the Service is not, at the outset, depressed as it is in the case of administrative sales.
>
> Q8. Will the Service foreclose the federal tax lien against entireties property?

---

[20] Note that had Mr. and Mrs. Craft been jointly liable for the tax debt, the federal tax lien would have encumbered the entire property, thereby allowing the IRS to levy and sell a fee simple interest in the property, pursuant to its administrative collection powers.

> A8. The Service will foreclose the federal tax lien against entireties property in appropriate cases. While in an administrative sale the Service can sell only the taxpayer's interest in entireties property (i.e., not the entire property itself), in a foreclosure action, pursuant to section 7403, the district court has discretion to order the sale of the entire property, even where a non-liable spouse has a protected interest in the property. *See* United States v. Rodgers, 461 U.S. 677 (1983) (principle applied with respect to the sale of homestead property). If the court orders the sale of the property, then the non-liable spouse must be compensated for his or her interest: section 7403 requires "a distribution of the proceeds of such sale according to the findings of the court in respect to the interests of the parties and the United States." Section 7403(c).

Id. at 645.

If the IRS were to file a foreclosure action and sell the Crafts' property, what amount would Mrs. Craft be entitled to receive for her interest? Valuing a spouse's interest in property held as tenants by the entireties has led to disagreement among the courts. The IRS's position in Notice 2003-60 is that, as a general matter, the value of the delinquent spouse's interest is deemed to be one-half. The district court in *Popky v. United States*, 326 F. Supp. 2d 594 (E.D. Pa. 2004), *aff'd*, 2005 U.S. App. LEXIS 8951 (3d Cir. 2005), adopted the IRS's 50-50 division of entireties property for valuation purposes and rejected the taxpayers' argument that the valuation process should take into account the different life expectancies of the two spouses.

> The IRS' proposed fifty-fifty division of the entireties property fails to account for the differing life expectancies of the spouses, and thus the value of each spouse's share fails to reflect the probability that either spouse will ultimately have a right to the whole of the entireties property. In *In re Basher*, 291 B.R. 357 (Bankr. E.D. Pa. 2003), the bankruptcy court refused to value each spouse's interest in the entireties property as fifty percent. Instead, the court valued the debtor's interest as fifty percent of the equity in the property adjusted to reflect the younger age and longer life expectancy of the debtor's wife. *Id.* at 364. The court held that the IRS' proposed fifty-fifty valuation had to be adjusted to consider the impact of the relative survivorship interests of the debtor and his wife. *Id.* at 365–66. The United States Bankruptcy Court for the District of Oregon followed a similar approach in *In re Pletz*, 225 B.R. 206, 209 (Bankr. D. Or. 1997), *aff'd*, 221 F.3d 1114 (9th Cir. 2000). "The entireties interest should be valued for purposes [of] determining the amount of the IRS's secured claim by determining the fair market value of the property and multiplying it by debtor's actuarially determined interest." *Id.*
>
> The government asserts that if I followed the reasoning of the bankruptcy court in *In re Basher*, the relative shares of the plaintiffs in the proceeds from the sale of the Margo Lane property would be 60.902% for Mrs. Popky and 39.198% for Dr. Popky. However, this approach relies on a speculative prediction that both spouses will have an average life span and it neither accounts for the health of the spouses nor for the likelihood of divorce or a sale of the property with the consent of both spouses which could break up the tenancy by the entireties. To include these factors would make valuation infinitely more complicated and would again reach a valuation based merely on speculation. I conclude the only equitable solution to the valuation of Mrs. Popky's interest in the entireties property is to divide the proceeds equally between her and Dr. Popky. The federal tax lien can therefore properly attach to one-half the value of the proceeds from the sale of the Margo Lane property.

Popky, 326 F. Supp. 2d at 602–03 (footnotes omitted); *see also* In re Gallivan, 312 B.R. 662 (Bankr. W.D. Mo. 2004) (following the valuation approach in *Popky*). *Cf.* In re Murray, 318 B.R. 211 (M.D. Fla. 2004) (following valuation approach applied in *Pletz* that determines the value of a taxpayer's interest in tenancy by the entireties property by taking into account the relative life expectancies of the two tenants).

[B] Judicial Proceedings Instituted by the Taxpayer

Reading Assignment: I.R.C. § 7421; 28 U.S.C. § 2410.

Because of its sovereign immunity, the United States cannot be sued in court without its specific consent. Although Code section 7421, referred to as the "Anti-Injunction Act," contains a specific prohibition against suits to restrain assessment or collection of any tax, it does not operate as an absolute bar. The Code itself lists a series of statutory exceptions, while the Supreme Court has created a judicial exception to the general rule prohibiting injunctions. The following case is typical of a taxpayer suit against the IRS to enjoin collection. How effective a remedy is it?

POWERS v. GIBBS

United States District Court, District of Columbia
1989 U.S. Dist. LEXIS 12302 (1989)

Thomas F. Hogan, United States District Judge:

This action is before the Court on defendants' motion to dismiss. Because the Court has considered matters outside of the pleadings, the motion shall be treated as one for summary judgment. Rule 12(b) Fed. R. Civ. P.

On July 14, 1988, plaintiff, a citizen of Ohio, filed this suit to enjoin the Internal Revenue Service (the "IRS") from seizing his property and from continuing to levy on his wages. In 1987, the IRS assessed a deficiency against the plaintiff to recover taxes owed in 1982 and 1983. Plaintiff alleges that the collection activities are void and violate his constitutional due process rights because the IRS failed to assess his deficiency or provide him with the required notice of assessment and demand for payment. In addition to the equitable relief, plaintiff requests $500,000 in compensatory damages and $500,000,000 in punitive damages. Defendants argue that the Court lacks subject matter jurisdiction to entertain plaintiff's claim for equitable relief and that defendants are immune from suit for damages. For the reasons stated below, the Court shall grant summary judgment to defendants and shall dismiss this case.

Plaintiff's suit is essentially one to enjoin the federal government from collecting revenue. Such suits are generally barred by 26 U.S.C. § 7421 (the "Anti-Injunction Act"). The Anti-Injunction Act states that "except as provided in sections 6212(a) and (c), 6672(b), 6694(c), 7426(a) and (b)(1), and 7429(b), no suit for the purposes of restraining the assessment or collection of any tax shall be maintained in any court by any person, whether or not such person is the person against whom such tax was assessed." The purpose of the Act is to permit the United States to assess and collect taxes without judicial interference and to require that disputes be determined in a suit for refund. The United States is thus assured of prompt collection of its lawful revenue. Enochs v. Williams Packing & Navigation Co., 370 U.S. 1 (1962).

The Anti-Injunction Act, however, does not bar suit in equity if the taxpayer establishes facts that bring him under one of the statutory exceptions. In addition, a judicially-created exception permits a federal court to entertain a suit to enjoin the IRS's tax collection activities, but only if the taxpayer can show: (1) that under the most liberal view of the law and facts available to the government at the time of the suit, it is apparent that the government cannot prevail on the merits; and (2) that irreparable injury will occur for which there is no adequate remedy at law. *Enochs v. Williams Packing & Navigation Co.*, 370 U.S. at 6–7.

Plaintiff does not allege any facts that bring him within any of the Act's exceptions. He contends merely that the levy and seizure are illegal because the IRS did not properly "assess" his deficiency. The plaintiff also contends that the IRS failed to notify him formally of the assessment and demand payment of the deficiency. Before these claim can be considered, a brief summary of the relevant IRS administrative procedures is necessary.

The IRS may not collect a tax deficiency until it sends, by certified or registered mail, a notice of deficiency to the taxpayer. 26 U.S.C. §§ 6212(a), 6213. The taxpayer has 90 days from the date the notice is mailed to petition the Tax Court for redetermination of the deficiency. Failure to file within the 90 day period deprives the Tax Court of jurisdiction to consider the deficiency. Keado v. United States, 853 F.2d 1209, 1212 (5th Cir. 1988). If the taxpayer does not file a petition with the Tax Court within 90 days, the IRS may assess the deficiency. Thereafter, the IRS must within sixty days notify the taxpayer of the assessment and demand payment of the unpaid tax. 26 U.S.C. § 6303. If the taxpayer neglects or refuses to pay within ten days after notice and demand, the IRS may commence collection action. 26 U.S.C. § 6331.[n.2] Once a notice of deficiency has been properly mailed to the taxpayer and the deficiency properly assessed, the taxpayer's only recourse to challenge the IRS's determination is to pay the deficiency and commence a refund suit in the district court. 26 U.S.C. § 7421–22; *Enochs v. Williams Packing and Navigation Co.*, 370 U.S. at 8.

The record shows that plaintiff did not petition the Tax Court for redetermination of his deficiency for either 1982 or 1983. Plaintiff does not contend that the IRS failed to properly mail the deficiency notices. However, he claims that the deficiency was not properly assessed because the defendants have not produced a document known as Form 23C, which must be executed if a deficiency is to be properly assessed. The relevant code provision requires "[t]hat assessment shall be made by recording the liability of the taxpayer in the office of the Secretary in accordance with rules and regulations prescribed by the Secretary." 26 U.S.C. § 6203. In addition, 26 C.F.R. 301.6203-1 provides that "[t]he assessment shall be made by an assessment officer signing the summary record of assessment. The summary record through supporting records, shall provide identification of the taxpayer, the character of the liability assessed, the taxable period, if applicable, and the amount of the assessment. . . . The date of the assessment is the date the summary record is signed by an assessment officer. . . ." The document described in the above regulation is known as "Form 23C." *United States v. Dixon*, 672 F. Supp. at 503, 504. Defendants have produced a "Certificate of Assessment and Payments" for each year's deficiency which plaintiff has not rebutted. The Certificate is signed by an IRS officer certifying that it is a true transcript of all the assessments, penalties, interests, and payments on record for the plaintiff. Specifically, the Certificate reflects that deficiencies were assessed on October 12, 1987, and October 26, 1989 (the "23C" dates) for 1982 and 1983. The Certificate is presumptive proof of a valid assessment in this case, notwithstanding the fact that the IRS has failed to produce the "23C" form. *See* United States v. Miller, 318 F.2d 637, 639 (7th Cir. 1983); United States v. Dixon, 672 F. Supp. 503, 505–506 (M.D. Ala. 1987). Furthermore, the Court takes judicial notice that the "23C" date in the Certificate refers to the dates on which the proper records were signed by the assessment officer. United States v. Posner, 405 F. Supp. 934, 937 (D. Md. 1975). The Court therefore finds that there is no genuine issue regarding whether or not a valid assessment was performed.

In addition to his claim of an invalid assessment, plaintiff contends that the levy and seizure must be enjoined because he was not provided a post-assessment notice and demand for payment as required by 26 U.S.C. § 6303. This claim also lacks merit. The

---

[n.2] The Court finds no merit to the plaintiff's argument that the IRS's prejudicial levy activities violate his Fifth Amendment due process rights. The constitutionality of the statutory levy procedures is well-established. Commissioner of Internal Revenue v. Shapiro, 424 U.S. 614, 630–32 n.12 (1976); Baddour, Inc. v. United States, 802 F.2d 801, 807 (5th Cir. 1986).

Court notes that the Certificate of Records and Assessments, which is a record of the transactions and correspondence following the assessment, reflects that the plaintiff received "first notices" for both the 1982 and 1983 assessments. The IRS's Notice of Levy on plaintiff's wages recites that notice and demand were made on the defendant pursuant to the Internal Revenue Code. Plaintiff made four payments following assessment of the 1982 deficiency. *See* Defendants' Motion to Dismiss, Exhibit B. The Court therefore also finds no genuine issue of fact on the present record that defendants fully complied with section 6303. *See* United States v. Lorson Electric Co., 480 F.2d 554 (2d Cir. 1973) (IRS complied with § 6303 requirements when its tax lien notice stated that there had been a demand for payment and the Certificate of Assessments and Payments stated that the taxpayer had received a first notice).

As the prior discussion makes clear, plaintiff's case does not fall within the *Enochs* exception to the Anti-Injunction Act because plaintiff has failed to satisfy the first prong of the *Enochs* test, as it is likely that the IRS will prevail on the merits. Notwithstanding that finding, however, the Court additionally finds that plaintiff has failed to satisfy the second prong of the *Enochs* test, as plaintiff has not shown that he will suffer irreparable injury.[n.3]

With respect to the second prong of the *Enochs* test, plaintiff has alleged that he is unable to provide for his family's basic needs as a result of the IRS's continuing to levy on his assets. Even if these unsupported claims were true, the Court finds that the plaintiff has an adequate remedy at law — namely, paying the delinquent taxes and filing a refund suit. Moreover, it is well established that financial hardship alone is insufficient to justify injunctive relief against IRS collection activities. Laino v. United States, 633 F.2d 626, 630 (2d Cir. 1980) ("[I]t is decisive that [plaintiff] failed to exhaust [his] legal remedies by neglecting to petition the Tax Court for redetermination of the deficiency . . . [Plaintiff] here [has] utterly failed to explain why [he] chose not to follow this generous avenue of relief. Under the circumstances, [plaintiff] cannot be heard to complain [he] now lack[s] an adequate remedy at law"); Lucia v. United States, 474 F.2d 565, 577 (5th Cir. 1973) (hardship alone is insufficient to justify injunctive relief).

The Court therefore lacks subject matter jurisdiction to entertain plaintiff's claim for equitable relief pursuant to the Anti-Injunction Act.

Plaintiff's remaining damages claims must also fail for the reasons stated above. The Court has found no genuine issue of material fact regarding whether or not defendants acted lawfully. Defendants are therefore entitled to immunity from such damages claims for acts taken in their official capacities. *See* Harlow v. Fitzgerald, 457 U.S. 800, 818 (1981).

Accordingly, the Court shall grant summary judgment for defendants and shall dismiss this action. An Order in accordance with this Memorandum Opinion shall be issued herewith.

* * *

Ordered that defendants' motion to dismiss, which the Court has treated as one for summary judgment, is hereby granted and this case is hereby dismissed.

Is the right to file a refund suit an adequate remedy at law for a taxpayer who does not have the funds to gain jurisdiction to a refund forum? And how would a court determine whether pre-payment followed by a refund suit is a viable remedy? Consider

---

[n.3] Both prongs of the *Enochs* test must be satisfied before the clear command of the Anti-Injunction Act can be overcome. Bob Jones University v. Simon, 416 U.S. 725, 745 (1974); Kemlon Products and Development Co. v. United States, 638 F.2d 1315 (5th Cir.), *modified on other grounds*, 646 F.2d 223 (1981).

the following excerpt from *MacKenzie v. IRS*, 2005 U.S. Dist. LEXIS 12437, a case in which the taxpayers sought an injunction to prevent the IRS from collecting tax:

> To prove an inadequate remedy at law, a taxpayer must show that payment of the disputed tax would deprive him or his family of the "necessities of life" Jensen v. I.R.S., 835 F.2d 196, 198 (9th Cir. 1987). To accomplish this, the taxpayer must submit detailed evidence of his financial situation, including evidence of his income, assets, liabilities, and expenses, so that the court can determine his ability to pay. *See id.* at 198–99; *Gibson v. United States*, 761 F. Supp. 685, 691–92 (C.D. Cal. 1991); *Hillyer v. C.I.R.*, 817 F. Supp. 532, 537–38 (M.D. Pa. 1993).
>
> * * *
>
> Plaintiffs fail to demonstrate the lack of an adequate remedy at law. Plaintiffs owe the IRS $13,179.00 in back taxes plus $18,154.77 in penalties and interest. . . . Plaintiffs recently possessed sufficient funds to pay these sums. According to plaintiffs, their family of three has been living off of approximately $20,000 a year. However, they earned an extra $50,000 in income in 2003. Plaintiffs do not account for how this additional income was spent.
>
> * * *
>
> Even if plaintiffs could adequately account for the use of these extra funds, plaintiffs still fail to provide an adequately detailed picture of their overall financial situation so as to provide a basis for determining their ability to pay. The record contains no information about plaintiffs' assets, including their interest in stocks, bonds, savings accounts, or other liquid or unliquidated assets. For example, it appears that plaintiffs own a home, but they do not inform the court of the equity they own in that home. . . . If this equity is reachable without irreparable consequences, plaintiffs may be required to use that equity to satisfy their tax debts prior to bringing a refund suit; therefore, this information is essential to a determination of plaintiffs' ability to pay. *See Shannahan v. United States*, 47 F. Supp. 2d 1128, 1144 (S.D. Cal. 1999) (declining to find that plaintiffs' loss of their home would deprive them of the necessities of life); *see also Hillyer*, 817 F. Supp. at 537 (finding that the loss of a home would cause irreparable injury where there was evidence that plaintiffs would be homeless without it). Plaintiffs' decision to place their child in a private school and pay school tuition cuts against their claim of inability to pay. . . . The amount of tuition is not provided.
>
> Plaintiffs assert that their various debts prevent them from paying the disputed taxes. . . . However, the evidence does not support this assertion. Plaintiffs admit that many of their debts, including those connected to their business, are collected on a flexible basis or are disputed by them. There is no evidence that plaintiffs will lose their business or home if they first honor their debt to the IRS. At most, the evidence shows that plaintiffs have found it difficult to juggle their various financial responsibilities and have put the tax deficiency at the bottom of the list. However, "[h]ardship in raising money with which to pay taxes is now common to all taxpayers." *Monge v. Smyth*, 229 F.2d 361, 368 n.8 (9th Cir. 1956) (quotation omitted). This hardship does not confer "equity jurisdiction on the courts to prevent collection by injunctive process." *Id.*

2005 U.S. Dist. LEXIS 12437.

Another type of proceeding that may involve the government, despite the Anti-Injunction Act prohibition, is a suit filed under 28 U.S.C. section 2410. This provision permits the United States to be joined as a party to a quiet title proceeding relating to property against which the United States holds a lien. Normally the suit is filed by a third party lienholder claiming priority over the government's lien in an attempt to obtain an adjudication confirming their superior status. The following case, brought by the taxpayers themselves, raises the question of whether the parties may litigate the validity of the government's tax lien as part of a quiet title suit.

ROBINSON v. UNITED STATES

United States Court of Appeals, Third Circuit
920 F.2d 1157 (1990)

Weis, Circuit Judge.

Asserting a procedural defect, taxpayers challenged an Internal Revenue Service lien via a suit under 28 U.S.C. § 2410(a). The district court dismissed for lack of jurisdiction concluding that the taxpayers' attack necessarily struck at the underlying assessment, a result it believed was barred by this Court's precedent. We reverse. Our prohibition against assaults on the "merits of an assessment" applies to the amount of tax due and does not prevent scrutiny of procedural lapses by the IRS.

In 1971 the Internal Revenue Service assessed plaintiffs for unpaid income taxes for the years 1968 and 1969. Because of taxes assertedly due for those years, the IRS filed liens in Montgomery County, Pennsylvania against the home that plaintiffs own.

Plaintiffs filed this action to quiet title under 28 U.S.C. § 2410(a). The complaint alleged that the government failed to comply with the statutory procedures for creating a lien, specifically that the IRS never issued a notice of deficiency to plaintiffs before assessing the tax due. For the purposes of its motion to dismiss, the IRS conceded that a notice of deficiency was not sent, but asserted that jurisdiction was lacking because sovereign immunity barred plaintiffs from attacking the merits of the assessment under section 2410(a). The district court agreed that the suit was essentially a challenge to the assessments, and dismissed for lack of jurisdiction.

I.

In the Internal Revenue Code Congress has specified steps for the creation of a lien arising out of unpaid taxes. After preliminary steps, when the IRS believes that the taxpayers have not paid all or any part of their income tax due, the following procedures apply.

1. The IRS mails a notice of deficiency to the taxpayers by certified or registered mail. 26 U.S.C. § 6212(a). Once this notice has been mailed, the taxpayers have ninety days in which to file a petition for redetermination in the Tax Court. 26 U.S.C. § 6213.

The notice of deficiency, sometimes called a "ninety day" letter, is the taxpayers' "ticket to the Tax Court" to litigate the merits of the deficiency determination, Delman v. Commissioner, 384 F.2d 929, 934 (3d Cir. 1967), *cert. denied*, 390 U.S. 952, 88 S. Ct. 1044, 19 L. Ed. 2d 1144 (1968), and is a jurisdictional prerequisite to a suit in that forum. Laing v. United States, 423 U.S. 161, 165 n.4, 96 S. Ct. 473, 46 L. Ed. 2d 416 (1976). Until ninety days have passed, the IRS can neither make an assessment nor utilize Court procedures for collection. Holof v. Commissioner, 872 F.2d 50, 53 (3d Cir. 1989). If the taxpayers file in the Tax Court within that period, the restraint on the IRS continues until the decision of the Court becomes final. 26 U.S.C. § 6213(a).

2. If the taxpayers do not file a petition in the Tax Court within the specified time, the IRS makes an assessment. 26 U.S.C. § 6213(c). A duly designated official for the district or regional tax center signs the summary record of the assessment, which identifies the taxpayers, the type of tax owed, the taxable period and the amount of the assessment. 26 U.S.C. § 6203; Treas. Reg. § 301.6203-1.

3. As soon as practicable and within sixty days after making the assessment, the IRS must issue a "notice and demand letter" to the taxpayers, specifying the amount due and demanding payment. 26 U.S.C. § 6303.

4. If the taxpayers do not pay after demand, the IRS may file a lien against their property. 26 U.S.C. § 6321. *See generally* Wilkens & Matthews, "A Survey of Federal Tax Collection Procedure: Rights and Remedies of Taxpayers and the Internal Revenue Service," 3 Alaska L. Rev. 269 (1986).

The first of these procedures — the provision requiring the IRS to issue a notice of deficiency — is the focal point of this case.

The notice is a "pivotal feature of the Code's assessment procedures," *Holof,* 872 F.2d at 53, because it serves as a prerequisite to a valid assessment by the IRS. The Internal Revenue Code is clear that "no assessment of a deficiency . . . and no levy or proceeding in court for its collection shall be made, begun, or prosecuted until such notice [of deficiency] has been mailed to the taxpayer, nor until the expiration of such 90-day . . . period." 26 U.S.C. § 6213(a). By providing an opportunity to litigate the merits of the deficiency in the Tax Court without requiring payment of the full amount allegedly owed, the statute provides substantial benefits to taxpayers.

Because this is an appeal from an order granting a motion to dismiss, we accept the plaintiffs' allegations that the IRS did not send a notice of deficiency but did file a lien in the county courthouse. *See* Matthews v. Freedman, 882 F.2d 83, 84 (3d Cir. 1989). Although these facts present a seemingly straightforward case of the IRS's failure to comply with the Code, the jurisdictional aspect of the suit in the district court must be resolved.

II.

In this appeal the IRS maintains that taxpayers' remedies are restricted to injunctive relief, refund actions or petitions to the Tax Court. Having "provided for situations such as this, and dictated the manner in which taxpayers should proceed," IRS Brief at 23, Congress did not intend to waive sovereign immunity in such cases brought under 2410(a). Plaintiffs point out that the absence of a notice of deficiency barred their right to proceed in the Tax Court, and that injunctive relief is not available.

III.

28 U.S.C. § 2410(a) provides that "the United States may be named a party in any civil action or suit in any district court . . . (1) to quiet title to . . . real or personal property on which the United States has or claims a mortgage or other lien."

Despite the broad wording of section 2410(a), courts have been cautious in permitting its use in tax cases. Recognizing that Congress has provided an elaborate system for litigating tax claims in the Tax Court before payment and in District Court and the Court of Claims for refunds, courts have hesitated to add to the remedies provided by the Internal Revenue Code. Section 2410(a) is a statute of general applicability, applying to all liens and not limited to those created by tax delinquencies, and therefore the courts have favored the specific procedures of the Code. *See e.g.,* Flora v. United States, 362 U.S. 145, 157, 80 S. Ct. 630, 4 L. Ed. 2d 623 (1960).

This attitude is reflected in the oft-cited opinion of *Falik v. United States,* 343 F.2d 38 (2d Cir. 1965). There, the IRS placed a lien on the taxpayer's home after determining that, as a responsible corporate officer, she was liable for social security and withholding taxes. The taxpayer attempted to use section 2410(a) to contest the validity of the lien on the ground that the IRS erred in holding her liable. The Court of Appeals concluded that Congress did not intend section 2410(a) to overturn the longstanding principle that except as to matters within the jurisdiction of the Tax Court, "a person whose sole claim is that a federal tax assessment was not well grounded in fact and law must 'pay first and litigate later.' " *Id.* at 42. Significantly, however, access to the Tax Court was not available to the taxpayer in that case.

The principle that a taxpayer cannot use section 2410(a) to challenge the extent of, or existence of, substantive tax liability is well-settled. In *Yannicelli v. Nash,* 354 F. Supp.

143, 151 (D. N.J. 1972), the district court noted that our Court has interpreted section 2410(a) to confer subject matter jurisdiction "provided that the plaintiff refrains from collaterally attacking the merits of the Government's tax assessment itself." In ruling on a motion for reconsideration, the district judge emphasized that "the 'merits' which the district court may not review in such an action include any issue touching upon the actual extent of the taxpayer's federal tax liability." *Id.* at 157 n.4.

The most significant case addressing the issue before us is *Aqua Bar & Lounge, Inc. v. United States*, 539 F.2d 935 (3d Cir. 1976). There, we confronted a challenge to the legality of the IRS's seizure and sale of a taxpayer's property because of nonpayment of taxes. The taxpayer admitted that the tax was due, but asserted that the IRS had failed to comply with the statutory requirements for a sale. We concluded that section 2410(a) waived sovereign immunity to a suit "which challenges the validity of a federal tax lien and sale so long as the taxpayer refrains from contesting the merits of the underlying tax assessment itself." *Id.* at 939–40.

In several instances in the *Aqua Bar* opinion the Court referred to disputes over the "merits of the underlying tax assessment" and determined that so long as no such attack was made, a suit under section 2410(a) did not "undermine the established administrative and judicial framework for resolving an individual's tax liability." *Id.* at 939. Significantly, the panel said "in the absence of a Congressional directive to the contrary, we refuse to place such a narrowing construction on § 2410 and thus deprive a taxpayer of any remedy against arbitrary administrative action." *Id.*

Other Courts of Appeals have cited *Aqua Bar* with approval. *See* Estate of Johnson, 836 F.2d 940, 944 (5th Cir. 1988) ("Several circuits have held that a taxpayer may use section 2410(a) to contest the procedural regularity of a lien."); Pollack v. United States, 819 F.2d 144, 145 (6th Cir. 1987) ("A suit under 28 U.S.C. § 2410 is proper only to contest the procedural regularity of a lien; it may not be used to challenge the underlying tax liability.").

IV.

Against this background we consider the issue raised by the parties. Any suit against the federal government must of course clear the hurdle of sovereign immunity and, in many tax cases, the Anti-Injunction Act, 26 U.S.C. § 7421(a). That statute provides that "except as provided in section[] . . . 6213(a), . . . no suit for the purpose of restraining the assessment or collection of any tax shall be maintained in any court by any person." Section 6213(a) states, "Notwithstanding the provisions of section 7421(a) [the Anti-Injunction Act], the making of such assessment or the beginning of such proceeding or levy during the time such prohibition is in force may be enjoined by a proceeding in the proper court."

Because section 6213(a), requiring a notice of assessment, provides an exception to the Anti-Injunction Act, at first glance it would appear that plaintiffs could have sought an injunction. However, "Congress, in enacting Section 6213(a), did not repudiate the principle that injunctive relief is an extraordinary remedy which is unavailable absent a showing of irreparable injury and no adequate remedy at law." Flynn v. United States, 786 F.2d 586, 590 (3d Cir. 1986). *See also* Commissioner v. Shapiro, 424 U.S. 614, 633, 96 S. Ct. 1062, 47 L. Ed. 2d 278 (1976).

Plaintiffs assert that it is unlikely that they could show the absence of a remedy at law, particularly because the option to file a refund action is available. The IRS seems to agree and, in addition, asserts that another remedy is available — a petition in the Tax Court. The IRS, however, has directed us to no authority on the latter point. We have found no instance in which the Tax Court has been granted jurisdiction over an income tax claim when a notice of deficiency was not sent. Indeed, the statutory language and case law are to the contrary. *Laing*, 423 U.S. at 165 n.4; *Delman*, 384 F.2d at 934 (3d Cir. 1967) ("It is true that unless a notice of deficiency is mailed to the taxpayer the Tax Court may not acquire jurisdiction.").

In the absence of a remedy in the Tax Court, the IRS argument seems to be reduced to the proposition that the possibility of filing a refund suit indicates that Congress did not intend to waive sovereign immunity in tax cases filed under section 2410(a). Because there is no evidence of such a Congressional intent and the IRS position is not supported by case law or logic, we reject that argument as not persuasive.

In addition, the IRS asserts that *Aqua Bar* does not apply because failure to send out a notice of deficiency inevitably undermines the procedures required to establish a valid assessment and, therefore, the challenge to the procedural integrity of the lien is in reality an attack on the substantive tax assessment. For the purpose of this suit, however, plaintiffs admit that the taxes are due and, consequently, they maintain there is no attack on the assessment. According to the district court, plaintiffs attacked the assessments: "If it were true that [plaintiffs] are challenging the tax liens on any basis which does not also amount to a challenge of the underlying assessment, their argument might be acceptable. But I am not persuaded that is the case."

Relying on *Aqua Bar*, plaintiffs maintain that a challenge to the procedural irregularity of the tax lien creates jurisdiction, particularly because they concede the amount owed. Certainly the plaintiffs' request for relief is based solely on the lien's procedural infirmity resulting from the failure to send the notice of deficiency. But, as the district court recognized, the theoretical prospect of remedying that procedural defect without altering the assessment itself presents some difficulties in practice. Although we think the distinction could be made in some highly sophisticated and rather unrealistic fashion, in the end we believe it is unnecessary to do so.

We reach that conclusion because the IRS has misconstrued the "merits of the underlying tax assessment" as articulated in *Aqua Bar*. A proper reading is that for jurisdictional purposes under section 2410(a), "merits" refers to the liability for the amount, if any, of tax due. *See Yannicelli*, 354 F. Supp. 143. *Aqua Bar* does not prohibit inquiry into procedural defects, and indeed the Court refused to adopt a narrow construction of section 2410(a) that would deprive taxpayers of a remedy against arbitrary administrative action.

Critical to our resolution of this issue is that the IRS's failure to send a notice of deficiency denied plaintiffs an opportunity to litigate the merits of the alleged deficiency in the Tax Court. This factor was not present either in *Aqua Bar* or in *Falik*. In both cases the Courts were concerned with preserving the expeditious methods of tax collection which Congress had created. Consequently, the taxpayers were not allowed to use section 2410(a) to evade "the pay first and sue later" refund suits — the only remedy authorized in the factual circumstances of those cases.

In the income tax case here, however, Congress has authorized an additional remedy, suit in the Tax Court before payment, and has clearly spelled out the prerequisites. Had the notice of deficiency been sent, plaintiffs would have had the right to file a petition in the Tax Court and under section 6213(a) no assessment could have been made before a decision by that Court. Opening the procedural deficiencies of the assessment to question under section 2410(a) in these circumstances, therefore, does not do violence to the collection system created in the Internal Revenue Code. Indeed, to read section 2410(a) in this manner preserves the options granted to the taxpayers and grants them the means, perhaps not otherwise available, to correct an arbitrary administrative action.

For these reasons we hold that in an income tax dispute cognizable in the Tax Court, jurisdiction under section 2410(a) is proper when the procedural error blocking access to the Tax Court may also impugn the procedural validity of the assessment. Consistent with the weight of authority we neither permit attacks on the amount of the assessment nor entertain assertions that no tax is owed.

We recognize that our decision on this point may seem to be at odds with those of the

Courts of Appeals for the Ninth and Tenth Circuits in *Elias v. Connett*, 908 F.2d 521 (9th Cir. 1990) and *Schmidt v. King*, 913 F.2d 837 (10th Cir. 1990), respectively. We are uncertain about the position of those Courts in those two cases because the opinions are unclear in discussing the governmental errors which are encompassed within section 2410(a) jurisdiction. To the extent, however, that those opinions may be understood to hold that the "merits of the underlying assessment" include procedural defects and prevents examination of such errors under section 2410(a), they are inconsistent with *Aqua Bar* and we find them nonpersuasive.

Congress has created an elaborate system for the collection and dispute of tax matters. Adherence to these procedures is required by both citizens and the IRS alike. As one commentator remarked, "The procedural provisions of the Code appear to be the creation of a scholastic, but whimsical, mind. In general, however, the courts take them literally: the game must be played according to the rules." Johnson, "An Inquiry Into the Assessment Process," 35 Tax L. Rev. 285, 286 (1980). In the factual situation assumed here, the IRS broke the rules.

Accordingly, the order of the district court will be reversed. The case will be remanded for further proceedings consistent with this Opinion, including a resolution of contested factual matters.

Procedurally, how might the plaintiffs in *Robinson* have litigated the issue of the validity of the tax lien in Tax Court? Also, why did the *Robinson* court distinguish between procedural defects and the substantive merits of the assessment? In this regard, consider *Koff v. United States*, 3 F.3d 1297 (9th Cir. 1993) (O'Scannlain, Circuit Judge, concurring), *cert. denied*, 511 U.S. 1030 (1994), which highlights the "split of authority" in the Ninth Circuit concerning whether a notice of deficiency represents a procedural or substantive question of law for purposes of 28 U.S.C. section 2410.

PROBLEMS

1. Is the collection of federal tax debts appropriate for a private enterprise or is this an inherently governmental function that should be carried out by IRS employees, in your opinion?
2. On May 1, Year 1, the IRS mailed to Molly's last known address a Notice and Demand for Payment of a $10,000 income tax liability. Two weeks later, Molly consented to the assessment of the liability by signing a Form 870. Accordingly, on February 1, Year 2 the IRS summarily assessed the liability.
   - A. On what date does the federal tax lien for the $10,000 unpaid tax liability arise?
   - B. Assuming Molly does not contest the IRS's collection actions, when is the last date that the IRS can collect the Year 1 tax liability?
   - C. To what property interests does the tax lien attach? What types of property that Molly may own would be exempt from the lien?
   - D. If the IRS decided to institute a levy proceeding in order to collect the unpaid amounts, what types of property that Molly may own would be exempt from levy?
3. The IRS has properly filed a Notice of Federal Tax Lien against Charlie's houseboat, the QE2. After the IRS filed the Notice of Federal Tax Lien, Charlie acquires another houseboat, the QE3.
   - A. Does the federal tax lien attach to the QE3? Does it matter whether the IRS has filed a Notice of Federal Tax Lien against the QE3?
   - B. Assume that the IRS has satisfied all the necessary prerequisites to seize the QE2. As part of that same levy proceeding, may the IRS also seize the

QE3?

C. If the IRS wrongfully levies against the QE3, what avenue of relief is available to Charlie?

4. Two years ago, the IRS assessed a $50,000 tax liability arising from Nathan's Year 1 tax return, and, shortly thereafter, sent him a Notice and Demand for Payment. At the time, Nathan owned no property. Instead, he lived with his grandfather who had a protracted illness that required constant care and attention, which Nathan provided. One year ago, Nathan's grandfather died. Nathan claims that he provided care and attention to his grandfather in exchange for his grandfather's promise to leave him a one-half interest in a piece of real estate that the grandfather owned. Nathan's grandfather died intestate in the state of Alabama, where the real estate is located.

   A. The IRS takes the position that Nathan owns a one-half interest as tenant in common in the real estate (the other one-half interest being owned equally by the grandfather's ten children) and that the federal tax lien attaches to that one-half interest. How would a court decide the extent of Nathan's interest in the property and whether it is subject to the federal tax lien?

   B. Assuming that a court would find that Nathan held a valid one-half interest as a tenant in common in the property, and assuming that the IRS followed all applicable procedural requirements, can the IRS levy against the property and administratively sell Nathan's interest in order to satisfy his outstanding tax liability? Does it matter whether the real property consists of a home that Nathan currently occupies as his primary residence?

   C. What other options does the IRS have to collect the unpaid liability based on Nathan's interest in the real estate?

5. Beth operates a local appliance store as a sole proprietorship. On June 1, Year 3, the IRS validly assessed a $25,000 liability arising from Beth's failure to pay income taxes during Year 1. On March 1, Year 4, after Beth repeatedly ignored IRS notices and demands for payment, the IRS properly recorded a Notice of Federal Tax Lien against all of Beth's assets.

   Six months prior to the recording of the federal tax lien, on September 1, Year 3, Beth borrowed $50,000 from the Third National Bank. To secure payment of the $50,000 advanced to Beth, the bank took a security interest in the inventory of Beth's appliance store. The bank made no effort to perfect its security interest until April 1, Year 4.

   A. Does the bank's security interest take priority over the government's federal tax lien?

   B. Would the answer to Part A change if the bank had perfected its security interest under state law on September 15, Year 3?

6. After Joel was audited by the IRS in early Year 3, the IRS assessed a $15,000 income tax liability arising from Joel's Year 1 tax year. At the conclusion of the audit, in March of Year 3, Joel moved from New York to California, and submitted his Year 2 return in April Year 3 using his new California address. In August of Year 3, the IRS mailed to Joel's prior address in New York a notice of deficiency setting forth the $15,000 liability. Months later, when Joel did not respond to the notice of deficiency, the IRS sent a Notice and Demand for Payment to the New York address. Because Joel did not respond to either notice, the IRS has sought to levy against an undeveloped tract of land Joel owns in California. What judicial remedies are available to Joel to prevent the IRS from collecting the tax liability by seizing and selling the California property?

Chapter 15

OFFERS IN COMPROMISE, INSTALLMENT AGREEMENTS, AND BANKRUPTCY CONSIDERATIONS

§ 15.01 INTRODUCTION

As a general proposition, the IRS does not take into account the taxpayer's ability to pay a tax debt when determining the extent of the taxpayer's liability. The IRS also typically does not consider ability to pay during settlement negotiations with the taxpayer. Even if the taxpayer or tax advisor is successful in negotiating a settlement totaling only a fraction of the originally asserted deficiency, this may be a hollow victory if the taxpayer cannot come up with the funds to pay the settled amount. Because the IRS's enforced collection procedures can seriously disrupt the taxpayer's business and employment relationships and jeopardize the taxpayer's credit rating, it is important for the taxpayer and his or her representative to attempt to negotiate the method of payment before the IRS files a Notice of Federal Tax Lien. This part of the negotiation can be just as important as settling the underlying tax liability.

All too often, however, an attorney may be called in to assist the taxpayer in a collection matter at the "last minute," after the IRS has already filed a Notice of Federal Tax Lien. Even at this late date, the representative should (1) confirm that the underlying liability has been properly assessed and (2) determine whether the statute of limitations on collection remains open. Both of these matters can be established by requesting from the IRS a copy of the taxpayer's transcript of account, obtained by filing Form 4506, Request for Copy or Transcript of Tax Form.[1] Identifying the assessment date is important not only for purposes of confirming whether the statute of limitations on collection has expired, but also because, as discussed in Chapter 14, the date of assessment fixes the date on which the federal tax lien arose. This latter determination may also be important should priority conflicts arise.

This chapter examines other procedures and options a taxpayer or representative should consider, including installment agreements and offers in compromise, once the IRS threatens collection proceedings. As a general matter, an installment agreement allows the taxpayer to pay an assessed liability over time, while an offer in compromise may permit the taxpayer to pay less than the total amount of the assessed deficiency. Both of these issues may be raised as part of a Collection Due Process (CDP) hearing, a topic discussed in detail in Chapter 16. The CDP procedures provide the taxpayer the opportunity for administrative review of his or her case before the IRS levies on the taxpayer's property, followed by judicial review of the Appeals Officer's determination in the Tax Court. *See* I.R.C. §§ 6320, 6330. Another option for some taxpayers faced with enforced collection action is the possibility of innocent spouse relief. The innocent spouse rules and procedures are discussed in Chapter 17.

---

[1] The exact date of assessment is determined based on the record of assessment signed by the assessment officer. *See* Treas. Reg. § 301.6203-1. The assessment date appearing in the taxpayer's transcript of account normally reflects the record date. A copy of the taxpayer's record of assessment may also be obtained through a FOIA request. *See* Powers v. Gibbs, 1989 U.S. District LEXIS 12302 (1989). The procedures for making a FOIA request are discussed in Chapter 6.

§ 15.02 TAXPAYER ASSISTANCE ORDERS AND AUDIT RECONSIDERATION

Reading Assignment: I.R.C. § 7811.

[A] Taxpayer Assistance Orders

Code section 7811 permits the Office of Taxpayer Advocate to suspend IRS collection activity as part of a Taxpayer Assistance Order ("TAO"), if to do otherwise would result in significant hardship for the taxpayer. I.R.C. § 7811(a). The taxpayer makes the request using Form 911, Application for Taxpayer Assistance Order to Relieve Hardship. "[I]rreparable injury to, or a long-term adverse impact on, the taxpayer if relief is not granted" is among the factors listed in section 7811 for determining whether a significant hardship exists. I.R.C. § 7811(a)(2)(D). Mere economic or personal inconvenience to the taxpayer, however, does not satisfy the standard. Treas. Reg. § 301.7811-1(a)(4). The Internal Revenue Manual also lists criteria the Taxpayer Advocate will use to decide whether a TAO should be issued in a taxpayer's case. One criterion is the following:

> The taxpayer is facing an immediate threat of adverse action. Most situations will involve an action by the IRS, such as the filing of a Notice of Federal Tax Lien, the service of a Notice of Levy or the seizure of property. Threat of adverse actions can also involve the taxpayer's personal situations, such as utility cutoffs or evictions. Such actions may result in negative financial consequences or economic burden to the taxpayer. A warning of impending action that will negatively impact the taxpayer is considered a "threat." An immediate threat is defined as an action that will take place unless there is an intervening action to stop the action.

I.R.M. 13.1.7.2.1.

A taxpayer might seek to utilize a TAO to prevent or stop a wage garnishment or to prevent seizure of a particular asset. *See* Treas. Reg. § 301.7811-1(c). If the TAO is granted, the statute of limitations on collection is suspended from the date the Taxpayer Advocate's office receives the application and ending on the date specified in the TAO. *See* I.R.C. 7811(d); Treas. Reg. § 301.7811-1(e).

In similar types of cases, the IRS may be willing, without a TAO, to declare the taxpayer's account "currently not collectible." *See* I.R.M. 5.16.1. This status causes the IRS to remove the account from its active inventory of collection cases. The status applies if, for example, the taxpayer cannot be located; the delinquent taxpayer's business has liquidated and no longer has assets; or the IRS determines that collection of the liability would create undue hardship for the taxpayer by leaving the taxpayer unable to meet necessary living expenses. I.R.M. 5.16.1.1(2).

[B] Audit Reconsideration

In some instances, a taxpayer who receives a Notice and Demand for Payment after the IRS assesses tax liability will maintain that he or she was never notified of the assessment or that the proposed assessment is incorrect. In limited instances, the IRS may allow the taxpayer to request audit reconsideration. *See* I.R.M. 4.13.1. If the taxpayer filed a return and has already been through the audit process, the IRS will allow audit reconsideration if the taxpayer can establish that the IRS made a computational or processing error in adjusting the taxpayer's liability. I.R.M. 4.13.1.7. In addition, audit reconsideration may be available when the taxpayer presents evidence that the IRS had not previously considered and that, if it had been considered, would have resulted in a change in the assessment. *Id.* If the taxpayer had the opportunity to present the evidence at an earlier time but did not, the IRS will likely deny audit reconsideration. In that case, the taxpayer could pay the resulting the liability and file a claim for refund or utilize other post-assessment dispute resolution procedures — such as the CDP process.

Another instance in which the IRS may allow audit reconsideration is when the taxpayer failed to voluntarily file a return. As explained in Section 3.02[A] of Chapter 3, the IRS has the authority under Code section 6020 to file a substitute return on the taxpayer's behalf. *See* I.R.C. § 6020(b). In that case, the IRS may allow audit reconsideration of an assessment based on the substitute return. I.R.M. 4.13.1.7.

§ 15.03 INSTALLMENT AGREEMENTS

[A] Application Process

Reading Assignment: I.R.C. §§ 6159, 7123; Prop. Reg. § 301.6159-1(d).

Although revenue officers are instructed to request immediate payment of an outstanding liability, it will be obvious to the IRS in many cases that the taxpayer is unable to comply with such a request. As an alternative to enforced collection action, the IRS may be willing to defer payment. If the taxpayer simply needs additional time to access funds to pay the amount owed, the revenue officer can grant an extension of time to pay for up to 120 days without any formalities or supervisor approval. *See* I.R.C. § 6161(a); I.R.M. 5.14.5.5. If a taxpayer has a more serious liquidity problem, the IRS will usually require the taxpayer to enter into a formal installment agreement. I.R.C. § 6159. Payments under the installment agreement will include an interest charge computed on the unpaid balance subject to the agreement, using the underpayment rate in Code section 6621. *See* I.R.C. § 6601(b)(1).

To apply for an installment agreement, the taxpayer typically must submit, in print or online, Form 9465, Installment Agreement Request. If the IRS accepts the installment agreement, it will charge the taxpayer a processing fee. *See* T.D. 9306 (Feb. 5, 2007). The charge is $105 for a basic agreement ($43 for taxpayers whose income falls at or below 250 percent of the poverty rate) and $45 for restructuring an existing agreement (regardless of income level).[2] *See* IR-2006-196. Taxpayers seeking to qualify for the reduced fee based on their income levels must complete Form 13844, Application for Reduced User Fee for Installment Agreements.

Although a taxpayer need not wait until collection proceedings begin to request an installment agreement, most taxpayers do. If the IRS rejects a proposed installment agreement, the taxpayer has 30 days in which to file an administrative appeal with the IRS Appeals Division. I.R.C. § 7122(e); Prop. Reg. § 301.6159-1(d). As explained in Chapter 16, if the IRS denies the taxpayer's request, the taxpayer can also raise the issue as part of a CDP hearing. While this is the route many taxpayers seeking appeals consideration take, the IRS also has procedures permitting early referral of a collection issue to the Appeals Division (the Collection Appeals Program or CAP). *See* I.R.C. § 7123. One of the issues that Appeals will consider as part of its CAP program is the denial of an installment agreement request. *See* I.R.M. 5.1.9.4.1.

---

[2] If the taxpayer agrees to allow the IRS to directly debit the installment payments from the taxpayer's bank account, the basic fee is reduced to $52.

[1] Automatic Acceptance

Reading Assignment: I.R.C. § 6159(c).

In limited instances, the Code *requires* the IRS to accept an individual taxpayer's installment agreement request. I.R.C. § 6159(c). If the unpaid amount is less than $10,000 (exclusive of interest and penalties), the IRS must accept the agreement if, among other requirements: (1) The taxpayer establishes that, during the preceding five years, he or she filed all required income tax returns and paid any tax shown on those returns; (2) the taxpayer agrees to pay the outstanding liability in full within three years; and (3) the taxpayer agrees to comply with all provisions of the Code while the agreement is in effect. *Id.*

The IRS also has a "streamlined" applications process that typically results in an automatic acceptance. Under this process, the IRS is generally willing to accept installment agreements if the taxpayer agrees to pay a balance due (including tax, interest, and penalties) of $25,000 or less within a five-year period. I.R.M. 5.14.5.2. For offers that fall within these parameters, the IRS has created an online process for approving installment agreement applications through its website. The Online Payment Agreement application is available on the IRS's website at http://www.irs.gov/individuals/article/0,,id=149373,00.html. The IRS processes streamlined requests, whether submitted by paper or online, without requiring that the taxpayer disclose financial information.

[2] Conditional Acceptance

Reading Assignment: I.R.C. §§ 6159(b), 6502(a)(2); Prop. Reg. § 301.6159-1(c), (e).

In those cases that fall outside the streamlined process discussed above, a taxpayer's ability to enter into an installment agreement is largely within the IRS's discretion. The IRS normally will not consider an installment agreement unless the taxpayer is otherwise compliant with filing and payment obligations for the current year. Furthermore, to ensure that the taxpayer is truly unable to make an immediate payment in full, the IRS requires the taxpayer to furnish a financial statement detailing the taxpayer's assets and liabilities, bank accounts, employment information, and future income prospects (usually Form 433-A, Collection Information Statement for Wage Earners and Self-Employed Individuals, reproduced below, and/or Form 433-B, Collection Information Statement for Businesses).

Based on this financial statement, the IRS will attempt to determine the taxpayer's equity in assets (and the taxpayer's ability to borrow against these assets from third parties in order to pay the liability); whether the taxpayer has any extravagant property (such as airplanes or yachts) that could be sold to satisfy the liability; and the taxpayer's cash flow. A determination of the taxpayer's cash flow, which will be used by the revenue officer to calculate the amount of the payments, is based on monthly income and expense information reported in Section V of the Collection Information Statement. The Statement provides the IRS levy source information (such as an employer's name and address and the existence of bank accounts and other asset information), which permits the IRS to more easily collect by levy should the taxpayer default on the installment agreement.

Form **433-A**
(Rev January 2008)
Department of the Treasury
Internal Revenue Service

Collection Information Statement for Wage Earners and Self-Employed Individuals

Wage Earners Complete Sections 1, 2, 3, and 4, including signature line on page 4. *Answer all questions or write N/A.*
Self-Employed Individuals Complete Sections 1, 2, 3, 4, 5 and 6 and signature line on page 4. *Answer all questions or write N/A.*
For Additional Information, refer to Publication 1854, "How To Prepare a Collection Information Statement"
Include attachments if additional space is needed to respond completely to any question.

Name on Internal Revenue Service (IRS) Account	Social Security Number SSN on IRS Account	Employer Identification Number EIN

Section 1: Personal Information

1a Full Name of Taxpayer and Spouse (if applicable)	**1c** Home Phone ( )	**1d** Cell Phone ( )
1b Address *(Street, City, State, ZIP code) (County of Residence)*	**1e** Business Phone ( )	**1f** Business Cell Phone ( )
	2b Name, Age, and Relationship of dependent(s)	
2a Marital Status: ☐ Married ☐ Unmarried *(Single, Divorced, Widowed)*		

	Social Security No. (SSN)	Date of Birth *(mmddyyyy)*	Driver's License Number and State
3a Taxpayer			
3b Spouse			

Section 2: Employment Information

If the taxpayer or spouse is self-employed or has self-employment income, also complete Business Information in Sections 5 and 6.

Taxpayer		Spouse	
4a Taxpayer's Employer Name		**5a** Spouse's Employer Name	
4b Address *(Street, City, State, ZIP code)*		**5b** Address *(Street, City, State, ZIP code)*	
4c Work Telephone Number ( )	**4d** Does employer allow contact at work ☐ Yes ☐ No	**5c** Work Telephone Number ( )	**5d** Does employer allow contact at work ☐ Yes ☐ No
4e How long with this employer *(years)* *(months)*	**4f** Occupation	**5e** How long with this employer *(years)* *(months)*	**5f** Occupation
4g Number of exemptions claimed on Form W-4	**4h** Pay Period ☐ Weekly ☐ Bi-weekly ☐ Monthly ☐ Other	**5g** Number of exemptions claimed on Form W-4	**5h** Pay Period ☐ Weekly ☐ Bi-weekly ☐ Monthly ☐ Other

Section 3: Other Financial Information *(Attach copies of applicable documentation.)*

6 Is the individual or sole proprietorship party to a lawsuit *(If yes, answer the following)* **Yes** ☐ **No** ☐

☐ Plaintiff ☐ Defendant	Location of Filing	Represented by	Docket/Case No
Amount of Suit $	Possible Completion Date *(mmddyyyy)*	Subject of Suit	

7 Has the individual or sole proprietorship ever filed bankruptcy *(If yes, answer the following)* **Yes** ☐ **No** ☐

Date Filed *(mmddyyyy)*	Date Dismissed or Discharged *(mmddyyyy)*	Petition No	Location

8 Any increase/decrease in income anticipated *(business or personal)* *(If yes, answer the following)* **Yes** ☐ **No** ☐

Explain *(Use attachment if needed)*	How much will it increase/decrease $	When will it increase/decrease

9 Is the individual or sole proprietorship a beneficiary of a trust, estate, or life insurance policy *(If yes, answer the following)* **Yes** ☐ **No** ☐

Place where recorded:		EIN:
Name of the trust, estate, or policy	Anticipated amount to be received $	When will the amount be received

10 In the past 10 years, has the individual resided outside of the United States for periods of 6 months or longer *(If yes, answer the following)* **Yes** ☐ **No** ☐

Dates lived abroad: from *(mmddyyyy)*	To *(mmddyyyy)*

Form 433-A (Rev. 1-2008) Page 2

Section 4: Personal Asset Information for All Individuals

11 **Cash on Hand.** Include cash that is not in a bank. **Total Cash on Hand**	$

Personal Bank Accounts. Include all checking, online bank accounts, money market accounts, savings accounts, stored value cards (e.g., payroll cards, government benefit cards, etc.) List safe deposit boxes including location and contents.

	Type of Account	Full Name & Address *(Street, City, State, ZIP code)* of Bank, Savings & Loan, Credit Union, or Financial Institution.	Account Number	**Account Balance** As of ______ mmddyyyy
12a				$
12b				$
12c	**Total Cash** *(Add lines 12a, 12b, and amounts from any attachments)*			$

Investments. Include stocks, bonds, mutual funds, stock options, certificates of deposit, and retirement assets such as IRAs, Keogh, and 401(k) plans. **Include all corporations, partnerships, limited liability companies or other business entities in which the individual is an officer, director, owner, member, or otherwise has a financial interest.**

	Type of Investment or Financial Interest	Full Name & Address *(Street, City, State, ZIP code)* of Company	Current Value	Loan Balance (if applicable) As of ______ mmddyyyy	**Equity** Value Minus Loan
13a		Phone	$	$	$
13b		Phone	$	$	$
13c		Phone	$	$	$
13d	**Total Equity** *(Add lines 13a through 13c and amounts from any attachments)*				$

	Available Credit. List bank issued credit cards with available credit. Full Name & Address *(Street, City, State, ZIP code)* of Credit Institution	Credit Limit	Amount Owed As of ______ mmddyyyy	**Available Credit** As of ______ mmddyyyy
14a	Acct No.:	$	$	$
14b	Acct No.:	$	$	$
14c	**Total Available Credit** *(Add lines 14a, 14b and amounts from any attachments)*			$

15a Life Insurance. Does the individual have life insurance with a cash value (Term Life insurance does not have a cash value.)
☐ **Yes** ☐ **No** If **Yes** complete blocks 15b through 15f for each policy:

15b	Name and Address of Insurance Company(ies):			
15c	Policy Number(s)			
15d	Owner of Policy			
15e	Current Cash Value	$	$	$
15f	Outstanding Loan Balance	$	$	$
15g	**Total Available Cash.** *(Subtract amounts on line 15f from line 15e and include amounts from any attachments)*			$

Form **433-A** (Rev. 1-2008)

Form 433-A (Rev. 1-2008) Page **3**

16 In the past 10 years, have any assets been transferred by the individual for less than full value
(If yes, answer the following. If no, skip to 17a) **Yes** ☐ **No** ☐

List Asset	Value at Time of Transfer	Date Transferred *(mmddyyyy)*	To Whom or Where was it Transferred
	$		

Real Property Owned, Rented, and Leased. Include all real property and land contracts

	Purchase/Lease Date *(mmddyyyy)*	Current Fair Market Value (FMV)	Current Loan Balance	Amount of Monthly Payment	Date of Final Payment *(mmddyyyy)*	**Equity** FMV Minus Loan
17a Property Description		$	$	$		$
Location *(Street, City, State, ZIP code)* and County			Lender/Lessor/Landlord Name, Address, *(Street, City, State, ZIP code)* and Phone			
17b Property Description		$	$	$		$
Location *(Street, City, State, ZIP code)* and County			Lender/Lessor/Landlord Name, Address, *(Street, City, State, ZIP code)* and Phone			
17c Total Equity *(Add lines 17a, 17b and amounts from any attachments)*						$

Personal Vehicles Leased and Purchased. Include boats, RVs, motorcycles, trailers, etc.

Description *(Year, Mileage, Make, Model)*		Purchase/Lease Date *(mmddyyyy)*	Current Fair Market Value (FMV)	Current Loan Balance	Amount of Monthly Payment	Date of Final Payment *(mmddyyyy)*	**Equity** FMV Minus Loan
18a Year	Mileage		$	$	$		$
Make	Model	Lender/Lessor Name, Address, *(Street, City, State, ZIP code)* and Phone					
18b Year	Mileage		$	$	$		$
Make	Model	Lender/Lessor Name, Address, *(Street, City, State, ZIP code)* and Phone					
18c Total Equity *(Add lines 18a, 18b and amounts from any attachments)*							$

Personal Assets. Include all furniture, personal effects, artwork, jewelry, collections *(coins, guns, etc.)*, antiques or other assets

	Purchase/Lease Date *(mmddyyyy)*	Current Fair Market Value (FMV)	Current Loan Balance	Amount of Monthly Payment	Date of Final Payment *(mmddyyyy)*	**Equity** FMV Minus Loan
19a Property Description		$	$	$		$
Location *(Street, City, State, ZIP code)* and County			Lender/Lessor Name, Address, *(Street, City, State, ZIP code)* and Phone			
19b Property Description		$	$	$		$
Location *(Street, City, State, ZIP code)* and County			Lender/Lessor Name, Address, *(Street, City, State, ZIP code)* and Phone			
19c Total Equity *(Add lines 19a, 19b and amounts from any attachments)*						$

Form **433-A** (Rev. 1-2008)

Form 433-A (Rev. 1-2008) Page **4**

If the taxpayer is self-employed, sections 5 and 6 must be completed before continuing.

Monthly Income/Expense Statement *(For additional information, refer to Publication 1854.)*

Total Income			Total Living Expenses			IRS USE ONLY
	Source	Gross Monthly		Expense Items [5]	Actual Monthly	Allowable Expenses
20	Wages *(Taxpayer)* [1]	$	**33**	Food, Clothing, and Misc. [6]	$	
21	Wages *(Spouse)* [1]	$	**34**	Housing and Utilities [7]	$	
22	Interest - Dividends	$	**35**	Vehicle Ownership Costs [8]	$	
23	Net Business Income [2]	$	**36**	Vehicle Operating Costs [9]	$	
24	Net Rental Income [3]	$	**37**	Public Transportation [10]	$	
25	Distributions [4]	$	**38**	Health Insurance	$	
26	Pension/Social Security *(Taxpayer)*	$	**39**	Out of Pocket Health Care Costs [11]	$	
27	Pension/Social Security *(Spouse)*	$	**40**	Court Ordered Payments	$	
28	Child Support	$	**41**	Child/Dependent Care	$	
29	Alimony	$	**42**	Life insurance	$	
30	Other (Rent subsidy, Oil credit, etc.)	$	**43**	Taxes *(Income and FICA)*	$	
31	Other	$	**44**	Other Secured Debts (Attach list)	$	
32	**Total Income** *(add lines 20-31)*	$	**45**	**Total Living Expenses** *(add lines 33-44)*	$	

1 Wages, salaries, pensions, and social security: Enter gross monthly wages and/or salaries. Do not deduct withholding or allotments taken out of pay, such as insurance payments, credit union deductions, car payments, etc. To calculate the gross monthly wages and/or salaries:
If paid weekly - multiply weekly gross wages by 4.3. Example: $425.89 x 4.3 = $1,831.33
If paid biweekly (every 2 weeks) - multiply biweekly gross wages by 2.17. Example: $972.45 x 2.17 = $2,110.22
If paid semimonthly (twice each month) - multiply semimonthly gross wages by 2. Example: $856.23 x 2 = $1,712.46

2 Net Income from Business: Enter monthly net business income. This is the amount earned after ordinary and necessary monthly business expenses are paid. **This figure is the amount from page 6, line 82.** If the net business income is a loss, enter "0". Do not enter a negative number. If this amount is more or less than previous years, attach an explanation.

3 Net Rental Income: Enter monthly net rental income. This is the amount earned after ordinary and necessary monthly rental expenses are paid. Do not include deductions for depreciation or depletion. If the net rental income is a loss, enter "0". Do not enter a negative number.

4 Distributions: Enter the total distributions from partnerships and subchapter S corporations reported on Schedule K-1, and from limited liability companies reported on Form 1040, Schedule C, D or E.

5 Expenses not generally allowed: We generally do not allow tuition for private schools, public or private college expenses, charitable contributions, voluntary retirement contributions, payments on unsecured debts such as credit card bills, cable television and other similar expenses. However, we may allow these expenses if it is proven that they are necessary for the health and welfare of the individual or family or for the production of income.

6 Food, Clothing, and Misc.: Total of clothing, food, housekeeping supplies, and personal care products for one month.

7 Housing and Utilities: For principal residence: Total of rent or mortgage payment. Add the average monthly expenses for the following: property taxes, home owner's or renter's insurance, maintenance, dues, fees, and utilities. Utilities include gas, electricity, water, fuel, oil, other fuels, trash collection, telephone, and cell phone.

8 Vehicle Ownership Costs: Total of monthly lease or purchase/loan payments.

9 Vehicle Operating Costs: Total of maintenance, repairs, insurance, fuel, registrations, licenses, inspections, parking, and tolls for one month.

10 Public Transportation: Total of monthly fares for mass transit (e.g., bus, train, ferry, taxi, etc.)

11 Out of Pocket Health Care Costs: Monthly total of medical services, prescription drugs and medical supplies (e.g., eyeglasses, hearing aids, etc.)

Certification: *Under penalties of perjury, I declare that to the best of my knowledge and belief this statement of assets, liabilities, and other information is true, correct, and complete.*

Taxpayer's Signature	Spouse's Signature	Date

Attachments Required for Wage Earners and Self-Employed Individuals:
Copies of the following items for the last 3 months from the date this form is submitted (check all attached items):

- ☐ Income - Earnings statements, pay stubs, etc. from each employer, pension/social security/other income, self employment income (commissions, invoices, sales records, etc.).
- ☐ Banks, Investments, and Life Insurance - Statements for all money market, brokerage, checking and savings accounts, certificates of deposit, IRA, stocks/bonds, and life insurance policies with a cash value.
- ☐ Assets - Statements from lenders on loans, monthly payments, payoffs, and balances for all personal and business assets. Include copies of UCC financing statements and accountant's depreciation schedules.
- ☐ Expenses - Bills or statements for monthly recurring expenses of utilities, rent, insurance, property taxes, phone and cell phone, insurance premiums, court orders requiring payments (child support, alimony, etc.), other out of pocket expenses.
- ☐ Other - credit card statements, profit and loss statements, all loan payoffs, etc.
- ☐ A copy of last year's Form 1040 with all attachments. Include all Schedules K-1 from Form 1120S or Form 1065, as applicable.

Form **433-A** (Rev. 1-2008)

If the taxpayer's assets do not provide a readily available source for payment (for example, the taxpayer has no equity in the assets or they are not readily disposable), the IRS will collect the tax through payments based on the taxpayer's disposable income, determined based on the information in the Collection Information Statement. When evaluating the amount to be paid, the revenue officer is instructed to make an objective economic judgment as to how much the IRS can collect without jeopardizing the taxpayer's ability to support his or her family, pay current taxes, and earn income from which to pay future installments. *See* I.R.M. 5.14.1.5. To help ensure consistency, the IRS has established uniform financial standards (based on local and national estimates for necessary and conditional expenses) to be used to determine the taxpayer's ability to pay. *See* I.R.M. 5.14.1.5(2).[3] The IRS's website, www.irs.gov, also include an interactive calculator that assists taxpayers who wish to file for an installment agreement to compute their expected monthly payments.

If the revenue officer agrees to an installment agreement, the officer will generally insist on an immediate payment of part of the outstanding liability, followed by equal monthly payments. Equal payments permit the IRS to monitor collection through its computer system and send reminders to taxpayers when an installment payment is due. If the scheduled payments extend beyond the statute of limitations on collection, the taxpayer may be asked to extend the limitations period for the duration of the installment agreement. I.R.M. 5.14.2.1; *see* I.R.C. § 6502(a)(2)(A).

If the installment payments are to continue for more than 12 months, the IRS may insist that the taxpayer provide follow-up financial information, which the IRS can use to modify or terminate the installment agreement if a significant change in the taxpayer's financial condition occurs. *See* I.R.C. § 6159(b)(3). If, for example, the taxpayer's financial status improves, the IRS has the option of increasing the monthly payments by modifying the installment agreement. *See* Prop. Reg. § 301.6159-1(c).

The IRS can also modify or terminate the agreement if the taxpayer provided inaccurate or incomplete information with the request, accrues additional tax liabilities, or fails to make scheduled installment payments. I.R.C. § 6159(b). Before doing so, the IRS must give the taxpayer 30 days' written notice, along with an explanation for the proposed action. I.R.C. § 6159(b)(5). The taxpayer then has 30 days after the modification or termination is to take effect in which to seek review of the decision with the IRS Appeals Division. *See* Prop. Reg. § 301.6159-1(e)(4).

[B] Partial Payment Installment Agreements

Reading Assignment: I.R.C. §§ 6159(a), (d), 7122(a).

In 2004, Congress amended section 6159 to permit the IRS to enter into installment agreements that do not provide for full payment of the taxpayer's liability. I.R.C. § 6159(a). As explained in the I.R.M. excerpt below, the circumstances under which the IRS will accept a partial payment installment agreement (PPIA) are limited:

(1) **No Asset/No Equity Cases**: A PPIA may be granted if a taxpayer has no assets or no equity in assets; or has liquidated available assets to make a partial tax payment.

(2) **Asset Cases**: A PPIA may be granted if a taxpayer does not sell or cannot borrow against assets with equity because:

a. the assets have minimal equity or the equity is insufficient to allow a creditor to loan funds; . . .

b. the taxpayer is unable to utilize equity;

Example: The property is held as a tenancy by the entirety when only one spouse owes the tax and the non-liable spouse declines to go along with the attempt to borrow, and the property does not appear to have been transferred into the tenancy to avoid the tax collection.

c. the asset has some value but the taxpayer is unable to sell the asset because it is currently unmarketable;

Example: The business taxpayer owns a vacant lot in a high-value area, but the lot cannot be sold until it meets certain environmental regulations.

---

[3] These collection financial standards are discussed in more detail in Section 15.04.

d. the asset is necessary to generate income for the PPIA and the government will receive more from the future income generated by the asset than from the sale of the asset;

e. it would impose an economic hardship on the taxpayer to sell property, borrow on equity in property, or use a liquid asset to pay the taxes.

Example: The taxpayer is on a fixed income, such as social security, and has the ability to make small monthly payments. The only other asset is the taxpayer's primary residence and there is equity in the property. The revenue officer does a risk analysis and determines that seizing the property would cause an economic hardship because the taxpayer cannot find suitable replacement housing and meet necessary living expenses if the property would be seized. . . .

f. The taxpayer's loan payment would exceed the taxpayer's disposable income and they would not qualify for a loan.

(3) The taxpayer will normally be required to make a good faith attempt to utilize equity before the Service will approve a PPIA. This includes applying normal business standards when applying for loans using equity as collateral. Taxpayers will also be required to submit copies of all documents that are used in the loan application process.

(4) If the taxpayer does not comply with the requirement of making a good faith attempt to use equity in assets or is not willing to make monthly payments consistent with ability to pay, the taxpayer will be considered a "won't pay" and seizure/levy action may be appropriate. If enforcement action is appropriate, a PPIA will not be granted. . . .

I.R.M. 5.14.2.2.2. If the IRS enters into a PPIA, the Code requires the IRS to review the taxpayer's financial situation at least every two years to determine whether modification or termination of the agreement is appropriate. I.R.C. § 6159(d); *see also* Prop. Reg. § 301.6159-1(a).

As explained in Section 15.04, a taxpayer who wishes to negotiate payment of an amount less than the taxpayer's entire assessed liability usually will apply for an offer in compromise under Code section 7122. While there may appear to be overlap between an offer in compromise and a PPIA, the two agreements are different. An offer in compromise is a contractual agreement between the IRS and the taxpayer under which the taxpayer pays an agreed-upon amount in full satisfaction of the taxpayer's liabilities. I.R.C. § 7122(a). A PPIA, by contrast, cannot be used to reduce or settle the taxpayer's final liability. It is merely an agreement that may allow the taxpayer to pay part of the liability over time. *See* Prop. Reg. § 301.6159-1(c)(1)(ii). Still, in many cases, a PPIA will allow the taxpayer to achieve the same ultimate goal, but without the finality associated with an offer in compromise and without having to go through the more rigorous offer in compromise application process, which is discussed below.

[C] Effect of Installment Agreement on Collection Activity

Reading Assignment: I.R.C. § 6331(k)(2); Prop. Reg. § 301.6159-1(g).

The statute of limitations on collection is suspended during the period that the proposed installment agreement is pending with the IRS. If the IRS rejects the proposed agreement, the limitations period remains suspended for 30 days following the rejection. Moreover, if the taxpayer defaults on an installment agreement and the IRS terminates it, the statute of limitations on collection tolls for 30 days following termination. If the taxpayer appeals the rejection or termination, the limitations period is suspended while the appeal is pending. *See* Prop. Reg. § 301.6159-1(g).

An installment agreement does not affect the IRS's right to file a Notice of Federal Tax Lien with respect to tax liabilities that are deferred under the agreement. Treas. Reg. § 301.6331-4(b)(1). However, the IRS may not levy on the taxpayer's property during any period that an installment agreement is pending or actually in effect. The levy prohibition also applies during the 30-day period after the IRS rejects the installment agreement request, during the 30-day period following termination of the agreement, and during the pendency of an appeal of the termination or rejection. I.R.C. § 6331(k)(2). The levy prohibition does not apply if the IRS determines that the proposed installment agreement was submitted solely to delay collection. Prop. Reg. § 301.6159-1(f)(2).

§ 15.04 OFFERS IN COMPROMISE

Reading Assignment: Skim I.R.C. § 7122.

Unless the taxpayer qualifies for a partial payment installment agreement, the IRS's willingness to enter into an installment agreement deferring payments over time is conditioned upon the taxpayer's payment of the entire liability. If, however, the taxpayer has few assets and little prospect of generating sufficient income to pay the liability in full, the taxpayer may be allowed to strike a settlement for less than 100 cents on the dollar through an offer in compromise agreement. An offer in compromise accepted by the IRS permits the taxpayer a fresh start by eliminating the excess liability over the payment amount agreed upon by the parties. *See* I.R.M. 5.8.1.1.4.

The statutory authority for making an "offer in compromise" is section 7122.[4] The conditions under which the IRS will accept a compromise offer are circumscribed. The IRS will compromise tax liability on three grounds: doubt as to liability, doubt as to collectibility, and the promotion of effective tax administration. Treas. Reg. § 301.7122-1(b). The IRS allows the taxpayer three different payment options: (1) a cash, lump sum offer, usually payable within 90 days; (2) a short-term periodic payment offer, payable over a two-year period; and (3) a deferred periodic payment offer, payable over the number of years remaining in the statute of limitations on collection. I.R.M. 5.8.1.9.4. The procedures for applying for an offer in compromise, the bases on which an offer will be accepted, and the effect of the offer in compromise on the collections process are discussed below.

[A] Offer in Compromise Application

The taxpayer requests an offer in compromise by submitting one of two forms: Form 656, a copy of which is set forth below, or Form 656-L. Taxpayers use Form 656 to request relief based on doubt as to collectibility and/or effective tax administration. Taxpayers wishing to strike a compromise based on doubt as to liability must use Form 656-L. Each form includes information relating to payment terms and submission rules. Form 656 also includes a checklist for the taxpayer to use to determine whether he or she is eligible to file an offer in compromise.

For most offer in compromise requests, the taxpayer must submit a $150 processing fee, which the IRS typically will apply against any amounts due. *See* I.R.C. § 7122(c)(2)(B). The processing fee does not apply to offers based on doubt as to liability. Further, the fee can be waived in the case of low-income taxpayers (those with income at or below 250 percent of the poverty rate). Proc. Reg. § 300.3(b). Form 656-A,

[4] An offer in compromise is not solely a tax collection tool. The taxpayer can request an offer in compromise at virtually any stage of an IRS proceeding, including during audit, at appeals, or even in Tax Court. However, offers in compromise based on doubt as to collectibility — the offers most commonly accepted — are usually negotiated in response to a Notice and Demand for Payment sent to the taxpayer after assessment, and often as part of a CDP hearing.

Offer in Compromise Application Fee Instructions and Certification, includes a worksheet that the taxpayer can use to determine whether he or she qualifies for an exception to the fee based on income. In most cases, the processing fee is not refundable, even if the IRS declares that the offer request is incomplete or incorrect and thus cannot be processed. However, the user fee may be refunded if either (1) the IRS accepts the offer based on effective tax administration, or (2) the IRS accepts the offer because of doubt as to collectibility and the IRS determines that collection of an amount greater than that offered would create economic hardship for the taxpayer. Proc. Reg. § 300.3(b)(2).

In addition to the processing fee, most taxpayers must submit a "down payment" before the IRS will process the application. In the case of any lump sum offer, defined in the Code as "any offer of payments made in 5 or fewer installments," the taxpayer must remit 20 percent of the amount of the lump sum offer. I.R.C. § 7122(c)(1)(A). For periodic payment offers, the taxpayer must remit the amount of the first proposed installment and comply with the taxpayer's own proposed payment schedule while the offer is being considered. I.R.C. § 7122(c)(1)(B). The advance payment generally is not refundable even if the IRS rejects the taxpayer's offer request. The IRS waives the down payment requirement in the case of low-income taxpayers, as defined above, and for offers based on doubt as to liability. *See* Form 656-L.

Form **656**
(February 2007)

Department of the Treasury — Internal Revenue Service

Offer in Compromise

Attach Application Fee and Payment *(check or money order)* here.

IRS RECEIVED DATE

Section I **Taxpayer Contact Information**

Taxpayer's First Name and Middle Initial	Last Name
If a joint offer, spouse's First Name and Middle Initial	Last Name

Business Name

Taxpayer's Address *(Home or Business) (number, street, and room or suite no., city, state, ZIP code)*

Mailing Address *(if different from above) (number, street, and room or suite no., city, state, ZIP code)*

DATE RETURNED

Social Security Number (SSN) *(Primary)*	*(Secondary)*	Employer Identification Number (EIN) *(EIN included in offer)*	*(EIN not included in offer)*
- -	- -	-	-

Section II **To: Commissioner of Internal Revenue Service**

I/We *(includes all types of taxpayers)* submit this offer to compromise the tax liabilities plus any interest, penalties, additions to tax, and additional amounts required by law *(tax liability)* for the tax type and period marked below: *(Please mark an "X" in the box for the correct description and fill-in the correct tax period(s), adding additional periods if needed).*

☐ 1040/1120 Income Tax — Year(s) ____________

☐ 941 Employer's Quarterly Federal Tax Return — Quarterly period(s) ____________

____

☐ 940 Employer's Annual Federal Unemployment (FUTA) Tax Return — Year(s) ____________

☐ Trust Fund Recovery Penalty as a responsible person of *(enter corporation name)* ____________,

for failure to pay withholding and Federal Insurance Contributions Act taxes (Social Security taxes), for period(s) ending ____________

____

☐ Other Federal Tax(es) [specify type(s) and period(s)] ____________

Note: If you need more space, use a separate sheet of paper and title it "Attachment to Form 656 Dated ____________." Sign and date the attachment following the listing of the tax periods.

Section III **Reason for Offer in Compromise**

I/We submit this offer for the reason(s) checked below:

☐ Doubt as to Collectibility — "I have insufficient assets and income to pay the full amount." You must include a complete Collection Information Statement, Form 433-A and/or Form 433-B.

☐ Effective Tax Administration — "I owe this amount and have sufficient assets to pay the full amount, but due to my exceptional circumstances, requiring full payment would cause an economic hardship or would be unfair and inequitable." You must include a complete Collection Information Statement, Form 433-A and/or Form 433-B and complete Section VI.

Section IV **Offer in Compromise Terms**

I/We offer to pay $__________ *(must be more than zero)*. Complete Section VII to explain where you will obtain the funds to make this offer.

Check **only** one of the following:

☐ **Lump sum cash offer** – 20% of the amount of the offer $__________ must be sent with Form 656. Upon written acceptance of the offer, the balance must be paid in 5 or fewer installments.

$__________ payable within ______ months after acceptance
$__________ payable within ______ months after acceptance
$__________ payable within ______ months after acceptance
$__________ payable within ______ months after acceptance
$__________ payable within ______ months after acceptance

☐ **Short Term Periodic Payment Offer** – Offer amount is paid within 24 months from the date IRS received your offer. The first payment **must** be submitted with your Form 656. You **must** make regular payments during your offer investigation. Complete the following:

$__________ will be submitted with the Form 656. Beginning in the month after the offer is submitted *(insert month __________)*, on the ______ day of each month, $__________ will be sent in for a total of ______ months. *(Cannot extend more than 24 months from the date the offer was submitted.)*

Catalog Number 16728N www.irs.gov Form **656** (Rev. 2-2007)

Section IV Cont.

☐ **Deferred Periodic Payment Offer** – Offer amount will be paid over the remaining life of the collection statute. The first payment **must** be submitted with your Form 656. You must make regular payments during your offer investigation. Complete the following:

$ ___________ will be submitted with the Form 656. Beginning in the month after the offer is submitted *(insert month ____________)*, on the _________ day of each month, $___________ will be sent in for a total of _______ months.

Optional - Designation of Required Payment under IRC 7122(c)

You have the option to designate the required payment you made under Section IV above. If you chose not to designate your required payment, then the IRS will apply your payment in the best interest of the government. Please complete the following if you choose to designate your payment.

$___________ paid under IRC 7122 (c) is to be applied to my ____________ Tax Year/Quarter*(s) (whichever is applicable)* for my/our tax form ___________

If you pay more than the required payment when you submit your offer and want any part of that additional payment treated as a deposit, check the box below and insert the amount. It is not required that you designate any portion of your payment as a deposit. **Note:** If the required payment is not paid, the offer will be returned even if you make a payment you designate as a deposit.

☐ I am making a deposit of $ __________ with this offer.

Section V **By submitting this offer, I/we have read, understand and agree to the following conditions:**

(a) I/We voluntarily submit all tax payments made on this offer, including the mandatory payments of tax required under section 7122(c). These tax payments are not refundable even if I/we withdraw the offer prior to acceptance or the IRS returns or rejects the offer. If the offer is accepted, the IRS will apply payments made after acceptance in the best interest of the government.

(b) Any payments made in connection with this offer will be applied to the tax liability unless I have specified that they be treated as a deposit. Only amounts that exceed the mandatory payments can be treated as a deposit. Such a deposit will be refundable if the offer is rejected or returned by the IRS or is withdrawn. I/we understand that the IRS will not pay interest on any deposit.

(c) The application fee for this offer will be kept by the IRS unless the offer was not accepted for processing.

(d) I/We will comply with all provisions of the Internal Revenue Code relating to filing my/our returns and paying my/our required taxes for 5 years or until the offered amount is paid in full, whichever is longer. In the case of a jointly submitted Offer in Compromise joint liabilities, I/we understand that default with respect to the compliance provisions described in this paragraph by one party to this agreement will not result in the default of the entire agreement. The default provisions described in Section V(i) of this agreement will be applied only to the party failing to comply with the requirements of this paragraph.

(e) I/We waive and agree to the suspension of any statutory periods of limitation (time limits provided by law) for the IRS assessment of the liability for the periods identified in Section II. I/We understand that I/we have the right not to waive these statutory periods or to limit the waiver to a certain length or to certain periods. I/We understand, however, that the IRS may not consider this offer if I/we refuse to waive the statutory periods for assessment or if we provide only a limited waiver. The amount of any Federal tax due for the periods described in Section II may be assessed at any time prior to the acceptance of this offer or within one year of the rejection of this offer. I/We understand that the statute of limitations for collection will be suspended during the period an offer is considered pending by the IRS (paragraph (k) of this section defines pending).

(f) The IRS will keep all payments and credits made, received or applied to the total original liability before submission of this offer and all payments required under section 7122(c). The IRS will also keep all payments in excess of those required by section 7122(c) that are received in connection with the offer and that are not designated as deposits in Section IV. The IRS may keep any proceeds from a levy served prior to submission of the offer, but not received at the time the offer is submitted. As additional consideration beyond the amount of my/our offer, the IRS will keep any refund, including interest, due to me/us because of overpayment of any tax or other liability, for tax periods extending through the calendar year in which the IRS accepts the offer. The date of acceptance is the date on the written notice of acceptance issued by the IRS to me/us or to my/our representative. I/We may not designate an overpayment ordinarily subject to refund, to which the IRS is entitled, to be applied to estimated tax payments for the following year.

(g) I/We will return to the IRS any refund identified in paragraph (f) received after submission of this offer.

(h) The IRS cannot collect more than the full amount of the liability under this offer.

(i) I/We understand that I/we remain responsible for the full amount of the liabilities, unless and until the IRS accepts the offer in writing and I/we have met all the terms and conditions of the offer. The IRS will not remove the original amount of the liabilities from its records until I/we have met all the terms and conditions of the offer. I/We understand that the liabilities I/we offer to compromise are and will remain liabilities until I/we meet all the terms and conditions of this offer. If I/we file for bankruptcy before the terms and conditions of this offer are completed, any claim the IRS files in the bankruptcy proceedings will be a tax claim.

(j) Once the IRS accepts the offer in writing, I/we have no right to contest, in court or otherwise, the amount of the liability.

(k) The offer is pending starting with the date an authorized IRS official signs the form. The offer remains pending until an authorized IRS official accepts, rejects, returns or acknowledges withdrawal of the offer in writing. If I/we appeal an IRS rejection decision on the offer, IRS will continue to treat the offer as pending until the Appeals Office accepts or rejects the offer in writing.

If I/we don't file a protest within 30 days of the date the IRS notifies me/us of the right to protest the decision, I/we waive the right to a hearing before the Appeals Office about the Offer in Compromise.

(l) If I/we fail to meet any of the terms and conditions of the offer and the offer defaults, the IRS may:

- immediately file suit to collect the entire unpaid balance of the offer;
- immediately file suit to collect an amount equal to the original amount of the liability, minus any payment already received under the terms of this offer;
- disregard the amount of the offer and apply all amounts already paid under the offer against the original amount of the liability; and/or
- file suit or levy to collect the original amount of the liability, without further notice of any kind.

The IRS will continue to add interest, as section 6601 of the Internal Revenue Code requires, on the amount the IRS determines is due after default. The IRS will add interest from the date the offer is defaulted until I/we completely satisfy the amount owed.

(m) The IRS generally files a Notice of Federal Tax Lien to protect the Government's interest on offers with deferred payments. Also, the IRS may file a Notice of Federal Tax Lien during the offer investigation. This tax lien will be released when the payment terms of the offer agreement have been satisfied.

(n) I/We understand that IRS employees may contact third parties in order to respond to this request and I/we authorize the IRS to make such contacts. Further, by authorizing the IRS to contact third parties, I/we understand that I/we will not receive notice, pursuant to section 7602(c) of the Internal Revenue Code, of third parties contacted in connection with this request.

(o) I/We are offering to compromise all the liabilities assessed against me/us as of the date of this offer and under the taxpayer identification numbers listed in Section II above. I/We authorize the IRS to amend Section II, above, to include any assessed liabilities we failed to list on Form 656.

Section VI Explanation of Circumstances

I am requesting an Offer in Compromise for the reason(s) listed below:

Note: *If you believe you have special circumstances affecting your ability to fully pay the amount due, explain your situation. You may attach additional sheets if necessary. Please include your name and SSN or EIN on all additional sheets or supporting documentation.*

____

____

____

____

____

____

____

Section VII Source of Funds

I / We shall obtain the funds to make this offer from the following source(s):

____

____

____

____

____

____

____

Page 4 of 4

Section VIII	Mandatory Signatures	
Taxpayer Attestation	**If I / We submit this offer on a substitute form, I/ we affirm that this form is a verbatim duplicate of the official Form 656, and I/we agree to be bound by all the terms and conditions set forth in the official Form 656.** **Under penalties of perjury, I declare that I have examined this offer, including accompanying schedules and statements, and to the best of my knowledge and belief, it is true, correct and complete.**	
	Signature of Taxpayer	Date
	Signature of Taxpayer	Date

Official Use Only

I accept the waiver of the statutory period of limitations on assessment for the Internal Revenue Service, as described in Section V(e).

Signature of Authorized Internal Revenue Service Official	Title	Date

Section IX	Application Prepared by Someone Other than the Taxpayer

If this application was prepared by someone other than the taxpayer, please fill in that person's name and address below.

Name

Address *(if known) (Street, City, State, ZIP code)*

Section X	Paid Preparer Use Only

Name of Preparer

Signature of Preparer	Date	Check if self-employed ☐	Preparer's CAF no. or PTIN
Firm's name (or yours if self-employed), address, and ZIP code			EIN
			Telephone number ( )

Section XI	Third Party Designee

Do you want to allow another person to discuss this offer with the IRS? ☐ Yes. Complete the information below. ☐ No

Designee's name	Telephone number ( )

Privacy Act Statement

We ask for the information on this form to carry out the internal revenue laws of the United States. Our authority to request this information is Section 7801 of the Internal Revenue Code.

Our purpose for requesting the information is to determine if it is in the best interests of the IRS to accept an Offer in Compromise. You are not required to make an Offer in Compromise; however, if you choose to do so, you must provide all of the taxpayer information requested. Failure to provide all of the information may prevent us from processing your request.

If you are a paid preparer and you prepared the Form 656 for the taxpayer submitting an offer, we request that you complete and sign Section X on Form 656, and provide identifying information. Providing this information is voluntary. This information will be used to administer and enforce the internal revenue laws of the United States and may be used to regulate practice before the Internal Revenue Service for those persons subject to Treasury Department Circular No. 230, Regulations Governing the Practice of Attorneys, Certified Public Accountants, Enrolled Agents, Enrolled Actuaries, and Appraisers before the Internal Revenue Service. Information on this form may be disclosed to the Department of Justice for civil and criminal litigation.

We may also disclose this information to cities, states and the District of Columbia for use in administering their tax laws and to combat terrorism. Providing false or fraudulent information on this form may subject you to criminal prosecution and penalties.

Catalog Number 16728N www.irs.gov Form **656** (Rev. 2-2007)

[B] Processing the Application

The IRS will process an offer in compromise only after the taxpayer remits the required payments and completes the application in full. *See* Rev. Proc. 2003-71, 2003-36 I.R.B. 517. In addition, the IRS will not begin to investigate an offer unless the taxpayer has filed all required tax returns. The taxpayer's offer is usually processed by an IRS employee who, after reviewing the application for completeness, may contact the taxpayer's representative to solicit additional information or explanations required to evaluate the offer.[5] *See* I.R.M. 5.8.5.2. For example, the employee may seek documents that verify the taxpayer's assets and ability to pay. Once an offer in compromise is accepted, the settlement will not be reopened unless the IRS discovers that the taxpayer falsified information, concealed assets, or there was a mutual mistake of fact by the parties.[6] Treas. Reg. § 301.7122-1(e)(5). Moreover, the taxpayer must agree that he or she will fully comply with all filing and payment requirements for a five-year period from the date the IRS accepts the offer. *See* Form 656. If the taxpayer fails to carry out the obligations under the compromise agreement, the IRS can terminate the agreement and proceed to collect the originally determined liability, reduced by any payments previously made. *See* I.R.M. 5.8.9.

If the IRS employee intends to reject the taxpayer's offer, an internal review procedure takes place, after which the taxpayer is informed of the rejection. At that point, the taxpayer is granted the right to Appeal the rejection to the IRS Appeals Division. *See* I.R.C. § 7122(e); *see also* I.R.M. 5.8.7. The taxpayer has 30 days from the date of the rejection letter to request an appeal. Treas. Reg. § 301.7122-1(f)(5). As noted above and discussed in Chapter 16, the Appeals Office may also be asked to consider the availability of an offer in compromise as part of a CDP hearing.

[C] Offers Based on Doubt as to Collectibility

Reading Assignment: I.R.C. § 7122(c).

The type of offer in compromise most often accepted by the IRS is an offer based on doubt as to collectibility. Doubt as to collectibility exists when the taxpayer cannot pay the full amount of tax liability owed within the remainder of the statute of limitations on collection. *See* Form 656. In evaluating offers on this basis, the IRS conducts a thorough examination of the taxpayer's assets, liabilities, and earnings potential. As with most installment agreements, the taxpayer must submit a financial statement on Form 433-A (Wage Earners and Self-Employed) or 433-B (Businesses), setting forth a description of the taxpayer's financial condition. I.R.M. 5.8.1.9. The standard the IRS uses to determine whether an offer amount based on doubt as to collectibility should be accepted is whether the amount reflects "reasonable collection potential." I.R.M. 5.8.4.4(2).

A taxpayer's collection potential depends primarily on a combination of the net value of the taxpayer's assets and the taxpayer's future ability to pay. More specifically, the offer amount must exceed the sum of (1) the taxpayer's "net realizable equity" plus (2) the taxpayer's "future income" determined over a four or five-year period, depending upon the terms of the offer. If the taxpayer intends to pay the offer amount within 5 months, the taxpayer calculates disposable income over a four-year period. If the payments will be spread over more than 5 months, the taxpayer typically uses a five-year period to calculate the taxpayer's future ability to pay. I.R.M. 5.8.5.5.[7] Form 656 includes a worksheet, a copy of which is set forth below, that the taxpayer can use to calculate an acceptable offer amount.

---

[5] The offer in compromise is deemed accepted if the IRS does not make a decision with respect to the offer within two years from the date that the offer was submitted. I.R.C. § 7122(f).

[6] When preparing the financial statement, taxpayers should consider Code section 7206, which makes it a felony to conceal property or falsify information on Form 656. The offer application also has a signature line for the preparer. The IRS now requires the preparer's signature in order to discourage unscrupulous practitioners from falsely marketing offers in compromise to taxpayers as a way of settling tax disputes for pennies on the dollar. *See* IR-2004-129 (Oct. 25 2004).

[7] A taxpayer seeking a deferred periodic payment offer that extends beyond two years typically calculates disposable income based on the number of years remaining in the statute of limitations on collection. I.R.M. 5.8.5.5.

Worksheet to Calculate an Offer Amount

For use by Wage Earners and Self-Employed Individuals.

Keep this worksheet for your records. Do not send to IRS.

Use this Worksheet to calculate an offer amount using information from Form 433-A.

1. Enter total checking account balances from Item 11c — A
2. Enter total other account balances from Item 12c — B (If less than 0, enter 0)
3. Enter total investments from Item 13d — C
4. Enter total cash on hand from Item 14a — D
5. Enter life insurance cash value from Item 16f — E
6. Enter total accounts/notes receivable from Item 23m — F

Subtotal: Add boxes A through F = G

7. Purchased Automobiles, Trucks, and Other Licensed Assets

	Enter current value for each asset			Enter loan balance for each asset	Individual asset value (if less than 0, enter 0)
From line 18a	$	x .8 =	$	—$	=
From line 18b	$	x .8 =	$	—$	=
From line 18c	$	x .8 =	$	—$	=

Subtotal = H

8. Real Estate

	Enter current value for each asset			Enter loan balance for each asset	Individual asset value (if less than 0, enter 0)
From line 20a	$	x .8 =	$	—$	=
From line 20b	$	x .8 =	$	—$	=

Subtotal = I

9. Personal Assets

	Enter current value for each asset			Enter loan balance for each asset	Individual asset value (if less than 0, enter 0)
From line 21b	$	x .8 =	$	—$	=
From line 21c	$	x .8 =	$	—$	=
From line 21d	$	x .8 =	$	—$	=
From line 21e	$	x .8 =	$	—$	=

Subtotal = J

From line 21a	$	x .8 =	$	—$	=

Subtract —$ 7720.00

Subtotal = K

10. Business Assets

	Enter current value for each asset			Enter loan balance for each asset	Individual asset value (if less than 0, enter 0)
From line 22b	$	x .8 =	$	—$	=
From line 22c	$	x .8 =	$	—$	=
From line 22d	$	x .8 =	$	—$	=
From line 22e	$	x .8 =	$	—$	=

Subtotal = L

From line 22a	$	x .8 =	$	—$	=

Subtract —$ 3860.00

Subtotal = M

11. Add amounts in Boxes G through M to obtain your total equity and assets = N

12. Enter amount from Item 34 $______
Enter amount from Item 45 and subtract — $______

Net Difference = O

This amount would be available to pay monthly on your tax liability

If Box O is 0 or less, STOP. Use the amount from Box N to base your offer amount in Section IV of Form 656. **Your offer amount must equal or exceed (*) the amount shown in Box N.**

13a.

If you will pay the offer amount in **5 months or less:**

Enter amount from Box O $______

Multiply by x 48 (or the number of months remaining on the ten-year statutory period for collection, whichever is less)

= P

Enter amount from Box N + Q

Add amounts in Box P and Box Q = R

Use the amount from Box R to base your offer amount in Section IV of Form 656.
Note: Your offer amount must equal or exceed (*) the amount shown in Box R.

13b.

If you will pay the offer amount in more than 5 months but less than 2 years

Enter amount from Box O $______

Multiply by x 60 (or the number of months remaining on the ten-year statutory period for collection, whichever is less)

= S

Enter amount from Box N + T

Add amounts in Box S and Box T = U

Use the amount from Box U to base your offer amount in Section IV of Form 656.
Note: Your offer amount must equal or exceed (*) the amount shown in Box U.

Note: Do not compute your offer amount using 13a or 13b if your statute expiration date(s) is less than five years from the date of your offer. Instead, refer to Page 6 under Deferred Payment Offer.

* Unless you are submitting an offer under effective tax administration or doubt as to collectibility with special circumstances considerations, as described on Page 1.

By law, the IRS has the authority to collect outstanding federal taxes for ten years from the date your liability is assessed. There may be circumstances that extend the ten year collection statute such as when a taxpayer files bankruptcy or an Offer in Compromise.

The IRS may adjust the RCP during the investigation to a higher or lower amount, depending upon the facts and circumstances of your individual case.

9

When calculating the taxpayer's realizable equity in assets, the taxpayer includes cash, amounts in checking and investment accounts, the cash value of any life insurance policies, and accounts receivable. *See* Form 656. The realizable value of the taxpayer's other real and personal property is normally its "quick sale" value, generally defined as 80% of the current fair market value of the assets. I.R.M. 5.8.5.3.1. Using a quick sale value takes into account the hardship caused when the taxpayer must sell an asset in a short period of time. The "net" realizable value of the taxpayer's assets is the quick sale value minus any amounts owed to creditors who have priority over the federal tax lien. Because of the unique nature of certain assets (such as going concern value and retirement plans), the IRS has established separate guidelines for determining whether these types of assets should be considered when calculating the minimum offer required. *See, e.g.,* I.R.M. 5.8.5.3.8 (pension and retirement plans).

To determine the taxpayer's future income, the IRS uses information set forth on the taxpayer's Collection Information Statement (Form 433), in combination with estimated national and local living costs, which it refers to as collection financial standards. *See* I.R.C. § 7122(d)(2)(A). The IRS relies upon these standards unless, based on the facts and circumstances of the taxpayer's case, the resulting amount would not leave the taxpayer with sufficient resources to provide for basic living expenses. I.R.C. § 7122(d)(2)(B). The IRS has posted these collection financial standards on its website at http://www.irs.gov/individuals/article/0,,id=96543,00.html.

A taxpayer's future income is the difference between the taxpayer's monthly income as reported on the Collection Information Statement minus "allowable expenses." *See* I.R.M. 5.15.1. Allowable expenses include four basic categories of expenses: (1) food, clothing, and other items; (2) out-of-pocket health care expenses; (3) housing and utilities; and (4) transportation. The first two categories of expenses are based on national standards — not the taxpayer's level of income. For example, in 2008, the allowable expense for food, clothing, and other items for a single taxpayer was $507 per month. The same number applies regardless of the geographic area in which the taxpayer lives. National standards are also used to calculate allowable health care expenses, which vary only by the taxpayer's age (for 2008, $57 per month for individuals under age 65 and $144 for those age 65 or older).

The IRS calculates expenses for housing and utilities based on standard living costs in the state and county in which the taxpayer resides. For example, the allowable expense for a family of four living in Manhattan, New York is $5,364 per month, while the allowable living expense for a family of four in Manhattan, Kansas is $1,364. Allowable expenses for transportation generally consist of ownership and operating costs associated with an automobile. Ownership costs are based on a national standard and operating costs are based on local standards.

When determining whether an offer should be accepted based on doubt as to collectibility, the IRS looks not only to the net realizable value of the taxpayer's assets and the taxpayer's disposable income, but may also consider the taxpayer's education, earnings potential, and likelihood of any increases in future income. *See* I.R.M. 5.8.5.5. Section 7122 specifically prohibits the IRS from rejecting an offer from a low-income taxpayer based solely on the amount of the offer. I.R.C. § 7122(c).

The following case, although somewhat lengthy, does a good job of illustrating the process for determining an acceptable offer amount. Procedurally, the case involves the Tax Court's review of an IRS Appeal Officer's determination, made as part of a CDP hearing, that the taxpayer's offer was not acceptable. Note that the process for calculating the taxpayer's future income, described above, was slightly different at the time the taxpayer's case was considered.

SAMUEL v. COMMISSIONER

United States Tax Court
T.C. Memo. 2007-312

NIMS, JUDGE:

This case arises from a petition for judicial review filed in response to a Notice of Determination Concerning Collection Action(s) Under Section 6320 and/or 6330. * * *

BACKGROUND

This case was submitted fully stipulated pursuant to Rule 122, and the facts are so found. * * *

Petitioner is a practicing physician specializing in adult and pediatric urology. He operates his own medical practice, David L. Samuel, M.D., A Professional Medical Corporation. Petitioner is also a partner in Pontchartrain Lithotripsy, LLC. Prior to starting his own practice, petitioner practiced with another urologist until sometime in 2002.

Beginning on February 3, 2003, petitioner began filing delinquent individual income tax returns for 1996–2002. * * *

Petitioner did not remit any payments for the amounts due on these returns when they were filed.

Respondent assessed the taxes shown on the * * * returns. Calculated as of January 1, 2005, petitioner owed in excess of $773,368 for the tax years 1996–2002, inclusive.

* * *

On July 8, 2004, petitioner submitted a Form 656, Offer in Compromise, along with two different Forms 433-A (both dated June 1, 2004) and a Form 433-B for his professional corporation. Petitioner submitted the offer on the basis of "doubt as to collectibility". Petitioner was not then, and is not now, contesting his 1996–2002 income tax liabilities. Petitioner offered to pay $30,000 to compromise his 1996–2002 tax liabilities. This was a short-term deferred payment offer payable in monthly installments of $1,250 for 24 months.

On one of the Forms 433-A, petitioner indicated that he operated David L. Samuel, M.D., P.C., and identified this corporation as his employer for the prior 4 years. Petitioner listed his assets as $1,409.89 in a checking account, a house valued at $330,000 (with a loan balance of $322,025), and furniture/personal effects worth $10,000. Petitioner indicated that he was the plaintiff in a $25,000 civil lawsuit for unpaid wages. Petitioner showed his only source of income as monthly wages of $7,963. Petitioner reported monthly expenses of: $976 for food, clothing, and miscellaneous (noted as the statutory allowance); $1,024 for housing and utilities (noted as the statutory allowance); $50 for health care; $2,470 for taxes; $2,750 for court-ordered payments (child support); and $250 for other expenses (later identified as attorney's fees for representation in the instant matter). The second Form 433-A contained the same information as the first, except that it reported gross monthly wages of $8,144.10 and monthly medical expenses of $41.20.

The Form 433-B for David L. Samuel, M.D., P.C., reflected that petitioner was the only shareholder. The total accounts/notes receivable of the medical corporation was shown as $87,388.73. The only other assets disclosed on the Form 433-B were $613.74 in a bank account, $200.22 of cash on hand, and office furniture valued at $4,000. In the "Investments" section, petitioner listed one share of Pontchartrain Lithotripsy, LLC, with a value of $10,000. Total monthly income for petitioner's professional corporation consisted of $26,435.20 in gross receipts and $4,416 in dividends for a total of $30,851.20. Petitioner reported monthly expenses totaling $33,523.93 for the professional corporation.

Petitioner's offer-in-compromise was accepted for processing and forwarded to respondent's New Orleans Compliance Office for investigation. Petitioner requested a face-to-face hearing at the New Orleans Appeals Office, to which the IRS agreed. The face-to-face hearing was conducted in New Orleans on January 31, 2005. During the face-to-face hearing, petitioner disclosed that he sold an interest in Fairway Medical Center (FMC) in June 2003, for $108,000 and refinanced his home in September 2003, for a net cash payment to him of $25,158. Petitioner also discussed his ownership interest in Pontchartrain Lithotripsy, LLC, from which he reported $51,922 of income in 2003, but which he designated on the Form 433-B as a $10,000 investment held by his professional corporation. Petitioner explained that his $10,000 initial investment in Sabine Lithotripsy, LLC (which dissolved into four entities, one of which was Pontchartrain Lithotripsy, LLC) entitles him to access a medical mobile unit for use in his medical practice. He also receives monthly income receipts, which he said are deposited into his business account. After the hearing, petitioner provided a list of the monthly income received from Pontchartrain Lithotripsy. This income totaled $61,440 for 2004.

On February 10, 2005, the settlement officer sent petitioner a letter with her preliminary determination. She stated her position that petitioner had "dissipated assets" with a disregard of his outstanding tax liabilities when he sold his interest in FMC and refinanced his home. She reasoned that at the time the transactions occurred, the outstanding assessed balances due to the IRS exceeded the amounts realized from the dissipated assets. In addition, she noted that none of the funds were remitted to the IRS, and she took the position that petitioner did not use any of the funds for necessary expenses. She said that unless petitioner increased his offer to $163,158 ($30,000 initial offer amount plus 100 percent of the dissipated asset values), she would assume that petitioner was not interested in pursuing the matter further, and that she would recommend that Appeals issue a notice of determination.

* * *

On March 2, 2005, petitioner responded to the preliminary determination letter. In his letter he said that when he "lost his job" practicing with another urologist in 2002, he accumulated substantial debt setting up his new medical practice and paying necessary living expenses and fell behind on his child support payments. The letter claimed that the payments made from the funds realized from the FMC sale in July and home refinancing in September 2003, were necessary to pay judgments rendered against him and to avoid additional legal proceedings.

* * *

From the refinance of his residence petitioner received a net amount of $25,158. Petitioner used $11,000 to pay delinquent child support and transferred the remaining $14,158 to his professional corporation (which was used to pay a supplier, malpractice insurance, delinquent telephone charges, and payroll).

Also in his response to the preliminary determination, petitioner asserted that the attorney's fees were an allowable necessary expense because they were necessary for his representation before the IRS with respect to his current tax matters. He closed the letter by saying he thought negotiation of an offer-in-compromise was possible given his belief that he did not dissipate assets and that he is allowed to claim attorney's fees as an expense.

On March 8, 2005, the settlement officer sent a letter to petitioner stating that her positions on the dissipated assets and attorney's fees remained unchanged. Petitioner did not respond to this letter and never increased his offer.

On April 8, 2005, Appeals issued petitioner a notice of determination sustaining the proposed collection actions. The summary of determination concluded that petitioner's proposed collection alternative was not a viable option. The notice indicated Appeals' finding that the IRS could collect more than the $30,000 offer. The notice referred to the discovery of the dissipated assets during consideration of the offer-in-compromise. The notice acknowledged the $15,600 payment to the IRS but pointed out that the remaining $117,558 was distributed to other creditors. It noted that petitioner was given the opportunity to increase his offer but declined to do so. * * *

The settlement officer's Appeals Case Determination (Case Determination) reflects that in recommending petitioner's offer based on doubt as to collectibility be rejected, she calculated petitioner's future income potential plus his net realizable equity (NRE) in assets to get the reasonable collection potential for the case.

In determining petitioner's NRE, the settlement officer decided that petitioner had dissipated assets in disregard of his tax liabilities when he sold his interest in FMC and when he refinanced his home. She considered the assets dissipated because petitioner realized the funds after his tax liabilities for 1996–2002 had accrued and after the amounts due for 1997–2001 were assessed, and he used all of the funds to pay other creditors, with the exception of the $15,600 payment to the IRS. She determined that 100 percent of the $133,158 received from the dissipated assets should be included in petitioner's NRE with the possible exception of the $15,600 paid to the IRS, the $5,000 legal fees incurred in the lawsuit against his former employer, and the $5,464 paid for child support. She reached this conclusion despite recognizing that the assets were dissipated before the offer-in-compromise was made. The settlement officer did not include any amount for the value of petitioner's residence in NRE, having determined that he had no equity. She also expressed doubt as to whether petitioner reported an accurate value for his interest in his medical corporation, noting the comparatively low value of equipment totaling $3,630 given that the business had gross income in excess of $300,000 in 2003. The settlement officer did not account for petitioner's interests in his medical corporation or Pontchartrain Lithotripsy in calculating NRE. The settlement officer determined petitioner's future income collection potential to be $946 per month, which, over 60 months (the multiplier for a short-term deferred payment offer) amounted to $56,760.[8]

In response to the notice of determination, petitioner filed a petition with this Court.

DISCUSSION

Before a levy may be made on any property or right to property, a taxpayer is entitled to notice of the Commissioner's intent to levy and notice of the right to a fair hearing before an impartial officer of the IRS Appeals Office. Secs. 6330(a) and (b), 6331(d). . . .

Where, as here, the underlying tax liability is not at issue, our review of the notice of determination under section 6330 is for abuse of discretion. *See Sego v. Commissioner*, 114 T.C. 604, 610 (2000); *Goza v. Commissioner*, 114 T.C. 176, 182 (2000). This standard does not require us to decide what we think would be an acceptable offer-in-compromise. *Murphy v. Comm'r*, 125 T.C. 301, 320 (2005), *aff'd*. 469 F.3d 27 (1st Cir. 2006). Rather, our review is to determine whether respondent's rejection of petitioner's offer-in-compromise was arbitrary, capricious, or without sound basis in fact or law. *Id.*

* * *

Section 7122(a) authorizes the Secretary to compromise any civil or criminal case arising under the internal revenue laws. * * *

The Secretary may compromise a tax liability based on doubt as to collectibility where the taxpayer's assets and income are less than the full amount of the liability. Sec. 301.7122-1(b)(2), Proced. & Admin. Regs. Generally, under the Commissioner's administrative procedures, an offer-in-compromise based on doubt as to collectibility will be acceptable only if it reflects the taxpayer's "reasonable collection potential". Rev. Proc. 2003-71, sec. 4.02(2), 2003-2 C.B. 517. Both parties appear to agree that petitioner's reasonable collection potential is substantially less than his tax liability which, as above noted, stood at more than $773,368, as of January 1, 2005. The parties obviously disagree as to petitioner's collection potential.

The IRS has developed guidelines and procedures for the submission and evaluation of offers to compromise under section 7122. Rev. Proc. 2003-71, *supra*. In furtherance thereof, the Internal Revenue Manual (IRM) contains extensive guidelines for evaluating offers-in-compromise. 1 Administration, Internal Revenue Manual (CCH), sec. 5.8, at 16,253. Both petitioner and respondent focus substantial attention in their briefs to the issue of "Dissipation of Assets", discussed below.

[8] [Note that the Worksheet to Calculate an Offer Amount refers to line numbers from a version of Form 433-A that is less recent than the one included in this chapter. In particular, the reference to "Item 34" in entry 12 of the worksheet should be to Item 32 of the Form 433-A included in this chapter. — Eds.]

The IRM provides in part, in "Dissipation of Assets", section 5.8.5.4, at 16,339-6, the following:

> (1) During an offer investigation it may be discovered that assets (liquid or non-liquid) have been sold, gifted, transferred, or spent on non-priority items and/or debts and are no longer available to pay the tax liability. This section discusses treatment of the value of these assets when considering an offer in compromise.
>
> * * *
>
> (2) Once it is determined that a specific asset has been dissipated, the investigation should address whether the value of the asset, or a portion of the value, should be included in an acceptable offer amount.
>
> (3) Inclusion of the value of dissipated assets must clearly be justified in the case file and documented on the ICS/AOIC history. * * *
>
> (4) When the taxpayer can show that assets have been dissipated to provide for necessary living expenses, these amounts should not be included in the reasonable collection potential (RCP) calculation.
>
> * * *
>
> (5) If the investigation clearly reveals that assets have been dissipated with a disregard of the outstanding tax liability, *consider including the value in the reasonable collection potential (RCP) calculation.* [Emphasis added.]

It is not totally clear how dissipated assets can be "no longer available to pay the tax liability" (see (1), above) while at the same time included in the "reasonable collection potential (RCP) calculation" (see (5), above).

The settlement officer apparently considered herself required to apply this rather cryptic guideline, and under an abuse of discretion standard we are not at liberty to challenge her judgment that it should be used. However, under the abuse of discretion standard, we must assure that the guideline is correctly applied.

The Appeals Case Determination states that:

> Appeals preliminary determination of Dr. Samuel's net realizable equity (NRE) in his assets is that it should include 100% of his dissipated assets totaling $133,158 with the possible exception of the $15,600 paid for his 2003 estimated tax payment, his legal fees of $5,000 incurred in association with his civil law suit against his prior employer and $5,464 paid for child support. He has no net realizable equity in his personal residence given that quick sale value (QSV) is used and offset against his mortgage of $322,000. Since his mortgage exceeds the QSV of $320,000 (80% of FMV determined to be at $400,000), he has no equity to include in his NRE. Appeals believes that his interest in his medical corporation exceeds that which was reported at the face-to-face hearing to be the value of the equipment totaling $3,630. This is an on-going business that had gross income in excess of $300,000 in 2003.

The Appeals Case Determination goes on to state that:

> Dr. Samuel was provided the opportunity to increase his offered amount to at least include amounts he realized pursuant to his dissipated assets in order that his offer receive further consideration. He declined to so do.

The $15,600 which Dr. Samuel paid for his 2003 estimated tax payment should have been excluded from the dissipated assets category, and if Appeals was in doubt about the includability of the $5,000 incurred in association with Dr. Samuel's civil law suit and the $5,464 paid for child support, these amounts should have been excluded also. It was an abuse of discretion not to do so.

It is represented in his brief that petitioner has been current on all of the filings and payments of his taxes, starting with 2003. It appears from the Appeals Case Determination that petitioner has in fact minimal assets from which cash could be realized, but that he has a medical practice that produces a fairly substantial amount of income. Clearly, then, any IRS recovery from petitioner would have to come principally, if not entirely, from his medical practice income.

* * *

Petitioner points out that 2 Administration, Internal Revenue Manual (CCH), section 5.15.1.10(3), at 17,662, allows as a necessary expense accounting and legal fees if representation before the IRS is needed or meets the necessary expense tests. The costs must be related to solving the current controversy. In calculating petitioner's future income potential, the settlement officer failed to allow monthly payments of $250 which petitioner was making to his tax attorney in connection with the current controversy. The corrected income potential would thus be $41,760.

The Appeals Case Determination takes the position that Appeals was not required to counteroffer petitioner's offer-in-compromise, but petitioner points out that 1 Administration, Internal Revenue Manual (CCH), section 5.8.4.6., at 16,308, provides that in the course of processing the case, if the taxpayer's offer must be increased in order to be recommended for acceptance, the taxpayer must be contacted by letter or telephone advising the taxpayer "to amend the offer to the acceptable amount". In the present case, petitioner should have been advised that instead of 100 percent of the dissipated assets, totaling $133,158, an acceptable amount would be $133,158 less $26,064 ($15,600 plus $5,000 plus $5,464), or $107,094. Appeals' failure to do so was an abuse of discretion, and we so hold.

Petitioner should be given the opportunity to revise his offer-in-compromise to reflect the $107,094, referred to above. However, since petitioner appears to lack any substantial assets outside his medical practice which could provide a source for paying any compromise amount, it is obvious, as previously observed, that any payments would come from his medical earnings. The [facts] unquestionably reveals that petitioner has ample income in excess of his $30,000 offer payable over 24 months.

We shall remand this case to Appeals for a 60-day period within which petitioner may, if he so chooses, revise the amount of his offer-in-compromise and suggest new terms of payment in accordance herewith.

An appropriate order will be issued.

Why, according to the court, should Dr. Samuel have to increase the net realizable value of his assets by $107,094? How did the court calculate that figure? Also, why did the IRS Appeals Officer not include Dr. Samuel's personal residence in the calculation of his net realizable equity when the residence had a gross current fair market value of $400,000?

[D] Offers Based on Doubt as to Liability

Given that a taxpayer has other avenues available to negotiate with the IRS over the extent of his or her tax liability, compromises on the basis of doubt as to liability are far rarer than those for doubt as to collectibility. The Treasury regulations provide that doubt as to liability exists "where there is a genuine dispute as to the existence or amount of the correct tax liability under the law." Treas. Reg. § 301.7122-1(b)(1). The regulations also provide that tax liability based on a final court decision cannot form the basis for an offer based on doubt as to liability. *Id.* In a case in which a deficiency assessment was made with little or no action by the taxpayer to defend against it, a representative may be able to compromise a previously assessed liability by raising the possibility that the taxpayer might prevail in a refund action following payment. An offer based on doubt as to liability might also relate to innocent spouse relief, discussed in Chapter 17, or the assertion of penalties.[9]

A taxpayer applying for an offer in compromise based on doubt as to liability files Form 656-L. The form does not require the taxpayer to submit a Collection Financial Statement, Form 433. If the IRS accepts the offer and the taxpayer satisfies all the obligations under the agreement, the IRS abates any tax liability in excess of the offer amount. *See* Form 656-L.

[E] Offers Based on Effective Tax Administration

Reading Assignment: Treas. Reg. § 301.7122-1(b)–(c).

Even if the taxpayer has assets and income that allow the taxpayer to pay the amount of tax liability owed, the IRS may still accept an offer in compromise if it promotes "effective tax administration" (ETA). *See* Treas. Reg. § 301.7122-1(b)(3). According to the regulations, an ETA offer may be allowed when collection of the entire liability would cause economic hardship for the taxpayer. Economic hardship might exist, for instance, if a taxpayer (or the taxpayer's dependent) faces a long-term illness, medical condition, or disability and it is foreseeable that the taxpayer's financial resources would be exhausted as a result. Economic hardship can also cover cases where the sale or liquidation of assets to pay a tax bill would prevent the taxpayer from meeting basic living expenses. *See* Treas. Reg. § 301.7122-1(c)(3)(i).

Even though economic hardship may not exist, the IRS may accept an ETA offer where "compelling public policy or equity considerations" provide a sufficient basis for compromising the liability. "Compromise will be justified only where, due to exceptional circumstances, collection of the full liability would undermine public confidence that the tax laws are being administered in a fair and equitable manner." Treas. Reg. § 301.7122-1(b)(3)(ii). No ETA offer will be accepted if to do so would undermine taxpayer compliance. Treas. Reg. § 301.7122-1(b)(3)(iii). Factors the IRS will consider when determining whether an ETA compromise agreement will have a negative impact on compliance are the requesting taxpayer's own compliance history, whether the taxpayer deliberately avoided paying taxes, and whether the taxpayer encouraged others to avoid paying their taxes. Treas. Reg. § 301.7122-1(c)(3)(ii). The regulations include several examples that explain these standards in more detail. *See also* I.R.M. 5.8.11.

If the IRS determines that the taxpayer also qualifies for an offer based on doubt as to collectibility, the IRS will not accept an ETA offer. If payment of the liability would still cause the taxpayer economic hardship, however, the IRS may treat the offer as one based on doubt as to collectibility with special circumstances. The same factors the IRS takes into account when processing an ETA offer are taken into account in a "special circumstances" offer. I.R.M. 5.8.4.3(4).

Some observers maintain that the IRS has interpreted the grounds for an ETA offer too narrowly. The following case, which involves the Tax Court's review of an Appeals Officer's determination to deny an offer as part of a CDP hearing, illustrates the IRS's approach to these types of offers and the Tax Court's reaction:

[9] The Code prohibits the IRS from rejecting an offer based on doubt as to liability because the IRS is unable to locate the taxpayer's return information. I.R.C. § 7122(d)(3)(B).

BARNES v. COMMISSIONER

United States Tax Court
T.C. Memo. 2006-150

LARO, JUDGE:

Petitioners petitioned the Court under section 6330(d) to review the determination of respondent's Office of Appeals (Appeals) sustaining a proposed levy relating to $342,012 of Federal income taxes (inclusive of interest) owed by petitioners for 1981 through 1986. Petitioners argue that Appeals was required to accept their offer of $32,000 to compromise what they estimate is their approximately $400,000 Federal income tax liability (inclusive of interest) for 1981 through 1998. We decide whether Appeals abused its discretion in rejecting that offer. We hold it did not.

FINDINGS OF FACT

The parties filed with the Court stipulations of fact and accompanying exhibits. The stipulated facts are found accordingly. When the petition was filed, petitioners resided in Pasco, Washington.

Beginning in 1984, petitioners' Federal income tax returns claimed losses and credits from their involvement in various partnerships organized and operated by Walter J. Hoyt, III (Hoyt) * * * . Hoyt was each partnership's general partner and tax matters partner, and the partnerships were all subject to the unified audit and litigation procedures of the Tax Equity and Fiscal Responsibility Act of 1982, Pub. L. 97-248, sec. 401, 96 Stat. 648. Hoyt was convicted on criminal charges relating to the promotion of these partnerships.

Petitioners' claim to the losses and credits resulted in the underreporting of their 1981 through 1986 taxable income. On August 16, 2003, respondent mailed to petitioners a Letter 1058, Final Notice of Intent to Levy and Notice of Your Right to a Hearing. The notice informed petitioners that respondent proposed to levy on their property to collect Federal income taxes that they owed for 1981 through 1986. The notice advised petitioners that they were entitled to a hearing with Appeals to review the propriety of the proposed levy.

On September 5, 2003, petitioners asked Appeals for the referenced hearing. On January 11, 2005, Linda Cochran (Cochran), a settlement officer in Appeals, held the hearing with petitioners' counsel. * * * The first issue concerned petitioners' intent to offer to compromise their 1981 through 1998 Federal income tax liability due to doubt as to collectibility with special circumstances and to promote effective tax administration. Petitioners contended that Appeals should accept their offer as a matter of equity and public policy. Petitioners stated that it took a long time to resolve the Hoyt partnership cases and noted that Hoyt had been convicted on the criminal charges. * * *

On February 15, 2005, petitioners tendered to Cochran on Form 656, Offer in Compromise, a written offer to pay $32,000 to compromise their approximately $400,000 liability. Petitioners supplemented their offer with a completed Form 433-A, Collection Information Statement for Wage Earners and Self-Employed Individuals, four letters totaling approximately 65 pages, and volumes of documents. The Form 433-A reported that petitioners owned assets with a total current value of $144,322 * * *.

* * *

As to the reported expenses, Cochran accepted all of those expenses except for the $500 "other expense" which petitioners failed to substantiate as to either its source or amount.[n.7] Cochran determined that petitioners' monthly excess income (i.e., monthly

---

[n.7] Cochran allowed petitioners' medical expenses in full, although she considered the amount to be greater

income less monthly expenses) was $501 ($4,707 − ($4,706 − $500)), that petitioners' income potential for the next 48 months was approximately $24,000 ($501 × 48 = $24,048), and that petitioners' reasonable collection potential was $163,617 (future income potential of $24,000 + net realizable equity of $139,617). As an alternate calculation, Cochran took into account petitioners' $500 other expense (so as to eliminate any consideration of future income potential) and recomputed their reasonable collection potential at their net realizable equity of $139,617.[n.9] Cochran performed the alternate calculation because she believed that the "other expense" could represent an otherwise allowable expense such as attorney's fees, although not reported as such.

On May 12, 2005, Appeals issued petitioners the notice of determination sustaining the proposed levy. The notice concludes that petitioners' $32,000 offer-in-compromise is not an appropriate collection alternative to the proposed levy. The notice, quoting in part Internal Revenue Manual (IRM) section 5.8.11.2.2.3, states that petitioners' offer does not meet the Commissioner's guidelines for consideration of an offer-in-compromise due to doubt as to collectibility with special circumstances. The notice, citing IRM sections 5.8.11.1.2 and 5.8.11.2.5, states that petitioners' offer also does not meet the Commissioner's guidelines for consideration as an offer-in compromise to promote effective tax administration.

* * *

OPINION

This case is one in a long list of cases brought in this Court involving respondent's proposal to levy on the assets of a partner in a Hoyt partnership to collect Federal income taxes attributable to the partner's participation in the partnership. * * *

* * *

Petitioners made their offer-in-compromise due to doubt as to collectibility with special circumstances and to promote effective tax administration. Petitioners reported on their Form 433-A that their reasonable collection potential was $140,462 (i.e., their assets' total reported current value of $144,322 less their $3,860 Buick LeSabre which was fully encumbered by debt). Cochran determined petitioners' reasonable collection potential by way of alternative calculations. Under each of those calculations, petitioners cannot fully pay their approximately $400,000 tax liability and thus do not qualify for an offer-in-compromise to promote effective tax administration. *See* sec. 301.7122-1(b)(3), Proced. & Admin. Regs.; *cf.* Fargo v. Comm'r, 447 F.3d 706 (9th Cir. 2006) (taxpayers made an offer-in-compromise to promote effective tax administration where they had sufficient assets to pay their tax liability in full). As to petitioners' offer-in-compromise due to doubt as to collectibility with special circumstances, the Commissioner evaluates such an offer by applying the same factors (economic hardship or considerations of public policy or equity) as in the case of an offer-in-compromise to promote effective tax administration. *See* IRM sec. 5.8.11.2.1 and .2. In accordance with the Commissioner's guidelines, an offer-in-compromise due to doubt as to collectibility with special circumstances should not be accepted even when economic hardship or considerations of public policy or equity circumstances are identified, if the taxpayer does not offer an acceptable amount. *See* IRM sec. 5.8.11.2.1.11 and .12.

Cochran considered all of the evidence submitted to her by petitioners and applied the guidelines for evaluating an offer-in-compromise due to doubt as to collectibility with special circumstances or to promote effective tax administration. As to the former,

---

than average. Cochran noted that petitioners' 2003 Federal income tax return claimed a deduction for $8,641 of medical expenses that they paid during that year.

[n.9] Cochran noted that the alternate calculations would be $131,617 and $107,617 were she to take into account the $32,000 proposed offer.

Cochran determined that petitioners' offer was unacceptable because they were able to pay more than the $32,000 that they offered to compromise their tax liability. As to the latter, Cochran determined that petitioners' offer did not qualify as an offer-in-compromise to promote effective tax administration because petitioners were unable to pay their liability in full. Cochran's determination to reject petitioners' offer-in-compromise was not arbitrary, capricious, or without a sound basis in fact or law, and it was not abusive or unfair to petitioners. Cochran's determination was based on a reasonable application of the guidelines, which we decline to second-guess. *See* Speltz v. Comm'r, 124 T.C. 165 (2005), *affd.* ___ F.3d ___ (8th Cir. 2006).

Petitioners make eight arguments in advocating a contrary result. * * *

* * *

Third, petitioners argue that Cochran inadequately considered their unique facts and circumstances. We disagree. Cochran reviewed and considered all information given to her by petitioners. On the basis of the facts and circumstances of petitioners' case as they had been presented to her, Cochran determined that petitioners' offer did not meet the applicable guidelines for acceptance of an offer-in-compromise due to doubt as to collectibility with special circumstances or to promote effective tax administration. We find no abuse of discretion in that determination.

Petitioners take exception to the fact that the notice of determination does not state specifically that petitioners are in their sixties and retired, speculating from this fact that Cochran did not adequately take into account their special circumstances. Petitioners also assert that Cochran failed to take their special circumstances into account because, they assert, she did not reflect that they both have "significant medical conditions" and that their medical expenses will increase in later years. Petitioners' assertions and speculation are without merit. We do not believe that Appeals must specifically list in the notice of determination every single fact that it considered in arriving at the determination. Nor do we find that Cochran inadequately considered the information actually given to her by petitioners. In fact, Cochran computed petitioners' future income potential by using the same income figures that petitioners reported on their Form 433-A, and the reported items of income were all types of retirement income that could reasonably be expected to remain constant over the next 48 months. Cochran's calculations also reflected her generous assessment that: (1) In the 48-month period, petitioners would pay $1,087 of medical expenses monthly, although she believed that amount to be greater than average, (2) petitioners had overstated the values of their vehicles and were entitled to a 20-percent reduction in those values, although petitioners had reported their vehicles at their trade-in values, (3) petitioners had properly valued their home and other real property at their assessed values, although appraisals or current market value may be higher, and (4) petitioners may be allowed to claim their $500 "other expense" as a monthly expense, although the nature of the expense had not been identified. Although petitioners believe that Cochran's calculation should have reflected increased medical expenses in the 48-month period and thereafter, we do not agree. We are unable to find that petitioners ever told Cochran with specificity that they would have to pay a greater amount of unreimbursed medical expenses in the future. Under the facts at hand, we consider it reasonable for Cochran to have used petitioners' $1,087 monthly estimate, particularly when the estimate, if annualized, exceeded petitioners' prior year's actual medical expenses. *See* Fargo v. Commissioner, 447 F.3d at 710 (it is not an abuse of discretion to disregard claimed medical expenses that are speculative or not related to the taxpayer).

Fourth, petitioners argue that Cochran did not adequately take into account the economic hardship they claim they will suffer by having to pay more than $32,000 as to their tax liability. We disagree. Section 301.6343-1(b)(4)(i), Proced. & Admin. Regs., states that economic hardship occurs when a taxpayer is "unable to pay his or her reasonable basic living expenses." Section 301.7122-1(c)(3), Proced. & Admin. Regs., sets forth factors to consider in evaluating whether collection of a tax liability would cause economic hardship, as well as some illustrative examples. One of the examples involves a taxpayer who provides full-time care to a dependent child with a serious long-term illness. A second example involves a taxpayer who would lack adequate means to pay his basic living expenses were his only asset to be liquidated. A third example involves a disabled taxpayer with a fixed income and a modest home specially equipped to accommodate his disability, and who is unable to borrow against his home because of his disability. *See* sec. 301.7122-1(c)(3)(iii), Examples (1), (2), and (3), Proced. & Admin. Regs. None of these examples bears any resemblance to this case but instead "describe more dire circumstances". Speltz v. Comm'r, ___ F.3d at ___.

Nor have petitioners articulated with any specificity the purported economic hardship they will suffer if they are not allowed to compromise their liability for $32,000. While petitioners claim generally that the sale of their residence would create an economic hardship in that they would be unable to afford paying either rent or a mortgage, this claim is vague, speculative, undocumented, and unavailing. Nor are we persuaded by petitioners' suggestion that their health is an "economic hardship" by virtue of section 301.7122-1(c)(3)(i)(A), Proced. & Admin. Regs. In this regard, petitioners have given us no reason to disagree with the essence of Cochran's determination that petitioners' health does not render them "incapable of earning a living", nor have we reason to conclude that petitioners' "financial resources will be exhausted providing for care and support during the course of the condition". *Id.*

* * *

Fifth, petitioners argue that public policy demands that their offer-in-compromise be accepted because they were victims of fraud. We disagree. While the regulations do not set forth a specific standard for evaluating an offer-in-compromise based on claims of public policy or equity, the regulations contain two illustrative examples. *See* sec. 301.7122-1(c)(3)(iv), Examples (1) and (2), Proced. & Admin. Regs. The first example describes a taxpayer who is seriously ill and unable to file income tax returns for several years. The second example describes a taxpayer who received erroneous advice from the Commissioner as to the tax effect of the taxpayer's actions. Neither example bears any resemblance to this case. Accord Speltz v. Comm'r, supra. Unlike the exceptional circumstances exemplified in the regulations, petitioners' situation is neither unique nor exceptional in that their situation mirrors numerous taxpayers who claimed tax shelter deductions in the 1980s and 1990s, obtained the tax advantages, promptly forgot about their "investment", and now realize that paying their taxes will require a change of lifestyle.

We also agree with a claim by respondent that compromising petitioners' case on grounds of public policy or equity would not promote effective tax administration. While petitioners portray themselves as victims of Hoyt's alleged fraud and respondent's alleged delay in dealing with Hoyt, they take no responsibility for their tax predicament. We cannot agree that acceptance by respondent of petitioners' $32,000 offer to satisfy their approximately $400,000 tax liability would enhance voluntary compliance by other taxpayers. A compromise on that basis would place the Government in the unenviable role of an insurer against poor business decisions by taxpayers, reducing the incentive for taxpayers to investigate thoroughly the consequences of transactions into which they enter. It would be particularly inappropriate for the Government to play that role here, where the transaction at issue is participation in a tax shelter. Reducing the risks of participating in tax shelters would encourage more taxpayers to run those risks, thus undermining rather than enhancing compliance with the tax laws.

* * *

We hold that Appeals did not abuse its discretion in rejecting petitioners' $32,000 offer-in-compromise. In so holding, we express no opinion as to the amount of any compromise that petitioners could or should be required to pay, or that respondent is required to accept. The only issue before us is whether Appeals abused its discretion in refusing to accept petitioners' specific offer-in-compromise in the amount of $32,000. *See* Speltz v. Comm'r, 124 T.C. at 179–180. We have considered all arguments made by petitioners for a contrary holding and have found those arguments not discussed herein to be without merit.

An appropriate order will be issued.

The Barneses were among several thousand investors in various cattle and sheep breeding activities marketed by Hoyt. After the Tax Court denied deductions and credits claimed by the investors, *see* Durham Farms # 1 v. Commissioner, T.C. Memo. 2000-159, *aff'd*, 2003-1 U.S.T.C. ¶ 50,391 (9th Cir. 2003), many of these investors received deficiency notices asserting penalties and interest well in excess of the actual deficiency amount. Why was the Tax Court so reluctant to approve an offer in compromise in this situation? If the investors reasonably relied on tax advice from Hoyt, wouldn't public policy be served by granting them some relief?

[F] Effect on Collection Activities

Reading Assignment: I.R.C. § 6331(i)(5), (k); Treas. Reg. § 301.7122-1(g), (i).

Once a taxpayer submits an offer in compromise, the IRS typically cannot levy against the taxpayer's property while it processes the offer.[10] Treas. Reg. § 301.7122-1(g); *see also* I.R.C. § 6331(k). Collection action is also postponed for 30 days following rejection of the taxpayer's offer, and during any appeal of that rejection. During these periods in which the IRS cannot enforce collection, the statute of limitations in section 6502 is tolled. I.R.C. § 6331(i)(5).

If an accepted offer is payable in installments, the taxpayer may be asked to extend the statute of limitations on assessment for the period the offer remains in force. Treas. Reg. § 301.7122-1(i). During the taxable year the offer is accepted, the IRS will also retain any refund to which the taxpayer would otherwise be entitled and apply that refund against the taxpayer's outstanding tax liability. *See* I.R.M. 5.8.1.9.5; Form 656. In some cases, the acceptance of the offer may be conditioned upon the taxpayer's execution of a collateral agreement to pay to the IRS a certain percentage of the taxpayer's future income over a specified number of years or waive current or future tax benefits (such as losses or deductions). *See* Treas. Reg. § 301.7122-1(e)(2); I.R.M. 5.8.6.3.

§ 15.05 THE BANKRUPTCY OPTION

Another alternative that may be available to a taxpayer facing the threat of enforced IRS collection proceedings is to file a petition in bankruptcy. The Bankruptcy Code, 11 U.S.C. § 101 *et seq.*, provides that certain tax liabilities are dischargeable in bankruptcy. Although a broad treatment of the bankruptcy rules relating to dischargeable tax debts is beyond the scope of this chapter, some understanding of which tax liabilities may be discharged is helpful to the tax practitioner.

The Bankruptcy Code lists those tax debts for which personal liability can and cannot be discharged. Once the debtor's tax liabilities are discharged in bankruptcy, the IRS is enjoined from seeking to collect any further amounts not recovered through the bankruptcy proceeding. 11 U.S.C. § 524. If the taxes are not dischargeable, the IRS can

---

[10] The IRS Reform Act added a rule prohibiting the IRS from levying against the taxpayer's property during the period that any offer in compromise is pending, during the 30-day period following rejection of the offer, or during the period any appeal of a rejected offer is pending. *See* I.R.C. § 6331(k). This prohibition does not apply if the IRS believes that the taxpayer is engaging in compromise negotiations primarily for delay, and that collection of the liability is in jeopardy. I.R.C. § 6331(k)(3), (i)(3)(A)(ii).

seek to collect the amounts as part of the bankruptcy proceeding or wait until the automatic stay is lifted and then collect the amounts directly from the taxpayer.

As a general rule, all tax claims except priority taxes are dischargeable. Thus, income taxes may be discharged if they were (1) due more than three years before the bankruptcy petition is filed and (2) assessed more than 240 days before such date. *See* Section 14.03[A][3] for a discussion of priority claims in bankruptcy. The employer's share of employment taxes (not trust fund taxes) that were due more than three years prior to filing the petition is also dischargeable. In addition to priority taxes, tax underpayments attributable to fraudulent returns or willful tax evasion, regardless of when the fraud or evasion occurred, and claims relating to taxes for which a required return was not filed or was filed late (but within two years before the bankruptcy petition date) are not dischargeable.[11] *See* 11 U.S.C. § 523(a)(1). Furthermore, the taxpayer's transfer of nonexempt assets in an attempt to delay or defraud creditors (including the IRS) will prevent his or her debts from being discharged in bankruptcy. 11 U.S.C. § 727(a).

The rules relating to dischargeability set forth above apply in Chapter 7 (liquidation) cases. The same general rules also apply in Chapter 11 (reorganization) and Chapter 13 (individual) cases, with certain exceptions. For example, in a Chapter 13 case, some priority taxes (other than trust fund taxes and taxes attributable to fraud) may be discharged if less than full payment of those tax debts is provided for in the plan and the IRS fails to object. *See* 11 U.S.C. § 1328(a)(2).

For a taxpayer whose total liabilities substantially exceed the taxpayer's assets and whose tax liability is presently dischargeable, a bankruptcy petition may present a viable option. However, because a bankruptcy action implicates important non-tax considerations, the taxpayer should consider this alternative carefully before deciding it is best. Faced with the possibility of seeking an offer in compromise or filing a bankruptcy petition, for instance, the taxpayer must weigh the discharged tax liabilities against the negative effect the bankruptcy filing may have on his or her credit rating.

The following excerpt raises some other considerations a taxpayer should think about when deciding whether to file for bankruptcy or request an offer in compromise.

Howard S. Levy, *Bankruptcy or Offer in Compromise? Where the Bankruptcy Code and IRS Policy Meet*
2 J. TAX PRAC. & PROC. 33 (Feb.–Mar. 2000)[12]

Timing Elements

Obtaining a bankruptcy discharge is often a waiting game, involving stringent adherence to multiple timing rules. A tax bankruptcy must be commenced more than three years after the tax returns were due to be filed (including extensions). If the returns were filed late, the bankruptcy must also be commenced more than two years from the date when the returns were filed. For example, if a return was filed four years after it was due, the client would then have to wait an additional two years after it was actually filed before becoming eligible for bankruptcy.

Additionally, a client must wait 240 days after a tax assessment to become eligible for a discharge. Where an offer in compromise has been submitted within 240 days after a tax assessment, the bankruptcy filing also will be delayed by the amount of time the compromise is pending plus 30 days. These periods operate independently of the

---

[11] For purposes of determining what constitutes a return for dischargeability purposes, a return prepared by the IRS pursuant to section 6020(a) and signed by the taxpayer is treated as a filed return. However, a substitute return prepared by the IRS under its authority in section 6020(b) is not considered a return for these purposes. *See* 11 U.S.C. § 523(a)(1)(B).

[12]

two-year/three-year rule. Bankruptcies and offers-in-compromise should be avoided 240 days after assessment.

In contrast to the stringent bankruptcy timing rules, an offer in compromise may be submitted at any time after assessment. No time constraints limit when an offer in compromise can be submitted, although the taxpayer must adhere to issues of processability.

* * *

Limitations on Type of Tax Involved

* * *

The IRS has greater latitude than the bankruptcy court to compromise tax debts. Under Code Sec. 7122(a), an offer in compromise can be used to settle any civil or criminal case before it is referred to the Department of Justice or after it has been referred to the Attorney General. This includes cases concerning dischargeable trust fund taxes, employment taxes, excise taxes and fraud, all of which are nondischargeable in a Chapter 7 bankruptcy.

* * *

Statute of Limitations

The filing of a bankruptcy petition or an offer in compromise gives the IRS more time to collect the tax in the event either is unsuccessful. When a bankruptcy petition is filed, the statute of limitations for collection is extended by the period the bankruptcy is pending (until dismissal or discharge) and for six months thereafter. Any offer in compromise pending on, or made after, December 31, 1999, automatically suspends the statue of limitations on collection for the period during which the IRS is investigating the offer, for 30 days after any rejection of the offer, and for any period during which the IRS is considering a timely filed appeal.

* * *

With the new Collection Due Process Appeals, avenues may exist to have the Tax Court review an offer-in-compromise issue properly included in a due process appeal that is filed in anticipation of submitting an offer. This would further extend the statute of limitations by the time of the Tax Court review. If the statute of limitations on collection is set to expire, it may be preferable to allow the statute to expire without the filing of a bankruptcy or a compromise.

* * *

Staying a Collection

When confronted with an IRS collection officer who is unwilling to release a property seizure, consideration should be given to using an offer in compromise or bankruptcy to stop IRS collection activity.

While an offer in compromise is pending, the IRS cannot engage in any action to collect the tax. The prohibition encompasses the period during which the IRS is evaluating and investigating the offer, the 30 days immediately following any rejection of the offer, and any period during which Appeals is considering a rejection.

Investigation and acceptance of a compromise take a minimum of six to nine months. If the offer is rejected and appealed, the time during which the appeal is being considered would extend the stay on collection to more than one year. However, the IRS may continue to pursue collection while an offer is being investigated if the offer is submitted solely for purposes of delay, does not contain adequate information to permit an investigation, cannot be processed, or jeopardizes collection of the tax.

* * *

When a bankruptcy petition is filed, the automatic stay provisions of 11 U.S.C. § 362(a) prevent the IRS from pursuing collection of outstanding taxes. The automatic stay provisions operate regardless of whether the underlying tax is dischargeable. The stay provisions operate to prevent the IRS collection activity from the date of filing until the earliest date on which the bankruptcy is closed, the bankruptcy is dismissed, or a discharge granted or denied.

The IRS may commence collection action on any property of the bankruptcy estate that the trustee abandons before the case is closed. Alternatively, the IRS may seek relief from the automatic stay provisions. Generally, a relief from stay is granted if a creditor can prove that it lacks adequate protection to assure that its interest in the bankruptcy estate will not decline in value during the bankruptcy.

* * *

Bankruptcy as Leverage in Compromise

An essential component to the value of an offer in compromise is the analysis of a client's disposable income. * * *

* * *

What if a client has disposable income that, if analyzed in a compromise, would result in a cost prohibitive administrative settlement? What if the tax liabilities were all dischargeable in the event a bankruptcy is filed? Of course, the client is ambivalent about filing for bankruptcy and prefers administrative settlement.

The IRS is permitted to consider the collection result of a potential bankruptcy discharge in evaluating the amount of a compromise. The Internal Revenue Manual provides that when a taxpayer threatens bankruptcy in an offer in compromise, the amount of the offer may be negotiated as a calculated business decision. Amounts that are negotiable based on a threatened bankruptcy include monies that may be collected from future income because the IRS would be barred from collecting from disposable income after a Chapter 7 bankruptcy against discharged liabilities.

Properly implemented, this provision can eliminate disposable income from an offer in compromise analysis. The result can be a compromise equal to only the value of exempt compromise assets, mirroring the result of a bankruptcy filing without the bankruptcy. In recognition of the benefit a client receives by getting a bankruptcy result without a bankruptcy, the IRS can request an amount in compromise that is slightly in excess of the amount that could be collected if bankruptcy is filed.

* * *

The IRS takes the position that it will not process the taxpayer's offer in compromise request if the taxpayer has already filed a petition in bankruptcy. *See* Form 656. Some bankruptcy judges have taken issue with the IRS's policy. In *IRS v. Holmes*, 309 B.R. 824 (M.D. Ga. 2004), for example, the bankruptcy judge issued an order directing the IRS to process and consider the debtor/taxpayer's offer in compromise even though the request was submitted after the debtor/taxpayer filed a petition. The district court affirmed the bankruptcy court's order, finding that the bankruptcy court did have the jurisdiction to require the IRS to process the offer in compromise request.

Why do you suppose the IRS has expressed an unwillingness to consider an offer in compromise during a bankruptcy proceeding? Would allowing the offer request to go forward give the taxpayer two bites at the same apple?

PROBLEMS

1. The IRS properly assessed and sent to Jennifer a Notice and Demand for Payment reflecting $15,000 of unpaid tax liability based on her Year 1 return. She was recently fired from her job and thus does not have the funds available to pay the entire liability within the 10-day period reflected in the notice.
   A. Would the IRS be willing to allow Jennifer to pay the tax debts in installments? How could she request such relief?
   B. Over how many years might the IRS allow her to spread the payments?
   C. How might your answer to Parts A and B change if the outstanding tax debt were $40,000?
   D. If the IRS accepts Jennifer's installment agreement request, is the IRS permitted to file a Notice of Federal Tax Lien during the time that the agreement is in effect? Could the IRS levy against Jennifer's property during the agreement period?
2. Tim was recently released from a drug rehabilitation program. While he was in the program, his former wife burned down his home (which was uninsured) and withdrew, without authorization, all of the funds in his checking account. Tim's only other asset is a rental home he owns with his ten siblings as tenants in common, which has a value of $300,000.
   A. If Tim currently owes $20,000 in tax liability, would the IRS consider allowing Tim to enter into an installment agreement under which he would pay $15,000 of that liability over a period of two years?
   B. If the IRS accepts the proposed agreement, and assuming the statute of limitations on collection remains open, could the IRS collect the remaining $5,000 from Tim after he pays the amounts under the proposed installment agreement?
3. Marge, who is 70 years old, is retired and living on her social security payments, which amount to $1,200 per month. Her only other means of support consists of $6,000 worth of annual dividend income from a minority stock interest she holds in Exx Corporation. Her Exx Corporation stock has an estimated value of $70,000. Her only other asset with any significant value is her home, which she owns free of debt, and which has a fair market value of $75,000. The IRS has validly assessed an unpaid tax liability of $4,000.
   A. Assuming that no doubt exists as to Marge's liability for the $4,000 assessment, what relief might be available to Marge to settle the debt for less than $4,000?
      i. What procedures would Marge need to follow in order to qualify for relief?
      ii. If Marge offers to make a lump sum payment of $2,000 in full satisfaction of the debt, what is the likelihood that the IRS would accept that offer? Assume for these purposes that Marge's allowable monthly expenses total $1,700.
      iii. How would you answer to ii change if Marge, before requesting relief, sold the Exx Corporation stock and used the sales proceeds to take an around-the-world cruise?
   B. How, if at all, would your answer to Part A.ii change if Marge's liability were $120,000 instead of $4,000?
4. Marge, the taxpayer in Problem 3, recently learned from her doctor that she needs to begin a course of treatment for a liver ailment. Marge anticipates that

the treatment will involve an expenditure of several thousand dollars that will not be covered by insurance.

A. Would an IRS agent be willing to consider this future expense when determining whether compromise of the tax liability is appropriate?

B. Assume that Marge's $4,000 tax debt arose from her failure to file a tax return for two consecutive years. She did not file because, at the time, she was dissatisfied with the amount of her social security check and figured she would "make up the difference" by not paying her federal income tax. How would this fact be taken into account when deciding whether she qualifies for the offer in compromise request she makes because of her liver ailment?

5. In Years 1 and 2, Candice, who is single, worked as an independent contractor providing management consulting services. Diamond, Inc. was her biggest client in both years. In Year 1, Candice earned a $200,000 fee from Diamond, Inc., which was paid to her in December of Year 1. When she had not received a 1099 form for Year 1 from Diamond, Inc. by late March of Year 2, she questioned her contact there who assured her that they were "working on it" and that she would receive the Form 1099 in time to file her income tax return by April 15. Candice followed up several times, but Diamond, Inc. never mailed her a copy of a 1099 form. When Candice prepared her Year 1 taxes in April of Year 2, she included only those amounts for which she had received Forms 1099, which totaled $40,000. Candice continued to work for Diamond, Inc. until May of Year 2, at which point, she billed them $150,000. They paid her the $150,000 in July Year 2. In February of Year 3, Candice received a Form 1099 from Diamond, Inc., reflecting payments to her of $350,000 for Year 2. Candice asked her contact to have the form corrected. After several phone calls, he told her that the company had decided it was too much trouble to correct the form and that it really should not matter to Candice because at some time or another she had been paid everything that was reflected in the Form 1099. Candice was frustrated because she had anticipated that only $150,000, plus about $80,000 from other jobs, would be reported to the IRS, and she therefore had not set aside enough money to pay the full tax liability. She received an automatic extension of time to file her Year 2 return. After procrastinating filing her return for several more months, Candice rationalized in December of Year 3 that there would be no harm to the IRS if she did not file a return for Year 2 and instead made it up to the IRS by not taking as many deductions as she legally could the following year.

In early Year 5, Candice received a notice of deficiency from the IRS with respect to her Year 2 tax year. The deficiency was for $115,000, which included unpaid taxes on the income that was reported to the IRS for Year 2, a negligence penalty, a failure to file penalty, an estimated tax penalty, and interest. Candice felt responsible for her lack of payment because it resulted from her failure to file, so she signed the included Form 870, reflecting her agreement to the amount stated, and wrote the IRS a note saying that she did not have the money to pay the tax liability. After sending the signed Form 870 and note back to the IRS, she realized that she might benefit from some legal advice, and consulted you about what she should do to resolve the matter with the IRS. She still has not filed a return for Year 2, though she did timely file for both Years 3 and 4. She also cannot afford to pay more than $15,000 of the $115,000 at this time. How would you advise Candice to proceed?

Chapter 16
THE COLLECTION DUE PROCESS PROCEDURES

§ 16.01 INTRODUCTION

As explained in Chapter 14, once the IRS assesses tax liability, attachment of the federal tax lien; levy; and possibly administrative sale of the taxpayer's assets may proceed without judicial review of the IRS's actions. As the Supreme Court noted early on in *Bull v. United States*, 295 U.S. 247 (1935), "in the field of taxation, . . . [t]he taxpayer often is afforded his hearing after judgment and after payment, and his only redress for unjust administrative action is the right to claim restitution." *Id.* at 260. The administrative collection procedures contained in the Code give the IRS significant advantages over other creditors, most of whom must obtain a court judgment before making efforts to collect amounts owed.

In response to criticisms of the IRS's collection practices, and in an effort to create a more typical debtor/creditor relationship between the taxpayer and the IRS, Congress created the Collection Due Process (CDP) procedures in 1998. *See* S. Rep. No. 105-174 (1998); IRS Reform Act § 3401. Under these procedures, before the IRS can levy on the taxpayer's property, it must give the taxpayer an opportunity for administrative review of the IRS's collections actions by the IRS Appeals Division. After the Appeals Officer renders his or her decision in the form of a notice of determination, the taxpayer has the right to appeal an adverse determination to the Tax Court. As explained below, the CDP procedures provide a meaningful opportunity for the taxpayer to resolve most concerns relating to the lien and levy process and to negotiate with the IRS over the how collection efforts will proceed.

This chapter examines both steps of the CDP process: administrative review at the Appeals level and judicial review of the Appeals determination, in that order. The material on administrative CDP determinations focuses on how to request CDP consideration, how CDP hearings are conducted by Appeals, and what types of issues the Appeals Officer must consider as part of the hearing. The discussion of court review in CDP cases examines such issues as (1) court jurisdiction over CDP appeals, (2) whether a taxpayer can voluntarily dismiss a CDP case, (3) the standard of review applicable in CDP cases, (4) whether review is or should be limited to the record of the CDP hearing at the administrative level, (5) the remedies available to the Tax Court in CDP cases, and (6) whether the Tax Court has refund jurisdiction in CDP cases.

§ 16.02 ADMINISTRATIVE CDP HEARING PROCEDURES

Reading Assignment: I.R.C. §§ 6320, 6330.

Code sections 6320 and 6330, which prescribe the collection due process procedures, are detailed, yet they leave many questions unanswered. Over the past 10 years, the Treasury Department has issued several sets of regulations that flesh out the procedures with more specificity. Judges have also struggled to fill gaps in the statute, arguing at length among one another about matters seemingly as trivial as whether the administrative hearing may be tape recorded and under what circumstances the hearing can take place over the telephone rather than face-to-face. When facing questions about the CDP procedures, the practitioner should consult the lengthy regulations under sections 6320 and 6330, which provide guidance in question and answer format. Another valuable source of information is the IRS's Collection Due Process Handbook, CC-2006-019 (Aug. 18, 2006), *available at* http://www.irs.ustreas.gov/pub/irs-ccdm/cc-2006-019.pdf, which contains information about both administrative and judicial CDP procedures.

[A] Requesting a CDP Hearing

Reading Assignment: I.R.C. §§ 6320(b), 6330(b); Treas. Reg. §§ 301.6320-1(b)–(c), (i), 301.6330-1(d).

Effective for collection activities initiated on or after January 19, 1999, the taxpayer is afforded an opportunity to suspend certain collection efforts in order to request a hearing with the Appeals Division. The Code requires the taxpayer to be notified of the right to request a CDP hearing in two separate instances: (1) After the IRS files a Notice of Federal Tax Lien with respect to the taxpayer's property, I.R.C. § 6320(b)(2), and (2) before the IRS levies on the property, I.R.C. § 6330(b)(2). The Collection Due Process Handbook clarifies how many CDP hearings the taxpayer is entitled to receive for any one taxable year:

> Sections 6320(b)(2) and 6330(b)(2) each provide that a taxpayer is entitled to only one CDP hearing with respect to the tax and tax period(s) covered by the CDP notice. This means that a taxpayer may have an opportunity for one CDP lien hearing, *see* Investment Research Associates, Inc. v. Commissioner, 126 T.C. No. 7 (2006) (upholds regulations only allowing hearing from filing of first NFTL), and one CDP levy hearing for each tax and tax period. Section 6320(b)(4) provides that, to the extent practicable, CDP hearings with respect to liens shall be held in conjunction with CDP hearings with respect to levies under section 6330. A taxpayer may receive more than one CDP hearing with respect to the same tax and period when there has been an additional assessment of tax (not including interest or penalty accruals) for that period or an additional accuracy-related or filing-delinquency penalty has been assessed. Treas. Reg. §§ 301.6320-1(d)(2) Q&A-D1, 301.6330-1(d)(2) Q&A-D1.

Collection Due Process Handbook, Part B.1; *see also* I.R.C. § 6330(b)(2); Treas. Reg. § 301.6330-1(d)(2).

A taxpayer seeking a post-lien CDP hearing under section 6320 must submit the request within 30 calendar days after the expiration of five business days from the date the Notice of Federal Tax Lien is filed. Treas. Reg. § 301.6330-1(b)(1). The request for a pre-levy CDP hearing under section 6330 must be filed no later than 30 days from the date of the pre-levy CDP notice. Treas. Reg. § 301.6320-1(b)(1). The hearing request must be in writing and signed by the taxpayer or the taxpayer's authorized representative. *See* Treas. Reg. § 301.6320-1(c)(2) Q&A-C1. The IRS has issued a special form for this purpose, Form 12153, Request for a Collection Due Process Hearing.

If the taxpayer fails to request the CDP hearing within the appropriate 30-day period, the IRS will permit an "equivalent" hearing. Treas. Reg. §§ 301.6320-1(i)(1), 301.6330-1(i)(1). Even though a hearing with the Appeals Division takes place, the IRS will not issue the taxpayer who participates in an equivalent hearing a notice of determination. Instead, the taxpayer will receive a "decision letter." The primary difference between a regular and an equivalent hearing is that the taxpayer has the right to appeal the Appeals Officer's decisions set forth in the notice of determination in Tax Court, but, in general, no appeal rights exist in the case of an equivalent hearing. *See* Treas. Reg. § 301.6320-1(i)(2) Q&A-I5. *But cf.* Craig v. Commissioner, 119 T.C. 252 (2002) (allowing appeal where Appeals issued a decision letter that erroneously denied the taxpayer's hearing request as untimely). *Craig* is discussed in Section 16.03[C].

[B] Effect of CDP Hearing on Statute of Limitations and Collection Actions

Reading Assignment: I.R.C. §§ 6320(c), 6330(e); review I.R.C. § 6502.

One of the few drawbacks for the taxpayer associated with the CDP process is that the statute of limitations on collection in Code section 6502 is suspended beginning on the date that the IRS receives the hearing request. I.R.C. §§ 6320(c), 6330(e)(1). The limitations period continues to be tolled until the date the IRS receives from the taxpayer a written withdrawal of the hearing request or until the determination resulting from the CDP hearing becomes final. The determination becomes final when either the time for seeking judicial review expires (generally 30 days after the date of the notice of determination) or the taxpayer exhausts his or her appeal rights following judicial review. The Code further provides that in no event does the limitations period expire before the 90th day after the date on which a final determination is made with respect to the hearing. *Id.* As a result, if fewer than 90 days remain in the limitation period after the tolling period ends, the difference between the number of remaining days and 90 days is added to the limitations period.

> *Example*: Assume that the statute of limitations on collection under section 6502 with respect to Alice's tax period listed in the CDP notice will expire on August 1, Year 12. The IRS sent Alice the CDP notice on April 30, Year 12. Alice timely requested a CDP hearing, which the IRS received on May 15. The Appeals Officer sent Alice a notice of determination on June 15. Alice timely seeks Tax Court review of that determination. In this case, the statute of limitations on collection would be suspended from May 15, Year 12 until the determination resulting from the CDP hearing becomes final, plus 90 days.
>
> If Alice had not sought judicial review of the notice of determination, because she requested the CDP hearing when fewer than 90 days remained on the statute of limitations on collection, the limitations period would be extended to October 13, Year 12 (90 days from July 15, Year 12 — 30 days after June 30). *See* Treas. Reg. § 301.6330-1(g)(3) Ex. 1–2.

Once the taxpayer files a request for a CDP hearing, certain collection actions are suspended. Section 6330(e)(1), for example, prohibits the IRS from instituting a levy action to collect the liabilities listed in the pre-levy CDP notice for the period during which the hearing and any appeals are pending. However, the IRS may levy while an appeal is pending as long as the underlying tax liability is not at issue in the appeal and the IRS shows good cause for doing so. In addition, the Tax Court has allowed the IRS to go forward with levy actions during the CDP process in cases in which the taxpayer raises only frivolous and groundless arguments as the basis for the taxpayer's appeal. *See* Burke v. United States, 121 T.C. 189 (2005). A taxpayer's request for a CDP hearing typically does not prevent the IRS from filing a Notice of Federal Tax Lien. Treas. Reg. § 301.6330-1(g)(2) Q&A-A-G3. The IRS can also initiate judicial proceedings to collect the tax covered by the CDP notice during the pendency of the hearing. *Id.*

[C] Conducting a CDP Hearing

Reading Assignment: I.R.C. §§ 6320(b)–(c), 6330(b)–(c).

The manner in which the Appeals Officer must conduct the CDP hearing has led to considerable litigation. The following excerpt from the Collection Due Process Handbook summarizes the relevant judicial decisions and explains the existing rules.

4. Hearing requirements

a. CDP hearings are informal

A CDP hearing is informal and the formal hearing requirements of the Administrative Procedure Act (APA), 5 U.S.C. § 551 *et seq.*, do not apply. Treas. Reg. §§ 301.6320-1(d)(2) Q&A-D6, 301.6330-1(d)(2) Q&A-D6. *See also* Robinette v. Commissioner, 439 F.3d 455 (8th Cir. 2006); Living Care Alternatives of Utica, Inc. v. United States, 411 F.3d 621 (6th Cir. 2005); Cox v. Commissioner, 126 T.C. No. 13 (2006); Davis v. Commissioner, 115 T.C. 35 (2000). Accordingly, recordings of telephone or face-to-face conferences are not required. Living Care Alternatives, 411 F.3d at 625; Rennie v. Internal Revenue Service, 216 F. Supp. 2d 1078, 1079 n. 1 (E.D. Cal. 2002). *See also* Jewett v. United States, 292 F. Supp. 2d 962 (N.D. Ohio 2003) (CDP hearing is informal and tape recording of all CDP hearings is not required); Kitchen Cabinets, Inc. v. United States, 2001-1 USTC ¶ 50,287 (N.D. Tex. 2001). *Contra* Mesa Oil, Inc. v. United States, 2001-1 USTC ¶ 50,130 (D. Colo. 2000) (suggests that CDP hearings must be recorded verbatim), *nonacq. at* AOD-2001-5, 2001-34 I.R.B. 174 (non-acquiescence on this point). While recording of all CDP conferences is not required, the taxpayer does have the right to record a face-to-face CDP conference in accordance with section 7521(a)(1). Keene v. Commissioner, 121 T.C. 8 (2003).

Taxpayers do not have the right to subpoena and examine witnesses at the hearing. Treas. Reg. §§ 301.6320-1(d)(2) Q&A-D6, 301.6330-1(d)(2) Q&A-D6; Robinette v. Commissioner, 123 T.C. 85, 98 (2004), *rev'd on other grounds*, 439 F.3d 455 (8th Cir. 2006). The appeals officer is not required to give the taxpayer a set of procedures governing the hearing. Lindsay v. Commissioner, T.C. Memo. 2001-285. Taxpayers do not have the right to subpoena documents, Barnhill v. Commissioner, T.C. Memo. 2002-116; Konkel v. Commissioner, 2001-2 USTC ¶ 50,520 (M.D. Fla. 2000), or examine them, Watson v. Commissioner, T.C. Memo. 2001-213. Section 6330(c)(1) does not require the appeals officer to provide the taxpayer with copies of the documents the appeals officer obtains to verify that the requirements of any applicable law or administrative procedure were met. Robinette v. Commissioner, *supra*; Nestor v. Commissioner, 118 T.C. 162 (2002); Brandenburg v. Commissioner, T.C. Memo. 2005-249; Gillett v. United States, 233 F. Supp. 2d 874, 883–884 (W.D. Mich. 2002); Danner v. United States, 208 F. Supp. 2d 1166 (E.D. Wash. 2002) (applying APA section 555(c) and section 6330); Reinhart v. Internal Revenue Service, 89 AFTR 2d 2517 (E.D. Cal. 2002). The court in Nestor wrestled with, but did not decide, whether an appeals officer is required by section 6203 to give a taxpayer a copy of his or her transcript of account if the taxpayer requests one. Since the Nestor opinion was issued, Appeals has decided to give a MFTRA-X (literal) transcript to each taxpayer who requests one.

Despite the informality of the hearing and the lack of a transcript and formal record, there must be a sufficient record, stating the appeals officer's findings and rationale, to permit review for abuse of discretion. The notice of determination must discuss all issues raised and should state why arguments and collection alternatives raised by the taxpayer were rejected. *See* Robinette v. Commissioner, 439 F.3d 455, 461–62 (8th Cir. 2006); Living Care Alternatives, 411 F.3d 621, 629 (6th Cir. 2005); Cavanaugh v. United States, 93 AFTR 2d 1522 (D.N.J. 2004); Cox v. Commissioner, 126 T.C. No. 13 (2006). There must be sufficient documentation in the record to show what happened at the administrative hearing. Cox, *supra* (administrative file . . . provides a singularly clear portrayal of administrative developments as "they occurred.") If the record is insufficient to permit abuse of discretion review, the case may need to be remanded to Appeals. . . .

The appeals officer has discretion regarding when to conclude a CDP hearing. In Murphy v. Commissioner, 125 T.C. 301 (2005), the Tax Court held that the appeals officer did not prematurely conclude the CDP hearing when the determination was made 8 months after the hearing commenced.

b. Face-to-face conference not required

The regulations provide that a CDP hearing may, but is not required to, consist of a face-to-face meeting, one or more written or oral communications, or some combination thereof. Treas. Reg. §§ 301.6320-1(d)(2) Q&A-D6, 301.6330-1(d)(2) Q&A-D6. *See* Olsen v. United States, 414 F.3d 144 (1st Cir. 2005); *see also* Katz v. Commissioner, 115 T.C. 329 (2000) (combination of telephone calls and written letters); Stephens v. Commissioner, T.C. Memo. 2005-183; Konkel v. Commissioner, 2001-2 USTC ¶ 50,520 (M.D. Fla. 2000) (solely written correspondence if the taxpayer consents). Therefore, all communications between the taxpayer and the appeals officer between the time of the request for the hearing and the issuance of the notice of determination are part of the CDP hearing. *See* TTK Management v. United States, 2001-1 USTC ¶ 50,185 (C.D. Cal. 2000).

If a taxpayer requests a face-to-face meeting, the regulations provide that the taxpayer should be offered one at the Appeals office closest to the taxpayer's residence or, if the taxpayer is a corporation, at the Appeals office closest to its principal place of business. Treas. Reg. §§ 301.6320-1(d)(2) Q&A-D7, 301.6330-1(d)(2) Q&A-D7. *See also* Parker v. Commissioner, T.C. Memo. 2004-226 (court remanded for new appeals hearing when CDP hearing was scheduled at appeals office 180 miles from taxpayer's residence, and there was a closer appeals office); Katz v. Commissioner, 115 T.C. 329 (2000).

The regulations do not require Appeals to offer the taxpayer a face-to-face or telephone conference in the absence of a request. Loofbourrow v. Commissioner, 208 F. Supp. 2d 698, 707 (S.D. Tex. 2002). *But see* Meyer v. Commissioner, 115 T.C. 417 (2000) (appeals officer erred in failing to offer a conference either in person or by telephone). Nevertheless, Appeals offers taxpayers a face-to-face or telephone conference in each nonfrivolous CDP hearing. Taxpayers who fail to avail themselves of an offered face-to-face or telephone conference cannot complain that they were denied the opportunity for such conference. Leineweber v. Commissioner, T.C. Memo. 2004-17; Moore v. Commissioner, T.C. Memo. 2003-1. *But cf.* Cox v. United States, 345 F. Supp. 2d 1218 (W.D. Okla. 2004) (hearing inadequate when taxpayer was not provided with notice that the telephone conference with Appeals constituted the CDP conference); Cavanaugh v. United States, 93 AFTR 2d 1522 (D.N.J. 2004) (court remanded to Appeals for new face-to-face CDP conference when taxpayer had requested a face-to-face conference and it was unclear whether taxpayer was advised that the telephone conference received instead constituted the CDP conference).

c. No face-to-face conference for taxpayers raising solely frivolous arguments

The face-to-face conference contemplated by the regulations is a conference for the purpose of addressing issues relevant to the taxpayer's CDP case — *e.g.*, the issues listed in section 6330(c)(2). A face-to-face conference serves no useful purpose if the taxpayer has no intention of discussing relevant issues, or if the taxpayer wishes to use the conference as a forum to espouse only frivolous and groundless arguments.

Accordingly, in CDP cases when the taxpayer raises only frivolous and groundless arguments, Appeals will not offer a face-to-face conference. Instead, the taxpayer will receive a hearing by telephone, correspondence, or some combination thereof. . . . The Tax Court has held in cases when a taxpayer raising only frivolous issues contests being denied a face-to-face conference that it would not be necessary or productive to remand the case to an appeals office for a new face-to-face hearing, citing Lunsford v. Commissioner, 117 T.C. 183, 189 (2001). *See* Ho v. Commissioner, T.C. Memo. 2006-41 (there is no requirement to offer a face-to-face conference to a taxpayer who raises only frivolous arguments); Wright v. Commissioner, T.C. Memo. 2005-291; Brandenburg v. Commissioner, T.C. Memo. 2005-249; Kozack v. Commissioner, T.C. Memo. 2005-246. *See also* Frese v. United States, 2006 USTC ¶ 50,169 (D.N.J.) (failure to provide face-to-face conference for the purpose of considering an offer-in-compromise not an abuse of discretion because taxpayer was making frivolous arguments and was not filing required returns and providing necessary financial information); Hinman v. Grzesiowski, 96 AFTR 2d 6788 (N.D. Ind. 2005) (mandamus relief improper to compel a face-to-face CDP hearing, when taxpayer did not appeal the Appeals determination).

d. Recording of CDP hearings under section 7521(a)(1)

The Tax Court has held that if a taxpayer is offered a face-to-face conference and requests to record the face-to-face CDP conference, in accordance with section 7521(a)(1), such recording must be allowed. Keene v. Commissioner, 121 T.C. 8 (2003).[1] However, when a taxpayer is improperly denied the right to record, the court will not remand to Appeals for a new recorded hearing when such a remand would be unnecessary or unproductive. Lunsford v. Commissioner, 117 T.C. 183, 189 (2001). *See, e.g.*, Carrillo v. Commissioner, T.C. Memo. 2005-290; Yazzie v. Commissioner, T.C. Memo. 2004-233; Kemper v. Commissioner, T.C. Memo. 2003-195; Pomeranz v. United States Department of Treasury, 2004-2 USTC ¶ 50,353 (S.D. Fla.).

e. Impartial appeals officer

Sections 6320(b)(3) and 6330(b)(3) require that the hearing be conducted by an officer or employee who has had no prior involvement with respect to the same unpaid tax. An appeals officer or employee will be considered to have had prior involvement with respect to the same tax if the taxpayer, the type of tax, and the tax period involved in the prior non-CDP hearing are identical to the taxpayer, the type of tax, and the tax period involved in the CDP hearing. Treas. Reg. §§ 301.6320-1(d)(2) Q&A-D4; 301.6330-1(d)(2) Q&A-D4.

Prior involvement includes participation in examination and collection activities (other than CDP appeals hearings) with respect to the same taxpayer, type of tax, and tax period. For example, an appeals officer has prior involvement under sections 6320(b)(3) and 6330(b)(3) if he served as a mediator during the examination of the same tax liability or was the revenue officer assigned to collect the same tax liability subject to the CDP hearing.

On the other hand, prior involvement does not generally include participation in prior CDP appeals hearings involving the taxpayer. For example, reviewing a taxpayer's 2001 and 2002 income tax liabilities as part of a CDP proceeding involving that taxpayer's 1999 and 2000 years does not constitute prior involvement for purposes of a subsequent CDP proceeding involving the 2001

[1] [The Tax Court has ruled that, while the taxpayer is allowed to record a face-to-face CDP hearing, the taxpayer is not allowed to record a telephone hearing. Calafati v. Commissioner, 127 T.C. 219 (2006). — Eds.]

> and 2002 tax years. Cox v. Commissioner, 126 T.C. No. 13 (2006) (" . . . both the statutory and the regulatory language suggest a relatively permissive standard under which participation in earlier collection proceedings would not constitute disqualifying prior involvement . . . ").

Collection Due Process Handbook, Part B.4.

[D] Scope of the CDP Hearing

[1] In General

Reading Assignment: I.R.C. § 6330(c).

During the CDP hearing, the Appeals Officer must first verify that the Code's procedures relating to the creation of the federal tax lien or the proposed levy have been satisfied (for example, that the IRS properly issued the notice of deficiency, the Notice and Demand for Payment, or the Notice of Intent to Levy). I.R.C. § 6330(c)(1). In addition, the taxpayer may raise any issue relevant to the lien or levy action, including innocent spouse claims; collection alternatives, such as offers in compromise and installment agreements; and suggestions as to which of the taxpayer's assets should be levied upon to satisfy the outstanding liability. I.R.C. § 6330(c)(2)(A). If the taxpayer has already raised an issue during the post-lien CDP hearing under section 6320, he or she is typically not permitted to raise the same issue during the pre-levy CDP hearing under section 6330. I.R.C. § 6330(c)(4). The Code instructs the Appeals Officer, when making the final determination in the taxpayer's case, to consider the issues the taxpayer raises as well as "whether any proposed collection action balances the need for the efficient collection of taxes with the legitimate concern of the person that any collection action may be no more intrusive than necessary." I.R.C. § 6330(c)(3)(C).

[2] When Can the Taxpayer Challenge the Underlying Tax Liability?

Reading Assignment: I.R.C. § 6330(c)(2)(B).

As a general matter, the taxpayer cannot use the CDP hearing to challenge the existence or amount of the underlying tax liability. An exception exists when the taxpayer "did not receive any statutory notice of deficiency for such tax liability or did not otherwise have the opportunity to dispute such tax liability." I.R.C. § 6330(c)(2)(B). The proper application of this limiting rule has been the subject of numerous judicial decisions. For example, in *Montgomery v. Commissioner*, 122 T.C. 1 (2004), the Tax Court considered the question of whether a taxpayer can challenge the amount of the taxpayer's self-reported liability as part of a CDP hearing. The taxpayers in *Montgomery*, husband and wife, filed their 2000 federal income tax return reporting a substantial tax liability but did not remit full payment of that liability. The IRS accepted the return as filed and, under the authority of Code section 6201(a)(1), summarily assessed the voluntarily reported tax liability. The IRS did not audit the taxpayers' return or issue a notice of deficiency.

After collection efforts failed, the IRS issued to the taxpayers a Notice of Intent to Levy and the taxpayers responded by requesting a CDP hearing under section 6330. Instead of scheduling a conference with the Appeals Officer, however, the taxpayers' representative contacted the Appeals Officer and explained that the taxpayers intended to submit an amended return that would request a refund of certain amounts they had already paid. The taxpayers did not follow up on their promise to submit the amended return and, after waiting what the Appeals Officer believed was a reasonable amount of time, the Appeals Officer issued a notice of determination allowing levy actions to proceed. A couple of weeks later, the taxpayers submitted their amended return for the tax year at issue showing a refund due[2] and instituted a proceeding in Tax Court challenging the Appeals Officer's determination and the amount of the underlying tax liability. *Id.* at 4–7.

The IRS moved for summary judgment in the case, maintaining that the taxpayers were barred from challenging the existence or amount of their tax liability as part of the CDP hearing because the tax liability in question was "self-assessed" on the taxpayer's original return. The IRS's motion read, in part:

> Respondent interprets section 6330(c)(2)(B) to mean that a taxpayer can challenge only those liabilities asserted by respondent that differ in amount from the taxpayer's self-determination. By granting taxpayers a right to contest the existence or amount of an underlying tax liability, Congress was concerned with tax liabilities asserted by respondent, rather than those originally computed and reported by the taxpayers themselves. This concern is evident in the phrasing of section 6330(c)(2)(B), which permits a taxpayer to contest an underlying tax liability in the event that he or she has been denied a prior opportunity to contest that liability in the form of a "statutory notice of deficiency" or "otherwise." It is nonsensical to permit taxpayers whose tax liabilities are self-determined to contest under section 6330 the liabilities they computed, voluntarily reported and declared to be correct under penalty of perjury.

Id. at 12–13.

The majority opinion rejected the IRS's arguments. The plain language of section 6330, the majority held, entitled the taxpayers to an opportunity to establish that they erred in their self-assessment because the IRS had not issued a notice of deficiency (which it was not required to do, of course, given that there was no tax deficiency) and the taxpayers had not had an opportunity to dispute their tax liability. According to the majority, this holding advanced the policies under sections 6320 and 6330 and was consistent with congressional intent that the IRS should collect the correct amount of tax. *Id.* at 21–22.

Judge Gerber, in his dissenting opinion, expressed a different concern:

> With due respect, I dissent from the holding of the majority. I agree that the majority's literal reading of the phrase, "underlying tax liability", is one possible way to interpret that phrase. It is my view, however, that the phrase "underlying tax liability", when considered in the context of section 6330 and specifically in context of section 6330(c)(2)(B), could also be read to not include a tax liability that a taxpayer has reported and admitted was owing.
>
> The intent of the statute was to give a taxpayer the right to challenge the "underlying tax liability . . . if the [taxpayer] . . . *did not otherwise have an opportunity to dispute such tax liability.*" Sec. 6330(c)(2)(B) (emphasis added). That phrase should not be interpreted to mean that a person could contest their own judgment as to the correct tax. The opportunity to contest tax liabilities is, without exception, granted by statute. If a person files a tax return and self-assesses or admits to owing a tax liability, but fails to pay the admitted liability, the statutory opportunity to contest such liability has traditionally been through a refund suit. Normally, with respect to an income tax liability, the right to sue for a refund requires full payment of the disputed liability. Under the majority's reading of section 6330(c)(2)(B), there would be no such requirement for payment prior to being able to contest the underlying merits of a

---

[2] The taxpayers' initial return reflected a tax liability of approximately $2.8 million and a payment of approximately $2.6 million. *Montgomery*, 121 T.C. at 3. Their refund claim, on their amended return, which was filed a year after their original return, was for $519,087. *Id* at 7.

> self-assessed amount in the context of a section 6330 hearing before this Court.
>
> The majority's interpretation results in a dramatic and improbable change from more than 75 years of established tax litigation procedure and precedent. If Congress had intended such a dramatic change, it certainly would have made some reference or modification to the existing statutory framework for refund claims and/or suits.
>
> Finally, I find it inconceivable that Congress intended that taxpayers who filed returns admitting that they owed tax are to be given the opportunity to contest their own "assessment" of the tax due, when the respondent seeks to collect it. It is my view that Congress intended to ensure that taxpayers had certain rights with respect to the collection process and to permit them to contest any changes respondent proposed, if they had not already had the opportunity to do so.

Id. at 45–47 (Gerber, J., dissenting).

What is Judge Gerber's concern with respect to refund suits? Keep in mind that the facts in *Montgomery* involve a tax *underpayment*, not a tax understatement (deficiency). That is why the opportunity to contest the correctness of the tax liability ordinarily would be through a refund suit, not a Tax Court suit (which would require a notice of deficiency). Does the majority's opinion in *Montgomery* allow a taxpayer to sue for a refund of an overpayment without having made full payment of the underlying liability?

Note that the IRS eventually acquiesced in the *Montgomery* decision, stating that the Tax Court's holding is not plainly inconsistent with the statute or legislative history. A.O.D. 2005-03 (Dec. 19, 2005), *available at* 2005 TNT 242-19 (Dec. 19, 2005). Treasury regulation section 301.6330-1(e)(1) now reflects the majority's view in *Montgomery*: "The taxpayer may also raise challenges to the existence or amount of the underlying tax liability, including a liability reported on a self-filed return, for any tax period specified on the CDP Notice if the taxpayer did not receive a statutory notice of deficiency for that tax liability or did not otherwise have an opportunity to dispute the tax liability." The fact that the taxpayer may contest a self-reported liability as part of a CDP hearing does not answer the question of whether the Tax Court has the authority to order the IRS to issue a refund to the taxpayer.[3] This question is considered below.

A taxpayer's efforts to contest the "underlying tax liability" — which, as indicated above, are viable only in limited circumstances — should be distinguished from the taxpayer's efforts to contest (1) the amount of tax liability that the IRS properly assessed and (2) the amount of tax liability that remains unpaid.[4]

> It is the position of Chief Counsel that "underlying tax liability" refers to the tax imposed by the Internal Revenue Code. Montgomery v. Commissioner, 122 T.C. 1, 7–8 (2004). Issues involving the expiration of statutes of limitations, application of payments and credits, and bankruptcy discharge are properly categorized as issues relating to the unpaid tax under section 6330(c)(2)(A), and should be reviewed for an abuse of discretion. *See, e.g.*, Eby v. Internal Revenue Service, 2006 U.S. Dist. LEXIS 14509 (S.D. Ohio 2006) (determination regarding expiration of collection statute of limitations is subject to abuse of discretion review); Comfort Plus Health Care, Inc. v. Internal Revenue Service, 2005-2 USTC ¶ 50,494 (D. Minn.) (determination with respect to application of credits reviewed for an abuse of discretion).

---

[3] Code section 6512(b), granting the Tax Court incidental refund jurisdiction and the jurisdiction to order the IRS to issue the taxpayer a refund, would not apply in *Montgomery* because the IRS never issued the taxpayers a notice of deficiency. Without a notice of deficiency, the taxpayers could not invoke the Tax Court's incidental refund jurisdiction.

[4] As explained below, challenges to the underlying tax liability under section 6330(c)(2)(B) are reviewed *de novo* while all other CDP appeals are reviewed for abuse of discretion.

Section 6330(b)(2)(B) does not preclude claims for spousal relief under sections 66 or 6015 because these claims do not dispute the existence of the liability but rather seek relief from the liability. Treas. Reg. § 301.6320-1(e)(3) Q&A-E3, 301.6330-1(e)(3) Q&A-E3. Claims for interest abatement under section 6404 are also not disputes about the existence of liability, because they seek relief from liability for interest.

Collection Due Process Handbook, Part IV.B.5.c.v.

What about a taxpayer who files an offer in compromise? Recall that Code section 6330(c)(2)(A) lists offers in compromise as a collection alternative that a taxpayer may raise at the CDP hearing. But what if the offer is based on doubt as to liability — is this a challenge to the "existence or amount of the underlying tax liability"? In *Baltic v. Commissioner*, 129 T.C. 178 (2007), the taxpayers received a notice of deficiency but failed to petition the Tax Court to challenge the IRS's deficiency determination. After collection actions began, the taxpayers requested a CDP hearing and, as part of the process, submitted an offer in compromise based on doubt as to liability. The Appeals Officer assigned to the CDP hearing forwarded the offer in compromise to another IRS employee for consideration. In the meantime, the Appeals Officer sustained the federal tax lien but postponed any levy action until the IRS had decided whether to accept the offer in compromise.[5] *Id.* at 179–80.

The taxpayers in *Baltic* challenged the Appeals Officer's refusal to consider their offer in compromise as part of the CDP hearing. The Tax Court held "unequivocally" that "a challenge to the amount of the tax liability made in the form of an [offer in compromise based on doubt as to liability] by a taxpayer who has received a notice of deficiency is a challenge to the underlying tax liability. Because the Baltics already had their chance to challenge that liability, section 6330(c)(2)(B) bars them from challenging it again." *Id.* at 183. The Tax Court further held that the Appeals Officer's decision to issue a notice of determination before the IRS had decided on the taxpayer's offer in compromise was not an abuse of discretion. According to the court, "Adding a desire to wait for consideration of [the offer] . . . adds nothing to the argument: The settlement officer here was just heeding the exhortation of the applicable regulation to issue a notice of determination as expeditiously as possible. . . ." *Id.*

[E] Penalties for Abusing CDP Procedures

Reading Assignment: I.R.C. §§ 6330(g), 6673, 6702(b).

Shortly after Congress enacted the CDP procedures, the IRS discovered that many taxpayers were using them primarily to delay and otherwise obstruct the IRS's legitimate collection actions. Many taxpayers, in fact, use the process to raise frivolous arguments that they have previously asserted during the audit and appeals stages. According to a General Accounting Office report, CDP cases "consume a disproportionately large amount of time because appeals personnel must often read lengthy frivolous submissions in search of any substantive issue that might be contained within the case file." Government Accountability Office, *Little Evidence of Procedural Errors in Collection Due Process Appeal Cases, But Opportunities Exist to Improve the Program*, GAO-07-112 (Oct. 2006) at 17.

The Tax Court has not been hesitant to impose penalties under section 6673 against taxpayers who raise only frivolous arguments during the CDP process. Section 6673 allows the court to penalize a taxpayer up to $25,000, if it appears that the taxpayer has instituted or maintained a proceeding primarily for delay or when the taxpayer advances frivolous or groundless positions. *See, e.g.*, Kemper v. Commissioner, T.C. Memo.

[5] As noted in Chapter 15, section 6133(k)(1) typically prevents the IRS from levying against a taxpayer's property while an offer in compromise is pending.

2003-195 (imposing $8,500 penalty on taxpayers for making frivolous arguments); Horton v. Commissioner, T.C. Memo. 2003-197 (granting IRS summary judgment and imposing $8,500 penalty for advancing frivolous contentions); *see also* IR-2005-64 (warning taxpayers and practitioners that Tax Court will impose penalties in the case of frivolous CDP appeals).

To discourage taxpayers from requesting CDP hearings in the first instance when they do not have legitimate concerns, in 2006, Congress added Code section 6702(b), which imposes a $5,000 penalty on any person who submits a "specified frivolous submission." I.R.C. § 6702(b)(1). A submission is a specified frivolous submission if it is a "specified submission" (defined in section 6702(b)(2)(B) to include a request for a CDP hearing and an application for an offer in compromise or installment agreement), and any portion of the specified submission: (1) is based on a position identified by the Secretary as frivolous; or (2) reflects a desire to delay or impede administration of the Federal tax laws. Section 6702(c) requires the Treasury Secretary to prescribe a list of frivolous positions. *See* 2007-14 I.R.B. 883, Notice 2007-30 (listing positions the IRS considers to be frivolous).

The same 2006 legislation also amended sections 6320 and 6330, both of which now require that CDP hearing requests be in writing and state the grounds for the requested hearing. I.R.C. §§ 6320(b)(1), 6330(b)(1). A request for a CDP hearing that includes a specified frivolous submission will be treated as if it were never submitted and will not be subject to further administrative or judicial review. I.R.C. §§ 6330(g), 6320(c) (as amended). Moreover, the taxpayer may not raise an issue as part of a CDP hearing if the issue involves a frivolous position. I.R.C. §§ 6330(c)(4), 6320(c) (as amended).

Whether the 2006 legislation will discourage taxpayers from instituting CDP actions solely for the purpose of delaying the inevitable remains to be seen. Does the legislation give the IRS too much power to decide whether the taxpayer is "due" a due process hearing?

§ 16.03 COURT REVIEW IN CDP CASES

As noted above, the results of the CDP hearing appear in a notice of determination prepared by the Appeals Officer, which is sent to the taxpayer. Treas. Reg. §§ 301.6320-1(e)(3) A-E8, 301.6330-1(e)(3) A-E8. The notice of determination must confirm that all procedural requirements were met in the taxpayer's case, and decide the merits of any issues raised by the taxpayer during the hearing. If the taxpayer does not obtain a favorable result in the administrative CDP hearing, judicial review of the decision is available. *See* I.R.C. §§ 6320(c); 6330(d)(1). Appeals are available from both post-lien and pre-levy administrative proceedings. *See* Tax Ct. R. 321(a).

In general, the taxpayer can raise the same types of issues in Tax Court that can be raised in a CDP hearing. *See* BNA Tax Mgmt. Portfolio 630-3rd T.M. IV-J. However, note that Treasury regulations limit the issues raised on appeal to those that were actually raised in the CDP hearing:

> In seeking Tax Court review of a Notice of Determination, the taxpayer can only ask the court to consider an issue, including a challenge to the underlying tax liability, that was properly raised in the taxpayer's CDP hearing. An issue is not properly raised if the taxpayer fails to request consideration of the issue by Appeals, or if consideration is requested but the taxpayer fails to present to Appeals any evidence with respect to that issue after being given a reasonable opportunity to present such evidence.

Treas. Reg. § 301.6320-1(f)(2) A-F3. In a court-reviewed opinion with a nine-judge majority opinion, the Tax Court followed the regulations' approach. *See* Giamelli v. Commissioner, 129 T.C. 107, 115 (2007) (reviewed by the court). A dissenting opinion authored by Judge Swift and joined by four other judges emphasized retention of "the latitude to deal with unusual situations as they arise rather than follow a wooden rule that may produce undesirable results." *Id.* at 123 (Swift, J., dissenting).

Note that the taxpayer has only 30 days within which to file a petition requesting review of a CDP hearing. I.R.C. § 6330(d)(1). Because spousal defenses are governed by the rules of Code section 6015, Treas. Reg. § 301.6320-1(e)(2), and section 6015(e)(1) provides 90 days to petition the Tax Court, two different time periods can apply when the taxpayer makes an unsuccessful innocent spouse argument at a CDP hearing.[6] The regulations provide:

> If the taxpayer seeks Tax Court review not only of Appeals' denial of relief under section 6015, but also of relief requested with respect to other issues raised in the CDP hearing, the taxpayer should request Tax Court review within the 30-day period commencing the day after the date of the Notice of Determination. If the taxpayer only seeks Tax Court review of Appeals' denial of relief under section 6015, then the taxpayer should request Tax Court review, as provided by section 6015(e), within 90 days of Appeals' determination. If a request for Tax Court review is filed after the 30-day period for seeking judicial review under section 6320, then only the taxpayer's section 6015 claims may be reviewable by the Tax Court.

Treas. Reg. § 301.6320-1(f)(2) A-F2.

[A] Forum Issues

[1] Which Court Has Jurisdiction Over a CDP Appeal?

Reading Assignment: I.R.C. § 6330(d)(1).

When Congress enacted the CDP provisions as part of the IRS Reform Act, it divided jurisdiction over appeals from CDP determinations between the Tax Court and the district courts, as follows:

> The person may, within 30 days of a determination under this section, appeal such determination —
>
> (A) to the Tax Court (and the Tax Court shall have jurisdiction with respect to such matter); or
>
> (B) if the Tax Court does not have jurisdiction of the underlying tax liability, to a district court of the United States.
>
> If a court determines that the appeal was to an incorrect court, a person shall have 30 days after the court determination to file such appeal with the correct court.

I.R.C. § 6330(d)(1) (1998). Thus, as originally enacted, the statute granted jurisdiction to the Tax Court over many CDP appeals but provided jurisdiction in the district courts over CDP appeals involving such taxes as employment and excise taxes. Accordingly, there are district court opinions in some CDP cases.

---

[6] Pursuant to CC-2006-019 (Aug. 18, 2006), *available at* http://www.irs.gov/pub/irs-ccdm/cc-2006-019.pdf:

> Similarly, if a taxpayer seeks review of a notice of determination which includes a determination not to abate interest under section 6404(e), the taxpayer must file an appeal within 30 days if the taxpayer also seeks review of other issues raised in the CDP hearing. If, however, a taxpayer seeks review only of the denial of the request for abatement of interest, the taxpayer must file an appeal with the Tax Court within 180 days after the notice of determination is mailed. *See* Section 6404(h)(1).

Id. at 41. Requests for interest abatement are discussed in Section 13.02[D][2].

Unfortunately, the provision in section 6330(d) allowing a taxpayer the opportunity to move the case to the proper court resulted in problems because tax protestors would intentionally appeal to the wrong court so as to delay proceedings. *See* Joint Comm. on Taxation, *Report of the Joint Committee on Taxation Relating to the Internal Revenue Service as Required by the IRS Reform and Restructuring Act of 1998*, at 88, app. 1 at 22 (2003), *available at* http://www.house.gov/jct/x-53-03.pdf; Hale E. Sheppard, *Where There's a Will, There's a Delay: Do Recent Legislative Changes to the CDP Rules Solve the Perceived Problems?*, 9 J. Tax Prac. & Proc. 41, 42 (2007). Responding to this and other concerns, Congress amended the statute in 2006 to provide the Tax Court with exclusive jurisdiction over CDP appeals. *See* I.R.C. § 6330(d)(1). The provision allowing a grace period to refile after filing in the wrong court was removed. *See* Chief Counsel Notice CC-2007-001 (providing guidance on how to proceed under the amended provision).

Note that, as discussed in Chapter 8, a taxpayer may pursue a CDP appeal as a small tax case, so long as "the unpaid tax does not exceed $50,000." I.R.C. § 7463(f)(2). The Tax Court has held that "the $50,000 limit in section 7463(f)(2) refers to the total amount of unpaid tax which the Commissioner has determined to collect. The fact that the unpaid tax for each year, period, or taxable event does not exceed $50,000 is irrelevant." Schwartz v. Commissioner, 128 T.C. 6, 12 (2007). Moreover, the court has held that conceding some of the unpaid tax will not make the case eligible for the small tax case procedure. *See* Leahy v. Commissioner, 129 T.C. 71, 76 (2007).

[2] Can the Taxpayer Obtain Dismissal Without Prejudice?

In *Wagner v. Commissioner*, 118 T.C. 330 (2002), the taxpayers filed a CDP petition in Tax Court, but sought to have the case dismissed without prejudice in order to pursue litigation in district court regarding net operating losses that the taxpayers sought to carry back to the year at issue in Tax Court. As indicated in Section 8.01[C] of Chapter 8, the Tax Court does not permit voluntary dismissal of a tax deficiency action. Consider the Tax Court's resolution of the dismissal issue in the CDP context:

WAGNER v. COMMISSIONER

United States Tax Court

118 T.C. 330 (2002)

Laro, Judge: Petitioners petitioned the Court under section 6320(c) to review a notice of a Federal tax lien placed upon their property. The lien arose from an assessment of Federal income taxes of $412,787.15 and $844.16 for 1991 and 1996, respectively. Petitioners now, after being served with respondent's answer and respondent's motion for summary judgment, move the Court to dismiss this case without prejudice to their right to seek in Federal District Court a determination that they incurred a net operating loss (NOL) in 1994 that may be carried back to 1991. We shall grant petitioners' motion.[n.2] * * *

The parties agree that the Court may dismiss this case pursuant to petitioners' request.[n.3] We distinguish this dismissal from our jurisprudence that holds that taxpayers may not withdraw a petition under section 6213 to redetermine a deficiency. That jurisprudence stems from the seminal case of Estate of Ming v. Commissioner, 62 T.C. 519 (1974).

In *Estate of Ming*, the taxpayers moved the Court to allow them to withdraw their

---

[n.2] In so doing, we, of course, leave to the District Court to determine whether petitioners are entitled to any relief there, and, if so, what type of relief.

[n.3] Respondent does not object to dismissal without prejudice to petitioners' filing a refund suit in District Court but takes the position that the dismissal should be with prejudice to their refiling a petition under sec. 6320(c) in our own Court based on the same claim as their existing petition.

petition for a redetermination of their 1964, 1965, and 1966 Federal income taxes. Presumably, they made their motion so that they could refile their lawsuit in District Court. We denied the motion. We noted that, whenever this Court dismisses a case on a ground other than lack of jurisdiction, we are generally required by section 7459(d)[n.4] to enter a decision finding that the deficiency in tax is the amount determined in the notice of deficiency. *Id.* at 522. We observed that entering such a decision would serve to preclude the taxpayers from litigating the case on its merits in District Court. *Id.* at 522–523. We noted that the Commissioner had been prejudiced by the taxpayers' filing of the petition by virtue of the fact that he was precluded from assessing and collecting the taxes which he had determined the taxpayers owed. *Id.* at 524.

In *Estate of Ming v. Commissioner, supra* 62 T.C. at 521–522, we also relied on our opinion in Dorl v. Commissioner, 57 T.C. 720 (1972), *affd.* 507 F.2d 406 (2d Cir. 1974), which held that a taxpayer may not remove a case from this Court in order to refile it in District Court. We observed in *Dorl* that the filing of a petition in this Court gives us exclusive jurisdiction under section 6512(a), which acts to bar a refund suit in the District Court for the same tax and the same year. We noted that this observation was supported by the legislative history accompanying the enactment of the predecessors of sections 6512(a) and 7459(d). That history states that, when a taxpayer petitions the Board of Tax Appeals, the Board's decision, once final, settles the taxpayer's tax liability for the year in question even if the decision resulted from a dismissal requested by the taxpayer. Estate of Ming v. Commissioner, *supra* 62 T.C. at 522.

We believe that our holding in *Estate of Ming* is inapplicable to the setting at hand where petitioners have petitioned this Court under section 6320(c). Section 7459(d) applies specifically to a petition that is filed for a redetermination of a deficiency and makes no mention of a petition that is filed under section 6320(c) to review a collection action. Section 6320 was added to the Code as part of the Internal Revenue Service Restructuring and Reform Act of 1998, Pub. L. 105-206, sec. 3401, 112 Stat. 685, 746, and that act made no amendment to section 7459(d), which finds its roots in section 906(c) of the Revenue Act of 1926, ch. 27, 44 Stat. 107. Nor do we know of any provision in the Code that would require us, upon a dismissal of a collection action filed under section 6320(c), to enter a decision for the Commissioner consistent with the underlying notice of determination. Whereas the relevant legislative history supported our holding in *Dorl v. Commissioner, supra,* we are unaware of any legislative history that would support a holding contrary to that which we reach herein.

Our granting of petitioners' motion is supported by rule 41(a)(2), which we consult given the absence in our Rules of a specific provision as to this matter.[n.6] *See* Rule 1. Under rule 41(a)(2), a plaintiff is not entitled as a matter of right to a dismissal after the defendant has served a motion for summary judgment but is allowed such a dismissal in the sound discretion of the court. Pontenberg v. Boston Scientific Corp., 252 F.3d 1253, 1255–1256 (11th Cir. 2001); LeCompte v. Mr. Chip, Inc., 528 F.2d 601 (5th Cir. 1976). In general, a court "should" grant a dismissal under rule 41(a)(2) "unless the defendant will suffer clear legal prejudice, other than the mere prospect of a subsequent lawsuit, as a result." McCants v. Ford Motor Co., Inc., 781 F.2d 855, 856–857 (11th Cir. 1986).

[n.4] Sec. 7459(d) provides in relevant part:

SEC. 7459(d). Effect of Decision Dismissing Petition. — If a petition for a redetermination of a deficiency has been filed by the taxpayer, a decision of the Tax Court dismissing the proceeding shall be considered as its decision that the deficiency is the amount determined by the Secretary. * * *

[n.6] Our Rule on dismissals, Rule 123(b), relates to dismissals "For failure of a petitioner properly to prosecute or to comply with these Rules or any order of the Court or for other cause which the Court deems sufficient". Pursuant to that Rule, "the Court may dismiss a case at any time and enter a decision against the petitioner." *Id.* Rule 123(b) does not apply to the setting at hand where petitioners voluntarily move the Court to dismiss their petition filed under sec. 6320(c) to review a notice of Federal tax lien.

"The crucial question to be determined is, Would the defendant lose any substantial right by the dismissal." Durham v. Fla. E. Coast Ry. Co., 385 F.2d 366, 368 (5th Cir. 1967). In making this determination, a court must "weigh the relevant equities and do justice between the parties in each case, imposing such costs and attaching such conditions to the dismissal as are deemed appropriate." McCants v. Ford Motor Co., Inc., *supra*, 781 F.2d at 857.

The statutory period in which petitioners could refile their lawsuit in this Court appears to have expired. Section 6330(d)(1) requires that a petition to this Court be filed within 30 days of the determination that is the subject of section 6320. *See also* sec. 6320(c). The rule is deeply embedded in the jurisprudence of Federal law that the granting of a motion to dismiss without prejudice is treated as if the underlying lawsuit had never been filed. Monterey Dev. Corp. v. Lawyer's Title Ins. Corp., 4 F.3d 605, 608 (8th Cir. 1993); Brown v. Hartshorne Pub. Sch. Dist., 926 F.2d 959, 961 (10th Cir. 1991); Robinson v. Willow Glen Acad., 895 F.2d 1168, 1169 (7th Cir. 1990); Long v. Board of Pardons and Paroles, 725 F.2d 306 (5th Cir. 1984); Cabrera v. Municipality of Bayamon, 622 F.2d 4, 6 (1st Cir. 1980); Humphreys v. United States, 272 F.2d 411, 412 (9th Cir. 1959); A. B. Dick Co. v. Marr, 197 F.2d 498, 502 (2d Cir. 1952); Md. Cas. Co. v. Latham, 41 F.2d 312, 313 (5th Cir. 1930). We conclude that respondent is not prejudiced in maintaining the subject collection action against petitioners as if the instant proceeding had never been commenced.

Accordingly, in the exercise of the Court's discretion, and after weighing the relevant equities including the lack of a clear legal prejudice to respondent, we shall grant petitioners' motion. In accordance with the foregoing,

An appropriate order of dismissal will be entered granting petitioners' motion to dismiss.

On what basis did the Tax Court distinguish *Estate of Ming*? Does that distinction make sense?

[B] Judicial Review of Administrative CDP Determinations

[1] Standard of Review

The legislative history of Code section 6330 provides the following with respect to the standard the Tax Court should use to review the Appeals Officer's determination in a CDP case:

> Where the validity of the tax liability was properly at issue in the hearing, and where the determination with regard to the tax liability is part of the appeal, . . . [t]he amount of the tax liability will . . . be reviewed by the appropriate court on a de novo basis. Where the validity of the tax liability is not properly part of the appeal, the taxpayer may challenge the determination of the appeals officer for abuse of discretion.

H. Conf. Rept. 105-599, at 266 (1998). The Tax Court applies that approach. *See, e.g.*, Goza v. Commissioner, 114 T.C. 181–82 (2000).

What is the "abuse of discretion" standard? Professor Danshera Cords explains:

> Abuse of discretion is often formulated as "arbitrary and capricious" action, without a sound basis in law. However, other formulations have been used. All of the formulations examine whether the action taken by the administrative agency was within the scope of its congressional delegation of authority.

Danshera Cords, *Collection Due Process: The Scope and Nature of Judicial Review*, 73 U. Cin. L. Rev. 1021, 1029 (2005) (footnotes omitted) (hereinafter *Collection Due Process Rights*). Yet, the Tax Court's approach in some abuse of discretion cases may resemble *de novo* review because, as discussed below, the Tax Court is willing to look beyond the administrative record and consider additional evidence. *See id.* at 1035; Leslie Book, *The Collection Due Process Rights: A Misstep or A Step in the Right Direction?*, 41 Hous. L. Rev. 1145, 1194–95 (2004); Bryan T. Camp, *The Failure of CDP, Part 2: Why it Adds No Value*, 104 Tax Notes 1567, 1572 (2004).

CDP appeals that raise multiple issues that are subject to different standards of review raise special difficulties:

> Mixed questions may appear in a single CDP appeal. For instance, a taxpayer may have properly challenged the underlying liability at the CDP hearing and also raised spousal defenses or proposed collection alternatives. Issues relating to the Appeals Officer's determination of the underlying liability and the proposed collection alternatives may be raised in the court, but what is the appropriate standard of review? Should the court use de novo review for only the underlying liability or also for the other issues raised in the hearing and on appeal?

Cords, *Collection Due Process Rights*, *supra*, at 1028 (footnotes omitted). Professor Cords points out that "[w]here challenge to both the underlying liability and other issues are properly presented in the CDP hearing on appeal, . . . [i]n some instances, de novo review has been made of the entire CDP hearing. In other instances, courts have concluded that de novo review is available only to the determination of the validity of the amount of underpayment." *Id.* at 1037 (footnote omitted). Which do you think is the better approach?

[2] Should Judicial Review Be Limited to the Administrative Record?

When the Tax Court reviews a notice of determination in a CDP case, should the Tax Court limit its review to the administrative record or may it consider evidence not presented during the CDP hearing? The Administrative Procedure Act (APA) provides, in part, that "the court shall review the whole record or those parts of it cited by a party . . . ." 5 U.S.C. § 706. In light of the APA, the IRS recognizes only limited exceptions to its view that review must be limited to the administrative record:

> Generally, review of the procedural aspects of a CDP hearing is limited to the administrative record. However, if the record does not adequately describe the hearing process or there is a dispute over what happened during the process, the reviewing court is permitted to supplement the administrative record with testimony or other evidence outside the record. Robinette v. Commissioner, 439 F.3d 455, 461 (8th Cir. 2006) ("Of course, where a record created in informal proceedings does not adequately disclose the basis for the agency's decision, then it may be appropriate for the reviewing court to receive evidence concerning what happened during the agency proceedings.") (citations omitted); Murphy v. Commissioner, 125 T.C. 301 (2005) (new evidence regarding an irregularity in the conduct of the hearing or some defect in the record may be presented at trial, even if the record rule is applied). *See also* James Madison Ltd. By Hecht v. Ludwig, 82 F.2d 1085,1096 (D.C. Cir. 1996) (courts may "need to resolve factual issues regarding the process the agency used in reaching its decision. . . . Although these facts are usually established by the administrative record or are otherwise undisputed, parties may occasionally raise an issue requiring district courts to engage in independent fact-finding.") Examples of factual disputes about the hearing process include a claim by a taxpayer that he requested a collection alternative despite the appeals officer's contrary finding in the notice of determination, and the taxpayer's claim that the appeals officer failed to inform him that the CDP hearing would be concluded if he failed to submit additional information by a certain date.

CC-2006-019, at 46 (Aug. 18, 2006), *available at* http://www.irs.gov/pub/irs-ccdm/cc-2006-019.pdf.

As the excerpt above indicates, the issue of whether judicial review in a CDP case is limited to the administrative record arose in *Robinette v. Commissioner*, 123 T.C. 85 (2004) (reviewed by the court), *rev'd*, 439 F.3d 455 (8th Cir. 2006), a case that generated seven separate opinions in the Tax Court and, eventually, a reversal of the court's majority opinion by the Eighth Circuit. In *Robinette*, the taxpayer had entered into an offer in compromise in 1995, the terms of which required that he timely file his 1995 through 1999 returns. The taxpayer claimed that his accountant mailed his 1998 return and stamped it using a private postage meter. However, the return was not received by the IRS, so the IRS declared the taxpayer in default of the compromise agreement and began levy proceedings. At the CDP hearing, the taxpayer offered alternative proof that he timely mailed the 1998 return, and claimed that he complied with the offer's terms in good faith. The Appeals Officer rejected the taxpayer's argument, stating that he would only accept certified or registered mail receipts as proof of mailing. *Id.* at 89–92.

Judge Vasquez (joined by five other judges) ruled that the Appeals Officer had abused his discretion by proceeding with a levy following what Judge Vasquez considered to be a minor breach of the offer in compromise. *Id.* at 112. More importantly, the judge held that the Tax Court could consider evidence presented at trial that was not in the administrative record of the CDP hearing. Although Judge Vasquez ultimately ruled that the new evidence proved unhelpful to the taxpayer's cause, he allowed the taxpayer to present evidence that he had signed and delivered the returns to his accountant for mailing, and also allowed testimony from the accountant regarding procedures used by the accountant to mail returns. This, and other related evidence presented at trial, was not in the administrative record. *Id.* at 105–07. According to Judge Vasquez, provisions of the APA that otherwise limit judicial review of administrative matters do not apply to the Tax Court's review of CDP hearings, which has always "applied [its] traditional de novo procedures in deciding whether an Appeals officer abused his or her discretion in determining to proceed with collection." *Id.* at 95.

Five concurring and two dissenting opinions were filed in *Robinette*. In lieu of reading those opinions, consider the following comments from Professor Leslie Book:

> I believe *Robinette* relates to a fundamental misperception about the means to protect taxpayer rights. *Robinette* reflects a judicial desire to correct for agency error, or at least maximize the potential to correct for agency error. In that way, *Robinette* can be seen as a taxpayer-friendly decision, yet I believe the decision for the court to consider evidence not before Appeals carries with it risks to taxpayer rights and risks usurping collection functions best left to the IRS.
>
> To appreciate that concern, it is again necessary to broaden the inquiry. In administrative law, different standards of review and how courts apply a particular standard can reflect a contradiction between the desire to ensure deference to agency expertise and a concern that the government does not erroneously deprive an affected party of a protected right. In administrative law, that contradiction has manifested itself in varying ways, including a historical toothless application of the abuse-of-discretion review standard. Over time, . . . abuse-of-discretion review became much more searching, resulting in courts taking a "hard look" at agency determinations reviewed even under an abuse-of-discretion standard, which is more deferential than de novo review. That evolution toward a less deferential application of the abuse-of-discretion standard reflected the courts' greater concern for reducing the risk of government deprivations or errors.
>
> In tax, deference was reflected not by a loose definition of abuse-of-discretion review, but rather, through the effect of the Anti-Injunction Act and the Declaratory Judgment Act, whole classes of IRS determinations have been

> exempt from judicial review. Essentially, with limited exceptions, IRS decisions regarding the manner of collecting taxes, and the appropriateness of collection alternatives, were exempt from judicial review. Until CDP, deference to the agency had been absolute. (Ironically, abuse-of-discretion review in tax cases has traditionally been more searching and similar in effect to de novo review.)
>
> The Tax Court's approach in *Robinette* is arguably taxpayer friendly, ... That in turn reflects the Tax Court's historical concern with providing itself with an opportunity to determine a correct tax liability, notwithstanding any agency practices before a tax's assessment. The right to a de novo scope of review in CDP cases also reflects the reality that many taxpayers before the IRS are not represented and may not be able to present sufficient evidence to Appeals, due to a number of reasons, including lack of sophistication and resources. Further, it also reflects the reality that informal procedures at Appeals may result in the IRS not considering information that might be relevant.
>
> Yet a failure to abide by the APA's general approach toward reviewing only material before an agency (called the "on the record" rule in administrative law) creates some risk that the IRS will take less care with its procedures at the hearing level. For example, the on-the-record rule creates incentives for the agency to conduct adequate procedures and provide sufficient explanations, so that a reviewing court will be able to perform its task of considering what an agency has decided, and the decision's rationale. Courts following the on-the-record rule may conclude that the agency has acted improperly, through a failure to consider relevant material or explain actions rationally, which should result in a remand and hopefully corrective agency practices. Often, better agency practice initially (compelled by the searching light of judicial review into what the agency did) provides more meaningful taxpayer protections than the possibility of more searching review.

Leslie M. Book, *CDP and Collections: Perceptions and Misperceptions*, 107 TAX NOTES 487, 490–91 (2005) (footnotes omitted).[7]

On appeal in *Robinette*, the Court of Appeals for the Eighth Circuit held that judicial review of a CDP determination should be limited to the administrative record, and thus reversed the Tax Court. Robinette v. Commissioner, 439 F.3d 455 (8th Cir. 2006). It went on to find that the administrative record in Robinette's case was adequate. The record consisted of the taxpayer's original offer in compromise, copies of IRS correspondence, the Appeals Officer's notes concerning communications with the taxpayer's representative, and a memorandum explaining the Appeals Officer's reasons for recommending the levy. Based on the record, the court concluded that the IRS did not abuse its discretion when it sustained the proposed levy. *Id.* at 464.

The Court of Appeals explained as follows its reasoning for limiting judicial review to the administrative record:

> Robinette argues, and a majority of the Tax Court held, that the Tax Court may receive new evidence in the course of reviewing whether an appeals officer abused his discretion in denying relief during a collection due process hearing. Indeed, a significant portion of the Tax Court's analysis that the appeals officer abused his discretion in this case was based on evidence not presented during the administrative appeal. The Commissioner contends this was error, and that consistent with general principles of administrative law and the Administrative Procedure Act ("APA"), judicial review of the agency's decision should be limited to the administrative record developed at the hearing before the appeals officer.

---

[7]

It is a basic principle of administrative law that review of administrative decisions is "ordinarily limited to consideration of the decision of the agency . . . and of the evidence on which it was based." United States v. Carlo Bianchi & Co., 373 U.S. 709, 714–15, 83 S. Ct. 1409, 10 L. Ed. 2d 652 (1963). Outside the context of the APA, the Supreme Court has held that where Congress simply provides for judicial review, without setting forth the standards to be used or the procedures to be followed, "consideration is to be confined to the administrative record," and "no *de novo* proceeding may be held." *Id.* at 715. . . .

Robinette's contention, therefore, is that the review of decisions by an IRS appeals officer under § 6330 should be exempt from both the statutory framework of the APA and from general principles of administrative law that limit the scope of judicial review to the administrative record. We are not persuaded that Congress endorsed such a departure when it authorized pre-deprivation judicial review of IRS levy activity in the Tax Court and the United States District Courts. . . .

Nothing in the text or history of the Restructuring and Reform Act of 1998 clearly indicates an intent by Congress to permit trials *de novo* in the Tax Court when that court reviews decisions of IRS appeals officers under § 6330. If anything, the available evidence suggests the opposite. The agreed-upon standard of review itself implies that review is limited to the administrative record, for as the Tax Court seemingly recognized in another case, it would be incongruous to hold that review is limited to determining whether an appeals officer "abused his discretion," but also to conclude that the appeals officer committed such an "abuse" by failing to weigh information that was never even presented to him. *See* Magana v. Comm'r, 118 T.C. 488, 493 (2002) ("It would be anomalous and improper for us to conclude that respondent's Appeals Office abused its discretion under section 6330(c)(3) in failing to grant relief, or in failing to consider arguments, issues, or other matter not raised by taxpayers or not otherwise brought to the attention of respondent's Appeals office."). Congress has employed the abuse of discretion standard of review in various settings, and in each case, judicial review under that standard has been limited to the administrative record. . . . We think it unlikely that Congress meant anything different here.

The Tax Court seemed to believe that because it traditionally has conducted *de novo* proceedings in deficiency proceedings, and because Congress did not change that practice when it passed the APA in 1946, Congress should likewise be presumed to have intended *de novo* proceedings in the Tax Court in connection with the review of decisions by an appeals officer under § 6330. We do not think the proposed conclusion follows from the history. Collection due process hearings under § 6330 were newly created administrative proceedings in 1998, and the statute provided for a corresponding new form of limited judicial review. The nature and purpose of these proceedings are different from deficiency determinations, and it is just as likely that Congress believed judicial review of decisions by appeals officers in this context should be conducted in accordance with traditional principles of administrative law. Indeed, that Congress provided for judicial review in either the Tax Court or a United States District Court, depending on the type of underlying tax liability involved, indicates that traditional principles of administrative law should apply.[8] Every district court to consider an appeal under § 6330 has limited its review to the record created before the agency, . . . , and it would be anomalous to conclude that Congress intended in § 6330(d) to create disparate forms of judicial review

---

[8] [As discussed above, in 2006, Congress gave the Tax Court exclusive jurisdiction over CDP appeals. — Eds.]

> depending on which court was reviewing the decision of an IRS appeals officer in a collection due process proceeding.
>
> That the collection due process hearings are informal does not suggest that the scope of judicial review should exceed the record created before the agency. "Agencies typically compile records in the course of informal agency action," and "the APA specifically contemplates judicial review on the basis of the agency record compiled in the course of informal agency action in which a hearing has not occurred." Fla. Power & Light Co. v. Lorion, 470 U.S. 729, 744, 105 S. Ct. 1598, 84 L. Ed. 2d 643 (1985). We thus find unpersuasive Robinette's reliance on *O'Dwyer v. Commissioner*, 266 F.2d 575 (4th Cir. 1959), which was premised on a now-outmoded understanding that informal agency action cannot be reviewed based on an administrative record. *Id.* at 580. Of course, where a record created in informal proceedings does not adequately disclose the basis for the agency's decision, then it may be appropriate for the reviewing court to receive evidence concerning what happened during the agency proceedings. Citizens to Pres. Overton Park v. Volpe, 401 U.S. 402, 420, 91 S. Ct. 814, 28 L. Ed. 2d 136 (1971). The evidentiary proceeding in those circumstances, however, is not a *de novo* trial, but rather is limited to the receipt of testimony or evidence explaining the reasoning behind the agency's decision. Camp [v. Pitts], 411 U.S. [138 (1973)] at 143.

Robinette, 439 F.3d at 459–62. Did the Tax Court or the Court of Appeals have the better approach? Do you agree with the taxpayer that "the review of decisions by an IRS appeals officer under § 6330 should be exempt from both the statutory framework of the APA and from general principles of administrative law that limit the scope of judicial review to the administrative record"?

Following *Robinette*, the Court of Appeals for the First Circuit followed its sister Circuit's holding. *See* Murphy v. Commissioner, 469 F.3d 27, 31 (1st Cir. 2006) ("Our decision to apply the administrative record rule in the context of district court appeals was premised on basic administrative law principles. . . . The reasons supporting application of the administrative record rule in district court CDP hearing appeals have equal force where the appeal takes place in the Tax Court.") (citation omitted).

[C] Tax Court Jurisdiction and Remedies

Reading Assignment: I.R.C. § 6330(b)–(d); Tax Court Rule 331.

Tax Court jurisdiction over a CDP appeal normally is premised on a notice of determination. *See* Craig v. Commissioner, 119 T.C. 252, 256 (2002); Goza v. Commissioner, 114 T.C. 176, 182 (2000). However, the Tax Court has ruled that it has jurisdiction where the IRS inadvertently denied the taxpayers' CDP request as untimely and issued a "Decision Letter Concerning Equivalent Hearing Under Section 6320 and/or 6330" following an "equivalent hearing," which is not a hearing subject to appeal. *See Craig*, 119 T.C. at 257. The court explained:

> Under the facts herein, where Appeals issued the decision letter to petitioner in response to his timely request for a Hearing, we conclude that the "decision" reflected in the decision letter issued to petitioner is a "determination" for purposes of section 6330(d)(1). *Cf.* Moorhous v. Comm'r, 116 T.C. 263, 270 (2001) (decision reflected in a decision letter was not a "determination" under section 6330(d)(1) where the taxpayer's request for a Hearing was untimely); Nelson v. Comm'r, T.C. Memo 2002-264 (same); Lopez v. Comm'r, T.C. Memo 2001-228 (same). The fact that respondent held with petitioner a hearing labeled as an equivalent hearing, rather than a hearing labeled as a Hearing, and that respondent issued to petitioner a document labeled as a decision letter, rather than a document labeled as a notice of determination, does not erase the fact

> that petitioner received a "determination" within the meaning of section 6330(d)(1). We hold that we have jurisdiction to decide this case.

Id. at 259.

[1] "Looking Behind" the Notice of Determination

The Tax Court Rule applicable to the commencement of what it terms a "lien and levy action" is Rule 331.[9] That Rule provides, among other things, for the content of the petition. *See* Tax Ct. R. 331(b). That section of the Rule is quite analogous to Rule 34(b), which provides for the content of the petition in deficiency actions. It is thus not surprising that, from a jurisdictional standpoint, the Tax Court has analogized the notice of determination issued at the conclusion of a CDP hearing to the statutory notice of deficiency that must be issued prior to a deficiency assessment.

Recall from Chapter 9 that a valid notice of deficiency is a prerequisite for Tax Court jurisdiction and that, as a general rule, the Tax Court will not "look behind" the notice of deficiency to question how or why the IRS asserted a deficiency. See *Greenberg's Express, Inc. v. Commissioner*, 62 T.C. 324 (1974), excerpted in Section 9.02[C] of Chapter 9. How far should the analogy between notices of determination and notices of deficiency extend? Consider the following case. Note that it was decided at a time when the district courts still had jurisdiction over some CDP appeals.

LUNSFORD v. COMMISSIONER
United States Tax Court
117 T.C. 159 (2001)

Ruwe, Judge.

This case arises from a petition for judicial review filed under section 6330(d)(1)(A). The issue for decision is whether this Court has jurisdiction to review respondent's determination to proceed with collection by way of levy. At the time petitioners filed their petition, they resided in Asheville, North Carolina. When this case was called for trial, the parties submitted the case fully stipulated. For convenience, we combine the facts, which are not in dispute, with our opinion.

Section 6331(a) authorizes the Commissioner to levy against property and property rights where a taxpayer fails to pay taxes within 10 days after notice and demand for payment is made. Section 6331(d) requires the Secretary to send notice of an intent to levy to the taxpayer, and section 6330(a) requires the Secretary to send a written notice to the taxpayer of his right to a hearing. Section 6330(b) affords taxpayers the right to a "fair hearing" before an "impartial" IRS Appeals officer. Section 6330(c)(1) requires the Appeals officer to obtain verification that the requirements of any applicable law or administrative procedure have been met. Section 6330(c)(2)(A) specifies issues that the taxpayer may raise at the Appeals hearing. The taxpayer is allowed to raise "any relevant issue relating to the unpaid tax or the proposed levy" including spousal defenses, challenges to the appropriateness of collection action, and alternatives to collection. Sec. 6330(c)(2)(A). The taxpayer cannot raise issues relating to the underlying tax liability if the taxpayer received a notice of deficiency or the taxpayer otherwise had an opportunity to dispute the tax liability. Sec. 6330(c)(2)(B).

Section 6330(c)(3), provides that a determination of the Appeals officer shall take into consideration the verification under section 6330(c)(1), the issues raised by the taxpayer, and whether the proposed collection action balances the need for the efficient collection of taxes with the legitimate concern of the person that any collection action be no more intrusive than necessary.

---

[9] Tax Court Rules 330 through 334 provide procedural guidance to taxpayers appealing the Appeals Officer's findings in the notice of determination.

* * *

[I]f we have general jurisdiction over the type of tax involved, a "determination" by Appeals and a timely petition are the only requirements for the exercise of our jurisdiction under section 6330. Temporary regulations promulgated under section 6330 [now final regulations — Eds.] require that the "determination" by Appeals be issued in the form of a "written" notice. Sec. 301.6330-1T(e)(3), Q&A-E7, Temporary Proced. & Admin. Regs, 64 Fed. Reg. 3411–3412 (Jan. 22, 1999). Thus, we have held that our jurisdiction under section 6330(d)(1) depends upon the issuance of a valid notice of determination and a timely petition for review. Sarrell v. Commissioner, 2001 U.S. Tax Ct. LEXIS 42, 117 T.C. 11 (2001); Offiler v. Commissioner, 114 T.C. 492, 498 (2000); Goza v. Commissioner, 114 T.C. 176, 182 (2000).

On April 30, 1999, respondent issued a notice of intent to levy to petitioners. The proposed levy was to collect unpaid income taxes of $83,087.85 for the taxable years 1993, 1994, and 1995. On May 24, 1999, petitioners filed a Form 12153, Request for a Collection Due Process Hearing, in which they raised the following issue regarding the validity of the assessments made by respondent:

> I do not agree with the collection action of levy and notice of intent to levy 4-30-99. The basis of my complaint is what I believe to be the lack of a valid summary record of assessment pursuant to 26 CFR 301.6203-1. Without a valid assessment there is no liability. Without a liability there can be no levy, no notice of intent to levy, nor any other collection actions.

On September 2, 1999, the Appeals officer wrote a letter to petitioners indicating that the validity of the assessments had been verified and attached a Form 4340, Certificate of Assessments and Payments, which clearly shows that the assessments in question were made and remained unpaid. The Appeals officer concluded the letter stating: "If you wish to discuss other matters, such as resolution of the liability please contact me by September 16, 1999. Otherwise, we will issue a determination." Petitioners made no response to this letter. No further proceedings or exchange of correspondence occurred prior to the Appeals officer's determination.

On November 3, 1999, a notice of determination was sent to petitioners by the IRS Appeals Office which sustained the proposed levy. The notice of determination included findings that: (1) All procedural, administrative, and statutory requirements were met; (2) the Form 4340 satisfied the requirements of section 6203;[n.4] (3) petitioners failed to present any collection alternatives; and (4) the proposed levy was justified. On December 2, 1999, petitioners filed a timely petition to the Tax Court.

Neither petitioners nor respondent has moved or argued that we lack jurisdiction in this case. However, questions regarding jurisdiction were raised by the trial judge at the time the case was called for trial. The specific jurisdictional question concerned whether petitioners were offered an opportunity for a hearing with an IRS Appeals officer. The trial judge's inquiry was based on our opinion in *Meyer v. Commissioner*, 115 T.C. 417, 422–423 (2000), which held that we lacked jurisdiction under section 6330(d) if the taxpayer was not given an opportunity for an Appeals hearing.

In *Meyer v. Commissioner, supra* at 422–423, we looked behind the notice of determination to find that the taxpayer was not offered an Appeals hearing. We then found that the notice of determination was invalid and that the Tax Court was without jurisdiction to review the Appeals officer's determination. *Id.* For the reasons discussed

[n.4] Sec. 6203 requires the Secretary to record the liability of the taxpayer and to furnish a copy of the record of assessment to the taxpayer on request. Sec. 301.6203-1, Proced. & Admin. Regs., provides that an assessment officer shall make the assessment and sign the "summary record of assessment. The summary record, through supporting records, shall provide identification of the taxpayer, the character of the liability assessed, the taxable period, if applicable, and the amount of the assessment."

below, we now conclude that our opinion in *Meyer* was incorrect.

As a preliminary matter, we point out that this Court should not have decided whether the notice of determination was valid in *Meyer v. Commissioner, supra*, because we did not have subject matter jurisdiction. We have held that we lack jurisdiction under section 6330(d) when the tax in issue is one over which we normally do not have jurisdiction. *See Johnson v. Commissioner*, 2001 U.S. Tax Ct. LEXIS 47, 117 T.C. ___ (2001); *Moore v. Commissioner*, 114 T.C. 171 (2000). The tax in *Meyer v. Commissioner, supra*, was a frivolous return penalty over which we normally have no jurisdiction. We therefore had no subject matter jurisdiction under section 6330(d). *Van Es v. Commissioner*, 115 T.C. 324 (2000). In that situation, section 6330(d) provides that "If a court determines that the appeal was to an incorrect court, a person shall have 30 days after the court determination to file such appeal with the correct court." Thus, in *Meyer v. Commissioner, supra*, we decided an issue regarding the adequacy of the hearing opportunity and its ramifications which should have been considered in the first instance by a district court with subject matter jurisdiction.

Secondly, in *Meyer v. Commissioner, supra*, our holding that the notice of determination was invalid was improperly predicated on facts regarding procedures that were followed prior to the issuance of the notice of determination rather than on the notice of determination itself. 115 T.C. at 422–423. Our analysis in *Meyer* improperly required us to look behind the notice of determination.

In *Offiler v. Commissioner*, 114 T.C. at 498, we analogized a notice of determination issued pursuant to section 6330(c)(3) to a notice of deficiency issued pursuant to section 6212, and said that the notice of determination is the jurisdictional "equivalent of a notice of deficiency."[n.6] In the context of a notice of deficiency, we have consistently held that as a general rule we do not look behind the notice to determine its validity. Pietanza v. Commissioner, 92 T.C. 729, 735 (1989), *affd. without published opinion* 935 F.2d 1282 (3d Cir. 1991); Riland v. Commissioner, 79 T.C. 185, 201 (1982); Estate of Brimm v. Commissioner, 70 T.C. 15, 22 (1978); Greenberg's Express, Inc. v. Commissioner, 62 T.C. 324, 327 (1974). It is well established that the Tax Court will generally examine only the notice of deficiency to determine whether the notice was valid for jurisdictional purposes. *See* Sealy Power, Ltd. v. Commissioner, 46 F.3d 382, 388 n.25 (5th Cir. 1995), *affg. in part and revg. in part* T.C. Memo. 1992-168; Clapp v. Commissioner, 875 F.2d 1396, 1402 (9th Cir. 1989).

We believe the same principles are applicable to a section 6330 determination. Our jurisdiction under section 6330(d)(1)(A) is established when there is a written notice that embodies a determination to proceed with the collection of the taxes in issue, and a timely filed petition. To the extent that *Meyer v. Commissioner*, 115 T.C. 417 (2000), holds that we must first look behind the determination to see whether a proper hearing was offered in order to have jurisdiction, *Meyer* is overruled.

We are, of course, cognizant of the role *stare decisis* plays in this Court and in other Federal courts, especially in the context of statutory construction. *See, e.g.*, Sec. State Bank v. Commissioner, 111 T.C. 210, 213–214 (1998), *affd.* 214 F.3d 1254 (10th Cir. 2000).

[n.6] In *Meyer v. Commissioner*, 115 T.C. 417, 421 (2000), we correctly stated the role that a notice of determination and timely petition play in our jurisdiction as follows:

> Section 6330(d) imposes certain procedural prerequisites on judicial review of collection matters. Much like the Court's deficiency jurisdiction, the Court's jurisdiction under section 6330(d) is dependent upon a valid determination letter and a timely filed petition for review. *See* Rule 330(b). Like a notice of deficiency under section 6213(a), an Appeals Office determination letter is a taxpayer's "ticket" to the Tax Court. *See* Offiler v. Commissioner, 114 T.C. 492, 498 (2000); *see also* Mulvania v. Commissioner, 81 T.C. 65, 67 (1983); Gati v. Commissioner, 113 T.C. 132, 134 (1999). Moreover, a petition for review under section 6330 must be filed with the appropriate court within 30 days of the mailing of the determination letter. *See* McCune v. Commissioner, 115 T.C. 114 (2000).

Nevertheless, when this Court decided *Meyer v. Commissioner, supra*, lien and levy cases under section 6330 were just starting to reach this Court. In the nascent stages of our section 6330 jurisprudence, we made a decision limiting our jurisdiction. After almost a year of experience in dealing with lien and levy cases, we have come to the conclusion that the jurisdictional analysis in *Meyer* was incorrect and has resulted in unjustified delay in the resolution of cases. Whether there was an appropriate hearing opportunity, or whether the hearing was conducted properly, or whether the hearing was fair, or whether it was held by an impartial Appeals officer, or whether any of the other nonjurisdictional provisions of section 6330 were properly followed, will all be factors that we must take into consideration under section 6330 in deciding such cases. But none of these factors should preclude us from exercising our jurisdiction under section 6330(d), in order to resolve the underlying dispute in a fair and expeditious manner.

In the instant case, there is nothing in the notice of determination which leads us to conclude that the determination was invalid. The notice of determination clearly embodies the Appeals officer's determination that collection by way of levy may proceed. Thus, regardless of whether petitioners were given an appropriate hearing opportunity, there was a valid determination and a timely petition. Those are the only statutory requirements for jurisdiction in section 6330(d)(1)(A). Accordingly, we hold that we have jurisdiction to review the determination in this case.

An appropriate order will be issued.

Reviewed by the Court.

* * *

WELLS, COHEN, SWIFT, GERBER, COLVIN, GALE, and THORNTON, JJ., agree with this majority opinion.

Read section 6330(b) through (d) carefully. As a matter of statutory construction, can the IRS issue a valid notice of determination if there has been no hearing? If the notice of determination is invalid, can the Tax Court take jurisdiction over the case? *See Lunsford*, 117 T.C. 159. Should the question of whether the Tax Court can "look behind" the notice of determination be affected by the standard of review applicable to CDP cases?

[2] Addressing an Inadequate Hearing

Having taken jurisdiction over the Lunsfords' appeal, the Tax Court, in a second court-reviewed opinion, reviewed the Appeals Officer's notice of determination for abuse of discretion. *See* Lunsford v. Commissioner, 117 T.C. 183 (2001) (reviewed by the court). Thus, instead of remanding the matter for an in-person CDP hearing, the majority resolved the case in favor of the Commissioner based on the record before it. According to the majority, the petitioners did not contest their failure to receive a CDP hearing, but instead raised only the issue of whether the Appeals Officer properly verified the underlying assessment. The majority rejected the petitioners' argument, finding it neither "necessary or productive" to remand the case for a hearing. *See id.* The three dissenting opinions (by Judges Colvin, Laro, and Foley) took issue with the majority's narrow reading of the case and the majority's failure to speak to the issue of whether the petitioners were entitled to a CDP hearing.

Professor Danshera Cords has explained the Tax Court's approach to insufficient CDP hearings as follows:

> In a number of cases, the Tax Court has concluded that it would be "neither necessary or productive" to send a case back for a hearing, concluding that, on the record before the court, the Appeals officer's CDP determination was

> justified even though no hearing had occurred. . . .
>
> Further complicating the issue, in some cases it is difficult to tell whether a CDP hearing took place, the correspondence was sufficient to constitute a correspondence hearing, or it was deemed unnecessary to consider whether a hearing had occurred. In some cases, the Tax Court has either refused to consider whether a hearing occurred or simply concluded that no hearing was held. In *Nichols v. Commissioner*, [T.C. Memo. 2002-17,] the court noted that "[n]o hearing was held with petitioners. Instead, on the basis of petitioners' letter and attached document, Appeals issued to petitioners . . . a Notice of Determination. . . ." The opinion moves from the assertion in the facts that there was no hearing to an analysis of the taxpayer's substantive arguments, without considering the consequences flowing from the absence of a hearing.
>
> It appears that the court in *Nichols* could have found a correspondence hearing, at least if review of the CDP request is sufficient to constitute a correspondence hearing. In addition, the Tax Court might have concluded that, pursuant to Tax Court Rule 331, the hearing issue was conceded because the taxpayer had not raised the issue. However, the opinion does not address either of these issues.
>
> Similarly, in *Robinson v. Commissioner*, [T.C. Memo 2003-77,] the Appeals officer "did not hold an Appeals Office hearing with [the taxpayer]. That is because the Appeals officer determined that the matters advanced in [the taxpayer's] attachments to Form 12153 did not require [the IRS] to hold a hearing to discuss those matters." The taxpayer was notified that the Appeals officer would "examine any information that [the taxpayer] wished to submit. . . . [The taxpayer] did not provide any information in response. . . ." The Tax Court did not address the fact that no meaningful hearing was held beyond this factual description. The taxpayer in *Robinson* was at least offered the opportunity to provide additional information and to discuss the matter with the Appeals officer in some fashion. Perhaps this is analogous to the situation where a taxpayer is offered the opportunity to schedule a CDP hearing and fails or refuses to do so. When a taxpayer fails or refuses to schedule a hearing, the Appeals officer has no choice but to issue a determination based on the available record so that collection can continue. If Mr. Robinson unreasonably failed or refused to schedule a hearing, the court could have concluded that a correspondence hearing was conducted, assuming that correspondence hearings are proper CDP hearings. Once again, the court did not address this issue.
>
> In *Nichols* and *Robinson*, the court did not even consider whether holding such a hearing would be "necessary or productive." Because the Tax Court acknowledges that it has upheld CDP determinations issued without a CDP hearing, it seems unlikely that the Tax Court was concerned about whether a hearing occurred in these cases. This is even more dangerous to taxpayer rights and the perception of fairness than the approach adopted in the *Lunsford* line of cases, which at least attempts to determine the likelihood that any relevant issues would be raised at a hearing.

Danshera Cords, *How Much Process Is Due? I.R.C. Sections 6320 and 6330 Collection Due Process Hearings*, 29 Vt. L. Rev. 51, 71–78 (2004) (footnotes omitted).[10]

If the court were to remand the matter to the IRS for a hearing, would it retain jurisdiction over the matter? Professor Cords has argued:

> If the court does not retain jurisdiction, who will ensure that the agency acts as it is directed? In recent cases, it has not been seriously questioned that the courts have the power to order further administrative consideration. The CDP

> provisions should clearly address retained jurisdiction, in the same way that IRC section 6330 currently addresses the retention of jurisdiction by the Appeals Office.

Cords, *Collection Due Process Rights*, *supra*, at 1040.

[3] Is There Refund Jurisdiction in CDP Cases?

Reading Assignment: I.R.C. § 6512(b)(1).

As discussed in Chapter 8, the Tax Court has overpayment jurisdiction in deficiency cases. *See* I.R.C. § 6512(b)(1). In a CDP case, can the Tax Court order a refund if the IRS offset an overpayment from another tax year to the year in question? The following case addresses that question.

GREENE-THAPEDI v. COMMISSIONER
United States Tax Court
126 T.C. 1 (2006)

THORNTON, JUDGE: Pursuant to section 6330(d), petitioner seeks review of respondent's determination to proceed with a proposed levy.

Background

* * *

Stipulated Decision for 1992 Taxable Year

On June 5, 1997, in a prior deficiency proceeding involving petitioner's 1992 taxable year, this Court entered a stipulated decision that petitioner had a $10,195 deficiency in income tax due but owed no additions to tax or penalties. The parties stipulated that interest would be assessed as provided by law and that effective upon entry of the decision by the Court, petitioner waived the restrictions contained in section 6213(a) prohibiting assessment and collection of the deficiency (plus statutory interest) until the decision of the Tax Court becomes final.

Collection Action on 1992 Liability

Respondent contends that on December 19, 1997, petitioner's 1992 deficiency was assessed and petitioner was sent a notice of balance due (including accrued interest) of $14,514.53. Petitioner disputes that any notice of balance due was ever sent. In any event, petitioner made no payment on her 1992 deficiency at that time.

On July 3, 2000, respondent sent petitioner a Form CP 504, "Urgent We intend to levy on certain assets. Please respond NOW." (Form CP 504), for taxable year 1992, indicating that she owed $23,805.53. By checks dated July 18, 2000, petitioner paid respondent $14,514.53 on her 1992 account; i.e., the amount of her balance as of December 19, 1997.[n.3] Contemporaneously, petitioner submitted to respondent a Form 12153, Request for a Collection Due Process Hearing, dated July 18, 2000, with respect to her 1992 tax year.[n.4] On the Form 12153, petitioner complained that the balance

---

[n.3] One of the checks was for $10,195; the memo line on the check states that it is for "Additional Tax 1992 Under Protest". The other check was for $4,319.53; the memo line states that this amount is for "1992 Interest Assessment Under Protest". A transcript of petitioner's account attached to the Form CP 504 sent to petitioner on July 3, 2000, showed the $4,319.53 amount as an interest assessment that was made on Dec. 19, 1997.

[n.4] The Appeals Office apparently treated this request as premature, on the ground that petitioner had not

shown on respondent's Form CP 504 included erroneous penalties and interest accruals.

On January 9, 2001, respondent issued petitioner a Final Notice—Notice of Intent to Levy and Notice of Your Right to a Hearing (the Final Notice) with respect to her 1992 income tax liabilities, showing an assessed balance of $4,992.70, and stating that this amount did not include accrued penalties and interest. Petitioner submitted another Form 12153, dated January 17, 2001, again requesting a hearing with respect to her 1992 taxable year and stating: "I do not owe the money. Notice improper".

Appeals Office Hearing and Notice of Determination

The Appeals Office hearing consisted of an exchange of correspondence and telephone conversations. During the hearing, petitioner contended that she was not liable for any interest accruals between December 19, 1997, and July 3, 2000, on the ground that she had not received the December 19, 1997, notice of balance due and was not notified of any balance due until July 3, 2000. By Notice of Determination dated May 22, 2001, respondent's Appeals Office sustained the proposed collection action.

Tax Court Petition

On June 22, 2001, petitioner filed her petition in this Court. The petition disputed, among other things, interest and penalties with respect to her 1992 income tax liability and requested this Court to order respondent to credit or refund what she alleged to be her tax overpayment for 1992. The petition also alleged that petitioner had failed to receive a meaningful Appeals Office hearing as required by section 6330.

Respondent's Motion for Partial Summary Judgment

On October 17, 2002, respondent filed a motion for partial summary judgment with respect to the issue of whether petitioner was afforded the opportunity for an Appeals Office administrative hearing under sections 6320 and 6330. By Order dated February 25, 2003, this Court granted respondent's motion for partial summary judgment, holding that "petitioner was provided with a meaningful opportunity for a collection due process hearing in this case."

Petitioner's Motion To Add 1999 Taxable Year to This Proceeding

Respondent's just-described motion for partial summary judgment indicated, among other things, that after the filing of the petition, respondent had offset a $10,633 overpayment from petitioner's 1999 income tax account against petitioner's 1992 tax liability, resulting in full payment of petitioner's 1992 liability. On December 3, 2002, petitioner filed a motion for leave to amend her petition to add taxable year 1999 to this proceeding. In her motion, petitioner stated that she had been "caught by surprise" by the information in respondent's motion that respondent had offset her 1999 overpayment against her alleged 1992 tax liability. By Order dated January 30, 2003, this Court denied petitioner's motion for leave to amend her petition. The Order stated:

> Respondent contends, and we agree, that petitioner is not permitted to dispute in this collection review proceeding respondent's application of an overpayment to offset all or part of the tax due for taxable year 1992 although the latter year is otherwise subject to review under section 6330. *See, e.g.*, Trent v. Comm'r, T.C. Memo 2002-285.

---

yet received any notice of Federal tax lien filing, final notice of intent to levy, or notice of jeopardy levy with respect to taxable year 1992.

District Court Refund Suit

Petitioner then filed a refund suit in the United States District Court, Northern District of Illinois, Eastern Division, claiming a refund of her 1999 overpayment. The United States moved to dismiss on the ground that as a matter of law petitioner has no claim for a 1999 overpayment because the credit against the 1999 tax year no longer exists, having been applied against petitioner's outstanding 1992 tax liability pursuant to section 6402(a). By memorandum opinion and order entered December 11, 2003, the District Court denied the Government's motion to dismiss, on the ground that it could not determine as a matter of law that petitioner's 1999 overpayment did not exceed her 1992 liability, so that the Government's section 6402(a) duty to "refund any balance to such person" would not arise in the District Court case. The District Court stated:

> Finally, the Court is mindful that although the Tax Court does not have concurrent jurisdiction over the issues in the present suit, which relates to the 1999 tax year, *see* Statland v. United States, 178 F.3d 465, 470–71 (7th Cir. 1999), the Tax Court proceedings related to Plaintiff's 1992 tax liability will likely resolve certain facts necessary to the resolution of the present litigation. Therefore, this matter is stayed pending the outcome of the Tax Court proceedings.

Amended Petition

Petitioner subsequently filed an unopposed motion for leave to file an amended petition in these Tax Court proceedings. In her amended petition, petitioner contended that the Appeals Office erred in determining that the proposed levy with respect to her 1992 taxable year should proceed. She also challenged her liability for the 1992 deficiency and associated interest on the ground that respondent had failed to make timely notice and demand for payment.

Discussion

* * * Sometime after the petition was filed, respondent applied petitioner's 1999 overpayment to offset her 1992 tax liability. Consequently, respondent no longer claims any amount to be due and owing from petitioner with respect to her 1992 income tax account. On supplemental brief respondent states that he "intends to take no further collection action with respect to * * * [petitioner's] 1992 tax liability". Accordingly, respondent contends that this case should be dismissed as moot. For the reasons described below, we agree.

The Tax Court is a court of limited jurisdiction; we may exercise jurisdiction only to the extent expressly authorized by Congress. *See, e.g.*, Henry Randolph Consulting v. Commissioner, 112 T.C. 1, 4 (1999). Our jurisdiction in this case is predicated upon section 6330(d)(1)(A), which gives the Tax Court jurisdiction "with respect to such matter" as is covered by the final determination in a requested hearing before the Appeals Office. *See* Davis v. Commissioner, 115 T.C. 35, 37 (2000). "Thus, our jurisdiction is defined by the scope of the determination" that the Appeals officer is required to make. Sklar v. Comm'r, 125 T.C. 281, 2005 U.S. Tax Ct. LEXIS 35, *25 (2005).

The Appeals officer's written determination is expected to address "the issues presented by the taxpayer and considered at the hearing." H. Conf. Rept. 105-599, at 266 (1998), 1998-3 C.B. 747, 1020. At the hearing, the Appeals officer is required to verify that "the requirements of any applicable law or administrative procedure have been met." Sec. 6330(c)(1); *see* sec. 6330(c)(3)(A).[n.10] The Appeals officer is also required to address whether the proposed collection action balances the need for efficient tax

[n.10] Although this language is somewhat open ended, the legislative history clarifies that this required collection with the legitimate concern that any collection action be no more intrusive than necessary. Sec. 6330(c)(3)(C). The taxpayer may raise "any relevant issue relating to the unpaid tax or the proposed levy". Sec. 6330(c)(2)(A). The taxpayer is also entitled to challenge "the existence or amount of the underlying tax liability" if he or she "did not receive any statutory notice of deficiency for such tax liability or did not otherwise have an opportunity to dispute such tax liability." Sec. 6330(c)(2)(B).

In *Chocallo v. Comm'r*, T.C. Memo 2004-152, the Commissioner had acknowledged that the tax liability he had been trying to collect by levy had been improperly assessed, had refunded previously collected amounts with interest, and had agreed that there was no unpaid tax liability upon which a levy could be based. Accordingly, this Court dismissed the case as moot. The Court stated: "Our jurisdiction under section 6330 is generally limited to reviewing whether a proposed levy action is proper." *Id.* The Court declined to entertain the taxpayer's motion for sanctions against the Government, reasoning that the taxpayer "has received all the relief to which she is entitled under section 6330". *Id.* Similarly, in *Gerakios v. Comm'r*, T.C. Memo 2004-203, we dismissed the collection review proceeding as moot where the parties agreed that there was no unpaid liability upon which a lien or levy could be based after the taxpayer had paid the liability in full.

In the instant case, as in *Chocallo* and *Gerakios*, respondent acknowledges that there is no unpaid liability for the determination year upon which a levy could be based and has stated that he is no longer pursuing the proposed levy. Accordingly, in this case, as in *Chocallo* and *Gerakios*, the proposed levy for petitioner's 1992 tax liability is moot.

In the instant case, unlike in *Chocallo*, respondent does not concede that the proposed levy was improperly made, nor has respondent returned to petitioner the disputed amounts that have been applied to satisfy petitioner's 1992 account. These circumstances, however, do not dictate a different result in this case. In this case, unlike in *Chocallo*, respondent has collected no amounts by levy. Respondent's offset of petitioner's 1999 overpayment against her 1992 tax account was pursuant to section 6402(a). An offset under section 6402 does not constitute a levy action and accordingly is not a collection action that is subject to review in this section 6330 proceeding. Bullock v. Comm'r, T.C. Memo 2003-5; *see* Boyd v. Comm'r, 124 T.C. 296, 300 (2005); sec. 301.6330-1(g)(2), Q&A-G3, Proced. & Admin. Regs. (an offset is a nonlevy collection action that the Internal Revenue Service may take during the suspension period provided in section 6330(e)(1)).

In the instant case, unlike in *Chocallo v. Commissioner*, *supra*, and *Gerakios v. Commissioner*, *supra*, there remains unresolved petitioner's claims for a refund. In her amended petition, petitioner contends that she is not liable for the 1992 deficiency and associated interest on the ground that respondent failed to assess the deficiency and mail her a timely notice and demand to pay; alternatively, she contends that pursuant to section 6601(c) she is not liable for interest accruals from the period from July 5, 1997 (when she claims respondent was required to make notice and demand for payment of her 1992 deficiency) to July 3, 2000 (when respondent sent her Form CP 504 requesting payment). On brief, petitioner contends that she is entitled to a refund for:

> all compound interest she paid for the period April 15, 1993 to July 18, 2000, all interest she paid for periods during which interest was suspended or [sic] July 5, 1997 to July 3, 2000; and for all sums that she paid for penalties and additions and interest on such, that were disallowed by the June 5, 1997 Tax Court decision.

Petitioner's claim for a refund arises, if at all, under section 6330(c)(2), as an outgrowth

verification pertains to legal and administrative requirements "for the proposed collection action". H. Conf. Rept. 105-599, at 264 (1998), 1998-3 C.B. 747, 1018.

of her challenge to the existence and amount of her underlying 1992 tax liability.[n.12] Pursuant to section 6330(c)(2), however, whatever right petitioner may have to challenge the existence and amount of her underlying tax liability in this proceeding arises only in connection with her challenge to the proposed collection action. Inasmuch as the proposed levy is moot, petitioner has no independent basis to challenge the existence or amount of her underlying tax liability in this proceeding.

More fundamentally, 6330 does not expressly give this Court jurisdiction to determine an overpayment or to order a refund or credit of taxes paid. This Court has not previously addressed the question as to whether such jurisdiction arises implicitly in collection review proceedings commenced in this Court pursuant to section 6330. The legislative history of this Court's overpayment and refund jurisdiction in deficiency proceedings is relevant in addressing this question.

When our predecessor, the Board of Tax Appeals (the Board) was created in 1924, it lacked jurisdiction to determine an overpayment for the year in question in a deficiency proceeding. * * * The Revenue Act of 1926, ch. 27, 44 Stat. 9, established the Board's jurisdiction to determine an overpayment in a deficiency proceeding. The Board still had no jurisdiction, however, to order payment of any resulting refund. *Id.* at 635–636; * * *. That situation persisted until 1988 when Congress enacted section 6512(b), giving the Tax Court jurisdiction to order the refund of overpayments determined in deficiency proceedings. Technical and Miscellaneous Revenue Act of 1988, Pub. L. 100-647, sec. 6244, 102 Stat. 3750. This legislative history makes clear that Congress believed that absent this legislative change the Tax Court lacked authority to order the refund of any overpayment. In this same legislation, the Senate proposed to expand the Tax Court's refund jurisdiction by granting the Tax Court jurisdiction over tax refund actions where the taxpayer already had a related deficiency proceeding pending in Tax Court. H. Conf. Rept. 100-1104 (Vol. II), at 234 (1988), 1988-3 C.B. 473, 724. This proposal was rejected in conference. *See id.* In describing "Present Law" as related to this proposal, the conference report stated: "The Tax Court has no jurisdiction to determine whether a taxpayer has made an overpayment except in the context of a deficiency proceeding." *Id.* at 233, 1988-3 C.B. at 723. In the Taxpayer Relief Act of 1997, Pub. L. 105-34, sec. 1451, 111 Stat. 1054, Congress enacted 6512(b)(4), which clarifies that in determining an overpayment pursuant to section 6512(b), the Tax Court has no jurisdiction to "restrain or review any credit or reduction made by the Secretary under section 6402." *See* H. Conf. Rept. 105-220, at 732 (1997), 1997-4 C.B. (Vol. 2) 1457, 2202 (stating that this amendment "clarifies that the Tax Court does not have jurisdiction over the validity or merits of the credits or offsets that reduce or eliminate the refund to which the taxpayer was otherwise entitled.").

Sec. 6512(b)(2), read in isolation, does not expressly confine to deficiency proceedings the Tax Court's jurisdiction to enforce overpayments; read in the context of sec. 6512 as a whole, however, that is clearly the effect. * * *

In sum, given that explicit statutory authority was required before this Court acquired jurisdiction to determine overpayments in deficiency cases, and given that additional explicit statutory authority was required before this Court acquired, decades later, jurisdiction to enforce such an overpayment, and given that Congress later clarified legislatively that this overpayment jurisdiction did not extend to reviewing credits under section 6402 (such as the credit of petitioner's 1999 overpayment against her 1992 tax liability), we do not believe we should assume, without explicit statutory authority, jurisdiction either to determine an overpayment or to order a refund or credit

[n.12] The right to challenge the existence and amount of underlying tax liability encompasses the right to challenge the existence and amount of disputed interest thereon. Urbano v. Comm'r, 122 T.C. 384, 389–390 (2004).

of taxes paid in a section 6330 collection proceeding.[n.19] As discussed below, this conclusion is reinforced by the absence in section 6330 of the traditional statutory limitations on the allowance of refunds or credits of taxes.

Section 6511 contains detailed limitations on the allowance of tax credits or refunds generally. Section 6511(a) sets out the requisite time periods for filing a claim for credit or refund. Section 6511(b)(2) limits the amount of tax to be refunded to two so-called look-back periods: (1) For claims filed within 3 years of filing the return, the refund is generally limited to the portion of the tax paid within the 3 years immediately before the claim was filed; (2) for claims not filed within 3 years of filing the return, the refund is generally limited to the portion of the tax paid during the 2 years immediately before the claim was filed. *See* Commissioner v. Lundy, 516 U.S. 235, 240, 116 S. Ct. 647, 133 L. Ed. 2d 611 (1996). Section 6512(b)(3) generally incorporates these rules where taxpayers who challenge deficiency notices in Tax Court are found to be entitled to refunds.

By contrast, section 6330 incorporates no such limitations on the allowance of tax refunds or credits. There is no indication that in enacting section 6330, Congress intended, sub silentio, to provide taxpayers a back-door route to tax refunds and credits free of these longstanding and well-established limitations. Nor, in light of the detailed and comprehensive codification of such limitations in sections 6511 and 6512(b), do we believe that Congress would have intended that such limitations should arise by inference in section 6330 with respect to claims for tax refunds or credits as to which our jurisdiction would similarly arise under section 6330, if at all, only by inference. Consequently, we are led to the conclusion that Congress did not intend section 6330 to provide for the allowance of tax refunds and credits.

Petitioner's claim for a refund is based at least partly on her claim that she does not owe at least some of the assessed interest, on the ground that respondent failed to make timely notice and demand for payment of her 1992 deficiency. This Court has held that in an appeal brought under section 6330(d), where the existence and amount of the taxpayer's underlying tax liability is properly at issue, our jurisdiction allows us to review the taxpayer's claim for interest abatement pursuant to section 6404, *see* Katz v. Commissioner, 115 T.C. 329, 340–341 (2000), as well as to redetermine the correct amount of the taxpayer's interest liability where the claim falls outside of section 6404, *see* Urbano v. Comm'r, 122 T.C. 384, 389–393 (2004). In interest-abatement proceedings brought under section 6404(h), this Court has held that we have jurisdiction to determine the amount of an overpayment pursuant to section 6404(h)(2)(B), which states: "Rules similar to the rules of section 6512(b) shall apply for purposes of this subsection." *See* Goettee v. Commissioner, T.C. Memo 2003-43.

We do not believe that petitioner's refund claim is properly construed as being predicated on a claim for interest abatement pursuant to section 6404. But even if petitioner's claim were so construed, that circumstance would not affect our conclusion that we lack jurisdiction under section 6330 to determine any overpayment or to order a refund or credit. Unlike section 6404(h), section 6330 contains no cross-reference to the rules of section 6512(b), nor does section 6330 cross-reference section 6404(h)(2)(B), which makes section 6512(b)-type rules applicable only "for purposes of this subsection" (i.e., subsection (h) of section 6404). Section 6404(h)(2)(B) illustrates that Congress has acted infrequently to extend this Court's overpayment jurisdiction, and then only in a deliberate and circumscribed manner. These considerations buttress our conclusion that

---

[n.19] We do not mean to suggest that this Court is foreclosed from considering whether the taxpayer has paid more than was owed, where such a determination is necessary for a correct and complete determination of whether the proposed collection action should proceed. Conceivably, there could be a collection action review proceeding where (unlike the instant case) the proposed collection action is not moot and where pursuant to sec. 6330(c)(2)(B), the taxpayer is entitled to challenge "the existence or amount of the underlying tax liability". In such a case, the validity of the proposed collection action might depend upon whether the taxpayer has any unpaid balance, which might implicate the question of whether the taxpayer has paid more than was owed.

we should not assume overpayment jurisdiction in a section 6330(d) proceeding absent express statutory provision.

We are mindful that the District Court has stayed petitioner's refund case with the expectation that this Court would resolve certain relevant facts in this proceeding. Because we lack jurisdiction in this proceeding to determine petitioner's 1992 overpayment or to order a refund or credit of petitioner's 1992 taxes, and because the proposed collection action for 1992 is now moot, no factual issue remains which would affect the disposition of the case before us. For us to undertake to resolve issues that would not affect the disposition of this case would, at best, amount to rendering an advisory opinion. This we decline to do. * * *

For the reasons discussed, we shall dismiss this case as moot.

* * *

GERBER, COHEN, WELLS, HALPERN, CHIECHI, LARO, GALE, HAINES, GOEKE, KROUPA, and HOLMES, JJ., agree with this majority opinion.

FOLEY, J., concurs in result only.

COLVIN, J., concurring: I accept as correct the majority's interpretation of the statute and our lack of jurisdiction in this case. However, I write separately to highlight the fact that the Commissioner's offset authority can cause undesirable consequences for taxpayers and the Court in collection review proceedings under sections 6320 and 6330.

The majority holds that petitioner properly invoked the Court's jurisdiction under section 6330 by filing a timely petition challenging respondent's notice of determination regarding the proposed collection of her tax liability for 1992. The majority also holds that action was rendered moot because petitioner later overpaid her Federal income tax for 1999, and the Commissioner offset that overpayment by the amount of her unpaid 1992 tax liability.

Typically in these situations, a taxpayer's only remedy may be to fully pay the tax, file a refund claim, and if unsuccessful, institute a tax refund suit in Federal District Court or the Court of Federal Claims. As a result, taxpayer protections provided in sections 6320 and 6330, that is, the right to administrative and judicial review of the Commissioner's collection actions, can quickly evaporate simply because the taxpayer overpaid his or her taxes for another year.

The circumstances present here may recur in future cases. The combination of the Commissioner's authority to offset an overpayment and the mootness doctrine may cause taxpayer frustration and waste judicial resources. The dismissal of a proceeding brought in this Court under section 6320 or 6330 due to the offset of an overpayment may convince taxpayers that their efforts during the administrative and judicial process were wasted. Taxpayers may draw little solace from the fact that they can reinstate their challenge to the Commissioner's collection action by filing a refund suit in another court.

MARVEL, WHERRY, and HOLMES, JJ., agree with this concurring opinion.

* * *

Recall the Tax Court's decision in *Montgomery v. Commissioner*, 122 T.C. 1 (2004), in which the majority concluded that a taxpayer could contest a self-reported liability as part of a CDP hearing when the taxpayer did not receive a notice of deficiency. Based on the Tax Court's holding in *Greene-Thapedi*, could the Tax Court have required the IRS to issue a refund to the taxpayers in *Montgomery* if the court had concluded that they had, in fact, overpaid their tax liability? In that regard, consider footnote 19 in *Greene-Thapedi*.

What do you think about the *Greene-Thapedi* majority's holding in light of the repetitive litigation it apparently requires? What does the concurrence say about this?

In *McGee v. Commissioner*, 123 T.C. 314, 317 (2004), discussed in Section 17.02[B][1] of Chapter 17, the Tax Court agreed with the IRS's position that an offset was a collection action, thus commencing the running of the two-year statute of limitations within which to file an innocent spouse request. Disagreeing with the IRS, the Tax Court further held that the notices sent to the taxpayer about the offset were collection-related notices that should have included notice of rights under section 6015, as required by the IRS Reform Act. *Id.* at 319–20. How does the majority's determination in *Greene-Thapedi* that an offset is not a collection action subject to review under Code section 6330 square with *McGee*?

In *Greene-Thapedi*, Judge Vasquez filed a lengthy dissent that was joined by Judge Swift. The dissent argued both that the Tax Court had jurisdiction under Code section 6330 to determine an overpayment and that the case was not moot. *Greene-Thapedi*, 126 T.C. at 15 (Vasquez, J., dissenting). In part, Judge Vasquez argued:

> I do not believe that the Commissioner can unilaterally deprive the Court of jurisdiction in section 6330 cases by merely stating that he no longer intends to proceed with collection. The congressional intent behind the enactment of section 6330 is frustrated if the Commissioner can unilaterally deprive the Tax Court of jurisdiction after directing the taxpayer to the Tax Court by issuing the notice of determination. *See* [Charlotte's Office Boutique, Inc. v. Commissioner, 425 F.3d 1203 (9th Cir. 2005), *aff'g.* 121 T.C. 89 (2003)].
>
> Respondent's statement that he will not proceed with collection is not a concession that the taxes are not due. *See id.* at 1208. A statement that does not change respondent's position on the amount of tax due for 1992 cannot deprive the Court of the jurisdiction we acquired when petitioner filed her petition for review of the notice of determination which challenged the amount of the underlying tax liability. *Id.* Although respondent states that he no longer intends to take further collection action against petitioner, respondent's statement has no bearing on our jurisdiction. *See id.* at 1209; LTV Corp. v. Commissioner [64 T.C. 589 (1975)].

Id. at 16.

He further explained that he believed that his view accorded with the purposes behind the CDP provisions:

> My view advances our established precedent that "In view of the statutory scheme as a whole, we think the substantive and procedural protections contained in sections 6320 and 6330 reflect congressional intent that the Commissioner should collect the correct amount of tax". Montgomery v. Commissioner, 122 T.C. at 10. In section 6330 cases, taxpayers should be able to claim an overpayment, and the Court should be able to enter a decision for an overpayment to ensure that the Commissioner collects no more than the correct amount of tax.
>
> Although the Tax Court has limited jurisdiction, section 6330 expanded the Court's jurisdiction. Robinette v. Commissioner, 123 T.C. at 99. The language of the statute provides a broader remedy than the majority's narrow interpretation allows. *Montgomery v. Commissioner*, *supra* at 9.
>
> The legislative history does not provide any specific expression of Congressional intent to bar taxpayers, such as petitioner, from raising an overpayment claim. *Id.* at 10. The majority limits the remedies available to taxpayers by holding that in section 6330 proceedings they cannot obtain a decision that there is an overpayment. Furthermore, the majority does not review petitioner's challenge to the amount of her tax liability for 1992 even though she properly raised this issue. Without a clear jurisdictional prohibition or inability, it would be most unjust to prohibit taxpayers from claiming an overpayment of the tax

> in this forum and require them to seek it in another. *See Estate of Baumgardner v. Commissioner*, 85 T.C. [445] at 446 [(1985)].
>
> I do not believe that Congress intended, when enacting section 6330, to expand this Court's jurisdiction and at the same time create a situation where choice of this forum would provide such unfair results. *See id.* at 453. To narrowly interpret the statute to prevent the Court from deciding an overpayment exists frustrates our congressionally conferred jurisdiction.
>
> As we noted in *Estate of Baumgardner v. Commissioner, supra* at 457: "it is hard to imagine that Congress could have intended to bifurcate an 'overpayment' " and that "It is equally hard to imagine that an 'overpayment' has a different meaning depending upon the forum. Either of those approaches would force some taxpayers to resolve a single tax controversy in two different forums", and this would duplicate costs for taxpayers. The majority's approach will force taxpayers to resolve a single tax controversy in two different forums — assuming arguendo that they were not so barred by the period of limitations, res judicata, or prejudiced by having their claim being reduced or eliminated by the look-back rules of section 6511(b).
>
> I seek to find harmony in the statutory framework in order to avoid acute injustice to taxpayers. "Considering the overcrowded dockets in most Federal courts, we cannot be insensitive to opportunities to avoid unnecessary litigation." *Id.* at 458. The majority merely punish (1) taxpayers whose cash reserves make it impossible for them to pursue relief in a District Court or the Court of Federal Claims, (2) taxpayers who are too unsophisticated to realize that a suit in District Court or the Court of Federal Claims could preserve his right to a refund, and (3) taxpayers whose expected refund is too small in relation to attorney's fees and other costs to justify a suit in District Court or the Court of Federal Claims. *See* Commissioner v. Lundy, 516 U.S. 235, 263, 116 S. Ct. 647, 133 L. Ed. 2d 611 (1996) (Thomas, J., dissenting).
>
> Petitioner has properly invoked the jurisdiction of the Court. By not deciding whether petitioner is entitled to an overpayment we are leaving an essential issue unaddressed. *See* Naftel v. Commissioner, 85 T.C. [527] at 535 [(1985)]. "The consequences of omitting consideration of this issue might well require additional hearings and evidence thus placing an undue burden on the Court as well as the parties." *Id.* "If we have jurisdiction to resolve the * * * issue, we should not ask the taxpayer who raises that issue at an Appeals Office hearing and in this Court to go to another court to resolve that issue". *Washington I*, 120 T.C. [114] at 134 [(2003)] (Beghe, J., concurring). This is "inconsistent with the goals of judicial and party economy embodied in the slogan 'one-stop shopping'." *Id.*

Id. at 24–25. Based on these limited excerpts, do you agree with the dissent's view or do you find the majority's view more compelling?

In *Freije v. Commissioner*, 125 T.C. 14, 26 (2005), the Tax Court held that its "jurisdiction is not confined to the year (or period) to which the unpaid tax relates, as respondent contends, but extends to facts and issues in nondetermination years where they are relevant to computing the unpaid tax." Thus, the court found that it could consider whether a remittance made for the tax year in question was improperly applied to a previous tax year. The IRS has stated that it "disagree[s] with *Freije* to the extent it may be read to support the position that a taxpayer may argue the entitlement to credits for non-CDP periods to decrease the amount of tax due for purposes of the CDP case." CC-2006-019, *supra*, at 36.

[D] Preparing for Tax Court Review

Based on the discussion above, how should a taxpayer approach preparation for Tax Court review of a CDP determination by the IRS? One commentator makes the following suggestions:

> You've prepared and presented your case all the way up to the Appeals Office, and your proposals on behalf of your client have been rejected. Many tax professionals figure the decision of the administrative appeal is the end of the road. Don't give up so easily. As we have seen in the cases discussed above, the notice of determination may be vulnerable on several grounds, all centering around the concept of arbitrary and capricious determinations. Examine the reasons given to justify the final determination. Look for weaknesses that may be identified by a Tax Court:
>
> • **Rejecting the offer without determining liability**. . . . [C]ollection activity without first fixing the correct amount owed could be deemed arbitrary.
>
> • **Failure to address all relevant factors**. . . . IRS Appeals may have simply left out consideration of a significant factor. . . .
>
> • **Inconsistent reasoning**. . . . [In one case,] the IRS was seen to stumble all over the place trying to come up with a reason to deny the taxpayer's requested installment plan, glaringly contradicting itself in several respects. Similarly, in other cases a search of the IRS offer-in-compromise file.[n.26] may reveal contradictions, inconsistencies or other grasping at straws in the rationale used for rejecting the requested relief.
>
> At the end of the day, it may not be necessary to roll over and accept a final determination by appeals. Appeals officers are human beings, and sometimes use poor judgment or unfairly gloss over important factors favoring the requested relief. Take a close look at it. You may find an Achilles' heel among the details.

Morgan D. King, *When the Tax Court Takes the Taxpayer's Side in Collection Disputes*, 9 J. Tax Prac. & Proc. 31, 37–38 (2007).[11]

[E] Appealing the Tax Court's Decision

Reading Assignment: I.R.C. § 7482(b)(1).

To which circuit does appeal from a Tax Court decision in a CDP case lie? Code section 7482(b)(1) provides that the Court of Appeals for the District of Columbia is the default venue if none of the subparagraphs in that paragraph apply. None of the subparagraphs list CDP proceedings. Should the default rule therefore apply? The IRS has argued otherwise:

> Although none of subparagraphs (A)–(F) expressly mentions a decision in a CDP case, we should not object to venue when a taxpayer appeals a CDP decision to the circuit court of appeals of the taxpayer's residence or principal place of business, which is the rule for deficiency cases. It is reasonable to believe that Congress intended the rules of section 7482(b)(1)(A)–(F) to apply to the appeal of CDP decisions, because section 6330(d)(1)(A) contemplates that the Tax Court should exercise jurisdiction over taxes being collected in the same manner as it exercises jurisdiction over deficiency cases.

CC-2006-019, *supra*, at 70. Do you agree, or do you believe that the IRS's interpretation contradicts the plain language of the statute?

---

n.26 Which may be obtained relatively easily with a Freedom of Information Request.

11

PROBLEMS

1. Dawn timely filed her Year 1 tax return reporting $20,000 of taxable income and showing a refund due of $1,000. Following an audit of her return, the IRS sent Dawn a notice of deficiency on March 1, Year 4 asserting a $3,000 deficiency arising out of income Dawn allegedly failed to report. Dawn ignored the notice. The IRS assessed the deficiency within the statute of limitations on assessment and filed a Notice of Federal Tax Lien on Tuesday, September 15, Year 4. Two days later, the IRS mailed to Dawn by certified mail the post-lien notice of her right to a CDP hearing under section 6320.
   A. When is the last day Dawn can file a request for a CDP hearing?
   B. How does she file the request and who will hear her case?
   C. Assuming Dawn wants to meet face-to-face with the hearing officer, must she specifically request such a hearing in advance? If she does, will the hearing officer have to grant her a face-to-face hearing?
   D. What impact does Dawn's CDP hearing request have on the running of the statute of limitations on collection, which otherwise would expire on April 15, Year 14?
2. Assume that Dawn, from Problem 1, ignored the post-lien notice she received from the IRS. In an effort to levy on her bank account, the IRS sends her a Notice of Intent to Levy notifying her of her right to a pre-levy CDP hearing under section 6330. Dawn timely filed a request for a CDP hearing.
   A. What impact will her request for a CDP hearing have on the IRS's ability to levy against her bank account?
   B. Can Dawn contest the existence of the unreported income as part of the CDP hearing?
   C. Assume that Dawn wishes to request an offer in compromise based on doubt as to collectibility. Will she be allowed to raise the issue as part of the CDP hearing?
3. Kenney properly filed a request for a CDP hearing relating to his income tax liability for Year 3. The hearing officer issued a notice of determination on April 1, Year 6 denying Kenney's request that the IRS not levy against his collection of vintage automobiles but instead levy against a piece of farmland he owns.
   A. How can Kenney obtain review of the hearing officer's determination? Which court will hear the appeal?
   B. What is the last day Kenney can file his petition for judicial review of the notice of determination?
   C. What standard of review will the court use when reviewing the hearing officer's decisions set forth in the notice of determination?
4. Mitchell timely filed his Year 1 return, which reflected $3,000 of tax due. Mitchell failed to remit the $3,000 with the return. After summarily assessing the $3,000 of tax due, the IRS filed a Notice of Federal Tax Lien against a parcel of real estate Mitchell owns in Oklahoma. One day later, the IRS sent Mitchell by certified mail the post-lien notice of his right to a CDP hearing under section 6320.
   A. Mitchell maintains that he misreported his Year 1 tax liability and that, in fact, he owed only $2,000. Can Mitchell raise the issue of his correct Year 1 tax liability as part of the CDP hearing?
   B. Assume that the IRS denies CDP relief to Mitchell. If, on appeal to the Tax Court, Mitchell can establish that his Year 1 liability was, in fact, $2,000, rather than the $3,000 amount he reported on his return, can the

Tax Court order the IRS to issue him a $1,000 refund?

5. Amber filed her Year 1 return, which reflected $10,000 of tax due, on December 1, Year 2, without having obtained an extension of time to file. She failed to remit any money with the return. The IRS assessed the $10,000 of tax due and filed a Notice of Federal Tax Lien against certain rental property Amber owns. The IRS also promptly sent Amber by certified mail the post-lien notice of her right to a CDP hearing. Amber made a request for a CDP hearing 45 days after she received the notice. She intends to propose an offer in compromise based on doubt as to collectibility.

   A. Is Amber entitled to a CDP hearing? If so, will the IRS consider her offer in compromise in the hearing?

   B. If the IRS conducts a hearing in Amber's case and she is unhappy with the resolution, can she appeal to the Tax Court?

6. Melanie was married to Ron from June of Year 1 until August of Year 2. They divorced when Melanie discovered that Ron's primary source of income was selling stolen car parts. Melanie and Ron filed a joint return for Year 1. Assume that Melanie has a viable "innocent spouse" claim to relief from joint and several liability from the Year 1 return.

   A. Can Melanie assert an innocent spouse defense in the CDP hearing?

   B. Assuming the IRS denies CDP relief, how much time will Melanie have to request court review? Assume that her claim for relief is based on her innocent spouse claim.

7. Vito, a sole proprietor of a small computer store, timely filed his Year 1 tax return reporting $55,000 of taxable income and showing tax due of $500, which he remitted with his return. The IRS audited Vito's Year 1 return and, without sending a 30-day letter, sent him a properly addressed notice of deficiency on April 1, Year 4, asserting a $25,000 deficiency. The notice of deficiency was misdelivered and Vito never received it. The IRS assessed the deficiency within the statute of limitations on assessment and filed a Notice of Federal Tax Lien on October 15, Year 4. The IRS promptly mailed to Vito by certified mail the required post-lien CDP notice. Vito requested a CDP hearing at which he made an offer in compromise based on doubt as to liability and doubt as to collectibility. After the hearing, the IRS sent Vito a notice of determination denying relief. Vito timely petitioned the Tax Court. What is the standard of review applicable in Tax Court to Vito's CDP hearing?

8. What is the rationale behind the notion of limiting CDP review in court to the agency record?

Chapter 17

JOINT AND SEVERAL LIABILITY AND THE "INNOCENT SPOUSE" PROVISIONS

§ 17.01 INTRODUCTION

[A] The Joint Return and Joint and Several Liability

Reading Assignment: I.R.C. § 6013(a)(1)–(2), (d)(3); Treas. Reg. § 1.6013-4(d).

Code section 6013(a) authorizes a joint return for husband and wife. In general, a husband and wife are jointly and severally liable for any tax for a year in which they filed a joint return, meaning that the IRS can pursue either spouse for any tax delinquencies.[1] I.R.C. § 6013(d)(3).

Why are married taxpayers jointly and severally liable for the taxes on their joint return? Professor Bryan Camp has argued that the notion that joint and several liability is the "price" spouses pay for filing a joint return does not comport with history, in part because "Congress made couples jointly liable in 1938 but waited 10 years to enact the supposed benefit of a separate rate structure for couples." Bryan T. Camp, *The Unhappy Marriage of Law and Equity in Joint Return Liability*, 108 Tax Notes 1307, 1308 (2005) (footnotes omitted). He further argues:

> I submit that the better explanation for, and understanding of, joint liability is the well-recognized tension in the tax code between treating individuals as individuals and treating them as part of a greater economic unit: the family. One sees the tension in the Revenue Act of 1913, the first revenue act under the modern income tax. . . . [T]he 1913 act did not permit couples to file jointly, yet allowed them to exempt $1,000 more than unmarried individuals. That additional exemption amount was made in recognition that marriage created an economic unit of more than one individual. That is, the additional exemption for married couples was based on the theory that "an American family of from three to five children living in decent comfort, and desirous of giving the children a college education would, it was maintained, need all of $4,000, or in the case of a widow, certainly all of $3,000, for meeting the necessary family expenses." . . .

Id. at 1309 (footnotes omitted).

[B] Innocent Spouse Relief: Historical Background

Although the Code has long provided for joint and several liability for a married couple filing a joint tax return, it has also provided an exception for an "innocent spouse." Relief from joint and several liability is particularly important if the spouses have divorced and the "innocent" spouse stands as the only viable collection source. Unless some form of liability relief applies, each divorced spouse remains liable for payment, even if the divorce decree specifies that one spouse is responsible for all tax liability arising from joint returns filed during the marriage. In such cases, while the innocent spouse may have a state law right of contribution against the other spouse to

[1] Note that joint and several liability applies only to joint tax returns. Under a Treasury regulation, if one spouse signed the return under duress, the return does not constitute a "joint return," and "[t]he individual who signed such return under duress is not jointly and severally liable for the tax shown on the return or any deficiency in tax with respect to the return." Treas. Reg. § 1.6013-4(d).

recover amounts paid to the IRS, such a remedy may be inadequate given the high costs of litigation and the poor prospects of collection in many cases.

The bulk of this chapter explores the contours and requirements of the statutory provisions for innocent spouse relief, which have evolved over time in favor of granting relief in more types of cases. This section provides some historical background and context. Professor Bryan Camp explains the origin of innocent spouse relief as follows:

> Most commentators trace the impetus for innocent spouse relief to the Supreme Court's 1961 decision in *James v. United States*, in which the Court, reversing a 15-year precedent, held that embezzlement income was indeed taxable. The paradigmatic cases prompting congressional action to modify the strict rule of joint liability seemed to be cases, like *James*, in which a husband embezzled or otherwise concealed income from his wife, got caught, and the IRS asserted a deficiency based on the omitted income. That, at least, is what the 1971 Senate Finance Committee report says.
>
> In many of the paradigmatic post-*James* cases in which the taxpayers raised an issue about the liability of the nonembezzling spouse, the husband and wife had already divorced. So it should come as no surprise that the three key cases immediately preceding the 1971 legislation involved divorced couples. . . .
>
> Marriage, of course, is a form of contract, and before the advent of no-fault divorce laws in the 1970s and 1980s, courts granted divorces only when one spouse breached the contract. The spouse seeking divorce would thus seek to prove that the other spouse breached the marriage covenant through some sort of bad behavior. . . . But divorce law required that the complaining spouse be innocent of that behavior. If both spouses were at fault, neither could be innocent and courts would not grant a divorce. Likewise, if both spouses were innocent, courts would not grant divorce. One had to be guilty and the other had to be innocent. That requirement was often justified by social policy: "It is one device for expressing the policy of the law against family disintegration and dissolution." . . .
>
> The divorce law notions of "fault" and "innocence" seemed particularly applicable to the kinds of tax cases in which one spouse concealed income not only from the government but also from the family unit, including the innocent spouse, who was equally defrauded and enjoyed no benefit. The first tax case in which a court applied the divorce law concept of "innocent spouse" was the 1958 opinion of the Ninth Circuit in *Furnish v. Commissioner*. There, the culpable husband significantly underreported income from his medical practice over the 10-year period at issue, and through use of nominees siphoned money from his practice into real estate holdings of which his wife knew nothing. She had divorced him after the fourth of those 10 years, but that did not stop the IRS from coming after her — 19 years later — to collect from her for the four years for which she had signed joint returns. The Tax Court rejected her argument that she had signed blank tax forms under duress but the Ninth Circuit remanded with instructions that if she could prove she had signed the blank forms "as an automaton, there could well have been no exercise of her free will."[n.34] The Ninth Circuit concluded its opinion with that rhetorical flourish, which is remarkable for how it contains the key ingredients of what was to be codified 13 years later in section 6013:
>
>> We agree with appellant Emilie Furnish Funk that the Tax Court here holds liable an innocent party for the fraudulent activities of a former spouse, when in fact said innocent party had no knowledge of, had not concurred in,

---

[n.34] [Furnish v. Commissioner,] 262 F.2d at 733. The duress argument is still a viable alternative to spousal relief. Treas. reg. section 1.6013-1(d); *see* Melvyn Frumkes, "Duress Diverts Dual Liability for Joint Returns," 19 J. Am. Acad. Matrimonial Law. 1 (2004) (collecting cases).

nor received benefit, direct or indirect, from said fraud.[n.35]

And so in *Furnish* the divorce law idea of "innocent spouse" was imported into tax law and became the underpinning of the statutory relief Congress enacted in 1971. The 1971 Senate Finance Committee's report explains its reasons for the law in terms that strongly echo the rationale of *Furnish*:

> Numerous cases have arisen in which the imposition of joint liability upon an innocent spouse has resulted in the committee's opinion, in grave injustice. . . . This liability may be imposed upon the spouse even though she had no knowledge of her husband's activities and the resulting omission from income, and even though she did not benefit in any way from the use of the funds. Several cases of this type have involved situations in which the innocent spouse has been deserted by her husband and the funds gained by embezzlement or theft have been squandered and spent by the wrongdoer.[n.36]

Id. at 1310–11. (footnotes omitted).[2]

The provision for relief from joint and several liability for tax obligations that was enacted in 1971, Code section 6013(e), was repealed in 1998 and replaced with Code section 6015, which is discussed further below. Prior to its repeal, section 6013(e) had four main requirements: (1) the spouses filed a joint return for the taxable year, (2) on the return there was a substantial understatement of tax attributable to grossly erroneous items of one spouse, (3) the other spouse established that in signing the return he or she did not know, and had no reason to know, that there was such substantial understatement, and (4) taking into account all the facts and circumstances, it was inequitable to hold the other spouse liable. I.R.C. § 6013(e)(1) (1998). In addition, in erroneous deduction cases, the understatement had to exceed a certain percentage of the purported innocent spouse's adjusted gross income for the "preadjustment year," a requirement that was overlooked all too often. As discussed below, many of these elements, including the knowledge element, were carried over to section 6015(b), though some of the elements were relaxed.

"Grossly erroneous items" meant any unreported item of gross income and any claim of a deduction, credit, or basis in an amount for which there was "no basis in fact or law." I.R.C. § 6013(e)(2) (1998). Taxpayers had a difficult time proving the presence of "grossly erroneous items" in erroneous deduction cases. *Crowley v. Commissioner*, T.C. Memo. 1993-503, provides an example. In that case, "Mr. Crowley was a partner in TSM Associates, Sinclair Securities Company, and APEX Associates, which were partnerships that had engaged in commodities straddle transactions involving Treasury bill options. Mr. Crowley, as an employee in James Sinclair Trading Corporation, arranged commodities straddle transactions for investors seeking 'tax-sheltered investments.'" *Id.* After Mr. Crowley and Ms. Cockrell divorced, the IRS audited their joint tax return for 1979 and disallowed the losses from the commodities straddles. However, the IRS later settled with them and other similarly situated taxpayers, allowing them to deduct 20 percent of the losses. Ms. Cockrell claimed innocent spouse relief, arguing that the statutory requirements were met. The Tax Court found otherwise on the "grossly erroneous" prong of former section 6013(e):

> Petitioner [Ms. Cockrell] contends that the fact that the parties entered into a compromise settlement is proof that the deductions in question are grossly erroneous items. Under the terms of the stipulated settlement, petitioner and Mr. Crowley were allowed to deduct 20 percent of the losses attributable to the commodities straddle transactions for the years in issue. The stipulations of

---

n.35 [*Furnish*, 262 F.2d at 733–34.]

n.36 S. Rep. No. 91-1537, reprinted in 1970 USCCAN (vol. 5) at 6089, 6090.

2

> settled issues filed in the instant case do not disclose the basis for the allowance of 20 percent of the deductions claimed by petitioner and Mr. Crowley. Consequently, we do not think that such compromise shows that the deductions in question were grossly erroneous items. To the contrary, the fact that respondent agreed to a compromise settlement suggests that the deductions in question were less than grossly erroneous. Anthony v. Commissioner, T.C. Memo. 1992-133; Neary v. Commissioner, T.C. Memo. 1985-261. * * *

Id., reconsid. den., T.C. Memo. 1995-551.

In addition to the difficult hurdle posed by the "grossly erroneous items" standard, because the innocent spouse issue usually was litigated in Tax Court as part of the underlying substantive proceeding, the spouse seeking innocent spouse relief would often be forced to argue both that the deduction was valid and that it had no basis in fact or law. Similarly, if one attorney represented both husband and wife, the attorney would be faced with the conflict inherent in making those contradictory arguments. Moreover, a substantive ruling that the deduction was invalid did not necessarily establish that it had no basis in fact or law.

In the *Crowley* case, Elizabeth Cockrell filed a petition for rehearing, in which she pointed out that two of the principals of her former husband's company, TSM Holding Company, had been convicted on tax fraud and conspiracy charges, which might indicate that the tax straddle deductions were grossly erroneous. The two attorneys representing the IRS in Cockrell's case were the same ones who had represented the IRS in the Tax Court case involving the two TSM Holding Company principals. Hearings Before the Committee on Finance, U.S. Senate on H.R. 2676, Appendix, Prepared Statement of Elizabeth Cockrell 262 (1998), *available at* http://books.google.com/books?id=3XTVPL0-zRwC&pg=PA262&lpg=PA262&dq=elizabeth+cockrell+irs+attorneys&source=web&ots=tDExtFf72e&sig=Yz7wD7iQ5Lv4--xl_JAyxKmyjG8&hl=en&sa=X&oi=book_result&resnum=1&ct=result. The Tax Court granted the rehearing petition.

On rehearing, the court decided the case on the "no reason to know" prong of the innocent spouse statute — an element that was carried over to section 6015(b) — again denying Ms. Cockrell relief:

> The Court of Appeals for the Second Circuit, the court to which an appeal in the instant case would lie, interprets subsection 6013(e)(1)(C) as requiring a taxpayer to establish that " 'she [or he] did not know and did not have reason to know that the deduction would give rise to a substantial understatement.' " Hayman v. Commissioner, 992 F.2d 1256, 1261 (2d Cir. 1993), (*quoting* Price v. Commissioner, 887 F.2d 959, 963 (9th Cir. 1989), *revg.* an Oral Opinion of this Court), *affg.* T.C. Memo. 1992-228.
>
> In the instant case, respondent contends that petitioner knew that the deductions in issue would give rise to substantial understatements when she signed the returns for the taxable years in issue. Respondent relies primarily on the testimony of Robert Kraft to support such contention. During the trial of the instant case, Mr. Kraft testified that he had received a law degree from Georgetown University Law Center. At a subsequent hearing, Mr. Kraft admitted that he has never received a law degree. In light of Mr. Kraft's admission, we regard his testimony as inherently untrustworthy and, therefore, do not accept his testimony. Respondent also argues that, because petitioner was a stockbroker who had passed the "series seven" stockbroker examination prior to the time she signed the returns in issue, she must have been exposed to the mechanics of commodities straddle transactions. Respondent, therefore, contends that petitioner knew that the deductions claimed on the returns for the taxable years in issue would give rise to substantial understatements. Nothing in the record, however, establishes that petitioner's studies or her work as a stockbroker exposed her to the intricacies of commodities straddle transactions.

Accordingly, we find that petitioner, when she signed the returns for the taxable years in issue, did not have actual knowledge that the deductions would give rise to the substantial understatements.

Even if a taxpayer does not have actual knowledge that deductions claimed on a return would give rise to a substantial understatement, a taxpayer who has reason to know of such an understatement is not entitled to innocent spouse relief. Sec. 6013(e)(1)(C). At the trial of the instant case, petitioner admitted that she signed the returns for the taxable years in issue without reviewing them. Nevertheless, she is charged with constructive knowledge of their contents. *Hayman v. Commissioner, supra* at 1262. Petitioner was educated and should have realized her responsibility for reviewing the returns she signed. Consequently, petitioner's failure to review returns that she signed under penalties of perjury cannot be excused. Terzian v. Commissioner, 72 T.C. 1164, 1170–1171 (1979).

The Court of Appeals for the Second Circuit has held that the magnitude of the deductions claimed on a return may give rise to a duty to inquire as to the propriety of the deductions. Friedman v. Commissioner, 53 F.3d 523, 531 (2d Cir. 1995), (*citing Hayman v. Commissioner, supra, affg. in part and revg. in part and remanding* T.C. Memo. 1993-549.) The duty of inquiry generally arises with respect to "tax returns setting forth large deductions, such as tax shelter losses offsetting income from other sources and substantially reducing or eliminating the couple's tax liability." *Hayman v. Commissioner, supra*, at 1262.

In the instant case, we believe that even a cursory review of the returns for the taxable years in issue would have alerted petitioner to the high probability that such returns contained substantial understatements. . . . Both the income and deductions with respect to Mr. Crowley's commodities straddle transactions reported on the 1980 and 1981 returns were larger than the other income and deductions reported by Mr. Crowley and petitioner. Under such circumstances, petitioner had a duty to look into the propriety of the deductions taken on the returns in issue, a duty she has failed to satisfy in the instant case. *Id.* Petitioner cannot obtain the benefits of section 6013(e) by simply turning a blind eye to facts that would reasonably put her on notice that further inquiry would need to be made. Bokum v. Commissioner, 94 T.C. 126, 148 (1990), *affd.* 992 F.2d 1132 (11th Cir. 1993). As we have previously noted, section 6013(e) is designed to protect the innocent, not the intentionally ignorant. Shannon v. Commissioner, T.C. Memo. 1991-207.

In deciding whether petitioner "had reason to know" of the substantial understatements when she signed the returns, we also take into account the factors that the Court of Appeals for the Second Circuit has held are to be considered in making such a decision: (1) The spouse's level of education; (2) the spouse's involvement in the family's business and financial affairs; (3) the presence of expenditures that appear lavish or unusual when compared with the family's past levels of income, standard of living, and spending patterns; and (4) the culpable spouse's evasiveness and deceit concerning their finances. *Friedman v. Commissioner, supra* at 531–532 (*citing Hayman v. Commissioner, supra* at 1261). The foregoing factors are considered "because, ordinarily, they predict what a prudent person would realize regardless of the other spouse's evasiveness or deceit." Bliss v. Commissioner, 59 F.3d 374, 379 (2d Cir. 1995), *affg.* T.C. Memo. 1993-390.

Applying such factors to the facts of the instant case, we conclude that petitioner had reason to know of the substantial understatements when she signed the returns for the taxable years in issue. Petitioner was a college-educated stockbroker who had passed the "series seven" examination. She was a former life insurance agent. Petitioner's involvement in the couple's business and financial affairs was also significant. Petitioner knew that Mr. Crowley was a "commodities trader." She traveled with him to several commodities seminars, where she attempted to attract clients for her husband at the hospitality suites provided by his employer after those seminars. They routinely entertained Mr. Crowley's clients at their apartment. Petitioner and Mr. Crowley lived lavishly during 1980 and 1981, the years for which petitioner seeks relief as an innocent spouse. They frequently dined at expensive restaurants during those years. During 1980, they vacationed in Canada, Vermont, and Florida. Mr. Crowley's American Express bill for that year was approximately $90,000, and a substantial portion of that amount was charged by petitioner. During 1981, petitioner and Mr. Crowley rented a two-bedroom apartment in Manhattan for approximately $1,400 or $1,500 per month and garaged Mr. Crowley's BMW automobile for approximately $250 to $300 per month. Finally, there is no evidence in the record that shows that Mr. Crowley was evasive or deceitful about their finances or that he attempted to conceal the fact that he had engaged in commodities straddle transactions. Based on the record in the instant case, we conclude that, at the time she signed the returns for the taxable years in issue, petitioner had reason to know of the substantial understatements in issue.

* * *

Petitioner claims that she signed the returns because she trusted Mr. Crowley. That trust alone, however, does not eliminate a spouse's duty to inquire when a perusal of the return would indicate that further inquiry is necessary. *Hayman v. Commissioner, supra* at 1262; Stevens v. Commissioner, 872 F.2d 1499, 1507 (11th Cir. 1989), *affg.* T.C. Memo. 1988-63. Consequently, we hold that petitioner has failed to prove that she did not know and had no reason to know that the deductions claimed on the returns for the taxable years in issue would give rise to substantial understatements.

Crowley v. Commissioner, T.C. Memo. 1995-551, *aff'd sub nom.* Cockrell v. Commissioner, 97-2 U.S.T.C. ¶ 50,549 (2d Cir. 1997) (unpublished op.), *cert. denied*, 522 U.S. 1147 (1998).

Elizabeth Cockrell's situation received considerable publicity. The notice of deficiency she had received was in the amount of $650,000, and related to tax liability resulting from her brief marriage to John Crowley, during which time she had earned only $9,000 per year. *You Think* You've *Got Problems*, New York Magazine 16 (April 10, 1995). Mr. Crowley had sent Ms. Cockrell a statement exculpating her, *id.*, but such agreements do not bind the IRS. In addition, in the initial *Cockrell* case cited above, the IRS's only two witnesses were John Crowley and Robert Kraft. Mr. Kraft was caught lying to the court, as described above.

§ 17.02 SECTION 6015

Elizabeth Cockrell later testified before Congress about the problems of women in her position. In response to her testimony and the testimony of others, Congress repealed subsection 6013(e) in 1998 and enacted Code section 6015. Section 6015 reflects a major overhaul of both the eligibility for and the procedures for obtaining relief from joint and several liability for taxes.

Due to political compromise among members of the Senate Finance Committee and House Ways and Means Committee, section 6015 contains a three-pronged approach to joint and several liability relief, with significant overlaps among the three categories. *See* H.R. Rep. No. 105-364; S. Rep. No. 105-174; H.R. Conf. Rep. No. 105-599. As discussed below, the three forms of relief are (1) "innocent spouse" relief under Code section 6015(b), which largely reenacts prior Code section 6013(e); (2) elective proportionate liability under section 6015(c); and (3) discretionary equitable relief under section

6015(f). This section of the chapter discusses those provisions, in that order, and then discusses the procedural issues that arise under section 6015.

[A] Substance

[1] Section 6015(b)

[a] Comparison with Former Section 6013(e)

Reading Assignment: I.R.C. § 6015(b); Treas. Reg. § 1.6015-2(c), -3(c)(2).

As indicated above, Code section 6015(b) is very similar to prior section 6013(e). For example, section 6015(b), like section 6013(e), includes an element that "taking into account all the facts and circumstances, it is inequitable to hold the other individual liable for the deficiency in tax for such taxable year attributable to such understatement." I.R.C. § 6015(b)(1)(D). This provision focuses, in part, on whether the spouse seeking innocent spouse relief (the requesting spouse) had received a benefit beyond normal support from the tax savings occasioned by the item or items in question. *See* Treas. Reg. § 1.6015-2(d). The standards for determining whether it would be inequitable to deny relief to the requesting spouse under section 6015(b) are similar to those used to determine relief under section 6015(f) and are discussed below in Section 17.02[A][3].

As explained above, the "knowledge" element also remains very similar. Former section 6013(e) required that "the other spouse establish[] that in signing the return he or she did not know, and had no reason to know, that there was such substantial understatement." I.R.C. § 6013(e)(1)(C) (1998). Similarly, section 6015 requires that "the other individual filing the joint return establishes that in signing the return he or she did not know, and had no reason to know, that there was such understatement." I.R.C. § 6015(b)(1)(C).

Note that, although the language relating to knowledge is unchanged, the "substantial understatement" requirement of old section 6013(e) was changed to merely require an "understatement," defined by cross-reference to section 6662 to mean essentially any amount by which the declared tax is less than the actual tax, regardless of the magnitude of that difference.

Under prior law, a $500 minimum understatement threshold, below which the requesting spouse could not qualify for relief, disproportionately affected lower-income taxpayers. In addition, section 6013(e)'s adjusted gross income-based limitations operated somewhat arbitrarily to deny relief to otherwise innocent spouses, and also required evidence regarding the requesting spouse's adjusted gross income for a tax year other than the one in question.

Case law interpreting former Code section 6013(e) can be used to interpret language that is identical in section 6015. *See, e.g.*, Doyle v. Commissioner, 94 Fed. Appx. 949, 951 n.2 (3d Cir. 2004) ("follow[ing] that interpretive guideline when applicable and appropriate."); Butler v. Commissioner, 114 T.C. 276, 283 (2000) (applying it to knowledge element); *see also* T.D. 9003 (July 18, 2002), *available at* 2002 TNT 140-9 (July 22, 2002) (Preamble to final section 6015 regulations, stating "the standards for knowledge or reason to know that were developed under former section 6013(e) should be used in determining a requesting spouse's knowledge or reason to know under section 6015(b).").

Note that in *Crowley*, excerpted above, the Tax Court considered a number of lifestyle factors in evaluating whether Ms. Cockrell had "reason to know" of the substantial understatements. Note also the court's statement that "trust alone . . . does not eliminate a spouse's duty to inquire when a perusal of the return would indicate that further inquiry is necessary." The Tax Court has held that, just as there was under section 6013(e), there is such a duty under section 6015(b). *See, e.g.*, Haltom v. Commissioner, T.C. Memo. 2005-209. The duty to inquire is discussed further in the next section.

Of course, section 6015(b) does vary from the old language in certain respects. Compare its language to the requirements of old section 6013(e), listed above in Section 17.01[B]. Note that, although the knowledge requirement remains the same, Congress mitigated it to some extent by providing that if a spouse "did not know, and had no reason to know, the *extent* of [the] understatement, then such individual shall be relieved of liability for tax (including interest, penalties, and other amounts) for such taxable year to the extent that such liability is attributable to the portion of such understatement of which such individual did not know and had no reason to know." I.R.C. § 6015(b)(2) (emphasis added). Accordingly, Congress provided for partial relief under section 6015(b). Notice also that "grossly erroneous items" was changed to "erroneous items," making that portion of the requirements easier to meet. Might that have made a difference with respect to the deductions disallowed in the *Crowley* case?

As under section 6013(e), relief under Code section 6015(b) is available only in tax understatement (deficiency) cases. In general, a tax understatement is the difference between the correct amount of tax less the amount of tax reported on the return. Accordingly, innocent spouse relief under section 6015(b) does not apply to a tax under*payment* (generally, an amount of tax liability reported on the return but not paid). If, for example, the joint return reflects the couple's correct tax liability but the taxpayers do not submit full payment with the return, innocent spouse relief under section 6015(b) is not available because there is no tax understatement. A spouse may qualify for *equitable* innocent spouse relief under Code section 6015(f) in the case of a tax underpayment, however. This form of relief is discussed below, in Section 17.02[A][3].

[b] The Knowledge Element in Section 6015(b)

Reading Assignment: I.R.C. § 6015(b)(1)(C); review Treas. Reg. § 1.6015-2(c), -3(c)(2).

As indicated above, one of the section 6015(b) requirements for relief is that the spouse seeking relief "establish[] that in signing the return he or she did not know, and had no reason to know, that there was [an] understatement" of tax. Treasury regulations provide the following guidance:

> A requesting spouse has *knowledge or reason to know of an understatement* if he or she actually knew of the understatement, or if a reasonable person in similar circumstances would have known of the understatement. For rules relating to a requesting spouse's actual knowledge, *see* § 1.6015-3(c)(2). All of the facts and circumstances are considered in determining whether a requesting spouse had reason to know of an understatement. . . .

Treas. Reg. § 1.6015-2(c) (emphasis added).

Note that regulation section 1.6015-2(c), paralleling the language of Code section 6015(b)(1)(C), refers to knowledge (or constructive knowledge) of the actual *understatement* of tax. The regulation it cross-references, however, section 1.6015-3(c), is a regulation under section 6015(c). The type of knowledge relevant under section 6015(c) is mere knowledge of the "item," not the understatement. As explained below, the difference between knowledge of the understatement and knowledge of the item can be very important. The former standard generally calls for more than mere knowledge of the item that gave rise to the understatement. It requires knowledge of the item's tax consequences before relief is barred.

Are the regulations thereby providing, contrary to the statutory language in section 6015(b), that knowledge of an erroneous item, without knowledge of the resulting understatement, constitutes the knowledge that poses a barrier to the application of section 6015(b)? The Preamble to the final section 6015 regulations suggests that the Treasury did not intend to be inconsistent with the statute:

> Section 1.6015-2(a)(3) of the proposed regulations provides that one of the requirements of relief under section 6015(b) is that the requesting spouse establish that he or she had no knowledge or reason to know of the item giving rise to the understatement. Two commentators pointed out that the underlined language is not consistent with section 6015(b)(1)(C), which articulates the requirement as knowledge or reason to know of the understatement. Both commentators suggested that the rules regarding knowledge under section 6015(b) should be consistent with the knowledge standard developed under former section 6013(e).
>
> The language in 1.6015-2(a)(3) of the proposed regulations was not intended to reflect a new standard of knowledge in section 6015(b) cases. . . . The Treasury and IRS did not intend to suggest a harsher standard of knowledge under section 6015(b) than that which existed under section 6013(e). Therefore, the final regulations adopt this recommendation by amending the language of 1.6015- 2(a)(3) of the proposed regulations to be consistent with the language of section 6015(b)(1)(C).

T.D. 9003 (July 18, 2002), *available at* 2002 TNT 140-9 (July 22, 2002). Given this statement, the reference in the section 6015(b) regulations to 1.6015-3(c)(2) is confusing.

Some courts apply the knowledge/reason to know standard differently depending upon whether the tax understatement arises from income omitted from the return, on the one hand, or an erroneous deduction or credit, on the other. What constitutes knowledge of the understatement in an omitted income case? Recall that case law on the knowledge element of former section 6013(e) remains relevant for the knowledge element of section 6015(b). *Cheshire v. Commissioner*, 282 F.3d 326 (5th Cir. 2002), explained: "Since the enactment of the original [innocent spouse] provision, courts have agreed that in omitted income cases, the spouse's actual knowledge of the underlying transaction that produced the income is sufficient to preclude innocent spouse relief (the 'knowledge-of-the-transaction test')." *Id.* at 333 (*citing* Reser v. Commissioner, 112 F.3d 1258, 1265 (5th Cir. 1997)).

Consider the regulation interpreting the provision in section 6015(b), discussed above, which allows for partial relief if the requesting spouse "did not know, and had no reason to know, the extent of [the] understatement. . . ." I.R.C. § 6015(b)(2). Treasury regulation section 1.6015-2 refers to "knowledge or reason to know of only a portion of an erroneous *item*. . . ." Treas. Reg. § 1.6015-2(e) (emphasis added). Does that once again shift the focus from understatement to item? The regulation provides the following example:

> H and W are married and file their 2004 joint income tax return in March 2005. In April 2006, H is convicted of embezzling $2 million from his employer during 2004. H kept all of his embezzlement income in an individual bank account, and he used most of the funds to support his gambling habit. H and W had a joint bank account into which H and W deposited all of their reported income. Each month during 2004, H transferred an additional $10,000 from the individual account to H and W's joint bank account. W paid the household expenses using this joint account, and regularly received the bank statements relating to the account. W had no knowledge or reason to know of H's embezzling activities. However, W did have knowledge and reason to know of $120,000 of the $2 million of H's embezzlement income at the time she signed the joint return because that amount passed through the couple's joint bank account. Therefore, W may be relieved of the liability arising from $1,880,000 of the unreported embezzlement income, but she may not be relieved of the liability for the deficiency arising from $120,000 of the unreported embezzlement income of

which she knew and had reason to know.

Treas. Reg. § 1.6015-2(e)(2) Ex.

Does this example suggest that W had actual or constructive knowledge of the *item* (embezzlement proceeds) or of the *understatement* (failure to report those proceeds)? Is a focus on the item simply consistent with the *Cheshire* knowledge-of-the-transaction approach to unreported income cases (cited above), in that knowledge of the income essentially constitutes knowledge of the understatement, given that the absence of the income on a tax return should be obvious? Does it matter if W knew of the $10,000 money transfers but not that they came from embezzlement? For example, if W thought the $10,000 transfers resulted from gifts from H's parents (which are excludible from income under Code section 102), would knowledge of $120,000 of transfers indicate that W had knowledge of the tax understatement relating to the $120,000?

Note that the regulations' example involves an omission of income case. What is the standard in cases involving erroneous deductions or credits, which, unlike income items, have to be claimed on a return in order to reduce tax liability? The Tax Court applies the knowledge-of-the-transaction test in both omission of income and erroneous deduction cases. *See* Jonson v. Commissioner, 118 T.C. 106, 116 (2002); Bokum v. Commissioner, 94 T.C. 126, 150-51 (1990), *aff'd on another ground*, 992 F.2d 1132 (11th Cir. 1993)). However, as noted above, some courts apply a different standard to erroneous deduction cases. The Court of Appeals for the Third Circuit has explained:

> In contrast [to the Tax Court], many circuits hold that in the erroneous-deduction context mere awareness of the underlying transaction that gave rise to an erroneous deduction does not alone cause the taxpayer to flunk Section 6015(b)(1)(C) (that view was first expounded in *Price v. Commissioner*, 887 F.2d 959, 964–65 (9th Cir. 1989)). Those circuits ask whether a reasonably prudent taxpayer could be expected to know that there was an erroneous deduction at the time she signed the return (*id.*). Any "yes" answer to that question triggers a duty of inquiry, and a taxpayer who then does not inquire further is denied relief under Section 6015(b)(1)(C) (*id.*).

Doyle v. Commissioner, 94 Fed. Appx. 949, 951 (3d Cir. 2004).

In *Doyle*, the court also elaborated on the duty to inquire into a possibly erroneous deduction, as follows:

> Various factors consistently play into the threshold determination as to whether a duty of inquiry arises as envisioned by *Price* and other cases following the same line. . . . Those factors include such matters as the taxpayer's level of education and involvement in the family's financial affairs, the size and nature of the deduction (particularly in relation to the couple's tax liability and gross income), the presence of comparatively large expenditures or an abrupt lifestyle change, and deception or evasion by the spouse with primary responsibility for the couple's finances (26 C.F.R. § 1.6015-2(c); *see also Hayman v. Commissioner*, 992 F.2d 1256, 1261–62 (2d Cir. 1993)).

Id. at 952. The Third Circuit found that "hiding her head in the proverbial sand" reflected a failure on the part of the purportedly innocent spouse to discharge her duty. *Id.*

Consider how the Tax Court in one case (involving an erroneous deduction and credit) allowed the duty to be satisfied:

> The Court has held that a requesting spouse may satisfy a duty to inquire by questioning his or her spouse about the accuracy of a joint tax return and receiving a plausible explanation. See, e.g., Foley v. Commissioner, T.C. Memo. 1995-16; Estate of Killian v. Commissioner, T.C. Memo. 1987-365. . . . Mr. Korchak testified credibly, and we have found, that if petitioner had questioned him before she signed the 1982 joint tax return, he would have assured her that the claimed $58,089 Madison Recycling loss and the claimed Madison Recycling

> credits of $114,407 were proper. We shall not penalize petitioner for failing to perform the act of asking Mr. Korchak about that claimed loss and those claimed credits where such an inquiry would have resulted in his assuring her that that claimed loss and those claimed credits were appropriate.

Korchak v. Commissioner, T.C. Memo. 2006-185, *68 n.28.

[2] Section 6015(c)

Reading Assignment: I.R.C. § 6015(c).

As discussed above, Code section 6015(b) updates the traditional standard for innocent spouse relief that existed prior to 1998. When Congress enacted section 6015 as part of the IRS Reform Act, it added two additional forms of relief, as well. One of those is in section 6015(c), which allows a spouse or ex-spouse to elect to allocate the deficiency between the spouses. Note that, unlike section 6015(b) relief, separate liability relief under section 6015(c) can only apply to taxpayers who are no longer married, legally separated, or not living together. This section thus applies a retroactive division of tax liability between taxpayers who are no longer a couple.

[a] The Knowledge Element in Section 6015(c)

The section 6015(c) election will not apply to any item of the other spouse with respect to which the electing spouse had *actual knowledge*. Section 6015(c) does not have a constructive knowledge provision. Furthermore, "a requesting spouse's actual knowledge may not be inferred when the requesting spouse merely had *reason to know* of the erroneous item." Treas. Reg. § 1.6015-3(c)(2)(iii) (emphasis added). Thus, the knowledge standard in section 6015(b) differs from the standard in section 6015(c) in two respects: (1) subsection (c) refers only to actual knowledge; and (2) the knowledge referred to in subsection (c) is knowledge of the *item*, rather than the understatement. Finally, note that, under section 6015(b), the requesting spouse must "establish[] that in signing the return he or she did not know, and had no reason to know, that there was such understatement," I.R.C. § 6015(b)(1)(C), whereas under section 6015(c), it falls to "the Secretary [to] demonstrate[] that an individual making an election under this subsection had actual knowledge . . . ," I.R.C. § 6015(c)(3)(C).

The reference in section 6015(c) to knowledge of the "item," rather than the "understatement," suggests that the spouse's knowledge of the tax consequences associated with the item is not required for relief to be barred. The Treasury regulations confirm that. Under the regulations, in cases of omitted income, "[actual] knowledge of the item includes knowledge of the receipt of the income. . . . " Treas. Reg. § 1.6015-3(c)(2)(i)(A) (adopting the holding of Cheshire v. Commissioner, 282 F.3d 326 (5th Cir. 2002), *see* Preamble to T.D. 9003, 2002 TNT 140-9 (July 22, 2002)). The regulations provide the following example:

> *Example 1.* Actual knowledge of an erroneous item. (i) H and W file their 2001 joint Federal income tax return on April 15, 2002. On the return, H and W report W's self-employment income, but they do not report W's self-employment tax on that income. H and W divorce in July 2003. In August 2003, H and W receive a 30-day letter from the Internal Revenue Service proposing a deficiency with respect to W's unreported self-employment tax on the 2001 return. On November 4, 2003, H files an election to allocate the deficiency to W. The erroneous item is the self-employment income, and it is allocable to W. H knows that W earned income in 2001 as a self-employed musician, but he does not know that self-employment tax must be reported on and paid with a joint return.
>
> (ii) H's election to allocate the deficiency to W is invalid because, at the time H signed the joint return, H had actual knowledge of W's self-employment income.

> The fact that H was unaware of the tax consequences of that income (i.e., that an individual is required to pay self-employment tax on that income) is not relevant.

Treas. Reg. § 1.6015-3(c)(4) Ex. 1.

Erroneous deduction and credit cases are a bit more complicated. The regulations provide that, in those types of cases, knowledge of the item "means knowledge of the *facts* that made the item not allowable as a deduction." Treas. Reg. § 1.6015-3(c)(2)(i)(B)(1) (emphasis added) (adopting the holding of King v. Commissioner, 116 T.C. 198 (2001), *see* Preamble to T.D. 9003, 2002 TNT 140-9 (July 22, 2002)). Thus, once again, relief can be barred even if the spouse has no knowledge of the tax law. The regulations provide the following example:

> *Example 5.* Actual knowledge of a deduction that is an erroneous item. (i) H and W are legally separated. In February 2005, a deficiency is asserted with respect to their 2002 joint Federal income tax return. The deficiency is attributable to a disallowed $1,000 deduction for medical expenses H claimed he incurred. At the time W signed the return, W knew that H had not incurred any medical expenses. W's election to allocate to H the deficiency attributable to the disallowed medical expense deduction is invalid because W had actual knowledge that H had not incurred any medical expenses.
>
> (ii) Assume the same facts as in paragraph (i) of this Example . . . except that, at the time W signed the return, W did not know whether H had incurred any medical expenses. W's election to allocate to H the deficiency attributable to the disallowed medical expense deduction is valid because she did not have actual knowledge that H had not incurred any medical expenses.
>
> (iii) Assume the same facts as in paragraph (i) of this Example . . . except that the Internal Revenue Service disallowed $400 of the $1,000 medical expense deduction. At the time W signed the return, W knew that H had incurred some medical expenses but did not know the exact amount. W's election to allocate to H the deficiency attributable to the disallowed medical expense deduction is valid because she did not have actual knowledge that H had not incurred medical expenses (in excess of the floor amount under section 213(a)) of more than $600.

Treas. Reg. § 1.6015-3(c)(4) Ex. 5.

As these examples may suggest, for "actual knowledge," the spouse's knowledge of the *source* of an item generally is not sufficient to deny relief. For example, if a spouse electing relief under section 6015(c) knew of the other spouse's equity interest in a certain corporation but did not actually know of dividend income received from the corporation, the electing spouse may still be entitled to relief. *See* Treas. Reg. § 1.6015-3(c)(2)(iii). However, a factor that may indicate actual knowledge is a deliberate attempt to remain ignorant with regard to the item at issue. Treas. Reg. § 1.6015-3(c)(2)(iv).

Section 6015(c) also provides that the "actual knowledge" prohibition on relief does not apply if the spouse with that knowledge establishes that he or she signed the tax return under duress. I.R.C. § 6015(c)(3)(C). However, Treasury regulation section 1.6013-4(d) provides that a return signed by one spouse under duress does not constitute a joint return. If the spouse is treated as if he she never signed the return, no joint and several liability results, so no liability relief is necessary. The regulations under section 6015(c) describe the exception to the actual knowledge test in terms of abuse, rather than duress: "If the requesting spouse establishes that he or she was the victim of domestic abuse prior to the time the return was signed, and that, as a result of the prior abuse, the requesting spouse did not challenge the treatment of any items on the return for fear of the nonrequesting spouse's retaliation, the limitation on actual knowledge . . . will not apply." Treas. Reg. § 1.6015-3(c)(2)(v). *Cf.* Rev. Proc. 2003-61, at § 4.01(d) (referring, in the equitable relief context, to "abuse not amounting to duress").

[b] Allocation

Reading Assignment: I.R.C. § 6015(d).

Section 6015(d) contains the allocation provisions applicable to section 6015(c) relief. In general, the separate liability election allows the parties to retroactively separate out the tax consequences for the year for which they filed jointly. In general, the requesting spouse bears the burden of proving how the items should be allocated. In other words, the requesting spouse has the burden of proving that the deficiency is *not* allocable to him or her. *See* I.R.C. § 6015(c)(2); Treas. Reg. § 1.6015-3(d)(3).

The Code sets out the broad outlines of the apportionment method, which is elaborated upon in the regulations. The general allocation method calls for proportionate allocation. *See* Treas. Reg. § 1.6015-3(d)(4). Under that method, the proportion of the deficiency that is allocated to a particular spouse is the same percentage as the ratio of the items allocable to that spouse is to the total amount of items giving rise to the deficiency. I.R.C. § 6015(d)(1). Subject to exceptions, "any item giving rise to a deficiency on a joint return shall be allocated to individuals filing the return in the same manner as it would have been allocated if the individuals had filed separate returns for the taxable year." I.R.C. § 6015(d)(3)(A). The ratio can be expressed as the following fraction:

$$\text{Deficiency} \quad \text{x} \quad \frac{\text{Net amount of erroneous items allocable to requesting spouse}}{\text{Net amount of all erroneous items}}$$

If the deficiency is attributable to an item of unreported income, the erroneous income item generally will be allocated to the spouse who earned the wages or who owned the business or investment that produced the income. Treas. Reg. § 1.6015-3(d)(2)(iii). If the deficiency is attributable to a disallowed deduction or credit, the erroneous deduction or credit item is attributable to the spouse to whom the item relates. Business deductions are generally allocated based upon the spouses' ownership interests in the business. Personal deductions are generally allocated equally between the spouses. Treas. Reg. § 1.6015-3(d)(2)(iv). Any accuracy-related or fraud penalties under Code sections 6662 or 6663 are allocated to the spouse whose items generated the penalty. Treas. Reg. § 1.6015-3(d)(4)(iv)(B).

> *Example.* Arthur and Beth timely filed their Year 1 joint return. In Year 3, the IRS assesses a $12,000 deficiency with respect to the return. The couple divorce shortly thereafter and Beth timely elects to allocate the deficiency under section 6015(c). Three erroneous items give rise to the deficiency: 1) a disallowed $15,000 business deduction from Arthur's business, reported on Schedule C; 2) $30,000 of unreported income generated in Arthur's business; 3) $15,000 of unreported wage income from Beth's employment.
>
> The $15,000 business expense deduction and the $30,000 of unreported business income will be allocated to Arthur. The $15,000 of unreported wage income will be allocated to Beth.
>
> In total, there are $60,000 worth of erroneous items, of which $45,000 are attributable to Arthur and $15,000 are attributable to Beth. The ratio of erroneous items allocable to Beth to the total erroneous items is 1/4 ($15,000/$60,000). Beth's liability is limited to $3,000 of the deficiency (1/4 of $12,000). The IRS may collect up to $3,000 from Beth and up to $12,000 from Arthur (the total amount collected, however, may not exceed $12,000). *See* Treas. Reg. § 1.6015-3(d)(5) Exs. 1 & 2.

Note that if Arthur also made an election under section 6015(c), there would be no remaining joint and several liability, and the IRS would only be permitted to collect $3,000 from Beth and $9,000 from Arthur.

An erroneous income or deduction item attributable to an asset that the spouses owned jointly is allocated 50 percent to each spouse, unless there is evidence that shows a different allocation is appropriate. Treas. Reg. § 1.6015-3(d)(2)(iii), (iv).

Example. Cathy timely elects to allocate a $3,000 deficiency on a joint return to her former husband, Dan. The entire deficiency arose from $11,000 of unreported interest income from the couple's joint bank account, of which Cathy had actual knowledge.

Generally, income, deductions, or credits from jointly held property that are erroneous items are allocable 50 percent to each spouse. However, in this case, both spouses had actual knowledge of the unreported interest income. Therefore, Cathy's election to allocate the $11,000 deficiency is invalid, and she and Dan remain jointly and severally liable for the entire deficiency. *See* Treas. Reg. § 1.6015-3(d)(5) Ex. 3.

An item otherwise allocable to the nonrequesting spouse is allocated to the requesting spouse to the extent the item created a tax benefit for the requesting spouse. I.R.C. § 6015(d)(3)(B). The requesting spouse is considered to derive a tax benefit, for example, if a deduction attributable to the nonrequesting spouse exceeds the nonrequesting spouse's income, so that the excess offsets the requesting spouse's income.

Example. In Year 1, Ed reports gross income of $5,000 from his business on Schedule C, and Fran reports $90,000 of wage income. On their Year 1 joint return, Ed deducts $20,000 of business expenses, resulting in a net loss from his business of $15,000. The couple divorce in Year 2, and in Year 3, the IRS assesses a $4,000 deficiency with respect to their Year 1 return. The deficiency results entirely from a disallowance of Ed's $20,000 of business expenses. Fran elects to allocate the deficiency under section 6015(c).

Because Ed used only $5,000 of the disallowed business deductions to offset gross income from his business, Fran benefitted from the other $15,000 of the disallowed deductions used to offset her wage income. Therefore, $5,000 of the disallowed business deductions are allocable to Ed and the remaining $15,000 of the disallowed deductions are allocable to Fran. Fran's liability is limited to $3,000 ($15,000/$20,000, or 3/4, of $4,000). *See* Treas. Reg. § 1.6015-3(d)(5) Ex. 5.

Note that if Ed also elected to allocate the deficiency, Ed's election to allocate the deficiency to Fran would be invalid because Ed had actual knowledge of the erroneous item.

Separate treatment items are removed from the allocation formula and separately allocated to the appropriate spouse. Treas. Reg. § 1.6015-3(d)(4)(i)(B)(2), (ii). Separate treatment items include tax credits (*e.g.*, child and dependent care credits, adoption credit, earned income tax credit, education credits) and taxes other than income taxes (*e.g.*, self-employment tax).

Example. In Year 3, the IRS assessed a $48,000 deficiency with respect to Gary and Helen's Year 1 joint return. The deficiency results from four erroneous items: (1) a $4,000 disallowed Lifetime Learning Credit attributable to Helen; (2) a disallowed business expense deduction of $16,000 attributable to Helen; (3) unreported income of $48,000 attributable to Gary; and (4) unreported self-employment tax of $28,000 attributable to Gary. Gary and Helen both elect to allocate the deficiency.

The $4,000 Lifetime Learning Credit and the $28,000 self-employment tax are separate treatment items, which total $32,000. The amount of erroneous items included in computing the proportionate allocation ratio is $64,000 ($48,000 of unreported income and the $16,000 disallowed business expense deduction). The amount of the deficiency subject to proportionate allocation is reduced by the amount of separate treatment items ($48,000 deficiency − $32,000 separate treatment items = $16,000).

Of the $64,000 of proportionate allocation items, $48,000 is allocable to Gary, and $16,000 is allocable to Helen. Gary's liability for the portion of the deficiency subject to proportionate allocation is limited to $12,000 ($48,000/$64,000, or 3/4, of $16,000) and Helen's liability for such portion is limited to $4,000 ($16,000/$64,000, or 1/4, of $16,000).

After the proportionate allocation is completed, the amount of the separate treatment items is added to each spouse's allocated share of the deficiency. Therefore, Gary's liability is limited to $40,000 ($12,000 + $28,000) and Helen's liability is limited to $8,000 ($4,000 + $4,000). *See* Treas. Reg. § 1.6015-3(d)(5), Ex. 4.

If a deficiency arises from two or more erroneous items that are subject to tax at different rates (*e.g.*, ordinary income and capital gain items), the deficiency will be allocated after first separating the erroneous items into categories according to their applicable tax rates. After all erroneous items are categorized, a separate allocation is made with respect to each tax rate category using the proportionate allocation method. Treas. Reg. § 1.6015-3(d)(6)(i).

Example. Ike and Janet divorce in Year 2 after having filed a joint Year 1 return. In Year 4, the IRS assesses a $10,000 deficiency with respect to the Year 1 return. Of this deficiency, $4,000 results from unreported capital gain income taxed at a 20 percent rate, arising from $12,000 of unreported capital gain income that is attributable to Ike, and $8,000 of unreported capital gain income that is attributable to Janet. The remaining $6,000 of the deficiency is attributable to $17,143 of unreported salary income of Janet that is subject to tax at a marginal rate of 35 percent. Both spouses timely elect to allocate the deficiency, and otherwise qualify under section 6015(c).

Because there are erroneous items subject to different tax rates, an alternative allocation method applies. The three erroneous items are first categorized according to their applicable tax rates (20% or 35%), then allocated between the spouses.

Of the total amount of 20-percent tax rate items (the $20,000 of capital gains), 60 percent ($12,000/$20,000) is allocable to Ike and 40 percent ($8,000/$20,000) is allocable to Janet. Therefore, 60 percent of the $4,000 deficiency attributable to these items (or $2,400) is allocated to Ike. The remaining 40 percent of this portion of the deficiency ($1,600) is allocated to Janet.

The only 35 percent tax rate item is allocable entirely to Janet. Accordingly, she is liable for $7,600 of the deficiency ($1,600 + $6,000), and Ike is liable for the remaining $2,400. *See* Treas. Reg. § 1.6015-3(d)(6)(iii) Ex.

The amount of the tax deficiency for which the requesting spouse remains jointly and severally liable is increased by the value of any "disqualified asset" that was transferred to the electing spouse. I.R.C. § 6015(c)(4); Treas. Reg. § 1.6015-3(c)(3)(i). A disqualified asset is any property that was transferred from the nonrequesting spouse to the requesting spouse if the principal purpose of the transfer was to avoid paying tax. I.R.C. § 6015(c)(4)(B); Treas. Reg. § 1.6015-3(c)(3)(ii). A rebuttable presumption exists that any asset transferred from the nonrequesting spouse to the requesting spouse is a disqualified asset if was transferred during the 12-month period before, and at any time after, the mailing of the first letter of proposed deficiency (*e.g.*, a 30-day letter). I.R.C. § 6015(c)(4)(B)(ii). This presumption does not apply to transfers made by reason of a divorce decree or separate maintenance agreement. Treas. Reg. § 1.6015-3(c)(3)(iii). Consider the following example:

> (i) H and W are divorced. In May 1999, W transfers $20,000 to H, and in April 2000, H and W receive a 30-day letter proposing a $40,000 deficiency on their 1998 joint Federal income tax return. The liability remains unpaid, and in October 2000, H elects to allocate the deficiency under this section. Seventy-five percent of the net amount of erroneous items are allocable to W, and 25% of the net amount of erroneous items are allocable to H.
>
> (ii) In accordance with the proportionate allocation method . . . H proposes that $30,000 of the deficiency be allocated to W and $10,000 be allocated to himself. H submits a signed statement providing that the principal purpose of the $20,000 transfer was not the avoidance of tax or payment of tax, but he does not submit any documentation indicating the reason for the transfer. H has not overcome the presumption that the $20,000 was a disqualified asset. Therefore, the portion of the deficiency for which H is liable ($10,000) is increased by the value of the disqualified asset ($20,000). H is relieved of liability for $10,000 of the $30,000 deficiency allocated to W, and remains jointly and severally liable for the remaining $30,000 of the deficiency (assuming that H does not qualify for relief under any other provision).

Treas. Reg. § 1.6015-3(c)(4) Ex. 6.

In addition, separate liability under section 6015(c) is not available at all if the IRS can prove that the taxpayers transferred assets between themselves as part of a fraudulent scheme to avoid liability. In the case of fraudulent transfers, joint and several liability applies to the entire return. I.R.C. § 6015(c)(3)(A)(ii). However, note that section 6015(c) poses no equity-based bar to separate liability relief. That is, a requesting spouse who benefitted from the understatement may still qualify for separate liability relief, so long as he or she did not have the prohibited actual knowledge and did not participate in fraudulent transfers.

[3] Section 6015(f)

Reading Assignment: I.R.C. § 6015(f).

Section 6015(f) provides a last-resort equitable relief provision. Consider the language of this provision. Does it explicitly require that the taxpayers have filed a joint return for equitable relief to be available? In *Raymond v. Commissioner*, 119 T.C. 191, 195 (2002), the Tax Court held that the spouses must have filed a joint return to be eligible for relief under section 6015(f). The Tax Court's analysis drew on a variety of factors, including legislative history and Revenue Procedure 2000-15, 2000-1 C.B. 447, which was subsequently superseded. *See id.* at 195–97. The current Revenue Procedure on equitable relief, Revenue Procedure 2003-61, retains that requirement. *See* Rev. Proc. 2003-61, 2003-32 I.R.B. 296, at § 4.01(1).

Revenue Procedure 2003-61 provides seven threshold conditions for relief; a description of the conditions under which the IRS ordinarily will grant equitable relief; and a nonexclusive list of factors for consideration in determining whether relief should be granted. *Id.* at § 4.01–.03. For example, abuse that does not rise to the level of duress is a factor that weighs in favor of relief. *See* Rev. Proc. 2003-61, 2003-32 I.R.B. 296, at § 4.01(7)(d). A significant benefit (beyond normal support) from the item in question is a factor that weighs against relief. *See id.* at § 4.03(2)(a)(v).

With respect to knowledge, which, as discussed above, is also important in section 6015(b) and (c) claims, the Revenue Procedure states:

> Reason to know of the item giving rise to the deficiency will not be weighed more heavily than other factors. Actual knowledge of the item giving rise to the deficiency, however, is a strong factor weighing against relief. This strong factor may be overcome if the factors in favor of equitable relief are particularly compelling. In those limited situations, it may be appropriate to grant relief

> under . . . section 6015(f) even though the requesting spouse had actual knowledge of the item giving rise to the deficiency.

Id. at § 4.03(2)(a)(iii)(B).

The following case applies the Revenue Procedure.

BANDERAS v. COMMISSIONER

United States Tax Court
T.C. Memo. 2007-129

WHERRY, JUDGE: This case arises from a petition for judicial review filed in response to a determination concerning relief from joint and several liability under section 6015. The issue for decision is whether denial by respondent of petitioner's request for relief from joint and several liability for the taxable years 1997 and 1999 constitutes an abuse of discretion.

FINDINGS OF FACT

* * *

Petitioner married Julio C. Banderas (Dr. Banderas) in March of 1972. For most of their married life, the couple resided in Georgia, where Dr. Banderas practiced medicine, specializing in orthopedic surgery, and petitioner stayed at home caring for their children and children from a previous marriage of Dr. Banderas. Petitioner later returned to school and in 1993 completed a registered nursing degree. Throughout the relevant period and at the time of trial, petitioner was employed in the nursing field, often working multiple jobs. During their marriage, petitioner and Dr. Banderas maintained and had equal access to a joint checking account, and both wrote checks on the account. Both also opened household mail. Dr. Banderas, however, assumed primary responsibility in handling the family's financial affairs.

In the mid-1990s, Dr. Banderas became involved in a contract dispute with a business associate, Alexander Doman (Dr. Doman), who was to purchase Dr. Banderas's medical practice in preparation for Dr. Banderas's retirement. The matter proceeded to litigation and resulted in a $832,447 civil judgment against Dr. Banderas on June 25, 1997. To collect on the judgment, the Banderases' joint checking account was levied in 1997. Petitioner then, in August of 1997, opened a separate checking account into which Dr. Banderas's Social Security checks and petitioner's income were deposited and out of which living expenses were paid.

During the pendency of the foregoing controversy, Dr. Banderas retired, and he and petitioner moved to Florida in early 1996. Thereafter, on October 3, 1997, Dr. Banderas filed a voluntary chapter 7 bankruptcy petition in the U.S. Bankruptcy Court for the Middle District of Florida. The bankruptcy case was closed by order of that court on July 21, 2005, after disbursement by the trustee of more than $2.37 million. Meanwhile, on October 15, 1998, petitioner and Dr. Banderas signed and timely filed a joint Form 1040, U.S. Individual Income Tax Return, for 1997. The return reflected total adjusted gross income of $304,673, consisting primarily of pension, annuity, and Social Security income of Dr. Banderas but also including $5,025 of wage income earned by petitioner. A reported $10,250 was shown as Federal income tax withheld, $250 of which represented withholding from petitioner's wages. The stated balance due was $64,767. Petitioner was aware of the balance due at the time she signed the return. No payment was submitted with the return. The Banderases' joint Form 1040 for 1998 was filed in late 1999 reporting a loss and is not at issue here.

By 1999, financial pressures had apparently led Dr. Banderas to return to work. Then, on September 16, 1999, Dr. Banderas was diagnosed with cancer. The cancer was terminal, and Dr. Banderas died of complications from the disease on November 16, 1999. On October 15, 2000, petitioner signed and timely filed a joint Form 1040 for 1999 as a surviving spouse. The return reflected total adjusted gross income of $121,326, which amount incorporated wage and Social Security income of Dr. Banderas totaling $84,089 and petitioner's wages of $37,068. After subtraction of $10,063 in Federal income tax withheld, $853 of which was attributed to petitioner's wages, the return reported a balance due of $10,262. No payment was submitted with the return.

On or about June 12, 2003, the Internal Revenue Service (IRS) received from petitioner a signed Form 8857, Request for Innocent Spouse Relief. Petitioner indicated on the Form 8857 that she was requesting equitable relief under section 6015(f) for underpayments of tax for 1997 and 1999, and she attached the following explanatory statement:

> Most of my married life — which was my entire adult life until my husband passed away — I was a "stay-at-home" wife and mother, with my husband working hard to support us and to build what we thought was our retirement plan.
>
> In 1997, as a result of an unjust judgement against my husband, an illegal hold was placed on our joint checking account, which caused our check to the IRS for the balance of our 1996 taxes to bounce due to "unavailable funds". Shortly afterwards, my husband was advised to file for bankruptcy.
>
> Before filing, we were reassured that the IRS would be the #1 creditor, and that all taxes would be paid before any other creditors. Had we not been assured of this, my husband would have gotten a distribution from the pension plan to pay any taxes before filing.
>
> During the bankruptcy proceedings, we realized that our retirement plan was, in reality, his retirement plan — and it was taken away. When my husband passed away, the proceeds of his life insurance policy also went to the bankruptcy court.
>
> So I found myself, at almost 50 years of age, not only without my beloved husband, but also with the urgent need to prepare financially for my future.
>
> In an attempt to pay off our debts, to support myself since he passed away, and to try to prepare for my future/retirement, I have been working 2-3 jobs at a time, 70-100+ hours/week, something that I cannot continue much longer.
>
> Finding myself now responsible for an additional bill of over $100,000 to the IRS, I am overwhelmed even by the idea of how to pay it off. Because almost all the taxes were based on my husband's income, etc., and the ensuing financial problems were a result of his petition of bankruptcy and the court's actions, I respectfully request that I be relieved of the responsibility of these debts as they present an unfathomable hardship to me.

Petitioner also submitted to the IRS a Form 12510, Questionnaire for Requesting Spouse, dated July 22, 2003. In response to a question asking her to explain when and how she thought reported balances due would be paid, petitioner wrote: "By proceeds from my husband's pension plan — never dreaming that the court would take it away". A further question asking what efforts were made to pay reported taxes after relevant returns were filed elicited the following answer:

> Everything (pension plan) was frozen by the court — we were waiting for the discharge to have the funds freed up — in 99 we found that was never going to happen — accountant said with such a loss we would not owe anything "ever again". Then my husband passed away; with $400,000 left in bankruptcy court they are telling me there will be none left for me or our kids.

Petitioner also on the Form 12510 completed a statement of her average income and expenses. She listed wage income of approximately $80,000 and monthly expenses totaling approximately $3,700.

Petitioner's request for relief was initially denied by the IRS Examination Division on April 29, 2004. Petitioner responded with a statement of disagreement requesting that the IRS reconsider the denial. Her reasons for the continued dispute paralleled those alluded to in her Forms 8857 and 12510, * * *.

Petitioner received the requested reconsideration of her claim by the IRS Office of Appeals. Appeals Officer Mark Pearce (Mr. Pearce) was assigned petitioner's case in July of 2004. His case activity records show that Mr. Pearce communicated with petitioner or her representative, James R. Monroe (Mr. Monroe), on a number of occasions and logged at least 8.75 hours specifically on her case. After his review of the case, Mr. Pearce concluded in an Appeals Case Memo prepared on February 22, 2005, that a weighing of the factors prescribed in Rev. Proc. 2003-61, 2003-2 C.B. 296, for evaluating claims under section 6015(f) did not support petitioner's request for equitable relief.

On March 3, 2005, the IRS issued to petitioner a notice of determination denying her request for section 6015(f) relief. The grounds listed in the notice for the denial were that petitioner had established neither a reasonable belief that the tax would be paid nor economic hardship. Petitioner filed a timely petition with this Court contesting the adverse determination and reflecting an address in Cape Coral, Florida.

* * *

OPINION

* * *

The Court reviews a denial of relief under section 6015(f) for abuse of discretion; i.e., whether respondent's determination was arbitrary, capricious, or without sound basis in law or fact. Jonson v. Comm'r, 118 T.C. 106, 125 (2002), affd. 353 F.3d 1181 (10th Cir. 2003); Butler v. Commissioner, 114 T.C. 276, 292 (2000). Except as otherwise provided in section 6015, the taxpayer generally bears the burden of proving such an abuse of discretion. Rule 142(a); Alt v. Comm'r, 119 T.C. 306, 311 (2002), affd. 101 Fed. Appx. 34 (6th Cir. 2004); Jonson v. Comm'r, supra at 113.

Relief under section 6015(b) or (c) is premised on the existence of an understatement or deficiency. Because the liabilities at issue in this case derive from unpaid taxes reported on the 1997 and 1999 returns, petitioner is not eligible for relief under subsection (b) or (c). Accordingly, there is no dispute that petitioner satisfies the criterion for equitable relief codified in section 6015(f)(2). The instant dispute thus centers on the facts and circumstances inquiry of section 6015(f)(1).

As directed by section 6015(f), the Secretary has promulgated guidance to structure the relevant facts and circumstances analysis, the applicable version of which is set forth in Rev. Proc. 2003-61, 2003-2 C.B. 296. Rev. Proc. 2003-61, sec. 4.01, 2003-2 C.B. at 297, first lists seven threshold conditions that must be met before the IRS will consider a request for relief under section 6015(f): (1) The requesting spouse filed a joint return for the year for which relief is sought; (2) relief is not available under section 6015(b) or (c); (3) the application for relief is made no later than 2 years after the date of the IRS's first collection activity; (4) no assets were transferred between the spouses as part of a fraudulent scheme; (5) the nonrequesting spouse did not transfer disqualified assets to the requesting spouse; (6) the requesting spouse did not file or fail to file the return with fraudulent intent; and (7) absent enumerated exceptions, the liability from which relief is sought is attributable to an item of the nonrequesting spouse. Respondent here concedes that petitioner meets these seven conditions.

Rev. Proc. 2003-61, sec. 4.02, 2003-2 C.B. at 298, then gives three circumstances under which, if all are satisfied, the IRS "ordinarily will grant relief" with respect to underpayments on joint returns. The first of these elements requires that, on the date of the request for relief, the requesting spouse be no longer married to, be legally separated from, or not have been a member of the same household as the nonrequesting spouse at any time during the preceding 12-month period. *Id.* sec. 4.02(1)(a), 2003-2 C.B. at 298. The death of Dr. Banderas in November of 1999 preceded petitioner's request by more than 12 months, and this element therefore raises no barrier. The remaining two elements, however, which address knowledge and economic hardship, are at the crux of the instant controversy.

The second, or knowledge, element requires that:

> On the date the requesting spouse signed the joint return, the requesting spouse had no knowledge or reason to know that the nonrequesting spouse would not pay the income tax liability. The requesting spouse must establish that it was reasonable for the requesting spouse to believe that the nonrequesting spouse would pay the reported income tax liability. If a requesting spouse would otherwise qualify for relief under this section, except for the fact that the requesting spouse's lack of knowledge or reason to know relates only to a portion of the unpaid income tax liability, then the requesting spouse may receive relief to the extent that the income tax liability is attributable to that portion. [*Id.* sec. 4.02(1)(b), 2003-C.B. at 298.]

Petitioner argues that respondent erred in concluding that she possessed knowledge or reason to know that the taxes would not be paid. As to 1997, petitioner contends that she had a reasonable belief that the taxes would be paid either out of the bankruptcy proceeding, from Dr. Banderas's pension plan, or from future earnings obtained through Dr. Banderas's returning to work. As to 1999, petitioner alleges that she reasonably believed that the taxes would be paid from funds remaining after the close of the bankruptcy proceeding, particularly in light of the additional $750,000 received by the bankruptcy estate from a life insurance policy on Dr. Banderas.

Petitioner testified regarding payment of the balances due on the 1997 and 1999 returns, of which she was concededly aware. * * *

With respect to 1999, counsel inquired: "what was your intent regarding the balance due that was shown on the 1999 tax return"? Petitioner replied: "I anticipated money coming from the Bankruptcy Court to pay it off", and she went on to cite the pension plan and life insurance.

The overarching general question raised by petitioner's contentions is one of timing. The standard suggested by petitioner on brief highlights this issue: "The test should be whether the requesting spouse had a reasonable belief that the taxes would *eventually* be paid by the non-requesting spouse." (Emphasis added.) Petitioner was clearly aware on the dates she signed the Forms 1040 that no liquid funds were available and on hand to be submitted with the returns. She knew that the bulk of Dr. Banderas's assets were tied up in the bankruptcy; there is no suggestion that any concrete steps had been taken, or were ever taken, to try to obtain a distribution from the pension plan; and Dr. Banderas had not yet returned to gainful employment at the time of filing the return for 1997 and was deceased at the time of filing the return for 1999.

It would thus appear that petitioner had not so much a reasonable belief that the taxes would be paid as an inchoate hope for a favorable change in circumstances that would, at some undefined future point in time, place moneys at Dr. Banderas's or her own disposal to pay the taxes. Petitioner has at no juncture made any attempt to identify when, in terms of a particular time period, she thought the taxes would be paid. Furthermore, although petitioner has generally alluded to being "told" that the IRS would be the number one creditor in the bankruptcy and that the pension plan was exempt, she did not call any witnesses to establish the specific information she was given. As much as we sympathize with the unfortunate, even tragic, string of events that befell the Banderas household, we cannot accept a test so nebulous as that proposed by petitioner. To do so would essentially eviscerate the reasonable belief standard. "Eventually" is simply too open-ended to place any meaningful or administratively workable limits on qualification for relief.

The Court concludes that a reasonable belief that taxes would be paid must at minimum incorporate a belief that funds would be on hand within a reasonably prompt period of time.[n.5] As just indicated, petitioner has failed to make such a showing here. Furthermore, because petitioner has never identified any timeframe, the Court need not probe the contours of the how soon question, or even whether the standard should be limited to situations where moneys were thought to be available at the time the relevant return was signed and filed.

* * *

The third and final element of section 4.02 of Rev. Proc. 2003-61 places a requirement that the requesting spouse will suffer economic hardship if relief is not granted. *Id.* sec. 4.02(1)(c), 2003-2 C.B. at 298. For purposes of making the hardship determination, Rev. Proc. 2003-61, supra, references the rules in section 301.6343-1(b)(4), Proced. & Admin. Regs. The cited provision defines economic hardship as an inability to pay "reasonable basic living expenses" and directs the Commissioner to consider factors such as, among other things, the taxpayer's age, employment status and history, ability to earn, number of dependents, and amount reasonably necessary for food, clothing, housing, utilities, medical expenses, insurance (including homeowner & health), transportation, current tax payments, etc. Sec. 301.6343-1(b)(4), Proced. & Admin. Regs.

The parties dispute what information the Court should consider in its analysis of this element. Respondent's position is that consideration should take into account only those materials provided to the Appeals Office during the underlying administrative process. Petitioner disagrees and has sought to supplement the administrative record in several respects. Petitioner suggests that a purportedly insufficient quantity of time spent by the Appeals officer in reviewing her case and the officer's failure to request updated financial information justify augmentation of the record.

The Court stated its position on this issue in Ewing v. Comm'r, 122 T.C. 32, 44 (in exercising our jurisdiction under section 6015(e)(1)(A) "to determine" whether a taxpayer is entitled to relief under section 6015(f), it is appropriate for this Court de novo to consider evidence beyond the administrative record), vacated on other grounds 439 F.3d 1009 (9th Cir. 2006). However, because here the outcome flowing from a limited review of the administrative record alone and that obtaining after taking into account all information proffered by petitioner are identical, the Court finds it unnecessary to comment further on the merits of the parties' differing views of the proper record for review.

During the administrative phase, petitioner submitted a Form 12510 dated July 22, 2003, showing an excess of income over expenses of approximately $2,980 per month. This portrayal clearly fails to reflect economic hardship, and we do not read petitioner's arguments to contend otherwise. Nor does petitioner suggest that she provided updated financial information to the Appeals officer at any time prior to his final recommendations on her case in early 2005. To the extent that petitioner intimates that the burden rested entirely on the Appeals officer to request new data, her point, in this particular context, is not well taken.

As a general matter, taxpayers are usually responsible for establishing their positions before the IRS. Second, on a more specific and practical level, petitioner, despite being

[n.5] Taxpayers are required to pay their taxes when due. A delay in payment not authorized by statute renders the Government an involuntary creditor without security or other assurance that the tax and interest thereon will be paid. When tax or interest due is not paid, the burdens of Government are transferred to other taxpayers, including those of future generations. Where all funds needed to pay the taxes for a year of bankruptcy will be trapped in the bankruptcy estate or for any other reason, the bankrupt taxpayer and spouse may, at the taxpayer's or spouse's option, elect to close their taxable years effective on the day before the bankruptcy case was commenced. Sec. 1398(d)(2). This election creates 2 short taxable years, the tax liability for the first of which is included as a claim against the debtor's estate and is payable from the estate. *Id.*; see also sec. 6161(c) (regarding authorized extensions of time to pay).

represented by counsel, apparently never alerted the Appeals officer of any relevant change in circumstances. Furthermore, the types of items reported on the Form 12510 were not inherently of a nature to raise a suspicion of dramatic change over the course of the ensuing period. The only likely difference hinted at on the face of the Form 12510 would have been a reduction in income, as petitioner appended a comment that she might be unable to continue to sustain multiple jobs. However, third-party payers reported to the IRS even higher wages of $87,925 for the completed taxable year of 2003 (the most recent year for which records would have been available during at least the majority of the time petitioner's case was before Mr. Pearce). This fact was noted by the Appeals officer in his recommendations. Third-party payers similarly reported still higher wages to petitioner of $90,974 for 2004. In this scenario, the Court, despite its admiration for petitioner's efforts to help herself, is unconvinced that petitioner may abdicate all responsibility for raising some issue of pertinent change or, conversely, that the Appeals officer acted arbitrarily or capriciously in relying on the information previously provided.

Additionally, the Court is not persuaded that petitioner's remarks concerning the quantum of time devoted to her case should have any bearing on our analysis. The recorded time is in no way patently insufficient, and the Court is not in a position to divine any type of arbitrary standard as to the time it might take an individual to properly evaluate a given set of facts.

At trial, petitioner sought to introduce three 1-page sheets of financial information, all dated November 14, 2005 (the date of the calendar call): (1) A listing of assets and liabilities; (2) a listing of purported actual current income and expenses; and (3) a listing of current income and expenses incorporating national, regional, and local IRS standards. The listings were not accompanied by any supporting documentation. Counsel for respondent objected on grounds, in part, that she was not provided with the exhibits until the morning of trial. The Court, in light of the Standing Pretrial Order and citing the prejudice to respondent's ability to prepare for cross-examination, sustained the objection, and the documents were not admitted. Instead, petitioner testified regarding her estimates of various assets, liabilities, income amounts, and expenses.

Petitioner then filed a posttrial brief and attached thereto three tables, purportedly summarizing petitioner's testimony and bearing striking similarity to the exhibits not admitted at trial (with the income and expense listings now bearing two columns, one labeled November 14, 2005, and the other labeled February 2005). However, the tables incorporate noticeably more detail and precision than can reasonably be gleaned from petitioner's often generalized approximations from the stand.

It is the status of the record as just described that precipitated the Court's comment that the outcome of the case is unaffected regardless of any proffered information considered in augmentation of the administrative record. The complete dearth of any documentation to corroborate or substantiate the figures renders petitioner's various estimates unpersuasive in any event. Moreover, the Court would observe that only the computations purporting to detail income and expenses as of February 2005 show an excess of expenses over income, and it is decidedly questionable whether all of those expenses shown are properly taken into account for purposes of section 301.6343-1(b)(4), Proced. & Admin. Regs. (for example, charitable contributions and payments on various liabilities).

The Court is therefore constrained to conclude that petitioner has failed to establish economic hardship within the meaning of Rev. Proc. 2003-61, sec. 4.02, 2003-2 C.B. at 298. Accordingly, on account of failure to satisfy two of the three elements enumerated as delineating those circumstances in which the Commissioner will ordinarily grant relief, petitioner does not qualify for equitable relief under Rev. Proc. 2003-61, sec. 4.02, 2003-2 C.B. at 298. Where relief is not available under section 4.02 of Rev. Proc. 2003-61, section 4.03 of the revenue procedure sets forth a list of nonexclusive factors that the Commissioner will consider in determining whether it would be inequitable to hold the requesting spouse liable for all or part of the unpaid income tax liability. As emphasized in Rev. Proc. 2003-61, sec. 4.03(2), 2003-2 C.B. at 298, no single factor is to be determinative; rather, all factors are to be considered and weighed appropriately.

Eight factors are listed, the latter two of which will weigh in favor of granting relief if present but will not weigh against relief if absent. The factors are directed toward whether: (1) The requesting spouse is separated or divorced from the nonrequesting spouse; (2) the requesting spouse will suffer economic hardship without relief; (3) the requesting spouse did not know or have reason to know that the nonrequesting spouse would not pay the liability; (4) the nonrequesting spouse had a legal obligation to pay the outstanding liability; (5) the requesting spouse received significant benefit (beyond normal support) from the enhanced assets or income resulting from the unpaid liability; (6) the requesting spouse has made a good faith effort to comply with income tax laws in subsequent years; (7) the requesting spouse was abused by the nonrequesting spouse; and (8) the requesting spouse was in poor mental or physical health when signing the return or requesting relief. Rev. Proc. 2003-61, sec. 4.03(2)(a) and (b), 2003-2 C.B. at 298–299.

As just described in connection with analysis of section 4.02 of Rev. Proc. 2003-61, the marital status factor weighs in favor of granting relief, while the economic hardship and knowledge elements weigh against granting relief. The remaining factors are considered below.

The legal obligation factor asks whether the nonrequesting spouse has an obligation to pay the outstanding liability pursuant to a divorce decree or separation agreement. *Id.* sec. 4.03(2)(a)(iv), 2003-2 C.B. at 298. Because petitioner and Dr. Banderas were never divorced or separated, this factor is neutral.

The significant benefit factor probes whether the requesting spouse received, directly or indirectly, from the assets or income resulting from the unpaid liability any benefit in excess of normal support. Sec. 1.6015-2(d), Income Tax Regs.; Rev. Proc. 2003-61, sec. 4.03(2)(a)(v), 2003-2 C.B. at 299 (referencing sec. 1.6015-2(d), Income Tax Regs.). Evidence of such benefit "may consist of transfers of property or rights to property, including transfers that may be received several years after the year of the * * * [relevant return]". Sec. 1.6015-2(d), Income Tax Regs. Normal support is measured by the circumstances of the particular parties. Estate of Krock v. Commissioner, 93 T.C. 672, 678–679 (1989); Levy v. Comm'r, T.C. Memo 2005-92.

Respondent notes that from 1999 to 2005, the Banderases or petitioner sold several parcels of real property and received approximately $8,000 to $10,000 on each of the three transactions. Petitioner testified that the proceeds were used primarily to pay living and moving expenses, to make a downpayment on a new residence, and to contribute to the cost of a daughter's wedding. In 2004, petitioner received a $60,000 distribution from her individual retirement account. Petitioner also acknowledged making a loan of conservatively at least $18,000 during 2004 to a friend whose whereabouts were unknown at the time of trial.

In the unique circumstances of this case, particularly the fact that the majority of the Banderases' assets were tied up in the bankruptcy litigation, the described uses of the relatively modest proceeds from the property transactions would not generally appear to rise to the level of excess benefit. The wedding costs, however, give us pause. Likewise, the $18,000 loan and the failure to apply any of the retirement account distribution to outstanding taxes could signal a more telling selective avoidance of tax liabilities. Nonetheless, the Court is also cognizant that, while the bankruptcy establishes reason to know that the taxes would not be paid at the time of filing, its pendency could have engendered a degree of confusion in petitioner's mind as to responsibility for the taxes and the eventual source of funds for their payment. The Court therefore is unconvinced that the substantial benefit prong weighs strongly either for or against relief.

The compliance with income tax laws factor addresses the good faith efforts of the requesting spouse in subsequent years. Rev. Proc. 2003-61, sec. 4.03(2)(a)(vi), 2003-2 C.B. at 299. The record indicates that petitioner's 2000 return was not timely filed and that amounts due remained outstanding until at least February of 2004. The 2001 and 2002 returns were timely filed, but the balance due for 2001 was not paid until January of 2003. The 2002 taxes were timely paid. As of the time of trial, IRS records did not reflect that petitioner had filed her 2003 or 2004 returns. Petitioner testified that she believed she timely filed the 2003 return but refiled it, in response to IRS inquiries, shortly before the trial in November of 2005, at which time she also filed her initial return for 2004. Petitioner also explicitly conceded at trial and on brief that various of her returns and related payments were delinquent on account of financial difficulties, moves, misplaced documents, etc.

Hence, petitioner's compliance with tax laws subsequent to the filing of the 1999 return reveals shortcomings. Additionally, petitioner's generalized allusions to financial pressures and information misplaced during moves are insufficient to establish good faith efforts with respect to the series of delinquencies occurring over a period of years. This factor weighs against relief.

The presence of abuse is a factor weighing in favor of relief, but its absence carries no contrary weight. Rev. Proc. 2003-61, sec. 4.03(2)(b)(i), 2003-2 C.B. at 299. Because petitioner has at no point alleged any abuse by Dr. Banderas, this factor is neutral.

The final factor enumerated in the revenue procedure, and again weighing only in favor of and not against relief, is directed toward whether the requesting spouse was in poor mental or physical health when signing the return or seeking relief. *Id.* sec. 4.03(2)(b)(ii), 2003-2 C.B. at 299. The nature, extent, and duration of illness are to be taken into account. *Id.* Petitioner's statements at trial and on brief incorporate general assertions of high blood pressure, depression, and bad knees. Nonetheless, the record is bereft of any corroborating medical documentation or any specific contentions regarding how such ailments might have impacted petitioner's ability to meet her Federal tax obligations. In fact, petitioner acknowledged that, except for her weight, she was in good health during the 1997 and 1999 years at issue and until 2000 when her blood pressure began rising. The Court observes that petitioner was able to work multiple jobs throughout much of the relevant period. Thus, while the Court does not doubt that petitioner bore substantial stress on account of the difficult circumstances besetting her family, the record does not enable us to find particular health issues of a nature that would affect the balancing of her claim for relief. This factor, too, is neutral.

Accordingly, of those factors identified in the pertinent revenue procedure, only one weighs clearly in favor of granting relief. The remainder are either negative or essentially neutral. The Court is therefore unable to conclude that respondent's denial of equitable relief under section 6015(f) was an abuse of discretion.

* * *

Decision will be entered for respondent.

Does *Banderas* present compelling facts for innocent spouse relief? If so, which facts are most compelling?

In *Banderas*, was the Tax Court willing to look beyond the administrative record in reviewing the IRS's section 6015(f) determination? Why do you think that the court noted that the outcome would be the same regardless? The IRS's position, as reflected in *Banderas*, is that the Tax Court can only consider the information in the administrative record. *See* CC-2007-013, 2007 CCN LEXIS 13 (June 8, 2007); CC-2005-011 Q&A 31, 2005 CCN LEXIS 9 (May 20, 2005); CC-2004-26, 2004 CCN LEXIS 19 (July 12, 2004).

As indicated above, "[s]ubsections (b) and (c) of section 6015 apply only in the case of 'an understatement of tax' or 'any deficiency' in tax and do not apply in the case of underpayments of taxes reported on joint tax returns." Hopkins v. Commissioner, 121 T.C. 73, 88 (2003). For example, if the IRS asserts a deficiency of $5,000 on a joint return, section 6015(b) or (c) may apply if the applicable requirements are met. However, if the joint return shows tax liability of $15,000 and only $9,000 is actually paid, neither section 6015(b) nor section 6015(c) can apply to the $6,000 balance.

By contrast, section 6015(f) can apply to underpayments of admitted liabilities, as well as to tax deficiencies. *See* Lily Kahng, *Innocent Spouses: A Critique of the New Tax Laws Governing Joint and Several Tax Liability*, 49 VILL. L. REV. 261, 269 (2004) ("The legislative history envisions the [section 6015(f)] relief provision possibly applying in the underpayment situation. The legislative history also makes clear that this is not the only instance where residual relief might be available."); *see also* Robert Nadler, *Equitable Relief: Time to Level the Playing Field*, 113 TAX NOTES 899 (2006) ("One of the first cases involving a claim for equitable relief arose in a deficiency proceeding.") (*citing* Butler v. Commissioner, 114 T.C. 276 (2000)). Thus, in the example above, if the requirements of section 6015(f) are met, it could apply to both the $5,000 deficiency and the $6,000 underpayment. This is an important difference between section 6015(f) and the other subsections of section 6015. Does the *Banderas* case involve an underpayment or understatement of tax?

[B] Procedure

A taxpayer may elect innocent spouse status on IRS Form 8857, Request for Innocent Spouse Relief (And Separation of Liability and Equitable Relief). The form is fairly lengthy and calls for explanations of answers to a number of questions, such as those relating to the requesting spouse's level of knowledge about the family's finances. The spouse may also attach to any request for relief from joint and several liability Form 12510, Questionnaire for Requesting Spouse. Form 12510 asks for information that helps the IRS process the request.

Treasury regulations provide that if a spouse requests relief under section 6015(b) or (c), the IRS will automatically consider whether that spouse qualifies under other relief provisions of section 6015. However, if a spouse elects relief under section 6015(f), relief will only be considered under that section. *See* Treas. Reg. 1.6015-1(a)(2). If the request for equitable relief is denied, the spouse may submit a timely request for relief under sections 6015(b) or (c). The IRS may also permit the spouse to amend the initial request to elect relief under those subsections.[3]

How does the IRS process innocent spouse claims? One scholar explains:

> The I.R.S. now has an entire processing center in Covington, Kentucky devoted to the processing of IS [innocent spouse] claims which was staffed as of 2001 by 157 employees. In all, it is reported that the equivalent of 953 full-time employees were expected to work exclusively on IS case processing in 2001, with most or all of them drawn from the ranks of auditing personnel. Despite this, claims processing is painfully slow, in part because of the unexpectedly large number of claims for relief, and in part because each claim must be decided on a case-by-case individual basis. In FY [fiscal year] 2005, the I.R.S. took an average 192 days to process IS claims which were ultimately allowed in full by the examination function, and 807 days for claims which went to the Appeals function.

---

[3] Further information relating to the qualifications for and procedures surrounding section 6015 relief is available in Publication 971, *Innocent Spouse Relief (And Separation of Liability and Equitable Relief)* (Rev. March 2004). Publication 971 also contains a number of flowcharts that may help a spouse and her representative determine whether she qualifies for relief from joint and several liability. The IRS has also created an online Innocent Spouse Tax Relief Eligibility Explorer that includes relevant questions and answers relating to liability relief. *See* http://www.irs.gov/individuals/article/0,,id=96727,00.html.

Richard C.E. Beck, *The Failure of Innocent Spouse Reform*, 51 N.Y.L. Sch. L. Rev. 928, 950–51 (2006).

[1] Timing of the Innocent Spouse Claim

A taxpayer need not wait for a notice of deficiency in order to make an innocent spouse election. However, the IRS will not consider a premature claim for relief. "A premature claim is a claim for relief that is filed for a tax year prior to the receipt of a notification of an audit or a letter or notice from the IRS indicating that there may be an outstanding liability with regard to that year." Treas. Reg. § 1.6015-5(b)(5).

An innocent spouse claim may be made with the IRS as late as the collections phase of the controversy.[4] *See* I.R.C. § 6015(c)(3)(B); I.R.C. § 6015(b)(1)(E) (election must be made "not later than the date which is 2 years after the date the Secretary has begun collection activities with respect to the individual making the election. . . ."). Although there is no statutory deadline to apply for equitable relief under section 6015(f), regulation section 1.6015-5(b)(1) applies the same deadline that applies to section 6015(b) and (c) requests, "two years from the date of the first collection activity against the requesting spouse after July 22, 1998, with respect to the joint tax liability."

Because many spouses have divorced or separated by the time the IRS seeks to assess an understatement relating to their jointly filed return, an innocent spouse may be largely unaware of the IRS's actions until the tax has been assessed and the IRS has begun collection enforcement. For those spouses who wait to request relief until after collection activity has begun, the best forum for doing so is the Collection Due Process (CDP) hearing. *See* I.R.C. §§ 6320, 6330. CDP hearings are discussed in Chapter 16.

What constitutes collection activities for purposes of section 6015? In *McGee v. Commissioner*, 123 T.C. 314 (2004), in May 1999, the IRS offset a refund owed the taxpayer against unpaid taxes from a year in which she had filed jointly with her ex-husband. The IRS sent her two notices about the offset, neither of which mentioned section 6015. More than two years later, the IRS filed a Notice of Federal Tax Lien on the taxpayer's residence. At that point, she hired an attorney and filed a request for equitable relief under section 6015(f) a few months later. The IRS's position was that the offset was a collection action, so it denied the taxpayer's request for relief because the request was filed more than two years after the first collection activity.

The Tax Court agreed with the IRS that the offset was a collection action. However, the Tax Court disagreed that the notices sent to the taxpayer were not collection-related notices, stating: "The incongruity of respondent's position is untenable. The offset was a collection action. *Campbell v. Comm'r*, 121 T.C. 290, 292 (2003). Accordingly, the notice of the offset was a collection-related notice and should have included the information required by RRA 1998 sec. 3501(b)." *Id.* at 319. That provision of the IRS Reform Act is an off-Code provision that requires collection-related notices to include notice of individuals' rights under section 6015. The Tax Court further stated:

> In this case, respondent's treatment of the offset as a collection action, coupled with his failure to send petitioner notice of her section 6015 rights as required by RRA 1998 sec. 3501, resulted in petitioner's failure to seek section 6015(f) relief within 2 years after the first collection action because she did not know of her rights. . . .
>
> It would be inequitable if respondent could prevent review of a request for relief under section 6015(f) by failing to inform petitioner of her right to relief in defiance of a congressional mandate. Such a result would be contrary to the very purpose of section 6015(f), which is to relieve inequitable situations involving joint liabilities. Respondent's administrative interpretations are given little weight when inconsistent with a statutory scheme. . . . Rev. Proc.

[4] Collection of taxes is discussed in detail in Chapters 14–16.

> 2000-15, sec. 5, should not be applied in a manner which frustrates the legislative intent of section 6015 and the related public law.
>
> Accordingly, we hold that the running of the 2-year period set forth in Rev. Proc. 2000-15, sec. 5, was not commenced by the collection activity in May 1999. Respondent's contrary interpretation of Rev. Proc. 2000-15, sec. 5, is an abuse of discretion.

McGee, 123 T.C. at 319–20.

The IRS responded to *McGee* with a Chief Counsel Notice. *See* CC-2005-010 (May 20, 2005), *available at* 2005 TNT 99-17. In the Notice, the IRS explained that because it "considered a refund offset notice to be an accounting notice and not a collection-related notice, the Service generally did not include a stuffer with refund offset notices." *Id.* The Notice also addressed how the IRS would treat pending and future cases:

> The Office of Chief Counsel and the Service agree that the Service should inform a taxpayer of the right to file a claim for relief under section 6015 if the Service sends a refund offset notice to the taxpayer. . . . The Service is changing its procedures so that in the future taxpayers will receive notice of their right to file a claim under section 6015 in refund offset cases. Once these changes in procedures are implemented, denials of claims for relief in cases involving claims filed more than two years after a refund offset should be defended. Until the changes in procedures are implemented, however, the Service should not deny, and Chief Counsel attorneys should not defend cases in which the requesting spouse filed the claim for relief more than two years after the refund offset unless the facts of the case are distinguishable from *McGee*.

Id. (footnote omitted).

Is innocent spouse relief available after death? Revenue Ruling 2003-36, 2003-18 I.R.B. 849, provides that an executor of a decedent's estate (1) may file a section 6015 request "as long as the decedent had satisfied any applicable requirements while alive" and (2) may "pursue a § 6015 request for relief . . . made during the decedent's lifetime." The Revenue Ruling explains that, although section 6015 does not expressly permit an executor to file a request for relief, an executor's authority to do so stems from both the "specific authority to make and disaffirm joint returns under § 6013(a)(3)" and his or her assumption of the rights of the decedent's estate under section 6903. Finally, an executor's authority to pursue existing section 6015 claims follows from the right to file a request for relief under section 6015.

[2] Court Jurisdiction Over Innocent Spouse Claims

Reading Assignment: I.R.C. § 6015(e).

Tax Court consideration of innocent spouse claims can arise in several contexts. The Tax Court has explained:

> One basis, which survives section 6013(e), is the traditional petition based on a notice of deficiency where the petition includes a claim by one or both spouses for relief from joint liability. Relief claimed in this context has traditionally been characterized as an affirmative defense, and the enactment of section 6015 has not negated this Court's authority to consider a claim for such relief in a "deficiency proceeding". . . .
>
> Another situation in which this Court has jurisdiction to review a claim for relief from joint liability involves the collection due-process procedures of sections 6320 and 6330. Among the issues that can be considered under sections 6320 and 6330 are "the underlying tax liability" and "appropriate spousal defenses". Sec. 6330(c)(2).

> Section 6015(e)(1)(A) also provides this Court with jurisdiction to consider a claim for relief from joint liability by specifically allowing a spouse who elects relief under section 6015 to petition this Court for review of the Commissioner's determination regarding an administrative claim for relief. Unlike a deficiency proceeding or a collection due-process proceeding, a proceeding under section 6015(e)(1)(A) is restricted to the issue of relief from joint liability for the individual electing such relief. A proceeding under section 6015(e)(1)(A) has been referred to as a "stand alone" proceeding. . . .

King v. Commissioner, 115 T.C. 118, 121–23 (2000).[5]

Under section 6015(e), stand-alone petitions may be filed no earlier than 6 months after the taxpayer filed the request for relief; the taxpayer need not continue to wait for an IRS determination of relief, once 6 months pass. I.R.C. § 6015(e)(1)(A)(i)(II). However, if the IRS does send a determination of relief, the Tax Court petition must be filed within 90 days of that mailing. I.R.C. § 6015(e)(1)(A)(ii). The Community Renewal Tax Relief Act of 2000 clarified that the 90-day period begins on the day *after* the IRS mails its denial, rather than the day of the denial. This makes the 90-day period parallel to the period for petitioning the Tax Court in response to a notice of deficiency.

In *Friday v. Commissioner*, 124 T.C. 220 (2005), a stand-alone case in which the IRS denied a requesting spouse relief under all subsections of section 6015, the IRS requested that the matter be remanded to the IRS's Cincinnati Centralized Innocent Spouse Operation Unit for further review of the claim under section 6015(f). The Tax Court refused to grant the motion. It noted:

> Even if the Commissioner fails to do anything for 6 months following the filing of an election for relief (where there is nothing to "review"), the individual may bring an action in this Court. See sec. 6015(b), (e)(1)(A)(i)(II). A petition for a decision as to whether relief is appropriate under section 6015 is generally not a "review" of the Commissioner's determination in a hearing but is instead an action begun in this Court. There is in section 6015 no analog to section 6330 granting the Court jurisdiction after a hearing at the Commissioner's Appeals Office.

Id. at 222.

What is the scope of Tax Court review in a stand-alone proceeding? In *Block v. Commissioner*, 120 T.C. 62 (2003), the taxpayer, having received from the IRS a notice of determination denying her request for relief from joint and several liability, filed a stand-alone petition under Code section 6015(e). She later sought to amend the petition to raise the expiration of the statute of limitations as an affirmative defense. The court denied the motion, holding that it lacked jurisdiction under section 6015(e) to consider the statute of limitations issue. *Id.* at 68–69. The court explained, "The relief from joint and several liability available in a section 6015(e) 'stand alone' petition does not

---

[5] Note that, in all three circumstances, the small tax case procedure, discussed in Chapter 8, may be available. That procedure generally allows disputes involving no more than $50,000 for each tax year to be resolved using less formal processes. The Tax Court has explained:

> [A] taxpayer may raise the matter as an affirmative defense in a petition for redetermination of a deficiency. Qualification to proceed as a small tax case would be governed by sec. 7463(a). Second, a taxpayer may request spousal relief in a sec. 6330 collection case. Qualification to proceed as a small tax case would be governed by sec. 7463(f)(2). Third, a taxpayer like petitioner may file a so-called stand-alone petition pursuant to sec. 6015(e) seeking spousal relief from joint and several liability on a joint return where the Commissioner has issued a final determination denying the taxpayer's claim for such relief or the Commissioner has failed to rule on the taxpayer's claim within 6 months of its filing. *Drake v. Comm'r*, 123 T.C. 320, 323 (2004). Qualification to proceed as a small tax case in this situation is governed by sec. 7463(f)(1).

Petrane v. Commissioner, 129 T.C. 1, 2 n.2 (2007).

incorporate preassessment procedures. Section 6015 assumes that the electing taxpayer is to be relieved from an existing joint tax liability, not whether the underlying joint tax liability exists." *Id.* at 68.

For a while, the Tax Court's jurisdiction to review denials of equitable innocent spouse relief under section 6015(f) was unsettled. In 2006, Congress cleared up any remaining issue, amending section 6015(e)(1) to read, "[i]n the case of an individual against whom a deficiency has been asserted and who elects to have subsection (b) or (c) apply, or in the case of an individual who requests equitable relief under subsection (f). . . ." The amendment thus expressly provides the Tax Court with jurisdiction over even non-deficiency section 6015(f) claims. It applies to "liability for taxes arising or remaining unpaid on or after" December 20, 2006. Tax Relief and Health Care Act of 2006, P.L. 109-432, Title IV § 408(c).

The Tax Court does not have exclusive jurisdiction over innocent spouse cases. If an innocent spouse case is docketed in Tax Court and either of the taxpayers on a joint return files a refund claim, the Tax Court loses jurisdiction over the innocent spouse proceeding. Section 6015(e) provides:

> If a suit for refund is begun by either individual filing the joint return pursuant to section 6532 —
>
> (A) the Tax Court shall lose jurisdiction of the individual's action under this section to whatever extent jurisdiction is acquired by the district court or the United States Court of Federal Claims over the taxable years that are the subject of the suit for refund, and
>
> (B) the court acquiring jurisdiction shall have jurisdiction over the petition filed under this subsection.

I.R.C. § 6015(e)(3). However, as in all refund cases, the tax must first be paid in full under *Flora v. United States*, 357 U.S. 63 (1958). *See* Andrews v. United States, 69 F. Supp. 2d 972, 978 (E.D. Ohio 1999), *aff'd*, 225 F.3d 658 (6th Cir. 2000) (unpublished op.). The bankruptcy courts also can hear innocent spouse claims. *See, e.g.*, Shafman v. United States Dep't of the Treasury, IRS (In re Shafman), 267 B.R. 709 (Bankr. N.D. W.V. 2001); French v. United States (In re French), 242 B.R. 369 (Bankr. N.D. Ohio 1999).

[3] Rights of the Other Spouse

In innocent spouse proceedings, the spouse (or ex-spouse) of the person requesting innocent spouse relief (the nonrequesting spouse[6]) also has rights. The nonrequesting spouse may wish to intervene in some cases to argue against removing liability from the requesting spouse. Code section 6015(h)(2) allows the nonrequesting spouse to be heard at the administrative level, and section 6015(e)(4) allows for participation in innocent spouse litigation.

[a] Participation in an Appeals Conference

Treasury regulations provide that the nonrequesting spouse must be given notice that the requesting spouse has filed a claim for relief and be given an opportunity to submit information for use in the administrative proceedings. Treas. Reg. § 1.6015-6(a)(1). The regulations further provide that:

> The Internal Revenue Service will consider all of the information (as relevant to each particular relief provision) that the nonrequesting spouse submits in determining whether relief from joint and several liability is appropriate, including information relating to the following —

---

[6] Note that the term "nonrequesting spouse," which is used in the Treasury regulations, simply refers to the spouse (or ex-spouse) other than the one whose innocent spouse claim is in question. It does not operate to preclude that spouse from also requesting relief under section 6015.

(1) The legal status of the requesting and nonrequesting spouses' marriage;

(2) The extent of the requesting spouse's knowledge of the erroneous items or underpayment;

(3) The extent of the requesting spouse's knowledge or participation in the family business or financial affairs;

(4) The requesting spouse's education level;

(5) The extent to which the requesting spouse benefitted from the erroneous items;

(6) Any asset transfers between the spouses;

(7) Any indication of fraud on the part of either spouse;

(8) Whether it would be inequitable, within the meaning of §§ 1.6015-2(d) and 1.6015-4, to hold the requesting spouse jointly and severally liable for the outstanding liability;

(9) The allocation or ownership of items giving rise to the deficiency; and

(10) Anything else that may be relevant to the determination of whether relief from joint and several liability should be granted.

Treas. Reg. § 1.6015-6(b). Thus, the submissions of the nonrequesting spouse can help establish or undermine the requesting spouse's claim for relief.

The rights of the nonrequesting spouse may raise safety issues in cases involving domestic violence. For example, if the requesting spouse is hiding from the other spouse, disclosure of the address of the requesting spouse could put that person in danger. Form 8857, *Request for Innocent Spouse Relief*, asks whether the requesting spouse has been a victim of domestic violence, and in IR-2001-23, the IRS announced a procedure to protect victims of domestic violence who claim innocent spouse relief. The Information Release explained the steps the IRS will take to protect the requesting spouse:

> [T]he IRS strictly adheres to tax law provisions that protect the confidentiality of sensitive information. This means the IRS will not release information that could endanger the safety of domestic violence victims.
>
> For example, the IRS will not release to a taxpayer's spouse (or former spouse) a new name, address, information about an employer, phone number or fax number or other information not related to making a determination about the innocent spouse claim.
>
> For potential abuse cases, the IRS also centralizes all correspondence in one location. This change means the other spouse can't guess the whereabouts of the domestic abuse victim through a postmark or the location of a local IRS office.

IR-2001-23, *available at* 2001 TNT 35-11 (Feb. 21, 2001).

Can the nonrequesting spouse appeal a decision by the IRS Appeals Division upholding the IRS's grant of relief to the requesting spouse? In *Maier v. Commissioner*, 119 T.C. 267 (2002), *aff'd*, 360 F.3d 361 (2d Cir. 2004), the Tax Court held that it lacked jurisdiction over Mr. Maier's petition contesting the IRS's administrative grant of relief from joint and several liability to Ms. Maier, his former wife. Mr. Maier had been allowed to submit information to the IRS but not to appear in person, and he remained dissatisfied at the level of participation he had been afforded.

The court pointed out that Ms. Maier had not petitioned the Tax Court, so there was no proceeding in which Mr. Maier could intervene. Accordingly, the court distinguished *King v. Commissioner*, 115 T.C. 118 (2000), *later proceeding* at 116 T.C. 198 (2001), which is discussed below, as well as *Corson v. Commissioner*, 114 T.C. 354 (2000). In addition, Mr. Maier had not requested innocent spouse relief for himself and the IRS had not mailed him a notice of deficiency. Thus, the court found no basis upon which to rest jurisdiction.

The Court of Appeals for the Second Circuit affirmed, also distinguishing *King* and *Corson*. *Maier*, 360 F.3d at 364–65. The Second Circuit held that the plain language of section 6015(e)(1)(A) means that only the requesting spouse can petition for review by the Tax Court. *Id.* at 364. The court also cited sections 6015(e)(4) and 6015(h) as reinforcing the notion that the non-requesting spouse "cannot independently invoke the jurisdiction of the Tax Court." *See id.* at 364.

Shortly after *Maier* was decided by the Tax Court, in Revenue Procedure 2003-19, 2003-5 I.R.B. 371, the IRS ruled that, when one spouse requests relief from joint and several liability and receives a preliminary determination issued on April 1, 2003 or later, the nonrequesting spouse may file a protest within 30 days and obtain a conference with the Appeals Division. Citing *Maier*, the Ruling notes that the IRS's decision with respect to the nonrequesting spouse is not appealable to the Tax Court but that, if the requesting spouse petitions the court, the Code and the Tax Court Rules permit the other spouse to intervene, as explained below. Had the procedures in Revenue Procedure 2003-19 been in place, would Mr. Maier have been able to be heard in Tax Court?

Recall that, if the requesting spouse does not petition the Tax Court, the nonrequesting spouse will not have an opportunity to be heard on the issue in court, at least if that spouse has not been mailed a notice of deficiency. That means that if, in the collection phase of a tax controversy, the IRS rules in favor of the requesting spouse, as the IRS did in *Maier*, the other spouse cannot obtain review of the decision. However, if the other spouse also makes a request for relief under section 6015, the Tax Court would be able to review denial of that request to the same extent it can with respect to any requesting spouse.

[b] Intervention in a Tax Court Proceeding

Reading Assignment: I.R.C. § 6015(e)(4).

The nonrequesting spouse is given an opportunity to become a party to the Tax Court innocent spouse proceeding. I.R.C. § 6015(e)(4). Accordingly, in *King v. Commissioner*, 115 T.C. 118 (2000), the Tax Court held that in any case in which an individual taxpayer seeks innocent spouse relief, the other spouse is entitled to notice and, if not already a party in the case, an opportunity to intervene to challenge the propriety of relieving the taxpayer from liability. *See also* Tax Ct. R. 325. However, if the intervenor, after being properly notified of the trial date, fails to appear, the Tax Court has held that the court may dismiss the intervenor's action for failure to prosecute, by analogy to Rule 41(b) of the Federal Rules of Civil Procedure. Tipton v. Commissioner, 127 T.C. 214, 218 (2007).[7]

What if the nonrequesting spouse seeks to intervene in *support* of the requesting spouse's request for relief? In *Van Arsdalen v. Commissioner*, 123 T.C. 135 (2004), a stand-alone section 6015 case, after the requesting spouse, Diana Van Arsdalen, petitioned the Tax Court, the IRS

> filed with the Court a notice of filing petition and right to intervene (the notice). The notice stated that respondent had informed Mr. Murray of the filing of the petition and of his right to intervene in the case. The notice stated in pertinent part: "Under T.C. Rule 325(b), Stanley D. Murray has a right to intervene in this matter for the sole purpose of challenging petitioner's entitlement to relief from joint and several liability."

Id. at 136–37. Ms. Van Arsdalen moved to strike the notice because of its limiting language, and Mr. Murray lodged a notice of intervention stating that he intended to

---

[7] If the nonrequesting spouse is deceased, does the right to intervene pass to his or her heirs? In *Fain v. Commissioner*, 129 T.C. 89 (2007), the Tax Court said yes. It continued the case to allow the parties to search for heirs. *Id.* at 92.

offer evidence in support of his ex-wife's claim for relief. The Tax Court allowed the intervention. *Id.* at 142. The court noted that its new procedural rule regarding intervention in section 6015 cases did not limit intervention in the way the IRS argued. *Id.* at 141. Subsequently, in Chief Counsel Notice CC-2005-11 (May 20, 2005), *available at* 2005 TNT 99-18 (May 24, 2005), the IRS stated that "[t]he standard language for the Notice of Filing has been revised to be consistent with the court's holding [in *Van Arsdalen*] by deleting the language 'for the sole purpose of challenging.' " *Id.* at Q&A 6.

[4] Credits and Refunds

Reading Assignment: I.R.C. § 6015(g)(1), (3).

In general, subject to several exceptions, a taxpayer who obtains relief under section 6015(b) or section 6015(f) can obtain a credit or refund of previously paid taxes. Thus, previously paid taxes for which the requesting spouse has been found not liable may be refunded. By contrast, no credit or refund may be made under section 6015(c). I.R.C. § 6015(g)(3).

In any refund context, the limitations periods of section 6511 and 6512(b), discussed in Chapter 10, apply. As a result, careful attention should be paid to time limitations. The Tax Court has held that the innocent spouse request on Form 8857 can constitute a refund claim. *See* Washington v. Commissioner, 120 T.C. 137, 161–62 (2003); *see also* Bartman v. Commissioner, T.C. Memo. 2004-93, *aff'd in part and rev'd in part*, 446 F.3d 785 (8th Cir. 2006). However, because Code section 6015(g) specifies that section 7122, relating to offers in compromise, overrides it, the Tax Court has held that a requesting spouse who signed an offer in compromise would "not be entitled to a refund or credit even if relief was ultimately granted under section 6015(b) or (f)." Dutton v. Commissioner, 122 T.C. 133, 140 (2004).

[5] Res Judicata

Reading Assignment: I.R.C. § 6015(g)(2).

Code section 6015 contains its own *res judicata* provision that generally precludes repetitive litigation of innocent spouse issues. Section 6015(g)(2) provides:

> In the case of any election under subsection (b) or (c), if a decision of a court in any prior proceeding for the same taxable year has become final, such decision shall be conclusive except with respect to the qualification of the individual for relief which was not an issue in such proceeding. The exception contained in the preceding sentence shall not apply if the court determines that the individual participated meaningfully in such prior proceeding.

Id.

The Tax Court has explained the purpose of this provision as follows:

> Before section 6015(g)(2) and its predecessor were enacted, if a court decision had become final as to a particular taxable year, the taxpayer could be barred under the doctrine of res judicata from seeking relief from joint and several liability in a later proceeding for the same taxable year. *See, e.g.*, . . . United States v. Shanbaum, 10 F.3d 305, 313–314 (5th Cir. 1994). . . . *See generally* Commissioner v. Sunnen, 333 U.S. 591, 92 L. Ed. 898, 68 S. Ct. 715 (1948). This was true whether or not relief from joint and several liability had been an issue in the prior court proceeding. *See* United States v. Shanbaum, *supra*. Section 6015(g)(2) and its predecessor change the result that obtained under prior law by permitting an individual who had not participated meaningfully in the prior court proceeding to elect relief under section 6015(b) or (c), as long as the

> individual's qualification for relief under section 6015(b) or (c) was not an issue in the prior court proceeding.

Vetrano v. Commissioner, 116 T.C. 272, 280 (2001). Section 6015(g)(2) thus modifies the common law doctrine of res judicata by allowing a taxpayer to make an innocent spouse claim after liability for the tax year has been decided, so long as the taxpayer did not meaningfully participate in the proceeding that determined liability.

Treasury regulations refer to the participation requirement as follows: "A requesting spouse is barred from relief from joint and several liability under section 6015 by res judicata for any tax year . . . if the requesting spouse meaningfully participated in that proceeding and could have raised relief under section 6015. A requesting spouse has not meaningfully participated in a prior proceeding if, due to the effective date of section 6015, relief under section 6015 was not available in that proceeding." Treas. Reg. § 1.6015-1(e). Thus, under the Treasury regulations, even if the requesting spouse meaningfully participated in the prior proceeding, section 6015(g)(2) will not apply if that spouse could not have raised the issue of relief under section 6015.

What constitutes material participation? In one case, the Tax Court ruled as follows:

> The record clearly establishes that petitioner Scott P. Thurner participated meaningfully in the District Court collection action. The documents that petitioners filed in the District Court collection action were signed by both petitioners and amply demonstrate that petitioner Scott P. Thurner was fully engaged in that proceeding. In addition, petitioner Scott P. Thurner acknowledged in the affidavit attached to his Objection that he maintained exclusive control over all tax matters including the handling of the District Court collection action. Accordingly, we hold that respondent is entitled to summary judgment that petitioner Scott P. Thurner is barred under section 6015(g)(2) from claiming relief under section 6015 for the years 1981, 1990, and 1992.
>
> In contrast, we are unable to conclude on this record that petitioner Yvonne E. Thurner participated meaningfully in the District Court collection action. Petitioner Yvonne E. Thurner's assertion that she merely complied with her husband's instructions to sign the pleadings and various other documents that were filed in the District Court collection action raises an issue of material fact as to her level of participation in that proceeding. Under the circumstances, drawing factual inferences in a manner most favorable to the party opposing summary judgment, see Dahlstrom v. Commissioner, 85 T.C. at 821, we conclude that respondent is not entitled to summary judgment that petitioner Yvonne E. Thurner is barred from claiming relief under section 6015 for the years 1981, 1990, and 1992. The question of the applicability of the bar of res judicata under section 6015(g)(2) as to petitioner Yvonne E. Thurner can be resolved only after further development of the record through discovery or trial of the case.

Thurner v. Commissioner, 121 T.C. 43, 53 (2003), *aff'd*, 2007 U.S. App. LEXIS 27176 (7th Cir. 2007).

In *Estate of Kanter v. Commissioner*, 337 F.3d 833 (7th Cir. 2003), *rev'd and remanded on another issue sub nom.* Ballard v. Commissioner, 544 U.S. 40 (2005), the Court of Appeals for the Seventh Circuit upheld the Tax Court's ruling that "any finding that a spouse had not 'meaningfully participated' in the litigation must occur in a subsequent, separate proceeding that could properly consider the matter now before [the Seventh Circuit] as a 'prior proceeding.' " *Id.* at 869. Thus, the court held, based in part on the plain language of the Code and in part on the general principle of res judicata, that section 6015(g)(2) could not be applied during the pendency of the judicial proceeding in question itself.

By its terms, section 6015(g)(2) applies only to claims under section 6015(b) and (c). Despite that wording, in *Thurner*, which was quoted above, the Tax Court determined that a claim brought under 6015(f) is subject to 6015(g)(2), *Thurner*, 121 T.C. at 51, thus allowing an earlier proceeding to have preclusive effect. *Thurner* involved a summary judgment motion in which the IRS asserted that it was entitled to summary judgment because 6015(g)(2) barred the taxpayer-husband's and taxpayer-wife's section 6015(b) and (f) claims as a matter of law. The taxpayers asserted that 6015(g)(2) did not apply to their claims under 6015(f). Following its rationale in *Fernandez v. Commissioner*, 114 T.C. 324 (2000), in which the court had reasoned that it had jurisdiction under 6015(e) to review denials of relief under 6015(f) despite statutory language that did not refer to section 6015(f), the Tax Court determined that, because "a claim for equitable relief under section 6015(f) is subordinate and ancillary to a claim for relief under section 6015(b) or (c)[,] . . . an express reference in subsection (g)(2) to a claim for equitable relief under section 6015(f) is not necessary to bring those claims within the purview of subsection (g)(2)." *Id.* at 51–52.

[6] Multiple Claims

Reading assignment: Treas. Reg. § 1.6015-1(h)(5).

Are taxpayers limited to one innocent spouse claim for a particular tax year? One commentator explains the complicated answer to this seemingly straightforward question and advocates for second claims for changed circumstances in section 6015(f) cases:

> Reg. section 1.6015-1(h)(5) limits taxpayers' claims for innocent spouse relief to the first timely claim for relief from joint and several liability, except for one group of taxpayers. The exception allows taxpayers who were not eligible to elect relief under section 6015(c) to make a timely claim later if at the later time the taxpayer is eligible for relief under reg. section 1.6015-3. Thus, under the regulation, taxpayers whose marital status changes, as defined by the statute, may file a second claim under section 6015(c), but taxpayers who later become unable to pay the tax because of changed circumstances (economic hardship, abuse, physical or mental illness) are not eligible to file a second claim for relief under section 6015(f). Not only does the IRS approach lack equity, the regulation may be unconstitutional.[n.54]
>
> Importantly, the statute does not limit a taxpayer to filing a single claim. Nor does the statute allow taxpayers whose marital status changes after they file the first claim to file a second claim. Interestingly, Congress provided limitations on multiple claims for innocent spouse relief. First, Congress limited claims under sections 6015(b) and (c) to the two-year period following the first collection activity. Second, section 6015(g)(2) bars claims following a final judicial decision in a case in which the taxpayer has participated meaningfully. But if the regulation is valid, section 6015(g)(2) becomes superfluous. Any time a claim for innocent spouse relief is timely filed, the regulation bars a second claim whether or not there is a final decision in the Tax Court. If the IRS is not going to consider second claims, why would Congress provide that claims that go to final decision are res judicata? To the extent the regulation overpowers the language of a statute, it may be vulnerable to attack.

[n.54] The regulation allows one class of taxpayers — those whose marital status changes — to file more than one claim while denying another class — those who become eligible for equitable relief under section 6015(f) — from filing further claims. It is arguable that this distinction violates the due process rights of the latter group. While the Fifth Amendment does not expressly contain an equal protection clause, the Supreme Court has held that in cases involving federal legislation, the Fifth Amendment encompasses the equal protection requirements of the Fourteenth Amendment. Weinberger v. Wisenfeld, 420 U.S. 636, 638 n.2 (1975); Johnson v. Robison, 415 U.S. 361, 364–365 n.4 (1974). The Fifth Amendment prohibits discrimination that is so egregious that it violates due process. Schneider v. Rusk, 377 U.S. 163 (1964).

> The policy reasons behind the "no second claims" in equitable relief cases are unclear. The IRS allows taxpayers to amend returns and to file more than one OIC [Offer in Compromise]. The IRS also has a good "audit reconsideration" program that allows taxpayers to present new information after the IRS has completed its examination and the tax has been assessed. But, if a final notice of determination is mailed in an innocent spouse case, regardless of the facts and circumstances, a taxpayer seeking equitable relief cannot file a second claim for relief.
>
> From a policy point of view, the "no second claim" policy conflicts with the overall legislative intent to expand innocent spouse relief, and it conflicts with the reality on the ground. For various reasons, a low-income taxpayer may need to file a second claim for equitable relief. Low-income taxpayers face challenges in filing for innocent spouse relief and providing information for the IRS determination. Those challenges include difficulties filling out forms and understanding instructions, moving to new residences, and taking time off from work to acquire records. Sometimes a low-income taxpayer does not provide enough information to convince the IRS that relief is justified. Later, after finding legal assistance, when they may be in a better position to present the information necessary to establish the facts and circumstances necessary for relief, the regulation prevents them from filing a second claim.
>
> But a second important reason exists for allowing additional claims for equitable relief. . . . [S]everal of the Rev. Proc. 2003-61 factors — economic hardship, illness, and abuse — may occur several years after a return is filed. If the facts and circumstances establish that it is inequitable to hold the taxpayer liable, the taxpayer should be granted equitable relief regardless of whether the taxpayer filed a previous claim. Collecting a joint liability from a taxpayer when the factors establish that it would be inequitable to do so falls squarely within the language of the statute and the legislative intent. The legislative goal was to relieve taxpayers if it was inequitable to hold them liable, not create barriers to relief.

Robert Nadler, *Equitable Relief: Time to Level the Playing Field*, 113 TAX NOTES 899, 904 (2006).[8]

§ 17.03 INJURED SPOUSE RELIEF

When a jointly filed return reflects an overpayment, the IRS normally issues a single refund check made payable to both spouses. *See* F.S.A. 200144030, *available at* 2001 TNT 214-20 (Nov. 5, 2001). However, the IRS is authorized to apply the overpayment against outstanding liabilities and other obligations owed by one or both of the spouses. See I.R.C. § 6402. A spouse is considered an "injured spouse" (as opposed to an innocent spouse) when an overpayment, instead of being refunded, is applied against the other spouse's past-due child support obligation; past-due federal or state tax liability; or federal nontax debt, such as an outstanding student loan. Rev. Rul. 80-7, 1980-1 C.B. 296; Rev. Rul. 74-611, 1974-2 C.B. 399. Injured spouse relief allows the spouse to claim his or her share of the refund.

To qualify for relief as an injured spouse, the requesting spouse must establish the following four conditions: (1) The requesting spouse filed a joint federal income tax return; (2) that spouse reported income, such as wages, on the joint return; (3) that spouse made and reported payments, such as federal income tax withheld from wages or estimated tax payments, *or* claimed the earned income tax credit or other refundable credit on the return; and (4) an overpayment was applied or is expected to be applied against the past due amount of the other spouse. *See* Internal Revenue Service,

---

Innocent Vs. Injured Spouse — Very Different Relief, 84 TAX NOTES 793, 793 (1999); IRS Publication 504, *Divorced or Separated Individuals* 3–4 (2007). The requesting spouse does not need to meet the second element if the spouse's permanent residence is in a community property state. IRS Publication 504, at 3–4.

The requesting spouse is not required to pay the past-due amount in order to qualify for relief. A spouse seeking injured spouse relief should file IRS Form 8379, Injured Spouse Allocation. Form 8379 may be attached to the federal income tax return to which it relates or it may be mailed in separately at a later date. Form 8379 must be filed when the requesting spouse becomes aware of the fact that an overpayment has or will be applied against the other spouse's past-due obligations. Form 8379 must be filed for each year for which a requesting spouse wishes to obtain injured spouse relief.

PROBLEMS

1. Ned and Stacey were married for three years. Last week, two years after their divorce, Stacey received a notice of deficiency with respect to a joint return Ned and Stacey filed for the last year of their marriage. The notice asserts a deficiency of $20,000 based on expenses from Ned's business that the couple deducted on the return. Stacey had reviewed and signed the return without any pressure from Ned. She has since remarried.
   A. Can the IRS pursue Stacey for the deficiency? Does it matter whether the IRS pursues Ned as well?
   B. If the IRS does pursue Stacey, would it be timely for her to make a claim for innocent spouse relief? If so, how would she go about doing so?
   C. Assume that Stacey makes a timely claim for innocent spouse relief under section 6015(b) on Form 8857. Will Ned be notified of her claim? If so, if he believes that she is ineligible for relief because she knew about the business deductions, what ability will Ned have to share that information with the IRS and, if necessary, the Tax Court?
2. What are the three ways that the Tax Court can obtain jurisdiction over an innocent spouse claim?
3. Sid, a financial consultant with a large firm, has been married for five years to Jeanne. Jeanne has a two-year Associates degree in bookkeeping from a local junior college. The couple has two young children, and Jeanne stays home with them. Sid is highly successful, but he is known for his violent temper.

   During Year 1, Sid received several fees, amounting to $50,000, "under the table." As in each year of their marriage, Sid prepared the couple's joint return. The Year 1 return reported $220,000 of gross income attributable to Sid's salary plus $5,000 of interest and dividend income. Thus, the return reported $225,000 of gross income. On April 15, Year 2, Sid handed Jeanne the return and told her that she had better sign it right away so he could send it in to the IRS on time. She questioned him about what was on the return, but he yelled at her to hurry up and sign it or she would be very sorry. Jeanne feared Sid's temper because of previous occasions during which he had assaulted and injured her, so she signed the return without asking any more questions. Sid mailed the return in from the U.S. Post Office later that day. A week later, Sid gave Jeanne a diamond bracelet and apologized to her for his behavior.

   The IRS recently sent the couple a notice of deficiency based on unreported income. Assume that the notice is timely. The deficiency amount is $30,000, which includes penalties. Sid and Jeanne divorced in Year 3, and Sid fled the country. The IRS is thus seeking to collect the entire $30,000 from Jeanne. How might she defend against payment of the $30,000 deficiency? Will she likely be successful?

4. Which subsection of section 6015 — (b), (c), or (f) — has the knowledge standard that is easiest for an innocent spouse to meet?
5. Carrie and John are legally separated. The IRS sent them a notice of deficiency in the amount of $12,000 with respect to a joint return they filed for a previous year. The notice of deficiency reflects two items, a disallowed business deduction of $30,000 attributable to Carrie and a disallowed charitable contribution of $10,000 attributable to John. Neither of them knew that the other's deduction was erroneous.
   A. Is Carrie eligible to make an election under section 6015(c)? Would she be eligible if she and John were not separated but instead were still happily married?
   B. Assuming that Carrie is eligible to make an election under section 6015(c) and she does so, whereas John does not, how much of the $12,000 deficiency will the IRS be entitled to collect from her and how much from John?
6. After reading the material in this chapter, does joint and several liability for amounts on joint returns seem justifiable? Do you think the innocent spouse provisions are appropriately tailored to providing exceptions from that liability?

Chapter 18
ETHICAL ISSUES IN TAX PRACTICE

§ 18.01 INTRODUCTION

Attorneys, certified public accountants, and enrolled agents may all practice before the IRS and the Tax Court.[1] Attorneys may also engage in other tax representation, such as litigating on behalf of clients in the district courts and Court of Federal Claims. Some ethical restrictions — such as the rules of Treasury Circular 230, which apply to practice before the IRS, and the tax penalty provisions in the Code — apply to all types of tax practitioners. Others, such as state ethical rules governing the professional conduct of attorneys, often patterned on the American Bar Association (ABA) Model Rules of Professional Conduct, apply only to attorneys. This chapter provides a discussion of selected ethical issues that arise in tax practice. The focus is on rules applicable to attorneys in private practice, although it draws on examples involving non-attorneys where appropriate.[2]

Over time, regulators have developed ethical restrictions that apply in various contexts, including tax advice given during tax planning; preparation of the client's return; and the tax controversy process. These contextual considerations, along with several conflict of interest issues that arise in tax practice, are discussed in more detail below. The chapter concludes with a discussion of how the Tax Court may discipline members of its bar.

§ 18.02 THE ROLE OF THE TAX PRACTITIONER IN PRESERVING TAX COMPLIANCE

Before contemplating any specific ethical considerations, consider the tax practitioner's role in the tax system. As discussed in Chapter 1, the latest estimate of the voluntary compliance rate in the United States is nearly 84 percent, meaning that approximately 84 percent of all federal income tax owed is timely and voluntarily paid. While this compliance rate is high compared to those of most other countries, the latest estimate of the annual income tax gap — the difference between what taxpayers owe in federal income taxes and the amount that taxpayers voluntarily pay on a timely basis — is $345 billion. *See* IR-2006-28 (Feb. 14, 2006).

What role do tax practitioners play in taxpayers' decisions to comply with the tax laws? Economic literature suggests that tax practitioners operate as rule enforcers and ambiguity exploiters. That is, most practitioners enforce clearly expressed rules, while some also exploit ambiguities in the law. In the role of a rule enforcer, a practitioner tends to serve a pro-compliance function. For example, a practitioner asked by client who has just won the lottery whether he or she needs to report the lottery winnings in gross income would likely advise the client to do so. If the taxpayer seems skeptical, most practitioners would counsel the client about both the clear law on this issue and the penalties associated with noncompliance. In most cases, this would convince the taxpayer that it is in the taxpayer's best interest to comply with his or her legal obligations.

---

[1] Attorneys may be admitted to practice before the Tax Court by filing a current certificate of good standing from a state bar along with the application form and the appropriate fee. By contrast, other applicants are required to pass a written examination and provide two letters of recommendation from persons admitted to practice before the Tax Court, in addition to completing the application and paying the appropriate fee. *See* Tax Ct. R. 200.

[2] Other practitioners are subject to generally applicable rules as well. For example, certified public accountants are subject to American Institute of Certified Public Accountants (AICPA) rules.

In cases in which the law is ambiguous or complex, and tax planning opportunities based on those ambiguities exist, some practitioners may take advantage of those opportunities by advising clients to take aggressive reporting positions. If so, the practitioner may be promoting noncompliance. How do we decide when the practitioner's advice is permissible or impermissible? Isn't minimizing the client's tax liability the practitioner's job? Does the practitioner, particularly an attorney, owe some duty to the "system" to ensure that his or her clients comply with the law? These issues are discussed below.

§ 18.03 TAX ADVICE AND RETURN PREPARATION

As any student of tax law knows, many tax questions do not lend themselves to precise answers. The facts underlying the client's transaction may be susceptible to more than one construction, the governing Code language may be unclear, or the applicable Treasury Regulations may reflect a dubious interpretation of the statute. If the attorney harbors doubt concerning an answer or interpretation, and believes that the IRS would ultimately prevail if the question were litigated, may the attorney nonetheless advise the client to take the doubtful position on a return? How much certainty must the practitioner possess before he or she may advise the client without violating the practitioner's professional obligations or running afoul of the applicable penalties in the Code?

[A] ABA Model Rules

As indicated above, attorneys are expected to follow state-level standards of professional conduct, most of which are based on ABA model rules. These standards are typically enforced by state licensing boards and state supreme courts. ABA Model Rule 1.2(d), for example, provides that "A lawyer shall not counsel a client to engage, or assist a client, in conduct that the lawyer knows is criminal or fraudulent, but a lawyer may discuss the legal consequences of any proposed course of conduct with a client and may counsel or assist a client to make a good faith effort to determine the validity, scope, meaning or application of the law." Model Rule 2.1 adds: "In representing a client, a lawyer shall exercise independent professional judgment and render candid advice. In rendering advice, a lawyer may refer not only to law but to other considerations such as moral, economic, social and political factors, that may be relevant to the client's situation."

These rules seem somewhat general, and thus not particularly helpful when applied to the tax context. The ABA's earliest effort to provide more specific advice to tax professionals relating to their ethical obligations in tax representation was ABA Formal Opinion 314, excerpted below.[3] Although subsequently revised, the opinion is important because of the way it characterizes the lawyer's relationship to the IRS.

ABA FORMAL OPINION 314

(1965)

In practice before the Internal Revenue Service, which is itself an adversary party rather than a judicial tribunal, the lawyer is under a duty not to mislead the Service, either by misstatement, silence, or through his client, but is under no duty to disclose the weaknesses of his client's case. He must be candid and fair, and his defense of his client must be exercised within the bounds of the law and without resort to any manner of fraud or chicane.

* * *

The Internal Revenue Service is neither a true tribunal, nor even a quasi-judicial

[3] ABA Opinions are not binding, but are considered a source of interpretive guidance.

institution. It has no machinery or procedure for adversary proceedings before impartial judges or arbiters, involving the weighing of conflicting testimony of witnesses examined and cross-examined by opposing counsel and the consideration of arguments of counsel for both sides of a dispute. While its procedures provide for "fresh looks" through department reviews and informal and formal conference procedures, few will contend that the service provides any truly dispassionate and unbiased consideration to the taxpayer. Although willing to listen to taxpayers and their representatives and obviously intending to be fair, the service is not designed and does not purport to be unprejudiced and unbiased in the judicial sense.

* * *

[W]hat is the duty of a lawyer in regard to disclosure of weaknesses in his client's case in the course of negotiations for the settlement of a tax case?

Negotiation and settlement procedures of the tax system do not carry with them the guarantee that a correct tax result necessarily occurs. The latter happens, if at all, solely by reason of chance in settlement of tax controversies just as it might happen with regard to other civil disputes. In the absence of either judicial determination or of a hypothetical exchange of files by adversaries, counsel will always urge in aid of settlement of a controversy the strong points of his case and minimize the weak; . . . Nor does the absolute duty not to make false assertions of fact require the disclosure of weaknesses in the client's case and in no event does it require the disclosure of his confidences, unless the facts in the attorney's possession indicate beyond a reasonable doubt that a crime will be committed. A wrong, or indeed sometimes an unjust, tax result in the settlement of a controversy is not a crime.

Similarly, a lawyer who is asked to advise his client in the course of the preparation of the client's tax returns may freely urge the statement of positions most favorable to the client just as long as there is a reasonable basis for those positions. Thus where the lawyer believes there is a reasonable basis for a position that a particular transaction does not result in taxable income, or that certain expenditures are properly deductible as expenses, the lawyer has no duty to advise that riders be attached to the client's tax return explaining the circumstances surrounding the transaction or the expenditures.

Do you agree with the ABA's characterization of the IRS as an adversary, even during the tax planning and return preparation stages? If so, which side — the IRS or the taxpayer — has the advantage?

Eventually, members of the tax bar became concerned that the "reasonable basis" standard in Formal Opinion 314 placed conscientious tax practitioners at a competitive disadvantage when compared to those willing to give more aggressive advice. In response, the ABA revised its formulation in 1985. The guidance relates specifically to tax preparation advice.

ABA FORMAL OPINION 85-352

(1985)

The Committee is informed that the standard of "reasonable basis" has been construed by many lawyers to support the use of any colorable claim on a tax return to justify exploitation of the lottery of the tax return audit selection process. This view is not universally held, and the Committee does not believe that the reasonable basis standard, properly interpreted and applied, permits this construction.

* * *

The ethical standards governing the conduct of a lawyer in advising a client on positions that can be taken in a tax return are not different from those governing a lawyer's conduct in advising or taking positions for a client in other civil matters.

Although the Model Rules distinguish between the roles of advisor and advocate, both roles are involved here, and the ethical standards applicable to them provide relevant guidance. In many cases, a lawyer must realistically anticipate that the filing of the tax return may be the first step in a process that may result in an adversary relationship between the client and the IRS. This normally occurs in situations when a lawyer advises an aggressive position on a tax return, not when the position taken is a safe or conservative one that is unlikely to be challenged by the IRS.

* * *

[A] lawyer, in representing a client in the course of the preparation of the client's tax return, may advise the statement of positions most favorable to the client if the lawyer has a good faith belief that those positions are warranted in existing law or can be supported by a good faith argument for an extension, modification or reversal of existing law. A lawyer can have a good faith belief in this context even if the lawyer believes the client's position probably will not prevail. However, good faith requires that there be some realistic possibility of success if the matter is litigated.

This formulation of the lawyer's duty in this situation addressed by this opinion is consistent with the basic duty of the lawyer to a client, recognized in ethical standards since the ABA Canons of Professional Ethics, and in the opinions of this Committee: zealously and loyally to represent the interests of the client within the bounds of the law.

Thus, where a lawyer has a good faith belief in the validity of a position in accordance with the standard stated above that a particular transaction does not result in taxable income or that certain expenditures are properly deductible as expenses, the lawyer has no duty to require as a condition of his or her continued representation that riders be attached to the client's tax return explaining the circumstances surrounding the transaction or the expenditures.

In the role of advisor, the lawyer should counsel the client as to whether the position is likely to be sustained by a court if challenged by the IRS, as well as of the potential penalty consequences to the client if the position is taken on the tax return without disclosure. . . . Competent representation of the client would require the lawyer to advise the client fully as to whether there is or was substantial authority for the position taken in the tax return. If the lawyer is unable to conclude that the position is supported by substantial authority, the lawyer should advise the client of the penalty the client may suffer and of the opportunity to avoid such penalty by adequately disclosing the facts in the return or in a statement attached to the return. If after receiving such advice the client decides to risk the penalty by making no disclosure and to take the position initially advised by the lawyer in accordance with the standard stated above, the lawyer has met his or her ethical responsibility with respect to the advice.

In percentage terms, how would you describe the "realistic possibility of success" standard adopted in Formal Opinion 85-352? Must the advisor believe that the taxpayer has a greater than 50-percent likelihood of success if the matter were litigated? Is a 50-50 chance of success sufficient?

Shortly after the ABA released Formal Opinion 85-352, an ABA Task Force issued a nonbinding report that attempted to quantify the level of doubt an attorney can hold about a reporting position and still recommend it to the client. According to the Task Force Report, a position having only a 5 percent or 10 percent likelihood of success, if litigated, should not meet the realistic possibility of success standard. As discussed below, a position having a likelihood of success closely approaching one-third should meet the standard. In determining whether a position meets the one-third standard, the likelihood of "concession in the bargaining process of settlement negotiations" may not be considered. ABA Special Task Force Report on Formal Opinion 85-352.[4] In applying the one-in-three standard, does the practitioner take into account the likelihood that the IRS will not audit the taxpayer's return? Why does the Task Force Report rule out the possibility of concessions on the part of the IRS when determining the likelihood of success? Given that most tax cases settle, would this not be a relevant consideration?

[B] Treasury Circular 230

[1] Background and Scope

Any person engaged in "practice before the IRS" is subject to the rules of Circular 230, which is promulgated by the Treasury Department under the authority of 31 U.S.C. section 330(a) and (b). The Circular 230 rules appear in Title 31 of the Code of Federal Regulations, Part 10. Circular 230 defines practice before the IRS as follows:

> *Practice before the Internal Revenue Service* comprehends all matters connected with a presentation to the Internal Revenue Service or any of its officers or employees relating to a taxpayer's rights, privileges, or liabilities under laws or regulations administered by the Internal Revenue Service. Such presentations include, but are not limited to, preparing and filing documents, corresponding and communicating with the Internal Revenue Service, rendering written advice with respect to any entity, transaction, plan or arrangement, or other plan or arrangement having a potential for tax avoidance or evasion, and representing a client at conferences, hearings, and meetings.

31 C.F.R. § 10.2(a)(4).

Any attorney or certified public accountant (CPA) who is not currently under suspension or disbarment from practice before the Internal Revenue Service may practice before the IRS upon filing with the IRS a written declaration that he or she is currently qualified as an attorney or CPA, as the case may be, and is authorized to represent the particular party on whose behalf he or she acts. *Id.* § 10.3(a), (b). Another category of practitioners, called enrolled agents, may also practice before the IRS. Enrolled agents are individuals who have been certified by the IRS after passing an examination or based on prior IRS service. *Id.* § 10.3(c). An individual who is enrolled in the Joint Board for the Enrollment of Actuaries may also practice before the IRS upon filing with the IRS a written declaration that he or she is currently qualified as an enrolled actuary and is authorized to represent the particular party on whose behalf he or she acts. Practice as an enrolled actuary is limited to representation with respect to issues involving certain statutory provisions. *Id.* § 10.3(d).

A practitioner subject to Circular 230 may be sanctioned for "incompetence and disreputable conduct." *Id.* § 10.51. This type of conduct includes (1) conviction of a criminal tax offense, *id.* § 10.51(a)(1); (2) giving false or misleading information to the IRS, *id.* § 10.51(a)(4); (3) willfully failing to file a federal tax return, *id.* § 10.51(a)(6); (4) assisting a client in violating the federal tax laws, *id.* § 10.51(a)(7); and (5) "giving a false opinion, knowingly, recklessly, or through gross incompetence, including an opinion which is intentionally or recklessly misleading, or engaging in a pattern of providing incompetent opinions on questions arising under the Federal tax laws," *id.* § 10.51(a)(13). A practitioner may also be sanctioned for willfully violating any of the Circular 230 regulations, as well as recklessly (or through gross incompetence) violating

---

[4] For a time, the one-in-three standard was consistent with the general reporting standard set forth in Circular 230, discussed below, and the standard for the return preparer penalty in section 6694, discussed in Chapter 12, as well as below. The Circular 230 and return preparer standards recently changed, but the ABA has shown no interest, thus far, in altering the one-in-three standard outside the context of tax shelter opinions.

standards in sections 10.34 (relating to return reporting positions), 10.35 (relating to opinion letters), or 10.37 (relating to other written advice), all of which are discussed later in the chapter.

Available sanctions against practitioners who violate the duties or prohibitions in Circular 230 include censure, as well as suspension and disbarment from practice before the IRS. *Id.* § 10.50(a). Congress has also authorized the Treasury to impose monetary penalties against a tax practitioner (and the practitioner's employer or firm) for violations of Circular 230. *See id.* § 10.50(c). The maximum monetary penalty is the "gross income derived or (to be derived) from the conduct giving rise to the penalty." *Id.* § 10.50(c)(2).

Subpart D of Circular 230 sets out the disciplinary procedures for violations. Enforcement authority rests with the Director of the Office of Professional Responsibility (OPR). The OPR Director may reprimand or institute a proceeding for sanction of any practitioner that the Director has reason to believe violated regulations governing practice before the IRS. *Id.* § 10.60. The OPR Director institutes the proceeding by filing a complaint with the OPR. *Id.* Before filing a complaint, the facts or conduct are brought to the attention of the practitioner in a written allegation letter. Except in limited cases, the practitioner is afforded an opportunity to demonstrate or achieve compliance with all lawful requirements. *Id.* If the OPR Director determines that no violation occurred, the Director dismisses the case. Special, expedited, disciplinary procedures exist for situations in which a practitioner has lost his or her license to practice as an attorney or CPA; has his or her license suspended or revoked for cause; or has been convicted of any crime under Title 26 of the United States Code or of a felony under Title 18 of the United States Code involving dishonesty or breach of trust. *See id.* § 10.82.

The complaint filed by the OPR Director provides a description of the allegations constituting the basis for the proceeding. *Id.* § 10.62(a). The complaint notifies the practitioner of the nature of the charges, the sanction being sought, the time within which to file an answer, and that a decision by default may be entered if the practitioner fails to file an answer as required. The deadline set for filing the answer must be at least 30 days from the date of service of the complaint. *Id.* § 10.62(b), (c). The answer must contain a statement of facts constituting the grounds of defense, and it must specifically admit or deny each allegation set forth in the complaint. The answer may also include affirmative defenses. *Id.* § 10.64. The OPR Director has discretion whether to file a reply. *Id.* § 10.66.

An Administrative Law Judge presides over the sanction hearings. *Id.* § 10.72(a). Except in cases in which the practitioner has failed to answer the complaint or where a party has failed to appear at the hearing, the Administrative Law Judge provides the parties, prior to making a decision, with a reasonable opportunity to submit proposed findings and conclusions. *Id.* § 10.75. After the Administrative Law Judge renders his or her decision, either party may appeal the decision to the Secretary of the Treasury within 30 days from the date of the decision. *Id.* § 10.77. The Secretary of the Treasury makes the final decision. *Id.* § 10.78.

If the final order against the practitioner is for suspension, the practitioner is not permitted to practice before the IRS during the suspension period. *Id.* § 10.79(b). If the final order is for disbarment, the practitioner is not permitted to practice before the IRS unless and until authorized to do so by the OPR Director. *Id.* § 10.79(a). Once five years elapse following the disbarment, the OPR Director can entertain a petition for reinstatement. The OPR Director cannot grant reinstatement to practice unless the Director is satisfied that the practitioner is not likely to conduct himself or herself in a manner contrary to the regulations in Circular 230, and that reinstatement would not be contrary to the public interest. *Id.* § 10.81. Details regarding monetary penalties for violations of Circular 230 are in 2007-20 I.R.B. 1243, Notice 2007-39.

[2] Advising Tax Positions and Preparing Returns

Circular 230 has its own set of standards for advising clients and preparing returns and documents submitted to the IRS; these standards appear in section 10.34. Before the Treasury proposed amendments to this section late in 2007, the general standard was as follows:

> (a) *Realistic possibility standard.* A practitioner may not sign a tax return as a preparer if the practitioner determines that the tax return contains a position that does not have a realistic possibility of being sustained on its merits (the realistic possibility standard) unless the position is not frivolous and is adequately disclosed to the Internal Revenue Service. A practitioner may not advise a client to take a position on a tax return, or prepare the portion of a tax return on which a position is taken, unless —
>
> (1) The practitioner determines that the position satisfies the realistic possibility standard; or
>
> (2) The position is not frivolous and the practitioner advises the client of any opportunity to avoid the accuracy-related penalty in section 6662 of the Internal Revenue Code [of 1986] by adequately disclosing the position and of the requirements for adequate disclosure." * * *
>
> (d) *Definitions* — For purposes of this section —
>
> (1) *Realistic possibility.* A position is considered to have a realistic possibility of being sustained on its merits if a reasonable and well informed analysis of the law and the facts by a person knowledgeable in the tax law would lead such a person to conclude that the position has approximately a one in three, or greater, likelihood of being sustained on its merits. The authorities described in 26 C.F.R. 1.6662-4(d)(3)(iii),[5] or any successor provision, of the substantial understatement penalty regulations may be taken into account for purposes of this analysis. The possibility that a tax return will not be audited, that an issue will not be raised on audit, or that an issue will be settled may not be taken into account.
>
> (2) *Frivolous.* A position is frivolous if it is patently improper.

How does this standard compare with the standard in ABA Formal Opinion 85-352?

In September of 2007, the Treasury proposed revisions to section 10.34 in response to amendments Congress enacted to the return preparer penalty in section 6694, discussed below. The proposed version of section 10.34 is slightly more specific and contains a higher reporting standard:

> (a) *Tax Returns* — A practitioner may not sign a tax return as a preparer unless the practitioner has a reasonable belief that the tax treatment of each position on the return would more likely than not be sustained on its merits (the more likely than not standard), or there is a reasonable basis for each position and each position is adequately disclosed to the Internal Revenue Service. A practitioner may not advise a client to take a position on a tax return, or prepare the portion of a tax return on which a position is taken, unless —
>
> (1) The practitioner has a reasonable belief that the position satisfies the more likely than not standard; or
>
> (2) The position has a reasonable basis and is adequately disclosed to the Internal Revenue Service.

* * *

[5] [The substantial authority standard applicable to the substantial understatement portion of the accuracy-related penalty in section 6662 is discussed in Chapter 12 and, in part, below. — Eds.]

(d) *Relying on information furnished by clients* — A practitioner advising a client to take a position on a tax return, document, affidavit or other paper submitted to the Internal Revenue Service, or preparing or signing a tax return as a preparer, generally may rely in good faith without verification upon information furnished by the client. The practitioner may not, however, ignore the implications of information furnished to, or actually known by, the practitioner, and must make reasonable inquiries if the information as furnished appears to be incorrect, inconsistent with an important fact or another factual assumption, or incomplete.

(e) *Definitions* — For purposes of this section —

(1) *More likely than not* — A practitioner is considered to have a reasonable belief that the tax treatment of a position is more likely than not the proper tax treatment if the practitioner analyzes the pertinent facts and authorities, and based on that analysis reasonably concludes, in good faith, that there is a greater than fifty-percent likelihood that the tax treatment will be upheld if the IRS challenges it. The authorities described in 26 CFR 1.6662-4(d)(3)(iii), or any successor provision, of the substantial understatement penalty regulations may be taken into account for purposes of this analysis.

(2) *Reasonable basis* — A position is considered to have a reasonable basis if it is reasonably based on one or more of the authorities described in 26 CFR 1.6662-4(d)(3)(iii), or any successor provision, of the substantial understatement penalty regulations. Reasonable basis is a relatively high standard of tax reporting, that is, significantly higher than not frivolous or not patently improper. The reasonable basis standard is not satisfied by a return position that is merely arguable or that is merely a colorable claim. The possibility that a tax return will not be audited, that an issue will not be raised on audit, or that an issue will be settled may not be taken into account.

(3) *Frivolous* — A position is frivolous if it is patently improper.

Why is Treasury willing to accept a lower standard of conduct ("reasonable basis" rather than "more likely than not") if the taxpayer adequately discloses the position? The more-likely-than-not standard is relatively easy to describe in percentage terms. What about the reasonable basis standard — based on the definition in section 10.34(e)(2), what percentage likelihood of success must the taxpayer have in order to satisfy this standard? Is it higher or lower than the realistic possibility of success standard?

[C] Return Preparer Penalties

Reading Assignment: I.R.C. §§ 6694(a)–(b), 7701(a)(36); skim Section 12.03 of Chapter 12.

Another limitation on the tax practitioner's conduct is the tax return preparer penalty in section 6694. As explained in greater detail in Chapter 12, violations of the section 6694 penalty standards give rise to a monetary penalty (the greater of $1,000 or 50% of the income to be derived from the subject transaction). Prior to its amendment in 2007, the threshold for advising undisclosed reporting positions was the "realistic possibility" standard, defined as follows:

> A position is considered to have a realistic possibility of being sustained on the merits if a reasonable and well-informed analysis by a person knowledgeable in the tax law would lead such a person to conclude that the position has approximately a one in three, or greater, likelihood of being sustained on its merits (realistic possibility standard). In making this determination, the possibility that the position will not be challenged by the Internal Revenue Service

(*e.g.*, because the taxpayer's return may not be audited or because the issue may not be raised on audit) is not to be taken into account.

Treas. Reg. § 1.6694-2(b)(1) (superseded by proposed regulations issued in 2008).

In 2007, Congress amended section 6694 to expand its scope (an issue discussed in Section 12.03 of Chapter 12) and to increase the expected reporting standard. For *undisclosed* positions, section 6694(a) replaced the realistic possibility of success standard with a requirement that the preparer reasonable believe that the tax treatment of the position would "more likely than not be sustained on its merits." For *disclosed* positions, section 6694(a) replaced the "not frivolous" standard with the requirement that the preparer have a "reasonable basis" for the tax treatment of the position. Thus, under the revised version of section 6694, a return preparer may be subject to a section 6694(a) penalty under the following circumstances:

Undisclosed Positions: If the position that creates the tax understatement is not disclosed, the preparer knew, or reasonably should have known of the position, and the preparer did not reasonably believe that the position would *more likely than not* be sustained on its merits.

Disclosed Positions: If the position that creates the tax understatement is disclosed, the preparer knew, or reasonably should have known of the position, and there was *no reasonable basis* for the position.

The more-likely-than-not standard applied to undisclosed positions is fairly easy to quantify in percentage terms; it means greater than 50 percent. *See* Prop. Reg. § 1.6694-2(b)(1). As noted in Chapter 12, determining whether a greater than 50-percent likelihood of success exists is made based on the regulations in section 6662 relating to the substantial understatement penalty. According to these regulations, the practitioner must consider both the surrounding law and the application of that law to the relevant facts. *See* Treas. Reg. § 1.6662-4(d)(2). The possibility that the return will not be audited is not taken into account. *Id.* Assume, for instance, that the return position at issue is the subject of a circuit split. If the taxpayer's case would not be appealable to any of the appellate courts that had already ruled on the issue, would it be possible for the return preparer to satisfy the more-likely-than-not standard? How does the more-likely-than-not standard relate to the "preponderance of the evidence" standard that typically applies to the burden of persuasion in civil tax cases?

The increased reporting standard has given rise to other questions. If the practitioner insists that the client disclose the return position, is the practitioner effectively conceding that the position does not satisfy the more-likely-than-not standard? How will the standard apply to valuation issues, given that courts often appear to "split the difference" between the taxpayer's claimed valuation and the IRS's valuation? Note also that section 6694 contains its own "reasonable cause" exception. I.R.C. § 6694(a)(3). Does this dilute the more-likely-than-not standard?

The more-likely-than-not standard is higher than the reporting standard in ABA Formal Opinion 85-352, which still applies the realistic possibility of success standard. What does it say about the legal profession when it sets a standard of professional conduct lower than the standard that could lead to a monetary penalty? Does this mean that the ethical standard is meaningless? The answer is no because the penalty in section 6694 applies only to a "tax return preparer." The Code defines a tax return preparer as any person who, for compensation, prepares or employs another to prepare all or a substantial portion of any return or claim for refund. I.R.C. § 7701(a)(36)(A). Regulations create an exception for some pre-transactional tax planning advice. According to proposed regulations, a person who does not sign the return but who gives advice on a specific issue of law is considered a tax return preparer only if the advice is given with respect to events that have occurred at the time the advice is rendered *and* the advice is directly relevant to the determination of the existence, characterization, or amount of an entry on a return or claim for refund. Prop. Reg. § 301.7701-15(b)(2), (3). If the planning advice relates to a proposed transaction, can the practitioner be subject to a return preparer penalty if the advice fails to meet the more-likely-than-not standard? What if the recipient of the advice consummates the transaction — would that cause the practitioner to be treated as a return preparer?

[D] Taxpayer Penalties

Reading Assignment: Skim Section 12.02[C][1]–[2] of Chapter 12.

Although the taxpayer-related penalties in the Code, such as the negligence and substantial understatement prongs of the accuracy-related penalty in section 6662, do not apply to tax practitioners in their capacity as such, the penalties do affect the type of advice a practitioner should be willing to give the client. If the practitioner intends to advise a reporting position that could lead to a taxpayer penalty, the practitioner should at least advise the client of that potential. Another connection between the taxpayer penalties and the practitioner's conduct relates to the reasonable cause defense in section 6664, which applies to many of the taxpayer penalties. Reliance on the advice of a professional may allow the taxpayer to avoid the penalty. See Section 12.02[C] of Chapter 12, which discusses this issue in detail.

Section 12.03 of that chapter highlights some potential conflicts of interest that may result from the fact that the penalty standards that apply at the taxpayer level differ from those that apply to the preparer. As explained in that section, the differing standards, particularly when it comes to disclosing the return position, could place the preparer in the position of urging the taxpayer to disclose the position in order to protect the preparer from a section 6694 penalty, even though the taxpayer would not risk a penalty if the position remained undisclosed.

The differing standards also raise other ethical considerations. For instance, if the return preparer insists on disclosure even though the taxpayer does not otherwise risk incurring a penalty, does the return preparer violate his or her ethical duties to the client given that disclosure will likely make the chances of IRS audit higher than they otherwise would have been? What if, in an effort to protect against a penalty, the return preparer attaches a disclosure statement to the taxpayer's return without the taxpayer's knowledge or consent — does this violate the preparer's duty of loyalty to the client?

§ 18.04 TAX SHELTER TRANSACTIONS AND TAX OPINION LETTERS

Reading Assignment: Skim Section 12.04 of Chapter 12.

The tax practitioner's role changes slightly when he or she is called upon by the client to issue a written opinion letter, particularly when the transaction involves an aggressive reporting position. Both the ABA and the Treasury (in Circular 230), have issued guidance that applies to a practitioner's obligations relating to tax shelter and other aggressive transactions.[6] These two sources of guidance are discussed below.

[A] ABA Standards

ABA Revised Formal Opinion 346, set out below, contains important guidance for the tax practitioner who renders an opinion letter relating to a tax shelter transaction. The ABA singled out tax shelter opinions for specialized guidance for a number of

[6] Congress has sought to regulate practitioner conduct relating to tax shelters through a series of mandatory disclosure rules, which are discussed in Section 12.04[A] of Chapter 12. As discussed in that section, the Code contains penalties for those practitioners who fail to comply with these rules. *See* I.R.C. §§ 6111, 6112.

reasons. At the time Formal Opinion 346 was drafted, abusive tax shelter investments were becoming an increasing concern for the government, as taxpayers sought to reap tax benefits (credits, losses, and deductions) from investments that were based on highly questionable factual assumptions and legal interpretations. Some of the blame for the proliferation of these abusive transactions was directed at the tax bar. Tax shelter promoters typically solicited opinion letters from tax attorneys, and then used the letters to market their investments to taxpayers who, often without reading the opinion letter in detail, viewed the attorney's opinion as a stamp of approval. In many cases, however, the tax shelter opinion contained inaccurate or hypothetical factual assumptions, or the opinion failed to draw any conclusion as to whether the expected tax benefits would be upheld if challenged by the IRS. Formal Opinion 346 sought to rectify some of these deficiencies.

FORMAL OPINION 346 (REVISED)*

(Jan. 29, 1982)

TAX LAW OPINIONS IN TAX SHELTER INVESTMENT OFFERINGS

An opinion by a lawyer analyzing the tax effects of a tax shelter investment is frequently of substantial importance in a tax shelter offering.[n.1] The promoter of the offering may depend upon the recommendations of the lawyer in structuring the venture and often publishes the opinion with the offering materials or uses the lawyer's name in connection with sales promotion efforts. The offerees may be expected to rely upon the tax shelter opinion in determining whether to invest in the venture. It is often uneconomic for the individual offeree to pay for a separate tax analysis of the offering because of the relatively small sum each offeree may invest.

Because the successful marketing of tax shelters frequently involves tax opinions issued by lawyers, concerns have been expressed by the organized bar, regulatory agencies and others over the need to articulate ethical standards applicable to a lawyer who issues an opinion which the lawyer knows will be included among the tax shelter offering materials and relied upon by offerees.

* * *

A "tax shelter opinion," as the term is used in this Opinion, is advice by a lawyer concerning the federal tax law applicable to a tax shelter if the advice is referred to either in offering materials or in connection with sales promotion efforts directed to persons other than the client who engages the lawyer to give the advice. The term includes the tax aspects or tax risks portion of the offering materials prepared by the lawyer whether or not a separate opinion letter is issued. The term does not, however, include rendering advice solely to the offeror or reviewing parts of the offering materials, so long as neither the name of the lawyer nor the fact that a lawyer has rendered advice concerning the tax aspects is referred to at all in the offering materials or in connection with sales promotion efforts. In this case the lawyer has the ethical

---

* This Opinion supersedes Formal Opinion 346 (June 1, 1981), which is withdrawn.

[n.1] A "tax shelter," as the term is used in this Opinion, is an investment which has as a significant feature for federal income or excise tax purposes either or both of the following attributes: (1) deductions in excess of income from the investment being available in any year to reduce income from other sources in that year, and (2) credits in excess of the tax attributable to the income from the investment being available in any year to offset taxes on income from other sources in that year. Excluded from the term are investments such as, but not limited to, the following: municipal bonds; annuities; family trusts; qualified retirement plans; individual retirement accounts; stock option plans; securities issued in a corporate reorganization; mineral development ventures, if the only tax benefit would be percentage depletion; and real estate where it is anticipated that deductions are unlikely to exceed gross income from the investment in any year, and that any tax credits are unlikely to exceed the tax on the income from that source in any year.

responsibility of assuring that in the offering materials and in connection with sales promotion efforts there is no reference to the lawyer's name or to the fact that a lawyer has rendered tax advice. The term also does not include the case where a small group of investors negotiate the terms of the arrangement directly with the offeror of securities and depend for tax advice concerning the investment entirely upon advisors other than the lawyer engaged to represent the offeror.

Disciplinary Standards

A false opinion is one which ignores or minimizes serious legal risks or misstates the facts or the law, knowingly or through gross incompetence. The lawyer who gives a false opinion, including one which is intentionally or recklessly misleading, violates the Disciplinary Rules of the Model Code of Professional Responsibility. Quite clearly, the lawyer exceeds the duty to represent the client zealously within the bounds of the law. *See* DR 7101; EC 710. Knowingly misstating facts or law violates DR 7102(A)(5) and is "conduct involving dishonesty, fraud, deceit, or misrepresentation," a violation of DR 1102(A)(4). The lawyer also violates DR 7102(A)(7) by counseling or assisting the offeror "in conduct that the lawyer knows to be illegal or fraudulent." In addition, the lawyer's conduct may involve the concealment or knowing nondisclosure of matters which the lawyer is required by law to reveal, a violation of DR 7102(A)(3).

The lawyer who accepts as true the facts which the promoter tells him, when the lawyer should know that a further inquiry would disclose that these facts are untrue, also gives a false opinion. It has been said that lawyers cannot "escape criminal liability on a plea of ignorance when they have shut their eyes to what was plainly to be seen." United States v. Benjamin, 328 F.2d 854, 863 (2d Cir. 1964). Recklessly and consciously disregarding information strongly indicating that material facts expressed in the tax shelter opinion are false or misleading involves dishonesty as does assisting the offeror in conduct the lawyer knows to be fraudulent. Such conduct violates DR 1102(A)(4) and DR 7102(A). * * *

* * *

Ethical Considerations

Beyond the requirements of the Disciplinary Rules, the lawyer who issues a tax shelter opinion should follow the Canons and the Ethical Considerations of the Model Code.[n.3] Although not constituting absolute requirements, the violation of which may result in sanctions, these Canons and Ethical Considerations constitute a body of principles which provide guidance in the application of the lawyer's professional responsibility to specific situations, such as the rendering of tax shelter opinions. The guidelines developed here are to be applied to each specific situation reasonably and in a practical fashion.

EC 722 says "a litigant or his lawyer may, in good faith and within the framework of the law, take steps to test the correctness of a ruling of a tribunal." *See also* EC 725. Principles similar to these are applied where the lawyer represents a client in adversarial proceedings before the Internal Revenue Service. In that case the lawyer has duties not to mislead the Service by any misstatement, not to further any misrepresentations made by the client, and to deal candidly and fairly. ABA Formal Opinion 314 (1965); * * *.

[n.3] Canon 1 says "[a] lawyer should assist in maintaining the integrity and competence of the legal profession." Canon 6 says "[a] lawyer should represent a client competently." The Ethical Considerations used to establish the guidelines in this Opinion are EC 15, EC61, EC64, EC65, EC71, EC73, EC75, EC76, EC78, EC710, EC722, EC725. *See also* Model Rules of Professional Conduct (ABA Commission on Evaluation of Professional Standards, Proposed Final Draft, May 30, 1981), Rule 2.3 at 116.

The lawyer rendering a tax shelter opinion which he knows will be relied upon by third persons, however, functions more as an advisor than as an advocate. *See* EC 73, distinguishing these roles. Since the Model Code was adopted in 1969, the differing functions of the advisor and advocate have become more widely recognized.

As advisor, a lawyer provides a client with an informed understanding of the client's legal rights and obligations and explains their practical implications. As advocate, a lawyer asserts the client's position under the rules of the adversary system.

The Proposed Model Rules specifically recognize the ethical considerations applicable where a lawyer undertakes an evaluation for the use of third persons other than a client. These third persons have an interest in the integrity of the evaluation. The legal duty of the lawyer therefore "goes beyond the obligations a lawyer normally has to third persons." Proposed Model Rules, *supra* note 3 at 117; *see also* ABA Formal Opinion 335 (1974). Because third persons may rely on the advice of the lawyer who gives a tax shelter opinion, principles announced in ABA Formal Opinion 314 have little, if any, applicability.

* * *

Making Factual Inquiry

ABA Formal Opinion 335 (1974) establishes guidelines which a lawyer should follow when furnishing an assumed facts opinion in connection with the sale of unregistered securities. The same guidelines describe the extent to which a lawyer should verify the facts presented to him as the basis for a tax shelter opinion:

> [T]he lawyer should, in the first instance, make inquiry of his client as to the relevant facts and receive answers. If any of the alleged facts, or the alleged facts taken as a whole, are incomplete in a material respect; or are suspect; or are inconsistent; or either on their face or on the basis of other known facts are open to question, the lawyer should make further inquiry. The extent of this inquiry will depend in each case upon the circumstances; for example, it would be less where the lawyer's past relationship with the client is sufficient to give him a basis for trusting the client's probity than where the client has recently engaged the lawyer, and less where the lawyer's inquiries are answered fully than when there appears a reluctance to disclose information.
>
> Where the lawyer concludes that further inquiry of a reasonable nature would not give him sufficient confidence as to all the relevant facts, or for any other reason he does not make the appropriate further inquiries, he should refuse to give an opinion. However, assuming that the alleged facts are not incomplete in a material respect, or suspect, or in any way inherently inconsistent, or on their face or on the basis of other known facts open to question, the lawyer may properly assume that the facts as related to him by his client, and checked by him by reviewing such appropriate documents as are available, are accurate.
>
> The essence of this opinion * * * is that, while a lawyer should make adequate preparation including inquiry into the relevant facts that is consistent with the above guidelines, and while he should not accept as true that which he should not reasonably believe to be true, he does not have the responsibility to "audit" the affairs of his client or to assume, without reasonable cause, that a client's statement of the facts cannot be relied upon. ABA Formal Opinion 335 at 3, 5–6.

For instance, where essential underlying information, such as an appraisal or financial projection, makes little common sense, or where the reputation or expertise of the person who has prepared the appraisal or projection is dubious, further inquiry clearly is required. Indeed, failure to make further inquiry may result in a false opinion. See *supra*, Disciplinary Standards. If further inquiry reveals that the appraisal or projection is reasonably well supported and complete, the lawyer is justified in relying upon the material facts which the underlying information supports.

Relating Law to Facts

In discussing the legal issues in a tax shelter opinion, the lawyer should relate the law to the actual facts to the extent the facts are ascertainable when the offering materials are being circulated. A lawyer should not issue a tax shelter opinion which disclaims responsibility for inquiring as to the accuracy of the facts, fails to analyze the critical facts, or discusses purely hypothetical facts. It is proper, however, to assume facts which are not currently ascertainable, such as the method of conducting future operations of the venture, so long as the factual assumptions are clearly identified as such in the offering materials, and are reasonable and complete.

* * *

Opinion as to Outcome — Material Tax Issues

Since the term "opinion" connotes a lawyer's conclusion as to the likely outcome of an issue if challenged and litigated, the lawyer should, if possible, state the lawyer's opinion of the probable outcome on the merits of each material tax issue. However, if the lawyer determines in good faith that it is not possible to make a judgment as to the outcome of a material tax issue, the lawyer should so state and give the reasons for this conclusion.

A tax shelter opinion may question the validity of a Revenue Ruling or the reasoning in a lower court opinion which the lawyer believes is wrong. But there must also be a complete explanation to the offerees, including what position the Service is likely to take on the issue and a summary of why this position is considered to be wrong. The opinion also should set forth the risks of an adversarial proceeding if one is likely to occur.

Overall Evaluation of Realization of Tax Benefits

The clear disclosure of the tax risks in the offering materials should include an opinion by the lawyer or by another professional providing an overall evaluation of the extent to which the tax benefits, in the aggregate, which are a significant feature of the investment to the typical investor are likely to be realized as contemplated by the offering materials. In making this evaluation, the lawyer should state that the significant tax benefits, in the aggregate, probably will be realized or probably will not be realized, or that the probabilities of realization and nonrealization of the significant tax benefits are evenly divided.

In rare instances the lawyer may conclude in good faith that it is not possible to make a judgment of the extent to which the significant tax benefits are likely to be realized. This impossibility may occur where, for example, the most significant tax benefits are predicated upon a newly enacted Code provision when there are no regulations and the legislative history is obscure. In these circumstances, the lawyer should fully explain why the judgment cannot be made and assure full disclosure in the offering materials of the assumptions and risks which the investors must evaluate.

The Committee does not accept the view that it is always ethically improper to issue an opinion which concludes that the significant tax benefits in the aggregate probably will not be realized. However, full disclosure requires that the negative conclusion be clearly stated and prominently noted in the offering materials.

* * *

Formal Opinion 346 states that an attorney's role changes from advocate to advisor when the attorney issues an opinion letter that will be relied upon by third parties. Why is that?

According to Formal Opinion 346, the attorney giving tax shelter advice that may be used by third parties should state in the opinion whether the tax benefits "probably will be realized or probably will not be realized." How would you describe this in percentage terms? How does that level of certainty compare with the general standard in Formal Opinion 85-352, which is excerpted in Section 18.03[A]? Also, is it permissible for an attorney to issue a tax shelter opinion that does not come to a conclusion about whether the tax benefits will or will not be realized? What about one that concludes that the tax benefits will *not* be realized? What use would such an opinion be to the client?

[B] Circular 230 Regulations Relating to Written Advice

Formal Opinion 346 responds primarily to the sorts of tax shelter transactions marketed to individual taxpayers in the 1970s and 1980s. As explained in Section 12.04[A] of Chapter 12, during the late 1990s, a new, more aggressive, form of tax shelter transactions was developed by unscrupulous attorneys and accountants. These new shelters were marketed not only to individuals, but also to corporations and other business entities. Many of these transactions were designed to generate losses and deductions through schemes that had no economic significance beyond the generation of tax benefits.

At the time, Treasury Circular 230 contained regulations that applied specifically to tax shelter opinion letters. Beginning in 2001, the Treasury began proposing new versions of those regulations. Each time, however, practitioners complained that the Treasury's definition of a "tax shelter" was too broad or was unworkable. Finally, in 2005, the Treasury issued the regulations that now appear in section 10.35. Instead of tailoring the regulations specifically to tax shelter opinions, the regulations cover a category of written advice known as a "covered opinion."

A covered opinion is any written advice, including electronic communications, concerning a federal tax issue arising in several specified types of transactions. One category of covered opinions includes written advice relating to an entity or arrangement the "principal purpose" of which is the avoidance or evasion of federal tax. 31 C.F.R. § 10.35(b)(2)(i)(B). An arrangement does not have the principal purpose of avoiding or evading tax if the purpose is to claim tax benefits in a manner consistent with the Code or Congressional intent. *Id.* § 10.35(b)(10).

Written advice that expresses a conclusion that promised tax benefits will "more likely than not" be sustained (a "reliance opinion") and advice that the practitioner knows or has reason to know will be used by a person other than the practitioner to promote or recommend a plan or investment (a "marketed opinion") may fall within the category of a covered opinion if the advice relates to a transaction the "significant purpose" of which is tax avoidance. *Id.* § 10.35(b)(4), (5). An issue is significant if the IRS has a reasonable basis for challenging the issue and the resolution could have a significant impact on the tax treatment of the transaction. *Id.* § 10.35(b)(3).

Section 10.35 contains detailed requirements relating to the content of a covered opinion, both in terms of factual and legal analysis.

(1) *Factual matters*

(i) The practitioner must use reasonable efforts to identify and ascertain the facts, which may relate to future events if a transaction is prospective or proposed, and to determine which facts are relevant. The opinion must identify and consider all facts that the practitioner determines to be relevant.

(ii) The practitioner must not base the opinion on any unreasonable factual assumptions (including assumptions as to future events). An unreasonable factual assumption includes a factual assumption that the practitioner knows or should know is incorrect or incomplete. For example, it is unreasonable to assume that a transaction has a business purpose or that a transaction is potentially profitable apart from tax benefits. A factual assumption includes reliance on a projection, financial forecast or appraisal. It is unreasonable for a practitioner to rely on a projection, financial forecast or appraisal if the practitioner knows or should know that the projection, financial forecast or appraisal is incorrect or incomplete or was prepared by a person lacking the skills or qualifications necessary to prepare such projection, financial forecast or appraisal. The opinion must identify in a separate section all factual assumptions relied upon by the practitioner.

(iii) The practitioner must not base the opinion on any unreasonable factual representations, statements or findings of the taxpayer or any other person. An unreasonable factual representation includes a factual representation that the practitioner knows or should know is incorrect or incomplete. For example, a practitioner may not rely on a factual representation that a transaction has a business purpose if the representation does not include a specific description of the business purpose or the practitioner knows or should know that the representation is incorrect or incomplete. The opinion must identify in a separate section all factual representations, statements or findings of the taxpayer relied upon by the practitioner.

(2) *Relate law to facts.*

(i) The opinion must relate the applicable law (including potentially applicable judicial doctrines) to the relevant facts.

(ii) The practitioner must not assume the favorable resolution of any significant Federal tax issue * * * or otherwise base an opinion on any unreasonable legal assumptions, representations, or conclusions.

(iii) The opinion must not contain internally inconsistent legal analyses or conclusions.

(3) *Evaluation of significant Federal tax issues.*

(i) In general. The opinion must consider all significant Federal tax issues * * * .

(ii) Conclusion as to each significant Federal tax issue. The opinion must provide the practitioner's conclusion as to the likelihood that the taxpayer will prevail on the merits with respect to each significant Federal tax issue considered in the opinion. If the practitioner is unable to reach a conclusion with respect to one or more of those issues, the opinion must state that the practitioner is unable to reach a conclusion with respect to those issues. The opinion must describe the reasons for the conclusions, including the facts and analysis supporting the conclusions, or describe the reasons that the practitioner is unable to reach a conclusion as to one or more issues. If the practitioner fails to reach a conclusion at a confidence level of at least more likely than not with respect to one or more significant Federal tax issues considered, the opinion must include the appropriate disclosure(s) * * * .

(iii) Evaluation based on chances of success on the merits. In evaluating the significant Federal tax issues addressed in the opinion, the practitioner must not take into account the possibility that a tax return will not be audited, that an issue will not be raised on audit, or that an issue will be resolved through settlement if raised.

* * *

(4) *Overall conclusion.*

(i) The opinion must provide the practitioner's overall conclusion as to the likelihood that the Federal tax treatment of the transaction or matter that is the subject of the opinion is the proper treatment and the reasons for that

> conclusion. If the practitioner is unable to reach an overall conclusion, the opinion must state that the practitioner is unable to reach an overall conclusion and describe the reasons for the practitioner's inability to reach a conclusion.

Id. at § 10.35(c).

How do the standards for factual and legal due diligence in section 10.35 compare with those in Formal Opinion 346, which is excerpted in Section 18.04[A]? How do they compare to the current return preparer penalty standards in section 6694?

The Circular 230 regulations also contain a series of mandatory disclosure requirements for covered opinions:

> (1) *Relationship between promoter and practitioner.* An opinion must prominently disclose the existence of —
>
> (i) Any compensation arrangement, such as a referral fee or a fee-sharing arrangement, between the practitioner (or the practitioner's firm or any person who is a member of, associated with, or employed by the practitioner's firm) and any person (other than the client for whom the opinion is prepared) with respect to promoting, marketing or recommending the entity, plan, or arrangement (or a substantially similar arrangement) that is the subject of the opinion; or
>
> (ii) Any referral agreement between the practitioner (or the practitioner's firm or any person who is a member of, associated with, or employed by the practitioner's firm) and a person (other than the client for whom the opinion is prepared) engaged in promoting, marketing or recommending the entity, plan, or arrangement (or a substantially similar arrangement) that is the subject of the opinion.
>
> (2) *Marketed opinions.* A marketed opinion must prominently disclose that —
>
> (i) The opinion was written to support the promotion or marketing of the transaction(s) or matter(s) addressed in the opinion; and
>
> (ii) The taxpayer should seek advice based on the taxpayer's particular circumstances from an independent tax advisor.
>
> * * *
>
> (4) *Opinions that fail to reach a more likely than not conclusion.* An opinion that does not reach a conclusion at a confidence level of at least more likely than not with respect to a significant Federal tax issue must prominently disclose that —
>
> (i) The opinion does not reach a conclusion at a confidence level of at least more likely than not with respect to one or more significant Federal tax issues addressed by the opinion; and
>
> (ii) With respect to those significant Federal tax issues, the opinion was not written, and cannot be used by the taxpayer, for the purpose of avoiding penalties that may be imposed on the taxpayer.

Id. at § 10.35(d).

Some written advice that might otherwise constitute a covered opinion is excluded from that definition (and thereby excluded from the section 10.35(c) requirements), in limited situations. For instance, advice given after the taxpayer files a tax return reflecting the tax benefits of the transaction described in the written advice does not constitute a covered opinion. *Id.* at § 10.35(b)(2)(ii)(c). Also, the practitioner giving the advice can, in some cases, "legend out" of the 10.35 regulations. For example, advice that might otherwise qualify as a reliance opinion is not subject to section 10.35 if the practitioner prominently discloses in the opinion that the advice cannot be used by the taxpayer to avoid penalties. *Id.* at § 10.35(b)(4)(ii). Similarly, advice will not be treated as a marketed opinion if the practitioner warns in the opinion that it cannot be used for penalty protection and that the taxpayer should seek advice from an independent tax adviser. *Id.* at § 10.35(b)(5)(ii). The disclosure exceptions do not apply to written advice relating to a "principal purpose" transaction.

Anyone who has received an e-mail from a tax practitioner within the last few years is likely familiar with Circular 230 disclosure legends. These boilerplate provisions typically state that the content of the e-mail cannot be used by the recipient to avoid a penalty. By placing the Circular 230 legend in the e-mail, the practitioner is attempting to avoid having the advice treated as a covered opinion, thus avoiding the legal and factual due diligence requirements associated with covered opinion advice.

Other written advice that does not fall within the category of a covered opinion is governed by a separate, and more limited, set of requirements in section 10.37.

> A practitioner must not give written advice (including electronic communications) concerning one or more Federal tax issues if the practitioner bases the written advice on unreasonable factual or legal assumptions (including assumptions as to future events), unreasonably relies upon representations, statements, findings or agreements of the taxpayer or any other person, does not consider all relevant facts that the practitioner knows or should know, or, in evaluating a Federal tax issue, takes into account the possibility that a tax return will not be audited, that an issue will not be raised on audit, or that an issue will be resolved through settlement if raised. All facts and circumstances, including the scope of the engagement and the type and specificity of the advice sought by the client will be considered in determining whether a practitioner has failed to comply with this section. In the case of an opinion the practitioner knows or has reason to know will be used or referred to by a person other than the practitioner (or a person who is a member of, associated with, or employed by the practitioner's firm) in promoting, marketing or recommending to one or more taxpayers a partnership or other entity, investment plan or arrangement a significant purpose of which is the avoidance or evasion of any tax imposed by the Internal Revenue Code, the determination of whether a practitioner has failed to comply with this section will be made on the basis of a heightened standard of care because of the greater risk caused by the practitioner's lack of knowledge of the taxpayer's particular circumstances.

Id. at § 10.37(a). Compare the language of section 10.37 to that of section 10.35. How do the factual and legal due diligence expectations differ?

Commentators have criticized the Circular 230 regulations relating to covered opinions both because of their complexity and their alleged intrusiveness into the private relationship between the practitioner and the client. The following excerpt raises some of these criticisms, as well as a potential solution to the problem of aggressive tax advice. Note also Professor Schenk's criticism of the use of tax opinions to provide a "reasonable cause" defense to the imposition of penalties.

Deborah H. Schenk, *The Circular 230 Amendments: Time to Throw Them Out and Start Over*

110 Tax Notes 1311 (2006)[7]

Introduction

Ever since Treasury issued amendments to Circular 230 covering formal opinions as well as other forms of written advice, there has been a torrent of objections from tax advisers. Some of the complaints were overblown — tax practice as we know it has not come to an end nor have all our clients abandoned us. Some of the complaints were trivial — the placement of a legend on e-mails did not disrupt practice and instead has become white noise. On the other hand, there is a good deal to be said for some of the complaints. Treasury has now made three attempts to draft the rules, but has steadfastly hewn to its original approach. Rather than spending untold additional hours fine-tuning the complex rules as initially issued, it is time for Treasury to admit that the amendments are simply wrongheaded. They do not accomplish what Treasury intended, they interfere with the attorney-client relationship where the government has no business interfering, and they raise a constitutional issue. Treasury should throw in the towel and switch courses.

* * *

Generally the government should regulate conduct in the least intrusive way. A regulation is justified when there is some behavior that is appropriate for the government to prevent or regulate. Thus the proper way to think about Circular 230 is to start with the government's objectives. What did the government want to regulate? Is it appropriate for the government to regulate that behavior? How good a job do the rules do in regulating that behavior?

The Government's Objectives

It is widely believed that one of the government's objectives was to limit the use of opinion letters in tax shelter offerings. The opinion letter is a key element in the marketing of tax shelters because it serves as insurance. There is some risk that the transaction will fail, that is, that on audit and subsequent litigation, the tax benefits promised by the shelter will not materialize. There is also a risk that a large penalty will be levied if the shelter fails. The investor effectively can ensure against that penalty by purchasing an opinion letter, because it is widely believed that the letter will trigger the reasonable cause exception of section 6664(c), thus negating the penalty. While Treasury and Congress have tried many ways to eliminate the current spate of tax shelters, none has been wholly successful. Treasury must have believed that attacking the opinion letter was an important arrow in its quiver in the tax shelter battle. Rather than eliminating the market for opinion insurance directly, it decided to try to stop the production of the opinions by regulating the writers.

Second, Treasury officials also have used a consumer protection argument to justify the regulation of written advice. The preamble to both the proposed and the final regulations includes this statement: "The tax system is best served when the public has confidence in the honesty and integrity of the professional providing tax advice." * * *

Are those two Treasury objectives appropriate? If a lawyer's opinion can be used to obtain a penalty waiver, Treasury obviously has a legitimate interest in that opinion. That presupposes that a "get-out-of-jail" option is a good idea. It even presupposes that a reasonable cause exception to a penalty is a good idea. Most people support a broad reasonable cause exception to tax penalties. I am not one of them. I'd favor a strict liability penalty in many cases. If Congress has decided that a penalty is an appropriate response to certain behavior on the part of a taxpayer (a wholly separate question from a waiver), there should be few circumstances in which the penalty should not apply, and if there are those circumstances, Congress should clearly delineate them.

But let's take the reasonable cause exception as a given. That still leaves open the question of the role of the attorney's opinion in proving reasonable cause. Keeping in mind that a penalty never applies if it turns out the taxpayer was right, per se penalty protection based on a legal opinion is a bad idea. I am unimpressed with the argument that a taxpayer should be able to rely absolutely on a lawyer's opinion. The many, many people I have heard utter that statement have never adequately explained why that is so. "My lawyer told me it was OK" does not strike me as a sufficient justification for avoiding penalties for behavior Congress has chosen to penalize, especially when that behavior is done by sophisticated taxpayers. The reliance-on-the-lawyer argument often is justified by the observation that taxes are so complex that taxpayers must rely on their lawyers for advice as to whether they are following the law. That surely is true. But it seems equally true of antitrust law or securities regulation. Moreover, the fact that you have to rely on the lawyer to understand your obligations does not support the assertion that the lawyer's advice should protect you from a penalty for violating those obligations. There is no reason why the government should bear the cost of the insurance. Usually, in exchange for a fee, the insurer agrees to bear the cost should the contingency occur. But here the government, which receives no fee, bears the entire cost, not the lawyer.

* * *

The government as well as the courts must shoulder the blame for the current state of affairs. Neither section 6664(c) nor the regulations provide that an opinion is per se protection against penalties. An attorney's opinion is one fact that must be considered along with other circumstances. Nevertheless, that is not the way it works in practice. The current practice is that an attorney's opinion is the most important factor in determining whether there was reasonable cause for a taxpayer's understatement of liability. A favorable opinion usually ensures that a penalty will not be imposed. Although that is not always the case, it is often enough that the opinion became the linchpin in tax shelters. Therefore, Treasury clearly has an interest in what that opinion actually says. The mere existence of an opinion is not sufficient; otherwise, the taxpayer can take significant steps to avoid the penalty simply by paying a fee, regardless of what the fee buys.

Thus, taking the current operation of the section 6664(c) exception as a given, there is a strong justification for Treasury to be involved in opinion-writing standards when those opinions are to be used to mitigate a penalty. How good a job do the Circular 230 amendments do in achieving that purpose?

The Rules Miss the Targets — Badly

The most obvious response is that they are largely overkill. The elaborate rules of section 10.35, and certainly section 10.37, catch much more than opinions used for penalty protection. It is true that section 10.35 contains an opt-out rule so that the elaborate requirements do not apply to opinions that will not be used as penalty protection. The opt-out rule, however, is not available for * * * principal purpose transactions. Realistically, there will not be many situations in which a taxpayer seeks an opinion about a transaction that does not have a principal purpose of avoiding tax — why else is he consulting a tax adviser? If so, the opt-out provision is narrow indeed and results in subjecting most formal opinions to section 10.35. Thus, most written communication between a tax lawyer and her client is subject to limitations imposed by section 10.35. That goes way beyond what is needed to rein in opinions used as insurance against penalties.

Not only do the amendments wildly overshoot the mark, it also seems likely that the rules will have a decidedly unintended negative effect. Many practitioners have reported that, contrary to their initial assumption that clients may be alarmed by the opt-out banners, they now view them as boilerplate that can be ignored. The regulations for section 6664(c), of course, include no mention of the legend. It seems entirely likely that a client faced with a substantial understatement penalty will continue to assert that she relied on an attorney's opinion despite a legend on the opinion. ("I did not understand it"; "It's on every e-mail I get"; How was I to know it actually meant something?"; "It may have said no reliance, but I in fact relied on it.") If a judge finds that that is reasonable cause for the understatement, the opt-out rule will have little meaning other than possibly eliminating the automatic finding of reasonable cause. In that case, Treasury will have accomplished nothing at all regarding penalty protection opinions. On the other hand, if the IRS and the courts actually enforced the opt-out rule, it might not be so bad. Because every document carries the warning, all taxpayers, sophisticated or not, have been warned not to rely on the opinion. The problem, of course, is the failure to include an opt-out provision for principal purpose transactions.

* * *

Treasury's second stated goal is consumer protection. Treasury has asserted that it has an interest in protecting consumers against unscrupulous attorneys who are issuing opinions or providing written advice that is not based on the facts, is not well-thought out, or draws unwarranted conclusions.

Leaving aside why that paternalistic interest would not apply equally well to oral advice (completely exempted from the Circular 230 amendments), the more basic question is whether it is appropriate for Treasury to monitor this activity. Historically, the regulation of lawyers has been left to the states, which impose standards in exchange for a license to practice law. (Similar regulations apply to CPAs.) Additional regulation by federal courts and agencies is appropriate when the court or agency is regulating the interaction with the court or agency itself. Thus, for example, the federal courts impose standards for practicing before those courts. The IRS and other federal agencies impose rules relating to submissions to or appearances before those agencies. Congress and the IRS have imposed standards on tax return preparers who are submitting documents to the government on behalf of taxpayers. Those are reasonable assertions of governmental power. In this case, however, Treasury is seeking to regulate the product of private contractual relationships, advice given by a tax adviser to a client, advice that will not be submitted to the government. The written advice provided by other professionals to their clients that is neither part of a government submission nor part of a public record usually is not regulated. Why is it necessary to regulate the written advice given by tax advisers? And if consumer protection is needed to protect unsophisticated individuals from their unscrupulous tax advisers, is the IRS really in the best position to provide that protection?

* * *

In summary, the case for Treasury's exercise of a consumer protection role is quite weak. Do sections 10.35 and 10.37 do a good job in protecting the consumer?

It appears that the section 10.35 rules perversely have had just the opposite effect. The amendments have created a number of incentives to avoid giving taxpayers both good advice or the advice they are willing to purchase. The irony is that many taxpayers may be getting worse advice after the advent of the Circular 230 rules than they would have in their absence.

* * *

[T]he rules substantially increase the cost of advice, thus discouraging some taxpayers from purchasing the advice. That may impose a barrier to procuring affordable, routine tax advice. This is not a new debate — whether clients should be able to purchase limited advice — but Treasury clearly seems to have come down on the side of no. Clients who want reasonably priced written advice regarding many transactions may forgo that advice if their only option is an expensive full-blown opinion. If a taxpayer wants to pay for only a limited three-sentence e-mail of the "maybe yes, maybe no, it depends on x" variety to decide whether to schedule a meeting on a transaction, why should the government insist that the taxpayer must obtain a formal opinion exploring and explaining every detail? That, in fact, may be a dumb thing to do, rife with risks, and could possibly lead the client to enter into a transaction he otherwise would not have done. But is that possibility so prevalent and so dangerous that the federal government is warranted in preventing all clients from obtaining that level of advice?

* * * [T]here is an increased incentive to use oral advice. The anecdotal evidence is that

no one is issuing a principal purpose covered opinion because the cost is prohibitive. An adviser who receives an e-mail or phone call asking for advice about a transaction designed to avoid federal taxes therefore is likely to deliver an oral response. That may be because he does not want to take the time (and may not be paid for the time) to determine whether the transaction is a significant purpose transaction with a more-likely-than-not confidence level — for which an opt-out banner could be attached — or is really a principal purpose transaction — for which an opt-out banner could not be used — and the adviser can respond only with a full-blown opinion that the client neither wants nor will pay for. It is not clear that this oral advice is better for the consumer. He has no record to review, no document on which to rely. If we are really interested in protecting the consumer, it seems odd that we would create an incentive for oral advice when there is more likely to be miscommunication and misunderstanding about the tax effects of a transaction. It is perverse that the rules push taxpayers to oral advice regarding the most aggressive tax planning.

* * *

Thus, as to the second goal, it is reasonably easy to conclude that the amendments to Circular 230 do a poor job of protecting consumers and may actually produce worse results for them.

Another reason to reject Treasury's approach is that it raises substantial First Amendment questions. The First Amendment prohibition on state regulation of speech is not absolute. Congress or the states can regulate some types of speech. For example, most state ethics rules prohibit lawyer advertising that is misleading or deceitful. An interference with legitimate speech, however, cannot be more than is necessary to achieve enforcement objectives (in this case tax enforcement). A Treasury regulation that penalizes an adviser for providing certain lawful communications to his client is suspect.

In summary, assuming opinions continue to have a role in mitigating penalties, Treasury has a reasonable basis for monitoring opinions used for penalty protection, but the current Circular 230 provisions do a poor job of carrying out that objective. And its regulation of other written advice provided by a lawyer to a client is an unwarranted intrusion into the tax adviser-client relationship that provides few, if any, consumer protection benefits. It's time to pull the plug on the current approach.

A Better Approach

How better to carry out the appropriate Treasury goal of regulating opinions used for penalty protection? I strongly favor an opt-in approach, that is, Treasury would provide detailed rules for the kind of opinion that would be taken into account as a factor in mitigating penalties. All other written and oral advice would be "regulated" by the market (or by other provisions in Circular 230 and state ethics rules). For the opt-in provision to have teeth, Treasury should amend the section 6664 regulations to provide that a tax adviser's opinion cannot be relied on for penalty protection unless it conforms to the Circular 230 requirements, states that it is intended to be relied on, and was received by the taxpayer before the return was filed. A limited scope opinion generally would not satisfy the tests for penalty protection, or at most would satisfy that the taxpayer had a reasonable belief regarding the issue addressed in the limited opinion but no protection for the overall results.

The opt-in approach would allow advisers to give opinions on tax avoidance transactions without following all of the requirements of Circular 230. There should be no objection as long as the adviser is not misleading or deceitful. If the opinion cannot be used for penalty protection, the client will want the best possible opinion to help him decide whether to invest. The adviser may decide that the transaction works or he may decide that it does not. Either way the client will pay for that advice but not insurance.

* * * If the opinion is bogus, the client should have recourse against the adviser.

Furthermore, the opt-in approach would eliminate much complexity engendered by the current rules. There are fine gradations in those provisions that an adviser realistically cannot distinguish. (Is it a principal purpose or a significant purpose?) (Do we stick a banner on every written communication and hope for the best?) Under an opt-in approach, only one decision would need to be made: Is penalty protection sought or not?

* * *

Many of Professor Schenk's reservations about section 10.35 relate to "principal purpose" transactions. As noted above, a covered opinion includes written advice concerned a federal tax issue arising from any "partnership or other entity, any investment plan or arrangement, or any other plan or arrangement, the principal purpose of which is the avoidance or evasion of any tax." Do you think the drafters intended this category of covered opinions to include advice relating to routine questions about whether the taxpayer must include a receipt in gross income or whether an expense is deductible? Also, what do you think about Professor Schenk's proposed "opt-in" approach as a replacement for the current Circular 230 rules?

§ 18.05 CONFLICTS IN REPRESENTATION

Circular 230 generally prohibits a practitioner from representing conflicting interests before the IRS without full disclosure and the consent of the affected client(s). According to section 10.29, a conflict exists when:

(1) The representation of one client will be directly adverse to another client; or

(2) There is a significant risk that the representation or one or more clients will be materially limited by the practitioner's responsibilities to another client, a former client or a third person, or by a personal interest of the practitioner.

Id. § 10.29(a). However, even if a conflict of interest exists, the practitioner may still represent the both clients if:

(1) The practitioner reasonably believes that the practitioner will be able to provide competent and diligent representation to each affected client;

(2) The representation is not prohibited by law; and

(3) Each affected client waives the conflict of interest and gives informed consent, confirmed in writing by each affected client, at the time the existence of the conflict of interest is known by the practitioner. The confirmation may be made within a reasonable period after the informed consent, but in no event later than 30 days.

Id. § 10.29(b).

Similarly, ABA Model Rule 1.7 provides:

> (a) Except as provided in paragraph (b), a lawyer shall not represent a client if the representation involves a concurrent conflict of interest. A concurrent conflict of interest exists if:
>
> (1) the representation of one client will be directly adverse to another client; or
>
> (2) there is a significant risk that the representation of one or more clients will be materially limited by the lawyer's responsibilities to another client, a former client or a third person or by a personal interest of the lawyer.
>
> (b) Notwithstanding the existence of a concurrent conflict of interest under paragraph (a), a lawyer may represent a client if:

(1) the lawyer reasonably believes that the lawyer will be able to provide competent and diligent representation to each affected client;

(2) the representation is not prohibited by law;

(3) the representation does not involve the assertion of a claim by one client against another client represented by the lawyer in the same litigation or other proceeding before a tribunal; and

(4) each affected client gives informed consent, confirmed in writing.

Why do these rules exist? In general, they reflect a concern for the consequences of conflicting loyalties on the part of the attorney. One scholar explains:

> In litigation, disputes over lawyers' professional conduct most frequently involve conflicts of interest, a subject addressed extensively by disciplinary rules. Although various purposes have been ascribed to them, the "conflict rules" are best understood as rules of "risk avoidance." They address situations in which there is a risk that a lawyer will not adequately carry out obligations to a present or former client because of competing obligations to another present or former client or because of the lawyer's own competing interests. Before accepting or continuing the representation in such situations, the lawyer must obtain the informed consent of the clients whose interests are put at risk; where the risk is unreasonably high, the lawyer must refrain from accepting or continuing the representation.

Bruce A. Green, *Conflicts of Interest in Litigation: The Judicial Role*, 65 FORDHAM L. REV. 71, 71–72 (1996) (footnotes omitted).

The Model Rules, like section 10.29 of Circular 230, provide an exception to the prohibition of representation where, among other things, the representative "reasonably believes" that he or she will be able to "provide competent and diligent representation to each affected client." What burden does this requirement place on the representative? One commentator argues:

> Rule 1.7 of the American Bar Association's . . . *Model Rules* states that a lawyer can represent a client with a conflicting interest if the lawyer reasonably believes he can competently and diligently represent the client and if he obtains the client's informed consent, which since the 2002 amendments, must be confirmed in writing. Because of the use of the term "reasonably believes," the lawyer's determination must be objectively reasonable. Rule 1.7 rests on the assumption that lawyers will disclose conflicts to their clients to obtain informed consent and that they will do so in a meaningful way so that the client will be able to make an intelligent decision as to whether to waive a conflict. However, social science literature suggests that a lawyer will rationalize his behavior as being ethical because of the innate human tendency to rationalize one's self-interest as being consistent with morality. Furthermore, he will attempt to persuade the client that he could effectively represent her despite any possible conflict. Finally, the client, who has already made a decision to trust the lawyer with her case, will be unlikely to question the lawyer's assertion that he could effectively represent her.

Leonard E. Gross, *Are Differences Among the Attorney Conflict of Interest Rules Consistent With Principles of Behavioral Economics?*, 19 GEO. J. LEGAL ETHICS 111, 113–114 (2006) (footnotes omitted).

Compare ABA Model Rule 1.7 with the analogous sections in the American Law Institute's *Restatement of the Law, Third, The Law Governing Lawyers*. Those sections provide:

§ 121 The Basic Prohibition of Conflicts of Interest

> Unless all affected clients and other necessary persons consent to the representation under the limitations and conditions provided in § 122, a lawyer may not represent a client if the representation would involve a conflict of interest. A conflict of interest is involved if there is a substantial risk that the lawyer's representation of the client would be materially and adversely affected by the lawyer's own interests or by the lawyer's duties to another current client, a former client, or a third person.

§ 122 Client Consent to a Conflict of Interest

> (1) A lawyer may represent a client notwithstanding a conflict of interest prohibited by § 121 if each affected client or former client gives informed consent to the lawyer's representation. Informed consent requires that the client or former client have reasonably adequate information about the material risks of such representation to that client or former client.
>
> (2) Notwithstanding the informed consent of each affected client or former client, a lawyer may not represent a client if:
>
> (a) the representation is prohibited by law;
>
> (b) one client will assert a claim against the other in the same litigation; or
>
> (c) in the circumstances, it is not reasonably likely that the lawyer will be able to provide adequate representation to one or more of the clients.

RESTATEMENT OF THE LAW, THIRD, THE LAW GOVERNING LAWYERS §§ 121–122.

Does the Restatement avoid the problem present in Model Rule 1.7 and Circular 230 of relying on the lawyer's reasonable belief as to whether a conflict exists? Note that Restatement section 121 provides that "[a] conflict of interest is involved if there is a substantial risk that the lawyer's representation of the client would be materially and adversely affected by the lawyer's own interests or by the lawyer's duties to another current client, a former client, or a third person." A comment to section 121 states:

> This Section employs an objective standard by which to assess the adverseness, materiality, and substantiality of the risk of the effect on representation. The standard of this Section is not the "appearance of impropriety" standard formerly used by some courts to define the scope of impermissible conflicts. That standard could prohibit not only conflicts as defined in this Section, but also situations that might appear improper to an uninformed observer or even an interested party.

Id. § 121 cmt. c(iv).

Some of the conflict of interest issues that may arise out of multiple representation are discussed in the following Tax Court case, which applies an earlier version of Model Rule 1.7, which is quoted in the case. Note who requested the disqualification of the attorney, Mr. Izen, and the Tax Court's reaction to that fact.

PARA TECHNOLOGIES TRUST v. COMMISSIONER

United States Tax Court
T.C. Memo. 1992-575

COHEN, JUDGE:

Each of these [consolidated] cases is before the Court for ruling on respondent's Motion to Compel Withdrawal of Petitioners' Counsel of Record for Conflict of Interest. The issue for decision is whether a conflict of interest exists that requires the disqualification of petitioners' counsel of record. * * *

BACKGROUND

Nassau Life Insurance Company, Ltd. (Nassau Life), promoted the use of domestic and foreign entities to shelter United States business and investment income from United States Federal income taxation. Nassau Life engaged in this activity through representatives known as "information officers" and through the dissemination of printed materials. From 1982 through 1988, Joe Alfred Izen, Jr. (Izen), was counsel to Nassau Life. In the course of that representation, among other services, he prepared and issued two opinion letters that related to the multiple-entity tax shelter promoted by Nassau Life. In a legal opinion letter dated September 26, 1983, Izen discussed the legal status of "contractual trust companies" that were being promoted by Nassau Life (the 1983 opinion letter).

[Petitioner] Ferber is a songwriter with a high school education. [Petitioner] Anderson completed the eighth grade. At the time of hearing on the pending motions, Ferber was 36 years old and Anderson was 30 years old.

Ferber and Anderson met in India in 1977 and became friends. In late 1984, Anderson began to engage in an electronics business, VideoLab, as a sole proprietor. Because of his limited education, Anderson wanted to adopt a structure for VideoLab that would minimize the amount of paperwork that was necessary to carry on the business. He discussed his plans with Ferber, who was then employed as an information officer for Nassau Life. Ferber, relying at least partially on the 1983 opinion letter, advised Anderson, who also had access to the 1983 opinion letter, to structure his business as a trust such as those promoted by Nassau Life.

In January 1985, Anderson formed Para Technologies (Para Tech) as a common-law business trust. From its creation and thereafter, Para Tech conducted the business in which VideoLab had previously been engaged. Ferber was the trustee of Para Tech. The beneficial owner of Para Tech was another trust, Atram Investment Group (Atram), formed under the laws of the Turks and Caicos Islands, British West Indies. Anderson was one of the beneficiaries of Atram.

In a legal opinion letter prepared for Nassau Life dated June 20, 1985, Izen discussed the tax aspects of contractual trust companies (the 1985 opinion letter). Among other things, the letter concluded that the grantor trust provisions of the Internal Revenue Code did not apply to "contractual trust companies." Izen's letter failed to discuss decided cases contrary to the positions he was espousing. Anderson and Ferber gained access to the 1985 opinion letter.

Respondent determined deficiencies in petitioners' Federal income taxes for 1987 and 1988. Respondent determined that Para Tech was an association taxable as a corporation for Federal income tax purposes and disallowed its claimed distribution deductions. Respondent determined that Anderson and Ferber were each taxable on an amount equal to the taxable income of Para Tech. Respondent asserted three alternative theories in support of this determination. First, because Para Tech should be taxed as a corporation and because of their control over Para Tech and Atram, Anderson and Ferber were in constructive receipt of dividend income equal to the amounts transferred from Para Tech to Atram. Second, if Para Tech was a trust, it was a grantor trust owned by Anderson and Ferber, who were therefore taxable on Para Tech's income. Third, because both Para Tech and Atram were sham entities that should be disregarded for Federal income tax purposes, Anderson and Ferber are taxable on the income from Para Tech's business. Respondent also determined that all three petitioners are liable for additions to tax for fraud.

Para Tech, Anderson, and Ferber filed petitions for redetermination with this Court. Izen is counsel of record for petitioners in these cases. Nassau Life is bankrupt. All legal fees are being paid by Para Tech. No discovery and no settlement negotiations have taken place, and none of the cases has been set for trial.

Respondent's counsel in these cases wrote letters to Izen dated September 19, 1991, and November 15, 1991, questioning Izen regarding possible conflicts of interest in his representation of petitioners. Izen did not respond to these letters. Respondent, therefore, moved the Court to compel withdrawal of Izen as petitioners' counsel.

DISCUSSION

Petitioners contend, based on *Appeal of Infotechnology, Inc.*, 582 A.2d 215 (Del. Super. 1990), that respondent lacks standing to make this motion because a nonclient litigant does not have the power to enforce a technical violation of the Model Rules of Professional Conduct (Model Rules). These cases, however, are distinguishable from *Appeal of Infotechnology, Inc., supra*, in which the court held that it had "become apparent that * * * [the opposing party] was seeking to use disqualification as a litigation tactic." *Id.* at 221. The Court is generally reluctant to disqualify counsel of a taxpayer's choice on motion of the adversary. *See* Alexander v. Superior Court, 685 P.2d 1309, 1317 (Ariz. 1984). In these cases, however, respondent promptly moved for disqualification prior to conducting discovery or engaging in settlement negotiations and before these cases were set for trial. *See* Duffey v. Commissioner, 91 T.C. 81, 84 (1988).

Rule 201(a) provides that "Practitioners before the Court shall carry on their practice in accordance with the letter and spirit of the Model Rules." This Court, therefore, has the power to compel withdrawal of petitioners' counsel if such representation would violate the Model Rules. Specifically, Rule 24(f) provides:[8]

> If any counsel of record (1) was involved in planning or promoting a transaction or operating an entity that is connected to any issue in a case, [or] (2) represents more than one person with differing interests with respect to any issue in a case, * * * then such counsel must either secure the informed consent of the client * * *; withdraw from the case; or take whatever other steps are necessary to obviate a conflict of interest or other violation of the ABA Model Rules of Professional Conduct, and particularly [Rule] 1.7 * * *

Rule 24(f), which became effective July 1, 1990, emphasizes the provisions of the Model Rules to which practitioners before this Court were already subject. Rule 24(f) was added "to insure that the bar of this Court disclose or rectify any conflict of interest." Rules of Practice and Procedure of the United States Tax Court, 93 T.C. 821, 858 Note.

Model Rule 1.7(b) provides:

> A lawyer shall not represent a client if the representation of that client may be materially limited by the lawyer's responsibilities to another client or to a third person, or by the lawyer's own interests, unless:
>
> (1) the lawyer reasonably believes the representation will not be adversely affected; and
>
> (2) the client consents after consultation. When representation of multiple clients in a single matter is undertaken, the consultation shall include explanation of the implications of the common representation and the advantages and risks involved.

Petitioners contend that Izen's representation of them does not violate Model Rule 1.7(b) because no potential conflict of interest exists among petitioners. Petitioners contend that each petitioner is contesting the deficiency and will argue that Para Tech should be recognized as a trust and that Para Tech's Federal income tax returns for 1987 and 1988 were correct.

Respondent contends that Izen's representation of each petitioner may be materially

---

[8] [Former Tax Court Rule 24(f) is now Rule 24(g). — Eds.]

limited by his responsibilities to the other petitioners and by his own interests. Respondent states:

> There are positions which can be advanced on behalf of each Petitioner which, if established, would enable that Petitioner to avoid liability for all or part of the deficiencies and additions to tax determined against that Petitioner, but which cannot be established without irreparably damaging some other Petitioner's case.

As set forth above, respondent determined that Anderson and Ferber were each taxable on an amount equal to the taxable income of Para Tech. One of respondent's alternative theories is that Para Tech is a grantor trust. Generally, the grantor trust rules apply to a person, such as Anderson, who created the trust. *See* secs. 671 through 678. Anderson formed the trust and transferred his business to it and is a beneficiary of the trust. Ferber, although serving as a trustee, is less likely to be a grantor. Ferber, and, hypothetically, Para Tech, would avoid taxation if respondent successfully established that the income was taxable to Anderson as the grantor.

Further, respondent has determined that each petitioner is liable for the additions to tax for fraud. In support of that determination, respondent's answer alleges that books and records made available to respondent during the examination of petitioners' returns were false and fraudulent, that petitioners "individually and in concert, refused to cooperate with Respondent's agents and attempted to obstruct Respondent's examination by various means," and that each petitioner understated or failed to report taxable income and tax due from them. In this regard, Anderson and Ferber can each argue that the other was responsible for maintaining the books and records of Para Tech and for preparing its tax returns and that each relied on the other. Each may also claim that he relied on Izen's opinion letters. In addition, Ferber, as trustee of Para Tech, is putatively making decisions for Para Tech, including using its funds to pay for litigation of these cases, while Anderson, not Ferber, has a beneficial interest in Para Tech.

Although it is too early in this litigation to anticipate all of the arguments that will be made, and the foregoing possibilities may not be the positions that petitioners should or will adopt at trial, there is a serious possibility that petitioners' positions may become adverse to each other. *See* Figueroa-Olmo v. Westinghouse Elec. Corp., 616 F. Supp. 1445, 1451–1454 (D. Puerto Rico 1985); Shadid v. Jackson, 521 F. Supp. 87, 89 (E.D. Tex. 1981).

* * *

We are not persuaded that Izen made a full and fair disclosure or that petitioners understood the inherent potential conflicts between them. The backgrounds of the individuals suggest a lack of sophistication in assessing matters such as these, and they relied solely on the advice of Izen in deciding to waive the conflicts of interest. *Compare* Adams v. Commissioner, 85 T.C. at 372–374 (holding that taxpayers could not be relieved of a settlement agreement based on their attorney's conflict of interest because taxpayers were sophisticated, knew all of the relevant facts, and had been advised by independent counsel before employing the author of an opinion letter). It appears to us that the waiver is not based on informed consent but on the cost of employing independent and separate counsel and having such counsel become familiar with the underlying facts of the cases.

Izen admitted during the hearing on respondent's motion that he had not secured written consents or waivers from petitioners and that he had not contacted Nassau Life or other beneficiaries of the Para Tech trust. Under these circumstances, we conclude that it is "more important that unethical conduct be prevented than * * * [that petitioners] have an unfettered right to counsel of * * * [their] choice." Kevlik v. Goldstein, 724 F.2d 844, 849 (1st Cir. 1984). The potential for unfairness to petitioners and damage to the integrity of the judicial process is too serious to permit Izen's representation of petitioners to continue, even in the face of an apparent waiver.

Figueroa-Olmo v. Westinghouse Elec. Corp., *supra* at 1451; Shadid v. Jackson, *supra* at 90; and Model Rules Rule 1.7 comment (1983) (stating that, "when a disinterested lawyer would conclude that the client should not agree to representation under the circumstances, the lawyer involved cannot * * * provide representation on the basis of the client's consent.")

Therefore, Izen must be disqualified from representing petitioners in these cases.

Respondent's motions will be granted.

Multiple representation is not the only ethical issue that was addressed by *Para Technologies Trust.* As the case indicates, Mr. Izen not only represented Mr. Anderson and Mr. Farber in Tax Court; he had also drafted the opinion letters on which they may have relied in creating the trust. Why might that give rise to a conflict of interest? The court addressed this issue as follows:

> Izen's personal interests in this case may also conflict with the interests of petitioners. Anderson and Ferber relied, at least partially, on opinion letters that Izen had written. Therefore, Izen has an interest in vindicating the positions he took in the opinion letters in order to maintain his professional reputation and to protect himself from any potential future liability to petitioners. *See, e.g.*, Eisenberg v. Gagnon, 766 F.2d 770, 779–780 (3d Cir. 1985) (holding that investors in a tax shelter could recover from an attorney who had misrepresented facts relating to the tax shelter). He would therefore be less likely to advise petitioners disinterestedly with regard to such matters as accepting a settlement offer. *See* Model Rules Rule 1.7(a) and 1.7 comment (1983) (stating that, "If the probity of a lawyer's own conduct in a transaction is in serious question, it may be difficult or impossible for the lawyer to give a client detached advice."). *See also* Adams v. Commissioner, 85 T.C. 359, 372–373 (1985). Izen's failure to advise petitioners of the potential adverse defenses or affirmative claims available to them would constitute a breach of his duty of loyalty to them. Figueroa-Olmo v. Westinghouse Elec. Corp., *supra* at 1453–1454; Eriks v. Denver, 824 P.2d 1207, 1211–1212 (Wash. 1992) (citing Model Rules Rule 1.7 comment (1984) and holding that as a matter of law there was a conflict of interest between promoters of and investors in a tax shelter). Finally, Izen is potentially a witness with respect to matters set forth in his tax opinion, and testimony on that subject could appropriately be obtained without violation of the attorney-client privilege. *See* In re Grand Jury Proceedings, 727 F.2d 1352 (4th Cir. 1984); and United States v. Jones, 696 F.2d 1069 (4th Cir. 1982).
>
> Izen and petitioners contend that petitioners have been informed of and waive Izen's conflict of interest. We are not persuaded, however, that the apparent consent of petitioners is informed and voluntary. * * *

Id.; *see also* Johnston v. Commissioner, T.C. Memo. 2000-315, n.13 (2000) (noting, in dicta, that if "[the Managing Agent for the Trustee,] Mr. Chisum[,] were a lawyer authorized to practice in this Court, there might well be grounds under Rule 24(g) for disqualifying him from representing petitioner and the other participants in the trust arrangements that Mr. Chisum has been promoting and operating . . . on the ground that Mr. Chisum has a conflict of interest.") (*citing Para Technologies Trust*).

Note the provisions in Model Rule 1.7(b) and Restatement Section 122 (as well as Section 10.29 of Circular 230) for informed consent by the client to the conflict of interest. May a client waive potential conflicts in advance? One commentator argues that doing so may offer advantages to both the attorney and the client:

> Allowing informed consent to conflicts of interest serves not only the interest of the lawyer, but those of his or her clients as well; the client who wants to hire

> the lawyer despite the lawyer's conflicting interests has an interest in being free to choose the representation of her choice. While a lawyer's loyalty to his clients is paramount, if the client who could be adversely affected by the lawyer's acceptance of a new client is willing to waive his objection to the representation, his interests are being protected as well. A waiver is a relinquishment by the client of his right to object to his lawyer's taking on additional clients with interests adverse to his own.

Alice E. Brown, *Advance Waivers of Conflicts of Interest: Are the ABA Formal Ethics Opinions Advanced Enough Themselves?*, 19 GEO. J. LEGAL ETHICS 567, 570 (2006) (footnotes omitted).

The ABA Model Rules and the Restatement differ in their approach to the question of general, or "open-ended" advance waivers of conflicts of interest — that is, a waiver of prospective conflicts that neither limits the waiver to specific matters nor identifies the party with the interest adverse to the client. *See* Nathan M. Crystal, *Enforceability of General Advance Waivers of Conflicts of Interest*, 38 ST. MARY'S L.J. 859, 864 (2007). Professor Crystal explains:

> The Model Rules and the Restatement provide materially different standards for permitting general advance waivers. The basic test under the Model Rules is whether "the client reasonably understands the material risks that the waiver entails." In deciding whether this requirement is met, Comment 22 to Model Rule 1.7 identifies several factors to be considered, including: the comprehensiveness of the explanation of possible types of representations that might arise in the future "and the actual [or] reasonably foreseeable adverse consequences of those representations"; whether "the client is an experienced user of the legal services involved"; whether "the client is independently represented by other counsel in giving consent"; and whether "the consent is limited to future conflicts unrelated to the subject of the representation." In other words, the Model Rules refuse to adopt a bright line test to determine whether a client has given informed consent to a future conflict. Instead, the validity of the consent turns on an analysis of various factors. If more factors are present, then "consent is more likely to be effective."
>
> The Restatement, on the other hand, appears to adopt a rule for determining the validity of consent to a general advance waiver. The Restatement provides: "A client's open-ended agreement to consent to all conflicts normally should be ineffective unless the client possesses sophistication in the matter in question and has had the opportunity to receive independent legal advice about the consent." Thus, under the Restatement, consent to a general advance waiver is valid if two requirements are met: (1) "the client possesses sophistication in the matter in question" and (2) the client "has had the opportunity to receive independent legal advice about the consent.["]
>
> * * *
>
> Aside from a fundamental difference in approach (multiple factors in contrast to a rule), the Model Rules and the Restatement contain a more substantive difference with regard to the role of independent counsel. The Model Rules state that whether "the client is independently represented by other counsel in giving consent" is an important factor in determining the validity of consent to an advance waiver. Thus, the Model Rules focus on actual representation by independent counsel. By contrast, the Restatement only refers to "the opportunity to receive independent legal advice about the consent."

Id. at 871–72 (2007) (footnotes omitted). Which do you think is the better rule?

§ 18.06 TAX COURT DISCIPLINARY ACTIONS

In Tax Court, unlike in district court and the Court of Federal Claims, taxpayers may be represented not only by attorneys admitted to practice before the Tax Court, but also by other individuals, including accountants, who have passed an examination. *See* TAX CT. R. 200. Under that Rule, "[a]n applicant for admission to practice before the Court must establish to the satisfaction of the Court that the applicant is of good moral and professional character and possesses the requisite qualifications to provide competent representation before the Court." TAX CT. R. 200(a). Moreover, Tax Court Rule 201(a) provides: "Practitioners before the Court shall carry on their practice in accordance with the letter and spirit of the Model Rules of Professional Conduct of the American Bar Association."

Tax Court Rule 202(a) provides that a member of its bar "may be disciplined" in the following circumstances:

> (1) Conviction in any court of the United States, or of the District of Columbia, or of any state, territory, commonwealth, or possession of the United States of any felony or of any lesser crime involving false swearing, misrepresentation, fraud, criminal violation of any provision of the Internal Revenue Code, bribery, extortion, misappropriation, theft, or moral turpitude;
>
> (2) Imposition of discipline by any other court of whose bar an attorney is a member, or an attorney's disbarment or suspension by consent or resignation from the bar of such court while an investigation into allegations of misconduct is pending;
>
> (3) Conduct with respect to the Court which violates the letter and spirit of the Model Rules of Professional Conduct of the American Bar Association, the Rules of the Court, or orders or other instructions of the Court; or
>
> (4) Any other conduct unbecoming a member of the Bar of the Court.

The discipline referred to "may consist of disbarment, suspension from practice before the Court, reprimand, admonition, or any other sanction that the Court may deem appropriate." TAX CT. R. 202(b).

The applicable Tax Court Rule distinguishes between suspension for more than 60 days or disbarment, on the one hand, and suspension for fewer than 60 days, on the other:

> The Court may, in the exercise of its discretion, immediately suspend a practitioner from practice before the Court until further order of the Court. However, no person shall be suspended for more than 60 days or disbarred until such person has been afforded an opportunity to be heard. A Judge of the Court may immediately suspend any person for not more than 60 days for contempt or misconduct during the course of any trial or hearing.

TAX CT. R. 202(b).

A practitioner suspended for 60 or fewer days is automatically reinstated to the Tax Court bar after the suspension period elapses. TAX CT. R. 202(d)(1). To initiate disciplinary proceedings in other cases, the Tax Court enters an order requiring the practitioner to show cause why the practitioner should not be disciplined. TAX CT. R. 202(c). The order also schedules a hearing. *Id.* The practitioner has the right to counsel, and the Tax Court may appoint counsel to assist it. TAX CT. R. 202(e), (f). A practitioner suspended for more than 60 days or disbarred from the Tax Court may not resume practice before the Tax Court until the practitioner is reinstated by a Tax Court order. TAX CT. R. 202(d)(2).

In some cases, a state may disbar an attorney. What effect should this have on the attorney's membership in the Tax Court bar? In *In re Winthrop Drake Thies*, 662 F.2d 771 (6th Cir. 1980), which involved an earlier version of the Tax Court Rules, the Tax

Court disbarred Mr. Thies, relying "exclusively on appellant's 1978 automatic disbarment from the New York State courts, which followed his 1976 felony conviction for assaulting a federal officer." *Id.* at 771–72.[9] That case explained the effect of a state disbarment action on a federal action:

> In *Selling v. Radford*, 243 U.S. 46 (1971), the Supreme Court considered the effect of disbarment from state court in a federal disbarment action. The Court found that although admission to a state bar may be a predicate to admission to a federal bar, a state disbarment order does not automatically bind a federal court. The Court reconciled the interest in judicial economy with the "quasi-criminal nature" of a disbarment proceeding, and concluded that a state disbarment gives rise to a rebuttable presumption that an attorney lacks the "private and professional character" to remain a member of the federal bar.
>
> The federal court should give conclusive effect to this presumption of unfitness
>
> > unless, from an intrinsic consideration of the state record, one or all of the following conditions should appear: 1. That the state procedure from want of notice or opportunity to be heard was wanting in due process; 2. that there was such an infirmity of proof as to facts found . . . that we could not . . . accept as final the conclusion on [the attorney's lack of character]; 3. that some other grave reason existed [which would make disbarment inconsistent with] principles of right and justice . . . [*Selling*, 243 U.S. at 51.]

Id. at 772 (footnotes omitted). *In re Thies* found that because the state court's process was inadequate — it held no hearing and made no factual findings, but rather disbarred Mr. Thies automatically upon his felony conviction — the Tax Court could not simply rely on that disbarment. *Id.* at 773.

Krouner v. United States Tax Court, 202 Fed. Appx. 470 (D.C. Cir. 2006) (unpublished), also involved an "automatic" New York disbarment. Consider the issue in that case.

KROUNER v. UNITED STATES TAX COURT

United States Court of Appeals, District of Columbia Circuit
202 Fed. Appx. 470 (2006)

HENDERSON, ROGERS AND GRIFFITH, CIRCUIT JUDGES.

AMENDED MEMORANDUM OPINION

On February 20, 2003, Krouner pled guilty to three felonies: insurance fraud in the third degree, *see* N.Y. Penal Law § 176.20, grand larceny in the fourth degree, *see id.* § 155.30, and workers' compensation fraudulent practices, *see* N.Y. Workers' Compensation Law § 96. *See In re Krouner*, 305 A.D.2d 932, 932, 759 N.Y.S.2d 402 (N.Y. App. Div. 2003) (per curiam). He was, apparently without being given an independent hearing, "automatically disbarred" from the practice of law in New York on the basis of these convictions. *See id.*

I.

On July 16, 2004, the Tax Court directed Krouner to show cause why he should not be suspended or disbarred from practice before the Tax Court.[n.1] After receiving

---

[9] The court noted: "The sentencing judge characterized the incident underlying this conviction as a 'kindergarten shouting and pushing match,' and concluded that 'a five hundred dollar fine would be sufficient punishment for Mr. Thies's fit of pique and temper. . . .' " *Thies*, 662 F.2d at 772 n.5.

[n.1] Rule 202 of the Tax Court's rules of practice and procedure, which was amended in September of 2005,

Krouner's written response, a hearing before a three-judge panel was held on September 14, 2004. After the hearing, Krouner was permitted to submit another brief. Krouner argued principally that (1) the Tax Court could not rely on the New York disbarment because the Supreme Court of New York, Appellate Division failed to provide him due process as it did not examine the mitigating circumstances of his various conditions, and (2) those conditions mitigate his crimes such that these convictions should not be grounds for disbarment from Tax Court practice. At the hearing, Krouner gave a somewhat incongruous account of his criminal convictions: He admitted that he pled guilty to crimes that the court described as "involv[ing] willfulness," but he described those offenses as "sort of like [] strict liability crime[s]" because of the interaction of certain "circumstantial evidence charges that are available in New York" and the sections of the N.Y. Penal Code under which he was charged. Krouner emphasized, however, that "I'm not trying to say [] that I wasn't guilty of the crimes that I pled to" and "I'm not here to say that I'm innocent of those crimes."

On October 22, 2004, the Tax Court issued its decision accompanying the disbarment order. The Tax Court treated Krouner's motion to reopen the record to consider the evidence from Krouner's Florida disciplinary proceedings in 2004 as a motion to vacate, *see* Tax Court Rule 162, and indicated that it would examine the evidence in that light. On January 27, 2005, the Tax Court, "[a]fter due consideration of the Confidential Record," denied Krouner's motions to vacate and for reconsideration.

II.

Krouner challenges the decision of the United States Tax Court to disbar him on the grounds that he was denied due process and that the court failed to credit sufficiently the "mitigating" effect of his evidence and based its disbarment upon the erroneous conclusion that the record demonstrated that he was aware that his guilty pleas to three felonies under New York law would result in disbarment in jurisdictions outside of New York. Whether our review is for abuse of discretion, *see Tulman v. Comm. on Admissions & Grievances*, 135 F.2d 268, 268, 77 U.S. App. D.C. 357 (D.C. Cir. 1943) (per curiam); *In re Cordova-Gonzalez*, 996 F.2d 1334, 1335–36 (1st Cir. 1993), or plenary, *see In re Grievance Comm. of the United States Dist. Court*, 847 F.2d 57, 61 (2d Cir. 1988); *see also* 26 U.S.C. § 7482(a) (2000), we hold that Krouner's challenges fail.

First, even assuming that the "automatic" New York disbarment fails the conditions set forth in *Selling v. Radford*, 243 U.S. 46, 37 S. Ct. 377, 61 L. Ed. 585 (1917), and followed in *Theard v. United States*, 354 U.S. 278, 77 S. Ct. 1274, 1 L. Ed. 2d 1342 (1957), the Tax Court's independent inquiry into Krouner's moral fitness afforded him due process of law. *See In re Ruffalo*, 390 U.S. 544, 551–52, 88 S. Ct. 1222, 20 L. Ed. 2d 117 (1968). The Tax Court allowed Krouner to present evidence mitigating the implication that his crimes evidenced an unfitness to practice before the Tax Court, *see* Tax Court Rule 202, including allowing the late submission of testimony from the Florida proceeding, and the Tax Court then based its disbarment upon its independent evaluation of Krouner's fitness. Although certain conditions may be sufficiently

---

see http://www.ustaxcourt.gov/notice.htm, provided at the relevant time that:

> The Court may deny admission to its Bar to, or suspend, or disbar, any person who in its judgment does not possess the requisite qualifications to represent others, or who is lacking in character, integrity, or proper professional conduct. Upon the conviction of any practitioner admitted to practice before this Court for a criminal violation of any provision of the Internal Revenue Code or for any crime involving moral turpitude, or where any practitioner has been suspended or disbarred from the practice of his or her profession in any State or the District of Columbia, or any commonwealth, territory, or possession of the United States, the Court may, in the exercise of its discretion, forthwith suspend such practitioner from the Bar of this Court until further order of Court.

mitigating to overcome the presumptive effect that a federal court must accord a state disbarment under *Selling*, 243 U.S. at 50–51; *see Theard*, 354 U.S. at 282, Krouner fails to show that he was denied procedural due process. His reliance on *In re Thies*, 662 F.2d 771, 773, 213 U.S. App. D.C. 256 & n.15 (D.C. Cir. 1980), where this court vacated a Tax Court order of disbarment predicated "exclusively" upon the state disbarment, is misplaced because the Tax Court's decision was based on an independent assessment of whether the New York proceedings afforded Krouner adequate process. Krouner contends that because the New York Appellate Division did not conduct an independent hearing prior to disbarring him, the Tax Court similarly denied him due process by relying upon the New York disbarment. However, the Tax Court — with the understanding that its actions were governed by *Selling* and *Thies* — inquired into, and allowed Krouner to explain, his guilty pleas. The Tax Court found that "the counts in this case all involved acts of dishonesty that raise questions of integrity and fitness to practice law"; that the criminal proceedings did not indicate any due process defect, and none was claimed by Krouner; and that Krouner admitted that he was guilty of the crimes and these crimes carried an element of "intent." It also examined the mitigating evidence presented by Krouner and "f[ound] [it] unpersuasive and insufficient to mitigate the effects of his guilty plea." Thus, the Tax Court did not repeat the core defect identified in *Thies*, 662 F.2d at 773, but independently inquired into the nature of the criminal activity and circumstances surrounding the guilty pleas, and thus of Krouner's fitness to practice before the Tax Court. Similarly, by independently inquiring into the mitigating effect of evidence identified by Krouner, the Tax Court provided the remedy that the Supreme Court found appropriate in *Theard:* an independent federal court examination of the grounds for disbarment with the understanding that some conditions may be insufficiently serious to indicate unfitness to practice law. *See Theard*, 354 U.S. at 282–83.

Second, the Tax Court also did not abuse its discretion, or otherwise err so as to require vacatur of the disbarment, in concluding that Krouner was not fit to practice before it. Krouner presents this legal contention in a number of ways, but in the end each fails. For instance, Krouner contends that the Tax Court did not examine the "real conduct" underlying his guilty pleas. He points out that the Tax Court stated that "[c]onduct such as that admitted by Mr. Krouner is a per se violation of the Rules under which practitioners in this Court operate." But the Tax Court's "per se" observation, contrary to Krouner's representations, does not indicate that the Tax Court allowed the fact of his conviction to suffice for his disbarment; rather, it viewed his conviction in the context of any mitigating circumstances and found these circumstances insufficient to avoid disbarment. Although Krouner points to cases where courts have imposed less severe sanctions, this argument simply seeks to have this court second-guess the Tax Court. Additionally, even assuming that the Tax Court erred in attributing to Krouner knowledge that his guilty pleas would result in his disbarment in jurisdictions outside New York, it would not constitute an abuse of discretion unless the Tax Court rested its decision on this fact, which it did not.

How can you explain the different holdings in *Krouner* and *Thies*? Based on the discussion in the two cases, do you believe that Mr. Krouner should have been disbarred by the Tax Court? What about Mr. Thies?

PROBLEMS

1. During the tax controversy process, the practitioner may act in the roles of advisor and advocate. According to the American Bar Association's ethical guidance, at what point in the process (planning, return preparation, filing, audit, appeals, litigation), does the practitioner's role switch from advisor to advocate? Do you agree with the ABA's position?

2. According to the ABA's ethical guidance, how much certainty must the practitioner have about a return position before the practitioner may advise a client to take that position?
   A. How does the ABA standard compare to the current standard for undisclosed positions in section 10.34 of Circular 230?
   B. How does the ABA standard compare to the reporting standard under section 6694 for undisclosed positions?
   C. Which of the various standards do you think is the most appropriate?
3. Both section 10.34 of Treasury Circular 230 and section 6694 contain reporting standards that differ for disclosed and undisclosed positions. How do the standards differ? Why impose a higher standard in one case and not the other?
4. The ABA, in the case of tax shelter opinion letters, and Treasury Circular 230 section 10.35, in the case of covered opinions, impose due diligence requirements on the drafter.
   A. How do those requirements differ in terms of (1) factual due diligence and (2) legal analysis?
   B. Given the similarities between the expected standards of conduct in Formal Opinion 346 and Treasury Circular 230 section 10.35, why not just rely on one or the other to regulate practitioner conduct, rather than both?
5. Are the Treasury Circular 230 standards relating to covered opinions an effective means of combating aggressive advice from tax practitioners? Would an "opt-in" system under which tax advice could be used for penalty protection only in cases in which the practitioner satisfied specific requirements be more effective?
6. Jones, a tax shelter promoter, advised Addison to invest in one of Jones's shelters. Addison did so, and the IRS subsequently audited Addison and disallowed all tax benefits relating to the shelter.
   A. Under what circumstances, if any, may Jones represent Addison before the IRS in the audit?
   B. Assume that Addison does not hire an attorney before receiving a notice of deficiency and petitioning the Tax Court. Under what circumstances, if any, may Jones represent Addison in the Tax Court case?
7. Bill and Carl are equal owners of a corporation engaged in the widget-making business. When they incorporated the corporation, Bill contributed a widget-making machine with a low basis and high value, and Carl contributed both (1) services and (2) supplies with a basis slightly in excess of value. They treated the transaction as a nonrecognition transaction under Code section 351. Bill, Carl, and the corporation have all been audited. The IRS contends that the incorporation of the corporation was taxable because of the magnitude of the services contributed by Carl. If the IRS's position is correct, Bill would owe substantial tax on the incorporation transaction, and the corporation would have a higher basis in the widget-making machine. Carl reported compensation income from the incorporation transaction, which would not be altered by the IRS's argument. Moreover, if the IRS's position is correct, Carl would be entitled to claim a small loss on the incorporation transaction. Bill and Carl contact Denise, an attorney.
   A. Under what circumstances, if any, may Denise represent Bill, Carl, and the corporation before the IRS?
   B. Under what circumstances, if any, may Denise represent Bill, Carl, and the corporation if the matter is docketed in Tax Court?
8. Walter, a tax attorney admitted to the Tax Court bar, was disbarred by the IRS for filing fraudulent tax returns. Will the Tax Court automatically disbar him based on the IRS disbarment?

Chapter 19
REPRESENTING CLIENTS IN TAX CASES

§ 19.01 INTRODUCTION

This chapter explains the basic skills an attorney will need to represent clients involved in tax controversies. It focuses on representation in a tax clinic setting because students may have an opportunity to participate in a clinic that represents low-income taxpayers.[1] However, the skills discussed in this chapter are equally relevant to private tax clients. In fact, a clinic is much like a small law firm. Nonetheless, clients of a low-income taxpayer clinic may present special challenges that other clients do not. In general, clinic clients may face financial, educational, cultural and/or linguistic barriers to resolving their tax problems. These special concerns are discussed further below.

Because effective representation requires a careful determination of the relevant facts, Chapter 19 begins, in Section 19.02, with a discussion of this fact-finding process, the initial client interview. Only after the relevant facts have been reviewed will the legal issues involved begin to appear. Researching these legal issues is the subject of Chapter 20, which describes the sources of federal income tax law and the process for locating those sources. Section 19.03 focuses on counseling the client at each stage of the controversy following analysis of the facts and applicable law. Finally, in Section 19.04, the chapter addresses the fundamentals of negotiation, a skill that is extremely important in tax controversy work.

§ 19.02 CLIENT INTERVIEWING

This section focuses on the content of the initial client interview. However, it is important to note that the attorney typically will conduct some preparation ahead of time. Many tax clinics ask the client to sign a power of attorney form in advance of the initial meeting to allow the clinic to retrieve the client's transcripts electronically from the IRS. *See* http://www.irs.gov/newsroom/article/0,,id=129058,00.html (Sept. 9, 2004). In this scenario, it is a good idea for the attorney to review the client's transcripts not only for the year in question but also for years before and after the year the taxpayer believes is the year for which there is a controversy. This may alert the attorney to related or ongoing problems that also need to be addressed.

[A] Goals and Structure of the Client Interview

The lawyer-client relationship begins with the initial client interview.[2] Therefore, the attorney should try to establish an initial level of trust and rapport by making his client as comfortable as possible.[3] Naturally, the attorney should introduce himself to the client using his first and last names, and generally should shake hands. Robert F. Cochran, Jr. et al., The Counselor-at-Law: A Collaborative Approach to Client Interviewing and Counseling 59, 64 (1999); *see also* David Binder et al., Lawyers as Counselors: A Client-Centered Approach 82–83 (2nd ed. 2004).

A client interview is composed of several parts, and the attorney will likely do a better job of obtaining the facts and establishing an initial level of trust if he has

---

[1] Low-income taxpayer clinics have proliferated since Congress authorized matching grants as part of the IRS Reform Act. *See* I.R.C. § 7526. Many tax clinics are located in academic settings, while others are run by not-for-profit organizations, including legal services organizations.

[2] For convenience, the chapter uses the terms "attorney" and "lawyer" to refer to the representative, even though the representative may be a student working under the supervision of a licensed attorney.

[3] For convenience, this chapter generally will refer to the taxpayer's lawyer as "he" and the taxpayer/client as "she." Other parties, such as IRS representatives, are referred to as "he or she."

organized the interview in advance. *See* STEFAN H. KRIEGER ET AL., ESSENTIAL LAWYERING SKILLS 87 (3rd ed. 2007). The seven main components of the interview are (1) the introductions and "small talk"; (2) routine collection of basic client information; (3) the information-gathering phase during which the client tells her story; (4) a goal-identification stage; (5) an informative stage in which the attorney conveys relevant tax law and tax procedure; (6) a discussion of strategy or possible courses of action; and (7) a closing stage in which attorney and client agree on the steps that will follow the interview. *See id.*; COCHRAN ET AL., *supra*, at 59–61. Some of these parts may be carried out in an interview subsequent to the initial one, particularly if the attorney is inexperienced and needs to consult with others first.

"Small talk" about a topic other than the client's case usually is a good way to begin the interview both because it helps put the client at ease, and also because it may actually elicit information relevant to resolving the client's tax problems.[4] *See* COCHRAN ET AL., *supra* at 65–69; BINDER ET AL., *supra*, at 83–84. For example, asking a client if she had any trouble finding the clinic might elicit a response that she used to work nearby. As this hypothetical response indicates, this "chit chat" may establish commonalities that help bridge any cultural gap between client and attorney.

The client may have been screened over the telephone before she was invited to an in-person interview. The screening may have included a brief discussion of the tax problem that prompted the client to call the clinic. However, the attorney should not assume that he already knows the nature of the problem. Instead, he should use the initial interview to find out the facts of the client's tax problem and what result she is looking for. Both goals are served by listening well to the client's story. Questions should therefore focus on developing that story. The attorney should also take detailed notes throughout the interview.

A number of routine matters should be addressed in the initial client interview. The attorney should ascertain or confirm that the client meets the income and amount-in-controversy guidelines of the clinic. *See* Christian A. Johnson & Mary Grossman, *The Tax Law Clinic: Loyola Chicago's Decade of Experience*, 50 J. LEGAL EDUC. 376, 380 (2000). The attorney should also confirm or ascertain the client's legal name, address, telephone number, social security number, employer's name and address, and the name and social security numbers of the client's spouse and any dependents she may have. *Id.* It is worth double-checking that all names are spelled correctly, and that social security numbers have been accurately recorded. Nina Olson with Michael A. Lormand, *Client Intake Interviewing and Preliminary Procedures in* EFFECTIVELY REPRESENTING YOUR CLIENT BEFORE THE "NEW" IRS § B.4.1 (Jerome Borison ed., 3rd ed. 2004). If a client interview will be videotaped, the attorney should make sure to receive the client's consent to the taping, after explaining how the videotape will be used by the clinic.

The client is likely to be unfamiliar with legal rules and doctrines. Therefore, the attorney should explain early in the interview the extent of the confidentiality of the initial interview, subsequent meetings, and any videotapes of the meetings. *See* COCHRAN ET AL., *supra*, at 61. The attorney should also be prepared for the possibility that the client may have brought another person to the interview, *see* Susan Bryant, *The Five Habits: Building Cross-Cultural Competence in Lawyers*, 8 CLINICAL L. REV. 33, 34 (2001), and should keep in mind that it is the client's decision whether to waive the confidentiality of the attorney-client relationship.

The attorney should also notify the client of any time constraints on the interview. COCHRAN ET AL., *supra*, at 69. The Cochran book provides the following sample statement to begin a client interview (the discussion of fees has been deleted):

> Before we get started, let me tell you about those papers you received in the waiting room. One paper describes what lawyers call the rules on confidential-

[4] For an excellent discussion of this phenomenon, with examples, see Gay Gellhorn, *Law and Language: An Empirically-Based Model for the Opening Moments of Client Interviews*, 4 CLINICAL L. REV. 321 (1998).

ity. That generally means that I cannot tell anyone what we talk about unless you give me permission, but that paper explains some of the exceptions to the rule. . . . Do you have any questions about . . . confidentiality?

Ok, I've set aside 45 minutes for this conference. If we need more time we can schedule another appointment at your convenience.

Id. at 73. The attorney should also discuss any fees or court costs that the case may involve. He should also ascertain whether the client has consulted with another lawyer or accountant about the problem, primarily to ascertain whether proceedings are already ongoing.

Throughout the interview, absent any special cultural concerns,[5] the lawyer should try to put the client at ease by listening, smiling, looking at the client, leaning forward, keeping his arms unfolded, speaking clearly, remaining genuine, and demonstrating that he is focused on and engaged by the interview. *See id.* at 59, 63. It may help to use the client's own terminology or phrasing when asking questions. *See id.* In addition, the attorney should avoid being distracted by ringing telephones or other people who may be walking nearby or talking in adjacent rooms.

To begin the fact-gathering portion of the interview, the lawyer may refer to the screening information he has but should ask the client what has prompted her to come to the clinic. This question should generally be broad and open-ended so that the client feels free to answer in the way she feels comfortable. *See id.* at 79. The tax problems of tax clinic clients frequently involve the earned income credit, filing status issues, dependency exemptions, and substantiation of deductions. Janet Spragens & Nina E. Olson, *Tax Clinics: The New Face of Legal Services*, 88 Tax Notes 1525, 1526 (2000).

> The LITCs are now seeing all of these issues and more: a steady stream of denied child care credits, home office deductions, start-up business expenses, unreported tip income, car expenses, substantiation (of cost of goods sold, interest payments, charitable contributions, etc.), worker classification issues, disability income, pensions, hobby losses, and self employment tax — to name just a few. The taxpayers are taxi drivers, maintenance workers, nurses, restaurant workers, bus drivers, artists, auto mechanics, hairdressers, retirees, agricultural workers, police officers, gas station attendants, teachers — even prisoners.

Id. In addition, tax clinic clients may have tax collection issues.

The client may be seeking advice because of a letter or notice she received from the IRS; it is a good practice to ask the client whether she received any such correspondence. Reviewing the letter may help the attorney determine the stage of the controversy (is it a 30-day letter, 90-day letter, Notice and Demand for Payment, or something else?) and whether immediate, emergency action must be taken. The letter

---

[5] "Appearing warm, reactive, and animated will not build trust in all cultural contexts. In many Asian cultures, expression of emotions is considered immature and a sign of weakness." J. Yamamoto & M. Kubota, *The Japanese American Family, in* The Psychosocial Development of Minority Group Children (J. Yamamoto, A. Romero & A. Moralse eds. 1983), quoted in Robert F. Cochran, Jr. et al., The Counselor-at-Law: A Collaborative Approach to Client Interviewing and Counseling 208 (1999). Another article explains:

> Cultural differences may . . . cause lawyers and clients to misperceive body language and judge each other incorrectly. For an everyday example, take nodding while someone is speaking. In some cultures, this gesture indicates agreement with the speaker; in others, however, it simply indicates that the listener is hearing the speaker. Another common example involves eye contact. In some cultures, looking someone straight in the eye is a statement of open and honest communication while a diversion of eyes signals dishonesty. In other cultures, however, a diversion of eyes is a sign of respect. Students need to recognize these differences and plan for a representation strategy that takes them into account.

Susan Bryant, *The Five Habits: Building Cross-Cultural Competence in Lawyers*, 8 Clinical L. Rev. 33, 48 (2001).

may also indicate the type of tax, tax years involved, and what the issue is. However, the attorney should make sure not to focus on letters and other documents to the detriment of listening to the client and developing rapport with her.

After identifying the basic nature of the tax problem, the attorney should elicit a narrative of it. For example, the attorney might start with, "tell me about the problem from the point it started to the present." Open-ended questions will advance the narrative while also providing the attorney with a sense of some of the causes of the client's problems. The attorney should be nonjudgmental, conveying acceptance of the problem so that the client feels comfortable making further confidences. A tax client is likely to be anxious about the tax matter and its implications for her financial wherewithal, and perhaps frustrated by ineffective attempts to resolve the problem with the IRS on her own. Supportive feedback can facilitate communication of all of the facts.

Therefore, during the narrative, the lawyer should avoid cutting off the client, limiting her responses, or "cross-examining" her. Many people have a natural tendency to interrupt others in conversation. Lawyers, in particular, tend to interrupt clients to elicit information in a particular order or to ascertain details they view as important. *See* COCHRAN ET AL., *supra*, at 88. By doing so, they may make clients uncomfortable in revealing relevant information, or go off on a tangent, thereby actually lengthening the interviewing process. *See id.* at 101–104. However, supportive "interruptions" such as expressions of understanding or agreement should facilitate communication.[6]

After the client tells her "story," the attorney may need to follow up with more specific, targeted questions to ascertain details the client may have omitted. *See id.* at 76. Drawing on the traditional reporters' questions of "who, what, when, where, why, and how" should help in covering all of the details. Make sure that the client is focused on the taxable year in question, which will likely be several years prior to the time the interview takes place. This may require prodding the client's recollection on issues as to the members of her household in that year, her employers, and the like. If the client cannot remember, the attorney should ask her to consult with others who might have the information, such as family members or former employers.

For a collections matter, one source, which does not focus specifically on low-income clients, recommends the following course of action:

> Whenever an IRS Collection Division matter arises, a client meeting needs to be arranged immediately to obtain the following key information:
>
> **What happened and why.** Ask the client what happened; why is the tax liability outstanding? . . . [K]nowing this information is critical when dealing with the Collection Division on the client's behalf. The most likely scenarios are:
>
> 1. The client filed his or her last income tax return showing a balance due and did not send in a check with the return. Possibly the client was self-employed and did not make sufficient estimated tax payments.
>
> 2. The client went through an IRS audit that resulted in a tax deficiency, which was never paid.
>
> 3. The client operates a small business with several employees and then fell behind in remitting payroll taxes.
>
> Knowing why it happened is equally as important:
>
> 1. Did the client have a significant reduction in income?
>
> 2. Did a new competitor take most of the customers away?
>
> 3. Was the client out of work for part of the year (perhaps due to sickness)?
>
> 4. Did the client expand too rapidly?

---

[6] This technique is termed "active listening." *See* STEFAN H. KRIEGER ET AL., ESSENTIAL LAWYERING SKILLS 84 (3rd ed. 2007).

5. Was the client simply living a more luxurious lifestyle than the client's income allowed?

Tax years involved. Determine whether the client owes money to the IRS for only one tax period, or whether a consistent pattern of not paying the IRS exists year after year.[7] Obviously, it is easier for the tax professional to deal with the IRS if the client is behind for only one income tax year (or one payroll tax quarter) and has always paid other past taxes on time.

If, on the other hand, the client consistently falls behind in paying taxes each and every year, then what is to prevent it from happening again? Corrective action by the client will need to be taken.

Review all notices. Review all IRS notices the client has already received to determine what stage the Collection Division process is at. For instance, the tax professional needs to determine whether the client has received only the initial Notice and Demand for Payment from the IRS Service Center, or whether the client has already received a more serious bank levy and possibly a Notice of Federal Tax Lien.[8]

Were all returns filed? Some taxpayers who owe the IRS money are also behind a year or two in filing their tax returns. Negotiating with the IRS on behalf of a client who is still behind in filing tax returns is difficult. Thus, immediate steps should be taken to prepare all late tax returns.

Review tax liability. A thorough review of the client's tax liability should be made. Possibly the underlying tax shown on the IRS notice is wrong — e.g., the IRS filed a substitute tax return (under Section 6020(b)(1)) that was inaccurate. Perhaps the IRS assessed payroll taxes for a business that actually closed months earlier without notifying the IRS. Also, check to determine whether all IRS penalties added on were proper. The IRS makes mistakes every day.

Review limitations period. A common misconception is that once a taxpayer owes the IRS money, the government can continue to collect on it forever. . . .[9]

Richard A. Carpenter, *Get the Best Deal for Clients from the IRS Collection Division*, 27 TAX'N FOR LAWYERS 77, 81 (1998).[10]

Once the attorney has what seems to be the complete story, he should summarize it for the client in order to be certain it is clear. This will also provide an opportunity for the client to mention additional facts that she may have forgotten to relate earlier. The attorney should be clear in the summary that these are the facts, as he understands them, for the taxable year in question, not the current year. If the attorney has not asked the client what her goals are before the client told her story, the lawyer generally should do so after he has determined what the tax problem is, allowed the client to tell the full story, and summarized it for the client.[11] However, some clinics may prefer that this step, and those following it, take place in a second interview, after the lawyer has had time to research the legal issues and discuss the case with others, such as a supervising attorney.

---

[7] [If the client has consistently underpaid taxes in the past, the attorney should be prepared to stress to the IRS the client's forward-looking compliance with the tax laws. — Eds.]

[8] [These notices are discussed in Chapter 14. — Eds.]

[9] [The statute of limitations on collections is discussed in Chapter 14. — Eds.]

[10]

[11] For an example of a client interview in which the attorney asks at the beginning of the interview what the client's goals are ("how I might be of help"), see David Binder et al., *Lawyers as Counselors: A Client-Centered Approach* 86 (2nd ed. 2004). The Binder book includes "clients' goals and expectations" as part of "preliminary problem identification." *Id.* at 87.

It is very important that the attorney ascertain the client's goals before focusing on courses of action because the client may have goals other than simply resolving the tax case. Those goals may include such things as demonstrating that she is not a "tax cheat," or keeping others, such as an employer or ex-spouse, unaware of her tax problem. If the lawyer does not find out the client's goals, what the lawyer might consider a "win" may actually disappoint or anger the client. *See* Clark D. Cunningham, *The Lawyer as Translator, Representation as Text: Towards an Ethnography of Legal Discourse*, 77 CORNELL L. REV. 1298, 1304 (1992).

For example, the client may have sought the clinic's help with filing tax returns for prior years.[12] The normal process is to mail the completed returns to the IRS, retaining a photocopy. However, if the client's reason for coming to the clinic is that she needs to prove in an upcoming immigration hearing that she has filed her tax returns, photocopies of completed returns will not be sufficient for the client's purposes. Instead, the client will need to have duplicate originals brought to the IRS in person, so that one original may be stamped "received" by the IRS and retained by the client.

As another example, the client's reason for enlisting the help of the clinic to obtain a tax refund retained by the IRS may be that she is facing eviction and urgently needs the money to pay her rent. If the attorney pursues audit reconsideration, for example, the process may take much longer than the client assumed, and the client may be furious even if she eventually receives the money. In this situation, the client's urgent need for the funds in order to avoid eviction would give rise to the right to seek the assistance of the Taxpayer Advocate Service to facilitate the receipt of the refund, which can be accomplished through the filing of Form 911. As these examples demonstrate, it is key that the attorney ascertain the client's goals, rather than assuming that the client's only goal is to pay the least amount of tax possible or obtain a refund.

Occasionally, clients may have goals that are not realistic, such as the desire to receive, in addition to a full concession by the IRS, a letter of apology. In those cases, the attorney might empathize with the client's situation and should try to diffuse the client's anger at the IRS and help the client develop more realistic goals. It may help to explain to the client that the audit rate on certain issues, such as the earned income credit, is relatively high.

In this regard, it may help to ascertain during the initial interview to what extent the client has already dealt with the IRS and the nature of those experiences. That is, if the client is extremely frustrated with the IRS, it is better to ascertain that early and try to diffuse the client's anger so that it does not pose a problem during the resolution of the controversy. The attorney might acknowledge the client's anger and feelings of being unfairly treated, and then redirect the client's attention to the client's primary concerns.

Some clients may push to take a case to trial in order to be able to tell their stories to a judge. The attorney might once again be empathetic, but explain to the client the disadvantages of pushing for a trial when the reality is that most tax cases settle, and that even the Tax Court discourages trials through its requirement of stipulations of the facts and techniques such as encouraging counsel to discuss settlement. The attorney may need to explain that it will only hurt the client's case if she insists on going to trial in spite of a reasonable settlement offer by the IRS. Moreover, if a client insists on making "tax protestor" arguments — for example, that the entire income tax is unconstitutional — the attorney must tell her that courts do not permit those arguments and very likely will impose monetary sanctions on the client if those arguments are

---

[12] "LITCs have been permitted to prepare tax returns because the IRS has taken the position that preparing tax returns for ESL [English-as-second-language] taxpayers constitutes a program to inform ESL taxpayers about their rights and responsibilities." *See* Leslie Book, *Tax Clinics: Past the Tipping Point and to the Turning Point*, 92 TAX NOTES 1089 (2001).

made. *See* I.R.C. § 6673(a) (discussed in Chapter 11); *see also* Philips v. Commissioner, T.C. Memo. 1995-540 (reproduced in Chapter 11). Similarly, an attorney cannot ethically make such arguments on a client's behalf.

On the other hand, some clients may wish to avoid making certain arguments, or may prefer to concede certain issues. For example, the facts of a client's case may suggest a compelling claim for innocent spouse relief. However, the client may be reluctant to portray her spouse or ex-spouse in a bad light. A victim of domestic violence may be extremely reluctant to testify to it in Tax Court, a public forum, even though the testimony would support the claim for innocent spouse relief. An attorney needs to be sensitive to this issue, and not simply assume that the client will be willing to tell her story to anyone. As another example, the client may be unwilling or unable to gather the documentation necessary to prove an issue such as "head of household" filing status, and prefer to move forward only on another issue, such as the earned income credit.

Once the client's goals have been identified, attorney and client can focus on possible ways to obtain that outcome. This will require a familiarity with tax procedure in general and specific options relevant to the client's situation in particular. For example, in a collections matter, options include making an audit reconsideration request; submitting an offer-in-compromise; entering into an installment agreement with the IRS; convincing the IRS that the account is uncollectible; paying the tax and conceding the case, perhaps by borrowing the money or selling assets; or, depending on the taxes involved, seeking bankruptcy protection. *See* Carpenter, *supra*, at 82–83 (footnotes omitted).

If Tax Court litigation is a possibility, the attorney should explain the basics of the court and its procedures, including those of the small tax case division. Very few tax cases go to trial, but Tax Court petitions are filed in many cases. The attorney should make the client aware that the taxpayer generally bears the burden of proving the facts in a litigated tax case. He should also explain to the client the importance of substantiating the relevant facts of the tax year in question. Records relating to the current year will not establish to the IRS where the client lived or the amount of her income or expenses from the tax year in issue. The client will need to understand that, without records, the resolution of factual questions will likely rest on the credibility of the client and her witnesses.

The discussion of possible ways of resolving the case should help the lawyer ascertain what resolution the client is seeking and what resolution, short of that, the client would be willing to accept. The lawyer should couch the available options in terms of those that occur to him off the "top of his head at this time" in case there are others as well or that subsequently become available. Note that, under legal ethics rules, the client is entitled to make most of the decisions in her case. *See* Model Rule of Professional Conduct 1.2(a). If the client is unsure of what resolution she wants, the attorney can ask the client to reflect both on the client's goals and on the desired outcome. *See* Cochran, et al., *supra*, at 107. He can also ask the client to think about possible ways to accomplish that outcome, which may help the client remain personally invested in the case. *Id.*

An experienced attorney may be able to assess the likely outcome of particular options. Inexperienced attorneys probably will be unable to evaluate the likely outcome, and should not make an uneducated guess. Instead, the attorney should tell the client that he will need to review the facts, perform research, and get back to her. Similarly, if the attorney does not know the length of time a particular course of action will take, he should not give one. Moreover, the attorney should avoid the temptation to promise a client a favorable outcome. Instead, he should make clear that he cannot guarantee any particular result.

If the attorney is experienced, and he knows the likely outcome of a particular option (such as an innocent spouse claim or a Tax Court trial), he should explain that to the client. If the likely outcome of a particular option is unfavorable, the attorney should communicate that and should not back off of the negative evaluation even if pressured by the client. *See id.* at 159 (*quoting* Linda F. Smith, *Medical Paradigms for*

Counseling: Giving Clients Bad News, 4 CLINICAL L. REV. 391, 391–93, 417–27, 430–31 (1998)). If the outcome of a particular course of action is uncertain, the attorney should convey that.

If the attorney, even an experienced one, does not perceive any way to obtain a desirable outcome in the client's case, it may be best to wait until after the interview to convey that. *See* KRIEGER ET AL., *supra*, at 271–72. First, reflection on the problem and consultation with others may suggest additional options.[13] In addition, as discussed below, people generally handle bad news better if they are given a complete explanation of why the news is what it is. Waiting before delivering the news provides time to prepare for likely client questions in that regard. *See id.*

At the close of the interview, the attorney should make sure that the client understands what will happen next. If additional information or documentation is needed from the client, the lawyer should explain what is needed, preferably providing the client with a written list.[14] If there are deadlines, including statutes of limitations, the attorney should inform the client about them and follow up with a letter that also provides the information. For example, if a client chooses not to pursue Tax Court litigation after receiving a notice of deficiency, the attorney should tell her the last day a petition may be filed so that the client knows the timetable under which she may change the decision not to petition the court. *See* COCHRAN ET AL., *supra*, at 108.

At the conclusion of the interview, the attorney should also tell the client how she may contact the attorney or the clinic as the case goes forward. This will assure the client of the clinic's continuing availability for follow-up interviews and counseling. *Id.* at 106–107. Once the clinic decides to take the case, the lawyer may need to ask the client to sign a representation agreement. That agreement should require clients to agree to maintain contact with the clinic and to update their contact information as it changes. Tax clinic clients may have financial problems that result in interruption of their telephone service and frequent moves. Regardless of whether a formal agreement is signed, the attorney should stress to the client how important it is that the clinic be able to contact her. Ascertaining the best way to contact the client may also elicit information about literacy problems the client may have.[15] In addition, once the clinic takes the case, the attorney should obtain a signed power of attorney if the clinic did not already obtain one in advance of the initial meeting.

As the discussion above indicates, the primary goals of an initial client interview are to establish rapport with the client and to understand the facts of the client's problem. Showing empathy, asking open-ended, broad questions, and listening closely are the attorney's best tools in this regard.

---

[13] Janet Spragens and Nina Olson provide an example of the creativity that may be necessary to resolve clients' tax problems:

> [T]his year the AU tax clinic successfully challenged the asserted tax on $10,000 of unreported lottery income won by one of its clients — by showing a pattern of regular gambling activity that produced offsetting losses. Even though the taxpayer, a construction worker, had thrown away his losing lottery tickets for the year in question, the student-attorney assigned to the case interviewed and obtained affidavits from the liquor store employees where the client had established a regular pattern of buying five tickets per day, six days per week (not Sundays), over several years. Indeed, in the initial client interview with the clinic, the taxpayer took out his wallet and pulled out the five tickets he had bought for that day, which the students immediately photocopied and later showed to the IRS.

Janet Spragens & Nina E. Olson, *Tax Clinics: The New Face of Legal Services*, 88 TAX NOTES 1525, 1527 (2000).

[14] If the client did not keep a copy of her tax return, the attorney will need to request it (or a transcript) from the IRS. If the client did not keep other documents, creativity may be necessary to find alternatives, as in the example regarding documenting lottery losses. *See* note 13, *supra*.

[15] The issues raised by illiterate clients are discussed further below, in Section 19.02[B].

[B] Special Challenges

[1] Generally

As indicated above, low-income clients may present special challenges caused by economic, educational, cultural, and/or linguistic barriers.

> Many LITC clients are those often least able to help themselves, including relative newcomers to the country who may speak English as a second language (ESL). These ESL taxpayers, while diverse in their backgrounds, often share significant language barriers, a fear of government, and fear of financial institutions. They also often have little understanding of our nation's voluntary system of tax self-assessment. Other clients include those who have reentered or just entered the workforce from the welfare rolls, and recently separated or divorced taxpayers. A significant number of LITC clients lack access to computers and to the Internet that many of us now take for granted in our lives, and have limited literacy skills and educational backgrounds. A large percentage of LITC clients has limited means of transportation, and are overextended, balancing the demands of both work and family in single-parent households.[16]

Leslie Book, *Tax Clinics: Past the Tipping Point and to the Turning Point*, 92 Tax Notes 1089, 1090 (2001) (footnote omitted). Thus, for example, even arranging a time for an interview may be difficult for a low-income client because the client may have an inflexible work schedule or transportation may be a problem. Olson with Lormand, *supra*, at § B.4.1. At times, the client may have no choice but to bring a child to the interview. *Id.*

Some clients may be illiterate. For those clients, it is important to explain everything orally. A complicating factor is that the client may be embarrassed about her illiteracy and reluctant to confide it. Therefore, the attorney should wait until he has developed an initial rapport with the client before asking questions related to literacy. He might start out by asking the client about her education level. He can then comment that the tax law is very complicated and many people have trouble understanding notices from the IRS. He can ask if the client has trouble with that as well, and if she has anyone who helps in this regard. This may not establish for the attorney whether the client has basic literacy and therefore can read letters from the clinic, but it may help. In addition, if the client admits to trouble reading or understanding IRS notices, the attorney should ask her to send or bring a copy of any such notices to the clinic immediately after receiving them.

Because the literacy issue may not be resolved in the first interview, it is important that the attorney follow up an interview with a new client not only with a representation letter but also with a telephone call that conveys the information. The attorney should document in the file when he called the client and what information he relayed.

[2] Language Barriers

Identifying the problem, ascertaining the facts, and developing rapport may be more challenging if the client and attorney have different cultural backgrounds, and even more difficult if they can communicate only through an interpreter. *See* Kevin R. Johnson & Amagda Perez, *Clinical Legal Education and the U.C. Davis Immigration Law Clinic: Putting Theory into Practice and Practice into Theory*, 51 SMU L. Rev. 1423, 1439 (1998). Inevitably, some tax clinic clients will not speak English well enough to communicate with an English-speaking attorney without an interpreter.

---

16 [In current literature, individuals with limited English ability may be referred to as "Limited English Proficient (LEP)." *See, e.g.*, Muneer I. Ahmad, *Interpreting Communities: Lawyering Across Language Difference*, 54 UCLA L. Rev. 999, 1000 (2007).]

A meeting with an interpreter present may take more time, so the attorney should plan accordingly. It is generally helpful to explain how the meeting will proceed and allow the client a chance to talk to the interpreter and raise any questions she has. When using an interpreter to communicate with a client, the lawyer should face the client and speak to her rather than to the interpreter. Questions should be addressed to the client directly (*e.g.*, "Where did you live in 2006?") rather than to the interpreter (*e.g.*, "Ask her where she lived in 2006."). It also helps to speak using fewer sentences at a time, so that the interpreter can more easily retain what was said.

The attorney should always be sensitive to communication barriers, including those posed by cultural differences, but these may be compounded if the client is speaking through an interpreter. For example, a Spanish-speaking client who is asked his marital status may say that he is "soltero" (which may be translated as "single") even if he is in fact divorced. Even if the client speaks English, cultural differences in the concept of marital status could result in the client saying that he is single. The distinction between being single and divorced may matter to the tax case because it may be important whether the client was married during the tax year in question. In such a case, the attorney may need to follow up a statement that a client is "single" with a question about whether he has ever been married. The following example from a law school clinic raises a similar issue.

> In . . . [one case] our client was charged with the misdemeanor of Operating a Vehicle While Under the Influence of Liquor . . . and a companion per se violation of operating a vehicle with a blood-alcohol level in excess of 0.10%. When the students presented the case to me after the intake interview, they reported that the client admitted that he was guilty. . . .
>
> The representation had an unusual complicating factor: the client's native language was Spanish and his ability to speak English was limited. Accordingly, we had arranged for a law student fluent in Spanish to attend the intake interview as a translator. As we reviewed the video tape, I noted that when the students asked the client, "What happened?" his first response was "Yo soy culpable." The translator paused for a moment and then said, for the client, "I'm guilty." . . . The students confirmed that this exchange was the basis for their report that the client "admitted" he was guilty.
>
> I was curious to find out why the client's words were translated as "I'm guilty," and so I sought out the translating law student. The translator confirmed my suspicion that the Spanish word used by our client, "culpable," was a close cognate of the English word bearing the same form. As a result, the client's statement could have also been translated: "I am culpable" or "I am blameworthy." Thus the client could have been saying something more like, "I feel bad about what I did," or "I accept personal responsibility for the consequences of my action." If the client's words had been given these latter possible translations, the students might well have reached a different conclusion about his admission of "guilt."

Clark D. Cunningham, *A Tale of Two Clients: Thinking about Law as Language*, 87 MICH. L. REV. 2459, 2464 (1989) (footnote omitted).

This example also reveals the importance of using a trained interpreter whenever possible. Interpretation is a skill that goes beyond the ability to speak two languages fluently. In part, it may require translating concepts rather than translating individual words. It may also require sensitivity to the fact that the meaning of words is influenced by cultural context, or call for proficiency in a particular dialect. In addition, tax cases present terms of art that may pose a challenge to an interpreter who is not familiar with them. For example, it may be particularly difficult to explain the difference between an IRS Appeals conference and an appeal from a court decision if the interpreter is not familiar with tax procedure.

Of course, it may not always be possible to use a professional interpreter. If that is the case, the attorney should consider who might serve as an interpreter. Sometimes the client will bring a family member to interpret, but that can pose additional problems. A client may bring a grade-school aged child to interpret for her, for example. A child is unlikely to be able to translate the legal and tax vocabulary necessary for attorney and client to communicate. Even an adult family member who serves as an interpreter may pose problems not present if an unrelated party interprets, because the family dynamic may hinder representation. For example, in an innocent spouse case, the client may be reluctant to talk about the details of her marriage in the presence of a family member.

If a non-professional interpreter is used, he or she should be instructed to tell the attorney if he or she is unsure of the meaning of a question or answer, rather than guessing at the translation. In addition, the interpreter should limit his or her interaction with the client to verbatim interpretation, so that the interpreter does not attempt to give legal advice to the client, insert the interpreter's own perspective or inadvertently hamper the attorney's development of rapport with the client. It may also be worth recording the interview if the client is comfortable with that and the clinic has appropriate safeguards to keep the recording confidential. That way, the lawyer can refer back to the recording and seek additional translation, if needed.

A client who cannot speak English likely cannot read it, either. It is therefore important to stress to a client who is not fluent in English that if she receives any mail from the government, or any other mail that may relate to her tax case, she should immediately send or bring a copy of it to the clinic. The IRS is not infallible, so filing a power of attorney under which the IRS sends copies to the clinic does not guarantee that the clinic will receive copies of everything.

[C] Following Up: Representation Letters and Retainer Agreements

After the initial interview, the attorney or the clinic should follow up with a letter to the client. The letter may include a retainer agreement, if that is the clinic's practice. Retainer agreements are discussed briefly below. The letter should be cordial, with an opening pleasantry and a closing expressing the attorney's interest in working with the client on the tax matter. In addition, the letter should avoid the use of legal jargon that the client might not understand. Furthermore, as indicated above, because of the possibility that the client is illiterate, it is worth telephoning her to convey the same information orally. The attorney should document the call in the client's file.

A representation letter should detail the facts of the case and ask the client to inform the attorney of any inaccuracies as soon as possible. It should also list any options summarized at the initial interview and any others that the attorney has thought of subsequently. In addition, it should reiterate that the attorney cannot guarantee any particular result. If the attorney needs particular documents from the client, the letter should list them. If a deadline, such as the deadline to file a Tax Court petition, has already passed, the letter should include that information. If there are deadlines that have not expired, the letter should specify them clearly. In addition, the letter should notify the client about the timing of the next contact between attorney and client, such as a statement that the attorney will contact the client if he has not heard from her by a certain date. The letter should also ask the client to inform the attorney as soon as possible if anything new happens with respect to the case.

A retainer agreement is a contract between the clinic and the client. It should specify the terms of the agreement, including (1) the clinic's fees, if any; (2) the extent to which the client is responsible for any costs incurred by the clinic on the client's behalf; (3) the client's obligation to notify the clinic of changes in her financial circumstances that may affect her eligibility for representation; (4) the clinic's right to retain any attorney's fees awarded in the case; (5) a confidentiality statement; (6) the clinic's right to withdraw from representation; and (7) the client's agreement to cooperate with the clinic. *See* Olson with Lormand, *supra*, Appendix H.

[D] Declining Representation

After the initial interview of the client, the clinic may decide to decline representation of the client for such reasons as (1) the client or her case does not meet the income level or other guidelines of the clinic, (2) the client seems uncooperative, unreliable, or untrustworthy, (3) the client's only case may consist of illegal "tax protestor" arguments, (4) the matter does not present a legal problem, (5) the situation may be simple enough that the client can handle it herself after some direction, (6) the clinic does not have the resources to provide quality representation of the client, (7) the client contacted the clinic too late for it to be able to help her, or (8) the matter presents a conflict of interest for the clinic. *See* Johnson & Grossman, *supra*, at 379–380; Olson with Lormand, *supra*, at B-2–B-3.

If the clinic declines representation, the clinic or the attorney who interviewed the client should inform the client both orally and in writing. This should forestall problems that could arise if the client were to believe or allege that the clinic had taken her case, and statutes of limitations were therefore allowed to run. Accordingly, the attorney should document in the file the oral communication with the client.

The letter declining representation should be as cordial as a representation letter, and similarly should avoid the use of legalese, even if it is a form letter. It should specify the reason that representation was declined. The letter should also inform the client that she may wish to seek other counsel promptly to avoid allowing any legal deadlines to lapse. However, the letter should be clear that its author has not researched what those deadlines might be.

§ 19.03 CLIENT COUNSELING

[A] Overview

The ultimate goal of client counseling by the attorney is to facilitate the client's process of deciding among various options as they present themselves throughout the pendency of the case. This will require the attorney (1) to ascertain the key facts and the client's goals, (2) to inform the client about applicable tax law and procedure, and (3) to provide advice to the client. *See* Robert F. Cochran, Jr. et al., The Counselor-at-Law: A Collaborative Approach to Client Interviewing and Counseling 132 (1999). These steps involve building rapport between the attorney and the client and negotiating the terms of the attorney-client relationship. Alex J. Hurder, *Negotiating the Lawyer-Client Relationship: A Search for Equality and Collaboration*, 44 Buff. L. Rev. 71 91 (1996). The attorney may have already completed part or all of one or more of the three steps during the initial client interview. However, it is likely that the client and attorney will need to talk additional times before the case is resolved.

A tax controversy may comprise several stages, each of which may warrant meeting with the client. Those stages may include an Appeals conference, negotiating with IRS counsel, Tax Court or other litigation, and resolution of collections issues. It is important that the attorney prepare for each meeting. Staying up-to-date on the case demonstrates a minimum level of professional competence and shows respect for the client by avoiding the need for her to repeat information previously conveyed. Thus, the attorney should review the facts of the client's case, the client's goals, and applicable substantive and procedural law. *See* Stefan H. Krieger et al., Essential Lawyering Skills 221 (3rd ed. 2007). He should also consider how to explain legal terms and concepts to a lay person. *Id.* at 262. In addition, the attorney should analyze the available options and their costs and benefits. *Id.* at 221–22. This will prepare him to assist client decisionmaking, as discussed below.

During each meeting with the client, the attorney should discuss the options presented, taking the lead on explaining the legal risks and benefits of each option, so as to inform the client fully. Some clients may benefit from seeing this information in writing. If the options are tentative because the next set of negotiations has not yet commenced, the attorney should make that clear to the client. Donald G. Gifford, *The Synthesis of Legal Counseling and Negotiation Models: Preserving Client-Centered Advocacy in the Negotiation Context*, 34 UCLA L. Rev. 811, 845 (1987).

As in the initial interview, during each encounter with the client, the attorney should avoid interrupting the client, and try to put the client at ease by demonstrating that he is focused on and engaged by the interview. Sitting together at a conference table or other table may make the client more comfortable than sitting with a desk between client and attorney. *See* Krieger et al., *supra*, at 263. In addition, the attorney should block out enough time for the meeting that the client is not rushed into a decision. Cochran et al., *supra*, at 153.

A lawyer effective at counseling clarifies his clients' goals, provides emotional support for his clients during the decisionmaking process, informs clients about available options, and encourages clients to organize the information in a way that facilitates decisionmaking. *Id.* at 113. The Cochran book suggests beginning follow-up discussions with a client with the open-ended question such as "Has anything happened that I should know about?" *Id.* at 135. In addition, specific, directed questions may be appropriate when the attorney knows that a particular event may have happened during the intervening time. *See id.* at 135–136.

As indicated above, legal ethics rules generally provide that the client, not the lawyer, is the decisionmaker. The lawyer is merely the client's agent in making those decisions. A client may choose to concede or settle a case that has a good chance at winning in court, or press to litigate a case with little chance of success. The client may want the lawsuit to go away as soon as possible, or may want a day in court. In general, those decisions are the client's, subject to the prohibitions against frivolous litigation. More typically, the client may be basing her decisions on how to proceed on the advice of her attorney. In this regard, preparation by the attorney, as discussed above, is key.

Following the initial question about whether anything has transpired since the last meeting, the attorney should propose an agenda for the conference. Hurder, *supra*, at 92. Once client and attorney agree on the agenda, the attorney should summarize the material to be discussed. This will help with efficient use of time. The summary should cover the key facts of the case, relevant tax law and procedure, and the options presented. *See* Cochran et al., *supra*, at 134. Note that these three parts of the summary correspond to the three points discussed at the beginning of this section. In addition, the attorney should ascertain whether the client's goals have changed since the last discussion. *Id.* at 135.

In presenting the available options, the attorney should list *all* options, even those he might dismiss if he were the client. *See id.* at 136, 138. Depending on the stage of the tax controversy, as discussed in Chapter 1 and subsequent chapters, these options may include requesting a settlement conference with the IRS Appeals Division, requesting mediation from the IRS, seeking to arbitrate with the IRS, petitioning the United States Tax Court, filing a refund claim, suing the government in a federal district court or the Court of Federal Claims, negotiating a collection dispute with the IRS, or requesting a Collection Due Process hearing. The attorney may suggest that some options are more feasible or appealing than others and explain why, but he should not eliminate options without at least mentioning them. Recall that the client, not the attorney, must make any decisions about her case. Without complete information, the client will not be able to make an informed decision.

Once all of the options are on the table, the client and attorney should discuss the pros and cons of each option, in light of the client's goals. *See id.* at 141. In establishing the criteria to be used to evaluate each option, the attorney should ask the client what criteria matter to her. The attorney can also assist the client in establishing the criteria by suggesting additional or different criteria that seem to reflect the client's goals and concerns. *Id.* at 144. If criteria emerge that seem inconsistent with the client's stated goals, the attorney should explore whether the client has additional, unarticulated goals. *Id.* at 145.

Once the criteria are established, they need to be applied to each available course of action. In order to apply the criteria systematically to each option, the attorney and the client should identify all of the consequences of each option, including consequences to third parties; assess both the positive and negative aspects of those consequences and the importance of each of these "pros" and "cons"; and evaluate the likelihood that each consequence will come to pass. *Id.* at 146–147. If the client states that she needs more information to evaluate the options, the attorney should provide it or arrange to get it to her. *Id.* at 155.

The attorney should also be prepared for the possibility that the client will try to avoid making a decision. If the client is unclear that the decision is hers, not the attorney's, the attorney should reiterate that the decision in the client's case belongs to the client. *See* KRIEGER ET AL., *supra*, at 264. However, it is human nature to avoid difficult decisions by procrastinating. The attorney can facilitate appropriate decisionmaking by establishing with the client the criteria to be used to evaluate each option under discussion and applying the criteria systematically to each option. *See* COCHRAN ET AL., *supra*, at 143. Having the client summarize the options and applicable criteria may also help the client take ownership of the decision. In addition, it may help to inform the client that, until the case is resolved, interest will continue to accrue on any amounts ultimately due to the IRS, as discussed in Chapter 13.

It is also possible that the client will disclaim responsibility for the decision, perhaps telling the attorney that she will do whatever the lawyer advises her to do or asking the attorney what he would do if he were the client. The attorney should try to assist the client in making the decision for herself. *See* DAVID BINDER ET AL., LAWYERS AS COUNSELORS: A CLIENT-CENTERED APPROACH 272 (2nd ed. 2004). He can tell the client that it is the client's decision because it is the client who will suffer the consequences; it is not the attorney who will have to pay the taxes. *See id.* The attorney can enumerate the options and ask the client which one looks best. If the client absolutely refuses to choose an option, and insists that the lawyer make the decision, the lawyer can specify which option he thinks best meets the client's goals and ask if the client agrees with that decision. In specifying the option that seems best, the attorney should be sure to specify the drawbacks and risks of that option, as well as the reasons the option seems to fit the criteria the client has established for the decision. Most importantly, he should prepare the client for the worst case scenario that could result from the choice. If the client agrees with the choice, the lawyer should record the decision in the client's file and follow up with a letter confirming that the client agreed to that choice during the meeting.

During the decisionmaking process, particularly if the client resists making a decision, the attorney should ascertain whether the client would like to discuss the options with someone else (such as a family member) before making a choice. Once the client has made a decision, the attorney may follow up with questions about whether the option satisfies the client's goals. *See* COCHRAN ET AL., *supra* at 155. This will help ensure that the client does not simply "settle" for a sub-optimal choice. *See id.* at 152. Finally, once the client has reached a decision, the attorney should discuss contingency plans in case the choice proves ineffective. *Id.* at 156.

If the client makes a decision that the attorney feels is extremely unwise given the facts, the client's stated goals, and the law, the attorney should question the client to ascertain the reasons for the client's decision. He should also warn the client of the likely negative consequences of that decision. *See* Krieger et al., *supra* at 275. The warning should be couched as concern for the client, rather than as a lecture. *Id.* It is not appropriate to argue with the client. Also, the attorney should make clear that he will follow through on the client's decision although he may disagree with it. *Id.*

[B] Delivering Bad News

Sometimes it will be necessary to give a client bad news. Before doing so, the attorney should gather all of the relevant information, so that he is prepared for any questions the client may ask. Cochran et al., *supra*, at 157 (quoting Linda F. Smith, *Medical Paradigms for Counseling: Giving Clients Bad News*, 4 Clinical L. Rev. 391, 430–31 (1998)). In general, bad news should be conveyed in person, not by telephone, and with adequate time for the client to process it. *Id.* at 158 (*quoting* Smith, *supra*). The attorney should be firm with the message, rather than hiding or burying the information or suggesting that the news could change. *See* Binder et al., *supra*, at 244. However, he should avoid "dropping a bombshell" on the client by conveying the bad news as soon as the counseling session begins. *Id.* Instead, the attorney should indicate that he has bad news to share and empathize with the client after relaying the bad news. *See* Krieger et al., *supra*, at 271–72; Cochran et al., *supra*, at 159 (*quoting* Smith, *supra*).

Depending on the type of bad news, the attorney may be able to continue to provide assistance to the client. For example, a client may come to a tax clinic with a legal issue on which the IRS is clearly right.

> In those cases, and there are many of them, the clinics perform an important "second opinion" service by helping the client evaluate the merits of the case and understand in fact that they do owe the money and that further litigation is just an exercise in building up interest charges. Often, the government attorneys have already told them this, but the clients are distrustful of the source of the information and tend not to believe it. Clinic attorneys can explain the law and the adjustments to the client in a way that often results in the taxpayer settling the case. In many instances, clients are not protesting the underlying liability but are simply unable to pay the tax. Clinics can then counsel and represent the client in the collection matter. . . .

Janet Spragens & Nina E. Olson, *Tax Clinics: The New Face of Legal Services*, 88 Tax Notes 1525, 1528 (2000).

The lawyer should also be able to help the client with bad news that arises later in the tax controversy process. For example, if a particular strategic choice did not resolve itself as attorney and client had hoped, they can turn to the contingency plan developed at the time the strategic decision was made. On the other hand, if the situation is such that there is nothing more that the attorney can do, he should consider whether there are other resources available to the client, and make an appropriate referral. He may also be able to advise the client how to handle the tax issue in the future so that the same problem does not arise again.

§ 19.04 NEGOTIATING A TAX CONTROVERSY

Given that more than 90 percent of all tax disputes settle prior to actual litigation, tax practitioners must constantly strive to improve their negotiation skills. Settlement-oriented negotiations may take place at various stages of the tax controversy process: at the conclusion of the audit, during the administrative appeal of an asserted deficiency or refund denial, during litigation, and during administrative collection proceedings. The goal in each case is to persuade the IRS representative that a settlement offer makes sense for both the client and the government.

While actual experience may be the best method for developing and improving one's negotiation techniques, there are aspects of the bargaining process in general, and the tax settlement process in particular, that a tax clinic student can learn through reading and study. This section is divided into two parts: first, a presentation of some basic considerations relating to negotiation and bargaining; and second, an examination of tactical issues tailored to each stage of the tax controversy process. The discussion assumes that the negotiation process can be broken down into identifiable steps. In reality, the steps commonly overlap and there can be movement back and forth from one step to another. Moreover, only parts of the negotiation process may be applicable to any given situation. As a result, the discussion serves primarily as a guideline for narrowing options, rather than an attempt to provide precise answers to all questions.

This section builds upon material discussed in other chapters. First and foremost, the chapter assumes an understanding of the various stages of tax controversies, explained in Section 1.04 of Chapter 1. In addition, knowledge of the examination process, discussed in Chapter 3, is helpful background information for this section. Finally, Chapter 5 raises some fundamental considerations concerning negotiations with the IRS Appeals Division, including how to draft a protest letter and whether to approach settlement negotiations at the Appeals level before or after filing a Tax Court petition.

[A] Negotiation Styles: Competitive and Cooperative

There are two basic negotiation styles: competitive and cooperative. A negotiator's style refers to his attitudinal approach or demeanor when interacting with the opposing party. Negotiation *style* is distinguishable from negotiation *strategy*. While style focuses on interpersonal behavior, strategy refers to the methods or tactics that the negotiator employs to reach the most favorable settlement possible. The distinction between style and strategy is often blurry, however. A negotiator may adopt a particular bargaining style in order to advance or camouflage his bargaining strategy. *See* ALI-ABA, SKILLS AND ETHICS IN THE PRACTICE OF LAW 61–62 (2nd ed. 2000).

As the name suggests, a cooperative negotiating style is characterized by courteous and tactful behavior, with a view toward an open and free flow of information between the parties. *See id.* at 64. A cooperative negotiator perceives the bargaining process as a joint effort in which both sides can succeed, or at least feel that they have succeeded. To achieve a joint solution, the attorney tries to develop a positive atmosphere of trust, conducive to finding common ground, shared interests, and compromise. Expressing a willingness to compromise does not mean that the cooperative negotiator should appear weak or uncommitted. He must still clearly identify the relevant issues and options and guard against sending conflicting signals to the other side.

A competitive negotiator, on the other hand, does not view the bargaining process as a joint effort, but instead as an adversarial proceeding in which the interests of his own client must prevail. The competitive style is characterized by firmness, aggressiveness, and a dominating attitude. *See id.* By seeking to control the negotiations, the competitive negotiator hopes to put his opponent on the defensive and force the opponent to make mistakes and unintentional concessions. A negotiator adopting the competitive style also is less likely to share information or ideas with the opposing side and more likely to use threats and arguments to attempt to force the other side to accept his bottom line position.

Each negotiation style, when carried out effectively, can lead to a successful result. In all cases, the negotiator should try to maintain a respectful and courteous attitude toward the IRS representative and avoid making personal attacks. As between the two types of behavior, competitive behavior carries a higher risk that settlement talks will fail. CHARLES B. CRAVER, EFFECTIVE LEGAL NEGOTIATION AND SETTLEMENT 19 (5th ed. 2005). A competitive negotiator who uses threats and intimidation may quickly lose objectivity, causing the process to degenerate into an ego contest between the participants. This tendency seems particularly strong among less experienced negotiators. Moreover, short-term successes using highly aggressive tactics may result in long-term damage to the negotiator's credibility, which may adversely affect the negotiator's ability to reach agreement with the IRS in future cases.

A purely cooperative style, however, carries its own risks. As noted above, an opponent may misinterpret a cooperative style as weakness or as a signal that the representative is willing to settle on any terms. *See* ALI-ABA, *supra*, at 64. A cooperative negotiator must also guard against making too many concessions and committing to an agreement that is, upon reflection, not in the client's best interests. Cooperative behavior is also less effective when the opponent adopts a non-cooperative attitude. *See* Craver, *supra*, at 20–21. A tax clinic student with little experience must be wary of IRS employees, especially those at lower levels, who feel no compulsion to achieve a result that is acceptable to both sides. Using a purely cooperative stance in these instances may be counter-productive.

It may be that adopting one style — purely competitive or purely cooperative — in any given case is a mistake. If it appears that the style initially chosen is not advancing the process, the negotiator should consider shifting to a different style in order to maintain control of the discussions. A shift in styles might be planned from the outset. A negotiator could decide to maintain a firm, competitive stance until such time as he is ready to make his final offer. To reach a final agreement, the negotiator might be willing to make a few last-minute concessions specifically contingent on the final agreement. Conversely, the negotiator might choose to make incremental concessions early in the negotiation process in a spirit of cooperation and good faith, and then rely on the resulting goodwill to justify holding firm on those issues that, unknown to the other party, are the most important to his client. This ability to adjust from one negotiating style to another is effective, but may not be possible for all negotiators. One's own personality and traits may dictate the approach. Attempting to use a competitive style when you are not comfortable with threats and conflict likely will lead to a disappointing result. *See generally* Paul M. Lisnek, Effective Negotiation and Mediation: A Lawyer's Guide §§ 4.1, 4.5 (1992).

[B] Negotiation Process

[1] Preparation and Planning

Whether the negotiator plans to adopt a cooperative or competitive style, planning and preparation are the keys to success. At the earliest stages, preparation involves thoroughly investigating the facts and carefully researching the underlying legal issues. Without an accurate and complete view of the facts and the law, a negotiator cannot properly evaluate the costs and benefits of a given settlement position.

Gathering all of the relevant facts requires good client interviewing skills, which are discussed in Section 19.02, above. The lawyer should encourage the client to be candid and to reveal to him any information that might be useful. The lawyer should also request that the client provide verification of those facts that she thinks the IRS will challenge. Even at this early stage of the process, the lawyer should start thinking about a bargaining range (maximum and minimum extremes) and how points along that range might be justified. One of the best sources for information that can be used to justify a bargaining position is the client herself. The lawyer might explore with the client such matters as industry-wide standards and the client's business and financial history. Information relating to the client's finances is particularly important when the lawyer is negotiating an installment agreement or offer in compromise in a collection case.

A lawyer who can adequately justify his own position can more easily change the opponent's perceptions about the dispute. Research in advance of settlement discussions should start with an exploration of arguments and legal theories supporting the client's positions. While developing justifications for a particular bargaining stance is important, an effective negotiator must also anticipate responses of the opponent and the legal theories the opponent will likely rely upon to support his own bargaining range. A lawyer who fails to delve into his opponent's expected bargaining stance may end up finding that his own position is unrealistically optimistic or, even worse, the lawyer's own settlement offer is much less favorable to his client than what the opposing party might otherwise have accepted. The process of researching tax law is discussed in Chapter 20.

Related to the idea of anticipating the opponent's response is identifying the client's external exposure. Through the same process of factual and legal research, the attorney should try to detect any liability exposure beyond amounts that are currently in issue. While a client with external exposure is at a disadvantage in the bargaining process, it is better to know and prepare for this potential liability than to be surprised by it during the actual negotiation. The best way to identify probable issues is to review the client's tax returns for the taxable year in issue, as well as those from prior years open under the statute of limitations. Common examples of external liability exposure include new issues, increased deficiencies, and fraud liability. The IRS may also bear some external exposure in the form of recoverable administrative costs, unexpected refunds, and new issues or theories supporting the taxpayer's position. These, too, should be identified and researched.

Preparing for negotiating also calls for ascertaining the extent of the authority the client will give the attorney to negotiate a settlement on her behalf. *See* STEFAN H. KRIEGER ET AL., ESSENTIAL LAWYERING SKILLS 308–09 (3rd ed. 2007). One author describes this process, which he calls "pre-negotiation," as follows:

> When you meet with your client to obtain settlement authority, you are counseling her, in the sense that you are learning from her what her preferences are, by comparing different alternatives, albeit hypothetical ones. But you are also deep into negotiation strategy thinking, and your meeting with your client is as much about how you will negotiate as about what your client ultimately wants. I list here some considerations for you to incorporate into your pre-negotiation counseling meeting and your planning for it. I note that these ideas will have relevance in all kinds of negotiations, whether litigation-based or transactional, distributive or integrative, as we see below.
>
> First, . . . obtaining some sensible bottom-line authority from your client does not mean that you will use that authority for your opening offer. While few things are firmly true in strategic law practice, it is accepted dogma that you do not make your bottom line your first offer. Also, in a related point, if you end up settling at your bottom line after a lot of negotiating in which you made demands or offers that were far more favorable to your client's bottom line, you can't always say that you have succeeded. Getting a deal within your client's authority range is not the same thing, necessarily, as getting a good deal.
>
> Second, there may be some situations where you will negotiate with an opposing lawyer or party before you have done any pre-negotiation counseling. This would be unusual, of course, but it is not unheard of. You could not settle in that negotiation, of course (you would have no authority to do so), but you could learn a great deal about the other side's power, strategy, and weaknesses. If the other side has performed its pre-negotiation counseling, and makes a demand or offer, you can then counsel your client about that discrete proposal in the fashion described in the conventional models. (If neither side has done any pre-negotiation counseling, then nobody can make any offers or demands or proposals, of course.)
>
> Third, let me emphasize the last parenthetical sentence of the previous paragraph. You cannot make a first offer if you have not had a pre-negotiation counseling meeting with your client. If you run into the emerging literature,

grounded in cognitive psychology, holding that those who make more favorable initial proposals tend to do better, you will want to be prepared to make an opening proposal if you believe your case's strategy calls for it. You cannot do so if you have not met with your client to learn her authority. . . .

Fourth, there is a fine tension between learning your client's true bottom line and giving you confidence to negotiate strongly. The less you know about your client's willingness to accept a lower figure, the better you may be able to negotiate. This is a critical insight about the interplay of the pre-negotiation counseling process and negotiation strategy, and one which invites a critique of pre-negotiation counseling which we will visit below.

Here's a brief example of this point. Let's assume you have a pre-negotiation counseling meeting with [your client] Lynn, who tells you (after some serious conversation) that she would accept a $150,000 settlement if that were the best you could get. If you end the meeting at that point, without pressing her downward, you may be a stronger negotiator with Alison [the opposing party's lawyer]. If Alison offers $140,000, you may confidently say that you have no such authority, and you may through your confidence persuade her that she has to pay $150,000 or above. If, on the other hand, you follow the counseling model suggested here to its logical conclusion, you may learn that Lynn, if really pushed, would accept $125,000 instead of going to trial. After that meeting, you may be a less effective negotiator with Alison, because you cannot honestly and confidently reject lower offers. . . . Even if you were willing to fib or mislead your partner while negotiating, possessing a lower reservation point means that proposals from the other side are more likely to fall within your range of acceptable settlements, and many observers of negotiation acknowledge the difficulty of holding out for more favorable terms when a proposal fits within your client's authority.

You therefore need to use your best judgment in seeking a bottom line of authority. Your opportunity to check back with your client before accepting any deal, your confidence in your ability to aim high even when you will be satisfied with low, your skill and experience as a negotiator, and your client's risk aversion all will factor into your choices.

Fifth, and finally, you may (and probably will) use this pre-negotiation counseling meeting to confer with your client about the nature of your opening proposal. I stressed above that your client's bottom authority is not the same thing, by any means, as your opening demand or offer. But choosing an opening demand or offer is a very important strategic judgment, and you often will involve your client in that decision making. If you shoot high, there is some (if perhaps less than conventionally thought) risk of deadlock and loss of credibility. Also, as offers seldom are one-dimensional, but instead consist of a package of terms, you will need some assistance in deciding which terms of your first proposal will be quite favorable and which will appear to be compromises.

Paul R. Tremblay, *"Pre-Negotiation" Counseling: An Alternative Model*, 13 Clinical L. Rev. 541, 557–60 (2006) (footnotes omitted).[17]

Preparation also involves learning as much as possible about the person with whom you will be negotiating and any limitations under which the opposing party will be bargaining. Without insights from prior interactions, determining the individual characteristics of the opponent (experience, skill, and honesty) can be difficult. As a general matter, auditors and agents at the examination level tend to have a firmer grasp of the facts (they performed the audit), but less understanding of detailed legal issues. Appeals

---

Officers, on the other hand, have more experience with technical legal arguments, but normally must rely on the examining agent's report to provide them with the facts.

The perspectives of the examining agent and the Appeals Officer may also differ. The examining agent may be more interested in defending the conclusions and arguments he plans to record in his report and, therefore, may be less willing to negotiate in the traditional sense. Furthermore, the examining agent and his or her supervisor are limited in their settlement authority: They may not strike a compromise that is contrary to a published IRS legal interpretation. Appeals Officers (and IRS Counsel) tend to adopt more of a "give-and-take" view of the negotiation process and, at least at the outset, want the case settled. As explained in Chapter 5, Appeals Officers have relatively broad settlement authority and must take the hazards of litigation into account when settling a case. The same is generally true of IRS Counsel.

The best source of information about the specific procedures and processes of the IRS at any stage of the controversy is the IRS's own Internal Revenue Manual. As discussed in Chapter 2, the Internal Revenue Manual is divided into major parts dealing with, among other topics, audits, appeals, refunds, and collection matters, and is further divided into separate handbooks addressing more specific topics.

As indicated above, although it is helpful conceptually to separate the preparation and planning phase of the negotiation process from later phases, it also may be a bit misleading. The planning processes discussed above must continue even after negotiation sessions begin. Every strategic and tactical move the negotiator employs should be carefully planned in advance and reassessed when conditions change.

[2] Information Exchange

The strengths and weaknesses of the client's case, which will ultimately guide the attorney's offer and concession strategy, should have been revealed during the research and investigation process. Once negotiations actually begin, the attorney typically wants to reveal to the opposing party the client's strengths, withhold any weaknesses, and determine the opposing party's weaknesses and concerns.

The negotiator's ability to withhold information during the audit phase of the controversy (prior to actual settlement talks) is limited by the IRS's broad summons authority in Code section 7602. As discussed in Chapter 4, during this pre-negotiation stage, the flow of information is one-sided — from the taxpayer to the IRS.[18] Once the audit concludes and the examining agent issues a revenue agent's report, the attorney can begin pursuing information held and created by the IRS. The attorney gains access to such information by requesting the client's administrative file or, if necessary, by making a Freedom of Information Act request, a topic discussed in Chapter 6.

An attorney's willingness to share information with the opposing party during the negotiation depends in part on whether he adopts a competitive or cooperative style. In almost all cases, however, the lawyer eventually wants to "share" the strengths of the client's position, usually at the beginning of the proceedings. Keep in mind that statements made on behalf of the client by a representative who acts under a power of attorney are not protected and may be used as admissions. As a result, the attorney must be extremely careful before making *any* representation, favorable or unfavorable, to the IRS. An experienced attorney double checks to ensure that the statements and information provided are accurate and do not unintentionally raise issues that are not already under consideration.

---

[18] *See* Chapter 3 for a discussion of IDRs (Information Document Requests) and other techniques for controlling the flow of information during the audit phase. After the taxpayer files a petition in the Tax Court or a complaint in one of the refund fora, the flow of information back and forth is largely controlled by that court's discovery rules.

Protecting sensitive, damaging aspects of the client's case from being revealed to the opposing party raises a more difficult issue. As a general matter, the lawyer has no obligation to correct an IRS employee's misunderstanding of the law or the facts, but he must be careful not to misrepresent the law or the facts. *See* Model Rule of Professional Conduct 3.3(a), 3.4. Misrepresentations threaten the lawyer's credibility with the opposing party. Once that credibility is lost, the negotiator may have difficulty persuading the opposing party that the client's position or settlement offer is valid.

A lawyer who is asked a direct question about a weakness in the client's case has another option that falls somewhere between answering truthfully and misrepresenting the client's position. The negotiator may try to "block" the opponent's inquiry. Listed below are some common blocking techniques:

Answer a Question with a Question. Responding to a question by posing another is the natural tendency of most lawyers anyway. The technique is effective because it is not merely a form of evasion, but is also a way to clarify or elaborate a position. The negotiator should formulate his follow-up questions in advance should the opposing party inquire about sensitive information.

Provide an Incomplete or Overly Broad Answer. The goal in this case is to respond with more information than has been asked for, or to respond to only the nonsensitive part of the topic contained in the question. In other words, respond to general questions with specific answers, and to specific questions with general answers.

Answer Another Question. If the opponent seems distracted, the negotiator can respond by answering a question that has already been asked, but with a slightly different response; or by reframing the question. The question might be reframed by using introductory phrases such as "I assume you're asking about . . . " or "If I understand your question correctly, you're looking for. . . ."

Claim that the Question is Out of Bounds. The negotiator can claim that the question delves into information protected by the attorney-client privilege or is irrelevant to the proceedings.

Change the Topic. The goal of this technique is to avoid the question asked by delving into a related topic in which the opponent has some interest. As with all these blocking techniques, the negotiator should plan this move in advance so that its execution is barely noticeable. Robert M. Bastress & Joseph D. Harbaugh, Interviewing, Counseling, and Negotiating: Skills for Effective Representation 422–425 (1990).

Overuse of these blocking techniques can backfire. If a lawyer consistently evades a particular question, it might eventually reveal to the opponent a weakness in the client's case. Before applying a blocking technique, the negotiator should carefully consider whether the information being protected is truly damaging to the client's case and whether it might be more advantageous to develop a truthful answer supported by a persuasive explanation.

[3] Offers and Concessions

In the opening moments of any face-to-face bargaining session, the parties typically try to establish some rapport with one another, and at the same time feel one another out for signs of bargaining style and strategy. Some negotiators suggest talking first about issues that are completely unrelated to the case, such as the weather or recent events. From there the lawyer can ease into a vague description of the client's case. Eventually, though, the parties must confront the specific issues involved. In almost all negotiations there will be controversial and noncontroversial issues. The lawyer's prior research should help him predict which issues will be controversial and which noncontroversial. During the actual negotiations, however, it is the opposing party's view of the issues that is important. In a surprisingly high percentage of cases, the IRS representative is willing to concede without a fight those issues that the lawyer initially believed would be the most contentious. Detecting agreement before launching any offer and concession strategy can save time and leave the lawyer in a stronger bargaining position. With respect to those issues upon which the opponent's initial view is at odds with the client's position, the negotiator should encourage the opposing party to acknowledge the strengths of the client's case and solicit the opposing party's perceptions about the weaknesses of his own case. Any resulting points of agreement can prove to be valuable bargaining chips if concessions eventually have to be made.

To the negotiator, the controversial issues — whether they be strengths or weaknesses — will typically be of greater importance than the noncontroversial issues. There is no clear answer as to whether noncontroversial or controversial issues should be discussed first. On the one hand, seeking agreement on minor issues at the outset establishes a climate of cooperation and builds trust between the participants. Early agreement also helps create momentum and allows a party to defer using competitive techniques, if they become necessary, until later in the process. There are, however, risks associated with putting controversial issues off until the end. Attorneys who isolate controversial issues for separate treatment later in the process may be left with no arguments or positions left to bargain with once those topics are eventually discussed. Despite any early agreements, the negotiations could end in deadlock. Taking up major, controversial issues early may also cause the parties to become more committed to the overall process. Once the larger issues are resolved, the lawyers may find that smaller points and details more easily fall into place. Whichever tack the negotiator decides to take, he should map out his agenda in advance.

Planning an agenda also involves creating an offer and concession strategy. At both the audit and appeals levels, the taxpayer's attorney is usually expected to make the first settlement offer. *See* IRS Reg. § 601.106(f). He should have developed, in consultation with the client, the client's minimum and maximum exposure. This information is crucial when deciding upon the opening offer. The attorney's initial offer will likely be rejected by the opponent, and it should, in some ways, reflect that eventuality. Proposing *too* outrageous an opening offer, however, could alienate the opposing party and stall the negotiations. The lawyer can also help decide upon an opening offer by predicting what his opponent might be willing to accept. Looking at the matter from the opponent's viewpoint will also allow the lawyer to recognize a favorable counteroffer from the opponent and be ready to act on it quickly before it is withdrawn.[19]

In addition to creating an offer strategy, the lawyer must also be prepared to make concessions. Concessions can play an important strategic role in reaching a final agreement. If movement toward a final agreement has begun to wane, a concession can jump start the negotiations or help reclaim some goodwill that may have been lost during prior adversarial bargaining. Deciding when and how much to concede must be considered in tandem with the offer strategy. One common tactic is to start with a relatively high opening offer, then make a series of small concessions until an agreement is reached. The attorney must employ this tactic carefully. Once the opposing party detects that the negotiator is readily making concessions, he may be inclined to raise his or her expectations and look for more concessions to follow. To avoid this, the attorney might make any concession on his part contingent upon a concession from the other side. Another tactic is to maintain a high unyielding position with a jump to an agreement at the very last minute. In this case the lawyer might make the concession specifically contingent upon a final agreement. Like any other

---

[19] The attorney's final settlement offer on behalf of the client, whether made during the Appeals process or just prior to litigation, should take into account Code section 7430, under which the taxpayer can make a "qualified offer" to settle the dispute. If the qualified offer is not accepted by the IRS and the taxpayer subsequently obtains a judgment that is as favorable as the taxpayer's offer, the taxpayer is deemed to be the prevailing party and therefore may be eligible to recover litigations costs from the IRS. Section 5.02[C][4] of Chapter 5 explains the requirements for making a qualified offer.

competitive technique, this tactic may increase tensions between the parties, cause delay, and eventually lead to breakdown of the negotiations. *See* I. William Zartman & Maureen R. Berman, The Practical Negotiator 166–175 (1982). In all cases, the concession strategy must be planned ahead. Once a concession has been made, it can be difficult to withdraw it later in the process.

Once a settlement has been reached, it will need to be reduced to writing. Many tax cases are not settled until after the matter is docketed in Tax Court. Tax Court settlements, though drawn up by the parties, must be accepted by the court and entered by a Tax Court judge as a "stipulated decision."[20] If a matter is not docketed in Tax Court, the agreement may be reflected on Form 870, Form 870-AD, or a closing agreement (Form 866 or 906), depending on the circumstances. Settlement with the Appeals Division is discussed in Chapter 5. Settlement more generally is discussed in Chapter 11.

[4] Responding to Deadlock

Even after the parties have made concessions, there may remain some areas of disagreement that prevent a final settlement. The lawyer must eventually decide, in consultation with the client, whether to agree to a proposed, but somewhat unfavorable, settlement, or to simply walk away from the negotiations with no agreement. Before doing either, he should consider the following techniques that can help break an impasse and move the proceedings along toward a final settlement.

Creating an Internal Deadline. Deadlines tend to encourage agreement. There are some timing deadlines, of course, over which the negotiating parties have little control — an approaching trial date, for instance. Alternatively, the parties might decide to create their own "internal" deadline, after which voluntary bargaining sessions cease. The internal deadline must be both reasonable and serious. An unreasonably short deadline might cause the parties to begin preparing for failure prematurely, rather than focusing on areas of agreement. If the deadline chosen is not taken seriously, it may also cause the parties to harden their positions in the hope that the other side concedes. *Id.* at 191–199.

Bluffing. When a lawyer bluffs, he concedes a position that he ostensibly values in order to achieve a position he actually wants to attain. Bluffing can relate not only to the importance that the negotiator places on a given settlement position, but also to the negotiator's commitment to seeing a final outcome. Bluffing raises ethical concerns, and also carries the risk that the opponent will call the bluff and expect the negotiator to follow through with his threat. When cooperative efforts have not resulted in an agreement, bluffing can be used to alter the opponent's perceptions in such a way that the opponent begins to believe that he has gained a bargaining position when, in fact, he has not. Lisnek, *supra*, Ch. 6.

Warnings and Threats. Highlighting the adverse consequences that will result from the opponent's failure to accept a final agreement (a warning) can help shape that party's perceptions. A threat is similar to a warning except that the negotiator vows to take some affirmative action against the opposing side if his demands are not met. Both techniques should be used sparingly and each must be credible if it is to be effective. In the case of a threat, the negotiator must be willing to back it up, and show at least some willingness to do so. *Id.*

Predictions and Promises. A prediction is essentially the inverse of a warning. Instead of accentuating the negative ramifications, a prediction focuses on the positive

---

[20] For example, a stipulated decision document in one case provided that the taxpayers "agreed: (1) to a deficiency of $26,955.75; (2) that they had no liability for the section 6662 accuracy-related penalty; and (3) that 'interest will be assessed as provided by law on the deficiency'." Goodman v. Commissioner, T.C. Memo. 2006-220.

outcomes that will flow from agreement. A promise, unlike a threat, carries the prospect of a reward rather than a punishment if the opponent takes certain action. It is often effective to combine a promise with a warning or threat: A promise of a satisfactory outcome if agreement is reached accompanied by a warning of an unsatisfactory outcome if agreement is not reached. *Id.*

[C] Tactical Issues at Each Stage of the Tax Controversy

The discussions above concerning negotiation styles and techniques are relevant to almost any bargaining situation, whether arising during audit, appeal, or as part of a collection matter. The material that follows examines tactical issues that are more specific to each stage of the tax controversy process. However, at whatever stage the attorney is first brought in, he must not overlook the importance of planning and preparation.

[1] Audit

The most common issues that arise during the examination phase relate to the taxpayer's ability to substantiate a return position, usually a deduction, through adequate documentation. These issues are also typical in tax clinic settings. If the revenue agent raises the issue, the lawyer should review the Code, Treasury Regulations, and Internal Revenue Manual for acceptable methods of substantiation,[21] and work with the client to gather the necessary receipts and supporting information.

Most audits that tax clinics participate in are correspondence audits. Only if the audit is an office or field audit will there be a face-to-face meeting with an IRS agent. In the examination context, most practitioners agree that the attorney should, at the outset at least, assume a cooperative attitude. Later in the process, if the risks associated with the competitive style (primarily, the prospect of deadlock) appear to be inevitable, then a more adversarial attitude may be appropriate. When choosing a negotiation style, the attorney must also be mindful early on of the potential for a burden of proof shift under Code section 7491. To cause the burden of proof to shift to the IRS during an eventual court proceeding, the taxpayer must establish, among other conditions, that she "cooperated" with reasonable requests for information and other documents. I.R.C. § 7491(a)(2)(B). Cooperation, for these purposes, focuses on the taxpayer's granting the IRS access to available information and exhausting administrative remedies. While establishing the cooperation element of section 7491 and maintaining a competitive negotiation style do not seem to be mutually exclusive, the attorney should bear section 7491 in mind if he plans eventually to make a case for the burden of proof to shift.

If the question is one of substantiation, negotiations with the revenue agent will likely focus on the scope and quantity of information the agent seeks. Before submitting any information to the IRS, the attorney should review it carefully to ensure that it does not raise additional issues that are not currently under consideration. Thomas C. Pearson & Dennis R. Schmidt, *Successful Preparation and Negotiation May Reduce the Time and Breadth of an IRS Audit*, 40 TAX'N FOR ACCT. 234, 236 (1988). If the client cannot locate the supporting documents, the lawyer should consider other sources of corroborating evidence, such as statements (and possibly affidavits) from third parties. If the client can generate no supporting evidence at all, conceding the issue and paying the resulting deficiency may be the best course of action.

Substantiating a return position primarily involves a question of fact. Factual questions, in a technical sense, are not subject to negotiation. Facts can, however, be perceived by the parties in different ways. The lawyer may find himself "negotiating"

---

[21] For example, Code section 274(d) and the accompanying Treasury regulations set forth specific substantiation requirements applicable to travel and entertainment expenses.

the importance of certain facts and their meaning in the broader context of the client's case. An examining agent's prior experience and level of training make him or her better equipped to understand factual arguments as opposed to complex legal theories. Even if questions of law hinder a satisfactory settlement, however, the attorney should ensure that the facts that are recorded in the revenue agent's report are accurate and, if at all possible, consistent with the client's position. A poor or inaccurate factual record will only make it more difficult for the attorney later in the process. If it appears that no progress is being made toward a final resolution, the attorney's best course of action is to begin preparing for the Appeals process.

[2] Administrative Appeal

The important strategic decision of whether to approach settlement negotiations with the Appeals Division on a docketed or nondocketed basis is discussed in Chapter 5. In short, negotiating with the Appeals Officer on a nondocketed basis avoids the time pressures associated with a looming trial date — which may or may not be advantageous to the taxpayer depending upon the issues involved — and preserves the possibility for the taxpayer to recover litigation costs from the IRS under Code section 7430. However, the nondocketed route is generally more time-consuming than the docketed route. Furthermore, negotiating with the Appeals Division before a statutory notice of deficiency has been issued raises the prospect that the Appeals Officer will include newly discovered issues in the deficiency notice sent to the taxpayer. If the same issues had been raised by the IRS after the notice of deficiency had been sent, the IRS would have borne the burden of proof in an ensuing Tax Court trial with respect to any "new matter." *See generally* Section 9.02 of Chapter 9. The attorney should discuss with the client how these considerations bear upon the client's specific case and help the client decide upon the appropriate route.

In many tax clinic cases, the case was already docketed before the client came to the clinic, so Appeals consideration will proceed on a docketed basis.[22] Settlement negotiations with the Appeals Officer will proceed in much the same manner whether the client chooses the docketed or nondocketed route. In both cases, the Appeals Officer, unlike the examining agent, must take account of the "hazards of litigation" when deciding whether to accept a settlement offer. The risk that the government will not prevail in litigation becomes the attorney's most important bargaining chip during the negotiations, and all effort should be made to highlight this risk to the Appeals Officer.[23] Appeals conferences themselves, as explained in the excerpt in Section 5.02[C][5] of Chapter 5, are conducted in an informal manner, yet this does not mean that the attorney should come to the table unprepared. The attorney's offer and concession strategy should be meticulously planned before any meeting takes place.

Most Appeals Officers do not have the time or the resources to prepare for the Appeals conference as well as they would like. They are heavily reliant on the examining agent for factual development, and on the taxpayer's protest letter, if one was submitted, to guide their legal research. As a result, they appreciate whatever cooperation they receive from the attorney, and most are willing to respond in kind when it comes to finding a satisfactory settlement.

An existing, favorable relationship between the attorney and the Appeals Officer, built on credibility and fair play, might encourage the Appeals Officer to give the client the benefit of the doubt. Barbara T. Kaplan, *Leveling the Playing Field in Federal Income Tax Controversies*, 56 N.Y.U. Ann. Inst. Fed. Tax'n § 32.10 (1997). When

[22] This is because the Tax Court will include a clinic "stuffer letter" in the envelope with the acknowledgment of receipt of the petition. For the format of such a letter, see http://www.ustaxcourt.gov/clinics stuffer_letter_acad/emic.pdf.

[23] If the negotiations take place on a nondocketed basis, the hazards of litigation should be explored in the protest letter. *See* Section 5.02[c][2] of Chapter 5 for suggestions on drafting protest letters.

choosing a style and strategy, the attorney should also consider the fact that the Appeals Officer normally must seek the approval of a superior before any settlement can be finalized. The Appeals Officer may have an easier time convincing the reviewer to accept the agreement if he or she can explain that the attorney for the taxpayer bargained in good faith and was willing to make concessions in order to reach an agreement.

[3] During Litigation

What has been said about negotiations with the Appeals Division applies just as well to negotiations with IRS Counsel and attorneys from the Department of Justice. Some experienced negotiators maintain that it is easier to strike a settlement at this late stage because the government attorney is keenly aware of the costs and time commitment associated with a trial. While the Appeals Officer must take litigation risks into account, the officer's knowledge of the subtle issues that can affect the outcome of a trial is limited. The government attorney will be more attuned to litigation-related issues such as burden of proof, admissibility of evidence, and discovery procedures. However, there are some issues for which the government will seek a judicial interpretation and therefore will not settle prior to trial. If, for example, courts have issued conflicting decisions with regard to the same issue, the government might seek further judicial review in an effort to achieve a uniformly accepted interpretation. *See* Peter R. Steenland, Jr. & Peter A. Appel, *The Ongoing Role of Alternative Dispute Resolution in Federal Government Litigation*, 27 U. Tol. L. Rev. 805, 809 (1996).

[4] Collection Process

Negotiations with the IRS after it has assessed a deficiency typically involve efforts by the attorney to suspend or otherwise lessen the impact of enforced collection action such as levy or seizure. Most often, the attorney will attempt to settle the client's unpaid account for less than the balance due (an offer in compromise) and/or spread payment of the accrued liability over a period of months or years (typically using an installment agreement, though, as discussed in Chapter 15, periodic payment offers in compromise are also possible, *see* I.R.C. § 7122(c)(1)(B)). Before the IRS will consider either form of collection relief, the taxpayer must be in current compliance, having filed all past and current tax returns. If this is not the case, the attorney should assist the client in rectifying the situation.

As noted in Chapter 15, the IRS may compromise a tax liability for one of three reasons: doubt as to liability, doubt as to collectibility, and for effective tax administration. I.R.C. § 7122. The attorney's approach will differ slightly in each case. A compromise offer based on doubt as to liability must be filed on Form 656-L (*Offer in Compromise Doubt as to Liability*) and cannot concurrently claim other grounds for compromise. *See* Internal Revenue Service, *Filing an Offer in Compromise*, http://www.irs.gov/businesses/small/article/0,,id=109628,00.html. Compromise offers based on doubt as to liability will end up in the hands of a revenue agent who will essentially "audit" the request. As in the case of a typical audit, preparation and information control are of key importance.

To obtain a compromise based on doubt as to collectibility, the taxpayer must establish that her existing assets and expected income do not permit her to pay the full assessed liability. To successfully negotiate an offer on this basis, the attorney must work with the client to meticulously prepare financial disclosure statements (Form 433-A, *Collection Information Statement for Individuals* or Form 433-B, *Collection Information Statement for Businesses*). On the disclosure forms, the client values her assets and liabilities (net worth) and lists her monthly income and expense figures. The financial information becomes the basis of the offer, which is made by submitting Form

656, *Offer in Compromise*. The attorney should carefully review the current offer in compromise regulations, Treas. Reg. § 301.7122-1, and the Internal Revenue Manual to determine an acceptable offer range.

Although the minimum acceptable offer will depend primarily upon a mechanical application of national and local personal expense standards, there is still room for negotiation.[24] In addition, with respect to an offer from a low-income taxpayer, the IRS is statutorily prohibited from rejecting it "solely on the basis of the amount of the offer." I.R.C. § 7122(d)(3)(A). Treasury regulations apply that standard in all cases. *See* Treas. Reg. § 301.7122-1(f)(3) ("No offer to compromise may be rejected solely on the basis of the amount of the offer without evaluating that offer under the provisions of this section and the Secretary's policies and procedures regarding the compromise of cases.").

In general, much of the attorney's time will be spent negotiating the adequacy and correctness of the financial statements. Two experienced practitioners suggest the following:

> The opportunity to provide the greatest benefit to the taxpayer in the [offer in compromise] process is in the valuation of assets for purposes of determining an acceptable offer amount. The lower the net realizable value of a taxpayer's assets, the smaller the offer needed to meet acceptance standards. On the other hand, grossly undervaluing an asset or assets will not be viewed favorably by the IRS. The IRS can and will perform its own valuations in complex cases and those involving substantial dollars.
>
> Taxpayers should use realistic valuations, and their practitioners should encourage this. In addition, seek the advice of knowledgeable valuation specialists where possible.
>
> * * *
>
> While unrealistically low valuations should be avoided, the submission of an [offer in compromise] requires the practitioner to be a strong advocate for the taxpayer and taking an aggressive stance on valuation matters should be both expected and respected by knowledgeable IRS personnel.
>
> Income-producing real estate, intangibles, and small closely held business or professional practices are all candidates for zealous valuation "advocacy" by taxpayer representatives. The practitioner should make sure to have good facts and sound arguments to support the valuations presented.

KIP DELLINGER & ROYAL DELLINGER, OFFER IN COMPROMISE PROCESS: INSIGHTS AND STRATEGIES 66–67 (1999).[25] Even when the client has few assets to report, careful completion of the financial disclosure statement can mean the difference between acceptance or rejection of the compromise offer. In the case of low-income clients, the attorney should question the client about outstanding loans from family members, overdue mortgage and credit card payments, and any other outstanding liabilities that affect the client's ability to pay.

To obtain a compromise based on effective tax administration, the taxpayer must prove that, in light of all the surrounding facts and circumstances, collecting the full amount owed would result in economic hardship or, regardless of the taxpayer's financial condition, would be detrimental to voluntary taxpayer compliance. The offer should explain the taxpayer's position in detail. The attorney must understand, however, that

---

[24] A more detailed discussion of permissible offer ranges and the role of personal expense standards can be found in Section 15.04 of Chapter 15.

[25] Reprinted with permission from Offer in Compromise Process: Insights and Strategies.

the IRS has been hesitant to grant this relief. Accordingly, creativity and factual investigation will be necessary if the taxpayer is to have a strong case.

In some circumstances, acceptance of an installment agreement is largely automatic. *See* I.R.C. § 6159(c); *Payment Plans, Installment Agreements*, at http://www.irs.gov/businesses/small/article/0,,id=108347,00.html#2. In other circumstances, negotiating an installment agreement with the IRS is similar to negotiating a compromise offer based on doubt as to collectibility. *See* I.R.C. § 6159. The same financial disclosure statements required when submitting an offer in compromise are also used to determine whether an installment agreement involving more than $25,000 in taxes, penalties, and/or interest will be accepted by the IRS, as well as to set the payments terms under that agreement. The attorney must also be familiar with the Internal Revenue Manual's standardized expenditure allowances, which the revenue agent will use to determine the client's ability to pay, and ultimately the minimum acceptable monthly installment amount. These standardized allowances are divided into "necessary expenses" and "conditional expenses." The attorney must negotiate with the IRS not only that the client will incur a particular necessary or conditional expense, but also the anticipated amount of the expense.[26] *See* Mark H. Ely, *Negotiating Installment Agreements with the IRS Collection Division*, TAX ADVISOR, Oct. 2000, at 742.

Typically, offers in compromise and installment agreement requests are made after the IRS begins collection enforcement action.[27] If the attorney has not previously been involved in the client's case, he should first review all notices sent to the client to determine where the case stands in the collection process. Of particular importance is the notice granting the client the right to request a Collection Due Process (CDP) hearing. The CDP notice must be sent once the IRS files a Notice of Federal Tax Lien or proposes to levy on the client's property, after which the taxpayer typically has only 30 days to request a hearing. I.R.C. §§ 6320, 6330. As explained in more detail in Chapter 16, a CDP hearing is conducted before a neutral Appeals Officer who must first confirm whether the IRS satisfied all Code procedures relating to the validity of the lien, including whether the IRS properly issued all the required notices and demands. This is an opportunity for the attorney to raise any procedural discrepancies. The Appeals Officer is not required to discuss the client's underlying tax liability, however, unless the client did not receive a notice of deficiency or has not otherwise had an opportunity to dispute the liability. The latter may be true of a tax clinic client who has allowed the case to proceed from audit to collection without making any efforts to question the IRS's asserted deficiency. If substantive liability is in issue, the negotiations will proceed much like any other Appeals hearing.

Even if the question of liability has already been determined, the attorney can raise any issue during the CDP hearing relating to the lien or proposed levy, including the appropriateness of an installment agreement or offer in compromise. If these issues have not been raised before, the Appeals Officer may refer the case to a revenue agent who will investigate whether such relief is warranted. If so, the negotiation will proceed as described above. If the prospect of an installment agreement or compromise has already been considered and rejected by a revenue agent earlier in the process, the Appeals Officer must judge whether the revenue agent's conclusion was correct. The attorney should point out any misinterpretations the revenue agent may have made when analyzing the taxpayer's financial statements, and if necessary update those statements to reflect the most current information available. If the Appeals Officer denies the taxpayer's request at the CDP phase, the taxpayer can seek review of the Appeals Officer's determination in the Tax Court. *See* I.R.C. § 6330(d)(1). As discussed in Chapter 16, the Appeals Officer's decision generally is reviewed using an abuse of

---

[26] The installment agreement procedure is explained in more detail in Section 15.03 of Chapter 15.

[27] The IRS will no longer accept offers in compromise before the tax has been assessed. *See Filing an Offer in Compromise*, *supra*.

discretion standard, except that issues of liability are subject to *de novo* review. Overturning the Appeals Officer's adverse determination will, therefore, be difficult.[28]

PROBLEMS

Problems 1 through 3 and 4B are role-playing problems.

1. You have been assigned to interview José Rodriguez, a new client of the tax clinic. Ascertain his tax problem and inform him of the next steps you plan to take in his case.
2. You were assigned to interview Ingrid Alfiori, a young woman who has an appointment with the clinic. Ascertain her tax problem and inform her of the next steps you plan to take in her case.
3. Sidney Smith has owned a small family restaurant as a sole proprietorship for many years. All of Sidney's assets are invested in the restaurant, which is slightly profitable; Sidney has income from it of about $25,000 per year, and has no income from other sources. Sidney was recently audited for the first time. The IRS agent concluded that Sidney was not reporting most cash receipts, and asserted a proposed deficiency of $22,000. Sidney came to the clinic with a 30-day letter from the agent to seek help resolving the dispute.
   A. Conduct an initial interview with Sidney.
   B. Assume that in the initial interview, you and Sidney decided to request an Appeals conference. Assume that, given the amount in dispute, you did not write a formal tax protest. Conduct the Appeals conference on Sidney's behalf.
   C. Assume that you were not able to reach a satisfactory settlement with Appeals, so you have scheduled a conference with Sidney to decide how to proceed with the case. Conduct that conference.
4. Jamie White, a teacher's aide, recently received a letter from the IRS denying her $2,328 earned income credit for her two children, Mary, age 5, and Donald, age 7. Apparently, her ex-husband, Daniel White, who does not live with them, also claimed the credit. Jamie receives $300 per month of child support from her ex-husband, a carpenter who earns approximately $15,000 to $18,000 per year. Jamie earns $12,000 per year from the school district, and has no other source of income. She told you in the initial interview that she spends most of that money on her children.
   A. Assume that the amount of the credit (if allowable) is correct and the only issue is whether Jamie may claim it. Draft a representation letter to send to Jamie. She resides at 100 April St., Apt. 3C, Aberdeen, New Jersey 07747.
   B. Assume that, after interviewing Jamie the first time, you checked the law and ascertained that it is Jamie, not her ex-husband, who is entitled to take the credit. Jamie was unsure of how far she wanted to pursue the matter, for fear of angering her ex-husband and thus jeopardizing the $300 per month of child support. You had agreed that you would call the IRS and try to resolve the matter by phone. The telephone calls proved unsuccessful, so you have scheduled a conference with Jamie to discuss how to proceed with the case. Conduct that conference.
5. Jack Pope owns a small hardware store in Lancaster, Pennsylvania through a

[28] For an example of a case finding abuse of discretion, see *Blosser v. Commissioner*, T.C. Memo. 2007-323 (settlement officer abused discretion in connection with taxpayer request to be placed in currently not collectible status due to failure to consider taxpayer's testimony regarding the lack of filing requirement and deteriorating financial circumstances).

closely-held C corporation, Pope Inc. Assume that Pope Inc. files its income tax returns on a cash method, calendar year basis. During Year 1, Pope Inc. paid $150,000 in salary to Jack and deducted that amount under Code section 162 as compensation. The $150,000 payment represented almost 90 percent of Pope Inc.'s total net earnings for the year. Pope Inc. also contributed some of its unsold inventory to a local church and claimed a charitable contribution on the corporation's return equal to $15,000. The tax-exempt charitable organization that received the gift failed to send Pope Inc. a notice reflecting the contribution as required by the section 170 regulations. The corporation also paid $50,000 for a new warehouse space constructed as an addition to the existing hardware store, and deducted the entire amount as a current business expense rather than capitalizing the expense.

The IRS audited Pope Inc.'s Year 1 income tax returns. Jack decided to handle the audit himself and not seek the advice of an accountant or attorney. At the conclusion of the audit, the corporation received a 30-day letter with the following proposed adjustments: (1) denial of the salary deduction in full on the basis that the payment represented an unreasonable compensation payment, resulting in a $30,000 asserted deficiency; and (2) denial of the charitable contribution deduction in full for failure to substantiate the amount, resulting in a $3,000 asserted deficiency. The 30-day letter made no mention of the warehouse addition.

Jack has hired you, on behalf of Pope Inc., to meet with the examining agent and attempt to work out a settlement. Assume for these purposes that, based upon the law and the facts, you predict that the corporation has a 40 percent chance of establishing to the IRS that the salary payment was fully deductible under section 162, and only a 10 percent chance that a court would deny the compensation deduction in full. You also believe that there is a 50 percent likelihood that a court would allow only a portion of the deduction — assume, for purposes of this problem, that if only a portion is allowed, that portion will be $80,000 and the resulting deficiency will be $14,000. Assume also that the charitable organization that received the inventory is unable to locate any documentation reflecting the gift, but that the organization's president is willing to draft a letter to the IRS, with the current date, stating that based upon his best recollection, Pope Inc. made the gift reflected on the corporation's return. Given this state of affairs, you predict that Pope Inc. has a 25 percent chance of prevailing on this issue and a 75 percent chance that a court would deny the charitable deduction.

A. How would you approach the negotiations with the examining agent?

B. Assume that the settlement negotiations in Part A end in deadlock. Jack, on behalf of the corporation, asks you to appeal the deficiencies asserted in the 30-day letter to the IRS Appeals Division. The case has been assigned to Doris Morgan, an Appeals Officer with whom you have had extensive and generally favorable dealings in the past. Having drafted a protest letter setting out the corporation's position on the compensation and charitable deductions, how would you approach the settlement negotiations with Ms. Morgan and what would be your opening settlement offer? Assume that the warehouse expenditure issue has not yet been raised by the IRS. How does this issue affect your approach to the negotiation?

6. Your client, Jim Wong, suffers from a lifelong neurological condition that has rendered him mentally challenged. For most of his life, Jim, an only child whose father passed away when he was young, lived with his mother in their family home. Following the death of his mother, Jim, then age 55, was left the family home, a run-down mobile home (on a lot under a 99-year ground lease), and an

annuity that his mother had hoped would provide for Jim's care for the rest of his life.

Shortly after his mother's death, a local contractor talked Jim into making numerous, but unnecessary, repairs to the home. To fund the repairs, Jim withdrew large amounts from his annuity in Year 1. When he filed his Year 1 income tax return, Jim failed to report the annuity withdrawals as income. He was not aware that the withdrawals would give rise to gross income. Two years after filing the return, the IRS mailed to Jim a notice of deficiency asserting a deficiency in the amount of $3,000, including interest but no penalties. Jim, unsure what to do, did not respond to the notice of deficiency. The IRS therefore assessed the tax.

After filing a Notice of Federal Tax Lien against Jim's home, the IRS sent him a Collection Due Process Notice under Code section 6320. Assume that as of the current date, Jim's house is valued at $70,000, and that the annuity generates $12,000 per year, which is just enough to cover Jim's annual living expenses. Assume also that the mobile home has been condemned as unfit for habitation and that the mobile home park where it is located has filed a $1,000 lien against the mobile home for Jim's failure to pay park association dues.

At the CDP hearing, you intend to make an offer in compromise on behalf of your client based on effective tax administration. How would you go about preparing the offer? How would you prepare for the CDP hearing?

Chapter 20
CONDUCTING TAX RESEARCH

§ 20.01 INTRODUCTION

By the conclusion of the client interview, the attorney is likely to have some general idea of the nature of the client's tax problem. Even experienced tax attorneys, however, are unable (and unwilling) to provide detailed answers to many substantive or procedural tax questions off the top of their heads. Before the attorney can accurately describe to the client her available options, including the potential for a negotiated settlement, the attorney must carefully research the specific legal issues involved in light of the facts the client has conveyed.[1] Because of the complex and ever-changing nature of federal tax law, tax research must be performed with a high degree of technical accuracy. And while the general research method is the same as in other areas of the law, some knowledge of specialized tax sources and research techniques is necessary.[2]

The discussion in this chapter focuses on how to research a civil, federal income tax question.[3] The chapter describes the primary and secondary sources of tax law, with special emphasis placed on identifying and locating those sources that are likely to be found in a typical law firm or law school library. While some mention is made of the precedential weight carried by each of the primary legal sources, reference should be made to Chapter 2 for a more in-depth discussion of that issue. The remainder of the chapter suggests a methodology that a student unfamiliar with tax research might use when researching a tax problem.

§ 20.02 PRIMARY SOURCES

There are three principal sources of federal tax law: (1) legislative; (2) administrative; and (3) judicial. This section discusses each of them, in turn.

[A] Legislative Sources

[1] Internal Revenue Code

Federal tax law may well be the purest form of statutory law.[4] The answer to almost any tax question will depend upon an interpretation of the statutory language. The main source of federal tax statutes is the Internal Revenue Code, which is Title 26 of the United States Code. The current version is officially titled the Internal Revenue Code of 1986 (the "Code"). The current Code was preceded by the Internal Revenue Code of 1954, and prior to that by the Internal Revenue Code of 1939. Before 1939, Congress enacted revenue acts, each constituting a complete body of federal tax law, every two to three years.

The Code is divided into eleven subtitles (designated by letter), each of which is further divided into chapters (designated by number), which in turn are divided into

---

[1] Like Chapter 19, this chapter generally will refer to the attorney as "he" and the taxpayer/client as "she."

[2] For a more detailed description of tax sources, see Gail Levin Richmond, Federal Tax Research: Guide to Materials and Techniques (7th ed. 2007); Robert L. Gardner et al., Tax Research Techniques (7th ed. 2005).

[3] The discussion assumes that the student is already familiar with traditional legal research methods, including the Westlaw Reporter System and the Shepard's and Key Cite citator services. The student is also assumed to have basic proficiency in computer-based research.

[4] In federal civil tax controversies, the United States Constitution plays a limited role and is, therefore, rarely consulted as part of the tax research process. In criminal tax proceedings, constitutional objections relating to such issues as self-incrimination, searches and seizures, and due process sometimes arise. Those issues are beyond the scope of this book.

variously designated subchapters, parts, subparts, sections, subsections, paragraphs, subparagraphs, sentences, and clauses. The attorney must be alert to these divisions, as some Code provisions apply throughout the entire Code, while others govern only a specific title, subtitle, or chapter. The scope of a particular provision is usually indicated by introductory language, such as "For purposes of this subtitle." Most of the income tax provisions are contained in Chapter 1 of Subtitle A. The procedural provisions that apply to all types of tax issues are located in Subtitle F.

[a] Current Version

While the Internal Revenue Code is included in the official United States Code set, it is most commonly accessed by tax practitioners through one of the commercially published looseleaf reporter services. The two most widely used services are published by the Research Institute of America (RIA) (formerly known as Prentice-Hall) and Commerce Clearing House (CCH). Each of them publishes the complete Code, updated on a regular basis, in a two-volume set. Both also publish an expanded multi-volume looseleaf reporter series organized by Code section. Following the official text of a Code section are the following: excerpts from selected legislative history; final, temporary, and proposed regulations; editorial explanations of the Code and regulation language; and digests of cases, revenue rulings, and letter rulings. The RIA income tax series, *United States Tax Reporter*, spans sixteen volumes, while the CCH equivalent, *Standard Federal Tax Reporter*, runs to nineteen volumes.

[b] Prior Code Versions

As explained in Chapters 7 and 10, respectively, the IRS normally has three years from the time the taxpayer files a tax return to assess a tax deficiency, and the taxpayer normally has three years after filing a return to claim a refund. In either case, the attorney often finds himself arguing about a Code provision that, at the time the controversy is joined by the IRS, has already been amended or repealed. Prior versions of the Code can also be important when doing substantive tax research, as interpretations of an amended Code section may inform the application of its current counterpart.

The attorney can find the full text of the Internal Revenue Code for any year after 1953 by looking in *U.S. Code Congressional & Administrative News — Internal Revenue Code*, published by Thomson Reuters/West. Pre-1954 Internal Revenue Code versions may be located in *Seidman's Legislative History of Federal Income and Excess Profits Tax Laws*. Non-current versions of the Code can also be found using an online service, Lexis (from 1978 forward) or Westlaw (from 1984 forward).

Tracking additions, deletions, and other amendments to the Code over a period of years presents more of a challenge. Although many of the old sections of the 1954 Code retained their same numbering in the 1986 version, all but one of the 1939 Code section numbers were changed in the 1954 version. Both the CCH and RIA looseleaf reporter series contain tables cross-referencing provisions of the 1939 and 1954 Codes, as well as amendment notes that describe prior changes to a particular Code section, but the coverage is limited. To help researchers identify specific amendments and changes in statutory language, RIA publishes a multi-volume looseleaf series titled *Cumulative Changes*. A separate set of volumes exists for the 1939, 1954, and 1986 Codes. *Cumulative Changes* volumes consist of a series of charts, one for each Code section. Each chart contains public law numbers for the original Act and any amendments, effective and enactment dates, as well as the full text of any amended or repealed provision. The charts also include internal changes within Code sections, such as redesignated subsections, added or repealed subsections, and rewritten subsections.

[2] Legislative History

Although the Code is highly detailed, many provisions may seem ambiguous when applied to a given set of facts. The meaning of an ambiguous Code section may be gleaned by resorting to legislative history to determine Congressional intent. The three principal sources of legislative history in the tax area are (1) hearings before Congressional committees; (2) debates on the floor of the House of Representatives and Senate; and (3) Congressional committee reports.

These three sources of legislative history are the by-products of the tax legislative process.[5] The legislative process usually originates with one or more proposals from the President delivered to Congress as part of the State of the Union Address in January. Written proposals from the President usually are issued in the form of general and technical explanations of proposed amendments, rather than in the form of a proposed bill. These explanations are prepared by the Assistant Secretary for Tax Policy in the Treasury Department.

The United States Constitution requires that bills for raising revenue originate in the House of Representatives. U.S. Const. Art. 1, § 7. Legislative counsel in the House, assisted by Treasury and IRS staff members, draft the initial language of a tax bill, which is then assigned a bill (H.R.) number. Once the bill is submitted in the House, it is referred to the House Ways and Means Committee. The Ways and Means Committee holds public hearings at which Treasury Department officials and representatives from private interest groups comment on the likely effect of the proposed legislation. The Ways and Means Committee eventually prepares a detailed House Report explaining the proposed legislation, and the bill is debated on the House floor. A similar process takes place in the Senate under the authority of the Senate Finance Committee. The Finance Committee holds its own set of hearings on the legislation (referred to as an Act at that point), publishes its own Senate Report, and makes whatever changes to the House version it deems appropriate.

After the Senate debates and passes its version of the legislation, the matter goes to a Conference Committee made up of House and Senate members who seek to iron out any differences and craft compromise legislation. The Conference Committee prepares its own report and sends the compromise version back to both houses. If passed by both, it is sent to the President for signature. Once the Act becomes law, it receives a public law (P.L.) number, which has no relation to the Act's earlier bill number.

Hearings before the House Ways and Means Committee and the Senate Finance Committee may help illuminate technical issues and offer insight into the meaning of the newly enacted legislation. Transcripts of selected hearings are published by the Government Printing Office (GPO) and are most easily obtained through the Library of Congress' website, thomas.loc.gov. Thomas also provides access to Committee Reports and the *Congressional Record* from the 104th Congress to the present.

Hearings transcripts are also available on microfiche from the *Congressional Information Service* (C.I.S.), a commercial publisher that also prepares a helpful finding index (*C.I.S. Index*) for these sources. Text of the House and Senate floor debates are published in the *Congressional Record*. Debate transcripts might be consulted to ascertain the policy behind a last-minute amendment that occurs on the floor of the House or Senate.

Of these three basic sources of tax legislative history, Committee Reports tend to be the most important. Committee Reports typically include a general explanation section that describes present law, the need for the legislation, and the expected impact the bill will have on various taxpayers. The report may also have a technical explanation of each

[5] The material in this section describes the typical or "historic" route of a tax bill from introduction to final passage. Numerous exceptions exist. *See generally* Bradford L. Ferguson et al., *Reexamining the Nature and Role of Tax Legislative History in Light of the Changing Realities of the Process*, 67 Taxes 804 (1989).

section of the bill. Committee Reports have become increasingly more detailed, many incorporating examples and instructions to the Treasury for drafting regulations. Courts frequently rely on Committee Reports to aid construction of the statute, and they can be valuable sources of guidance for taxpayers, particularly with respect to Code sections for which regulations have not been issued. Among the House, Senate, and Conference Committee Reports, the Conference Report (which is assigned a House Report number) is usually the most helpful, as it highlights areas of disagreement between the House and Senate versions and describes the legislation that may eventually become law.

Selected Committee Reports are reprinted in the *U.S. Code Congressional and Administrative News* (U.S.C.C.A.N.), published by Thomson Reuters/West, as well as the *Cumulative Bulletin*. Reprints in the *Cumulative Bulletin* are generally more complete and, if available, should be consulted first. A compilation of Committee Reports for all revenue acts from 1913 to 1938 is contained in a separate edition of the *Cumulative Bulletin*, 1939-1 C.B. Part 2. Selected Committee Reports for revenue legislation from 1939 until 1953 are scattered throughout the *Cumulative Bulletin* for the relevant years. The *Cumulative Bulletin* did not reprint legislative history surrounding the enactment of the 1954 Code. This material is found in Volume 3 of the *U.S.C.C.A.N.* for 1954. Most Committee Reports relating to revenue legislation after 1954 can be found in the *Cumulative Bulletin*, including the House, Senate, and Conference Committee Reports surrounding the Tax Reform Act of 1986, which are contained in 1986-3 C.B. Volumes 2–4.

Several commercial publishers have issued special compilations of tax legislative history. These include: *Seidman's Legislative History of Federal Income Tax and Excess Profits Tax Laws* (through 1953); Reams & McDermott, *Legislative History of the Internal Revenue Acts of the U.S.* (1950 to present). Legislative history is also included in BNA's *Tax Management Library* (1969 to present).

[3] Joint Committee Explanation ("Bluebook")

Following enactment of major tax legislation, the staff of the Joint Committee on Taxation (composed of representatives of the House Ways and Means Committee and the Senate Finance Committee) may issue a single-volume "general explanation" of newly enacted or amended Code sections. These post-enactment explanations are organized in much the same way as Committee Reports: Prior Law; Reasons for Change; Explanation of Provision. Typically bound in a blue cover, these sources are known, colloquially, as "Bluebooks" and are published by several commercial publishers.

Because Bluebook explanations are written after the bill is made law, they are not technically legislative history. Nonetheless, courts routinely cite Bluebook explanations just as they would other Committee Reports. When the Bluebook explanation is consistent with the other legislative history, this may be appropriate. However, when the Joint Committee Staff expresses an opinion on an issue left unresolved by the Committee Reports, the precedential weight of these comments is debatable. *Compare* Alfaro v. Commissioner, 349 F.3d 225, 230 (5th Cir. 2003) ("The Taxpayers are correct that, inasmuch as the Blue Book was prepared following the adoption of the statute that it explains, this publication is not binding authority. As the Eleventh Circuit said . . . , however, the Blue Book provides 'a valuable aid to understanding the statute.' The Commissioner properly reminds us that, in the absence of definitive legislative history . . . substantial weight should be given to the Blue Book."), *with* Robinson v. Commissioner, 119 T.C. 44, 95 (2002) (J. Thornton, concurring) ("Where, as here, a Blue Book explanation does more than merely collate materials from the official committee reports or clarify inconsistencies therein, and instead purports to add a new gloss to the statute, we should be free to disregard the Blue Book explanation or at least accord it greatly reduced interpretive weight."). *See also* Treas. Reg. § 1.6662-4(d)(iii) (including the Bluebook in the list of authorities that may be relied upon by taxpayers to avoid the substantial understatement penalty in Code section 6662(b)(2)).[6]

[B] Administrative Sources

The IRS, alone or in conjunction with other Treasury Department divisions, issues a wide variety of pronouncements pursuant to its administrative rule-making authority. These pronouncements are discussed below.

[1] Treasury Regulations

Treasury Regulations represent formal and authoritative interpretations of the Code. The Treasury Department officially releases all final regulations, although responsibility for initially drafting the regulations rests with the IRS Office of Chief Counsel. As explained in more detail in Chapter 2, most courts accord regulations a significant degree of deference, although a regulation may be declared invalid if the agency's interpretation is inconsistent with Congressional intent or is otherwise unreasonable. *See* Section 2.02[A] of Chapter 2 (discussing the differences between legislative and interpretive regulations and the amount of deference accorded to each). Regulations help explain complex statutory provisions, resolve doubtful questions of interpretation, and often include specific examples of how a Code section should operate. Of all the administrative sources of tax law, regulations are the most important and should be consulted whenever available. Not all Code sections, however, have corresponding regulations.

Regulations issued under both the 1986 and 1954 versions of the Internal Revenue Code are numbered by a prefix designation and then by the Code section number that the regulation interprets. A regulation's prefix indicates its basic subject matter: Income tax regulations have the prefix "1," estate tax have the prefix "20," gift tax have the prefix "25," and procedural and administrative regulations have the prefix "301." Regulations relating to income tax provisions of the 1939 Internal Revenue Code were issued in sets, with the prefix designation being determined by the location of that regulation in the official *Code of Federal Regulations*. Income tax regulations under the 1939 Code carried the prefix "29."

The Administrative Procedure Act, 5 U.S.C. § 553, obligates government agencies to issue most regulations first in proposed form and to solicit comments from the general public before the regulations are finalized. Proposed regulations, along with the invitation to make comments, are published in the *Federal Register* as Notices of Proposed Rulemaking. Before being finalized, proposed regulations do not carry the force and effect of law. Nonetheless, they cannot be ignored because if they are eventually made final, they are usually made effective retroactively to the date on which they where originally proposed. *See* I.R.C. § 7805(b)(1). In addition, the IRS has stated that it will follow proposed regulations if no other version of the regulations is in force. *See* Chief Counsel Notice CC-2003-014 (May 8, 2003) ("If there are no final or temporary regulations currently in force addressing a particular matter, Chief Counsel attorneys may not take a position that is inconsistent with proposed regulations."). If proposed regulations are not finalized, courts need not accord them any deference, but may do so if the regulation represents a reasonable interpretation of the statute. *See* Vanscoter v. Sullivan, 920 F.2d 1441 (9th Cir. 1990).

When Congress enacts a new Code provision and taxpayers need immediate guidance in order to comply with the newly enacted law, regulations may be issued in temporary form. Unlike proposed regulations, temporary regulations have the same force and effect as final regulations from the date of original issuance. The Code now requires temporary regulations to be issued simultaneously with proposed regulations

---

[6] The substantial understatement penalty is discussed in Chapter 12.

in order to comply with notice and comment procedures in the Administrative Procedure Act. *See* I.R.C § 7805(e)(1). Temporary regulations retain their legal effect for a period of three years from the date of issuance, or until superceded by final regulations, whichever first occurs. I.R.C § 7805(e)(2).

Final and temporary regulations, and any amendments thereto, are officially issued in the form of Treasury Decisions (T.D.s), which are eventually codified into Title 26 of the *Code of Federal Regulations* (26 C.F.R.). T.D.s are reprinted in the *Cumulative Bulletin*, an official publication of the IRS released at least twice a year.[7] Instead of looking in the *C.F.R.* or *Cumulative Bulletin* for the text of a regulation, practitioners usually rely on one of the looseleaf tax services, which include proposed, temporary, and final regulations in the material following the Code section to which the regulation relates.

When reading regulations, be aware that many have not been updated to reflect subsequent amendments to the underlying Code section. *See, e.g.*, Treas. Reg. § 1.351-1(a) (still referring to stock *or securities* as permissible consideration when determining the 80 percent control requirement, even though the reference to securities has been eliminated from the statute). To the extent that the regulation is still consistent with the Code, it retains its value. Both of the major looseleaf tax services make an effort to warn readers of regulations that have not been updated to reflect Code changes, but the warnings are in very general terms.

Proper analysis of a regulation provision also requires the attorney to determine whether the regulation has been upheld, invalidated, or otherwise commented upon by a court. To do so, the attorney can consult one of a number of tax citator volumes: RIA, *United States Tax Reporter — Citator*; CCH, *Standard Federal Tax Reporter — Citator*; *Shepard's Federal Tax Citator*. These volumes list cases (and in the case of the RIA and CCH services, rulings and other pronouncements) that have cited the regulations, and whether the citing authority's analysis follows, invalidates, or criticizes the regulation.

If the attorney needs to obtain the text of a prior version of a regulatory provision, he can do so by using RIA's *Cumulative Changes* series, discussed above in the context of prior versions of the Code. The *Cumulative Changes* regulation volumes include charts tracing amendments to the regulatory language, along with T.D. cites, enactment dates, and cross-references to the *Cumulative Bulletin*.

[2] IRS Pronouncements

[a] Procedural Regulations

An attorney can better represent a client if the attorney knows, before the fact, how the IRS will approach a particular issue or controversy. One source of information about the IRS's internal operations is the Statement of Procedural Rules. The regulations included in the Statement of Procedural Rules are issued by the IRS, without the need for Treasury Department approval, and are included in Title 26 of the *Code of Federal Regulations*. IRS procedural regulations carry the prefix "601." Some procedural regulations describe general IRS processes that may affect the rights and duties of taxpayers, *see, e.g.*, Proc. Reg. § 601.105 (examination of returns and claims for refund), while others instruct taxpayers as to how to gain the consent of the IRS to make changes in reporting methods, *see, e.g.*, Proc. Reg. § 601.204 (changes in

---

[7] Most Treasury Decisions begin with a Preamble, which can be an important source of regulatory intent. The Preamble summarizes the regulation and often explains why the proposed version of the regulation may have been changed before being finalized.

accounting periods and in methods of accounting). The full text of the IRS Statement of Procedural Rules may also be located in either of the looseleaf reporter series (RIA Volume 28; CCH Volume 18).

[b] Internal Revenue Manual

Another important source of information about how the IRS implements the law is the *Internal Revenue Manual* (I.R.M.). The I.R.M. includes detailed instructions for IRS personnel on such topics as corporate and individual audits, the Appeals process, and collection procedures, just to name a few. A separate subpart of the I.R.M., the Chief Counsel Directives Manual, is a multi-volume portion that covers procedures for the Office of Chief Counsel. While the I.R.M. is written specifically for the IRS's own employees, the material is equally valuable to practitioners because it alerts the practitioner to issues of IRS concern. Once the client receives notice of an impending audit, for example, the attorney would be well advised to review the audit guidelines for the issues that are, or likely will be, under examination. These guidelines catalog audit procedures, along with exhibits and instructions to the examining agent for gathering information from the taxpayer. By reviewing these guidelines in advance, the attorney can better prepare the client for questioning and can begin compiling the documentation that the IRS will likely request.

The material in the I.R.M. can also assist the attorney when advising the client during the planning phase of transaction, before it is reported on the client's return. In this instance, the attorney can use the information in the I.R.M. to assess the risk that the IRS will challenge the tax consequences of a reporting position. In light of this information, the attorney might suggest that the client alter the transaction to conform to the IRS's views expressed in the I.R.M. or, alternatively, counsel the client to compile documentary evidence supporting the client's tax treatment, which can be used should the IRS eventually question the taxpayer's reporting position.

CCH issues the entire I.R.M. in a two-part looseleaf series, along with a cumbersome index system. The three Audit volumes contain guidelines relating to the IRS's examination function. The six Administrative volumes include I.R.M. parts relating to Appeals, Exempt Organization, Collection, Criminal Investigation, and Penalties. The I.R.M. can also be accessed and searched using Lexis or Westlaw, as well as the IRS's website.

[c] Revenue Rulings and Revenue Procedures

Revenue Rulings (Rev. Ruls.) represent the IRS's official interpretation of the Code as it applies to a given set of facts. IRS examining agents and Appeals Officers will normally follow the IRS's own Revenue Rulings and, as a result, taxpayers generally may rely upon them to support a reporting position if the taxpayer's facts are substantially identical to those in the ruling. *See* Estate of McLendon v. Commissioner, 135 F.3d 1017 (5th Cir. 1998) (IRS will not be permitted to depart from a Revenue Ruling in an individual case where the law is unclear). Beyond that, the precedential weight accorded Revenue Rulings is somewhat uncertain. *See id.* at 1023–24 ("[R]evenue Rulings are odd creatures unconducive to precise categorization in the hierarchy of legal authorities. They are clearly less binding on the courts than treasury regulations or Code provisions, but probably . . . more so than the mere legal conclusions of the parties."). *See also* Section 2.02[B][2] of Chapter 2.

Revenue Procedures (Rev. Procs.) describe IRS practices in relation to specific issues and provide taxpayers with instructions for requesting information from the IRS. As noted in Chapter 2, the first Revenue Procedure of each year lists the general guidelines for requesting a letter ruling or determination letter. *See* Section 2.04 of Chapter 2. While many Revenue Procedures are merely directive, others necessarily affect the application of substantive tax law. For example, Revenue Procedure 89-30,

1989-1 C.B. 895, as updated, outlines the detailed information that the taxpayer must submit in order to obtain a letter ruling confirming the status of a transaction as a corporate reorganization. The detailed representations required by the Revenue Procedure incorporate the IRS's views on substantive matters such as business purpose, continuity of interest, and continuity of business enterprise.

Revenue Rulings and Revenue Procedures are both issued bi-weekly in the *Internal Revenue Bulletin* (I.R.B.) and are reprinted in a consolidated, semi-annual *Cumulative Bulletin* (C.B.) volume. Revenue Rulings and Procedures are numbered based upon the year of issuance and order of issuance within that year. A typical cite, Rev. Rul. 2007-39, 2007-1 C.B. 1449, refers to the 39th Revenue Ruling issued in 2007, published in the first volume of the 2007 Cumulative Bulletin, on page 1449. Within any given C.B. volume, Rulings and Procedures are organized by Code section, rather than in numerical order. The C.B. includes a numerical finding index at the beginning of each volume, which allows the attorney to find the specific page number for a given Ruling or Procedure. The spine of each volume includes the inclusive numbers for Rulings and Procedures, which allows the attorney to quickly choose the correct volume from the shelf.

Before relying on a Revenue Ruling to support the client's position, the attorney must ensure that the ruling has not been modified or otherwise declared invalid by the IRS. Changes in the Code, regulations, or a subsequent court decision may affect all or a portion of the Revenue Ruling or Procedure. Each volume of the C.B. contains a *List of Current Action* that catalogs Revenue Rulings and Procedures that have been superseded by announcements within that particular C.B. volume. Using the *List of Current Action* to update a Ruling or Procedure, therefore, would require that the attorney review the *List* in every C.B. volume subsequent to the one in which the Ruling or Procedure was initially published. This would be unnecessarily time-consuming.

If the attorney is only concerned with the current administrative status of the Revenue Ruling or Procedure, he can check that status using either of the looseleaf reporter services, both of which include tables of obsolete, revoked, and superseded Rulings and Procedures. A better method, however, would be to use one of the tax citators noted above. Not only does the citator specify whether the Ruling or Procedure has been superseded, it also lists cases and other pronouncements that cite the Ruling or Procedure, along with an analysis of whether the citing material approves or criticizes the Ruling or Procedure being researched. The Shepard's citation service can also be accessed online through Lexis.

[d] Letter Rulings

Letter Rulings (often called "private letter rulings" or "PLRs") are written responses from the Office of Chief Counsel to a taxpayer who formally requests advice concerning the tax consequences of a specific transaction. As explained in more detail in Section 2.04 of Chapter 2, a taxpayer often requests a letter ruling to assure herself of the tax results of a transaction before consummating or reporting the transaction on her return.[8] During the research process, the attorney may discover a series of letter rulings all dealing with a single point of law. Although a letter ruling may be cited as precedent only by the taxpayer to whom the ruling was issued, I.R.C. § 6110(k)(3), a series of similar letter rulings might help the attorney predict for the client the IRS's probable approach in a given situation. Letter rulings also constitute authority for avoiding the substantial understatement penalty in Code section 6662. *See* Treas. Reg. § 301.6662-4(d)(iii).

[8] Section 2.04 of Chapter 2 also discusses the administrative process for requesting private guidance.

Letter Rulings are numbered according to the year of issuance, the week of issuance, and the order within that week. PLR 200839025, for instance, was the 25th letter ruling issued during the 39th week of 2008. Code section 6110 requires that the IRS release letter rulings to the public after identifying details have been redacted. While letter rulings are not officially reported, several commercial publishers obtain copies from the IRS and print the full text of letter rulings in looseleaf and microfiche form. These include RIA, *Private Letter Rulings*, and CCH, *IRS Letter Rulings Reporter*. To locate a ruling that involves the application of a specific Code section, the attorney should consult a tax citator volume. Both the *Shepard's Federal Tax Citator* and *RIA's United State Tax Reporter — Citator* include letter rulings within the scope of their coverage. Given the sheer number of these rulings, probably the best way to access and search for letter rulings is through Lexis. Many private letter rulings are also available on the IRS's website.

[e] Other IRS Pronouncements

The IRS National Headquarters releases a host of other pronouncements that address both substantive and procedural issues. Some represent formal legal opinions that could affect an entire category of taxpayers, while others provide individualized guidance.[9] None constitutes precedent for anyone other than the taxpayer in issue, if any, yet they often reveal to the attorney the IRS's position and litigation strategy with respect to important issues or transactions. Listed below is a description of some of these pronouncements and how they may be accessed.

Technical Advice Memoranda (TAM) — TAMs are similar to letter rulings, described above, except that the request for guidance from the Office of Chief Counsel is made during the examination or appeals process, rather than prior to filing the return. In most cases, it is the IRS representative who initiates the request for advice, in which case the taxpayer is given the opportunity to submit information in support of the taxpayer's interpretation of the issues involved. *See* Rev. Proc. 2008-2, 2008-1 I.R.B. 90. TAMs are numbered like letter rulings and can be accessed and researched just like letter rulings. A short-lived variation of technical advice, Technical Expedited Advice Memoranda (TEAM), was introduced by the Office of Chief Counsel in 2002 to speed the guidance process, but their use has been eliminated. *See* Chief Counsel Notice CC-2006-013, *available at* 2006 TNT 88-40 (May 8, 2006).

General Counsel Memoranda (GCM) — GCMs are a historical form of guidance. There were released by the Office of Chief Counsel and set forth the reasoning underlying a Revenue Ruling, letter ruling, or TAM. A taxpayer can rely on the analysis and conclusions in a GCM as authority to avoid the substantial understatement penalty. Treas. Reg. § 301.6662-4(d)(3)(iii). GCMs were numbered sequentially, with no reference in the number to the year of issuance. CCH's *IRS Positions* contains full text versions of GCMs, along with a Code section finding list and a table that cross-references a ruling with its underlying GCM. They are also available on Lexis or Westlaw, and some are also available on the IRS's website.

Actions on Decisions (AOD) — AODs are issued by the Office of Chief Counsel and explain the IRS's decision to acquiesce (Acq.) or nonacquiesce (Nonacq.) in a judicial determination adverse to the government. An acquiescence does not necessarily mean that the IRS agrees with the court's reasoning, but only that, in the future, the IRS will treat similar disputes in a manner consistent with the conclusions reached in the acquiesced case. A nonacquiescence reflects the possibility that the IRS will pursue the issue in other cases, notwithstanding the adverse determination by a court. While AODs are intended for internal IRS guidance and may not cited as precedent by the taxpayer, the AOD conveys to the public the IRS's current litigating position on many

---

[9] *See generally Inventory of IRS Guidance Documents — A Draft*, 88 Tax Notes 305 (2000); Sheryl Stratton & Judy Parvez, *IRS Guidance 1980–2003: An Ever-Changing Landscape*, 105 Tax Notes 985 (2004).

important issues. They can also be used as authority for avoiding the substantial understatement penalty in Code section 6662. *See id.* AODs are numbered based on the order of issuance within a given year. AOD 2008-032 would be the 32nd AOD issued in 2008. Full text versions of AODs are available in CCH's *IRS Positions*, as well as from the online services.

Chief Counsel Advice (CCA) — As discussed in both Chapters 2 and 6, Chief Counsel advice encompasses a wide variety of documents that must be released by the IRS under Code section 6110(i). The types of documents that fall within the scope of CCA has varied over the years as the IRS Office of Chief Counsel has sought to increase the pace at which it releases legal guidance to IRS attorneys and field personnel. Some observers also believe that the frequent changes in the types of guidance reflect efforts on the part of the IRS to avoid the disclosure mandate in section 6110. While no form of CCA carries precedential weight, they remain important research tools. CCA often reveals the IRS's interpretation of its own regulations and procedures. Most forms of CCA are available through Lexis or Westlaw, as well as on the IRS's website. The prior and current forms of CCA are discussed below.

Early Forms of CCA — Until recently, one of the most common types of CCA was Field Service Advice (FSA). FSA was similar to technical advice except that the IRS representative could request the advice from the Office of Chief Counsel without the knowledge or involvement of the taxpayer. *See, e.g.*, FSA 200122002 (concluding that cost of tires having a useful life of greater than one year must be capitalized). At one time, the IRS published several categories of FSA: Strategic Advice Memoranda (SAM), Background Advice Memoranda (BAM), and Reviewed Advice Memoranda (RAM). The IRS began phasing out FSAs of all forms in 2002.

Litigation Guideline Memoranda (LGM) was another format by which the Office of Chief Counsel provided information and instructions to IRS Counsel outside the National Headquarters relating to litigation methods and procedures. LGMs often included discussions of cases and precedents the attorney should follow. *See, e.g.*, LGM 1994 TL100 (explaining the IRS's litigation position with respect to whether the IRS may rely on an information return when determining whether the taxpayer failed to report income). Their use also has been eliminated.

Current Forms of CCA — In 2006, the Office of Chief Counsel announced efforts to revitalize the way it provides legal advice to IRS employees. *See* Chief Counsel Notice CC-2006-013 (May 5, 2006), *available at* 2006 TNT 88-40 (May 8, 2006). The initiative included two new types of nonprecedential legal advice. The first, Generic Legal Advice memoranda, are designed to help IRS personnel resolve audit issues that affect multiple taxpayers in a single industry. *See* CC-2007-003 (Jan. 17, 2007) (containing procedures for issuing general advice). The second, Case-Specific Legal Advice memoranda, are designed to provide the Office of Chief Counsel with a way to issue timely advice to IRS personnel concerning the development of a specific case. The advice does not involve legal determinations but instead relates primarily to strategic and tactical issues.

The term Chief Counsel advice also describes a separate type of written advice (C.C.A.) from the Office of Chief Counsel containing the analysis and legal conclusions of the Chief Counsel with respect to the resolution of a specific taxpayer's case. *See, e.g.*, C.C.A. 200043006 (interpreting the 7122 regulations relating to the economic hardship basis for an offer in compromise). Individual C.C.A.s are numbered like letter rulings and are available through electronic sources. A related form of advice, Chief Counsel Notices, represents temporary directives from the National Headquarters used to disseminate instructions, policies, and procedures to IRS personnel.

Bulletins (Collection, Bankruptcy, and Summonses (formerly General Litigation); Criminal Tax; Disclosure Litigation) — These Bulletins are published monthly by the IRS National Headquarters and summarize for IRS attorneys recent developments in their respective areas. The Bulletins may include matters of substantive importance or matters of more general interest, such as recent court decisions, law review articles, and advisory opinions. The IRS considers Bulletins to be informational only, and instructs its attorneys not to cite the pronouncements as authority for any proposition of law. I.R.M. 34.11.2.1. Both Lexis and Westlaw have files for the various types of Bulletins, and some are available on the IRS's website.

[f] IRS Forms and Publications

The IRS issues a variety of tax forms to help taxpayers comply with the law. The forms and accompanying instructions explain the requirements of the Code and regulations and guide taxpayers as to how to report items of income, deduction, and the like. In addition, the IRS drafts Publications to help taxpayers meet their reporting obligations. IRS Publications explain the reporting requirements applicable to different groups of taxpayers and provide more specific guidelines concerning important areas of the law. *See, e.g.*, IRS Pub. 594, *The IRS Collection Process*; IRS Pub. 596, *Earned Income Credit*. The IRS website includes forms and Publications that can be downloaded and printed.

IRS Publications provide the attorney with an easy-to-use source of information about commonly encountered questions and filing issues. The attorney must be careful, however, when relying on discussions of substantive law in IRS Publications. The Publications rarely include citations to authority, nor do they indicate whether the position asserted in the Publication has been disputed. Moreover, while the IRS anticipates that taxpayers and their representatives will make use of these Publications when preparing tax returns, the IRS is not bound by statements made in the Publications.

[C] Judicial Sources

The Tax Court, the Federal district courts, and the Court of Federal Claims all handle the trial of tax cases, all of which may be appealed to the appropriate Federal Circuit Court of Appeals and then, upon grant of certiorari, to the United States Supreme Court. In addition, as indicated in Chapter 11, the bankruptcy courts may also consider tax issues in bankruptcy cases.

Opinions in federal tax cases generally interpret and apply the Internal Revenue Code, and in the process consider Treasury Regulations, Revenue Rulings, and many of the other administrative authorities discussed above. Judicial decisions in the tax area have also generated a number of common law doctrines, including the "assignment of income doctrine," *see* Lucas v. Earl, 281 U.S. 111 (1930), and the "step transaction doctrine," *see* American Bantam Car Co. v. Commissioner, 11 T.C. 397 (1948), *aff'd* 177 F.2d 513 (3rd Cir. 1949), *cert. denied*, 339 U.S. 1920 (1950), which now pervade many areas of tax law. *See generally* Martin D. Ginsburg, *Making Tax Law Through the Judicial Process*, 70 A.B.A. J. 74 (1984).

Tax opinions are published in a variety of different places. As discussed below, the reporter in which a court case will be published generally depends on which court issued the opinion. However, both CCH and RIA publish annual compilations of tax decisions issued by federal district courts, the Court of Federal Claims, the Courts of Appeals, and the Supreme Court, all within a single set of volumes. These compilations may also contain "unpublished" decisions of the Court of Appeals. RIA's service is titled *American Federal Tax Reports* (A.F.T.R.), while CCH's service is *U.S. Tax Cases* (U.S.T.C.). These commercial publishers created the compilations to work in conjunction with their respective looseleaf reporter services, discussed above. CCH's looseleaf service, *Standard Federal Tax Reporter*, contains citations to the U.S.T.C., using paragraph numbers, while RIA cites cases in its looseleaf service, *United States Tax Reporter*, using the A.F.T.R. Thus, *Commissioner v. Glenshaw Glass Co.* may be cited as 348 U.S. 426 (1955), 75 S. Ct. 473 (1955), 99 L. Ed. 483 (1955), 55-1 U.S.T.C. ¶ 9308, 47 A.F.T.R. (P-H) 162, and 1955-1 C.B. 207.

[1] The Principal Judicial Fora

[a] Tax Court

As indicated in Chapter 8, the United States Tax Court hears the overwhelming majority of litigated tax cases. Tax Court opinions fall into three principal categories, regular Tax Court opinions, Memorandum Opinions, and Summary Opinions.[10] The first two types of opinions apply to those decisions made outside the small tax case division of the court. Summary Opinions are those issued in small tax cases.[11] Tax Court opinions, regardless of type, are styled "[Taxpayer name] v. Commissioner."

For each case other than a small tax case, the Chief Judge of the Tax Court decides whether the opinion will be issued as a regular Tax Court opinion or as a Memorandum Opinion. Theodore Tannenwald, Jr., *Tax Court Trials: A View from the Bench*, 59 A.B.A. J. 295, 298 (1973). Only regular Tax Court opinions have unquestioned precedential value and are officially published. These regular opinions are sometimes called "division" opinions, *see* Meade Wittaker, *Some Thoughts on Current Tax Practice*, 7 VA. TAX REV. 421 (1988), because the Tax Court is divided into divisions. *See* I.R.C. § 7460 (referring to divisions of the Tax Court). In addition, they are also sometimes referred to as "T.C." opinions because, as noted below, the official reporter that publishes these opinions is abbreviated "T.C." for "Tax Court." Most regular opinions are authored by a single judge speaking for the entire Tax Court. However, a small percentage of these opinions is reviewed by all 19 judges of the Tax Court in a court conference. Court-reviewed opinions state that they were "reviewed by the court." Because multiple judges review those opinions, there may be concurring and dissenting opinions.

The Chief Judge of the Tax Court generally designates as Memorandum Opinions those that apply well-settled law to the particular facts of the case.

> The memorandum opinions, that is, the ones that are not printed, are supposed to be limited to those having no value as a precedent. They include any case decided solely upon the authority of another, cases involving subjects already well covered by opinions appearing in the bound volumes of the reports, failure of proof cases, and some others. . . .

J. Edgar Murdock, *What Has the Tax Court of the United States Been Doing?*, 31 A.B.A. J. 297 (1945). The memorandum designation, however, is sometimes misleading. There are Memorandum Opinions that appear to contain the Tax Court's first analysis of an issue, and some that become leading cases. *See* Mark F. Sommer & Anne D. Waters, *Tax Court Memorandum Decisions — What Are They Worth?*, 80 TAX NOTES 384, 384 n.10 (1998) (discussing Bardahl Mfg. Corp. v. Commissioner, T.C. Memo. 1965-200). The Tax Court's official policy is that it does not cite its Memorandum Opinions, *see* McGah v. Commissioner, 17 T.C. 1458, 1459 (1952), *rev'd on other grounds*, 210 F.2d 769 (9th Cir. 1954), and that it does not consider them to be "controlling precedent," *see* Nico v. Commissioner, 67 T.C. 647, 654 (1977), *aff'd in part and rev'd in part*, 565 F.2d 1234 (2d Cir. 1977). Nevertheless, the Tax Court has cited Memorandum Opinions, even in its regular opinions. *See, e.g.*, Compaq Computer Corp. v. Commissioner, 113 T.C. 214 (1999) (*citing* UPS of Am. v. Commissioner, T.C. Memo. 1999-268, as well as other Memorandum Opinions), *rev'd*, 277 F.3d 778 (5th Cir. 2001).

---

[10] Pre-1942 decisions of the Tax Court's predecessor, the Board of Tax Appeals, are contained in the *Board of Tax Appeals Reports* (B.T.A.).

[11] The Tax Court's small tax case procedure is discussed in Section 8.06 of Chapter 8.

Attorneys can locate regular and Memorandum Opinions in a variety of sources. Only regular opinions are officially reported by the Tax Court. The official reporter service is the *United States Tax Court Reports*, which, as noted above, is cited as "T.C." Cites are to volume number, the reporter abbreviation, page number, and year. Regular opinions also appear in one of two commercially published compilations, RIA's *Tax Court Reported and Memorandum Decisions* and CCH's *Tax Court Reports*. Memorandum Opinions, although not officially published by the Tax Court, are privately published by RIA and CCH, both of which use the name *Tax Court Memorandum Decisions* for their reporter volumes. Memorandum Opinions are numbered by year, in the order of issuance. For example, the first memorandum opinion of 2001 was *Lawrence v. Commissioner*, T.C. Memo. 2001-1 (decided on January 3, 2001). In addition, the Tax Court releases all of its opinions, including Summary Opinions, on the court's website, located at www.ustaxcourt.gov.

Summary Opinions are the opinions issued in small tax cases. *See* I.R.C. § 7463(a) ("A decision, together with a brief summary of the reasons therefor, in any such case shall satisfy the requirements of sections 7459(b) and 7460."). They may cite regular Tax Court opinions and Memorandum Opinions, among other authorities. *See, e.g.*, Ramey v. Commissioner, T.C. Summary Op. 2001-156. Summary Opinions have no precedential value for other cases, and decisions in Summary Opinions may not be appealed. I.R.C. § 7463(b). However, they may illustrate how the Tax Court's small case division or particular special trial judges tend to decide certain issues. As stated above, Summary Opinions are available on the Tax Court's website. They are also published online by Tax Analysts.

Tax Court cases, other than small tax cases, which are not reviewable, generally are appealable to the Court of Appeals for the circuit in which the taxpayer resided at the time the taxpayer filed the Tax Court petition. I.R.C. § 7482(b)(1). Under *Golsen v. Commissioner*, 54 T.C. 742, 756 (1970), *aff'd*, 445 F.2d 985 (10th Cir.), *cert. denied*, 404 U.S. 940 (1971), if that circuit has precedent "squarely in point," that precedent applies in Tax Court. Otherwise, the Tax Court will apply its own rule. Therefore, in reading Tax Court cases to determine the court's approach to an issue, it is important to determine whether the Tax Court reached a decision constrained by binding circuit precedent. If that is the case, the court will almost certainly cite *Golsen*.

[b] United States District Courts

As discussed in Chapter 10, the federal district courts have trial-level jurisdiction over federal tax refund cases. The opinions generally are styled "[Taxpayer name] v. United States." District court opinions in tax cases have no more precedential value than they do in other areas of the law, but they may be persuasive even to other courts. Some district court opinions are not officially published, though they may be reproduced online. Those that are published are included in the *Federal Supplement*, a case reporter published by Thomson Reuters/West.

[c] Court of Federal Claims

Just like the federal district courts, the Court of Federal Claims has trial-level jurisdiction over federal tax refund suits. The opinions are also styled "[Taxpayer name] v. United States." Decisions in these cases may be appealed to the Court of Appeals for the Federal Circuit. In addition to that Circuit precedent, the Court of Federal Claims is bound by decisions of its predecessor courts, the United States Court of Claims and the United States Court of Customs and Patent Appeals. *See* Maniere v. United States, 31 Fed. Cl. 410, 415 (1994); *see also* South Corp. v. United States, 690 F.2d 1368, 1370 (Fed. Cir. 1982) (*en banc*). Since 1992, decisions of the Court of Federal Claims have been reported in the *United States Court of Federal Claims Reporter* (Fed. Cl.).

[d] Courts of Appeals and United States Supreme Court

There are 13 Circuit Courts of Appeals, including the Court of Appeals for the D.C. Circuit and the Court of Appeals for the Federal Circuit. *See* 28 U.S.C. § 41. Cases decided by each Court of Appeals provide precedent for cases that fall within that circuit. They also provide persuasive authority for cases in other circuits.

There are special rules for two circuits. First, courts in the Eleventh Circuit follow Fifth Circuit precedents through September 30, 1981, when the Fifth Circuit was divided into two circuits. Bonner v. City of Prichard, 661 F.2d 1206, 1207 (11th Cir. 1981). Second, the decisions of the Court of Appeals for the Federal Circuit's "predecessor courts, the United States Court of Claims and the United States Court of Customs and Patent Appeals, announced by those courts before the close of business September 30, 1982," are binding precedent in the Court of Appeals for the Federal Circuit. *South Corp.*, 690 F.2d at 1369.

Some Circuit Court opinions are not officially published, though they may nonetheless be reproduced online. Thomson Reuters/West has begun to publish all "unpublished" opinions in a reporter entitled the *Federal Appendix*. As explained in Chapter 11, different circuits, for a time, had different rules about citing their unpublished opinions. *See, e.g.*, Anastasoff v. United States, 223 F.3d 898, 905 (8th Cir. 2000) (declaring unconstitutional under Article III its rule permitting unpublished opinions). For "unpublished" opinions issued after January 1, 2007, Federal Rule of Appellate Procedure 32.1 now provides that a court may not prohibit or restrict their citation by a party.

The United States Supreme Court hears few tax cases each year. A Supreme Court opinion provides the highest form of case law authority. However, it is important to check whether the Code section or regulation analyzed by the Court has been amended or otherwise modified since the Supreme Court's decision. Sometimes Congress overrules a Supreme Court decision by statute. For example, *Commissioner v. Lundy*, 516 U.S. 235 (1996), which applied a two-year statute of limitations to an overpayment claim made in Tax Court when no return had been filed prior to the mailing of a notice of deficiency, was overruled by language added to Code section 6512(b)(3). *Lundy* and section 6512 are considered in Chapter 10.

Court of Appeals' decisions appear in the *Federal Reporter*, while Supreme Court decisions are officially reported in the *United States Reports* (U.S.), and unofficially reported in the *Supreme Court Reporter* (S. Ct.) and the *United States Supreme Court Reports, Lawyers' Edition* (L. Ed.). Supreme Court opinions are also published in the *Cumulative Bulletin*.

[2] Locating Relevant Case Law — Citators

There are several ways to locate relevant tax cases. One common way is to perform a key-word search (using relevant terms, phrases, or Code section numbers) using Lexis or Westlaw. Another way, which does not require online resources, is to consult secondary sources to identify the major cases on a particular topic. Helpful secondary sources are discussed below. Once the researcher has identified a case on a topic, he can use a "citator" to find additional cases. A citator service provides a list of cases and other legal documents, followed by a list of cases and other authorities that cite the main case or other document. If the attorney has the citation of even one relevant case, he can use a citator to find cases citing that case, cases citing those cases, and so on. The attorney can use this to locate a body of relevant cases, including those most on point.

The best known citator series is *Shepard's Citations*, which is available in hard copy or online through Lexis. The Westlaw alternative, Key Cite, is only available online. In the field of federal tax law, the principal citators are *Shepard's Federal Tax Citator*,

CCH's *Standard Federal Tax Reporter — Citator*, and RIA's *United States Tax Reporter — Citator*, all of which were mentioned above.

[3] Updating Case Research

A citator service not only lists cases and other documents that cite the principal case or document, it also indicates how the later source has treated the principal one. For example, a citator will indicate if a case has been affirmed, overruled, or questioned by a subsequent case. This is extremely valuable for ascertaining the state of the law and avoiding the potentially costly mistake of relying on cases that are no longer good law. Lexis and Westlaw each provide a service that performs only the specific function of checking the validity of a citation, without listing all authorities citing the principal one, as Shepard's does. The Lexis service is called Auto-Cite. The Westlaw service is part of Key Cite and is called Key Cite History.

§ 20.03 SECONDARY SOURCES

Because of the breadth of federal tax law, secondary (unofficial) sources play an important role in the research process. As discussed in more detail below, the attorney may find it helpful to begin with a general discussion of the law in a secondary source, and then move to primary sources to find a specific answer. The number and variety of secondary sources dealing with federal tax law is almost overwhelming, and this section makes no attempt to discuss every one available. Listed below, however, are the most widely used and, therefore, the ones most likely to be found in a law school or law firm library. Because the organization of each varies, many of these sources have their own set of instructions, which the attorney should consult in order to make efficient and effective use of the source.

[A] Tax Reporter Services

For many tax attorneys, a tax reporter service (commonly called a looseleaf service) is the most valuable and often-used research tool. Tax services allow the attorney to quickly access up-to-date versions of the Code and regulations, read expert commentary, and research cases and rulings interpreting a Code section, all within a single source.

As noted above, the two most popular reporter services are RIA's *United States Tax Reporter* and CCH's *Standard Federal Tax Reporter*, both of which issue their services in multi-volume, looseleaf binders. The services generally are organized in Code section order. With respect to each Code section, the reporter service includes (1) the Code text; (2) citations to, and in some cases, excerpts from selected legislative history; (3) texts of proposed, temporary and final regulations promulgated under the Code section (if any); (4) editorial commentary and planning tips; and (5) abstracts of cases, Revenue Rulings, Revenue Procedures, and letter rulings, organized by topic sub-headings. The editorial explanations scattered throughout the material following the Code language are well-written and extensive, yet the attorney should avoid relying on them as a substitute for reading the primary authority. The attorney should also avoid relying upon the case and ruling abstracts for guidance and should instead read the cited authority itself. *See* I. Richard Gershon & Jeffrey A. Maine, A Student's Guide to the Internal Revenue Code § 8.02 (5th ed. 2007).

The looseleaf volumes can be accessed in one of two ways. If the attorney already knows the particular Code section he needs to research, he can choose the appropriate volume number by looking at the bindings, which indicate each volume's scope of coverage. If the attorney is unsure which Code section controls, he should consult the comprehensive subject matter Index Volume. The indices refer to paragraph numbers within the Code volumes. Although the Code volumes also include consecutive page numbers, references and cross-references are always made to paragraph numbers, a system that may take the attorney some time to become accustommed to. In addition to the Index Volume, the reporter services incorporate a number of other devices that allow the attorney to locate information he needs, including tables of cases; finding lists of rulings and other pronouncements; charts; and material on IRS organization.

The looseleaf services are kept current by weekly update pages. Once new legislation is enacted or new regulations issued, for example, the publisher quickly incorporates the new material (sometimes in a matter of days) into revised looseleaf pages that are forwarded to the subscriber. The old material must be removed and the new pages inserted. Each service also publishes a separate binder that contains recent developments. (RIA Volume 16; CCH Volume 19). Included are full texts of recently released Revenue Rulings and Procedures, Treasury Decisions, Letter Rulings, and Tax Court decisions, accompanied by an index and finding list.

[B] Tax Management Portfolios

When researching a Code provision with which he is unfamiliar, an attorney may discover that a broader discussion of the purpose and application of the Code language is more helpful, at least initially, than merely reading the Code in isolation. In those cases, the attorney has his choice of a number of tax compilations organized by subject matter, rather than by Code section. Probably the most popular topic-based source is the *Tax Management Portfolios* series, published by the Bureau of National Affairs (BNA). The Portfolio series is divided into five major categories — U.S. Income; Estates, Gifts and Trusts; Compensation Planning; Real Estate; and Foreign Income. Within each category are a series of separate, spiral-bound Portfolio volumes (over 300 in total).

Each portfolio volume represents an individual treatise on a specific tax topic authored by a practitioner with recognized expertise in the area. Portfolios are organized in a standard pattern. The Detailed Analysis Section in Part A provides a narrative explanation and analysis of the topic in question, supplemented by extensive footnotes to statutory, administrative, and judicial sources. Many authors focus their discussion on tax planning opportunities and approaches the attorney might take to counter an expected IRS position. Part B of each Portfolio contains Worksheets which, depending upon the issues involved, might include procedural checklists, IRS forms and documents, sample letters and documents, and related IRS information. The Portfolio on Collection Procedures, for instance, reprints the national and local collection financial standards that the IRS will use in deciding whether to accept an offer in compromise. Each Portfolio concludes with a bibliography and reference list in Part C with citations to the Code, regulations, legislative history, and administrative sources, as well as cites to tax articles. A separate Index binder allows the attorney to access the Portfolios by topic, key word, or Code section. The Portfolios are updated on a regular basis, with New Developments pages located at the beginning of each volume.

[C] Tax Treatises

A Tax Management Portfolio's depth of coverage is usually exceeded only by a tax treatise. One or more tax treatises exists for virtually every area of tax specialization. They, too, provide the attorney with in-depth, narrative discussion of specialized and general areas of the law. Most also provide extensive citations and references to primary source materials. The following is a list of frequently cited treatises, all of which are kept current with supplements.

- Boris I. Bittker & James S. Eustice, Federal Income Taxation of Corporations and Shareholders (7th ed. 2001) (single volume treatise on corporate tax issues).
- Boris I. Bittker & Lawrence Lokken, Federal Taxation of Income, Estates, and Gifts (3rd ed. 1999) (multi-volume treatise covering a wide range of tax

areas, including individual, corporate, and partnership tax, as well as international tax and estate planning).

- Kevin Hennessey et al., The Consolidated Tax Return: Principles, Practice, Planning (6th ed. 2002) (consolidated returns).
- Joel D. Kuntz & Robert J. Peroni, U.S. International Taxation (1996) (three-volume treatise on international tax).
- William S. McKee et al., Federal Taxation of Partnerships and Partners (4th ed. 2007) (two-volume treatise on partnership tax).
- Ann Murphy, Federal Tax Practice and Procedure (2003) (tax procedure).
- Michael I. Saltzman, IRS Practice and Procedure (Rev. 2nd ed. 2003) (IRS procedure).
- Deborah H. Schenk, Federal Taxation of S Corporations (1985) (Subchapter S corporations).

[D] Tax-Related Periodicals

Journal articles devoted to tax issues range in scope from surveys of recent developments to analyses of sophisticated transactions. The attorney researching a given issue is likely to find one or more articles that bear upon the client's case

The following journals publish mostly practitioner-oriented articles: *Tax Lawyer*; *The Tax Adviser*; *Taxes — The Tax Magazine*; *Journal of Taxation*; *Practical Tax Strategies*; and *Real Estate Taxation*. Other tax journals concentrate on tax policy-oriented articles. These include New York University's *Tax Law Review*; *Virginia Tax Review*; and *Florida Tax Review*. In addition, *Tax Notes*, mentioned below in connection with daily tax services, publishes articles on tax law and policy authored by tax professors as well as practitioners, as do related titles such as *State Tax Notes* and *Tax Notes International*.

Tax Institutes associated with various law schools, including New York University, the University of Southern California, Tulane University, and the University of Miami, conduct annual seminars addressing current tax topics. The proceedings of these tax institutes are published in separate volumes. *See, e.g., Annual New York University Institute on Federal Taxation*.

A researcher can locate relevant tax articles in a number of ways. Tax articles are commonly referenced in the footnotes of tax treatises and in the bibliography sections of Tax Management Portfolios. The attorney can also research articles addressing a particular topic by using one of the tax article indices. The *Index to Federal Tax Articles*, published by Warren Gorham & Lamont, allows the attorney to search for tax articles by subject matter or author. Cited articles are followed by a short description of the article's subject matter. A similar service published by CCH, *Federal Tax Articles*, also includes summaries of tax articles, but is organized in Code section order rather than by topic. Because the number of journals cited and the years of coverage differ between the two sources, to be thorough, the attorney may wish to consult both sources. Many tax publications, including all of those noted above, except *Taxes*, may also be found online on Lexis and/or Westlaw, although historical coverage is limited.

[E] Daily/Weekly Tax Reports

The prior discussion has stressed the attorney's need to stay up-to-date on developments in the law. Given the speed with which changes take place in the tax area and the number of legal sources that must be monitored, this is not an easy task. In the area of tax planning in particular, the attorney not only must be aware of recent changes, he must also factor into his advice pending developments in the law that might affect the client's transaction. Responding to this need to remain current, a number of publishers have developed daily and weekly tax services that report developments in statutory, administrative, and judicial authority.

Many tax attorneys begin their mornings by scanning the contents of a daily reporter service, typically Tax Analysts's *Tax Notes Today* series or BNA's *Daily Tax Report*. Both sources report on legislative and judicial developments in the law and reprint full text versions of selected cases, rulings, committee reports, proposed regulations and other matters. *Tax Notes*, a weekly magazine published by Tax Analysts, includes both that information and informative articles on substantive and procedural tax law. Many of these articles also appear in *Tax Notes Today*. *Tax Notes* and the *Daily Tax Report* are available in both print and online form, while *Tax Notes Today* is an online-only publication.

§ 20.04 DEVELOPING A RESEARCH METHODOLOGY

Whether the attorney is rendering advice on the tax consequences of a proposed transaction, preparing a return, or preparing a case for trial, the first step in any research project is to obtain all the facts that might bear upon the ultimate solution to a tax problem. Section 19.02 of Chapter 19 describes the process by which the attorney gathers facts from the client during an initial interview. Once the attorney begins searching for authority, it may become clear that the attorney failed to obtain facts that are critical to the final outcome. In such cases, the attorney may have to conduct follow-up interviews with the client in order to collect additional facts or re-check facts in light of the substantive law that the attorney uncovered during the research process.

Once the attorney establishes the initial facts, he can begin researching the law that applies to those facts. Before delving into a particular source of law, however, he should have in mind a research strategy or methodology.[12] The attorney who does not consider in advance how he should approach a research question is likely to waste time and resources reviewing the same sources over again or, more seriously, risk reaching an incorrect conclusion because he failed to locate sources that bear directly upon his client's case. There are, of course, many different methods for conducting tax research. With practice and experience, the attorney will naturally begin to develop a method that works for him. For those who have not yet developed their own method, we offer the following two general strategies for approaching a tax question.

As noted initially in this chapter, the answer to almost any tax question will derive from an interpretation of the Code. If the attorney is aware, or believes he is aware, of the principal Code sections involved, then the Code language is the obvious place to start. The looseleaf reporter services provide the best source for Code language, as they are updated more quickly than any other print source. Congress drafts most Code sections so that they have broad applicability, so it is not surprising that the client's facts may not fit neatly within the statutory language. After reading the statutory language, however, the attorney should have some understanding of the essential rules or elements applicable to the client's case. If the attorney determines that the answer to the client's tax question depends on the meaning of a particular word in the statute, he should review the legislative history following the Code language in the reporter service. Committee Reports and other sources can sometimes reveal why Congress chose to employ a specific term.

---

[12] The research methodology the attorney chooses to employ may vary depending upon the goal of the project. An attorney may go about researching a question of tax policy differently than he would if he were researching the tax consequences of a specific transaction. The method may also vary depending upon whether the client expects only a general opinion relating to an area of the law, as opposed to a specific opinion relating to the client's own tax return. The discussion of the research process in this section focuses on answering interpretive questions; that is, how the Code applies to a specific fact situation. The method used to answer interpretive questions is generally the same whether the question arises before the taxpayer reports the item on the return or after the IRS questions the return position during an audit.

If the legislative history does not provide any helpful insight, the attorney should review the regulations accompanying the Code section. In many cases, the editors of the looseleaf reporters will have included editorial explanations of the regulatory language, which can help the attorney identify relevant material. Even after reviewing the regulations, a precise answer still may not have revealed itself. At this point, the attorney should consult the case and ruling annotations in the looseleaf service. The annotations are organized by topic, and the editors have included, in most cases, short descriptions of the opinion's holding. Once a case or ruling that seems to fit the client's fact pattern is identified, the attorney should read the item in its entirety. As discussed above, the attorney can then use a citator service to locate additional cases and rulings.

Throughout this process, the attorney should keep a written record of what he has consulted so that he does not repeat his efforts should he return to the same research project at a later time. The attorney must also keep in mind the precedential weight of the source he is consulting and ensure that the source's effective date matches with his client's transaction. If the attorney discovers a case, ruling, or other pronouncement that he believes controls his client's case, he must update the item using the techniques described above to ensure that the item has not been overruled or otherwise declared invalid.

A second research approach applies when the attorney is unfamiliar with the area of tax law involved and therefore does not know the controlling Code section. One option would be to refer to the subject matter index of the reporter service, which will cross-reference paragraph cites within the reporter volumes. Once the relevant Code provision is found, the attorney can approach the research task as described above. In other cases, the attorney may find it helpful to familiarize himself with the broader subject matter area involved. Tax treatises and Tax Management Portfolios are each excellent sources for gaining an understanding of the underlying legal issues. They can also point the attorney towards Code references that apply to his case. Equally as important, these secondary sources highlight related issues that the attorney may not have considered and that may not have revealed themselves if the attorney had focused only on a single Code section. Because of the extensive use of detailed footnotes in these sources, in many cases the treatise or Portfolio will provide an quick answer to the client's specific question. If not, the attorney will at least have an idea of relevant Code or regulation sections, which he can access using the looseleaf reporter services.

Given the number of primary sources that may bear, directly or indirectly, on the client's case and the number of secondary sources that might provide helpful commentary, the attorney could spend several days compiling and reading all the relevant material. External time limitations and mounting fees that the client might not be willing to shoulder often require the attorney to formulate an answer or opinion based upon a limited amount of research. For the inexperienced attorney, knowing when he has adequately exhausted the available research sources can be difficult. Consider the following advice:

> One important rule is that the laws of probability apply to searches (*i.e.*, it is virtually impossible to find every *potentially* relevant document). . . . This usually occurs because one or more of the following:
>
> - The difficulty of the research question.
> - The depth and quality of the available electronic and hard-copy tax libraries.
> - The adequacy of time and budget to devote to the research problem.
> - The researcher's skill and experience.
>
> A second important rule is that there is always an answer, with varying degrees of certainty in its relevance to the research question. Tax practitioners reason by analogy, relying on precedent and making conclusions that are seldom absolutely certain. What does the researcher do when the question

seems not to have been completely answered? At some point, a judgment has to be made. Sometimes the answer is arrived at simply by using the *best* reasoning and related available authority to generate an *acceptable* conclusion. Not every answer will be based on tax authority on point with the client's facts and research issue.

If it is rare to find all documents relevant to the research question, how does one determine when the search is sufficient and should be concluded? Obviously, if there is certainty that the correct answer has been discovered, the research should stop. Certainty, however, is only relative, and what may appear complete to one researcher could seem incomplete to another. Therefore, in addition to the criteria discussed above, the following signs indicate that the research is complete (or at least adequate).

What level of relevant tax authority was obtained during the research? Do the Code and underlying regulations provide the answer or has only a district court case in a circuit other than the client's been found?

Has the "loop been closed?" Do different tax services, treatises and/or primary authority keep pointing to the same tax authority in support of an answer?

Robert L. Black, *Tips, Tricks and Traps of CD-ROM Tax Research (Part II)*, 27 TAX ADVISER 23, 26 (1996).

§ 20.05 COMPUTER-ASSISTED RESEARCH

The discussion so far has focused largely on print sources of tax law commonly found in public and private library collections. Most of the primary and secondary sources noted above are now available online through Lexis or Westlaw, although the dates of coverage are limited. These sources can be researched using the key-word search engines associated with each service. Whether the attorney chooses to approach the research project using online sources will depend upon a number of factors, not the least of which is the cost associated with online research.

Given the breadth of tax sources available online, one can easily become overwhelmed searching for background research. In many cases it is more cost-effective to use print sources first, and access online sources to update one's research or to retrieve specific items. It is particularly important when doing online research to organize the process. When searching for a specific answer, the tendency among many inexperienced researchers is to create a broad search query, combining many different files, with no consideration given to the relative precedential authority of each source. Even when using an online source, therefore, the attorney should formulate a research methodology and avoid the temptation to read only cases and rulings, rather than the Code and regulations.

The attorney can also use the Internet to research and access tax sources. In recent years, the availability of tax resources on the Internet has greatly expanded. The websites listed below provide access to tax-related materials. Bear in mind, however, that, as extensive as some of these online research services may be, many of them allow limited access to sources issued before 1954, and some even later than that.

- *CCH Tax Reasearch Network*: tax.cchgroup.com (fee-based online tax library consisting of CCH Standard Federal Tax Reporter, along with key-word search capabilities).
- *RIA Checkpoint*: checkpoint.riag.com (fee-based tax research system including searchable primary sources and federal tax analysis and explanations).
- *IRS Website*: www.irs.gov (information concerning organization and operations of the IRS, as well as IRS Forms and Publications that can be downloaded and printed).

- *Tax Analysts Online*: www.tax.org (news and information).
- *Tax Resources*: www.taxresources.com (index of tax forms, cases and professional articles).

Full text versions of the Code and Regulations, Revenue Rulings and Procedures, Letter Rulings, IRS Publications, and other primary authorities are also available from tax service providers in a CD-ROM or DVD format. In addition, many of the secondary sources mentioned above, including the RIA and CCH looseleaf services, have been issued in electronic form. Those just beginning tax research should first use the hard copy versions to familiarize themselves with what each contains and how the services are organized. Most CD-ROM and DVD products have key-word search features, as well as "hyperlinks" that permit the researcher to instantly access the full text of Code sections, regulations, rulings, and cases by clicking on highlighted text. Some of the products, by publisher, are:

- CCH Incorporated, *Standard Federal Tax Reporter on CD-ROM* (full text).
- LexisNexis, *Tax and Estate Planning Library* (compilation of tax-related treatises, handbooks, and forms).
- Tax Analysts, *OneDisc* (full text of primary sources with commentary and analysis).

PROBLEMS

1. Elinor graduated from law school two years ago and immediately began working for Stickley & Brandt as an associate attorney in their general business division. Her duties at the firm included corporate transaction work as well as the occasional project dealing with the tax consequences of mergers and acquisitions. Elinor took a 6-month leave of absence from the firm in order to have her first child. Instead of returning to the law firm, she decided to enroll in New York University's Master's Degree in Taxation (LL.M.) program on a full-time basis. She completed the program in 9 months and immediately afterwards began working for a tax boutique firm in New York. Elinor incurred $35,000 in LL.M. tuition expenses and an additional $26,000 in living expenses (meals and lodging) during the 9-month term of the program. Locate relevant case law dealing with the issue of whether the educational expenses Elinor incurred to obtain the LL.M. are deductible under Code section 162.
   A. Begin your research using the CCH *Standard Federal Tax Reporter* looseleaf service. Keep a log of the sources you consulted.
   B. Begin your research using the *Tax Management Portfolios*. Which portfolios did you consult?
   C. Begin your research using one of the online services. Keep a log of the databases you consulted.
2. Jerry Porter, a new client, contacts you regarding an audit of his calendar year 1992 return, which, because of numerous extensions of the statute of limitations, is still on-going. One of the issues raised in the audit concerns whether property sold by Jerry during the 1992 taxable year gave rise to capital gain or ordinary income. What tax rate(s) applied to capital gain income generated by an individual taxpayer as a result of sales of capital assets made during calendar year 1992? How did you ascertain that?
3. Your first assignment as a new associate is to write a memorandum on Subpart F income. You did not take an international tax course in law school and, therefore, do not know the applicable Code section involved. How might you begin researching this issue?
4. While preparing for a Collection Due Process (CDP) hearing on behalf of a client, you come across a Field Service Advice memorandum (FSA) that contains an

interpretation of Treasury Regulation section 301.7122-1(c)(3), which permits the IRS to compromise a tax liability if to do so would promote effective tax administration. The Office of Chief Counsel's interpretation in the FSA is favorable to your client's case. How might you use the FSA when negotiating with the Appeals Officer during the CDP hearing?

5. Jamie White, the teacher's aide discussed in Problem 4 of Chapter 19, recently received a letter from the IRS denying her $2,328 earned income credit for her two children, Mary, age 5, and Donald, age 7. Apparently, her ex-husband, Daniel White, who does not live with them, also claimed the credit. Jamie receives $300 per month in child support from her ex-husband, a carpenter who earns approximately $15,000 to $18,000 per year. Jamie earns $12,000 per year from the school district, and has no other source of income. She told you in the initial interview that she spends most of that money on her children. Research the earned income credit to determine whether Jamie may be entitled to it. What facts would Jamie need to prove, and how could she prove them?

6. Acme, Inc. ("Acme"), a calendar-year, subchapter C corporation, engages in a variety of businesses, both domestically and overseas. As more fully described below, the IRS has filed a summons enforcement action in a local district court (in the district in which Acme's document storage facility is located). Acme's outside counsel, Grungee & Bungee, a large Seattle-based firm, has appointed you as local counsel. The partner in charge of the case for Grungee & Bungee is Kirk Cobain, Esq.

   One of Acme's wholly owned subsidiaries is the Giant Widget Investment Zone, Inc. ("GWIZ"), a Delaware company. Starting in Year 5, GWIZ formed a joint venture with a British corporation, Widget Enterprise Technology, PLC ("WET"). The idea of the joint venture was first proposed in Year 4 by Diana Rossi, the President and CEO of Acme. Rossi's idea was to form a joint venture to compete with the huge Japanese widget conglomerate, Hiabachi. Rossi approached WET and convinced its CEO to participate. In deciding what structure to use for the joint venture, Rossi asked her Vice President for Taxes, I.M. Heigh, to come up with the structure that would minimize the overall United States and British tax burden on the two companies. Heigh is a Certified Public Accountant and an attorney licensed to practice in California; she works out of Acme's Seattle Headquarters. Heigh wrote her counterpart at WET, U.R. Kute, Vice President of Inland Revenue, and proposed three possible structures: a joint venture, a Swiss partnership, and an Irish corporation. Kute is an attorney and a member in good standing of the British bar.

   On September 2, Year 4, Kute responded to Heigh's request in a letter ("Kute letter") entitled "Possible Structures for Widget Collaboration — U.S., U.K. Tax Treatment." It explained how each of the proposed structures would be treated under British law and analyzed the interplay of British and American tax law. The letter pointed out several possible problems with the joint venture model that, if either the British Inland Revenue or the IRS were to take certain positions about certain transactions, would make the joint venture model considerably less attractive. The letter also discussed certain proposed provisions that the IRS could use to greatly increase both Acme and WET's U.S. tax liabilities. Heigh used the Kute letter to help prepare a recommendation to Rossi.

   During an audit of Acme's Year 1-Year 4 tax years, before the joint venture started, Acme gave the IRS an index of files relating to various collaboration agreements it had entered into with other corporations, both domestic and foreign. On November 10, Year 6, using that index, the IRS requested files that appeared relevant to the open examination. Acme and GWIZ attorneys and their paralegals then went through the files and, after removing documents they thought were protected by a privilege, provided the IRS with a list of withheld documents and allowed the IRS examination team access to the remainder. The examiners then reviewed the files, took notes, and selected certain documents to be copied. Under this process, files became available to the IRS piecemeal.

One file that the IRS asked to see was listed in the index as "File #70." The description of that file included a reference to a "Acme Tax Dept. memo — structures of Int'l collaborations." As with other files, the IRS was allowed to review the documents in File #70 after a GWIZ paralegal had pre-reviewed the file for privileged documents. On January 9, Year 7, GWIZ attorney Brittney Spares, Esq., signed a memorandum (the "Spares memo"), prepared by the paralegal, that notified Revenue Agent Ricardo Nunzio that files #69–89 were ready for examination but that 21 documents from those files were being withheld. Nunzio then reviewed the files.

One of the documents Nunzio selected for copying was a November 15, Year 4 memo to I.M. Heigh prepared by M.T. Cann (the "Cann memo"), an accountant in the Acme Tax Department who worked under Heigh. The Cann memo provided an overview and history of various international agreements that Acme had been party to over the years. A number of documents were attached to the Cann memo, including a copy of the Kute letter. When Nunzio reviewed the Cann memo, he found the Kute letter. Based on that letter, he recommended that the IRS open audits for Acme and WET for Year 5-Year 8.

Nunzio also asked about the disposition of several other files (#41–43) that he had wanted to review but had not been provided. He was told that those files had been moved from the GWIZ offices to the Acme's Tax Department for review. Acme's Tax Department decided to withhold documents in those files and listed 40 documents withheld in a February 15, Year 7, memorandum from Paul Bouquet to Revenue Agent Nunzio (the "Bouquet memo"). Document #25 was described as "Letter dated September 2, Year 4 from U.R. Kute to I.M. Heigh Re: Widget Collaboration — U.S. and U.K. Income Taxes."

On February 29, Year 7, Nunzio told Heigh's secretary that he already had document #25. On March 13, Year 7, Nunzio received a letter from Kirk Cobain, dated March 10, Year 7, asserting that the Kute letter was not supposed to have been attached to the Cann memo and demanding the return of the Kute letter. Revenue Agent Nunzio made no response to the letter. Instead, Nunzio recommended to the Office of Chief Counsel that the IRS seek to enforce the summons as to the withheld documents. Accordingly, the IRS has filed a petition in District Court for enforcement of the summons requesting the documents withheld by Acme's Tax Department. Nunzio has filed a standard declaration that meets the requirements set forth in *United States v. Powell*, 379 U.S. 48 (1964).[13]

A. Is the Kute letter protected by the attorney-client privilege? Prepare a 5–7 page single-spaced research memo addressed to Kirk Cobain of the Grungee & Bungee law firm that gives your best legal analysis and advice. Confine your recitation of the facts to no more than one page, and focus your analysis on the law applicable in your Circuit. Do not consider the issue of whether the privilege, if applicable, has been waived.

B. Assuming that the Kute letter is protected by the attorney-client privilege, can Acme get the letter back, or has the privilege been waived? Prepare a 5–7 page single-spaced research memo, addressed to Kirk Cobain of the Grungee & Bungee law firm, giving your best legal analysis and advice. Confine your recitation of the facts to no more than one page, and focus your analysis on the law applicable in your Circuit.

C. Assume that (1) Acme is legally entitled to return of the Kute letter

---

[13] This problem is copyrighted by Bryan Camp and is used, as adapted, with permission.

because the letter was subject to the attorney-client privilege and (2) the privilege has not been waived by the inadvertent disclosure of the letter to the IRS. What procedure should Acme follow to obtain an order requiring the government to return the letter? What issues of law does the procedure raise? Confine your recitation of the facts to no more than one page, and focus your analysis on the law applicable in your Circuit.

TABLE OF CASES

[References are to pages. Principal cases appear in capital letters.]

A

B

[References are to pages. Principal cases appear in capital letters.]

C

[References are to pages. Principal cases appear in capital letters.]

D

E

[References are to pages. Principal cases appear in capital letters.]

[References are to pages. Principal cases appear in capital letters.]

[References are to pages. Principal cases appear in capital letters.]

[References are to pages. Principal cases appear in capital letters.]

N

[References are to pages. Principal cases appear in capital letters.]

[References are to pages. Principal cases appear in capital letters.]

S

T

[References are to pages. Principal cases appear in capital letters.]

U

V

W

Y

Z

TABLE OF STATUTES

[References are to pages.]

[References are to pages.]

CONGRESSIONAL RECORD

COURT OF FEDERAL CLAIMS RULES

FEDERAL RULES OF APPELLATE PROCEDURE

FEDERAL RULES OF CIVIL PROCEDURE

FEDERAL RULES OF EVIDENCE

GULF OPPORTUNITY ZONE ACT OF 2005

IMPROVED PENALTY ADMINISTRATION AND COMPLIANCE ACT

INTERNAL REVENUE CODE

[References are to pages.]

[References are to pages.]

[References are to pages.]

[References are to pages.]

[References are to pages.]

[References are to pages.]

[References are to pages.]

[References are to pages.]

[References are to pages.]

INTERNAL REVENUE MANUAL

[References are to pages.]

IRS LEGAL MEMORANDUM

IRS REFORM ACT

MODEL RULES OF PROFESSIONAL CONDUCT

PENSION PROTECTION ACT OF 2006

PRIVATE LETTER RULINGS

PROCEDURAL REGULATIONS

[References are to pages.]

PROPOSED REGULATIONS

RESTATEMENT (SECOND) OF JUDGMENTS

RESTATEMENT (THIRD) OF THE LAW GOVERNING LAWYERS

RESTRUCTURING AND REFORM ACT OF 1998

REVENUE ACT OF 1926

REVENUE ACT OF 1928

REVENUE ACT OF 1934

REVENUE PROCEDURES

[References are to pages.]

REVENUE RULINGS

SMALL BUSINESS AND WORK OPPORTUNITY TAX ACT OF 2007

SOCIAL SECURITY ACT

TAX COURT RULES

[References are to pages.]

TAX EQUITY AND FISCAL RESPONSIBILITY ACT

TAX REFORM ACT OF 1969

TAX REFORM ACT OF 1976

TAX REFORM ACT OF 1984

TAX REFORM ACT OF 1986

TAX RELIEF AND HEALTH CARE ACT OF 2006

TAXPAYER RELIEF ACT OF 1997

TECHNICAL AND MISCELLANEOUS REVENUE ACT OF 1988

TEMPORARY REGULATIONS

TREASURY CIRCULARS

TREASURY REGULATIONS

[References are to pages.]

[References are to pages.]

[References are to pages.]

UNITED STATES CODE

[References are to pages.]

VICTIMS OF TERRORISM TAX RELIEF ACT OF 2001

STATE STATUTES

ARIZONA REVISED STATUTES ANNOTATED

ARKANSAS CODE ANNOTATED

CALIFORNIA FAMILY CODE ANNOTATED

IDAHO CODE

KANSAS STATUTE ANNOTATED

LOUISIANA CIVIL CODE ANNOTATED

NEW YORK PARTNERSHIP LAW

NEW MEXICO STATUTES ANNOTATED

NEVADA REVISED STATUTES

UTAH CODE ANNOTATED

UTAH RULES OF CIVIL PROCEDURE

WASHINGTON REVISED CODE

INDEX

[References are to pages.]

A

B

C

[References are to pages.]

[References are to pages.]

[References are to pages.]

[References are to pages.]

[References are to pages.]

[References are to pages.]

[References are to pages.]

[References are to pages.]